THE LIGHT *of* THE WORLD

THE LIGHT
of
THE WORLD

by

Rt. Rev. BENEDICT BAUR, O.S.B.

translated by

Rev. EDWARD MALONE, O.S.B.

BENEDICTUS BOOKS
Manchester, NH

Dom Benedict Baur's *Light of the World* was first published in 1952 by B. Herder Book Co. The present edition by Benedictus Books® prefers fidelity to the original over modernized diction, and so contains only minimal formatting and editorial changes that do not affect the original content or style. Citations have been added or amended where necessary.

Approbations from the original:
Imprimi Potest: Stephanus Schappler, O.S.B., Abbas Coadjutor
Conception Abbey, March 23, 1952
Imprimatur: Carolus Hubertus LeBlond, Episcopus Sancti Joseph
St. Joseph, March 26, 1952

Scripture quotations are either the author's original translations from the Latin Vulgate, or drawn from the Challoner version of the Douay-Rheims Bible, per the imprint of John Murphy Company (Baltimore, 1899).

Cover design by LUCAS Art & Design, Jenison, MI
Front cover art: Jesus Resurrected (Getty 538198794)

Benedictus Books
Box 5284, Manchester, NH 03108
1-800-888-9344

www.PrayBenedictus.com

ISBN 978-1-64413-594-5

eBook ISBN 978-1-64413-595-2

Library of Congress Control Number: 2022946952

first edition

CONTENTS

PART TWO
THE EASTER CYCLE

PART THREE
THE TIME AFTER PENTECOST

PUBLISHER'S PREFACE

Light of the World was first published in German as *Werde Licht*! (Herder, 1937), the fruit of several decades spent in teaching and retreat direction by the esteemed author, Dom Benedict Baur. Although his theological and pastoral efforts were deservedly known and praised in his own day, a brief word of introduction seems appropriate.

In addition to serving over two decades as Archabbot of Beuron, Dom Baur (born Karl Borromäus Baur, December 9, 1877) was a German Benedictine theologian, professor, and retreat master of renown among the parishes and religious houses of Germany and Italy in the early 20th century.

Dom Baur professed his monastic vows at the Archabbey of Beuron in 1898, and was ordained to the priesthood there some five years later. He was appointed to the house professorships of dogmatic theology and canon law in 1905, and his gifts in these disciplines, coupled with his keen pastoral insight and formation within the Benedictine school of liturgical prayer led to his being frequently sought as a director of spiritual retreats in both Germany and Italy. He was later recruited as professor of dogmatics at the Pontifical Athenaeum Sant'Anselmo in Rome, where he taught from 1931 to 1938 before being named Archabbot of Beuron by Pope Pius XI. He reigned as Archabbot until 1955, successfully steering the Beuron Congregation through the stormy years of war as an opponent to the Nazi regime. Nearly eighty, he then retired to teaching and retreat work from the quiet of the Beuron cloister, passing to his eternal reward there on November 10, 1963.

During his life, Dom Baur distinguished himself among the various Rhineland Benedictine houses for his work in the liturgical movement — a theological and pastoral programme which, by that time, was beginning to adopt a character far different from the one championed by its saintly grandfather, Dom Prosper Guéranger of Solesmes. Although generally committed to promoting liturgical prayer as the central element of Christian prayer life, the movement that began with an intention to explain and unfold the richness of the Church's sacred rites had in many places shifted to experimentation and adaptation of the liturgical forms themselves. A fundamental change in principle was in fact underway: from a disposition that reverently received the liturgical patrimony of the Church, to one of refashioning it to better suit contemporary preference.

Of the two dispositions, Dom Baur was decidedly of the former, as may be evinced from his excellent introduction to the present work. "We have simply allowed ourselves to be guided and instructed by the liturgy," insists the author, "and we rest satisfied that we are thus following the right way and that we are receiving wholesome spiritual nourishment." This attitude of devout receptivity to the Church's liturgical tradition — that which nourished countless saints and mystics throughout her history — may be found informing Dom Baur's meditations in *Light of the World* no less than it did those of Dom Guéranger, and with equally inspirational effect. Rather than modify or attenuate the splendor of the Catholic ritual and doctrinal heritage, Dom Baur's aim in *Light of the World* is to help us enter into it, like a grand cathedral, and make it our own:

> The present work is intended to increase the reader's acquaintance with the feasts of the Church and with her teaching as found in the missal, so that these may become a fruitful background for mental prayer, and a help and protection for Christian life. The doctrine and inspiration of the Mass and of the Mass formulas are inexhaustible.

Just a few years after his death, Dom Baur's brilliant liturgical meditations had the misfortune of being lost under a sweeping tide of liturgical innovation, as the close of the Second Vatican Council saw *Light of the World* pass out of print and almost completely out of knowledge in the English-speaking world. We are grateful to restore the original edition of this title to circulation, in the kind of typesetting and binding merited by so worthy a work. Excepting a few corrections to the citations and typography, no alterations have been made to the body text from the original.

In turning these pages, the reader will find himself in the hands of a true spiritual master; one who balances dogmatic precision with pastoral sensitivity, practical wisdom, and spiritual insight that soars to the sublime. We hope and pray that Dom Baur's profound erudition and years of instructing others in the things of God may now serve thousands more in this new printing of his work, and that the divine radiance manifest in the Roman Rite may continue to spread abroad. "The light shineth in darkness, and the darkness did not comprehend it" (Jn 1:5).

Introduction

"Arise, be enlightened, O Jerusalem: for thy light is come and the glory of the Lord is risen upon thee. For behold darkness shall cover the earth, and a mist the people: but the Lord shall arise upon thee, and His glory shall be seen upon thee. And the Gentiles shall walk in thy light, and kings in the brightness of thy rising" (Is 60:1–3). This Jerusalem is our Holy Mother the Church of the New Covenant. She is the city of light, filled with the magnificence of Christ, the supernatural Sun who enlightens her. We enter this Holy City by liturgical prayer and liturgical offerings, for we desire to be filled with her light.

"But we all, beholding the glory of the Lord with open face, are transformed into the same image from glory to glory, as by the Spirit of the Lord" (2 Cor 3:18). Piety may be called liturgical when its attention is fixed on the splendor of Christ. Such piety is occupied with the thought of what Christ is, what He has done for us, and what He continues to do for us. It expresses itself in acts of thanksgiving, praise, and petition. It is ever conscious of the fact that the Father has given us and continues to give us all that He has, in the person of His only-begotten Son. It knows that Christ lives in us, and that in Him we can do all things (Phil 4:13).

Liturgical piety is a piety which delights in God and His providence, and which for this reason is confident of victory. It is attuned to the sentiment expressed by the Apostle, writing to the Romans: "If God be for us, who is against us? He that spared not even His own Son but delivered Him up for us all, how hath He not also with Him given us all things?... Who then shall separate us from the love of Christ? Shall tribulation? or distress? or famine? or nakedness? or danger? or persecution? or the sword?... In all these things we overcome because of Him that hath loved us" (Rom 8:31 ff.). If we thus keep our attention fixed on the face of the Lord when celebrating the holy liturgy, we ourselves shall be illuminated by the brilliance which proceeds from Him.

The present work is intended to increase the reader's acquaintance with the feasts of the Church and with her teaching as found in the missal, so that these may become a fruitful background for mental prayer, and a help and protection for Christian life. The doctrine and inspiration of the Mass and of the Mass formulas are inexhaustible. What we offer here is merely an attempt to direct and stimulate investigation on the part of the reader. We are under no delusion that we have exhausted the subject.

Following the liturgical sequence freely and without constraint, we have carefully refrained from attempting to force the thoughts and teachings found in the texts of the Mass into a prearranged scheme or into a system of the spiritual life. We have simply allowed ourselves to be guided and instructed by the liturgy, that is, by the praying and offering Church, and we rest satisfied that we are thus following the right way and that we are receiving wholesome spiritual nourishment.

We treat of the Sunday Masses and also of the weekday Masses. The feast days belonging to the structure of the ecclesiastical year and likewise certain important feasts of the Blessed Mother and of the saints are also included.

The treatment of the Sunday Mass has a more detailed liturgical introduction. This introduction will explain the inner meaning of the Sunday Mass and is intended as a preparation for the celebration of the Holy Sacrifice rather than as a meditation.

Strict adherence to the text creates no small difficulty. The liturgy makes frequent use of repetition, even delights in repetition. In fact, this is not harmful to our life of prayer. We are more likely to get results if we are not given new material for thought each time. We can and should always exercise a new faith, confidence, and love, and offer ourselves anew to God; with joy we should adore, thank, and praise God, repent of our sins, and pray for pardon, light, and grace. Generally the liturgy follows the manner of affective prayer rather than that of mental exercise.

Prayer is not in the first instance a matter of doctrine or knowledge, but an action. It is the continuation of our Lord's life in His mystical body, the Church. The members of this body continue to pray and struggle, and He who is the head gathers them together and offers them to His Father in His own prayers and offerings. Hence the piety of the liturgy is regulated by externals, by objective facts, by the supernatural relationship of God with humanity. It deals with the fact of the Incarnation of the Son of God, with the mysteries of His life and death, with His humiliation and exaltation, and particularly with His continued operation in His mystical body, the Church. Liturgical prayer is, therefore, primarily a matter of contemplation, adoration, thanksgiving, and participation in the life of Christ. The soul that is nourished by the liturgy must soon become absorbed with Christ in God and yet remains intimately bound to the Church. It cannot fail to make fruitful in its own life what it has observed and learned to treasure in the life of Christ. It will make use of what it learns for its own spiritual advantage, for the sanctification of the whole Church, with the growth of whose life it is intimately associated. Through beholding the glory of the Lord it will be transformed into the same image.

Christian Life and the Ecclesiastical Year

The spiritual life of the Christian is merely the participation in divine life. It is God living in us. We obtain this life through a spiritual rebirth in the sacrament of baptism.

The world came to know this divine life for the first time in the Incarnation of the Son of God, when Mary spoke her fiat at Nazareth. Since that time this life has continued to come to us through Christ. He came that we "may have life and may have it more abundantly" (Jn 10:10). The germ of this divine life is planted in our soul at baptism, but this germ must be developed and brought to perfection. Both in our conduct and in our character we must be transformed into the likeness of the Son of God (Rom 8:29). Christian holiness consists primarily in the perfect development of the germ that was planted in our soul at baptism. This development may be accomplished by perfect participation in the life of Christ. He who is the vine gives life to us who are the branches (Jn 15:5). Our personal task in this work is to prepare ourselves with joy and confidence for the reception of a full measure of this life. We must protect it, nourish it, and perfect it.

The divine life that we received at baptism is nourished and developed by our participation in the sacramental life of the Church. Christ opens the fountains of the supernatural life for us by the sacraments and particularly by the Eucharist and the Sacrifice of the Mass. Sanctity on earth and its consummation in the eternal bliss of heaven are both within the reach of the soul through the Church. In her Christ continues to live visibly in the world. In fact, the life of the Church and the life of Christ are one, and there can be no supernatural life that is not in some sense a participation in the life of the Church.

All life, even spiritual life, is organic rather than mechanical; a tree must develop roots before it can grow a trunk. As in nature life is measured in terms of years, so in the providence of God the life of the Church here on earth, the Christian life, is fashioned on this same pattern, a holy year, or year of grace.

In the course of a year Christ relives His liturgical life in the Church. Through His sacramental presence His life begins, develops, and draws to a close in that period of time. He who wishes to live with Christ and in Christ must participate in His liturgical life by means of the liturgical year. Each year we begin anew. Each year we seek to attain perfection but we do not reach it. Then God gives us a new year of salvation. We attempt it again, and each year by our union with Christ in His Church we endeavor to perfect the seed that was planted in our soul at baptism. Thus our human will, which by itself would fail, is borne along by the power of Christ's spirit and life.

In our continual search for holiness we discover an unfailing source of inspiration in the life of Christ and His saints as reviewed in the Church year. We enter into the spirit and piety of the Church, which is pervaded with the life and spirit of Christ. We let ourselves be guided through the ecclesiastical year by her prayers, her feelings, and her spirit. In Christ, our glorified Master, we have infallible guidance. As members of Christ's mystical body we submit ourselves, in the course of the Church year, with faith and confidence to the power of the Master. Thus the ecclesiastical year accomplishes its work in us and leads us on to Christian perfection.

We persuade ourselves too readily that by our own intelligence, judgment, and effort, we can master the life which God alone can give, and that we can of ourselves fulfill the commandments He has ordained for us. We cannot go astray if we adopt as a guide the axiom which St. Benedict in his *Rule* laid down as the guiding principle for the recitation of the Divine Office: "Let our mind be in harmony with our voice" (chap. 19). This same sentiment is expressed by St. Paul, writing to the Corinthians: "But we all, beholding the glory of the Lord with open face, are transformed into the same image from glory to glory as by the Spirit of the Lord" (2 Cor 3:18). The devout contemplation of the Lord, whose glory vivifies the sacred liturgy, gives us a new character and gradually transforms us into the likeness of Christ. But we must be transformed through the Spirit of the Lord, not through our own judgment and effort.

Liturgical Meditation

Liturgical meditation, like liturgical piety, is based on the objective facts of the operation of God's grace on humanity, on the Church, and on the individual soul. It concerns itself first of all with what God has become for our sake, what He has done for us, and what He continues to do for us. In liturgical meditation our minds are occupied with the sublime truths which God has revealed to His Church and its members. The model of the soul engaged in liturgical meditation is the Blessed Virgin, who, being overshadowed by the Spirit of God, sings: "My soul doth magnify the Lord, and my spirit hath rejoiced in God my Savior.... Because He that is mighty hath done great things to me; ... and His mercy is from generation unto generations" (Lk 1:46 ff.).

Like all other prayer, liturgical prayer requires an appropriate preparation. The remote preparation is our entire daily life, which must be so regulated that it contributes to our prayer life. It must concentrate on the destruction of sinful habits and illicit passions, and prompt us to submit with resignation to the ordinances and commandments of God. The proximate preparation is made by reading over carefully and thoughtfully the material on which we are to meditate. When beginning the meditation itself, we must lay aside all work that may distract us and separate us from God and Christ, and through earnest prayer call down help from above upon our undertaking.

There are several approved methods of meditation. The method of St. Ignatius and the method of St. Sulpice are both well adapted to the practice of liturgical meditation.

The Method of St. Ignatius

The exercise of the memory. We exercise our memory by recalling the material we have prepared for our meditation the night before, and read it through again slowly and thoughtfully.

The exercise of the understanding. We ask ourselves whether in this mystery or happening there is anything significant for us. What practical conclusions must we draw from it? How must we act in the future? What obstacles must we remove? What means have we at our disposal for this purpose?

The exercise of the will. This should result in a clear, definite resolution, flowing from the affections that accompanied the exercise of the understanding. The conclusion consists of a childlike colloquy with God, Christ, Mary, or the saints.

The Method of St. Sulpice

Adoration. We raise our eyes to Christ the Lord, and behold Him in His person, in His mysteries, in His members, and in ourselves. We consider Him in His life, His virtues, His teachings, and His works. We contemplate Him in His works, particularly in the Sacrifice of the Mass, and in His saints. As a result our hearts are stirred to adoration, wonder, gratitude, praise, and love.

Participation. We long to share the life of Christ and to transplant His spirit, His virtues, and His sanctity into our soul. We desire to share His life and His sufferings, His death and His glorification. We examine ourselves and repent of our past negligence and faults. We humble ourselves because of our present unworthiness and resolve to improve our lives in the future. To have some assurance of this improvement, we devote ourselves to meditation and pray earnestly for pardon, light, strength, and grace. We ask for an increase in virtue and for a growth of love for Christ, our head.

Cooperation. As a result of our meditation we formulate a clear definite resolution for the day that is before us and for our future life. At the conclusion of our meditation we thank God for the grace and enlightenment we have received, and ask for pardon for the mistakes and faults of our meditation, and beg His blessing upon the tasks of the day.

PART ONE

The Christmas Cycle

Advent

In the liturgy of Advent the Church distinguishes, without separating them, two comings of Christ. His first appearance on earth was in His Incarnation, when He was conceived by the power of the Holy Ghost in the womb of His virgin mother. The same Son of God, who became man two thousand years ago, will be born again in the Church and in each individual soul this morning, and every morning, as long as the story of the redemption of man continues. For the Church and for each soul, every moment of earthly existence is an advent, a time of expectation and longing, in which Christ seeks to establish Himself in our heart, to fill us with His spirit and His light. It is a time set aside as a preparation for His second coming.

In His second coming on the last day, Christ will come with power to complete the work of redemption on earth and to summon the elect on earth to share in the completion of His work, the enjoyment of eternal life.

The dominating thought of the season of Advent is that of His first coming, that is, of His appearance in the world two thousand years ago, and of His continued presence in the souls of men through His redeeming power. This first coming of Christ is likewise a preparation for and an introduction to His second coming in the eternal Christmas of heaven.

In the liturgy the coming of Christ in grace is an event both of the past and of the present. In the Mass, Christ comes every day to His Church and to the souls of men. In His birth the Church sees at the same time His rebirth in the soul through the sacraments. In this sense the coming of Christ is always of the present. The liturgy leads us to the altar and tells us that here we shall await, with faith and longing during the Mass of the catechumens, the coming of Christ in the Consecration and Communion which are to follow. The liturgy seeks to impress on us the importance of preparing our souls with zeal for the coming of the Lord. During the season of Advent we are to purify and sanctify our heart that it may become a worthy birthplace for Him. This we do by self-denial, penance, prayer, and vigilance. We must stir up in our hearts a longing for light, grace, and sanctification.

The coming of Christ is of the present in so far as He who appeared for the first time at Christmas and who appears daily in the Mass, continues to live in the entire Church without interruption. He continues to live and work as the head lives and works in its members, as the vine continues to nourish the branches. Christ lives in the entire Church in the person of the pope, the bishop, the priest, and of each member of the Church. We believe that Christ is thus always mystically near at hand. We thank Him and adore Him for His ever-abiding presence. We open our hearts and our souls to Him and renounce earthly vanities and follies. We allow ourselves to be completely possessed by Christ so that He may be born again in our heart and establish Himself in our soul. "Put ye on the Lord Jesus" (Epistle of the first Sunday of Advent).

The liturgy of Advent sets before us the picture of John the Baptist, the forerunner of Christ, preaching penance in the wilderness, and of the Virgin Mother at Nazareth. During Advent we are to imitate John the Baptist and the Blessed Virgin.

"Do penance." In this holy season we acknowledge that we are sinners. We are aware of our weakness, of our sinfulness, of our unworthiness, and we feel unable to free ourselves from the misery of our present state. Of ourselves we cannot avoid sin, we cannot master our passions or control our evil impulses. We need a Savior and we cry out when we realize how great is our need of redemption. "Stir up Thy might, O Lord, and come to our aid." We go to meet the Savior and, like other Johns, we prepare the way for Him in our souls. John is our guide and model. We are to imitate him in penance, renunciation, vigilance, and prayer.

Behold the Virgin who spoke her fiat in humility and faith, and with complete resignation to the will of the Almighty. "And the Word was made flesh." How marvelous was the state of the Virgin at Nazareth! She became the instrument of salvation, the cause of our joy, the Mother of God, and the means of our redemption. In her purity and her union with God, in her obedience and love, Mary sums up perfectly the spirit of Advent. Behold the Virgin. She is the symbol and model of the Christian soul.

Thus Advent opens to our mind a rich field of mysteries, provides us with food for thought and motives for action. These thoughts and motives should plant the spirit of Advent in our heart, and deepen and nourish that spirit in us.

First Sunday of Advent

The Mass

"Stir up the wills of Thy faithful people, O Lord." Thus we prayed on the last Sunday of the ecclesiastical year. With the same words on our lips we begin the new liturgical year. "Stir up Thy might, we beseech Thee, O Lord, and come." The last days of the Church year which has just passed were marked by an intense longing for the coming of Christ. This same intense longing accompanies us across the threshold of the new year and becomes a mighty prayer: "Come, O Lord, come." During Advent we expect His coming in grace. We need a Redeemer; we need additional strength and help; no one can supply this strength but He in whom alone the world may find salvation and redemption. We practice piety during Advent not merely to provide for our own personal needs; we feel also the need for redemption on the part of our brethren in Christ. We share their spiritual needs and unite their petitions to our own when we call out to heaven for a Redeemer.

We have already pointed out the similarity between the Collect of the last Sunday after Pentecost and that of the first Sunday of Advent. There is also a remarkable similarity between the Gospels of the two Sundays. Both speak of the terror that is to accompany the last days. But in the midst of the darkness and the catastrophe threatening all humanity, the light of redemption breaks through. "But when these things begin to come to pass, look up and lift up your heads, because your redemption is at hand." Full of faith and confidence, we look forward to the day of redemption which is now approaching.

"To Thee I have lifted up my soul. In Thee, O my God, I put my trust" (Introit). With these words we express our joy as we fix our eyes on the Gospel which promises us the Redeemer. "Show, O Lord, Thy ways to me and teach me Thy paths" (Introit), for Thou alone canst redeem me. The Kyrie is an ardent expression of sorrow for sin and of our intense longing for the coming of the Savior and the kingdom of God. "Stir up Thy power, O God, and come." Only a divine power can accomplish our redemption and rescue us, individually and as a race, from the perils threatening our salvation. Great indeed are the things that the work of redemption is to accomplish in us.

In the Epistle we learn that we must cast off the works of darkness. We must put aside rioting, drunkenness, chambering and impurities, contention and envy. Having rid ourselves of these things, we are to put on Jesus Christ. When Christ has been so firmly established in our hearts that we can say with St. Paul, "I live, now not I; but Christ liveth in me," then truly the kingdom of God has been perfectly established in our souls. May God give all of us the grace to reach that state of perfection. In the Gradual and in the Alleluia verse we pray that this may come to pass.

Our hearts should be filled with joy at the good tidings that Advent brings to us. "Lift up your heads, because your redemption is at hand." In the quiet weeks of Advent we become aware of the mystery that surrounds the Blessed Virgin. She prepares for the journey to Bethlehem. In the city of David a Savior will be born unto you, "your redemption is at hand." The Virgin approaches us again now in the Holy Sacrifice in another way, but with an equal measure of grace. Blessed is the moment when the priest bends low over the host and, falling on his knees, adores the fruit of his priestly words. At that moment both the priest and the altar become sanctuaries of the Most High. "Your redemption is at hand." With earnest longing we approach the Redeemer with the words, "To Thee I have lifted up my soul."

With our gift of bread and wine we offer up to Christ the Lord our soul with all its powers and all its aspirations. We are no longer engaged in the "works of darkness," for we have rejected everything that is opposed to the operation of grace in our souls. We have "put on Christ" and, having thus united ourselves to Him in spirit, we become priests and victims of the sacrifice. Clothed with the sacred garment of His priesthood, His purity, His virtues, His complete submission to the divine will, our minds and hearts must be in harmony with the will of the eternal and holy Father. With this thought in mind, we can say in all sincerity: "Hallowed be Thy name; Thy kingdom come."

"To Thee I have lifted up my soul." In the mind of the Church the participation of the faithful in the celebration of the Mass should not be an empty ceremony. She desires that they cooperate with all their mental and spiritual powers. She seeks to lay hold on the whole man, on his heart, his inclinations, on all that is dearest to him, and to offer them up to God as a holocaust. Only in this way can she free us from the entanglements of the world and the flesh. "The kingdom of God, your redemption, is at hand."

A wonderful blessing results from the devout attendance at Mass. "Your redemption is at hand" when you begin to make a fervent use of Holy Communion. "The Lord will give goodness, and our earth shall yield her fruit" (Communion). This prayer makes a delicate allusion to the Mother of God. She was united in her first great communion with God at the moment when the angel announced to her that she was to be the mother of Christ. In the person of Mary, the earth, that is, the human race, brings forth its most precious fruit, Christ. When we receive the

Holy Eucharist during Mass we, too, experience the effects of grace upon our souls. Our universe, that is, our soul, is enriched by Christ, by His grace and His redemption. The things promised us in the Gospel of the Mass are fulfilled in the Communion. "The kingdom of God is at hand." We have put away for the rest of the week the works of darkness, and have put on Christ. We have put on the armor of light and, like Mary, we have become sanctuaries of the Most High.

Meditation

"Lift up your heads, because your redemption is at hand" (Gospel). The coming of Christ, which is spoken of in the Gospel, will also mean our redemption. Oppressed by evil on all sides and burdened with the sins of her children, the Church looks forward to the day of salvation with great longing. This day had its beginning the moment Christ was conceived by the Blessed Mother. It will endure till the end of time, even till the coming of Christ for the Last Judgment. "Lift up your heads, because your redemption is at hand." Our life is a continual Advent during which we are always on the road to salvation.

"I have lifted up my soul" (Introit). Advent implies a turning toward God with fervent longing. "Stir up Thy might, we beseech Thee, O Lord, and come, that from the threatening dangers of our sins we may be rescued by Thy protection" (Collect). In many ways we are still in need of redemption. We are still in danger of committing sin; we often misuse the grace of God; we may yet become victims of our own unruly passions. We are repeatedly beset by the temptation to reason and act in a purely natural way, to ignore the supernatural, to go astray, and thus to lose God. The Apostle's earnest warning applies to all of us as long as we live: "Wherefore he that thinketh himself to stand, let him take heed lest he fall" (1 Cor 10:12).

In the face of this terrible possibility and against the allurements of the flesh, who can give us assurance that we shall not fail? When we consider the strength of our self-love and self-will, how can we be sure that we shall not fall into sin? Our human foresight, our scant prudence, and our faltering resolutions are not a sufficient guarantee; only the grace of God can give us this assurance. Only "with the Lord there is . . . plentiful redemption" (Ps 129:7). Feeling the need of this assurance we turn to the coming Redeemer. "To Thee I have lifted up my soul; in Thee, O my God, I place my trust. . . . Show, O Lord, Thy ways to me, and teach me Thy paths" (Introit).

"It is now the hour for us to rise from sleep" (Epistle). During the season of Advent we should put away all sin. "The night is passed, and the day is at hand. Let us therefore cast off the works of darkness and put on the armor of light. Let us walk honestly as in the day; not in rioting and drunkenness, not in chambering and impurities, not in contention and envy, but put ye on the Lord Jesus Christ" (Epistle).

Hitherto we have been asleep in sin. "It is now the hour for us to rise from sleep," time to put away all that is earthly, all that will displease the Lord when He comes. It is now the hour for us to arise by penance and self-denial from our former sins and infidelities. We must arise to a tireless struggle against all that is unclean, depraved, superficial, and worldly. Advent is the time for us to purge our souls from the spirit of the world, from the spirit of impurity, from all that does not lead to God and promote His interests.

"Prepare ye the way of the Lord, make straight His paths. Every valley shall be filled and every mountain and hill shall be brought low; and the crooked shall be made straight and the rough ways plain. And all flesh shall see the salvation of the Lord" (Lk 3:4–6).

"Prepare ye the way of the Lord." He celebrates His coming today when He descends on our altars at the Consecration of the Mass. He celebrates His coming by His union with the soul in Holy Communion. He comes to us each time He knocks at our soul with grace. "Behold I stand at the gate and knock" (Apoc 3:20). Since Christ is continually supplying us with grace, our whole life may be said to be an advent. There is scarcely a moment of our life when we could not exclaim with justice: "The time has come for us to rise from sleep. Let us lay aside the works of darkness; prepare ye the way of the Lord."

"Do penance, for the kingdom of heaven is at hand" (Mt 3:2). This is the message of John the Baptist in the wilderness. It is also the beginning of the gospel of Christ: "Do penance, for the kingdom of heaven is at hand" (Mt 4:17). In former times good Christians sanctified the season of Advent by increasing their prayers, their penances, and their self-denial. We should at least try to improve our lives during this season by a more conscientious performance of the duties of our state of life, and by a wholesome self-examination. We should now take a more serious view of the state of our soul, and make a better use of our time. During this period the devout Christian will make a more consistent effort to fight against his natural slothfulness and indolence, and attempt to improve his character and dispositions. He will be more patient and charitable toward his neighbor, and thus mortify his self-will and self-love. In this way he will truly be preparing the way of the Lord.

"Your redemption is at hand." "The Holy Ghost shall descend upon thee, O Mary; fear not, for thou shalt have the Son of God in thy womb" (Benedictus antiphon at Lauds). In the liturgical sense this reference applies not only to Mary, the mother of Jesus, but also to the Church and to each individual soul. "Fear not, for in Holy Communion thou shalt have in thy bosom the Son of God."

"Your redemption is at hand." This coming of the Redeemer is but a step toward His final coming at the end of time. On that day our bodies, too, will share the fruits of the redemption. The bonds of death will be broken. Our bodies are to rise from the grave clothed with garments of heavenly splendor. In the mansions of heaven Christ will celebrate with us an eternal and happy redemption.

Prayer

To Thee, O Lord, have I lifted up my soul. In Thee, O my God, I put my trust; let me not be ashamed. Neither let my enemies laugh at me; for none of them that wait on Thee shall be confounded.... Show, O Lord, Thy ways to me and teach me Thy paths. Direct me in Thy truth and teach me; for Thou art God my Savior.... Remember, O Lord, Thy bowels of compassion, and Thy mercies, that are from the beginning of the world. The sins of my youth and my ignorances do not remember. According to Thy mercy remember Thou me.... All the ways of the Lord are mercy and truth to them that seek after His covenant and His testimonies. For Thy name's sake, O Lord, Thou wilt pardon my sin. (Ps 24:1–11.)

Stir up Thy might, we beseech Thee, O Lord, and come, that from the threatening dangers of our sins we may be rescued by Thy protection and saved by Thy deliverance, who livest and reignest world without end. Amen.[1]

[1] Usually the prayer at the end of each meditation is the Collect of the Mass under consideration.

Monday

"Knowing that it is now the hour for us to rise from sleep; for now our salvation is nearer than when we believed. The night is passed, and the day is at hand. Let us therefore cast off the works of darkness, and put on the armour of light. Let us walk honestly, as in the day; not in rioting and drunkenness, not in chambering and impurities, not in contention and envy; but put ye on the Lord Jesus Christ" (Epistle).

"The day is at hand." It is the day on which Christ is to return, the day on which He is to reappear with power and glory to judge the living and the dead (2 Tm 4:1). The first week of Advent fixes firmly in our minds the thought of the Last Judgment. Let us make a good use of the time that is given to us. "It is now the hour for us to rise from sleep.... Our salvation is nearer than when we believed," that is, when we were but recently baptized. The Day of Judgment is at hand, for each moment slipping by brings the Judge nearer. As the days and the years and the centuries glide silently by, we approach ever nearer to the moment that will see the resurrection of the body from the dead, and the beginning of eternal life and everlasting glory. With each return of the season of Advent the words of the Apostle are verified, "our salvation is nearer than when we believed." Our life is marching inevitably toward its end. The hours and the days that we have squandered in sleep will not return. The time that we have failed to use profitably during our lifetime must remain eternally unprofitable. It is indeed time for us to arise from sleep.

"Leave off your dreaming,
Put sleep to flight,
For Christ appears
From out the night."
—Advent hymn

It was not only the foolish virgins who slept when the bridegroom was long in coming (Mt 25:5). Even zealous souls may become drowsy, sleepy, negligent, and halfhearted, fulfilling their duties mechanically and imperfectly. For this reason the Church admonishes us at the beginning of Advent, "It is now the hour for us to rise from sleep."

"The day is at hand." In the Epistle this phrase may be understood in another sense also. Our present life as Christians differs from our former life as pagans as the day differs from the night. When the liturgy speaks of the day's being at hand, it means that now as Christians our lives begin to be illuminated by the rays of the rising Sun, which is Christ. Or is it not rather the beginning of our glorified life that is promised us when the fullness of time has come? On the far horizon of our Christian life the day of our resurrection is already dawning. The pagan Gentiles are still living in the darkness of spiritual night. We Christians live in the full, clear light of day. It behooves us, therefore, to make a profitable use of the time given to us; "Let us therefore cast off the works of darkness," the works of paganism, the works of an unchristian life, and put on the armor of light. The works of darkness are rioting and drunkenness, inordinate love of pleasure, chambering and impurities, sensuality and all other forms of immorality. Contention and envy are likewise the works of darkness, since they are violations of our obligations to practice charity toward our neighbor.

Since we are Christians, we must make an unqualified renouncement of the works of darkness. Our task requires only that we "put on the Lord Jesus Christ." We must think and reason as Christ thinks and reasons; we must love what He loves: the will of His Father, the salvation of souls, poverty, humility, suffering, and the cross. We are to live our lives on earth as He lived His life, in simplicity, with our heart and mind fixed on God. Our life should be a continual prayer and a continuous act of consecration to duty. All our actions should be marked by a complete surrender to the overpowering love of the Father. Whoever lives thus is truly a Christian; he is another Christ.

It is to such a life that the liturgy invites us so insistently during Advent. Our aim at the beginning of the new Church year should be to "put on Christ."

"The day is at hand," the Day of Judgment. With every moment that passes we come nearer to that dread day. The first judgment comes at the moment of our death. This judgment will bring us peace and consolation if, while there is yet time, we rise from the sleep, from the sluggishness, from the inactivity of our present life, and return to our first fervor. In the monotony and trials of the spiritual life, sensible devotion may indeed fail us, but our will to serve God must remain constant. A properly ordered will can keep us punctual and devoted even when we have lost all taste for prayer, and when we are oppressed by the many sacrifices and sufferings of the day. Even when we are weary and tired, and seem to have failed in our attempts to serve God, the will can remain fixed on its purpose. Does it actually do so in our case?

How far have we succeeded in putting on Christ? It may indeed be true that we make our meditation and devote some time to spiritual reading daily; we receive Communion frequently; we are much given to prayer; we have had an abundance of grace. But have we actually "put on Christ"? Have these practices led us to think as Christ thinks, to live as He lived, to love as He loved? It is time that we rise from sleep and begin anew to strive earnestly to "put on Christ."

"The Lord will give goodness; and our earth shall yield her fruit" (Communion). We are invited to begin the new year of grace with renewed confidence. In Holy Communion, God the Father bestows on us His choicest gift, Christ Jesus, His dearly beloved Son. Christ nourishes us with His flesh and blood, and fills us with His spirit and His life. Thus strengthened by Holy Communion, our earth, that is, our soul, brings forth its fruit of virtue: holiness and union with God.

The Church urges us to make use of the Holy Eucharist as a means to perfection. In this sacrament we shall find motivation and help in the task awaiting us. Let us receive Christ daily, and each day offer him a purer and more devoted heart.

Prayer

Stir up Thy might, we beseech Thee, O Lord, and come, that from the threatening dangers of our sins we may be rescued by Thy protection and saved by Thy deliverance, who livest and reignest world without end. Amen.

Tuesday

"To Thee I have lifted up my soul" (Introit). In the desolation of our present state and in our great need of redemption we cry out to heaven for help. We know well that no created power can redeem us and free us. Christ, the incarnate Son of God, alone is able to redeem us. Now He stands at the threshold. In the mystery of Christmas He comes to be our Savior. With faith and confidence we call out to Him: "To Thee I have lifted up my soul." We shall consider now the offering we must make during Advent and the fruit that we may expect from it.

Our task during Advent. At the Offertory of the Mass, while the priest raises the paten and the chalice, we say: "To Thee I have lifted up my soul." In spirit we place on the paten our soul with all its powers, our heart with all its affections, and our whole being. We wish to become, like the bread and wine, a complete offering to God. As the bread and wine are to be changed into the body and blood of Christ at the moment of consecration, so we desire to be changed at the beginning of the new Church year. We wish to die to self, to earthly desires and thoughts, to worldly designs and ambitions. We desire to be changed into Christ and to imitate His actions and His methods. "Put ye on the Lord Jesus Christ" (Epistle). Overwhelmed by the spirit of Christ, we will know nothing but God and His holy will. God alone can satisfy us. "To Thee I have lifted up my soul."

The fruit of Advent. "The Lord will give goodness, and our earth shall yield her fruit" (Communion). This is God's answer to our cry, "To Thee I have lifted up my soul." The fruit that our earth is to bring forth at Christmas is of immeasurable value. It is the fruit which the most pure Virgin already bears in her womb. It is the fruit of the bread and wine that we have already offered. It is the blessing that God returns for the gift we gave Him. It is Jesus Christ, the Son of God.

"Hath He [the Father] not also, with Him, given us all things?" (Rom 8:32.) What are all worldly goods and possessions, what are the choicest of Christmas gifts that men exchange, when compared with the gift of the Father, His Son Jesus Christ?

"He who soweth sparingly, shall also reap sparingly, and he who soweth in blessings, shall also reap blessings" (2 Cor 9:6). In making our offering to God we have withheld nothing. At the Offertory we placed on the paten our time, our understanding, our health, our thoughts, our whole future. But this offering was merely a beginning. "To Thee I have lifted up my soul" every moment of the day. In spirit and in fact we are to see Christ in all things. We feel His continual presence, we submit to His holy will, we are ever aware of His guidance and His providence. In the spirit of living faith we submit with confidence and without reservation to His guidance and protection. Our love and trust in Him are such that we confidently embrace whatever sacrifices, whatever humiliations, and whatever sufferings may be required of us. We embrace Him with a love that avoids all that is opposed to Him, that includes all that leads to Him, that subjects self to Him in all things.

"To Thee I have lifted up my soul." We see in His first coming the beginning of His second advent, when He is to come with power and glory to judge both the living and the dead, to reward the good and punish the wicked. That day will be the day of perfect redemption. Heaven awaits us. "Blessed are the poor in spirit; blessed are they that suffer persecution for justice's sake; rejoice, for your reward is very great in heaven" (Mt 5:3–12).

Prayer

To Thee, O Lord, have I lifted up my soul. In Thee, O my God, I put my trust; let me not be ashamed. Neither let my enemies laugh at me; for none of them that wait on Thee shall be confounded.... Show, O Lord, Thy ways to me and teach me Thy paths. Direct me in Thy truth and teach me; for Thou art God my Savior, and on Thee have I waited all the day long. Remember, O Lord, Thy bowels of compassion, and Thy mercies, that are from the beginning of the world. The sins of my youth and my ignorances do not remember. According to Thy mercy remember Thou me; for Thy goodness' sake, O Lord. (Ps 24:1–7.)

Wednesday

"Lift up your heads because your redemption is at hand" (Gospel). These are the glad tidings of Advent. "We look for the Savior" (Phil 3:20), in the "blessed hope and coming of the glory of the great God and our Savior, Jesus Christ" (Ti 2:13). Christmas will bring us redemption and pardon for our sins.

"He shall save His people from their sins" (Mt 1:21). By committing sin men have inflicted insult on God. Sin is a disgraceful attack upon God, a foolish attempt to cast Him from His throne and to banish Him from the world which He created. He, the almighty Creator, is to have no place in the world He created. Who is capable of making satisfaction to Him for this insufferable insult? No man is capable of it. How, then, is satisfaction of an infinite value to be made for the infinite offense? The good works of all men and of all generations would not suffice. What reparation they would be capable of making would be limited and therefore inadequate, and could not repair the offense to the infinite majesty of God. Even God Himself could not satisfy for the sins we have committed. Infinite majesty cannot lower itself sufficiently to make satisfaction commensurate to the offense. And so we should have remained in our sins, the children of wrath, unless there was found one who is at one and the same time God and man, and who is willing to take our sins upon Himself.

Christ "emptied Himself, taking the form of a servant, being made in the likeness of men, and in habit found as a man. He humbled Himself, becoming obedient unto death, even to the death of the cross" (Phil 2:7 f.). By His death He blotted out "the handwriting of the decree that was against us, which was contrary to us. And He hath taken the same out of the way, fastening it to the cross" (Col 2:14). He offers His blood as the price of our redemption. All the tears, the prayers, the works of penance, the sufferings, and the satisfactions of the entire race cannot be compared in value with one drop of His precious blood. Christ and Christ alone can redeem us from our sins.

He could have left us in our sins. We were all eternally lost and eternally separated from God. But Christ's love for us constrained Him to come and make reparation for His people. How deep should be our gratitude! "I will heal thee of thy wounds" (Jer 30:17). Christ comes to heal our wounds. He is the good Samaritan who finds the poor man that was left half-dead by the wayside. He pours the oil of His grace into the wounds of the sufferer and gives Himself no rest until the victim of this attack is completely recovered.

Christmas heals the mortal wound of our spiritual blindness, which for so long has kept us occupied with earthly things and has driven us to the worship of false gods, which

Scripture calls our adulteries. Christmas rescues us from these inordinate pleasures, from covetousness, from our tepidity, from our unchecked sensuality and self-complacency, from our eagerness for power and honor. Christ brings us relief from all the ills that trouble humanity. He establishes us in the only soil in which we may expect spiritual growth, in the hidden life with God.

In the modern world, almost anything may serve as a god. Money, sensual pleasure, beauty, and athletics all have their worshipers. God appears to be the only thing that can be readily dispensed with. God is a tiresome burden. At Christmas time He appears among us as a man and offers us the truth. His own life furnishes us with a living example of the complete, true, and happy way of life. He shows us the way, and the only way, out of the confusion that bewilders the world today. He infuses into our souls a divine light and a divine strength. He pours oil and wine into our wounds and is tireless in His efforts to help us. With His plan of redemption He returns to us each year, just as He appeared on the first Christmas Day. "On earth peace to men of good will." Blessed be the coming of the Lord!

Acutely aware of the need of this godless and irreligious generation, and feeling the needs of the race as well as those of our immediate friends and neighbors, we seek to serve as intercessors and advocates for wretched humanity. "To Thee I have lifted up my soul" (Introit). We cry out in our own name and in the name of all men for the coming of the Savior. "Show us, O Lord, Thy mercy, and grant us Thy salvation" (Ps 84:8). "Stir up Thy might, we beseech Thee, O Lord, and come." Thou shalt save Thy people from their sins; Thou shalt heal their wounds.

In the Mass we lift up to the Father our pure, holy, and immaculate gift, the body and blood of the Savior. In the name of all our brethren we ask mercy through the sufferings and death of Jesus Christ. We ask God to forgive our sins and to "lead us not into temptation," but to deliver us from the evil of the neglect of God and His commandments. We ask Him to deliver us from the evils of impenitence, spiritual blindness, and eternal damnation.

"To Thee I have lifted up my soul." In praying thus, the Church teaches us that God will deliver us from the threatening dangers of our sins, and that He will shield us and deliver us from eternal damnation. Out of love He comes as our Redeemer and Savior. We believe in Him, we trust in Him, we thank Him and prepare His way before Him.

Prayer

Stir up Thy might, we beseech Thee, O Lord, and come, that from the threatening dangers of our sins we may be rescued by Thy protection and saved by Thy deliverance, who livest and reignest world without end. Amen.

Thursday

"Lift up your heads, because your redemption is at hand" (Gospel). We live in expectation of the Savior and of our coming redemption. The birth of Christ will bring us the assurance that God "hath sent redemption to His people; He hath commanded His covenant forever" (Ps 110:9). Crying out from the depths of our misery and spiritual need, we trust that the coming Savior will bring us the needed help, "because with the Lord there is mercy, and with Him plentiful redemption" (Ps 129:7).

"He shall save His people from their sins." The angel Gabriel approached St. Joseph with the words: "Fear not to take unto thee Mary thy wife, for that which is conceived in her is of the Holy Ghost. And she shall bring forth a son; and thou shalt call His name Jesus. For He shall save His people from their sins" (Mt 1:20 f.). Jesus has come into the world to redeem His people from their sins. He has destroyed sin and has appeased the wrath of His Father. He has broken the power of hell and has cast forth the prince of this world. Hell has been conquered, and once again the gates of heaven are open. All this has been wrought through the life and death of the Savior. This is the sublime and consoling message that the Christmas season brings to us: We are rescued, we are redeemed.

"And you, when you were dead in your offenses and sins, wherein in time past you walked according to the course of this world, according to the prince of the power of this air, of the spirit that now worketh on the children of unbelief; in which also we conversed in time past, in the desires of our flesh, fulfilling the will of the flesh, and of our thoughts, and were by nature children of wrath, even as the rest; but God (who is rich in mercy) for His exceeding charity wherewith He loved us, even when we were dead in sins, hath quickened us together in Christ (by whose grace you are saved) and hath raised us up together and hath made us sit together in the heavenly places through Christ Jesus. That He might show in the ages to come the abundant riches of His grace, in His bounty toward us in Christ Jesus. For by grace you are saved through faith, and that not of yourselves, for it is the gift of God" (Eph 2:1–8). Without doubt we are redeemed. How can we fail to rejoice and thank God for this assurance? We have been saved from hell, and heaven awaits us.

"Lift up your heads, because your redemption is at hand." We are already redeemed; yet Scripture merely says, "Your redemption is at hand." Does this perhaps mean that many men need yet to be reconciled to God; that many men still labor under the burden of sin and guilt, and are still under the power of Satan? We must remember that there still remains in man the power to sin. Although we have been redeemed, the strength of human passion still remains; there is still the barrier of pride, and many of us may yet be the children of wrath. Our guilt in the eyes of God still remains to be destroyed by the application of the merits of Christ. Is the Church not right, then, when she places before us during Advent the redemption as something yet to be accomplished? Undoubtedly this applies to many of us. Many men are still at enmity with God and are spiritually dead because of their sins. Even though we may not actually be in the state of sin, we are still subject to the effects of sin. We are still bound by the servitude to the goods and allurements of the world and to our own selfish interests.

"Lift up your heads, because your redemption is at hand." Have confidence, for in the coming of Christ we shall find salvation. Our spiritual need is great, our tendency to evil is persistent, and our attempts at virtue are weak and ineffective. We are slow to respond to the call of grace, and we shrink from sacrifice; we crave the esteem of men, and we are bound by many other chains to the things of earth. Who can save us from ourselves? The Savior alone can do this, and He is now approaching to redeem us. He comes for no other purpose than this, that He may supply the help we need. He comes as one possessed of "all power . . . in heaven and in earth" (Mt 28:18). He is the strong one who crushes the power of Satan (Lk 11:22). He comes as one "who loved me and delivered Himself for me" (Gal 2:20). He appears as the shepherd who gives His life for His sheep (Jn 10:11). "Greater love than this no man hath, that a man lay down his life for his friends" (Jn 15:13). Should I not expect all things from Him and place my complete trust in Him? "To Thee I have lifted up my soul. In Thee, O my God, I put my trust; let me not be ashamed" (Introit).

How wonderful is the mystery of Advent! We are already redeemed, and yet in a real sense we remain in need of redemption. Our sins have been destroyed, and God has been reconciled with His rebellious children. The power of Satan has been broken, and heaven is again attainable; grace is now within easy reach of all men. We have been redeemed as a race, and as members of that race we have only to reclaim our share of that redemption. We have now merely to cooperate with God's plan of redemption and we shall be saved. The merits of the redemption have been deposited by Christ in the treasury of the Church. Each of us must, however, assert his claim to membership in the kingdom of Christ in order to profit by the fruits of the redemption.

We are indeed redeemed, but in our present state our personal salvation is not assured. We are children of God, children of grace, branches of the vine that is Christ; and we draw upon that vine for spiritual life and vigor. Yet we are by no means perfect. We still need an increase of grace, of virtue, of union with God. Our faith needs to be strengthened, our hope needs to become more unwavering, our love must become more fervent. For an increase of these virtues we pray earnestly and perseveringly during the season of Advent. Perfection is our goal, and we must not be satisfied with less. Our spiritual life must never be allowed to become stationary.

We are redeemed, and yet have need of redemption. Even when we have become perfect, with the help of divine grace, we shall still be subject to the power of death. But from this we are to be freed when Christ appears on the last day. He will summon our wretched bodies and bid them to be joined again to our souls, that they may share in the eternal happiness we have merited by our lives. Only when this has been accomplished will our redemption be complete. "Eye hath not seen, nor ear heard, neither hath it entered into the heart of man, what things God hath prepared for them that love Him" (1 Cor 2:9). "Your redemption is at hand."

Prayer

Establish in our hearts, we beseech thee, O Lord, the mysteries of the true faith, and lead us to eternal life. Through Christ our Lord. Amen.

Friday

"It is now the hour for us to rise from sleep.... Let us therefore cast off the works of darkness and put on the armor of light" (Epistle).

"It is now the hour for us to rise from sleep." The time has come. The Apostle admonishes not merely the heathens and the unbelievers, but us also who have been baptized, who have received the gift of faith, and who should of ourselves see the necessity of arising from our sins. Even for those who practice daily meditation, who attend Mass regularly, who receive Holy Communion frequently, and who engage in other pious practices, this admonition is timely. In spite of all these good works, we are still asleep. Perhaps our sleep is not that of grievous sin, but we are retarded in our spiritual progress by tepidity, by the routine of our daily life, and by our negligence. We lack zeal for the interests of God, we are slothful in our search for union with Him. We must strive to purify our intentions and perfect our prayer. By the judicious practice of penance we must strive to make satisfaction for our own sins and for those of our brethren. Our lives ought to be characterized by a burning zeal for the salvation of all men. If God has promised us eternal life, is He not entitled to our entire service? Has He not a right to our complete subjection to His holy will? As a matter of fact, what is the measure of the sacrifices we make? Indeed, it is time that we rise from sleep, today at the beginning of the new ecclesiastical year, during this holy season of Advent.

"Put ye on the Lord Jesus Christ" (Epistle). We must put off the old man and put on the new. This new man must share the life of Jesus Christ in spirit and in truth. Christ did not intend to be merely an exemplar and a model for us. No, He wishes to be much more than that. He is the vine giving life to the branches and making it possible for them to bloom and to bring forth fruit.

"Put ye on the Lord Jesus Christ." We understand this as meaning that we are to live His life, that we are to love what He loved, that we are to cherish poverty, self-denial, the cross, and intimate union with the Father. We are to fashion our life after His. We are to seek the will of the Father in all things, to strive ceaselessly to promote His honor, and to work continually for the salvation of souls. We should imitate His virtues, especially His humility and His modesty, and should copy His goodness and mildness toward all men. We should reproduce in ourselves His love for His enemies and His horror for sin and for all that may displease the heavenly Father.

"Put ye on the Lord Jesus Christ." Let us understand that He wishes us to be real members of His body, living branches of the vine, in order that His holiness, even His very thoughts, may become ours and live in us. This is the true message that Advent brings to us. "Today if you shall hear His voice, harden not your hearts" (Ps 94:8). It is time for us now to rise from sleep and be renewed in Christ Jesus.

To "put on the Lord Jesus Christ" is an ambitious program, but it is my task for the coming year. Everything I encounter during the coming year should be used to advance my perfect union with Christ. During the coming ecclesiastical year I shall share in the grace and the redemption of Christ to the extent to which I incorporate myself in Christ and live in union with Him. My progress in the spiritual life will be measured by the degree of my incorporation in the life of Christ, by my success in my attempts to "put on the Lord Jesus Christ." "Put ye on the Lord Jesus Christ." The liturgy of the Church year will help me to accomplish this program. It will place in my hands the means necessary for this purpose; foremost among these means are the Sacrifice of the Mass and Holy Communion. We understand clearly the magnitude of the task that lies before us, but we see also the efficacy of the means placed at our disposal: "The Lord will give goodness," that is, Christ in the Holy Eucharist, "and our earth [our soul] shall yield her fruit" (Communion). Why, then, should I shrink before the magnitude of the task? "I can do all things in Him who strengtheneth me" (Phil 4:13). I shall draw near to the Church and her holy liturgy, and she will unite me more closely to Christ, and open to me the fountains of His grace.

Prayer

Protect us, O Lord, who devote ourselves to Thy holy mysteries, that we may give ourselves up entirely to the things of God, and serve Thee with our whole body and soul. Amen.

I beseech Thee, O Lord, send Him whom Thou hast promised. See the great need of Thy people. Come and redeem us as Thou hast promised. (Responsory at Matins.)

Saturday

The station for the Mass during the first week of Advent is the Church of St. Mary Major in Rome. Entering into the holy shrine, the house of the Mother of God, we recall with her the holy mystery of the Incarnation. "The angel of the Lord declared unto Mary, and she conceived of the Holy Ghost." Salvation is brought to us by the Church through Mary.

"The angel of the Lord declared unto Mary." In Mary, the Mother of God, in whose house we are now assembled, we shall find Christ, and with Him salvation. The Virgin believes; she speaks her fiat with complete resignation to the message of the angel; and the Word was made flesh in the womb of the Virgin. "Hail Mary, full of grace, the Lord is with thee; blessed art thou among women." Mary is the Mother of God, the bridge by means of which Christ brings us salvation. He who desires salvation and the forgiveness of his sins, he who seeks the truth and the grace of eternal life, will find it in the Virgin Mary. "He that shall find me shall find life" (Prv 8:35). "Hail Mary, full of grace, the Lord is with thee. The Holy Ghost shall come upon thee, and the power of the Most High shall overshadow thee; and the Holy that shall be born of thee shall be called the Son of God" (Responsory at Matins).

In the liturgy, Mary is not merely an eminent personality of the past; she is also a type and a symbol of the Church; she is a present reality and enjoys a mysterious life in the Church today. In the person of Mary, the Church prepares for the feast of Christmas. Through her the Church has conceived salvation. By means of her the Word was made flesh in the Church and has taken up His abode among us.

Of the Church it may be said, as it was said of the Virgin Mother, "The Lord is with thee." The Church is the Mother of God during the season of Advent. He who wishes to find Christ and the truth, he who desires to obtain grace and share the life of God, will find these things in the Church.

Today we abide in the house of Mary and await in the quiet of Nazareth the approach of the Son of God. The angel, in the person of the priest, comes and brings us the message: "Behold, the Virgin, the Church, will conceive in this hour." He bends low over the bread and the chalice. "This is My body; this is My blood." The Holy Spirit overshadows the bread and the chalice. The Church believes and prays and acknowledges gratefully: "The Word was made flesh and dwelt among us." What a blessed advent! What a blessed appearance of the Lord in the house of Mary, the holy Church! Soon He will enter our souls in Holy Communion and take up His abode in our hearts as He once did in the bosom of Mary at Nazareth. "The Lord is with thee."

You and I are united, not so much by the fact of salvation, grace, and redemption, as by the fact that we enjoy membership in the communion of the Church. So intimately are we united by reason of the supernatural life and calling that we could not be more closely united in desire and feeling if we were bound together by chains. So complete is our solidarity as a group in our life, our virtues, and even in our sins, that we think of salvation principally as it applies to the whole Christian community. We share Christ and His redemption in the measure in which we are united to Mary and the Church. Only by praying, believing, and hoping with the Church can we find an escape from the narrowness and isolation of ourselves as individuals. Only by our membership in the Church and through our association with her may we hope to grow to our true stature and enlarge our capacity for grace at the coming of Christmas. "He that shall find me shall find life." Indeed, we should submit ourselves entirely to the Church. It is she who is "full of grace." We unite our weakness to her strength, and thus strengthened, we become profitable servants.

In our union with the Church we may expect the grace of final perseverance. How the Church longs for the second advent of Christ! The feast of Christmas stirs again in her heart that longing for completion of the work of redemption. "Show us Thy salvation" in the eternal life of heaven. This we can obtain only through Mary and the Church. Sorry indeed is the state of the man who separates himself from the communion of the Church and from her mystical life. If we unite ourselves daily to the Church in faith and prayer, we may expect to find Christ a Redeemer instead of a Judge.

Prayer

Hail Mary, full of grace, the Lord is with thee; blessed art thou among women, and blessed is the fruit of thy womb.

Show us Thy mercy, O Lord, and send us Thy salvation. Through Mary and through Thy holy Church manifest Thyself, and we shall be saved. Amen.

Second Sunday of Advent

The Mass

The stational church for the second Sunday of Advent is the church of the Holy Cross in Jerusalem. Of old, salvation was of the Jews, and through them it was given to the Gentiles. The Jerusalem of today's liturgy is the Holy Catholic Church, but through it salvation is made available to all men.

Today we enter the chambers of the house of God (Jerusalem) and join in the triumphant song: "People of Sion, behold the Lord shall come to save the Gentiles" (Introit). The Redeemer, sprung from the blessed race of Israel, the Savior promised by the prophets, advances beyond the borders of the land of the Israelites into the land of the Gentiles. "The Lord shall come to save the Gentiles" and complete the redemption of mankind, in the Church, in us, and among the heathen.

In the Kyrie and the Collect we pray for the salvation of the entire Church, for the sick, the blind, the lame, and the unredeemed. In the Epistle, Paul, the Apostle of the Gentiles, informs us of their call to salvation. "Christ Jesus was minister of the circumcision for the truth of God, to confirm the promises made unto the fathers. But the Gentiles are to glorify God for His mercy." The Jews, therefore, had a right to expect the coming of Christ and salvation. This the Gentiles cannot expect in justice. If Christ visits them and brings them salvation, it is a singular grace, an act of pure mercy. For this reason we look forward to the coming of Christ with deep gratitude. His glory already shines on us from the heavenly Sion. We have already received the invitation to assemble and prepare ourselves for His coming (Alleluia verse). John, the forerunner, already stands at the portals. "Behold I send My angel before Thy face, who shall prepare Thy way before Thee" (Gospel).

In a few moments Christ Himself will appear in our midst in the Holy Sacrifice of the Mass. At the Offertory we begin to prepare for His coming. With John the Baptist we put aside our ordinary occupations and withdraw into the wilderness to purify our spirit and our heart. "Behold the Lord shall come to save the Gentiles." We are the blind, the lame, the sick, and the dead of the Gospel. Now He is coming to help us. "Thou wilt turn, O God, and bring us to life" (Offertory). Burdened with the consciousness of our sinfulness, burning with desire for the completion of our redemption, and eager to be freed from our sins, our faults, and our negligences, we look forward to the coming of the Savior with faith and confidence. He will heal our wounds and regenerate us so that we shall live in God and by God.

We learn the full extent of the blessing of His coming in the Communion prayer: "Arise, O Jerusalem, and stand on high; and behold the joy that cometh to thee from thy God." The coming of Christ to Jerusalem, the Church, and to the soul in Holy Communion, is likewise a preparation for that final coming of Christ when He will lead the Church and all its members into the world beyond. There we shall enjoy the happiness of the possession of God and eternal salvation. "I rejoiced at the things that were said to me: we shall go into the house of the Lord" (Alleluia verse). This means that we shall enjoy membership in the mystical body of Christ and salvation through Christ, who was born of the Virgin of Nazareth. We shall go into the house of God and celebrate the Mass and receive Holy Communion. We shall eventually go into the heavenly house of God and enjoy the blessed vision of God and eternal salvation.

Meditation

"People of Sion, behold the Lord shall come" (Introit). In the liturgy Sion is Jerusalem, the new Jerusalem of the Church, the Jerusalem of the eternal glory of heaven; likewise God's kingdom of Christian souls. In addressing the people of Sion, the Church in reality is addressing her own members. As the second Sunday of Advent dawns, the Church is possessed by the thought that Christ is coming to His holy city to reign over the kingdom which He has established. This kingdom is composed of the souls of the Christian men and women whom He has redeemed. "Prepare ye the way of the Lord." Prepare the streets of the city of God for the great moment when Christ, the divine King and Master, will come to His holy city (at Christmas and Epiphany).

The Lord shall visit the people of Sion, that is, His Church. "People of Sion, behold the Lord shall come to save the Gentiles; and the Lord shall make the glory of His voice to be heard in the joy of your hearts" (Introit). "I rejoiced at the things that were said to me: we shall go into the house of the Lord" (Alleluia verse), to Sion of the New Law, into God's kingdom, the Church, to which we have been called. Here in the Church we shall find Him; here we shall see and hear His gentle voice; here we shall obtain forgiveness for our sins and the grace we need. Christ and the redemption He accomplished for us is made available to us through the Church that He established. Moreover, by membership in the Church we share in the merit of the prayers of Christ, in the salvation purchased by His suffering, in the work of His apostolate. "I rejoiced at the things that were said to me: we shall go into the house of the Lord," for we are members of the Church and of the mystical body of Christ.

"The Lord shall come to save the Gentiles." Christ is the Savior of the people of Israel. To them was the promise made that from their seed would be born the Savior of the world. They had a right to the Savior. "But the Gentiles are to glorify God for His mercy" (Epistle). The Gentiles had no claim to the promise made to the patriarchs, nor were they included in the covenant made with Abraham. They could not claim the law of Moses, and no promise of redemption had been specifically made to them. They did not belong to the chosen people, but were strangers and had no claim to the Redeemer. Nevertheless He has come to redeem them and us, and for this very reason we should rejoice the more in His mercy. The Gentiles give glory to God because of the mercy He has shown them. And I also "rejoiced at the things that were said to me: we shall go into the house of the Lord" (Alleluia verse). We rejoice because we, too, are now called to membership in the Jerusalem of the New Covenant, and we are made members of the mystical body of Christ.

"People of Sion, behold the Lord shall come to save the Gentiles." God willed to have all men saved, and "to come to the knowledge of the truth" (1 Tm 2:4). In His love God included even the Gentiles. "God is charity. By this hath the charity of God appeared toward us, because God hath sent His only-begotten Son into the world that we may live by Him. In this is charity; not as though we had loved God, but because He hath first loved us, and sent His Son to be a propitiation for our sins" (1 Jn 4:8–10). We have good reason to praise God and thank Him for His mercy. But this praise should not be merely a lip service, but rather a continual praise of God by the preservation of the purity of life which we were given at baptism. "Now the God of hope fill you with all joy and peace in believing; that you may abound in hope and in the power of the Holy Ghost" (Epistle).

"God shall come manifestly" (Gradual). The Lord has come to reign in the kingdom of His Church, and here He will relive His life. Whoever wishes to share His life must participate in the sacramental life of the Church. "We shall go into the house of the Lord." During Advent our participation in the life of the Church must become deeper and more active, "that with one mind and with one mouth you may glorify God and the Father of our Lord Jesus Christ" (Epistle). We must unite ourselves to the Church in faith, in hope, in love, and in sacrifice. Only when we are united in the bonds of love with our brethren in Christ, can we make a perfect oblation to God. When we have accomplished such a union with God, we can honor the Father perfectly and obtain the joy which He has promised us in the celebration of Christmas on earth, and in the possession of the eternal Christmas in heaven.

God sent His only-begotten Son into the world that we might have life through Him. "In Him was life, and the life was the light of men" (Jn 1:4). He came and gave even to the Gentiles "the power to become the sons of God." From His fullness we have all received. In giving us this divine life, God bestowed upon us a treasure that surpasses all understanding. In comparison, the life we enjoyed heretofore is little better than death. "We know that we have passed from death to life" (1 Jn 3:14). Let us walk in the newness of life as children of God, sharing the life of the divinity. It is possible for us to share in the life of God by reason of our membership in the Church. Let us show great reverence for that life. "Arise, O Jerusalem, and stand on high; and behold the joy that cometh to thee from thy God" (Communion).

This new life that is promised to us has already begun. Whoever as a member of the Church possesses Christ, enjoys this life. Such a soul will enjoy this life in all its splendor and fullness when Christ comes to judgment on the last day. The Church longs for the arrival of that day.

"Behold the joy that cometh to thee from thy God" when at the end of time He will take you to Himself in heaven. We look forward to that blessed day.

Prayer

Teach us, we beseech Thee, O Lord, through our participation in the mystery of the Holy Eucharist, earthly prudence and heavenly life. Amen.

Monday

"When John had heard in prison the works of Christ, sending two of his disciples he said to Him: Art Thou He that art to come?" (Gospel.) Today John the Baptist appears in the liturgy for the first time. He was imprisoned because he had declared to the adulterous Herod, "It is not lawful for thee to have her," thy brother's wife (Mt 14:4). In thought he was living with Christ, whose way he had been sent to prepare.

John had gathered about him a group of disciples when he was preaching at the Jordan, and it was from among these that he sent messengers to Jesus. He intended to divert their attention from himself to Christ. A few of them attached themselves to Jesus, but the others remained aloof. Christ was more winning in His ways than John. He engaged the confidence of the people even more fully than John had done. John had settled near the Jordan, and the people had sought him out; but Christ journeyed from place to place in search of them. John was austere and ascetic; Jesus was gentle and mild. The Pharisees complained because Christ ate with publicans and sinners (Mt 9:11). He performed countless miracles for the benefit of the sick. But many people preferred a harsh and severe master such as John had been. Many of them were displeased with Christ's mildness and began to make comparisons between Him and John.

They came to John and complained: "We can no longer make progress with your work. This man is drawing all the people after Him." John did not let himself be deceived. His first concern is to direct the attention of his disciples to Jesus. He is above all envy and flattery and will not allow his disciples to become so attached to him that they will lose Christ. He chooses two of the dissatisfied ones and sends them to Christ to inquire: "Art Thou He that art to come, or look we for another?" John's sole concern is that his disciples discover Christ and in Him the truth and everlasting life. He seeks nothing for himself, but only the glory of Christ and the salvation of his disciples. John, the forerunner of Christ, is a symbol of the Church. She directs our attention to Christ, the Savior who is to come.

"Art Thou He that art to come, or look we for another?" This is the great question that perplexes John's disciples and still puzzles the world. Jesus gives the answer in a way that cannot be misunderstood. His works proclaim it, for "the blind see, the lame walk, the lepers are cleansed, the deaf hear, the dead rise again, the poor have the gospel preached to them." The kingdom of God is distinguished by the works of charity it performs. In Jesus the truth of the kingdom of God appears on earth. He is the personification of the infinite love which assumes the poverty of the poor, which destroys the miseries of the sick, which does not shrink from the lepers, and which conquers even death itself. Even thus He comes to us today in Mass and in Holy Communion, and lives day and night in the tabernacle to comfort us with His holy love. We are, in the mind of the liturgy, the blind, the lame, the lepers, and the dead. He comes to us each day to continue the marvelous works of His love. "The blind see, the lame walk, the lepers are cleansed, the dead rise again." Indeed we need expect no other. Christ is He that is to come; He is here. We receive Him in our hearts with joy and thanksgiving. We unite ourselves to Him in the Sacrifice of the Mass and in Holy Communion; in order to share His life more intimately here in the Holy Sacrifice, in Holy Communion, and at His feet in the tabernacle, we learn each day anew that it is He who works and lives in us. He it is whom we were to expect and whom we need so much. He alone is all that we need. In Him we possess all things: truth and life, God and heaven.

"Arise, be enlightened, O Jerusalem; … the Lord shall arise upon thee, and His glory shall be seen upon thee" (Is 60:1 f.). By Jerusalem the liturgy has in mind Mary, the Mother of God, the Church, the religious community, the Christian family, the convent. "The Lord shall arise upon thee" in Mass, in Holy Communion, and at Christmas. The fruit of this? "His glory," His spirit, His life, His virtues, His patience, His charity, His love, enlivens the Church and each of its members. The Christian is another Christ.

"Now the God of patience and of comfort grant you to be of one mind one towards another, according to Jesus Christ; that with one mind and with one mouth you may glorify God and the Father of our Lord Jesus Christ. Wherefore receive one another as Christ also hath received you unto the honor of God" (Epistle). Would that these words of the Epistle fell not on deaf ears. How far removed are we still from the true spirit of Advent!

Prayer

Stir up our hearts, O Lord, to prepare the way for Thy only-begotten Son, that we may be able to serve Thee with clean hearts purified by the coming of Him who liveth and reigneth with Thee forever and ever. Amen.

Tuesday

During this week the liturgy reveals the imposing figure of John the Baptist. He is cast into prison, but even there he continues his mission of preparing the way for Christ and seeks to direct his own disciples to Christ. He knows Jesus, and only Jesus.

Even in his youth John had forsaken all and had withdrawn into the silence of the desert. "And the child grew and was strengthened in spirit; and was in the deserts until the day of his manifestation to Israel," says St. Luke (1:80). He is a man given to the spirit, to the inner life, to silence, and the company of God. He never left his beloved solitude to seek his relatives or Him whose way he had been sent to prepare. Yet how devoted he was to Christ! He is conscious of only one force, and that is the will of God and the voice of the Holy Spirit that accompanies him. He wears a garment of camel's hair and a leathern girdle. His food is wild honey and locusts, the only fare afforded by the desert. He indulges in no comforts; his home is a cave, and his bed is a stone.

The day comes when he is to manifest himself to Israel, and he appears on the banks of the Jordan. He preaches penance, for the kingdom of God is at hand. He baptizes the multitudes that come to him. By receiving this baptism they acknowledge their willingness to do penance for their sins. They flock to him by the thousands to hear him. They believe he is the promised Messiah or the prophet Elias, but he acknowledges frankly: "I am the voice of one crying out in the wilderness; make straight the way of the Lord.... I indeed baptize you in water,... but He that shall come after me is mightier than I, whose shoes I am not worthy to bear. He shall baptize you in the Holy Ghost and fire" (Jn 1:23; Mt 3:11).

Christ calls our attention to this same John in the Gospel. "What went you out into the desert to see? A reed shaken with the wind? But what went you out to see? A man clothed in soft garments?... A prophet? Yea, I tell you, and more than a prophet. For this is he of whom it is written: Behold, *I* send My angel before Thy face, who shall prepare Thy way before Thee" (Mt 11:7–10). John is a man of retirement, a man of God, a man given to penance and self-denial, a man devoted to Christ, a man of deepest humility. Behold, then, the man who prepares the way for Christ, first in his own heart, and then in the hearts of others. John is surely an example for us, and personifies the spirit of Advent.

The Baptist is a symbol of the Church. John is long since dead, beheaded by the cruel Herod. He fell a victim to the revengeful spirit of a woman, but he lives on in the Church to which he passed on his mission. In the liturgy it is the Church that now prepares the way for Christ on the Jordan. When Advent comes, she also withdraws into the wilderness to live alone with God a life of abnegation and recollection, and to preach penance to men. "Bring forth therefore fruit worthy of penance," she cries to all her children. "And think not to say within yourselves: We have Abraham for our father [for we have been baptized]. For I tell you that God is able of these stones to raise up children to Abraham. For now the ax is laid to the root of the trees. Every tree therefore that doth not yield good fruit shall be cut down and cast into the fire" (Mt 3:8–10). Do penance, for the Lord is nigh; "Whose fan is in His hand, and He will thoroughly cleanse His floor and gather His wheat into the barn; but the chaff He will burn with unquenchable fire" (Mt 3:12).

John is again manifested to us in the Mass and in the appearance of Christ at Christmas and Epiphany. "Behold the lamb of God, behold Him who taketh away the sin of the world" (Jn 1:29). The Church offers us Christ and His grace in the sacrament of baptism and in the Blessed Sacrament of the tabernacle. Through her teachings and dogmas and morals, through her sacraments and in her liturgy and in her spirit, we come, to Christ, the Redeemer. We must listen attentively to her teachings during Advent and enter with a determined will into the spirit of the season. Through the Church we come to Christ.

Each of us should be a forerunner of Christ. Of each of us Christ should be able to say: "He is not a reed shaken with the wind." He is established by the Spirit and immovable in his Christian principles and faithful to his mission. Whether men ridicule him or praise him, whether His affairs prosper or fail, he does not waver. He is firmly established in his faith and in the love of God and of Christ. He is not clothed in soft garments. He is a true John, a man of penance, of self-denial, of self-control. Like another Baptist, like men of true Christian character, we should go forth to meet Christ as often as He comes to us in the Mass and in Holy Communion. During these weeks let us live in the spirit of the liturgy and of the Church. Thus we may be sure of preparing for a fruitful Christmas and of making the graces of the season more complete and more effective.

Prayer

Stir up our hearts, O Lord, to prepare the way for Thy only-begotten Son, that we may be able to serve Thee with clean hearts purified by the coming of Him who liveth and reigneth with Thee forever and ever. Amen.

Wednesday

"People of Sion, behold the Lord shall come to save the Gentiles. And the Lord shall make the glory of His voice to be heard in the joy of your heart" (Introit). This is the sign of the redemption: "The blind see, the lame walk, the lepers are cleansed, the deaf hear, the dead rise again, the poor have the gospel preached to them" (Gospel). This is a consoling thought for us. In the mind of the Church we are the blind, the lame, the deaf. We long for the Redeemer and pray in the Mass today: "Thou wilt turn, O God, and bring us to life; and Thy people shall rejoice in Thee" (Offertory).

"Thou wilt turn, O God, and bring us to life." Never do we experience the longing for the Redeemer and feel the need of redemption as deeply as during this week of Advent. At no time in our lives do we feel so much like the blind, the lame, and the lepers, the deaf, and the dead of today's Gospel. But now we are redeemed. Now we are inspired by the hope that we are in the state of grace and in union with God. We are living branches of that organism of grace, the mystical body of Christ. We acknowledge gratefully what grace has done for us. Nevertheless it is true that we are not all that we should be, and that we should make a better use of the abundant graces that we are continually receiving from Christ our head. We are by no means perfect. In many things we are still blind and are deceived by the false pleasures of the world, by the devil, and by our self-love. In many ways we are still lame, hindered by our passions, by human respect, by bad habits and other external influences.

We must rid ourselves of our inconstancy, of our ill temper, of our restlessness, and of the scruples that may worry us. We must purify our thoughts, our intentions, our motives. Even our prayers and our efforts at perfection are tainted by our vanity, our self-love, our ambition, and our complacency. There is much in us that is degenerate and unclean. From the depth of our misery we look up with trust and confidence to Him who is promised to the people of Sion at Christmas, and in the Mass and Communion. "Thou wilt turn to us, O God," in Thy descent upon our altars and into our hearts. Send us all, the Church as a whole and each of us individually, Thy mercy and Thy salvation.

"And bring us to life." From the fountains of the Redeemer we draw forth new blood, new strength, and new joy. These things flow to us from the altar. By the hands of the celebrating priest we lay our gifts on the altar at Mass. Our gift is bread and wine. With this bread and wine we mean to include our heart, our life, our whole person. In a few seconds the power of the Most High will overshadow the bread and wine. They are presently to be changed into the body and blood of the living, life-giving, and glorified Christ. What is done to the bread and wine in the Mass is accomplished in a mysterious way also in us. The Lord comes to us in the Holy Sacrifice, in Holy Communion, at Christmas, to fill us with this life. His life is the light that heals our blindness, the strength and refreshment that supports us in our lameness. His life is purity and innocence, and removes from us all uncleanness. His life of self-sacrifice and His subjection to the will of His Father heals our deafness. His life is immortality, endless fulfillment, and wakens us to the fullness of a holy life. "I am come that they may have life and may have it more abundantly" (Jn 10:10). We are indeed possessed of grace and virtue, but not yet in its entirety. It will and it must grow in us, in our family, and in the entire mystical body of Christ. "He that is just, let him be justified still; and he that is holy, let him be sanctified still" (Apoc 22:11). How much stronger and more gloriously should the life of grace flourish in our souls! Our dedication to God, our self-denial, and our obedience must become still more perfect. Our charity must increase. How acutely we feel this need during Advent! The fresher and more vigorous spiritual life that we need, Advent will awaken in us.

"Now if we be dead with Christ, we believe that we shall live also together with Christ; knowing that Christ, rising again from the dead, dieth now no more, death shall no more have dominion over Him. For in that he died to sin, he died once; but in that he liveth, he liveth unto God. So do you also reckon that you are dead to sin, but alive unto God, in Christ Jesus our Lord" (Rom 6:8–11). We are to share Christ's life with Him. He is the vine, and we are the branches. The life of the vine and of the branches is one and the same life. It is incumbent upon us to open our life to Him, to stir up in our hearts a longing for Him. We are bound to remove all obstacles that might hinder Him when He seeks to enter our hearts with His grace at Christmas time and at Holy Communion. "He hath filled the hungry with good things; and the rich He hath sent empty away" (Lk 1:53).

Prayer

Thou wilt turn, O God, and bring us to life, and Thy people shall rejoice in Thee. Show us, O Lord, Thy mercy, and grant us Thy salvation. (Offertory.)

We beseech Thee, O Lord, spare us through our humble works and prayers; and since of ourselves we deserve nothing, grant us Thy protection. Through Christ our Lord. Amen. (Secreta.)

The Immaculate Conception

Vigil of the Immaculate Conception

"Who is she that cometh forth as the morning rising, fair as the moon, bright as the sun, terrible as an army set in array?" (Communion.) The dawn of redemption now appears in the person of Mary Immaculate. We greet her with joy. "I will put enmities between thee and the woman and thy seed and her seed; she shall crush thy head" (Gn 3:15).

"Wisdom hath built herself a house" in Mary Immaculate. "She hath hewn her out seven pillars" (Gradual). They are the seven pillars of virtue and grace — the three theological virtues of faith, hope, and charity, and the four cardinal virtues: wisdom, justice, fortitude, and prudence. "The foundations thereof are in the holy mountains." Our Lord's whole human existence, work, and suffering were established by Him on a holy mountain in the person of Mary Immaculate, since He chose her as His mother and condescended to take His human nature through her. Mary is the holy mountain which towers immeasurably over all the other mountains and hills, men and the angels. Indeed, "The Lord loveth the gates of Sion above all the tabernacles of Jacob" (Gradual). He has greater love for Mary and does more for her than for anyone else, be it angel or man. Mary is to be His mother. We rejoice because of the greatness that God has bestowed upon our beloved mother.

"As the vine I have brought forth a pleasant odor, and my flowers are the fruit of honor and riches. I am the mother of fair love, and of fear, and of knowledge, and of holy hope. In me is all grace of the way and of the truth; in me is all hope of life and virtue. Come over to me all ye that desire me, and be filled with my fruits; for my spirit is sweet above honey, and my inheritance above honey and the honeycomb. My memory is unto everlasting generations. They that eat me shall yet hunger; and they that drink me shall yet thirst. He that hearkeneth to me shall not be confounded; and they that work by me shall not sin. They that explain me shall have life everlasting" (Epistle).

Mary is the house which eternal Wisdom has built for itself, and the vine that brings forth wonderful fruit. She has brought forth Christ and His salvation. "Come and hear, all ye that fear God" (Introit). We shall go to Mary to see her and to find in her Jesus, our God and our all. "Who is she that cometh forth as the morning rising, fair as the moon, bright as the sun, terrible as an army set in array?" Thus the Church speaks of her in the Communion prayer of today's Mass. Mary Immaculate is the dawn; through her, the most pure one, we have the Eucharist and Holy Communion.

"The foundations thereof are in the holy mountains." When God sought a habitation for Himself, he wished that it be pure. What should He find if He were to take up His abode in my soul today in Holy Communion? I will turn to my most pure mother, that she may establish me in purity.

"The foundations thereof are in the holy mountains." What will He find when, at the end of time, He comes to call us to the abode of light and holiness in the heavenly Sion? In heaven there is holiness unalloyed. Nothing unclean can ever enter there. How pure and how holy must also be the advent of our earthly life if we seek to enjoy the blessed Christmas of heaven!

Prayer

O God, who in a wonderful way didst preserve the mother of Thy only-begotten Son from all taint of Original Sin, grant, we beseech Thee, that, strengthened by her prayers and being made clean of heart, we may devoutly assist in the keeping of her holy festival. Through Christ our Lord. Amen.

Feast of the Immaculate Conception

The liturgy places the beautiful feast of the Immaculate Conception in the middle of the Advent season. In the person of Mary, the sun of the redemption and salvation dawns, and through her Christmas is brought to us. Through her, Christ the Son of God announces His coming.

"Thou art all fair, O Mary, and the stain of Original Sin is not in thee" (Alleluia verse). Since we are children of Adam, the moment we are conceived we contract the guilt of Original Sin. From the first moment of our existence we are children of wrath, an object of abhorrence to God. Original sin has made us so ugly, so hateful, and so worthless, that its defilement has covered our whole soul and our whole person. Mary has been preserved from all this. From the first moment of her existence she was full of grace, perfectly pure and holy, and most pleasing to God in her heavenly beauty and holiness. She alone of all mankind has been preserved from the stain of Original Sin. She is the spotless lily, full of purity and light. "Thou art all fair, O Mary, and the stain of Original Sin is not in thee. Thy vesture is white as snow; and thy face is as the sun. Thou art the glory of Jerusalem [the Church]; thou art the joy of Israel; thou art the honor of our people" (Antiphons at Vespers). "There is no defilement in her; she is a ray of the eternal sun, a mirror without spot; she is brighter than the sun, whiter than snow" (Responsory at Matins). So also must each one be in whom God will take up His abode; bright, pure, spotless, a clear mirror of the glory and holiness of God. God comes only to the pure.

"I will greatly rejoice in the Lord" (Introit). Joyfully we add our prayers of thanksgiving to those the Church sends up to the throne of God in thanksgiving for Mary's Immaculate Conception. Her gratitude is ours also. We realize that the immaculate Mother, like ourselves, is a member of the mystical body. Her purity, her abundant grace, her virtues, belong also to us. She has received this immense treasure, not so much for her own benefit as for that of her children and for that of the entire mystical body. By reason of her stainless and matchless purity she dared to conceive the Son of God. By virtue of her Immaculate Conception, this second Eve, the spotless helpmate of the second Adam, shared with her Son in the work of redemption and helped us to obtain the mercy of God, forgiveness for our sins, and temporal and eternal salvation. All the spiritual favors we obtain from God come to us through Christ and His blessed mother.

Mary's Immaculate Conception, her purity, and her abundant graces, therefore, belong also to us who are members of the mystical body of Christ. Since we are united to her through the mystical body, we may truly sing with her and with the Church: "I will greatly rejoice in the Lord, and my soul shall be joyful in my God; for He hath clothed me with the garments of salvation, and with the robe of justice He hath covered me, as a bridegroom decked with a crown, and as a bride adorned with her jewels" (Introit).

"Thou art all fair, O Mary, and the stain of Original Sin is not in thee." "Hail Mary, full of grace, the Lord is with thee; blessed art thou among women" (Offertory).

Hail Mary, full of grace, holier than the saints, more exalted than the heavens, more glorious than the cherubim, more honorable than the seraphim, and of all creatures the most worthy of veneration. Hail, O dove, who brings to us the fruit of the olive and announces to us a Savior from the spiritual deluge and a harbor of safety.... Hail, glorious paradise of God, planted today in the East by His most benevolent and omnipotent hand,... and producing the matchless rose for the cure of those who have drunk the destructive and bitter potion of death.[2]

"Thou art all fair, O Mary." The soul that is to be the dwelling place of God must indeed be pure. "Holiness becometh Thy house, O Lord" (Ps 92:5). Purity, holiness, and sanctifying grace are the things that have value in the sight of God. The position we hold in life, earthly greatness, bodily beauty, the esteem of men, honor and earthly glory, all these have little importance in the eyes of God. "Draw us to thee, O immaculate Virgin." We long for purity. Grant us purity, O pure Virgin.

Prayer

O God, who by the Immaculate Conception of the Virgin, didst make ready a worthy dwelling place for Thy Son: grant, we beseech Thee, that, as through the foreseen death of the same Son, Thou didst preserve His mother from all stain of sin, so may we likewise be pure in heart through her intercession and may come to Thee. Through the same Jesus Christ Thy Son, our Lord. Amen.

[2] St. Germanus; lesson at Matins.

First Day in the Octave

"Thou art all fair, O Mary, and the stain of Original Sin is not in thee, alleluia." Thus sings the Church today, and gratefully we join our voices to hers.

"The Lord possessed me in the beginning of His ways, before He made anything, from the beginning" (Epistle). Mary is likewise contained in the eternal Wisdom, who is to become man in time, who adorns her with His person, His purity, and His glory, and is most intimately united with her in His work on earth. God ordained the creation of Mary with the same act by which He willed the Incarnation of His Son. "The Lord possessed me in the beginning of His ways." God chose Mary from all eternity as the one from whom His Son, the eternal Wisdom, was to take His sacred humanity. By virtue of this intimate union with divine Wisdom and divine purity, she is herself possessed of unlimited purity, wisdom, and holiness.

In the liturgy she is presented to our wondering eyes clothed with divine wisdom, as the Seat of Wisdom. "Now, therefore, ye children, hear me.... Blessed is the man that heareth me, and that watcheth daily at my gates, and waiteth at the posts of my doors. He that shall find me shall find life, and shall have salvation from the Lord" (Epistle).

In today's liturgy Mary is the woman of fortitude who will crush the head of the serpent and will overcome singlehanded the ancient enemy of the Church and of the kingdom of God. Mary is the Judith of the new chosen people. She it is who rescues beleaguered souls from the hand of Holofernes. With hearts filled with joy and gratitude, we greet her on the day of her triumph over Satan and Original Sin. "Blessed art thou, O Virgin Mary, above all women upon the earth. Thou art the glory of Jerusalem, thou art the joy of Israel" (Gradual). Today thou shalt crush the head of the vile serpent who rages against thy Son and His people. We fly to thy patronage, O immaculate and victorious Virgin.

The liturgy presents Mary to us as full of grace. "At that time the angel Gabriel was sent from God into a city of Galilee, called Nazareth, to a virgin espoused to a man whose name was Joseph, of the house of David; and the virgin's name was Mary. And the angel being come in, said unto her: Hail, full of grace, the Lord is with thee: blessed art thou among women" (Gospel). "Full of grace." "He hath clothed me with the garments of salvation, and with the robe of justice He hath covered me, as the bride adorned with her jewels" (Introit). From the first moment of her conception she is enriched with more grace than the most highly favored angel or archangel in heaven. Richer in grace and more resplendent with supernatural beauty than the holiest of the saints of the Church, is this immaculate mother of ours. "Thou art all fair, O Mary."

"The stream of the river [the fullness of grace] maketh the city of God [Mary] joyful; the Most High hath sanctified His own tabernacle. God is in the midst thereof, it shall not be moved; God will help it in the early morning [at her conception].... Come and behold ye the works of the Lord, what wonders He hath done upon earth [in Mary] making wars to cease even to the end of the earth. He shall destroy the bow and break the weapons [Satan and Original Sin], and the shield He shall burn in the fire. Be still and see that I am God. I will be exalted among the nations, and I will be exalted in the earth. The Lord of armies is with us [in Mary]; the God of Jacob is our protector" (Ps 45:5 ff.).

Purity is union with God. Purity is the strength that brings victory. Purity is the most precious of graces. "Blessed are the clean of heart" (Mt 5:8). "Draw us, O immaculate Virgin."

Prayer

O God, who by the Immaculate Conception of the Virgin, didst make ready a worthy dwelling place for Thy Son: grant, we beseech Thee, that, as through the foreseen death of the same Son, Thou didst preserve His mother from all stain of sin, so may we likewise be pure in heart through her intercession and may come to Thee. Through the same Jesus Christ Thy Son, our Lord. Amen.

Second Day in the Octave

The mystery of the Virgin Mother which gives us the Redeemer at Christmas is based on the Immaculate Conception and on purity. Christmas demands pure hearts and pure intentions.

"O God, who by the Immaculate Conception of the Virgin, didst make ready a worthy dwelling place for Thy Son" (Collect). Mary, who was worthy to be a dwelling place for God, is free from all personal sin, from all inordinate inclinations. She was not merely cleansed immediately after her conception, but she is exempt from all stain from the first moment of her existence. "I will put enmities between thee and the woman" (Gn 3:15). Thus Mary, stainless in her purity and heavenly in her beauty, from the first moment of her existence was a worthy habitation for the most high God. The Lord comes to the pure. Christmas demands pure hearts.

"Thou art all fair, O Mary." Mary's soul was enlightened by the light of purity, her will was perfectly united to God's will, her heart was free from every inordinate inclination and desire. She had the greatest dread of all sin, the most ardent love of every virtue, the most intimate union with God, and a complete forgetfulness of self. "Thou art all fair, O Mary, and the stain of Original Sin is not in thee." "Hail, full of grace." Because thou art pure, thou art full of grace; because thou art full of grace, the Lord is with thee, and thou art blessed among women. Hail, Mary, for through thee we possess purity, life, salvation, Christ, and heaven. Fruitful purity!

"Blessed are the clean of heart, for they shall see God." They shall see God at Christmas time, in their daily Holy Communion, and in the uninterrupted union of their soul with His. Their vision of God will be complete and perfect when their eyes close upon this world and open upon the eternal life beyond. "They shall see God."

Advent and Christmas require purity of heart in us. "I will put enmities between thee [Satan, sin] and the woman." This applies to us and to the Church as well as to Eve and Mary. We swore such enmity in baptism when we said, "I renounce Satan." We then swore enmity, unremitting enmity, to Satan, sin, and the world.

God wills to take up His abode in our souls at Christmas. He seeks a worthy dwelling place such as He prepared for Himself by Mary's Immaculate Conception. Am I such a dwelling place? Mary Immaculate, be thou our model and ideal.

Mary is also our most powerful intercessor. We should beseech her to obtain from God for us the graces necessary to make us worthy dwelling places for the Lord who is coming. In the Mass of the feast we pray: "Grant, we beseech Thee, that ... we may likewise be pure in heart through her intercession and may come unto Thee." Mary is our mediator. We go to her to obtain the grace to become ever more pure and holy in thought and work, so that we may look forward with joy and confidence to Christ's coming on the Day of Judgment.

Prayer

Deliver us from our sins, O Lord, and let us come unto Thee with pure souls, through Christ our Lord. Amen.

Third Day in the Octave

With Holy Mother the Church, we exclaim in admiration: "Thou art all fair. Thy vesture is white as snow, and thy face is as the sun. Blessed art thou, O Virgin Mary, by the Lord, the most high God, above all women upon the earth. Draw us, O immaculate Virgin; we will run after thee in the odor of thy ointments" (Antiphons at Vespers).

"The things that are contemptible hath God chosen,... that He might bring to nought things that are" (1 Cor 1:28). Men place great importance on talent, intelligence, art, and invention; God prizes more the possession of sanctifying grace, union with God, and supernatural riches. Before God the great are they who are pure of heart, free from inordinate passions and desires. They are great in the sight of God who are children of God and are rich in virtue, faith, and love, as Mary was. We become truly great before God when Christ lives in us and we in Him. Our greatness depends on our being branches of the tree, Christ, having one will, one spirit, and one love with Him. "The Lord is with thee," and therefore "blessed art thou among women." "Behold from henceforth all generations shall call me blessed" (Lk 1:48). Draw us to thee, O Virgin Mary, and bring us to that true greatness, greatness before God.

"Full of grace." Mary is the acme of human greatness and beauty because of the plenitude of her graces and the perfection of her union with God. "Thou art all fair." Her beauty consists in the perfect harmony between her soul and her body, her heart and her spirit, her will and her affections, her nature and her grace. Mary, full of all grace, is the new man in whom there is nothing wanting, whose soul and body are perfectly formed, and in whose thoughts, desires, and character there is no defect. Hers is a beauty and perfection without blemish, a beauty and perfection never before found in man. Grace perfects and elevates our nature in that way. "Thou art all fair, O Mary. Draw us, O immaculate Virgin."

Yet men place so much importance in mere human greatness. We should strive rather for supernatural greatness, and seek to excel in faith, in grace, and in union with God. "Seek ye therefore first the kingdom of God and His justice [that is, be justified in the eyes of God], and all these things shall be added unto you" (Mt 6:33). "Draw us, O immaculate Virgin." Thou wilt lead us to that true greatness, union with God.

"But the foolish things of the world hath God chosen, that He may confound the wise; and the weak things of the world hath God chosen, that He may confound the strong. And the base things of the world and the things that are contemptible hath God chosen, and things that are not, that He might bring to nought things that are" (1 Cor 1:27–28). Yet we shun these things that God has chosen, that seem foolish in the eyes of the world. We fear being forgotten; we dread to be thought unimportant; we shrink from being despised. How unenlightened we still are! "Draw us, O immaculate Virgin." Pray for us, most wise Virgin, that we may be wise.

In these references to Mary we may also see the Church, the deep interior life of our Holy Mother the Church, despised and held in contempt by the world. "And the base things of the world and the things that are contemptible, hath God chosen, and the things that are not, that He might bring to nought things that are." Her very existence is greatness before God. Her promise of life is, "The Lord is with thee." Heal us, O Lord, who acknowledge and love her as our mother, and who live and love, trust and pray, and sacrifice with her.

Prayer

Hail Mary, full of grace, the Lord is with thee; blessed art thou among women, and blessed is the fruit of thy womb, Jesus. Holy Mary, Mother of God, pray for us sinners now and at the hour of our death. Amen.

Fourth Day in the Octave

In the Collect for the feast we pray: "through the foreseen death of Thy Son, Thou didst preserve His mother from all stain of sin." We should meditate on these words.

Mary's Immaculate Conception is the first fruits of the redemption and of Christ's death on the cross. She has been redeemed in a different and much more perfect sense than we were. Original sin poisoned our existence from the first moment of our life and destined us for hell. In baptism, through the infinite mercy of God, this sin is taken away. Mary was preserved from all such sin. The vile stain of Original Sin, which made every other child of Adam abhorrent to God, would also have affected Mary had not the infinite power and mercy of God preserved her from it. In this way Mary was preserved from all stain through a special privilege of God. We rejoice exceedingly that Mary was redeemed in this singular way, and we congratulate her on the great things that grace has accomplished in her. We admire the power and wisdom and love of God as reflected in the soul of Mary.

Mary is the first and most noble fruit of the redeeming death of Christ. Her Immaculate Conception means her preservation from the stain of Original Sin and from some of its sad consequences. Our souls are freed from this sin by baptism, and thus we escape eternal punishment. We, too, are redeemed; but in us the consequences of that sin remain. And how heavily they weigh upon us! Our understanding is obscured in its search for truth, hampered particularly in its search for truth in matters of religion; we are so easily led into error. The will is sluggish in the performance of good works, and ever inclined toward evil; it shrinks from discipline, sacrifices, and struggle, and is pitifully weak in time of temptation. Besides, our evil inclinations obstruct grace and the guidance of reason, and lead men into countless sins. So powerful was the working of grace in Mary that she was spared all this. Is there, then, any child of Adam more glorious and more pure and fair than she?

In the Immaculate Conception of Mary the liturgy shows us what the Redeemer, who is to come at Christmas, will work in our souls also. We shall be freed from sin, made safe from error, and liberated from the spiritual weakness that has overtaken us. We shall find the grace we need to overcome our evil desires and inclinations. Therefore we pray in today's Mass: "As through the foreseen death of Thy Son, Thou didst preserve His mother from all stain of sin, so may we likewise be pure in heart through her intercession and may come to Thee."

"Draw us, O immaculate Virgin." We are still completely under the tyranny of sin and its consequences; but draw us that we may faithfully respond to the grace of God and obtain perfect purity.

PRAYER

O Lord, as through Thy prevenient grace Mary was preserved from all stain, so through her intercession may we be freed from all sins. Through Christ our Lord. Amen. (Secreta.)

Fifth Day in the Octave

As the priest and the faithful are receiving Holy Communion, the liturgy greets the immaculate Mother with the words: "Glorious things are said of thee, O Mary; for He who is mighty hath done great things unto thee" (Communion). As we receive Holy Communion the liturgy sees in us another Virgin of Nazareth blessed by God.

"Glorious things are said of thee, O Mary." She was immaculately conceived and by the grace of God was endowed with an unclouded intellect and preserved from all evil inclinations and from weakness of will. To this singular privilege was added the fullness of grace and the gifts of the Holy Ghost: understanding, wisdom, knowledge, justice, prudence, temperance, and the fear of God. She had also the gift of prayer, spiritual insight, and perfect love and faith. All this was crowned by her being chosen the Mother of God. Mary is indeed the stainless one, full of grace, destined to become the Mother of God by the message brought to her by the angel. In obedience and humility she spoke her fiat: "And the Word was made flesh and dwelt among us." Indeed, glorious things are said of thee, O Mary, and the Lord hath done great things unto thee.

In the liturgy Mary is the symbol of the Christian soul. What it says of her in the Communion prayer of the Mass, it says also of me when I receive Communion: Glorious things are said of thee, O Christian soul. Thou art, like Mary, a temple of the Most High; like Mary, a second Virgin of Nazareth. The Almighty hath done great things unto thee. As a pledge of His love and blessing He has sent you His only Son. "Hath He not also with Him given us all things?" (Rom 8:32.) In Christ He has given us the forgiveness of sin and the strength to live our lives in purity, virtue, and holiness. He has given us the assurance of victory over evil, the right to unlimited grace, and He has made us coheirs with His saints to the treasures of His love. Glorious things are planned for thee, O Christian soul. Holy Communion is the pledge and the source of all the rich blessings promised to you.

The Church in her liturgy looks upon the Christian soul as another Virgin of Nazareth each time it receives Holy Communion. Let us consider seriously what that means. Let us meditate on Mary. When I receive Holy Communion, I should be like her in my desires, my thoughts, my affections, and my works. I should be pure, stainless, and devoted to God as she is. How miserably I fail in all this!

What should the frequent reception of Holy Communion accomplish in my soul? Let us consider the Virgin of Nazareth after she had conceived the divine child. She was absorbed in a life of prayer, humility, patience, and suffering. And we? What causes the difference? Certainly it cannot be the fault of our divine guest, who wishes to do great things to us. No, the fault must be our own.

"Glorious things are said of Thee," O holy Church, O Christian soul. "Come, ye blessed of My Father, possess you the kingdom prepared for you from the foundation of the world" (Mt 25:34). O blessed day of the coming of the Lord! He offers to the Church and to all of us the perfect and eternal possession and enjoyment of God, a blessed, eternal, perfectly satisfying participation in the pure, holy life of God. Come O Lord, give us Thy salvation in the endless communion of eternal life.

Prayer

Inviolate and inviolable and all pure art thou, O Mary, shining gate of heaven. O exalted mother of Christ, mother most beloved, graciously accept our praise. We fly to thee with heart and mind; make us pure in body and soul. Through thy all-powerful intercession obtain for us mercy, O beloved queen, O Mary free of all stain. Hail Mary, full of grace, the Lord is with thee.

Sixth Day in the Octave

"I will greatly rejoice in the Lord, and my soul shall be joyful in my God" (Introit). Thus the Church rejoices when contemplating the Immaculate Conception. "Glorious things are said of thee, O Mary; for He who is mighty hath done great things unto thee" (Communion).

On December 8, 1854, Pope Pius IX declared to the universal Church: "The doctrine which teaches that the Blessed Virgin Mary in the first instant of her conception, by a singular privilege and grace granted by God in view of the merits of Jesus Christ, was preserved exempt from all stain of Original Sin, is revealed by God and is a dogma of faith for all the faithful." Mary owes this singular privilege to the merits of the death of her Son as foreseen by God. She, like ourselves, was redeemed by Christ's death; that is, redeemed in the sense that she was preserved from Original Sin in virtue of His death. She was free not only of Original Sin, but also of all personal sin throughout her life. She was perfectly pure in all her thoughts, feelings, inclinations, and desires. Since she was preserved from the sin of Adam, she was a virgin in body and in spirit. "This gate shall be shut. It shall not be opened and no man shall pass through it, because the Lord, the God of Israel hath entered in by it, and it shall be shut for the Prince. The Prince Himself shall sit in it" (the womb of the Virgin) (Ez 44:2 f.).

Since she was without sin, she was restored to life a few days after her death and was taken up into heaven. "And a great sign appeared in heaven: a woman clothed with the sun, and the moon under her feet, and on her head a crown of twelve stars" (Apoc 12:1). She is the one who has overcome sin, Satan, death, and the world. "I will put enmities between thee and the woman, and ... she shall crush thy head" (Gn 3:15; Benedictus antiphon). Indeed, "glorious things are said of thee, O Mary." We rejoice in the belief of the Church. "He who is mighty hath done great things unto thee."

The Church today makes a single moving plea, a plea for purity. She prays for purity in the Collect, the Secreta, and the Postcommunion. The Church is not satisfied with praising and admiring the virtues of Mary; we must indeed strive to reproduce in ourselves the spirit and the virtues of her whom we admire, love, and venerate. The liturgy leads us even further;

it recognizes in the immaculate Virgin a powerful intermediary who pleads the cause of her impure and sinful children before the most pure God. The moment our prayers reach God, she joins to them her intercession. Thus our prayers reach the ears of God, not from the lips of unworthy sinners, but from the lips of our pure and stainless mother. Thus the liturgy lives in the conviction that on the feast of the Immaculate Conception this wonder shall be accomplished, that we sinners, too, "may be pure in heart through her intercession and may come" to God pure and unsullied (Collect). It believes, too, that "through her intercession we may be freed from all sins" (Secreta) and that "the sacrament which we have received [will] repair in us the wounds of that sin from which Thou didst in a singular manner preserve the Immaculate Conception of Blessed Mary" (Postcommunion).

In virtue of this feast, the Church and every soul which by degrees clothes itself in the resplendent garment of that purity, will reflect the beauty and splendor which is so remarkable in the Immaculate Conception. The wounds made by Original Sin shall be healed; the concupiscence of the eyes, the concupiscence of the flesh, and the pride of life, will be destroyed in us on the feast of the Immaculate Conception. Thus the Church believes and prays. Our life, too, our prayers, and our works should be based on this conviction.

The Church must be pure. It is the virgin bride of Christ. Her garment is purity and sanctity. She is to be pure, not only as an ideal and in her glorified members in heaven, but also as an organism on earth and in all her members, particularly in consecrated souls. She must also be pure in me, and that is why she prays so persistently for this holy virtue.

Purity is the ideal of the Church. We must make our ideals and our life conform to those of the Church, particularly now as Christmas approaches. Christ will come to pure, virgin souls, and they will be a delightful Bethlehem for Him.

Prayer

May the sacraments which we have received, O Lord our God, repair in us the wounds of that sin from which Thou didst in a singular manner preserve the Immaculate Conception of Blessed Mary. Through Christ our Lord. Amen. (Postcommunion.)

Octave of the Immaculate Conception

"My soul doth magnify the Lord.... Because He that is mighty hath done great things to me, and holy is His name" (Lk 1:46, 49). "I will greatly rejoice in the Lord, and my soul shall be joyful in my God: for He hath clothed me with the garments of salvation, and with the robe of justice He hath covered me, as a bride adorned with her jewels" (Introit).

Mary's first prerogative is declared to us by the liturgy in the words of St. Epiphanius:

With the exception of God alone, Mary stands above all others; she is more grand by nature than the cherubim and seraphim themselves and all the angelic army; no heavenly or earthly tongue is in the least able to praise her, not even the tongue of angels. O Blessed Virgin, pure dove and heavenly spouse; Mary, heaven, temple, and throne of the Divinity, who hast Christ, the Sun radiant in heaven and on earth!... The Virgin is an immaculate lily, who begot an undying rose, Christ.... Marvelous is the miracle in the heavens, the bridal chamber of a virgin bearing the Son of God.... The Lord of angels has become the infant of a virgin.... Hail, full of grace, a virgin adorned with many virtues. Hail, full of grace, you are a golden vessel containing heavenly manna. Hail, full of grace, you satisfy the thirsty by the sweetness of an everlasting fountain. Hail, most holy Mother Immaculate, you have given birth to Christ, who was before you. Hail, royal robe of purple which clothed the King of heaven and earth. Hail, unfathomable book, you have produced the Word to be read by the world, the Son of God.

Mary's prerogative. Mary knew no pride, she had no disorderly trust in her own will and ability. From the moment of her conception, Mary was endowed with an abundance of all graces, but the plan of the all-knowing God concerning Mary requires a special grace, the deepest humility, a grace of complete trust in Him, a grace of watchfulness, foresight, and seclusion. Amazing wonder on earth! Mary knows no pride. She is perfectly humble and aware of her own nothingness, completely forgetful of self. Elizabeth reminds her of her high calling, "Blessed art thou." But Mary turns to the Lord, "My soul doth magnify the Lord.... Because He that is mighty hath done great things to me." Nothing for herself, nothing from herself; all for God, all from Him. To Him be all praise; for herself only the recognition of her own frailty and nothingness, and therefore that mistrust in self, the drawing back, the flight. In such a soul grace can take root and grow.

Today we praise her in the liturgy, saying: "Hail Mary, full of grace, the Lord is with thee; blessed art thou among women" (Offertory). By the abundance of grace which was given her, Mary believes that she can be faithful to grace only by watchfulness, retirement, and renunciation. And we? Do we not possess great riches of grace? Are we humble enough to protect this treasure and make it possible for more grace to enter our souls?

Mary knows no pride, no self-conceit, no self-presumption, no great spiritual hallucination. And we? Not without reason has the great author of *The Spiritual Combat*, Scupoli, said: "If a soul had such great mistrust of herself as Mary had, it would persevere in grace without ever committing the slightest fault."

Prayer

O Mary conceived without sin, pray for us who flee to thy protection.

Mother of our Redeemer, give us the Savior who will free us from sin, who will protect us from ourselves, from our inborn pride, from our self-presumption; who will cleanse us and keep us clean.

Hail Mary, full of grace, the Lord is with thee.

December 13, St. Lucy

St. Lucy is a figure of Advent. She looks for the coming of the bridegroom, whom she cherishes. She awaits Him anxiously; she hastens to meet Him with the lamp of love in her hand. "We should live soberly and justly and godly in this world, looking for the blessed hope and coming of the great God and our Savior Jesus Christ" (Ti 2:12 f.).

St. Lucy made a pilgrimage with her sick mother to the grave of St. Agatha. Her mother recovered her health, and in gratitude St. Lucy begged her mother to be allowed to live as a virgin and to distribute her possessions to the poor. When she had returned to her native city, Syracuse, she sold all that she possessed and gave it to the needy. She renounced marriage with a man to whom she had been promised against her will. The disappointed suitor accused her to the authorities for being a Christian. In 304 A.D. she suffered martyrdom without flinching.

This blessed martyr withdrew from everything that did not come from her beloved bridegroom, Christ. "Thou hast loved justice and hated iniquity" (Introit). Thou hast given up everything that does not come from Him, or which might hinder thy approach to Him.

In the sacred liturgy St. Lucy is a type and a symbol of Holy Mother the Church and of the Christian soul. With St. Lucy the Church and the soul of man advance to meet the heavenly bridegroom, through the reception of Holy Communion, at the moment of death, and finally in the Last Judgment. St. Lucy, and with her the Church and the soul of man, has lifted her gaze from purely temporal affairs to contemplate the things of heaven. She is concerned now with her union with God, with her betrothal with Christ, with the kingdom of grace and holiness, and with the time of her eternal nuptials with Jesus, her beloved. She has understood that the kingdom of God is like a hidden treasure, for which a man, discovering it, will dispose of all that he has that he may buy it. She knows that the kingdom of heaven is the priceless pearl which a man should acquire at the cost of all his other possessions (Gospel).

May St. Lucy be our model in her eagerness to sacrifice her life for Christ, in the impetuosity of her search for betrothal with Christ. "After her shall virgins be brought to the king" (Offertory). In the Offertory of the Mass, St. Lucy leads the chorus of virgins to the King. By this group of virgins is meant the Church and all Christian souls. At the hour of sacrifice we wish to be offered with St. Lucy as a sacrifice of love. And the offering we make of ourselves during the Mass should be continued in the trials, sufferings, and exertions of the day. Today we wish to be offered to almighty God, together with St. Lucy and with Christ the King of martyrs, as a holocaust of love. "Thou hast loved justice and hated iniquity." I must be another St. Lucy; that must be the true inspiration of the present feast.

Free from all earthly attachments, we hasten forward with St. Lucy and with Holy Mother the Church, in this advent period of our earthly life, to meet the bridegroom who is approaching. For He is the hidden treasure, the priceless pearl. No one else and nothing else has any value or attraction in our eyes. "I count all things to be but loss for the excellent knowledge of Jesus Christ my Lord; for whom I have suffered the loss of all things, and count them but as dung, that I may gain Christ" (Phil 3:8).

Prayer

Graciously hear us, O God of our salvation, and grant that we who keep with rejoicing the festival of blessed Lucy, Thy virgin and martyr, may profit by the devout fervor we feel in so doing. Through Christ our Lord. Amen.

Third Sunday of Advent[3]

The Mass

The spirit of the season progresses with the third Sunday of Advent. We no longer hear, "The Lord shall come," but rather, "The Lord is nigh." The liturgy now releases its pent-up spirit in childlike joy. It seems that the Christmas bells are already ringing. The liturgy of the Mass is filled with psalms of the redemption. Psalm 84 is frequently used, and we find it especially in the Introit and the Offertory. The rose-colored vestments breathe a spirit of joy.

"The Lord is nigh." This thought is the guiding motif of today's Mass as well as that of the Ember days which occur during the week. Clearly and definitely the Introit announces the theme, "Rejoice in the Lord always.... The Lord is nigh." Do not be sad, but in prayer cast all your sorrow on Him. He is nigh as the Savior and Redeemer. "Thou hast blessed Thy land; Thou hast turned away the captivity of Jacob" (Introit). Thou hast visited Thy people who were languishing in the captivity of Babylon. He who in former days was born a Redeemer in Bethlehem, will at His second coming "reform the body of our lowness, made like to the body of His glory" (Phil 3:21). "Maran-antha" — come, O Lord (1 Cor 16:22); thus the Christians prayed to God in former times. Today we pray in a similar spirit in the Kyrie and the Collect: "Incline Thy ear to our prayers, we beseech Thee, O Lord, and enlighten the darkness of our minds by the grace of Thy visitation," which we now await.

The Epistle repeats with assurance, "The Lord is nigh." At the same time it teaches us how we should be disposed toward the coming of our redeeming God. In the first place, we should have kindness and love for all our neighbors. We should withdraw our hearts from all miserable worldly concerns, and let our soul dwell on God. Finally, our mind and heart should be transformed by the blessed peace of God. "O Lord, stir up Thy might and come" (Gradual). Behold, He comes, He is very near. Already He is made known by His herald, John the Baptist. The voice of John at the Jordan is so insistent that it has stirred Jerusalem. Such crowds of people come to John that the government is obliged to send officers to keep order. John clearly declares his mission to the world. Now it must be evident to everyone that the Lord is nigh.

He is nigh; yes, He "stands in the midst of you" now in the Holy Sacrifice of the Mass. We await Him and we possess Him, the Savior and the Redeemer. "Rejoice in the Lord always; again I say, rejoice.... The Lord is nigh" (Introit). Already He abides among us. He abides among us in the person of His forerunner, who acknowledges himself unworthy to loosen the latchet of His shoe (Gospel). At length He appears to us in person. "Rejoice in the Lord." It is imperative that we free ourselves from all worldly thoughts and fix our attention on Him. At so important a moment we should not be occupied with excessive solicitude about the things of this world, but should keep our attention fixed on Him who stands in our midst. "Through Him and with Him and in Him, all honor and glory is given unto Thee, O God," but to us every means of salvation and grace.

[3] Meditations on the "O" antiphons, which occur in the office of Vespers from December 17 to December 23, are given on, pp 57–65.

"The Lord is nigh." He comes into our very soul in Holy Communion. In our admiration of the humility of the Baptist, we may wonder about our own worthiness to receive Him. But the Church says "to the fainthearted: Take courage and fear not. Behold our God will come and will save us" (Communion). The petition which we made to God in the Gradual, "Stir up Thy might and come," has been heard. Our desire is fulfilled; we are redeemed. His coming in Bethlehem some two thousand years ago is now to be repeated in our soul. Our souls have become another Bethlehem.

Meditation

The stational church for this Sunday is that of St. Peter in Rome. Here Peter established his see, and where Peter is, there is Christ also. "The Lord is nigh," and we are not lost. We have nothing to fear but our own weakness, our own unworthiness and sinfulness. We have a Redeemer who will satisfy for our past sins. The Lord is nigh and is always concerned about the work of our salvation and sanctification.

"Rejoice in the Lord" (Introit). The spirit most characteristic of the Christian is joy. When he was made a child of God on the day of his baptism, the Church prayed "that he may joyfully serve Thee in Thy Church." In a sense, then, the Christian is commanded to be joyful. Joy is the badge of his state of life, the pledge of his lasting incorporation in Christ. Why should the Christian be sad? Hath not God "with Him given us all things?" (Rom 8:32.) Through baptism and the possession of sanctifying grace a man becomes a member of the true vine, which is Christ, and a child of God. Our heavenly Father takes us gently by the hand and leads us on. He keeps us in His infallible truth. He strengthens us in Holy Communion; He gives us the promise of eternal happiness to come. From God we have the privilege of Holy Communion, the guarantee of infallible truth, and the promise of an eternal and blessed life in the home of the Father. Should we not rejoice in the Lord our Redeemer?

"Rejoice in the Lord always." Always rejoice, even in grief and sorrow, in care and solicitude, in difficulties and trials, and in all the trying tasks of this present life. "To them that love God, all things work together unto good" (Rom 8:28). Labor and effort are essential if we are to attain to a holy life, growth in grace, and eternal blessedness. Suffering, too, we may expect — suffering with Christ, who by His own suffering makes ours fruitful. Christ fights with us and in us, that through us He may conquer Satan, and that by Him we may gain eternal happiness. Our own poverty of soul should teach us to distrust our own strength. Our past failures should make us turn to Him when our virtue is tested. "To them that love God, all things work together unto good," the good of our salvation.

"The Lord is nigh." No man can bear the sufferings and trials of life alone. When we view the forces arrayed against us, the prospect is frightening. But it need not be so if we understand our position. Once we have acquired membership in Christ, the Lord is nigh. We live by the life of Christ, our Redeemer, as children in the house of their father. Once we understand our union with our Lord and realize that His strength is our strength and that our cause is His cause, we shall have good reason to rejoice. He is as close to us as the vine is to its branches. He is our life. For one who has grasped this idea, there is no reason to be sad, no matter what dangers threaten. Every situation in life will find such a one rejoicing in the glory of the Lord (Phil 4:4; 1 Cor 1:31).

"The Lord is nigh." We are redeemed, and we have been incorporated into the mystical body of Christ. It would be strange to find in a Christian a consciousness of this incorporation in Christ and at the same time any kind of sadness or sorrow; the two are incompatible. Such a state of mind would show a lack of appreciation for what Christ has done for us, or a great indifference and ingratitude toward the Savior.

"The Lord is nigh." If we could only grasp this idea and regulate our lives by it! "May he serve Thee joyfully in Thy Church." Perhaps the reason we fail to reach this blessed state of mind is that we are so reluctant to separate ourselves from the specious joys of the world. The price of the peace and joy that Christ brings is mortification, death, sacrifice, and the renunciation of worldly pleasure.

Prayer

Incline Thy ear to our prayers, we beseech Thee, O Lord, and enlighten the darkness of our minds by the grace of Thy visitation. Amen.

Monday

The liturgy is aware how near God is and confidently reminds us: "Be nothing solicitous; but in everything, by prayer and supplication with thanksgiving, let your petitions be made known to God" (Epistle).

"Be nothing solicitous." A strange command! Are we, then, able to work out our own salvation? Is our eternal salvation assured? Do we not need the light and grace and guidance of God to be redeemed from a single grievous sin? Are we not always in danger of falling back into sin? We know that for every increase of grace, for every meritorious work, for every meager act of virtue, we must depend on the help of God. Indeed, our Lord has told us, "Without Me you can do nothing" (Jn 15:5). Grace must begin and perfect all things in us. Of ourselves we are unable to do any good whatsoever; and yet the liturgy tells us, "Be nothing solicitous." Why is this? "The Lord is nigh." He is here to redeem us and to give us the light and the strength that we need. Look upon Him, believe in His nearness, in His love, in His solicitude for you.

Unfortunately we are the more occupied with the thought of our own misery than we are with the mystery of God's love for us. Because we have our mind fixed on our own insufficiency rather than the powerful help that God offers us, we are sad. The contemplation of our own misery will bring us only confusion, discouragement, and regret. Such is certainly not the proper spirit for the season of Advent. Let us rather "be nothing solicitous."

In heartfelt prayers of thanksgiving and contrition we should make our petitions known to God. Such is the message of today's liturgy. Prayer is the all-powerful weapon that is placed in our hands. If we have need of anything whatsoever, we know that "the Lord is nigh." He is near with His love and His mercy. Therefore cast your solicitude on the Lord. The more miserable we are of ourselves, the more confidently we should turn to Him. The misery and wretchedness of our state prompts God to help us more readily. And the Lord, as the Introit tells us, will bless His land, His inheritance, and will free us from our captivity, our sorrow, our evil habits, and will lead us home. "The Lord is nigh."

"The Lord is nigh" to him who prays to the Lord with a clean heart, with humility and perseverance, and with trust in God. "Seek and you shall find, knock and it shall be opened to you" (Mt 7:7). The Lord is nigh in the celebration of the Mass. There He appears in our midst, the high priest and mediator, in order that we may put all our petitions into His priestly hands. He will present them to His heavenly Father and intercede for us. Let us cast all our solicitude on the Lord, who has offered Himself for us in the Mass. He is continually pleading in our behalf, and now He beseeches the Father in the celebration of the Holy Sacrifice. All the merit of His life and the satisfaction made to His Father on the cross are now again offered to God to obtain the graces we need.

Why, then, are you yet solicitous? If you resign yourself completely into His hands, and bury your fears and hopes in His heart, all will be well. "The Lord is nigh; be nothing solicitous."

PRAYER

Incline Thy ear to our prayers, we beseech Thee, O Lord, and enlighten the darkness of our minds by the grace of Thy visitation. Amen.

Tuesday

"Let your modesty be known to all men. The Lord is nigh" (Epistle). This is the urgent warning of the Introit and the Epistle of the Mass for the third Sunday of Advent.

"Let your modesty be known to all men." The Epistle admonishes us to express our joy outwardly by kindness toward all our fellow men. "Let your modesty be known to all men." By being kind to others we are only sharing with others the love Christ expressed for us by becoming man. The more we exert ourselves to attain union with God, the more difficult this fraternal charity becomes; for an intensive striving for God makes us more critical of others. We acquire new standards, to which we expect others to conform. We see, as it were, with sharpened vision, and we are, therefore, liable to form hasty and unkind opinions of others. We fail to understand the importance of winning the love of our fellow men by means of forbearance and love. Men immediately observe in us a definite coldness, an aloofness from our surroundings, a lack of interest, a certain amount of affectation, and a tendency to faultfinding — an unwarranted eagerness to teach and criticize others.

"Let your modesty be known to all men. Instead of criticizing others, we should let all men see and experience our goodness; we should be charitable in our thoughts and words. We must control our tongue, and when we are called upon to speak of others, we should call attention only to the good things they may have said and done. Let us, then, be charitable when we speak; let us always try to praise the virtues of others and excuse their faults, rather than indulge in petty criticism. Our own conduct, too, should be characterized by kindness. The third Sunday of Advent invites us to undertake this program of kindness.

"The Lord is nigh." He is near us by reason of His conception in the womb of the Virgin Mary. He is near us in the Mass and in Holy Communion, but we too easily forget that He is also present in our fellow man, even in the man whom we meet in the street. "There hath stood one in the midst of you whom you know not, . . . who is preferred before me [from all eternity], the latchet of whose shoe I am not worthy to loose" (Gospel). I may find Him in the people I meet during this day, in the men and women with whom I live and work. Unfortunately, I do not recognize Him; nevertheless, He does live in my fellow man as the head lives in the body and the vine lives in its branches.

Poor, blind creatures that we are, we observe only what is superficial; we see only flesh and blood, but miss the God who lives within. "As long as you did it to one of these, My least brethren, you did it to Me.... As long as you did it not to one of these least, neither did you do it to Me" (Mt 25:40, 45). How forgetful we are! If we had only the faith and spiritual vision of the early Christians. Their whole life was dominated by this thought: "If you see your brother, you see the Lord." If we could make this idea a part of our life, we should no longer be harsh, cold, and unsympathetic with our fellow men, but kind, gentle, and tolerant.

The Virgin who conceived the Son of God from that moment was completely dominated by the Spirit of God. She hastens at once to the mountain country to assist Elizabeth, her cousin, and to exercise herself in love and charity. The first fruit of Mary's charity and love is the sanctification of John the Baptist in his mother's womb.

"Let your modesty be known to all men. The Lord is nigh." He is nigh in our fellow men, who are members of Christ. Since He lives in us as the head lives in its members, He sees that His goodness and mildness becomes manifest in us also. The holy season of Advent demands of us a Christian life that is unselfish, charitable, and all-embracing, since Christ wishes to live in us and make His life manifest in us. How little we understand the nature of Christianity and the art of living with Christ in His Church! This condition is undoubtedly the result of our individualism, our narrowness and selfishness.

The liturgy of the third Sunday of Advent reminds us continually, "Let your modesty be known to all men. The Lord is nigh," in our fellow men and in us. We must, in a sense, become as the Virgin of Nazareth, and make the mildness and goodness of Christ shine forth in our life. Today's Mass furnishes us with a powerful means of grace. We feel our need for redemption, our lack of virtue, and our sloth. We know how sadly we fail to realize in our lives the unlimited goodness of Christ, who lives in us. We cry out to Christ and ask Him to free us from our narrowness, from our coldness, and from our individualism. We take to heart the words of the Communion: "Say to the faint-hearted: Take courage and fear not; behold our God will come and will save us."

Prayer

Thou, O Lord, that sittest upon the cherubim, stir up Thy might and come. Give ear, O Thou that rulest Israel; that leadest Joseph like a sheep. Stir up Thy might, O Lord, and come to save us. Convert us, O God, and show us Thy face, and we shall be saved. (Gradual; Ps 79:2–4.)

Ember Wednesday

The stational church for Ember Wednesday in Advent is the church of St. Mary Major in Rome. The liturgy invites us to visit the home of the Virgin of Nazareth and presents us the scene of the Annunciation. Reverently beholding the holy Virgin, we contemplate the great mystery of the Incarnation.

The angel of the Lord declared unto Mary: "Behold, thou shalt conceive in thy womb and shalt bring forth a son, and thou shalt call His name Jesus. He shall be great and shall be called the Son of the Most High" (Gospel). How is this to be? "The Holy Ghost shall come upon thee, and the power of the Most High shall overshadow thee." Mary believes. She recognizes this as the will of God and submits herself to His designs with complete surrender and self-forgetfulness. "Behold the handmaid of the Lord; be it done to me according to thy word." In that moment "the Word was made flesh," and the Virgin's obedience, purity, and love bore fruit. "Blessed art thou that thou hast believed" (Lk 1:45).

"The Word was made flesh" in the womb of the Virgin, in whose house we are today assembled. Mary has become a new heaven, a heaven on earth, and we cry out: "Drop down dew ye heavens, and let the clouds rain the Just One." Mary is the "earth" which is to "be opened and bud forth a Savior"; she is the "heavens" which "show forth the glory of God" (Introit). In the Incarnation was fulfilled the prophecy made by Isaias seven hundred years before the birth of Christ. "The Lord himself shall give you a sign: Behold a virgin shall conceive and bear a son, and His name shall be called Emmanuel," God with us (Epistle). "And the Word was made flesh" (Jn 1:14) through the Virgin Mary, who conceived by the Holy Ghost.

Come let us adore the Word Incarnate. Mary is the tabernacle of the covenant in which God draws near to men. "In the last days, the mountain of the house of the Lord shall be prepared on the top of the mountains [that is, Sion, Mary, the dwelling place of God], and it shall be exalted above the hills, and all nations shall flow unto it. And many people shall go and say: come and let us go up to the mountain of the Lord, and to the house of the God of Jacob [to Mary] and He will teach us His ways, and we will walk in His paths, for the law [that is, the Word, Christ] shall come forth from Sion, and the word of the Lord [Christ] from Jerusalem [Mary].... O house of Jacob, come ye and let us walk in the light of the Lord our God," which is brought to us by Mary (First lesson). We contemplate with faith and devotion the mystery that is accomplished in the Virgin Mary. "The angel of the Lord declared unto Mary, and she conceived of the Holy Ghost." In adoration and wonder we bend our knee, for "the Word was made flesh and dwelt among us."

Today we celebrate the Holy Sacrifice in the church of St. Mary Major, the house of Mary. Mary is the new Jerusalem, the dwelling place of the divine Savior. In a few short days she will bring forth the fruit of her blessed womb.

At the Communion we sing, "Behold a virgin shall conceive." At the moment when the angel brought her the message and Mary conceived of the Holy Ghost, she experienced, as it were, her first Holy Communion. This blessed communion was full of blessing for Mary herself and for the whole human race. As often as the children of the Church approach the Communion rail to receive the body of the Lord, the message of the angel is, in a sense, again repeated: "Behold a virgin shall conceive." When we receive the Holy Eucharist, we are, in the mind of the liturgy, the Virgin of Nazareth, and we experience in ourselves the blessed conception which we celebrate today in the church of St. Mary Major. We share with Mary the experience of conceiving the Son of God and having Him as truly in our hearts as she had. "Behold a virgin shall conceive.... His name shall be called Emmanuel," God with us. Oh, that we might realize in ourselves the wonderful teaching of the liturgy.

"Behold a virgin shall conceive." The virgin soul lives united to God and Christ. The door of our hearts should be wide open to receive the King of Glory. Such a soul the Gradual calls the "innocent in hands and clean of heart." Such a soul has only one answer to the message of the angel: "Behold the handmaid of the Lord; be it done to me according to thy word." Each time we approach Holy Communion we should receive Christ with the sentiments which Mary had when she conceived Him at Nazareth.

"Behold a virgin shall conceive." With the liturgy we recognize here a reference to the Church. In her bosom the Church bears Christ, the author of grace and salvation. Only in the Church will mankind be able to find Christ. "Come and let us go up to the mountain of the Lord." There in His holy temple, in the Church, He will teach us His ways.

PRAYER

O God, who didst will that Thy Word should be conceived in the womb of the Virgin Mary, be attentive to our prayers and assist us through her intercession, whom we believe truly to be the Mother of God. Through Christ our Lord. Amen.

Thursday

"At that time the angel Gabriel was sent from God into a city of Galilee called Nazareth, to a virgin espoused to a man whose name was Joseph, of the house of David; and the virgin's name was Mary" (Lk 1:26 f.; Gospel of Ember Wednesday).

"To a virgin." Nowhere else in the Gospels is there given such a detailed and solemn account of the sending of an angel to men. Why such an account on this occasion? The angel was sent to a virgin, and "the virgin's name was Mary." Here lies the superiority of our religion over every other religion both before and after it. Christianity differs from the other religions of the world in the heavenly purity of its first hour of life. A pure angel of God approaches the purest of virgins. Here victory is achieved over the flesh and over the spirit of impurity so common among men. This victory is assured by the announcement which the angel makes to the virgin. The designs of the pure God depend on the will of the pure virgin. God assumes humanity by way of purity and virginity.

"Hail, full of grace, the Lord is with thee; blessed art thou among women.... Behold thou shalt conceive in thy womb and shalt bring forth a son" (Lk 1:28, 31). "Hail, full of grace." Mary does not answer. She considers well what the message of the angel may mean. The Virgin's peace of mind is disturbed by the word of the angel. The honor and the dignity offered here seem almost too great. However, the angel has more to say to her. First she receives the assurance, "Fear not"; then she is told, "Thou shalt conceive in thy womb and shalt bring forth a son." Finally the wonderful plan of redemption is revealed to her. "He shall be great and shall be called the Son of the Most High; and the Lord God shall give unto Him the throne of David, His Father; and He shall reign in the house of Jacob forever, and of His kingdom there shall be no end" (Lk 1:32 f.). Not only does Mary learn that she is to be the Mother of God, but the whole marvelous plan of redemption is laid before her. How greatly God has honored Mary! And how greatly in her has He honored the state of virginity! How generous He is with her, for

He has given her everything! To virginity and purity God reveals His mysteries. "Blessed are the clean of heart, for they shall see God" (Mt 5:8).

"Behold a virgin." A virgin stands at the portals of our redemption. In a sense, the accomplishment of our redemption depends on her alone, for it depends on her giving her consent to the plan proposed by God. She gives her consent when she replies to the message of the angel: "Behold the handmaid of the Lord; be it done to me according to thy word" (Lk 1:38). But before giving her consent she inquires cautiously, "How shall this be done, because I know not man?" Observe Mary's high regard for her virginity. She is determined to remain a virgin. She had previously accepted the life of virginity as God's will in her regard, and in the fullness of understanding which God had given her, had recognized the value of this state of life. Now she desires with her whole soul to remain a virgin if this be the will of God. A person who gives himself freely to the life of virginity for the love of God, has given to God all that it is possible to give. He has given God the highest expression of pure love and of perfect faith.

"Behold the handmaid of the Lord." Mary need not fear for her virginity, for God is also concerned that she remain a virgin. He does not intend to violate her virginity; on the contrary, He will sanctify her virginity by divine maternity. The power of the Holy Ghost will come upon her, and the power of the Most High will overshadow her, and the Son of God will descend and take up His abode in her virginal body. She becomes His handmaid and His mother. Her concern is that the will of God be accomplished in her. She stands there at the turning point of history to point out the way of salvation for men. "Behold the handmaid of the Lord."

In our daily Holy Communion we, too, experience the conception of Christ in our own lives. What a privilege and honor is ours! How great, then, should be our purity and devotion when we approach this holy sacrament! Like Mary, we should declare ourselves the handmaid of the Lord and imitate the virtues of the Virgin of Nazareth.

Prayer

Hail, Virgin Mother, Star of the Sea,
O Gate of Heaven, we come to thee;
The joy the angel brought is mine,
The name of Eve is changed for thine.
You free th' earth's slaves and bring them light,
You put the hellish hordes to flight.
Now prove thyself our one true mother
Left to us by Christ our brother.
O ever virgin, fair and pure,
When thou art near we feel secure.
Now give thy faltering children strength,
And take us to our home at length,
That we may join in praising thee
Both now and in eternity.
Amen.

Ember Friday

"Thou art near, O Lord, and all Thy ways are truth" (Introit). God is near today in the Virgin Mary. She has conceived the Son of God in order to bring Him to us. We are witnesses of the blessings which she brings today to the house of Elizabeth; she brings Christ with her. Through her Elizabeth is filled with the Holy Ghost, and John the Baptist is sanctified in his mother's womb. Mary is the Mother of God and the channel of all grace.

Mary, having conceived the Son of God, hastens to the hill country, to the city of Juda, and greets her cousin, Elizabeth. At Mary's greeting, Elizabeth feels the infant whom she has conceived (John the Baptist) leap for joy in her womb. Elizabeth is herself filled with the Holy Ghost and learns the secret that has been confided to Mary: "Blessed art thou among women, and blessed is the fruit of thy womb. And whence is this to me, that the mother of my Lord should come to me?... And blessed art thou that thou hast believed" (Gospel). Mary is the living monstrance that presents Christ and His grace to men. Through Mary, John the Baptist is sanctified in his mother's womb, cleansed from the stains of Original Sin, and clothed with the garment of sanctifying grace. Mary would gladly have withdrawn from the world to live in the solitude and obscurity of Nazareth after having conceived the Son of God, but God calls her to the service of charity, and she recognizes no call but the will of God. She does not shrink from any exertion; she is not dismayed by any obstacle or difficulty. He who is filled with Christ is filled with zeal and love and determination. How do we stand in this regard?

The stational church for today's Mass is the church of the Twelve Apostles in Rome. Mary is the apostle of the liturgy, the Mediatrix of all grace. She is the root from which springs the full bloom, Christ. "And of His fullness we all have received, and grace for grace" (Jn 1:16). But all of this grace we receive through the instrumentality of Mary. Today we, like John the Baptist, are sanctified by Mary's visit. With hearts full of thankfulness we say with the Gradual: "Lord, Thou hast blessed Thy land [Mary and through her the Church and its members]; Thou hast turned away the captivity of Jacob" (the captivity of sin, the devil, and eternal damnation). Everything through Mary.

"Behold the Lord shall come, and all His saints with Him: and there shall be in that day a great light" (Communion). The coming of Christ in Holy Communion is the prelude to the coming of Christ at the end of time, when He will appear accompanied by His saints and angels to lead us and the Church to an eternal communion with Him in heaven. Holy Communion is for us a pledge of the possession of God in the eternal light of heaven.

Through Mary Christ accomplishes the salvation of many souls. He took her as His mother in order that in His earthly life He might have a new Eve to assist Him, the new Adam. As she cooperated in the winning of all the graces which Christ has merited for us, so now that she is in heaven she enjoys the privilege of dispensing all the graces which Christ wishes to give us. Every grace which we receive, Mary helped to win for us. For this reason she is also charged with the dispensation of these graces. We receive all grace from God through Christ and His Blessed Mother. Thus Christ wishes to honor His mother, and we should gratefully seek from her all the graces that we need. She is the humble, obedient handmaid of Christ, the pure Virgin.

In the liturgy the blessed Mother of God, the Mediatrix of grace, is a symbol of the Church. The Church bears Christ in her virginal bosom (the Blessed Sacrament in the tabernacle). She gives Him to us in the sacraments, in the Holy Sacrifice of the Mass, and in His abiding presence in the tabernacle. "Hail, full of grace, the Lord is with thee," O Holy Mother the Church.

The first fruit of the Incarnation and of Holy Communion is Christian charity. Mary "conceived of the Holy Ghost," and at once set out to visit her cousin Elizabeth. Likewise in us fraternal charity should be inseparable from Holy Communion.

Mary is like the Ark of the Covenant. She is clothed with the Spirit of God within and without. She is inwardly occupied in divine contemplation, and outwardly in the practice of fraternal charity. She unites in her own person the virtues of both Mary and Martha. In the case of the Virgin, the service of her neighbor is the direct result of her complete devotion to the service of God. She is the handmaid of the Lord because of her union with God and because of her complete dependence on His grace and His holy will. Everything she does is regulated by the grace of God in accordance with His will.

Prayer

Stir up Thy power, we beseech Thee, O Lord, and come, that they who trust in Thy goodness may be more speedily freed from all adversity.

Mary, Mediatrix of all grace, pray for us that we may be delivered from our sins, our weaknesses, and our imperfections, and may begin to live a holy life.

Hail Mary, full of grace, the Lord is with thee; blessed art thou among women, and blessed is the fruit of thy womb, Jesus.

Ember Saturday

On this day in ancient times, the Church celebrated the vigil, which ended in the celebration of Mass early Sunday morning. The vigil is a symbol of the Church, which brings to us the light of Christ out of the night.

We stand in need of redemption. Today we feel like a people that has lived in darkness and in the unfruitful wastes of the desert; we are like the lame and the blind and those who are bound by chains. We are, in truth, bound by the chains of sin, self-love, and weakness. We feel the full weight of our sins and bow under the yoke of Satan and struggle in the misery of our servitude. The chains wrought by Original Sin bind all of us, the priests who celebrate Mass daily, the religious and the pious laymen who receive Holy Communion daily. Even though we pray much and meditate frequently, we are far from what we should be, and we are still closely bound by our self-love and by our blindness and hesitancy in the spiritual life. No one stands in need of redemption so much as we. "Drop down dew, ye heavens, from above, and let the clouds rain the just; let the earth be opened and bud forth a Savior, and let justice spring up together. I the Lord have created Him" (Fourth lesson).

The Lord is to come now in the Mass. He is to come at Christmas to give sight to the blind and those that live in darkness. The earth "shall bud forth and blossom, and shall rejoice with joy and praise; the glory of Libanus is given to it, the beauty of Carmel and Saron. They shall see the glory of the Lord and the beauty of our God.... Then shall the eyes of the blind be opened, and the ears of the deaf shall be unstopped" (Second lesson). The chains of servitude fall from the afflicted members of humanity. Grace and the forgiveness of sin are given to men, and the night of sin and blindness depart. A new life is given to us: "I am come that they may have life and may have it more abundantly" (Jn 10:10).

The new life which is given to us is a participation in the divine life. It is a share in the pure and blessed life which the Holy Trinity lives in heaven. By reason of our adoption as sons of God we may hope to share and enjoy this life. The Son of God in His Incarnation has taken us to Himself and made us members of His mystical body, and has thus lifted us up so that it is possible for us to enjoy the life of God. Could anything more sublime have happened to us? The Father, the Son, and the Holy Ghost share with us their blessed and ineffable life. Indeed, we have been redeemed, and that redemption means not only freedom from our sins, but also the privilege of living henceforth the life of the divinity. We have been made the beloved children of God.

"By this hath the charity of God appeared towards us, because God hath sent His only-begotten Son into the world that we may live by Him. In this is charity; not as though we had loved God, but because He hath first loved us, and sent His Son to be a propitiation for our sins" (1 Jn 4:9 f.).

We are redeemed. The God of heaven comes to us, and we are elevated to a participation in the divine life. The divine life, which flows from the Father to the Son, is communicated to men also through the humanity of Christ. By faith, reverence, and love, we open our hearts to the benign influence of this divine life. God clothes our soul in His love, His purity, His holiness. For these divine favors we are grateful. We know by these favors that we are truly redeemed and that we are now raised to a new life through Christ, who has purchased them for us.

Prayer

Grant, we beseech Thee, almighty God, that we who are oppressed by the former servitude under the yoke of sin, may be delivered by the new birth of Thy only-begotten Son, which we await, who livest and reignest with Thee forever and ever. Amen.

Hymn (Dn 3:52–59)

Blessed art Thou, O Lord, the God of our fathers: and worthy to be praised and glorified and exalted above all forever.

And blessed is the holy name of Thy glory: and worthy to be praised and exalted above all in all ages.

Blessed art Thou in the holy temple of Thy glory: and exceedingly to be praised and exceeding glorious forever.

Blessed art Thou on the throne of Thy kingdom: and exceedingly to be praised and exalted above all forever.

Blessed art Thou that beholdest the depths and sittest upon the cherubims: and worthy to be praised and exalted above all forever.

Blessed art Thou in the firmament of heaven: and worthy of praise and glorious forever.

All ye works of the Lord, bless the Lord: praise and exalt Him above all forever.

O ye angels of the Lord, bless the Lord: praise and exalt Him above all forever.

O ye heavens, bless the Lord: praise and exalt him above all forever.

Fourth Sunday of Advent

The Mass

In the early ages of the Church the celebration of Ember Saturday continued until the following morning and terminated with the Sunday Mass. The evening service in St. Peter's in Rome consisted of the recitation of psalms, the reading of lessons and prophecies, the sermon by the pope, the collection of the tithes, the celebration of the Holy Sacrifice, and the seven blessings. In later centuries the night vigil was abolished, and the services were reduced to what we now have on Ember Saturday. For this reason a new Mass had to be composed for the following day, the fourth Sunday of Advent. This new Mass does not introduce any new liturgical idea, but continues the thought of the Mass for Ember Saturday and sums up the ideas of the preceding week. It takes up again the idea proposed to us on the first Sunday of Advent, the idea of purifying our lives as a preparation for the coming of Christ.

We patiently await the coming of the Lord. "Drop down dew, ye heavens, from above, and let the clouds rain down the just. Let the earth be opened and bud forth a Savior" (Introit). Heaven has already descended to the Virgin of Nazareth, and the power of the Most High has overshadowed her. She has conceived the Savior by the power of the Holy Ghost. The heavens, indeed, have opened and have rained down the Just One. In a few days the earth will bring forth its fruit: the virginal womb of Mary will bring forth the Savior. We humbly beseech God to hasten that day, for we are greatly in need of the Savior and His grace. "Stir up Thy might and come, we beseech Thee, O Lord, and succor us with great power; that by the help of Thy grace the forgiveness of Thy mercy may hasten what our sins impede" (Collect).

The Epistle turns our attention to the newly ordained priests. By their ordination they have become "ministers of Christ and dispensers of the mysteries of God," called, like Mary, to bear Christ in their purified hands and to bring Him to men through prayer, the sacraments, and the Holy Eucharist. Men look upon us as the servants of Christ, full of grace and responsibility. God's consecrated servants are accountable to Him. "Therefore judge not before the time," that is, before the coming of the Lord. "Leave judgment of His servants to the Lord, for He will bring to light the hidden things of darkness, and will make manifest the counsels of the heart." Christ will appear on the last day as the Judge, to whom all will have to give an account. The coming of Christ in Bethlehem, and His coming upon the altar in the Mass, and His coming into our hearts in Holy Communion, all point to His second coming at the end of the world, when He will come with power and majesty to judge and set all things right. "The Lord is nigh" (Gradual) in His servants. He is now ready to celebrate His holy sacrifice. In holy impatience we cry, "Alleluia! Come, O Lord, and tarry not, forgive the sins of Thy people Israel."

The Lord is indeed coming, for John the Baptist, His forerunner, is already preaching penance in the name of Christ, whose way he has come to prepare. The Evangelist gives the time and the circumstances of the Baptist's preaching with unusual exactness and detail. We feel that we are standing at the turning point of history. The Lord is near. In the Offertory we greet her who is full of grace: "The Lord is with thee; blessed is the fruit of thy womb."

"The Lord is nigh unto all them that call upon Him" (Gradual). We turn, now, from all that is past, all that is evil, and look forward to the redemption. In the Offertory we are the Church, Mary, the virgin and handmaid. As virgin we have been freed from everything that is not from God and for God; we have offered ourselves up to Him as handmaids with deep humility; therefore, we are prepared to receive Him and His gifts. Now He can fill our souls with His grace. "Drop down dew, ye heavens." In the Consecration of the Mass the heavens drop down upon Mary and the whole Church. The heavens rain down the Savior upon the Church as they once rained manna upon the chosen people. Now He is in our midst with the fullness of grace to free us from our sins. He prays for us, offers Himself up for us, and will Himself be the expiation for all the offenses of which we have been guilty in the eyes of the Father. We unite ourselves to Him and offer up His body and blood and His soul to the Father as our offering of praise, thanksgiving, petition, and expiation.

What our hands and hearts offer to the Father, again descends upon us. in the form of grace and blessing. "Let the clouds rain down the Just One" into our hearts. In Holy Communion the Church shares the blessed conception of the Virgin. "His name shall be called Emmanuel," God with us (Communion). "The Lord is nigh unto all them that call upon Him in truth," in honest acknowledgment of their own nothingness, in detachment from all things that are not of God, and in the spirit of the virgin and handmaid.

Meditation (1)

Three heralds of Advent appear in the Mass today: Isaias the Prophet in the Introit (on the way to the Sanctuary), John the Baptist in the Gospel (in the vestibule), and the Blessed Virgin in the Offertory and the Communion chant (at the place of sacrifice in the holy of holies). All three remind us that the Lord is nigh and that we must prepare the way for Him; they explain the meaning of the Mass to us.

In the instructional part of the Mass, grace knocks at our soul. The call of grace reaches us through Isaias and John the Baptist, through the texts and the songs, through the Epistle and the Gospel. They remind us significantly, "The angel of the Lord declared unto Mary." Grace knocks at our hearts and with an Ave on its lips seeks entrance into our souls. It comes to us in the plain garb of human language; chants, prayers, and stories. Like Mary we listen with attention and wonder what this greeting of grace may mean, and what the lessons, the admonitions, and the prayers may signify.

The Offertory is our fiat, the joyful assent of the soul in answer to the Ave of the angel; our assent to the call of grace that reaches us in the Mass. In the offering of the bread and wine, the Church and the Christian soul echoes Mary's words: "Behold the handmaid of the Lord." The faithful offer up to God their souls and their bodies to be used at His good pleasure. Upon the altar they lay their souls and their bodies, their strength, their talents, and all that they have, as a complete holocaust to the will of God. "Prepare ye the way of the Lord." We turn away from all that is sinful, from all that can in any way displease Him, in order that our thoughts, our plans, our works, and our hopes may prepare the way for Him; we level all the hills of self-esteem and pride in order that we may live, no longer to ourselves, but to God. "Behold the handmaid of the Lord." We place ourselves in the hands of God with complete subjection: "Be it done to me according to thy word."

At the Consecration of the Mass we shall see the "salvation of God," Christ, the Son of God, the Emmanuel. "And the Word was made flesh," once in the womb of Mary, but now every day in the womb of the Church; on the altar, at the Consecration of the Mass, He becomes mine, as once He became Mary's child. With firm faith we take Him into our trembling hands and offer Him up to the heavenly Father. In Holy Communion we may even receive Him into our hearts.

"Behold a virgin shall conceive" (Communion). The Christian soul, the Church, is that virgin. It might be said of us, as it was said of Mary, "Blessed art thou." We are, indeed, full of grace, for now we have the grace that we need for our present life; we are assured of the resurrection at the last day, and of our eternal salvation in the world to come. In the possession of this grace we have the guarantee of the salvation of God. The liturgy looks forward to the birth of Christ with this hope and prayer: "Show us, O Lord, Thy mercy, and grant us Thy salvation" (Ps 84:8). God will show us the mercy of the resurrection of the dead and the beatific vision in heaven. The Christmas which we now await is only the beginning of and the preparation for the eternal joys of heaven.

"The Lord is nigh." John, the forerunner who is to prepare His way, has already begun the work that was given him. "Now in the fifteenth year of the reign of Tiberius Caesar, Pontius Pilate being governor of Judea, and Herod being tetrarch of Galilee, and Philip his brother tetrarch of Iturea and the country of Trachonitis, and Lysanias tetrarch of Abilina, under the high priests Annas and Caiphas, the word of the Lord was made unto John, the son of Zachary, in the desert" (Gospel). John preaches penance to the people: "Do penance, for the kingdom of heaven is at hand.... Prepare ye the way of the Lord" (Mt 3:2 f.).

"Prepare ye the way of the Lord," that He may come to you without hindrance. "The crooked shall be made straight, and the rough ways plain." We are to prepare for His coming by a lively faith in Him who is to come, by purifying our souls from all that is sinful and unworthy of Him; we prepare by acts of penance, by sorrow and humility, and by a humble and worthy confession of our sins. "The Lord is nigh."

"Behold a virgin shall conceive," the liturgy cries out to us at the time of Communion. We should approach the holy table with pure hearts and clean hands, and with the firm resolution to live only for Him who is now come to live in us. The fruit of the Incarnation should make us new men, men filled with the life of God and the love of Christ.

Prayer

Stir up Thy might and come, we beseech Thee, O Lord, and succor us with great power; that by the help of Thy grace the forgiveness of Thy mercy may hasten what our sins impede. Amen.

Meditation (2)

"A virgin shall conceive and bear a son, and his name shall be called Emmanuel" (Communion). In today's liturgy the virgin is both the Church and our soul. Year after year the Church, and with it the Christian soul, renews itself in the fire of penance and sorrow, that it may become a pure holocaust to God; she becomes a more perfect virgin, and thus becomes more fruitful in the things that are of God. "The Lord is nigh unto all them that call upon Him" (Gradual); that is, God is near all those who humbly and truthfully acknowledge their own nothingness and sinfulness; God is near all those who recognize their own worthlessness and place all their trust in Him. God loves the humble man.

"Hail Mary, full of grace" (Offertory). Today the Church makes her offering to God with this greeting to Mary on her lips. Mary spoke her fiat with deep humility and faith, and thus opened wide her soul to God. When she had spoken her assent, the power of the Most High could overshadow her and she could conceive the Son of God. The Fathers of the Church tell us that she conceived Him first of all in spirit; that is, by faith, virginal purity, humility — by her complete conformity to the designs of God and by the frank acknowledgment of her own unworthiness. Only after she had thus been prepared in spirit did she conceive Him in the flesh. It was necessary that she first detach herself from all that is not godly and conform her will and her desires to those of the Almighty. Only then could God take complete possession of her and man could address her: "Hail Mary, full of grace, the Lord is with thee; blessed is the fruit of thy womb."

"Behold a virgin shall conceive" (Communion). To properly celebrate Christmas and enjoy the full fruit of the Incarnation, we must, like Mary, become virgins and handmaids of the Lord. We must emulate her purity, her sinlessness, her freedom from pride and self-love, her complete conformity to the will of God. We must recognize our complete dependence on the power of the Most High for light, guidance, and help from above. We must open our hearts to Him and imitate Mary in her complete offering of self to the designs of God. We must, like her, eradicate from our lives all willful faults, and be unwavering in our service of God and devotion to Him. We must be prepared to sacrifice all that we have without asking what return will be made to us. We must not falter when we are misunderstood, when our actions are falsely construed, and when we are falsely accused by others.

"He that judgeth me is the Lord, [therefore] to me it is a very small thing to be judged by you or by man's day; but neither do I judge my own self." For we are the handmaids of the Lord, "the ministers of Christ and the dispensers of the mysteries of God" (Epistle). The Church sees in her ministers and her people, not merely fallen men, but men who are called by Christ to act in His name and to offer to God the Holy Sacrifice and administer the sacraments. Christ lives in them, and through them He purifies souls, sanctifying them and leading them to God. Like Mary, we are handmaids since we are members of the mystical body of Christ. The more closely we unite ourselves to the mystical body, the more fully is Christ's divine life realized in us.

"Behold a virgin shall conceive." With ardent desire we cry out with the liturgy today: "Let the clouds rain the just." Ye heavens, rain down Christ, the Just One, and with Him His grace, His strength, and the divine life. "Let the earth be opened and bud forth a Savior" (Introit). By the earth is meant our soul, which during Advent is prepared to bring forth the Savior by penance, self-denial, and an intense desire for the coming of the Redeemer. Now that the soil of our soul has been thus prepared, it can receive the seed of Christ and bring forth its fruit. The fruit which our soul is to bear is the Emmanuel, God with us, the new man.

"Prepare ye the way of the Lord; make straight His paths. Every valley shall be filled, and every mountain and hill shall be brought low, and the crooked shall be made straight, and the rough ways plain; and all flesh shall see the salvation of God" (Gospel).

Prayer

Drop down dew, ye heavens, from above, and let the clouds rain the just. Come, O Lord, and tarry not; forgive the sins of Thy people Israel. (Introit; Alleluia verse.)

Stir up Thy might and come, we beseech Thee, O Lord, and succor us with great power; that by the help of Thy grace the forgiveness of Thy mercy may hasten what our sins impede. Amen.

December 21, St. Thomas the Apostle

"Fear not, for the fifth day our Lord will come to you" (Benedictus antiphon at Lauds). This is the message which the liturgy brings us today, and with the apostle Thomas we fall on our knees and exclaim, "My Lord and my God." The answer of Christ to the apostle applies also to us: "Blessed are they that have not seen and have believed." O Lord, increase our faith.

"And you, when you were dead in your offenses and sins, wherein in time past you walked according to the course of this world, according to the prince of the power of this air [that is, Satan], of the spirit that now worketh on the children of unbelief; in which also we all conversed in time past, in the desires of our flesh, fulfilling the will of the flesh in our thoughts, and were by nature children of wrath even as the rest" (Eph 2:1–3) — in such a state we should have remained had Christ not come to free us from the slavery of sin and to lead us back to God.

"You are no more strangers and foreigners, but you are fellow citizens [by reason of your membership in the Church] with the saints and the domestics of God, built upon the foundation of the apostles and prophets, Jesus Christ Himself being the chief cornerstone.... In whom you also are built together into an habitation of God in the Spirit" (Epistle). All these things were accomplished by the first Christmas: Christ redeemed us and through baptism makes us members of His body, therefore children who have the right to address God as "our Father." We are now members of the family of God; that is, we are members of His holy Church and have a right to all the goods and possessions which He has bestowed upon His Church. As children of the Church we are the living stones from which the Church is constructed. Christ is the cornerstone of this building, and the apostles are the foundation; all of these are formed into one magnificent structure by the master builder, the Holy Ghost. He hews and shapes us by means of His graces and by temptations and trials of all kinds, that we may daily become more suitable for the place we are to fill in the building of the Church.

"For God so loved the world as to give His only-begotten Son; that whosoever believeth in Him may not perish, but may have life everlasting" (Jn 3:16). "God is love." How unworthy we are of that love! What have we done to merit it? For it is only through the "mercies of the Lord that we are not consumed" (Lam 3:22). O God, I trust in Thy love.

Today we are another Thomas. The Lord appears and tells us, "Be not faithless, but believing" (Gospel). Let us go forward to meet the Lord when He comes at Christmas and in Holy Communion, that the words of the Epistle may be more perfectly realized in us. He will come with great power and majesty to accomplish the work which He began at His first coming and which He has begun in us.

"My Lord and my God." Yes, Christ, the tiny baby of the crib, is our Lord and our God. He is the offering which we make upon our altars, and the food which we receive in Holy Communion.

He enlightens us with His grace and love during those precious moments when He rests in the tabernacle of our soul. My Lord and my God for time and eternity! "Blessed are they that have not seen and have believed." The day will come when the veil that conceals His glory from our eyes is to be taken away. Then we shall see Him face to face. Such will be the reward of our faith.

Prayer

Grant us, we beseech Thee, O Lord, to glory in the feast day of Thy blessed apostle, Thomas, that we may be ever assisted by his patronage and may at all times imitate his faith with fitting devotion. Through Christ our Lord. Amen.

The "O" Antiphons

December 17, O Sapientia

"O Wisdom, who camest out of the mouth of the Most High, reaching from end to end and ordering all things mightily and sweetly, come to teach us the way of prudence."

O Wisdom! The Savior whom we shall find as a weak babe in the crib is the Wisdom which from eternity proceeds from the Father. The eternal Wisdom which comes to us in the person of the Savior, has devised everything that is: heaven and earth, angels and men, matter and spirit, the entire universe. It has formed all creatures and given them their outward form and their place in the order of creation. It has fixed the wonderful order of nature, and it governs its laws. Its power guides and directs all creation, even to the last particle of dust. The power of this gentle and mighty Spirit has its eternal designs upon the world and pervades and governs all that exists. Eternal Wisdom, resting as a child in the lap of Thy mother, I believe in Thee. How great Thou art in the works of Thy creation, how wonderful is the order of Thy universe, how merciful in the work of redemption, how sublimely humble in Thy crib, how divinely wise in the teachings of Thy gospel, how provident in the work of Thy holy Church! O divine Wisdom, let me understand Thee.

Divine Wisdom clothes itself in the nature of a man. It conceals itself in the weakness of a child. It chooses for itself, infancy, poverty, obedience, subjection, obscurity. "I will destroy the wisdom of the wise and the prudence of the prudent I will reject.... Hath not God made foolish the wisdom of this world? For seeing that in the wisdom of God the world by wisdom knew not God, it pleased God, by the foolishness of our preaching, to save them that believe. For both the Jews require signs, and the Greeks seek after wisdom; but we preach Christ crucified, unto the Jews, indeed, a stumbling block, and unto the Gentiles foolishness; but unto them that are called, both Jews and Greeks, Christ, the power of God and the wisdom of God.... But the foolish things of the world hath God chosen, that He may confound the wise; and the weak things of the world hath God chosen, that He may confound the strong. And the base things of the world and the things that are contemptible, hath God chosen, and the things that are not, that He might bring to nought things that are" (1 Cor 1:19 ff.).

Come, O divine Wisdom, teach us the way of knowledge. We are unwise; we judge and speak according to the vain standards of the world, which is foolishness in the eyes of God. Come, O divine Wisdom, give us the true knowledge and the taste for what is eternal and divine.

Inspire us with a thirst for God's holy will, help us seek God's guidance and direction, enlighten us in the teachings of the holy gospel, make us submissive to Thy holy Church. Strengthen us in the forgetfulness of self, and help us to resign ourselves to a position of obscurity if that be Thy holy will. Detach our hearts from resurgent pride. Give us wisdom that we may understand that "but one thing is necessary" (Lk 10:42). "For what doth it profit a man if he gain the whole world and suffer the loss of his own soul?" (Mt 16:26.) The Holy Spirit would have us know that one degree of grace is worth more than all worldly possessions.

"The sensual man," with only his natural ability, his unaided human talents, "perceiveth not these things that are of the Spirit of God" (1 Cor 2:14). Eternal Wisdom is foolishness to such a man. He cannot understand because he is not spiritually minded. The spiritual man who is guided by the Holy Ghost, penetrates and values all things in the light of divine Wisdom, who "Himself is judged of no man. For who hath known the mind of the Lord, that he may instruct Him? But we have the mind of Christ," the eternal Wisdom (1 Cor 2:15 f.).

The wisdom of God appears to us in the crib, in poverty, in silence, in the weakness of childhood, in the gospel message: Blessed are the poor in spirit, the meek, those who suffer persecution for Christ's sake. The wisdom of God is made manifest in the foolishness of the cross.

Prayer

O Wisdom, who camest out of the mouth of the Most High, reaching from end to end and ordering all things mightily and sweetly, come to teach us the way of prudence.

O Mary, virgin most prudent, pray for us.

December 18, O Adonai

"O Adonai (O almighty God), and leader of the house of Israel, who didst appear to Moses in the burning bush and didst give him the law on Mount Sinai, come with an outstretched arm to redeem us."

O Adonai! The Redeemer whom we await was already the Redeemer in the Old Testament. He it was who appeared to Moses in the burning bush in the desert and gave him the commission to lead Israel out of the bondage of Egypt. Through Moses, He wrought great signs in Egypt and rescued His people from the power and the tyranny of the Pharaohs. He led His people with power through the Red Sea and gave them the Ten Commandments on Mount Sinai. He led them through the desert, provided food and drink, and ushered them into the Promised Land. He appears now also as the Redeemer of the Church of the New Law. He is the Savior and guide of those who have been baptized in the Church. Little child of the crib, so small, so weak, so silent, how mighty must You be to rescue us from passion, from temptation, and from the power of Satan! We believe in Your power, we trust in the strength of Your arm, we follow with confidence Your leadership and Your guidance.

O Adonai, O almighty God, stretch forth Thy arm and save us. The enemy of our salvation, the enemy of souls, the enemy of the Church rises with great power seeking to destroy belief in God, in Christ, and in the Christian religion. Men have wandered far from the true God; they have turned their backs on Him and have made for themselves graven images. They have banished God from their thoughts and from their lives. God is a disturbing element which they would be glad to be rid of. Any other molestation they will gladly suffer, no matter how foolish and disturbing it is.

"Be astonished, O ye heavens, at this, and ye gates thereof be very desolate, saith the Lord. For My people have done two evils: they have forsaken Me, the fountain of living water, and have digged to themselves cisterns, broken cisterns, that can hold no water" (Jer 2:12 f.). Both men and nations have lost all peace and tranquility. All virtues, innocence, fidelity, honor, honesty, and even a man's word may be bought for gold. Scarcely one man can be found who trusts another. Nation has risen against nation, and man against man. Few are they who are faithful to their duty. The spirit of self-sacrifice is rarely to be found. Whether men read, study, or work, their actions are characterized by a spirit of restlessness and disquietude. All their striving produces few results, except to make them more tired, empty, and soulless. And yet they persist in their efforts to do without God and without Christ. Thus they live in spite of the fact that "there is no other name under heaven given to men whereby we must be saved" (Acts 4:12). Only He, the almighty God, can save us.

Thou art He "who didst appear to Moses in the burning bush." "I have seen the affliction of My people in Egypt, and I have heard their cry because of the rigor of them that are over the works. And knowing their sorrow, I am come down to deliver them out of the hands of the Egyptians and to bring them out of that land into a good and spacious land, into a land that floweth with milk and honey" (Ex 3:7 f.). Thus spoke the Lord to Moses from the bush which burned but was not consumed, which is a figure of God's condescension to assume the weakness of human nature. The human nature of Christ is united to the burning divine nature, and yet it is not consumed.

As Moses approached the burning bush, so we approach the divine Savior in the form of a child in the crib, or in the form of the consecrated host, and falling down we adore Him. "Put off the shoes from thy feet, for the place whereon thou standest is holy ground.... I am who am" (Ex 3:5, 14).

O Adonai, almighty God! Mighty in the weakness of a child, and in the helplessness of the Crucified! Thou, almighty God, mighty in the wonders that Thou hast worked! Mighty in guiding, sustaining, and developing Thy Church! "The gates of hell shall not prevail against it" (Mt 16:18). Thou art mighty in the healing and redemption of souls, mighty in Thy love for us, who are so unworthy of Thy love. Instant are Thou in mercy, and all-sufficient in every need. Come and save us.

"Come with an outstretched arm to redeem us." This is the cry of the Church for the second coming of Christ on the last day. The return of the Savior brings us plentiful redemption. "Come, ye blessed of My Father, possess you the kingdom prepared for you" (Mt 25:34).

Prayer

O Adonai, O almighty God, who didst appear to Moses in the burning bush and didst give him the law on Mount Sinai, come with an outstretched arm to redeem us. Amen.

December 19, O Radix Jesse

"O Root of Jesse, who standest as an ensign of the people, before whom kings shall keep silence and the Gentiles shall make supplication, come to deliver us and tarry not."

Christ the King, the Lord! Divine Wisdom, Adonai, the powerful God, is at the same time man with flesh and blood of the house of Jesse, the father of King David. Verily, the right of kingship has now passed from the house of David. The glory that once clothed the royal family has faded and withered, leaving only a blighted and withered root. But from this root is to spring a glorious blossom, the King of the world. "He shall rule from sea to sea and from the river unto the ends of the earth. Before Him the Ethiopians shall fall down and His enemies shall lick the ground. The kings of Tharsis and the islands shall offer presents: . . . all nations shall serve Him" (Ps 71:8–11). To Him God has said, "Thou art My Son. . . . I will give Thee the Gentiles for Thy inheritance, and the utmost parts of the earth for Thy possession" (Ps 2:7 f.).

"He shall be great, . . . and the Lord God shall give unto Him the throne of David, His father, and He shall reign in the house of Jacob forever. And of His kingdom there shall be no end" (Lk 1:32 f.). In the face of Roman power He shall declare, "I am a King" (Jn 18:37). On the throne of the cross they shall proclaim His kingship in the three universal languages of the time: "Jesus of Nazareth, the King of the Jews" (Jn 19:19). He will send forth apostles, for all power is given Him "in heaven and in earth. Going, therefore, teach ye all nations, . . . teaching them to observe all things whatsoever I have commanded you" (Mt 28:18–20). Before Him a Herod, a Domitian, and a Diocletian shall tremble. A Julian will be obliged to confess, "Galilean, Thou hast conquered."

He will establish His kingdom in the world, a kingdom of truth, of justice, and of grace. He who was cast off by men and fastened to the cross, will make that cross a throne. The Lord rules as a king from His cross. He is remembered gratefully and loved by millions who leave all earthly things, father and mother and all else, to follow Him. They devote their health and their life, even their blood, to His service. Root of Jesse, Thou standest as an ensign of the nations, and kings are silent in reverence before Thee.

"Come to deliver us and tarry not." The world cries out for Christ its King, who shall cast out the Prince of this world (Jn 12:31). The prince of this world established his power over men as a result of Original Sin. He exercises his lordship very efficiently, and has led many men into apostasy and idolatry, and has brought them into the temples where he himself is adored. He even dared to approach our Lord, after His fast of forty days in the desert, to tempt Him to fall down before him and adore him. Even after we had been delivered from the servitude of Satan through the death of Christ on the cross, the prince of this world attempts to exercise his power over us. "The devil, as a roaring lion, goeth about seeking whom he may devour" (1 Pt 5:8). Like a bird of prey he hovers above us waiting for a favorable opportunity to seize us and lead us into sin. Often enough he transforms "himself into an angel of light" (2 Cor 11:14). The sworn enemy and adversary of Christ and of all that is good, he devotes his entire energy and his great intelligence to the task of establishing a kingdom of sin and darkness which is opposed to God and to Christianity.

Satan establishes his power over deluded men in a way that is perfectly obvious. When he has gained control over the body of a man, he uses it for his own purposes, as though it were he who actually controls and animates the body in place of the human soul. He often exerts his influence over men by harassing them and hindering them by his external works, as is so evident in the lives of some holy men and women. In these trying times, when faith in Christ and in God has largely disappeared, when the propaganda of a pagan culture is broadcast everywhere, and the forces of evil and falsehood rise up to cast God from His throne, who does not feel the power of the devil? Does it not appear that we are approaching that time when Satan will be released from the depths of hell to work his wonders and mislead, if possible, even the elect? (Apoc 20; Mt 24:24.)

"Come, tarry not." Observe how thoroughly the world of today has submitted to the reign of Satan. Mankind has abandoned the search for what is good and holy. Loyalty, justice, freedom, love, and mutual trust are no longer highly regarded. Establish, O God, Thy kingdom among us, a kingdom established upon truth, justice, and peace. "Come, tarry not." "Thy kingdom come."

Prayer

O Root of Jesse, who standest as an ensign of the people, before whom kings shall keep silence and the Gentiles shall make supplication, come to deliver us and tarry not. Amen.

December 20, O Clavis David

"O Key of David, and Scepter of the house of Israel, who openeth and no man shutteth, who shutteth and no man openeth, come and bring forth from his prison house the captive that walketh in darkness and in the shadow of death."

O sublime majesty of the coming Redeemer! To Him has been delivered the key, the government of the house of David (Is 22:22). Boundless is His power over the graces and privileges of the Church; over the souls and hearts and the wills of men. He holds the destiny of the Church in the palm of His hand. He is Master of the storms that arise to destroy the Church and the souls committed to her. He is capable of dealing with the false principles and the errors that threaten her doctrines. He has overcome the devil and his associates, the world, the flesh and its tribulations. To Him all power is given (Mt 28:18). "He shall open and none shall shut" (Is 22:22). Against the power that is His all other forces are powerless. The destiny of souls and the government of the Church is placed in His hand. He is the Lord of all. O Key of David, I believe in Thy power; and in the many difficult situations that confront the Church and my own soul, I place my trust in Thee. Come, lead the captives from their prison. With the key of His almighty power, the Redeemer has opened the prison in which poor, sinful man was languishing in darkness and in the shadow of death. Those who were held captive by Satan and by sin, who were degraded and dishonored, are now given the power to become the children of God. They are rescued from the beast who would degrade them; their good inclinations and desires are strengthened; and they are made a dwelling place of the Holy Spirit. Men were slaves of passion; they were bound and fettered by concupiscence of the eyes, the concupiscence of the flesh, and the pride of life.

Key of David, come and deliver the captives from their prison. The Church wishes that by the practice of virtue we should free ourselves from sin and unfaithfulness. She asks God that He may spare us from punishment, deliver us from His wrath, from an evil death, and from hell. The Church prays that God may free us from a heart that clings to the world, from a spirit that is pleased with worldliness, from a human respect that degrades us. She urges us to return kindness and affection for scorn, love and compassion for persecution. Our Holy Mother the Church prays that we may be delivered from ourselves, from our self-love, and from all our secret sins. She prays that God may detach our hearts from all that can bind them to earth, for he who has been freed from the things of the earth is free with the freedom of Christ.

Key of David, come and deliver the captives from their prison. By Thy coming free us from all that separates us from God. Bring us freedom and redemption; incline us to surrender ourselves completely to God.

Fortunate is the soul that has been led from the prison of passion to this perfect freedom of Christ. Such a soul breathes the air of heaven. Its will is always accomplished, for it is one with the will of God, who ordains and permits all things. Its knowledge is heavenly and above all the things of earth. Its freedom is deep and is assured against all disturbance. Its joy is complete in the eternal company of God. Key of David, come, give us all the freedom to live entirely for God and Christ, and to stand aloof from all that is not of God and of Christ our Lord.

When shall we achieve this perfect freedom? Only when in the resurrection of the dead the last enemy has been conquered, and when the last fetter has fallen from our limbs, will our freedom be perfect. Victory and triumph will come for the Church and her teaching when, at the Last Judgment, she is recognized for what she really is. On that day all creation will acknowledge her to be the mystical body of Christ, the ark which has saved mankind. Her children, too, will triumph on that day, for Christ will say to them, "Come, ye blessed of My Father, possess you the kingdom prepared for you from the foundation of the world" (Mt 25:34). "Lift up your heads, because your redemption is at hand" (Lk 21:28).

Prayer

O Key of David, and Scepter of the house of Israel, who openeth and no man shutteth, who shutteth and no man openeth, come and bring forth from his prison house the captive that sitteth in darkness and in the shadow of death. Amen.

December 21, O Oriens

"O Dawn of the East, brightness of light eternal and Sun of Justice, come and enlighten all who sit in darkness and in the shadow of death."

"You were heretofore darkness" (Eph 5:8). The sun awakens life; it brings vitality, beauty, and health to the material world. Should this light fail, the world would languish and wither away; all creatures would be struck with consternation. A similar happening occurs in the soul that has been cut off from grace. That soul sits in the shadow of death. It is afflicted by doubts, and as the light of grace wanes, it is plunged into the black night of despair. It deteriorates morally; it trembles with anxiety at the thought of the future. Its life, yes, its very existence is a mystery. It is uncertain of its origin, ignorant of its future. The existence of suffering and death are for it a complete mystery. Such is the state of a soul cut off from Christ. For ages mankind has puzzled over the mystery of life. It has worshiped at the shrine of idols fashioned by its own hand. It has run the gamut of idolatry from the worship of serpents to the worship of self. It has sought light in sacrifice, even in the sacrifice of human life; yet it has found no enlightenment; it has attained no peace or freedom. The sun has been obscured, the light of Christ has not been revealed to it.

It is the Sun, the Redeemer, whom we await. "I am the light [the sun] of the world" (Jn 8:12). Christ is the light of the world because of the faith which He has infused into souls. He has enlightened the world by His teaching and by the example of His life. In the crib, in Nazareth, on the cross on Calvary, in the tabernacle of our churches, He answers the eternal questioning of the benighted soul.

By the light of this Sun all is made clear. Men come to a new knowledge, a true and certain knowledge of their origin and their destiny. From Christ they learn that God is a loving Father who recognizes them as His children, and who wishes them to be eternally happy with Him. Man comes to a correct knowledge of himself and his relationship to God. He learns the worthlessness of all that is passing and temporal. He begins to understand the value of obscurity, the joy of suffering, the regenerative power of charity. But Christ gives more than knowledge; He gives new strength, new hope, new ideals. "I am the light of the world." From Christ comes all true life: all understanding, all happiness, all prosperity, all power.

O eternal Sun, come and enlighten us, for where Thou art not, there is darkness, death, and wickedness. "Come and enlighten all who sit in darkness and in the shadow of death."

"But now [you are] light in the Lord" (Eph 5:8). In the Church the light has now appeared to us on the first Christmas night, on the day of our baptism, daily in the Mass and at the time of Holy Communion, and in the many inspirations and promptings of grace. How thankful we should be for this light, which is Christ.

But we have yet to reach the full measure of the stature of Christ. Alas! we let ourselves be burdened by earthly sorrow, we are distracted by the excitement of the moment, and our spiritual growth is hampered by our attachment to the things of this world. Fervently we should repeat that plea of Holy Mother the Church, "O dawning Sun of righteousness, come and enlighten us, who yet sit in the darkness of suffering, of human reasoning, and of self-love."

The light of Christ will be revealed perfectly only when we meet Him at the time of His second coming. Then we shall be brought into the light of glory, and we shall "shine as the sun in the kingdom of their Father" (Mt 13:43).

Prayer

O Dawn of the East, brightness of eternal light and Sun of Justice, come and enlighten all who sit in darkness and in the shadow of death. Amen.

December 22, O Rex Gentium

"O King of the Gentiles and their desired one, Thou corner-stone that maketh both one, come and save man, whom Thou hast made out of dust."

"A certain nobleman went into a far country to receive for himself a kingdom and to return" (Lk 19:12). This nobleman is Christ, the Son of God, King of all nations. His kingdom is over all men and over all things, both material and spiritual. He has everything in His hand as God and man. But another, Satan, has broken into His kingdom and has made himself master of many of Christ's subjects. In the old dispensation only a small part of humanity, the chosen people, remained faithful to the almighty King.

Christ, the Son of God, came into this "far country" in order to become man and, by means of humility, obedience, and poverty, to cast out the usurper who had taken His subjects. He came to reassert His dominion over all those who had left Him, both Jews and Gentiles.

"Come and save man, whom Thou hast made out of dust." What is man? He is but a particle of dust, an insignificant creature who has further separated himself from God through sin. He has been cut off from the fountain of truth and banished from God to darkness and misery. Still in the ruins there dwells a spirit that possesses a capacity for truth. In these ashes there is yet a spark that may be fanned to life to burn with the brilliance of divine life. But only God can revive this flame. For this reason the Church cries out, "Come and save man, whom Thou hast made out of dust." Save him who is so weak, so miserable and helpless. Remember his nothingness. Consider the many enemies who lay snares to rob him of divine life and to entice him into sin. Think of his obscured knowledge and his proneness to evil, of his tendency to error, and his weakness in the face of temptation. Guard him from the enticements of the world; shelter him from the poison of erroneous teaching; deliver him from the devil and his angels.

During these days before Christmas, the Church contemplates the overwhelming misery of unregenerated mankind. She cries out, "Come and save man, whom Thou hast made out of dust." She cries out to heaven with the Psalmist, "Have mercy on me, O God, according to Thy great mercy; and according to the multitude of Thy tender mercies blot out my iniquity. Wash me yet more from my iniquity, and cleanse me from my sin.... For behold I was conceived in iniquities, and in sins did my mother conceive me.... Turn away Thy face from my sins, and blot out all my iniquities" (Ps 50:3 f., 7, 11). Let us join fervently in this request.

Jesus is King of all nations. "The kings of the earth stood up and the princes met together against the Lord and against His Christ. Let us break their bonds asunder, and let us cast away their yoke from us. He that dwelleth in heaven shall laugh at them, and the Lord shall deride them. Then shall He speak to them in His anger and trouble them in His rage. But I am appointed king by Him over Sion, His holy mountain.... The Lord hath said to Me; Thou art My Son; this day have I begotten Thee. Ask of Me and I will give Thee the Gentiles for Thy inheritance, and the utmost parts of the earth for Thy possession" (Ps 2:2–8). Well may Herod seek the life of the newborn king. Indeed, many kings and tribes and nations in the course of time shall deprecate the divine King, Christ. But to Him has been given all power in heaven and on earth (Mt 28:18). Before Him every knee shall bend, and every tongue shall confess that He is the Lord (Phil 2:10 f.). The more the mighty contemn the kingship of Christ, the more shall He be exalted by the Father.

Now He comes to us in the form of a lovely child. One day in the presence of the Roman governor He will assert His right to kingship. But after this one public confession of His royal origin He withdraws again into the obscurity which He had freely chosen. For the present He is satisfied with this manifestation of His royal dignity. The day will come, however, when He will manifest it with power and majesty as He comes again on the clouds of heaven. Before all nations God will declare: "I have anointed Him King of Sion, My holy mountain." All men shall pay Him homage as king; all nations shall acclaim Him the King of Glory.

Prayer

O King of the Gentiles and their desired one, Thou cornerstone that maketh both (the Jew and the Gentile) one, come and save man, whom Thou hast made out of dust. Amen.

December 23, O Emmanuel

"O Emmanuel (God with us), our King and Lawgiver, Thou expected one of the nations and their Redeemer, come and save us, O Lord our God."

Now we are about to receive the Savior, Emmanuel, God with us. God's only-begotten Son, born of the Father before all time, God of God, light of light, true God of true God, one being with the Father, is about to be born in time. For the salvation of men, He has come down upon earth and is conceived by the Holy Ghost in a virgin. He shall be called God with us, and yet He will be one in nature with us. He is to be like to us in all things except sin. He wills to share our poverty and to pray and suffer with us; He assumes our guilt. He is God with us in every phase of our life; He even takes our place on the cross, he remains with us in Holy Communion, in our daily Mass, and in our tabernacles. At some time in the future He will still be God with us in His beautiful heaven. All this He has done for us even though we have repeatedly turned our back on Him.

"Come and save us." The great God is with us. He has come, not to destroy the sinful world, as He once destroyed Sodom and Gomorrha, but to redeem it from its sins. This redemption is to be accomplished at the cost of great personal sacrifice to Him. As if this did not satisfy the burning ardor of His love, He wills to remain with us in our tabernacles. He incorporates us into Himself and shares His very life with us. We are engrafted in Him as a branch might be grafted to a new tree. "I am the vine, you the branches" (Jn 15:5). God with us! Was ever a God closer to His creatures or more truly one with them? We now belong to God and not to ourselves. We are, so to speak, one with the consecrated host. The Father, looking upon us, no longer sees us as mere creatures, but as part of His only-begotten Son, Jesus. If He sees Christ as the vine, He sees us as the branches. Even the smallest leaf fluttering on the farthest branch belongs to the tree and lives by the sap of the tree. Could Christ have redeemed us more completely than He has by engrafting us into His own divine life?

We are a part of Christ; but we still have much to do to perfect our union with Him. The Christian is another Christ. His thoughts, his judgments, his actions must be fashioned after those of Christ. His subjection to the will of God must be simple and complete; his horror of sin must be instant and compelling; his separation from the world and all that does not lead to God must be unreserved.

God with us! God wished to be with us in order that He might lift us up from our nothingness and incorporate us into His divine life. He comes to us each Christmas to stimulate our growth. In every Mass, in every Holy Communion, in the promptings and stirrings of grace, He draws us yet closer to Himself. In His second coming we shall share His life of transfiguration in heaven.

Prayer

O Emmanuel, our King and Lawgiver, Thou expected one of the nations and their Redeemer, come and save us, O Lord our God. Amen.

Christmastide

The climax of the Christmas season is the birth of Christ. He who is awaited during the season of Advent with such great longing arrives on Christmas Day. He who comes is true God and true man, our Savior, "full of grace and truth; . . . and of His fullness we all have received" (Jn 1:14, 16).

Christmas is the feast of the mercy and love of God. "For God so loved the world as to give His only-begotten Son, that whosoever believeth in Him may not perish, but may have life everlasting" (Jn 3:16). Such is the importance which God places on our salvation and our eternal happiness.

In the liturgy of Advent, Christ is not so much the weak, helpless babe, as the divine King, the heavenly Lord and Savior. Christmas has its own peculiar dogmatic character, which differs from the ideas many pious Christians have of it. Both liturgical piety and popular piety have a place at the crib of the Savior. The liturgy sees the Son of God in the crib at Bethlehem, a King and Master, who appears now in His Church to win a place in the souls of men and to establish His throne in their hearts. He is and must be King. For this reason the liturgy of Christmas and Epiphany both emphasize the idea of the eternal birth of Christ as God as much as the kingship of the child who is born to us.

What happened at Bethlehem is for the liturgy a matter both of the past and the present. Each time the host is consecrated at Mass, the liturgy celebrates Christmas. Our Bethlehem is the altar and the Christian soul. Like the shepherds of Bethlehem, we bring our gifts to Him at the Offertory. In a holy exchange He takes those gifts, transmutes them, and gives them back to us at the time of Holy Communion, that through this exchange we may become like unto Him in all things (Secreta of the first Mass of Christmas). In Holy Communion the Church places Him in our hearts as His mother once laid Him in the manger at Bethlehem. The Lord will be born again in our soul and will take up His abode there. The old man must be put away and a new life must take possession of us as a result of the Incarnation of the Son of God. The Lord sets up His throne in our hearts and fills us with His life, His strength, and His grace. "And I live, now not I; but Christ liveth in me" (Gal 2:20). That is the purpose and the gift of Christmas.

Christmas is also a symbol and a pledge of the glorious coming of Christ which all mankind will witness at the end of the world and which each person will experience individually at the moment of his death. At Christmas He appears among us as the heavenly, glorified Christ, in which form He is once to come to judge the living and the dead. Moreover, this glorification of the humanity of Christ is fulfilled before our eyes. Now we behold it in symbol and in faith; we behold it in the brightness of the light with which the Church illuminates the Holy Night.

We experience also on the feast of Christmas the coming of the divine King in the flesh. Then He comes to us in the Bethlehem of our churches and our souls. He comes to us, too, in the Parousia at the end of the world, when the coming of Christ will find its completion and perfection. In that day the redeemed will experience the joy of victory and the glory which is to have no end.

The liturgy of Christmas first of all sets before us Christ, the divine King, as the object of our contemplation; in second place the Virgin Mother is to occupy our thoughts. It was she who gave birth to the divine King, nourished Him as a child, and watched over Him during the flight into Egypt. She offered Him to God in the temple, and after watching Him grow to manhood, elicited from Him His first miracle at Cana in Galilee. Mary is a type of the Church, which in its turn relives all these mysteries and passes on to her children the graces she receives. Mary is also a type of the individual Christian soul, which should enter with the Church into the feelings and sentiments of the Blessed Mother as presented by the liturgy during the Christmas season. The Christian should become another Mary, doing all things for Christ and in Christ.

Christmas should accomplish in us a new birth. As Mary gave birth to the human nature of Christ and presented Him to the Church, so the Church also, in the power of the Holy Spirit, gives her children a new life in Christ. It is for this reason that the liturgical texts of the Christmas cycle dwell continually on the birth of Christ. He is actually born in us for the first time at the moment of our baptism. He is reborn daily and more perfectly in our souls each time we receive Him in Holy Communion, in the fruit of the Holy Sacrifice of the Mass, and in the unending stream of grace that is poured out upon us.

The birth of Christ through the Virgin Mary is a pledge and a guarantee of the reality of His birth in us, a pledge of our incorporation in His divine life. It assures us of the reality of our function as a branch on the vine of divine life, and is a pledge of our eventual resurrection to eternal life and the possession of eternal happiness.

Vigil of Christmas (1)

Today the liturgy takes us into the sanctuary of the Blessed Mother in the church of St. Mary Major in Rome. She directs our attention to Mary, who is on the point of bringing salvation to us. "In the morning you shall see His glory" (Introit).

Mary conceived of the Holy Ghost. "That which is conceived in her is of the Holy Ghost" (Gospel). This conception is exalted above all others; it is completely beyond the grasp of human intelligence and human experience. Faith alone can grasp the marvel that is transpiring here, and faith exclaims: "Blessed art thou among women." Mary had freely renounced all merely human relationships; this renunciation raised her to a plane on which she was worthy to conceive and bring forth the Son of God. From her substance alone the Holy Spirit would draw material for the body and blood, the heart and the hands and the eyes of the incarnate Son of God. "He hath regarded the humility of His handmaid.... He that is mighty hath done great things to me" (Lk 1:48 f.). Blessed art thou, O handmaid of the Lord. Blessed is he who for the love of God can renounce all things, for "he that shall lose his life for Me shall find it" (Mt 10:39).

Mary conceived the Son of God and gave Him to us. She has already withdrawn from Nazareth to Bethlehem. Here she awaits the hour in which she is to give us that which is to her most precious and most dear. For me and for my salvation she conceived Him and bore Him in her holy bosom for nine months. How she longs to bring Him to me, and what sacrifices she undergoes that He may be mine! She must undertake a long, hard journey in the middle of winter; she is refused a place of rest in Bethlehem, and must withdraw to a rude, cold stable to bring forth her son. But all this she does gladly in order to bring the Savior and His redemption to mankind. These sacrifices are the measure of her love for us, and of her longing to share with us her good fortune.

"Lift up your gates, O ye princes; and be ye lifted up, O eternal gates, and the King of Glory shall enter in" (Offertory). He who has taken up His abode in the bosom of the Virgin, is soon to appear on our altar, in order that He may offer Himself up as a sacrifice for us. He will be born again daily in our hearts in Holy Communion to cleanse us yet more perfectly from our sins. At the moment of Holy Communion I am to receive Him whom Mary loved and bore in her bosom, whom she served, and to whom her whole life was dedicated. How I should strive to imitate the virtues of Mary, now that the holy season of Christmas is approaching! Her heart is filled with faith, longing, and love. She is pure, detached from all things that savor of this world; she is living in perfect union with God.

When I receive Christ in Holy Communion, should He not become for me, as He did for Mary, the center of all my thoughts and desires and my love? Should I not, like Mary, devote to Him my entire life, my strength, my time, and my heart?

"This day you shall know that the Lord will come and save us, and in the morning you shall see His glory" (Introit). These words were first spoken by Moses when he promised the manna to the chosen people. Christ is the true manna which descends from heaven upon Bethlehem and upon the chosen people of the Church of God. He comes to save us. Christmas is a day of forgiveness, and mercy, and grace. For this reason the vigil of Christmas should be a day of penance and self-denial, a day of prayer and pious recollection.

Prayer

O God, who dost gladden us with the yearly expectation of our redemption, grant that we who now joyfully receive Thy only-begotten Son as our Redeemer, may also without fear behold Him coming as our Judge, our Lord Jesus Christ, Thy Son, who with Thee liveth and reigneth world without end. Amen.

Vigil of Christmas (2)

"This day you shall know that the Lord will come and save us, and in the morning you shall see His glory" (Introit). The motif of the liturgy of the day is expectation. Tomorrow is to be the day of fulfillment.

Tomorrow you shall see His glory with your bodily eyes, in reality and truth. "You shall find the infant wrapped in swaddling clothes and laid in a manger" (Lk 2:12). Near His crib, in silent prayer and adoration, you will find His virgin mother. There, too, you will find, silent and absorbed in prayer, the blessed Joseph. Silent night, holy night! There you will find the child, nestling in the forbidding straw, deprived of all comforts which an ungrateful people might have given Him. "He came unto His own, and His own received Him not" (Jn 1:11).

We shall see Him also with the eyes of faith. "In the beginning was the Word, and the Word was with God, and the Word was God.... And the Word was made flesh and dwelt among us (and we saw His glory, the glory as it were of the only-begotten of the Father), full of grace and truth" (Jn 1:14). In this child in the manger are hidden all the treasures of wisdom and knowledge. "For in Him dwelleth all the fullness of the Godhead corporeally" (Col 2:9). He is the one "who is the image of the invisible God, the first-born of every creature. For in Him were all things created in heaven and on earth, visible and invisible, whether thrones, or dominations, or principalities, or powers; all things were created by Him and in Him. And He is before all; and by Him all things consist. And He is the head of the body, the Church, who is the beginning, the first-born from the dead; that in all things He may hold the primacy. Because in Him it hath well pleased the Father that all fullness should dwell; and through Him to reconcile all things unto Himself, making peace through the blood of His cross, both as to the things that are on earth, and the things that are in heaven" (Col 1:15–23).

We behold the child. His human soul is completely immersed in the majesty and the glory of the Godhead. Since He is in continual possession of the vision of God, He has all the treasures of wisdom and knowledge. His soul possesses the vision of the future; it is continually concerned with my salvation, and offers itself up for me and prays for me continually. In the hands of this child is placed the government of the heavens and the earth; His power extends over angels and men, over spirits and hearts. "All power is given to Me in heaven and in earth" (Mt 28:18).

This is He "who was made to Him of the seed of David according to the flesh; who was predestinated the Son of God in power according to the spirit of sanctification by the resurrection of our Lord Jesus Christ from the dead; by whom we have received grace and apostleship for obedience to the faith in all nations for His name, among whom are you also the called of Jesus Christ our Lord" (Epistle). We rejoice in the honor that is bestowed on us in our election to the faith in Jesus Christ. With our whole soul we believe in Him who has become true man and our brother in the flesh. We believe, too, that He is the Son of God, for He convincingly proved His divinity by His resurrection from the dead.

The King of Glory will come to mankind, to the family of nations, and to the hearts of all men, in order to bring them salvation. "Be ye lifted up, O eternal gates"; be opened to Him in faith and longing that you may receive His rule. For it is a rule of grace, of love, and of peace — peace for man with God and with himself. Today we prepare ourselves for His blessed rule by purifying our hearts, our souls, and our thoughts. We shall make our hearts a crib in which He may rest secure.

"The King of Glory shall enter in." He comes now in the lowliness of suffering in order to overcome death, He will one day come in glory as Judge and Ruler of the world. Christmas is the complement of the coming of the Lord on the last day. Blessed are they who now share His lowliness, for they may look forward to His coming as Master and Judge with confidence and hope.

Prayer

O God, who dost gladden us with the yearly expectation of our redemption, grant that we who now joyfully receive Thy only-begotten Son as our Redeemer, may also without fear behold Him coming as our Judge, our Lord Jesus Christ, Thy Son, who with Thee liveth and reigneth world without end. Amen.

Vigil of Christmas (3)

"Be ye lifted up, O eternal gates" (Offertory). Such is the cry that ascends from mankind weeping before the eternal gates. Behind those gates stands the promised Redeemer. He is the one who is to lift up these gates and bring to men the salvation so ardently desired.

The holy gate which conceals the expected Redeemer whom we so much desire is Mary, the Virgin. In the mind of the liturgy she is the *Regis alti janua et porta lucis fulgida,* the gates through which the light of the rising sun, Christ, is to reach mankind. Mary appears in the Mass today as the gate of light through which the Redeemer will come to open for us the gates of paradise, which have been closed to us for so long. She has conceived by the Holy Ghost, not by man. We are assured by the angel that what is born of her is of the Holy Ghost. He who is conceived in the Virgin by the Holy Ghost, is to redeem His people from their sins. We gather about the gate through which He is to come to us. We raise our voices and cry to Mary, the tabernacle in which He is now enthroned: "Show unto us the fruit of thy womb, Jesus, O clement, O loving, O sweet Virgin Mary."

The Redeemer stands behind the holy gate, ready to come. This is He who is the Son of God, "who was made to Him of the seed of David according to the flesh" (Epistle). He is God and man united in one person. He is the Son in whom the Father is well pleased (Mt 3:17). All things are given into His hands by the Father (Mt 11:27). Before Abraham was, He is, and He was possessed of glory before the world was made (Jn 8:58; 17:5). All power in heaven and earth is given to Him (Mt 28:18). Heaven and earth will pass away, but His word will not pass away (Mt 24:35). He is God, and God He will ever remain. It is His will that we become perfect, even as His heavenly Father is perfect. He has a just claim to our faith, our service, and our love. Salvation is possible to us in His name, and there is no other name under heaven whereby we can be saved (Acts 4:12). He is God and at the same time man, the son of the Virgin, flesh of our flesh, like to us in all things, sin excepted (Heb 4:15). He is the Son of Man, a term which He liked to apply to Himself; He is our high priest, our brother, and our Redeemer.

He is full of grace and wisdom, "and of His fullness we all have received" (Jn 1:16). He is the God-man, to whom the winds and the waves are obedient, before whom all human ailments disappear. When the moment of His great humiliation is come, all nature expresses its grief: the sun hides its face, the earth trembles, the stones burst asunder. This is the one who now stands behind the eternal gates and is ready to come to us. Tomorrow He will pass through the gates and come to us to redeem us.

The Mass of the vigil gives us a threefold promise that tomorrow the Redeemer will come and save us. We receive this assurance in the Introit, the Offertory, and the Communion. The event which we have awaited with such great longing all during Advent will become a reality tomorrow. Tomorrow he comes to us through Mary. Lift up the gates of your churches, the gates of your hearts, that the King of Glory may enter.

"Today you shall know that the Lord shall come." His coming in the Mass and in Holy Communion is our best assurance that we shall see His glory tomorrow, as we are promised in the Introit of this Mass. Christmas is the great revelation of His glory, which is revealed in His virgin birth, in the rejoicing of the angels on Christmas morning, in the voluntary poverty of the manger, and in the loving benevolence with which He, God, looks upon men. This is the one who was promised by the prophets of the Old Testament. This is He who is born to us from "the seed of David according to the flesh. Who was predestinated the Son of God in power according to the spirit of sanctification by the resurrection of our Lord Jesus Christ from the dead" (Epistle). In the fullness of time He will certainly come in all His power and majesty to judge the living and the dead. Then all men shall behold His glory. We should have deep faith in Christ, for He is God and man, our Savior, our King, our Master, and our Judge. Let His glory shine upon us, for He is the "only-begotten of the Father, full of grace and truth" (Jn 1:14).

Prayer

O God, who dost gladden us with the yearly expectation of our redemption, grant that we who now joyfully receive Thy only-begotten Son as our Redeemer, may also without fear behold Him coming as our Judge, our Lord Jesus Christ, Thy Son, who with Thee liveth and reigneth world without end. Amen.

Christmas Week

The Three Christmas Masses

Since the time of Pope Gregory the Great (604 A.D.), it has been the custom in the Roman Church to celebrate three Masses on Christmas Day. In Rome the first Mass is celebrated in St. Mary Major during the night; the second, in the church of the Resurrection, St. Anastasia, at the break of day; and the third, in St. Peter's later in the morning. The obscurity and semi-darkness that characterizes the season of Advent, is still found in the first of the Christmas Masses. Mankind still stands in the darkness of the night, filled with expectation. The angels hover brightly over the earth; only Mary is close to the incarnate Son of God. But in the early morning the darkness recedes, and the Sun, the true Sun, Jesus Christ the Redeemer, appears on the horizon. He reaches the zenith in the third Christmas Mass. There we shall behold what we longed for so ardently during Advent. The Son of God comes, and the government of the world is upon his shoulders. He is Christ, the Lord and Master of the universe.

The fundamental thought of the liturgy of the day is the expression, "A child is born to us." The child we behold in the crib is the Lord and ruler of the world; "the government [of the world] is upon His shoulders, and His name shall be called the angel of the great council" (Introit, third Mass). He is the one who is to unfold the great plan of redemption. In gratitude and joy we recite Psalm 97, which tells us of His world dominion. The Kyrie is a plea to the universal King for His mercy and grace. We greet Him joyfully in the Gloria: "Thou art the Son of the Father; Thou who takest away the sins of the world; Thou who sittest at the right hand of the Father. Thou alone art holy, Thou alone art the Lord, Thou alone, O Jesus Christ, art most high with the Holy Ghost in the glory of God the Father."

In the Collect of the Mass we repeat our petition to be freed from the chains of Satan and from sin and to be incorporated into the kingdom of Christ. St. Paul then appears in the Epistle to unfold for us the fullness of the majesty that belongs to the Christ child, who lies before us in the crib. Christ is the Son, the heir of all that the eternal Father possesses; and all things are placed in His hands. He is Master of all that exists, and has placed His throne at the right hand of the Father on high. His reign is eternal and is a reign of justice. Heaven and earth are to pass away, but Christ and His kingdom shall remain.

The Gradual of the Mass is a commentary on the theme that St. Paul introduces. Christ's reign is a reign of grace and will accomplish the redemption of the human race. "All the ends of the earth have seen the salvation of our God.... The Lord hath made known His salvation.... This day a great light hath descended upon the earth." The Gospel continues this thought. Blessed are they who receive the light. To them will be given the grace and the strength to become the children of God. This is the great mystery of Christmas: the Son of God becomes man in order that men may share the life of God.

At the Offertory we approach with gifts in our hands to lay them at the feet of the divine King, Christ. The heavens and the earth are Thine. Thine, too, is my heart, my body, my soul, all that I am and all that I possess. My gift is the bread and wine which will be offered by the priest. To this gift I add my heart, which I wish to unite to Christ, who is my real gift to God; I wish to join with the whole Church triumphant and the Church militant in making the holocaust to the heavenly Father.

Heaven will soon descend upon the altar, "for this day a great light hath descended upon the earth" (Alleluia verse). The altar becomes a throne, and the dominion of this throne extends over all men and all the kingdoms of the earth. "A child is born to us, whose government is upon His shoulders" (Introit). We are not only privileged to see this child, but He is ours to take in our hands and offer to the heavenly Father as a sacrifice of praise, thanksgiving, petition, and reparation. "Hath he not also with Him given us all things?" (Rom 8:32.) Above our own hearts, too, the heavens have opened. At Holy Communion heaven will descend upon us, and Christ will begin the reign of grace in our hearts. "All the ends of the earth have seen the salvation of our God" (Gradual). Be thou, O Christ, King and Lord of all nations, and Lord and Master of my heart.

Christmas (1)

Today the liturgy takes us to Bethlehem, to the crib of the newborn King. There we cast ourselves on our knees in adoration and contemplate the words of the Credo and the Gospel.

"I believe ... in the one Lord Jesus Christ, the only-begotten Son of God, born of the Father before all ages. God of God, light of light, true God of true God. Begotten, not made; consubstantial with the Father; by whom all things were made. Who for us men and for our salvation came down from heaven; and was incarnate by the Holy Ghost of the Virgin Mary, and was made man" (Credo).

In the Gospel of the third Mass, St. John announces the Incarnation of the Son of God:

In the beginning was the Word; and the Word was with God; and the Word was God. The same was in the beginning with God. All things were made by Him, and without Him was made nothing that was made. In Him was life; and the life was the light of men. And the light shineth in darkness, and the darkness did not comprehend it. There was a man sent from God whose name was John. This man came for a witness, to give testimony of the light, that all men might believe through him. He was not the light, but was to give testimony of the light. That was the true light, which enlighteneth every man that cometh into this world. He was in the world, and the world was made by Him, and the world knew Him not. He came unto His own, and His own received Him not. But as many as received Him, He gave them power to be made the sons of God, to them that believe in His name; who are born, not of blood, nor of the will of the flesh, nor of the will of man, but of God. And the Word was made flesh and dwelt among us (and we saw His glory, the glory, as it were, of the only-begotten of the Father), full of grace and truth.... And of His fullness we all have received, grace for grace (Jn 1:1–14, 16).

How can we fail to become inflamed with love for Him who for love of us poured Himself out and humbled Himself even to the death of the cross? And yet we love Him so little.

Should not a living faith in the mystery of Christmas fill us with unspeakable joy and inflame our hearts with love? The Son of God has given us the power to become with Him children of God and to share in the divine life. This life comes from the Father to the Son, and, by reason of the Incarnation, from the Son to us. "Of His fullness we all have received." Yet we profit so little from this great truth.

The Son of God came to us, became one of us, and shared our human nature in order to make it possible for us to share with Him the sonship of God. Of ourselves we have no claim to this exalted dignity, for our natural inheritance is the sin of Adam. We had been disinherited by our Father and were children of wrath. But God sent His Son to follow us into our exile and call us back to the adoption of the sons of God.

Since Christ is our brother, we share the love, protection, and care which His Father showers upon Him. How significant for us, then, are these words, "children of God," when we recall the words of the Father on the banks of the Jordan and on Mount Tabor: "This is My beloved Son, in whom I am well pleased" (Mt 3:17; 17:5). At baptism the heavenly Father addresses these same words to us: "This is My beloved son." By these words we are "translated... into the kingdom of the Son of His love" (Col 1:13) and partake of the nobility, joy, and inheritance of the Son of God. We are "heirs indeed of God, and joint heirs with Christ" (Rom 8:17); we are His "brethren" (Rom 8:29). He is God's Son by generation and nature; we are His sons by grace and adoption.

"Behold what manner of charity the Father hath bestowed upon us, that we should be called and should be the sons of God" (1 Jn 3:1). Are we not amazed that we who are dust and ashes should now become the children of God, brothers of the Word Incarnate, and heirs of the kingdom of heaven? Sad to say, many of us esteem the goods of this earth and the affection of men above this marvelous brotherhood and this glorious inheritance.

O child of God, quickened by the spirit of Christ, think, live, and love with the spirit of Christ. Study this spirit as you gaze upon Him in His crib. He will come, too, to the crib of your heart, and here He will seek to free you from the spirit of pride, from the spirit of selfishness, and from your sins.

Our fellow men are also the children of God and the brethren of Christ. Let us not forget that our neighbor is as much the son of God as we are. How, then, can we despise a child of God, a brother of Christ? We may despise his faults, it is true, but not the man himself, for he, too, is a brother of Christ.

Prayer

Grant, we beseech Thee, almighty God, that the new birth in the flesh of Thy only-begotten Son may set us free, whom the old bondage doth hold under the yoke of sin. Amen.

Christmas (2)

In the second Mass on Christmas the liturgy directs our attention to the crib of the Savior. "A light shall shine upon us this day, for the Lord is born to us; and He shall be called Wonderful, God, the Prince of Peace, the Father of the world to come; of whose reign there shall be no end. The Lord hath reigned, He is clothed with beauty; the Lord is clothed with strength and hath girded Himself" (Introit of the second Mass).

With our gaze fixed on the crib which has become the throne of the God-man, we rejoice in the words of the Apostle: "For we ourselves also were some time unwise, incredulous, erring, slaves to diverse desires and pleasures, living in malice and envy, hateful and hating one another" (Ti 3:3). "And you, when you were dead in your offenses and sins, wherein in time past you walked according to the course of this world, according to the prince of the power of this air, of the spirit that now worketh on the children of unbelief; in which also we all conversed in time past, in the desires of our flesh, fulfilling the will of the flesh and of our thoughts, and were by nature children of wrath, even as the rest" (Eph 2:1–3). We were all of us at one time unredeemed, far from God, separated from Christ, and wanting the grace and sonship of God.

"But when the goodness and kindness of God our Savior appeared, not by the works of justice which we have done, but according to His mercy He saved us by the laver of regeneration and the renovation of the Holy Ghost, whom He hath poured forth upon us abundantly, through Jesus Christ our Savior; that being justified by His grace, we may be heirs according to hope of life everlasting" (Ti 3:4–7; Epistle of the second Mass). We are redeemed. That is the glad tidings which the Savior has brought us through His Incarnation and birth of the Virgin Mary.

We are redeemed. This redemption is accomplished through Christ Jesus, the infant in the crib. He has won for us all the benefits of the redemption. We have only to believe in Him, think of Him, and unite ourselves to Him. Because of His great mercy, God has delivered us from the reign of the powers of darkness — from sin, the tyranny of passion, Satan, and hell — and has made us coheirs of the kingdom of His divine Son, "in whom we have redemption through His blood, the remission of sins" (Col 1:14).

The chains by which Satan held us captive have been broken, and we have escaped from his power. We have become incorporated into the kingdom of the Son of God and entitled to the fruits of the redemption. Among these fruits are the possession of truth and grace, the indwelling of the Holy Spirit in our souls, the love of God, and complete incorporation into Christ and His Church. By means of the redemption we may now take part in the life of the vine which is Christ, and we have the assurance of our eventual resurrection and the possession of eternal life. All these things are now ours, brought to us by the child in the crib, not because of our good works, but because of His great mercy. "By this hath the charity of God appeared towards us, because God hath sent His only-begotten Son into the world that we may live by

Him. In this is charity; not as though we had loved God; but because He hath first loved us, and sent His Son to be a propitiation for our sins" (1 Jn 4:9 f.).

Christ "gave Himself for us, that He might redeem us from all iniquity, and might cleanse to Himself a people acceptable, a pursuer of good works" (Ti 2:14). In order to accomplish God's purpose, the purification and sanctification of the world, the Son of God has delivered Himself up for us by His suffering, death, and resurrection. By means of the waters of baptism, the celebration of the Eucharistic sacrifice, and the other sacraments, God makes it possible for us to take part in this mighty work. With the Apostle and Holy Mother the Church we say: "And I live, now not I; but Christ liveth in me" (Gal 2:20). We are redeemed. But we must allow Him to accomplish in us the fullness of His redemption. On His part nothing is lacking.

The Christian is another Christ. To accomplish reality, Christ comes daily upon our altars, and into our souls in Holy Communion; He wishes to communicate to us the fullness of His divine life and transform us unto His own likeness. How far I have drifted from Him! How little I really resemble Him! How little I resemble Him in the poverty of His crib, in His abnegation and love of poverty, in His devotion to the cross, and in His love for souls!

Prayer

Grant, we beseech Thee, almighty God, that the new birth in the flesh of Thy only-begotten Son may set us free, whom the old bondage doth hold under the yoke of sin. Amen.

December 26, St. Stephen

The liturgy places St. Stephen first among the saints who stand about the crib of the Savior. Stephen is a man full of grace and the Holy Spirit, the first martyr to bear witness to the faith in Jesus Christ. In the liturgy St. Stephen is not only a historical person; he is at the same time the embodiment of an idea. Every Christian must work out his redemption as St. Stephen did; he must first of all become filled with grace and the Holy Spirit, and outwardly this spirit must manifest itself by a steadfast faith in Christ and a willingness to testify to the divinity of Christ, even by martyrdom if necessary.

At the command of the apostles, the faithful chose seven men "full of the Holy Ghost and wisdom," among whom was Stephen, "a man full of faith and of the Holy Ghost" (Acts 6:5). The seven were brought to the apostles, who prayed over them and laid hands upon them, ordaining them deacons. The most distinguished of these is Stephen, who, "full of grace and fortitude, did great wonders and signs among the people" (Epistle; Acts 6:8). Courageously he acknowledges Christ. In the true spirit of detachment he endures the death of stoning at the hands of the very men whom he desired to bring to the love of Christ. Drenched in blood and on the point of death he prays, "Lord Jesus, receive my spirit.... Lord lay not this sin to their charge" (Epistle). Thus died Stephen, a man full of faith and love, who lays down his life with a prayer on his lips for the forgiveness of his murderers. Thus the mystery of Christmas and the redemption was worked out in the life of St. Stephen.

St. Stephen is a type of the Church and of the true Christian. The coming of the Son of God is not merely a lovely idyll, a pastoral scene, or an idle play; it is a reality which must be accomplished in the life of the Church and in the life of each Christian. The Christian who wishes to celebrate Christmas in the proper spirit must become like St. Stephen, a man of faith and wisdom, a man of grace and fortitude in the Holy Spirit. He must place his life and his strength at the service of the Son of God and, becoming an apostle of Christ, dedicate himself to the salvation of the souls of his fellow men. For it will come to pass that the Christian, too, will come "unto his own, and his own received him not" (Jn 1:11); then he will have acquired the spirit of Christ. The Christian, too, must become a martyr for Christ, for Christ came, not to bring peace, but the sword (Mt 10:34). Christ will and must be a king. He turns away resolutely from the old man, from all that is worldly and all that is sinful. "He that is not with Me is against Me" (Lk 11:23). Those who accept Christ completely will themselves soon experience that which was written of the Son of God, "His own received Him not." This repudiation has been the experience of the Church, and it will be the experience of each faithful Christian. This is the idea which St. Stephen personifies in the liturgy of today.

"Princes sat and spoke against me, and the wicked persecuted me.... [But] I see the heavens opened and Jesus standing on the right hand of the power of God" (Gradual). Stephen is a type of the Church and the true Christian. "The torrent of stones was sweet to him" (Antiphon at Lauds). Stephen is a symbol of the Church, for his spirit is in her and in all true Christians.

In the Offertory of the Mass we bring forward our gifts of bread and wine; we bring to the altar our body and soul, our heart and our life, and we say as other Stephens: "Lord Jesus, receive my spirit." Take all that I am and all that I have, O my King and my God.

In the Communion today we identify ourselves with Stephen. We await the second coming of Christ at the moment of our death with the words, "Lord Jesus, receive my spirit." Take from me everything, that I may live only to Thee.

Prayer

Grant us, we beseech Thee, O Lord, so to imitate what we revere that we may learn to love even our enemies; for we celebrate the day of his birth to immortality, who could plead with our Lord Jesus Christ, Thy Son, even on behalf of his persecutors. Who with Thee liveth and reigneth world without end. Amen.

December 27, St. John the Apostle

Today at the side of the newborn King we find, with the Virgin Mother, the virgin apostle, John, adoring in the house of Mary in Bethlehem — the stational church of St. Mary Major.

John is the living expression of the blessings that have been brought to us by the redemption. John is a man of virginal purity, the man who rested on the breast of the Master, who is filled with divine wisdom. "In the midst of the Church the Lord opened his mouth and filled him with the spirit of wisdom and understanding; He clothed him with a robe of glory" (Introit). His life is absorbed in Christ, the incarnate Wisdom. "She will meet him as an honorable mother. With the bread of life and understanding she shall feed him, and give him the water of wholesome wisdom to drink. And she shall be made strong in him, and he shall not be moved; and she shall hold him fast, and he shall not be confounded;

and she shall exalt him among his neighbors, and in the midst of the Church she shall open his mouth, and shall fill him with the spirit of wisdom and understanding, and shall clothe him with a robe of glory. The Lord our God shall heap upon him a treasure of joy and gladness, and shall cause him to inherit an everlasting name" (Epistle). These are the works which Christ, the child in the manger, the eternal Wisdom, accomplishes in John, His disciple, and in His Church. These, too, the fruits of the Incarnation, He would accomplish in our lives if we would permit it.

John is the unerring witness of the Incarnation and of the birth of Christ, the God-man. Yesterday St. Stephen, by his words and by laying down his life for his faith, bore witness to the child we see here in the crib. Today we receive the testimony of John, the apostle and Evangelist. He has given us his testimony in his Gospel. "In the beginning was the Word, and the Word was with God, and the Word was God.... And the Word was made flesh and dwelt among us (and we saw His glory, the glory as it were of the only-begotten of the Father), full of grace and truth" (Jn 1:14). "And we know that his witness is true," cries the liturgy today in the Gospel and in the Alleluia verse.

Because of his virginal purity and his spirituality, John drew closer to the person of Christ and had a keener insight into the mysteries of His life than any other apostle. He rested upon the breast of the Master and drew the riches of his Gospel from the heart of Christ Himself. In his writings he poured forth upon the world the riches of the Word of God. As a result of his contemplation and of his great personal love for the Savior, he is full of wisdom and initiated into all the mysteries of Christ. In St. John we have a reliable witness; we know that his testimony is true. "In the beginning was the Word.... And the Word was made flesh."

In St. John is fulfilled the promise of the Epistle: "He that feareth God will do good; and he that possesseth justice shall lay hold on her.... With the bread of life and understanding she shall feed him, and give him the water of wholesome wisdom to drink; and she shall be made strong in him, and he shall not be moved" (Epistle). In John we recognize ourselves, for in the Holy Sacrifice of the Mass our Lord feeds us with the bread of life and wisdom.

In the house of Mary, in Holy Mother the Church, we have infallible truth. John gives us this truth in his Gospel and in his life. This truth radiates from the incarnate Wisdom which we see in the manger on Christmas Day; its fruits are a life of purity, the forsaking of all that is sinful and unholy, and a life centered on God.

When we celebrate Christmas in the proper spirit, we, too, add our testimony to that of St. Stephen and St. John. "The light shineth in darkness, but the darkness did not comprehend it" (Jn 1:5). We should add to the testimony of John the testimony of our own faith. Still more should we bear witness to Christ by the purity of our lives, by the strength of our love of Christ, and by forsaking all that cannot with propriety be seen at the side of the crib and in the house of Mary.

Prayer

Do Thou, O Lord, in Thy goodness shine upon Thy Church; that enlightened by the teaching of blessed John, Thy apostle and Evangelist, she may attain to the everlasting gifts. Through our Lord Jesus Christ. Amen.

December 28, Feast of the Holy Innocents

With St. Stephen and St. John the Apostle, the Holy Innocents today bear witness to the newborn King. "Out of the mouth of infants and of sucklings, O God, Thou hast perfected praise, because of Thy enemies" (Introit). Children and those with the simplicity of children are dear to the heart of Christ. "Suffer the little children and forbid them not to come to Me" (Mt 19:14).

Christ, indeed, has enemies. "He was in the world, . . . and the world knew Him not" (Jn 1:10). "Behold this child is set for the fall and for the resurrection of many in Israel" (Lk 2:34). The enemy (Herod) already lurks in nearby Jerusalem. He is determined to destroy the child and orders the brutal murder of the children of Bethlehem and its environs. Wherever Christ is reproduced, in His Person, in His teaching, in His spirit and His commandments, in His Church, and especially in His holy members, He finds contradiction and hatred. "If they have persecuted Me, they will also persecute you" (Jn 15:20). Persecution is characteristic of true Christianity; it is the mark of the Church and of the true Christian: "If you had been of the world, the world would love its own; but because you are not of the world, but I have chosen you out of the world, therefore the world hateth you" (Jn 15:19).

Christ has many witnesses: the prophets, the angels, John the Baptist, the shepherds, the star, the wise men of the East, the Holy Innocents. All of these are willing and joyful witnesses of the Savior. Through their untimely death and the ceaseless wail of their distracted mothers, the Holy Innocents of Bethlehem proclaim far and wide the birth of Him whom Herod sought to kill. Of them Christ has said: "You shall be witnesses unto Me" (Acts 1:8). One must be with Christ or against Him. One must be a witness to Him or an enemy to Him. There can be no neutrality in the service of Christ.

Happy were the children of Bethlehem who were privileged to offer their lives for the persecuted and despised Savior. They belong now to the multitude of the elect who have "His name and the name of His Father written on their foreheads. . . . And they sung, as it were, a new canticle before the throne and before the four living creatures. . . . These were purchased from among men, the first fruits to God and to the Lamb. And in their mouth there was found no lie; for they are without spot before the throne of God" (Epistle).

The devil could have conferred upon the Holy Innocents no greater favor than that accomplished by his hatred of them. To live, to suffer, and to die for Christ and His cause, is not a loss, but a privilege. "He that hateth his life in this world, keepeth it unto life eternal. If any man minister to Me, let him follow Me; and where I am, there also shall My minister be" (Jn 12:25 f.).

In the Offertory of the Mass the Holy Innocents represent us. At Mass we bring forward all that we are and have — our life, our body and soul, and all our goods — and offer them freely in witness to the divinity of Christ. We are indeed privileged to thus offer ourselves for Christ; for through this offering and through the union of our life with His, we shall be freed from the slavery of sin and of the flesh. For this reason we rejoice with the Holy Innocents in the Offertory prayer: "Our soul hath been delivered as a sparrow out of the snare of the fowlers. The snare is broken, and we are delivered."

"A voice in Rama was heard, lamentation and great mourning; Rachel bewailing her children, and would not be comforted because they are not" (Communion). These children, however, now live and have communion with the glorified Christ. We, too, shall share this divine life if we share in His passion.

PRAYER

O God, whose praise the martyred Innocents confessed this day, not by speech, but in their death; mortify in us all the evils of vice, that Thy faith which our tongues profess, our lives also may by their actions confess. Through our Lord Jesus Christ. Amen.

Sunday within the Octave of Christmas (1)

In the middle of the night the Word of God descended into the homes of the Egyptians and slew every first-born among them. Israel was then freed from the Egyptian captivity. The Introit of the Mass for this Sunday reminds us of this marvelous delivery. "While all things were in quiet silence and the night was in the midst of her course, Thy almighty Word leapt down from heaven from the royal throne" (Ws 18:14 f.) and released Israel from the chains of the Egyptians from which they yearned so long to be freed. This descent of the angel among the people of Israel is a foreshadowing of the descent of the Son of God to free mankind when He comes to us at Christmas.

"God sent His Son, made of woman, made under the law, that He might redeem them who were under the law; that we might receive the adoption of sons" (Epistle). This is the mystery of Christmas, the mystery of the love, wisdom, justice, and mercy of God. We were slaves to the Egyptians; we served the severe taskmasters of this life: the world, the flesh, and the devil. God, looking upon our misery, sends His Son to become a slave, to assume our bondage, to purchase our freedom. Christ becomes subject to all the ills to which the human race is subject; He must be born as men are born, He must grow to manhood, He must suffer, He must die. He must be like to us in all things except sin. He is subject even to the law of Moses, since He is a Hebrew. He faithfully observes this law, which was fashioned for a sinful and stiff-necked people, and which had become for them an insufferable burden.

On this Sunday we find the Son of God, the almighty Word, with His mother and His foster father in the temple, humbly submitting to the prescriptions of the law of Moses, as if He had been conceived in sin like His fellow men. From His submission to the law one might suppose that He, too, had been conceived in a natural way, by the desires of man and by a human father, not by the will and power of God. For Him the law was not necessary, but He submits to it joyfully and willingly. He has become a slave for us in order to free us from our bondage. Surely there has never been a more sublime example of perfect love and condescension. The Son of God descends from His royal throne and exchanges His divine freedom for the chains of men in order that men may be free. Such an act of divine condescension demands our careful contemplation.

"God sent His Son" to redeem us "that we might receive the adoption of sons." This is freedom, indeed. Not only are we freed from the bondage of sin, but we are made sons of God and share the majesty of the Son of God. "And because you are sons, God hath sent the Spirit of His Son into your hearts, crying: Abba, Father. Therefore now he is not a servant, but a son; and if a son, an heir also through God" (Epistle). But this redemption which the Son of God has wrought in us is not merely a liberation from the slavery of the world, the flesh, and the devil; it elevates us to a higher sphere and introduces us to a new life. "But as many as received Him,

He gave them power to be made the sons of God, to them that believe in His name; who are born, not of blood, nor of the will of the flesh, nor of the will of man, but of God" (Jn 1:12 f.).

We are, then, the children of God, born to Him through the virginal birth of baptism, and are filled with the spirit of His life, by which we are entitled to cry out to God and call Him our Father. "Hallowed be Thy name; Thy kingdom come; Thy will be done." Thy will be done in us and through us. A redemption such as this could have been conceived only by the infinite wisdom of God and executed only through His almighty power. A new race comes into being at Christmas, a race born of the strength of the incarnate Word of God. The child who is born to us at Christmas is born under the law, but holds the scepter of omnipotence in His tiny hands.

The Gospel of the day describes the members of the family who surround the throne of the newborn King. Grouped about His throne we find the Virgin Mother and her virginal spouse, St. Joseph. There, too, is the aged Simeon, now filled with the Spirit of God and uttering his great prophecy: "Behold, this child is set for the fall and for the resurrection of many in Israel, and for a sign which shall be contradicted. And thy own soul a sword shall pierce." Nearby lingers the chaste widow, Anna, the prophetess, whose days and nights were spent in prayer and the service of God. These are the first members of the new race raised to a new life by the Spirit of God. Theirs is the new age, the age in which men will live by the Spirit of God, abounding in all good works (Collect).

The Incarnate Word of God became subject to the law in order to free us from the servitude of the law and to establish His sovereignty over us. Though subject to the law, He is above the law and confers upon our fallen nature a royal freedom that makes us the children of God.

With profound gratitude we cry out to Him, "The Lord hath reigned; He is clothed with beauty; the Lord is clothed with strength and hath girded Himself" (Introit). "Thou art beautiful above the sons of men; grace is poured abroad in Thy lips" (Gradual). The glory of the divine King, of the Word of God, the reflected splendor of the Father, shines in the eyes and upon the lips of the child in the manger at Bethlehem. He is our brother and our Savior, who for our sake was subject to the law of childhood and childhood's weaknesses. Yet He is the only-begotten of the Father.

"My heart hath uttered a good word, I speak my works to the King" (Gradual). The Church, the bride of the divine King, presents herself to Him as a victim. In the celebration of the Holy Eucharist, the almighty Word of God descends upon the altar (into the womb of His bride), and in Holy Communion takes up His abode in the hearts (His crib) of her children, to fulfill what was announced in the Epistle and Gospel. He becomes subject to the law, as our sacrifice and sacrificial meal, "that He might redeem them who were under the law, that we might receive the adoption of sons. And because you are sons, God hath sent the Spirit of His Son into your hearts, crying: Abba, Father. Therefore now he is not a servant, but a son; and if a son, an heir also through God" (Epistle).

"Learn of Me" to be resigned to the law of obedience, to the requirements of your vocation, to the call of duty, to the will of God. "He that humbleth himself shall be exalted" (Lk 14:118:14).

Prayer

Almighty and everlasting God, do Thou direct our actions according to Thy good pleasure, that we may deserve to abound in good works, in the name of Thy beloved Son, who reigneth with Thee forever. Amen.

Sunday within the Octave of Christmas (2)

"Take the child and His mother and go into the land of Israel, for they are dead that sought the life of the child" (Mt 2:20). Joseph listens attentively to the words of the angel, and taking the child and His mother, he returns to the land of Israel. The Church uses these words in the Communion prayer of today's Mass and applies them to the Eucharist.

"Take the child." The time of the exile in Egypt is passed. It was a time of trial and hardship. Joseph and Mary and the child live in a foreign land, among a people whose religion, customs, and tastes differed from their own. They were undoubtedly subjected to many discomforts and humiliations. Before they fled into Egypt, Joseph had been instructed to "be there until I shall tell thee" (Mt 2:13). Joseph and Mary do not attempt to shorten the time of their exile; they wait in patience and longing for the call which will bring them back to the land of Israel. They have resigned their wills completely to the will of God. Now the angel appears and says, "Arise and take the child and His mother and go into the land of Israel, for they are dead that sought the life of the child" (Mt 2:20). Joseph responds immediately to the command. Both he and Mary carry out with childlike simplicity and complete confidence whatever God commands them to do.

"Go into the land of Israel." Christ's reason for coming into the world was to free us from our exile and to lead us back to the promised land of eternity. "Take the child and His mother," the liturgy urges us in the Communion prayer. United with Christ and supported by His strength, we shall find our way back to the blessed land of eternity, for "except you eat the flesh of the Son of Man and drink His blood, you shall not have life in you. He that eateth My flesh and drinketh My blood, hath everlasting life" (Jn 6:54 f.).

The Eucharist is the sacrament of life and grace. The other sacraments also produce life in us, but only because of their connection with this sacrament, the most sublime of the lifegiving channels of grace. "Except you eat the flesh of the Son of Man and drink His blood, you shall not have life in you" (Jn 6:54). Only if we have the strength provided by this marvelous food shall we be able to survive the hardships of the long and arduous journey to eternity. We must remember that we are commanded by the Church to "take the child," to receive Him frequently in the Eucharist.

"This is the bread which cometh down from heaven, that if any man eat of it, he may not die" (Jn 6:50). This is the bread which gives us the strength to withstand all temptations, to overcome all the enemies of grace and virtue. It is at the same time the antidote which preserves us from mortal sin (Council of Trent). This bread nourishes the soul and strengthens it against its own evil inclinations. It cannot be otherwise, for when we receive the body of Christ, we become one with Him. When we receive Him into our heart in Holy Communion, He is like a holy fire that burns in our heart. He desires to draw us to Him and transform us. By receiving this bread, all the obstacles that hinder our return to the land of Israel — our pride, our self-will, our evil passions — are subdued and cleared away.

"Take the child and His mother and go into the land of Israel." If we wish to return to the blessed land of our Fathers, there is no other way except in company with the child. And we must take not only the child, but also His mother. Mary, the mother of Christ according to the flesh, is our mother according to the spirit. It was she who brought forth the body and the blood which we receive in Holy Communion.

She was the divinely appointed helper of the new Adam, and by her humility and resignation to the will of God, she cooperated in the salvation of the human race. By her intercession she obtains for us every grace that we receive from God. Whoever desires grace from God may turn to Mary with confidence. God gladly gives His grace through her. To seek graces that do not come to us through her hands would be a fruitless task. "So mighty art thou, O Lady, and so great, that he who desires grace and comes not to thee for aid, would have his desires seeking to fly without wings."[4]

"Take the child and His mother." Christ in the Eucharist is the center of devotion in the Church, and near Him is His mother. Christ in the Eucharist should also be the center of devotion for every Christian. More important than all other devotions is the Mass and the reception of Communion. But Mary, too, must find a place in our devotions, for she is the Mediatrix of all graces. Let us be sure that we assist devoutly at Mass, that we understand the mysteries of the Eucharist, and that we appreciate the privilege of being children of Mary and members of the mystical body of her divine Son.

Prayer

O almighty and everlasting God, do Thou direct our actions according to Thy good pleasure, that we may deserve to abound in good works, in the name of Thy beloved Son, who reigneth with Thee forever. Amen.

At the Manger (1)

With the liturgy we acknowledge the helpless child in the manger to be the strong one, the almighty and divine King, the Lord of all, the founder and Master of the "kingdom of truth and life." His is "a kingdom of holiness and grace, a kingdom of justice, love, and peace" (Preface for the feast of Christ the King). Faith sees a crown and scepter that are invisible to corporeal eyes.

We gaze in wonder at the enthronement of this King. God the Father proclaims Him King over Sion, the Church; and the new King announces to the whole world: "I am appointed King by Him over Sion, His holy mountain, preaching His commandment" (Ps 2:6). Though we find Him here apparently helpless in the manger, all power is given to Him in heaven and on earth (Mt 28:18). I believe in Thy kingship O Lord; I submit to Thy rule; I am fortunate to be ruled by so gracious a King. Unreservedly I trust in Thy authority. In the service of Thee and Thy kingdom I wish to live and die.

The foundations upon which this King builds His empire are not those of flesh and blood. He depends on no mighty armies and sets no value on nobility of birth. He is not dependent on the fickle attachment of men, and has no need of the intelligence and talents of those who serve Him. Money and wealth are not the means of advancement in His kingdom, but the possession of grace is all-important. "No man can come to Me except the Father, who hath sent Me, draw him" (Jn 6:44). The ideal courtier is he who listens eagerly to the promptings of grace and follows them. "Every one that hath heard of the Father and hath learned cometh to Me" (Jn 6:45). These are the true children of God. "Every one that is of the truth heareth My

[4] Dante, *Paradiso*, canto 33, lines 13ff.

voice" (Jn 18:37). Everyone who is "clean of heart," whose heart is open to the truth, who has good will and is prepared to accept this truth, comes to the kingdom of God. The fundamental principles of this king are far reaching, simple, and universal. This fact is a great consolation for distracted men, for good will is all that is necessary for obtaining membership in this holy kingdom, in the Church of God. "Unless you be converted and become as little children, you shall not enter into the kingdom of heaven" (Mt 18:3). Our membership in the kingdom of heaven depends on our becoming little children like the child of Bethlehem. We must open our eyes to "the true light which enlighteneth every man that cometh into this world."

God "will have all men to be saved and to come to the knowledge of the truth" (1 Tm 2:4). God gives grace to all in due season, unless they harden their hearts and make themselves blind to it. Perhaps because we are but dust and ashes, because of ourselves we are so worthless, He gives His truth to us. Is it not marvelous that he makes us the object of His love, who are so wicked and evil? He wishes to fill us with the Holy Spirit, that thus being sanctified we may become partakers of the divine nature and of eternal life. What a grace is the possession of the love of God!

In addition to all that He has already done for us, He now confides to our faltering hands the task of completing the work which He has begun. We are permitted to cooperate with Him in this work. We should share the divine life, not only by the possession of sanctifying grace, but we should also "put on Christ" and reproduce His holiness in our own lives.

In this work of our sanctification God will not fail, but we readily do so. "And the light shineth in darkness, and the darkness did not comprehend it. He came unto His own and His own received Him not" (Jn 1:5, 11). Men fail in humility, for they are pleased with their own strength and knowledge. They are foolish in their wisdom; they lack the simplicity and humility of childhood which Christ requires.

We place our faith in the words of St. John: "Behold what manner of charity the Father hath bestowed upon us, that we should be called and should be the sons of God" (1 Jn 3:1). Let us pray today for the many who do not enjoy the sonship of God and do not understand its value. Let us give them an example of childlike simplicity. This is true Catholic action; it is the duty which the mystery of Christmas imposes upon us.

Prayer

Stretch forth from heaven, O Lord, Thy helping hand, that we may search for Thee and desire Thee with our whole heart. Through Christ our Lord. Amen.

At the Manger (2)

Today we kneel at the foot of the manger in holy admiration. The King whom the heavens cannot contain is there confined to a tiny crib; from the lowliness of His crib His power stretches to the uttermost heavens. He is laid in the straw of the manger, and does not shrink from His lowly bed. He who feeds the birds of the air today depends on His mother's milk for sustenance.

We have inherited from Adam a threefold disorder, which is at the root of all our difficulties: the concupiscence of the eyes, that is, our attachment to earthly things; the concupiscence of the flesh, that is, our inclination to sensuality in its various forms; and the pride of life, which is our insatiable thirst for honor, riches, fame, and power. The new Adam, the child who lies in the manger before us, shows us the way to escape these evils. He teaches us that by voluntary poverty, by humble submission to the suffering that God sends us, and by suppressing our evil inclinations, whatever they may be, we may escape from this disastrous threefold disorder.

"Take up My yoke upon you and learn of Me because I am meek and humble of heart; and you shall find rest to your souls" (Mt 11:29). We are reminded, too, of the words of St. Paul to the Philippians: "For let this mind be in you which was also in Christ Jesus. Who, being in the form of God, thought it not robbery to be equal with God, but emptied Himself, taking the form of a servant" (2:5–7). When we gaze upon "the infant wrapped in swaddling clothes and laid in a manger" (Lk 2:12), how ridiculous is our pride and how futile our thirst for riches in the light of this divine example. Where shall we ever learn wisdom and humility if this example of the infant Jesus does not inspire us?

We cast ourselves down in adoration before the child in the manger and implore: "O Wisdom, come and teach us the way of prudence." Teach us that all that is not in conformity with Thy teaching and example is loss and not gain. Let us have the insight to understand that what is worldly and human is vain. "But the things that were gain to me, the same I have counted loss for Christ. Furthermore, I count all things to be but loss for the excellent knowledge of Jesus Christ, my Lord; for whom I have suffered the loss of all things and count them but as dung, that I may gain Christ and may be found in Him, not having my justice, which is of the law, but that . . . which is of God, justice in faith: that I may know Him and the power of His resurrection and the fellowship of His sufferings, being made conformable to His death. If by any means I may attain to the resurrection which is from the dead" (Phil 3:7–11).

This, then, is the example that is given us. The divine King, the Word of God, voluntarily chooses poverty as His lot; He seeks the seclusion of Nazareth and the weakness and suffering of men in order to teach us divine wisdom. Those who truly seek Him will follow Him in that way, for He has assured us: "I am the way" (Jn 14:6). We need not be ashamed of the poverty and weakness of the Church. Her divine founder chose these things voluntarily for Himself and for all her children.

Prayer

Child of the manger, Thou begotten of the Father before all ages, Thou didst choose to be born in a stable. Thou didst possess glory in heaven and didst deign to come down to the earth. Thou whom the angels serve and praise, didst make Thy abode in a stable and wast found by shepherds. Deliver our hearts from all inordinate, temporal attachments, that we may by faith find Thee and ever remain close to Thee. Amen.

At the Manger (3)

"O wondrous exchange! The Creator of the human race, taking unto Himself a living body, deigns to be born of a virgin; and becoming man from no human generation, He hath bestowed upon us His divinity" (Antiphon for the octave of Christmas).

The Son of God takes upon Himself the wretchedness of the human race and becomes a child at Bethlehem. At His side stand Mary and Joseph, descendants of David, who had come to the city to be enrolled in obedience to the ordinance of Caesar. While fulfilling this duty, Mary gives birth to her Son, wraps Him in swaddling clothes, and cares for Him as any other mother would have done. Faith shows us the fullness of the divinity behind this outward appearance of weakness and helplessness. "The Lord hath said to Me: Thou art My Son; this day have I begotten Thee" (Introit of the first Christmas Mass). We see a weak, newborn babe, but we acknowledge Him to be the Son of God, one in nature and essence with the all-knowing, all-powerful God.

"O wondrous exchange!" The Son of God partakes of our human nature. He is fitted with a body such as ours, and is subject to the hunger, thirst, and other annoyances and sufferings which all human beings undergo. He has a soul like ours, with all its delicate sensibilities, its love of beauty and truth, its sense of man's degradation by Original Sin. "Wherefore it behooved Him in all things to be made like unto His brethren, that He might become a merciful and faithful priest before God, that He might be a propitiation for the sins of the people" (Heb 2:17). He partakes of our human nature in order to cleanse it and make it worthy to participate in the divine nature. Child of the crib, how shall we thank You for this wondrous fellowship?

"O wondrous exchange!" We give the Son of God our misery and our nothingness, and He shares with us His divine nature. In exchange for what we give Him, He adorns us with sanctifying grace, calls us to the sonship of God and the resurrection to eternal life, and assures us of our possession of bliss for eternity. For what we have given Him, He tells us "that eye hath not seen, nor ear heard, neither hath it entered into the heart of man, what things God hath prepared for them that love Him" (1 Cor 2:9).

"O wondrous exchange!" In the Offertory procession of the Mass we bring the elements of bread and wine, and with them offer up our bodies and our souls, our hearts, our miseries, our sins, and our needs. *Suscipe, Domine:* "Receive, O Lord, our gifts." He accepts them and in the Consecration transforms them and fills them with His divine nature, with His light and His life, and He gives them back to us in Holy Communion, no longer bread and wine, no longer our own unworthiness and nothingness, but His own flesh and blood, His own divine nature and human nature, pure, holy, full of divine power and divine life. "He that eateth My flesh and drinketh My blood abideth in Me, and I in him.... He that eateth this bread shall live forever" (Jn 6:57, 59).

Prayer

May the oblation of this day's festival be pleasing to Thee, we beseech Thee, O Lord; that of Thy bountiful grace we may, through this sacred exchange, be found conformed to Him in whom our substance is united to Thee. Who with Thee liveth and reigneth forever. Amen.

At the Manger (4)

"O wondrous exchange! The Creator of the human race, taking unto Himself a living body, deigns to be born of a virgin; and becoming man from no human generation, He hath bestowed upon us His divinity" (Antiphon for the octave of Christmas). In the Incarnation there takes place a marvelous exchange; on the one hand, God assumes our human nature; on the other, He permits us to share in His divine nature.

"He hath bestowed upon us His divinity." God would owe us nothing at all even if we should place all that we have at His disposal. All God's actions are directed by divine wisdom, and if He chose to assume our nature, He must have done so for a worthy purpose. His purpose was to enable us to share in His divine nature and to enjoy His divine life. What a marvelous exchange! In exchange for the human nature which He borrows from us, He gives us the privilege of participating in His divine nature.

In the child in the crib dwells the fullness of divinity: "For in Him dwelleth all the fullness of the Godhead corporeally" (Col 2:9). "In Him was life, and the life was the light of men" (Jn 1:4). O wondrous exchange! We possess the divine life when we possess sanctifying grace. We share His life when we practice His virtues, that is, when we express our love for the Father and for our fellow men, and when we practice obedience, purity, and humility.

Man is but dust and ashes (Gn 18:27). He is subject to vanity (Rom 8:20) and is "bent upon evil at all times" (Gn 6:5); yet to him it is given to participate in the life of the divinity. His sins are destroyed, and he is clothed with the splendor and beauty of the divinity. The life which the Son derives from the Father and imparts to His own assumed humanity, is imparted in turn to His fellow men. Christ is the vine, and His life is imparted to us, who are the branches. "I am the vine, you the branches; he that abideth in Me, and I in him, the same beareth much fruit; for without Me you can do nothing" (Jn 15:5).

With this incorporation into the life of Christ, we are lifted above the needs and interests of the life we once led; we are given a new insight and a new knowledge, and our will is constrained to strive toward a higher ideal. "And I live, now not I, but Christ liveth in me" (Gal 2:20). This new ideal governs my thoughts, my motives, and every phase of my life. It consecrates me and my service to the things that pertain to the sacred vine of which I am a living branch. O wondrous exchange! We give God our miserable human nature and receive in turn a participation in His divine nature and divine life. This is the lesson we learn as we kneel devoutly at the crib and contemplate the great mystery of Christmas.

Therefore, dear brethren, let us render thanks to God the Father through His Son, in the Holy Spirit; who, because of His great love with which He hath loved us, has had mercy on us and, when we were dead in our sins, has given us life in Christ, that in Him we might be a new creature, a new image. Let us, then, put off the old man with all his works, and now that we participate in the regeneration of Christ, let us renounce the works of the flesh. Recognize, O Christian, thy own dignity; and having been made a partaker of the divine nature, return not to the vile state in which you once lived. Remember of whose body and whose head you are a member. Remember that you have been snatched from the power of the prince of darkness and have been made to share in the light and kingdom of Christ.[5]

As Christ lives a twofold life, so also does the Church and each soul that is baptized. The divine element dominates the life of Christ; so, too, it must be the ruling element in our lives. Everything that pertains to our natural life should now be directed to the proper supernatural end. Confidence in God should bear us up in time of trial; love should be the motive of all our works; resignation should temper our trials; and purity should mark us as the children of God. The most insignificant action performed with this supernatural attitude is of much greater value than all the knowledge, talent, honor, and success that we obtain in the merely natural order.

[5] Sermon of St. Leo; lesson at Matins of Christmas.

Our spiritual life really consists in a growth in Christ. For this reason all worldly and carnal desires and ambitions must be set aside. The life of the Christian must be modeled after the life of Christ.

Prayer

Grant, we beseech Thee, almighty God that we who are bathed in the new light of Thy Word made flesh, may show forth in our actions that which by faith shineth in our minds. Through the same Christ our Lord. Amen.

Second Week after Christmas

January 1, Our New Year Program

Although the liturgy of the Church does not provide for the celebration of New Year's Day, we should not for this reason pass over it lightly. We should at this time reconsider the program which the Church outlined for us at the beginning of the liturgical year, a program both positive and negative. We are to renounce all worldly lusts and practice piety.

The Redeemer who came to live among us makes it clear to us that in the sight of God only one thing is necessary: the salvation of our immortal soul. All the actions of our life, then, should be directed to the salvation of our own soul and that of our neighbor. Indifference to the claims of God and to the fate of the soul in the world to come, is the besetting sin of our age. Life in our times is so clamorous and so urgent in its solicitations that it threatens to blind us and close our eyes to our true destiny. Our lives become worldly and we neglect the needs of our soul. The Church shows us how to avoid this danger, and in the Epistle for the feast of the Circumcision we are directed to renounce all "ungodliness and worldly desires" that might captivate us and interfere with the salvation of our soul.

Not only must we avoid those things that might harm us, but we must also do something positive: "We should live soberly and justly and godly." We must live soberly, that is, be moderate in our thoughts, words, and actions, making them conform to the truths of our faith; justly, that is, giving every man what is due him, but not forgetting the claims of God and our fellow man, the claims of nature, grace, and our own soul, and even the just claims of our body. We must live "godly," that is, we must be sustained by a childlike confidence in the heavenly Father, whose children we have become by reason of our brotherhood with Christ. We must live with the conviction that His fatherly care and loving hand are always guiding us, protecting us, and sanctifying us.

"Looking for the blessed hope and coming of the glory of the great God and our Savior, Jesus Christ" (Epistle). All temporal things must pass away, but they point the way to that which is enduring and eternal, which alone can satisfy our souls. Now we wait for the day when eternity will begin for us and the Lord will return in majesty. Thus He shall come to us at the moment of our death and on the day of the Last Judgment. Our faith teaches us to believe that death merely opens for us the gates of eternity. If our lives have been worthy, the Lord upon His return will unite our transfigured souls to our bodies. This holy hope prompts us to long joyfully for the return of the Lord and for the blessed eternity that will follow. This hope sustains us and gives us the strength to conquer. The sacrifices and the good works which we undertake at the beginning of the new year will increase our merit for eternity if we persevere in them.

Shun all ungodliness and worldliness; "live soberly and justly and godly," sustained by the loving hand of a devoted Father; long for the blessed day of eternity with holy hope. This is the program the Church sets before us at the beginning of the new year.

The liturgy shows us also where we shall find the strength to do these things. "A child is born to us and a Son is given to us, whose government is upon His shoulders; and His name shall be called the Angel of great counsel" (Introit). Christ, the Lord of all things, is born to us. He, the Son of God, has assumed a human nature and in the Mass has become our sacrificial meal and at the same time the spotless oblation which we offer to God. With His help we shall be able to accomplish our program. "I am the vine, you the branches. As the branch cannot bear fruit of itself unless it abide in the vine, so neither can you unless you abide in Me" (Jn 15:5, 4).

On New Year's Day we should renew the promises we made at our baptism. "I renounce Satan and all his works and pomps. I believe in God the Father, the Son, and the Holy Ghost, and in the Holy Catholic Church." We should resolve that all we do, we will do for God and in accordance to the holy will of Jesus. Lord, take me to Thyself, take me to Thyself.

Prayer

Protect us, O Lord, who dedicate ourselves to Thy service, that we who have received divine things may faithfully serve Thee with body and soul throughout this new year.

"Thine are the heavens, and Thine is the earth. The world and the fullness thereof Thou hast founded" (Offertory). Thine I am also, and Thine I wish to be every moment of the new year. I place the entire coming year, with all its duties, trials, difficulties, sufferings, and sacrifices, on the paten today and unite them to Thy sacrifice in honor of God for the good of the Church, for the salvation of souls, and for an increase of grace and virtue. Amen.

January 1, Feast of the Circumcision

Today the Church celebrates the octave of the birth of Christ and the feast of the Circumcision. At the Circumcision the child received the name Jesus, Savior and Redeemer, and for the first time shed blood for the redemption of men.

Although He was Lord of the Sabbath and in no way subject to the law of Moses, Christ freely and willingly submits to the prescriptions of the law. Although entirely sinless, He who is the Holy of Holies desires to appear before men as a sinner and to bear the mark of sin on His own holy body. He conceals the fullness of grace and holiness which He possesses, and subjects Himself to the law of circumcision, to which the other children of Israel were obliged. What sublime humility He shows by this act of submission! Such is the way of eternal wisdom.

"His name was called Jesus." He humiliates Himself by submitting to circumcision, and God exalts Him because of this sublime humility. At the moment of this humiliation, when He is being circumcised, He receives the name of Jesus, "the Savior." "For which cause God also hath exalted Him and hath given Him a name which is above all names" (Phil 2:9). Every man who is born into this world is born in the state of Original Sin, since he is a son of Adam. Likewise, all who escape from this curse that was leveled at Adam, do so through the saving merits and the humility of Jesus. Those who receive grace from God, who perform any meritorious act, who attain to the sonship of God, do so only by virtue of the merits and the humility of Christ. "He is before all, and by Him all things consist. And He is the head of the body, the Church, who is the beginning, the first-born from the dead; that in all things He may hold the primacy. Because in Him it hath well pleased God the Father that all fullness should dwell" (Col 1:17–19). This is the first law of the supernatural life: "He that shall humble himself shall be exalted" (Mt 23:12).

The Church is deeply stirred by this voluntary humiliation of the incarnate Word of God. She listens as He declares: "I am the way, the truth, and the life" (Jn 14:6). "He that followeth Me walketh not in darkness, but shall have the light of life" (Jn 8:12).

"Learn of Me." Neither miracles, nor deeds of great valor are required of us, but only a deep and true humility. That is the first lesson our Lord wishes us to learn. He knows that the cause of our unfruitfulness is our pride, and in His divine wisdom He tells us through St. Peter: "In like manner, ye young men be subject to the ancients. And do you all insinuate humility one to another, for God resisteth the proud, but to the humble He giveth grace" (1 Pt 5:5).

This axiom, then, should light our way as we enter the new year. "He that humbleth himself shall be exalted" (Lk 14:118:14). Let us choose the path which Christ points out to us, the way of humility. We will possess the spirit of Christ in the measure that we imitate His humility. Today He gives us a sublime example of His humility in the Gospel; and in Holy Communion, He furnishes us with the strength to follow where He has led. Humility is the way to grace and to a life in union with God. Let us try to understand the lessons of the liturgy and practice them in our daily life.

Prayer

O God, who withstandest the proud and givest grace to the humble, grant us the spirit of true humility in accordance with the example of Thy Son. Let us never through pride turn from Thy will, but by our submission make us worthy to receive the gifts of Thy grace. Through Christ our Lord. Amen.

January 1, The Circumcision of Christ

Mary's place in the liturgy of the feast of the Circumcision is so prominent that this feast may be considered as much a feast of the Blessed Mother as it is of our Lord.

Mary took an intimate and motherly part in the events celebrated in this feast. We feel her compassion for her Son. But following the guide of the liturgy, we can hardly feel that this is a feast of the "sorrowful" Mother. We see her, rather, as the valiant Virgin Mother renewing her fiat and joining in the sacrifice of her child. On this day Jesus makes the first offering of His blood for the redemption of mankind. Mary suffers with Him, but she does so with joy, for she knows that in this way the redemption of the race is being accomplished. Her love is heroic and disinterested, for she is not concerned with her own suffering, but looks upon it as a necessary sacrifice for the salvation of men.

Mary is here a type of the Church. The Church, too, looks on at this first offering of the blood of Jesus with compassion and love. This most precious blood for the redemption of mankind she offers up with Jesus and Mary daily and hourly and without interruption. She knows that the shedding of His blood is for the redemption of men. No one understood better than she the immense value of a human soul and the terrible tragedy of the damnation of a single soul.

Like Mary, looking on and yet suffering with Christ, the Church has worked with diligence, suffered with patience, and has striven for two thousand years for the salvation of men. Thousands upon thousands of her priests daily approach the altar to renew this sacrifice in the interest of the salvation of the race. Daily they pray for themselves and for the Church: "Forgive us our trespasses; ... lead us not into temptation, but deliver us from evil." She invites the faithful to the sacrament of penance, where these graces are freely dispensed. She urges them to receive the body of the Lord, that their souls may abound in grace and grow strong against the temptations of the world. Her liturgy is a continual appeal on the part of priests and religious for the salvation of men. Under the inspiration of the Holy Spirit, she has instituted various confraternities of prayer, societies given to the practice of good works and penance, that souls may advance in holiness and grace. In fact, she exists only for the salvation of souls, and is ever restless until they rest in God.

We can well imagine the motherly compassion Mary endured with her Son at His circumcision. Our hearts should be filled with admiration and gratitude for this forgetfulness of self which makes her suffer so willingly for us.

Perhaps too few of us appreciate the great privilege that is ours in being members of the Church. She is a second Virgin Mary, animated by the Holy Spirit, and she has only one aim and ambition: the salvation of the souls of her children. Her principal work is the salvation of the souls of men. Her dogmas, her moral teaching, and her sacred liturgy are all directed toward this end. A man has no better assurance of his salvation than his loyalty and devotion to the Church.

Every true son of Holy Mother the Church will share in this zeal for the salvation of souls. If the love of Christ resides in the soul of man, that man must of necessity thirst with Christ for the salvation of souls. We may well test the genuineness of our love for Christ by asking ourselves whether we are really devoted to the work of saving our own soul and that of our neighbor.

Today we also celebrate the octave of the feast of St. Stephen. We may take him as a model of zeal for the work of the Church. He was entirely devoted to the work of saving the souls of his fellow men. In the pursuit of this purpose he even sacrificed his life. His labor and His suffering bore abundant fruit, among which must be counted the young man who held the coats of those who cast the stones at the martyr. The glorious transformation which changed Saul into Paul was due in great measure to the zeal and suffering of Stephen.

Prayer

O God, who through the fruitful virginity of the Blessed Mary didst bestow on mankind the rewards of eternal salvation, grant, we beseech Thee, that we may experience her intercession for us, through whom we were made worthy to receive the Author of life, Jesus Christ, Thy Son our Lord. Who liveth and reigneth with Thee, world without end. Amen.

Feast of the Holy Name

The Church celebrates the feast of the Holy Name of Jesus shortly after the feast of the Circumcision, for He received this name when He was circumcised in the temple.

"In the name of Jesus let every knee bow of those that are in heaven, on earth, and under the earth; and let every tongue confess that the Lord Jesus Christ is in the glory of God the Father" (Introit). The heavenly Father has elevated the name of Jesus above all others. The will and intellect of every man should bow in reverence at the mention of this holy name. Christ is the "stone which the builders rejected, the same is become the head of the corner.... For other foundation no man can lay, but that which is laid, which is Christ Jesus" (Mt 21:42; 1 Cor 3:11). This name was given in heaven, announced by the angel Gabriel, and made known to the Virgin at the time of the Annunciation. "Thou shalt conceive in thy womb and shalt bring forth a Son; and thou shalt call His name Jesus" (Lk 1:31).

Jesus means Savior. His very name bespeaks the infinite love which He bears for us. We are to understand that He is a Savior whose works are of infinite value, whose authority is unlimited, and whose fondest desire is to reconcile us with His Father and to make us His coheirs to the kingdom of heaven. "O Lord, our Lord, how wonderful is Thy name!" (Ps 8:2.) Truly wonderful is His name, for it shields us from the wrath of an angry God, and by it we may ask for light and grace and virtue.

"O Lord, our Lord, how wonderful is Thy name!" This is the name of the eternal high priest who became man for us. This is He who offered upon the altar of the cross, and offers daily on the altars of our churches, the only sacrifice that is entirely pleasing to the Father. This is He who by reason of His humanity can offer sacrifice in the name of man, and who by reason of His divinity can offer a sacrifice worthy of the majesty of God. This is He who, by uniting the divine nature and the human nature in Himself, can so elevate the degraded nature of men that they may hope to participate in the divine life and enjoy the majesty of God.

"Thou art sweet and mild, and plenteous in mercy" (Offertory). The name of Jesus is the sweetest of all names, and He who bears it is most worthy of all love. He who calls Jesus his friend can be assured that this friend is the most devoted and unselfish of all friends. Jesus is always solicitous for the welfare of His friends, and by means of the daily Sacrifice of the Mass and by His continual intercession for us in heaven, He devotes Himself to our salvation.

Christ has chosen other names for Himself which, although contained in the name of Jesus, emphasize particular aspects of His love for us. He is the Father of the Poor, the Good Shepherd who goes in search of the lost sheep; He is the Son of Man; He is the way, the truth, and the life. St. Bernard said of the name of Jesus, "It is like honey in the mouth, like music in the ear, like gladness in the heart."

Jesus is our all. In His name we may pray to the Father with assurance of being heard (Jn 16:23). In His name the Church administers all her sacraments. In His name she offers all her prayers and blesses homes, the fields, and the sick. In the name of Jesus she casts out evil spirits, and at the hour of our death bids us, "Go forth, Christian soul." She assures us that whoever shall call upon this name will be saved (Acts 2:21). When our soul has departed this life to seek its eternal home, the Church asks in the name of Jesus, "Eternal rest give unto him, O Lord."

The lessons at Matins and the Epistle for this feast, taken from the Acts of the Apostles, relate the cure of a lame man wrought by St. Peter in the name of Jesus. "But Peter said: Silver and gold I have none; but what I have I give thee; in the name of Jesus Christ of Nazareth, arise and walk" (Acts 3:6). Peter seizes this opportunity to announce the name of Jesus to the people and to show them its great power. The people are amazed, but Peter hastens to assure them that by no excellence or power of his own is this miracle wrought. He attributes all to the power of the name of Jesus. "Be it known to you all and to all the people of Israel, that by the name of our Lord Jesus Christ of Nazareth, whom you crucified, whom God hath raised from the dead, even by Him this man standeth here before you whole" (Acts 4:10).

The feast of the holy name of our Savior is a day of mercy and forgiveness. The Offertory instructs us to pray, "I will praise Thee, O Lord my God, with my whole heart, and I will glorify Thy name forever; for Thou, O Lord, art sweet and mild and plenteous in mercy to all that call upon Thee."

Prayer

Jesus, the very thought of Thee
With sweetness fills my breast,
But sweeter far Thy face to see
And in Thy presence rest.

Nor voice can sing nor heart can frame
Nor can the memory find
A sweeter sound than Thy blest name,
O Savior of mankind.

O hope of every contrite heart,
O joy of all the meek,
To those who fall, how kind Thou art,
How good to those who seek!

But what to those who find? Ah this
Nor tongue nor pen can show;
The love of Jesus, what it is
None but His loved ones know.

Jesus our only joy be Thou
As Thou our prize wilt be;
Jesus, be Thou our glory now
And through eternity.
Amen.

January 3, Octave of St. John

"Do Thou, O Lord, in Thy goodness shine upon Thy Church; that enlightened by the teaching of blessed John, Thy apostle and Evangelist, she may attain to the everlasting gifts" (Collect). Today we sit at the feet of John the Evangelist to receive the instruction which he has given to the Church and to us through his Gospel.

"Amen, Amen, I say to thee, that we speak what we know, and we testify what we have seen, and you receive not our testimony. If I have spoken to you earthly things, and you believe not, how will you believe if I shall speak to you heavenly things? And no man hath ascended into heaven but He that descended from heaven, the Son of Man, who is in heaven. And as Moses lifted up the serpent in the desert, so must the Son of Man be lifted up; that whosoever believeth in Him may not perish, but may have life everlasting. For God so loved the world as to give His only-begotten Son, that whosoever believeth in Him may not perish, but may have life everlasting. For God sent not His Son into the world to judge the world, but that the world may be saved by Him. He that believeth in Him is not judged. But he that doth not believe is already judged, because he believeth not in the name of the only-begotten Son of God. And this is the judgment: because the light is come into the world and men loved darkness rather than the light; for their works were evil" (Jn 3:11–19).

"And for them do I sanctify myself, that they also may be sanctified in truth. And not for them only do I pray, but for them also who through their word shall believe in Me; that they all may be one, as Thou, Father, in Me and I in Thee; that they also may be one in Us; that the world may believe that Thou hast sent Me. And the glory which Thou hast given Me, I have given to them: that they may be one, as We also are one. I in them and Thou in Me, that they may be made perfect in one; and the world may know that Thou hast sent Me and hast loved them, as Thou hast also loved Me. Father, I will that where I am they also whom Thou hast given Me may be with Me: that they may see My glory which Thou hast given Me because Thou hast loved Me before the creation of the world. Just Father, the world hath not known Thee; but I have known Thee; and these have known that Thou hast sent Me. And I have made known Thy name to them, and will make it known; that the love wherewith Thou hast loved Me may be in them, and I in them" (Jn 17:19–26).

God loved the world and He has loved me. For a long time He has sought man. He sought him out in paradise, in the burning bush in the desert, in the thunder and lightning on Mount Sinai, in the pillars of fire in the desert, and in the preaching and miracles of the prophets in the Old Testament. Now He Himself comes in the form of man. It is no longer difficult for man to find God or for God to find man. The threats hurled from Mount Sinai and the fire called down from heaven by Elias are forgotten. God no longer needs to use threats and terror to keep man mindful of Him. He stands before us now in the form of a little child. Could He have done yet more to convince us of the sincerity of His love for us?

"That they may be one." We had been separated from God by sin; but the Word of God came to free us, that we might again be united to God in heart and in spirit. In fact, this very union of heart and will with God and our neighbor is the distinguishing mark of the Christian. "By this shall all men know that you are My disciples, if you have love one for another" (Jn

13:35). Christ proved His love for us, not merely by word of mouth, but by the supreme test of works and deeds. The same expression of love He expects of us.

PRAYER

Do Thou, O Lord, in Thy goodness shine upon Thy Church; that enlightened by the teaching of blessed John, Thy apostle and Evangelist, she may attain to the everlasting gifts. Through our Lord Jesus Christ. Amen.

January 4, Octave of the Holy Innocents

The Church is filled with admiration today as she contemplates the providence and foresight of the heavenly Father. "O Lord, our Lord, how admirable is Thy name in the whole earth!" (Introit psalm.) Dramatic is the scene which is presented to us by the liturgy today. The loathsome King Herod is filled with anger and fear; he sends his heartless soldiers to destroy all the male children in the vicinity of Bethlehem who are less than two years old. The distracted mothers of these helpless victims bewail the loss of their innocent ones. The slain children, true soldiers of Christ, march triumphantly into the presence of God wearing the crown of martyrdom and bearing in their hands the palms of victory. "O Lord, our Lord, how admirable is Thy name in the whole earth!"

The children of Bethlehem had not yet reached the age when they could freely choose to love God; yet the providence of God watches over them. In the opinion of men, their fate was a sad and gruesome one. Their lives, begun so propitiously, have been destroyed without reason by a wanton murderer. Life has given them nothing. Only grief can be felt for them. "A voice in Rama was heard, lamentation and great mourning: Rachel bewailing her children, and would not be comforted because they are not" (Gospel). But what is a loss in the estimation of men, is in the providence of God a great gain. "Our souls hath been delivered as a sparrow out of the snare of the fowlers" (Gradual). The evil machinations of Herod and the cold steel of his soldiers are the means that have wrought the salvation of these children. "O Lord, our Lord, how admirable is Thy name in the whole earth." In the providence of God all things work for the good of men. "To them that love God, all things work together unto good" (Rom 8:28). Man proposes, but God disposes; the ways of God are not the ways of men.

"To them that love God, all things work together unto good." Though the design of God is frequently hidden from our sight, we may be sure that He is using all that enters into our life for our own good. All that concerns our physical health, our worldly possessions, even our good name, God uses for our good. If our heavenly Father deprives us of these things for a time, it is merely that they may not stand in the way of our salvation. The discomforts and failures and sufferings of our daily life God uses that He may detach our hearts from the world and drive us back into His sheltering arms. He may at times humiliate us by sending us spiritual dryness and temptations that we may more surely place our trust in Him. Even the sins that we have committed and for which we are truly sorry, God may use for our spiritual advancement, even as He used David's sin and Peter's denial to spur them on to more fervent and devoted service. In every event of our life we may detect the fatherly hand of God. He controls all things, He directs all things with divine wisdom and love. For this reason we may say with truth, "To them that love God, all things work together unto good." "O Lord, our Lord, how wonderful is Thy name in the whole earth!"

"To them that love God, all things work together unto good." If this statement of the Apostle is true, then it behooves us to surrender ourselves completely to the providence of our heavenly Father. "He that findeth his life, shall lose it; and he that shall lose his life for Me, shall find it" (Mt 10:39).

We may be sure, then, that God weighs, measures, and directs all the events of our life in order that His plan of salvation for our soul may be fulfilled. How different life becomes for the man who views everything in the light of faith! How bitter and hopeless life would be if man were not persuaded that whatever happens to us is directed by the providence of a loving Father who is seeking our salvation!

Would that we might submit ourselves to the providence of God as the children of Bethlehem surrendered to Him! A child makes no plans for the future; it has no worries about the conduct of its affairs, but looks to its father with complete confidence for the provision of all the necessities of life. A child has no fear as long as its father lingers near; it is not anxious about its welfare, but trusts its father completely. This, too, is the disposition we should cultivate toward our heavenly Father. "Out of the mouth of infants and of sucklings, O God, Thou hast perfected praise" (Introit). "Suffer the little children to come unto Me,... for of such is the kingdom of heaven" (Mk 10:14).

Prayer

O God, whose praise the martyred Innocents confessed this day, not by speech, but in their death; mortify in us all the evils of vice, that Thy faith which our tongues profess, our lives also may by their actions confess. Through our Lord Jesus Christ. Amen.

Epiphany

In the early Church the birth of Christ was celebrated on the feast of Epiphany, a feast that is much older than Christmas. Today the feast of Epiphany occupies the place of a second Christmas. More properly, Epiphany completes the Christmas solemnities. Christ entered the world in the silence of the night, as an insignificant child born in a stable. At Epiphany His identity is revealed and He appears now in His majesty and royal splendor. By His passion and resurrection He has entered into His glory (Lk 24:26); that is, His humanity is raised to the position of Lord and King of all creation. As Ruler and as King he enters today into His city (mankind, the Church) and celebrates the triumph of His omnipotent and majestic love for men. It is the marriage feast of Christ and His bride, the Church. The wise men from the East are present, representing the Gentiles, whom He has invited into His kingdom. We should all participate in this splendid feast. The way to the eternal feast in heaven is through the Eucharistic banquet which we now enjoy each day in the Church.

The feast of Epiphany, the manifestation of the Lord, makes known to the world the divinity of the child who was born in the crib at Bethlehem. This revelation is made to the world in the persons of the three wise men who came to attend His birth as the representatives of the Gentile nations. The heavenly Father will confirm this revelation at the baptism of Christ: "This is My beloved Son, in whom I am well pleased" (Mt 3:17). Christ Himself will further manifest His divinity at the marriage feast of Cana.

The feast of Epiphany reveals Christ's mission as King and Ruler of the world. The child of Bethlehem shall come on the last day as King and Ruler of all, "with much power and majesty" (Mt 24:30). Then all men will finally recognize Him as King and will fall on their knees to acknowledge His dominion. On the feast of Epiphany the liturgy begins to pay Christ the homage that is due to Him as King. In the persons of the three wise men we approach to offer our gifts and to acknowledge Him as King of the world. We unite with the Church in submitting ourselves to Him as His subjects. Unlike earthly kings, He is not satisfied with a lofty acceptance of our submission. He is capable of divine condescension, and in Holy Communion stoops down to press us to His breast and fill us with His spirit and majesty. Thus we, too, become an "epiphany," a manifestation of the divinity and majesty of Christ.

The saints, in whom Christ's grace has worked such wonders, are also a manifestation of the divinity and majesty of Christ. In the liturgy they represent the concrete examples of what Christ meant to accomplish through His entry into the world. They are reflections of the great light that arose over Bethlehem and which now brightens the eternal mansions. "Then shall the just shine as the sun in the kingdom of their Father" (Mt 13:43).

Vigil of Epiphany

Tomorrow we celebrate the feast of Epiphany, the solemn entrance of the King and Lord into His kingdom, the Church, and into the hearts of men. The heart of each individual soul is rightfully His domain, and there He must rule. Herod, the enemy who sought His life, is dead (Gospel), and now the way is clear.

"While all things were in quiet silence, and the night was in the midst of her course, Thy almighty Word, O Lord, came down from heaven, from Thy royal throne" (Introit). God works His wonders in silence and in secret. Peace and silence must characterize the Church as a whole and each soul as a member of the Church. Our eyes, our tongues, our inclinations, our impulses and passions, must all be subject to rest, quiet, and peace; only then can the divine King enter into His kingdom. This was the manner in which the Word of God came into the world from His royal throne in heaven. When He came, He chose a place far from the noise and bustle of the restless city of Jerusalem, which at that time was filled with strangers. In silence and in peace the Spirit of the Lord had overshadowed the Virgin Mary, who had been freed from all disorderly passions and impulses. "And His place is in peace, and His abode in Sion" (Ps 75:3).

"The Lord hath reigned, He is clothed with beauty; the Lord is clothed with strength, and hath girded Himself" (Introit psalm). Even in the abandoned stable, in the poverty and secrecy of His birth, even in the helplessness and weakness of His childhood, Christ is King, the strong one. His strength He will manifest when He sets forth to redeem men. Hopelessly lost in the mire of sin and exhausted by the struggle with the prince of this world, men will be victorious by virtue of the strength of this divine child. So strong is He that He will raise us up to be the children of God and heirs of the kingdom of heaven. We embrace Him now in His poverty, in His obedience, and in His weakness. This submission to His apparent weakness will make us strong. "But the foolish things of the world hath God chosen, that He may confound the wise; and the weak things of the world hath God chosen, that He may confound the strong" (1 Cor 1:27). "For when I am weak, then I am powerful" (2 Cor 12:10).

The vigil of Epiphany is a day of holy silence and of great expectation. God works His marvels in silence and in peace. "When Herod was dead, behold an angel of the Lord appeared in sleep to Joseph in Egypt, saying: Arise, and take the child and His mother, and go into the land of Israel, for they are dead who sought the life of the child. Who arose and took the child and His mother, and came into the land of Israel" (Gospel). In the silence of the night St. Joseph received the joyful news that he and the child and His mother could now return to their home; their sojourn in Egypt was over. In silence and in watching the Christian soul is prepared for the communications and the enlightenment of God. In silence the soul is strong and disposed to accept the will of God without murmuring and without question. "Who arose and took the child and His mother, and came into the land of Israel." How different is the attitude of the soul that is worldly, restless, and inquisitive.

Our whole Christian life is, in a sense, a vigil. In seclusion and prayer, in detachment from the world and its pleasures, the Christian should await the appearance of the Lord at the hour of death. In the middle of the night, when we least expect Him, He will appear to lead us home to the eternal marriage feast in heaven. Happy are those souls who, like the wise virgins, are found watching when the Lord appears. Happy are they if they have not become involved in worldly vices and temporal affairs, but hold their lamps burning in their hands when the coming of the Lord is announced.

At the end of the world the Lord will appear with power and majesty. Then He will raise us to life again, and those who have been faithful He will invite to share with Him the glory and the majesty that He has received from His heavenly Father. The whole life of a Christian, then, must be a vigil on the threshold of eternal life. For this reason the Church prays continually, with eyes and heart uplifted, that Christ will come and receive His bride. How little we understand the significance of the feast of Epiphany! We are too much concerned about the things of this world to understand the meaning of this "manifestation" of the Lord.

Prayer

O almighty and eternal God, do Thou direct our actions according to Thy good pleasure, that we may deserve to abound in good works in the name of Thy beloved Son, who with Thee reigneth forever and ever. Amen.

Feast of Epiphany

Christmas brought us a new light. As the sun after dawn climbs to the zenith, so in the sacred liturgy in the time after Christmas the spiritual Sun, Christ, rises higher and begins to enlighten and bless the world. Christ resides in His Church; He "is risen upon her" like the sun. Yet more than that, He has become one with His Church; Christ and His Church now form one being, one organism of grace. As theologians put it, Christ and His Church form one mystical body.

"Today the Church is betrothed to her heavenly spouse, for in the river Jordan Christ washed away her sins; and the wise men bearing gifts hastened to the royal wedding; and the guests refreshed themselves with water made wine" (Benedictus antiphon at Lauds). What a charming picture of the wedding feast! "Lift up thy eyes round about and see; all these are gathered together, they are come to thee; thy sons shall come from afar, and thy daughters shall rise up at thy side. Then shalt thou see and abound, and thy heart shall wonder and be enlarged" (Epistle).

Baptism is the door by which we enter the Church (first Sunday after Epiphany). In the Gospel of the second Sunday after Epiphany, we reach the climax of the theme of Epiphany. This Gospel recounts the story of the wedding feast at Cana. Men enter the Church through baptism, and in union with her they are espoused to Christ and are thus able to partake of the wedding feast. Presently the wedding feast represents the reception of Holy Communion, and it symbolizes the eventual union with Christ in heaven. There we shall experience the perfect epiphany, the complete revelation of Christ.

The feast of Epiphany is a mystical betrothal, and for this reason the Church sings the song of the bride today at Matins: "I will greatly rejoice in the Lord, and my soul shall be joyful in my God; for He hath clothed me with the garments of salvation; and with the robe of justice He hath covered me, as a bridegroom decked with a crown, and as a bride adorned with her jewels" (Is 61:10). Here is the mystery of the Church, the mystery of human life, the secret of human greatness. The Church, and we ourselves with her, are caught up into a vital and mystical union with Christ. We, together with Christ, form the whole Christ through a holy betrothal. An earthly betrothal can achieve only a union of effort, of will, of love, and of purpose. But the union of Christ with His Church and with us produces a union like that of a head with its members, or like the union of a vine with its branches — a true and vital union. The union of Christ with His members surpasses every earthly union as heaven surpasses earth. Christ and His Church, Christ and His members live one and the same life. What a marvelous grace this is! How sublime is our destiny! *Gaudens gaudebo:* "I will greatly rejoice in the Lord, and my soul shall be joyful in my God" (Is 61:10). I have been united to the life and the person of Christ in the Church and through the Church.

"Lift up thy eyes round about and see." Understand this mystery. It is Christ who lives and works in the Church. His divine Spirit animates and joins the souls of all believers to Himself. It is His Spirit which is the principle of life in the Church, which makes it one living organism, and which makes the redemption of mankind effective. The Church is Christ Himself; she is the real manifestation of His divinity on earth. The Church is not a mere mediator between Christ and the soul, not a mere intermediary between God and man. The Church is the form in which Christ the Mediator and Redeemer draws near to men and accomplishes His work of redemption. The Church is the ever present epiphany, the abiding presence of Christ on earth. The Church can no more be separated from Christ, from His Spirit and His person, than a living body can be separated from its soul. In spite of her earthly appearance, she is elevated into the sphere of divine being. In her works we recognize the priesthood of Christ, the truth of Christ, the grace of Christ, the power and authority of Christ. "He that heareth you, heareth Me" (Lk 10:16).

"Behold the Lord the Ruler is come; and the kingdom is in His hand, and power and dominion" (Introit). The divine bridegroom has been betrothed to His Church. Through the Church, He makes our life His, and His life ours. He lives in His Church, and He lives in each and every one of us who are children of the Church. "I am the vine; you the branches" (Jn 15:5). The vine lives in its branches; it sustains them, animates them; its life pulsates through them, vitalizes them, nourishes them, and makes them fruitful. The branches share the life of the vine. That is the secret of the Church, and the secret of our greatness. "Arise and be enlightened, O Jerusalem, for the glory of the Lord is risen upon thee" (Gradual). Arise and be enlightened, O Holy Mother the Church, and thou, O happy Christian soul.

"Behold the Lord the Ruler is come." Behold, He lives in each and every member of the Church, in your neighbor as well as in yourself. In our neighbor we behold a manifestation of Christ. We must see Christ in our neighbor, honor Christ in our neighbor, and love Christ in our neighbor. We serve Christ in our neighbor. "Amen, I say to you, as long as you did it to one of these my least brethren, you did it to me" (Mt 25:40).

"Behold the Lord the Ruler is come." Clearly the liturgy has in mind that glorious day when Christ will return in all His glory to summon His bride, the Church, and every Christian soul to the heavenly nuptials in the kingdom of heaven. "Arise and be enlightened, O Jerusalem."

Prayer

Grant unto us, we beseech Thee, O almighty God, by purity of heart to attain to the understanding of that which with solemn worship we venerate. Through Christ our Lord. Amen.

Feast of Epiphany (2)

"Behold the Lord the Ruler is come; and the kingdom is in His hand, and power and dominion" (Introit). On the obelisk which stands in the plaza of St. Peter's in Rome, the following words are emblazoned in great, golden letters: *Christus vincit, Christus regnat, Christus imperat:* "Christ has conquered, Christ reigns, Christ commands."

Christ is King of all visible creation. "All power is given to Me in heaven and in earth" (Mt 28:18). "Thou hast subjected all things under His feet" (Ps 8:8; Heb 2:8). By virtue of this plenitude of power He established His kingdom on earth, the Church. He chooses His disciples and apostles, and sends them forth endowed with His power to teach and with the power to loose and to bind. Then He gives up His life, and through His death and resurrection He conquers death, sin, hell, and the prince of this world, and acquires that perfection and glorification which will be displayed before all His creatures. The glory that is His, He will communicate to all who belong to Him. His victory over death and the powers of hell will become their victory. In a little while all creation will share His victory, "and of His kingdom there shall be no end" (Lk 1:33).

"And behold, I am with you all days, even to the consummation of the world" (Mt 28:20). "For where there are two or three gathered together in My name, there am I in the midst of them" (Mt 18:20). He is the King of all realms and kingdoms, and governs all by means of His Spirit. Whatever any creature on earth seeks and desires, conceives and accomplishes, undergoes and suffers, believes and trusts, has its source in Him. He, the King, leads and governs all His subjects. He fondly cherishes all His creatures and sends forth His Spirit into their hearts and rules their souls with His divine strength. "Behold the Lord the Ruler is come." Come let us seek Him, greet Him, adore Him, and serve Him.

Christ is the King of our soul. He inspires the soul to search for that which is good. He penetrates the spirit with His light, and subjects it to His truth and to the precepts of our holy faith. He rules in the consciences of men, and metes out the proper rewards and punishments. It is He who lays down the principles by which the human will must be governed and by which it will be judged. He guides and directs the steps of every soul and watches over them at every moment with an all-seeing eye and a mighty arm. There are no pure accidents in the life of the soul. Everything is subject to the touch of His hand. He rules with a benevolent providence in every soul that He has destined for eternal happiness. With His all-powerful graces He illumines the eyes, sways the heart, and floods the soul with a supernatural light. He moves the will to attain the precious fruits of salvation. "But to every one of us is given grace according to the measure of the giving of Christ.... From whom the whole body, being compacted and fitly joined together, by what every joint supplieth, according to the operation in the measure of every part, maketh increase of the body unto the edifying of itself in charity" (Eph 4:7, 16). How wonderfully the power of His rule is manifested in the souls of the saints! They are the product of the irresistible grace of Christ. His kingdom will not be fully revealed until the time of the general judgment, when He will return with power and majesty. What a revelation when the full glory of His kingdom is revealed in eternity, and we are permitted to gaze upon it forever!

Christ is King. All creation is His kingdom. All that exists in heaven and on earth is His and is subject to the divine King who rules from the crib and the tabernacle. All things are laid at

His feet by His heavenly Father, and He guides and controls all by the touch of His hand. All this we believe, and for this we adore Him. Christ "is the image of the invisible God, the first-born of every creature. For in Him were all things created in heaven and on earth, visible and invisible, whether thrones, or dominations, or principalities, or powers; all things were created by Him and in Him. And He is before all, and by Him all things consist. And He is the head of the body, the Church, who is the beginning, the first-born from the dead; that in all things He may hold the primacy; because in Him it hath well pleased the Father that all fullness should dwell [the fullness of divine life, of grace, and of glory]. And through Him to reconcile all things unto Himself" (Col 1:15–20).

Prayer

All ye works of the Lord, bless the Lord; praise and exalt Him above all forever. O ye angels of the Lord, bless the Lord; praise and exalt Him above all forever. O ye heavens bless the Lord; praise and exalt Him above all forever. O all ye waters that are above the heavens, bless the Lord; praise and exalt Him above all forever. O all ye powers of the Lord, bless the Lord; praise and exalt Him above all forever. O ye sun and moon, bless the Lord; praise and exalt Him above all forever. (Dn 3:57–62.)

Feast of Epiphany (3)

Today by means of the sacred liturgy we relive the manifestation of Christ to the Gentiles at Bethlehem. "When Jesus was born in Bethlehem of Juda, in the days of King Herod, behold there came wise men from the East to Jerusalem, saying: Where is He that is born King of the Jews?... The chief priests and the scribes of the people ... said to them: In Bethlehem of Juda; for so it is written by the Prophet.... Having heard the king, [the wise men] went their way.... And entering into the house, they found the child with Mary, His mother, and falling down they adored Him" (Gospel).

In the wise men who were summoned to the crib of Christ, we are to see the peoples of all past, present, and future generations; but more especially we are to see ourselves. It is we who have been enlightened and aroused by the grace of God to go in search of Christ. Our holy faith is the guiding star which leads through the darkness and the troubles of our earthly sojourn so that the wickedness of Herod can neither misdirect us nor terrify us. Our faith is an unmerited grace. "You have not chosen Me; but I have chosen you" (Jn 15:16). Grace has led us to Him; grace has further revealed Him in the Gospel, in His Church, in the holy sacraments, and particularly in the Holy Eucharist. We are ever conscious of His living presence and His ever-present guidance. By means of grace we discover Him each day more perfectly within ourselves, operating in us as a vine operates in its branches, or as the head operates in its members, animating them with its own vigor and life. Yet a little while and this star will lead us to a place where we shall find Him with His mother, sitting upon the throne of His majesty, at the right hand of the Father. "The Lord hath appeared to us, come let us adore Him." How glorious will be that day when we shall be allowed to gaze upon His majesty, without reservation, with complete security, and for all eternity! This will be the true epiphany, and the consummation of our Christmas.

We rejoice with all our hearts at the glorious destiny that is ours. We greet the star of faith with hearts full of confidence, and we follow faithfully its light and its guidance. We rejoice in our holy baptism, by means of which we were first united to Christ. We exult in our holy Church, which is the house in which we "found the child with Mary, His mother." With the wise men of the East let us lay aside those comforts which the earth could offer us, and turn resolutely aside from all that might detain us in our search for Christ, and hasten to meet Him that we may lay our gifts at His feet. The gifts which we bring are the gold of our faith and devotion, the incense of our veneration and adoration, the myrrh of our willingness to accept all manner of discomfort, sacrifice, labor, suffering, crosses, and humiliations for His sake.

"We have seen His star in the east and are come to adore Him." He unites the human nature and the divine nature in one person, and, "as the Father hath life in Himself, so He hath given to the Son also to have life in Himself" (Jn 5:26). One and the same life is possessed by the Father and by the humanity of Christ. In the child to whom the star has guided us there resides "all the fullness of the Godhead corporeally" (Col 2:9).

This fullness of divine life which is possessed by the child in the manger is to be communicated to us and to all men upon the earth. The sonship of God, which is His by nature, He is to extend to us by means of grace, so that Christ, according to the divine plan, is to be "the first-born amongst many brethren" (Rom 8:29). As He is the Son of God by nature, so we become the sons of God by grace. This sonship we receive from Christ. Through Him and through Him alone can we receive grace and eternal life. To be a Christian means to share the sonship of God with Christ, the Son of the eternal Father, to whom we are united as members of a body are united to their head. Only those who possess Christ, only those who come to Him, can share in the life of the children of God, in the grace of God, and in the enjoyment of eternal life. It is the star of faith that has led us to Christ. We have found Him, not by any effort of our own nor because we were more worthy than others, but because of a gratuitous grace of the infinite mercy of God the gift of faith was imparted to us. For this tremendous gift we are thankful, for "by the grace of God I am what I am" (1 Cor 15:10).

How rich we are in the possession of Christ, who has appeared to us! "That Thou wouldst recall to the unity of the faith all those who are in error, and bring all unbelievers to the light of the gospel: We beseech Thee hear us" (Litany of the Saints).

Prayer

O God, who by means of a star didst this day manifest to the Gentiles Thy only-begotten Son; grant that we to whom Thou hast already made Thyself known by faith, may come at last to the vision of the beauty of Thy majesty. Through Christ our Lord. Amen.

Sunday within the Octave of Epiphany (1)

Today the sacred liturgy allows us to witness the first Offertory procession when she shows us Jesus at the age of twelve setting out for His first visit to the temple at Jerusalem. He must "be about My Father's business." He goes to make an offering of Himself to His heavenly Father. Then He returns to Nazareth to continue His offering in the tranquil atmosphere of His family circle. There He "was subject to them." Twenty years later He will complete His sacrifice on the cross in Jerusalem. Today we join the Offertory procession led by the child Jesus; as the Epistle admonishes us: "Brethren, I beseech you by the mercy of God, that you present your bodies a living sacrifice, holy, pleasing unto God, your reasonable service" (Epistle).

Jesus goes to Jerusalem to make His offering. For many centuries the Jews from all parts of the land have made pilgrimages to Jerusalem to offer sacrifice in the temple, where the holy sacrificial fire burned continually in the courtyard. Animals were continually slaughtered and their blood was sprinkled on the altar of sacrifice. But these sacrifices were not fully pleasing to God. They had no power to free men from sin, nor to justify them in the sight of God; neither could they bring to God the honor that was His due. A new kind of sacrifice must be found, and it would be found. "I have no pleasure in you, saith the Lord of hosts; and I will not receive a gift of your hand. For from the rising of the sun even to the going down, my name is great among the Gentiles, and in every place there is sacrifice, and there is offered to my name a clean oblation; for my name is great among the Gentiles, saith the Lord of hosts" (Mal 1:10 f.). Today the incarnate Son of God goes up to the mountain of the temple for the first time as a full grown Israelite, and there quietly and unnoticed He makes His offering. With Mary and Joseph He offers the humble gift of the poor; but together with this humble external gift He adds His inner self, His entire being, His willingness to undertake whatever the heavenly Father desires of Him. "Behold I come. In the head of the book it is written of me that I should do Thy will, O God" (Heb 10:7). This is the perfect offering in which the Father is well pleased.

Jesus takes us with Him when He goes to make His offering. "Brethren, I beseech you by the mercy of God, that you present your bodies a living sacrifice, holy, pleasing unto God, your reasonable service" (Epistle). To the offering of the Savior we add the offering of ourselves. At the Offertory of the Mass we give everything that we have. We offer ourselves, body and soul, as a pure and sinless sacrifice to God. We are to offer to God our "reasonable service"; that is, we are to make an offering that has been sanctified by the spirit, by grace, faith, and love.

Our offering does not begin with the Offertory of the Mass, and it does not end there; it must include every action of the day and everything we do as Christians. This truth we learn from the Epistle, which continues: "And be not conformed to this world [that is, to its motives, its point of view, its works], but be reformed in the newness of your mind, that you may prove what is the good, and the acceptable, and the perfect will of God." A new spirit must be born in us; the spirit of Christ must envelop us. We must learn to love what He loves and hate what He hates, to do what He wishes, and to model our lives after the example which He has given us. In this spirit we will understand, love, and do what is "the good, and the acceptable, and the perfect will of God" (Epistle). "Present your bodies a living sacrifice, holy, pleasing unto God," in union with the sacrifice of Christ, who this day is in our midst and offers Himself up with us.

To be a Christian means that we must make the pilgrimage to Jerusalem with Jesus, that we must offer ourselves up with Him in the Holy Sacrifice of the Mass and in all our daily actions. "For I have given you an example, that as I have done to you, so you do also" (John 13:15).

"Present your bodies a living sacrifice, holy, pleasing unto God." Our bodies are something more than a base prison for our souls, something more than the corrupt source of evil and wickedness, something more than the base material which is the source of all sin. It has the honor and the duty of being a holy offering made to God. By means of a new spirit we can make it a host which will undergo an eternal consecration with the resurrection of the dead. "So also is the resurrection of the dead. It is sown in corruption, it shall rise in incorruption" (1 Cor 15:42).

Prayer

Protect us, O Lord, who have consecrated ourselves to Thy service, that we may be concerned with divine things, and live united with Thee in body and soul. Amen.

Sunday within the Octave of Epiphany (2)

"Christ has appeared to us" as the divine King. The sacred liturgy today leads us to Him that we may pay Him homage. He is seated upon His exalted throne, and the angels are adoring Him. "Upon a high throne I saw a man sitting, whom a multitude of angels adore, singing together: Behold Him the name of whose empire is forever. Sing joyfully to God all the earth; serve ye the Lord with gladness" (Introit).

We stand in wonder at this appearance of God in the form of a twelve-year-old boy in the temple. He has not returned to Nazareth, as Joseph and Mary supposed, but has remained in the temple. There He mingled with the aged doctors of the law of Israel and astonished them by the sagacity of His questions and the wisdom of His answers. "And all that heard Him were astonished at His wisdom and His answers" (Gospel). Even Joseph and Mary are astonished at finding Him in the temple. His mother speaks to Him and asks: "Son, why hast Thou done so to us?" Thus she reminds Him of His duty as her child. But Jesus reminds His mother that He has a higher duty to perform as the Son of the eternal Father. "Did you not know that I must be about My Father's business?" These are the first spoken words of Christ that are recorded in the Gospels; these are the only words that have been recorded of His childhood. These words, like the last words He was to speak on the cross, are of His heavenly Father. These words are a clear and enlightening revelation of His consciousness that He is the Son of the Father, and that He shares the divine nature of the Father. It reveals to us further that He belongs entirely to the Father and He has surrendered Himself completely to the will of the Father. The child in the midst of the learned doctors of the law reveals His hitherto hidden wisdom. He is the Son of God. And this child who is the Son of God retires with Joseph and Mary to the seclusion of Nazareth, where He is "subject to them." Astonished, deeply moved, and in adoration the sacred liturgy stands in wonder at this revelation of God in the form of a twelve-year-old child. "Sing joyfully to God, all the earth, serve ye the Lord with gladness; come in before his presence with exceeding great joy, for the Lord He is God" (Offertory). At this very hour He will appear in our midst in the Holy Sacrifice of the Mass. This is the blessed epiphany of the altar. "Behold Him whose rule endureth forever."

The feast of Epiphany is and should be a feast which is celebrated in honor of Christ the divine King. We pay our homage to Him by our prayers and by our celebration of the liturgy, which we share with the Church in heaven and on earth. We pay homage to Him by submitting our intelligence to faith, to His words, to His teachings, to His gospel, to His Church and its dogmas. And even if all others were to desert Him, yet we should remain true to Him and cry out with St. Peter, "Thou hast the words of eternal life" (Jn 6:69). We honor Him by subjecting our wills to His ordinances and commands, to His sacraments, and to His Church. "He that hath My commandments and keepeth them; he it is that loveth Me" (Jn 14:21). "He that heareth you [the Church], heareth Me; and he that despiseth you, despiseth Me" (Lk 10:16). We pay homage to Him by subjecting ourselves to His operation in us. We honor Him by our resignation and subjection in afflictions and humiliations, by our inner purification and mortifications, and by the duties and obligations of our everyday life. We glorify Him by not attributing to ourselves, to our own good will, to our own efforts or strength, the good works which we perform. With the Apostle we humbly acknowledge, "For it is God who worketh in you both to will and to accomplish, according to His good will" (Phil 2:13). With grateful hearts we cry out, "Not to us, O Lord, not to us; but to Thy name give glory" (Ps 113:9). We honor Him by applying to our own lives the admonition of the Epistle of today's Mass: by making our bodies and souls a living sacrifice, holy, pleasing to God. We glorify Him if we transform ourselves by His spirit and shape our lives according to the pattern He has given us, doing only that which is in accord with the will of God and is perfect and pleasing to Him, living in union with Holy Mother the Church.

Christ is King. That is the theme of the feast of Epiphany. "And we saw His glory, the glory as it were of the only-begotten of the Father, full of grace and truth" (Jn 1:14). This glory Christ has won through His victory on the cross. For this reason neither the Church nor the members of the mystical body can achieve glory without a sacrifice and a cross. "Ought not Christ to have suffered these things and so to enter into His glory?" (Lk 24:26.)

Therefore we bring our bodies and all that we possess and present them as an offering on the altar. With Stephen we share the passion of Christ, and thus we go to attain our glory in the Offertory, in the Consecration, and in Holy Communion.

We are to present our bodies as a living sacrifice, holy, pleasing to God, on the altar. This we are to do not only at the time of the Holy Sacrifice of the Mass, but at every hour of the day and in the ordinary affairs of our everyday life. We must not be conformed to the manner of this world, but we must reform ourselves through the renewal of our spirit. We are thus to prove what is the good and the acceptable, the perfect will of God. We are to live in the consciousness that all of us together form one living organism, the body of Christ (in the community of the Church), and that we are members of one another and of Christ our Lord (Epistle). We live the life of the whole, the life of the community, the life of the mystical body of Christ. That is the Lord's command. "This is My commandment: that you love one another as I have loved you" (Jn 15:12).

May Christ be King of my whole being, of my thoughts, my will, my affections, and of my desires. May His will be done in all things. That is my ambition when I celebrate the Holy Sacrifice with Him today. I consecrate myself to Him, and through Him and in Him I consecrate myself to the Father.

Prayer

In Thy loving kindness, O Lord, graciously hear the prayer of Thy suppliant people; and grant that they may perceive what they ought to do, and may have the strength to do it. Through Christ our Lord. Amen.

Feast of the Holy Family

Today the liturgy takes us back to Nazareth, that we may catch a glimpse of the life of the Holy Family. We are begotten in the bosom of our family; in the midst of our family we grow to maturity. We are all called to live a family life, whether it be the life of a human family in this world, or the life of the supernatural family, which is the Church (through baptism), or the life of a religious family (through religious profession). Thus we may all go to Nazareth and with profit observe the model that is offered to us, so that we may shape our lives after that example.

The life of the Holy Family at Nazareth is sketched for us in the Gospel of the feast. The entire family goes up to Jerusalem to offer the prescribed sacrifice. There Joseph and Mary lose the child and return to Jerusalem in deep sorrow searching for Him. Eventually they find Him in the temple, and Jesus becomes subject to them. The life of the Holy Family is characterized by zeal for religion and prayer, and by the love that binds it together. Moreover, Jesus, the Son of God, shows a respectful obedience to Joseph and Mary. "And He was subject to them." Come and observe, and learn to imitate this divine model.

The spirit of the Holy Family and its characteristic virtues are pictured for us in the Epistle of the Mass. "Brethren, put ye on, therefore, as the elect of God [through holy baptism], holy and beloved, the bowels of mercy, benignity, humility, modesty, patience; bearing with one another and forgiving one another if any have a complaint against another; even as the Lord hath forgiven you, so do you also. But above all these things, have charity, which is the bond of perfection; and let the peace of Christ rejoice in your hearts, wherein also you are called in one body; and be ye thankful. Let the word of Christ dwell in you abundantly, in all wisdom; teaching and admonishing one another in psalms, hymns, and spiritual canticles, singing in grace in your hearts to God" (Epistle).

An inspiring model, a precious instruction! The sacred liturgy, however, is not satisfied with this. She opens to us the sources of strength which are needed for a good, Christian family life. She opens these to us through the Holy Sacrifice of the Mass, Holy Communion, and prayer.

A devoted family spirit and these family virtues are a precious possession both for the human family and for the supernatural family. Among these virtues we may call attention especially to the will and effort to be of one heart and one soul in chaste love; to the disposition of devotion to one another, bearing each other's faults and forgiving each other's mistakes; to the disposition to serve one another and to subject one's own interests to the common good of the family; to the disposition to do whatever is necessary for mutual understanding and mutual appreciation. To live a good, Christian family life requires sacrifice, the renunciation of one's own wishes, and a reasonable mortification of self. If it is to be perfect, it requires complete victory over self-love. It requires a high degree of virtue, deep piety and living faith, much prayer, and a close union with God.

Prayer

O almighty God, we offer Thee this victim of atonement, humbly entreating that through the intercession of the Virgin Mother of God, and of the Blessed Joseph, thou wouldst establish our families firmly in grace and peace. Through Christ our Lord. Amen.

O Lord Jesus Christ, who was subject to Mary and Joseph, and who hast thus sanctified domestic life with ineffable virtues; grant that we, with their aid, may be guided by the example of the Holy Family and thus attain to eternal fellowship with them in heaven. Amen.

First Day in the Octave

The three wise men open their treasures and make their offering. The liturgy imitates this example daily in the Offertory of the Mass. The Offertory for the feast of Epiphany refers to the Church, to us:

"The kings of Tharsis and the islands shall offer presents; the kings of the Arabians and of Saba shall bring gifts; and all kings of the earth shall adore Him; all nations shall serve Him."

In the offerings which the faithful formerly brought to the altar in the Offertory procession and which the priest now, in the name of the sacrificing Church, brings to the altar as the bread and wine, we give ourselves as sacrifices to God. These sacrificial gifts are a substitute for those who offer them. Instead of gold, we offer the best and most precious thing we have: ourselves, our heart with its desires and inclinations, our will, our freedom, and our actions. "Behold, I come to do Thy will" (Heb 10:9). To Him belongs all we have and are. When we offer incense, we acknowledge Him to be our God, our all. Our whole life should be a prayer and a continual elevation of our thoughts and affections to our Lord and God. "Let my prayer be directed as incense in Thy sight" (Ps 140:2). With our offering of myrrh we renounce, as did the wise men at the crib, the inordinate attachment to flesh and blood; we leave father and mother in order to live for Him. We renounce the inordinate desires of earthly life and willingly share the poverty of the divine King in the manger. We choose a life of penance and resolve to mortify the internal and external man.

At the Consecration of the Mass, our gifts of bread and wine become the living Christ. "Graciously regard, we beseech Thee, O Lord, the gifts of Thy Church, in which gold, frankincense, and myrrh are no longer offered, but He whom those mystic offerings signified is immolated and received, Jesus Christ, Thy Son, our Lord" (Secreta). Then with the Church we offer this unspotted, holy, and immaculate gift to the Father. It is our gold, frankincense, and myrrh. The gold is the divine person of the incarnate God. The incense is His endless holiness, which alone can pay worthy adoration, homage, praise, and thanksgiving to God. The myrrh is His holy love for God and man which prompted Him to suffer death on the cross. By means of this most perfect offering we give "to God the things that are God's" (Mt 22:21). "By Him, and with Him, and in Him, is to Thee, God, the Father Almighty, in the unity of the Holy Ghost all honor and glory," and to us the forgiveness of sin and the fullness of grace.

"The kings of Tharsis and the islands shall offer presents; the kings of the Arabians and of Saba shall bring gifts." How zealous these kings were! How much they have sacrificed in order to make an offering to the Lord! How great and generous was their faith! With what joy they gave the best they had! And when we come to Mass, what do we have to offer? What do we finally give? Have we ever given all that we have: our entire will without restriction? Have we forsaken every selfish wish, every selfish demand, in order to live according to His will and desire? Have we really offered, given all, renounced all, as the Lord demands of us?

Our participation in the sacrificial offering of the Church consists of more than words and prayers. What we do in the Offertory procession of the Mass and in the Consecration is merely a beginning, the first step. We should continue our self-offering, but in a different way. The three kings who offered the gifts in Bethlehem returned home "by a different way." They became new men; they broke with the old way which they had hitherto taken. The true co-offering of the Mass creates a new spirit, a new man, who goes forth and offers every day to the Lord and Savior. He recognizes the Lord in his brothers and sisters and in all with whom he comes in contact. He opens the treasures of his heart and inspires the members of Christ with his love, his talent, and his strength. He gives to those in need and freely opens his hand to share his goods. In the spiritual and corporal works of mercy which he performs, one may discern the extent of his sincerity at the Offertory of the Mass.

PRAYER

Graciously regard, we beseech Thee, O Lord, the gifts of Thy Church, in which gold, frankincense, and myrrh are no longer offered, but He whom those mystic offerings signified is immolated and received, Jesus Christ, Thy Son, our Lord. Amen.

Second Day in the Octave

For the reception of Communion, the liturgy for the feast of Epiphany places the words of the three wise men on our lips: "We have seen His star in the East and are come with gifts to adore Him." These words take on a Eucharistic meaning.

"We have seen His star." In the star the liturgy recognizes the Holy Eucharist. "We have seen His star" in the celebration of Mass, in the reception of Holy Communion, and in the visits we make to the tabernacle. The altar is our Bethlehem. By the light of faith we have been led here and we have found Him. He is the Star of the East, the Eucharistic sun, from whom all life and blessings proceed. "He that eateth My flesh and drinketh My blood hath everlasting life, and I will raise him up in the last day. For My flesh is meat indeed, and My blood is drink indeed. He that eateth My flesh and drinketh My blood abideth in Me and I in him. As the living Father hath sent Me, and I live by the Father, so he that eateth Me, the same also shall live by Me" (Jn 6:55–58).

Christ is the source of all supernatural life and grace. Daily He enlightens us in the Mass, in Holy Communion, and in our visits to the tabernacle. May the Eucharist be our star. Let us turn our eyes to it often during the day. We should visit the tabernacle frequently in order to study the star and to be enlightened and penetrated by its light. This is the crowning point in the life of the three wise men: they have seen the star. May this good fortune be ours daily. "We have seen His star ... and are come with gifts to adore Him," Jesus, our all, in the Holy Eucharist.

We "come with gifts to adore Him." In the light and strength of the star which has risen for us early in the morning in Mass and Communion, the day will be filled with holy thoughts, holy affections, and good deeds. The love aroused in our heart by the sacraments penetrates all our deeds and bestows a priceless value on all our works. Every morning the Holy Eucharist will enkindle in our hearts a greater and purer love. If we have adopted this attitude, every thought, every deed, every sacrifice we make, becomes a gift which we may offer to the newborn child.

With gifts in our hand, in the strength of the Holy Eucharist, we approach the Lord. In the holy Bethlehem of heaven, our homeland, we shall love, adore, and possess Him eternally.

"We have seen His star." From the Offertory and from our sacrificial meal we return to our daily occupations. The star which we saw early in the morning follows us everywhere. By recalling to mind our part in the Mass and Holy Communion, we shall be able to renew our strength and courage when our tasks become burdensome.

"We have seen His star in the East and are come with gifts to adore Him." The star of the Holy Eucharist has also risen over our neighbor; he has partaken of the same sacrificial meal we have. We have shared in offering the same divine victim; we have been enlightened by the same star. Its light has guided and strengthened both of us. We should soon be able to see Christ in each of our fellow men. Then we shall honor our neighbor because we see Christ in him. We shall best serve and worship Christ when we have learned to love our neighbor for His sake. "As long as you did it to one of these My least brethren, you did it to Me" (Mt 25:40). The fruit of our daily sharing in Mass and Holy Communion should be a persevering and efficacious love of the members of Christ's mystical body.

Prayer

Grant, we beseech Thee, almighty God, that what we celebrate with solemn office, we may attain by the understanding of a purified mind. Through Christ our Lord. Amen.

Third Day in the Octave

"Christ has appeared: come let us adore Him" (Invitatory at Matins). The liturgy for today is filled with admiration for the divine King. "Behold the Lord the Ruler is come; and the kingdom is in His hand, and power and dominion" (Introit). In the Epistle the Gentiles come to the city of the divine King to pay Him homage; in the Gospel and Offertory the wise men come from the East. Let us also pay our homage with the liturgy.

Our mind falters when it contemplates this mystery; our reason cannot comprehend it. But the eyes of faith recognize in the weak child in the manger the eternal Son of God, the Ruler, the Lord of all, the one to whom "all power is given, … in heaven and in earth" (Mt 28:18). "I believe in Jesus Christ, God of God, light of light, one in substance with the Father, who for us men and for our salvation came down from heaven and became incarnate by the Holy Ghost of the Virgin Mary; and was made man." He suffered, died, and was buried, but rose again and ascended into heaven, where He "sitteth at the right hand of the Father." We believe in His person, in His words, in all His promises, in His Church and her teachings and sacraments. We believe in the resurrection of the body and in life everlasting. We build all things on this foundation, "for other foundation no man can lay" (1 Cor 3:11).

We must also submit our will to the designs of the divine King and accept His commandments, His laws, His gospel, and His visible representatives on earth, the pope and the bishops. We submit confidently to the designs of His providence, and conform ourselves to His plans in our regard. In spite of the labors, trials, discouragements, and sufferings these plans may hold in store for us, we acknowledge His right to make them, and we are persuaded that they are for our best interest. Our human weakness will rebel at the temptations, misfortunes, and trials that will overtake us, but we shall embrace them because it is His will.

We ourselves are the Gentiles, who in the Epistle send their kings to worship the divine King. The wise men of the Gospel, who come from the East, are our ambassadors. In the Offertory the kings of Tharsis and the islands make their submission in our name. Like the wise men, we now approach Christ humbly and in the spirit of reverent prayer. Only in this way can we hope to learn to know Him and to find grace to fulfill His will. "Put ye on the Lord Jesus Christ" (Rom 13:14). Let us put on Christ externally by giving ourselves to unceasing prayer, by Christian mortification, and by continual self-forgetfulness. We must achieve self-control and meekness of heart, "that the life also of Jesus may be made manifest in our bodies" (2 Cor 4:10). We are to put on Christ internally by directing all our thoughts and desires according to the will of the heavenly Father. The degree of our success in this effort will be gauged by the measure of our love of our neighbor, and by the extent of our submission to the will of God. We should look forward to the time when we shall be so firmly established in Christ that we may say with St. Paul, "I live, now not I, but Christ liveth in me" (Gal 2:20).

In every Mass that we attend we should renew our resolution to put on Christ. When we offer the bread and wine, we should think of ourselves as wise men bringing gifts to the divine King. At the Consecration of the Mass, the infant King will come down to us to accept our gifts and consecrate them by this prayer. In this way the value of our offering is made acceptable to God. At the time of Holy Communion, He will leave His manger and set up His throne in our heart and rule over our thoughts and actions during the day. The heavenly Father will bless all that we do, in Him and by Him and through Him. No situation can arise in our daily life that He cannot sanctify and turn to the advantage of our soul, to the benefit of the Church, and the honor of God. All that is required of us is that we make an efficacious intention to perform all our actions in conformity with the will of Christ and for the honor and glory of God. By our possession of Christ we have become precious in the eyes of God, and we are rich beyond all understanding.

Prayer

Grant, we beseech Thee, almighty God, that what we celebrate with solemn office, we may attain by the understanding of a purified mind. Through Christ our Lord. Amen.

Fourth Day in the Octave

The wise men of the East found the child, offered their gifts, and returned to their homes. "And having received an answer in sleep that they should not return to Herod, they went back another way into their country" (Mt 2:12).

"By another way." St. Gregory the Great explains in a homily, used in the office today, the meaning of this Gospel.

The wise men teach us a great lesson in that they return by another way into their own country. By thus doing as they had been warned, they make known to us what we, too, should do. Our country, to be sure, is paradise, and since we now know Jesus, we are forbidden to return thither along the same way by which we left it. For we departed from our own country by pride, disobedience, the love of visible things, by tasting the forbidden food; but we must return thither by the way of tears, obedience, contempt of visible things, and by curbing the desires of the flesh.

Let us, then, return to our own country by another way; and since we left the joys of paradise for the sake of pleasure, we are bidden to regain them by pain. And therefore, dearly beloved, we must ever be fearful, ever on the watch, as we set before the eyes of our heart, on the one side, our sinful deeds, on the other, the severity of the Last Judgment. Let us consider how severe a judge is coming, who even now threatens us unseen; who strikes terror into sinners, but nevertheless still forbears and delays to come quickly that He may find less to condemn.

Let us expiate our sins with tears, and in the words of the Psalmist, let us come before His presence with thanksgiving. Let no appearance of pleasure deceive us; let no vain joy seduce us. For the Judge is at hand who said: "Woe to you, that now laugh; for you shall mourn and weep" (Lk 6:25). Hence did Solomon say, "Laughter shall be mingled with sorrow, and mourning taketh hold of the end of joy." And again: "Laughter I counted error, and to mirth I said: Why art thou vainly deceived?" And yet again: "The heart of the wise is where there is mourning, and the heart of fools where there is mirth" (Prv 14:13; Eccles 2:2; 7:5).

Pensemus. Let us consider carefully, says the great St. Gregory. Epiphany reminds us vividly of the Lord, who will return in His majesty to judge the living and the dead.

He who once has learned to know Christ, becomes a new man. He sets out on "another way." He begins to separate himself from the joys and vanities of the present life and to devote himself to the things that are eternal. He escapes from Herod and the Jews and fixes his gaze on heaven that he may live a holy and supernatural life. He came to God a sinner, but like the wise men of the Gospel, he returns by "another way."

The knowledge and insight which led the Magi to the crib of Christ found little appreciation among their contemporaries. When they returned to their own country, great demands were made on their fidelity. In the midst of heathen surroundings, among skeptical relatives and acquaintances, they must hold fast to the Lord. They are met by ridicule, contradiction, and criticism. They are looked upon as weak-minded old men who were led astray by a star. But they remain faithful to Jesus, Mary, and Joseph, and they become holy. That is the way of God's grace. Virtue is tried in the fire.

Daily we visit the Lord in the Mass. We open our treasures and offer Him gold, incense, and myrrh. In Holy Communion we receive Him and He receives us. If we are wise, we also will return by another way and abandon the reckless, earthbound way which we have been following. "We have seen the Lord." We should now live for Him, and for Him alone, in spite of all difficulties.

Prayer

Grant, we beseech Thee, almighty God, that what we celebrate with solemn office, we may attain by the understanding of a purified mind. Through Christ our Lord. Amen.

Octave of Epiphany

Today we celebrate the baptism of Christ in the Jordan. The heavens opened above Him, the Holy Ghost descended upon Him in the form of a dove, and the Father glorified Him: "This is my beloved Son, in whom I am well pleased" (Mt 3:17). This is the second epiphany, or manifestation, of the Lord. The past, the present, and the future are made manifest in this epiphany.

Christ was baptized. The most holy one placed Himself among us, the unclean and sinners. The Son of God freely humbled Himself at the hand of the Baptist. By His baptism in the Jordan, Christ manifests His humility and dedicates Himself to the redemption of man. "Behold the Lamb of God. Behold Him who taketh away the sin of the world" (Jn 1:29). He takes upon Himself the sins of the whole world and buries them in the waters of the Jordan. He answers the call of the Father with a divine energy, and is prepared to die even the death on the cross for the salvation of our soul. He knows that He is destined for another baptism, a baptism of blood, and yet He exclaims: "How am I straightened until it be accomplished?" (Lk 12:50.) At this moment the great manifestation takes place. The heavens open above Him, and the voice of the Father declares: "This is My beloved Son, in whom I am well pleased."

Today we are witnesses with St. John the Baptist of this great manifestation of God at the Jordan. We rejoice that our Lord and Savior is proclaimed from heaven the Son of God before the whole world. We express our adoration in the Gloria of the Mass: "O Lord God, Lamb of God, Son of the Father, who takest away the sins of the world, have mercy on us. Who takest away the sins of the world, receive our prayer."

The epiphany at the Jordan continues even to this day. It is recalled every time a person receives the sacrament of baptism. In baptism we bury our guilt in the baptismal water, and we are cleansed of all sin. We arise to a new life as the children of God, who says of us: "This is My beloved child; in him I am well pleased." The Holy Spirit enters the soul with the fullness of grace and many spiritual gifts.

Christ's baptism is repeatedly recalled in the celebration of Mass. There we become one with Him in His death, and with Him die to sin and perversity. With the substance of the bread we become transformed and we are consecrated men, sanctified by God and offered up in the divine manifestation of the sacred Consecration. Baptism bears its fruit in the sacrificial meal of Holy Communion. There Christ fills us with His life and spirit, and draws us into His person, into Himself. We become one with Him, with Him children of the Father. And the voice of the Father declares, "This is My beloved child; in Him I am well pleased."

There will be another epiphany, or manifestation, of God in heaven. After the struggle with death, after we have used up the time that is allotted to us, we shall enter the eternal life and enjoy the perfect harmony of the children of God. Then heaven will again open for us; it will open its treasures and we shall again behold God in all His glory. The voice of the Father will proclaim unceasingly, "This is My beloved Son, in whom I am well pleased."

Where Jesus humbled Himself, there the heavens exalted and glorified Him. God treats us in the same manner. "He that humbleth himself shall be exalted" (Lk 14:11).

We believe in Christ, the Son of God, and we consider ourselves fortunate to be permitted to witness daily the manifestation of God in the celebration of Mass and in the reception of Holy Communion. We pray that we may be permitted to continue witnessing this miracle. We desire this privilege for our brethren also, for we may not come to the Father without them.

Prayer

Grant, we beseech Thee, almighty God, that what we celebrate with solemn office, we may attain by the understanding of a purified mind. Through Christ our Lord. Amen.

Second Sunday after Epiphany

The Mass

On the feast of Epiphany, Christ revealed His glory for the first time. When He came into the world, it was in the silence and secrecy of Bethlehem. At Epiphany, however, He asserts His right to dominion over men and over His Church by accepting the submission of the three kings. The Church, into whose fold are gathered the nations of all ages, seeks Him out to offer Him gifts in acknowledgment of His right to rule. These are the thoughts which the liturgy develops from the story of the visit of the Magi.

Christ manifests Himself a second time at His baptism in the Jordan. There the heavens open, and He is publicly proclaimed the Son of God. A third manifestation of His divinity will be made at the marriage feast at Cana. "This beginning of miracles did Jesus in Cana of Galilee; and manifested His glory. And His disciples believed in Him" (Jn 2:11).

This third manifestation of Christ's divinity is the theme of the liturgy on the second Sunday after Epiphany. As we enter the house of God on this day to attend Mass, the Gospel calls attention to the miracle of the wedding feast at Cana. With the eyes of faith we see the splendor of our hidden God, and we adore Him. About us we hear the children of God cry out for mercy, "Lord have mercy on us." Then they burst into song, the song of the angels, "Glory to God in the highest, and on earth peace to men of good will." After this song of exultation the liturgy prays, "O almighty and eternal God, who rulest all things both in heaven and on earth, mercifully hear the prayers of Thy people and grant us Thy peace in our days" (Collect).

The peace of God produces concord in the hearts of men and gives them the strength to continue in the practice of virtue. One who possesses the peace of Christ is borne up by His spirit and His strength, and makes Him manifest by good works. In such a Christian life, as described in the Epistle, the power and glory of Christ are made manifest. Verily, "the Lord sent His Word, and healed them" (Gradual), reformed them in a new life, and established them in the fullness of divine strength. "Praise ye the Lord, alleluia."

The devout Christian heart is touched by the story of the miracle at Cana. The Lord with His divine power commands the water, and it ceases to be water; it becomes wine, excellent wine, fit for a wedding feast. All nature is subject to Him. The elements do His bidding and adore Him. At the Offertory of the Mass, drops of water are mingled with the wine, and in the Consecration both are changed into the blood of Christ. So, too, all our labors, prayers, and sufferings, unless they be mingled with those of Christ, are as worthless and meaningless as water. At the Consecration of the Mass, the Lord renews the miracle of Cana. The water which was poured into the chalice becomes with the wine the blood of Christ. Our rebellious wills, our wandering thoughts, our puny labors, our distracted prayers, our meager sufferings, are consecrated and become immensely precious in the eyes of God when united to those of Christ. They now bear the mark of Christ. The Father recognizes in them the work of His divine Son. Because of this union they are worthy to be offered to the Father in thanksgiving and adoration. Thus by the sacred consecration we are able to unite our offerings, deeds, and prayers to the offerings, deeds, and prayers of Christ. Thus begins the transformation of the earthly man into the heavenly man, the eternally sanctified man.

One day we shall partake of the "good wine" in eternal union with our heavenly bridegroom, Christ. While we are still on earth, the Mass is the beginning and guarantee of the heavenly wedding feast. Christ's manifestation of Himself at the heavenly Cana will be perfect and eternal.

Meditation

The third manifestation of Christ's divinity took place at the wedding feast in Cana, where Christ changed water into wine. He "manifested His glory, and His disciples believed in Him" (Gospel).

After the epiphany in Bethlehem and at the Jordan, we witness the epiphany at Cana. The first miracle in the life of Christ was inspired by the need of His friend, the poor bridegroom, and performed at the request of Mary, His mother. The disciples who had gathered about Him were today to catch a glimpse of the glory and power that were really His. For a moment His divinity is revealed, and He exercises His almighty power, which had hitherto been concealed under a humble exterior. "What He shall say to you, do ye," the solicitous mother told the servants of the bridegroom. Jesus told them to "fill the waterpots with water." The servants thereupon prepared six pots and filled them to the brim with water. Jesus drew near and commanded them: "Draw out now and carry to the chief steward." The steward tasted the water made wine, and he was astonished. Whence came this wine? Quietly and without a word or gesture Christ had changed the water into wine. Thus Jesus "manifested His glory."

The liturgy recognizes in this miracle a figure of what the Church accomplishes in the Mass. A more wonderful transubstantiation occurs daily at Mass in our churches: bread and wine are changed into the body and blood of Christ. Like His disciples, we also are witnesses of His divine power and majesty. We, too, believe in Him and follow Him with unfaltering confidence and trust. "And we saw His glory, the glory as it were, of the only-begotten of the Father" (Jn 1:14). "Let all the earth adore Thee, O God, and sing to Thee; let it sing a psalm to Thy name, O Most High" (Introit).

"Thou hast kept the good wine until now," the steward exclaimed when he met the bridegroom. This was not the usual custom, for "every man at first setteth forth good wine, and when men have well drunk, then that which is worse; but thou hast kept the good wine until now" (Gospel). For the liturgy the "good wine" which has been saved until now is the Holy Eucharist. It has been saved until now, that is, until the new dispensation, until the time of the mystical wedding of Christ with His Church. Many precious gifts God gave to His Chosen People in the

Old Testament; but this, His most precious gift, is reserved for the day when His only-begotten Son should take flesh in the womb of the Virgin.

"Thou hast saved the good wine until now." The holy Eucharist is another manifestation, or epiphany, of Christ. Here God reveals Himself in the form of bread and wine. Having partaken of this miraculous "wine," we also experience a change. We are strengthened, cleansed, and purified. "Shout with joy to God, all the earth, sing ye a psalm to His name. Come and hear all ye that fear God, and I will tell you what great things the Lord hath done for my soul" (Offertory). In the Eucharist we see His glory. We believe in Him; we follow Him. Let us each day in the Holy Eucharist be filled with His grace and divine presence, and become ever more intimately united with Him. What a holy, grace-filled wedding feast! It is the introduction to and the preparation for the eternal wedding feast in heaven.

"At that time there was a marriage in Cana of Galilee; and the mother of Jesus was there. And Jesus also was invited, and His disciples, to the marriage" (Gospel). This union of man's soul with God was ordained by the Father that we might be lifted up from our lowliness and partake of the fullness of His divine life. With grateful hearts we acknowledge: "The Lord sent His word and healed them, and delivered them from their destruction. Let the mercies of the Lord give glory to Him" (Gradual).

He who wishes to attend the wedding feast must come attired in a wedding garment. St. Paul explains what this means: "Let love be without dissimulation: hating that which is evil; cleaving to that which is good; loving one another with the charity of brotherhood; with honor preventing one another. In carefulness not slothful; in spirit fervent, serving the Lord; rejoicing in hope; patient in tribulation; instant in prayer; communicating to the necessities of the saints; pursuing hospitality. Bless them that persecute you; bless and curse not. Rejoice with them that rejoice; weep with them that weep, being of one mind, one towards another; not minding high things, but consenting to the humble" (Epistle). Thus clothed with virtue must he be who would attend the heavenly wedding feast. Is my soul so attired when I partake of the Eucharistic wedding feast? Let us examine ourselves according to the instructions of St. Paul in the Epistle.

Prayer

O almighty and eternal God, who rulest all things both in heaven and on earth, mercifully hear the prayers of Thy people and grant us Thy peace in our days. Through Christ our Lord. Amen.

Monday

"Let all the earth adore Thee, O God, and sing to Thee" (Introit). We praise Thee because Thou dost celebrate daily Thy epiphany in our midst in the Sacrifice of the Mass, because in the miracle of the consecration, Thou dost transform bread and wine into Thy body and blood, and because Thou dost give them to us in Holy Communion. "May the operation of Thy power be increased within us, we beseech Thee, O Lord, that being quickened by Thy divine sacraments, we may by Thy bounty be prepared to receive what they promise" (Postcommunion).

What takes place in reality at Mass is symbolic of what happens when we take off the old man and put on the new. We change from sinful, earthly, passionate, imperfect creatures to sons of God, living a divine and holy life. Thus we may understand the Epistle and the story of the miracle at Cana. If we assist devoutly at Mass today and receive Communion fruitfully, we shall return home as new men. Then we will live a life such as that outlined for us by St. Paul in the Epistle. We shall hate what is evil and cleave to what is good. We shall love one another with the charity of brotherhood, and anticipate one another in honor. Avoiding all sloth, we shall be fervent in spirit and serve the Lord. We shall rejoice in hope, be patient in tribulation, and instant in prayer. We shall contribute to the necessity of the saints (our fellow Christians), and pursue hospitality. With them that rejoice we shall rejoice, with them that weep we shall weep. We shall turn from high things and consent to that which is humble.

The change that takes place in the Mass must find a parallel in our own lives if we are to be properly prepared for the coming of Christ in His majesty on the last day. On that day He will appear before the whole world in majesty and power. At His final coming the final transformation will take place. "And as in Adam all die, so also in Christ all shall be made alive.... So also is the resurrection of the dead. It is sown in corruption; it shall rise in incorruption. It is sown in dishonor; it shall rise in glory. It is sown in weakness; it shall rise in power. It is sown in a natural body; it shall rise a spiritual body.... For this corruptible must put on incorruption; and this mortal must put on immortality" (1 Cor 15:22, 42–44, 53). Christ "will reform the body of our lowness, made like to the body of His glory, according to the operation whereby also He is able to subdue all things unto Himself" (Phil 3:21). With the same ease with which He performs the miracle of Cana and the daily miracle of the Mass, He will one day transform our bodies so that we may share His eternal glory. Rejoice in hope; God "hath regenerated us unto a lively hope, by the resurrection of Jesus Christ from the dead" (1 Pt 1:3). "So also you now indeed have sorrow. But I will see you again and your heart shall rejoice; and your joy no man shall take from you" (Jn 16:22). "And I dispose to you, as My Father hath disposed to Me, a kingdom" (Lk 22:29). "Be glad and rejoice, for your reward is very great in heaven" (Mt 5:12).

What now is, will pass. God will renew all things. "He who soweth sparingly shall also reap sparingly, and he who soweth in blessings shall also reap blessings" (2 Cor 9:6). "Now the God of hope fill you with all joy and peace in believing, that you may abound in hope and in the power of the Holy Ghost" (Rom 15:13).

Prayer

May the operation of Thy power be increased within us, we beseech Thee, O Lord, that being quickened by Thy divine sacraments, we may by Thy bounty be prepared to receive what they promise. Through Christ our Lord. Amen. (Postcommunion.)

Tuesday

"At that time there was a marriage in Cana of Galilee; and the mother of Jesus was there. And Jesus also was invited, and His disciples, to the marriage" (Gospel). The liturgy of the second Sunday after Epiphany gives us a picture of the union of the divine King with humanity, with the Church. This is a favorite theme of the liturgy: the Church is the bride of Christ. To this union the liturgy applies the Canticle of Canticles, which the Holy Ghost inspired in the Old Testament. The Canticle expresses the unceasing solicitations of God for the love of His chosen people. Many of the prophets, too, sang of this wonderful union of God with His beloved. The symbol they find most fitting is that of a betrothal. (Cf. Ez 16:8; Is 54:6.) The liturgy applies these references to the union of Christ with His Church. God in the person of Christ is the bridegroom of the Church and humanity.

Of the royal bridegroom the Psalmist sings: "Thou art beautiful above the sons of men; grace is poured abroad in Thy lips; therefore hath God blessed Thee forever. Gird Thy sword upon Thy thigh, O Thou most mighty. With Thy comeliness and Thy beauty set out, proceed prosperously, and reign. Because of truth and meekness and justice: and Thy right hand shall conduct Thee wonderfully. Thy arrows are sharp; under Thee shall people fall, into the hearts of the king's enemies. Thy throne, O God, is forever and ever; the scepter of Thy kingdom is a scepter of uprightness. Thou hast loved justice and hated iniquity; therefore God, Thy God hath anointed Thee with the oil of gladness above Thy fellows. Myrrh and stacte and cassia perfume Thy garments, from the ivory houses, out of which the daughters of kings have delighted Thee in Thy glory. The queen stood on Thy right hand in gilded clothing, surrounded with variety" (Ps 44:3–10).

This royal bridegroom unites divinity and humanity in one person, in whom the divine nature permeates the human nature with its light and glory. His lips announce the condescension and goodness of God, which has appeared to us in Him (Ti 3:4). In His hand rests the sword of righteous power, with which He strikes down all that is opposed to God. He is the champion of truth and the protector of all those predestined by God. He overcomes the resistance of men and of evil spirits. He is a source of consolation for the kingdom of God, the Church. He is the defender of the lowly, and He shall lift up him who has been crushed. The bent reed He shall straighten, and the dying flame He shall rekindle. He administers justice and reconciles men to God. He is the divine Ruler, the Lord of all, the absolute Master of angels and men. No one can withstand Him; all must do His will. He is holy and He hates all injustice; therefore God has blessed Him with the fullness of grace. From His human nature flows the sweetness of myrrh, stacte, and cassia, the perfumes of heavenly majesty. His companions are the daughters of kings, who await the call of the kingdom of God. They stand arrayed in the precious jewels of sanctifying grace, which the Lord has earned for them by His death on the cross. The place of honor at the right hand of the King is occupied by His bride, the queen, the Church.

The royal bride is the Church. "The daughters of kings have delighted Thee in Thy glory. The queen stood on Thy right hand in gilded clothing, surrounded with variety. Hearken, O daughter, and see and incline thy ear; and forget thy people and thy father's house. And the King shall greatly desire thy beauty, for He is the Lord thy God, and Him they shall adore. And the daughters of Tyre with gifts, yea, all the rich among the people shall entreat thy countenance" (Ps 44:10–13). In the New Testament, in the union of Christ with His Church, flesh and blood and descent from Abraham are no longer important, but rather a life of grace and virtue, the love of Christ and personal holiness. The Church is the only bride of Christ. Dressed in glowing garments, she will be led to her bridegroom. But the beauty of the King's bride is not an earthly beauty; it does not lie in ostentatious display, nor in the splendor and glory with which her friends surround her. Her beauty is supernatural and lies in her fullness of grace, virtue, and holiness. In this holy attire she will be led into the presence of the King.

As the royal bride is escorted from her father's house by a resplendent procession, she is followed by so vast a multitude that the Psalmist sees before his eyes the peoples of all nations. All the cities of the world are represented. Led by the queen, the Church, they will be brought to the palace of the King. To her, sons will be born of water and the Holy Ghost. She will be the mother of many children, the Church of innumerable saints, who will carry the message of the royal bridegroom to the ends of the earth. As the years pass, more men and nations will join the long procession which is marching to Sion to pay homage to the divine King. They, too, are to enjoy His love and generosity. "Let all the earth adore Thee, O God, and sing to Thee; let it sing a psalm to Thy name, O Most High" (Introit).

The various dioceses of the world, the parishes, the religious communities, the individual souls of men are also daughters of the King. The more intimately united they are with the bride of Christ, the queen, the Church of Rome, the more fruitful will be their union with Christ.

The palace in which the bride is united to the bridegroom is the house of God. The throne at which the marriage takes place is the altar. "Forget thy people and thy father's house." Leave all, offer all, give all that you have. Then thou canst partake of the wedding feast of Holy Communion, which is the foundation of our participation in the eternal and blessed life that is to come.

The escort of the bride is the Holy Spirit. He it is who forges the bond of love between the bride and the bridegroom. He clothes the soul in the wedding garment of sanctifying grace and makes her fit to become the bride of Christ. "The charity of God is poured forth in our hearts, by the Holy Ghost who is given to us" (Rom 5:5). Blessed art thou, O heavenly bride. Thou art obedient to Him in all things, completely possessed by Him, giving undivided affection to Him; thou art fruitful to Him in spiritual children, in virtue, in good works. "Forget thy people, and thy father's house." Leave all earthly things, leave flesh and blood, and live for Him alone.

Prayer

Shout with joy to God, all the earth, sing ye a psalm to His name. Come and hear, all ye who fear God, and I will tell you what great things He hath done for my soul, alleluia. (Offertory.)

Wednesday

"At that time there was a marriage in Cana of Galilee; and the mother of Jesus was there. And Jesus also was invited, and His disciples, to the marriage" (Gospel). In the union of Christ, the Son of God, to humanity, Mary played a leading role. In the liturgy she herself is the bride whom the Lord chose, the new Eve alongside the new Adam, Christ. In admiration the Church in her liturgy gazes untiringly on Mary, on the picture which the Psalmist describes: "The daughters of kings have delighted Thee in Thy glory. The queen stood on thy right hand in gilded clothing, surrounded with variety" (Ps 44:10).

Mary is the royal bride to whom the Father entrusted His Son, the King of Glory. From the very first moment of her existence, the Father began to prepare her for her union with His Son. Never did the stain of sin touch the future bride. Immaculately she was conceived, free from all inordinate passions, shining with the brilliance of the choicest gifts of mind and heart. The

Holy Ghost gave her as jewels the fullness of His gifts; the Son clothed His future mother in the bridal attire of complete holiness and the richest virtues. "All beautiful art thou, Mary, and there is no stain in thee." Therefore "the King desires thy beauty." He sends the angel Gabriel as matchmaker to ask Mary's consent to the marriage. The bride gives her answer: "Be it done to me according to thy word" (Lk 1:38). Mysteriously the union of the eternal Son of God and Mary, the virgin bride, takes place. This union, full of grace, endured on earth for thirty-three years. The new Eve took her place at the side of the new Adam, and became His trustworthy assistant in the work of our redemption.

The first Eve lost our inheritance for us; the second Eve returns us to Christ, the new Adam. As the new Eve, Mary stands under the cross, shares the pains with the new Adam, and courageously offers Him to the Father. In like manner she is His helpmate in the painful regeneration of the children of salvation. "Woman, behold Thy son." She is the mother of the living, the mother of those redeemed on the cross. By her assumption she became queen of heaven and earth. She is the mistress, the queen of all, the bride of Him to whom all power in heaven and on earth has been given. As bride and queen she has been made protectress of His treasures and dispenser of all His graces. She is enthroned at the right hand of the King, attired in the gold of God's glory, surrounded by choirs of angels and saints, with power over the heart of her bridegroom and King. We rejoice that the Lord has chosen her as His bride. We congratulate her; we pay her homage. With boundless confidence we turn to her, the bride of the omnipotent God, our powerful intercessor.

"They have no wine." Mary is the virgin bride, the mighty helpmate of the new Adam. She has a quick perception and an eager eye for the necessities of those around her. She grasps the situation at once and does the right thing. She notices before anyone else that the wine is short. "They have no wine." The first recorded words of Mary, the royal bride, at the wedding feast in Cana are spoken to relieve the need of her host — a human and superficial need, but she is aware even of these. In the mouth of the bride of Christ, this plea to Christ has a symbolic meaning. We hear this plea and recognize it as a symbol of the requests she makes for us before the throne of Christ. "They have no wine." If Mary had such sympathy for the needs of the couple at the feast of Cana, how much more will she heed our more pressing needs? All the necessities of men, their cares and sufferings, she will carry to the Lord of heaven: "They have no wine." Upon her request, what we have need of will be given to us.

"Whatsoever He shall say to you, do ye." The second words of Mary are directed toward us. Hardly has she made known our needs to the Lord, when she turns to us and makes known to us what God wishes of us. Just as she noted quickly what men were in need of, so, too, she perceives what God demands of His children. "Whatsoever He shall say to you, do ye." The servants do as Mary advised them. They listen to the words of Jesus: "Fill the waterpots with water." Now Mary's petition will be heard. The need of the wedding couple is satisfied. "Blessed is the man that heareth Me" (Prv 8:34). Mary demands that we do what Jesus bids us and wishes us to do. She is one with Him and conforms in all things to His will.

"All the glory of the king's daughter is within golden borders, clothed round about with varieties. After her shall virgins be brought to the king" (Ps 44:14 f.). Mary is the royal bride enthroned above all other creatures. In external life she is so humble, so poor, so insignificant in the eyes of men; and yet she is of royal birth. But that which is unnoticed by men is the very thing that

God chooses in His work. "He hath regarded the humility of His handmaid. For behold, from henceforth all generations shall call me blessed, because He that is mighty hath done great things to me, and holy is His name; and His mercy is from generation unto generations" (Lk 1:48–50). Mary desires to be nothing more than a handmaid, yet God elevates her to the position of Queen of Heaven. This is the mystery of humility: "He that humbleth himself shall be exalted" (Lk 14:11; 18:14).

"After her shall virgins be brought to the king; ... they shall be brought with gladness and rejoicing" (Ps 44:15 f.). They are the companions of the royal bride, her honored escort, themselves brides of Christ, noble daughters of the King. "These are they who were not defiled with women, for they are virgins" (Apoc 14:4). They leave earthly pleasures and take flight to the heavenly bridegroom. Rejoice at the hour when He shall take you home to the blessed wedding feast in heaven. Virginity and chastity are raised to the highest dignity. "Blessed are the clean of heart" (Mt 5:8).

"After her shall virgins be brought to the King." Blessed are those souls called to the religious life. "And I will espouse thee to Me forever, and I will espouse thee to Me in justice and judgment, and in mercy and in commiserations" (Os 2:19). Truly He has "blessed thee forever" (Ps 44:3). "See" the bridegroom; to Him alone "incline thy ear.... Forget thy people and thy father's house" (Ps 44:11). Give up everything to gain all in Christ, imitating Mary, the royal bride.

"After her shall virgins be brought to the King." Great as their number may be, do not take heed to those who are concerned only with the things of the flesh. Learn to treasure, honor, and love Christ.

PRAYER

Protect us, O Lord, and grant that we may seek the things of God and serve Thee with body and soul. Through Christ our Lord. Amen.

Thursday

"At that time there was a marriage in Cana of Galilee" (Gospel). At this wedding the bride and the groom are not important. The groom is spoken to, but the Evangelist does not regard it worthwhile to record what the bridegroom replies to the chief steward. We feel, when reading this story, that the wedding feast itself is of little concern to the Evangelist. He uses it as the background for another wedding feast, the marriage of Christ the King to His Church and to the Christian soul. These thoughts are proposed to us by Epiphany.

Christ, the divine King, is the bridegroom of the soul. He is not satisfied with becoming our brother, our Redeemer, the vine which upholds the branches and fills them with life; He desires to be united in the most intimate union of which man is capable. "Wherefore a man shall leave father and mother and shall cleave to his wife; and they shall be two in one flesh" (Gn 2:24). "This is a great sacrament; but I speak in Christ and in the Church" (Eph 5:32). St. Paul points out the great mystery in this union of a man and wife. But he also proclaims very clearly that this union is great and holy because it is a symbol of the union of Christ the Lord with His Church and with our souls. In this light the words of the Apostle take on a wider and deeper meaning: "The husband shall leave father and mother and cling to his wife," and the two shall become one in spirit, one in thought, one in desire and will. They shall have one heart and one understanding and one soul, loving and possessing one another completely. Sweet is the name father, and sweet is the name mother and the name friend, but sweetest of all is the name husband and wife. Husband and wife have everything in common and nothing of their own. They have one inheritance, one house, one table, one bridal chamber, one heart, and one will. The Apostle desires to lead us into such a holy union with Christ. "I am jealous of you with the jealousy of God. For I have espoused you to one husband, that I may present you as a chaste virgin to Christ" (2 Cor 11:2). The Lord desires to take our soul unto Himself as the clean and unspotted bride. He desires to be the bridegroom of our soul.

"All I have is thine" (Lk 15:31). The union of Christ with our soul produces three characteristics, the first of which consists of the sublime gift of sanctifying grace, supernatural virtue, and the gifts of the Holy Ghost. We receive the plenitude of supernatural life when our soul is in union with Christ. "All the glory of the king's daughter is within golden borders, clothed round about with varieties" (Ps 44:14–15).

The second characteristic of this union is that the soul possesses all the good things that Christ possesses. "All I have is thine," the divine bridegroom says to the soul. He gives it His merits, His prayers, His heart, His humanity. He gives it His divinity, His mother, His inheritance in heaven, so completely does He love the soul.

The third characteristic is that the soul shares with Christ His royal dignity, His power, and His majesty. The bride, the individual soul, shall also be queen and share in the sovereign power of the bridegroom, elevated above all that is earthly. It shall lose its fear of men and of the world. It will be freed from lust, from the pride of life, and shall overcome all human suffering and all sinful attachments. It will escape Satan and hell.

Our soul must be consumed by a burning desire to be joined to the heavenly bridegroom, who has done so much for us. He desires to belong entirely to us, to fill us with His grace. How fortunate we are because we have been entrusted to Him who has loved us with an eternal love and has undergone death and has poured forth His blood to purify us! "Hearken, O daughter, and see and incline thy ear; and forget thy people and thy father's house. And the king shall greatly desire thy beauty" (Ps 44:11 f.). "All I have is thine."

"Shout with joy to God, all the earth; sing ye a psalm to His name. Come and hear, and I will tell you what great things the Lord hath done for my soul" (Offertory). Betrothal to Christ! Could the Lord have done greater things for His Church, or for us, than to raise us to this union? How heartily we should thank Him for uniting Himself with humanity in a nuptial union when He became man! What can we offer in return for His desire to die for us, to unite us with Himself? What return can we make for the regeneration of baptism and for the more intimate union accomplished through our religious profession? He comes to us daily in the Mass and in Holy Communion to unite Himself more closely with us. He wishes to share with us His possessions, His power, and His majesty. "Forget thy people and thy father's house." Give all in order to possess Him alone.

"In all things you are made rich in Him" (1 Cor 1:5). We are indeed made rich by this nuptial union with Christ. Why are we yet so depressed, so weak, so perplexed and despondent? Why do we cling to the earth, to our petty sufferings? Why do we struggle so in our own small miseries? Is it not because we do not consider our riches in Christ and our union with Him? Epiphany must make us conscious of this inheritance. The Lord must appear anew as the bridegroom of the Church and of our soul.

Prayer

May the operation of Thy power be increased within us, we beseech Thee, O Lord, that being quickened by Thy divine sacraments, we may by Thy bounty be prepared to receive what they promise. Through Christ our Lord. Amen. (Postcommunion.)

Friday

The changing of the water into wine at the wedding feast is of great significance for the liturgy. At the celebration of Mass water is mixed with wine. As the water is mingled with wine and consecrated and changed into the precious blood, so we are united with Christ in the Holy Sacrifice, and are united, and changed, and consecrated, and sanctified with Him. The Epistle presents to us mankind offered and consecrated by the participation in the celebration of Mass.

"Brethren, having different gifts, according to the grace that is given us, either prophecy, to be used according to the rule of faith; or ministry, in ministering; or he that teacheth, in doctrine; he that exhorteth, in exhorting; he that giveth, with simplicity; he that ruleth, with carefulness; he that showeth mercy, with cheerfulness" (Epistle).

We should be content with our condition in life and with the position in which God has placed us. We should rest satisfied with the talent God has provided and with the state of health in which we find ourselves. We must be faithful to the duties of our station, and zealous for the tasks assigned to us by our position in the body of Christ, the Church. In this way we shall be an epiphany, a manifestation of the spirit of Christ. Thus we shall become "other Christs" and shall win souls for Christ. That should be the fruit of our assistance at Mass. We do not stand alone, but we live in union with Christ and with our brethren. "For we are the good odor of Christ unto God, in them that are saved and in them that perish" (2 Cor 2:15). Such is the exterior life in the man consecrated to God.

"Loving one another with the charity of brotherhood; with honor preventing one another. In carefulness not slothful; in spirit fervent, serving the Lord; rejoicing in hope; patient in tribulation; instant in prayer; communicating to the necessities of the saints; pursuing hospitality. Bless them that persecute you; bless and curse not. Rejoice with them that rejoice; weep with them that weep, being of one mind, one towards another; not minding high things, but consenting to the humble" (Epistle). Such is the interior life of the man consecrated to Christ at Mass.

This perfect Christian, both in his exterior life and in his interior life, in his thoughts and deeds regarding Christ, his neighbor, and himself, is the fruit of assisting properly at Mass and of offering himself with Christ's sacrifice. Christ lives in us, and we become other Christs.

This exercise in virtue must not be confined to the Church or to the family circle. The perfect Christian must go out and face life and give an example to those with whom he lives. In the eyes of the world he must show forth Christ in his life. Such a Christian will excel in kindness, in virtue, in charity for those about him. He will surpass others in culture and proficiency; he will be more farsighted in business, kinder and more just in his dealings with others, whether in the office, factory, or store. He will accept the happenings of the day, not as the result of chance or of his own planning, but in every event he will see the hand of providence. If he desires to rejoice, he will, like the wedded couple at Cana, invite Christ to be his guest. He is another Christ.

True Christianity produces honorable men, men of solid virtue. It promotes honest self-denial, propriety, independence, courage, valor, truth, and an abiding sense of peace. These are all too often forgotten virtues.

Prayer

O God, who in creating human nature didst marvelously ennoble it, and hast still more marvelously renewed it; grant that by the mystery of this water and wine, we may be made partakers of His divinity, who vouchsafed to become partaker of our humanity, Jesus Christ, Thy Son our Lord, who liveth and reigneth with Thee in the unity of the Holy Ghost, one God world without end. Amen.

Saturday

The miracle of Cana is an epiphany, a manifestation of the miraculous power of the Savior, and it is also a revelation of His divine love for man.

The Lord attends the wedding of simple, humble people. He wishes to honor and please them; He likes to be with the humble. It happened that the supply of wine did not suffice for the wedding celebration, which in Palestine lasts for several days. By a miracle of His power the Savior comes to the assistance of the embarrassed bridegroom. But the miracle of power has its foundation in Christ's love, in His sympathy with these poor people who are in need. We are told that He went about "doing good" (Acts 10:38). He is the incarnate divine mercy, the love descended from heaven. His love is not confined to a small circle of the faithful; it embraces the whole world. He rejoices when we rejoice, He suffers when we suffer, He unites Himself to us in all things.

"This is My commandment, that you love one another as I have loved you" (Jn 15:12). How does He love us? In the manger, on Olivet, on the cross, in the tabernacle, in Holy Communion. He "loved them unto the end" (Jn 13:1), until His last drop of blood had been shed. Thus He loves men who so often offend Him and forget what He has done for them. Yet He prays: "Father, forgive them" (Lk 23:34). We should love Him as He has loved us. He has made our love of neighbor a sure sign of our being His disciples (Jn 13:35). This is the "new commandment" He has given us. I must be a manifestation, a revelation of His love for others; I must offer myself for the brethren in Christ as He offered Himself for me. I must forgive as He forgave; I must pray and sacrifice and be zealous as He was for the salvation of others. Thus I shall win grace for my neighbor and inherit heaven with Him. That is His "new commandment."

The Epistle speaks emphatically of this epiphany of love. "Loving one another with the charity of brotherhood,... bless them that persecute you,... being of one mind, one towards another" (Epistle). True Christian life is enduring, patient, indefatigable, forgiving, peaceful, loving toward enemies as well as friends. "A new commandment I give unto you" (Jn 13:34), who have been established in Me by My spirit and My strength.

Standing in partnership, joined to one another, for one another, and with one another, we approach the altar. Christ our high priest, our head, leads; with Him the family of God in heaven and on earth, all together with one heart and one soul, one in faith and desires, comes to praise, thank, petition, sacrifice, and atone, to ask for light and grace.

No one can offer himself for himself without the others, separating himself from the community, being at variance with the brethren, turned away from them, filled, perhaps, even with hate for them. Only he who is in heart and soul one with the community of Christ is a true partaker of the sacrifice and heir of the fruit of the Mass. "Above all these things have charity" (Col 3:14).

"Fervent in spirit." Nowadays there are many flames in the world; the flame of hate, passion, self-love. But the Church calls on us Christians to be fervent in spirit, to glow with a heavenly flame, to be enkindled by the flame of the Holy Ghost. By this flame of love which the Holy Ghost places in us, we serve the Lord "rejoicing in hope, patient in tribulation, instant in prayer, communicating to the necessities of the saints, pursuing hospitality" (Epistle). The fruit of the Holy Sacrifice and of the wedding banquet of Holy Communion is the Christian enkindled by the Spirit of Christ, an image of the Lord, full of zeal, enthusiasm, and life for all that pertains to God, to the Church, and to souls.

Prayer

May the operation of Thy power be increased within us, we beseech Thee, O Lord, that being quickened by Thy divine sacraments, we may by Thy bounty be prepared to receive what they promise. Through Christ our Lord. Amen. (Postcommunion.)

Third Sunday after Epiphany

The Mass

The adoring angels approach the throne of His Majesty and the earth stands in awe, for the Lord has manifested His kingship at Epiphany. "And the daughters of Juda rejoiced" (Introit). In the Holy Sacrifice the Church makes her complete submission to the sovereignty of the King. "Graciously look upon our infirmities and stretch forth the right hand of Thy majesty to protect us" (Collect). Christ the King rules in His kingdom, and yet there are many provinces that do not recognize His authority. The Epistle characterizes these rebellious people as conceited, self-seeking, and vain. "Graciously look upon our infirmities." We seek only to be saved from ourselves, and only Christ and His grace can save us. He is the King of the Church and the sovereign of each soul.

"The Lord hath built up Sion: and He shall be seen in His glory" (Gradual). Sion is the Church, the kingdom of His grace in souls, where He rules over our corrupted nature. "Stretch forth the right hand of Thy majesty to protect us." The Gospel illustrates these words of the Collect. "Lord, if Thou wilt, Thou canst make me clean," cries the afflicted leper. Christ wills, and the leper is cleansed, for Christ has power over the ills of the body. He wills that we, too, be cleansed from our afflictions. For are not we ourselves the sick of the Gospel? The Gentile centurion besought Christ for the cure of his sick servant because he knew that Christ was the Master of life and death. He knew that it was not even necessary for Christ to come down to his house. "Lord, I am not worthy that Thou shouldst enter under my roof" (Mt 8:8). So great faith Christ had not found even in Israel, and He rewards it by healing the man's servant from afar. Truly,

"The Lord hath reigned" (Alleluia); "the right hand of the Lord hath exalted me; I shall not die, but live" (Offertory).

In the Offertory we draw near to Christ like one of the afflicted men of the Gospel. We have been prostrated by sickness, and we now long to live a strong, healthy, normal life. We approach Christ and cry out, "Stretch forth the right hand of Thy majesty to protect us." We recognize Christ as our King and wish Him to rule over us completely, even over our mind and heart and will. Let us offer all that we have and place it on the paten today. Soon He will come to offer His own sacrifice to the Father, and He will unite to this whatever we have placed at His disposal. He will free us from our sickness and consecrate and sanctify our life. "The right hand of the Lord hath exalted me." In the sacrificial offering He joins our works and prayers and sufferings with His own. In this manner our works and prayers acquire a supernatural value in the sight of God. "I live, now not I; but Christ liveth in me" (Gal 2:20). Christ asserts His right to reign over us in Holy Communion. At this moment He comes and takes up His abode in our hearts. He places His hand on our soul and nourishes it and consecrates it, that it may be restored to health, resemble His soul, and show forth His life in its works. "All wondered at these things which proceeded from the mouth of God" (Communion), concerning God's Eucharistic power in souls. "Thy kingdom come."

Meditation

"The Lord hath built up Sion [His Church]; and He shall be seen in His glory" (Gradual). This is the feast of the Epiphany, the manifestation of Christ, the divine King, in His Church. He has always manifested Himself in His Church and will continue to live there and carry on His works of love and mercy. Today we acknowledge His royalty. "The Lord hath reigned; let the earth rejoice" (Collect).

"The Lord hath built up Sion" (Gradual). Sion is the Church, the congregation of the faithful gathered about the altar of sacrifice. They draw close to the altar, for there the Lord is soon to appear in their midst. They approach with a faith like that of the centurion of the Gospel: "Lord, only say the word and my servant shall be healed." Whatever their afflictions may be, they are confident with the leper: "Lord, if Thou wilt, Thou canst make me clean." The Apostle of the Gentiles admonishes them in the Epistle: "Brethren, be not wise in your own conceits. To no man rendering evil for evil; providing good things not only in the sight of God, but also in the sight of all men.... Revenge not yourselves, my dearly beloved, but give place unto wrath. For it is written: Revenge is mine, I will repay, saith the Lord. But if thy enemy be hungry, give him to eat; if he thirst, give him to drink; for doing this, thou shalt heap coals of fire upon his head. Be not overcome by evil, but overcome evil by good."

The kingdom of God is within the hearts of men. Christ puts aside His divine estate for the moment that He may minister to the needs of souls. "And Jesus, stretching forth His hand, touched him, saying: I will. Be thou made clean. And forthwith his leprosy was cleansed" (Gospel). It is not difficult for us to recognize ourselves in the leper of the Gospel. In His boundless love for us, Christ stretched forth His hand at baptism and said: "I will. Be thou made clean." It is His love that has moved Him to cleanse us. He is the manifestation of God's love for us. He demands of us only what He demanded of the leper and the centurion — faith. We have this faith when we cry out, "Lord, if Thou wilt, Thou canst make me clean."

"The right hand of the Lord hath wrought strength; the right hand of the Lord hath exalted me. I shall not die, but live, and shall declare the works of the Lord" (Offertory). These works the Lord has shown us in His sacraments. In baptism and in the sacrament of penance He cleanses our souls; in Mass and Holy Communion He strengthens us to keep us well. "I shall not die, but live," by the mercy and power of God.

I believe and I hope that I also shall be numbered among those who "shall come from the east and the west and shall sit down with Abraham, and Isaac, and Jacob in the kingdom of heaven" (Gospel). With us, the Gentiles, "the Lord hath built up Sion," the Church. "The Gentiles shall fear Thy name, O Lord, and all the kings of the earth Thy glory" (Gradual). We are thankful for His grace and unmerited love; but we should regret that we have not always responded to His grace and love.

PRAYER

Almighty and eternal God, graciously look upon our infirmity and stretch forth the right hand of Thy majesty to protect us. Through Christ our Lord. Amen.

Monday

"Amen I say to you, I have not found so great faith in Israel" (Gospel). The chosen people had received revelations, the prophets, and the Law; they had the Scriptures, the temple, and their sacrifices. All these things should have prepared them for the Savior; but most of the Jews did not believe in Him. Many of the Gentiles, however, of whom the Roman centurion is an example, had faith in Him. The centurion did not feel that it was necessary for Christ to visit his servant in order to cure him. "Only say the word, and my servant shall be healed." And our Lord, admiring his faith, replies: "Amen, I say to you, I have not found so great faith in Israel."

Jesus requires faith of those who would serve Him. He has hidden his divinity under the veil of His humanity. He is dependent on His mother and His friends for the necessities of life; He is subject to poverty and suffering. His divinity is discernible only to the eye of faith; and such faith He requires of all His disciples. "Blessed are they that have not seen and have believed" (Jn 20:29). He has not found this kind of faith among the chosen people. The Jews were anticipating a Savior who would free them from the galling yoke of the Roman army. They sought a Messias who could re-establish their political independence and promote their material prosperity. In the many trials and sufferings which the nation had undergone, it had lost sight of its true purpose. Absorbed in its temporal cares, it had forgotten, in spite of the Scriptures and all the prophets, that it had been chosen for a divine and eternal destiny. So far had their unbelief gone that, when they were called upon to acknowledge their King, the Jews demanded His death from Pilate, a Gentile. The chosen people gave up their inheritance, and it was transferred to the Gentiles, to whom we belong.

The Roman officer, like the Magi at Epiphany, speaks as the representative of the Gentile world. With them we confess today, "Thou art Christ, the Son of the living God" (Mt 16:16). We give our complete assent to His divinity, to His right to the title of King, to the doctrine which He has preached, and to His commandments and His sacraments. We are not alone in this acknowledgment, for "many shall come from the east and the west, and shall sit down with Abraham, and Isaac, and Jacob in the kingdom of heaven" (Gospel).

Today the Church admires the faith of the Roman centurion. He has not been prepared for the coming of Christ by the prophets, the Scriptures, or the miracles wrought by God to strengthen the faith of His people. And yet he believes. He not only believes that Christ can heal his servant, but is persuaded that it is not even necessary for Christ to come down to his house; His mere word will suffice. In fact, his great reverence for the person of Christ leads him to believe that it would be an indignity for Christ to enter his house.

How different is the attitude of the Jews! They have closed their eyes to the wonders that Christ works; they have forgotten the prophecies of the Old Testament. The workings of grace are indeed mysterious. "I will have mercy on whom I will have mercy; and I will show mercy to whom I will show mercy" (Rom 9:15). And the Apostle continues: "So then it is not of him that willeth, nor of him that runneth, but of God that showeth mercy" (Rom 9:16). If, then, we have been called to the kingdom of God, it is not of our own doing nor because of our worthiness, but because of the mercy of God. How wonderful is God's mercy toward us!

To whom does God show this mercy? It is to little ones, the patient ones. "I confess to thee, O Father, Lord of heaven and earth, because Thou hast hid these things from the wise and prudent, and hast revealed them to the little ones" (Mt 11:25). The wise and the learned in Israel, who trust in their knowledge of the Scriptures, are left to perish in their own conceit. To the little ones who can rely on no earthly wisdom it is given to know the mysteries of God. "God resisteth the proud, but to the humble He giveth grace" (1 Pt 5:5).

"He that thinketh himself to stand let him take heed lest he fall" (1 Cor 10:12). If the chosen people could misuse the grace of God, may not we do the same? Indeed, how often have we not failed to respond to grace! How little effort we put forth to repel venial sins! Often enough to place mere whims and personal preferences before the will of God. "And if some of the branches be broken and thou, being a wild olive, art ingrafted in them and art made partaker of the root and of the fatness of the olive tree, boast not against the branches. But if thou boast, thou bearest not the root, but the root thee. Thou wilt say then: The branches were broken off that I might be grafted in. Well! because of unbelief they were broken off. But thou standest by faith. Be not high minded, but fear. For if God hath not spared the natural branches, fear lest perhaps He also spare not thee" (Rom 11:17–21).

Prayer

O Lord, Thou hast made us participate in so great a mystery; grant, we beseech Thee, that our lives may be an example of gratitude. Amen.

Tuesday

"The Lord hath built up Sion," His Church (Gradual). The kingdom of God is the kingdom of the spirit, a kingdom of peace and love. Thus we are assured by the Epistle of the third Sunday after Epiphany.

"To no men rendering evil for evil." Unredeemed men, the world, seek revenge. The world sees no virtue but only weakness in the practice of self-control, forgiveness, and charity. It has retained the spirit of the Old Law: "An eye for an eye and a tooth for a tooth." This is not the spirit of the Christian, for he is bidden, "If one strike thee on thy right cheek, turn to him also the other" (Mt 5:39). Christ was not satisfied merely to leave this instruction to His disciples; He gave them a sublime example when He allowed Himself to be scourged and sentenced to death without resisting. When He was spit upon and struck, He suffered all His torments in silence. For those who persecuted Him He prays, "Father, forgive them, for they know not what they do" (Lk 23:34). This, too, is the spirit on which He has established His kingdom, the kingdom of the spirit.

"Overcome evil by good." This is the spirit of Christ and of true Christian piety. "If thy enemy be hungry, give him to eat" (Epistle). The only revenge permitted to the Christian is the return of good for evil. He is to overcome evil only by doing good. "Do good to them that hate you and pray for them that persecute … you" (Mt 5:44). This disposition must be universal. The Christian must do good to everyone, even to those who persecute him and hate him; he must repay evil with good. This is the spirit of Christ, the spirit every member of Christ must have.

"The Lord hath built up Sion." He builds up His kingdom by means of His graces, dispensed in the Mass and in Holy Communion. His task is not an easy one. The material which He uses is the cold, vindictive hearts of men. These hearts are narrow, selfish, proud, and unbending. They are given to bickering, faultfinding, criticism, and slander. The Lord must shape these living stones to fit the design of the Sion He has planned. The Epistle of the day shows us how deficient we are in the qualities which Christ desires of us. We perceive our misery, but we cry out to Him, "Lord, Thy kingdom come." Fill our hearts with Thy spirit, our minds with Thy thoughts, our souls with Thy love.

"Overcome evil by good," with unfeigned charity for all men. This virtue has been called the milk of human kindness. Kindness is the most pleasing adornment of the Christian personality. "Put ye on, therefore, as the elect of God, holy, and beloved, the bowels of mercy, benignity, humility, modesty, patience" (Col 3:12). In this spirit the true Christian must grow, especially if he wishes to profit from his attendance at Mass.

The Mass is a communal act of worship. We cannot assist at it with profit unless our heart is at peace with God and our neighbor. The Mass is the supreme act of public worship in the Church. To offer worthily the Holy Sacrifice, we must be united in heart and in soul with our brethren in Christ. But this does not mean merely the bodily union of the faithful in offering their gifts. We must be united in spirit, too, for we pray not merely for our own needs, but for all our brethren: "Give us this day our daily bread; forgive us our trespasses, as we forgive those who trespass against us. And lead us not into temptation." That is the language of Christian brotherhood, Christian charity.

Prayer

O Lord, Thou hast given us participation in the graces of Mass and Communion; grant, we beseech Thee, that our lives may be regulated in conformity with these graces. Amen.

Wednesday

"The Lord hath built up Sion." The Lord has built a new city, in which He is to appear in His majesty. The old Jerusalem has fallen, but a new city has risen on the ruins of the old, and its inhabitants are the nations of the Gentiles. To the inhabitants of the new city He has given new life and strength, as He gave them to the leprous man and to the centurion of the Gospel. "I shall not die, but live, and shall declare the works of the Lord" (Offertory).

This new life is a participation in the life of the Divinity. Our life as Christians is not merely a matter of calling on Christ as our Redeemer in our necessities. Much less does it consist in honoring Him as a mere man who by the power of His example has taught the world to live a life of virtue and holiness. Christ was more than a teacher of a new and excellent philosophy; He was the author of an entirely new life, a life that was to share in the divine life. This life is to begin for men even while they are still on earth; they are to will what God wills; they are to understand as God understands; they are to enjoy the blessedness of the Father and the Son and the Holy Spirit in the world to come. "Behold what manner of charity the Father hath bestowed upon us, that we should be called and should be the sons of God" (1 Jn 3:1).

This new life is a life in union with God. "If any one love Me, he will keep My word, and My Father will love him, and We will come to him and will make Our abode with him" (Jn 14:23). After this union is effected by Christ, human life is charged with a new sensibility and a new felicity, and is born to an inexhaustible fullness of life. A Christian comes to know himself, no longer as a mere man, but as a child of God. His mind is occupied with the thought of the goodness of God, and his soul is enthralled by the charm of His love. Man now converses with God as a child with its father. God in turn enlightens the intellect of His child and fortifies the will of His beloved one with His own divine strength. In all His dealings with the soul, God is most wise. At times He fills it with an ineffable sweetness; at times He leaves it to wander in spiritual dryness; but He is always there. He guides the faltering soul through the darkness as a skillful pilot guides his boat through the surf. We have only to follow the direction of the pilot to arrive safely at port.

"The Lord hath built up Sion." The liturgy is here referring to the new race that is born by baptism, which has been filled and permeated with the spirit of Christ. This new race can be brought forth only from the divine life. Christ alone can give it to us, and He gives it gladly. All power is given Him by the Father, and He gives this life to all who confide in Him.

"He that eateth of this bread shall live forever" (Jn 6:59). The sacraments are the divinely instituted means by which the soul obtains the new life of grace. The Christian soul should feel deep gratitude for this wonderful gift of God. Let us rejoice, then, with the holy liturgy, for "The right hand of the Lord hath wrought strength; the right hand of the Lord hath exalted me; I shall not die, but live, and shall declare the works of the Lord" (Offertory). Let us be confident. We have been engrafted on the vine from which the divine life flows. We may be sure, then, with the Apostle of the Gentiles, "I can do all things in Him that strengtheneth me" (Phil 4:13). But without Him we can do nothing.

Prayer

Almighty and eternal God, graciously look upon our infirmity and stretch forth the right hand of Thy majesty to protect us. Through Christ our Lord. Amen.

Thursday

As Jesus descended from the mountain, a great multitude followed Him and a leper came and fell at His feet and cried out, "Lord, if Thou wilt, Thou canst make me clean. And Jesus, stretching forth His hand, touched him, saying: I will. Be thou made clean" (Gospel). Christ thus manifested both His goodness and His power over nature.

"Lord, if Thou wilt, Thou canst make me clean." Leprosy is the figure of sin, which defiles the soul. Leprosy is a disease that is particularly horrible because of the disfigurement that it produces in its victims. The effect of leprosy on the body gives us a tangible impression of the effect of sin on the soul. Passion is so deeply rooted in our natures that, unless it is ruled with a firm hand, it may destroy and disfigure the beauty both of our body and of our soul. This passion is insatiable and will not rest until it has destroyed our soul and the souls of others. Any soul that wishes to become a member of Christ must first cleanse itself from the vices of passion. "Lord, if Thou wilt, Thou canst make me clean." Jesus wills to make us so. "I will. Be thou made clean." We must be clean in our thoughts, actions, and desires. How could it be otherwise, since by baptism we have become living members of His body? The body and soul of man belong to Christ and are part of Him since He has by His death snatched them from the hands of the enemy. But even after our incorporation in the body of Christ, the deeply rooted evil of our animal passions remains with us, and we must wage a continual war against it. "Lord, if Thou wilt, Thou canst make me clean."

"Blessed are the clean of heart" (Mt 5:8). Christ expects not only that the soul be clean of actual sins of impurity, but also that the heart be clean. No attachment to sin can be allowed to grow up in the soul, and everything that fosters such an attachment must be cut off. The Christian must always keep in mind the end for which he was created, and with a determined will strive continually to attain that goal. He must be prepared for trials and difficulties, for the way is not easy, and trials, suffering, and self-denial mark the way that leads to salvation. Only when the soul has detached itself from all that might tarnish its beauty can it fulfill its proper function of reflecting the beauty of God. To accomplish such detachment is the work of continual mortification and earnest sacrifice. "Blessed are the clean of heart, for they shall see God." Blessed are they who by continual self-control have overcome all that is earthly and human, and have made themselves a holocaust to God.

"Lord, if Thou wilt, Thou canst make me clean." "The Lord hath built up Sion [His Church] and [there] He shall be seen in His glory" (Gradual). Christ loved chastity, and He desires to see this virtue reproduced in His disciples. He wishes us, as members of His body, to manifest the splendor of His purity. You are "now light in the Lord. Walk, then, as children of the light" (Eph 5:8). We pray, not only for ourselves, but also for our brethren: "Lord, if Thou wilt, Thou canst make me clean."

Nothing can satisfy the heart of man but life in union with God and the blessed company of the saints. Our souls are vessels into which the divine life is poured. Like the shining vessels of a great king, our souls should be dipped into the majesty of God and come forth overflowing with the sweetness of divinity. They should be a delight to the angels and the saints. But God cannot draw to Himself anything that is unclean. Only they who have achieved purity of soul may approach close to the divinity. "Blessed are the clean of heart, for they shall see God."

Today as we approach the Holy Sacrifice, we cry out with the leper of the Gospel, "Lord, if Thou wilt, Thou canst make me clean." We kneel with the leper at the roadside, and the Lord comes to us in the Mass. At Holy Communion He presses us to His breast and stirs our soul with His grace as though we were not loathsome, vile creatures, the outcasts of men. He whispers into our ear, "I will. Be thou made clean." We rest satisfied, for the holy liturgy assures us: "The right hand of the Lord hath wrought strength; the right hand of the Lord hath exalted me; I shall not die, but live, and shall declare the works of the Lord" (Offertory).

Prayer

Almighty and eternal God, graciously look upon our infirmity and stretch forth the right hand of Thy majesty. Through Christ our Lord. Amen.

Friday

Today the liturgy continues to consider the healing of the leper. The faithful are invited to assist at the Holy Sacrifice with the object of preparing themselves for the worthy reception of Holy Communion. In order to approach worthily, we must be clean of heart. "I will. Be thou made clean" (Gospel).

"Who shall ascend into the mountain of the Lord; or who shall stand in His holy place. The innocent in hands and clean of heart, who hath not taken his soul in vain nor sworn deceitfully to his neighbor. He shall receive a blessing from the Lord and mercy from God his Savior" (Ps 23:3–5). If such dispositions were required for the worthy approach to the temple at Jerusalem, how much more worthy they should be who approach the Holy Sacrifice of the Mass and Holy Communion. Perhaps our disposition when approaching Mass and Communion will ever fall short of the ideal, for evil habits and inclinations cling to us persistently. We shall always have to struggle with our self-love, which tends to separate us from God and our neighbor; our thoughts ever tend toward that which is worldly and human; the spirit of pride tends to dominate all our thoughts and actions. We are still much attached to the pleasures and joys and lusts of the world, and persistently seek that which is to our own advantage. Self, and not God, is still the center of all our actions. Though we may have avoided grievous sins, we are still the victims of habitual venial sins. Do we wonder, then, why we have not profited in greater measure from our frequent reception of the sacraments? Let us ask Him fervently: "Lord, if Thou wilt, Thou canst make me clean." Today when He appears on our altar, let us ask Him, "Create a clean heart in me, O God, and renew a right spirit within my bowels" (Ps 50:12).

Only "the innocent of hands and the clean of heart" may approach the Lord. A high degree of purity is required of those who receive Him daily. The reception of any sacrament is always a matter of great moment. No action of human life is more sublime than the reception of the body and blood of the Lord. The reception of the Eucharist is the most fruitful and most powerful means of obtaining an increase of grace and holiness. "A soul that is well prepared for the reception of the Sacrament, obtains by this one reception an incomparably greater grace than is given to all the saints together in their visions and revelations" (Lallenmant).

If one is to receive the Eucharist with profit, one must be properly prepared. The Church requires of us, not only that we be in the state of grace, but also that we approach with the proper motives and the proper dispositions. If we receive from the force of habit, out of mere vanity, because we wish to enjoy the esteem of other men, or for any other human motive, we are not properly disposed. The proper motive for the reception of Holy Communion is the desire for a closer union with God. Another good motive is that we may gain strength to overcome our evil habits and free ourselves from all our faults. We may be sure that, whatever the evil habit that binds us, we shall be able to free ourselves from it if we persist in the frequent and worthy reception of the Sacrament. If in spite of our struggles and the frequent reception of the Sacrament, we find that we still fall back frequently into the same sins, we may be fairly sure that we have not prepared ourselves sufficiently and that we need to improve our disposition for receiving Holy Communion.

We should examine ourselves frequently and discover whether we are approaching the Sacrament with a sincere desire to achieve purity of heart. Much of the fruit of the Mass and Holy Communion depends upon the disposition of our soul. Let us, then, approach the Lord again and ask Him humbly, "Lord, if Thou wilt, Thou canst make me clean." Without Thy help the task is too great for me. "Stretch forth the right hand of Thy majesty" and heal me as Thou didst heal the leper, and say to my troubled soul, "I will. Be thou made clean."

Prayer

Almighty and eternal God, graciously look upon our infirmity and stretch forth the right hand of Thy majesty to protect us. Through Christ our Lord. Amen.

Saturday

The disposition of the Roman centurion is worthy of our admiration. He explains briefly his servant's condition to the Lord. Christ answers him, "I will come and heal him." But the centurion had not asked for this favor and even feels that he is unworthy of so great a favor. "Lord, I am not worthy that Thou shouldst enter under my roof; but only say the word, and my servant shall be healed." The Church has found no words more fitting than these for the soul approaching the Eucharist.

"Lord, I am not worthy." The dwelling place of Christ must be free from all sin. The only one who was truly worthy to receive Christ was His immaculate mother, who by a special grace had been preserved even from Original Sin. From the first moment of her existence she was free from all stain. She was so firmly established in grace and virtue that during her entire life she was never guilty of the least fault. Her every thought, word, and deed was performed in the most perfect conformity to the will of God and in the most perfect purity. In the eyes of God she remained the spotless one, the single example of perfect virtue. Her motives were never tainted with self-seeking; her prayers sought only what was the will of God; her works were performed only that He might be glorified. So great was her purity of heart that the human mind can scarce conceive it. God's kindly providence watched over the days of her childhood and her sojourn in the temple. She and she alone was worthy to become the dwelling place of the Most High.

In Holy Communion we await the coming of this same God. Although He does not come to us to assume a human nature, as He did when He came to dwell in the breast of Mary, He is nevertheless the same holy, eternal, and mighty God. Though we cannot duplicate the spotless holiness of Mary, we nevertheless have the obligation of making our hearts as pure and spotless as possible. But, alas, how great is the difference between our heart and Mary's heart! How far from the holiness and purity of the Virgin of Nazareth! When we reflect upon the matter, we must confess with the centurion: "Lord, I am not worthy that Thou shouldst enter under my roof." My mind is tainted with unclean thoughts; my will seeks what is displeasing to Thee; my desires are imperfect and degraded. In my service of Thee I have been guilty of countless acts of infidelity. My soul is utterly unworthy of the sanctity of Him who is about to enter it.

"But only say the word, and my soul shall be healed." In spite of our unworthiness we lift our eyes to Christ. We have faith in His love, and we trust in His mercy. "Have mercy on me, O God, according to Thy great mercy; and according to the multitude of Thy tender mercies blot out my iniquity" (Ps 50:3). As a final preparation for the coming of the most holy One, we repeat the Confiteor and beg the Virgin Mother, the apostles, and the saints to intercede for us.

In the Mass we have also asked the priest to intercede for us, and through him the Church has given us assurance of the forgiveness of our sins. The Lord has promised to hear the prayer of His Church, and our soul has been healed. The way is now opened for the coming of the divine King. "May the body of our Lord Jesus Christ keep thy soul unto life everlasting." So great is Christ's love for us that He Himself has prepared our soul as He prepared His virgin mother. The better the preparation we make for His coming, the more fruitful His grace will be in us.

"Lord, I am not worthy." Like the centurion of the Gospel, we feel that our very unworthiness gives us a special claim to His grace and mercy. Christ marveled at the faith of the centurion, and turning to His disciples said, "Amen, I say to you, I have not found so great faith in Israel." It was not the state of the man's soul so much as his great faith that moved the Lord to help him. "Go, and as thou hast believed, be it done to thee."

"Lord, I am not worthy." To receive Holy Communion with greater profit, we should be conscious of our own unworthiness. We know that in spite of our unworthiness Christ came to call, not the just, but sinners. The best proximate preparation for the reception of the Eucharist is a faith and confidence similar to that of the Roman centurion. With the centurion we ask no questions, for we are convinced that Christ has only to say the word and our soul shall be healed. We should dwell less upon our own unworthiness than upon His great goodness and mercy. A good act of faith includes all the other acts of preparation that are required. "Only say the word, and my soul shall be healed."

Prayer

Almighty and eternal God, graciously look upon our infirmity and stretch forth the right hand of Thy majesty to protect us. Through Christ our Lord. Amen.

Fourth Sunday after Epiphany

The Mass

Today the glory of the Lord is again proclaimed, this time by the tempest on the sea. The apostles' boat is tossed to and fro as if there were no one at the helm. The boat and its occupants are engulfed by the darkness of the night. The disciples, seeing the violence of the wind and the waves, fear that they are lost. There is no one to save them, for the Master is asleep. He sleeps as if their danger — and it is His danger as well — means nothing to Him. The disciples find no alternative but to approach Him and awaken Him. "Lord, save us, we perish." Christ rises and manifests to His disciples His sovereign power over the raging elements. He gives a sign, and there is a great calm. The disciples are amazed and ask themselves: Who is this man, that the wind and the waves obey Him?

With this picture in mind we approach the Church today. We are impressed, as we were on the preceding Sunday, with the majesty of the kingship of Christ. The angels fall down before Him and adore Him; the earth looks up to Him. The Church cries out with joy at the possession of Him, and her children rejoice in the Holy Sacrifice by which they are redeemed, for this sacrifice is the means of their salvation (Introit). Thou "knowest that we are beset by perils such as our human frailty cannot withstand" (Collect). The boat that is being tossed about by the waves of the sea is the Church. We who occupy the boat, the members of the Church, are in danger of being lost unless the protecting hand of the Lord rescues us. Christ remains in the boat with us as long as we have love for Him and for one another. "Love thy neighbor as thyself," and "where there are two or three gathered together in My name, there am I in the midst of them" (Mt 19:19; 18:20). A church without love would be a church without Christ. A church, a community, a parish that is not bound together with the bond of love, does not satisfy the condition of the Epistle. Where love dwells in the heart, there is Christ.

Love drew the Savior into the boat on the tossing sea of Galilee; it is this same love that has caused Him to remain in the bosom of His Church. The Church is His kingdom, and in it He exercises His power, not to bring souls into subjection, but to save them. "The Lord hath reigned; let the earth [the Church] rejoice" (Introit). By these words we are carried back in memory to the time He arose in the foundering boat and commanded the waves to be calm. On another occasion He rebuked the enemies of His Church and warned them, "The gates of hell shall not prevail against it" (Mt 16:18). We can undoubtedly remember many times when He appeared in the tossing boat of our soul and commanded the winds and the waves of temptation to be calm, and "there came a great calm." On those occasions we experienced in ourselves the glory of Christ. "The right hand of the Lord hath exalted me" (Offertory).

With a lively faith in the power of the hand of the Lord, which has saved us in the trials of this life, we begin the Offertory procession. On the altar He permits His majesty to be manifest, although His real presence is veiled under the appearance of bread and wine. We discern no life; He is, as it were, asleep in the boat (the Church), resting while awaiting the exertions and the experiences of the new day. Yet in His sacramental presence on the altar the Church possesses Him in all His strength and power, in His eternally precious life. In Holy Communion He enters into each individual soul as into a boat, to act as its protector and guide. While He remains there, no malicious enemy may enter in. The heart in which He dwells may turn to Him and cry, "Lord, help us." Such a soul does not hope or cry out in vain. But Christ will remain only in those souls who fulfill the great commandment, "Love one another. For he that loveth his neighbor hath fulfilled the law."

Meditation

This Sunday brings us to another manifestation of Christ. Christ lives in His Church. He governs and guides it, and protects and helps the head of the Church, as He directs the storm-tossed boat of Peter to the shores of eternity. Rejoice, O holy Church, for your divine and mighty King is with you. "God is in the midst thereof, it shall not be moved; God will help it in the morning early" (Ps 45:6).

"When Jesus entered into the boat, His disciples followed Him" (Gospel). In the sacred liturgy the Church is the boat into which Christ entered. "The Lord hath built up Sion; and He shall be seen in His glory" (Gradual). She is filled with the strength of God through her possession of the body of Christ. He, the Lord, is her head. He is her life and fills her with His own strength, holiness, and truth. Christ is the real person of the Church, in a most intimate and substantial union with her. Anyone who desires the truth and grace of Christ, who seeks the forgiveness of sins, peace of heart, and the fullness of all good things, will find them only where Christ is, in His Church. "His disciples followed Him" into the boat. We are His disciples and we have entered into His boat, the Church, to cross the tempestuous sea that separates us from eternity. He is there in our midst. He is among us through His representatives, the pope, the bishops, and the priests. He makes His presence felt by means of His sacraments and the Holy Sacrifice of the Mass. His grace operates in us secretly and mysteriously and gives us divine life as the vine gives life to its branches.

"A great tempest arose in the sea so that the boat was covered with waves." From the beginning the history of the Church has been a stormy one. The kingdom of God, the true Church, will always be attacked in this world by storms and waves. It will always be the target of suspicion, calumny, hatred, and persecution. The mighty ones of the world, the unbelieving, the immature scientist, the prejudiced historian, the godless press, will all hurl themselves against the boat of Christ. If the Church were not exposed to these storms and trials, if she were not hated and not humiliated, suppressed and persecuted, she would not be the bride of Christ, the crucified One. "If they have persecuted Me, they will also persecute you" (Jn 15:20). The fisherman's boat, the Church, is exposed to the winds and the waves, the persecutions and the injustices of the world; but we need not fear, for there in the boat is Christ with us, His apostles and disciples.

In the daily celebration of the Mass, Christ enters into the boat, His Church, with renewed love and majesty. He never leaves her. "Behold I am with you all days, even to the consummation of the world" (Mt 28:20). Thus each day we behold a new epiphany, a new appearance of the King, Christ the Lord, in His Church.

"And His disciples followed Him." We are the disciples, and in following Him into the boat we are taught to undergo the trials, storms, temptations, and sufferings of life. This is a trying experience, but we have Him always with us, and we may turn to Him whenever we have need of Him. "Lord, save us, we perish." In the time of our necessity He arises from His sleep and rebukes the waves. "The right hand of the Lord hath wrought strength; the right hand of the Lord hath exalted me; I shall not die, but live, and shall declare the works of the Lord" (Offertory).

Today we are to stir up again our faith in the Church and in Christ the King, who lives and works in her, who guides and protects her. We have nothing to fear, for He is in the midst of His Church, and "the gates of hell shall not prevail against it" (Mt 16:18). The Lord hath built up Sion, His Church, and He shall be seen in His glory. We may be sure that He will appear at the proper time to rebuke and calm the storm, but we must not wait until that time to cry out to Him, "Lord, save us, we perish."

PRAYER

O God, who knowest that we are beset by perils such as our human frailty cannot withstand: grant us health of mind and body, that by Thy help we may overcome the things which we suffer for our sins. Through Christ our Lord. Amen.

Monday

"Jesus entered into the boat." In the sacred liturgy this boat is the Church; it is also our soul. Christ lives in us, works in us, guides and protects us. "The right hand of the Lord hath wrought strength; the right hand of the Lord hath exalted me; I shall not die, but live, and shall declare the works of the Lord" (Offertory).

Christ lives in our soul. He penetrates our very being even as the life of the vine penetrates the branches. Christ forms with us one organism, even as the vine and its branches are one organism. According to the Council of Trent, His light, His strength, and His life penetrate our innermost being. He is bound to us with an interest that is divine, a love that is boundless, and a mercy that is inexhaustible. We can never be alone or forsaken, for He is always with us. He is always at our side, understanding, sympathetic, and powerful. He works silently, but the effect of His work is the cleansing and healing of our soul, and the infusion of a new and divine life. He appears to sleep in the boat of our soul, so silent and unobtrusive is He. But this sleep is only apparent, for He is there guiding our boat. He gives us strength and courage to weather the storms of temptation and suffering. In our fear and anxiety we turn to Him: "the right hand of the Lord hath wrought strength; . . . I shall not die, but live, and shall declare the works of the Lord."

Christ placed His seal upon us when we were baptized. It was then that He first entered into our boat and said, "Thou art mine." Ever since that day He has been leading us, guiding us, protecting us. Each morning He comes to us again in Holy Communion to guide us through the heat and the burden of the day. We are safe in His strong hands; He gives us a sure course and a safe journey. The more completely we place our trust in Him and the more fully we free ourselves from fear and solicitude, the more surely will He take the direction of our lives into His own hands. "The right hand of the Lord hath wrought strength."

It is true that we are aware that the Lord is in the boat with us when the storms arise; yet we are troubled and anxious. The howling of the winds and the violence of the storm seem not to disturb Him; but we are filled with fear and solicitude. That is His mysterious way. Even in the midst of the storm He holds the universe in the palm of His hand. Not even a sparrow shall fall from the roof without the will of the Father; "the very hairs of your head are all numbered" and not one shall perish (Mt 10:29 f.; Luke 21:18). "Why are you fearful, O ye of little faith?" (Mt 8:26.)

Unless the darkness had engulfed us, Christ could not enlighten us. There must be a storm in order that our steadfastness of soul may be tried. But when the storm does come, how our peace of mind and our soul are troubled! How easily our confidence is destroyed! Sometimes when we lose confidence we lose love also. We learn that our confidence and love were, after all, very shallow. Our soul had taken root in earthly things, in the shifting sands of human affection, in our own fickle self-love and self-will. When the storm comes, we are easily dislodged. We did not let love take root deeply. Our confidence was not born of the consciousness that Christ slept and watched in the depth of our soul. "Lord, that I may see."

In these storms much that was cumbersome and useless in our lives is destroyed. It is good that it should be so. In these storms we exercise our strength; our faith and trust in God are strengthened, and we pray with renewed fervor. Do we not wish to grow in these virtues? Why, then, do we fear the storm? "This is the victory which overcometh the world, our faith" (1 Jn 5:4).

Prayer

May Thy gifts, O God, detach us from earthly pleasures and ever strengthen us with heavenly nourishment. Through Christ our Lord. Amen. (Postcommunion.)

Tuesday

"Rising up, He commanded the winds and the sea, and there came a great calm" (Gospel). Christ the Lord is Master of the universe. Even the winds and the waves obey Him.

Christ the Lord is in the boat with us. This fact should be our greatest consolation, for all power is given to Him. There is nothing that happens in the life of the individual soul or in the life of the Church which is not known to Christ. His divine wisdom embraces and measures all things. He is Master of all that transpires in nature and in the life of nations and states, Master even of the most insignificant events in the daily lives of individuals. He is the cause of all that comes to pass, even though our meager human understanding is unaware of this relationship. He often appears to be sleeping, idle, or impotent in the midst of us. He permits many things that puzzle our shortsighted intellects and cause us to regard the future with doubt and mistrust. We are persuaded that He should immediately arise at the sight of injustice and speak the word which would destroy evil and the evildoer. "Lord, wilt Thou that we command fire to come down from heaven and consume them? And turning He rebuked them, saying: You know not of what spirit you are. The Son of Man came not to destroy souls but to save" (Lk 9:54 f.). He remembers all, loves all, and knows how; He can, in His plan of redemption, save all. Yes, we believe He is in the boat with us, directing and guiding the destiny of each of us.

"Why are you fearful, O ye of little faith?" (Gospel.) The soul of Jesus is deeply wounded by any lack of faith in Him. Not blind necessity, nor fate, nor any combination of chance and the natural law governs the affairs of men, and the universe; but the providence of God rules all things. "Why are you fearful, O ye of little faith?" How can anyone fear when he realizes that God is with him in the boat? Only one thing is expected of us, that we believe in Him and place ourselves completely in His keeping. We must surrender ourselves to Him with complete confidence and allow Him to dispose of us as He wishes. Everything that He does is done for our best interest. Our faith and our reason command us to submit to Him; yet how often we do so with doubt, with fear and hesitation! This is not the kind of trust He desires; He wishes a faith and a confidence in Him that does not falter, that does not hesitate, that asks no questions and feels no anxiety.

Why so many considerations? Why do we have so much anxiety and restless solicitude for our own welfare? We wish to sanctify ourselves by our own exertion and effort; but God wishes to accomplish this Himself, and He requires of us our complete submission to His plan. He desires nothing so much as our sanctification, but He insists on accomplishing it in His way. That is the sacred law of the spiritual life. "When thou wast younger thou didst gird thyself and didst walk where thou wouldst. But when thou shalt be old, thou shalt stretch forth thy hands, and another shall gird thee and lead thee whither thou wouldst not" (Jn 21:18). That is the secret of Christian life.

If we surrender ourselves completely to God, we shall make rapid progress. If we work by ourselves, our progress will be slow and toilsome. If God works with us and in us, we shall advance rapidly. "He must increase, but I must decrease" (Jn 3:30).

Prayer

O God, our salvation, hear us and protect us from all the enemies of body and soul. Grant us Thy grace in this life and eternal happiness in the next. Through Christ our Lord. Amen.

Wednesday

"Adore God, all you His angels.... The Lord hath reigned; let the earth rejoice" (Introit). Christ is the divine King who works wonders both in nature (Gospel) and in the hearts of men whom He unites in brotherly love (Epistle). "That they all may be one" (Jn 17:21).

"Owe no man anything, but to love one another.... Love, therefore, is the fulfilling of the law" (Epistle). We cannot free ourselves from this obligation of love so that at any time we may be free not to love one another. "He that loveth his neighbor hath fulfilled the law. For thou shalt not commit adultery; thou shalt not kill; thou shalt not steal; thou shalt not bear false witness; thou shalt not covet; and if there be any other commandment it is comprised in this word: Thou shalt love thy neighbor as thyself. The love of our neighbor worketh no evil. Love, therefore, is the fulfilling of the law" (Epistle). True love of neighbor rests on the love of God. In its essence the love of neighbor does not differ from the love of God, for we can love our neighbor only in so far as we love God. Without the love of God, the love of neighbor cannot exist. In all nature, any impediment placed in the way of full self-gratification results in hatred and strife. Among men, too, hatred and strife are inevitable unless the associations of one man with another are founded on the love of God and of one another. For this reason the love of neighbor fulfills the entire law, even the first three commandments, which deal with the honor of God Himself. Therefore charity, the love of one's neighbor, is the most fundamental principle of the spiritual life, around which all else centers; it is the standard by which our progress in holiness is measured. We can never have too much love for our neighbor.

"The right hand of the Lord hath wrought strength" (Offertory). Christ the Lord founded the Church on love. On Pentecost He sent the Holy Spirit upon His entire Church. Now "the multitude of the believers had but one heart and one soul.... All things were common unto them" (Acts 4:32). After Christ's ascension the brethren persevered in brotherhood and in prayer. "Fear came upon every soul.... All they that believed were together and had all things in common,... praising God and having favor with all the people" (Acts 2:43 ff.).

Charity soon became the distinguishing mark of the Christians, for the pagans pointed to them and said: "See how they love one another." Shortly before Christ began His passion, He besought the Father: "That they all may be one as Thou, Father, in Me and I in Thee; that they also may be one in Us; that the world may believe that Thou hast sent Me" (Jn 17:21). "Every kingdom divided against itself shall be brought to desolation, and house upon house shall fall" (Lk 11:17). The kingdom of Christ, the Church, must therefore be united in love. For "the glory which Thou hast given Me, I have given to them; that they may be one, as We also are one" (Jn 17:22). The "glory" which Christ had from His Father before all time, He has given us in sanctifying grace, "that they may be one as We [the Father and the Son] also are one." Sanctifying grace makes us children of God and unites us in love. Men are to love one another and to be united in heart and soul, not for any mere human motive, but because they are children of the same Father, and it is the will of the Father that they be one, "as Thou Father in Me, and I in Thee." Who can work this miracle of grace in our hearts? Only Christ, the divine King. "The right hand of the Lord hath wrought strength."

If the love of neighbor is the fulfilling of the law, then we fulfill the great commandment of the love of God only in so far as we love our neighbor. The two are really one and the same virtue and have one and the same motive, which is God Himself.

Love of neighbor is not an isolated part of Christian piety; it is the whole life of the Christian. The true state of our soul is more plainly discernible in our attitude toward our neighbor than it is in our external works of piety. External works of piety and virtue may give the impression of holiness where it does not actually exist. Where genuine charity is practiced, no such mistake can be made.

The Church calls the attention of the faithful to the duty of practicing charity at each celebration of the Holy Sacrifice. The faithful gather about the altar in the true spirit of brotherhood. Anyone who bears hatred or enmity toward his neighbor in his heart, can hardly join with sincerity in the sacrifice, and certainly not in the union that is realized in the reception of Holy Communion.

"Owe no man anything, but to love one another." Perhaps the practice of charity even among Christians falls far short of the ideal. Not enough importance is attached to the inward quality of our charity. Sins against charity are perhaps more frequent than any others among the chosen ones of God, both priests and religious. The lack of charity is often the besetting sin of the pious. What wonder, then, that grace is not more fruitful in their hearts when they fail in the first and greatest commandment, which is that of love. That is undoubtedly the reason why the Church today in the name of Christ asks for an increase of charity.

Prayer

O God, who knowest that we are beset by perils such as our human frailty cannot withstand: grant us health of mind and body, that by Thy help we may overcome the things which we suffer for our sins. Through Christ our Lord. Amen.

Thursday

The Gospel narrative about the storm on the Sea of Galilee gives us a picture of what we may expect in our life as Christians. Since man in this world is surrounded with difficulties and threatened by so many dangers, the Church prays: "O God, who knowest that we are beset by perils such as our human frailty cannot withstand: grant us health of mind and body, that by Thy help we may overcome the things which we suffer for our sins" (Collect).

"We are beset by perils such as our human frailty cannot withstand." We should never allow ourselves to lapse into a false sense of security. When the apostles entered the boat to cross the Lake of Genesareth, they certainly knew how to operate their boat even in the face of the approaching storm. But even their skill and experience were not sufficient to avert the danger. Our situation is even more precarious, for we are threatened by dangers from all sides. Our self-seeking, our spiritual pride, our evil desires, yes, even our natural gifts and the good works we perform may place us in grave danger of losing the friendship of God. The world about us and the men with whom we come in contact offer additional pitfalls which may lead us astray. No man is immune from the environment in which he lives, and sometimes the love and esteem of other men may be as dangerous to our spiritual welfare as their open antagonism.

The world in which we live, its ideals and its ambitions, are not those of the true Christian, and may even be a grave threat to his salvation. We have, moreover, a great enemy in the devil, the traditional enemy of God and men, who from the beginning has been the father of lies and a murderer. He goes about "as a roaring lion,... seeking whom he may devour" (1 Pt 5:8). He is not an enemy to be underestimated, for he "transformeth himself into an angel of light" (2 Cor 11:14). He is clever and knows how to deceive men. He leads astray, not only those whom he has enslaved by sin, but even those who know their danger and are earnestly seeking to walk the path of virtue.

Because of "our human frailty" we are unable to withstand these dangers. "Behold, Thou hast made my days measurable, and my substance is as nothing before Thee. And indeed all things are vanity; every man living. Surely man passeth as an image; yea, and he is disquieted in vain" (Ps 38:6 f.). Indeed, how weak and timid we are in the presence of physical pain and suffering! A slight fever, and we are confined to our bed. How easily we persuade ourselves of the need of additional sleep and rest and ease! How ingenious we are in finding excuses for departing from our schedule of prayer, work, and duty! What difficulty we find in curbing our curiosity, in ruling our tongue, and in guarding our eyes! We seize eagerly on the first opportunity to depart from our good resolutions. Our bad habits reassert themselves and go unchallenged; our vanity increases, and we foster its growth; we become indolent and distracted, and will not turn from our evil ways. One day we are despondent, and the next we are lifted up to the heights. Today we are generous and magnanimous, and tomorrow we shall be selfish and irritable. No thoughtful man needs to be convinced of his frailty. His daily imperfections and his repeated departures from his good resolutions have convinced him of his human weakness.

What, then, can we do? We must turn to Him who alone can rescue us from this frailty. "The right hand of the Lord hath wrought strength; the right hand of the Lord hath exalted me; I shall not die, but live, and shall declare the works of the Lord" (Offertory). With this prayer on our lips we await the coming of Christ in the Consecration and in Communion. By ourselves we are small, miserable, and insignificant; but in Holy Communion, He draws us to Himself, and His strength becomes our strength, His life becomes our life. When He is with us, we may well say, "I shall not die, but live"; and in spite of the dangers that threaten us, we may assert with full confidence, "I can do all things in Him that strengtheneth me" (Phil 4:13).

This is, indeed, a manifestation of the Lord and His power. "Power is made perfect in infirmity" (2 Cor 12:9). "Why are you fearful, O ye of little faith? Then rising up, He commanded the winds and the sea, and there was a great calm. But the men wondered, saying: What manner of man is this, for the winds and the sea obey him?" (Gospel.) "The Lord hath built up Sion." Christ has regenerated men who, distrusting their own frailty, have turned to Him for help.

Prayer

O God, who knowest that we are beset by perils such as our human frailty cannot withstand: grant us health of mind and body, that by Thy help we may overcome the things which we suffer for our sins. Through Christ our Lord. Amen.

Friday

The Gospel gives a full account of the Lord's intervention during the storm which was threatening to sink the boat in which He and His disciples were crossing the Lake of Genesareth. A word from Him, and a great calm comes over the sea. Amazed like the apostles, we now stand waiting for the appearance of this same Lord, who is about to return to us in the Holy Sacrifice of the Mass. "The right hand of the Lord hath wrought strength.... I shall not die, but live" (Offertory).

"Without Me you can do nothing." "As the branch cannot bear fruit of itself, unless it abide in the vine, so neither can you unless you abide in Me. I am the vine, you the branches; he that abideth in Me, and I in him, the same beareth much fruit; for without Me you can do nothing" (Jn 15:4 f.). Of ourselves we can accomplish nothing, but with God we can live His life, know with His divine knowledge, see with His eyes. He stirs up in us the desire to make our wills conform to His divine will. By His holiness we are purified, and in His strength we become strong. This transformation can be accomplished, however, only if we are prepared to abandon our own will and subject ourselves completely to Him. If we seek our own will, we shall find only ourselves. As long as we rely on our own strength, we shall be too weak to raise ourselves to God. But by means of His graces He makes it possible for us to participate in His life and to live supported by His strength. If we fail to make use of this opportunity, we are left to our own devices and accomplish nothing. We are like the dry branches of a vine which receive no nourishment from the vine. No branch can hope to produce fruit if it is separated from the vine of which it is a part. Neither can we make any progress in the spiritual life or bring forth fruit of good works unless we are united to the source of all good, Christ our Savior.

The first principle of the spiritual life is the realization that of ourselves we are unable to accomplish anything. Until the soul has learned to mistrust itself and place its complete reliance on God, it will make no progress. "God resisteth the proud, but to the humble He giveth grace" (1 Pt 5:5). The man who relies on his own strength is like him of whom Isaias says, "Lo, thou trustest upon this broken staff of a reed, upon Egypt; upon which if a man lean it will go into his hand and pierce it" (Is 36:6).

"The right hand of the Lord hath wrought strength; the right hand of the Lord hath exalted me; I shall not die, but live" (Offertory). "He that abideth in Me, and I in him, the same beareth much fruit" (Jn 15:5). Distrust of ourselves leads us naturally to trust in God, who then supplies us with life-giving strength, as the vine supplies its branches with nourishment. "I can do all things in Him who strengtheneth me" (Phil 4:13). Our true strength lies in our confidence in His mercy and in our reliance on His divine providence. His power is infinite, His will to help us is constant and unchangeable, and we never ask in vain for that which is conducive to our salvation and sanctification. By sanctifying grace He has made us members of His mystical body, and what He has so propitiously begun, He will bring to perfection.

Even when we have sinned we may yet place our trust in God. His love and His mercy are inexhaustible. "The right hand of the Lord hath wrought strength," wonders of love and mercy in the souls of His creatures. God lives in our souls, and we may submit ourselves to Him with full confidence.

The most fatal mistake that we can make in the spiritual life is to delude ourselves by thinking that we can accomplish good by ourselves. Such an illusion is born of pride and a misplaced confidence in our own powers. Only when we come to understand fully the truth of our Lord's assurance, "without Me you can do nothing," can we begin to make spiritual progress. Reliance on ourselves is our greatest weakness; complete dependence on God is our strength. "When I am weak, then I am powerful" (2 Cor 12:10).

"The right hand of the Lord hath wrought strength." We approach the altar today with the hope that our disposition may invite Him to work His wonders in our soul. Our very nothingness draws down upon us the stream of life-giving grace. "The right hand of the Lord hath exalted me" and given me the privilege of participating in the life of Christ. "I shall not die, but live"; I shall live the life of Christ on earth and eternally in heaven, where I shall fully understand that all credit is due to the power of the right hand of God, and I shall announce the works of the Lord forever.

Prayer

O God, who knowest that we are beset by perils such as our human frailty cannot withstand: grant us health of mind and body, that by Thy help we may overcome the things which we suffer for our sins. Through Christ our Lord. Amen.

Saturday

"The right hand of the Lord hath wrought strength" (Offertory). God works wonders in the order of grace as well as in the order of nature. Therefore in the Postcommunion we pray: "May Thy gifts, O God, detach us from earthly pleasures and ever strengthen us with heavenly nourishment." Detachment from earthly pleasures and spiritual nourishment and strength are the fruit of the devout assistance at Mass and frequent Communion.

"May Thy gifts detach us from earthly pleasures." The world offers many pleasures: sinful pleasures, about which we shall say nothing here, and necessary, legitimate pleasures, with which we are here principally concerned. The organs of pleasure are the senses, which are refreshed and delighted by the ever-recurrent beauties of nature, by the fragrance of flowers, by the beauty of great works of art, by the subtle charms of fine literature, by the grace and movement of good music, and even by the enjoyment of delicate foods and beverages. Noble and worthwhile pleasure may be found in the enjoyment of family life, in the attachment of true friends, and in the devotion of those who love us. We experience pleasure in the service of others, in our work, in the feeling of accomplishment, in the advancement of science, and in the pursuit of truth. These pleasures were created by an all-wise providence, and man needs them; they refresh his energy and strength and keep the human organism working smoothly just as oil does in a machine. And yet in the Mass today we pray that we may be detached from earthly pleasures. Are we to suppose that these legitimate pleasures are no longer permitted to us? Surely that is not the mind of the liturgy.

God has strewn these pleasures abundantly through life, but we should not rest satisfied in them or cling to them obstinately, or seek them exclusively and inordinately. They should serve the purpose which God had in mind in creating them; they should lead us more surely and more sweetly to God, their Author. The fruit, then, of our prayer and of the Mass and Communion should be this, that we do not become attached to these pleasures after they have served their purpose. The delight we find in legitimate pleasures should arouse in us the desire to pass on from them to God, who is their source.

A soul that rests satisfied with these pleasures, legitimate though they may be, makes a grave mistake, for they are so easily lost. Natural beauty, the fruit of our study and toil, the pleasures and satisfactions of life, may all slip from our grasp before we have begun to enjoy them. We should use these things as a means of lifting ourselves to a greater and imperishable good. This, then, is the gift asked for in the Communion prayer, that we be detached from the pleasures of the world and be lifted beyond them to God, who is "all in all" (1 Cor 15:28). We should come to seek for nothing for ourselves, but all for God.

"May Thy gifts . . . ever strengthen us with heavenly nourishment." We pray here for the countless gifts of God, the gifts designed by His eternal wisdom for our body and soul, for our mind and our spirit. The most marvelous of these gifts, the gift that contains them all, is the gift of the Eucharist. The reception of the Eucharist should always furnish us with new strength and courage; it should always renew the ardor of our love for God and our neighbor. If our disposition is good, the result can hardly be otherwise. The life of the eternal Word of God, which we receive in the Eucharist, is the real source of all love. The life of the Word consists in loving the Father and all things which proceed from Him. The Word was made flesh to manifest this love to men, and by this manifestation to lead men themselves to love the Father. Love called the Word of God into the world; love took Him from the world through the suffering of the cross; love calls Him back daily to our altars and confines Him to our tabernacles. When we receive Him in Holy Communion, He gives Himself to us in His entirety and fills us with His own being. How can a soul fail to love God with all its strength when the source of love dwells within it? Its thoughts, words, and deeds should now be centered upon the love of God.

Holy Communion should enkindle in us the ardor of love and prompt us to direct all the acts of our life, even the most insignificant, toward the love of God. It should inspire us to be instant in our prayer, prompt in the practice of charity, firm in our works of mortification, and ever concerned about the salvation of our soul. Holy Communion should lead us eventually to be so occupied with God that we forget ourselves and no longer know or recognize anything but Him, His will, and His honor. "I live, now not I, but Christ liveth in me" (Gal 2:20).

We need the pleasures and satisfactions of this life which God has provided for us. But how often we rest satisfied with these things for their own sake! Who can free us from this danger? "The right hand of the Lord." We should examine ourselves to learn whether our attachment to our work and the pleasures which God allows us are sane and healthy. Are they leading us to God, or are we seeking pleasure for its own sake?

Do we trouble ourselves after receiving Communion in the morning to ask ourselves whether our actions are being given the proper direction? Is the love of God the motive for our work? This consideration is important, for the motive for which we perform an action is more important than the success or failure of the work itself. It is important, therefore, that we attempt to motivate our work properly. All our actions, even the most insignificant, should be performed with the purpose of honoring God, for the most commonplace action, the most trifling sacrifice, the smallest victory, becomes great when accomplished with this disposition. But the motive of all must be love.

Prayer

May Thy gifts, O God, detach us from earthly pleasures and ever strengthen us with heavenly nourishment. Through Christ our Lord. Amen.

Fifth Sunday after Epiphany

The Mass

Just as the power and majesty of the Lord was illustrated last Sunday during the storm at sea, so today it is shown in His control of the cockle which the enemy sowed in the field of the Church. The cockle and wheat represent the forces of good and evil, which oppose each other here on earth. They form two mighty armies, the army of Christ and the army of the Antichrist, struggling for mastery in the same field, the soul of man. It was to be expected that the establishment of the kingdom of God on earth would meet with opposition, contradiction, and persecution. But both the cockle and the wheat, the opponents of the kingdom of God and the proponents of grace, virtue, and holiness, are subject to the divine power and must serve the ends of the divine King and His plan of salvation. "The Lord hath reigned" (Introit).

The Church is confident in the power of Christ. "Adore God, all you His angels; Sion heard and was glad" (Introit). In her struggle against the powers of evil, the Church implores God: "Since Thy family depends entirely on the hope of Thy heavenly grace, defend it always by Thy protection" (Collect). The Church has a perfect right to depend on the benevolent providence of God, for it is God's family. Her children are the children of God and partakers of the divine life. At her head stands Christ, who prays and intercedes for His members. By baptism the faithful are engrafted on Christ and become members of one mystical body, by which they are sustained and nourished. This union of the members with Christ is as vigorous and as real as the union of Christ with the Father; it also effects a union of the members with one another, which is expressed by acts of compassion, by goodness toward our fellow men, by sharing our goods with them, by patiently bearing the faults of others. Our union with God is expressed by the joy and gratitude so evident in the hymns and psalms which the soul sings to God, and by a life of complete dedication to God through Christ Jesus our Lord (Epistle). Indeed, we acknowledge the words of the Epistle thus: "The Gentiles shall fear Thy name, O Lord, and all the kings of the earth Thy glory" (Gradual). We praise God, and in love and patience we suffer the cockle that springs up about us.

By the wheat we understand those who follow Christ the King, that is, the baptized. The cockle represents those who are opposed to God and to Christ, the enemies of God and His Church, and even those who, although they are Christians, do not lead a true Christian life, or who do not live according to their faith. "Suffer both to grow until the harvest" (Gospel). The Lord bears with us patiently and lovingly, and we should imitate Him. We must be compassionate and forgiving, knowing that "the Lord hath reigned." He is Lord and has power even over the cockle, and He knows how to make it serve the kingdom of God and the good and salvation of souls (Gospel). We respond to the sentiments of the Gospel: "I believe." "The right hand of the Lord hath wrought strength; the right hand of the Lord hath exalted me" (Offertory). "The Lord hath reigned."

With a firm faith in the omnipotence of the divine King, we approach to make our offering. We offer to the Father the sacrifice of propitiation, and He releases us from our sins and "sanctifies us in mind and body" (Secreta) because of our sacrifice. At the time of Holy Communion the Father sows the good seed of the Eucharist in His field, which is the Church and the souls of men. When the seed has sprung up, it becomes apparent that the enemy has sown his seed also. But the wheat of the Eucharist sown by the divine King gives the Church and the Christian soul the strength to withstand the encroachments of the cockle, the attacks of all enemies from within and without. The Church and the Christian soul will have a most certain proof of the wisdom, power, and strength of Christ, in the continuous growth and the unconquerable fruitfulness of the Church. They "all wondered at these things, which proceeded from the mouth of God" (Communion). All will wonder at the power of the words of Christ which are spoken by the lips of the priest, "This is My body; this is My blood."

Meditation

"Adore God, all you His angels; Sion [the Church] heard and was glad; the daughters of Juda rejoiced. The Lord hath reigned; let the earth rejoice; let many islands be glad" (Introit). "And we saw His glory" (Jn 1:14). He permits His glory to shine in each of His members and in His Church as a whole.

The glory of the Lord is made manifest in individual Christians (Epistle). Before baptism they were worldly men, given to "fornication, uncleanness, lust, evil concupiscence, and covetousness" (Col 3:5). But now by the power of God they are "the elect of God," filled with "mercy, benignity, humility, modesty, patience, bearing with one another" (Epistle). In their hearts the power of God has conquered, and they now experience peace, a peace which the world cannot give, a peace which embraces God, their neighbor, and themselves. They now love God and praise Him with sacred hymns and canticles. Whatever they say or do, they do in the name of Jesus Christ (Epistle). They are now, in truth, new men, reborn according to the righteousness and goodness of God.

"Beholding the glory of the Lord with open face, [we] are transformed into the same image from glory to glory, as by the Spirit of the Lord" (2 Cor 3:18). This transformation is the work of God. He has poured forth His Holy Spirit into our hearts, and we have become the children of God. He has endowed our souls with new virtues, the virtues of faith, hope, charity, justice, and fortitude. These virtues have flowed into our souls from Him as the sap flows out into the branches from the vine. The withered branches again come to life. The Lord rebuilds the city of Sion (the Jerusalem of the Church); there "He shall be seen in His glory" (Gradual).

In the Gospel the Lord manifests His majesty to the Church. "The kingdom of heaven is likened to a man that sowed good seed in his field. But while men were asleep, his enemy came and oversowed cockle among the wheat and went his way. And when the blade was sprung up and had brought forth fruit, then appeared also the cockle" (Gospel). The Lord has thus forewarned us that cockle would spring up in His Church. But "Christ also loved the Church and delivered Himself up for it, that He might sanctify it, cleansing it by the laver of water in the word of life; that He might present it to Himself a glorious Church, not having spot or wrinkle or any such thing, but that it should be holy and without blemish" (Eph 5:25 ff.). The Church, then, is a holy institution, holy in her faith, holy in her dogmas, holy in her sacraments, her liturgy, and her prayers. She seeks also to sanctify and make holy the millions of souls who are her children. Through her Christ sows good seed in the souls of men, but the enemy has not been idle and has sown the cockle, the seeds of evil, in their hearts also.

In the early days of the faith, the disciples suffered with joy for the love of Christ. They were abused, despoiled of their property, persecuted from city to city; but they suffered all this with joy, knowing that they were to receive an eternal reward for their faithfulness (Heb 10:32 ff.). But this spirit did not long endure. Many found their way into the fold who had not learned what it meant to put on Christ. When they had received baptism they had boldly declared that they would follow Christ, but they did not fully understand what Christ meant when He said, "If any man will come after Me, let him deny himself" (Mt 16:24). The sacrifices imposed by the carrying of the cross they were not willing to undertake. The humility, poverty, and submission often demanded of the Christian they looked upon as foolishness. Thus the cockle entered into the field of the Lord. This spirit quietly grew, and worldliness spread from individuals to communities, and eventually invaded even the communities of religious. Even today the spirit of the world, the fruit of the cockle, is widespread in the Church.

"Wilt thou that we go and gather it up?" The servants of the lord are eager to destroy the cockle; but the lord answers: "No, lest perhaps gathering up the cockle, you root up the wheat also together with it. Suffer both to grow until the harvest; and in the time of the harvest I will say to the reapers: Gather up first the cockle and bind it into bundles to burn, but the wheat gather ye into my barn" (Gospel).

The Lord is also Master of the cockle. He has the power to make use of it for the salvation of the wheat among which it grows. "Think not that the evil of this world is without purpose, or that God cannot change it into something good. The evil one is permitted to live, either that he may thereby better his own condition, or that others may be helped to become holy by him" (St. Augustine). The history of the Church furnishes many consoling illustrations of this truth. Every period of laxity in the church is followed by a period of reform and fervor. There is always much of the world and its spirit among the members of the Church, but Christ and His spirit are there also. "Jesus Christ, yesterday, and today, and the same forever" (Heb 13:8), is still living in the Church and ruling it. He makes His presence known in many marvelous ways. "The right hand of the Lord hath wrought strength; the right hand of the Lord hath exalted me; I shall not die, but live, and shall declare the works of the Lord" (Offertory).

"Power is made perfect in infirmity" (2 Cor 12:9). It is true that the Church does suffer much because of the cockle that grows within her, but composed as she is of a human element and a divine element, she will never be without the cockle. She does not become despondent because of the evil that she sees in her children. Although many of her children are recalcitrant, she bears with them patiently, trusting in Him who commanded, "suffer both to grow." The Church knows that Christ will ensure the growth of her virtuous members in spite of the evil brethren who surround them. We share this faith and confidence of Holy Mother the Church. We may deplore the fact that there are many in the Church who are not virtuous, but we remember the promise of our blessed Savior, "I am with you all days, even to the consummation of the world" (Mt 28:20).

Prayer

O Lord, we beg Thee in Thy never-failing goodness to guard Thy family, and since it depends entirely on the hope of Thy heavenly grace, defend it always by Thy protection. Through Christ our Lord. Amen.

Monday

The Lord sowed good seed in His field, but the enemy came and sowed cockle among the wheat. Yet the Lord commanded, "suffer both to grow."

The field in the Gospel is an image of my soul. Christ the Savior has chosen this field for Himself. He blessed it and prepared it for cultivation and sowed good seed in it. He prepared it for growth in virtue with the infusion of the virtues of faith, hope, and charity, and with other supernatural favors. He nourishes this field with the dew of grace, and lets the light of His love shine upon it. Lord, "didst Thou not sow good seed in Thy field? Whence, then, hath it cockle?" Do we not find much cockle in our souls? Whence the corrupt thoughts and desires, the perverted weaknesses that are continually drawing us toward sin? We see our souls choked with pride, self-love, conceit, laziness, and a petty human respect. Lord, "didst Thou not sow good seed in Thy field?"

"Wilt thou that we go and gather it up?" No, "suffer both to grow until the harvest." God's way is to let the cockle grow until the time of the harvest. We would not have it so. We in our impatience would be at once rid of everything that humiliates us or troubles us. Men naturally are reluctant to admit their failures and would free themselves from their inclination toward evil. They would have their souls be a good field with only good seed and without cockle. But that is an idle dream. Many men would like to picture themselves in this way, but the ways of men are not the ways of God. "Suffer both to grow" does not mean, however, that we should allow the evil we see in ourselves to grow unopposed. We must continually struggle against it and continue until the hour of our death to beg our Lord to "deliver us from all evil." Indeed, we need His help if we are to be delivered, for we are truly a field with much cockle among the wheat.

"It is good for me that Thou hast humbled me" (Ps 118:71). Why is the cockle allowed to grow in our souls? Virtue is perfected in infirmity. Our weaknesses keep us at all times conscious of our unworthiness and make us understand how sinful we really are. When we learn what manner of men we are, we say in truth and sincerity, *Domine non sum dignus:* "Lord I am not worthy." Have mercy on me, O Lord, according to Thy great mercy.

"Suffer both to grow." The good seed finds nourishment and room to grow even among the cockle. When we see evil about us, we also appreciate more the virtue that we find in us. Living as we do in the midst of evil, we see the need of prayer; we flee to Him who alone can protect us and help us. The battle against evil is an exercise of virtue and an occasion for spiritual progress.

Sooner or later the day of the harvest will be at hand. Then only the good wheat will be allowed to remain in the sight of God. How thankful and grateful we shall be that we have managed, with the help of grace, to overcome the evil cockle with which we were obliged to struggle! Then we shall perceive how wonderful was the providence of God, and we shall exclaim, "O the depth of the riches of the wisdom and of the knowledge of God! How incomprehensible are His judgements, and how unsearchable His ways!" (Rom 11:33.) How wonderful is the manifestation of the power of the divine King in the souls of the redeemed!

Prayer

O Lord, we beg Thee in Thy never-failing goodness to guard Thy family, and since it depends entirely on the hope of Thy heavenly grace, defend it always by Thy protection. Through Christ our Lord. Amen.

Tuesday

"Suffer both to grow" (Gospel). However mysterious it may seem to us, it is universally true that there is cockle among the wheat. This fact is true of the Church as a whole and of all its parts. Every diocese, every parish, every religious institution has its spiritual cockle. "Suffer both to grow."

In spite of the cockle sown by the enemy, it is evident that the Lord has sown good seed in His Church. She possesses, in the first place, divine truth; she has the sacraments, especially the Blessed Eucharist, and an impressive list of saints both in heaven and on earth. In spite of all these spiritual treasures, there is also much evil. The history of the Church records many grave scandals among its members, many great schisms and heresies, and grave moral guilt on the part of its children. Even the religious houses record the sad story of the appearance of the cockle which the devil has sown among the wheat of the Lord. Many religious soon allow their fervor to grow cold; many of them are fainthearted and timorous; very often they fail in charity, or even desert the religious life altogether. Lord, how is this possible in Thy Church? Dost Thou not behold the cockle that the enemy hath sown in Thy field? But the Lord replies: "Suffer both to grow."

It seems as if the presence of cockle is part of the plan of divine providence. In any event, the divinity of the Church appears more clearly when we understand how much evil she has managed to survive. An institution so human and so weak could hardly have survived so long had it not been sustained by a divine element. If we had been founding a Church, we should have undoubtedly striven vigorously to exterminate the cockle from the beginning. Like the Sons of Thunder, James and John, we should have called down lightning from heaven to destroy everything that was not to our liking. "Lord, wilt Thou that we command fire to come down from heaven to consume them?" (Lk 9:54.) There have been many reformers in the Church who had this spirit. Montanus and Tertullian longed for such a Church, a Church of the elite, a Church of "pure ones," a Church composed only of those who were wise and holy and free from all blemish. Such is the spirit of men, but it is not the spirit of God.

Those who would have a perfect Church, fail to consider our defective human nature. Christ deals with frail and sinful man. Knowing man's need of redemption, Christ came as the adequate Redeemer. He established a Church which provides us with the means of sanctification no matter what our individual weakness may be. Even though many of those who find their way into the Church are cockle in the wheat, it is the way of God to let both grow until the time of the harvest.

O God, almighty King, how marvelous Thou art in spite of the cockle that grows in Thy field! "Adore God, all you His angels" (Introit). O Lord, the cockle in Thy Church is widespread; yet it is Thy Church. Give enlightenment to our minds that we may see Thy divine hand in the growth of the cockle. Thy hand is in all things that are: "The right hand of the Lord hath wrought strength" (Offertory).

O great and holy Church, how marvelous thou art in spite of all the evil that is allowed to grow in thee! In obedience to the command of thy divine founder, thou dost embrace all men, whatever their weaknesses, that they may be saved. Thou dost undergo a continual martyrdom at the hands of thy unworthy children. "I came not to call the just, but sinners to penance" (Lk 5:32).

PRAYER

O Lord, have mercy and forgive us our sins, and direct our wayward hearts. Through Christ our Lord. Amen.

Wednesday

Christ, the Lord and Master, lives in His kingdom, the Church. It is our privilege to associate ourselves with this divine kingdom. But this privilege carries with it certain obligations, which are explained to us in the Epistle of the Mass for this Sunday.

The privilege that is ours when we become members of the Church is this: we become "the elect of God, holy and beloved." We have been chosen out of millions of souls for this great privilege; we are the adopted children of God and heirs of an eternal inheritance. God has taken us as we were and has made us "holy and beloved." Through the sacraments of baptism and penance He has cleansed us from all our defects; He has transformed us by means of grace. He has united us to Himself as His beloved. "But God (who is rich in mercy) for His exceeding charity wherewith He loved us, even when we were dead in sins, hath quickened us together in Christ (by whose grace you are saved) and hath raised us up together and hath made us sit together in the heavenly places, through Christ Jesus. That He might show in the ages to come the abundant riches of His grace in His bounty towards us, in Christ Jesus. For by grace you are saved through faith, and that not of yourselves, for it is the gift of God" (Eph 2:4 ff.).

But we who are so highly privileged also have certain obligations. "Brethren, put ye on as the elect of God, holy and beloved, the bowels of mercy, benignity, humility, modesty, patience; bearing with one another and forgiving one another if any have a complaint against another; even as the Lord hath forgiven you, so do you also" (Epistle). Above all else, we must put on the mantle of charity. "This is My commandment, that you love one another as I have loved you" (Jn 15:12). Even the least act of charity shown to our neighbor for the love of Christ is meritorious and will bring us an eternal reward. When we fail in charity toward our neighbor, it is as though we had refused an act of kindness to Christ Himself. Whatever bitterness or cruelty we practice on those about us is really practiced on the person of our Savior. Let us examine ourselves honestly and consider whether our Lord could be satisfied with the charity we show toward our neighbor. Charity is the "bond of perfection." Our love of God is just as extensive as is our love of our neighbor. We shall be judged according to the measure of our love. If the chief privilege of the Christian is to be a child of God, the chief obligation is to love.

Christ has truly manifested Himself among men and taken up His abode among them in human form in order that He may build up Sion. This new Sion is the kingdom of love. "That they all may be one, as Thou, Father, in Me, and I in Thee" (Jn 17:21).

"I in them, and Thou in Me; that they may be made perfect in one" (Jn 17:23). Through baptism we become one with Christ by grace, as the Father, Son, and Holy Ghost are one by nature. He has incorporated us into Himself as branches on a vine. He lives in us continually that we may be one with Him even as He is one with His heavenly Father and the Holy Ghost. We should try to understand this great truth and understand how pleased Christ is when we love our neighbor and are one in heart and spirit with Him.

The Lord came upon earth to establish a kingdom among men. Opposed to this kingdom is the kingdom of the Antichrist. These two kingdoms are distinguished chiefly by two different species of love. The kingdom of Christ is characterized by the love of God and the love of our neighbor for God. The kingdom of the Antichrist is characterized by a selfish self-love which separates from God and turns in scorn from all that God has promised. Today we renew our determination to remain firmly united to the kingdom of Christ. We shall remember that Christ has said, "This is My commandment, that you love one another as I have loved you" (Jn 15:12).

The fruit of Holy Communion should be an increase of love for God and our neighbor. We deceive ourselves if we think that we can unite ourselves to Christ in Holy Communion and at the same time feel enmity for our neighbor. If we treat our neighbor with harshness or bitterness, we can hardly receive Holy Communion with fruit. "By their fruits you shall know them" (Mt 7:16). Let the fruit of our Holy Communions be an increase in our love for our neighbor.

Prayer

Pour forth, O Lord, the Spirit of Thy love, that we may become one in heart through the grace of Thy Father, with whom Thou livest and reignest forever. Amen.

Thursday

The sacred liturgy today asks us to be an epiphany, a manifestation of the Lord. The Christian is another Christ, "made conformable to the image of His Son" (Rom 8:29). "Even as the Lord hath forgiven you, so do you also.... And let the peace of Christ rejoice in your hearts, wherein also you are called in one body" (Epistle).

"Let the peace of Christ rejoice in your hearts." Whenever the bishop turns to the people during Mass to say, "Peace be with you," and whenever the priest turns to say, "The Lord be with you," our Holy Mother the Church reminds us of the peace of Christ that should reign in our hearts. "May the peace of the Lord remain with you," the priest says immediately before the Agnus Dei. The Agnus Dei itself is a prayer for peace.

This longing for peace reaches its climax in the prayer for peace which precedes Communion. "Lord Jesus Christ, who has said, My peace I leave with you, My peace I give you, give peace and unity to Thy Church." The kiss of peace, commonly known as the "Pax," immediately follows this prayer in the Solemn Mass. This ceremony signifies the unity of the mystical body of Christ, the Church. This insistence of the liturgy on the peace of Christ should impress us with its importance. The peace of Christ will regain in our hearts when we have freed ourselves from sin, from self-love, from evil habits, and from our evil inclinations.

The peace of Christ means union with God and progress in virtue; it characterizes those Christian communities which are "one heart and one soul," as were the assemblies of apostolic times (Acts 4:32). This peace displaces all selfishness and enmity. For this reason "you are called in one body" that all may be one in Christ. Let us strive to achieve peace, unity, and harmony in our lives; that is the spirit which Christ would have reign in our hearts.

What hinders us most in acquiring this peace of Christ? The first obstacle is our attachment to earthly things. For some men this may assume the form of earthly possessions; for others it may be an attachment to their work; while still others may be hampered by ambition, pride, or self-love. These faults make us critical, proud, quarrelsome, passionate, and impatient; they make us unwilling to make sacrifices, and without the sacrifice of our self-love, perfect love of God and of our neighbor is impossible. If we were true Christians, we would despise all earthly possessions. With St. Paul we would consider all things as loss which do not lead us directly to Christ. "But the things that were gain to me, the same I have counted loss for Christ. Furthermore, I count all things to be but loss for the excellent knowledge of Jesus Christ, my Lord; for whom I have suffered the loss of all things and count them but as dung, that I may gain Christ and may be found in Him, not having my justice, which is of the law, but that which is of the faith of Christ Jesus, which is of God: justice in faith. That I may know Him and the power of His resurrection and the fellowship of His sufferings, being made conformable to His death. If by any means I may attain to the resurrection which is from the dead" (Phil 3:7–11).

Those are the sentiments of a true Christian. Can we speak in like manner? Most of us fail to realize the value of the things that God has promised us, and thus fail to direct all our energies toward obtaining them. We take a very human view of our fellow man. We see in him only another creature like ourselves, and not a member of the mystical body of Christ. The living faith which enables us to see Christ in our fellow man is wanting in us. For the true Christian there is "neither Gentile nor Jew,… barbarian nor Scythian, bond nor free" (Col 3:11). The Christians of apostolic times used to say, "If thou see thy brother, thou hast seen Christ." How little that spirit has penetrated even the most pious of us.

"Let the peace of Christ rejoice in your hearts." The struggle to obtain this peace and harmony will stamp out our self-love and free us from our solicitude for earthly goods. Christ wishes to live His life in us in all its fullness. He is incarnate Love in the souls of men; He is the enemy of all discord and dissension. He judges everything in the light of eternity. His chief concern is to see us united to the Father and the Holy Ghost. Four things, says the *Imitation of Christ*, lead us on the way of peace and unity: "Study, my son, to do the will of another rather than thy own. Ever choose rather to have less than more. Always seek the lowest place, and strive to be subject to everyone. Desire and always pray that the will of God may be entirely fulfilled in thee. Behold such a one entereth within the borders of peace and rest" (III, chap. 23).

Prayer

O God, from whom proceed all holy desires, all right counsels, and just works, grant unto us, Thy servants, that peace which the world cannot give, that our hearts may be devoted to Thy service, and that being delivered from the fear of our enemies, we may pass our time in peace under Thy protection. Through Christ our Lord. Amen.

Friday

"The kingdom of heaven is likened to a man that sowed good seed in his field. But while men were asleep, his enemy came and oversowed cockle among the wheat" (Gospel). Truly, God sowed the best of seed in our souls at baptism. The seed sown there is the seed of sanctifying grace and the seed of the virtues of faith, hope, and charity. Daily He cares for the field of our soul and nourishes by Holy Communion the seed planted there. He gives us the grace to suffer, to grow, and to endure. In spite of the fact that He sowed good seed, and in spite of the fact that He continuously watches over us, the cockle is always there too. When we ask, "Wilt Thou that we go and gather it up," He answers, "Suffer both to grow."

"But while men were asleep, his enemy came and oversowed cockle among the wheat." Every day we examine our conscience, and we go to confession weekly. We are continually making new resolutions to amend our lives and to root out our faults. We study the example of our Lord and the lives of His saints, and pray frequently to be freed from our self-love and from our inordinate attachment to the things of this world. In spite of all this effort, we seem unable to uproot the cockle of our daily faults. It is true that not all of our faults are deliberate, yet neither are they entirely blameless. Somehow, when we reflect upon them, we always feel that we could have avoided them if we had been more vigilant. There appears to be no end to our weaknesses, and we appear to make so little progress. At least outwardly we strive to do our duty and to conform to what is expected of us; yet we are continually discovering that our motives are not always pure. If we have conformed to the will of God and our rule of life, our actions are more often motivated by human respect than by our devotion to God. We may ask ourselves: Where does all this lead to? Are we really preparing for a holy death by daily advancing in perfection? We fear that such is not the case in spite of all our firm resolutions to begin now to live entirely for God.

When we engage in some important worldly affair in the success of which we are intensely interested, no care or trouble or exertion is too great for us. But for the things that concern God and our eternal salvation, we can muster very little zeal and hardly any enthusiasm. How eagerly we grasp for excuses that will free us from the onerous task of mastering ourselves! How gladly we embrace exceptions that liberate us from the little sacrifices of regular life and allow us to associate slyly with the world! The cockle is still among the wheat. In spite of all our striving we have actually made little progress in virtue.

"Suffer both to grow." The servants of the Lord were displeased at finding the cockle and wished to uproot it immediately. The Lord, however, is wiser and counseled them, "Suffer both to grow until the harvest." All this cockle serves a purpose. Even the faults which we consider involuntary, faults of character and faults resulting from our natural weaknesses, are not without a purpose and play a definite part in our spiritual life. If we consider them in their true light, they are really opportunities for spiritual growth. They keep us conscious that we have yet far to go to approach the holiness of our Lord and His saints. When we gaze upon ourselves and see ourselves as we really are, we become humble. It is easier for us to embrace the cross when we understand that our own miserable weaknesses require this bitter remedy. Like the servants of the Lord, our willfulness and self-love prompt us to destroy all our faults (our cockle) by one grand gesture. But God is wiser than we: "Suffer both to grow." He would have us grow strong in virtue by a patient and persistent struggle against our faults. God does not will the faults that He sees in us any more than we do, but He knows that their presence will keep us humble and prompt us to strive incessantly to increase in virtue and strength.

Furthermore, our faults will prompt us to turn to God for help in time of need. Seeing our own weakness, we shall learn to turn at once to God, the source of all strength. Let us ask God for help, for we know that He is ever ready to assist us. Let us ask with confidence for the grace to serve Him faithfully. Our faults serve this purpose, at least: they convince us that of ourselves we cannot succeed, and must turn to Christ for aid.

"Suffer both to grow." This does not mean that we should be indifferent to the cockle which we find in our field. It is a great accomplishment if we can truly say that we have not of ourselves added new faults to the cockle sown by the enemy. When we can say that we have in some measure mastered our weaknesses, when the faults that we have are no longer multiplied, when we no longer commit them willingly, when we meet all trials and temptations with courage and confidence, we shall know that we are dealing with the cockle in the way our Lord approves.

"Suffer both to grow." Spiritual growth is possible only when there is inner peace, which is most necessary if we wish to pray. Restlessness, violence, and impetuosity are not conducive to the practice of virtue. Such a spirit is more characteristic of pride and self-love. Our love of God and our neighbor must be tranquil and stable. Let us deal with the cockle in our field with patience, perseverance, and determination. Above all, let us trust in the Lord, who is aware of the cockle growing in our souls, and wait for His grace.

PRAYER

O Lord, we beg Thee in Thy never-failing goodness to guard Thy family, and since it depends entirely on the hope of Thy heavenly grace, defend it always by Thy protection. Through Christ our Lord. Amen.

Saturday

"The kingdom of heaven is likened to a man that sowed good seed in his field" (Gospel). Hardly had the man sown good seed in his field when his enemy came and sowed cockle among the wheat. Wherever Christ has sown good seed in the field of the world, there also the devil sows the seed of evil. The seed of the devil is the temptations which he uses to entice men away from God.

"My brethren, count it all joy when you shall fall into divers temptations" (Jas 1:2). No man is ever free from temptation, which may arise from our past sins, from our evil fantasies, from our various passions, or from our own perverted inclinations. The devil may use the things around us and the men and women with whom we live as a means of tempting us to sin. Temptations come, finally, from the devil himself, who, "as a roaring lion, goeth about seeking whom he may devour" (1 Pt 5:8). He lies in wait for us like a serpent seeking a favorable moment to strike us swiftly and silently. The devil is very clever and makes use of a multitude of devices to tempt us.

Whenever the devil attempts to lead us astray, we may be sure that God is also at hand; for no temptation can come to us which He has not permitted. Temptations are not God's work, but He permits them that we may be strengthened in virtue. He weighs and measures every temptation to which we are subject and makes use of it to advance us in holiness. He has foreseen the effects of the temptation upon us, and in His infinite wisdom has permitted us to suffer the trial. The devil cannot come near us until the Lord has first set the conditions and has provided us with the grace we need to resist the temptation. Why, then, should we fear temptation? "Let no temptation take hold on you, but such as is human. And God is faithful who will not suffer you to be tempted above that which you are able; but will make also with temptation issue, that you may be able to bear it" (1 Cor 10:13).

"Suffer both to grow." Temptations are beneficial to the soul and help it to grow in virtue. They prove, refine, and strengthen our loyalty to God and His commandments. There is no real virtue that is not tried virtue. We are so attached to the world that temptations are necessary to convince us that the world is not the greatest and highest good. By suffering trials and temptations valiantly and patiently, we may also make satisfaction for our past failures. We may also shorten the time of temporal punishment due to sin more easily by meeting and conquering temptations than we ever could in purgatory. Temptations also keep us conscious of our inner weakness and preserve us from pride when we might be tempted to think that we have attained a high degree of virtue. These temptations give us an occasion to practice virtue and make it a permanent part of our character. Not only is our strength and virtue increased and proved by temptation, but our merit also is greatly increased when we make a successful conquest of temptations. A man who knows his own weaknesses is zealous in prayer. If we suffered no temptations, we should become easygoing and slothful in the spiritual life, and should make very little progress. One grows strong only by frequent and regular exercise, and this fact is as true of the spiritual life as it is of physical life. We should take comfort, then, in the words of the Apostle: "Count it all joy when you shall fall into divers temptations" (Jas 1:2).

"The kingdom of heaven is likened to a man that sowed good seed in his field. But while men were asleep, his enemy came and oversowed cockle among the wheat, and went his way. And when the blade was sprung up and had brought forth fruit, then appeared also the cockle. And the servants of the good man of the house coming said to him: Sir, didst thou not sow good seed in thy field? Whence, then, hath it cockle?" (Gospel.) Like the servants of the good man, we may be greatly surprised to discover the cockle in the field of our soul. We become restless and fear lest we should be overcome by temptation. Immediately we ask, "Shall we go gather it up?" We wish to be entirely free from temptation, rid of it for good. Probably we are wishing merely to avoid the struggle necessary to overcome the temptation. Our zeal is often merely another form of self-love.

The closer the Lord wishes to draw us to Himself, the more pure we must be; and we can become pure only by being tried as gold is tried in the fire. "All the saints passed through many tribulations and temptations and profited by them. And they that could not support temptation, became reprobate and fell away. There is no order so holy nor place so retired where there are not temptations and adversities."[6]

"Suffer both to grow until the harvest." By the time of the harvest is meant the time of our death. If our strength in virtue and our reward in heaven are to increase, then the temptations by which we acquire our virtue and reward must also increase. The devil is more eager to tempt the holy and pious soul so that he can decrease its reward, or if he finds it possible, deprive it of its eternal happiness altogether.

The pious soul does not consider sins of omission as serious as sins of commission, and therefore falls more readily into them. Sins of omission are also less apt to arouse real contrition in the sinner. If the soul is truly pious, however, it will be wary of all sins, and therefore immediately on the alert when temptations of any kind arise. "The right hand of the Lord hath wrought strength; I shall not die, but live, and shall declare the works of the Lord" (Offertory). God strengthens the soul by trying it with temptations.

Prayer

O Lord, we beg Thee in Thy never-failing goodness to guard Thy family, and since it depends entirely on the hope of Thy heavenly grace, defend it always by Thy protection. Through Christ our Lord. Amen.

[6] *Imitation of Christ*, bk. 3, chap. 13.

Sixth Sunday after Epiphany

The Mass

This week introduces us to a new aspect of the power of the divine King. In spite of its humble beginning, the kingdom of God swept all opposition before it and established itself firmly in the hearts of men. Although apparently weak and helpless, the Church has been sustained through the centuries by the almighty power of God. The Church has been endowed with a subtle power to attract the hearts of men, and when they have submitted to her gentle rule, she proceeds to sanctify them. "The Lord hath reigned." The Church is an epiphany of the Lord, a manifestation of His overwhelming power.

Conscious of the strength and vitality which God has given her, the Church approaches the altar of the Lord. "Adore God.... The Lord hath reigned; let the earth rejoice" (Introit). The Church asks only that she may be faithful to the service which God expects of her. "Grant us, we beseech Thee, O almighty God, ever to fix our thoughts on reasonable things and to do what is pleasing to Thee both in words and in deeds" (Collect). The Church has no doubt about her divine commission or her power; she asks only that her children concern themselves with the things of God, both in word and in deed. She knows that if they have their minds and hearts fixed on the things that pertain to God, they will be filled with Christ and will grow in spirit. Like the Thessalonians, they will live by faith and perform the works of love. They will depend on the power of God for all things, and rest satisfied with the reward that is promised them in the kingdom of Christ that is to come. They have turned away from the false gods which they once served, and are now devoted to the service of the living God (Epistle). Only the power of the divine King could have accomplished this transformation, and for this reason the Church rejoices when she sings, "The Gentiles shall fear Thy name, O Lord, and all the kings of the earth Thy glory" (Gradual).

The strength of the Lord which has been planted in the Church is like the grain of mustard seed which was sown in a field. The mustard seed is the smallest and most insignificant of all seeds; yet it grows into a mighty tree. So, too, the seed which God has planted in the Church. This seed is again compared to the leaven which a woman hid in three measures of meal. In a short time the whole was leavened. In like manner the power and the strength of God penetrates the whole Church until it is filled with the spirit of Christ. "The right hand of the Lord hath wrought strength" (Offertory).

In the Offertory the Church places her prayers of praise and thanksgiving upon the altar. The most precious offering which she can make is the offering of her heart, and this she makes by uniting it to the sacred offering of Christ in the Mass. That she may be worthy to associate her offering with His, she prays in the Offertory prayer for purity of heart and for inward and outward renewal. Presently the Lord Himself will appear in the midst of His faithful to offer Himself up for them, and to be offered by them to His heavenly Father.

In Holy Communion He presents Himself to the soul and fills it with His own life. The sacred host is the mustard seed which God plants in the souls of men; it will soon grow into a mighty tree. The sacred host is the leaven which the woman hid in three measures of meal. The almighty Father hides His power in the person of His divine Son, which the soul receives in

Holy Communion. If we but allow Him to do so, Christ will penetrate our thoughts, our motives, our actions, and our works, as leaven penetrates the meal. As all the meal soon becomes leavened, so, too, the human soul will become permeated with the divine presence, and an epiphany, or manifestation of the Lord, may truly be said to have taken place in our soul. All those who see us will recognize the work that God has accomplished in our souls. They will be amazed at the power of the words that proceed from the mouth of the Lord: "The kingdom of heaven is like a grain of mustard seed,... like leaven."

Meditation

The Lord manifests Himself to the world at Epiphany. He comes into the world at Christmas as a helpless child; but now He is made known to the world. He grows to full maturity and in due time will gather all men to Himself, as the mustard tree gathers the birds of the air in its branches. He compares Himself to the mustard seed, which in itself is very insignificant, but which possesses the power to produce a flourishing plant. He is the leaven with which the whole human race is to be permeated until it has been transformed by the power of God. "Adore God all you His angels; Sion heard and was glad; and the daughters of Juda rejoiced. The Lord hath reigned, let the earth rejoice, let many islands be glad" (Introit).

"The kingdom of God is like to a grain of mustard seed, which a man took and sowed in his field; which is the least indeed of all seeds; but when it is grown up, it is greater than all herbs and becometh a tree; so that the birds of the air come and dwell in the branches thereof" (Gospel). The mustard seed mentioned in the Gospel is a symbol of Christ. For thirty years He lives in obscurity before He manifests His hidden power and strength to the world. When He does manifest Himself to the world, He is persecuted, rejected by His people, and finally crucified. Yet from this apparent failure springs the great tree, the Church, which gathers the children of men into her many branches.

The leaven, too, is a symbol of Christ. "The kingdom of heaven is like leaven, which a woman took and hid in three measures of meal until the whole was leavened" (Gospel). Christ will spread His influence until it penetrates the hearts and souls of all men and fills them with His strength and spirit. No one is refused admission to this blessed union; no one is too insignificant to escape the love and attention of God. Even I may become a branch of the great tree which springs from the mustard seed. I, too, may be permeated with the leaven of Christ's love and power. How wonderful is the condescension and solicitude of God!

The Epistle shows us the practical application of the parable of the Gospel. The Apostle of the Gentiles points out to the Christians of Thessalonike how the mustard seed, the Word of the Lord, has grown in them until it has become a mighty tree. "Brethren, we give thanks to God always for you all, making a remembrance of you in our prayers without ceasing, being mindful of the work of your faith and labor and charity, and of the enduring of the hope of our Lord Jesus Christ before God and our Father; knowing, brethren, beloved of God, your election.... And you became followers of us and of the Lord, receiving the word in much tribulation, with joy of the Holy Ghost; so that you were made a pattern to all that believe.... For they themselves relate of us what manner of entering in we had unto you, and how you turned to God from idols to serve the living and true God, and to wait for His Son from heaven (whom He raised up from the dead), Jesus, who hath delivered us from the wrath to come" (Epistle).

Would that someone could testify to our fruitfulness as Paul testified to that of his disciples! Christ, the mustard seed, wishes to take root in our hearts. The Church continues to nourish the seed which God has planted in our hearts; she nourishes it with the grace which she dispenses through her sacraments. God grant that we may not prove unfertile soil.

In the Offertory procession the Church expresses her gratitude for the works that the Lord has accomplished in her. In union with the offering of Christ, she offers whatever the seed of the Lord's word has produced in the heart of her children. In the Secreta she asks that "this offering cleanse and renew us, govern and protect us." In the Mass, Christ will place Himself in the hands of the Church to be offered to the Father for all her needs. In the sacrificial repast of Holy Communion, He will become the food of our souls and will renew them with His life. Holy Communion now becomes the mustard seed that is sown in the souls of men.

Like the leaven which the woman hid in the meal, the Spirit of God is planted in the erring soul of man that it may fill that soul with its life. The Spirit of Christ must penetrate all our thoughts, all our desires, and all our actions. Christ will not rest until He has transformed us entirely into Himself. Each day, if we cooperate with the grace of Christ, we become an epiphany, a manifestation of the power of Christ. All who see us will know and recognize the wonderful power of Christ in us.

In the Holy Eucharist, Christ is the mustard seed and the leaven which the woman hid in three measures of meal. The Church plants the word of God in the deepest part of our soul; but it must spread its influence to every part of our being until we can say with St. Paul, "And I live, now not I, but Christ liveth in me" (Gal 2:20). This should be the fruit of our daily Mass and Communion: our soul should grow strong on the bread with which it is fed.

Prayer

Grant us, we beseech Thee, O almighty God, ever to fix our thoughts on reasonable things and to do what is pleasing to Thee both in words and in deeds. Through Christ our Lord. Amen.

Monday

"The kingdom of God is like to a grain of mustard seed, which a man took and sowed in his field; which is the least indeed of all seeds; but when it is grown up, it is greater than all herbs and becometh a tree; so that the birds of the air come and dwell in the branches thereof" (Gospel). The kingdom of heaven mentioned in the Gospel is the Church. "Fear not, little flock, for it hath pleased your Father to give you a kingdom" (Lk 12:32).

It "is the least indeed of all the seeds." The kingdom which Christ established was indeed unimpressive and small. It was quite different from the kingdom which the Jews had anticipated. They had hoped for a Messias who would help them throw off the hated yoke of the Roman power and establish the kingdom of Israel. They had prepared for a Messias who would come with great earthly power, pomp, and majesty. Such was their purely human conception of the mission of the Messias. But the thoughts of God are not the thoughts of man. The kingdom of God was to be very insignificant in its beginning, as was the life of its divine Founder. Although He was the Son of God and the splendor of the Father, Christ humbled Himself and became obedient, even unto the death of the cross (Phil 2:8). This same sacrifice He was to impose on His Church and on all who were redeemed by His grace. This is the law of grace. "For both the Jews require signs and the Greeks seek after wisdom. But we preach Christ crucified: unto the Jews indeed a stumbling block and unto the Gentiles foolishness. But unto them that are called, both Jews and Greeks, Christ the power of God and the wisdom of God. For the foolishness of God is wiser than men; and the weakness of God is stronger than men. For see your vocation, brethren, that there are not many wise according to the flesh, not many mighty, not many noble. But the foolish things of the world hath God chosen, that He may confound the wise" (1 Cor 1:22 ff.). This is not the wisdom of the world, but the foolishness of God; the weak, the ignorant, the poor, and those whom the world despises, these hath God chosen. "Suffer the little children and forbid them not to come to Me, for the kingdom of God is for such" (Mt 19:14).

"But when it is grown up, it is greater than all herbs and becometh a tree" (Gospel). It was a small and unimpressive group of disciples which Christ gathered about Him in the days of His preaching. Yet He can assure them that "it hath pleased your Father to give you a kingdom" (Lk 12:32). The Lord had scarcely left them when on Pentecost this small group of disciples was augmented by three thousand others. "And by the hands of the apostles were many signs and wonders wrought, among the people.... And the multitude of men and women who believed in the Lord was more increased" (Acts 5:114). From this small beginning the Church spread rapidly throughout Judea and Samaria. Soon the faith in Jesus spread to Damascus, Antioch, Asia Minor, and Rome, in spite of the opposition of the civil power. "He that humbleth himself shall be exalted" (Lk 14:11). Thus the Apostle of the Gentiles explains the mystery of the kingdom of God: "But the foolish things of the world hath God chosen, that He may confound the wise; and the weak things of the world hath God chosen, that He may confound the strong. And the base things of the world and the things that are contemptible, hath God chosen, and the things that are not, that He might bring to nought things that are" (1 Cor 1:27 f.).

Thus the Church of Christ is stronger than any earthly power and more durable than any mere earthly kingdom. In spite of all the force that is brought to bear on her for her destruction, she lives and prospers and grows. In spite of the persecutions which she has suffered, in spite of the false teachers who have arisen within her, she continues her way serenely and unperturbed. False philosophies arise to undermine her doctrine, but she conquers them all with her wisdom. Her enemies continually oppose her, but she silences them all with the example of her purity, and virtue, and holiness. Indeed, the mustard seed has become the greatest of all herbs. "The right hand of the Lord hath wrought strength; the right hand of the Lord hath exalted me. I shall not die, but live, and shall declare the works of the Lord" (Offertory).

The above principles apply not only to the Church, but also to every individual soul. This universal law of grace was exemplified by Christ in His own birth as a helpless babe in Bethlehem. "He that humbleth himself shall be exalted," is the first law of all spiritual growth. "Blessed are the poor in spirit, for theirs is the kingdom of heaven" (Mt 5:3). In spite of the perverted teachers of Israel, the scribes and Pharisees, He gathers His disciples about Him and invites them to learn of Him "because I am meek and humble of heart" (Mt 11:29). He rejoices "because Thou hast hid these things from the wise and the prudent and hast revealed them to the little ones. Yea, Father, for so hath it seemed good in Thy sight" (Mt 11:25 f.).

We rejoice at the privilege of being members of this holy Church. We are like birds that come to rest in the sheltering arms of the tree which has grown up from a tiny seed. It is good to live as a Catholic; it is good to die as a Catholic.

Prayer

Grant, we beseech Thee, O almighty God, ever to fix our thoughts on reasonable things and to do what is pleasing to Thee both in words and in deeds. Through Christ our Lord. Amen.

Tuesday

"The kingdom of heaven is like to a grain of mustard seed" (Gospel). It is small and insignificant; yet, when planted in good soil, it springs to life and grows rapidly until it has become a tree. How appropriate this parable is! Everything that God means to prosper must make a humble beginning; but good soil is necessary in which God can plant His seed.

The kingdom of Christ, the Church, is like a mustard seed in the simplicity of its teaching. She preaches humility, subjection, poverty, detachment from the world. Her doctrine includes the creation of the world by God, the reality of sin, the redemption of men through Christ, and their sanctification by the Holy Ghost. She insists on the reality of the resurrection and the fatherhood of God. She explains the fallen nature of man by pointing out his present sinfulness, his injustice, and his lack of charity. She points to the life of eternity as the end of man's existence. It is all very simple; even a child can understand it. Years of study are not necessary for the fundamental understanding of her dogmas. Even the first exponents of the Gospel were the most simple and humble of men, unlettered and simple Galilean fishermen. The historians of the early Church, the Evangelists, gave the world their story in simple, straightforward language which everyone could grasp. Like the mustard seed, the Church had a simple and small beginning.

"But when it has grown up, it is greater than all herbs." Although the doctrine which Christ preached appears simple in the eyes of men, it has worked miracles in their souls. She allows man to see and understand his environment and the purpose for which he exists. Under the guidance of grace, the human intellect reaches a level which it could never have attained without divine assistance. The soul which lives in the light of faith acquires a strength and courage which it could not otherwise have attained. Enlightened by faith, the Christian finds courage to face temptation, persecution, sickness, and even death without murmuring. When oppressed with suffering, or when smarting with the contempt which the world shows her, such a soul suffers silently and calmly, not because of pride or stubbornness, not because she is indifferent to suffering, but because she has an unshakable confidence in the abiding presence of Christ. She finds a precedent for the treatment she is receiving in the suffering and ignominy of her Lord and Master, Jesus Christ.

Inspired with confidence in Christ's abiding presence, St. Lawrence, the martyr, was able to lie down on his red-hot griddle as if it were a soft bed. Similar heavenly wisdom inspired St. Catherine of Siena to choose a crown of thorns when she might very well have chosen a crown of gold. St. Paul and his disciples gloried in the sufferings which they had been allowed to undergo for Christ. Inspired by the love of Christ, Christians of all ages have gone bravely to meet whatever indignity the world held for them. Sin and any sort of disloyalty they could not endure, but no sacrifice could frighten them if they felt that it would increase their holiness. Christianity has inspired thousands of young men and women to leave father, mother, home and family, and all that is dear to the heart of men, to live lives of self-denial and sacrifice. Chastity, poverty, and obedience become sweet when inspired by the example of the Savior and when undertaken in His interest. The saints undertook what seem to us tremendous hardships and unbearable mortifications because of the supernatural courage and wisdom which the faith inspired in them. Surely there is no higher kind of courage than that shown by the lives of the saints. The teachings of the Church are indeed simple, but what marvelous works they produce!

God builds on a simple foundation. "The right hand of the Lord hath wrought strength." When the doctrine of Christ is accepted with childlike simplicity, there "the Lord hath built up Sion, and He shall be seen in His glory" (Gradual).

The teaching of our faith is like the mustard seed; it is disregarded, underrated, misunderstood, and contemned by the world. Things that are novel, sensational, and impressive, such as the discoveries of science, easily attract the attention of men. But they know very little about the fundamental truths of their existence; truths which a child learns in his catechism. Many men are not greatly interested in the end and purpose of their existence; they are too much concerned with the distractions and pleasures which it now furnishes. How can the mustard seed become a great herb in such soil as this?

"All wondered at these things which proceeded from the mouth of God" (Communion). For sheer want of effort we have lost our understanding of the wonders of the Gospels and the mysteries of our faith. Our life, our prayer, our meditations, are dry, uninteresting, and unfruitful. We have good reason to pray in the Postcommunion "that we may ever hunger after those things by which we truly live."

Prayer

Having been fed, O Lord, with Thy heavenly delights, we beseech Thee that we may ever hunger after those things by which we truly live. Through Christ our Lord. Amen. (Postcommunion.)

Wednesday

"The kingdom of heaven is like to leaven, which a woman took and hid in three measures of meal until the whole was leavened" (Gospel). The parable of the mustard seed shows the rapidity with which the unimpressive beginnings made by Christianity were to grow to their full stature. The parable of the leaven shows how the kingdom of God penetrates and absorbs all that it touches. By its ability to transform all things, the Church proves its claim to divine origin. "The Lord hath built up Sion; and He shall be seen in His glory" (Gradual).

"The kingdom of God is like to leaven." The leaven which the woman placed in the three measures of meal was very small; yet it expanded and was absorbed by the meal until all was leavened. As soon as one places leaven in a pan of dough, the latter begins to rise. The working of the leaven in the dough is silent and invisible, but it soon increases the dough threefold and prepares it for the baking. The kingdom which Christ established on earth is similar. The beginnings of the Church were quiet and unimpressive. Its divine Founder came quietly into the world at Bethlehem and began His work in complete seclusion, in silent prayer and sacrifice. Humanly speaking, the success which Christ achieved in His life was unimpressive. He had not even succeeded in completely changing the inner dispositions of the apostles on whom He established His Church. This Church was established on the feast of Pentecost, when the Holy Spirit descended upon the apostles in the form of fiery tongues. From that moment the Church is the leaven which is to change mankind into the children of God.

St. Luke paints for us a vivid picture of the power and vitality of the infant Church. "And they were persevering in the doctrine of the apostles, and in the communication of the breaking of bread, and in prayers. And fear came upon every soul. Many wonders also and signs were done by the apostles in Jerusalem, and there was great fear in all" (Acts 2:42 f.). And again in a later chapter of the Acts of the Apostles he relates: "And the multitude of believers had but one heart and one soul; neither did any one say that aught of the things which he possessed was his own; but all things were common unto them. And with great power did the apostles give testimony of the resurrection of Jesus Christ, our Lord; and great grace was in them all. For neither was there any one needy among them. For as many as were owners of lands or houses, sold them and brought the price of the things they sold, and laid it down before the feet of the apostles, and distribution was made to every one according as he had need" (4:32 ff.). Thus did Christianity penetrate and elevate everything that it touched.

"The kingdom of heaven is like to leaven." The chief purpose of the Church is the religious and moral regeneration of the human race. She also undertakes to improve the social, economic, and cultural standards of the world. Even the heathens worshiped a divinity, but their reason for worship was usually a fear of the gods or a desire to wring some favor from them. Their religions did not pretend to work a moral reform in their lives. The religion of the Jews was vastly superior to the religions of the pagans; it was based on divine revelation and insisted on the adoration of the one true God. It was, nevertheless, a religion of fear, and remained a national religion, confined, for the most part, to the Jewish people. The religion of the Jews served primarily as a preparation for the perfect religion which came only with Christ and His Church. Christ replaced the law of fear with the law of love. "Thou shalt love the Lord thy God with thy whole heart" (Mt 22:37). Christ's law of love requires also the love of neighbor — a supernatural love based on our love of God. The law embraces all men, and there is no circumstance when one may be excused from this universal law of love.

Christianity gives a supernatural direction to all the activities of man and inspires him with the desire to possess God both in this life and the next. What a harvest of good works this influence has produced! What a treasure of sacrifice, patience, and virtue has been produced by the millions of souls who have been leavened by the spirit of love! For two thousand years the law of Christ has been cultivating these virtues in the hearts of the saints. The kingdom of God is within us, and there the Church hides the leaven of divine love until our souls are completely absorbed by it. Indefatigably and without ceasing she continues to work in the souls of men in spite of all opposition and persecution.

The Church began the work of regeneration in us when we were baptized. In that holy sacrament we became "a new creature" (2 Cor 5:17) "and put on the new man, who ... is created in justice and holiness of truth" (Eph 4:24). Then we "received the spirit of adoption of sons, whereby we cry Abba (Father)" (Rom 8:15).

Every day the Church invites us to celebrate the Holy Sacrifice with her and to participate in the fruits of the sacrifice by Holy Communion. The Holy Eucharist is the divine leaven which penetrates our souls and rejuvenates them. All the other sacraments and sacramentals of the Church are instituted for the same purpose. If we make use of the means which she places at our disposal, the leaven of divine grace will completely transform us. Then the words of the great Apostle will be true of us also: "I live, now not I, but Christ liveth in me" (Gal 2:20).

Have we allowed the Church to work this transformation in us? Have we really managed to put off the old man with his habits of thought, his manner of acting, his selfishness, and his self-love? Have we really "turned to God from the idols to serve the living and true God, and to wait for His Son from heaven (whom He raised up from the dead), Jesus, who hath delivered us from the wrath to come" (Epistle)?

Prayer

Grant us, we beseech Thee, O almighty God, ever to fix our thoughts on reasonable things and to do what is pleasing to Thee both in words and in deeds. Through Christ our Lord. Amen.

Thursday

"The kingdom of heaven is like leaven" (Gospel), which, although very small in quantity, very soon leavens the whole mass. This parable is an image of the fruitfulness of the doctrine of Christ, which is the leaven which penetrates all our thoughts and actions, and makes them fruitful in Christ. When this spirit has completely penetrated our soul, then the kingdom of God is realized in us.

He who studies his fellow men without the light of faith, is considering them in an entirely false light. Such a man is bound by earthly considerations and soon becomes impatient with the imperfections which he sees. His vision is impaired, and he sees all things only in the light of human wisdom. God's purposes and ways are unfamiliar to him. He judges only that to be important which will win the favor of his fellow men; the approval of God does not concern him. His life is a confusion of fears, hopes, plans, and disappointments. He wanders through life, insecure in his possessions, confused in his objectives, restless and without peace. He cannot understand the existence of suffering, hardship, and disappointment, and life itself becomes a riddle. The greatest enigma of all is the end of life, death, beyond which he cannot see. He has achieved very little peace or happiness in this world, and he has performed no works that are of value for eternity. "You have sowed much, and have brought in little; you have eaten, but have not had enough; you have drunk, but have not been filled with drink" (Agg 1:6).

"The kingdom of God is like to leaven, which a woman hid in three measures of meal until the whole was leavened." If our thoughts and actions and desires are permeated with the love of Christ, then we live continually in the kingdom of Christ. When we have reached this stage, we live more truly in the world of faith than in the world about us. Our life is changed from an earthly plane to a heavenly plane, and we recognize the hand of God in all that happens to us. We see the hand of providence in every event of our life. Even the misfortunes which befall us we accept with resignation as part of the kindly providence of our Father. Even the malice of men can become for us an instrument in the hand of God for our sanctification. The loss of our earthly possessions is not of great moment as long as our heavenly inheritance is not endangered. We measure all things with the measure of eternity and study them in the light of the Gospel. Everything which we encounter is a creature of God and is to be used for the purpose which God intended. We lay up a treasure, not upon earth, but in heaven, where the moths will not devour nor the thieves break through to steal (Mt 6:19). We know that we have God for our Father and that we have been incorporated in Christ as living members of His mystical body. In this manner the teaching of Christ permeates and elevates all our human actions, as the leaven permeates the meal with which it is mixed. A soul who is thus inspired has already begun the life of heaven on earth and makes progress according to the degree of his faith in Christ.

"The Lord hath reigned" (Introit). Christ wishes to reign in our hearts to permeate them with the leaven of faith. But our actions are still too human, too earthly, too imperfect. We still rely too much on our own strength and not sufficiently on the power and wisdom of God. We still place too high a value on the things of this world, and not enough on the things that are eternal. The words of the Gospel remain for us mere printed words and not a part of our very being. "The Lord hath reigned." But if the Lord is to reign in our hearts, His thoughts, His motives, and His ambitions must become ours too. The Christian is another Christ. Christ established His holy Church and the sacraments, especially the Eucharist, for the express purpose of making us one with Him. The better we prepare ourselves for Holy Communion, the more perfectly will His work be accomplished in us.

Prayer

Grant us, we beseech Thee, O almighty God, ever to fix our thoughts on reasonable things and to do what is pleasing to Thee both in words and in deeds. Through Christ our Lord. Amen.

Friday

"The kingdom of heaven is like to leaven, which a woman took and hid in three measures of meal until the whole was leavened" (Gospel). This leaven we understand to be the grace of Christ, which leavens all mankind.

"In three measures of meal." The meal is a symbol of our heavily burdened human nature, which needs the elevating power of grace. Pride is one of the most deep-seated of human vices. It poisons all our thoughts and contaminates our most generous actions; it draws us slowly but surely away from God. Even our inborn sensuality, which continually molests the spirit and draws us with a strange hypnotic power toward evil, is really the result of our pride. By ourselves it is impossible to conquer this vice of pride and sensuality, for man is inclined by nature toward evil. As a matter of fact, all our actions, when not tempered by divine grace, are sensual and worldly. "For all that is in the world is the concupiscence of the flesh, and the concupiscence of the eyes, and the pride of life, which is not of the Father, but is of the world" (1 Jn 2:16). Men thirst for pleasure, sensuality, covetousness, and the fulfillment of their own will. Such is the meal of human weakness in which the woman, the Church, hid the leaven.

St. John mentions three sources of evil in the world; the more important are the concupiscence of the flesh and the pride of life. The more a man loses himself in his own pride, the further he is driven from God and truth. Sensuality is like a great weight on the shoulders of men; each time they yield to it, the more firmly it becomes fixed in their soul and the heavier the burden becomes. Sensuality stirs up the flesh to rebellion against the spirit, and as the gap widens between them, men become more and more miserable. Unless the flesh and the spirit can be brought to work in harmony, there can be no peace or rest for either. Men at times try to bridge this gap by plunging headlong into vice, never satiated and never at rest. This violent separation of the spirit and the flesh is the chief obstacle the soul meets in giving itself entirely to God.

In this terrible struggle the woman, the Church, intervenes by mixing the leaven of grace with the meal of human passions. By means of grace she seeks to aid the spirit in subduing the passions. Her task is not to settle the case of one or the other soul, but to bring about the triumph of the spirit over the flesh in the entire human race: "Until the whole is leavened."

The first step in elevating the soul is taken by God Himself. Knowing as He does that of ourselves we can accomplish nothing, He takes the first step and infuses His gifts into our soul. He lightens the burden of passions and quells the conflict between the spirit and the flesh. Grace, the decisive factor in the struggle, tempers our proneness to evil and strengthens the powers of our soul for the performance of good. Grace elevates the soul and strengthens the powers of understanding, will, and memory. It accomplishes the work of restoration in a twofold manner, as sanctifying grace and as actual grace.

As sanctifying grace it penetrates the soul as the heat of fire penetrates iron. The soul is made to resemble its Creator; we become children of God and obtain possession of divine life, and thus a new relationship is set up between us and God and between us and our fellow man. By sanctifying grace we become incorporated in the body of Christ and live by Him as the branch lives by the vine. As grace transforms and elevates the soul, so, too, its powers are refined and strengthened so that we now see that we are able to perform actions that could not be performed by merely human strength. With the infusion of the grace of faith, we obtain an entirely new outlook on life. From that moment we see the world and all it contains, as it were, through the eyes of God. We come to participate in the knowledge of the divinity. With the infusion of sanctifying grace, divine love, too, is infused into our souls. God Himself is the source of this divine love, and He is Himself consumed by it. With sanctifying grace we also receive the virtue of hope, which comes to the assistance of our will. The virtue of hope counsels us in time of doubt, strengthens us in time of weakness, fills us with confidence when we hesitate, and urges us onward. This divine hope bolsters up our courage and keeps us aloof from all things that would lead us away from God; it prompts us to depend on God's strength. With these three divine virtues, all other supernatural virtues are also infused into our souls, and we are raised to a supernatural plane, far above the sordid surroundings into which we were born.

The second form of elevating grace is actual grace, which assimilates whatever is good in our nature and perfects and supernaturalizes all the various elements of our being, directing them toward the last end: the possession of God. It is distinct from our natural life, but penetrates and leavens all the actions of our daily life. Even our habits of mind, the vagaries of our fancy, are tempered by this grace and directed toward God. Grace is continually at work healing, shaping, and transforming our fallen nature. Our hearts, even while on earth, must be fixed in heaven, where God rules and Christ reigns as King.

"The kingdom of heaven is like to leaven, which a woman took and hid in three measures of meal until the whole was leavened." In the kingdom of Christ, the Church, this leavening process is accomplished by the operation of grace. God has placed in her custody the holy sacraments, which are the normal channels through which grace is given to men. How fortunate we are to be members of God's instrument of salvation, the Church! Let us remain ever faithful to her.

Grace is the leaven that will prepare our souls for heaven; however, our cooperation also is required. Unless we permit ourselves to be leavened by it, grace cannot accomplish its purpose in us. If we place no obstacle in the way of grace, it will transform us and lift us up to God. The obstacle we most frequently place in the way of grace is the attitude of indifference.

Prayer

Grant us, we beseech Thee, O almighty God, ever to fix our thoughts on reasonable things and to do what is pleasing to Thee both in words and in deeds. Through Christ our Lord. Amen.

Saturday

At the close of the season of Epiphany, the Church begs God for the grace to be spiritually disposed to accomplish whatever He requires of it.

Grant, O God, that we may ever meditate on spiritual truths; for "it is the spirit that quickeneth; the flesh profiteth nothing. The words that I have spoken to you are spirit and life" (Jn 6:64). The liturgy attempts to enlighten our mind and heart and to elevate them to God. Liturgical prayer is the effort of the soul to lift its eyes to the source of all enlightenment, to Christ, the splendor of the Father. "For you were heretofore darkness, but now light in the Lord. Walk, then, as children of the light" (Eph 5:8). When we were baptized, the priest prayed: "O almighty and eternal God, ... drive out from him all blindness of heart, ... that having been impressed with the sign of Thy wisdom, he may progress from day to day. Enlighten him with the light of Thy wisdom, ... and give him true knowledge." In the daily celebration of the Mass this same theme is presented to us in the Epistles and Gospels in order that the supernatural light may penetrate our soul; thus we come eventually to view all things as they appear in the eyes of God and of our blessed Savior. "Therefore, if you be risen with Christ, seek the things that are above, where Christ is sitting at the right hand of God. Mind the things that are above, not the things that are upon the earth; for you are dead, and your life is hid with Christ in God" (Col 3:1–3).

We should be spiritually minded, as our Lord pointed out to us in the beautiful Sermon on the Mount. "Blessed are the poor in spirit; ... blessed are the meek; ... blessed are they that mourn; ... blessed are they that hunger and thirst after justice; ... blessed are the merciful; ... blessed are the clean of heart; ... blessed are the peacemakers; ... blessed are they that suffer persecution for justice' sake" (Mt 5:3 ff.). He is spiritual who plucks out his eye or who casts away his hand if they lead him into sin. He is spiritual who, when his coat is taken, offers his cloak also. The spirit of God abides in the man who truly loves his neighbor, and who for the love of Christ loves not only his friends, but his enemies also, and who finds the courage to love even those who persecute him (Mt 5:29 ff.). We are spiritual when we have become followers of the Lord, when we receive with joy the word of the Gospel in spite of persecution, when we turn "to God from idols to serve the living and true God, and to wait for His Son from heaven,... Jesus, who hath delivered us from the wrath to come" (Epistle).

"Grant us ... to do what is pleasing to Thee" (Collect). Then we are truly spiritual when we accomplish what is pleasing to God. The slightest trial or tribulation, when accepted with the proper motive, is pleasing to God. If we have the proper spirit, we accept all things that He sends us, suffer joyfully all trials that we meet, and according to our light do all things that are pleasing to Him in our state of life. All our actions will be pleasing to Him if we perform them with the purpose of doing His holy will. A true Christian sets aside his own will and seeks first what may be the will of God. He no longer lives for himself, but for God alone. He seeks perfect cooperation between his own will and the will of God, and seeks to live in the most intimate union with Christ. The chief purpose of our liturgy is to establish this disposition in our souls. It would have us say with Christ, "My meat is to do the will of Him that sent Me" (Jn 4:34).

In the daily Sacrifice of the Mass the liturgy instructs us systematically in the Christian life. The Epistles and Gospels give us the principles and the application of these principles to our daily lives. Every Christian who makes a serious effort to apply the principles of the Gospel to his life becomes, in a sense, an epiphany, a manifestation of Christ in the world. Christ manifests Himself in their lives; in them He "hath built up Sion and He shall be seen in His glory" (Gradual).

The liturgy concerns itself chiefly with those who have been baptized. Having restored us to the supernatural life through baptism, Holy Mother the Church seeks to transform us, to fill us with grace, to enlighten us, and to perfect our union with Christ. Let us examine ourselves and learn how far this transformation has been accomplished in our soul. If we have not made progress, it is because we have placed some obstacle in the path of grace.

Many of us, perhaps, will discover that we have made very little progress. We may discover, upon investigation, that we are still more concerned about the things of this world than we are about the things of God (Col 3:1 f.). We may learn that our yearning "to be dissolved and to be with Christ" is very weak indeed (Phil 1:23). The thirst for holiness and the desire to become detached from the things of earth may hardly have touched our soul. The spirit of faith and of complete dependence on God may scarcely have moved us at all. How far we still are from that disposition of soul which made St. Paul cry out: "We know that to them that love God, all things work together unto good"; for He has predestined us "to be made conformable to the image of His Son" (Rom 8:28 f.). Therefore He has justified us.

"What shall we then say to these things? If God be for us, who is against us? He that spared not even His own Son, but delivered Him up for us all, how hath He not also with Him given us all things? Who shall accuse against the elect of God? God is He that justifieth. Who is he that shall condemn? Christ Jesus that died, yea, that is risen also again; who is at the right hand of God, who also maketh intercession for us. Who, then, shall separate us from the love of Christ? Shall tribulation? or distress? or famine? or nakedness? or danger? or persecution? or the sword?... But in all these things we overcome because of Him that hath loved us" (Rom 8:31–37).

Prayer

Grant us, we beseech Thee, O almighty God, ever to fix our thoughts on reasonable things and to do what is pleasing to Thee both in words and in deeds. Through Christ our Lord. Amen.

O God, our refuge and our strength, Thou art the Author of all righteousness. Give answer to the earnest pleadings of Thy Church, that we may truly acquire what we ask for with earnest faith. Through Christ our Lord. Amen.

Feasts of the Saints during the Time after Epiphany

January 17, St. Anthony

The feast of the holy hermit St. Anthony is, in a sense, an epiphany also, for the influence of Christ is made manifest in the life of this saintly recluse.

One day St. Anthony heard these words of our Lord read in church: "If thou wilt be perfect, go sell what thou hast and give to the poor, and thou shalt have treasure in heaven; and come follow Me" (Mt 19:21). St. Anthony, taking the admonition to heart, understood these words to apply to him personally, and he followed them literally. Without hesitation he disposed of his property, applied the proceeds to the relief of the poor, and retired to the desert. "Blessed is the rich man ... that hath not gone after gold nor put his trust in money nor in treasures" (Ecclus 31:8). A man whose heart is detached from the goods of this world has a higher ideal. "Let your loins be girt and lamps burning in your hands; and you yourselves like to men who wait for their lord when he shall return from the wedding, that when he cometh and knocketh, they may open to him immediately. Blessed are those servants whom the Lord, when He cometh, shall find watching" (Gospel). These words were verified in the life of St. Anthony. He has set aside all worldly occupations and awaits the coming of his Lord and Master. Having girded his loins with the girdle of chastity, poverty, mortification, and penance, he holds the lamp of love in his hand and stands gazing steadfastly, expecting momentarily the coming of the Lord. "What doth it profit a man if he gain the whole world and suffer the loss of his own soul?" (Mt 16:26.)

Anthony has made a complete conquest of the world and of himself. "Thou hast given him his heart's desire, O Lord" (Offertory). In the silence of the desert the hermit learned true wisdom. He learns to weigh all things in the light of his eternal destiny. All that is temporal and earthly appears to him as dung and waste. "But one thing is necessary" (Lk 10:42). "The mouth of the just shall meditate wisdom, and his tongue shall speak judgment; the law of his God is in his heart" (Introit). He was "beloved of God and men, whose memory is benediction. He made him like the saints in glory.... He sanctified him in his faith and meekness, and chose him out of all flesh; for He heard him and his voice, and brought him into a cloud" (Epistle), into the ecstasies of contemplation and loving intercourse with God, like Moses on Mt. Sinai. Nights he spent in prayer; for Anthony the sun rose all too soon and called him away from his prayer. St. Anthony asked God for divine life, and God was generous: "Thou hast given him length of days forever and ever" (Gradual).

The contemporaries of St. Anthony were astonished at the miracle of grace that had sprung up in their midst; thousands of them, inspired by his example, disposed of their earthly goods and retired to the desert to learn the way of salvation from him. He became the father and teacher of a great army of ascetics, hermits, and monks, who made their study of God and of divine ways without the help of books and in the deep silence of the desert. "Thou hast given him length of days forever and ever." At first the life of the desert was hard and difficult; it required great sacrifice and heroic virtue; but its reward was the possession of God and the revelation of His beauty. Anthony sacrificed all that he might gain all. What he lost became his reward. Through his foolishness he gained eternal wisdom.

"For he that will save his life, shall lose it; and he that shall lose his life for My sake, shall find it. For what doth it profit a man if he gain the whole world, and suffer the loss of his own soul? Or what exchange shall a man give for his soul?" (Mt 16:25 f.) "Then Jesus said to His disciples: If any man will come after Me, let him deny himself and take up his cross and follow Me" (Mt 16:24).

In the Mass today we surrender all things, following the example given us by St. Anthony. We wish to be a complete holocaust to God. The more we offer now, the more we shall receive in return at the time of Holy Communion. We shall enjoy, above all, the eternal communion in heaven.

PRAYER

May the intercession of the blessed abbot Anthony, we beseech Thee, O Lord, commend us unto Thee, that what we cannot have through our own merits, we may obtain through his patronage. Through Christ our Lord. Amen.

January 21, St. Agnes

Agnes, a mere child of thirteen years, when accused of being a Christian, repulsed all attempts to make her unfaithful to Christ, and for her steadfastness she was beheaded. To earthly lovers she cried out: "Away from me, for another has become my lover."

Agnes' loyalty to her lover, Christ, stirs our admiration. Christ is her world: she lives only to contemplate Him, and she is loved by Him. "With His ring the Lord Jesus Christ has betrothed Himself to me" (Antiphon at Vespers). "Honey and milk I have received from His mouth, and with His blood He has reddened my cheeks."[7] "When I love Him, I am chaste; when I touch Him, I am clean; when I receive Him, I am a virgin" (Responsories at Matins). "In Him I have confidence; to Him I surrender myself with perfect resignation" (Antiphon at Matins). Thus Agnes lives in heavenly union with the divine bridegroom, not in a temporal union, not occupied with herself, her health, or her beauty. Agnes knows only Christ and the wonderful works He has accomplished in her. When she receives Holy Communion, she understands the treasure which she possesses in her faith in Christ and in the Church, and this consciousness makes her strong and steadfast.

For the liturgy St. Agnes is a type of the Church. In this maiden the Church and the Christian soul recognize themselves called to a loving union with Christ. Today we approach the Holy Sacrifice with St. Agnes, leaving behind the things that in this godless world tend to spoil us. We look upon all that is transitory and frivolous as "the food of death." With Agnes we have fixed our gaze on Christ, the heavenly bridegroom, who in Holy Communion daily gives Himself to us and joins Himself with us, preparing us for our eternal home of love. We look at

[7] In early Christian times the newly baptized received milk and honey immediately after receiving Holy Communion. In former times the Christians also moistened their foreheads and cheeks with the Eucharistic blood.

the eternal reward which awaits us. "Behold, what I desired I now possess; I am already joined to Him in heaven, whom I so ardently desired on earth" (Benedictus antiphon).

Christianity made Agnes so happy that she gladly surrendered human love, parents, possessions, and even her life. She gives an inspiring example to us Christians who laboriously perform our duties with fear and anxiety, lacking the courage, joy, and the spirit of sacrifice that Agnes had.

Why this difference? Agnes rose to the level of Christ. Now she looks above herself at Christ, her all. She is fully aware of her richness and strength and the eternal reward to which she is entitled by reason of her baptism and Holy Communion. She knows that she is loved, that Christ belongs to her, and she to Him. We look only to ourselves; we measure everything according to our own strength and effort. We adhere to our own methods, and consider only our own progress, restraints, and difficulties. We do not see further than ourselves; we do not live in Christ. For us, Christ, the Sun, has not yet risen. Therefore we do not find that boundless, triumphant confidence in Him that inspired Agnes. Even in our piety, self comes first; it obstructs in us the free, joyful view of Him who is our all. Epiphany! May the Lord manifest Himself in us as He did in Agnes, the youthful martyr.

Prayer

O almighty and eternal God, who has chosen the weak things of the earth to confound the strong; grant us, we beseech Thee, that we who devoutly celebrate the feast of Thy martyr Agnes, may profit by her intercession. Through Christ our Lord. Amen.

January 25, Conversion of St. Paul

The conversion of St. Paul is also a manifestation of the power of God. A change as wonderful and sublime as the transformation of water into wine takes place in this transformation of Saul into Paul; the fiercest enemy and persecutor of Christ and His Church becomes His most zealous follower and apostle, a vessel of election for the conversion of the Gentile world (Acts 9:15). In the words of the Introit of the Mass, we rejoice: "For I know whom I have believed, and I am certain that He is able to keep that which I have committed to Him against that day" (2 Tm 1:12).

"In those days Saul, as yet breathing out threatenings and slaughter against the disciples of the Lord, went to the high priest and asked of him letters to Damascus" (Epistle). Fanatical in his devotion to his race and religion, Saul hated the Christians and spared no means to destroy them. He took part in the stoning of Stephen, the deacon; then he began to search out the Christians as far as Damascus, in Syria, in order to bring them back to Jerusalem to appear bound in chains before the council of the Jews. That is the man Saul, full of violence and intolerance, yet in good faith; he hated Christ and His followers because he thought it the duty of a zealous Jew to do so. But Christ appeared to him on the way to Damascus. A marvelous epiphany! Paul has but one question: "Lord, what wilt Thou have me to do?" Saul, the persecutor, is changed into Paul, the apostle of Christ. This change is wrought by the appearance of the Lord and by the grace of the crucified Christ.

Paul recognized the grace which he undeservedly and unexpectedly received on the way to Damascus. He surrendered all, even what he had up to this time considered most sacred: his religion, his former convictions, his ideals, and his reputation among his fellow men. He knew how they would slander and detract him, and would consider him a traitor; but this thought does not deter him. To serve his Master is his only concern. "I know whom I have believed" and in whom I have trusted. With Christ I have won all things; by Christ I shall not be betrayed. With Christ alone my life and undertakings have merit and shall be eternally rewarded. By that which I hitherto considered worthy, I was deceived. Only in Christ is there salvation and every good. To Him I give myself, Him I shall serve, for Him I shall live, for Him I shall die. Paul realized the value of the promises made by Christ to those who leave all things and follow Him: they "shall receive a hundredfold [in this world] and shall possess life everlasting" (Gospel). Indeed, in Christ, who has appeared to him and whom he follows, he receives a hundredfold.

On the road to Damascus, Christ appeared to Saul, the persecutor. A crucial experience for Saul! Thereby he became an entirely new man, with new ideas and new ideals, a new goal, and a new strength. He withdrew to pray and fast, permitted himself to be baptized, and lived in complete resignation to the will of God. Henceforth he would labor for Christ, for the Church, and for souls. We thank God for St. Paul. In this apostle we honor the selected tool, the chosen vessel of grace, and respectfully listen to his words, which are so frequently used in the liturgy of the Mass.

Today we see ourselves in Paul. His experience at Damascus is reenacted in us at baptism, which is an unmerited grace and blessing given by the Lord to an unworthy sinner. We ask, "Lord, what wilt Thou have me to do?" And we accept Him: "I believe in God,... in Jesus Christ,... in the Holy Ghost." Christ's appearance on the road to Damascus has often been repeated in many hours of grace we have experienced. Often we chose the wrong way. Then suddenly and unexpectedly He appeared before the eyes of our spirit. "Why persecutest thou Me?" At once we asked, "Lord, what wilt Thou have me to do?" and He said to us, "Go into the city," turn to the Church, to the priesthood of the Church. "There it shall be told thee what thou must do." The priest raised his hand in blessing and spoke the following consoling words over us: "I absolve thee of all thy sins."

St. Paul's experience at Damascus is re-enacted daily for us in the Mass. Sacrificially (symbolically) we leave all things and in the bread and wine place ourselves on the altar. "Lord, what wilt Thou have me to do?" After we have given all in the Offertory, we receive a hundredfold in return at Communion; we receive Christ, His life, His merits, His love of the Father. Christ gives us the strength to conquer ourselves. Like Paul, like one filled with Christ, like a manifestation of Christ, we return from the altar to our daily duties. We become apostles of Christianity, bringing Christ to all men as Paul did, becoming all for all in order to win all for Christ (1 Cor 9:19 ff.). Like St. Paul, we should not shun any difficulty or trial, but courageously face every adversity in our zealous service of Christ (2 Cor 11:24 ff.). Then, confident of victory, we can say with Paul: "I know whom I have believed, and I am certain that He is able to keep that which I have committed to Him against that day," when He shall call us to eternal union with Himself (2 Tm 1:12). Eternally we shall enjoy what Christ has promised: "You who have left all things and followed Me, shall receive a hundredfold, and shall possess life everlasting" (Communion). Yes, I will go with Paul. "I know whom I have believed."

Prayer

O God, who hast taught the whole world by the preaching of blessed Paul the apostle, we beseech Thee to grant that we who this day celebrate his conversion may advance toward Thee by following his example.

Sanctified by this saving mystery, we beseech Thee, O Lord, that he under whose patronage Thou hast vouchsafed to place us may not fail to intercede for us. Through Christ our Lord. Amen. (Postcommunion.)

January 29, St. Francis de Sales

Today we celebrate with the liturgy the feast of the great St. Francis de Sales, doctor of the Church, bishop of Geneva, author of *An Introduction to the Devout Life* and other spiritual works. He died December 28, 1622.

St. Francis continues to live in the Church: *in medio ecclesiae*. Even today his voice, filled with the spirit of wisdom and understanding, is raised in the midst of the congregation of the Church (Introit). He is the salt of the earth, the light of the world; and his light, his teachings, and his virtues enlighten us in order that, seeing them, we may praise the Father, who works such wonders in His saints. With loving zeal he fulfills the commands of the Lord, even the least and most insignificant ones; and as he teaches, so he lives. "He that shall do and teach, he shall be called great in the kingdom of heaven" (Gospel), both in the Church here on earth and in heaven. In the Church, the mysterious organism of grace in which Christ, the vine, lives and nourishes His saints, St. Francis became what he is today. Only in the Church and through the Church could he have attained his present glory.

St. Francis continues to live in the Church and for the Church. Therefore the liturgy celebrates the feast of this doctor of the Church who possessed such supernatural wisdom and understanding. The Church commemorates him as the high priest who, certainly united with the saints, celebrates with us the Holy Sacrifice and adds to our gifts his own virtues, merits, and intercession. She commemorates him as a true and wise dispenser of grace whom God has appointed as a gracious and mighty intercessor for "His family," the Church.

"You are the salt of the earth; but if the salt lose its savor, wherewith shall it be salted? It is good for nothing any more but to be cast out and to be trodden on by men. You are the light of the world. A city seated on a mountain cannot be hid. Neither do men light a candle and put it under a bushel, but upon a candlestick, that it may shine to all that are in the house. So let your light shine before men that they may see your good works and glorify God" (Gospel). St. Francis has been placed on a candlestick and enlightens "all that are in the house" of the Church. We see his good works, his accomplishments in souls, the thousands who were led back from Calvinism to the truth of Christ, and many thousands for whom he has become a leader and savior by his writing; we see the marvelous virtues and the richness of grace which he received from the Lord. We acknowledge him as an epiphany of the Lord's wisdom, strength, and grace, and therefore in the Sacrifice of the Mass we praise and thank our heavenly Father for this manifestation of His goodness and grace.

We look at the light which the Lord has placed on the candlestick in His holy Church, and we come to this light to enkindle and replenish our own little light. St. Francis de Sales is one of the great saints in the kingdom of heaven, one of the masters and teachers of the Christian life. He is one of those who "do and teach" (Gospel).

"The just shall flourish like the palm tree; he shall grow up like the cedar of Libanus" (Offertory). In the same spirit of resignation to God in which St. Francis de Sales once approached the altar and now continues to offer to the Lord in heaven, we bring to the altar our own offering — ourselves. We are like branches and twigs of the palm tree striving for heaven, nourished by the strength, teaching, example, and intercession of this saintly bishop, Francis de Sales. Thus he grows as a cedar of Libanus and bears us up with himself as an offering to God. Thus are we, in the thoughts of the liturgy, one in spirit with the communion of saints.

At the sacrificial meal of Holy Communion, we see in the priest who distributes Communion the bishop and high priest, Francis de Sales. As the trusted servant of Christ, whom the Lord has placed as father over us, he dispenses to us "in due season," today, the food of doctrine and the Holy Eucharist (Communion).

Prayer

O God, who for the saving of souls didst will that blessed Francis, Thy confessor and bishop, should become all things to all men, be pleased to grant that we, being filled with the sweetness of Thy love, guided by his teachings, and helped by his merits and prayers, may attain to the joys of everlasting life. Through Christ our Lord. Amen.

February 1, St. Ignatius of Antioch

In St. Ignatius, bishop of Antioch in Syria, who shed his blood, we have an example of a hero burning with true love for Christ. He died at Rome about the year 107, torn to pieces by lions.

In his *Epistle to the Romans* St. Ignatius expresses his great desire to suffer and die for Christ:

Suffer me to become food for the wild beasts, through whose instrumentality it will be granted me to attain to God. I am the wheat of God, and am ground by the teeth of the wild beasts, that I may be found the pure bread of God.... I pray that they may be found eager to rush upon me,... and not deal with me as with some, whom, out of fear, they have not touched. But if they be unwilling to assail me, I will compel them to do so.... Now I begin to be a disciple, and have no desire after anything visible or invisible, that I may attain to Jesus Christ. Let fire and the cross; let the crowds of wild beasts; let breakings, tearings, and separations of bones; let cutting off of members; let shatterings of the whole body; and let the very torment of the devil come upon me: only let me attain to Jesus Christ.[8]

Here we find an echo of those glorious words of St. Paul: "God forbid that I should glory, save in the cross of our Lord Jesus Christ, by whom the world is crucified to me, and I to the world" (Introit). "According to my expectation and hope, that in nothing I shall be confounded, but with all confidence as always, so now also, shall Christ be

[8] Chaps. 4 f.; trans. from *The Ante-Nicene Fathers*, I, 75.

magnified in my body, whether it be by life or by death" (Phil 1:20). Thus the Christian thinks, lives, and dies.

How did St. Ignatius acquire such heroism? He acquired it from the vivid consciousness of his being united with Christ. Christ is the "grain of wheat" that (in suffering, death, and burial) falls into the earth and dies, but "bringeth forth much fruit" (Gospel). St. Ignatius knows that he belongs to this grain of wheat, that he is part of it, and that he must therefore be one with Christ in humiliation and suffering, in captivity and in bloody death. The grain of wheat is the entire Christ: head, body, and members. Christ in His members, in those baptized, must also fall into the ground, "for we are buried together with Him by baptism into death" (Rom 6:4). We, the members, stand in fruitful union with Christ, the grain of wheat; for "if it die, it bringeth forth much fruit." Therefore Ignatius is glad to meet his death. He longs to suffer and die for Christ, for he understands his union with Christ, his oneness with Christ. He knows what he has in possessing Christ. He knows that the Father has given us all things by giving us Christ. He knows that Christ died and rose again and is now seated at the right hand of the Father making intercession for us.

If God and Christ be for us, there is no force in the world strong enough to rob us of the love God has for us because of His Son. Ignatius knows that he is loved by God in Christ with a divine, all-powerful love. "Brethren, who shall separate us from the love of Christ? shall tribulation? or distress? or famine? or nakedness? or danger? or persecution? or the sword?... I am sure that neither death, nor life, nor angels, nor principalities, nor powers, nor things present, nor things to come,... nor any other creature shall be able to separate us from the love of God, which is in Christ Jesus our Lord" (Epistle).

"Behold a great priest, who in his day pleased God. There was not found any like him who kept the law of the Most High" (Gradual). "With Christ I am nailed to the cross. I live, now not I, but Christ liveth in me" (Alleluia verse). Ignatius had offered the Eucharistic sacrifice so often and had longed so ardently to make an adequate return for Christ's love that on the eve of his passion he naturally thought of himself as wheat to be ground for Christ. "I am the wheat of Christ; may I be ground by the teeth of wild beasts that I may be found pure bread" (Communion). His desire was fulfilled when the lions tore him to pieces and he suffered a bloody martyrdom.

By assisting at Mass, Christians are united to Christ as grains of wheat are united to make bread. What they begin in the liturgical sacrifice they perfect by their daily sufferings and hardships: they permit themselves to be offered with Christ. "He that loveth his life, shall lose it; and he that hateth his life in this world, keepeth it unto life eternal" (Gospel). Every day the hour of eternal union draws nearer. We who have suffered here as members of Christ, shall rise and be glorified as He was. "Where I am, there also shall My minister be" (Gospel).

"O Lord, remember David and all his meekness" (Introit). Let us pray with the Church: O God, remember today Thy holy bishop and martyr, Ignatius, and all that he prayed, suffered, and offered Thee. On account of him look graciously upon Thy holy Church and grant us forgiveness for our sins and imperfections; grant us the grace to die to the world as Ignatius did, and to search for nothing but Christ. "If only I may win Christ."

Prayer

Have regard to our weakness, O almighty God, and since the burden of our deeds is heavy upon us, let the glorious intercession of blessed Ignatius, Thy martyr and bishop, be our protection. Through Christ our Lord. Amen.

February 2, The Purification of Mary (1)

Today the liturgy has a candle procession in order that we may accompany Mary on her pilgrimage to Jerusalem. In the temple we shall find the blessed Simeon waiting to receive the holy child from the arms of Mary. We, too, share his rapture: "My eyes have seen Thy salvation, which Thou hast prepared before the face of all peoples"; and we listen to his prophetic words to Mary: "Behold this child is set for the fall and for the resurrection of many in Israel" (Lk 2:30 f., 34).

By the lighted candles we carry in our hands we acknowledge the arrival of the true light of the world, Jesus Christ. By means of this symbol of light, we carry Christ in our hands today with deep reverence. With Mary and Simeon we feel that we are blessed bearers of Christ, and we acknowledge joyfully, "My eyes have seen Thy salvation." We possess Christ, who is "full of grace and truth" (Jn 1:14). He is the fullness of all truth, purity, holiness, and happiness. He alone can fully satisfy our heart and all our desires. We possess Him, we believe in Him, we trust Him, and we dedicate ourselves to Him with all our hearts. We carry Him with us as a light through life, as a light that illuminates our way, guides us, comforts us, and gives us joy. We carry this light with us into our family, into our place of business, on the street, and in all our actions, and thus we lend to our surroundings a joyful and fruitful Christian atmosphere. "You are the light of the world" (Mt 5:14). We carry the light, Christ, in our hands, and thus we become confessors, apostles, and missionaries of Christ, "a light to the revelation of the Gentiles" (Lk 2:32).

From the hands of the Church we receive the lighted candle, which is a symbol of Christ, the light of the world. The Church alone has the power to bless these candles and to place them in our hands as Mary laid the infant Christ in the arms of Simeon. Only Mary can bring Christ to us, and only in Christ can we have light, grace, and life.

For the liturgy Mary is a type and symbol of the Church. In the blessing of the candles the Church places the truth before our eyes: the Church, and only the Church, has the power to give us Christ, His truth, His graces, and His sacraments. If we desire to receive grace, if we wish to possess Christ, and in Christ life and salvation, then we must turn to the Church. She is "His temple," into which the Lord shall come (Epistle). In this temple we shall find the mercy of God; that is, the merciful, incarnate Christ, the Savior, as we acknowledge in the Introit: "We have received Thy mercy, O God, in the midst of Thy temple," in Thy holy Church.

Candlemas is past, yet still with us. We ourselves have been strengthened in baptism, incorporated in Christ, the light. "For you were heretofore darkness, but now light in the Lord [that is, members of Christ]. Walk, then, as children of the light," as bearers of Christ, called to announce Him and His spirit (Eph 5:8).

Candlemas! We walk to the temple with the light in our hands, with Mary. We proceed with Christ in our soul by faith, in our heart by love, and in our work by resignation to His holy will and the things He permits us to undergo. We walk hand in hand with Mary, the Church, the temple of the heavenly Jerusalem. Mary, the Church, guides us safely. Above, Christ, the light, awaits us in all His splendor. There we shall eternally thank Him and rejoice with Him. "My eyes have seen Thy salvation."

Prayer

O Lord Jesus Christ, who on this day appeared among men in the substance of flesh and was presented by Thy parents in the temple, and whom the venerable old man, Simeon, being filled with the light of Thy Spirit, recognized, took up, and blessed: be pleased to grant that, enlightened and taught by the grace of the same Holy Spirit, we may know Thee rightly and love Thee faithfully, who with God the Father livest and reignest in the unity of the same Holy Spirit, God, world without end. Amen. (Prayer at the blessing of the candles.)

The Purification of Mary (2)

Today we accompany Mary, the Mother of God, from Bethlehem to the temple in Jerusalem. She carries the child in her arms and offers Him to the Lord God.

Jesus offers. The law which bound the Jewish mother to offer her first-born male child to the Lord in the temple had no binding force in this case. Jesus Himself was God, the lawgiver; His birth was sacred. Since He was the only-begotten of the Father, there was no need for His being taken to the temple to be sanctified. Nevertheless, He permitted Himself to be taken to the temple by Mary and Joseph. The great moment foretold by the prophet has come: "Behold I send My angel, and he shall prepare the way before My face. And presently the Lord, whom you seek,... shall come to His temple" (Epistle). It is "His temple" because the temple belongs to Him. By right, all the offerings made there should be given to Him. But He comes as a child in the arms of His mother, quiet, unnoticed, secretly. Nothing betrays the holiness of His soul. Concealing the glow of His divinity here in His temple, Jesus renews every blessing of the Father which He received at the moment of His conception in the womb of the Virgin Mary: "I come to do Thy will, O God" (Heb 10:9). Today He makes that same great, holy sacrifice of adoration, thanksgiving, atonement, and petition. This is the first perfect sacrifice which the temple of Jerusalem ever witnessed. The sacrifices of rams and oxen need be no more; the only sacrifice worthy of God has been offered in the temple. "We have received Thy mercy, O God, in the midst of Thy temple.... Great is the Lord, and exceedingly to be praised; in the city of God, in His holy mountain" (Introit). This sacrifice is a prototype of the daily Sacrifice of the Mass, at which we are now permitted to assist.

Mary offers. The offering of Jesus in the temple is accomplished by the hands of Mary. Enlightened by the light of the Holy Ghost, Mary realizes at this moment what she must undergo in the future. She perceives the magnitude of the sacrifice she must make. With the same disposition of submission to the Father which Jesus has in His heart, she offers her child. With a wholehearted and disinterested fiat in her heart and on her lips, she presents her most precious and beloved Son as an offering. She makes her offering in the name of all men and as the representative of all mankind. This is a great moment in Mary's life, in the life of all mankind, in the life of each individual soul. Mary, bringing her child, at the same time brings the first fruits of the future sacrifice to be offered to God on Golgotha. She is a cooperator in the work of our redemption. In admiration we look at Mary offering her beloved Son and, united in spirit with Jesus, presenting herself for the legal purification as a sacrifice to the Father. As the one offering and as the one offered, she today begins her life of sacrifice. Simeon makes known to her the sufferings she must undergo: "Behold this child is set for the fall and for the resurrection of many in Israel and for a sign which shall be contradicted. And thy own soul a sword shall pierce" (Lk 2:34 f.). Mary speaks her fiat; she desires to be a sacrifice. Soon the day will come when at the foot of the cross she will witness the completion of the sacrifice of Jesus which has begun today: "Be it done to me according to thy word" (Lk 1:38).

Daily our Savior offers Himself in our midst in the celebration of the Mass. Thus His presentation in the temple is continued. He offers Himself through the hands of Mary, that is, the Church. The Church also takes holy offerings, His body and His blood, His heart and His soul, and with all His merits presents them as gifts to the Father. This holy sacrifice of adoration, thanksgiving, atonement, and petition is worthy in the sight of God. We unite ourselves with this sacrifice of Christ; we also desire to make our daily life a real sacrifice.

"We have received Thy mercy," the incarnate mercy of God, our Savior, "in the midst of Thy temple," in the celebration of the Mass. We believe; we are thankful. We desire to be like Mary, offering sacrifice and being offered at the same time.

Prayer

Almighty and eternal God, we humbly beseech Thy majesty that as Thy only-begotten Son was this day presented in the temple in the substance of our flesh, so Thou mayest cause us to be presented to Thee with purified minds. Through Christ our Lord. Amen.

The Purification of Mary (3)

On Candlemas Day the Church places burning candles in our hands. She thereby calls us to be bearers of Christ, to bear Christ in our souls and in our wills.

We must bear Christ in our souls, that is, in our thoughts, words, and deeds. We are Christians and conscious of being filled with the spirit and life of Jesus. Therefore we no longer see things from a natural, mundane point of view, but from the same point of view as Jesus sees them. We see the great and small things through the eyes of Christ. They become for us a revelation of the wisdom, power, and love of God. With the eyes of Jesus we see the hand of almighty God upholding all creation. We recognize Him in all men, in all creatures. We penetrate accidents of things and see them in their real value. With the eyes of Jesus we see beyond the present day into the world to come, firmly believing in the principles announced in the Sermon on the Mount: "And opening His mouth he taught them saying: Blessed are the poor in spirit; for theirs is the kingdom of heaven.... Blessed are they that mourn; for they shall be comforted. Blessed are they that hunger and thirst after justice; for they shall have their fill.... Blessed are the clean of heart; for they shall see God" (Mt 5:2 ff.). There will be an eternity and a just judgment; everyone will receive what he deserves. In all the decisions which we must make, let us ask ourselves: "What doth it profit a man if he gain the whole world and suffer the loss of his own soul?" (Mt 16:26.) Let us live in accordance with this principle: "But one thing is necessary" (Lk 10:42). And thus we will possess Christ in our souls as a guiding light. "You are the light of the world.... Let your light shine before men" (Mt 5:14, 16).

We must carry Christ in our will, in our heart, our deeds, and our life. We live with Him, in accordance with His words and example, aware that His union with us is as real as that of the body with its members and the vine with its branches. "I can do all things in Him who strengtheneth me" (Phil 4:13), who lives in me, who upholds me and fills me with His strength. We live with Him and carry in our hearts a holy desire to love Him. In the strength of His love we bring forth every sacrifice and strive to conquer the power of self-love. We live with Him in blind confidence in His love, in His nearness, in His guidance, in His grace. The Lord is ever with us to help us. We live with Him in a spirit of detachment from self and created things, in a spirit of fearlessness of the world and the scorn and ridicule of men, with boldness for the interests of Christ and souls.

On Candlemas Day we renew in ourselves the significance of our calling to be Christ-bearers and to bring Christ to the world. Men today need Christ; they yearn for Christ. Our calling is to be apostles of Christ, everyone in his proper station. The candle which we have in our hands on Candlemas Day reminds us of our duty to be Christ-bearers.

If only we were upright, perfect Christians! But there we fail. Christianity is, for the majority of men, a life of anxiety, uncertainty, fear, and slavishness to formula and method. Our Christianity is burdened by so much mistrust of ourselves and others, by so much self-love, self-seeking, and selfishness. We are Christians only in form and rule; Christians of habit, anxious about little things. We are all too little Christian at heart, enkindled by no great desire of doing things for Christ. Seldom are we the Christians St. Paul desires us to be: "And let the peace of Christ rejoice in your hearts, wherein also you are called in one body; and be ye thankful" (Col 3:15). This joyful, grateful Christianity has become strange to us.

Prayer

Send forth Thy light and Thy truth to me, that they may lead me unto Thy holy hill and into Thy tabernacles. Amen.

The Purification of Mary (4)

"Now Thou dost dismiss Thy servant, O Lord, according to Thy word in peace, because my eyes have seen Thy salvation" (Gospel). The Church places these words on the lips of the priest at Compline, the evening prayer of the Church.

The day is drawing to a close. As we say Compline, our night prayers, our mind wanders back over the day to make thanksgiving for the blessings of the morning, the midday, and the afternoon. We recall the privileges that were ours at Mass, at the time of Holy Communion, and at the hours of prayer. We remember the hours of work, the toils, temptations, and acts of self-denial which the day has brought. We are not unmindful of the joys that were ours. Recalling all these things at the close of day, in the spirit of faith and in the words of the holy liturgy, we say with deep gratitude: "Now Thou dost dismiss Thy servant, O Lord,... because my eyes have seen Thy salvation."

The day has brought us the grace, love, help, and mercy of our God and Savior. "To them that love God, all things work together unto good" (Rom 8:28). Even our many failures, the indeliberate and half-deliberate faults, even sins for which we have immediately been sorry, which we hate, which we desire never to commit again, may become an occasion of grace for us, a way of knowing ourselves, accusing ourselves, humiliating ourselves, and making us desire to live in complete resignation to God's holy will. Today "my eyes have seen Thy salvation."

The evening of our life is ever drawing nearer. The years of our childhood, adolescence, middle age, and old age all pass before us. Looking back, we see stains, sins, and faults as numerous as the sands on the seashore. Then we glance upward. In His infinite mercy and love we see the Lord exchanging our stained robe for the immaculate garment of salvation. From the first grace of baptism until the last grace we shall ever receive, our life is nothing but a work of salvation and grace from the Lord. Our sinfulness and weakness, our unfaithfulness and unworthiness, He has endured with divine patience and fatherly mercy. Though we were unworthy, yet He has led us through many dangers and pitfalls into which we surely would have fallen without His guidance and assistance. He has given us as a possession the many prayers, examples, and merits of the saints in heaven and on earth. He has placed over us a guardian to accompany us and lead us in the way of salvation. With grateful hearts we look back at our life and, thanking Him, see the salvation which He has made possible for us. Only the mercy of God has kept us from being eternally lost. Our prayer is a Miserere, a call for mercy and grace. But the Miserere enters into the joyful prayer of Simeon: "Now Thou dost dismiss Thy servant... in peace, because my eyes have seen Thy salvation."

"My eyes have seen Thy salvation." Yes, Lord, teach us to see Thy salvation, Thy merciful, loving, holy dealing with us and in us. Heal us from the habit of looking at ourselves alone, at our deeds and troubles and sufferings, and cure us of our unworthiness. Help us in the battle against sin, and grant us the grace ever to increase in all virtue. Grant that our eyes may see our salvation, You, our Redeemer.

Lord, give us the spirit of Thy great apostle Paul. He was tempted by human desires even more than we are. His trials and troubles were numerous and great, but he always turned to Thee, the Redeemer. "For which cause we faint not; but though our outward man is corrupted, yet the inward man is renewed day by day. For that which is at present momentary and light of our tribulation, worketh for us above measure exceedingly an eternal weight of glory. While we look not at the things which are seen, but at the things which are not seen. For the things which are seen are temporal; but the things which are not seen are eternal" (2 Cor 4:16–18).

Prayer

O Lord Jesus Christ, the true light who enlightenest every man that cometh into this world, pour forth Thy blessing upon these waxen candles and sanctify them with the light of Thy grace; and mercifully grant that, as these lights enkindled with visible fire dispel the darkness of night, so our hearts, being enlightened with invisible fire, even the brightness of the Holy Spirit, may be delivered from the blindness of every vice; that with the eye of the mind purified, we may be able to discern those things which are pleasing to Thee and useful for our salvation; whereby after the dark trials of this world, we may be found worthy to arrive at the never-failing light. Through Thee, Christ Jesus, Savior of the world. Amen. (Prayer at the blessing of the candles.)

PART TWO

The Easter Cycle

Introduction

During the season of Christmas and Epiphany, the Redeemer made His appearance among us. Awed by our nearness to the Divinity, we cast ourselves down in adoration at His feet. "Adore Him all you His angels" (Ps 96:7). "Behold the Lord, the Ruler, is come, and the kingdom is in His hand, and power and dominion" (Introit for Epiphany). "Come let us adore Him."

Now the scene is suddenly changed. On Septuagesima Sunday, the picture of Christ as the King of Glory is withdrawn. Now He stands before us as the suffering and dying Redeemer. Holy Mother the Church will accompany Him on the sorrowful journey through His passion, will suffer and die with Him, and will arise again with Him at Easter.

During Lent we, too, shall "die." We shall die to sin and to the world and all its vanities. This death will impose on us a relentless and bitter struggle against our passions, our worldliness. It will require of us much suffering and much self-restraint. Through the privations of this life we shall gain the glory of the life to come.

Of this much we can be certain, that in this struggle we shall win, that by dying to the life of this world we shall make sure the life to come. Our confidence arises from our knowledge that Christ is our head, who lives in us and fights for us. Because of His abiding presence we are confident of victory, of resurrection, and of life eternal. During the time from Septuagesima to Easter we must wage an unceasing battle with nature that we may overcome sin, the flesh, and the world. Through the holy liturgy we carry on this battle daily. Through strife we achieve victory; by dying we live. "I shall not die, but live" (Ps 117:17).

Septuagesima Sunday

The Mass

Septuagesima Sunday ushers in the Easter cycle, and our thoughts dwell on the blessed mystery of Easter. The Easter cycle includes Christ's passion, resurrection, and glorification. The devout Christian soul will accompany the Church as she contemplates Christ in His passion, death, resurrection, and eternal glorification. Through struggle to victory is the universal law. Through suffering, tribulation, and death the soul achieves self-mastery, resurrection, and life. This struggle valiantly waged in this life will bring the soul to the resurrection and eternal life in heaven.

On Septuagesima Sunday in the ancient Church, the candidates who were to receive baptism at Easter were selected from those who had presented themselves for instruction. This practice should remind us also that we once were presented for baptism, and as members of Christ's mystical body we should renew our resolution to accompany Him on His sorrowful journey. We shall accompany Christ through His struggles to victory. Having resolved to acquit ourselves manfully in the struggle for the glory of God, and having concentrated all our energies for that task, we shall eventually achieve a glorious victory and a blessed Easter. Our model of mortification during this season is the martyr St. Lawrence. We gather around him in his church at the beginning of Lent to prepare for the struggle. Dimly in the background we catch a glimpse of the greatest of all martyrs, Jesus Christ, clothed in garments crimsoned with His own blood. With Him and His holy Church we press forward for the struggle. "The sorrows of death surrounded me, the sorrows of hell encompassed me; and in my affliction I called upon the Lord, and He heard my voice from His holy temple" (Introit). Feeling the burden of our sinfulness, we cry out: "Graciously hear, we beseech Thee, O Lord, the prayers of Thy people, that we who are justly afflicted for our sins, may mercifully be freed for the glory of Thy name" (Collect).

Having made our humble plea for mercy, we arise to gird ourselves for the struggle that lies ahead of us. The goal which we expect to reach is the eternal resurrection. But to attain our goal we must chastise our bodies and bring them into subjection (Epistle). The strength to persevere in this life of self-denial we must seek from God, who will not deny His help to those who seek Him (Gradual). With the catechumens let us present ourselves again as laborers in the vineyard of the Lord. In this vineyard we shall work out our own salvation and that of our neighbor, and shall contribute to the success of the Church on earth. We have been called into the vineyard at the eleventh hour, that is, in the era of Christ, in the era of the new dispensation. God has given us a sublime calling. Since He also gives us strength and directs our labors, we can hardly refuse to labor zealously.

When we make our offering in the Mass today, we do so in the spirit of the willing laborers in the vineyard of the Lord. As the paten is raised by the priest, we offer with the spotless wafer our determination to struggle against the weakness of the flesh, the allurements of the world, and sin. We unite to this offering all the trials and sufferings that the days may bring us, and beg the grace of sustaining them in the spirit of St. Lawrence and in union with the suffering of our Redeemer.

Thus we begin Mass by renewing our belief that this sacrifice is truly a renewal of the offering on Calvary, and we declare ourselves ready to follow Him to death. The consummation of this sacrifice will not be death, but life; we look forward, not to Good Friday, but to Easter Sunday; not to the darkness of the grave, but to the brilliance of the resurrection; we are interested, not in the struggle, but in the victory. Christ now offers Himself, not as the suffering Redeemer, but as the living, glorified conqueror of death and sin. Through the Holy Sacrifice of the Mass, He makes us partakers of this resurrection and glorification. We share also in His love of the Father, His sanctity, His perfect prayer, His union with God; and thus we become most pleasing to His heavenly Father. Although He is now risen and glorified, He descends to give Himself to us in Holy Communion, and shares His glorified life with us. We are now enlightened by the glory that is His, and we begin to share His glorified life. A soul thus favored is, in a sense, already adorned with the crown of victory, and has placed in its hands already in this world the penny that is the reward for faithful service in the vineyard of the Master. The favors enjoyed by such a soul are an earnest of the crown of victory that is to be its reward in heaven. Through its sufferings it will conquer.

Meditation

Easter, the day of victory, the day of resurrection and redemption, is already beginning. We gather at the stational church of the martyr St. Lawrence, who was tortured on the gridiron. We feel that we are united to him, and this union gives us strength for the struggle. Victory may be gained only through strife. At Easter we shall renew that spirit of our baptism and rise to a new life. But the road to Easter leads over Golgotha.

"The kingdom of heaven is like to an householder who went out early in the morning to hire laborers into his vineyard" (Gospel). He begins his search for laborers early in the day and visits the market place again at the third, the sixth, the ninth, and the eleventh hour. At each visit he finds unemployed laborers idling in the market place, unconcerned about the work in the vineyard of souls. So, too, the Lord approaches us with the question, "Why stand you here all the day idle?... Go you also into My vineyard." We have as yet done very little for the salvation of our own souls or for those of others. We must now take up the task earnestly and zealously. The Lord has given us the call: "Go you also into My vineyard," work for the salvation of souls. Today at this very hour the invitation is given to us. For us it is not yet too late; it is never too late for any soul that is willing to turn from its evil ways and make an earnest effort. It is too late only for those who abandon the struggle. "Why stand you here all the day idle?" God calls us today to bear patiently the heat and the burden of the day in His vineyard; He invites us to strive in the arena of the world for the incorruptible crown of eternal life. We must struggle valiantly for the crown of victory.

The liturgy places St. Lawrence before us as a model for our conduct during Lent. While suffering on his bed of fire at the time of his martyrdom, he cried out: "The sorrows of death surrounded me, the sorrows of hell encompassed me; and in my affliction I called upon the Lord, and He heard my voice from His holy temple" (Introit). A second model is given us in the Epistle in the person of St. Paul, the valiant champion of the Church: "Brethren, know you not that they that run in the race, all run indeed, but one receiveth the prize? So run that you may obtain. And every one that striveth for the mastery refraineth himself from all things; and they indeed that they may receive a corruptible crown, but we an incorruptible one. I therefore so run, not as at an uncertainty; I so fight, not as one beating the air; but I chastise my body and bring it into subjection, lest perhaps when I have preached to others, I myself should become a castaway" (Epistle).

The chosen people, the Israelites, provide a third example of the preparation we should make for Easter. The thought of our baptism and of the Holy Eucharist dominates the Easter cycle, which we are now beginning. But the liturgy warns us to remember that the chosen people, too, had a baptism and a Eucharist. They "were all under the cloud, and all passed through the sea, and all in Moses were baptized, in the cloud and in the sea; and did all eat the same spiritual food, and all drank the same spiritual drink (and they drank of the spiritual rock that followed them; and the rock was Christ). But with most of them God was not well pleased" (Epistle). Only a small remnant of the chosen people reached the Holy Land. The majority of them were unfaithful to God in spite of their baptism and the heavenly manna. Woe be to us if we should prove unworthy of our baptism and of the Holy Eucharist. Even the most holy things can be misused.

"Every one that striveth for the mastery refraineth himself from all things." That should also be our program at the beginning of Lent. Why must we give up everything? That Christ the conqueror may conquer again in us and have the honor that is His due. We must reject everything and purify ourselves, so that nothing may hamper Christ's work in us. We die, and yet we live. We must die to all sin and to all willful imperfections. We must abandon all desires and thoughts that are not in conformity with God's holy will. We must die to our own will in order that the will and the spirit of Christ may dominate us completely. This is what the holy season of Lent wishes to accomplish in us. Are we prepared to sacrifice everything? "Know you not that they that run in the race, all run indeed, but one receiveth the prize?" (Epistle.)

Only "one receiveth the prize." This one is Christ, the conqueror of sin and death. We shall win only in so far as we are united to Him as members of His mystical body. Living in union with Him, making use of this strength, we, too, shall conquer. That He may triumph in His members He must live in us and we in Him. In the Holy Sacrifice of the Mass today we shall enter more fully into His life and He into ours. In Him we shall receive the prize, the possession of eternal life.

Prayer

Thou art a helper in due time in tribulation; let them trust in Thee that know Thee, for Thou hast not forsaken them that seek Thee, O Lord. For the poor man shall not be forgotten to the end; the patience of the poor shall not perish forever; arise, O Lord, let no man prevail (Gradual).

Graciously hear, we beseech Thee, O Lord, the prayers of Thy people, that we who are justly afflicted for our sins, may mercifully be freed for the glory of Thy name. Through Christ our Lord. Amen. (Collect.)

Monday

"Go you also into My vineyard" (Gospel). Where were we idling before He called us into His vineyard? The lessons at Matins answer this question for us; during the week following Septuagesima Sunday, they relate the story of creation and of Original Sin. We see the effects of Original Sin and of separation from God, in which state we should have remained had not God called us into His vineyard.

"The serpent was more subtle than any of the beasts of the earth.... And he said to the woman: Why hath God commanded you that you should not eat of every tree of Paradise? And the woman answered him, saying: Of the fruit of the trees that are in Paradise we do eat; but of the fruit of the tree which is in the midst of Paradise God hath commanded us that we should not eat, and that we should not touch it lest perhaps we die. And the serpent said to the woman: No, you shall not die the death. For God doth know that in what day soever you shall eat thereof, your eyes shall be opened; and you shall be as Gods, knowing good and evil. And the woman saw that the tree was good to eat and fair to the eyes, and delightful to behold; and she took of the fruit thereof, and did eat, and gave to her husband, who did eat" (Gn 3:1–6).

This action of our first parents was fatal. The serpent had made a true but tragic prophecy. "Your eyes shall be opened." Eve toyed with temptation. She believed the tempter and violated the commandment of God. She preferred her pride, her disobedience, her own will, to that of God.

"And the Lord God called Adam, and said to him: Where art thou?... Thou hast eaten of the tree whereof I commanded thee that thou shouldst not eat. And Adam said: The woman, whom Thou gavest me to be my companion, gave me of the tree and I did eat. And the Lord God said to the woman: Why hast thou done this?... I will multiply thy sorrows and thy conceptions; in sorrow shalt thou bring forth children, and thou shalt be under thy husband's power, and he shall have dominion over thee. And He said to Adam: Because thou hast harkened to the voice of thy wife, and hast eaten of the tree whereof I commanded thee that thou shouldst not eat, cursed is the earth in thy work. With labor and toil shalt thou eat thereof, all the days of thy life. Thorns and thistles shall it bring forth to thee; and thou shalt eat the herbs of the earth. In the sweat of thy face shalt thou eat bread till thou return to the earth out of which thou wast taken; for dust thou art and to dust thou shalt return" (Gn 3:9 ff.). Severe punishment! Adam was cast out of Paradise and condemned to a life of toil and suffering, and in the end to a bitter death. And what of the eternity that was to follow this death?

Sin means a separation from God, a desertion of God and His law; it is the setting of our will against His. Sin means so many things. It means preferring a created good to the uncreated God, a momentary pleasure to a divine love. I place my own whim before God's will; God receives second place.

Today we unite ourselves with all sinful mankind and say in its name and for its intention the prayer at the Introit of the Mass: "The sorrows of death surrounded me, the sorrows of hell encompassed me" (Introit).

Woe to us should the Master of the vineyard fail to visit the market place and invite us to labor in His vineyard, if He should fail to call us to membership in His holy Church. How thankful we should be today that He has already called us! In order to show our gratitude, we should labor faithfully in His vineyard and do His will in all things.

"In my affliction I called upon the Lord, and He heard my voice from His holy temple" (Introit). Thus we approach the altar today and take the precious body and blood of Christ in our hands and offer them to the heavenly Father: Father for the sake of Thy Son, have mercy, pardon our sins, and restore us to grace. "Make Thy face to shine upon Thy servant," upon Thy Church, upon all mankind, "and save me in Thy mercy" (Communion). "If Thou, O Lord, wilt mark iniquities, O Lord who shall abide it?" (Tract.)

Prayer

Out of the depths I have cried to Thee, O Lord; Lord hear my voice. Let Thy ears be attentive to the prayer of Thy servant. (Tract.)

Graciously hear, we beseech Thee, O Lord, the prayers of Thy people, that we who are justly afflicted for our sins, may mercifully be freed for the glory of Thy name. Through Christ our Lord. Amen. (Collect.)

Tuesday

"Go you also into My vineyard" (Gospel). In the vineyard of the Lord you will find work enough to occupy you for the rest of your life, if you will only do the work.

God calls us first of all to work in the garden of our own soul. Sanctify and save thy soul. "For what doth it profit a man if he gain the whole world and suffer the loss of his own soul?" (Mt 16:26.) Let us look first to the salvation of our own soul, our one immortal soul. All other tasks must give way and be subservient to this one all-important duty. Our first thought should always be: "My soul and eternity." We are occupied with many things. A continual round of duties claims our attention, and we live in continual unrest and haste. Our life is one continuous succession of projects, schemes, plans, books, and formulas without end and without measure. Yet we find no time for our soul, for self-examination, or for a restful quarter of an hour before the tabernacle. We are too busy for mental prayer or for a quiet moment with God. We have no time for the urgent work in the vineyard of the Lord, where we were to acquire virtue and free our soul from its vices. O ye of little faith! The Son of God becomes man, dies upon the cross, founds His Church, establishes the sacraments, and lives continually in the tabernacle. All this He has done for us and for the salvation of our souls. All His thoughts are concentrated on this task. "Seek ye therefore first the kingdom of God and His justice, and all these things shall be added unto you" (Mt 6:33). Christ lives in us. He draws us to Himself with promises, with trials, with consolations, and He seeks to make us share His work and live united to Him. He has really only one objective — the salvation of our soul. What are we doing to cooperate with Him?

God calls us to labor in the vineyard of the Church. The heart of Jesus is the center of the world. By the fire of its all-consuming and life-giving love, He unites all hearts in one. He fills up the great void between Himself and the heart that abandons itself to Him. Through the medium of the Sacred Heart of Jesus, Christian hearts communicate their light and their love to one another, and maintain a loving contact with one another. They live for one another, they bear each other's burdens, and share their riches and virtue. Such is the communion of saints. What one accomplishes in the vineyard of his own soul, he accomplishes in the souls of others, in the souls of his brothers and sisters.

"Go you also into My vineyard." We are invited to share in the redemption of the souls of our brothers and sisters. We are urged to share with our neighbor the strength, the life, and the spirit that Christ has infused into our souls. "You are the light of the world" (Mt 5:14). He who labors faithfully in the vineyard of Christ for the salvation of his own soul, labors also for the souls of others who are members of the kingdom of Christ. The rose that adorns itself adorns also the garden in which it grows. The same is true in the order of grace. Nothing is ever lost. I have in me the power to bring about the salvation or ruin of the world. I must of necessity either contribute to the edification of the world, or I will be a scandal to it. He who fails to edify scandalizes. Either I must live the life of grace and practice virtue, and then I live for the whole, or I am sick, blind, and lame, and then I am a burden on society, a hindrance exposing the whole to the danger of ruin. I am either a servant of God or a menial of Satan. There can be no neutrality in the life of grace. I am responsible, not only for my own virtue, but for the virtue of others also. Thus we see how vast is the vineyard in which Christ has invited us to work. He has given me a task of great importance to accomplish. Have I given serious thought to my obligations?

"Go you also into My vineyard." Septuagesima cries out to me to bestir myself. It charges me to be a true soldier and commands me to work harder than before. Such faithful service I owe to God, who has called me. I owe it to my own soul, and to each and every one of my fellow men.

Behold those who strive for the mastery in the arena. They withhold themselves from all things harmful. We have a crown of much greater value to strive for. Consider the disposition of St. Paul, "I so fight, not as one beating the air; but I chastise my body and bring it into subjection lest perhaps when I have preached to others, I myself should become a castaway" (Epistle). Do

I dare act otherwise? "If any man will come after Me, let him deny himself and take up his cross and follow Me" (Mt 16:24).

PRAYER

O God our refuge and our strength, be attentive to the prayers of Thy Church, and grant that we may seek the things that are of God, and serve Thee in body and soul. Through Christ our Lord. Amen.

Wednesday

"The kingdom of heaven is like to an householder, who went out early in the morning to hire laborers into his vineyard" (Gospel). At the third, the sixth, and the ninth hour he returns to the market place in search of laborers. At the eleventh hour, that is, at the time of the New Covenant, he called us. "Why stand you here all the day idle?... Go you also into my vineyard," we are told in the Gospel on Septuagesima Sunday.

The first call. The householder, the heavenly Father, calls us to labor in His vineyard early in the morning, that is, in our youth. At the time of our baptism He said to us, "Go you also into My vineyard." He enclosed us in His holy vineyard, the Church, and set us to work. "Thou shalt love the Lord thy God with thy whole heart and with thy whole soul and with thy whole mind and thy whole strength" (Mk 12:30). "I am the Lord thy God,... thou shalt not have strange gods before Me" (Ex 20:2 f.). We have declared ourselves ready to serve Him. We have entered into a solemn agreement to obey God, to observe His commandments, to promote His honor and glory, and to extend His kingdom. We are obliged to deny ourselves, to labor for Him, to pray to Him, to suffer for Him, and to fight for Him. We should use our hands only to execute His will, our tongue only to speak what He wills. Our feet must carry us only to those places where He would have us be. Our hearts should love Him alone. All our strength, our powers, our talents, should be consecrated to His service. He will allow us no other gods. We have the duty to give up our own will and to live for Him alone. We must forsake our own desires and plans and preferences. He must be our whole life. We are on earth for only one reason — to know God, to love Him, and to serve Him. That is our calling.

The second call. With Septuagesima Sunday we enter the Easter cycle. The center of this division of the Church year is the resurrection of Christ on Easter morning and our resurrection from sin through baptism. Our preparation for Easter is the renewal of our baptism, which should bring us a new and more perfect realization of the importance of the call we have received and of the value of the precious gifts that came to us at baptism. It should renew and deepen our consciousness also of the obligations we have undertaken. It should make us ask ourselves seriously whether we have been faithful to these obligations. "I am the Lord Thy God,... thou shalt not have strange gods before Me." Have we accomplished the task for which we were called into the vineyard? Could God still not say to us with truth: "Why stand you here all the day idle?" Why are you occupied with so many vain and useless things? Why do you serve so many false gods? Why are you so covetous of gold, solicitous for your body and for its comforts? Why are you chasing so many vain shadows? Why are you so eager to enjoy the esteem of others? Why are you so desirous of honor and of the empty glamour and show of the world? Why are you so careless of sin and so insistent on your own will and your own ambitions? The householder comes out to call us again today. Today we again renew our contract with God. From this day forward we shall serve more faithfully and more zealously Him into whose vineyard we have been called.

At the Offertory of the Mass we place on the paten our will and the promise of a more faithful service. "I will love Thee, O Lord, my strength. The Lord is my firmament, my refuge, and my deliverer" (Introit). "It is good to give praise to the Lord, and to sing to Thy name, O Most High" (Offertory). But our praise must be not merely a lip service. Our life, our works, and our service must also be worthy of Him. We should seek nothing for ourselves, but everything for Him. With this disposition we begin the Holy Sacrifice today.

The reward, the penny promised us, is given in Holy Communion. "He that eateth My flesh and drinketh My blood, hath everlasting life, and I will raise him up in the last day" (Jn 6:55). We shall be awakened to the perfect life in heaven. This is the reward we seek by our labor in the vineyard of the Lord. "Many are called, but few chosen" (Gospel). Only a few are found worthy of their vocation. I am determined to be among those few, cost what it will.

Prayer

May Thy faithful people, O God, be strengthened by Thy gifts; that in receiving them, they may seek after them the more, and in seeking them, may receive them forever. Through Christ our Lord. Amen. (Postcommunion.)

Thursday

We stand now on the threshold of Easter. Our eyes contemplate the mystery of Christ's passion and resurrection, of the darkness of Good Friday and the brilliance of Easter morning. In the suffering and the triumph of St. Lawrence we acknowledge with the liturgy the dominion of Christ. We pray in the Introit: "The sorrows of death surrounded me, the sorrows of hell encompassed me; and in my affliction I called upon the Lord, and He heard my voice from His holy temple."

"The sorrows of death surrounded me." These words apply to Christ in His suffering. We accompany Him on His sorrowful journey to the Mount of Olives. We are to witness the terrible agony that caused Him to break out in a bloody sweat. "Father, if it be possible, let this chalice pass from Me. Nevertheless, not as I will, but as Thou wilt" (Mt 26:39). We accompany Him also to the hall of judgment and stand with Him before the Sanhedrin. We are present, too, when He is dragged before Pilate, the pagan judge. We contemplate His terrible suffering at the pillar, and see Him crowned with thorns and derided by the Roman soldiers. With heavy hearts we follow His bloody footprints on the way of the cross, and share His agony as He hangs in torture for three hours on the cross. "The sorrows of death surrounded me, the sorrows of hell encompassed me."

"In my affliction I called upon the Lord, and He heard my voice," Christ cried out in His struggle. Thou art "a helper in due time, in tribulation; ... for Thou hast not forsaken them that seek Thee" (Gradual). On Easter morning He will rise in glory. He has won the reward of victory: resurrection and glorification. He has conquered Satan, sin, and death. Now He possesses dominion over our spirits and over our hearts. Since He became obedient unto death, "God also hath exalted Him and hath given Him a name which is above all names: that in the name of Jesus every knee should bow, of those that are in heaven, on earth, and under the earth: and that every tongue should confess that the Lord Jesus is in the glory of God the Father" (Phil 2:9–11). "I called upon the Lord, and He heard my voice."

Christ the Lord is the head that directs the body, the vine that nourishes the branches. He lives in us who are His members. By reason of our baptism we share His life with all its vicissitudes. While He is on earth, He remains the suffering and struggling Redeemer, and He renews His passions and trials in us. We are in a real sense His body and members of His body. The experiences of His physical body must now be repeated in us. By virtue of our baptism we are called to relive His life, to share His sufferings and exertions, to participate in His resurrection and glorification. Christ lives in me. I can do all things in Him who lives within me.

Today as we attend Mass we witness the renewal of the mystery of His death and resurrection on our altar. We will not allow Him to undertake this renewal alone. We unite ourselves to Him and resolve to make ourselves a holocaust to the Father. We resign our claim to all things: to our will, our earthly possessions, our health, our strength, our body, our soul, and all that we possess. All this we place on the paten with the altar bread, as a pure and holy offering to the Father. We die, but we arise again when He comes to us in Holy Communion to fill us with His life and His strength. Supported by His strength we go forth to meet the tasks of the day, to "fight the good fight of faith" (1 Tm 6:12). We call out to the Lord and He hears us. We shall conquer, and we shall win the crown.

Prayer

Graciously hear, we beseech Thee, O Lord, the prayers of Thy people, that we who are justly afflicted for our sins, may mercifully be freed for the glory of Thy name. Through Christ our Lord. Amen.

Friday

"I therefore so run, not as at an uncertainty; I so fight, not as one beating the air" (Epistle). St. Paul, who here also speaks to us, knows what he is working for. He is conscious of his aim, and that aim is the winning of an imperishable crown. He is determined that nothing shall prevent his obtaining it.

"I believe in life everlasting." This eternal life is our objective. This life will be the rest due to the weary soldier after battle. It is the possession of every good that the heart of man could desire, the possession of the highest and most desirable good conceived by the spirit and heart of man. The crown we shall win is an imperishable crown, not a mere perishable wreath. It will be the possession of complete inner happiness and an abode of bliss. Our crown shall be the clear vision of the living God, and a sharing of His divine life and of that of the glorified Christ. It is the being honored by God and by all the inhabitants of heaven, both men and angels. This crown we shall possess, not for one brief moment, but for all eternity. It is the perfection of the entire man, the perfection of his will, his heart, his strength, his character, and his personality, which has an inborn capacity for enjoying the company of God and the saints. Is not this reward worth the striving? Should we not put aside everything that does not help us to win this crown? "Every one that striveth for the mastery refraineth himself from all things" (Epistle).

"Bodily exercise is profitable to little, but godliness is profitable to all things, having promise of the life that now is and of that which is to come" (1 Tm 4:8). Godliness gives promise of a reward even in this life. The reward of virtue in this life is a perfect soul, which knows but one law: the will and honor and glory of God. Its perfection consists in nothing more than perfect conformity to the will of God. It seeks but one thing, and that is to do what is pleasing to God. When such a soul is persuaded that a certain task is the will of God, nothing is too difficult for it. It sets about its work without haste, without anxiety, undisturbed and confident in the possession of God. Come what will, it seeks only to do the will of God though men oppose it on all sides. It has only one rule — the will of God. It fears the loss of nothing but the approval of God. It is prepared at all times to sacrifice its harmless and well-intentioned pleasures, the occupations to which it is attached, and even that to which most men cling passionately, the hope of reaping the fruit of the seed they have sown. Such a soul conducts itself with equanimity in all undertakings and sufferings, in honor or in disgrace, in success or in failure, when praised or when condemned; yes, even when it has actually made a mistake, the attitude of such a soul does not change. It is attached to its own works, of course, but the honor of God comes before all these. It is good to every man, and prizes truth and virtue above all else. It offers correction without bitterness, but speaks the truth without respect to persons. It weeps with the sorrowful and rejoices with those that rejoice. It fulfills the commandments faithfully, but is not slavishly attached to them. It is prepared at every moment to forsake anything and everything for the love of God, and to fulfill the will of God. It is delighted with every opportunity to work and sacrifice to accomplish the will of God. Having found God, it has found itself and true freedom of spirit. "So shall it be in the soul; God's will is accomplished in it. God gives Himself to the soul, and the soul gives itself to God. All other desires are put aside" (Mechtilde of Magdeburg).

The childlike spirit which God develops in such a soul, drives out all fear, all uneasiness and severity. A wonderful peace of soul is one of the rewards of virtue even here on earth. This peace elevates the soul above the restlessness and turmoil of the world. It is a peace that pervades the soul to its very depths, and in this peace God alone dwells. A soul which has obtained this peace desires nothing else, and complains of nothing. This peace tempers all suffering, controls the inordinate wandering of our minds, strengthens the will, and protects the soul in all its vicissitudes. Whatever life brings, the soul accepts as coming from God and as a manifestation of His love. The reward of virtue is reaped already in this life.

But there can be no victory without a struggle. The kingdom of God is not for the lazy, the indolent, the sentimental, the timid lovers of ease. It has place only for those who are prepared to fight. Those who would belong to it must fight for that which is heavenly against that which is earthly, for the light against the darkness, for Christ against Belial.

He who would win the crown of victory must have courage. Only those who have the courage to deny themselves and endure hard things will win this crown. They must be prepared to reject all that is contrary to Christ and His law. They must disengage their hearts from self-will, from all that is transitory, from all that threatens to separate them from God.

PRAYER

Hear us, we beseech Thee, O Lord: cleanse our hearts and grant us Thy grace. Through Christ our Lord. Amen.

Saturday

"Every one that striveth for the mastery refraineth himself from all things.... I therefore so run, not as at an uncertainty; I so fight, not as one beating the air; but I chastise my body and bring it into subjection, lest perhaps when I have preached to others, I myself should become a castaway" (Epistle). The season that precedes Lent and the lenten season itself are seasons for serious and earnest self-denial. Even St. Paul feared that he might be lost should he fail to practice mortifications and bring his spirit into submission.

"If any man will come after Me, let him deny himself" (Mt 16:24). No man in this world is so perfect that he can afford to neglect self-denial; that is, no man can afford to neglect the task of subjecting his senses and his passions to his will. No one has the garden of his soul so thoroughly cleansed of weeds that it needs no further weeding. Scarcely has a person finished his work before the weeds spring up again. A man never reaches so great a height of perfection in this world that he destroys the roots of sin. For this reason there can never be any secure virtue unless it is accompanied by true self-denial. He who has not gained control over his self-will, can never practice perfect obedience. He who has not brought his passions firmly under the control of his will, can never practice perfect chastity. No man can practice fraternal charity and love even his enemies unless he has first overcome himself and mortified his own desires. Self-denial is especially necessary for those who seek to practice virtue. "You will progress in virtue in the measure in which you gain control of yourself."[9] Why do we remain stationary so long in one degree of perfection? Why are we so lacking in strength and initiative? It is simply because we fail in self-denial. Without mortification we can have no taste for meditation, no fervor in prayer, no strength in the face of temptation, no power of resistance to the seduction of the flesh, and finally, no true virtue. Therefore, "If any man will come after Me, let him deny himself."

"I say then: Walk in the spirit, and you shall not fulfill the lusts of the flesh. For the flesh lusteth against the spirit, and the spirit against flesh; for these are contrary one to another; so that you do not the things that you would.... Now the works of the flesh are manifest, which are fornication, uncleanness, immodesty, luxury, idolatry, witchcrafts, enmities, contentions, emulations, wraths, quarrels, dissensions, sects.... They who do such things shall not obtain the kingdom of God. But the fruit of the spirit is charity, joy, peace, patience, benignity, goodness, longanimity, mildness, faith, modesty, continency, chastity" (Gal 5:16 ff.).

"Walk in the spirit." On this principle our mortification should be grounded. If we walk in the spirit, we shall be able to free our fallen nature from the domination of our inordinate passions and regulate it according to grace. By means of mortification we subject our lower

[9] *Imitation of Christ*, bk.1, chap. 25.

nature to the spirit. Mortification is a powerful remedy for the weaknesses and ills of the spirit. It is indispensable as a means of acquiring perfection and union with God. "And they that are Christ's, have crucified their flesh with the vices and concupiscences" (Gal 5:24). Can this be said of the followers of Christ today? Very few of them prize mortification, and most of them flee from it. Are we, then, still really Christians?

In the prelenten season and during Lent, the liturgy centers our attention on mortification and self-denial. Daily it calls to our attention in the Preface for Lent the value of mortification: "By the fasting of the body Thou dost curb our vices, elevate our minds, and bestow virtue and reward." Do we live according to this principle? The mortification urged by the liturgy is required, not merely of great sinners, penitents, novices, and newly ordained priests, but even of those advanced in virtue; those advanced in age also need mortification both of body and mind. These, too, need to mortify their pride and self-will, their unruly passions, their dissatisfaction, their bitterness, and their self-seeking. Even those advanced in age and virtue daily experience how prone the human spirit is to evil. Age is no protection against foolishness or temptation; for temptation follows us always, and even an old man may easily fall unless he unceasingly practices self-control by all manner of mortification. "We suffer with Him [Christ] that we may be also glorified with Him" (Rom 8:17). We die in order to live. Without death through mortification during Lent, there can be no resurrection at Easter, or eternal life.

Prayer

We beseech Thee, O Lord, graciously to hear our prayers. Deliver us from our sins; protect us from all evil. Through Christ our Lord. Amen.

Sexagesima Sunday

The Mass

The stational church for Sexagesima Sunday is St. Paul's in Rome. St. Paul speaks today for the assembled faithful. Their needs are his needs, their griefs his griefs, their cries his cries. He has experienced in his own person all the bitterness and weakness and the sufferings of the Church, and here where we are assembled today he allows us to share his struggles again with him.

"Arise, why sleepest Thou, O Lord? Arise and cast us not off to the end" (Introit; Ps. 43:23). O suffering Church of Christ! Psalm 43 recounts for us the wonders and miracles God worked on behalf of His people; it relates His intervention and the destruction of their powerful enemies. Today His people cry out, "Our belly hath cleaved to the earth" (Introit). Yes, O Lord, Thou dost lift Thy eyes to behold Thy children, the children born to Thee in baptism, nurtured and raised for God, and instructed in holy wisdom. Thou hast healed their wounds with Thy holy sacraments and nourished them with the Holy Eucharist. In these days of licentiousness, when men dance and sing, when the world is steeped in materialism and sensuality, and nations live at enmity with God and His Christ, Thou standest before us as before so many living corpses. In so many of Thy children Thou cleavest to the earth.

"Arise, why sleepest Thou, O Lord?" A sincere cry for mercy rises from the bosom of the Church. Oh, that the world had the grace of understanding the words of St. Paul, around whose tomb the faithful are assembled today! St. Paul tells us that he who would serve Christ must undergo hardships of all kinds, and be prepared to fight the good fight for Christ. He must not expect to find his way to Christ by an easy way, but by way of hardships, self-denial, toil, patience in suffering, fidelity under temptation, and in an unwavering reliance on supernatural grace. What would Paul have been without his sufferings, his chains, and his martyrdom? But where would he have found strength to endure these things except in the all-powerful help from above? (Gradual.)

But grace alone is not enough. Grace must fall on good ground to be fruitful, on ground such as the soul of Paul. When the seed of enlightenment of the spirit and of the guidance of the will falls by the wayside, it is trampled upon and destroyed. When it falls on stony ground, it can strike no root and will wither away. When it falls among thorns, the tender shoots will be strangled. Only when the seed falls on good ground can it bring forth fruit (Gospel). How many there are who belong to the church, who are immersed in a veritable sea of grace, and yet bring forth no fruit! Is this because God fails to give them the seed of grace? No, indeed; it is the earth that is found wanting, not the seed.

It behooves us therefore to follow in the footsteps of the blessed apostle Paul, in the way of voluntary self-denial and penance. We should detach our heart from all earthly things and from all unnecessary occupations. We shall prove fruitful ground only if we devote ourselves entirely to Christ and His interests. We should crucify our vices by earnest works of Christian mortification, that having cast out the old man, we may live a new life in union with God. We shall then bring forth fruit a hundredfold when Christ unites Himself to us in Holy Communion and fills us with His life and His strength. "He that abideth in Me and I in him, the same beareth much fruit; for without Me you can do nothing" (Jn 15:5).

This new life itself is the seed for the bearing of another fruit, the fruit of eternal union with God. In that life our resurrection will be to a life of unending bliss, an eternal Easter in heaven. But as yet "our belly hath cleaved to the earth." "O Lord, arise and cast us not off to the end.... Help us and deliver us" (Introit) now in the Mass and Communion and again when we shall "go in to the altar of God [in heaven], to God who giveth joy to my youth" in the resurrection of eternal life (Communion).

Meditation

Today we celebrate the Holy Sacrifice of the Mass at the tomb of the great Apostle of the Gentiles, Paul. Today he becomes a type of the Church. He is persecuted and tried on all sides, and yet he is filled with the strength of Christ, "for power is made perfect in infirmity" (Epistle).

"Our belly hath cleaved to the earth.... Arise, why sleepest Thou, O Lord" (Introit). That is the cry of unredeemed mankind. It is likewise the prayer of the Church militant although it is now redeemed. However, even as Christ, the head of the Church, was not exempt from suffering during His earthly life, neither are His members exempt from suffering. The Epistle gives us a picture of the suffering Church in the sufferings of the Apostle. We see in St. Paul the suffering priests and the suffering faithful. He suffered many things, "in many more labors, in prisons more frequently, in stripes above measure, in deaths often." He was "in perils of robbers, in perils from my own nation, in perils from the Gentiles, ... in perils from false brethren; in labor and painfulness, in much watching, in hunger and thirst, in fastings often, in cold and nakedness" (Epistle). Thus, too, the Church must suffer. She is contradicted, slandered, misrepresented, and persecuted by those outside her fold. She suffers much from her own children also. Many of her priests prove unfaithful; her princes and her religious often fail her; her children are often given to bitter and unjust criticism, to distrust and worldliness. We feel her suffering and grief when she cries out to God today, "Arise, why sleepest Thou, O Lord? Arise and cast us not off to the end. Why turnest Thou Thy face away and forgettest our trouble? Our belly hath cleaved to the earth; arise, O Lord, help us and deliver us" (Introit). We cannot free ourselves or raise ourselves from the earth because we are so weak and wayward and helpless.

"Thou hast moved the earth, O Lord, and hast troubled it. Heal Thou the breaches thereof, for it has been moved" (Tract). These breaches are the sufferings and struggles of the Church and her children on earth. These sufferings are part of the plan of God. They are trials through which He purifies His Church. Through these sufferings, trials, temptations, and humiliations, the earth (the Christian soul) is "moved" and troubled. God takes the soul in His strong hands, shakes and moves it until it is prepared to admit its own helplessness and worthlessness. Now it will recognize and declare its abject poverty and unworthiness. Once it has made this acknowledgment, it is prepared to receive the good seed. From this point on it attempts nothing of itself, but depends on God for grace and on the love of Christ for everything. The seed that God sows in the humbled and troubled soul falls on good ground. The souls that receive this seed "in a good and perfect heart ... bring forth fruit in patience" (Gospel). The strength of Christ is perfected through the weakness of humanity. The soul is prepared for receiving the strength of Christ by the recognition of its own weakness and unworthiness.

Having been humiliated by the hand of God through suffering and labor, the soul is exalted. The more it is torn, and the more thorough and complete this humiliation, and the more docile the soul is under the hand of God: the deeper the seed of grace sinks into it, and the more fruitful it becomes. The Church and the truly Christian soul is therefore thankful for the trials that come from the hand of God. The blood of martyrs is still the seed of the Church. Salvation still comes through the cross. It is still true, as our Lord tells us, that "he that humbleth himself shall be exalted" (Lk 14:11). St. Peter, too, urges us: "Be you humbled, therefore, under the mighty hand of God, that He may exalt you in the time of visitation" (1 Pt 5:6). The secret of the vigor and growth of the Church may be found in humiliations, sufferings, and trials which God allows to overtake her. The more she is tried, the deeper she becomes rooted in Christ, and the greater becomes her ability to triumph over all difficulties. What is true of the Church is true of each individual soul. This is the teaching of the liturgy. "Every branch in Me that beareth not fruit He will take away; and every one that beareth fruit He will purge it that it may bring forth more fruit" (Jn 15:2).

Christ comes to us in the Holy Sacrifice and at the time of Holy Communion. He sows His seed in our soul. In the soil of the soul that has been prepared to receive it by humiliation and suffering, the seed sown by Christ will bring forth rich fruit. "Power is made perfect in infirmity (Epistle). But this is true only if the soul submits to the trials and sufferings that God sends it.

These sufferings are profitable only for the soul that embraces them willingly and receives them blindly from the hand of God with complete and perfect confidence in His providence. If we are wanting in faith and confidence in God, these visitations will fail in their purpose.

God influences the Church and the souls of men in various ways, but the one He uses most frequently is that of inflicting suffering from within and from without. No other method has proved so fruitful for the Church and for souls. God sends sufferings to His Church and to souls precisely because He loves them. He must send them trials if they are to grow strong, become perfect, and bear fruit. "Thou hast moved the earth, O Lord." Only when the Lord has moved it can the earth (the soul) become fruitful.

"Perfect Thou my goings in Thy paths, that my footsteps be not moved. Incline Thy ear and hear my words. Show forth Thy wonderful mercies, Thou who savest them that trust in Thee" (Offertory). With this prayer we surrender ourselves to the strength of Christ which flows from the Mass. The weakness of men will be perfected by the strength of Christ. Sharing the strength of Christ, the Church and the soul of the Christian will be faithful in the way of the Lord. Christ gives the soul a new life (Secreta), holy joy (Communion), and a devout way of life (Postcommunion). That is the substance of our thoughts and prayers as we celebrate the liturgy today.

Prayer

O God, who seest that we put not our trust in anything that we do of ourselves; mercifully grant that by the protection of the Doctor of the Gentiles, we may be defended against all adversities. Through Christ our Lord. Amen.

Monday

The lessons read at Matins during this week relate the story of the Deluge. During the whole week the liturgy dwells on the terrible judgment passed by God on sinful mankind.

"And after that men began to be multiplied upon the earth and daughters were born to them. The sons of God [the descendants of God-fearing Seth], seeing the daughters of men [the descendants of Cain] that they were fair, took to themselves wives of all which they chose.... And God, seeing that the wickedness of men was great on the earth and that all the thought of their heart was bent upon evil at all times, it repented Him that He had made man on the earth" (Gn 6:1 ff.).

God then considered destroying man, but He waited patiently for one hundred and twenty years. He commanded Noe to build an ark which could be seen by all men, and charged him to tell them that God would destroy the world should men fail to give up their evil ways. Erring men had only ridicule and derision for Noe, his ark, and his fantastic story. God then carried out the threat He had made. "And the flood was forty days upon the earth, and the waters increased and lifted up the ark on high from the earth. For they overflowed exceedingly; and filled all on the face of the earth, and the ark was carried upon the waters. And the waters prevailed beyond measure upon the earth; and all the high mountains under the whole heaven were covered.... And all flesh was destroyed that moved upon the earth, both of fowl, and of cattle, and of beasts, and of all creeping things that creep upon the earth; and all men.... And Noe only remained and they that were with him in the ark" (Gn 7:17 ff.). God will not be mocked. "But except you do penance, you shall all likewise perish" (Lk 13:5).

Salvation can be found only in the Ark, in Christ. The normal approach to Christ is through the Church, which is the body of Christ. Only if we associate ourselves with the Church can we share in the redemption and obtain salvation. "No one can have God for his Father who does not have the Church for his mother" (St. Cyprian). The same saint compares the Church to the ark of Noe. Only he who enters the Church can be saved. Only those who are guided by the infallible authority of the Church, who are submissive to her teachings, and who make use of her sacraments with faith and humility, can escape eternal death.[10] "Amen I say to you, whatsoever you shall bind upon earth, shall be bound also in heaven; and whatsoever you shall loose upon earth, shall be loosed also in heaven" (Mt 18:18). "He that heareth you heareth Me; and he that despiseth you despiseth Me; and he that despiseth Me despiseth Him that sent Me" (Lk 10:16). Salvation is only in the Ark, in the Church of God.

"And all the thought of their heart was bent upon evil at all times." We all know from our own past experiences how terrible and how persistent is the power of sin in man. With St. Paul we may all say: "For I know that there dwelleth not in me, that is to say, in my flesh, that which is good. For to will is present with me; but to accomplish that which is good, I find not. For the good which I will, I do not; but the evil which I will not, that I do. Now if I do that which I will not, it is no more I that do it, but sin that dwelleth in me. I find then a law, that when I have a will to do good, evil is present with me.... But I see another law in my members, fighting against the law of my mind, and captivating me in the law of sin, that is in my members" (Rom 7:18 ff.).

We should acknowledge our inborn perversity with all humility and fight against the roots of evil that are embedded in our soul. "Unhappy man that I am, who shall deliver me from the body of this death? The grace of God, by Jesus Christ our Lord" (Rom 7:24 f.). We shall seek this grace, then, in our Lord Jesus Christ, through His holy Church. In this Ark we shall find salvation.

"Unless you shall do penance, you shall all likewise perish" (Lk 13:3). The Deluge was a punishment sent by God because of sin and man's impenitence. "Delay not to be converted to the Lord, and defer it not from day to day" (Ecclus 5:8). "Knowest thou not that the benignity of God leadeth thee to penance? But according to thy hardness and impenitent heart, thou treasurest up to thyself wrath, against the day of wrath, and revelation of the just judgment of God" (Rom 2:4 f.). In the name of the whole sinful race we cry out in the Introit of today's Mass: "Arise and cast us not off to the end. Why turnest Thou Thy face away and forgettest our trouble?... Arise, O Lord, help us and deliver us." Let us not become the victims of sin. Give to each of us the grace to perform sincere and adequate penance.

Today we thank God that he has called us, unworthy as we are, into His Ark, the Church, in which we shall most certainly be saved.

[10] However, the grace of God is not restricted. Pope Pius IX, while reiterating the traditional teaching, "Outside the Roman Church no one can be saved," nevertheless adds: "It must likewise be held as certain that those who live in ignorance of the true religion, if it is invincible, are guilty of no fault in this matter before the eyes of God" (Denzinger, no. 1647). –Fr. Malone

Prayer

O God, who seest that we put not our trust in anything that we do of ourselves; mercifully grant that by the protection of the Doctor of the Gentiles, we may be defended against all adversities. Through Christ our Lord. Amen.

Tuesday

The stational church for Sexagesima Sunday is the basilica of St. Paul in Rome. We assemble there in the house of the holy Apostle and feel ourselves united to him in the closest fellowship as "companions of the saints." He is filled with the spirit of Christ, burning with zeal for Christ, and prepared to undergo all sufferings and hardships for Him (Epistle).

"I know a man in Christ" (Epistle). This man is St. Paul himself. We are amazed when we read today his account of the sufferings and labors he undertook to win souls to Christ. He has suffered in many labors, in frequent imprisonment, from abuse without measure; often in danger of death, five times he was beaten with rods. Once he was stoned, three times he suffered shipwreck; his travels were endless; he endured hunger, thirst, fastings, cold, blows, and unrelenting persecutions. This is the "man in Christ" who was "caught up into paradise and heard secret words which it is not granted to man to utter" (Epistle). To this same man is given a sting of the flesh, an angel of Satan to buffet him. "Gladly therefore will I glory in my infirmities, that the power of Christ may dwell in me." This is "a man in Christ," a man of courage, of self-sacrifice, of heroic zeal for souls. What kind of men are we? We are so weak, so querulous, so timid in our piety, so self-centered, so miserly in our dealings with God and our fellow man, so unskilled in the practice of virtue.

How has Paul acquired this breadth and profundity of holiness? He has identified himself with Christ and united himself to Him in all things. He feels the strength of Christ in his veins; Christ's aims and objectives live in him; he is inflamed with a love of Christ and of souls which gives him no rest, but drives him on to undertake all sacrifices, sufferings, and labors; and each new trial and persecution only serves to renew the fire of that love. St. Paul is no longer conscious of anything but Christ; everything else is vanity in his eyes. He has only one ambition, and that is to gain Christ and to have Christ take complete possession of him. "For to me, to live is Christ, and to die is gain" (Phil 1:21).

By baptism we too have been incorporated in Christ and have become living members of His body, the Church. "I am the vine, you the branches. He that abideth in Me and I in him, the same beareth much fruit" (Jn 15:5). By the daily reception of Holy Communion this union is intensified and perfected. In this manner the "man in Christ" is created.

The true Christian has a profound faith in his incorporation with Christ, and is sincerely grateful for the favor of having been made a branch of the vine, and for the privilege of sharing the life and strength of the vine. "I can do all things in Him who strengtheneth me," in Him whose life fills me and vitalizes me. He shares His life with me through Holy Communion.

Today we assemble in the house of St. Paul to join him in offering the Holy Sacrifice and in receiving Holy Communion, and to become like him, a "man in Christ." We return to our daily tasks and carry with us to all our undertakings the strength of St. Paul and Christ. "I can do all things in Him who strengtheneth me" (Phil 4:13).

PRAYER

O God, who seest that we put not our trust in anything that we do of ourselves; mercifully grant that by the protection of the Doctor of the Gentiles, we may be defended against all adversities. Through Christ our Lord. Amen.

Wednesday

"The sower went out to sow his seed." Three fourths of the seed will be unfruitful because it falls on barren soil. That which falls on fertile ground, however, will bring forth fruit thirtyfold, sixtyfold, and a hundredfold (Gospel).

We are dependent on the divine sower. The soil of our hearts (our spirit, our thoughts, our will) can of itself produce nothing. Of ourselves we are incapable of the least good thought or resolution, or of the smallest act of Christian virtue. "Not that we are sufficient to think anything of ourselves as of ourselves; but our sufficiency is from God" (2 Cor 3:5). "For it is God who worketh in you, both to will and to accomplish according to His good will" (Phil 2:13). We are so entirely dependent on the sower that He assures us, "Without Me you can do nothing" (Jn 15:5). Without Him we are incapable of anything but sin, and we sink in our misery as a stone sinks in water. Without His help we are as abandoned as the victims of the Deluge, of whom Holy Scripture says: "All the thought of their heart was bent upon evil at all times" (Gn 6:5). "Or what hast thou that thou hast not received? And if thou hast received, why dost thou glory as if thou hadst not received it?" (1 Cor 4:7.) We depend entirely on the divine sower to sow the seeds of good in our hearts.

The sower comes to us to sow good seed in our hearts. First of all He plants the seed of virtue by baptism, incorporating us in His mystical body, the Church. How often He has planted and replanted these seeds in our hearts! He has planted it through the word of God, which is given to us through the Church and her priesthood. He has planted again through the example of a perfect life, in the person of His own divine Son, who is placed before us as a model: "This is My beloved Son, ... hear ye Him" (Mt 17:5). He has touched our hearts with grace by means of His holy sacraments, which are the ordinary means used by God to nourish virtue. In the sacrament of baptism our soul was bathed in the redeeming blood of the Savior and cleansed from all stain of Original Sin, so that we might arise as new men reborn to a new life and the sonship of God. In the sacrament of confirmation Christ renewed His grace in us and gave us the power to grow to our full stature as children of God and heirs to the kingdom of heaven. In the sacrament of the Eucharist, He gives us his very self; His flesh and blood become our daily bread. He now no longer merely helps and strengthens us, He Himself lives within us by a true physical union of His flesh and blood with ours. He has become as close to us as a vine is to its branches. At every crucial turning point in our lives, at the moment of our greatest successes and failures, from our youth to our old age, from the moment of our baptism to our last illness, Christ is near, concealed in the Blessed Sacrament, but ever ready to sow the seed of His grace in our hearts. Oh, that we had the eyes of faith to see Him sowing His seed by whispering His divine counsel into our ear, and that we had the wisdom to profit by His advice and to heed His warnings! Would that we had the gracefulness to thank Him for His help and the wisdom to open our hearts wide so that the seed He sows might take deep root!

"At that time, when a very great multitude was gathered together and hastened out of the cities unto Jesus" (Gospel). The people mentioned in the Gospel today are these people who are assembled here today to offer up the Holy Sacrifice. We have the sower in our midst; today He will sow this good seed in our hearts through the lessons taught by the Epistle and Gospel of the Mass, through the edifying example set for us by St. Paul in the Epistle, through the example He Himself gave us by His death on the cross, and by the unbloody renewal of that death in the Mass today. He became "obedient unto death, even to the death of the cross" (Phil 2:8).

"The sower went out to sow his seed." The seed which Christ today sows in the Mass is, in the mind of the sacred liturgy, especially the Holy Eucharist, Holy Communion. This seed cannot fail to reproduce itself sixtyfold if it falls on fertile soil. Yet in the soil of our soul it so often fails to bear fruit at all. The soil has not been properly prepared. We are too preoccupied by worldly cares and burdens of our life. We are too concerned about that which is worldly and transitory and too little interested in that which is divine and eternal. Thus the soil of our soul becomes rocky ground, so hard and forbidding that the seed can strike no roots. The holy sacraments produce fruit, the Council of Trent tells us, according to our preparation and dispositions.

Prayer

Perfect Thou my goings in Thy paths, that my footsteps be not moved; incline Thy ear and hear my words; show forth Thy wonderful mercies, Thou who savest them that trust in Thee, O Lord. (Offertory.)

Thursday

Lent, the spring and seeding time of the soul, is near at hand. In the Mass and in the Holy Eucharist good seed will be sown in our soul. The divine sower strews His seed with a prodigal hand. Is the soil of our soul prepared to receive it?

"Some fell by the wayside; and it was trodden down, and the fowls of the air devoured it.... And they by the wayside are they that hear; then the devil cometh and taketh the word out of their heart" (Gospel). These are the souls which are dissipated and unmortified. They no longer have taste for anything but that which is superficial and worldly; they have abandoned the practice of recollection; they preserve no watch over their senses and over the desires and movements of their heart. They are they who hear the word of God; "then the devil cometh and taketh the word out of their heart."

"And other some fell upon a rock. And as soon as it was sprung up, it withered away because it had no moisture." This seed sprang up, but it soon withered because it could not fix its roots in the soil. These are the souls who receive the seed with good will, but as soon as they are subject to temptation or are required to make sacrifices, they weaken and submit. "In time of temptation they fall away."

"And other some fell among thorns.... And that which fell among thorns are they who have heard and, going their way, are choked with the cares and riches and pleasures of this life, and yield no fruit." The soul tends naturally toward God and earnestly receives His grace. But at the same time it is troubled by various illicit desires and the cares of its station in life; it is troubled about its past and worried about its future. It is concerned about its health, frightened by the prospect of humiliation, depressed by the injuries it has suffered, terrified by uncertainties and hardships; and amid all these trials the seed can neither strike roots nor bring forth fruit.

"I will go in to the altar of God; to God who giveth joy to my youth" (Communion). I will go to the altar of God and obtain the good seed, Holy Communion, and plant it today in the good soil of my heart. I will open wide the furrows of my soul and prepare in my heart good ground, free of stones and thorns, so that the seed may take root and bear fruit a hundredfold.

In Holy Communion, Christ gives us His flesh and blood, and with them and through them His spirit. His spirit operates in our soul and performs the same service for it that the blood performs for the body. His spirit fills us completely, and He lives in us. If we listen to His inspirations, He will soon bring us to a perfect union with Himself. Then we shall see all through the eyes of Christ and shall will what He wills. Then we shall desire only what He desires, love only what He loves. Then our heart will be one with the heart of Christ, and we shall be able to say with St. Paul, "And I live, now not I, but Christ liveth in me" (Gal 2:20). Christ then will completely occupy our heart, and we may then truly be said to be "another Christ," because of the union of His heart and soul with ours. Then we shall have lost our own life, but we shall have acquired the life of Christ. Then the prophecy of Christ will be fulfilled in us: "And I live by the Father, so he that eateth Me, the same also shall live by Me" (Jn 6:58). This is the hundredfold fruit of Holy Communion.

In order that our soul may reap this fruit, the Lord has "moved the earth" (our soul) "and hast troubled it" (Gradual) through humiliation, trials, and sufferings of all sorts. The "power [of God] is made perfect in [our] infirmity" (Epistle).

Prayer

We humbly beseech Thee, O almighty God, to grant that we who have been refreshed by Thy sacraments may so live as to do Thee worthy and acceptable service. Through Christ our Lord. Amen. (Postcommunion.)

Friday

"The sower went out to sow his seed. And as he sowed, some fell by the wayside; and it was trodden down, and the fowls of the air devoured it.... And they by the wayside are they that hear; then the devil cometh and taketh the word out of their heart" (Gospel). The devil removes the word from their heart by holding them bound by venial sins. By such sin the inspirations of grace are prevented from germinating and growing.

Deliberate venial sin ruins the soil of the soul so that it cannot bring forth abundant fruit. Such sin does not separate the soul from God, but attaches itself like a dead weight to the soul and spirit, so that a man is hindered from living for God. Such a soul is like an eagle whose wings have been clipped. Venial sin shows a neglect of God and a contempt for Him, even though such neglect and contempt are not directly intended. By such sins we set up our own will against the will of God for the sake of some desire, some need, some temporal advantage which we prefer to the command and will of God. We thereby reject the inspirations of grace by our venial sins. Then we return to seek an increase of grace and love. Will God again offer us the grace which we once rejected? Since we have already misused the grace He gave us, God is likely to be less prodigal with His grace, and we shall receive it less frequently and in smaller measure. We shall easily fall into new faults, and thus the will becomes accustomed to giving way to venial sin. Our mental powers will be darkened; our faith will be weakened; the soul will become indifferent. If we are not on our guard and if we do not make strenuous efforts at the first sign of unfaithfulness, we are in danger of becoming spiritually blind and hardened. "And as he sowed, some fell by the wayside; and it was trodden down."

Our ruin is completed by habitual venial sin. There are many pious people who murmur and criticize others and never make an effort to cure this fault, never strive earnestly against it, and never feel sorrow for having given way to it. They are disobedient in little things, impatient and uncharitable in their thoughts and in their dealings with others, untruthful in speech, lazy and indolent in their religious duties, unmortified and insolent in speech. They treat lightly the good name and the good works of others, and are not always honest in their dealings with others. They know that they have these faults and bemoan them, but they are not really sorry for them, nor do they make use of the proper means for correcting them. They are not convinced that each of these faults and imperfections is a millstone about their neck which drags them ever downward. They do not consider that they began to fall into these faults by allowing their thoughts to become worldly. They do not remember that they began by neglecting and misusing the grace that was given them. The seed that was sown was good seed, but it fell by the wayside. "I would thou wert cold or hot. But because thou art lukewarm ... I will begin to vomit thee out of My mouth" (Apoc 3:15–16). Such is the fate of those who are indifferent to venial sin.

The seed fell by the wayside and on stony ground. How can it strike roots in such soil? How can grace produce fruit in a soul that is given up to habitual venial sin, that is overcome by sleep and indifference, and abuses grace? How can the seed bring forth fruit in such a soul? How can grace be fruitful in a soul that scarcely ever prays, that is entirely occupied with creatures, and that withstands the Holy Spirit? (Acts 7:51.)

"Arise, why sleepest Thou, O Lord? Arise and cast us not off to the end.... Our belly hath cleaved to the earth. Arise, O Lord, help us and deliver us" from the evil of habitual venial sin (Introit). Who can deliver us once we have become victims of this baneful vice? Only the mercy of God. But what if the mercy of God should be inclined to vomit us out of its mouth? We may be sure that during the holy season of Lent, God will show His mercy.

What should our lives as Christians be if not a life of living submission to God through Christ Jesus? But how is this possible when even those who are priests and religious consecrated to God continue to oppose God, trifle with the things that are displeasing to Him, and thus place themselves in danger of turning their back on Him entirely? It is high time that we break away completely from venial sin.

What prevents the divine seed from bringing forth fruit in our soul? Is it our unrestrained selfishness that revolts at the thought of any mortification? Is it our vanity which can bear no rebuke? Is it our self-sufficiency that spoils all our good works? Is it an attachment to our secret desires and secret passions that holds us back? Is it possibly our natural temperament, which we refuse to mold and change, that makes our progress so slow. Perhaps it is our neglect of prayer, or our haste and distraction in prayer. May God give us the grace to recognize the habitual venial sins that have bound our soul to earth. That we may obtain this grace we pray in the Offertory: "Perfect Thou my goings in Thy paths, that my footsteps be not moved; incline Thy ear and hear my words; show forth Thy wonderful mercies, Thou who savest them that trust in Thee, O Lord."

Prayer

Thou hast moved the earth, O Lord, and hast troubled it. Heal Thou the breaches thereof, for it has been moved, that they may flee from before the bow, that Thy elect may be delivered. (Tract.)

Deliver us from the bonds of venial sin. Amen.

Saturday

Today we listen with astonishment as the words pour forth from the mouth of the apostle Paul telling of the wonderful fruit borne by the seed the Lord placed in his soul on the way to Damascus. "But that [which fell] on the good ground are they who in a good and perfect heart, hearing the word, keep it and bring forth fruit in patience" (Gospel). St. Paul received the word of God into his heart, nourished it with grace, and brought forth fruit in patience.

"The sower went out to sow his seed" (Gospel). "Saul, as yet breathing out threatenings and slaughter against the disciples of the Lord," set out from Jerusalem to Damascus with the intention of bringing the disciples back to Jerusalem in chains. His heart was fixed with zeal for the Law and for the religion of his fathers, and in this heart God sowed the seed of His word. "And suddenly a light from heaven shined round about him. And falling on the ground, he heard a voice saying to him: Saul, Saul, why persecutest thou Me? Who said: who art Thou, Lord? And He: I am Jesus, whom thou persecutest. It is hard for thee to kick against the goad. And he, trembling and astonished, said: Lord what wilt Thou have me to do? And the Lord said to him: Arise and go into the city, and there it shall be told thee what thou must do" (Acts 9:1, 3–7). The seed has been sown. Saul received it willingly "Lord what wilt Thou have me to do?" He does as he has been directed, and enters the city. He remains there waiting patiently in his blindness, without eating or drinking. He prays and abandons himself entirely to the direction of Ananias, who restores his vision and baptizes him. He retires to solitude and to prayer that the seed may take root deeply in his soul. It springs up vigorously, and Saul becomes Paul. From that moment on he is obsessed by one idea: Christ, His Church, and the salvation of souls. "Forgetting the things that are behind" (Phil 3:13), he now knows only Christ and Him crucified. "For to me, to live is Christ; and to die is gain.... But I am straightened between two: having a desire to be dissolved and to be with Christ, a thing by far the better" (Phil 1:21, 23).

A soul so fully occupied with Christ, so full of zeal for the salvation of souls and the welfare of the Church, a soul that has broken with all that is not of Christ, is certainly good soil. We need not wonder, then, that St. Paul's life and labors were so marvelously fruitful and that he bore suffering and trials with such heroism. Neither are we surprised that he so soon reached such sublime heights of prayer and contemplation that he was "caught up to the third heaven"

(Epistle). "But that [which fell] on the good ground are they who in a good and perfect heart, hearing the word, keep it and bring forth fruit in patience."

"In a good and perfect heart." We have received the word of God, and we shall continue to receive it. But shall we continue to preserve it in a perfect heart? Shall we receive it and protect and nourish it as St. Paul did? Why do we not experience a growth in holiness such as Paul experienced? There are three things that interfere with our growth in holiness. "Some fell by the wayside," in a soul distracted and dissipated by idle fancies and futile plans. Such a soul is barren of spiritual fruit, because it must investigate every new face that appears, read every item in the papers, and know and listen to everything that goes on about it. Its energies are dissipated by the pursuit of temporal things and has no time for God, for prayer, or meditation. It walks so much in the world that it has no time to walk with God.

"Some other fell upon a rock." This is the timid or selfish soul that shrinks from any sacrifice. It may be pious and religious, but as soon as it is called upon to undergo hardships or temptation, it renounces the word for its own peace and comfort. "And some fell among thorns." These souls receive the word of God, and by the grace of God are determined to become pious and virtuous. In spite of their good resolutions, however, they allow bad habits and unmortified passions to grow up in their hearts. They retain a passionate attachment to their worldly goods, to the comforts of life, to the esteem of their fellow men, to their profession, their studies, and their hobbies. They insist on their own will, they fail to improve their traits of character, they insist on their own opinions, and waste much time and effort pampering their bodies and providing for their own comfort. These unmortified habits, which they refuse to correct, are the thorns which choke out the good seed in their souls. This dissipation, lukewarmness, and attachment to the world are the obstacles that hinder the growth of the word of God in our souls. Any lack of fruitfulness in us is not the fault of the seed, but the fault of the soil in which it is planted.

Today we are assembled at the tomb of St. Paul. We feel ourselves united with him, and as we gather in his church today, we long to be filled with his strength and his spirit. Oh, that like him we might prove good ground, in which Christ, the divine husbandman, sows the seed so abundantly!

We will have to improve ourselves in many ways if the seed is to bring forth fruit in our souls. Above all, we must prepare the soil of our soul. We must remove all that can prevent or impair the work of grace in our hearts. Indifference, lukewarmness, and attachment to the world must go. Above all, we must cast off all ill-regulated attachments and unbecoming activities.

The words of the Apostle apply to us: "For the earth that drinketh in the rain which cometh often upon it, and bringeth forth herbs, meet for them by whom it is tilled, receiveth blessing from God. But that which bringeth forth thorns and briers, is reprobate and very near unto a curse, whose end is to be burnt" (Heb 6:7 f.).

Today, as we gather to celebrate the holy mysteries, we place our petitions on the paten and beg God, for the sake of Christ's offering, to give us the strength to renounce perfectly everything that would hinder the growth of His grace in our soul.

Prayer

We humbly beseech Thee, O almighty God, that we may be enlightened by Thy grace, that we may know what we must do, and do what is right. Through Christ our Lord. Amen.

Quinquagesima Sunday

The Mass

In the Gospel of today's Mass the Church reveals the mystery of the approaching lenten and paschal seasons. "Behold, we go up to Jerusalem, and all things shall be accomplished, which were written by the prophets concerning the Son of Man. For He shall be delivered to the Gentiles, and shall be mocked and scourged and spit upon; and after they have scourged Him they will put Him to death" (Gospel). The apostles, even St. Peter, whose church is the stational church today, "understood none of these things, and this word was hid from them." Nevertheless they bravely accompany Jesus to Jerusalem.

In the liturgy of the Mass which we are about to celebrate, we go along with Christ to Jerusalem and to the Calvary of the altar. There the mystery of which Christ spoke shall be re-enacted before our eyes. We join ourselves to the offering of our great high priest, and accompany Him on the path that He has chosen. That path will lead us through strife and struggle to victory, to the eternal Easter. So we pray with our Savior in the Introit, which represents His journey to Jerusalem: "Be Thou to me a God, a protector, and a place of refuge to save me." With these words we enter prayerfully with the Church into the arduous struggle of Lent. It will be a struggle against our passions and temptations, against the solicitations of the world and hell. Lord have mercy upon us. "Guard us from all adversity, who have been loosened from the bonds of sin" (Collect).

Renunciation, sacrifice, and heroic struggle: that is our program for Lent. These difficulties must be borne patiently and in the spirit of love. Our works and sufferings will be to no avail unless they are performed with love. For this reason the Apostle in the Epistle speaks of love in such glowing terms. It was love that drew Christ to Jerusalem to offer Himself up for us. It is His love that makes Him share with us the fruits of His suffering and death. With gratitude we acknowledge in the Gradual: "Thou art the God that alone dost wonders; Thou hast made Thy power known among the nations. With Thy arm Thou hast redeemed Thy people, the children of Israel and of Joseph."

Love must rule all our actions also. With love we accompany Him; with love we offer with Him; with love we offer all we have, our bodies and our souls, our time, our health, and all that we possess. In this spirit we join with our Lord in the Offertory procession this morning. We are prepared to share His suffering with Him, to be reviled, to be scourged, yes, even to accompany Him to death. "Teach me Thy justifications" (Offertory). Heal us of the blindness that makes us fail to appreciate the mystery of the cross, the mystery of the sacrifice and death of our high priest, and give us the grace to understand Him, to follow Him, and to live with Him. Through death to life! "He that loveth his life shall lose it; he that hateth his life in this world, keepeth it unto life eternal" (Jn 12:25). If we offer ourselves with Christ in the Offertory, life will be given to us in Communion. "They did eat and were filled exceedingly" (Communion). St. Peter, in whose house we are assembled, leads us along the way we must follow. At first he, too, failed to understand the word; but love opened his eyes. It obliged him to follow his Master and to share His crucifixion. Love opened to him the door to life and to the eternal Easter.

Meditation

Struggle and labor are the lot of Christ and His Church. We know that because of our weakness we could expect nothing but defeat and disillusionment. But our very weakness is our strength. The more we humble ourselves and the greater our trust in the Lord, the surer we are of victory. From Him we shall obtain the strength for victory. For this reason we cry out with the Church today, like the blind man in the Gospel: "Be Thou unto me a God, a protector, and a place of refuge to save me; for Thou art my strength and my refuge; and for Thy name's sake Thou wilt lead me and nourish me" (Introit).

"And when He drew nigh to Jericho, a certain blind man sat by the wayside begging. And when he heard the multitude passing by, he asked what this meant. And they told him that Jesus of Nazareth was passing by. And he cried out, saying: Jesus, Son of David have mercy on me.... And Jesus, standing, commanded him to be brought unto Him. And when he was come near He asked him, saying: What wilt thou that I do to thee? But he said: Lord, that I may see. And Jesus said to him: Receive thy sight; thy faith hath made thee whole. And immediately he saw and followed Him, glorifying God; and all the people, when they saw it, gave praise to God" (Gospel).

The blind man of the Gospel is, in the eyes of the liturgy, the Church of the Gentiles. Abandoned to itself, it is the blind man sitting by the wayside in misery and poverty. How it longs for the ability to see! The power of vision would be its most priceless possession. But who can and who will give it the power of sight? The Son of God descends from heaven and meets it on the wayside. It learns that the Lord is passing by and cries out to Him from the depths of its misery, its poverty, and its helplessness: "Son of David, have mercy on me." The Lord is disposed to grant mercy. "What wilt thou that I do to thee?" "Lord, that I may see." Only let me see; only give me light. Give me that, and I shall be rich and possess all things. The Lord gives it the desired grace, the grace of faith. Now its desires are satisfied, and in the possession of the faith it possesses all things: God, the world, time, eternity, light, and love. With joy and gratitude it cries out: "Thou art the God that alone dost wonders; Thou hast made Thy power known among the nations. With Thy arm Thou hast redeemed Thy people, the children of Israel and of Joseph" (Gradual). "Sing joyfully to God, all the earth; serve ye the Lord with gladness.... We are His people and the sheep of His pasture" (Tract).

We are the Church. In baptism Christ heals our blindness. The Fathers were wont to call baptism "the enlightenment." In this sacrament we receive the gift of faith and Christ, the truth, our God and our all. Would that it could be said of us, as it was of the blind man, "And immediately he saw and followed Him, glorifying God"!

In the mind of the liturgy, today should be a day of thanksgiving for the gift of faith. How often has it been necessary for Christ to restore our "inner sight" since the time of our baptism? How little we treasured it! How carelessly we cared for it! We should imitate the liturgy, which never wearies of thanking God for this marvelous gift. "Blessed art Thou, O Lord; teach me Thy justifications. With my lips I have pronounced all the judgments of Thy mouth" (Offertory).

Until now we were helpless, poor, and blind. Then through Christ we received our sight. We now behold the marvelous world of His gifts and His grace, the most resplendent of which is the Holy Eucharist. He comes to us again today in the Eucharist to bring us new light, a deeper insight. "They did eat and were filled exceedingly; and the Lord gave them their desire; they were not defrauded of that which they craved" (Communion). Who is so fortunate and rich as the children of the Church? Indeed, in the Church, in Christ, we are not defrauded.

In our weakness lies our strength. It is our very weakness that draws us to Christ, to baptism, to the Holy Eucharist, to the altar, to the unceasing search for God. "Thou art my strength and my refuge; and for Thy name's sake Thou wilt lead me and nourish me" (Introit) with Thy strength and Thy life. "And I live by the Father; so he that eateth Me, the same also shall live by Me" (Jn 6:58).

Prayer

Graciously hear our prayers, we beseech Thee, O Lord, and guard us from all adversity, who have been loosened from the bonds of sin. Through Christ our Lord. Amen.

Monday

With heartfelt gratitude the Church praises God today for having been cured of its blindness. Christ has given her the light of faith, and with it the gift of love. Love rules the world and all mankind. But there are two kinds of love. There is a love that is impure and unholy, a love of self that degrades, a love that seeks the things that God has condemned and forbidden. This is the love that fills man with the concupiscence of the flesh and the pride of life. This love degrades man, separates him from God, and plunges him into misery (Jn 2:16). There is also a pure love, a holy love that seeks God, elevates the soul, and induces man to forget self and dedicate himself entirely to God. For this love the liturgy thanks God today. This is the kind of love that God gave to His Church when He enlightened her. This is her wealth, that she loves God, and in God her neighbor. This is the theme of the Epistle of Quinquagesima Sunday, which is a canticle of love for God and our neighbor.

"Brethren, if I speak with the tongues of men and of angels, and have not charity, I am become as sounding brass or a tinkling cymbal. And if I should have prophecy and should know all mysteries and all knowledge, and if I should have all faith so that I could remove mountains, and have not charity, I am nothing. And if I should distribute all my goods to feed the poor, and if I should deliver my body to be burned, and have not charity, it profiteth me nothing" (Epistle). Everything depends on our having charity. But what kind of charity must we have?

"Charity is patient, is kind. Charity envieth not; dealeth not perversely; is not puffed up; is not ambitious; seeketh not her own; is not provoked to anger; thinketh no evil; rejoiceth not in iniquity but rejoiceth in the truth; beareth all things, believeth all things, hopeth all things, endureth all things." See here the inner life of the Church, her heart, her love of God and her love of men.

"Charity never falleth away, whether prophecies shall be made void, or tongues shall cease, or knowledge shall be destroyed. For we know in part, and we prophesy in part. But when that which is perfect is come, that which is in part shall be done away. When I was a child, I spoke as a child, I understood as a child, I thought as a child; but when I became a man, I put away the things of a child. We see now through a glass in a dark manner; but then face to face. Now I know in part; but then I shall know even as I am known. Now there remaineth faith, hope, and charity, these three; but the greatest of these is charity" (Epistle).

These virtues are the treasures of the Church: She possesses faith; she has hope; she has, in the person of many of her children, knowledge and the gifts of prophecy and of miracles. But above all these treasures is the gift of love — the pure and perfect love of God. This love fulfills perfectly the will of God, not out of fear or because it is constrained, not for the sake of any reward, but simply in order to be pleasing to God and to give joy to Him who has first given Himself to us. This love controls all thoughts and desires, directs them to God in prayer, in work, and in service. This love makes its possessor strong and eager to bear all sacrifices and trials for love of Him.

This love of God makes the Church inexhaustible in her works of charity. The history of the Church is one uninterrupted epic of heroic fraternal charity. She has been unremitting in her service of the orphans, the poor, the widows, the slaves, the exiled, the imprisoned, the wretched, and the helpless. What is the life of her priests, her missioners, her religious of both sexes, but a marvelous story of lives devoted to the spiritual and corporal works of mercy.

We should examine ourselves carefully according to the maxims of the Epistle. Have we the spirit of charity? In baptism the spirit of charity was planted in our soul. By the offering of the Holy Sacrifice and the reception of Communion the flame of charity is stirred to life and increased. Do we live and practice fraternal charity? Have we not lost many opportunities to practice it? Let us beg our Lord, "Enkindle in us the fire of Thy love."

PRAYER

Graciously hear our prayers, we beseech Thee, O Lord, and guard us from all adversity, who have been loosened from the bonds of sin. Through Christ our Lord. Amen.

Tuesday

Today we stand silent before the beginning of the lenten season. The Church has prepared us for it in three stages. In the lessons at Matins she presents the three great patriarchs, Adam, Noe, and Abraham. Adam, who is the author of Original Sin, is also a figure of Christ; Noe, having been rescued from the Deluge by the ark, is a figure of mankind rescued from sin through the Church by means of baptism. Abraham, offering up his son on Mount Moriah, is a figure of the sacrificial death of Christ on Calvary. Three great figures of the New Testament appear in the three stational churches on each of these three Sundays, St. Lawrence, St. Paul, and St. Peter. Three main thoughts dominate the Gospels for these three Sundays: the invitation to the laborers to work in the vineyard of the master (Septuagesima); the sowing of the seed of the word and of grace in the Church (Sexagesima); the healing of the blind man (the Church) by baptism, the beginning of our enlightenment in the eternal Easter of heaven (Quinquagesima).

"At that time Jesus took unto Him the Twelve and said to them: Behold, we go up to Jerusalem, and all things shall be accomplished which were written by the prophets concerning the Son of Man; for He shall be delivered to the Gentiles and shall be mocked and scourged and spit upon; and they will put Him to death, and the third day He shall rise again" (Gospel). With a deep earnestness and a quiet determination the Lord goes to meet His death. His disciples (His Church) are to go with Him. They are one with Him. "Behold, we go up to Jerusalem" (to Holy Week, to Easter). Of every Holy Sacrifice of the Mass it could be said: "Behold, we go up to Jerusalem," to the mount of Calvary, to relive there with our Lord the mystery of His suffering and death. Our whole life as Christians is nothing else but an ascent to Jerusalem and the sharing of His painful journey. During the season of Lent the liturgy will banish all our doubts and scruples and will clearly show us the path. "Behold, we go up to Jerusalem," to suffer with our Master, to die with Him, and to rise with Him to eternal life. "Through battle to victory" must not remain empty words. By dying we live. "Yet so, if we suffer with Him, that we may be also glorified with Him" (Rom 8:17).

"And they understood none of these things, and this word was hid from them, and they understood not the things that were said." The apostles had now been with Him for three years. He had taught them carefully, and as the incarnate Son of God, He had given them an example of humility, patience, and zeal. Still their thoughts are earth-bound. Their hopes are still based on a national hero to throw off the Roman yoke and establish a Jewish kingdom. And these twelve apostles dream of obtaining the preferred places and honors in this kingdom. "They understood none of these things" when He spoke to them of the kingdom of God and told them that His kingdom is not of this world but is founded, not on national or political power, but on suffering and the cross. They are still blind although they have been so long in the company of Him who came to be the light of the world. The doctrine of suffering and of humility is often an unwelcome doctrine even to pious souls. The blindness of the apostles afflicts us also.

We are now approaching the season of Lent, Good Friday, the cross and suffering. The Church bears witness to the fact that the contemporary world has lost the spirit of true penance. The world lets Christ make His painful journey unaccompanied. We beg Him to spare us suffering. We admire the Christian heroes of the cross, the martyrs and saints of the Church, and celebrate their feasts. Yes, they are wonderful, we say, but we are incapable of their heroism and love of the cross. Modern Christians, both in the world and in the cloister, have forgotten how to appreciate and love the cross. The love of the cross has too small a place in our spirit, in our life, in our heart (1 Cor 1:17). We have forgotten how to treasure the cross of Christ (Gal 6:14). We would be ashamed to have it said of us that we knew nothing "but Jesus Christ, and Him crucified" (1 Cor 2:2). We read and meditate devoutly on the chapter from the *Imitation of Christ*, "The Royal Way of the Cross," but it remains for us just a beautiful theory. We read and sing the formula: *Nos autem gloriari oportet in cruce Domini nostri Jesu Christi* ("We ought to glory in the cross of our Lord Jesus Christ"). We sing, "I am dead to the world and the world to me"; but it is all merely a theory. For most of us the axioms remain mere axioms. We join our Lord daily in His mystical suffering and death in the Sacrifice of the Mass; yes, we even receive the sacrificed God in our heart that He may fill us with the spirit of sacrifice, with His love of suffering. Every day we encounter Christ in His suffering, but we understand "none of these things," not even those of us who are baptized Christians, priests, and religious.

"Lord, that I may see" (Gospel), the Church cries out when the Lord appears in our midst in the Mass today. "Lord, that I may see." She begs that her children may learn to understand again the mystery of the cross and the lesson of Good Friday.

"Lord, that I may see." Lord, that we may know and acknowledge that there is no salvation except by sharing the suffering and the cross of Christ. If we would be saved, we must accompany Him not only to the cenacle, but also to the Mount of Olives, to the hall of scourging, and to Calvary. "Lord, that I may see" that penance and self-discipline are proper to the true servant of God and are the only true mark of the follower of Christ.

"Lord that I may see." This is our prayer today for ourselves and for all the children of Holy Mother the Church. What we need most is a love of the cross, of penance, of self-control, and of self-sacrifice.

Prayer

Graciously hear our prayers, we beseech Thee, O Lord, and guard us from all adversity, who have been loosened from the bonds of sin. Through Christ our Lord. Amen.

Lent

Holy Mother the Church is about to "go up to Jerusalem" with the Lord. With Him she will suffer and die and rise again from the dead. She longs to obtain the light of the Resurrection, and she can attain it only if she shares the passion and death of Jesus. The more she shares His passion and death, the more perfectly will she share His life. With this end in view, the Church and we her children with her enter into the holy season of Lent, which originally began on the first Sunday of Lent.

"Behold, now is the acceptable time, behold, now is the day of salvation" (Epistle of the first Sunday of Lent). "Now is the acceptable time." The Church here refers to the jubilee year of the Israelites, for whom every fiftieth year was a year of grace. During this year all debts which had been contracted and were as yet unpaid, were canceled. All Jewish slaves received their freedom, and all possessions that had been purchased from other Jews were returned to their original owner. Even the land enjoyed a rest, for there was no work in the fields, and men lived on what had been produced in the preceding years. This was the jubilee year, the year of grace, when God was again acknowledged as the real Lord and Master of all things on earth, and His people acknowledged His right to dispose of their goods as He saw fit. By this practice the people were reminded that they were to be always in readiness to serve God and to expend themselves in His praise and honor. The Jews were thus reminded that their first duty was to live for God, and that all concern for earthly possessions was secondary.

The jubilee year is a figure of the "restitution of all things" (Acts 3:21) and of man's final redemption. It is also a figure of the coming of the Savior and of the New Dispensation in which we live. In this New Dispensation the sins of men were to be forgiven by virtue of the sacrifice of the Son of God. We have thus been redeemed from the bondage of Satan. We are now the children of God, members of His family, and we are nourished by the bread of life, the Holy Eucharist. Our first and most essential duty, then, is to show our gratitude to God by praising and honoring Him. For this purpose the Church has provided us with the psalms and hymns of the Divine Office. But she does even more: She places in our hands the bread and wine which are to become the body and blood of Christ, so that we may offer to the Father a "pure, holy, and unspotted sacrifice." "Behold, now is the acceptable time, behold, now is the day of salvation," the year of grace, the jubilee year.

"But we have this treasure in earthen vessels, that the excellency may be of the power of God and not of us. In all things we suffer tribulation, but are not distressed; we are straitened, but are not destitute; we suffer persecution, but are not forsaken; we are cast down, but perish not; always bearing about in our body the mortification of Jesus, that the life also of Jesus may be made manifest in our bodies" (2 Cor 4:7–10). "In all things let us exhibit ourselves as the ministers of God; in much patience, in tribulations, in necessities, in distress,... by honor and dishonor, by evil report and good report, as deceivers, and yet true; as unknown, and yet known; ... as needy, yet enriching many; as having nothing and possessing all things" (2 Cor 6:4–10).

The true Christian, as described by the Epistle of the first Sunday of Lent, is rich in God and united to Him, and by His strength lifts himself above the world, its goods, and its ideals. And yet the Church knows that many of her children will be unable to attain to this high goal. They are still attached to the world, sharing its viewpoint, cherishing its maxims, anxious and concerned about temporal affairs. She knows that in many of her children she is still stained and tainted. Realizing this, she has provided the season of Lent as a time for cleansing and purification: "O God, Thou dost purify Thy Church with the annual observance of Lent" (Collect of the first Sunday of Lent). During this holy season perfect harmony should be re-established between God and all the children of the Church.

We enter this season in the spirit of the Church and of her liturgy. We seek to wash away the stains of sin and to rid ourselves of our inordinate attachment to all that is temporal and worldly. We renounce everything that hitherto has prevented us from reaching the heights of a truly Christian life. This renunciation will cost us effort, strife, and suffering. Yet we unite ourselves to our suffering Savior, persuaded that He who is our head will triumph in His members. The more perfect our union with Him in the Holy Sacrifice and in the sacrificial banquet of Holy Communion, the more certainly shall we share His new life and His glorification at Easter. Then we shall, as men risen from the dead, dedicate our lives to God anew in this year of grace.

Three prominent ideas are proposed for our contemplation by the liturgy of Lent: the passion and the resurrection of Christ; baptism; penance. During Lent we are to think of ourselves as living with Christ, the innocent one, who is to be condemned, disgraced, persecuted, and finally delivered up to death. We are to share His labors, His sacrifices, and His humiliations as He relives them during this season. Following the suggestion of the lenten liturgy, we renew the promises which we made at baptism. We renew our profession of faith and our renunciation of sin. We join the ranks of the penitents and seek by our good works to atone for our past sins and negligences. We withdraw from the world and devote more of our time than is customary to recollection, prayer, holy reading, and meditation. One of the best good works for the season of Lent is the daily attendance at Mass.

Ash Wednesday

We receive from the hands of the Church the cross of ashes, and with it we join the ranks of the public penitents, who during Lent, in the early days of the Church, publicly performed severe penance for their sins. They were excommunicated, excluded from Holy Communion; then on Holy Thursday they were again readmitted into full communion with the Church. The cross of ashes is a sign of our readiness to lead a life of penance. "Remember, O man, that thou art dust, and into dust thou shalt return."

"Be converted to Me with all your heart, in fasting and in weeping and in mourning. And rend your hearts and not your garments, and turn to the Lord your God; for He is gracious and merciful, patient and rich in mercy, and ready to repent of the evil.... Blow the trumpet in Sion; sanctify a fast; call a solemn assembly; gather together the people; sanctify the Church.... Between the porch and the altar the priests, the Lord's ministers, shall weep and shall say: Spare, O Lord, spare Thy people, and give not Thy inheritance to reproach" (Epistle). Such is God's appeal to the Church of the Old Testament. God first asks for penance, the interior sentiments of penance, sorrow, contrition; the external works of penance, fasting and self-denial, are to follow. Through sin we have turned away in disobedience to His commandments and deprived Him of the honor and recognition due to Him. We have gone after something else, a creature, and made it our god. Penance must make recompense for our departure from God and our service of creatures. In repentance the soul must turn back to God: "Be converted to Me with all your heart." Because it has given itself up to the service of a creature and preferred it to God, the soul must in penance subject itself to a punishment, a privation, an act of self-denial. Only in this way does man free himself from sins which he has committed, and places himself in a position to receive pardon for his sins. "Be converted to Me with all your heart."

"When you fast, be not as the hypocrites, sad. For they disfigure their faces that they may appear unto men to fast.... But thou, when thou fastest,... appear not to men to fast, but to thy Father who is in secret, and thy Father who seeth in secret will repay thee" (Gospel). St. Augustine comments on these words of the Gospel in the lessons at Matins:

According to these precepts, it is clear that all our attention should be directed to acquiring interior joys; lest, while seeking external rewards, we conform ourselves to this world and lose the promise of that blessedness which is the more solid and stable as it is more interior, in which God has chosen us to be made like to the image of His Son. We must especially note in this chapter that pride is to be found, not only amid the splendor and pomp of material things, but even in sadness and squalor; and it is then even more dangerous because it hides under the name of the service of God.

Christianity is the religion of the inner self, not of external greatness before men nor of outward appearance. Christian piety keeps its eyes fixed on God and His holy will. Its motive is the love of God, of which we are reminded, not without cause, at the beginning of Lent. No one should be able to notice our fasting. But we should be more recollected than usual, more strict with ourselves than during the rest of the year. We should deprive ourselves somewhat of sleep, devote more time to prayer, and observe more carefully the virtue of silence. But towards others we should be more charitable, all the more ready to serve, all the more pleasant, cheerful, and cordial. No one should know that during these weeks we practice more mortification than usual. "Lay not up to yourselves treasures [honor, recognition, praise] on earth, where the rust and moth consume.... But lay up to yourselves treasures in heaven," before God, with the intention of pleasing Him alone. According to these directions of the Gospel, let us take upon ourselves the work of Lent.

"Let us change our garments for ashes and sackcloth; let us fast and lament before the Lord; for our God is plenteous in mercy to forgive our sins."

"Let us amend for the better in those things in which we have sinned through ignorance, lest, suddenly overtaken by the day of death, we seek time for penance and be not able to find it. Attend, O Lord, and have mercy; for we have sinned against thee. Help us, O God, our Savior; and for the honor of Thy name, O Lord, deliver us" (Antiphons before Mass).

"By the fasting of the body Thou dost curb our vices, elevate our minds, and bestow virtue and reward" (Preface for Lent).

We pray and do penance in the name of the community, for the entire Church militant. We know we are united with all our brothers and sisters in Christ, and we implore, one for all and all for one: "Have mercy on me, O God, have mercy on me; for my soul trusteth in Thee. Thou hast mercy upon all, O Lord, and hatest none of the things which Thou hast made, overlooking the sins of men for the sake of repentance, and sparing them; because Thou art the Lord our God" (Introit).

PRAYER

Grant to Thy faithful, O Lord, that they may undertake the venerable solemnities of fasting with piety and carry them through with unwavering devotion.

Look with favor, O Lord, on those who bow before Thy majesty, that they who have been refreshed with the divine gift (the Holy Eucharist) may ever be strengthened by heavenly aid. Through Christ our Lord. Amen.[11]

Thursday after Ash Wednesday

We gather for the divine services in the sanctuary of the soldier and martyr, St. George. Together with us he prays the Introit: "When I cried to the Lord, He heard my voice from them that drew near to me.... Cast thy care upon the Lord, and He shall sustain thee." Let us pray like King Ezechias in the Epistle and like the Roman officer in the Gospel. Lent is a time for prayer.

"In those days Ezechias was sick even to death; and Isaias, the son of Amos the prophet, came unto him and said to him, Thus saith the Lord: Take order with thy house, for thou shalt die, and not live. And Ezechias turned his face towards the wall and prayed to the Lord and said: I beseech Thee, O Lord, remember how I have walked before Thee in truth and with a perfect heart, and have done that which is good in Thy sight. And Ezechias wept with great weeping. And the word of the Lord came to Isaias, saying: Go and say to Ezechias, Thus saith the Lord, the God of David thy father: I have heard thy prayer and I have seen thy tears; behold I will add to thy days fifteen years; and I will deliver thee and this city out of the hand of the king of the Assyrians, and I will protect it" (Epistle). Ezechias begged for a favor, and more was granted him than he had dared ask for. "Ask and it shall be given you" (Lk 11:9). "Cast thy care upon the Lord, and He shall sustain thee" (Introit).

The Roman soldier comes with great faith to Jesus, urged on by a loving care for his ill servant (Gospel). He besought the Lord; "Lord, my servant lieth at home sick of the palsy, and is grievously tormented. And Jesus saith to him, I will come and heal him. And the centurion, making answer, said: Lord, I am not worthy that Thou shouldst enter under my roof; but only say the word, and my servant shall be healed. For I also am a man subject to authority, having

[11] Where two prayers are given during Lent, the second one is usually the Prayer over the People for that day.

under me soldiers; and I say to this: Go, and he goeth; and to another: Come, and he cometh; and to my servant: Do this, and he doeth it." Such confidence moves the Lord, who answers the prayer of the centurion, "Go, and as thou hast believed, so be it done to thee. And the servant was healed at the same hour." "And all things whatsoever you shall ask in prayer, believing, you shall receive" (Mt 21:22).

The sacred liturgy sees in the Roman centurion of the Gospel the stational saint, St. George. He comes today to the Lord and implores for his sick servant; that is, for the congregation which is present in his house. He comes with the love and the solicitude of the centurion of the Gospel and makes a plea for us, his congregation. We have confidence that his plea will be answered.

Joined with the holy martyr, George, let us sing the Offertory chant: "To Thee, O Lord, have I lifted up my soul; in Thee, O my God, I put my trust." St. George gave his life's blood for the Lord; we also give up everything in the Holy Sacrifice of the Mass and offer ourselves a holocaust to the Lord. Dead to sin, dead to the world and worldliness, dead to self-love and self-seeking, we tread the way of the martyr, the path of self-denial and of the holy love of God and Christ. We live only for the sake of God's holy will and His good pleasure, not for ourselves or for any creature for its own sake.

The liturgy exhorts us urgently today to prayer of petition. We are urged to pray for ourselves, as Ezechias did, and for others, as the centurion of the Gospel did. "Ask and it shall be given you," reads that great command of the order of grace. The one, then, who does not ask, does not receive. He who asks for little, receives little; who asks for much, receives much. "He hath filled the hungry with good things, and the rich [who do not ask] He hath sent empty away" (Lk 1:53). "All [adults] who are saved, are saved because they have prayed. And all who are damned, are damned because they have not prayed" (St. Alphonsus Liguori). Prayer is the ordinary means of obtaining grace from God.

In the days of faith and devotion, Christians frequently prayed the seven penitential psalms and the way of the cross, and daily assisted at Mass and performed other special works of penance during Lent. We also should pray more during Lent than is our wont.

In the celebration of Mass we enter with heart and soul into the prayers which the priest from Ash Wednesday on daily recites for the intercession of the saints (*A cunctis*) and for the living and dead (*Omnipotens sempiterne Deus*).

Prayer

O God, who art offended by sin and appeased by penance, graciously regard the prayers of Thy people making supplication to Thee, and turn aside the scourge of Thy anger, which we deserve for our sins. Through Christ our Lord. Amen.

Friday after Ash Wednesday

The liturgy today leads us into the house of the "two men of mercy," the holy martyrs John and Paul. They had distributed their large possessions to the poor, so that they could follow the way to heaven without impediment. On account of their charity "the Lord hath heard them and hath had mercy on them" (Introit). From the example of these two saints of effective brotherly love, the Church teaches us today the third aspect of our lenten work and baptismal renewal; it consists in the perfecting of the spirit of active Christian, brotherly love. "He that loveth not, abideth in death" (1 Jn 3:14).

"Is not this rather the fast that I have chosen? Loose the bands of wickedness, undo the bundles that oppress; let them that are broken go free, and break asunder every burden. Deal thy bread to the hungry, and bring the needy and the harborless into thy house; when thou shalt see one naked, cover him, and despise not thy own flesh [your fellow man]. Then shall thy light break forth as the morning, and thy health shall speedily arise.... Then shalt thou call, and the Lord shall hear; thou shalt cry, and He shall say: Here I am. Because I the Lord thy God am merciful" (Epistle). "Blessed are the merciful, for they shall obtain mercy" (Mt 5:7). Fasting, mortification, works of penance are good and necessary, but only when they are preceded by the observance of the first commandment, the love of God and of one's neighbor, and serve love and kindness. "And if I should distribute all my goods to feed the poor, and if I should deliver my body to be burned, and have not charity, it profiteth me nothing" (1 Cor 13:3).

"He that loveth his neighbor hath fulfilled the law." Every other commandment is contained in this precept. "Thou shalt love thy neighbor as thyself.... Love therefore is the fulfilling of the law" (Rom 13:9–10). Dispensation can be given from fasting; but from love, never. "Love thy neighbor as thyself" (Mt 19:19). Do we observe this command?

"You have heard that it hath been said: Thou shalt love thy neighbor and [the Pharisees added this] hate thy enemy. But I say to you: Love your enemies; do good to them that hate you; and pray for them that persecute and calumniate you; that you may be the children of your Father, who is in heaven, who maketh His sun to rise upon the good and bad, and raineth upon the just and the unjust" (Gospel). To the sanctification of Lent belongs the will of brotherly love and the act of this love, even of the love of one's enemy. "Forgive us our trespasses as we forgive those who trespass against us." "Be ye therefore merciful as your Father also is merciful. Judge not, and you shall not be judged. Condemn not, and you shall not be condemned. Forgive, and you shall be forgiven. Give, and it shall be given to you" (Lk 6:36–38).

"A new commandment I give unto you; that you love one another as I have loved you" (Jn 13:34). "He that saith he is in the light [in possession of sanctifying grace] and hateth his brother, is in darkness [of sin] even until now. He that loveth his brother, abideth in the light.... But he that hateth his brother, is in darkness and walketh in darkness" (1 Jn 2:9–11). "We know that we have passed from death [sin] to life [grace] because we love the brethren. He that loveth not, abideth in death" (1 Jn 3:14). How is true penance or the forgiveness of sin possible if we are not diligent in the practice of brotherly love?

Today's liturgy reminds us of two special fields of brotherly love: almsgiving and the love of one's enemies. In the liturgy the stational saints, John and Paul, are the men of mercy, men of good deeds to the poor. If the Church today takes us into their house, she wishes that we enter into their spirit and perform works of mercy, especially almsgiving. Are we doing our duty in this regard? Have we not much to make good during the holy season of Lent? "He that hath the substance of this world, and shall see his brother in need, and shall shut up his bowels from him; how does the charity of God abide in him?" (1 Jn 3:17.) How can he obtain forgiveness from God if he attend not to his brother's need?

How about our love of our enemies? "Love your enemies; do good to them that hate you; and pray for them that persecute and calumniate you; that you may be the children of your Father who is in heaven, who maketh His sun to rise upon the good and bad, and raineth upon the just and the unjust." Love of our enemies is not merely a counsel, it is a holy, positive command of the Lord. It is a proof of the genuineness of our love for our neighbor and for God. If the love of enemies, which the Gospel asks for, is to be found so seldom even among us Christians, that is an indication that among us Christians — it is unfortunately true — very little love is to be found.

Herein lies the principal weakness in our Christian life: we lack sufficient love of our neighbor, both inwardly and outwardly. Our lives are full of self-love and self-seeking. Here our lenten activity must begin its work. The effort that the holy season of Lent asks of us is: "Love your enemies. Do good to them that hate you, and pray for them that persecute and calumniate you." Die to self-love and to self-seeking. That is the most important mortification.

Prayer

O God, strength of those who hope in Thee, be propitious to our prayers; and because without Thee human weakness can do nothing, grant us the assistance of Thy grace, so that we may be pleasing to Thee by the fulfillment of Thy commandments both in desire and in act. Through Christ our Lord. Amen.

Saturday after Ash Wednesday

It is night, and we labor at the oars, struggling to bring our faltering ships to land through the troubled waters of our daily life. On the shore, waiting to receive us, is Jesus. At the time of the fourth watch of the night, that is, toward morning, He enters into our boat by means of Holy Communion, and guides our troubled craft to the desired goal (Gospel). The struggle to preserve our souls from every sin and to practice the penance imposed on us for past offenses, has been a trying experience. Nevertheless we place all our trust in Christ. In the Holy Eucharist we shall find the strength to finish successfully the works of penance undertaken during Lent.

Beautiful is the fruit which is produced during the season of Lent. "If Thou will take away the chain out of the midst of thee, and cease to stretch out the finger and to speak that which profiteth not. When thou shalt pour out thy soul to the hungry and shalt satisfy the afflicted soul, then shall thy light rise up in the darkness, and thy darkness shall be as noonday. And the Lord will give thee rest continually, and fill thy soul with brightness, and deliver thy bones. And thou shall be like a watered garden, and like a fountain of waters, whose waters shall not fail. And the places that have been desolate for ages shall be built in thee; thou shalt raise up the foundations of generation and generation" (Epistle).

When the true spirit of Lent prevails, the divine life of grace flourishes in the soul, and all virtues and good works come rapidly to perfection. When the Christian acquires this spirit, he becomes a co-worker with Christ in building the kingdom of God, both in his own soul and in the Church. He contributes to the salvation of the whole race by his example, by his prayers, and by his merits. He becomes a rugged stone upon which the rest of the structure can be built. His good works during Lent support the other members of the Church and furnish them with grace for enlightenment, strength, and conversion. We are a part of the whole, and the whole depends on us.

The converse is true if we fail to bring forth good works of penance during Lent. What a loss to ourselves and to the whole Church! In the story of salvation we must be either builders or destroyers; either we gather or we scatter. There can be no neutrality. This is the mystery of the body of Christ. For this reason our Holy Mother the Church takes a serious view of the season of Lent. Would that we shared her concern!

Both the desire to perform good works and the strength necessary to complete them comes from Christ. We are like the apostles in today's Gospel, confronted with adverse winds and unable to make progress in spite of our work at the oars. We shall ever have adverse winds and shall ever find obstacles to the spiritual life within ourselves. We possess a fallen nature, prone always toward evil and lacking an appreciation of the one thing necessary, divine life. In addition to our fallen nature, we must face the world with its enticements, its false principles, and its faulty reasoning. To these obstacles Satan will add the weight of his cunning and immense power. How can we hope to overcome such great obstacles? The Gospel of today gives us cause for hope, for "He [Christ] went up to the mountain to pray" (Mk 6:46). He is in heaven and in our tabernacles waiting to join our prayer to His to obtain for us the necessary help.

In the early morning Christ will come into our tiny ships in Mass and in Holy Communion. "And the wind ceased." Borne onward by His prayers and by those of His Church, strengthened by His coming to us in Holy Communion, we shall complete successfully our trying journey through the season of Lent, through the time of our earthly sojourn, and arrive one day at the blessed shores of eternity to enjoy an eternal Easter.

"Serve ye the Lord with fear, and rejoice unto Him with trembling; embrace discipline lest you perish from the just way" (Communion). Although we believe firmly in the merit of our good works during Lent, we trust more in the merits of Christ and His prayers and those of His Church. His infinite wisdom and His omnipotence are always with us. He brings them to us daily in the Mass and in Holy Communion.

"The Lord [in Holy Communion] became my helper. I will extol Thee, O Lord, for Thou hast upheld me" in Thy holy Church (Introit). "One thing I have asked of the Lord, this will I seek after: that I dwell in the house of the Lord" (Gradual).

Prayer

O Lord, give ear to our supplications and grant that we may keep with devout service this solemn fast, which has been wholesomely instituted for the healing of our souls and bodies. Through Christ our Lord. Amen.

First Sunday of Lent

The Mass

Today we gather with the faithful of the early Church in the Lateran basilica, the church of the Savior in Rome. In the apse of the basilica we see the venerable mosaic of the divine Savior. We gather at His feet, conscious of His presence and of our union in spirit with Him. At His side for the ensuing forty days we shall practice self-denial and penance. From the heavens above us we hear the consoling promise of the Father, "He shall cry to Me, and I will hear him. I will deliver him and I will glorify him" (Introit). Thus, full of confidence, we send up our cry for mercy, *Kyrie eleison,* and unite our prayers to those of the Church.

The path which we are to follow during Lent is one of self-denial, of voluntary mortification, and of patient acceptance of crosses, sufferings, and humiliations. It is a time of grace, a time of salvation. We die, and yet we live (Epistle). The more we die to ourselves during Lent, the more surely shall we live to God. We should begin Lent full of confidence, for God's help and grace are at our disposal (Gradual and Tract). When nature becomes incapable of further sacrifice, grace supports it. Thus we are invited by the Gospel to undertake a fast of forty days with our Lord. He who so triumphantly overcame Satan and all his temptations, fights and conquers in us also. He makes us strong and invincible. We shall conquer even as He conquered, but we must undertake the struggle of Lent if we would rise at Easter. At the Offertory we bring our good resolutions to the altar and resolve to tread the path of suffering with our Master. These resolutions we lay on the paten as the priest offers up the host, and thus enter into the closest sacrificial union with our blessed Savior. We wish to be made a sacrificial victim with Him.

At the Consecration of the Mass, He will come among us and become our sacrificial gift to the Father. He becomes our own possession, and we take Him in our hands to offer Him up as our sacrifice to the heavenly Father. We offer His merits, His forty days of fast in the desert, His self-denial, His suffering, and His death. He represents us and the whole Church; but with Him we offer ourselves also as a sacrificial gift. Henceforth we shall live, not for ourselves, but as men dedicated to God. We have dedicated ourselves to Him; we have become victims with Him; we are now dead to sin and the world.

At the sacrificial banquet of Holy Communion we receive grace and salvation in return for what we offered at the Consecration. "He will overshadow thee with His shoulders, and under His wings thou shalt trust. His truth shall compass thee with a shield" (Tract). The mighty hero, Christ Himself in the Eucharist, will be our protection and shield against Satan and his attacks, against the world and sin. Should we not, then, enter Lent with courage and hope? The Holy Eucharist which we have received gives us the assurance that we shall rise again to an eternally blessed life for the enjoyment of perfect happiness (Postcommunion).

Full of gratitude for what we have received from the Holy Sacrifice of the Mass, we breathe forth our thanks, *Deo gratias.* Armed with the blessing of Christ through the hands of His priest, we withdraw to our homes to take up alone the battle of the spirit against the flesh. The spirit of the world still lives in us, and we must fight against it. Christ the conqueror lives in us, and we must not waver. "He hath given His angels charge over thee, to keep thee in all thy ways" (Tract).

Meditation

There is joy in the song of the liturgy today. "He shall cry to Me, and I will hear him" (Introit). Christ is in the desert, praying and fasting. The Church has gone into the desert with Him. "He shall cry to Me" during the holy season of Lent, "and I shall hear him. I will deliver him and I will glorify him; I will fill him with length of days" at Easter, at our resurrection to the everlasting life of heaven. The season of Lent is a preparation for the glory of Easter morning, and the beginning of our glorified life in heaven. The season of Lent gives us the assurance of salvation and of our deliverance from sin through Christ. As Christ rose from the dead and was exalted, so shall we also rise and be exalted. Truly this is a time of grace. For this reason the liturgy of the first Sunday of Lent is characterized by joy, confidence, and longing for Easter.

"At that time Jesus was led by the spirit into the desert to be tempted by the devil. And when He had fasted forty days and forty nights, afterwards He was hungry. And the tempter [came] to Him" (Gospel). Like Christ, the Church and her children are led into the desert during the season of Lent. Lent is a time of self-denial and of suffering. During this time we, too, shall be tempted by the devil, the flesh, and the world. Three times the tempter approached Christ. "If Thou be the Son of God, command that these stones be made bread." Then the devil took Him up to the pinnacle of the temple in Jerusalem and said to Him: "If Thou be the Son of God, cast Thyself down; for it is written: That He hath given His angels charge over Thee." On the third attempt the devil took Christ up to a high mountain. There he showed him all the kingdoms of the world and their glory. "All these will I give Thee if falling down Thou wilt adore me." But all these temptations were futile, for "behold, angels came and ministered to Him" (Gospel). In Christ, His Church and we His members were also tempted. Christ's victory over the temptations of the devil was really our victory. His victory prefigures and assures our victory over sin and the devil. Such a victory, however, can be assured only to those who are closely united to Christ through His Church. As living branches of the vine, filled with His vitality and strength, they share in His victory. If we are thus united to Christ, we have little to fear from the tempter, for His strength supports us. Of ourselves we are weak and easy victims of Satan, but in Christ we are strong and invincible. The closer our union with Christ, the greater our strength.

The liturgy of the Mass today offers us two excellent helps in our struggle with the temptations of Satan, the world, and the flesh. The two weapons offered to us are the word of Christ and the body of Christ. Christ's body is offered in the oblation and the Communion of the Holy Sacrifice. From the altar on which the Holy Sacrifice is celebrated springs the fountain from which we drink in Holy Communion the strength of Christ. Strengthened by this nourishment, we answer the solicitations of the devil, "Begone Satan." Here at the altar the Church and her children draw the strength to resist the tempter and his enticements. "It is written," and we are confident that the enemy will not overcome.

The liturgy of Lent also offers us the word of Christ in Holy Scripture. In every Mass new texts and maxims are presented to us. Holy Scripture is our spiritual food. "Not in [earthly] bread alone doth man live, but in every word that proceedeth from the mouth of God" (Gospel). Every word of Holy Scripture which the liturgy presents to us in the lessons of the Divine Office and the chants of the Mass, comes from the mouth of God. Every word is issued by the Spirit of God and helps to bring the tempter to nought. Can the tempter, the world, and the flesh injure us if we take refuge in these means provided for us, in the word of God and in the Eucharist?

During Lent we retire for forty days to fast and to fight against our evil inclinations and against the devil if God should allow him to tempt us. If we cannot observe so severe a fast as our Lord observed, let us do at least as much as we can. In the desert of Lent to which we have withdrawn, let us show ourselves in all things the servants of God. Let us serve God "in much patience, in tribulation, in necessities, in distresses,... in labors, in watchings, in fastings, in chastity, in knowledge, in long-suffering, in sweetness,... in charity unfeigned; ... by honor and dishonor, by evil report and good report" (Epistle). We must preserve this attitude without becoming impatient, without complaint, without giving in to ill-humor, without exonerating ourselves, keeping the spirit of sacrifice at all times for the love of Christ.

During the trying season that is before us, our lives should be characterized by a firm confidence in God, who lives in us, fights in us, and conquers again in us. "Thou art my protector and my refuge; my God, in Him will I trust. For He hath delivered me from the snares of the hunter.... He will overshadow thee with His shoulders, and under His wings thou shalt trust. His truth [grace] shall compass thee with a shield; thou shalt not be afraid of the terror of the night.... For He hath given His angels charge over thee, to keep thee in all thy ways.... Because he hoped in Me, I will deliver him; I will protect him because he hath known My name. He shall cry to Me, and I will hear him; I am with him in tribulation. I will deliver him and I will glorify him; I will fill him with length of days, and I will show him My salvation" (Tract; Psalm 90). So we believe and trust.

Prayer

O God, who dost purify Thy Church with the annual observance of Lent, grant to Thy household that what it strives to obtain from Thee by abstinence, it may secure with good works. Through Christ our Lord. Amen.

Monday

Like the neophytes of the early Church, we now seek to stir up in our hearts the grace which we received at our baptism. At baptism we were chosen to be the children of God and were received into the number of the "blessed of the Father." The stational church for the Mass today is that of St. Peter in Chains. In the person of St. Peter, who was bound with chains and miraculously delivered by Christ, we recognize ourselves. We, too, were bound by the chains of sin and were miraculously delivered by Christ through our second baptism in the holy sacrament of penance. The Mass today reminds us of the grace of our baptism and the obligations it imposes.

The grace of baptism. "I will bring [my sheep] out from the peoples [the heathens] and will gather them out of the countries, and bring them to their own land [the Church]. And I will feed them in the mountains of Israel; ... I will feed them in the most fruitful pastures.... I will seek that which was lost; and that which was driven away I will bring again. And I will bind up that which was broken, and I will strengthen that which was weak" (Epistle). At the time of our baptism Christ lovingly and mercifully segregated us from the pagan world and placed us in His Church. Thus He manifested Himself as the good shepherd who leads His sheep to good pastures (to grace, truth, and the sacraments, particularly the Holy Eucharist). By means of

His Church and His grace He leads us to the great day when the goats shall be separated from the sheep. "When the Son of Man shall come in His majesty,... all nations shall be gathered together before Him, and He shall separate them one from another, as the shepherd separateth the sheep from the goats. And He shall set the sheep on His right hand, but the goats on His left. Then shall the King say to them that shall be on His right hand: Come ye blessed of My Father, possess you the kingdom prepared for you" (Gospel). "He that believeth and is baptized shall be saved" (Mk 16:16).

We have been baptized; we are the children of God and the heirs of the kingdom of heaven. If we prove true to the vows we made at our baptism, we shall hear that blessed invitation on the day of judgment: "Come ye blessed of My Father, possess you the kingdom prepared for you from the foundation of the world." How eternally thankful to God we shall then be for having incorporated us into Himself and His Church through baptism!

Obligations of the baptized. By baptism we were incorporated in Christ as a member of His body, or as a branch of the vine. Christ lives in His members as a vine lives in its branches. What is done to the members of Christ, then, is done also to Him. "I was hungry, and you gave Me to eat; ... sick, and you visited Me. I was in prison, and you came to Me." But what we should do to His members and fail to do, we fail to do to Him. "I was hungry, and you gave Me not to eat; I was thirsty, and you gave Me not to drink. I was ... sick and in prison, and you did not visit Me." Therefore, "Depart from Me, you cursed, into everlasting fire, which was prepared for the devil and his angels." Why is this penalty inflicted upon men? "Amen I say to you, as long as you did it not to one of these least, neither did you do it to me. And these shall go into everlasting punishment; but the just into life everlasting" (Gospel).

At baptism we enter into a union with Christ's body, a union of love. The responsibilities of our baptism must be fulfilled. We must cherish our neighbor for the sake of Christ, who prayed "that they all may be one, as Thou, Father, in Me and I in Thee; that they also may be one in Us; that the world may believe that Thou hast sent Me.... I have made known Thy name,... that the love wherewith Thou hast loved Me may be in them and I in them" (Jn 17:22, 26). "This is My commandment, that you love one another as I have loved you" (Jn 15:12). We shall all be judged by the degree of charity we practiced with regard to our neighbor.

"As the eyes of servants are on the hands of their masters, so are our eyes unto the Lord our God, until He have mercy on us. Have mercy on us, O Lord, have mercy on us" (Introit). Thus we implore with the catechumens, who said this prayer looking forward ardently to the time of their baptism. This should be our prayer also for all those who stand in need of reconciliation through the sacrament of penance. We feel their need of help and we pray with them and for them that they may find their way back to God during the holy season of Lent. This is a season of grace even for those who have abandoned God. In their name we cry out to God: "As the eyes of the servants are on the hands of their masters, so are our eyes unto the Lord our God, until He have mercy" and grant them pardon and grace. "Have mercy on us, O Lord, have mercy on us."

"As long as you did it to one of these My least brethren, you did it to Me" (Gospel). It is a spiritual work of mercy to pray for sinners and to undertake sacrifices for them that they may find the grace to return to God. Since they are still members of the same body, although diseased, we feel a responsibility for their conversion. We become even more conscious of this responsibility during Lent. The Lord has assured us, "I desire not the death of the wicked, but that the wicked turn from his way and live" (Ez 33:11).

In the Communion prayer of the Mass the liturgy reminds us again, "Amen I say to you: What you did to one of My least brethren, you did to Me. Come ye blessed of My Father, possess you the kingdom prepared for you from the foundation of the world." The Church never tires of repeating this truth. The first fruit of Holy Communion should be an abiding love for others. "By their fruits you shall know them" (Mt 7:16). The fruit of Holy Communion is love. Love is tolerant, it forgives easily, it places itself at the service of the one beloved. Love covers the multitude of sins and faults in the one loved with a veil of charity. Has our frequent reception of Holy Communion produced this spirit of charity in us?

"I will lift up my eyes and consider Thy wonders, O Lord" (Offertory). The wonders here referred to are the wonders worked by the love of Christ, who has offered Himself up for us in the Sacrifice of the Mass. We have also the wonders of His love in the sacraments of baptism, penance, and Holy Communion. "Teach me Thy justices; give me understanding, and I will learn Thy commandments" (Offertory), especially Christ's commandment of love.

Prayer

Convert us, O God, our salvation, and that the lenten fast may profit us, instruct our minds with Thy heavenly instructions.

Loose the bonds of our sins, we beseech Thee, O Lord, and do Thou mercifully avert whatever we deserve for them. Through Christ our Lord. Amen.

Tuesday

Renounce whatever displeases God or prevents your approach to Him. This is the invitation extended to us by the liturgy in today's Mass. We celebrate the divine mysteries in the church of the holy martyr and virgin, St. Anastasia. We pass down the crooked little street through the noisy, boisterous cattle market which now lies near the church, to the home of the virgin martyr. We brush aside the turmoil of the mundane things going on about us, and press forward to the *Anastasis,* the resurrection of Easter.

"Seek ye the Lord while He may be found; call upon Him while He is near. Let the wicked forsake his way, and the unjust man his thoughts; and let him return to the Lord, and He will have mercy on him; and to our God, for He is bountiful to forgive" (Epistle). Jesus enters solemnly into Jerusalem. "The whole city was moved, saying: Who is this? And the people said: This is Jesus, the prophet from Nazareth of Galilee" (Gospel). They recognized Him to be the Messias. Jesus enters the temple and there finds the money changers, the merchants, and those who bought and sold the animals of sacrifice. They are too absorbed by their worldly occupation to observe that the Lord has appeared among them. They ignore Him; they cannot be bothered with Him. Christ turns on them with wrath and drives them all from His temple. "It is written, My house shall be called the house of prayer, but you have made it a den of thieves" (Gospel).

Having disposed of the money changers, Christ turns His attention to the Pharisees. These are the wise ones of Israel, the self-satisfied teachers, who look upon themselves as divinely inspired. They indeed have heard of Him and do not fail to notice His approach.

But they murmur against Him and reproach Him; they determine to cast Him out of the temple and to put Him to death. He interferes with their plans: "And leaving them, He went out of the city."

"Seek ye the Lord while He may be found." He is here and may be found, but those who buy and sell in the temple will not find Him, for they are too preoccupied with other things. He is here, but the Pharisee will not find Him; rather, he deliberately turns from Him. Let this warning guide us during Lent. Only those will find Him who seek Him sincerely. Not only those who offer Him active opposition, but those also who fail to look for Him will be condemned. "Seek ye the Lord while He may be found." "Behold now is the acceptable time, behold, now is the day of salvation" (Epistle, first Sunday of Lent). Now, during Lent, the Lord is near. Seek Him while He may be found.

"And there came to Him the blind and the lame in the temple, and He healed them." At His approach the children cried out, "Hosanna to the Son of David." To the Pharisees, who were indignant at this acclamation and who asked Him, "Hearest Thou what these say?" He answered: "Yea. Have you never read: Out of the mouth of infants and sucklings Thou hast perfected praise?" (Gospel.) The blind, the lame, and the children recognize Him when He comes. They seek Him and gather around Him. They are not absorbed by the cares and occupations of the world; the noise and bustle and unrest of the world has not destroyed their sense of values. In the eyes of the world they are the outcasts, the useless, the worthless. They can produce nothing, and yet they seek the Lord. With faith and confidence they gather around Him, crying out their hosanna. Should we not be as the blind, the lame, and the children? When shall we put aside our vain occupations? When shall we see the emptiness and vanity of all transitory things? When shall we find the grace to withdraw from the busy market place of the world to see the Lord? "Hosanna to the Son of David. Blessed is He who cometh in the name of the Lord," we sing now and at the Consecration of the Mass. Under the inspiration of grace we repeat this song at the time of Holy Communion. But we must renounce what is not of God and whatever hinders our approach to God. We must renew our baptismal vows. "I do renounce sin," we said at our baptism; and we must now renew our promise and turn with our whole heart to the Lord. "Seek ye the Lord while He may be found."

"And leaving them, He went out of the city into Bethania, and remained there" (Gospel). The Lord comes to all during the lenten season; but He will turn away from the man who trifles with grace. Will He come a second time?

"He went out of the city into Bethania." The Lord is not pleased with the man who is absorbed by the business of the world. He turns away from the man who is excessively concerned about the things of time, who is enslaved by worldly passions. In the heart of such a man there is no room for God. "You have made [My house] a den of thieves." The soul of the Christian is the temple of God, a house of prayer, and it must not be profaned by sin or worldly occupations. Christ came to take up His abode in our souls and thus to complete the work of His redemption. We must assist Him by purifying our hearts, by casting out of this temple the idols that make it a place of pagan worship. Our soul must be a house of prayer. It must reproduce the quiet and peace of Bethania, a penitential spirit, a spirit of recollection and seclusion. Let us then seek the Lord while He may be found.

"I have put my trust in Thee, O Lord. I said, Thou art my God, my times are in Thy hands" (Offertory). "Thou art my God." I renounce all others. Now that I am no longer burdened by the cares of this world or by inordinate attachments, I may seek Thee.

"Seek ye the Lord." We have no work more important than to please God and to do His holy will. If only I please Him, then nothing else matters. God alone suffices.

Prayer

Look down upon Thy household, O Lord, and grant that our minds, having been chastened by the mortification of the flesh, may glow in Thy sight by the desire for Thee. Through Christ our Lord. Amen.

Ember Wednesday

"As He was yet speaking to the multitudes, behold His mother and His brethren stood without, seeking to speak to Him" (Gospel). With Mary, the mother of Jesus, who today gathers us about her in her sanctuary (the stational church for the Mass today is St. Mary Major in Rome), we come to Jesus as He speaks to the multitudes in the Holy Sacrifice of the Mass. We must listen carefully to His words. He tells us of the high vocation to which we are called by baptism, and He warns us lest we should prove unworthy of this high calling.

"The men of Ninive [the pagans] shall rise in judgment with this generation [the chosen people of Israel] and shall condemn it; because they did penance at the preaching of Jonas; and behold a greater than Jonas here. The queen of the South [of Saba] shall rise in judgment with this generation and shall condemn it; because she came from the ends of the earth to hear the wisdom of Solomon; and behold a greater than Solomon here" (Gospel). The chosen people would have nothing to do with their Savior when He came to them. They rejected Him, and therefore they themselves were rejected. We who are of the Gentiles have been chosen in their place. Mary and our Holy Mother the Church lead us to Him. In baptism we were made His brothers and sisters and were joined to Him in a union of prayer, in a union of life and spirit. From that moment we are bound to do the will of the Father.

"Behold the handmaid of the Lord" (Lk 1:28). Christ and His blessed mother had but one ambition, and that was to do the will of the Father. When Mary asked to see her Son, Jesus stretched forth His hand toward His disciples and says, "Behold My mother and My brethren; for whosoever shall do the will of My Father that is in heaven, He is My brother and sister and mother" (Gospel). To be a Christian is to be the brother of Christ, to have the same will, the same desires, the same burning zeal to accomplish the will of the Father. Have we really understood the implications of our baptism? Have we sought the will of the Father before all else?

The chosen people renounced their inheritance in spite of the abundant graces and the miraculous guidance they had received from God. In spite of the preaching of the prophets and the frequent warning of God, in spite of the revelations of the holy books and their possession of the true faith, they failed to recognize and accept the promised Messias. The long awaited Redeemer "came unto His own; but His own received Him not" (Jn 1:11). Israel repudiated its Savior and condemned Him to a most cruel death. How could such an action be possible? Yet it is possible and is a warning to us. Our having been called by baptism, our possession of faith and membership in the true Church, is no guarantee against infidelity or apostasy. "He that thinketh himself to stand, let him take heed lest he fall" (1 Cor 10:12). The enemy, the impure spirit, never sleeps. "Your adversary, the devil, as a roaring lion, goeth about seeking whom he may devour" (1 Pt 5:8). "And when the unclean spirit is gone out of a man [at the time of baptism or after a good confession], he walketh through dry places, seeking rest, and findeth none. Then he saith: I will return into my house from whence I came out; and coming he findeth it empty, swept, and garnished [by grace and the beginning of virtue]. Then he goeth and taketh with him seven other spirits more wicked than himself, and they enter in and dwell there; and the last state of that man is made worse than the first. So shall it be also to this wicked generation" (Gospel).

We, too, can prove unfaithful to our vocation, lose our faith, and fall away. How many examples of apostasy do we not have in the history of the Church, in the annals of religious houses, and even among the clergy! For this reason the Church presses upon us the urgency of self-examination, penance, and meditation during the holy season of Lent. In the lessons of Matins, two excellent examples are presented for our imitation. They are Moses and Elias. Moses withdraws from the world to the heights of Sinai. There amid the clouds, high above the lowly plains where other men idle away their time, he gives himself to fasting for forty days. In quiet communion with God he receives the Ten Commandments. Elias also fasts for forty days, and then food is given to him that enables him to make a pilgrimage to the mountain of God. During Lent we should, like Moses, withdraw from the world to spend our time in conversation with God. Like Elias, strengthened by the divine food of the Eucharist, we should abstain from the pleasures and vanities of secular life, and make our way steadfastly and courageously to the Mountain, which is Christ.

Our hearts are filled with gratitude for the great grace that has been given to us in baptism. We should renew our desire and our resolution to accomplish the will of the Father. "I will meditate on Thy commandments which I have loved exceedingly; and I will lift up my hands to Thy commandments, which I have loved" (Offertory). Let God's will be done in all things and before all things. Then we shall truly be the brothers and sisters of Christ, one in spirit with Him. In our prayers today we include all of our brethren, that God may give them the grace to prove faithful to their vocation and to remain faithful children of the Church, unflinching in their devotion to her.

"He that thinketh himself to stand, let him take heed lest he fall" (1 Cor 10:12). "Be sober and watch; because your adversary, the devil, as a roaring lion, goeth about seeking whom he may devour. Whom resist ye, strong in faith.... But the God of all graces, who hath called us to His eternal glory in Christ Jesus, after you have suffered a little will Himself perfect you and confirm you and establish you" (1 Pt 5:8–10). Give us the strength, O God, to resist all temptation, to escape all sin, and to embrace every grace.

Prayer

Mercifully hear our prayers, we beseech Thee, O Lord, and stretch forth the right hand of Thy majesty against all things that work against us.

Enlighten our minds, we beseech Thee, O Lord, with the light of Thy brightness, that we may be able to see what we ought to do and have the strength to do what is right. Through Christ our Lord. Amen.

Thursday

Today we are urged to do penance. The Church leads us to the place where the blessed martyr St. Lawrence suffered, the Church of St. Lawrence in Panisperna. On this spot St. Lawrence suffered his passion on the glowing coals and attained the crown of glory. During Lent we can share his struggles and his martyrdom by our self-denial, and thus atone for our past sins and negligences.

"The soul that sinneth, the same shall die" (Epistle). The sinner must not place the blame for his sins on others. He may not say that, because the father hath eaten sour grapes, the teeth of the children are set on edge. "As I live, saith the Lord, ... behold all souls are Mine; as the soul of the father so also the soul of the son is Mine. The soul that sinneth, the same shall die." Such a one can live only if he does penance for his sin and if the sin be forgiven. "And if a man be just and do judgment and justice, ... and hath not wronged any man, but hath restored the pledge to the debtor; ... hath given his bread to the hungry and hath covered the naked with a garment; hath not lent upon usury, nor taken any increase; ... hath walked in My commandments and kept My judgments, to do truth: he is just, he shall surely live, saith the Lord Almighty" (Epistle). The soul that would be saved must practice justice, forgiveness, charity, and fidelity to the commandments of God.

"At that time Jesus went forth and retired into the coasts of Tyre and Sidon. And behold a woman of Canaan [a heathen woman] who came out of these coasts, crying out, said to Him: Have mercy on me, O Lord, Thou Son of David; my daughter is grievously troubled by a devil. Who answered her not a word.... But she came and adored Him, saying: Lord, help me. Who answering, said: It is not good to take the bread of the children [the chosen people of Israel] and to cast it to the dogs [the heathens]. But she said: Yea, Lord, for the whelps also eat of the crumbs that fall from the table of their master. Then Jesus answering said to her: O woman, great is thy faith; be it done to thee as thou wilt. And her daughter was cured from that hour" (Gospel). This is a picture of the Church in action. She is the woman of Canaan who moves the Lord by her urgent entreaties. "Have mercy on me, O Lord, Thou Son of David; my daughter is grievously troubled by a devil." The Church beseeches the Lord for pardon and grace for her sinful children, who until the feast of Easter stand at the church door with the penitents. They have been separated from the altar, excluded from offering their gifts and from receiving Holy Communion; they are the "whelps" who may not share the bread at the table with the children, but who are fed from the crumbs that fall from the table. "It is not good to take the bread of the children and to cast it to the dogs." The Church continues to pray for sinners even though the Lord pretends not to hear. She will move Him with her importunity. "Woman, great is thy faith; be it done to thee as thou wilt."

"The soul that sinneth, the same shall die." But it has still a means of salvation. Its mother, the Church, still prays for it: "Have mercy on me, O Lord, Thou Son of David." The Church makes the concerns of her sinful children her own concern. She has committed her official prayer, the Divine Office, to her priests and religious, who as a body raise their hands together to ask the Lord for grace and mercy for those who live in sin. We should have full confidence in the intercession of the Church. What a consolation for us to remember that we never pray alone, that we are not alone in our anxiety for the conversion of those dear to us! Holy Mother the Church is also aware of their needs and is solicitous for them. And the Church will surely be heard.

Today in the spirit of the liturgy it behooves all of us to assume the attitude of penitents. With the Canaanite woman we should pray fervently and perseveringly: "Have mercy on me, O Lord; … my daughter [my soul] is grievously troubled by a devil." Bowed down and full of remorse we pray at the foot of the altar: *Mea culpa, mea culpa, mea maxima culpa.* Turning from our own unworthiness we approach the heavenly mother, Mary, the holy apostles Peter and Paul, blessed John the Baptist, and all the saints in heaven, and implore them to ask God to forgive us our sins. Then we turn to the celebrating priest and through him to the whole Catholic Church that they also may include us in their prayers to God. And the Church answers through her priests, "May the almighty God have mercy on you and forgive you your sins." "Show us O Lord Thy mercy, and grant us [in this holy season of Lent] Thy salvation." *Kyrie eleison; Christe eleison; Kyrie eleison.* The Church's prayer for mercy is heard.

The Church offers the Holy Sacrifice to the blessed Trinity as an act of propitiation for our sins and the sins of other men. After the Consecration she offers the blood of the Redeemer to the Father, begging Him to forgive us our sins.

Prayer

Behold with kindness, we beseech Thee, O Lord, the devotion of Thy people, that they who are now mortified in the flesh by abstinence, may be refreshed in mind by the fruit of their good works.

Grant to all Christian peoples, we beseech Thee, O Lord, to understand what they profess and to love the heavenly gifts to which they have recourse. Through Christ our Lord. Amen.

Ember Friday

Ember Friday finds us assembled in the church of the Twelve Apostles. The Mass has in mind both the penitents and the neophytes. We join ourselves to them at the Introit and pray, "Deliver me, O Lord, from my necessities, see my abjection and my labor, and forgive me all my sins. To Thee, O Lord, have I lifted up my soul; in Thee, O my God, I put my trust."

"If the wicked do penance for all his sins, which he hath committed, and keep all My Commandments, and do judgment and justice, living he shall live, and shall not die. I will not remember all his iniquities that he hath done; in his justice, which he hath wrought, he shall live. Is it My will that a sinner should die, saith the Lord God, and not that he should be converted from his ways and live? But if the just man turn himself away from his justice, and do iniquity according to all the abominations which the wicked man useth to work, shall he live? All his justices which he hath done shall not be remembered; … in his sin which he hath committed, in them he shall die. … And when the wicked turneth himself away from his wickedness, which he hath wrought, and doeth judgment and justice; he shall save his soul alive. Because he considereth and turneth away himself from all his iniquities which he hath wrought, he shall surely live and not die" (Epistle). Blessed penance! God rejoices in the opportunity we give Him for forgiving our sins. He is eager to forgive the sins of anyone who will turn away from his evil ways and do penance. "The days of penance have come," the liturgy admonishes us every day at Tierce. "The days of penance have come to us, to redeem our sins and save our souls." The chapter at Sext continues: "Let the wicked forsake his way and the unjust man his thoughts, and let him return to the Lord; and He will have mercy on him" (Is 55:7).

"Jesus went up to Jerusalem." Christ came to Jerusalem on a Sabbath and approached the pool of Bethsaida. The pool was surrounded by a building having five porches, where lay a great multitude of the sick who were waiting for the movement of the water. He who first reached the water after it had been moved by the angel, was freed from whatever infirmity troubled him. Here Jesus met a man who had suffered for thirty-eight years. "Wilt thou be made whole? The infirm man answered, "Sir, I have no man, when the water is troubled, to put me into the pond; for whilst I am coming, another goeth down before me. Jesus saith to him: Arise, take up thy bed and walk. And immediately the man was made whole, and he took up his bed and walked." What the Gospel records becomes for us a reality in the holy liturgy. The porches of the pool of Bethsaida are for us the world in which we live. Here on every hand lie the sick, the halt, and the lame. The pool is the Church with its fountains of grace which spring up eternally. We are the sick man of the Gospel. Our sickness is described by the number thirty-eight. Forty, according to St. Augustine, is the number of perfection. Our number is lacking two of reaching perfection. The two things that we lack are the love of God and the love of our neighbor. The Sabbath on which the Lord comes to us is the moment of our baptism. In gratitude we recall our first meeting with the Savior, when He asked us if we would be whole, and He healed us from Original Sin. We remember also the many other Sabbaths on which He came to us in the sacrament of penance to free us from our infirmities, when He again asked us, "Wilt thou be made whole?" We replied to Him through His representative, the priest, and we acknowledged our misery. But he consoled us and said, "Arise ... and walk." Thy sins are forgiven thee. "Behold thou art made whole. Sin no more, lest some worse thing happen to thee" (Gospel).

"Deliver me, O Lord, from my necessities; see my abjection and my labor, and forgive me all my sins" (Introit). "Behold thou art made whole." With a grateful heart we recite the Offertory prayer, "Bless the Lord, O my soul, and never forget all He hath done for thee; and thy youth shall be renewed like the eagle's." During this Mass and at the time of Holy Communion we shall be made whole. "Thou art made whole. Sin no more, lest some worse thing happen to thee."

The liturgy insists on penance, and justly so. We Christians of the twentieth century are lacking in a real understanding of the necessity, purpose, and value of penance. A true penitential spirit and real works of penance are for the most part unknown to us; we shy away from mortification and privation. We have no patience with suffering and seldom have control over our desires and impulses. We fail to recognize the danger of too much sleep, luxurious dress, and sumptuous meals; and we seek to avoid every inconvenience and spiritual burden. It is a grave burden on us if we are required to fix an hour for rising and for performing our duties. We fret at the loss of our trivial pastimes, and at the sacrifice of empty pleasures. We find it difficult to control our tongues, to guard our eyes, to temper our curiosity, to refuse some dainty morsel, to omit some slight diversion, to give up even some sinful habit that has been dominating us. If this is our disposition, how shall we overcome temptation? "The kingdom of heaven [of virtue and perfection] suffereth violence, and the violent bear it away" (Mt 11:12). "Enter ye in at the narrow gate; for wide is the gate and broad is the way that leadeth to destruction, and many there are who go in thereat. How narrow is the gate and strait is the way that leadeth to life, and few there are that find it" (Mt 7:13–14).

PRAYER

Be gracious to Thy people, O Lord, and as Thou dost make them devoted to Thee, mercifully cherish them with Thy benign assistance.

Hear us, O merciful God, and show to our minds the light of Thy grace. Through Christ our Lord. Amen.

Ember Saturday

The liturgy of the Mass today again recalls the early ages of the Church. The stational church is St. Peter's in Rome, and the divine services begin at night. Early Sunday morning, at sunrise, we bring the service to a close with the Eucharistic sacrifice and the reception of Holy Communion. Thus we pass the lenten night of our earthly existence to our real life after the resurrection of Easter.

The liturgy attempts to arouse in us a longing for redemption and the brightness of Easter morning. We return to the hour when for the first time, at the moment of our baptism, the heavenly light shone upon us. We cast off at that moment the darkness of sin and freed ourselves of Satan and his pomps. We turned to Christ, the light of men, the sun of life, and promised: I believe; I dedicate myself to God; I dedicate myself to Jesus Christ; I dedicate myself to the Holy Spirit and to the Church. Today we relive that moment. "This day the Lord thy God hath commanded thee to do these commandments and judgments [baptismal vows], and to keep and fulfill them with all thy heart and with all thy soul. Thou hast chosen the Lord this day to be thy God, and to walk in His ways, and keep His ceremonies and precepts and judgments, and obey His commands. And the Lord hath chosen thee this day to be His peculiar people and to keep all His commandments, ... that thou mayest be a holy people of the Lord thy God" (First lesson). As the people of the Lord, we make our journey through the night of our earthly life toward the light. We are surrounded on all sides by hostile adversaries (Second and third lessons). We see ourselves menaced by Satan, by the world, by our base passions, by the perversity of our own heart. We therefore cry out to God, "Have mercy upon us, O God of all, and behold us in the light of Thy mercies" (Fourth lesson). "Look down, O God our protector, and grant us who are burdened with the weight of our sins, to obtain mercy and thus serve Thee with a tranquil mind" (Second Collect). The liturgy here expresses its longing for light, freedom, and resurrection from the death and bondage of sin. It longs for the coming of the angel of the Lord, who will snatch us from the darkness of the night and lead us to the brightness of eternal day, as he saved the three young men from the fiery furnace (Fifth lesson).

The Mass shows us how this longing may be fulfilled. In the Gospel we are led up to Mount Tabor so that with Peter, in whose church we celebrate the holy mysteries today, we may be witnesses of the transfiguration of the Lord. The path of our life leads through the night of our earthly pilgrimage, and as we follow it we must embrace the cross, mortification, humiliation, and suffering; but it will lead us finally to the heights of Mount Tabor and transfiguration. Christ is the head and we are the members of one body. Today He appears in the splendor of His transfiguration on Mount Tabor and in the Holy Sacrifice; we who are members of His body will one day share in that glorification, and with the Church we shall live eternally united to Him. The transfigured host on the Tabor of the altar is our certain assurance of the future glorification and transfiguration of the Church. With confidence we dwell, not on the night that surrounds us now, but rather on the glory of the awakening that awaits us in the eternal transfiguration of the everlasting Easter. "Lord, it is good for us to be here."

Today we renew our baptismal vows. At the celebration of the Mass we should repeat our *Abrenuntio:* "I renounce." With the gifts of bread and wine which we bring to the altar, we join ourselves to the sacrifice and pledge: "Receive my liberty, my memory, my understanding, my will. I give Thee all that I am so that You may do with me what You will."

Transfiguration! After the lenten trials and sacrifices of our earthly life, we may look forward to transfiguration in heaven. Now we see only the hard, stony path that stretches out before us. We are so absorbed by the struggle with ourselves, so busy with the sacrifices, prayers, and works that are imposed on us, that we are prone to lose sight of the glory that awaits us. If we could keep the thought of our future glory before us, we should find new courage and strength to bear our trials and hardships more joyfully. If only the glorified Savior were more truly a part of our conscious life! Today the holy liturgy urges us to acquire such an awareness.

"That thou mayest be a holy people of the Lord" (First lesson). Baptism, religious profession, and holy orders make us the holy people of the Lord. How easily we forget that we are His chosen people! How readily we forsake Him and turn to lesser gods!

Prayer

Look favorably upon Thy people, we beseech Thee, O Lord, and by Thy mercy turn aside from them the scourges of Thy wrath.

Direct our actions, we beseech Thee, O Lord, by Thy inspiration and further them with Thy continual help; that every prayer and work of ours may begin always from Thee and through Thee likewise be ended. Through Christ our Lord. Amen.

Second Sunday of Lent

The Mass

In early Christian times, when the fervor and heroism of the first converts was still ardent, the Ember celebration began late on Saturday evening. On this day the faithful in Rome gathered at the Church of St. Peter. Since there were many lessons to be read before the conferring of holy orders, and since there were to be lengthy sermons by the bishops, and the alms were to be distributed to the poor, the services lasted until the next morning. Thus it happened that the Mass which we now have on Ember Saturday was actually said on the following Sunday morning. As men grew to dislike the long services, however, they were shortened and were transferred to the morning of Ember Saturday. A new Mass was then composed for the Sunday which followed. This Sunday Mass was more or less a substitution for the Mass of Ember Saturday and was made up largely from that Mass. The Mass for the second Sunday of Lent, therefore, breathes the spirit of Ember Saturday. It centers about the transfiguration on Mount Tabor. Our Savior in His transfiguration is the first gleam of light in the gloom of the lenten season. Thus we are reminded that we go through darkness to light, through suffering and death to life and resurrection, and eventually to transfiguration.

We are conscious of our many sins, and in the Introit we cry out for God's mercy, for the remission of our sins, for the cleansing even from all sinful thoughts (Collect). We long for the light of the resurrection which illuminates Christ in His transfiguration. "What fellowship hath light with darkness?" (2 Cor 6:14.) We are the children of light, and therefore we should not linger in the mire of passion, lust, and avarice. "God hath not called us unto uncleanness, but unto sanctification" to walk in the light (Epistle). Walking in the light of the transfiguration today are the apostles (Gospel). Filled with reverence and awe they fall on their faces and exclaim, "Lord, it is good for us to be here." In the mind of the liturgy today we are the apostles.

As we gaze upon the splendor of the scene, we express our faith in the transfiguration. We know that all too soon we shall see this same Christ in shame and humiliation on the Mount of Olives and on Golgotha. We know that we, too, shall one day be transfigured after we have suffered a similar passion and struggle in our earthly life. Through the night of this suffering we shall pass to the light. This belief leads us to recite the Credo with joy. "I look for the resurrection of the dead and the life of the world to come." We are strengthened in our resolutions. "I will meditate on Thy commandments, which I have loved exceedingly; and I will lift up my hands to Thy commandments, which I have loved" (Offertory).

In the Consecration of the Mass, that which was related in the Gospel becomes a reality. Our altar is Mount Tabor. On this altar is enthroned the transfigured God. The apostles heard a voice from heaven saying, "This is My beloved Son, in whom I am well pleased." To Him we are now closely united in the Holy Sacrifice of the Mass, and with Him we become one victim, one host, one sacrifice offered to the Father. With Him and through Him we, too, are the sons of God. Through His lips we can cry, *Pater noster:* "Our Father." Truly the Father hears in our prayers and supplications the voice of His beloved Son, and He is well pleased. We may expect, then, that He will shower His blessings and His graces upon us in Holy Communion. There our hearts become a Mount Tabor, the scene of a delightful transfiguration. The light surrounding this transfiguration dispels the darkness within our soul. The beloved Son becomes our most treasured possession. We live, now not we, but Christ lives in us. He implants in our hearts the seed of a future transfiguration. Let us then, advance through the night of our earthly life, bravely, firmly, and with confidence that we may one day reach the brightness of the eternal Easter. "Walk then, as children of the light" (Eph 5:8).

Meditation

Last Sunday we considered the temptation of Christ in the desert. Today His triumph is acknowledged on the heights of Mount Tabor by Moses and Elias (the Old Testament), and God rewards it by the Transfiguration. Today the Father in heaven acknowledges Christ as His Son. "This is my beloved Son, in whom I am well pleased; hear ye Him" (Gospel).

"At that time Jesus taketh Peter and James and John his brother, and bringeth them up into a high mountain apart; and He was transfigured before them. And His face did shine as the sun; and His garments became white as snow. And behold, there appeared to them Moses and Elias talking with Him. And Peter answering, said to Jesus: Lord, it is good for us to be here.... And as he was yet speaking, behold a bright cloud overshadowed them. And lo! a voice out of the cloud saying: This is My beloved Son, in whom I am well pleased: hear ye Him" (Gospel). In Peter and James and John we recognize our Holy Mother the Church. During the season of Lent, Christ takes His Church aside to the mount that He may reveal to her His glory and His essence. In view of His approaching passion, His apostles, His Church, must be strengthened by the vision of His transfiguration. By this revelation it is made aware of His divinity and immortality. Today we take the place of His apostles, and we climb Mount Tabor in order to see Him transfigured. We shall not lose faith in Him when we see Him descend to suffering and humiliation. "Brethren: We pray and beseech you in the Lord Jesus, that as you have received from us how you ought to walk and to please God, so also you would walk, that you may abound the more. For you know what precepts I have given you by the Lord Jesus. For this is the will of God, your sanctification, that you should abstain from fornication.... God hath not called us to uncleanness, but unto sanctification in Christ Jesus our Lord" (Epistle).

Bright heights of Tabor! On all sides yawn the abysses of darkness and sin. The Epistle mentions especially the abyss of fornication and sins of lust and all dishonest dealings with our fellow men. Then St. Paul warns us: "The Lord is the avenger of all those things, as we have told you before and have testified. For God hath not called you to uncleanness, but unto sanctification." Thus the lesson we have to learn during Lent is that we must allow the transfigured one to lift us up and to transfigure us, not only in the next life, but here on earth — now. We must struggle now to sanctify our thoughts, our affections, our intentions, and our motives. Our prayers and labors and sufferings must be transfigured while we are still in this life, or they will be worthless. "This is the will of God, your sanctification." We shall be transfigured when we have obtained the mastery over our sensual appetites, over the lust of the eyes, the desires of the flesh, and the pride of life. Everything that is dishonorable in our life must be cast off. The transfiguration of the outward man is achieved by disciplining the tongue, the senses, and the whole body. The transfiguration of the inner man is brought about by the cultivation of purity of thought and motives. Thus in the eyes of the true Christian there already shines some of the brilliancy of the transfigured Christ. Something of the whiteness of His garments and the brilliancy of His face as it appeared on Mount Tabor is already shared by the Christian who leads a pure life in this world. Such a transfiguration is the purpose of all our lenten practices.

Today we see Christ transfigured on Mount Tabor, and by this vision we are strengthened and confirmed in our belief in Him. We look up to Him, and having been strengthened by the vision of His power and glory, we go bravely on our way. Dead to our sensual passions and to unjust dealings with our fellow men, we walk as we have been taught to walk in order that we may please God and advance in perfection. This is the will of God, our transfiguration, our sanctification, that we may arise new and perfect men. During the season of Lent we ardently desire to escape from the mire of lust, worldliness, and self-love, and to ascend the mountain of the transfiguration. "Remember, O Lord, ... Thy mercies that are from the beginning of the world.... Deliver us, O God of Israel, from all our tribulations" (Introit). Deliver us from the slavery of all that is sinful, worldly, and unjust. "Harken to the voice of my prayer, for to Thee will I pray, O Lord" (Communion). Transform my soul through Holy Communion, that it may be purified from all uncleanness and may be transfigured by sanctifying grace, by the gifts of the Holy Spirit, by virtue, and by good works.

Today we see Christ transfigured again on the Tabor of our altars. His face shines like the sun. His garments are white as snow. Reverently we prostrate ourselves with Peter, James, and John, and adore Him. Christ comes to us in Holy Communion; He touches us and says to us, "Arise, and fear not." We should be strengthened by this assurance of the Master and go forth bravely to meet the trials and tribulations of our daily life. Supported by His strength, we are prepared to meet the temptations of the world, the flesh, and the devil. Holy Communion gives us the strength to walk as we were taught to walk, that we may please God and sanctify our souls. The inner purity which Holy Communion produces in us shines in our faces and makes known to the world the transfiguration that has taken place in us.

Our Holy Mother the Church, however, is grieved at the sight of so many of her children who do not walk as they were taught to walk, who are not pleasing to God, who do not keep themselves clean, but give themselves up to impurity and lust. They are like the Gentiles who know not God. They were invited and were given the grace to walk with Christ in the splendor of Mount Tabor, in purity, in holiness, and in a transfigured life. But instead they have given themselves up to sensuality and uncleanness. Their lives are a source of great sadness to the Church. "The troubles of my heart are multiplied," she prays to the Lord. "Deliver me from my necessities, O Lord. See my abjection and my labor, and forgive me all my sins" (Gradual). See my sorrow and grief over my many straying children. In the Mass we cry out, "Forgive us our trespasses, ... and lead us not into temptation, but deliver us from evil," the evils of sensuality, sin, and eternal death.

Prayer

O God, who seest that we are wholly without strength in ourselves, keep us both within and without; that we may be protected in body from all adversity, and cleansed in mind from every evil thought. Through Christ our Lord. Amen.

Monday

Today for the first time the theme of Christ's passion enters the lenten Masses. Christ is persecuted by the Jews. We take an active part in this persecution which reached its climax in the crucifixion; but it continues in His mystical body, the Church; and only on the last day will it finally be overcome, and Christ and His Church will be triumphant.

In the Epistle, Daniel represents Christ. Our Savior has taken upon Himself the sins of the world. By His suffering He expiated them, and on the cross His blood pleaded for forgiveness for His brethren. "O Lord, our God, who hast brought forth Thy people out of the land of Egypt, with a strong hand [through baptism], . . . we have sinned, we have committed iniquity, O Lord, against all Thy justice; let Thy wrath and Thy indignation be turned away, I beseech Thee, from Thy city Jerusalem [the Church]. . . . For by reason of our sins and the iniquities of our fathers, Jerusalem and Thy people are a reproach to all that are round about us. Now therefore, O our God, hear the supplications of Thy servant and his prayers; and show Thy face upon Thy sanctuary which is desolate. . . . O Lord, hear; O Lord, be appeased; harken and do; delay not for Thy own sake, O my God; because Thy name is invoked upon Thy city and upon Thy people, O Lord our God." Thus our Lord prays for us, His people. Once He prayed for us on the cross; now He prays for us each day in the Mass, which is a sacrifice of propitiation and of petition for pardon and for grace. Alas, the many sins and injustices that are committed by the holy people of God! What would have happened to us if Christ had not taken our sins upon Himself? How should we be saved if He had not interceded for us? In spite of our unworthiness, He offered Himself for us on the cross, and continues to do so daily in the Mass.

"I go" (Gospel). Christ clearly foresaw the sufferings that awaited Him. He knew beforehand that He would be obliged to submit to the scourging and the disgraceful mockery before the judges and the soldiers of Herod. He knew that the people whom He loved so tenderly would reject Him. Nevertheless He says, "I go." His love of the Father and His intense desire to make reparation for the sins of men urge Him on. Love moves Him to redeem men and thus transform them from the children of wrath into the sons of God. Because He wishes to share with us the blessedness of His life in God, He can say: "I go" to offer Myself up for all men.

The Son of Man, in the name of penitent sinners, now goes before His father in the Holy Sacrifice. He makes petition for His Church, humiliated by the sins of so many of her children. On the altar He repeats in an unbloody manner the sacrifice which He offered on the cross, that He might earn pardon, grace, and help for His Church. Everything that He did while He was on earth, He now offers for this intention. He repeats His prayers, His sufferings, and His works, and offers them for each one of us. He goes, and we go with Him. We recognize in the Mass the repetition of His sacrifice on the cross, inspired by the same love and by the same desire to redeem and save us. The Son of Man goeth, and we join ourselves to Him and to the offering of bread and wine, that we may become one sacrifice of expiation and immolation with Him. Having prepared ourselves to sacrifice everything for Him, we also become holocausts of love. We also are prepared to be rejected, judged unjustly, humiliated, and crucified with our Lord and Savior.

We join our prayers to those of the Savior who today lifts His voice to plead for His Church. We read the touching words of the Epistle and offer them as our prayer for all humanity.

Today we have met in the church of St. Clement. High up in the apse there is a beautiful mosaic cross which reminds us of His prophecy, "When you shall have lifted up the Son of Man [on the cross], then shall you know that I am He" (Gospel). During Lent we should learn to recognize Him in His passion, in His self-immolation, in His humiliation, and in His charity.

"He that sent Me is with Me, and He hath not left Me alone; for I do always the things that please Him" (Gospel). Would that we could truly say with our Savior, "I do always the things that please Him"!

PRAYER

Grant, we beseech Thee, O almighty God, that Thy people, while afflicting the flesh by fasting from food, may follow after justice by abstaining from sin.

Hear our supplications, O almighty God, and kindly grant the effect of Thy wonted mercy to those whom Thou dost permit to rely confidently on Thy goodness. Through Christ our Lord. Amen.

Tuesday

"I have sought Thy face; Thy face, O Lord, I will seek; turn not away Thy face from me" (Introit). With this longing for the countenance of the Lord, we make our way with the penitents and the neophytes to the sanctuary of St. Balbina. In order to appear properly in the presence of the Lord, whose image looks down upon us from the apse of this basilica, we leave behind us all that pertains to the world. The leading thought of the liturgy of the day is that the life of the Christian should be one of humble service offered as a gift of love to God.

The gift of love. St. Balbina was one of those heroic Roman virgins who gave themselves up entirely to the practice of works of charity. She devoted her fortune, her energy, and her full time to the care of the Christians confined to prison, to the sick, the poor, and the oppressed. St. Balbina has a prototype in the kind widow of Sarephta, the pagan woman of whom the Epistle speaks today. Elias the prophet is sent to Sarephta and by chance he meets the widow gathering wood. He addresses her and makes the request: "Give me a little water in a vessel, that I may drink,... and a morsel of bread." The widow promptly shares with the prophet her last morsel, which she had intended for herself and her son. The widow's charity and her generous alms are promptly rewarded. "The pot of meal shall not waste, nor the cruse of oil be diminished.... And from that day the pot of meal wasted not, and the cruse of oil was not diminished." Almsgiving always brings blessings, whether to the widow of Sarephta or to St. Balbina. Therefore in your almsdeeds give gladly and generously. "Give and it shall be given to you; good measure and pressed down and shaken together and running over shall they give into your bosom. For with the same measure that you shall mete withal, it shall be measured to you again" (Lk 6:38).

Humble service. "He that is greatest among you shall be your servant" (Gospel). The pagan, the unbaptized, the scribes and the Pharisees are of another opinion. They sit on the chair of Moses. They are the teachers and set the standard for others. They love to be heard, to be seen, to be admired, and they require others to listen to their wisdom. They allow themselves to be called Rabbi, Master. Be not thus, you who are baptized. "He that is the greatest among you shall be your servant." The greatness of a Christian does not consist in the adulation of men, but rather in the humble service of his brethren in Christ, for which St. Balbina has given us a sublime example. Her greatness consists in the humble service of others. "He that shall humble himself shall be exalted" (Gospel). We are to see in our brother, who is a child of God and a brother of Christ, another Christ. When we find an opportunity to serve our brother, we should congratulate ourselves that we have found an opportunity to serve and help Christ, for out of love and reverence for Him we should do the deed. "As long as you did it to one of these, My least brethren, you did it to Me" (Mt 25:40).

The liturgy urges us to perform good works during Lent and particularly to give alms to the needy. "Cast thy care upon the Lord, and He shall sustain thee" (Gradual). He sustained the widow of Sarephta, who had "only a handful of meal in the pot, and a little oil in a cruse" (Epistle). She had intended to prepare a little hearth cake for herself and her son, "that we may eat it and die." Although there was a great famine in the country, the prophet tells her, "fear not... but first make for me of the same meal a little hearth cake, and bring it to me; and after make for thyself and thy son." The widow obeys the word of the prophet, and behold, "From that day the pot of meal wasted not, and the cruse of oil was not diminished." Thus does God reward alms given for His sake and for the sake of Christ. "Cast thy care upon the Lord, and He shall sustain thee."

"Deal thy bread to the hungry and bring the needy and the harborless into thy house; when thou shalt see one naked, cover him and despise not thy own flesh" (Is 58:7). These words, which the liturgy speaks to us daily during Lent (at None), the early Christians understood literally and fulfilled literally. It was their custom to share, not only their bread, but all their personal property as well. They brought to the apostles even the wages they received for their labor and the money received from the sale of their property, so that none of their fellow Christians should be in want. That is the spirit of true Christianity.

"Have mercy on me, O Lord, according to Thy great mercy; O Lord, blot out my iniquity" (Offertory). In almsdeeds we have an excellent means of atoning for our sins.

"He that is the greatest among you shall be your servant.... And he that shall humble himself shall be exalted" (Gospel). In the Sacrifice of the Mass we behold Him who "humbled Himself, becoming obedient unto death, even to the death of the cross. For which cause God also hath exalted Him and hath given Him a name which is above all names" (Phil 2:8 f.). We are to follow Him on this path of humiliation by humbling ourselves, by submitting to the will of God, and by the charitable service of our fellow men.

Prayer

We beseech Thee, O Lord, kindly to support us in this holy observance, that what we know by Thy authority should be done, we may accomplish with Thy help.

Mercifully listen to our supplications, O Lord, and heal the maladies of our souls, that having received the remission of our sins, we may ever rejoice in Thy blessing. Through Christ our Lord. Amen.

Wednesday

Before going up to Jerusalem with His disciples, Christ predicts to them His passion and death. "The Son of Man shall be betrayed to the chief priests and the scribes, and they shall condemn Him to death, and shall deliver Him to the Gentiles to be mocked and scourged and crucified; and the third day He shall rise again" (Gospel). Then the mother of two of the apostles, James and John, approached Him with the request: "Say that these my two sons may sit, the one at Thy right hand and the other at Thy left, in Thy kingdom. And Jesus answering said: You know not what you ask. Can you drink the chalice that I shall drink? They say to Him: We can." This Gospel is read today in the stational church of St. Cecilia. Just as Salome, the mother of James and John, brought her sons to Christ, so St. Cecilia brought her spiritual sons, Valerian and Tiburtius, to Christ, to baptism, and to martyrdom. Salome and Cecilia are types of the Church, who during Lent leads her children, the neophytes, to baptism, to Christ, and to participation in the sufferings and resurrection of Christ.

The Church prays for her children. In the Gospel of the Mass today, Salome leading her sons to Christ represents the Church praying for her sons. The mother of James and John forgets herself and casts herself down at the feet of the Lord to make a request for her children. In the Epistle, too, we find a picture of the Church praying for her children. Esther the queen entreats King Assuerus in behalf of her people who had been condemned to destruction. Esther finding favor in the sight of the king, is a picture of the Church, who is all-powerful in her prayers to God. She prays day and night through her priests and religious, through her saints in heaven and on earth. "O Lord, all things are in Thy power and there is none that can resist Thy will, if Thou determine to save Israel [souls].... And now, O Lord, O King,... have mercy on Thy people, because our enemies resolve to destroy us and extinguish Thy inheritance. Despise not Thy portion, which Thou hast redeemed for Thyself out of Egypt. Hear my supplication and be merciful to Thy lot and inheritance, and turn our mourning into joy, that we may live and praise Thy name, O Lord; and shut not the mouths of them that sing to Thee, O Lord our God" (Epistle). Thus the Church prays during Lent for her children, the neophytes, the sinners, the penitents, and for all of us. The world owes its continued existence to the continual prayer of the Church.

The Church leads souls to Christ as did St. Cecilia, who led her pagan friends, Valerian and Tiburtius, to Christ. We see the Church also exemplified in Salome in the Gospel. She has no other mission than to point the way to Christ. Through her sacraments and her sacrifices, in life and in death, she leads men to Christ. She takes her children by the hand and leads them to Christ, who is the fountain of truth, of life, and of grace. She and she alone can lead us to Christ and to eternal salvation. Lead us, O Holy Mother the Church, for thou alone dost know the way to Christ.

The Church also induces her children to participate in the chalice of the Lord. When a man becomes a Christian through baptism, he begins to taste the chalice of Christ. "Can you drink the chalice that I shall drink?" the Lord asks us. With James, and John, and Valerian, and Tiburtius we answer, "We can." We are determined to share everything with Christ, into whose body we have been incorporated by baptism. We accompany Him and turn away steadfastly from the world and its vanities. We wish to share His love of poverty, His privations, His mortifications, His self-denial, by patiently bearing the hardships of our state of life. We follow Him by a willing acceptance of difficulties, sufferings, troubles, and reverses. Thus we become martyrs of love, confident of His love and providence.

The Church prays for her children and leads them to Christ and makes them share His suffering and humiliation. We should not fear when she invites us to share with Him fasting, self-denial, and the cross. By thus inviting us she proves that she is from above and not of the earth. She is filled with the spirit of God, not with the spirit of the world.

The Church leads us to Christ especially in the celebration of Mass and in the reception of Holy Communion. We participate in the Mass in order that we may drink His chalice with Him. We place ourselves on the altar next to the Lamb of God, and with ourselves we offer everything that we possess, everything that we are. In all sincerity we wish to be offered with

Him and to share His chalice completely. For this reason in Holy Communion He fills us with a consuming desire to make sacrifices for Him. Now we feel strong enough to drink His chalice throughout the day in whatever form it may appear. To attend Mass and to live in a spiritual atmosphere now means that we, too, are a sacrifice to God. It means the acceptance of trials sent by God and the search for voluntary mortification. It means that we must surrender ourselves unconditionally to the will of God, becoming like grains of wheat that are ground between the millstones of the duties of our state of life. It means that we must become a bread which at the moment of consecration will cease to be bread; that is, we shall cease to live for our own sake and begin to live for Christ.

Prayer

Look upon Thy people with favor, we beseech Thee, O Lord, and grant that they whom thou dost command to abstain from food may also refrain from baneful vices.

O God, the restorer and lover of innocence, direct the hearts of Thy servants unto Thee, that being filled with the fervor of Thy spirit, they may be found steadfast in faith and efficacious in works. Through Christ our Lord. Amen.

Thursday

Our lives should be devoted to penance. Today we join the penitents at St. Mary's in Trastevere. They are allowed to assist at the celebration of Mass only "at the gate" and are excluded from the reception of Holy Communion. They are like the miserable Lazarus and wait for "the crumbs that fell from the rich man's table"; that is, from the Christians who are permitted to receive Holy Communion. Today we shall meditate on the curse of sin in this life, and the wages of sin in the next; meanwhile let us earnestly perform penance in expiation for our sins.

What should the true Christian be like? He should be like "a tree that is planted by the waters, that spreadeth out its roots towards moisture.... And the leaf thereof shall be green, neither shall it cease at any time to bring forth fruit" (Epistle). The Christian should be a tree planted by the waters of grace in the fruitful soil of the Church. He should be a branch of the true vine, Christ, and live by the strength and vigor of the vine. When we commit sin, we cease to be green and to bear fruit. We become like withered and barren trees, fit only to be burned. By sin we voluntarily separate ourselves from God. The veins through which the life blood of Christ reached us are now severed, and we are dead to grace and dead to God. Holy love has been banished from our soul. Only the divine virtues of faith and hope remain behind as mute witnesses of the desolation of a holy place. These virtues, too, may die as a result of frequent sin. The yoke of sin becomes heavier with the passing years. Evil habits bind the soul in iron bands and rob her of all freedom. Thus she loses courage to resist and becomes an easy prey to temptation and to her own passions. That is the penalty for sin already here on the earth.

The final wages of sin is the eternal punishment of hell. Hell is the exclusion of the soul from God, from all light, from all satisfaction, from the one true good. It tortures the soul with unhappiness and merciless flames, in which, according to today's Gospel, the glutton languishes. This desolate soul craves a drop of water to moisten his tongue; but his longing is in vain. He suffers unspeakable pain and looks about him for help. He looks in vain, for the time for mercy, the time for repentance and conversion, the time of grace, is past. Only one thing remains, and that is an eternity in hell. This is the eternal penalty of sin. While man is still on earth, sin can be expiated; once he has passed into eternity, it is too late. Let us, then, do our good works and perform our penances while we have time. Let us "commend ourselves to God in much patience, in fasting, in the armor of justice" (Antiphon for Sext); that is, through a holy Christian life.

In the Offertory we are reminded of the true Moses, Christ. He comes in the Mass to offer Himself to the Father as a victim for our sins. He comes to make satisfaction for us, to pacify His Father, and to obtain forgiveness for men. At the Consecration we receive Him into our hands and raise Him up to heaven saying: "Why, O Lord, art Thou angry with Thy people? Let the anger of Thy soul be appeased." Remember Thy Son, who on the tree of the holy cross poured out His blood; and for His sake have mercy on us. "And the Lord was appeased from the evil which He had threatened to do to His people" (Offertory). At the Communion the Father gives His Son the kiss of peace; now we, too, have peace, for we are again the children of God, living members of Christ. At Easter, Christ will be able to take us with Him to the Father. "He that eateth My flesh and drinketh My blood, abideth in Me and I in him" (Communion).

Which was the more fortunate, the poor Lazarus or the rich worldling? What has happened to the riches and the pleasures of the rich worldling? Money and riches led him astray, and now he is buried in hell. "Woe to you that are rich" (Lk 6:24). There is indeed great danger in wealth. "Cursed be the man that trusteth in man and maketh flesh his arm [the perishable goods of this earth, such as money, pleasure, and position], and whose heart departeth from the Lord. For he shall be like a tamaric in the desert" (Epistle). O unhappy worldling!

"Blessed be the man that trusteth in the Lord, and the Lord shall be his confidence. And he shall be as a tree that is planted by the waters, that spreadeth out its roots towards moisture; and it shall not fear when the heat cometh. And the leaf thereof shall be green, . . . neither shall it cease at any time to bring forth fruit" (Epistle). Such is the poor, sick Lazarus.

"The heart is perverse above all things, and unsearchable; who can know it? I am the Lord who search the heart and prove the reins, who give to every one according to his way, and according to the fruit of his devices; saith the Lord Almighty" (Epistle) both to the glutton and to Lazarus.

He who humbles himself, as did poor Lazarus, he who does penance for his sins, acknowledges them with humility, and performs good works to expiate them, will be heard. "Do penance."

Prayer

Grant us, we beseech Thee, O Lord, the assistance of Thy grace, that being duly intent on fasting and prayer, we may be delivered from the enemies of soul and body.

Hear, O Lord, Thy servants, and shower perpetual kindness upon those who ask it; that to those who glory in Thee, their Creator and Ruler, Thou mayest restore an abundance of good things, and preserve what Thou dost restore. Through Christ our Lord. Amen.

Friday

Four weeks from today will be Good Friday. In the Collect of the Mass today we pray that we may receive the grace to prepare ourselves for the coming solemnities with sincere minds. Thus our thoughts today are carried forward to the passion and death of our Lord. The atmosphere of Good Friday hovers over the liturgy today and takes possession of our soul.

The liturgy furnishes us with an image of the suffering Savior in the person of Joseph in Egypt. Joseph is the favorite son of Jacob, but he is hated by his brethren. Jacob sends Joseph to his brothers in Sichem, where they have been pasturing their sheep. Joseph carries out the wish of his father and finds his brethren, not in Sichem but in Dothain. They see him coming from afar and say, "Let us kill him and cast him into some old pit, and we will say: Some evil beast hath devoured him" (Epistle). Ruben, one of the brethren, is opposed to this plan, and they are content to cast him into a dry cistern; later they decide to sell him as a slave for thirty pieces of silver, to a group of merchants who are making their way into Egypt. Then they tell their father that Joseph has been slain by a wild beast.

Meanwhile Joseph, who was rejected and sold into captivity by his brethren, is wonderfully exalted by the Lord in Egypt. He becomes the first minister to the king of Egypt and saves the country from famine. When his brethren come to pay their respects to the King and obtain grain, Joseph reveals his identity, and his aged father hastens to his son, whom he had thought to be dead, and finds a home and needed assistance. "In my trouble I cried out to the Lord; and He heard me. O Lord, deliver my soul from wicked lips and a deceitful tongue" (Gradual). Thus the liturgy wishes us to pray to the Savior, of whom Joseph is a figure.

"A householder ... planted a vineyard, and made a hedge round about it, and dug in it a press, and built a tower [for protection], and let it out to husbandmen, and went into a strange country. And when the time of the fruit drew nigh, He sent his servants to the husbandmen that they might receive the fruits thereof; and the husbandmen, laying hands on his servants, beat one and killed another." Again the householder sent other servants, who also were treated cruelly. "Last of all he sent to them his son, saying: They will reverence my son. But the husbandmen, seeing the son, said among themselves: This is the heir; come, let us kill him and we shall have his inheritance. And taking him, they cast him forth out of the vineyard and killed him" (Gospel). The householder is God, who sent His prophets and servants to His chosen people. But Israel rejected the messengers whom He sent to them, and even stoned them and put them to death. Then God sent his own divine Son. "He came unto His own, and his own received Him not" (Jn 1:11). Like Joseph, He is sold to his enemies by one of His own disciples for thirty pieces of silver. He has rendered nothing but good to His people, but they reject Him as their Savior, turn from Him, and shout to His judges, "Crucify Him; crucify Him.... His blood be upon us and our children" (Lk 23:21; Mt 27:25). Betrayed, despised, disgraced, and burdened with the curse of His people, He staggers painfully toward the heights of Calvary. There He will be crucified and His blood will be shed. But on "the third day He shall rise again" (Mt 20:19). "The stone which the builders rejected, the same is become the head of the corner. By the Lord this has been done and it is wonderful in our eyes" (Gospel).

Today we gather in the sanctuary of St. Vitalis, who, like Joseph, was thrown alive into a pit and then covered with stones and earth. In this martyr Jesus continues His passion and death. In the passion of St. Vitalis, the Church participates in the passion, humiliation, and death of the Lord. Really the Church herself is a martyr and treads the path of Christ. She allows herself to be hated by the world, to be calumniated and crucified and abused by her enemies. In this way she proves that she belongs entirely to Christ, that she is His bride, His true Church. The word of the Psalmist is true of her. "The stone which the builders rejected, the same is become the head of the corner" (Ps 117:22).

When we celebrate Mass in the church of St. Vitalis, we likewise choose to follow the path of suffering with Christ. At the Consecration we will be sanctified and crucified with Him. In Holy Communion we receive the flames of the martyr's love and the strength to share faithfully and steadfastly the way of the cross. With Him whose disciples we are, we may expect to be hated, calumniated and persecuted. "But if doing well you suffer patiently, this is thankworthy before God. For unto this are you called" (1 Pt 2:20).

Through baptism we are called upon to suffer with Christ. We renew our choice in every Mass and Communion. Now is the time to share the sufferings of Christ, and we pray: "In my trouble I cried to the Lord" (Gradual). Now is the hour of suffering, but when that hour has passed, the day of exaltation will come. "Thou, O Lord, wilt preserve us and keep us from this generation for ever" (Communion); in virtue of Holy Communion, may we remain faithful to You in our suffering, and thus also arrive with You at a common glorification. Yes, we must be faithful to our suffering Savior, that we may be glorified with Him.

Prayer

Grant we beseech Thee, O almighty God, that with the sacred fast to purify us, Thou mayest cause us to come with sincere minds to the holy things that are before us.

Grant unto Thy people, we beseech Thee, O Lord, health of soul and body, that by persevering in good works we may deserve to be defended by the protection of Thy power. Through Christ our Lord. Amen.

Saturday

The stational saints, Peter and Marcellinus, remind us of the two brothers of the Old Testament, Esau and Jacob, and of the two brothers mentioned in today's Gospel. The story of Esau and Jacob reminds us of the mystery of our being called to membership in the Church. The parable of the prodigal son reminds us of our call to conversion. "The law of the Lord is unspotted, converting souls.... The heavens show forth the glory of God, and the firmament declareth the work of His hands" (Introit).

By the mysterious operation of God, Jacob, the younger son, is preferred to Esau, the first-born. Jacob receives the great blessing of his dying father Isaac: "God give thee the dew of heaven and of the fatness of the earth, abundance of corn and wine; and let people serve thee, and all tribes worship thee. Be thou lord of thy brethren, and let thy mother's children bow down before thee. Cursed be he that curseth thee, and let him that blesseth thee be filled with blessings" (Epistle). Here Jacob represents the Church, which comprises souls taken from the pagan nations. We are Gentiles; but we are preferred to the chosen people, Israel, without any merit on our part and in spite of our unworthiness. We have received the blessing of our heavenly Father in the possession of Christ and eternal salvation.

O blessed mercy of God! Without any merit on our part He has shown us mercy. Why have the first-born, the people of Israel, been rejected? Why has redemption been withdrawn from them and offered to the Gentiles? Why has God called me to membership in His Church, while passing by so many who are perhaps more worthy than I? "How incomprehensible are His judgments and how unsearchable His ways!" (Rom 11:33.) How does it come about that "two women shall be grinding at the mill; one shall be taken [into the kingdom of God] and one shall be left" (Mt 24:41)? Why is one man given light and another left in darkness? Whoever has the light of grace, has received it by an infinite, loving, and completely mysterious election. Jacob has been chosen instead of Esau. In gratitude the liturgy confesses: "It is good to give praise to the Lord, and to sing to Thy name, O Most High. To show forth Thy mercy in the morning and Thy truth at night" (Gradual). Let us consider this truth and give thanks to God. "What hast thou that thou hast not received?" (1 Cor 4:7.)

How have we responded to this love of our Father? Have we proved worthy of our election? The Gospel gives us the answer. Like the younger of the two sons we come to our Father and ask, "Father, give me the portion of substance that falleth to me." After a few days the younger son, the prodigal, takes all his possessions and goes into a far country. There he wastes his substance, living riotously. A famine comes, and he cleaves to one of the citizens of that country, who sends the prodigal to his farm to tend the swine. The foolish young man suffers great hardships and returns to his senses. He says to himself, "How many hired servants in my father's house abound with bread, and I here perish with hunger? I will arise and go to my father's house and say to him: Father, I have sinned against heaven and before thee. I am not worthy to be called thy son. And rising up he came to his father." His father, recognizing him already from a distance, is moved with sympathy, hastens toward him, embraces him, and kisses him. The repentant son falls at his father's feet. "Father, I have sinned.... I am not worthy to be called thy son." But the father forgives him, and calling one of his servants, says to him, "Bring forth quickly the first robe and put it on him, and put a ring on his hand, and shoes on his feet; and bring hither the fatted calf, and kill it, and let us eat and make merry; because this my son was dead, and is come to life again; he was lost, and is found."

This story is repeated again today. It is the history of the Church; it is the history of our own desertion. In this Gospel we are given an urgent call to repentance and conversion. "Father, I have sinned." Penance alone can save us. Our Father welcomes us with mercy. The sin and its eternal punishment are forgiven; the good works which we did before sin and the merits which we lost through sin are revived. The Father receives us again as His children, and celebrates a joyful banquet with us at Holy Communion.

In the story of each human life, God's mercy stands on one side and the unfaithfulness of man on the other. Will God have to cast us off as He did the people of Israel? Have we not fully deserved it? Sometimes it appears that God wishes to allow our faithless generation to go its own way. If He does, it will merit a well-deserved punishment.

What can save us from rejection? Only penance, self-examination, and conversion. "Be converted to Me with all your heart, in fasting and in weeping and in mourning" (Chapter at Tierce; Jl 2:12). "Let the wicked forsake his way and the unjust man his thoughts, and let him return to the Lord, and He will have mercy on him; and to our God, for He is bountiful to forgive" (Chapter at Sext; Is 55:7).

Prayer

Grant salutary effects to our fasts, we beseech Thee, O Lord, that the chastisements of the flesh which we have undertaken, may bestow more life to our souls.

Keep Thy household, we beseech Thee, O Lord, with continual loving kindness, that as it relies only on the hope of heavenly grace, it may also be fortified by heavenly protection. Through Christ our Lord. Amen.

Third Sunday of Lent

The Mass

The liturgy for the third Sunday of Lent has been arranged with the catechumens in mind, that is, those who are to receive baptism on the vigil of Easter. We who have already been baptized unite ourselves to them and relive the great event of our baptism, which is the basis of our whole life as Christians. We gather together in the church of St. Lawrence, under whose protection the catechumens were placed on Septuagesima Sunday. Today the first act of their solemn baptism is anticipated: the first exorcism of the evil spirit. Filled with an ardent longing for freedom from the slavery of Satan and inspired by a desire of ranging themselves on the side of Christ, the catechumens, and we with them, pray: "My eyes are ever toward the Lord, for He shall pluck my feet out of the snare." Filled with longing we cry out with the catechumens: "Look Thou upon me and have mercy on me" (Introit). In the Collect we pray, "Have regard to the desires of the lowly, we beseech Thee, O almighty God, and stretch forth the right hand of Thy majesty in our defense."

What do the catechumens seek? What are they trying to accomplish? The answer is given in the Epistle: "Brethren, be ye followers of God as most dear children.... But fornication and all uncleanness or covetousness, let it not so much as be named among you, as becometh saints.... For you were heretofore darkness, but now light in the Lord. Walk then as children of the light." Here we find clearly explained the meaning of the baptism we have received.

It is imperative that we grasp what the Epistle tells us with regard to the effects of our baptism and the obligations we assumed. Should we not arouse ourselves to a manner of life such as our baptism requires? For this we pray when we say, "Arise, O Lord, let no man be strengthened.... To Thee I have lifted up my eyes who dwelleth in heaven.... Have mercy on us O Lord, have mercy on us" (Gradual and Tract). Give us light and strength.

The poor man in the Gospel, from whom the devil was driven, is a figure of the baptized. "The strong one" has been driven out of our hearts by one who is stronger, by Christ. Christ has deprived him of his armor, so that he no longer has any power over the baptized. Truly the kingdom of God, the kingdom of grace and salvation, is at hand. But the work of salvation is not yet finished. The operation of grace in our souls requires our full cooperation. It is for this reason that the candidates for baptism, and we the baptized, are admonished: "He that is not with Me is against Me." There can be no neutrality with Christ. There can be no halfway mark between the service of two masters. We must choose the one or the other. This is the charge laid upon the baptized: they must be entirely devoted to Christ. We must believe in Him implicitly, imitating His example and obeying His commands. If one is not with Christ, one is against Him and drives Him out of his heart. Satan then enters into such a man and takes with him seven other spirits worse than himself, and the last condition of the man is worse than the first. In gratitude for our baptism we assent to it again when we recite the Credo, and thus we renew our baptismal promises and submit to the judgments of Christ, which are "sweeter than honey and the honeycomb" (Offertory).

When we make our offering we place ourselves on the side of Christ. "He that is not with Me is against Me." As the drops of water used at the Offertory mingle with the wine in the chalice, so we wish to be united with Christ in the Mass. With Him we wish to be crucified to sin and to the world. We offer ourselves with Him, dedicating to God our thoughts, our works, and our deeds, thus becoming with Him one holy and immaculate offering. Our offering will be sealed by Holy Communion. The stronger one enters our hearts and subdues by His power the strong one who lives there. He stretches forth the right hand of His majesty to protect us. We are made secure in Christ. This is the fruit of our offering and of our baptism. "Blessed are they that dwell in Thy house" (Communion). Through our baptism, our Mass, and our Communion we are bound to Christ and filled with Him. Renewed by His spirit we repeat with all our heart our baptismal promises; with Christ and for Christ we work, suffer, and pray. "My eyes are ever toward the Lord, for He shall pluck my feet out of the snare" (Introit). From the struggle of Lent in this world we shall make our way to the light and glory of eternity.

Meditation

The stational church today is that of St. Lawrence, the patron of neophytes. On his glowing gridiron he attains his transfiguration. He looks at us also with a burning desire for our salvation. We, too, must purify ourselves for the transfiguration of Easter morning. "My eyes are ever toward the Lord.... To Thee, O Lord, have I lifted up my soul" (Introit). We beseech Him during this holy season of Lent to perfect in us and in all faithful children of the Church the work of regeneration.

"At that time Jesus was casting out a devil, and the same was dumb. And when He had cast out the devil, the dumb spoke and the multitude were in admiration at it" (Gospel). In former times the driving out of the evil spirits from those to be baptized, was undertaken in the sanctuary of St. Lawrence. The very incident recorded in the Gospel of the Mass today, took place in our own lives when we were baptized. In the person of the priest, who represents Him, Christ came to us and drove out the evil spirit who had possessed us from our entry into the world. "I command you, every unclean spirit, in the name of the Father Almighty, and in the name of Jesus Christ, His Son, our Lord and Judge, and by the power of the Holy Ghost, to depart from this creature of God, which our Lord has deigned to call His temple, that it may be a temple of the living God, and that the Holy Ghost may dwell in it. Through the same Christ our Lord, who shall come to judge the living and the dead and the world by fire. Amen."

Christ, who is stronger than Satan, has driven the mighty adversary from our souls. When we renounce Satan and all his pomps, we do so with perfect freedom and we undertake a life-long struggle against him. We are incorporated in the living Christ and share in the life of the "strong one." The strength of Christ, which made St. Lawrence victorious on his burning griddle, operates in us also. Thus we approach the battle of life for the decisive meeting with Satan. "He that is not with Me is against Me" (Gospel). We place ourselves under the banner of Christ, for there can be no neutral position. We have devoted all our energies to the struggle, and today in the middle of the lenten season we look back on what has been accomplished. Have we been faithful to our baptismal promises? Has Satan and sin and the powers of darkness made no inroads upon us? The liturgy rightly reminds us today: "But fornication and all uncleanness or covetousness, let it not so much as be named among you, as becometh saints; or obscenity, or foolish talking, or scurrility, which is to no purpose; but rather giving of thanks. For know ye this, and understand, that no fornicator, or unclean or covetous person, which is a serving of idols, hath inheritance in the kingdom of Christ and of God" (Epistle).

Let us therefore examine ourselves seriously. "Today if you shall hear His voice, harden not your hearts" (Ps 94:8). Woe to us if the unclean spirit should return to our souls and bring with him seven other spirits worse than himself. The last condition of that man is worse than the first. "For you were heretofore darkness; but now light in the Lord. Walk then as children of the light, for the fruit of the light is in all goodness and justice and truth" (Epistle). We are children of the light and should no longer know darkness; we should walk always with our gaze fixed on God, in unfaltering faith and in unceasing praise of our Creator. What are the fruits that may be expected of the children of light? Their lives must be characterized by unfailing charity towards their fellow men, by an upright life and a ceaseless search for that which is most in conformity to the will of God and conducive to the salvation of one's neighbor and of one's own soul. The children of light can have nothing in common with wickedness. They cannot share the passions and jealousies and affectations of men of the world.

The essence of a true Christian life lies in an unfailing love of God and our neighbor. The life of the Christian is a life of love. That love obliges him to separate himself completely and effectively from all that is sinful; not only from that which is mortally sinful, but from every venial sin and imperfection that is in any way deliberate. This love can endure no willful imperfection. It knows and desires only what is pleasing to God. Its every action is performed out of pure love of God and of Christ. This love seeks to give to God and to the Savior everything that it has, even to the last drop of its blood. It is prepared to suffer all trials and humiliations for the love of God, and even rejoices that it is permitted to undertake this suffering for the love of God.

Today in the Holy Sacrifice of the Mass we renew our struggle for virtue. We unite ourselves to the suffering Christ as He offers Himself to the Father, and strive to enter more intimately into His life. Aided by His strength, we take up again the struggle against evil and renew our efforts to acquire solid virtue. As children of the light we go forward to Easter and our eternal transfiguration.

"Blessed are they who hear the word of God and keep it" (Gospel). That is the way of light and love. Only he who loves can fulfill the law of God perfectly. To this commendation of Christ the true lover replies: "The justices of the Lord are right, rejoicing hearts, and His judgments are sweeter than honey and the honeycomb; for Thy servant keepeth them" (Offertory).

PRAYER

Have regard to the desires of the lowly, we beseech Thee, O almighty God, and stretch forth the right hand of Thy majesty in our defense. Through Christ our Lord. Amen.

Monday

Naaman, a heathen officer of the king of Syria, comes to the prophet Eliseus and humbly submits himself to the direction of the servant of God. He bathes in the Jordan, and while sojourning in Israel (that is, in the Church) he is cleansed of his leprosy (Epistle). While the heathen finds a cure in Israel, the people of Israel, the inhabitants of Nazareth, reject the "prophet" (Christ), and seek to put him to death. The chosen people reject their Savior, and we, the Gentiles, are called to Christ and salvation. Such thoughts fill our minds as we gather at the church of a holy pope, Mark, to celebrate the Holy Sacrifice.

"He came unto His own and His own received him not" (Jn 1:11). Christ visited His home in Nazareth, where He was well known. Since the time He began His public life, the people of Nazareth had been hearing of the miraculous cures He had worked in Capharnaum and in the other cities of Galilee. But his fellow townsmen ridiculed His miraculous power. Why does He not perform in Nazareth the wonderful things He has been performing in the other cities of Israel? He answers their mockery, "Amen I say to you, that no prophet is accepted in His own country.... There were many widows in the days of Elias in Israel, ... and to none of them was Elias sent but to Sarephta of Sidon, to a widow woman. And there were many lepers in Israel in the time of Eliseus the prophet, and none of them was cleansed but Naaman the Syrian." They understand very well the indictment implied in these words, and they become very angry. They drive Him out of the city, and leading Him to a high hill on which their city was built, they seek to cast Him headlong over the cliff. "But He, passing through the midst of them, went His way" (Gospel).

Israel, and particularly Nazareth, did not recognize the time of grace. They had only a shallow ridicule and a bitter hatred for Christ, and sought to dispose of Him. "But He ... went His way." Christ will not force His grace upon those who do not wish to receive it. Through their own fault "the children of the kingdom shall be cast out" (Mt 8:12). Here again the liturgy earnestly admonishes us not to turn away from Christ and His call to penance, but to be converted to do penance and to prepare for Easter.

"There were many lepers in Israel in the time of Eliseus the prophet, and none of them was cleansed but Naaman the Syrian." (Gospel). The kingdom of God slips through the fingers of the proud, the unbelieving, the self-satisfied, and falls into the hands of him who believes and seeks God. Naaman, the heathen, longed for a new, vigorous life. He came from far off, from Damascus to Samaria, and humbled himself by submitting to the directions of Eliseus and by descending into the waters of the Jordan. His faith, his humility, and his submission to the prophet bring him the cure of his leprosy. "There were many lepers in Israel in the days of Eliseus the prophet, and none of them was cleansed." The heathens believed and received salvation; the Israelites lost the kingdom of God through their unbelief. The inheritance that was the portion of the chosen people, is offered to us who are members of the Church, but only on condition that we have faith and submit humbly to the teaching and commandments of Christ and His Church. We shall be saved only if we are conscious of our unworthiness and frailty, and confidently seek help from Him. "Hear, O God, my prayer, and despise not my supplication; be attentive to me and hear me" (Offertory). "Have mercy on me, O Lord, for man hath trodden me underfoot; all the day long he hath afflicted me" (Gradual).

Today in the liturgy we are like the heathen Naaman. In the celebration of the Holy Sacrifice we come to the great prophet, Christ. We submit ourselves in faith, humility, and confidence to His grace, which we are to receive when He comes to us in Holy Communion. "He that eateth My flesh and drinketh My blood, abideth in Me and I in him" (Jn 6:57). "In God I will trust. I will not fear what man can do against me" (Introit), because by virtue of my baptism Christ lives in me as the head lives in its members. In Him "I can do all things" (Phil 4:13).

Whatever we obtain now from Christ is only the beginning. Our salvation will be assured only when we have entered safely into eternity and have arrived at the eternal Easter. To that happy day we look forward when we say the Communion prayer: "When the Lord shall have turned away the captivity of His people, Jacob shall rejoice and Israel shall be glad." With firm confidence in God we repeat: "I look for the resurrection of the dead and the life of the world to come." To obtain this resurrection, we must come to the great prophet in the land of Israel, to Christ in His holy Church.

"He that thinketh himself to stand, let him take heed lest he fall" (1 Cor 10:12). If the chosen people could lose the salvation that had been promised them, why cannot the same happen to us? What is our protection against such a catastrophe? It is humility. If we have faith and submit humbly to Christ and His Church, we shall not fall. We must cling to Christ and to the things of God with faith and reverence.

Prayer

We beseech Thee, O Lord, pour forth Thy grace into our hearts, that as we abstain from carnal food, so also we may withdraw our senses from harmful excesses.

Let Thy mercy, O Lord, succor us, that we may be worthy to be snatched by Thy protection from the dangers that threaten us, and to be saved by Thy deliverance. Through Christ our Lord. Amen.

Tuesday

The Sacrifice of the Mass today is celebrated in the church of the holy virgin St. Prudentiana, on the spot where St. Peter once lived and worked in Rome. The virgin Prudentiana carries in her hand the vessel of oil, the vessel of the love of God. "She overcame numberless trials, provided an honorable burial for a large number of holy martyrs, and distributed her entire fortune to the poor for the love of Christ" (Martyrology).

"In those days a certain woman cried to the prophet Eliseus saying: Thy servant, my husband is dead.... And behold the creditor is come to take away my two sons to serve him. And Eliseus said to her: ... Tell me, what hast thou in thy house? And she answered: I thy handmaid have nothing in my house but a little oil to anoint me. And he said to her: Go borrow all thy neighbors' empty vessels, not a few. And go in and shut thy door; ... and pour out thereof into all those vessels; and when they are full take them away." The woman did as she was told, and when all the vessels were full of oil, the prophet commanded her: "Go sell thy oil and pay thy creditor; and thou and thy sons live of the rest" (Epistle). This miracle is meant to be a figure of the blessings wrought by our lenten penances. The widow mentioned in the Epistle is our Holy Mother the Church. Her spouse has ascended into heaven and has left her, and since that day she has been persecuted. The creditor, Satan, seeks to take from her the children who have been born to her by baptism; and now Satan would give them over to destruction. She turns to the great prophet, Christ, and obtains help. During the season of Lent, He pours out abundantly the oil of grace that will pay off her indebtedness. Now is the time of grace. Now, by baptism and penance, He breaks the bonds by which the creditor holds her captive. Not in vain, therefore, we cry out, "I have cried to Thee, for Thou, O God, hast heard me; O incline Thy ear unto me and hear my words. Keep me, O Lord, as the apple of Thy eye; protect me under the shadow of Thy wings" (Introit). "From my secret sins cleanse me, O Lord, and from those of others spare Thy servant" (Gradual). Now our prayers shall be heard and we shall obtain forgiveness.

"Amen, I say to you [the apostles], whatsoever you shall bind upon earth, shall be bound in heaven. And whatsoever you shall loose upon earth, shall be loosed also in heaven" (Gospel). Peter is near at hand in the house of Prudentiana. To him and to the other apostles Christ entrusted the power to bind and to loose. Peter is in our midst. We have come to him and to the Church to obtain the forgiveness of our sins. The creditor, Satan, can no longer press his claims upon us. The Church through her priesthood possesses the power to forgive sins, even the greatest. What she forgives will be forgiven also in heaven. "Whose sins you shall forgive, they are forgiven them" (Jn 20:23) in the sacrament of penance. We need only to come to Peter, to the Church, and make a humble confession of our guilt. If we do that, the Church assures us: "I absolve thee from thy sins." When this grace has been given to us, we may truly say, "The right hand of the Lord hath wrought strength; the right hand of the Lord hath exalted me; I shall not die, but live, and shall declare the works of the Lord" (Offertory). Lent offers us an excellent opportunity to do penance for our sins and to receive the sacraments fervently and worthily.

The Church today prays for her children, and her prayer is always efficacious. "If two of you shall consent upon earth concerning anything whatsoever they shall ask, it shall be done to them by My Father, who is in heaven; for where there are two or three gathered together in My name, there I am in the midst of them" (Gospel). The Lord Himself, whose petitions are most efficacious, prays with His Church.

"The right hand of the Lord hath wrought strength, the right hand of the Lord hath exalted me; I shall not die, but live, and shall declare the works of the Lord" (Offertory). The Church prays continually for the forgiveness of sins; as often as we confess them with humility and contrition to the representative of the Church, we are assured of forgiveness. "I shall not die, but live," because I have, as my most precious possession, the Church, her prayers, and her sacraments.

When we offer the Mass today, we offer to the Father the greatest sacrifice, Christ, with all His prayers, His sufferings, and His death. "From my secret sins, cleanse me, O Lord." For the sake of Thy Son be merciful and grant to sinners that they may be converted and live. We perhaps have the responsibility for seeing that some particular person finds his way to the Church and her sacraments so that he may be converted and live. We share the responsibility of the Church for the conversion and salvation of our brothers in Christ. Much depends on our prayers and good works during Lent. Every Christian should be like St. Prudentiana, bearing always the vessel of mercy and fraternal charity.

Prayer

Hearken unto us, O almighty and merciful God, and favorably grant us the gifts of saving self-denial.

Defend us, O Lord, with Thy protection and keep us forever from all iniquity. Through Christ our Lord. Amen.

Wednesday

Today we stand at the tomb of the holy pope and martyr, St. Sixtus, and receive the Ten Commandments, which in the early Church were given to the neophytes on this day that they might learn them by heart and meditate on them.

In spirit we are on Mount Sinai. Peals of thunder and flashes of lightning and the glare of the burning mountain announce the presence of Jahve. Like the Israelites, we are seized with terror. "Thus saith the Lord God; Honor thy father and thy mother; ... thou shalt not kill.... You shall not make gods of silver.... You shall make an altar of earth unto me," and you shall offer sacrifice. The Ten Commandments, which we accepted when we were baptized, are nothing but the expression of the will of God, holy, wise, and as immutable as God Himself. These commandments result from the providence, wisdom, and holiness of God. There can be nothing more reasonable, more important, more holy, than the will of God as expressed in the Ten Commandments, which we vowed to keep at the moment of our baptism, when we dedicated ourselves to the service of God. Today we renew this dedication and renew our resolution to keep the Ten Commandments. In one way or another they all concern themselves with the great commandment: "Thou shalt love the Lord thy God, with thy whole heart and with thy whole soul and with all thy strength,... and thy neighbor as thyself" (Lk 10:27).

How have we observed the commandments of God? Let us hope that we have observed them with more sincerity than had the Pharisees of today's Gospel. They twist the meaning of the immutable commandments so that they can fulfill them outwardly, yet accomplish their own will in the end. They "transgress the commandments of God for your tradition" (Gospel). They substitute human wisdom for the commandments of God. May such an observance of the law of God be far from us who are baptized.

We should receive the commandments of God in reverence and in faith, because we believe that they express the will of God. We keep them because we wish to conform our wills to His; because we love God and our blessed Savior. We observe the commandments because we believe their observance is pleasing to Him. The will of God is our joy. "My meat is to do the will of Him that sent Me" (Jn 4:34). In baptism we died to ourselves and to the desires of the old man; we gave up our right to direct our own activities and to live according to our own desires. We dedicated ourselves unconditionally to the will of God and to a blind trust in His providence. "Thy will be done." I was baptized "not to do my own will, but the will of Him" who called me (Jn 6:38). To do God's will is the essence of a good Christian life. The devout Christian submits to the holy will of God in all things. Are we so disposed? Do we seek first the will of God and look to Him for guidance in all things?

At the Offertory of the Mass today we place our heart and our will on the paten. We will die to ourselves in order to rise again with Christ and live according to the divine will. In Holy Communion He inspires us with His spirit and supports us by His strength. We conform ourselves to Him who followed, not His own will, but the will of His Father. "My meat is to do the will of Him that sent Me." In our lives, as in the life of Christ, there must be a complete conformity to the will of the Father. This should be the fruit of our reception of Holy Communion.

Christians often show irreverence to God and a distrust of His providence by their neglect of His commandments. They often attach too little importance to them, readily transgress them, and show them little reverence. Thus they enter on a path which leads them to sin and to eventual ruin. This ruin, which is caused by sin, affects not only the individual soul, but also families and nations. "O Lord, be merciful to me for Thy name's sake" (Offertory). Make known to me the ways of life when You come to me in Holy Communion; "fill me with joy with Thy countenance" already here on earth, then forever in heaven (Communion).

Prayer

Grant us, we beseech Thee, O Lord, that being disciplined by salutary fasting and abstaining from baneful vices, we may the more easily obtain Thy merciful forgiveness.

Grant, we beseech Thee, O almighty God, that we who seek the favor of Thy protection, may be delivered from all evil and serve Thee with a quiet mind. Through Christ our Lord. Amen.

Thursday

Today at the tomb of the holy physicians, Cosmas and Damian, the Church implores God that we may have the strength to keep holy the second half of Lent, and continue our penance with courage and fidelity.

Jesus enters into the house of Simon Peter. "Simon's wife's mother was taken with a great fever, and they besought Him for her. And standing over her, He commanded the fever, and it left her. And immediately rising, she ministered to them" (Gospel). Christ was moved to perform this act of charity by the pressing desire of His heart to help those who suffer. He is in name and by His very essence a Savior. St. Augustine, in explaining this Gospel, says that we are afflicted by the fever of avarice, passions, lust, ambition, and anger. We are sick and acknowledge with humility that we are weak and that we have been guilty of sins and imperfections of all kinds. Only Christ can cure us. We hasten to Him now in the Mass and at the time of Holy Communion, in the reception of the sacrament of penance, by our acts of contrition. "The eyes of all hope in Thee, O Lord; and Thou givest them meat in due season. Thou openest Thy hand and fillest every living creature with blessings" (Gradual). Thou art the Savior. Thou dost come to us during the holy season of Lent, and particularly at the time of Mass and Holy Communion, to be a savior for Thy people and for Thy Church. "The eyes of all hope in Thee." "There is no other name under heaven given to men whereby we must be saved" (Acts 4:12). "I am the salvation of the people, saith the Lord; from whatever tribulation they shall cry to Me, I will hear them; and I will be their Lord forever" (Introit).

In the house of Peter (in the Church) the divine physician carries on His works. "Hear ye the word of the Lord, all ye men of Juda that enter in at these gates [through baptism] to adore the Lord.... And I will dwell with you in this place," in the house of Peter, the Church (Epistle). The more intimately we enter into the life of the Church, the closer the Savior comes to us. We draw close to Him by faith, by obedience to His Church, by submission to her authority, and by the devout use of her sacrifice and her sacraments. Our attitude toward the body of Christ, the Church, is the determining factor in our relationship to Christ Himself. Here in the family of the Church we shall find salvation after the Lord has died and returned to His Father.

Jesus, our Savior, appears in the house of Simon Peter, the Church. "Blessed are they that dwell in Thy house, O Lord" (Ps 83:5). The Epistle addresses us earnestly: "Make your ways and your doings good.... For if you will order well your ways and your doings, if you will execute judgment between a man and his neighbor, if you oppress not the stranger, the fatherless, and the widow,... and walk not after strange gods to your own hurt, I will dwell with you in this place," in the community which is the Church. "Trust not in lying words, saying: The temple of the Lord, the temple of the Lord, it is the temple of the Lord"; that is, do not assert foolishly: "I am a Catholic, therefore I shall be saved." God demands more than mere membership in His Church; He demands also a holy life within the Church.

Who will measure the extent of the sacrifices made by the Son of God for the salvation of men? Let us consider well His Incarnation, His poverty, His degradation, and His humiliation. How cruelly He was calumniated! and how persistent is that calumny even today! Who can weigh the depth of the ingratitude of His people, who called upon the Roman governor to "crucify Him"? He who would understand the suffering and the love of Christ, must consider His agony in the Garden of Olives, His cruel scourging at the pillar, the pain of the crowning with thorns, the bitterness of the mockery when the soldiers thrust the reed into his hands as a scepter. He who would understand the love of God must follow Him on the way of the cross and watch Him die on Calvary. All these sufferings He accepted to accomplish our salvation. How grateful we should be for such a Savior!

We should offer the Holy Sacrifice today primarily as an act of thanksgiving to the Father, who "so loved the world, as to give His only-begotten Son" (Jn 3:16) that He might save us. At Holy Communion we should unite ourselves to our Savior. "Thou hast commanded Thy commandments to be kept most diligently; O that my ways may be directed to keep Thy justifications" (Communion). That should be our program for life.

Prayer

May the blessed solemnity of Thy saints, Cosmas and Damian, magnify Thee, O Lord, for by Thy ineffable providence Thou hast granted eternal glory to them and assistance to us.

May heavenly favor increase the people subject to Thee, O Lord, and make them always obey Thy commandments. Through Christ our Lord. Amen.

Friday

We assemble again today in the sanctuary of St. Lawrence, the patron and model of catechumens. Near the church there stood, in ancient times, an open fountain. Today's liturgy refers to the waters of baptism, "springing up into life everlasting" (Gospel). Today we join the newly baptized Christians and stir up the grace of baptism within ourselves.

Moses struck the rock in the desert, and water flowed forth to relieve the thirst of the people of Israel and to save them from death in the desert (Epistle). The rock is an image of Christ (1 Cor 10:4). The rod which Moses used to strike the rock is a figure of the cross upon which Christ died. The water which flowed from the rock, foreshadowed the grace which flows from the sacraments. We receive first the graces of the sacrament of baptism, which the neophytes now await with great longing.

Just as the water from the rock refreshed the Israelites in the desert and saved them from a terrible death from thirst and gave them the strength to continue and finish their perilous journey to the land of promise, so the waters of baptism strengthen and refresh us, the new Israel, that we may continue our journey through the wilderness of our earthly life to the promised land of heaven, guided and protected by the pillar and the cloud of God's providence. Christ the rock accompanies us. Day by day we may refresh ourselves at the life-giving waters which Christ earned for us by His life and death. This lifegiving water comes to us through the Mass and the sacraments. From the precious wounds opened in His sacred body by the scourge, by the nails of the crucifixion, and by the lance of the centurion, this lifegiving water flows down upon us in a continuous stream. Deprived of this water from the Rock (Christ), men would languish and die in the wilderness. "He that shall drink of the water that I will give him, shall not thirst forever" (Gospel). What a wonderful promise! We discover the Rock which gives this precious water when we are baptized. It is the water of salvation. The devout Christian believes and is grateful. Let us engrave the image of this Rock in our hearts.

Jesus explained to the Samaritan woman the mystery of the water that gives eternal life (Gospel). Fired by a zeal for the salvation of souls, He seats himself by Jacob's well to await the approach of the Samaritan, the sinner. He offers her the water which He alone can give. He assures her that he who drinks of this water will not thirst again. It is the water of eternal life, which He gives to the soul of the Samaritan woman, changing her from a sinner into a disciple. The woman leaves her waterpot standing by the well; she no longer has any thought of the natural water she came to draw. After she has tasted the living water which Christ gives her, the natural water no longer has any attraction for her. A new world has been opened before her eyes. She breaks with sin and becomes a new creature, nourished by the spirit of Christ. This Samaritan woman is an image of the catechumens and of us who have been baptized.

At Jacob's well, which for us is the sacraments and the tabernacle, Christ waits for us, who are unworthy sinners. He wishes to save us by means of the living water which He will give us. Having been allowed to drink from this water, we leave our pot standing at the well, as did the Samaritan woman. We leave behind us the old man with his outlook on life, his ambitions, and his base motives. Only one thing now has any value in our eyes: the life of grace as children of God, a life filled with love for God and for souls. We wish to become disciples of Christ and apostles of His grace and His doctrine. We indeed are like the Samaritan woman, who found Christ at the well of Jacob; henceforth we shall live by His grace and His spirit.

Now during the Holy Sacrifice of the Mass, Jesus stands at the well of Jacob, the fountain of grace. There He waits for me, the Samaritan, that He may teach me by means of the Epistle and Gospel. He has been waiting for me at the well of Jacob that He might lead me to the Father through the Holy Sacrifice of the Mass, that He might apply to my soul through this means the graces that He has merited for me, and that He may even give Himself to me in Holy Communion. In the Communion we sing: "He that shall drink of the water that I will give him, saith the Lord, it shall become in him a fountain of water springing up unto life everlasting." He gives us this water to drink in Holy Communion. Thus we have within ourselves the fountain which springs up into life everlasting.

"Show me, O Lord, a token for good; that they who hate me may see and be confounded, because Thou, O Lord, hast helped me and has comforted me. Incline Thy ear, O Lord, and hear me, for I am needy and poor" (Introit). The Church wends her way over the long desert road of her earthly pilgrimage, poor and helpless, deprived of all human support, persecuted, and hated by the devil, the prince of this world, and by all his minions. She has only one support: the rock that she finds in the desert, the life-giving rock, Christ in the Holy Eucharist. God entrusted to her the Holy Eucharist as a sign of His goodness. She will not fail, but she will live, pursuing her way confidently to eternal life, serene in the possession of Christ in the Eucharist. "In God hath my heart confided, and I have been helped; and my flesh hath flourished again, and with my will I will give praise to Him" (Gradual).

Here with Jesus in the splendor of the radiant host, our flesh flourishes again. We come here with the people of Israel, languishing and near death from the trials of the desert; we come with the sinner, the Samaritan woman. Here He works each day a sign of His goodness.

"Hearken to the voice of my prayer, O my King and my God; for to thee will I pray, O Lord" (Offertory). He heard the prayer of the people of Israel in the desert; He heard the prayer of the sinner at the well of Jacob. He will also hear the Church and us, her children, daily in the Holy Sacrifice of the Mass. "Give us this day our daily bread; and forgive us our trespasses.... And lead us not into temptation, but deliver us from evil." Only with the Lord is there salvation and life. "Come to me,... and I will refresh you" (Mt 11:28).

Prayer

Look down with merciful approval on our fasts, we beseech Thee, O Lord, that as we abstain from food with our body, so too may we refrain from sin in our minds.

Grant, we beseech Thee, almighty God, that we who trust in Thy protection, may by Thy help overcome all things standing in our way. Through Christ our Lord. Amen.

Saturday

Today we devote ourselves entirely to penance. We acknowledge the sins by which we have proved ourselves unfaithful to God, and we pray to the Lord in the Introit of the Mass: "Give ear, O Lord, to my words; understand my cry; harken to the voice of my prayer, O my King and my God."

During the days of the Feast of Tabernacles, an adulterous woman was brought before our Lord, who had come to the temple early in the morning and was preaching to the people, who flocked to hear Him. The scribes cast before Him a poor woman they had just taken in adultery, and said: "Master, this woman was even now taken in adultery. Now Moses in the law commanded us to stone such a one. But what sayest Thou?" (Gospel.) For the Jews adultery was one of the basest of sins, and in the Old Testament it was punishable by death.

In the liturgy the adulterous woman is a figure of the sinful Christian soul. By our sins we, too, have been unfaithful to God, to our Savior, and to the Church. We have turned our back on Him who from the moment of our baptism has not ceased to shower us with love and grace. We have withdrawn our heart and our love from God, its true spouse, and have given it to another. We have pandered our love to a base desire, to an empty pleasure, to the prince of this world, who seeks only our destruction. This is indeed spiritual adultery. The adulterous woman was cast before Jesus, and He received her kindly. What will He say to those who have accused her? They have quoted Moses. Will He uphold them? Jesus says not a word, but bows down and silently writes with His finger in the sand, as if to indicate that He wishes to have nothing to do with the persecution of this poor woman. The scribes insist on an answer to their question. Jesus rises and gives them an answer they were not expecting: "He that is without sin among you, let him cast the first stone." Are they without sin who wish now to stone her? One after another they slip away to hide their shame. The sinful woman is left alone with Jesus. "Woman, where are they that accused thee? Hath no man condemned thee?" "No man, Lord." "Neither will I condemn thee" (Gospel).

Jesus forgives this shameful sin, but not without the admonition, "Sin no more." This is a consoling thought for us. We, too, have been guilty of many sins, but we are not lost if only we come to Jesus with sorrow and contrition, confess our guilt to the representative of Christ, and resolve to give up our sins in the future. Christ is always ready to receive the penitent sinner. "For though I should walk in the midst of the shadow of death [as did the adulterous woman], I will fear no evil; for Thou art with me, O Lord" (Gradual). Thou dost not will the death of the sinner, but that he be converted and live (cf. Ez 18:23, 33:11).

The Pharisees, zealous for the law, consider how they may hand the adulterous woman over to death. They are without feeling and without mercy. But Jesus is of a different disposition. He will not destroy, but save. He receives the sinner back again. He reveals in His passion and death how vigorously He condemns and rejects sin; but the sinner He will save. We must acknowledge our sins, do penance for them, and avoid them in the future. "Direct my steps,… and let no iniquity have dominion over me, O Lord" (Offertory).

The Epistle of this Mass is the complement of the Gospel. Susanna, the wife of Joakim, is falsely accused of adultery by the two wicked elders. She is being led out to death when Daniel, enlightened by the Spirit of God, brings the truth to light. Through the wisdom of Daniel, the innocence of the chaste Susanna is proved, and she is saved from death. The Old Testament is the testament of justice, in which sin is punishable by death; the New Testament is the testament of mercy, in which the sinner may find forgiveness through penance. The New Testament gives the sinner strength to overcome passion and sin, and to raise himself to a life of virtue and holiness. How grateful we should be for having learned to know Christ, and for the opportunity of coming to Him through penance! We should be grateful, too, for the Eucharist.

In virtue of this sacrament we may unite ourselves to Him ever more intimately, and partake of His life and His strength.

"He that is without sin among you, let him cast the first stone." How shall we fare in the final judgment if He applies to us the code that we use in the judgment of our neighbor? We frequently and unjustly condemn the faults of our neighbor, and cast stones at him for his least faults. Are we acting within our rights? We must change our attitude if we hope to find mercy. We are too much like the two elders who accused Susanna, and like the scribes who accused the woman of the Gospel. We should be more like Christ, who forgave the adulterous woman and all sinners who came to Him.

Prayer

Grant, we beseech Thee, O almighty God, that they who mortify the flesh by abstaining from food, may observe justice by refraining from sin.

Stretch forth to Thy faithful, O Lord, the right hand of Thy heavenly aid, that they may seek Thee with all their hearts and may be worthy to obtain what they ask. Through Christ our Lord. Amen.

Fourth Sunday of Lent

The Mass

"I rejoiced at the things that were said to me; we shall go into the house of the Lord" (Gradual). Today we go into the house of the Lord, known as the Church of the Holy Cross in Jerusalem. Jerusalem! Here the catechumens and the faithful (the baptized) touch the holy ground upon which they stand. In Jerusalem, Christ was crucified and buried, and there He arose from the dead. But for the faithful and for the catechumens, Jerusalem is more than a mere reminder of these holy events; for the faithful it is a reality, it is the Catholic Church of which they are members; for the catechumens it is the holy Church which soon shall receive them through baptism. "I rejoiced at the things that were said to me; we shall go into the house of the Lord." "Rejoice with joy . . . and be filled from the breasts of your consolation" (Introit). The Church unlocks the fountains of grace and happiness. How exalted the new Jerusalem stands before us! In the old Jerusalem the Synagogue is only a shadow of the law of dread and servitude. In the new Jerusalem, the Church of the New Dispensation, we become the children of God; we are brothers and sisters of the Son of God and heirs of the kingdom of heaven; we eat at the family table of our mother, the new Jerusalem (Epistle). What happiness to be incorporated in this new Jerusalem! Thus we read with joy the theme of this Sunday. "I rejoiced at the things that were said to me; we shall go into the house of the Lord" (Introit). "He shall not be moved forever that dwelleth in Jerusalem" (Tract).

Christ now lives and works in the Jerusalem of the Church. The Church is also the mount which Christ ascends in today's Gospel. Many people accompany Him, following Him "up into a mountain," far away from the bustle of the world, far from the wild disorder of town and city. But how shall this multitude be fed? They have followed Him into the desert and up the mountain, renouncing the world and its pleasures (through baptism), and they now receive from Christ's own hands a new bread that contains all sweetness. He gives them bread and fish — the Eucharist. On the mount of the altars of the Catholic Church that bread is prepared for the multitude. "Praise the Lord for He is good; sing ye to His name, for He is sweet; whatsoever He pleased, He hath done in heaven and in earth" (Offertory).

Now He comes in person into our midst. Today we are of the multitude which followed the Lord, as the Gospel tells us. We desire to be with Him. What we once vowed in holy baptism — "I do renounce Satan" — we promise again today in the Mass. We leave the path of sin, the indulgence of our inordinate passions, the joy of the world. Together with our Savior we enter upon our lifelong lenten journey and withdraw from the world of pleasure into the desert of mortification. We have Christ; that is enough for us. We will keep Him, listen to Him; we will fill ourselves with His spirit. We shall live a new life, an inspired life, a life dedicated to God. This life in union with Christ we undertook when we were baptized, and we renew our promise again in the Mass today. To offer up the Holy Sacrifice of the Mass with Christ means to die to the world and to live with Christ. "For in that He [Christ] died to sin, He died once; but in that He liveth, He liveth unto God. So do you also reckon that you are dead to sin, but alive unto God, in Christ Jesus our Lord" (Rom 6:10 f.). When we have entered into the consecration, when we have made a step forward in the work of our inner "transubstantiation," we become capable of fruitful participation in the sacrificial meal of Holy Communion. Oh, the happiness produced by a worthy Communion! One must have experienced it to understand this happiness that can be had only in the Jerusalem of our Holy Mother the Church. There alone Christ gives Himself to us in Holy Communion. "Rejoice with joy you that have been in sorrow, that you may exult and be filled from the breasts of your consolation" (Introit).

Meditation

Laetare Sunday. Today is the Sunday of joy which has been placed in the middle of the austere season of Lent. We are on our way through the desert. In fasting and prayer we have given ourselves to penance. We have been longing for release from our sins, from the tyranny of our senses, from the tedium of our life. We long to renew our spirit with Holy Mother the Church, and to put on the new man. Today we pause momentarily to look ahead toward our destination. A few weeks ago we set out for Jerusalem, the City of God, the city into which, once our work is over, we shall enter. "I rejoiced at the things that were said to me; we shall go into the house of the Lord" (Gradual).

"It is written that Abraham had two sons, the one by a bond woman [Agar] and the other by a free woman [Sara].... Which things are said by an allegory. For these are the two testaments. The one [the Old Testament] from Mount Sinai, engendering unto bondage.... But that Jerusalem which is above is free, which is our mother" (Epistle). O Jerusalem, holy city of Israel, within whose walls lies the temple of God! To Jerusalem the pilgrim of Israel brought his offerings to thank God, to atone, to entreat, and to sit at the same table of sacrifice with the Lord. Because of this intimate union with the living God, the Holy City was called the bride of the Most High. He guarded and protected her with His special love.

In Jerusalem the kingdom of God, the kingdom of the promised Messias, was to be erected. From Him salvation was to come to men. Truly the prophet had good reason to cry: "Rejoice, O Jerusalem." But this bride of Christ, this favorite of God, proved unfaithful. The Lord, the bridegroom, came. "He came unto His own, and His own received Him not" (Jn 1:11). She became the harlot; the slave woman; she became a captive of the Pharisees, a puppet in the hands of the politicians and scribes. She scoffed at those who loved God, and she crucified her bridegroom and Savior. "His blood be upon us and our children" (Mt 27:25). To this unfaithful city is addressed the words: "Cast out the bondwoman and her son; for the son of the bondwoman shall not be heir with the sons of the free woman" (Gal 4:30). In place of the faithless Jerusalem, Christ raised up a new Jerusalem.

"But that Jerusalem which is above is free, which is our mother" (Epistle). The Church is His body, His visible form, His spouse whom He loves. The Church is she for whom He "delivered Himself up that He might sanctify it; ... that He might present it to Himself a glorious Church, not having spot or wrinkle or any such thing" (Eph 5:25 ff.). The Church is "a chosen generation, ... a holy nation, a purchased people, ... who in times past were not a people, but are now the people of God, ... who hath called you out of darkness into His marvelous light" (1 Pt 2:9 f.). "I rejoiced at the things that were said to me; we shall go into the house of the Lord." We shall go into the house built on faith, built on one Lord and one God. There is a firm union between the foundation and all the stones that go to make the walls of this structure, between Christ and us. We form one unit, one family, having one faith and one sacrifice, all receiving the same holy sacraments. To this Church will come the nations from the four corners of the earth. They will enjoy a unity of life with her; they will receive a rich share of her fullness of grace and truth. Each year will see the spread of her dominion.

The rocks which are taken from the quarry of the human race are shaped by baptism so that they may be used to build the structure of the Church on the cornerstone which is Christ. Having been baptized, the soul becomes a living rock. Thus we become "fellow citizens with the saints and the domestics of God" (Eph 2:19). In this house there is peace and abundance (Gradual). The Lord has deposited in His Church the fullness of His goods, His truth, His grace, and His life. He gives to all who are living in that house the bread of the Eucharist that they may be filled. To this holy repast come the people of God (Communion). Let us rejoice, O Jerusalem, O holy Church; come together all you that love the Church. "Rejoice with joy, you that have been in sorrow, that you may exult and be filled from the breasts of your consolation," the Church (Introit).

"Jerusalem, ... thither did the tribes go up, the tribes of the Lord, to praise Thy name, O Lord" (Communion). The Jerusalem of the Church points today to the Jerusalem in heaven. There we shall find the fulfillment of all our desires. There we shall find peace and abundance of happiness (Gradual). Banished will be every anxiety, everlasting our union with the highest good, uninterrupted our beatific vision. From God and Christ glory will be communicated to the blessed, who shall be transfigured by the divine splendor flowing through them and shall be satiated with His delights. "We shall go into the house of the Lord."

When we received baptism, we were allowed to go into the house of the Lord. Today we thank God for the grace of baptism. "Praise ye the Lord, for He is good; sing ye to His name, for He is sweet" (Offertory).

Let us adhere to the Church. She is the holy city of Jerusalem, the bride of Christ, our mother. She will lead us by the hand through the Lent of our earthly sojourn to the heavenly Jerusalem.

Today we think also of the many people who do not know the new Jerusalem, the Church. Poor, misguided people! They do not have a mother at whose breasts they may be filled with consolation.

PRAYER

Grant, we beseech Thee, almighty God, that we who rightly suffer for our deeds, may be relieved by Thy consoling grace. Through Christ our Lord. Amen.

Monday

Today the story of our Lord's suffering for the first time appears prominently in the liturgy. We are now called upon to share His suffering and death. "Can you drink the chalice that I shall drink?" (Mt 20:22.) Yes, we feel that we can drink the chalice of Christ, and we desire most earnestly to do so. For this reason we assemble in the church of the Four Crowned Martyrs for Mass today. Christ, the great martyr, has drawn us here. We wish to share His martyrdom, His humiliation, His rejection, His crucifixion, that we may share also His resurrection.

Jesus is the true Solomon. The Epistle tells us of the two mothers who came to Solomon for justice. They were both living in the same house. Each of them gave birth to a child, but one of these women overlaid her child in her sleep. She took the dead child and placed it in the arms of the other woman while she slept. She then claimed the living child as her own. In the morning the mother of the living child notices that the infant in her arms is not her own. Both women come now to Solomon that he may judge their dispute. With the wisdom that God had given him, Solomon decides the case and determines who is the mother of the living child, which he returns to its true mother. In this story we find another significant figure of things that were to come. The two women represent the Synagogue and the Church of Christ. The Synagogue, the Old Testament, can no longer save souls after the coming of Christ. It can bring only death and ruin to those who remain attached to it. But the Church can save souls. She snatches them from the grasp of the robber, death. Christ is the judge between the two women. From the cross He assigns to the Church the souls which He has redeemed through His blood. The veil of the temple is rent; the Old Testament has no more to give. "Give the living child to this woman [the Church of the New Testament] and let it not be killed; for she is the mother thereof" (Epistle). Christ not only pronounces judgment, as Solomon did, but takes the cross upon His shoulders and submits to a disgraceful death in order to save us and give us to our true mother. He also provides her with all that is necessary for her role as mother of mankind and our guide to eternal life. By His death He gave us our mother, the Church, and in her He gave us eternal life.

Jesus is the living temple (Gospel). Israel built the temple for herself. Forty-six years she worked to erect it. Now she has disgraced it and degraded it by the worldly traffic which she carried on in its courts. Then Christ came, and taking cords, made a scourge with which He drove the merchants and money-changers out of the temple. The Jews were incensed by this act and demanded of Him, "What sign [miracle] dost Thou show unto us, seeing Thou dost these things?" He points to His own person, to the temple of His body, and says to them: This is the sign which I shall show you. "Destroy this temple, and in three days I will raise it up" (Gospel). Here there was question of two temples, the temple of stone in which they stood, and the temple of Christ's body. The Jews had already disgraced the stone temple of Jerusalem, and they were soon to destroy the temple of Christ's body. But Jesus has given them the sign they demanded. After three days He raised up, by His glorious resurrection from the dead, the temple which they had destroyed. The Jews did not understand what He meant. At the moment not even the apostles understood Christ in the sense that He intended. But the apostles held their peace, and "when therefore He was risen again from the dead, His disciples remembered that He had said this"; that is, that He had prophesied His resurrection from the dead after three days. Through their unshakable faith in their Master they are led to a more perfect understanding of Christ. The Jews, on the other hand, because of their unbelief sank deeper and deeper into their blindness. Men are divided in their attitude toward Christ, and consequently "this child is set for the fall and for the resurrection of many" (Lk 2:34).

"Destroy this temple." Jesus proves Himself by the cross: for the first time on Good Friday, and daily in the Holy Sacrifice of the Mass, which is the living representation of His death and resurrection. He proves Himself by the cross in the history of the Church and in the lives of His saints. How are we to prove ourselves? By the amount of worldly goods that we accumulate? By the honors and the temporal success we achieve? No, indeed. "If any man will come after me, let him… take up his cross daily and follow me" (Lk 9:23). "With Christ I am nailed to the cross" (Gal 2:19). This is the essence of Christianity. This is the Christianity of Christ, the proof of the true Church of Christ. How little this truth is understood! How seldom do men live in accordance with it! Do I myself really understand it and live by it?

"Save me, O God, by Thy name, and in Thy strength deliver me; O God, hear my prayer; give ear to the words of my mouth" (Introit). This is the prayer of the Savior on the Mount of Olives, at the pillar of the scourging, during the way of the cross, and on the cross itself. It is the prayer of the suffering and persecuted Church. Today we unite ourselves and our prayers with those of the suffering Savior.

In the Sacrifice of the Mass we enter into a union with the suffering Christ. We wish to be true Christians; that is, martyrs. We are prepared to give up all things in order to be with Him. We wish to renounce our passions, the world, and all that is evil, that we may be a pure oblation to the Father. We wish to be martyrs to the love of God, and we wish to submit ourselves perfectly to all His desires.

We thank God today that He has given us so good a mother at the moment of our baptism. We have faith in her and surrender ourselves to her completely. We shall not be deceived when we see her ill-treated and persecuted. On the contrary, her suffering is our most certain proof that she is the spouse of Christ Crucified.

Prayer

Grant, we beseech Thee, O Lord, almighty God, that by keeping the sacred observance with devotion year by year, we may be pleasing to Thee both in body and soul.

Graciously hear our supplications, we beseech Thee, O Lord, and grant the help of Thy protection to those to whom Thou dost give the spirit of prayer. Through Christ our Lord. Amen.

Tuesday

Lawrence, the stational saint, directs our attention to the great martyr, Christ. "Hear, O God, my prayer, and despise not my supplication; be attentive to me, and hear me. I am grieved in my exercise; and I am troubled at the voice of the enemy, and at the tribulation of the sinner" (Introit). There He hangs on the cross in an unspeakable agony, the "mediator of God and men" (1 Tm 2:5). His blood cries out for mercy on sinners. "Let Thy anger cease, and be appeased upon the wickedness of Thy people" (Epistle). The Church unites herself with the Lord, praying and offering Himself for His people. "Be appeased," she cries out to heaven, "upon the wickedness of Thy people." Now, in the celebration of the Holy Sacrifice of the Mass, the Lord has been appeased.

The Lord is praying for us. Moses, the Epistle continues to inform us, spent forty days on the heights of Sinai. At the foot of the mountain the people who had just received the Ten Commandments amid thunder and lightning, were making themselves an idol. They danced about their idol and thus broke their covenant with Jahve. Descending the mountain, Moses sees what has happened and in his anger he breaks the tables of stone on which the commandments have been engraved. God will destroy this generation. "I see that this people is stiff-necked; let Me alone that My wrath may be kindled against them, and that I may destroy them." God promised Moses that he would make him the father of "a great nation" if He destroyed this people. But Moses besought God for mercy for his erring people. "Why, O Lord, is Thy indignation enkindled against Thy people.... Let Thy anger cease, and be appeased upon the wickedness of Thy people." "And the Lord was appeased from doing the evil which He had spoken against His people" (Epistle).

The liturgy recognizes in Moses a figure of Christ our Lord. We are the sinful people of Israel. By our baptism the Lord led us out of Egypt and snatched us from the slavery of Satan and sin. He received us into His kingdom, and blessed us with the benefits of supernatural life as children of God. But we soon proved unfaithful to the things which Christ had taught us by His word and example. We allowed our hearts to become attached to the vain goods of this life, and we made for ourselves idols, which we adored and to which we offered sacrifice. God became angry with us for this breach of loyalty. Then the Son of God descended from the mountain (from heaven) to plead for His sinful people. He prays to the Father: "Why O Lord, is Thy indignation enkindled against Thy people, whom Thou hast brought out of the land of Egypt with great power and with a mighty hand?... Let Thy anger cease, and be appeased upon the wickedness of Thy people." Thus He prayed in the first moment of His Incarnation when He entered into the world. Thus He prayed without interruption during His earthly life; thus He prayed in the Garden of Olives, at the pillar of the scourging, and as He was being rejected and condemned by the judges of His nation. His prayer continued as He began His painful journey to Calvary; it was not interrupted by His agony on the cross. Now, before the throne of His Father in heaven, He repeats the same prayer unceasingly, "always living to make intercession for us" (Heb 7:25). In the silence of the tabernacle He prays continually to His heavenly Father, "Be appeased upon the wickedness of Thy people," "Hear, O God, my prayer, and despise not my supplication; be attentive to me, and hear me" (Introit).

With grateful hearts we draw near to the Savior who sacrificed Himself for us. We will accompany Him on His way of suffering, into the Garden of Olives, into the house of the high priest, into the prison in which He was held captive during the night. We follow Him as He is dragged to Pilate, and from Pilate to Herod, and from Herod back to Pilate. We suffer with Him when the pagan judge has Him brought forth before the people, who cry out: "Crucify Him." We share His shame when a common murderer is preferred before Him. We follow Him through the cruel scourging, the shameful mockery, and the painful crowning with thorns. We follow in sorrow as He begins His dreadful journey up the mount of Calvary, for we wish to share also in the redemptive act He is about to perform. He is praying and offering Himself up for us. "Be appeased upon the wickedness of Thy people.... And the Lord was appeased" by the death of His son, our Redeemer and our mediator.

With the same intention of making atonement for our sins and of reconciling us with the Father, He offers Himself up for us daily in the Holy Sacrifice of the Mass, which is the mysterious repetition of His passion and death on the cross. By this means also the grace won for us on Calvary is applied to our souls. In the Holy Sacrifice of the Mass He prays for us: "Let Thy anger cease, and be appeased upon the wickedness of Thy people." "Forgive us our trespasses.... And lead us not into temptation; but deliver us from evil." Deliver us from impenitence, from inconstancy, and from an evil death.

Jesus is praying for us and offering up His sacrifice for us. This does not mean that there is nothing left for us to do. We must not suppose that we may continue in sin. Having seen in the death of Christ the malice of sin, we must separate ourselves from it and give ourselves up to penance, fasting, and mortification. We must now take part in His sufferings and perform works of expiation for our own sins and for those of our neighbor. We are responsible, not only for our own souls, but also for those of our neighbors. We are, in a sense, coredeemers and partially responsible for their salvation. We shall perform our share of the work of redemption in so far as we penetrate into the sufferings of our Lord, who prayed and suffered for us. We shall share in His redemptive work in the measure in which we share His spirit.

Inspired by the spirit of Christ, we go forth now to our daily tasks and seek to sanctify them by prayer and sacrifice. We may thus obtain for our brethren in Christ the strength to overcome all their temptations in matters of faith and morals.

Prayer

May the facts of the sacred observance, we beseech Thee, O Lord, make us grow in holiness and procure for us the continual help of Thy favor.

Have mercy on Thy people, O Lord, and from the unceasing tribulation under which they labor, grant them relief in Thy mercy. Through Christ our Lord. Amen.

Wednesday

Today we accompany the catechumens to the Basilica of St. Paul, the Apostle of the Gentiles. During the early years of Christianity, the catechumens were on this day subjected to a severe scrutiny to determine whether they could be admitted to baptism. On those who passed the scrutiny successfully, the ceremony of the "opening of the ears" was performed. They were then given the book of the Gospels, the confession of faith, and the Our Father, all of which remind us of our own baptism.

"At that time Jesus, passing by, saw a man who was blind from his birth" (Gospel). Born blind! Eternal night! The beauty of the world is entirely hidden from the blind man. How sad an affliction! But Christ happens to pass the blind man. He forms a paste out of spittle and dust, and rubs it into the eyes of the blind man, and commands him, "Go, wash in the pool of Siloe." The blind man does as he is told and returns with his vision restored. Spiritually we are all like the man born blind. Original sin has cast the spell of night over us. We are blind and deprived of all supernatural light. But Jesus passed us in the way and sent us to bathe in the pool of the baptismal font, and our spiritual sight was restored to us. A new world was opened to us, just as a new world was opened to the man born blind. The vision that was restored to us was the vision of faith, the vision of truth. In the light of faith we gaze into God's world of thought, and we begin to think the thoughts of God. We now have the "light of life" (Jn 8:12). We can now understand the important issues of life in the light of God's eternal wisdom. We are now in a position to understand whence we came, why we came, and where we are going. We know now with certainty why we dwell in this world, what we have to do while here, and what will be our destiny when this life is finished. We were blind, but now through baptism we have been made to see.

"I will pour upon you clean water [baptism]; you shall be cleansed from all your filthiness [sin].... And I will give you a new heart and put a new spirit within you; and I will take away the stony heart out of your flesh, and will give you a heart of flesh. And I will put My spirit in the midst of you, and I will cause you to walk in My commandments and to keep My judgments and do them. And you shall dwell in the land [heaven] which I gave to your fathers, and you shall be My people, and I will be your God" (Epistle). Behold here the new man who has been cured of his blindness through baptism.

"I am the light of the world" (Gospel). The warm, spring sunshine calls the beautiful plants of the earth, but it also arouses the poisonous serpents from their hiding places. Jesus heals the blind man, and wicked and envious men appear at once to condemn Him for His good work. But the blind man no longer has any fear. With a charming simplicity, complete frankness, and without respect to persons, he tells truthfully and with gratitude and joy, of the wonderful things that have happened to him. Do we live continually in grateful remembrance of our baptism? The Lord gloriously reveals Himself in the cure of the blind man. This miracle is a figure of the mercy and love of our Lord. The poor blind man gives us an example of faith. He was a beggar, an outcast from society; and yet he is a hero and a confessor of the faith. He is a teacher and an apostle for Christ. The Pharisees cast him out of the synagogue because of his adherence to Christ; they excommunicate him from their church. But he is received with favor by Christ. "Dost thou believe in the Son of God?" The blind man asks, "Who is He, Lord, that I may believe in Him? And Jesus said to him: Thou hast both seen Him, and it is He that speaketh with thee. And he said: I believe Lord. And falling down he adored Him."

"Blessed is the nation [the baptized] whose God is the Lord; the people whom He hath chosen for His inheritance. By the word of the Lord the heavens were established; and all the power of them by the spirit of His mouth" (Gradual). And this same God has chosen us for

His special inheritance. "O ye nations, bless the Lord our God, . . . who hath set my soul to live, and hath not suffered my feet to be moved" (Offertory).

"The Lord made clay from spittle and anointed my eyes; and I went and I washed, and I saw, and I have believed in God," the Church sings at the Communion of the Mass today. These are the fruits of Holy Communion: "I saw and I have believed." May this fruit be realized in us also.

Prayer

O God, who dost vouchsafe to the just the reward of their merits, and to sinners pardon through fasting, have mercy upon Thy suppliant people that the confession of our guilt may have power to obtain for us forgiveness for our misdeeds.

May the ears of Thy mercy, O Lord, be opened to the prayers of Thy suppliants, and that thou mayest grant their desires to them that petition Thee, make them ask the things that are pleasing to Thee. Through Christ our Lord. Amen.

Thursday

It is appropriate that the story of the raising to life of the youth of Naim be told in the stational church of St. Martin of Tours, for he also was gifted with the power to restore life to the dead. "Seek ye the Lord, and be strengthened; seek His face evermore" (Introit).

As Jesus was passing by the city of Naim with His disciples, they encountered a funeral procession at the gates of the city. A young man was being carried out to his last resting place. This young man had been the hope and the support of his widowed mother, who followed the bier in tears. Christ was moved with pity, and He approached the bier and commanded the dead man, "Young man, I say to thee, arise" (Gospel). The dead man sat up, and Jesus gave him back to his mother. Yes, that is the heart of our loving Savior, full of understanding and sympathy. He restores to the sorrowing mother the son she had lost. How good He is! He provides us with joy, help, and happiness. His arrival at the city at the time of the funeral appeared to be mere chance, but it was not mere chance. He came there with the intention of saving this young man and of raising him from the dead.

What the Epistle and the Gospel relate of the past, becomes for the liturgy a reality of the present. For the liturgy the dead child of the Sunamite woman and the young man of Naim are figures of the souls of men who, through Original Sin or actual sin, are without the life of grace. Our ill-regulated passions, our sloth concerning the things of God, are carrying us out from our city to bury us with the eternally dead in hell. Our passions, our pride, our avarice, our self-love, the world, the flesh, and the devil, all join in the procession that would lead us to destruction. We are yet young men and should be in the full vigor of life, but these enemies carry us out as one dead. Weeping and sorrowful, our mother, the Church, follows this sad procession. She knows the sad state of these souls, for she gave them life, and they were her hope and support, and she would have led them to eternal life. But now they are dead in sin. Then Christ appears. He beholds her tears, and these tears touch His heart. "Weep not." He approaches the dead soul in the sacrament of penance and commands the sinful soul, "I say to thee arise." "I absolve thee from thy sins." The soul lifts itself up, abandons the path of sin, and is given back to its mother. The mother rejoices particularly when these children are restored to her by their Easter confession.

This restoration of life is worked by the prayers and tears of the Church. The grace of repentance, the conversion from our evil ways, the forgiveness of our sins, has been obtained for us by the prayers, sacrifices, and works of penance performed by the Church. "She shed tears over each of her children, as if it were her only child. She suffers the most pain when she sees that her children fall victims to death through sin" (St. Ambrose).

The tears and prayers of our Holy Mother the Church have not been in vain. We rely upon the prayers of the Church when we intercede for those of our friends who have wandered from the straight and narrow path. Sin results in estrangement from God and induces death. The mouth is dead, for it is no longer open to prayer and conversation with God; the eyes are dead, for they no longer behold God, but only creatures; the hands are dead, for they work no longer for God, but against Him; the feet are dead, for they carry us not to God, but down the path of destruction. There is only one who can help us, only one who can restore life to our members. In the fullness of His divinity He assumes human nature and becomes like unto us in all things except sin (Heb 4:15). He is a second Eliseus, He lays His mouth upon our mouth, His eyes upon our eyes, His hands and feet upon our hands and feet. He who is the origin of all life puts on the appearance of death; He sanctifies the dead soul; He opens the silent lips so that they may praise God; He restores light to the failing eyes so that they may behold the glory of God; He reactivates the stiffened hands so that they may be lifted to defend the honor of God, and the feet, that they may tread the way of salvation. The soul thus restored cries out, "Bless the Lord, O my soul, and let all that is within me, bless His holy name" (Ps 102:1). Jesus is for us the prophet Eliseus. How grateful we should be for our restoration to the life of grace!

The Church weeps for the sinner. With this holy mother we, too, grieve for our wayward brothers and sisters who through sin have died and are being carried slowly to their ruin. We share the anguish of the sorrowing mother, and join her in her impetuous prayer for their salvation. We, too, can share the redemptive work of the new Eliseus. We can take upon ourselves the burden of the sins, the errors, the blindness, and the perversity of our neighbors. With the prophet Eliseus we seek the dead man in his chambers and lay our eyes on his eyes, our mouth on his mouth, our arms on his arms, in heartfelt love and sympathy. We must not avoid him or despise him, for we see in him a soul sick unto death. We can offer for him our prayers, our sacrifices, our works of penance, with the intention of bringing him to salvation. We thus become all things to all men. "I desire not the death of the wicked, but that the wicked turn from his way and live" (Ez 33:11).

Prayer

Grant, we beseech Thee, O almighty God, that chastened by the facts of our devotion, the devotion itself may also gladden us so that, with our earthly affections subdued, we may the more easily lay hold on heavenly things.

O God, the Creator and Ruler of Thy people, drive away the sins which beset them, that being pleasing unto Thee, they may be secure under Thy protection. Through Christ our Lord. Amen.

Friday

Today in a festive spirit we assemble for Mass at the church of St. Eusebius. We are among the tombs where the ancient Romans used to bury their dead. In our midst is Christ, who is the Author of life, and who raises the dead to life. We offer Him our congratulations in the Introit of the Mass. "The meditation of my heart is always in Thy sight, O Lord, my helper and my Redeemer." Thou hast raised me from the death of sin, and on the last day Thou wilt raise me again to eternal life. "The heavens show forth the glory of God, and the firmament declareth the work of Thy hands," the miracles of the raising of the dead to life (Introit).

The raising of Lazarus to life was one of the most important miracles Christ performed during His lifetime. We are astonished at it. But St. Augustine teaches us:

If we are astonished at Him who worked this miracle, still we should rather rejoice than be amazed. He who brought the dead man back to life is the same who created him, the Son of the Father. What miracle is that if one should be restored to life by Him through whom so many daily are called into life? If He wished, could He not in an instant raise all the dead? But He has reserved this event for the end of the world. The hour will come in which all shall hear His voice, as the dead Lazarus once heard it, and will come forth from their graves (Jn 5:28). Through the miracle performed for Lazarus we should also be prepared for the great mystery of the general resurrection, so that we will rise to life and not to death.

Jesus is the one who raises the dead to life. What He does for Lazarus, He does for all of us spiritually in baptism and in the sacrament of penance. In Holy Communion He plants in our bodies the germ of a future resurrection so that the poor body may also live eternally and enjoy the happiness of heaven. "I am the resurrection and the life. He that believeth in Me, although he be dead, shall live" (Jn 11:25).

Jesus restores life to those who are spiritually dead. When Jesus saw the sister of Lazarus weeping, He was deeply moved and said, "Where have you laid him? They say to Him: Lord, come and see. And Jesus wept. The Jews therefore said: Behold how He loved him" (Gospel). Why did the Lord weep, and why was He troubled? The liturgy shows us the meaning of this figure, through the mouth of St. Augustine:

The dead man, who lay in the tomb already four days, is a figure of the sinner, whom the burden of sins weighs down. Thus he gives an indication how you, too, should be troubled when a grievous sin weighs you down. If you acknowledge your guilt, if you say: I have done this evil thing, and God has had mercy on me; I transgressed, and God has spared me; I am baptized, and yet have fallen again into sin; where should I begin? Where should I go? Where can I flee? If you confess contritely, then the Savior weeps with you in sympathy.

"Where have you laid him?" He knows all things. Why then, does He ask? He asks in order to teach us that, when we have sinned, we are strangers. Sin has so disfigured us that He no longer recognizes us. We are cast off as a rotting, decaying corpse. "Come and see." He sees the misery of our sins and weeps over us. "Be hold how He loved him." Then Christ draws near to the sinner with the sacrament of baptism, or with the sacrament of penance, and commands with authority, "Come forth." Break with death; leave behind all sin and corruption. "Come forth" to live the life of grace, the life of a child of God. Thus a resurrection from the dead occurs each time the sacrament of baptism or the sacrament of penance is administered.

Today we rejoice over the restoration of the dead; that is, over the precious graces of baptism and penance. It is a time of earnest petition for the catechumens and for the many unfortunate sinners who are dead in their sins. May they receive the grace to come forth from the darkness of sin, and henceforth to walk steadfastly in the light of faith. Our prayers and sacrifices can obtain this grace for them.

This is also a day for firm resolutions. "Let us also go that we may die with Him," we resolve today with the apostle Thomas (Gospel). We shall have life if we die with Him. If we would achieve union with Christ, if we wish to devote ourselves entirely to the Father, then we must die to sin. The true Christian life and also the daily Mass demands that we die to sin. "So do you also reckon that you are dead to sin, but alive unto God in Christ Jesus our Lord" (Rom 6:11). Our program for Lent also demands that we die to sin.

Prayer

O God, who dost renew the world with ineffable sacraments, grant, we beseech Thee, that Thy Church may profit by Thy eternal institutions and not be lacking in temporal assistance.

Grant, we beseech Thee, O almighty God, that being conscious of our own infirmity and confiding in Thy power, we may ever rejoice under Thy tender care. Through Christ our Lord. Amen.

Saturday

This is a day of holy exultation. The catechumens have assembled in the sanctuary of the holy bishop St. Nicholas. Here they are to undergo their examination before baptism. After this examination they hear the invitation: "All you that thirst, come to the waters [of baptism].... Come and drink with joy" (Introit). What will they obtain in baptism, in Christianity, in the Church?

In the sacrament they will find the Lord, the shepherd of their soul. "Thus saith the Lord [the Messias, the Christ]: ... In the day of salvation I have helped thee, and I have preserved thee and given thee to be a covenant of the people, that thou mightest raise up the earth, and possess the inheritances that were destroyed" (Epistle). The Father has delivered humanity, particularly the heathen world, to us and to His incarnate Son, not only that He may judge the world, but that He may also save it (Jn 3:16). The Savior thus sent by God calls all men to salvation. "Say to them that are bound: Come forth; and to them that are in darkness: Show yourselves. They shall feed in the ways, and their pastures shall be every plain. They shall not hunger nor thirst, neither shall the heat nor the sun strike them; for He shall give them drink.... Behold these shall come from afar, and behold these from the north and from the sea, and these from the south country.... Because the Lord hath comforted His people and will have mercy on His poor ones" (Epistle). All this He has done out of love. "Can a woman forget her infant, so as not to have pity on the son of her womb? And if she should forget, yet will not I forget thee." The Father, without any merit on our part, has entrusted us to His Son, the Savior, through baptism. He is the Good Shepherd, who will lead us to green pastures. He is the bread of life (the Eucharist) and the fountain of living waters (baptism). Therefore let us go to Christ, the Good Shepherd. "To Thee, O Lord, is the poor man left: Thou wilt be a help to the orphan" (Gradual). "Give praise, O ye heavens, and rejoice, O earth; . . . because the Lord hath comforted His people, and will have mercy on His poor ones" (Epistle). He shows His mercy in the sacraments of baptism, penance, and the Eucharist. "The Lord is become my firmament and my refuge and my deliverer: and in Him will I put my trust" (Offertory).

"I am the light of the world; he that followeth Me, walketh not in darkness, but shall have the light of life" (Gospel). How unfortunate are those who have not received baptism! Unfortunate, too, are those who, having received baptism, relapse into sin and separate themselves from Christ, the light. Like the Jews of today's Gospel, they walk in the darkness of night, having turned away from the light. They cannot, in fact, bear the light. They would even extinguish it, "but His hour was not yet come." The light was withdrawn from the Jews, they walked in darkness. Only a few days yet, and they would ask a pagan judge to nail their Savior to the cross. In the presence of the pagan judge and before the eyes of the world they were to reject Him whom their fathers had so eagerly longed for, and who had been promised them by their prophets through the centuries that had gone before. They were to reject Him to whom all their religious worship and their sacrifices had been offered. "Give us Barabbas." "What, then, shall I do with Jesus, the king of the Jews?" Pilate asks. Screaming they cry out: "Crucify Him, crucify Him. . . . His blood be upon us and our children" (Lk 23:21; Mt 27:25). They indeed walked in the darkness. Can a greater misfortune happen to a nation, to humanity, to a soul than to be visited with spiritual blindness? How fatal the blindness that will not see Christ! Pride, self-sufficiency, and perverse adherence to the Mosaic law made Israel blind to Christ, the true light.

"I am the light of the world." Israel turned away from the light, and it was given to us who were chosen from among the pagans. We were selected through baptism and by our adherence to Christ, "Who hath delivered us from the power of darkness, and hath translated us into the kingdom of the Son of His love, in whom we have redemption through His blood, the remission of sins. . . . And He is the head of the body, the Church, who is the beginning, the first-born from the dead" (Col 1:13 ff.). We have been incorporated into Him in a living union. "I am the light of the world," the Sun of truth and justice.

Are we truly walking in the light? The reception of baptism in itself is not enough. Our life must be a continual renunciation of all that is evil, of all that is in opposition to God. We must believe in Christ, in eternity, in the resurrection of the dead to eternal life. Because we believe these things, we must accept His commandments and keep them. What is the unmistakable test to determine whether we are walking in the light or not? "He that saith that he is in the light, and hateth his brother, is in darkness even until now. He that loveth his brother abideth in the light, and there is no scandal in him. But he that hateth his brother is in darkness, and walketh in darkness and knoweth not whither he goeth, because the darkness hath blinded his eyes" (1 Jn 2:9 ff.). When we receive Holy Communion today we acknowledge gratefully: "The Lord ruleth me, and I shall want nothing; He hath set me in a place of pasture; He hath brought me up on the water of refreshment" (Communion).

Prayer

Vouchsafe, O Lord, by Thy grace to make fruitful the fervor of our devotion; for the fasts we have undertaken shall profit us only if they be pleasing to Thy goodness.

O God, who dost choose rather to have pity on them that hope in Thee than to be angry, grant that we may duly lament the evils we have done, that we may deserve to find the favor of Thy consolation. Through Christ our Lord. Amen.

Passiontide

Today we enter a new phase of the holy season of Lent. From *Septuagesima* until today we have striven to purify our own life. The liturgy has directed us toward this end during the last seven weeks. By disciplining our passions, by mortification, fasting, prayer, and almsgiving, we have prepared ourselves for the great task that now awaits us. We are to share in the death and resurrection of Christ. This theme pervades the liturgy throughout Passiontide. Our hearts now long for the graces which this season will provide.

During Passiontide the cross occupies the central place in the liturgy. We must learn to love, understand, and reverence the cross, for it is the source of our salvation. The tree of Paradise brought forth death, but the tree of the cross gives life. By means of the tree in Paradise, Satan overcame men; by means of the cross Christ overcame Satan (Preface of the Holy Cross). In understanding and loving the cross of Christ, we must learn also to understand and treasure our own cross. "If any man will come after Me, let him deny himself and take up his cross and follow Me. For he that will save his life, shall lose it; and he that shall lose his life for My sake, shall find it" (Mt 16:24 f.).

"Behold, in the cross all doth consist, and all lieth in our dying; and there is no other way to life and to true interior peace but the way of the holy cross and daily mortification. The more one dies to self, the more one lives to God. If indeed there had been anything better and more beneficial to man's salvation than suffering, Christ would certainly have shown it by word and example."[12]

Passion Sunday

The Mass

Today we see Christ beginning His sacrificial mission. With loving understanding the Church presses close to Him that she may accompany Him through the ordeal of His passion and death. She dons her mourning apparel; she hides the beauty of her ornate crosses and images, and even omits the *Gloria Patri* from the Mass. In the breviary the series of readings taken from the books of Moses are interrupted to make place for the writings of Jeremias, who gives us a vivid picture of the sufferings of Christ. Holy Mother the Church cries out repeatedly to the Father, "From the mouth of the lion deliver me, O Lord." She lives and shares intimately the suffering of her beloved Savior. This spirit must fill our heart during Passiontide.

[12] *Imitation of Christ*, bk. 2, chap. 12.

The Introit shows us the high priest, Christ, at the foot of Calvary. We join Him as He cries out in anguish: "Judge me, O God, and distinguish my cause from the nation that is not holy" and that is trying now to destroy me. We who are faithful are not mere spectators, for we know that we are one with Him. We unite ourselves with Him and with the whole Church and make His distress and prayer our own. The result is the mighty plea for mercy which surges up to heaven through the somber strain of the Kyrie and the Collect.

Christ now turns His steps toward the altar of sacrifice. He does not walk now as the high priest of the Old Law, who brought only the blood of animals into the holy of holies, but He goes clothed in His own priestly robes, and offers His own blood to the last drop. He offers now, not an animal as a victim, but Himself as the unspotted and holy victim; He reconciles man with God and establishes a new race, a holy Church. The way is not an easy way, but a way of pain and sorrow. As we accompany Christ, we pray with Him the stirring words of the Gradual and the Tract: "Deliver me, O Lord, from my enemies.... Often they have fought against me from my youth." In the Gospel we see His enemies surrounding Him, reviling Him and ridiculing Him. They take up stones to cast at Him; but "Jesus hid Himself, and went out of the temple." The incident is full of meaning. He forsakes the Synagogue, which despised and rejected His person and His doctrine, and turns to the Church of the New Law. This new Church gladly hears His word and shares His life. "If any man keep My word, he shall not see death forever" (Gospel). We are a holy Church, and we keep His word. We express our determination to do this in the Credo of the Mass. We believe and we will live as we believe. "I shall live and keep Thy words" (Offertory).

Christ approaches our altar to renew His redeeming sacrifice in an unbloody and mysterious manner. Spiritually and mysteriously we follow Him and take part in this redeeming act. With thankful hearts we await the coming of our pure, holy, and unspotted victim. We offer it to God with our thanks, our adoration and petitions, and as a satisfaction for our sins. But we do more. We do not allow Christ to offer Himself alone. We enter with Christ into the holy of holies to offer our own blood before the face of the Father. As the substance of the bread and wine becomes the body and blood of Christ, so we, too, are made one with Christ. We put off the old man and put on the new man; we think new thoughts, we strive for a new goal, we live a new life. We have been lifted up and out of the world, and now we belong to God. We have been crucified with Christ, and now we are dead to sin and evil; we have been made an offering with Christ, and now belong to God (Rom 6:11). When we depart from Mass, we are new men, for we have been joined in the closest union with God. We pray with childlike confidence, for we pray with Christ the "Our Father," a prayer which expresses childlike confidence and self-surrender. "Give us this day our daily bread." How can He refuse us now that we have been so intimately united to His Son? As a proof of His fatherly care and friendship, God gives us the very essence of all good, His only Son, and with Him, His holy and divine life. "This is My body.... Do this, as often as you receive it, in commemoration of Me" (Communion). We must share this action with Him by living with Him and dying with Him. Full of confidence we await the fulfillment of the words of the Gospel: "If any man keep my word, he shall not see death forever."

Meditation

"Judge me O God, and distinguish my cause from the nation that is not holy. Deliver me from the unjust and deceitful man; for Thou art God my strength" (Introit). "Deliver me, O Lord, from my enemies.... Often have they fought against me from my youth.... The wicked have wrought upon my back. They have lengthened their iniquities; the Lord who is just will cut the necks of sinners" (Gradual, Tract). Thus the Church prays from the depths of her heart, feeling the anxiety and suffering of her bridegroom.

"Brethren: Christ being come, an high priest of the good things to come, by a greater and more perfect tabernacle, not made with hands, that is, not of this creation; neither by the blood of goats or of calves [as the high priest of the Old Law], but by His own blood, entered once into the Holies, having obtained eternal redemption" on the cross (Epistle). The animal sacrifices of the Old Law could not work justification; but "the blood of Christ... shall cleanse our conscience from dead works [the works of sin] to serve the living God. And therefore He is the Mediator of the New Testament, that by means of His death, for the redemption of those transgressions which were under the former Testament, they that are called may receive the promise of eternal inheritance, in Christ Jesus our Lord" (Epistle). The high priest of the Old Law took the blood of animals into the holy of holies of the temple at Jerusalem; he himself suffered no harm through the offering of the sacrifice. Not so with Christ. He offers His own blood to the last drop. He endures shame and pain, indescribable humiliation and torture; He suffers in the garden, at the pillar of the scourging, on the way to Calvary, and on the cross. He took upon Himself this suffering to purchase for us freedom from sin and an eternal inheritance.

"They took up stones therefore to cast at Him; but Jesus hid Himself and went out of the temple" (Gospel). The Jews were unable to seize Him, for He was more powerful than they. They were burning with hatred, and they misconstrued His words; yet He assures them, "I do know [the Father] and do keep His word. Abraham your father rejoiced that he might see My day; he saw it and was glad." This assertion drives the Jews to distraction. "Thou art not yet fifty years old; and hast Thou seen Abraham?" He answers them; "Amen, amen I say to you, before Abraham was made, I am." At this point they took up stones to cast at Him. But His time is not yet come, and they cannot injure Him. He quietly leaves the temple, for they will apprehend Him, judge Him, and put Him to death only when He has determined to permit it, for He is to undertake His passion and death freely. "He was offered because it was His own will" (Is 53:7). His power is supreme, and He knows the desires and the intentions of His enemies. His knowledge is infinite, and He knows all the details of His coming passion. He knows that by submitting to the defeat of the cross He will be victorious. "Father, forgive them, for they know not what they do" (Lk 23:34). Christ faces His passion as a conqueror.

The passion and death of our Lord on the cross is not merely a human sacrifice, but a manifestation of the divinity through the sacrifice of the crucified body of the Savior. His death is not marked by groaning, hatred, or self-pity; there is only the quiet and peaceful assurance of His victory over the blindness, weakness, and passion of men. The heart of the Savior overflows with love. "Father, forgive them, for they know not what they do." The divinity achieves victory through the death of the God-man. "Indeed this man was the Son of God" (Mk 15:39).

"By His own blood," out of the depths of His love, He redeemed us. Today the Church veils the cross. Is it perhaps because we are not worthy to see it? Is it possible that we are His enemies, who wish to stone Him in return for His love? For our salvation He undertook the bloody ordeal in the Garden of Olives, the cruel scourging at the pillar, the ignominious crowning with thorns, and the death on the cross. Yet for the most part we have remained cold and indifferent. What do we do for the salvation of souls? It is true that we pray for one another, offer a few words of comfort, and do each other slight favors; but we do little more. Christ was more generous. He endured the crowning of thorns and dragged the heavy cross to Calvary. We pamper our bodies as if they were our last end. We prefer to have our heads crowned with laurels and roses. We are impatient and consider ourselves unfortunate whenever we are called on to carry a mere splinter of the cross of Christ. Are we one in spirit with Him? Do we love what He loves and hate what He hates? Are we His friends? He lives for God and for sinners; we live for ourselves, for pleasure, and for the satisfaction of our passions.

Christ and His members must be one. They must walk the same road, not only during the liturgical service, when they are lifted up together in the mysteries of the sacrifice, but also in every event of life. Christ welcomed suffering, and accepted it freely; He did not flee the hardships of life. He makes suffering in us, His members, serve the spirit; He uses it as a means of freeing us from the world and all that is temporal, and thus raises us from things of this world to the things that are eternal.

Now, during Passiontide, we must begin to love and treasure pain and suffering. In the cross, in suffering, in our crucifixion with Christ, we shall find salvation. For Him and with Him we should bear all the slight injustices committed against us. For Him we should suffer freely and willingly the unpleasant and disagreeable things that occur to us. But our faith is weak. We flee from the cross instead of holding it dear, instead of loving it and welcoming it as our Savior did.

Prayer

We beseech Thee, almighty God, mercifully look upon Thy family, that by Thy bounty it may be governed in body, and by Thy protection be guarded in mind. Through Christ our Lord. Amen.

Monday

Christ issues an urgent invitation today to become sharers of His passion in order that what is "wanting of the sufferings of Christ, [may be filled up] in my flesh" (Col 1:24). Hence the liturgy takes us today to the holy martyr Chrysogonus, after whose example we should undertake to suffer with Christ.

"The rich He hath sent empty away" (Lk 1:53). Those unfortunate rich are pictured in the Gospel today. They have heard of Christ, they have heard many things of Him, they have shown an interest in Him; but they find that they have no need for Him. He has nothing to give them, for they are sufficient in themselves and have all that they desire. They live happily without Him. He may even be a disturbance in their lives, a reproach, a thorn in the side, pricking their vanity and their pride. But eventually they find that one cannot ignore

Christ nor take a neutral stand with regard to Him. Having made this discovery, most of the rich hate Christ. Today the rich, the rulers, the high priests, send out their minions to arrest Christ. Christ speaks to them thus: "Yet a little while I am with you; and then I go to Him that sent Me. You shall seek Me, and shall not find Me. And where I am, thither you cannot come" (Gospel). Such is the terrifying judgment on the wicked. They will have need of Him; in time of trouble they will seek Him; but they shall not find Him. They will be separated from Him forever, for, "Where I am, thither you cannot come." "He hath filled the hungry with good things; and the rich He hath sent empty away" (Lk 1:53). That is a fundamental law of the Christian order of grace.

"He hath filled the hungry with good things." The Lord turns from the self-sufficient Jews to the pagans. Even the inhabitants of Ninive are called (Epistle). Jonas the prophet came to them and preached penance. "Yet forty days and Ninive shall be destroyed. And the men of Ninive believed in God, and they proclaimed a fast and put on sackcloth, from the greatest to the least. And the word came to the king of Ninive, and he rose up out of his throne, and cast away his robe from him, and was clothed with sackcloth, and sat in ashes." He commanded that men and beasts should fast and "be covered with sackcloth, and cry to the Lord with all their strength." We are like the people of Ninive, thirsting for salvation. The Lord has called us. We must have faith, we must do penance, we must follow the Lord wholeheartedly. We must not confine our works to meditation on the passion of Christ, and prayers and protestations; we must put on sackcloth and perform works of self-denial and penance. We should become sharers of the passion of Christ and be nailed to the cross with Him. And we must not undertake penance reluctantly, only because we are obliged to do so or out of fear of losing our souls; the Lord is seeking those who desire to participate in His passion, who appreciate His cross, and who love it for what it is. He seeks the courageous, self-sacrificing souls, men like St. Chrysogonus.

Today in the sanctuary of St. Chrysogonus we begin the journey down the sorrowful path that will make us sharers of the passion of Christ. We are to help Him carry His cross and we shall be with Him all the day long, afflicted and trodden under foot (Introit). We shall persevere in this path and adhere to Christ with all our hearts, that we may be scourged with Him, unjustly accused and condemned with Him, and classed with criminals. With Him we shall hear the cruel mob crying out for our crucifixion. Daily in the Mass the Christian follows the path trodden by His savior and is nailed to the cross with Him. "Have mercy on me, O Lord, for man hath trodden me under foot; all the day long he hath afflicted me, fighting against me" (Introit). Thus Jesus prayed during His passion; thus the Church prays, and we pray with her. The Lord gives us the strength to drink the chalice of suffering. "The Lord of hosts, He is the King of Glory" (Communion).

"Jesus has many lovers of His heavenly kingdom, but very few are they who carry His cross with Him. He has many who long for consolation, but few who long for suffering. All wish to rejoice with Him hereafter, but only a few wish to suffer something with Him. Many follow Him in the breaking of bread, but only a few share the drinking of His chalice. Many praise His wonderous deeds, but very few follow Him in the degradation of His cross."[13]

[13] *Imitation of Christ*, bk. 2, chap. 11.

Prayer

Sanctify our fasts, we beseech Thee, O Lord, and mercifully grant us the forgiveness of our sins.

Give Thy people, we beseech Thee, O Lord, health of soul and body, that by persevering in good works we may ever deserve to be defended by Thy protection. Through Christ our Lord. Amen.

Tuesday

The divine services today are held in the sanctuary of the martyr St. Cyriacus. He brought help and comfort to the Daniel of the New Testament, Christ, held captive in His members. He brought help and food to the prisoners of Christ, just as the prophet Habacuc brought help to Daniel in the lion's den in Babylon.

In Daniel the liturgy recognizes Christ, surrounded on all sides by unbelief, ridicule, and by the unfaithfulness of His brethren in Galilee, who go to Jerusalem earnestly seeking to put Him to death. Some of them say that He is a good man, but others say that He is a seducer of the people (Gospel). After a few days they will call upon false witnesses and drag Him before Annas and Caiphas; they will hand Him over to the pagan judge, Pilate, and seek His condemnation. They will help stir up the mob to demand His death. He is like Daniel among the lions. They are not satisfied merely with destroying Him; they must have Him put to death on the cross to satisfy their thirst for revenge. They will stand under His cross and in their hatred will deride and torment Him even in His disgrace and agony. They will shake their heads and say, "Vah, Thou that destroyest the temple of God and in three days dost rebuild it, save Thy own self. If Thou be the Son of God, come down from the cross.... He saved others, Himself He cannot save. If He be the king of Israel, let Him now come down from the cross and we will believe Him" (Mt 27:40 ff.). He is like the innocent Daniel among the lions. He dies on the cross, and His body is laid in the tomb. Like lions guarding their prey, His enemies seal the tomb where they have laid Him.

"Distinguish my cause, O Lord; deliver me from the unjust and deceitful man" (Gradual). The enemies of Daniel believed that they had destroyed him, but he was miraculously saved. So, too, the enemies of Christ thought that they had destroyed Him; but God put them to shame. By His death He lays the foundations of His kingdom. He sends forth His apostles, and soon all nations flock to Him, to love Him and serve Him. Men leave father and mother, give up earthly possessions, earthly love and companionship, and embrace a life of mortification, privation, and labor for the love of souls. They give up all things to follow Christ. "He humbled Himself; ... for which cause God also hath exalted Him and hath given Him a name which is above all names." All creatures shall bow to His name and acknowledge that Christ has been glorified by God (Phil 2:8 ff.).

"And upon the seventh day the king came to bewail Daniel; and he came to the den and looked in, and behold Daniel was sitting in the midst of the lions. And the king cried out with a loud voice, saying: Great art Thou, O Lord, the God of Daniel. And He drew him out of the lions' den. But those that had been the cause of his destruction, he cast into the den, and they were devoured in a moment before him. Then the king said: Let all the inhabitants of the whole earth fear the God of Daniel; for He is the Savior, working signs and wonders in the earth, who hath delivered Daniel out of the lions' den" (Epistle). In like manner Christ was sealed in the den of the tomb, and although He surrendered to death, God raised Him up to victory. He has triumphed through His cross. "Let them trust in Thee who know Thy name, O Lord; for Thou dost not forsake them that seek Thee. Sing ye to the Lord who dwelleth in Sion [in His Church], for He hath not forgotten the prayers of the poor" (Offertory).

Daniel in the lions' den is a figure of Christ persecuted by His enemies. His person, His doctrine, His commandments, His moral precepts, His holy sacraments, His Church with its supreme ruler, His bishops, and His priests are all attacked and slandered. So it must be, for Christ is like Daniel in the lions' den. Daniel is also a figure of the Church, persecuted and hated like its Master. Christ and His Church must suffer persecution and hatred and so enter into glory (Lk 24:26).

"Go into Judea, that Thy disciples also may see Thy works which Thou dost," His brethren urge Him. "For there is no man that doth anything in secret, and He Himself seeketh to be known openly.... Manifest Thyself to the world" (Gospel). Thus is Christ advised by worldly men, even His friends and members of His own family, for the world has only ridicule and misunderstanding for Christ and His mission. With divine consideration Jesus answers them, "My time is not yet come; but your time is always at hand." They would have Christ seek a career of earthly honor; but Christ seeks only the path of humiliation. Exaltation and glory are His, but they are deferred to another time. "Lofty is the home; but lowly the way to it.... The home is Christ's repose (at the right hand of the Father); the way to it is by suffering" (St. Augustine).

"My time is not yet come." Thus we also speak, the members of Christ's mystical body. If the lovers of this world tempt us, we answer, "My time is not yet come." When, then, will our time come? "When Christ shall appear, who is your life, then you also shall appear with Him in glory" (Col 3:4). That indeed will be our time.

We shall therefore gladly follow Christ in His humiliation. His time came at Easter. Our time will also come in the blessed Easter of our eternal glorification. "Let them trust in Thee who know Thy name, O Lord; for Thou dost not forsake them that seek Thee" (Offertory).

Prayer

May our fasts be acceptable to Thee, O Lord; may they atone for our sins and render us worthy of Thy grace; and may they lead us to eternal remedies.

Grant us, we beseech Thee, O Lord, persevering service in Thy will, that in our time the people that obey Thee may increase both in merit and number. Through Christ our Lord. Amen.

Wednesday

Today with the holy pope and martyr, St. Marcellus, we take part in the *scrutinium*, the examination of the catechumens. They are to be examined regarding the commandments of God, which fourteen days ago they were given to learn. This is a day of examination for us also. We must inquire of ourselves how we have kept the commandments which we vowed to keep at the time of our baptism.

"My sheep hear My voice,... and they follow Me" (Gospel). Christ is the shepherd; the Church is the flock. She listens to His voice, and for two thousand years she has conformed herself to

His wishes. He commanded her, "Going, therefore, teach ye all nations, baptizing them in the name of the Father" (Mt 28:19). The Church has conscientiously carried out this command of the Lord. "This is My body.... This is the chalice of My blood.... Do this in commemoration of Me." This commission she fulfills faithfully in the daily celebration of the holy mystery of the Eucharist. She receives His word, His teachings and admonitions, from the lips of His apostles through the Gospels. She accepts them in humble faith and obedience.

"My sheep hear My voice." Through baptism we become members of the flock of Christ, and as members of His flock we listen to His voice and follow Him. We follow Him in His commandments, in His love of poverty, humiliation, and suffering, and in His love of the cross. We should examine ourselves in all sincerity to see if we have listened to His voice in all things. We ask ourselves if we have been faithful to His will and His commandments, or whether we have been listening rather to the voice of the world and arranging our life according to its spirit, its principles, and its allurements. "My sheep hear My voice,... and they follow Me."

"And I know them." He is concerned about all His sheep, about all those who are baptized. He cares for them that He may not lose one of them, but that they may all have eternal life. "No man shall pluck them out of My hand" (Gospel). Christ's sheep are so dear to Him because they have cost Him so dearly. He won them by much toil, by terrible suffering, by immeasurable sacrifices. He sacrificed His life in order to win for them the grace of baptism. "I give them life everlasting" (Gospel). "I know them"; I love them. I give them My merits, My satisfactions, My blood, My life. "My deliverer from the angry nations, Thou wilt lift me up above them that rise up against me.... I will love Thee, O Lord, my strength; the Lord is my firmament, and my refuge, and my deliverer" (Introit). "I will extol Thee, O Lord, for Thou hast upheld me, and hast not made my enemies to rejoice over me" (Gradual).

Today is a day of earnest self-examination. "My sheep hear My voice." Do we listen to His voice? Are we numbered among His sheep? Does St. Augustine's description of Christ's sheep apply to us?

The sheep of Christ are those who believe in Him; the sheep of Christ are those who follow the shepherd; the sheep of Christ are those who do not turn away from the Redeemer, who enter the sheepfold at the gate, who go out and find pastures; they will enjoy eternal life.... They have entered by faith; they will go out by the door of death. In the same way we have entered through the door of faith, and will in faith leave the body in order to find the heavenly pastures, eternal life.

Today the Epistle is applied to the catechumens and to us: "I am the Lord.... Thou shalt not calumniate thy neighbor, nor oppress him by violence.... Respect not the person of the poor [to treat him unjustly], nor honor the countenance of the mighty; but judge thy neighbor according to justice. Thou shalt not be a detractor nor a whisperer among the people.... Thou shalt not hate thy brother in thy heart; but reprove him openly, lest thou incur sin through him.... Thou shalt love thy friend as thyself. I am the Lord. Keep ye My laws; for I am the Lord your God."

This is a day of thanksgiving. Christ knows us and gives us eternal life through the ministration of the sacraments of the Church. I "will compass Thy altar,... that I may... tell of all Thy wondrous works" (Communion).

This is a day of salutary fear in view of what the Gospel relates to us concerning the Jews. They see Christ and hear His words; they behold His miracles, His virtue, His holiness, His freedom from sin; yet they do not believe in Him but turn away from Him. We, too, can abuse the grace that is given us. "He that thinketh himself to stand, let him take heed lest he fall" (1 Cor 10:12). Lord, protect us from the evil of the abuse of grace, from the evil of spiritual blindness, from the spirit of unbelief. Grant that we may always and everywhere listen to Thy voice and follow Thee, our true shepherd.

Prayer

Enlighten the hearts of Thy faithful by this sanctified fast, O God of mercy, and in Thy kindness turn a pitying ear to the suppliants to whom Thou givest the spirit of devotion.

Give ear unto our supplications, O almighty God, and benignly grant the effect of Thy accustomed mercy to those whom Thou hast allowed to be confident in the hope of Thy good will. Through Christ our Lord. Amen.

Thursday

On the last Thursday before Holy Thursday, the day of the reconciliation of penitents, we celebrate Mass in the church of the holy bishop and martyr, St. Apollinaris. Today we are the sinner who sheds tears and confesses her sins in penance and contrition at the feet of the Savior.

"At that time one of the Pharisees desired Jesus to eat with him; and He went into the house of the Pharisee, and sat down to meat. And behold a woman that was in the city, a sinner," learned that Jesus was in the house of Simon. She came to Christ, for her conscience was giving her no rest. She was not invited to this banquet; but she came in and in the sight of all present she cast herself down and washed Christ's feet with her tears and dried them with her hair; she then kissed His feet and anointed them with oil. Simon, the host, looked upon this scene with suspicion and said to himself: "This man, if He were a prophet, would know surely who and what manner of woman this is that toucheth Him; that she is a sinner," a fallen woman (Gospel).

The Lord knew very well the thoughts of His host and spoke a parable: "A certain creditor had two debtors; the one owed five hundred pence, and the other fifty. And whereas they had not wherewith to pay, he forgave them both. Which therefore of the two loveth him most? Simon answering, said: I suppose that he to whom he forgave most. And He said to him: Thou hast judged rightly.... Dost thou see this woman? I entered into thy house, thou gavest Me no water for My feet; but she with tears hath washed My feet and with her hairs hath wiped them. Thou gavest Me no kiss; but she, since she came in, hath not ceased to kiss My feet. My head with oil thou didst not anoint; but she with ointment hath anointed My feet. Wherefore I say to thee: Many sins are forgiven her because she hath loved much; but to whom less is forgiven, he loveth less." Then Christ turned to the sinful woman. "Thy sins are forgiven thee.... Thy faith hath made thee safe. Go in peace" (Gospel). We, too, are like the sinner at the feet of our Lord. We acknowledge with tears of sorrow and love our many sins, and with the sinner of the Gospel we beg to be forgiven. "Deliver us not up forever, for Thy name's sake, and abolish not Thy covenant.... In a contrite heart and humble spirit let us be accepted" (Epistle).

"Give glory to Thy name, and deal with us according to the multitude of Thy mercy" (Introit). The grace and mercy of the Lord works in the sinner the miracle of conversion. Through the mysterious working of His graces He opens the eyes of the unfortunate woman and allows her to see the baseness and shamefulness of her life. He implants in her heart the thought of changing her life, of seeking pardon, and of doing penance for her past offenses. He gives her the courage to brave the wrath of the Pharisee, and the humility to cast herself down and confess her guilt before all who are present. How graciously and lovingly Christ received her confession of guilt! He offers her no reproach, He uses no harsh words, but sends her away with the assurance, "Thy sins are forgiven thee.... Thy faith hath made thee safe. Go in peace." How full of understanding He is! He longs to forgive us and make us happy. "I am not come to call the just, but sinners" (Mt 9:13), those who admit their guilt and are sorry.

"Bring up sacrifices [of penance, sorrow, and satisfaction for sins; of prayer, fasting, and almsgiving] and come into His courts. Adore ye the Lord in His holy court. The Lord will discover the thick woods; and in His temple all shall speak His glory" (Gradual). Today we are penitent, like the sinful woman of the Gospel. We come with her to the feet of the Lord, in the congregation of the Church, to hear His consoling words, "Thy sins are forgiven thee."

"Because she hath loved much," Magdalen received pardon. "But to whom less is forgiven, he loveth less." Precisely because his love is meager, little is forgiven him. The remission of sin depends on the degree of love. Perfect love, with a contrite heart, is capable of remitting all sins and the temporal punishment due to them, both here and in purgatory.

"Thy faith hath made thee safe. Go in peace." In the spirit of faith we approach the representative of Christ to ask for forgiveness. In faith we confess our sins; and in faith we receive the words of the priest, "I absolve you from your sins." In the person of the priest, Christ stands before us just as he stood before Magdalen. "Go in peace"; be at peace with yourself, with your neighbor, and with God. The bonds of your sins have been broken, and the tears that you have shed have extinguished the flames of hell. You were sick when you came, but now you are cured. You leave the priest with a new life. "Thy sins are forgiven thee.... Thy faith hath made thee safe. Go in peace." O wonderful sacrament of penance!

Magdalen brought with her a box of ointment to anoint the feet of Jesus. Previously she had used this precious ointment only for her own adornment, that she might please men. Today she lays at the feet of Christ that which she had formerly squandered on her body, on vanity, on sin. With perfect sincerity she sets aside her old life of sin. Her perfect conversion and repentance is a model for us also.

Prayer

Grant, we beseech Thee, O almighty God, that the dignity of humanity, impaired by excessive indulgence, may be restored by the earnest practice of healing restraint.

Be merciful, we beseech Thee, O Lord, to Thy people, that rejecting the things which displease Thee, we may rather be filled with the delights of Thy commandments. Through Christ our Lord. Amen.

Friday

Eight days remain before we shall behold the spectacle of the God-man bleeding and dying on the cross. Today Good Friday already casts its shadow over us. We are led to the sanctuary of St. Stephen, the first martyr; today we should live with Christ the martyr.

Today the enemies of Christ have decided to put Him to death. The Pharisees have assembled, and they ask of one another, "What do we, for this man doth many miracles? If we let Him alone so, all will believe in Him." Christ therefore must die. "It is expedient for you that one man should die for the people, and that the whole nation perish not," the high priest points out. "From that day, therefore, they devised to put Him to death" (Gospel). One week later they will have accomplished their wicked plan. In the Garden of Olives they will apprehend Him; they will produce false witnesses to accuse Him; they will abuse Him with their mockeries; they will drag Him before the tribunal of the Roman governor and demand His death. They will follow Him up to Calvary; they will gloat over His fall, taking a fiendish delight in His agony. They will abuse and mock Him even as He prays for them on the cross: "Father, forgive them, for they know not what they do" (Lk 23:34). Too often we also place ourselves among the enemies of Christ. Is not every sin a rejection of Christ, a mockery of His commandments, and a condemnation of His principles? How often we allow our passions to overcome us and cause us to reject the commandments of Christ! We desert Him and adopt the attitude of the world and of the enemies of Christ. Lord, give me light that in the light of Thy passion I may recognize the malice and shamefulness of my sins and infidelities. Give me the grace of true sorrow for sin, and that I may never again make common cause with Thy enemies.

Christ knew all the plans of His enemies and knew exactly what the future held in store for Him. By the beatific vision, which He always enjoyed, He was fully aware of what awaited Him in His passion. He could foresee the treason of Judas and the denial of Peter; every detail of His suffering and His humiliation was ever present to Him and caused Him sorrow. "Have mercy on me, O Lord, for I am afflicted; deliver me and save me out of the hands of my enemies and from them that persecute me. Let me not be confounded, O Lord, for I have called upon Thee" (Introit). "O Lord, deliver me not over to the will of them that trouble me; for unjust witnesses have risen up against me" (Communion).

Now "Jesus walked no more openly among the Jews; but He went into a country near the desert, unto a city that is called Ephrem" (Gospel). In solitude and seclusion He prepares Himself for the task that lies before Him. The same spirit of self-surrender which characterized His entry into the world, He now brings to the struggle which will force Him out of the world: "Not My will, but Thine be done" (Lk 22:42). Everything He does, He does of His own free will and because it is the will of His Father. "I do always the things that please Him" (Jn 8:29). Second only to His love for the Father is His love for men, whose salvation He most earnestly desires.

After a few days of seclusion He will return to Jerusalem, and men will rejoice. The hour is approaching when He will allow His enemies to exercise power over Him. But during this period of seclusion we should live with Jesus and share His silence and His prayer. In this solitude we shall find the strength and the light to accompany Him when the day of His suffering arrives.

In the church of St. Stephen we join ourselves to Christ to share His condemnation and His death with the entire Church, which is despised and persecuted on earth. With Christ we, too, shall be martyrs; we shall suffer and die. In our own name and in that of the whole Church we pray: "Have mercy on me, O Lord, for I am afflicted. Deliver me and save me out of the hands of my enemies and from them that persecute me. Let me not be confounded, O Lord, for I have called upon Thee. In Thee, O Lord, have I hoped" (Introit).

The more violent the persecution of Christ and His Church, the more faithful must be His friends. With the Epistle we say, "O Lord, all that forsake Thee shall be confounded; they that depart from Thee, shall be written in the earth; because they have forsaken the Lord, the vein of living waters. Heal me, O Lord, and I shall be healed; save me, and I shall be saved. Behold, they say to me [in scorn]: Where is the word of the Lord? Let it come. And I am not troubled, following Thee for my pastor; and I have not desired the day of man, Thou knowest.... Let them be confounded that persecute me; and let me not be confounded. Let them be afraid, and let not me be afraid; bring upon them the day of affliction, and with a double destruction destroy them, O Lord our God." A ray from the sun of Easter already breaks through the night of Good Friday.

Prayer

Mercifully pour Thy grace into our hearts, we beseech Thee, O Lord, that curbing our sinful propensities with voluntary chastisement, we may suffer in this life and not be condemned to eternal punishments.

Grant, we beseech Thee, O almighty God, that we who seek the favor of Thy protection, being delivered from all evils, may serve Thee with a quiet mind. Through Christ our Lord. Amen.

The Feast of the Seven Sorrows

On the Friday before Good Friday our Holy Mother the Church sympathetically directs our attention to the Sorrowful Mother. What Simeon predicted of her in the temple really came to pass: "And thy own soul a sword shall pierce, that out of many hearts thoughts may be revealed" (Lk 2:35). Through her participation in the sufferings of her Son, Mary is the representative of the Church and of every Christian soul.

"At that time, there stood by the cross of Jesus, His mother, and His mother's sister, Mary of Cleophas, and Mary Magdalen" (Gospel). Mary could not be separated from her Son in His hour of suffering. From the moment she offered Him in the temple she knew that He was to be sacrificed as a victim for the sins of the world, and that she as His mother must share in that sacrifice. From that day onward she kept ever before her eyes the picture that Simeon had painted for her. Hers was a long-enduring martyrdom. Each day she knew that the moment was approaching nearer when He must begin His passion. Each day brought new sufferings, until now she stands beneath the cross. She is near at hand when the cruel soldiers tear His clothing from His bleeding body and stretch Him on the cross and fasten Him with nails driven through His hands and feet. She presses close to the cross upon which her Son is dying. She stands there in the deepest sorrow, yet resigned and courageous. She unites her sufferings to those of her Son, who is offering His suffering to the Father. She joins herself to the sacrifice of her Son, and offers all this to the heavenly Father for the salvation of the world—for each of us. The offering which the Son makes to the Father is likewise the offering of the mother. They are most intimately united in their suffering and in their sacrifice. "O all you that pass by the way, attend and see if there be any sorrow like to my sorrow" (Tract).

"Woman, behold thy son." Looking down from the cross, Jesus beholds His mother and His beloved disciple, St. John. Then He addresses Himself to His mother: "Woman, behold thy son," and to John He says, "Behold thy mother" (Gospel). This is the highest point in Mary's suffering. At the moment when she has given her Son the greatest possible proof of her mother love; when she is sharing His suffering and His death agony, and lingers with Him in His last moments, and when He, seeing her suffering, might have been expected to give her the most perfect proof of His filial devotion, He addresses her merely as "Woman." Now she is to accept another as her son. Not only is she to lose her own Son through death — as if that were not suffering enough — but instead she is to be the mother of a stranger. What an exchange! She must accept John in exchange for Jesus, the servant for the Master, the son of Zebedee in exchange for the Son of God (St. Bernard). But such is the will of God. Just as the offering of Jesus was made perfect and complete by His Father's abandonment of Him on the cross, so, too, the offering of the mother received its crowning perfection when Jesus abandoned her as He hung on the cross. The forsaking of the Son on the cross by the Father had its counterpart in the forsaking of the mother by the Son. And as the greatest pain and suffering of the Son consisted in His abandonment even by the Father; so the deepest pain of the mother as she stood under the cross consisted in her abandonment by her Son. "Woman, behold thy son." He has torn Himself away from her completely in order that her cup of suffering may be filled. "O all you that pass by the way, attend and see if there be any sorrow like to my sorrow."

Mary has followed her Son to the very foot of the cross. She is the true mother, the valiant mother, the mother prepared for any sacrifice. She shared with Jesus all His sufferings and humiliations. She will not allow Him to drink His chalice of humiliation alone. She does not shrink from approaching the very foot of His cross, thus making it known to all that she is the mother of the condemned one. She is prepared for any suffering. She does not cry out, "This is too much." In spite of all the bitterness which life brings she has but one guiding principle: "Behold the handmaid of the Lord. Be it done to me according to thy word" (Lk 1:38).

Mary gives up her son. Every sweet memory that remains to her from her motherhood she now joins to the offering she is making at the foot of the cross. This abandonment of every earthly tie with Jesus only tends to make her more truly the mother of the Lord. Now she is no longer merely the mother of the incarnate Jesus, as she had been at the time of His conception and birth; she has become the mother of His mystical body, the mother of His holy Church. Now she no longer knows "Christ according to the flesh" (2 Cor 5:16), but according to the spirit, having become the mother of "a new creature" (2 Cor 5:17), who is born through Christ's death on the cross. She is now the mother of the whole Christ, the new Eve, the mother of the living, the mother of us all. Mary gave birth to us spiritually at the foot of the cross, and that birth was accompanied by unspeakable labor and pain. On Easter she will receive Jesus again, but she will not forget that He has given her to us in His stead, and that she must love us as she loved Him. Christ bound us intimately to His blessed mother as she stood beneath the cross. The cost of becoming our mother was tremendous. We are indeed the children of pain, and for that reason the more dear to her. The same consideration should make us the more grateful and devoted to her.

As she stands beneath the cross, suffering and offering her sacrifice with Christ, Mary is the symbol and the type of the Church. During Passiontide the liturgy sees in Mary the Church and each of its members. The Church, the living, trusting bride of Christ, accompanies her bridegroom bravely and faithfully to the end. Down through the ages she shares His ignominy and His humiliations at the hands of wicked men. She enters with her bridegroom into His deepest sufferings and shares His death with Him. Each day in the celebration of the Holy Sacrifice she repeats the self-immolation of Christ, and adds to it the offering of another Mary at the foot of the cross — the offering of herself. She is joined in a most intimate union of mind and heart with Him. The life of the Church and that of every devout Christian must of necessity follow the *via dolorosa* of the Sorrowful Mother. The closer she presses to the cross, the more fruitful is her motherhood of souls. "He that shall lose his life for Me shall find it" (Mt 10:39).

Prayer

O God, in whose passion the sword of sorrow foretold by Simeon did pierce the most sweet soul of Mary, the glorious Virgin and Mother: mercifully grant that we who reverently meditate on her anguish and suffering may, through the glorious merits and prayers of all the saints standing faithfully by Thy cross, obtain the blessed fruit of Thy passion. Who livest and reignest forever. Amen.

Saturday

In today's Gospel we read about the triumphant entry of our Lord into Jerusalem. "Hosanna, blessed is He that cometh in the name of the Lord, the king of Israel." The bringing of Lazarus back to life had set the crowd on fire with enthusiasm for Christ. Even the pagans were flocking to see this wonder-worker. But through this thin veil of triumph, Christ sees the truth. The Jews will forsake Him, and the pagans will accept Him.

A group of pagans comes to the apostles Andrew and Philip, and asks to be introduced to Christ. Jesus takes this opportunity to point out the glory that will come to Him through the conversion of the Gentiles. "The hour is come that the Son of Man should be glorified." But Christ must win this glorification through His suffering and death. "Unless the grain of wheat falling into the ground die, itself remaineth alone; but if it die, it bringeth forth much fruit" (Gospel). Jesus is the grain of wheat. He had to die, says St. Augustine, through the infidelity of the Jews, and rise through the faith of the pagans. "The death of the grain of wheat is therefore not its death; it is the development of its life and the creation of a new life. We, too, together with Jesus are the grains of wheat." "If it die, it bringeth forth much fruit. He that loveth his life shall lose it; and he that hateth his life in this world keepeth it unto life eternal" (Gospel). We shall obtain the fruit of Christ's passion and achieve glorification with Him in the measure that we are as grains of wheat with Him: "If it die, it bringeth forth much fruit." Without apparent death the grain of wheat remains barren and sterile.

"Now [in the passion of the Lord] is the judgment of the world; now shall the prince of this world be cast out. And I, if I be lifted up from the earth, will draw all things to Myself" (Gospel). From the cross the crucified Savior will draw all things to Himself; He will overcome all opposition and will draw the spirits and hearts of all peoples to Himself. Generation after generation of the pagans will come to the crucified Christ, "unto the Jews indeed a stumbling block, and unto the Gentiles foolishness; but unto them that are called, … the power of God and the wisdom of God" (1 Cor 1:23 f.). All hasten to Him who was crucified, and confess, "Thou wast slain and hast redeemed us to God in Thy blood, out of every tribe and tongue and people and nation" (Apoc 5:9).

"It is truly meet and just … that we should at all times and in all places give thanks to Thee, O holy Lord, Father Almighty, eternal God; who didst set the salvation of mankind on the tree of the cross, so that whence came death [into the world], thence also life might rise again, and that He who overcame by the tree, might also be overcome on the tree, through Christ our Lord" (Preface of the Mass). At the foot of the cross spring up unceasing fountains of grace, the sacraments. From the cross we obtain enlightenment and inspiration. From the cross we obtain the grace for victory over evil, the power to perform good, hope for the pardon of our sins, and the assurance of grace in the future. In the cross we find consolation in trouble and suffering. The cross is the key to the kingdom of heaven.

O cross, our only hope, all hail!
This Passiontide thy balm exhale;
In loving hearts augment thy grace,
The sinner's stains entire efface.

Christ the Savior gave a new meaning to suffering and sorrow. For Christ the passion is "the price of redemption." "The Son of Man [came] to give His life a redemption for many" (Mk 10:45). Through baptism we "are baptized in His death" (Rom 6:3). Our sufferings, then, are joined to His and have the same meaning His had. They are made to serve the work of redemption. It is true that Christ's work of redemption was completed with the sacrifice of Calvary; but it must be continued by us in the unbloody Sacrifice of the Mass, and in the suffering undertaken by each man. By our sufferings we "fill up those things that are wanting of the sufferings of Christ, … for His body, which is the Church" (Col 1:24). Our suffering has its purpose in the redemption of the world. Because we love men and the souls of men, we love the sufferings of Christ, which wrought their redemption.

"And I, if I be lifted up from the earth, will draw all things to Myself." Many of the baptized become sick of soul, broken in spirit, and weak in faith when they are confronted with a cross. These are the weak Christians who refuse to allow themselves to be lifted up on the cross; they have failed to understand what it means to be allowed to "partake of the sufferings of Christ" (1 Pt 4:13). Neither do they understand Paul when he is filled with joy over his tribulations (2 Cor 7:4). For the good Christian, suffering on the cross means that he becomes fruitful, truly great in the eyes of God. "If I be lifted up from the earth, I will draw all things to Myself," is true of us too. Even if life offers us nothing but toil and worry, let us be content. Even if we have showered love and care on others and receive nothing but ingratitude, let us not be overcome; we must lift ourselves above all these disappointments and above the fickleness and faithlessness of men. By accepting our daily crosses we draw down upon ourselves the grace and blessing of God. We must therefore embrace the cross that we may be drawn to Christ, and may in turn draw all things to ourselves. The cross is our salvation.

Prayer

Let the people consecrated to Thee, we beseech Thee, O Lord, grow unceasingly in the spirit of loving devotion, that being taught by sacred rites, they may abound in more precious gifts as they become more pleasing to Thy majesty.

Let Thy right hand, we beseech Thee, O Lord, guard Thy suppliant people and duly teach those purified that by present consolation they may attain the good things to come. Through Christ our Lord. Amen.

Palm Sunday

The Mass

Today we stand at the threshold of Holy Week. In the stirring events of the next few days the most important event of all history will be enacted before us: the suffering and death of Christ. On Palm Sunday, Christ made His triumphal entry into Jerusalem from Mount Olivet. As early as the fourth century the Christians, and particularly the Church at Jerusalem, celebrated the entry of Christ into the Holy City. They gathered on Mount Olivet and marched into the city singing and holding in their hands boughs cut from trees. The Roman Church borrowed this procession from the Church in Jerusalem. The church of St. Silvester in Rome represented Mount Olivet, and here the Christians gathered on Palm Sunday. In this church the palm branches were blessed. Amidst the jubilant shouts of "Hosanna! Blessed is He that cometh in the name of the Lord," everyone went to the church of the Holy Redeemer (the Basilica of St. John Lateran). When the procession approached the Lateran Basilica, the clergy and singers of this church came out to meet the faithful, and then all sang hymns. Afterwards they entered the church and celebrated Mass.

Today we perform a similar ceremony. The priest blesses the palms and gives them to us. The procession then begins. We, the faithful, form an escort for the priest, who represents Christ in our midst. We wave our palms and thus confess our belief in Christ, the King of martyrs, our victorious champion. Yes, we wish to be in the entourage of Christ. The palms in our hands indicate that we are prepared to follow Him to death if necessary. In holy joy we shout, "Hosanna! Blessed is He that cometh in the name of the Lord." Let us sing this hymn with joy and with hearts filled with true contrition. "All glory, praise, and honor be to Thee, O King, Christ the Redeemer.... Thou art the king of Israel" (Hymn). Would that we had the faith and spirit of the martyrs and holy confessors, our forebears in the faith! Put your heart into every word and every action that is performed in today's liturgy. Let all your actions in this holy ceremony be founded on a firm faith and an unshakable conviction. Let your spirit be like that of the martyrs, joyful and ready for any sacrifice.

After the procession of the palms is finished, the scene changes completely. The divine King, whom we have just greeted with a triumphal hosanna, is now cast into bitter sorrow and agony. He now sees Himself devoured by the jaws of the lion; abandoned by God; in His agony He cries out to His heavenly Father (Introit). He who cannot deceive or be deceived, He who confesses Himself equal to the Father, is now humiliated, trampled in the dust, loaded with the sins of His fellow men. He is about to atone for the pride and the rebellion of men, for which purpose He became obedient unto death, even to the painful and disgraceful death of the cross. But death, disgrace, and humiliation are not ends in themselves; they are only the means of His exaltation, glorification, and glorious resurrection (Epistle). For this reason the suffering soul finds these words of the Gradual so consoling, "Thou hast held me by my right hand; and by Thy will Thou hast conducted me, and with Thy glory Thou hast received me." The Tract speaks of the Easter light which shines in the darkness of tribulation.

And now we are shown the whole passion of the God-man. We see the accusers full of injustice and wickedness, the unjust judges, Barabbas, the murderer who is to be pardoned, and Christ, who is to be condemned. Deeply moved, we sink to our knees at the words, "And Jesus, again crying with a loud voice, yielded up the ghost." We see now what man can do. We hold the palms in our hands and proclaim that we are resolved to share the cross of Christ. We resolve to die to everything that is not Christ, and to live for Him alone.

At the Offertory we who have resolved to die with Christ unite ourselves to Him. In the bread and wine which we offer, we see a union of ourselves with Christ. We die to the old man and enter into union with Christ in the Consecration, when He renews His death on the cross in a mysterious and unbloody manner. But without death there can be no life; without the cross there can be no salvation and no Easter.

We are joined with Christ in death when we receive Holy Communion. Then we seal our agreement to die with Christ. He is the victim and He draws us to Himself so that we share in His death and in His divine life. We are offered up with Him; we are crucified with Him, and for that reason we live for Him. With Him we now know only one thing: to do the will of the Father. "Thy will be done" (Communion).

Meditation

Today in the church of the Holy Redeemer (the Lateran Basilica) we gather about our Savior. With our palms and olive branches in our hands we follow Him in His triumphal entry into Jerusalem. He enters today the great city that is to be the scene of His conflict, His passion, His death, His victory, and His resurrection. We know that we are one with Him, and we must not let Him enter alone.

Christ the King of martyrs. Today the Church blesses the palms and olive branches and gives them to us. "The branches of palms signify His triumphs over the prince of death, and the olive branches proclaim in some way the coming of a spiritual unction" (that is, the fullness of God's mercy). Palm and olive branches signify "that our Redeemer, compassionating the miseries of mankind, was about to fight with the prince of death for the life of the whole world, and by dying was to triumph.... And we humbly beseech Thee, O holy Lord, almighty Father, eternal God, through the same Jesus Christ our Lord, that in Him and through Him, whose members Thou hast pleased to make us, we may become victorious over the empire of death, and may deserve to be partakers of His glorious resurrection" (Prayer for the blessing of palms).

The palm in the hand of the Christian signifies his desire to share the martyrdom of Christ. The Preface of the martyrs which is sung at the blessing of the palms, clearly declares:

"Thy creatures serve Thee because they acknowledge Thee as their only Creator and God; and Thy whole creation praises Thee, and Thy saints [the blessed martyrs] bless Thee; for with fearless voice they confess the great name of Thy only-begotten Son before the kings and powers of this world." We take the palms in our hands to signify that we, too, are united to Christ and His martyrs. We acknowledge Christ before the powers of the world, and follow Him to martyrdom, victory, and resurrection. We are "the children of the Hebrews" and we sing to Him our hosanna. We sing to Christ our King: *Gloria, laus, et honor tibi sit* ("All glory, praise, and honor be to Thee, O King, Christ the Redeemer"). We rejoice today, for we know that this entry into Jerusalem merely foreshadows His victorious entry into the heavenly Jerusalem. We hurry to meet Him with palm branches in our hands, which represent the good works which we have performed, our victories over sin, the flesh, and the world. Seeing these, He will usher us in with Him into the heavenly bridal chamber to an everlasting betrothal. The cross, and only the cross, can open to Christ the splendor of heaven; neither can there be any other way of entry for us. Borne along by His strength, we take up the cross, confident that we will be glorified with Him.

The way of victory is the road of the martyrs. With deep emotion we follow the Church today in the words of the Epistle: "Brethren, let this mind be in you, which was also in Christ Jesus; who, being in the form of God thought it not robbery to be equal with God; but emptied Himself, taking the form of a servant, being made in the likeness of men, and in habit found as a man. He humbled Himself, becoming obedient unto death, even to the death of the cross." Thus the liturgy gives us a vivid picture of the humiliation and the suffering of our Lord. The way of Christ is our way too. "My heart hath expected reproach and misery; and I looked for one that would grieve together with Me, but there was none" (Offertory). We, too, must share His disgrace and suffering, as we have promised Him in our baptism. We attend the Mass now to accompany Him on the way of suffering that lies before Him. "He humbled Himself, becoming obedient unto death, even to the death of the cross." May that be our way too. The Mass will supply us with the courage and the strength to follow it.

Today Christ is greeted with a shout of joy; tomorrow He will hear the cruel mob cry, "Let Him be crucified." Today we receive the blessed palms in our hands, and the liturgy explains to us the meaning of this action. But too many of us lay aside the spirit of martyrdom when we lay down the palms that we have received. This is not the spirit of the true follower of Christ.

"I looked for one that would grieve together with me, but there was none. I sought for one that would comfort me, and I found none." Few are they who love the cross; but many are they who hate Christ and His cross. He who loves not the cross cannot love the crucified One.

Prayer

Almighty and eternal God, who didst cause our Savior to take upon Him our flesh and to suffer death upon the cross that all mankind might imitate the example of His humility; mercifully grant that treasuring the lessons of His patience, we may deserve to have fellowship in His resurrection. Through Christ our Lord. Amen.

Monday

Like the Master, the Church is maligned and persecuted by her enemies. "My face I did not turn away from those who struck Me and spit upon Me. For thirty pieces of silver I was appraised by them. Look, O Lord, to the lips of those who hate Me, and see what they plot against Me" (Antiphons at Lauds). Today the Church gathers her children for the celebration of the holy mysteries in the church of the holy virgin St. Praxedes, who, with St. Prudentiana, devoted herself to the service of Christ in the poor. Mary anointing the feet of the Lord in the Gospel of the Mass represents St. Praxedes, who anointed the feet of the Lord in the person of the poor. Judas protests at this extravagance and at the waste of the precious ointment. The liturgy is moved by Christ's twofold offering of His body: to His enemies that it might be tortured, and to Mary that it might be anointed and prepared for burial.

"The Lord God hath opened my ear, and I do not resist; I have not gone back. I have given my body to the strikers and my cheeks to them that plucked them; I have not turned away my face from them that rebuked me and spit upon me. The Lord God is my helper" (Epistle). With deep sympathy we watch Him as He offers His cheek to the traitor to be kissed. "Dost thou betray the Son of Man with a kiss?" (Lk 22:48.) He offers His hands to those who come to the Garden of Olives to take Him; He offers His body to those who would scourge Him; He bows His head as they offer Him the crown of thorns. His hands and feet He extends willing that they may be nailed to the cross. His heart is bared for the soldier who lifts up his spear to pierce it. Now He has given up everything in obedience to His Father. "By His bruises we are healed" (Is 53:5).

Mary, the sister of Lazarus, today brings precious ointment that she may anoint the feet of Jesus in Bethany. She presses forward lovingly to the Lord and shares most intimately His sufferings. Even when He is taken prisoner by His enemies, even when He is being put to death, she does not desert Him, but draws still nearer to Him. We, too, should anoint the feet of Jesus. During these days more than ever we should draw nearer to Him and assure Him of our faith, our devotion, and our loyalty. With Mary and St. Praxedes we should serve Him and "anoint His feet" in the person of His poor. "As long as you did it to one of these My least brethren, you did it to Me" (Mt 25:40).

Judas and Mary are both with Christ, and to both He gives His body. Today Mary anoints His body; in a few days Judas will greet Him with a treasonable kiss. We should emulate the conduct of Mary. We come to Him during these days to participate in His sufferings and to comfort Him with our tears of love and gratitude. Thus we help Him carry His cross and imprint His image upon our soul.

The abuse of Christ and His body did not cease with His passion and death. The abuse continues in the persecution of His Church. His teaching, His Church, His priests, His faithful followers, still suffer from the enemies of Christ. We can prove our love for Christ by remaining all the more faithful and loyal to Him when these persecutions come.

"I have given My body to the strikers, and My cheeks to them that plucked them." With unshakable patience, without complaint, without becoming angry or impatient, Christ submitted to these indignities. His only word is the prayer, "Father, forgive them, for they know not what they do" (Lk 23:34). "Learn of Me, because I am meek and humble of heart" (Mt 11:29).

Prayer

Grant, we beseech Thee, O almighty God, that we who in our many adversities faint through our own weakness, may take heart anew through the pleading of the passion of Thy only-begotten Son.

Help us, O God, our salvation, that we may celebrate with joy the memory of those benefits by which Thou hast deigned to restore us to a new life. Through Christ our Lord. Amen.

Tuesday

Today we see the Lord surrounded by His enemies. Like a lamb He is led to the slaughter. His apostles have fled; Peter, the chief of the apostles, has denied Him. The Lord lifts His eyes to His Father, who must guide Him through the night of suffering to the light of the resurrection. "But it behooves us to glory in the cross of our Lord Jesus Christ" (Introit). We are happy that we are allowed to share His chalice and to carry His cross.

The enemies of Christ have surrounded Him. Christ knew perfectly well from the first moment of His Incarnation that He was destined to suffer and die. His passion and His coming death were always before Him. "And I was as a meek lamb that is carried to be a victim; and I knew not [I did not resist] that they had devised counsels against Me saying: Let us put wood on His bread and cut Him off from the land of the living, and let His name be remembered no more" (Epistle). Christ goes to His death like a lamb that is led to the slaughter. He makes no protest; He does not murmur or complain. Thus He allowed Himself to be taken prisoner by His enemies, to be condemned by the high priests and Pilate, to be scourged, crowned with thorns, and nailed to the cross. Through all this suffering He remains silent. He prays: "For to Thee have I revealed My cause, O Lord My God" (Epistle). The more completely He entrusts His affairs to the care of His heavenly Father, the more certainly the Father will bring to nought all the plans of His enemies. They will succeed in putting Him to death, but by this very death He will be victorious. Above all this injustice from Christ's enemies stands God, the Lord of hosts; "Thou who judgest justly and triest the reins and the hearts, ... to Thee have I revealed My cause, O Lord My God" (Epistle). The cross thus becomes the way of salvation, the way to resurrection and glorification.

Even the faithful Peter denies the Lord. While standing in the courtyard of the high priest, Peter is accosted by a maidservant with the words, "Thou also wast with Jesus of Nazareth." Peter vehemently denies this charge: "I neither know nor understand what thou sayest." Then he flees to the outer court, where he is again challenged by the maidservant, "This is one of them." Peter again denies this accusation; but "after a little while they that stood by said again to Peter: Surely thou art one of them, for thou art also a Galilean." Still Peter denies: "I know not this man of whom you speak." Then the cock crew for the second time, and Peter remembered the words which Christ had spoken, "Before the cock crow twice, thou shalt thrice deny Me." And He began to weep bitterly.

Peter never forgot during the rest of his life that he had once denied his Savior. Neither did he cease to worry about it, nor to confess it openly before the world and do penance for his sin. Peter himself in his preaching in the various countries he visited, told frankly what Mark reports in his Gospel. With touching candor and humility he confessed before all the great sin that he had committed and the kindness with which Christ had forgiven him.

The more closely the enemies press about Christ, the more confidently He turns to His Father. "My prayer shall be turned into my bosom. Judge Thou, O Lord, them that wrong me; ... rise up to help me" (Gradual). "Keep me, O Lord, from the hand of the wicked; and from unjust men deliver me" (Offertory). "They that sat in the gate [in a public place] were busied against me; and they that drank wine made me their song; but as for me, my prayer is to Thee, O Lord" (Communion). Overwhelmed in the blackest night of suffering, surrounded by enemies on every side, Christ thinks not of His suffering nor of His enemies; He turns to the Father; He prays: "Keep Me, O Lord, from the hand of the wicked; and from unjust men deliver Me" (Offertory); that is, raise Me up from the dead on the third day, and exalt Me as the King and Lord of all.

"It behooves us to glory in the cross of our Lord Jesus Christ" (Introit). We stand at the side of the crucified Lord and consider it true happiness to share in the cross of the Lord and to drink His chalice. "Know you not that all we who are baptized in Christ Jesus, are baptized in His death," crucified with Him (Rom 6:3)? If we were real Christians, we would rejoice that we are allowed to share in the disgrace of Christ's cross, to lead a life of sacrifice and self-denial, of privation and humiliation. Unfortunately we think of the passion of Christ in a selfish manner and consider only the benefits that it conferred upon us.

Prayer

Almighty and eternal God, grant that we may so celebrate the Lord's passion that we may deserve to obtain Thy pardon.

May Thy mercy, O God, purify us from every deceit of our old nature and make us ready to receive a holy renovation. Through Christ our Lord. Amen.

Wednesday

In St. Mary Major in Rome, we recall the passion and death of the Lord in company with His sorrowful mother. In a special way the Church reminds us of the treason of Judas. From ancient times the Church has set aside Wednesday of Holy Week to commemorate the betrayal, and she keeps a penitential fast in memory of this event.

Judas approaches. The Garden of Olives was the foot of the altar where Christ prayed before He ascended the great altar of Calvary. He suffers unspeakable anguish of soul. So intense is His interior suffering that His blood is forced through His pores in a bloody sweat. He turns to His apostles, whom He has left at a short distance; "Arise, pray," He admonishes them. While He is yet speaking, the band sent to apprehend Him approaches. At the head of this motley crew is the apostle Judas. He approaches Christ and greets Him with a kiss. "Dost thou betray the Son of Man with a kiss?" What a spectacle! Christ betrayed by one of His own apostles and handed over to His enemies. That act sounded the depths of ingratitude, hypocrisy, and baseness. The act was made more despicable by the fact that it was performed for money.

The Church suffers with Christ. She has suffered similar experiences, for often in the course of her history many of her children have proved traitors to their Lord and Redeemer. This is as mysterious as it is terrifying — an apostle turned traitor. He who had been selected from among millions for the special love and esteem of Christ, sells his benefactor for thirty pieces of silver. He who stands, "let him take heed, lest he fall" (1 Cor 10:12). "Watch ye and pray that ye enter not into temptation" (Mt 26:41).

Christ sees the traitor approaching, and although He knows his foul plan, He does not withdraw. He offers His cheek to be kissed. He has feelings only of love and kindness even for this traitor. He even calls him friend. In effect He says: Even if you no longer love Me, I still love you and am prepared to forgive you the injury you are doing to Me. Christ shows no bitterness; He has no harsh reproach even for Judas. For this fallen apostle He has only sympathy. What did Judas gain? Thirty pieces of silver and the curse of God. He received a small temporal reward for his treachery and was burdened with a remorse of conscience that drove him to eternal damnation. This is the *mysterium iniquitatis,* the mystery of iniquity. Sin, the blindness and perversity of the human heart, is indeed a mystery. If the Lord were not so full of kindness and understanding, if He did not love us much beyond our deserts, what would become of us? Even an apostle can become a traitor.

The Church makes a recompense to Christ for the disgrace heaped upon Him by Judas. "In the name of Jesus let every knee bow, of those that are in heaven, on earth, and under the earth; for the Lord became obedient unto death, even the death of the cross. Therefore the Lord Jesus Christ is in the glory of God the Father" (Introit). He is obedient to the Father, even submitting to the traitor. That was the will of the Father, and it was sufficient for Christ.

Why has the traitor come to betray Christ? What has brought Him? Poor blind apostle! Poor blind Christians! Why do they expend their energies on everlasting worries? Why do they toil so eagerly for money? Why do they seek so avidly for offices, high positions, and the esteem of men? Very often to achieve their ambitions they jeopardize their chances for eternal happiness. Often they forsake religion and neglect the sacraments. What remains to them from all the temporal advantages they may gain? They soon prove empty; this discovery drove Judas to despair and suicide.

"Simon, sleepest thou? Couldst thou not watch one hour with Me?" With these words, spoken by Christ to Peter, the Church calls upon us at Lauds not to leave the Savior alone in His suffering and humiliation. At least during Holy Week let us remain close to Christ. That this may be easier for us, we are led to St. Mary Major. Behold the mother. Behold how Mary suffers with Jesus. Mary represents the Church suffering with Christ. Each of us should imitate Mary in her suffering with her Son. With her we should follow Him with sympathetic hearts and stand under His cross on Calvary. May not Christ address to us the sad words, "Couldst thou not watch one hour with Me? . . . He does not sleep, but hastens to betray Me to the Jews" (Responsory at Matins). It is often true that the friends of Jesus sleep while His enemies are hard at work.

PRAYER

O God, from whom Judas received the punishment of his crime and the thief the reward of his confession, grant us the effect of Thy clemency, that as Jesus Christ our Lord in His passion gave to each a different recompense according to his merits, so may He bestow the grace of His resurrection on us who have been delivered from past sins. Who liveth and reigneth with Thee forever. Amen. (Collect for Holy Thursday.)

Holy Thursday

At the Lateran Basilica, the church of the Holy Redeemer, we are to witness today the readmission of the penitents into the community of the faithful. They have been excluded from the Offertory procession and from Holy Communion. But the time of their penance is now ended, and they may again approach the altar with their gifts and receive Holy Communion. We share in their joy and gratitude. The prayer they say when they offer their gifts, we make our own. "I shall not die, but live" (Offertory). We recall today also the events of the life of Jesus that distinguish Holy Thursday. We commemorate this day Jesus' departure from Bethania, the Last Supper, the washing of the feet, the institution of the Holy Eucharist and of the priesthood, Christ's farewell discourse, the journey to the Garden of Olives, the agony in the Garden, the betrayal by Judas, and the apprehension of Christ. Holy Thursday is particularly dedicated to the memory of the institution of the Holy Eucharist.

"Having loved His own who were in the world, He loved them unto the end" (Jn 13:1). He continues to love them in the Holy Eucharist. His love was not satisfied by His suffering and death on the cross; He wished to remain with us always. Yes, he wished to do more: He wished to become the nourishment of our souls, to fill us with His own life, and to unite Himself to us. He is the vine, we are the branches. Christ loved His own to the end—the end of the cross; He will continue to love them until the end of time in the tabernacle. This is a love without bounds; this is our treasure in our poverty. This is the extraordinary good fortune of Christians, that Christ loves them with an infinite love. "As the Father hath loved Me, I also have loved you. Abide in My love" (Jn 15:9). We, too, must love Him with all our strength.

Christ gave the apostles an additional proof of His love in the washing of their feet. Today the liturgy closely associates the washing of the feet with the reception of Holy Communion; when Holy Communion is distributed to the faithful, she uses this prayer: "The Lord Jesus, after He had supped with His disciples, washed their feet, and said to them: Know you what I, your Lord and Master, have done to you? I have given you an example, that you also may do likewise" (Communion). Daily Holy Communion and the love of our neighbor are complementary. "If we love one another, God abideth in us, and His charity is perfected in us.... If any man says: I love God, and hateth his brother, he is a liar. For he that loveth not his brother whom he seeth, how can he love God, whom he seeth not?" (1 Jn 4:20.) How can such a man receive Holy Communion worthily? On the other hand, the worthy reception of Holy Communion impels us to love the other members of the mystical body of Christ. The antiphons sung during the washing of the feet show this connection: "A new commandment I give unto you: that you love one another as I have loved you, says the Lord. Blessed are the undefiled in the way, who walk in the law of the Lord." "If I your Lord and Master have washed your feet, how much more ought you to wash one another's feet. Hear these things, all ye nations; give ear, all ye inhabitants of the world. If I your Lord and Master have washed your feet, how much more ought you to wash one another's feet." "By this shall all men know that you are My disciples, if you have love one for another." The Holy Eucharist is a gift of love. Love becomes an obligation: "A new commandment I give unto you, that you love one another as I have loved you." Let us examine ourselves to see if we really keep this commandment to love one another always.

"Where charity and love are, there God is." The love of Christ has brought us together. Let us exult and be joyful in Him. Let us fear and love the living God, and love one another with sincerity. Where charity and love are, there God is. Having assembled here to worship God, let us beware of divisions among ourselves. Let malicious upbraidings cease; let there be no wrangling. And may Christ our God be in our midst; for where charity and love are, there God is. "Together with the blessed may we also see Thy face in glory, O Christ God.... Through endless ages. Amen" (Antiphon at the washing of the feet).

The Holy Eucharist is the fruit of the cross. The more closely we press to the cross, the more fully we shall profit by the reception of Holy Communion. "It behooves us to glory in the cross of our Lord Jesus Christ" (Introit). But probably we flee from the cross and seek to escape it whenever we can. We chafe under the cross that has been laid on our shoulders. What Christians we are! As long as we have this spirit, the mystery of the cross will ever remain a mystery for us. We shall never have the perfect love which we should have for the Eucharist.

"In whom is our salvation, life, and resurrection" (Introit). Our salvation is in Him who dwells in the tabernacle, who prays for us and offers Himself for us daily. "Blessed are they that dwell in Thy house, O Lord" (Ps 83:5).

Prayer

O God, who in this wonderful sacrament has left us a memorial of Thy passion; grant us, we beseech Thee, so to venerate the sacred mysteries of Thy body and blood that we may ever feel within us the fruit of Thy redemption. Who livest and reignest world without end. Amen. (Collect for Corpus Christi.)

Good Friday

This is a day of mourning for the Church and for the faithful. The cross occupies the most prominent place in the liturgy of the day. It was on the cross that the Lord carried out the will of the Father to its last detail by giving up His life for our sins. He "loved me and delivered Himself for me" (Gal 2:20).

"And when they were come to the place which is called Calvary, they crucified Him there; and the robbers, one on the right hand and the other on the left. And Jesus said: Father, forgive them, for they know not what they do. But they, dividing His garments, cast lots. And the people stood beholding, and the rulers with them derided Him saying: He saved others; let Him save Himself, if He be Christ, the elect of God. And the soldiers also mocked Him, coming to Him and offering Him vinegar, and saying: If Thou be the king of the Jews, save thyself. And there was also a superscription written over Him in letters of Greek and Latin and Hebrew: this is the king of the Jews. And one of those robbers who were hanged blasphemed him, saying: If Thou be Christ, save Thyself and us.... And it was almost the sixth hour; and there was darkness over all the earth until the ninth hour. And the sun was darkened, and the veil of the temple was rent in the midst. And Jesus crying out with a loud voice, said: Father, into Thy hands I commend My spirit. And saying this, He gave up the ghost" (Lk 23:33 ff.). "He humbled Himself, becoming obedient unto death, even to the death of the cross" (Phil 2:8). "Oh all ye that pass by the way, attend and see if there be any sorrow like to my sorrow" (Lam 1:12).

The holy body has been torn by the cruel scourge until it is one mass of burning and bleeding wounds. The terrible crown of thorns has pierced His head, and He is consumed by thirst. To this unspeakable physical pain is added an anguish of soul that is even more terrible. He hears the shocking cry of His blinded people: "His blood be upon us and our children" (Mt 27:25). He hears the exultant yells of His enemies, and He looks into the future and sees that millions of men will repay His suffering and His love with the basest ingratitude and the cruelest indifference. Why do they act thus? They have no time to attend to Christ. The grace which He won for them with such prodigal suffering and with so much love they neglect or abuse, and thus run the risk of losing their immortal souls. The immense inheritance which He purchased by His blood they allow to slip through their fingers. How this ingratitude and blindness tortures Him! With Mary and John we stand under His cross today to share His agony.

Christ died in our stead. "Surely he hath borne our infirmities and carried our sorrows; and we have thought him as it were a leper, and as one struck by God and afflicted. But he was wounded for our iniquities; he was bruised for our sins; the chastisement of our peace was upon him, and by his bruises we are healed. All we like sheep have gone astray, every one hath turned aside into his own way; and the Lord hath laid on him the iniquity of us all" (Is 53:4–6). No mortal man could satisfy for the insult offered to God by sin; not even the highest of the angels could make adequate satisfaction. "Search not for a man to redeem you; Christ the God-man alone can perform works of sufficient value" (St. Basil). He takes our indebtedness upon Himself and lifts it up to His cross. "Knowing that you were not redeemed with corruptible things, as gold or silver, from your vain conversation of the tradition of your fathers; but with the precious blood of Christ as of a lamb unspotted and undefiled" (1 Pt 1:18 f.). The penalties which Christ suffered should have been our penalty. "Greater love than this no man hath, that a man lay down his life for his friends" (Jn 15:13).

Christ has died for each one of us personally. The wages of sin is death. All the penalties of sin press upon us at death. God's justice has not prepared anything so frightening as the prospect of death. Every creature shrinks from the thought of it. Nothing is so surely a punishment for sin as is death. Death cuts the bonds that secure the body and soul to the earth, just as sin first severed the bond which bound men to God. Christ the Lord delivers Himself up freely to death for our sake. His love is "strong as death." His submission to this most terrifying of God's punishments is the highest token of His love. He chooses the most terrible prospect of death that He may give me the surest sign of His love.

In giving over His body to death, He destroys the body of sin and death on the cross. Having bathed mankind in His precious blood, He has provided humanity with a new and holy body. Men thus reborn are worthy to become the sons of God and merit eternal life and eternal glory.

Christ died for us on the cross. What a mysterious dispensation of God's providence! The unjust man commits the sin, but the Just One satisfies for it. The guilty one escapes the penalty of sin, but the Innocent One pays the penalty. The Lord and Master pays the debts which were contracted by the servant. What a contrast between the wickedness of man, and the goodness and justice and mercy of God! God has done all this for us; what have we done for Him?

Prayer

We beseech Thee, O almighty God, to look down upon Thy family, for whom our Lord Jesus Christ freely delivered Himself into the hands of sinners, and for whom He suffered the martyrdom of the cross. Who liveth and reigneth world without end. Amen.

Holy Saturday

The impressive baptismal ceremonies, which were once performed on Holy Saturday night before the Easter services, are now anticipated Holy Saturday morning. A distinctive feature of the Holy Saturday services is the blessing of the Easter candle. The Church confesses her amazement at the relationship between the miracles of the Old Testament and the events of the New Testament. The miracles of the Old Testament were types of things that were to transpire in the New Testament. "For it would have profited us nothing to have been born unless we had also been redeemed. O wonderful condescension of Thy mercy towards us! O inestimable affection of charity, that to redeem a slave Thou didst deliver up Thy Son! O truly necessary sin of Adam, which was blotted out by the death of Christ! O happy fault that merited so great a Redeemer!" (*Exultet.*)

"O happy fault!" In the light of the resurrection of Christ (symbolized by the Easter candle), man finds a solution to a problem which had puzzled him for ages. Why has God allowed evil to occur when He could so easily have prevented it? Even though evil is entirely the work of man, it is still subject to the power and providence of God; He could prevent it. Why has He not done so? Because by overcoming evil, God manifests His power. By destroying evil in us, God demonstrates His love for us. His victory over evil is a more convincing proof of His power than all the works of creation. In this victory the various aspects of the divine essence are revealed to us. Without the existence of evil, we should never have known the depth of God's wisdom and mercy. It was the mercy of God that sent the Lamb to the sacrifice. Incarnate mercy offers itself as a sacrifice, and the sacrifice is accepted by the divine mercy. Thus in the death of Christ the greatest of all miracles was performed. Omnipotence itself made itself powerless; life was given over to death. God permitted evil in order to bring about a higher good, namely, the Incarnation, and through the Incarnation the kingdom of the redeemed. "O happy fault that merited so great a Redeemer!"

Both in Holy Scripture and in the teaching of the Fathers there is a foundation for the doctrine that Christ would not have become incarnate had not Adam sinned. This view is also defended by the majority of theologians. The Credo, which we sing at Mass as the avowal of our faith, teaches that Christ, the Son of God, descended from heaven and became man to redeem us from sin. Deeply moved by this manifestation of the love, mercy, power, and justice of God, we sing with the Church in the Exultet: "For it would have profited us nothing to have been born unless we had also been redeemed. O wonderful condescension of Thy mercy towards us! O inestimable affection of charity, that to redeem a slave Thou didst deliver up Thy Son! O truly necessary sin of Adam, which was blotted out by the death of Christ! O happy fault that merited so great a Redeemer!" Sin, the greatest evil performed by men, becomes the occasion for God's greatest work, the Incarnation of Christ and the redemption of humanity. Evil must be made to serve God; and since it can be made to serve Him, He allows it to happen.

In the cross is salvation. Yet a single drop of Christ's blood, a solitary prayer, a single request for pardon and grace made by Christ, would have been sufficient for the redemption of men. "As much as the ocean exceeds a drop, so much does the merit of Christ exceed our sins" (St. Chrysostom). Even though the justice of God required full satisfaction for sin, it could not have demanded the passion and death of Christ for this purpose. Full satisfaction could have been given by a lesser act. But Christ undertook this excess of suffering that we might understand the extent of His love. The mystery of the cross and the existence of evil and suffering are hidden from the worldly man, but they should be perfectly clear to the Christian. If we understand Christ and His mission, we will understand that poverty, humility, misery, and suffering recommend us to the mercy and love of God. They are the sign and seal of His love; they are a pledge that He wishes us to resemble His Son.

Suffering is the gate of eternal life. Suffering cheerfully and freely borne is a proof of our surrender to God. Such suffering glorifies God. No love can be more sincere, no surrender more heroic and complete than that which manifests itself in voluntary suffering. Christ, our Lord and Master, embraced suffering instead of pleasure; but the spirit of the world cultivates pleasure, honor, and indulgence. Christ frees men from the bonds of the world, from the weaknesses of the flesh, and from self-indulgence. Whomever the Lord wishes to raise to sanctity, He raises on the cross. The soul, then, that wishes to be filled with grace must first be crucified. The most sublime form of knowledge is that which is based on suffering. The truest and the greatest good fortune of man on earth is the privilege to suffer for Christ. By means of the cross the Lord places His seal upon us. The cross purifies and prepares the soul for the pure love of God. He who flees from suffering impedes the progress of love, for in the cross is salvation.

Wherever injustice raises its head, it will be subdued. He whom injustice thought to destroy and drive from the world, has raised Himself triumphantly from the grave. His Church must also be persecuted and tried. But when her enemies believe that they have destroyed her and are beginning to raise a funeral mound over her, she springs miraculously to a new life. From death comes life. "The blood of martyrs is the seed of Christians."

"To them that love God, all things work together unto good" (Rom 8:28). Those who love God may be hated and trampled by men, but in all this persecution God has His own designs, which are hidden from wicked men. The good Christian will await patiently the revelation of God's designs in the sufferings that are imposed upon him; for he is confident that "to them that love God, all things work together unto good."

Prayer

Almighty and eternal God, who art wonderful in the ordering of all Thy works, let them whom Thou hast redeemed understand that to have made the world in the beginning was a no greater work than to have immolated at the end of time Christ our pasch. Who with Thee liveth and reigneth forever. Amen.

Feasts of the Saints during Lent

February 5, St. Agatha

St. Agatha, who was born of a noble Sicilian family, is noted for her valiant fight to preserve her chastity, and for her steadfastness in the faith. She remained true to Christ, consistently refusing to offer sacrifice to the gods, and obtained the crown of martyrdom during the persecution of Decius, about the year 250. Today we are witnesses of her struggle and of her victory.

"But the foolish things of the world hath God chosen that He may confound the wise, and the weak things of the world hath God chosen, that He may confound the strong; and the base things of the world, and the things that are contemptible, hath God chosen, and things that are not, that He might bring to nought things that are; that no flesh should glory in His sight" (Epistle). God "hast granted even to the weaker sex the victory of martyrdom" (Collect).

What a singular victory this delicate and defenseless young virgin, Agatha, won over the mighty Roman governor, Quintianus! "Why do you who are born of a noble family," he asked of her, "seek to lead the ignoble and servile life of a Christian?"

"I am the servant of Christ," Agatha replied, "and for this reason I clothe myself in the garments of a servant. There can be no greater honor than to serve as the servant of Christ." Although Quintianus threatened her with the most severe tortures unless she would agree to deny Christ, she remained steadfast. "If you threaten to cast me to the wild beasts, know that they will become gentle in the name of Christ. If you will make use of fire, then the angels will cause the healing dew of heaven to descend upon me." Forthwith Agatha was beaten with rods, and when she was led away to prison, she went as one proceeding to a festive banquet.

Shortly thereafter she was again summoned before the judge. "If you fail to see that the executioners lacerate my body, my soul cannot enter into the paradise of the Lord with the martyrs," she told him. Agatha was tortured on the rack, branded with glowing irons, and finally her breasts were cut off. During the ensuing night the apostle Peter appeared to her and healed her. Then once more she bore witness to Christ, and after further tortures she was brought back to her prison more dead than alive. There she offered the following prayer for death: "O Lord Jesus Christ, good Master, I thank Thee that Thou hast given me victory over the tortures of the executioners; now let me attain to Thy imperishable glory." O miracle of Christian fortitude!

"There are eunuchs who were born so from their mother's womb; and there are eunuchs who were made so by men; and there are eunuchs who have made themselves eunuchs for the kingdom of heaven. He that can take it, let him take it" (Gospel). Agatha the virgin, the eunuch for the sake of the kingdom of heaven! Quintianus was inflamed with love for her, but Agatha would hear nothing of a union with him. She sought a greater good, holy virginity, for the sake of the kingdom of God. The governor spared no means to overcome her resolution to preserve her virginity. Nevertheless Agatha remained firm and unshaken in her resolution. She knew well what was necessary for the true happiness of man. Resplendent with the double crown of virginity and bloody martyrdom, she advanced to meet her heavenly bridegroom.

"Let us all rejoice in the Lord, celebrating a festival day in honor of blessed Agatha, virgin and martyr, at whose passion the angels rejoice and give praise to the Son of God" (Introit). The joy of victory today fills the Church on earth and in heaven. Agatha's victory is indeed the victory of Christ; it is the triumph of His power and His grace; it is the triumph of the head in His members, the triumph of Christ in His Church. In the person of Agatha the power of Christ, the power of Christianity, becomes manifest. That same power and grace is always at our disposal also. Like Agatha we are members of the body of Christ, and His grace and strength flow through our members.

The life that Agatha lived, the works that she wrought, the sufferings she endured, the prayers she offered, and the victory she won, belong to me and to the entire Church of Christ. Today in the Holy Sacrifice of the Mass we offer the sufferings, merits and victory of Agatha as a reparation and compensation for our own deficiencies and faults, as an atonement and satisfaction for our failings and our sins, as a petition for additional help and grace. We rejoice in the victory of our sister in Christ. We thank Him that He has given her the strength and fortitude necessary for victory.

In the liturgy Agatha is a type of the Church and of the Christian soul. For this reason she is today the bridesmaid of those who celebrate the Mass with her. In the Offertory we behold the virgins in her train, and by her we are ushered into the presence of Christ in the celebration of the Mass. Today with St. Agatha we are determined to be faithful in love and purity, and for this reason we offer our gift of bread and wine, and with it our very selves, that we may live like other Agathas.

Prayer

O God, who among other miracles of Thy power hast granted even to the weaker sex the victory of martyrdom, grant, we beseech Thee, that we who celebrate the festival of blessed Agatha, Thy virgin and martyr, may walk to Thee by her example. Through Christ our Lord. Amen.

February 10, St. Scholastica

St. Scholastica (d. about 542), the beloved sister of St. Benedict, was consecrated to Christ the Lord from early childhood. The liturgy honors her today especially as a type of the consecrated bride burning with love for her divine spouse.

Scholastica is the bride of Christ. The Gospel of the Mass describes the virgin awaiting the arrival of the bridegroom with a burning lamp in her hand. Her heart belonged to her spouse, and for this reason Scholastica, from her early childhood, turned her back on the world and centered her undivided interest on the heavenly bridegroom. She lived a life of seclusion and of prayer, communing unceasingly with her spouse. It is not surprising that she manages to exercise such a great influence over His heart and hand.

As was her custom once a year, she visited her brother, St. Benedict, a few days before her death. The day was spent in pious conversation, and as evening approached, St. Benedict wished to depart and return to his monastery on the mountain. But St. Scholastica wanted to prolong the heavenly conference into the night, for she seemed to be living already in the world beyond. This request, refused by her brother, she besought of her bridegroom. Hardly had she addressed a few words to Him for this purpose, when a violent storm broke forth, a storm so violent that St. Benedict was unable to leave the house. The heavenly bridegroom had fulfilled the wishes of His bride. St. Scholastica died a few days later, and St. Benedict saw her soul ascending to her heavenly spouse in the form of a dove.

Scholastica is a type of the Church and of the Christian soul. We who form the Church are the virgins who await the coming of the bridegroom. In the Epistle the Apostle is jealous with the "jealousy of God" for the Church, for the Christian soul, that it may be true to Christ and consecrate its love and its heart to Him alone. "For I have espoused you to one husband, that I may present you as a chaste virgin to Christ." It is our vocation to live as brides of the divine bridegroom, to whom we were espoused at our baptism. In the person of St. Scholastica, the Church and Christian souls await the bridegroom, ever in readiness for the hour when He will come to escort them home for the eternal nuptials. Like St. Scholastica, the Church "hast loved justice [Christ] and hated iniquity." Like her I should "speak [consecrate] my works to the king" (Introit).

"The kingdom of heaven [the Church] shall be like to ten virgins who, taking their lamps, went out to meet the bridegroom" (Gospel). We now await the bridegroom with lighted lamps in our hands, and we have with us the oil of our good works. We are ready with our offerings when He comes in the Holy Sacrifice to lead us to the bridal banquet of Holy Communion. Holy Communion is for us a blessed wedding feast.

The bridegroom will come again at the hour of our death. The whole life of the Christian on earth can scarcely be anything else but one long vigil in expectation of the coming of the bridegroom, who will come at the moment of death to draw us home for the eternal nuptials in heaven. But how miserably we fail to conform to the thought proposed by the liturgy in today's Gospel when we cling to what is temporal and live for worldly things as did the foolish virgins of the Gospel! "Watch ye, therefore, because you know not the day nor the hour" (Gospel). Are we truly vigilant?

O bride of Christ, go forth to meet the bridegroom. St. Scholastica leads the way. We form part of her bridal company, and she will lead us to Christ, the heavenly bridegroom. She will lead us now in the Holy Sacrifice and at the hour of our final departure. How different our lives would be were we truly conscious of our espousal to Christ!

Prayer

O God, who didst cause the soul of blessed Scholastica, Thy virgin, to enter heaven in the form of a dove to show us the way of innocence, grant that by her merits and prayers we may live in such innocence as to deserve to attain eternal joys. Through Christ our Lord. Amen.

March 19, St. Joseph

During the course of the liturgical year the Church celebrates two feasts of St. Joseph. One is celebrated during the third week after Easter, when he is honored as the protector of the Church. On March he is honored as the blessed and divinely chosen spouse of the Mother of God, Mary, who shared with him the custody of the divine child.

"The just shall flourish like the palm tree; he shall grow up like the cedar of Libanus" (Introit). St. Joseph stands before us, endowed by God with all the graces and gifts which were necessary to make him worthy of his position as consort and husband of the virginal mother of Jesus. He was one in soul and in spirit with her. His was a singular privilege. He is the husband of the Mother of God, bound to her in true and lawful wedlock. She is entrusted to him and subject to him and united to him by the most profound veneration and love. After Jesus Himself, no one is nearer to her than St. Joseph, and no one is more perfectly cognizant of her mystery. No one knows her better, no one loves her more dearly or is united to her more intimately, than St. Joseph. The Gospel of today's Mass shows us how much he loved and appreciated her. Mary had conceived by the Holy Ghost, but as yet St. Joseph was unaware of this mystery. "Whereupon Joseph her husband, being a just man and not willing publicly to expose her, was minded to put her away privately." Those were bitter days for St. Joseph, and he suffered greatly. Then God, through His holy angel, reassured him: "Joseph, son of David, fear not to take unto thee Mary thy wife, for that which is conceived in her is of the Holy Ghost." Joseph now understood what God required of him. With complete self-effacement he placed himself at the service of the Virgin Mother, and with unfailing devotion and fidelity shared with her a life of poverty, her seclusion, her exile in Egypt, her work, her life of contemplation, and her blessed communion with Jesus at Nazareth. "Lord, Thou hast prevented him with blessings of sweetness; Thou hast set on his head a crown of precious stones" (Gradual).

"And she shall bring forth a son; and thou shalt call his name Jesus" (Gospel). Among the Hebrews the privilege of bestowing a name on a child belonged to the father. St. Joseph had the full rights of a father over the child Jesus. He whom Mary had conceived by the Holy Ghost belonged most properly also to St. Joseph, who was her legitimate spouse. By his marriage to Mary, he had full rights over Jesus. He was in a true sense of the word His father, and he possessed all the rights and duties of a father with regard to the Son of God made man. Who among us can understand or fully appreciate the dignity and the significance of such a virginal fatherhood? Jesus recognizes and honors St. Joseph as His father. He wishes to be subject to him, to be dependent upon him, to be his child, to be obedient to his every word and wish. He desires to be in the company of St. Joseph, to love him, to work at his side, to join him in his prayers, to share his life most intimately. How holy and pure St. Joseph must have been! He lived continually in the presence of God Himself. Such was the sanctity of St. Joseph. Like the palm, so flourishes the just man, St. Joseph, who was planted in the fullness of grace and virtue in the house of God in the midst of the Holy Family at Nazareth.

In the celebration of the Holy Sacrifice today, St. Joseph is our intercessor with Jesus. He is even more than that, for he joins us in our offering. He places himself at the head of our Offertory procession. The Offertory says of him and of us, since we are united with him: "My truth [God's grace] and My mercy shall be with him; and in My name shall his horn be exalted." In the strength of our union with St. Joseph, we shall find in the Mass deliverance from our sins. We shall be "exalted," borne aloft with the offering of Christ, and shall share in the precious fruits of the sacrifice. We shall share the purity, the justice, the holiness of St. Joseph. This is the mind of the liturgy with regard to the communion of the saints.

"That which is conceived in her is of the Holy Ghost" (Communion). As St. Joseph believed, so we, too, must believe that that which we receive in Holy Communion is the Son of God, born of the Virgin Mary. If only we, at the time of Communion or on the occasion of one of our visits to the Blessed Sacrament, would commune with God with the deep and powerful faith of St. Joseph! We would indeed be healed by such an association.

How different are the thoughts of God from the thoughts of men! Men would have selected one of their great leaders, one of royal ancestry or of spiritual prominence, to be the foster parent of the Son of God. But what is great in the eyes of men has little meaning in the eyes of God. God chose a man who was pure, virginal, poor, and humble. That is God's manner of thinking. That is true greatness.

Prayer

We beseech Thee, O Lord, that we may be helped by the merits of the spouse of Thy most holy mother, so that what we cannot obtain by ourselves may be given to us through his intercession. Who livest and reignest with the Father in the unity of the Holy Ghost now and forever. Amen.

March 21, St. Benedict

St. Benedict, who was born in Umbria about the year 480, consecrated himself to the monastic life in the wilderness near Subiaco while he was still a youth. Through the Rule which he composed, he became the founder of monastic and religious life in the Western Church. Through his order the conversion of the Germanic tribes and the Christianization of all central and northern Europe was accomplished. A great number of the monastic rules of later ages are based on the Rule of St. Benedict. St. Benedict died at Monte Cassino about the year 543.

"The mouth of the just shall meditate wisdom, and his tongue shall speak judgment" (Introit). Thus the liturgy sketches the portrait of St. Benedict. He is first of all a just man. In his heart and in his mouth are wisdom. Even while he was pursuing his studies at Rome, he was, according to the testimony of St. Gregory, wise beyond his age. He indulged in none of the worldly enjoyments and practices common among his fellow students. For him the world was but a faded flower. He was impelled to live for God and for God alone. Benedict was a man of character, conscientiously pursuing his purpose, serious in his outlook on life. This seriousness of purpose impelled him to leave Rome, as St. Gregory says, "knowingly ignorant and wisely unlearned." Benedict possessed a true supernatural wisdom, the spirit of true Christian wisdom. He judged all things by the light of divine wisdom and in their relationship to eternity. He knew that God had chosen precisely those things which the world considers foolish, to confound those things which the world considers wise (1 Cor 1:26 ff.). Inspired by this spirit of wisdom, Benedict chose to live a mortified life in a cave at Subiaco. Separated from the company of men, deprived of the comforts of life, he endured hunger and the heat and cold. He had chosen to live a life of prayer in continual union with God, a life of silence in continual conflict with his passions and with all that could in any way hinder his advance in godliness. "The law of his God is in his heart" (Introit). He sought only to do God's will, to comply fully with the law of God; such was his rule and norm of life. Thus he lived with God at Subiaco in holy solitude, "under the eyes of the heavenly spectators" (St. Gregory). Therefore God "heard him and his voice, and brought him into a cloud," the cloud of His holy presence, the cloud of divine union, as once He led Moses into a cloud on Mount Sinai. "And He gave him commandments before His face, and a law of life and instruction" (Epistle).

Eventually God led Benedict from the seclusion of his valley at Subiaco to the towering mountain of Monte Cassino, that his light might illuminate the whole world. Here, inspired and guided by the spirit of God, he wrote his Rule, through the observance of which countless souls have been sanctified and have found a "law of life and instruction." "Lord, Thou has presented him with blessings of sweetness" (Gradual). "The just shall flourish like the palm tree; he shall grow up like the cedar of Libanus" (Alleluia verse). Through St. Benedict a mighty stream of grace and blessing flowed out upon the world, upon many nations and ages, and enriched them with countless blessings.

"Behold we have left all things and have followed Thee" (Gospel). St. Benedict, too, abandoned all things to follow Christ: his father and mother, his home, his family, his position of honor, his worldly possessions, and all that belonged to him as the son of a patrician. He abandoned even his studies at Rome, since he saw how many others had suffered injury to their souls through the pursuit of such studies. He had only one ambition, and that was to gain Christ, to share His life of voluntary poverty, to subject his own will, and to suppress the desires and longings of his own heart. He longed for a life of obedience, of prayer, of consecration to God. He sought a life of strenuous labor, a life of self-abnegation, a life in a community of brethren, full of mortification and suffering, providing an ample opportunity to practice humility and to fulfill the law of charity: to love God and one's neighbor. "Behold we have left all things and have followed Thee." For this reason Benedict was "blessed by God both in name and in grace" (St. Augustine). "He who soweth sparingly shall also reap sparingly, and he who soweth in blessings shall also reap blessings" (2 Cor 9:6). Such a one "shall receive a hundredfold [in this life] and shall possess life everlasting" (Gospel). On earth he will enjoy a life of inner tranquility, the reputation of a noble, pure, and well ordered character, a life fruitful for the salvation of his own soul and for the eternal welfare of his neighbor and of all humanity. And in addition "he shall possess life everlasting." "He asked life of Thee, and Thou hast given him length of days forever and ever" (Gradual). "Thou hast given him his heart's desire, O Lord, and hast not withholden from him the will of his lips. Thou hast placed on his head a crown of precious stones" (Offertory).

"He who soweth in blessings shall also reap blessings." It is the planting which determines the difference in the richness of the harvest, and this truth was recognized by St. Benedict. If we would receive, we must first give. If we would gain all, we must first abandon all. "If any man will follow Me, let him deny himself and take up his cross and follow Me. For whosoever will save his life shall lose it; and whosoever shall lose his life for My sake and the gospel shall save it. For what shall it profit a man if he gain the whole world and suffer the loss of his soul? Or what shall a man give in exchange for his soul?" (Mk 8:34–37.)

In the liturgy St. Benedict is the "faithful and wise servant whom his lord setteth over his family, to give them their measure of wheat in due season" (Communion). He is the lawgiver, the father and the leader of a great family of monks and religious. Through his example, through his Rule, through his intercession with God, he gives us in due season the bread which we require. He obtains for us wisdom, guidance, and strength, that we may leave all things and follow the Lord, so that we may obtain the hundredfold in this world and "life everlasting."

Prayer

O almighty and eternal God, who this day hast released from the prison of the body and taken into heaven the soul of Thy confessor St. Benedict, grant unto Thy servants who celebrate his feast the remission of all sins, that they who rejoice in his glory may, through his intercession before Thee, also partake in his merits. Through Christ our Lord. Amen.

March 25, The Annunciation

Nine months before the feast of Christmas our thoughts turn to that day on which the eternal Word, at the message of the angel, assumed human nature in the womb of the most holy Virgin in order that He might redeem man from his sins and from eternal damnation. This day was the most memorable day in the history of the human race, since on this day the divinity was united with humanity in a manner more perfect than ever before; in fact, in the most perfect manner possible. This was the day of the betrothal of the Son of God with humanity.

Today the angel comes to the Virgin and tells her: "Fear not, Mary, for thou hast found grace with God. Behold thou shalt conceive in thy womb and shalt bring forth a son, and thou shalt call His name Jesus. He shall be great and shall be called the Son of the Most High." The virgin is to remain a virgin and yet become a mother. "The Holy Ghost shall come upon thee and the power of the Most High shall overshadow thee. And therefore also the holy one which shall be born of thee shall be called the Son of God." Then Mary replies, "Behold the handmaid of the Lord; be it done to me according to thy word" (Gospel). "And the Word was made flesh" in the womb of the Virgin. In the Offertory of the Mass we use the words of the angel to address Mary. Ave Maria: "Hail Mary, full of grace, the Lord is with thee. Blessed art thou among women." Mary, the Mother of God, is the masterpiece of God's creation. Like Christ, the God-man, she stands alone, and there could never be another like her.

"Behold the handmaid of the Lord." Mary is truly the handmaid of the Lord, for she conforms perfectly to God's will and is completely dependent on His designs; her will is one with the divine will. In reply to the glorious message of the angel and the singular honor and distinction that is conferred upon her, Mary says humbly: "Behold the handmaid of the Lord; be it done unto me according to thy word." At the moment when heaven itself awaits her consent, at the moment when the uncreated Word of the Father descends to become incarnate through her, Mary will look upon herself merely as the handmaid of the Lord. The more she is honored by heaven, the more she humbles herself. Such is the fruit of the greatness that comes to us from God; we must recognize our own unworthiness and insignificance in all humility. A low opinion of self brings with it the gift of greatness which is given by God. Humility brings us close to God and unites us with Him. "He that shall humble himself shall be exalted" (Mt 23:12). "Be it done to me according to thy word." Mary freely gives her consent, and at that very moment she conceives the Son of God. He at once floods her soul with His light and pours forth upon her all the riches of His grace. She is united with Him most intimately. The feelings and dispositions of the Son become immediately those of the mother, for Jesus and Mary have become intimately united. Mary has no thoughts or impulses that are not in conformity with His. She lives with Him and in Him. In becoming the Mother of God, she subordinates herself completely. She is honored by the eternal One she bears in her womb, and she loses herself in the abyss of divinity. Her exaltation is the result of her humility: "Behold the handmaid of the Lord; be it done unto me according to thy word." "Hail Mary, full of grace, the Lord is with thee."

"Behold a virgin shall conceive and bear a son, and his name shall be called Emmanuel [God with us]" (Epistle). In the womb of the Virgin the Son of God is wedded to humanity. The liturgy treats this union of humanity with the divine King with the greatest reverence. "Hearken, O daughter, and see, and incline thy ear; for the King hath greatly desired thy beauty" (Tract; Ps. 44:11 f.). Already the nations approach to pay homage to the queen on the day of her nuptials. The daughters of Tyre lead the way, and in her train in an unending procession follow the representatives of the richest kingdoms of the earth, bearing gifts in their hands as a sign of their homage. "All the rich among the people shall entreat thy countenance.... After her shall virgins be brought to the King" (Introit; Tract). These are the men and the nations which shall be converted to Christ. With joy they follow the queen (Mary, the Church) and enter into the chambers of the King. They shall share with her now her supernatural gifts and graces as they will one day share with her forever and ever the joys of eternity. "They shall be brought with gladness and rejoicing; they shall be brought into the temple of the King" through Mary and through the Church (Introit; Tract).

The Son of God desires to be wedded to the human race through His love. Mary is the representative of the whole race. In Mary we and every member of the race were asked to decide whether or not we would accept the offer of almighty God; whether or not we wished to be redeemed. Through Mary we and the whole race of men gave an affirmative answer to God's proposal. "And the Word was made flesh." Today we thank the Blessed Virgin for having spoken her fiat as our representative.

Now we, too, must eagerly accept every grace which God offers to us. "After her virgins shall be brought to the King." That is, pure souls, souls which have been cleansed from everything that could interfere with their spiritual union with God, shall be brought before the throne of God.

"Behold a virgin shall conceive," the holy liturgy sings in the Communion prayer. The virgin lives again each day in our Holy Mother the Church. Each day in Holy Communion we relive the blessed Incarnation of Christ in the Virgin Mary. Would that we were as pure and as holy as she!

Prayer

O God, who didst will that at the message of an angel Thy Word should take flesh in the womb of the Blessed Virgin Mary; grant unto Thy suppliants that we who believe her to be truly the Mother of God, may be assisted by her intercession before Thee. Through the same Christ our Lord. Amen.

Eastertide

Easter is the Solemnity of Solemnities, the center and climax of the Church year. All the mysteries that we have commemorated from Advent until now have pointed toward Easter; all that we shall yet celebrate in the weeks that follow has its foundation in the mystery of Easter, and receives its meaning and importance from this mystery.

The resurrection of Christ is the consummation of the Incarnation (the Christmas mystery) and of the Passion. St. Paul reveals the meaning of Easter when he writes to the Corinthians, "And if Christ be not risen again, your faith is vain, for you are yet in your sins. Then they also that are fallen asleep in Christ are perished" (1 Cor 15:17 f.). Even the Incarnation and the Passion are not sufficient in themselves. Christ became man and died to deliver us from the death of sin. But that was not enough. In order to give us immortal life, He rose from the dead. He "rose again for our justification" (Rom 4:25). He rose that He might bring us the perfect and eternal life which He merited for us by His death and which shines so brightly in Him. By the mystery of Easter we are able to enter into the splendid life of His glorified body. We were created for glory from the beginning, but we lost it with the sin of Adam. We won it back through the resurrection of Christ. For this reason Easter is a time of joy. Through Christ we have all risen from sin and have access to immortal and eternal life.

The life which we obtain at Easter is already a foretaste of the everlasting, heavenly life which we shall eventually enjoy. The prayer said in the Easter Mass assures us that "God, who on this day by Thy only-begotten Son has overcome death, has opened to us the gate of eternity." Over and over again in the liturgy of the Easter season we are reminded of this truth, that in the temporal celebration of Easter we already touch the reality of the eternal life of glorification. "I live, and you shall live" (Jn 14:19).

The joy of Easter finds its natural expression in the joyous banquet of Holy Communion, the Easter banquet, the paschal meal. Holy Communion is the food upon which this new life is nourished. He who rose from the dead enters our soul in person, and illuminates it with the fullness of His new life. What He is, we are also, as He rose from the dead, so shall we rise. We now walk "in newness of life" (Rom 6:4).

The spirit of Eastertide is a spirit of sincere gratitude to the risen Christ, through whom we possess eternal life. "I live, and you shall live." We should acquire this spirit of joy, a spirit which will lift us above sin and the world and death. The risen Christ will give us the strength to overcome the powers of darkness and death. We must have a spirit of hope. We shall, since Christ rose, most certainly rise on the last day, and our bodies shall be awakened to eternal life. "I shall not die, but live." We should have an unshakable faith, for Christ arose from the dead. His resurrection attests to His divinity and the truth of His doctrine.

Easter sets a new task before us. We must now begin to live the life of the new man. We rose with Christ in baptism. "If you be risen with Christ, seek the things that are above, where Christ is sitting at the right hand of God. Mind the things that are above, not the things that are upon the earth. For you are dead [to the world, to sin, to temporal things], and your life is hid with Christ in God" (Col 3:1–3). "Purge out the old leaven, that you may be a new paste, as you are unleavened.... Let us feast, not with the old leaven ... of malice and wickedness, but with the unleavened bread of sincerity and truth" (1 Cor 5:7 f.; Epistle of Easter Sunday). Daily during the Easter season the liturgy reminds us, both in the Mass and in the Divine Office, of the words of the Apostle: "Christ, rising again from the dead, dieth now no more." He died to sin once for all; He lives now for God (Rom 6:9 f.). Christ, the whole Christ (the Church, all of us), now lives for God.

We are the "Christ" who is risen. We died to sin in baptism. We live now for God. "Christ, rising again from the dead, dieth now no more." We have put an end to our sinning, and we live now only for God and for the performance of His holy will. "Our conversation is in heaven" (Phil 3:20). We must acquire a spirit of self-denial, and be willing to carry the cross of Christ. We can share in the life of the risen Christ only if we have been willing to share his humiliation and crucifixion.

The time from Easter to Pentecost is merely an extension of the feast of Easter, forming a continuous, uninterrupted Easter feast. In various forms recur thoughts that deal primarily with Christ's resurrection and our call to share His new life with Him. "I live, and you shall live" (Jn 14:19).

The period from Pentecost to Advent also bears a close relationship to Easter. It will develop and perfect the life which was given to us at Easter. Christ lives in us, and we live in Him. He lives on in His members; and we, the members, share His life. He lives in our body as well as in our soul, for the body, too, shall rise and be restored to life and share the life of Christ in the blessed Easter of eternal life. "I believe in the resurrection of the body and life everlasting. Amen."

Easter Sunday

The Mass

Resurrection, victory, light, life — that is the joyous message of Easter. Christ rises from the dead first in His person and then in His members. The resurrection of Christ is the resurrection of His Church, too; His victory is a victory for His members. This doctrine is made clear to us through the close association of baptism with the celebration of Easter.

In ancient times there was no celebration on Holy Saturday as there is today. This day was a day of silent mourning for the dead. Only late in the evening, at dusk, the faithful and the catechumens assembled in the house of God. They proceeded at once to bless the light with which the church was illuminated (now the blessing of the fire). From the new light the Easter candle and the other lights in the church were lighted. Readings from Scripture followed.

The meaning of Christian baptism became clearer with the reading of the twelve prophecies from the Old Testament. The catechumens were to receive baptism at dawn. They watched with throbbing hearts as the water was blessed in the baptismal font. One after another they descended into the baptismal water, were submerged three times, and received the sacrament of baptism from the hands of the bishop. With Christ they had descended into the tomb (the baptismal water) and had obtained new life. They were now Christians, new men with a new faith, a new plan of life, and new ideals. They now had a new spirit and had obtained a new strength, for they had been reborn of the Holy Ghost. In their garments of light, their new, white baptismal robes, the catechumens participated in the Mass of the faithful and received Holy Communion for the first time. This is Easter, a time of resurrection, an experience of eternal importance.

Today we are assembled in the church of St. Mary Major, the church of the Mother of God, in which the Christmas mysteries were celebrated. On Christmas we celebrated the birth of Christ; now we celebrate His resurrection, which for the early Christians was the rebirth of Christ. Two thoughts dominate the text of the Mass today: Christ's resurrection, and Christ, the Easter Lamb; in the background is the thought of baptism. The paschal lamb of the people of Israel found its fulfillment in the sacrifice of Christ. This celebration recalls the redemption of the people from the slavery of Pharao (Satan), their deliverance from destruction in the passage through the Red Sea (baptism), and their entrance into the Holy Land (the Church, heaven, eternal life). In Him who rose from the dead we have the lamb that was slaughtered and at the same time gives life, redemption, deliverance, eternal life.

With the banner of victory in His hand, the risen Christ presents Himself to His Father in the Introit: "I rose up and am still with Thee." You laid your hand upon Me to strike Me with suffering and death, but You also helped Me, protected Me, and delivered Me. In Your divine wisdom You led Me through night to light, through death to life. The Church prays these words with Christ: "I rose up and am still with Thee"; that is, the Church rose through the death of Christ from the night of sin and was freed from the power of Satan. "I am still with Thee"; that is, I possess eternal life since I am united to Christ. "Thou hast laid Thy hand upon me"; You still lay Your hand heavily on me, striking me with tribulation while protecting me and guarding me. Thy hand still leads me, the Church, through death to life, to victory over sin, the world, and death. In the Kyrie we beg for this Easter grace, for this new life, that it may flow out to all the children of the Church. "Lord have mercy on us."

Easter means new life. Before an Israelite could eat the paschal lamb, he had to rid his house of all leaven. The Apostle concluded that only he may eat the paschal lamb of the Christians who has put off the old man (Epistle). He must become a new man who feasts "with the unleavened bread of sincerity and truth." Only if he has overcome the darkness of sin can he gaze on the glory of the risen Christ, who appears in our midst in the celebration of the Mass. As Magdalen found Him in the garden on Easter morning, so we find Him this morning in the house of God. Here on our altar He becomes our paschal lamb. We take Him into our hands and offer Him to the Father as our Easter gift, "a pure, holy, and unspotted host." But we know that this gift of ours, pure and holy as it is, can profit us only if we are united to it spiritually; that is, only in so far as we share in the life of the risen Christ, having overcome sin, the world, and the devil.

Easter reminds us not only of the paschal lamb, but also of our baptism. It commemorates not only something that happened to Christ, but also something very important that happened to us. By baptism we obtained a new life, the life Christ merited for us by His death; and we nourish it by the reception of Holy Communion. We are no longer what we were yesterday.

We have been changed, we have risen from the grave of our sins, our negligence, our avarice, our selfishness, and our past life. We have died to sin once for all; and now we live to Christ. We lift ourselves above the purely natural thoughts and acts of the present to turn our attention to the "things that are above, not the things that are upon the earth" (Col 3:2). The proof of our union with Christ is in our reception of Holy Communion, by virtue of which we are "of one heart" with one another, and filled with the "spirit of Thy love." In the Postcommunion we ask that this spirit may be increased.

Meditation

In ancient times the catechumens were baptized early Easter morning in the church of the Holy Redeemer (the Lateran basilica in Rome). For the celebration of the Easter Mass we accompany the catechumens to the church of St. Mary Major. Mary, to whom this church is dedicated, was bequeathed to redeemed humanity as she stood under the cross on Calvary. After greeting the risen Christ, we congratulate Mary: "Rejoice, O Queen of heaven, alleluia."

Christ rose from the dead, and He turns first to His heavenly Father. "I rose up and am still with Thee" (Introit). Thus He casts Himself in devoted and grateful love on the bosom of His Father. "Thou hast laid Thy hand upon Me" through the shame and humiliation I suffered during My passion. Now this same hand is held out to glorify Him and cover Him with splendor; "Thy knowledge is become wonderful" (Introit). Yesterday the humiliation and bitterness of the cross, today the splendor of heavenly glory!

We can have no doubt concerning Christ's resurrection. "The Lord is risen indeed" (Lk 24:34). Heretofore the divinity of Christ appeared only in His miracles; now it shines in its fullness. From Him who yesterday died on the cross, now comes grace, life, and pardon. By the resurrection of Christ, God set the seal of divine approval on all that Christ had taught, on all that He had done, and on the Church which He had established. "This Jesus hath God raised again" (Acts 2:32). Every word, then, that He spoke is infallibly true. Therefore men must submit to Christ and accept His commandments without question. "I am the way, the truth, and the life" (Jn 14:6). The Resurrection settles all our doubts and makes us inconceivably rich. How wonderfully God glorified Christ in the Resurrection! We must place all our faith in Him and rejoice from the bottom of our heart.

With Christ we, too, have risen. Christ not only redeemed us, the living, from sin; He redeemed also the dead. He "hath raised us up together and hath made us sit together in the heavenly places" (Eph 2:6). Our future is most intimately joined to that of Christ. He is risen; so we, too, must rise. Because we belonged to the race of Adam, we shared death with him. Because we now belong to the new Adam, we shall also share His resurrection to eternal life. "When Christ shall appear, who is your life, then you also shall appear with Him in glory" (Col 3:4). "For if the dead rise not again, neither is Christ risen again. And if Christ be not risen again, your faith is vain, for you are yet in your sins. Then they also that are fallen asleep in Christ are perished. If in this life only we have hope in Christ, we are of all men most miserable. But now Christ is risen from the dead, the first fruits of them that sleep. For by a man came death, and by a man the resurrection of the dead. And as in Adam all die, so also in Christ all shall be made alive. But every one in his own order; the first fruits, Christ, then they that are of Christ" (1 Cor 15:16–23).

The lessons of Holy Saturday and the blessing of the baptismal font announce the resurrection of the soul from sin. The entire season of Lent prepared the soul for this rebirth. The Church compares the emergence of the Christian from the baptismal font to the resurrection of Christ from the tomb. In this sense St. Paul declares: "If you be risen with Christ [that is, baptized], seek the things that are above,... not the things that are upon the earth. For you are dead [to sin], and your life is hid with Christ in God" (Col 3:1 ff.). Because you have risen with Christ, "purge out the old leaven [from your soul], that you may be a new paste, as you are unleavened [new, reborn].... Therefore let us feast, not with the old leaven, nor with the leaven of malice and wickedness, but with the unleavened bread of sincerity and truth" (Epistle).

"I rose up and am still with Thee" (Introit). After His labors and His humiliations, Christ finds rest with His Father. "I am still with Thee." This is perfect beatitude. Through His cross He entered into the possession of eternal glory. Christ has gained the crown of victory;[14] through Christ men also win their crowns of victory. Humanity was under a curse and subject to the wrath of God. Now that they have risen with Christ, their guilt has been destroyed. "I rose up and am still with Thee." The liturgy places these words in the mouth of the Church that she may pray them with Christ.

"The earth trembled and was still when God arose in judgment" (Offertory). The resurrection of Christ is the judgment and condemnation of those who have turned away from God. This judgment was prefigured by the angel who passed through the land of Egypt destroying the first-born of the Egyptians. The Israelites marked the doors of their houses with the blood of the paschal lamb. We are the new Israel, and "Christ our Pasch is sacrificed" (Gradual). We mark ourselves with His blood, which we enjoy in the Holy Eucharist. We have been pardoned, we are saved, we shall live.

"He is risen." The resurrection of Christ is a pledge of our own resurrection. It is the foundation upon which our faith rests. It is the guarantee of our redemption and God's assurance that our sins are forgiven and that we are called to eternal life. "This is the day which the Lord hath made; let us be glad and rejoice therein. Give praise to the Lord, for He is good, for His mercy endureth forever. Alleluia" (Gradual). "Christ our Pasch is sacrificed.... The Lamb redeems the sheep. Christ, the innocent One, hath reconciled sinners to the Father" (Alleluia verse, Sequence).

Prayer

O God, who on this day by Thy only-begotten Son hast overcome death and opened to us the gate of eternity, help us to attain the desires which Thou hast inspired in us. Through Christ our Lord. Amen.

Monday

Today the neophytes are led to the stational church of St. Peter. Peter presents himself to them and to us as a witness of the resurrection. He has been commissioned by Christ to "preach to

[14] Cf. the Epistle of Septuagesima Sunday.

the people and to testify that it is He who was appointed by God to be judge of the living and of the dead" (Epistle). He lives and He will come again with power and glory. He will awaken all those who slumber in their graves and call them before His righteous judgment. Happy will be those who have risen with the Lord in baptism and who by virtue of their baptism "deserve to attain perfect liberty and advance to life everlasting" (Collect).

"In those days Peter, standing in the midst of the people, said: Men, brethren, you know ... how God anointed Jesus of Nazareth with the Holy Ghost and with power, who went about doing good and healing all that were oppressed by the devil, for God was with Him. And we are witnesses of all things that He did in the land of the Jews and in Jerusalem; whom they killed, hanging Him upon a tree. Him God raised up the third day, and gave Him to be made manifest, not to all the people, but to witnesses preordained by God; even to us, who did eat and drink with Him after He arose again from the dead. And He commanded us to preach to the people, and to testify that it is He who was appointed by God to be judge of the living and of the dead. To Him all the prophets give testimony, that by His name all who believe in Him receive remission of sins" (Epistle).

Peter was an eyewitness of Christ's resurrection just as he was of the other events in Christ's life. The Church is aware of the value of Peter's testimony. Not all men can be eyewitnesses of Christ; all but a few must depend on the testimony of a few witnesses. For this reason today we come directly to Peter, an eyewitness, to receive his testimony. Today we join the uncounted millions who for centuries have believed so firmly in his testimony that they have been willing to give their life in support of it. We have faith. Our salvation depends on our faith, not on our learning and knowledge. "For it is written: I will destroy the wisdom of the wise.... Where is the wise? Where is the scribe? Where is the disputer of this world [the philosopher]? Hath not God made foolish the wisdom of this world? For, seeing that in the wisdom of God the world by wisdom knew not God, it pleased God, by the foolishness of our preaching, to save them that believe" (1 Cor 1:19 ff.). We believe that "God raised up [Jesus] on the third day, and gave Him to be made manifest ... to witnesses preordained by God." Because of our faith in Peter's testimony, "we receive remission of sins" (Epistle). "He that believeth and is baptized shall be saved. But he that believeth not shall be condemned" (Mk 16:16).

"The Lord is risen indeed and hath appeared to Simon" (Gospel). The testimony which St. Peter gives us in the Epistle is supported by statements of the other apostles. Christ revealed Himself also to the two disciples who were making their way to the village of Emmaus. Overjoyed by this appearance of Christ, the two disciples hastened back to Jerusalem and "found the eleven gathered together, and those that were with them."

Even before these two disciples could announce their marvelous experience, they are told by the apostles, "The Lord is risen indeed and hath appeared to Simon." To Peter! If, then, Peter asserts, "Him God raised up the third day," there can no longer be any doubt. "The Lord is risen." If He has risen, then the just and holy God has reversed the cruel judgment of the men who condemned Him. God has placed His approval on His life and on every word that He spoke. He, the crucified One, has been recognized by God as "the way, the truth, and the life" (Jn 14:6). Surely then, men must recognize Him, believe in Him, and unite themselves to Him through baptism. This may require of them humiliations and suffering, but it will eventually lead them to glory, resurrection, and eternal happiness.

"This is the day which the Lord hath made; let us rejoice and be glad therein" (Gradual). The Lord leads us by means of baptism to a land flowing with milk and honey. "May the law of the Lord be always in your mouth" (Introit); that is, announce all the great things which God has done to you, especially that He has led you to believe in Christ.

"The Lord is risen and hath appeared to Peter" (Communion). Christ appears to us today in the form of Holy Communion. With Peter, in whose house we celebrate today's mysteries, we are now witnesses of the resurrection. We shall bear witness to this resurrection by word of mouth, by our lives, and if it should be necessary, even by our blood.

Prayer

O God, who by the paschal solemnity hast blessed the world with remedies, pour forth Thy heavenly gifts, we beseech Thee, on Thy people, that it may deserve to attain perfect liberty and advance toward life everlasting. Through Christ our Lord. Amen.

Tuesday

During this period the Church is greatly concerned that the neophytes and the faithful be filled with efficacious faith in the risen Christ. "If Christ be not risen again, then is our preaching vain, and your faith is also vain.... Then they also that are fallen asleep in Christ are perished" (1 Cor 15:14, 18).

Christ is indeed risen. We hear the glad news today from the mouth of the Apostle of the Gentiles, in whose sanctuary we celebrate the sacred liturgy. He speaks to his brethren of the race of Abraham. The inhabitants of Jerusalem did not recognize Christ as the Messias; although they could find no fault in Him, they demanded His death. "But God raised Him up from the dead the third day; who was seen for many days by them who came up with Him from Galilee to Jerusalem, who to this present time are His witnesses to the people" (Epistle).

The apostles were among the first to whom Christ appeared. The evening of Easter Sunday, "Jesus stood in the midst of His disciples and saith to them: Peace be to you. It is I, fear not. But they, being troubled and frightened, supposed that they saw a spirit. And He said to them: Why are you troubled, and why do your thoughts arise in your hearts? See My hands and My feet, that it is I Myself; handle Me and see, for a spirit hath not flesh and bones as you see Me to have. And... He showed them His hands and His feet" (Gospel). The apostles are full of amazement and joy, and yet they do not fully believe. Then He consumes food before their eyes and gives them to eat from what remains of the fish and the honeycomb. He reminds them that He had already spoken to them about His passion and resurrection when He was still with them. Then He explains to them the Scriptures: "Thus it is written; and thus it behooved Christ to suffer and to rise again from the dead the third day; and that penance and the remission of sins should be preached in His name unto all nations."

The risen Christ stands in our midst today in the celebration of the Eucharistic mysteries. He salutes us, "Peace be to you." We are allowed to see Him, to touch His glorified body, and to take it in our hands to offer it to the Father. He is our pure, unspotted victim. He opens our understanding that we may comprehend the Scriptures, wherein we see that it was prophesied that Christ should suffer and on the third day rise again. He hands us the fish and the bread of Holy Eucharist. In the reception of Holy Communion He fills us with His spirit and His life. We have risen with Him, and now we seek the things that are above, where He sits at the right hand of God. We think now of the things that are above, not of worldly things (Communion). "Lift up your hearts." Christ, the risen Christ, must dominate our thoughts, as He dominated the thoughts of the apostles in the supper room.

"See My hands and My feet." The Mass which we are attending is the repetition of His sacrifice on Calvary. When He comes to us at the Consecration of the Mass, He shows us His hands and His feet. Christ glorified suffering. For this reason He will bear His glorified wounds for all eternity. They will remind us that He has redeemed us from pain. Easter proclaims to the world: "The sufferings of this time are not worthy to be compared with the glory to come" (Rom 8:18). The Easter joy causes the Christian to forget that He has carried the cross, for he knows that he has been redeemed. Christ was "obedient unto death, even to the death of the cross. For which cause God also hath exalted Him and hath given Him a name which is above all names" (Phil 2:8 f.). "See My hands and My feet," and know that the sufferings of this time are not worthy to be compared with the glory that awaits us. "See My hands and My feet," and know that the chalice of suffering is the chalice of salvation.

Christ is indeed risen. Our faith, then, is certain. We are redeemed. In Him we have the pardon of our sins. He has won for us the grace of becoming the children of God and heirs to the kingdom of heaven. "This is the day which the Lord hath made; let us rejoice and be glad therein. Let them now speak that have been redeemed by the Lord" (Gradual).

The words of the Introit are true of us: "He gave them the water of wisdom [baptismal grace] to drink; it shall be made strong in them [confirmation],... and it shall exalt them forever." This grace is the result of the death and resurrection of Christ, for which we offer Him our thanksgiving today. "Give glory to the Lord, and call upon His name; declare His deeds among the nations" (Introit). "The Lord thundered from heaven, and the Most High gave His voice; and the fountains of waters appeared, alleluia" (Offertory).

Prayer

O God, who dost continually enrich Thy Church with new offspring, grant to Thy people that they may by their good life hold fast to the sacrament which they have received by faith. Through Christ our Lord. Amen.

Wednesday

1. The liturgy today recalls the third appearance of Christ after His Resurrection, when we gather with the neophytes in the church of St. Lawrence.

"Come, ye blessed of My Father, receive the kingdom which was prepared for you from the foundation of the world, alleluia" (Introit). With these words the Lord receives the newly baptized Christians as they present themselves at the threshold of the church of St. Lawrence. "Receive the kingdom" by reason of your membership in the Church, which is the kingdom of God on earth. In the Church, which the neophytes have entered by the gate of baptism, they receive supernatural gifts from heaven. Here they sing a "new canticle," the song of the baptized, the song of the beloved children of God who have arisen from sin. Here in the celebration of Mass the Lord appears to us. We are like the apostles fishing in their fragile boat, while He appears to us walking on the firm shore of eternity. In the fire of His passion He has prepared for us fish and bread, which He offers us in the form of the Eucharist. By this means we become new creatures, cleansed from sin, and the seed of immortality is implanted in our souls. "Christ, rising again from the dead, dieth now no more, alleluia; death shall no more have dominion over Him, alleluia, alleluia" (Communion). We are now one with Him. By virtue of Holy Communion we share His immortality. Death shall no more have dominion over us. Death must release us when Christ calls us to eternity. Then we shall enter into the blessed kingdom of eternal life. "Come, ye blessed of My Father, receive the kingdom which was prepared for you from the foundation of the world."

"Ye men of Israel, and ye that fear God [among the heathens], hear. The God of Abraham, and the God of Isaac, and the God of Jacob, the God of our fathers hath glorified His Son Jesus, whom you indeed delivered up and denied before the face of Pilate, when he judged He should be released. But you denied the Holy One and the Just, and desired a murderer [Barabbas] to be granted unto you. But the Author of life you killed, whom God hath raised from the dead, of which we are witnesses" (Epistle). We, the baptized, are also witnesses of this miracle. Baptism imposes on us the duties of a witness, a martyr for Christ. Therefore we celebrate the holy mysteries today with the holy martyr St. Lawrence. He reminds us of the fish and bread on the hot coals in today's Gospel. He is the patron and the model of the baptized, the living representation of the ideal for which we should all strive. Like St. Peter and St. Lawrence, we live among unbelievers and those who have gone astray. We are witnesses of the risen Christ. We have been inspired by His example and filled with grace by the reception of His holy body. We have become new men, risen men. We now have new ideals, new strength, and a new outlook on life. We are, as it were, a living testimony to Christ; He lives and works through us. We must bear witness to Christ's resurrection, not with empty words, but by the testimony of a holy life. "I live, now not I, but Christ liveth in me" (Gal 2:20).

"Come, ye blessed of My Father." Baptism gives us the right to expect that Christ will address these words to us and that we shall stand at His right hand on the day of judgment. It gives us the right to expect that we shall enter heaven triumphantly with Christ. Do we appreciate the benefits of baptism and live worthy of so great a grace?

Baptism is not an empty ceremony. It is a call to martyrdom for Christ. Are we strong enough for this? Are we detached from the things of the world? Are our lives truly mortified? Can we say with St. Paul: "I count all things to be but loss for the excellent knowledge of Jesus Christ my Lord; for whom I have suffered the loss of all things and count them but as dung, that I may gain Christ, and may be found in Him, not having my justice which is of the law, but that which is of the faith of Christ Jesus, which is of God, justice in faith; that I may know Him and the power of His resurrection [that is, the glorious life which He now lives and which He imparts to His own] and the fellowship of His sufferings [that is, to suffer with Christ], being made conformable to His death, if by any means I may attain to the resurrection which is from the dead" (Phil 3:8–11)?

"Christ, rising again from the dead, dieth now no more, alleluia; death shall no more have dominion over Him, alleluia, alleluia" (Communion). In the mind of the liturgy, the mystical Christ, the Church, now dies no more. To be a good Christian, to receive Holy Communion worthily and frequently, implies the complete separation from sin. This idea is impressed upon us by the Easter liturgy. "If you be risen with Christ [through baptism], seek the things that are above.... You are dead [to sin], and your life is hid with Christ in God" (Col 3:1 ff.; Epistle of Holy Saturday). "Purge out the old leaven that you may be a new paste.... Let us feast ... with the unleavened bread of sincerity and truth" (1 Cor 5:7 f.; Epistle of Easter Sunday).

Prayer

O God, who dost gladden us with the yearly solemnity of the Lord's resurrection, grant in Thy loving kindness that through the temporal feast which we keep we may be worthy to reach eternal joys. Through the same Christ our Lord. Amen.

Thursday

Eight days ago the penitents received absolution and were readmitted to communion with the Church. This reconciliation took place in the church of the Twelve Apostles. In this same church we gather every ember Friday to weep over our sins with Magdalen, the penitent. The church of the Twelve Apostles has a close relationship with St. Mary Magdalen, for at the tomb of the risen Savior, Mary was made an apostle: "Go to My brethren [the apostles] and say to them: I ascend to My Father and to your Father." The liturgy lingers about the tomb today with the penitent Magdalen, to whom Christ first appeared after appearing to His mother. At Mass the Lord comes to us as He came to Mary at the tomb.

"Mary stood at the sepulcher without, weeping. Now as she was weeping, she stooped down and looked into the sepulcher; and she saw two angels in white.... They said to her: Woman, why weepest thou? She saith to them: Because they have taken away my Lord, and I know not where they have laid Him. When she had thus said, she turned herself back and saw Jesus standing; and she knew not that it was Jesus" (Gospel). St. Gregory thus comments on this touching incident:

Mary Magdalen, who had been a sinner in the city, by loving the Truth washed away the stains of her crime with her tears.... "Many sins are forgiven her, because she has loved much" (Lk 7:47). She who formerly had remained cold in her sin, afterwards became fervent with holy love.... Of the disciples [who had come to the tomb] it is written: "The disciples therefore departed again to their home" (Jn 20:10). And then is added: "But Mary stood at the sepulcher without, weeping." What a great love glows in the heart of this woman, who did not leave the tomb even though the disciples left!... She sought Him in tears, and inflamed with the fire of love, she burned with yearning for Him whom she thought had been taken away. Thus it happened that she alone then saw Him, she who alone had remained to seek Him.

The former sinner, the penitent, is the chosen one of the Lord. She is allowed to see Him because she has loved much and because she remained to seek Him. The sign of real virtue is perseverance. "He that shall persevere to the end, he shall be saved" (Mt 24:13). Would that we had such a longing for Christ as Magdalen had! Would that we could love as she loved! Our hearts are filled with worldly desires, and we have little room left for Christ. We are so attached to the foolishness and emptiness of the world that we have no love for Christ.

"Why weepest thou? Whom seekest thou?" Christ asks Magdalen. She thinks that it is the gardener addressing her, and she says to Him, "Sir, if thou hast taken Him hence, tell me where thou hast laid Him, and I will take Him away. Jesus saith to her: Mary. She, turning, saith to Him: Rabboni (which is to say, Master)." She then casts herself at His feet, seeking to kiss and embrace them. Now she thinks she will never lose Him whom she has found. Christ does not permit this expression of her love. She has more important duties now. "Go to My brethren and say to them: I ascend to My Father" (Gospel). Mary obeys at once. She tears herself away from Him whom she loves and brings the glad news to the apostles. "Congratulate me, all you who love the Lord; for He whom I sought has appeared to me. And I saw the Lord as I wept at the tomb, alleluia, alleluia. Although the disciples went away, I did not leave, and glowing with the fire of love for Him, I burned with longing for Him. And I saw the Lord as I wept at the tomb, alleluia, alleluia" (Responsory at Matins).

Today the Lord appears to us in the Mass and calls us by name as He once called Magdalen. He called us by this name first when we were baptized. Today we should come to the Communion rail with a longing similar to Mary's. We must persevere even when He appears to withdraw from us and when He no longer allows us to experience the comfort of His presence. We should submit our heart to all His wishes and all His desires.

When we have recognized Him and received Him in Holy Communion, we also become apostles. Our mission is to love our neighbor. By our zeal in the practice of fraternal charity we give testimony to the world that Christ is risen and that He continues to live and work in us, the members of His mystical body. Having done penance, Magdalen now knows only the joy of possessing Jesus. We must share her joy.

Prayer

O God, who hast united different peoples in the confession of Thy name, grant that there may be one faith in the mind and one piety in the deeds of those born again in the waters of baptism. Through Christ our Lord. Amen.

Friday

Today we are led by the neophytes to the church of St. Mary of the Martyrs. Here we behold Mary surrounded by a glorious group of martyrs. She is the same one whom we greeted a few days ago under the cross on Calvary as the Sorrowful Mother, the Queen of martyrs. Today we take part in spirit in the appearance of Christ which is related in the Gospel.

Jesus appears to His disciples. "At that time the eleven disciples went into Galilee, unto the mountain where Jesus had appointed them; and seeing Him, they adored; but some doubted.

And Jesus, coming, spoke to them, saying: All power is given to Me in heaven and on earth. Going, therefore, teach ye all nations, baptizing them, . . . teaching them to observe all things whatsoever I have commanded you. And behold I am with you all days, even to the consummation of the world" (Gospel). The disciples, following His orders, gathered there at the mountain which He had designated beforehand. They were rewarded by seeing Him. They recognize Him as the same Jesus with whom they had lived so intimately for several years, whom the Jews had rejected and put to death so cruelly. But now He is risen, and He lives. He speaks to them these consoling words: "All power is given to Me in heaven and on earth." He has unlimited power, to which He is entitled not only as God, but also as man, for He is the Lord and shares the authority and the glory of the Father. We congratulate Him on this glorification and confess in the Gloria of the Mass: "Thou alone art the Lord. Thou alone art the Most High, together with the Holy Ghost, in the glory of God the Father."

Christ passes His authority on to His apostles. "Teach ye all nations." The apostles and their successors, the bishops, are the official teachers of the Church, duly appointed and commissioned by Christ for that purpose. They are the custodians of the truth which He brought, and the guardians of His doctrine. "He that heareth you, heareth Me; and he that despiseth you, despiseth Me" (Lk 10:16). They have been sent to save men and to lead them to eternal life. For this work Christ gave them His authority and assured them of His continual assistance. "Behold I am with you all days, even to the consummation of the world." The risen Christ lives in His Church. He to whom all power is given in heaven and on earth abides with His Church and guarantees her infallibility, integrity, and holiness. He is with His Church to defend her from all her enemies. "The gates of hell shall not prevail against [her]" (Mt 16:18). Storms will buffet the Church, but we must have confidence in her, for "I am with you all days even to the consummation of the world." We confess our faith in the Credo of the Mass.

Christ appears to us in the Church. Today in the liturgy we are the disciples whom the Lord is to meet at the mountain (the altar, the tabernacle). We received His command and followed Him to the mountain, and we shall be rewarded, for at the Consecration He will appear to us. We fall down and adore Him. This is indeed He whom we saw hanging on the cross in pain and agony, the man of sorrows. But He is risen, and from our altar He speaks to us: "All power is given to Me in heaven and on earth." He has power over the elements, over all human ills, over the hearts of men, and over the evil spirits. He has power over the enemy of our salvation, over our passions, and over our self-love. "All power is given to Me." From the mountain of our altar He reassures us, "Behold I am with you all days." He is with us, for His love and His kindly providence accompany us everywhere. He is with us, for His strength helps us to overcome evil and to practice virtue. He is with us, enlightening us and inspiring us to virtue. What have we to fear? We may always come for help to the mountain He has pointed out to us. We believe in His readiness to help us, in His unlimited power, and His undying love. We are confident of His ability to protect us, and of His will to sanctify us.

"Going, therefore, teach ye all nations . . . to observe all things whatsoever I have commanded you." When we receive baptism, we become subjects of the Church, and she has authority to teach us all things whatsoever Christ has commanded her, and to require our obedience.

She cannot make exceptions with regard to His laws and commandments. For if she did, she would cease to be the Church of Christ. We who have accepted baptism from her are subject to her rules and commandments as well as to those of Christ. We cannot appeal from the Church to Christ. We cannot withdraw from her authority or reject her teaching without withdrawing from Christ. "He that heareth you, heareth Me; and he that despiseth you, despiseth Me." Christ and His Church are one. I am loyal to Christ in the measure that I am loyal to His Church. I can depend on His guidance and presence in so far as I submit to the Church.

"Going, teach ye all nations," the Communion tells us. We who have received the body of Christ are called upon to be apostles and missionaries; we are to be apostles of prayer, and missionaries through our works of expiation, our holy life, and our good example. We receive the grace to carry out our mission in Holy Communion, when He comes to us with the fullness of His power and fills us with His life. His power must go out from us to sanctify and enlighten others as often as we go to Holy Communion.

Prayer

Almighty and eternal God, who in the covenant of man's atonement hast bestowed the paschal sacrament, grant that what we outwardly celebrate we may imitate effectually. Through Christ our Lord. Amen.

Saturday

In ancient times the neophytes gathered on this day in the Lateran Basilica, the church in which they were baptized on Holy Saturday. In this same church they laid aside the white baptismal robes, which were then put away in the treasury of the church to be preserved as a pledge of the loyalty of those who had worn them, and to be produced as evidence against those who proved unfaithful to their baptismal promises. The baptismal garment symbolized the putting off of the old man and the putting on of the new.

"Laying away all malice and all guile, and dissimulations and envies, and all detractions" (Epistle). Thus also did the Lord at His resurrection leave behind Him the garments in which He had been wrapped. From the linens left behind, the apostles Peter and John recognized the place where He had lain, when they visited the tomb on Easter morning. "And they both ran together, and that other disciple did outrun Peter and came first to the sepulcher. And when he stooped down, and saw the linen cloths lying, but yet he went not in. Then cometh Simon Peter, following him, and went into the sepulcher and saw the linen cloths lying, and the napkins that had been about His head, not lying with the linen cloths, but apart, wrapped up into one place. Then that other disciple also went in, who came first to the sepulcher, and he saw and believed" (Gospel). The liturgy wishes to tell us that we Christians must lay aside all malice and guile and evil detraction. When we have done this, the Church will acknowledge that we have laid aside the old man in the waters of baptism and have risen with Christ. The liturgy wishes us to be true Christians. She wishes us to prove our Christianity by deeds, "laying away all malice and all guile, and dissimulations and envies, and all detractions."

The Epistle describes in detail the characteristics of the new man which we must put on, the ideal Christian. "As newborn babes, desire the rational milk [of Christian doctrine and Christian principles] ... that thereby you may grow unto salvation; if so be you have tasted that the Lord is sweet. Unto whom coming as to a living stone, rejected indeed by men but chosen and made honorable by God; be you also as living stones built up, a spiritual house, a holy priesthood, to offer up spiritual sacrifices, acceptable to God by Jesus Christ.... The same is made the head of the corner; and a stone of stumbling and a rock of scandal to them who stumble at the word [the gospel of Christ], neither do believe.... But you are a chosen generation, a kingly priesthood, a holy nation, a purchased people [by the death of Christ]; that you may declare His virtues, who hath called you out of darkness into His marvelous light; who in time past were not a people, but are now the people of God." This is the ideal Christian. This is the new man who is incorporated in Christ through baptism. Would that we could shape our souls after the model given us in the Epistle! Would that we truly understood our dignity as Christians, the importance of our incorporation in Christ, the sublimity of our kingly priesthood! It is our vocation to declare His wondrous deeds and to proclaim that He has called us to His wonderful life.

Full of joy the Church greets the neophytes as they offer their gifts at the altar. "Blessed is He that cometh in the name of the Lord. We have blessed you out of the house of the Lord" (Offertory). To Him I consecrate myself; for Him I shall live. "He hath shone upon us, alleluia." We walk in His life. "The Lord brought forth His people with joy, alleluia; and His chosen ones with gladness, alleluia" (Introit). "This is the day which the Lord hath made; let us rejoice and be glad therein, alleluia. Praise the Lord, O ye His servants" (Gradual).

"All you who have been baptized in Christ, have put on Christ, alleluia" (Communion). For the liturgy the reception of Holy Communion is putting on Christ. We laid aside the visible baptismal garments; but in place of them we make our whole life an invisible garment that should never be laid aside. "You have put on Christ." As in baptism we have become a branch of the vine, so in the reception of Holy Communion this union is deepened and renewed. In virtue of this Communion we shall live the life of Christ and put on His manner, His virtue, His purity. "I live, now not I, but Christ liveth in me" (Gal 2:20). This new life the liturgy expects of the baptized.

Prayer

Grant, we beseech Thee, O almighty God, that we who have kept the Easter festivities with veneration, may by them be found worthy to come to eternal joy. Through Christ our Lord. Amen.

First Sunday after Easter

The Mass

The Masses of Easter week refer frequently to the newly baptized. Clothed in their white robes, the neophytes have been coming daily to the Holy Sacrifice. Yesterday, on Saturday of Easter week, they laid aside these garments, which are still preserved in a nearby room as mute but eloquent witnesses of their baptism and of the obligations thereby undertaken. Today, on what is known as Alb Sunday, they appear for the first time without the baptismal robes. The Holy Sacrifice of the Mass is celebrated in the church of St. Pancratius, the youthful martyr who sealed his baptismal vows with his blood. Pancratius died at the age of fourteen years. Those who gather in his church today see his image looking down at them from the walls of his church and feel his spirit hovering over them. All those who have just received baptism, and we also, should feel inspired to keep our baptismal vows as faithfully as Pancratius did his.

The Church addresses the neophytes today with motherly tenderness and thinks of them as "newborn babes, desiring the rational milk" (Introit) of the Holy Eucharist, the fruit of the Holy Sacrifice. This thirst is created in those who receive baptism, who long for the time of Mass that they may participate in the sacrificial meal of Holy Communion. From their lips breaks forth the song, "Rejoice to God our helper; sing aloud to the God of Jacob" (Introit). This should be our song, too, on Alb Sunday, when we renew our baptismal vows. Today, full of joy, we gather with the newly baptized and sing the Gloria: "Glory to God in the highest."

In the Collect we pray that we may keep faithfully and seal with our lives what was wrought in us by baptism and by Holy Communion. In baptism we received the gift of faith, of whose power the Epistle reminds us today: "Who is he that overcometh the world, but he that believeth that Jesus is the Son of God?" We profess our faith in that doctrine when we receive baptism. We also have the means of strengthening us in the faith and the help to overcome the most powerful weapons of the enemy. We receive the strength to overcome the temptations which weaken and crush other men. With St. Thomas the apostle we fall on our knees and confess Christ, "My Lord and my God." "Blessed are they that have not seen and have believed" (Gospel).

Having professed our faith in the Credo, we are ready for the Offertory procession and for the act of sacrifice. We now approach the altar as the holy women approached the sepulcher on Easter morning. We bring as our gift our hearts filled with love and faith. The angel greets us. "He whom you seek is risen" (Offertory). In the Consecration of the Mass He will appear in our midst as the living God. As an expression of our faith in Him we sing the Sanctus, greeting Him as the Savior who comes in the name of the Lord.

As He greeted the apostles gathered in the upper room, He greets us now, "Peace be to you" (Gospel). He shows us His hands and His feet. Joyfully we confess Him to be the risen Christ, the source of all grace and all salvation. "My Lord and my God." Full of faith we take Him in our hands as our offering. At the altar we offer Him to God as our gift. "Through Him, and with Him, and in Him is to Thee, O God, the Father Almighty, in the unity of the Holy Ghost, all honor and glory." Having become so perfectly united to Him, we may now pray with Him and through His lips. "Our Father, who art in heaven.... Give us this day our daily bread" in Holy Communion. In Holy Communion we touch the wounds of Christ with St. Thomas the apostle, and through this contact we receive divine life in proportion to our faith. Thus is satisfied the yearning for the rational milk, of which the Epistle speaks. With grateful hearts we answer the deacon's *Ite missa est* with a joyful *Deo gratias:* "Thanks be to God." Blessed are they that believe.

Meditation

Yesterday the neophytes laid aside their white garments, and today they appear for the first time in their ordinary clothes. They are now full-fledged Christians. Their last stational procession leads them to the sanctuary of St. Pancratius, the youthful martyr who sealed his baptism with his blood. Here they promise to keep their baptismal vows faithfully until death.

"Whatsoever is born of God overcometh the world" (Epistle). In baptism we are "born of God." We must overcome the world; that is, we must stand aloof from the world. "All that is in the world is the concupiscence of the flesh, and the concupiscence of the eyes, and the pride of life" (1 Jn 2:16). But we are born of God; we are of a divine race, of heavenly nobility. Therefore we must rise above what is earthly. Indeed we scorn the world and what it offers. We know that we are the children of God. God is for us; who, then, in the world can harm us? "If God be for us, who is against us?... Who, then, shall separate us from the love of Christ? Shall tribulation, or distress, or famine, or nakedness, or danger, or persecution, or the sword?... In all these things we overcome because of Him that hath loved us" (Rom 8:335, 37). What can the things of this world profit us? "He who knows that he is the child of God can have no regard for human greatness and immense wealth. He who admires anything less than God falls from the heights of his nobility" (St. Cyprian). Because we are born of God, we must lift ourselves above the world, its goods, and its interests. We must not let our ideals degenerate, and we must not lower ourselves from the lofty position which is ours as children of God. We have overcome the world; for "whatsoever is born of God overcometh the world."

"This is the victory which overcometh the world, our faith. Who is he that overcometh the world, but he that believeth that Jesus is the Son of God?" (Epistle.) There are men who allow themselves to be led and directed by their senses; others are led by their reason. But neither of these know the sublimity and riches of the children of God. This can be understood only by those who have a lively faith in Jesus, the Son of God. Such men desire only what God desires. They know no higher destiny than to follow in the footsteps of Christ, to follow Him who is the way, the truth, and the life, "in whom are hid all the treasures of wisdom and knowledge" (Col 2:3). They love what Christ loves. They choose what Christ chose — voluntary poverty, suffering, privation, and the cross. To them Jesus is the Son of God, the infallible truth, the Wisdom of God. The deeper this faith becomes, the higher it lifts us above the transitory and trivial things of this world. "The just man liveth by faith" (Rom 1:17). "I live, now not I; but Christ liveth in me. And that I live now in the flesh; I live in the faith of the Son of God, who loved me and delivered Himself for me" (Gal 2:20).

The apostle Thomas could not believe that the Lord was truly risen and that He had appeared to the apostles. He insisted on seeing His wounds and touching them with his hands. "Except I shall see in His hands the print of the nails, and put my finger into the place of the nails, and put my hand into His side, I will not believe" (Gospel). Eight days after this avowal by St. Thomas, Christ appeared again to the apostles, and calling to Thomas, He said: "Put in thy finger hither, and see My hands, and bring hither thy hand and put it into My side, and be not faithless but believing" (Gospel). Thomas fell to his knees, exclaiming, "My Lord and my God." And our Lord replied, "Because thou hast seen Me Thomas, thou hast believed; blessed are they that have not seen and have believed." Christ demands faith. Only he who has a strong faith can conquer the world.

The Easter garments have been laid aside. Now the Church prays for the newly baptized and for us, that we may retain the graces we received at Easter, and practice them in our daily life. Easter is a feast that should not be allowed to pass away. We must conquer the selfish desires that come to us daily. Resurrection! To be risen means to be free, independent, and detached from the world and all it can offer. To be risen means to rejoice in the belief that He is risen to whom is given all power in heaven and on earth. To be risen means to share the victorious power of God, and to be convinced that Christ is God. The prince of this world and all his minions are already judged and condemned. If we are risen, then we must remember that we have received pardon for our sins and that we enjoy the sonship of God. This sonship is the pledge of eternal life and an earnest of our heritage in heaven. Once we have risen, we must know that God is our Father and that His power rules the world. He knows every plot and every scheme that the impure evil one has concocted against the pure ones of the earth. If our Easter is to be perfect, it must transfigure our lives and soothe our troubles and cares.

Prayer

Grant, we beseech Thee, O almighty God, that we who have celebrated the paschal solemnity, may by Thy bounty show forth its effects in our life and conduct. Through Christ our Lord. Amen.

Monday

Today with grateful hearts we recall the joy and graces of our first Holy Communion. Our first Holy Communion was most intimately connected with our baptism. On Low Sunday we should renew our baptismal vows: "I renounce Satan, and sin, and the world with all its vanities." And "I believe in God the Father, and in Jesus Christ, and in God the Holy Ghost, and in the Holy Catholic Church." For this great day the liturgy proposes for our consideration at Matins the words of St. Paul to the Colossians:

"Therefore, if you be risen with Christ, seek the things that are above, where Christ is sitting at the right hand of God. Mind the things that are above, not the things that are upon the earth. For you are dead; and your life is hid with Christ in God. When Christ shall appear, who is your life, then you also shall appear with Him in glory. Mortify therefore your members which are upon the earth: fornication, uncleanness, lust, evil concupiscence, and covetousness, which is the service of idols. For which things the wrath of God cometh upon the children of unbelief; in which you also walked some time, when you lived in them. But now [since you have been baptized] put you also all away: anger, indignation, malice, blasphemy, filthy speech out of your mouth. Lie not one to another; stripping yourselves of the old man with his deeds, and putting on the new, him who is renewed unto knowledge, according to the image of Him that created him.... Put ye on therefore, as the elect of God, holy and beloved, the bowels of mercy, benignity, humility, modesty, patience; bearing with one another, and forgiving one another, if any have a complaint against another; even as the Lord hath forgiven you, so do you also. But above all these things have charity, which is the bond of perfection. And let the peace of Christ rejoice in your hearts wherein also you are called in one body; and be ye thankful. Let the word of Christ dwell in you abundantly, in all wisdom, teaching and admonishing one another in psalms, hymns, and spiritual canticles, singing in grace in your hearts to God. All whatsoever you do in word or in work, do all in the name of the Lord Jesus Christ, giving thanks to God and the Father by Him" (Col 3:1–17).

Our reception of Holy Communion, like our reception of baptism, should not be a mere passive reception. We must also give something, make our contribution to the offering made by the Lord in the Holy Sacrifice. In order to receive worthily, we must place ourselves in a sacrificial state of mind, as St. Paul so often reminds us. Just before the Christians in the ancient Church received the sacred host from the priest in their outstretched hand, they crossed both arms on their breasts in the form of a cross. Thus they reminded themselves of their duty to offer themselves as a sacrifice when they received Holy Communion. In Holy Communion we receive all and we must give all. Is that truly our attitude? We should make our own the sentiments expressed by the famous French bishop, Bossuet:

Come to me, O holy body of my Redeemer. Come, O burning coal, and purge my lips. Inflame my soul with the love that impelled You to accomplish my redemption. Come, O precious blood which flowed forth from the sacred body, and envelop my heart with Your fire. O my Savior, this is truly Thy body which was so cruelly lacerated. Would that I might share each of Thy wounds with Thee! For through them Thou hast poured forth Thy blood for me. The world will have none of me, and it were much better for me had I nothing to do with it. We two are estranged, the world and I. Now I live for Christ, and He lives in me. At least it should be so. This should be the fruit of my Holy Communion. Alas, that I am yet so far from this ideal!

There is the tragedy. We receive Holy Communion so often, and yet offer to God and our Savior little more than a negligent, worldly life.

Prayer

We beseech Thee, O Lord, that through the reception of Thy most holy sacrament we may be made into a new creature in Christ our Lord. Amen.

Tuesday

"As newborn babes, alleluia, desire the rational milk without guile" (Introit). Thus the Church addresses the newly baptized on Low Sunday; thus she speaks to those who communicate and to all the faithful. To the Church we are throughout our lives merely "newborn babes."

"Unless you ... become as little children, you shall not enter into the kingdom of heaven"; that is, you cannot reach perfection. Such was Christ's answer to the question proposed by the apostles: "Who, thinkest thou, is the greater in the kingdom of heaven? And Jesus calling unto Him a little child, set him in the midst of them and said: Amen I say to you, unless you be converted and become as little children, you shall not enter into the kingdom of heaven. Whosoever therefore shall humble himself as this little child, he is the greater in the kingdom of heaven" (Mt 18:1–4). On another occasion Christ pointed to the Father in heaven saying: "Be you therefore perfect as also your heavenly Father is perfect" (Mt 5:48). We must all become like the pure, living God, and at the same time remain like the innocent child which reposes on the breast of its mother. The greatest man in the world is not the intellectual, nor the scholar, nor the performer of great deeds, nor the ruler, nor the man of wealth; but rather he who is in all appearances the most unimportant, the most unassuming, the most childlike — he who remains most like what he was when he proceeded from the hands of his heavenly Father. The greatest accomplishment in the life of a man, and in the life of a Christian, is to become humble and childlike. God treasures not our great accomplishments, our pretentious plans, and our mighty undertakings, nor even our great works of self-denial and penance, nor our lengthy prayers, nor even our many pious works. In themselves all these things do not honor God. All these can easily be poisoned and ruined by our pride and ambition and self-will. What God prizes most and what makes us truly great in the eyes of God, what opens to us the gates of the heavenly kingdom of grace, virtue, and perfection, is the possession of a childlike spirit.

Not without reason God began the great work of redemption by becoming a child. All sound spirituality begins with the spirit of childhood, and is based on that foundation. For this reason the liturgy cries out to us: "As newborn babes, desire the rational milk without guile." "Whosoever therefore shall humble himself as this little child, he is the greater in the kingdom of heaven." This is the viewpoint of God, of Holy Mother the Church, and of all the saints. We, too, should choose for ourselves the way of spiritual childhood, the way of simplicity.

He possesses this spirit of childhood and humility who, recognizing his own limitations and weaknesses, submits himself completely to those who occupy God's place in his regard. Such a one desires to be small, dependent, and unimportant. In the spirit of simplicity he believes what is told to him by others. He executes without question the commands given him by his superiors, and does not inquire why a thing should be done. He carries out without question the tasks imposed on him. Since he is filled with the spirit of faith, he does not exhaust himself with worrying about ways and means of accomplishing his tasks. The spirit of childhood causes him to die to his own wishes and to forget himself completely. Our spiritual progress depends largely on our ability to forget ourselves, not on our profound insight, lofty meditations, and great enlightenment. We advance in truth in the measure in which we renounce the world and even our own wishes and desires. Once we have reached spiritual childhood, we no longer view things with our own eyes. We abandon ourselves completely to the hand of providence. We proceed on our way without bothering to observe whether the way is precipitous, stony, or smooth; we look only at the hand that leads us, and pay no heed to the question of where or how we are being led. We forget ourselves completely, and rest secure in the arms and on the heart of our heavenly Father, just as the child rests secure on the bosom of its mother. If we have really reached spiritual childhood, we seek no opportunity to display our striking virtues before others. In this state we follow with heroic fidelity and self-sacrifice every inspiration of grace, every command of our superiors, every opportunity to undergo hardship, every occasion for mortification which God sends to us; we recognize the hand of God in everything that the day may bring, and we accept it all with complete and joyful self-sacrifice. For the sake of God we are filled with a spirit of kindness and friendliness no matter what our surroundings may be. God alone and what is pleasing to Him become our sole interest.

"Perfection appears easy to me. I see that it suffices to recognize one's own nothingness and to rest in the arms of God like a child. I rejoice in being small, for it is the children alone and those who become like little children who will be permitted to frequent the heavenly banquet."[15]

In the state of spiritual childhood, God is everything and man is nothing. In such a "child" God accomplishes all that He desires precisely as He desires it. In such a soul God finds no obstacle and no opposition. For this reason all true spiritual progress depends on the acquisition

[15] St. Theresa of the Child Jesus.

of the state of spiritual childhood. "God rejoices more over what He accomplishes in a soul that surrenders itself humbly in its poverty than He does in the creation of a million suns."[16] The state of spiritual childhood is a more perfect state even than that of patient suffering, since nothing subdues a man so thoroughly as the earnest and peaceful desire to be humble. By becoming as little children we shall reach the state of perfection. "Whosoever therefore shall humble himself as this little child, he is the greater in the kingdom of heaven."

Prayer

Grant, we beseech Thee, O almighty God, that we who have celebrated the paschal solemnity, may by Thy bounty show forth its effects in our life and conduct. Through Christ our Lord. Amen.

Wednesday

"As newborn babes, desire the rational milk without guile, that thereby you may grow unto salvation" (1 Pt 2:2). This is a forceful admonition to us that we should grow in the spiritual life.

"Being born again, not of corruptible seed, but incorruptible, by the word of God, who liveth and remaineth forever" (1 Pt 1:23). As a consequence of our spiritual rebirth, St. Peter concludes: "Wherefore, laying away all malice and all guile and dissimulations and envies and all detractions, as newborn babes, desire the rational milk without guile, that thereby you may grow unto salvation,... purifying your souls in the obedience of charity [that is, according to the prescriptions of the gospel], with a brotherly love, from a sincere heart, love one another earnestly" (1 Pt 2:1 f.; 1:22).

Rebirth in Christ eradicates in us the old man with his vices and self-seeking, with his malice and hypocrisy. It produces in us the new man, stifling self-love and implanting in our soul a love which binds us as brothers in Christ and unites us by an inner bond of charity. To the extent that we embrace this new life and let it operate in us, this rebirth makes us men of strength and heroism, men of patience, kindliness, and stability, men who are considerate and helpful, who are zealous in the practice of fraternal charity. "By this shall all men know that you are my disciples, if you have love one for another" (Jn 13:35).

"As newborn babes, desire the rational milk without guile." The positive element in this rebirth calls for a growth in the life of grace. Just as newborn babes long for their mother's milk, so should we long with a burning desire for spiritual food through which the life of the soul is strengthened and nourished. It is not enough to be born or reborn; we are born and then reborn that we may achieve our salvation and holiness and reach the full stature of our being. The nourishment by which we achieve this growth is the "rational milk without guile." the word of God which is revealed to us in the gospel and is presented again continually by the Church. The more readily we accept this word of the gospel, the more certain and the more rapid is our growth to full spiritual manhood. Thus we attain our full perfection in heaven.

"Desire the rational milk without guile." Just as the child longs eagerly for its mother's milk, once it has tasted its sweetness, so you also will long for the word of the gospel "if so be you

[16] Ibid.

have tasted that the Lord is sweet" (1 Pt 2:3). The rebirth which we experienced through our baptism is nourished in the steadfast and living desire for the word of the gospel, and by means of the nourishment thus obtained, we shall grow in holiness.

How does this spiritual rebirth affect our lives? Negatively, it cleanses us from all self-seeking and from everything within ourselves that hinders the practice of fraternal charity; positively, it arouses in us the burning desire for inner growth and a persistent and ever-increasing thirst for the word of the gospel. These desires are increased daily through the celebration of the liturgy, through which the Church seeks to enlighten us by the gospel. Here we shall find the nourishment without guile, which will serve our spiritual growth. The strength gained from this nourishment made the early Christians strong and heroic, and prepared them to be always ready to sacrifice their lives for Christ and their faith.

"Desire the rational milk without guile." Holy Mother the Church offers this milk of doctrine to us. To her Christ gave the commission, "Going therefore, teach ye all nations,... teaching them to observe all things whatsoever I have commanded you" (Mt 28:19 f.). The doctrine of the Church consists in those things "whatsoever I have commanded you"; it is the uncontaminated doctrine of Christ. For this reason Christ gave her the assurance of His abiding presence: "Behold I am with you all days even to the consummation of the world" (Mt 28:20). For this purpose He sends the Holy Spirit, the "Spirit of Truth" (Jn 15:26): "But when He, the Spirit of Truth is come He will teach you all truth.... He shall receive of Mine and shall show it to you" (Jn 16:13 f.). "He shall abide with you and shall be in you" (Jn 14:17). Christ assures the Church that "He that heareth you, heareth Me" (Lk 10:16).

Error is rampant in the world. False doctrines and divergent schools of thought seek to lead men away from God, from Christ, and from the gospel. They alienate men from the Church and leave them miserable. We are assured that we are in possession of the unadulterated truth as long as we cling to the Church, to her teachings, and her principles, and her liturgy. "Desire the rational milk without guile."

Prayer

We beseech Thee, O Lord our God, to make the most holy mysteries, which Thou hast given us to ensure our salvation, a remedy for us both now and in the future. Through Christ our Lord. Amen. (Postcommunion.)

Thursday

During the second week after Easter the liturgy lays great emphasis on the virtue of faith. "As newborn babes, desire the rational milk without guile" (Introit). "And this is the victory which over-cometh the world, our faith... [in the fact] that Jesus is the Son of God" (Epistle). In the Gospel the Lord reproaches the apostle Thomas for his unbelief. Thomas, falling on his knees before the Lord, confesses, "My Lord and my God." Jesus replies, "Because thou hast seen Me, Thomas, thou hast believed. Blessed are they that have not seen and have believed." The Communion prayer resumes the theme of the Gospel and calls out to us when we receive the Lord, "Put in thy hand and know the place of the nails, and be not faithless, but believing."

As newborn babes, yet wise by reason of faith! In the measure in which we acquire a childlike spirit, our faith becomes proportionately stronger and more perfect. Christianity is founded on faith. Faith is the beginning of salvation and the basis of all Christian thought. All Christian reasoning, all Christian values, all Christian undertakings, all Christian life, spring from the virtue of faith. Faith includes more than the mere conviction that God, the Supreme Being, exists. Faith requires that we accept and conform our lives to all those things which God has commanded us to accept. We must accept all His commands on faith, simply because God has spoken. By faith we make an offering of our whole being to God and subject ourselves to Him in the spirit of sacrifice. We make a voluntary renunciation of our own understanding and accept all that God reveals, out of a deep veneration for His infallibility. It is indeed no small matter to consecrate oneself to God as a sacrifice, together with all one's thoughts and desires; yet we do this by our faith. We do even more. To believe in God means to make Him our highest and greatest goal, the goal upon which we center all our thought and actions, all of our strivings, our whole life. We make ourselves and our whole life completely dependent on Him, and strive with all the strength of our heart and mind to serve Him. To believe in God means that a man must give himself and all that he is over to God and serve Him with a service that can be rendered to God alone. Only he can believe in God in this manner who possesses the Christian faith; and he who possesses this faith must make God the center of all his thoughts and desires. He must subject himself to God, to His every word and command, to His inspirations and guidance. Do we have such a faith?

"This is the victory which overcometh the world, our faith." But our faith in God has various degrees and stages of perfection. We should strive to attain to perfect faith, that "which overcometh the world." We have reached the first degree of faith when we live according to the maxims of the faith. "Faith ... if it have not works, is dead in itself" (Jas 2:17). He who knows the will of his master, but fails to carry it out, he who has the name of the Lord on his lips, but dishonors Him by his deeds, is worthy of greater punishment than he who has learned nothing of the faith. "Not every one that saith to Me, Lord, Lord, shall enter into the kingdom of heaven; but he that doth the will of My Father who is in heaven, he shall enter into the kingdom of heaven" (Mt 7:21).

To be joyful and free in our faith is the second degree of faith. He who lives by faith as the child in the house of his father, as the free man in his home, feels nothing of the burden of faith which the slave finds so onerous. The realms of faith become for him a familiar region, and he moves about in the light of faith with a naturalness and ease which others would find difficult or impossible. Even the regulations of spirit and heart, which faith imposes, become familiar and do not become burdensome.

To live by faith is the third and final stage in our growth in faith. Faith lives in us, and we live by faith. "In the head of the book it is written of me that I should do Thy will; O my God, I have desired it, and Thy law in the midst of my heart" (Ps 39:8 f.). Those who live according to faith need make no laborious search to discover the will of God. Without compulsion and, as it were, by instinct they sense God's presence and recognize the hand of God in everything that befalls them, be it sweet or bitter, welcome or unwelcome. They have no need of artificial means for placing themselves in the presence of God. They feel themselves in the presence of God even when they are engaged in the most absorbing work, or when they are surrounded on all sides by men of the world. Their life, both day and night, is a burning flame of love that consumes them in the service of God. Faith is no longer something exterior to them, but becomes the very soul of their life. It is this kind of faith that makes saints. Once we possess such faith, we readily overcome the world with its lusts and its self-love, and we allow ourselves no rest until we have complied with every law and every counsel which faith presents to us to arouse our love and our generosity.

Because we live by faith and according to the rules of faith, the world attacks us who are Christians. The world cannot endure the spirit which inspires us as Christians, because our world is in the realm of faith. The knowledge of it is not "found in the land of them that live in delights" (Jb 28:13). The more we are misunderstood and abused by the world, the more we ought to thank God, for persecution is a good indication that God has endowed us with His spirit.

We must treasure and love the faith with which we were filled at the time of our baptism. We must not rest until it has pervaded our very flesh and blood, until we live by faith alone.

Prayer

Grant, we beseech Thee, O almighty God, that we who have celebrated the paschal solemnity, may by Thy bounty show forth its effects in our life and conduct. Through Christ our Lord. Amen.

Friday

"At that time, when it was late that same day [Easter Sunday], the first of the week, and the doors were shut, where the disciples were gathered together for fear of the Jews, Jesus came, and stood in the midst, and said to them: Peace be to you. And when He had said this, He showed them His hands and His side. The disciples therefore were glad when they saw the Lord. He said therefore to them again: Peace be to you. As the Father hath sent Me, I also send you. When He had said this, He breathed on them, and He said to them: Receive ye the Holy Ghost; whose sins you shall forgive, they are forgiven them, and whose sins you shall retain, they are retained" (Gospel).

The sacrament of penance is the gift of the risen Christ to His Church. St. Jerome calls it a "second plank after our shipwreck," and Tertullian refers to it as "an arduous baptism." It is a marvelous means of salvation for those baptized.

"Whose sins you shall forgive, they are forgiven them." Christ sacrificed even His life for the salvation of men. Could He have done more for us? Should not the remembrance of the crucified One and the memory of His death for us inspire us with so great a love that we could never sin again? We have, moreover, the strength and the grace provided by the Eucharist, through which He gives Himself to us for the nourishment of our souls. Does not the Eucharist have the power to sanctify us so that we can overcome all sin, so that sin can no longer have any part in us? But Christ, knowing the weakness and the wickedness of men, approaches His Church on Easter night and provides her with yet another means for the remission of sin, for the healing of the wounds caused by sin, and for strengthening us against sin. He gives us the sacrament of forgiveness, of mercy, of reconciliation, a means whereby we may regain peace with God and with ourselves. "Peace be to you." This holy sacrament is His Easter greeting to His apostles, to His Church, and to us. He thus provides a new proof of His love and solicitude for us. He wishes to enrich us with grace and grant us forgiveness, even when we have been unfaithful.

"Peace be to you." He sets no limits to the number of times we may receive this sacrament, for He knows only too well our weakness and our instability. Neither does He set any limit on His mercy in this sacrament. There is no sin, however frightful, which cannot be forgiven. Even venial sins and the daily minor failings of which we are guilty, are matter for this sacrament. "Whose sins you shall forgive, they are forgiven them." Christ's mercy in giving us this sacrament shows us how concerned He is that we become incorporated in Him through baptism and the Eucharist. He wills that we be free from all sin and live as pure children of God. He desires that we begin a new life, free of all sin or infidelity to the Father. Would that we might carry out His designs!

Mortal sin breaks and interrupts the organic and vital union of the baptized with Christ; it separates the member from the head; it shears off the branch from the vine. Just as baptism unites us to Christ the head, and elevates us so that we can participate through Christ in the divine life of the Father and the Holy Spirit, so grievous sin destroys our vital union with Christ the head, and thus also our union with God. In the moment of sin we cease to be children of God, the objects of His benevolence and loving providence. We become loathsome and displeasing to Him. He can no longer take up His abode in our souls. He is obliged to cast us off as once He turned His face from Adam and Eve in Paradise and drove them from His presence. We are cast forth from the kingdom of light; we cease to be children of God; we are hurled down into the ugly abyss of sin. Our "end is destruction" (Phil 3:19).

But the Lord came in order that we "may have life" (Jn 10:10), that holy life that overcomes the world and death; the same life that He had after His Resurrection. On Easter day He instituted the holy sacrament of penance, through the power of which our union with Christ, broken by sin, is re-established. By this means we are reinstated in grace and become again living members of the mystical body of Christ. "I desire not the death of the wicked, but that the wicked turn from his way and live" (Ez 33:11).

We acknowledge with gratitude and faith the precious Easter gift which the Lord has given us in the sacrament of penance. We recognize the apostles and their successors, the bishops and priests, as having the commission and the power to forgive or retain our sins. They are, therefore, placed over us as judges of our conscience. Because of these Easter gifts we subject ourselves in obedience and with confidence to the priests who have been placed over us. From them we seek and receive the forgiveness of our faults.

Since the Lord receives us in the sacrament of His mercy with so much love and solicitude, it is fitting that we respond to His advances with a like generosity. Knowing the importance and the efficacy of this sacrament, we should be eager to use it for the salvation of our soul and the enrichment of our spiritual life.

Prayer

Grant, we beseech Thee, O almighty God, that we who have celebrated the paschal solemnity, may by Thy bounty show forth its effects in our life and conduct. Through Christ our Lord. Amen.

Saturday

"Except I shall see in His hands the print of the nails, and put my finger into the place of the nails, and put my hand into His side, I will not believe." Thomas must see to believe. The Lord deals with this weakness in His disciple with a condescension that is striking. Nevertheless He does not fail to admonish him, "Because thou hast seen Me, Thomas, thou hast believed; blessed are they that have not seen and have believed" (Gospel).

Thomas is the representative of that vast throng of men who refuse to accept the testimony of the gospel or of the Church. They accept nothing but that which they can see with their own eyes and touch with their own hands. Thomas is also typical of all those who, though they accept the testimony of the gospel and of the Church, yet in practical life never rise above a purely natural level in their thinking and in their outlook on life. They recite the Creed with the Church, but they lack the spirit of faith. Many Christians and many Catholics have such an attitude. They reason, judge, speak, and act in exactly the same manner as the world about them thinks and acts. Practically speaking, they have no higher ideal than any other man of the world. They are satisfied with health, prosperity, a livelihood, an interesting occupation, and amusing pastimes. When they encounter anything unpleasant or when they suffer hardships, they look about for a scapegoat, disclaiming all personal responsibility, and exhaust all the means at hand to escape from that which is hard or unpleasant. There is nothing supernatural in their point of view or in their manner of acting.

The majority of Christians and of Catholics who subscribe fervently to the creed of the Church, allow themselves to be governed by worldly considerations, by the opinion of their superiors, or by the claims of their worldly occupations, or the needs of their human career. Their actions are governed by human respect; they are swayed by any emotion; and they are covered with a mantle of self-love and pride. Even those consecrated to God and living behind the walls of the cloister are often ruled by purely natural motives far more than they themselves suspect. More than they are aware of it, their actions are governed by self-love in its manifold forms, rather than by motives of faith and the love of God. They live lives that are far from being supernatural. They do not live, as they should, by faith, with their gaze fixed on Christ, on God, and on His holy will. For this reason they experience so much unrest, so much uncertainty, such instability, weakness, and emptiness in their spiritual life. "Blessed are they that have not seen and have believed."

"Know also this, that in the last days shall come dangerous times. Men shall be lovers of themselves, covetous, haughty, proud, blasphemers, disobedient to parents, ungrateful, wicked, without affection, without peace, slanderers, incontinent, unmerciful, without kindness, traitors, stubborn, puffed up, and lovers of pleasures more than of God; having an appearance indeed of godliness, but denying the power thereof" (2 Tm 3:1–5). We are tempted to believe that the evil times described here by St. Paul have already arrived. Even in the very strongholds of piety, many pious and spiritual persons have become worldly and exert themselves only in the search for pleasure. They measure life in terms of the senses. Theirs is a piety which is little more than a continuous interplay of sensations and emotions. Such piety naturally shrinks from difficulties, exertions, and self-sacrifice. It occupies itself with spiritual things, even with prayer and the sacraments, only as a means of satisfying its emotional needs. The soul is thus deprived of the benefits it should reap from these exercises. The reward of such effort is merely a desolate spiritual dryness and an enduring emptiness. "One encounters scarcely a single person," says St. John of the Cross, "who escapes this tyranny of the senses."

Such souls barely scratch the surface of life; superficiality rules their life of prayer, their work, and their fulfillment of the duties of their state of life. They cannot rise to God, for they are bound to earth by fetters of superficiality. They can never look into the depths, because their attention is always distracted by trivialities. They are warped and become such slaves of minor details that their condition is often ridiculous. They are cast about from side to side, and become continually weaker. They multiply their prayers, increase their efforts and their spiritual exercises; but all this serves merely to dissipate their strength and squander their energy. They have "an appearance indeed of godliness, but deny the power thereof." Such miserable, unfruitful souls have built their spiritual edifice on feelings and emotions rather than on the spirit and the firm foundation of faith. Since they live without having fixed their gaze on God and His love, since they neglect His providence and His will, there is no depth to their piety, no strength or security or stability in their souls. "Blessed are they that have not seen and have believed."

"This is the victory which overcometh the world, our faith" (Epistle). The spirit of faith makes us consider everything we encounter in the light of God and His divine providence. It makes us accept everything as coming from His eternal solicitude and by His divine appointment. Faith gives us enlightenment, solidity, understanding, and peace. "Blessed are they that … have believed."

That new life which we received at Easter (that is, when we were baptized), we should strive to increase daily through the celebration of Mass and the devout reception of Holy Communion. We may enrich our spiritual life further by holy reading and the practice of other spiritual exercises. Even when we have done these things, we shall yet remain far from our goal, which is to live entirely by faith. Only when we have reached that goal will we be able to truly celebrate "the paschal solemnity" (Collect).

Prayer

Grant, we beseech Thee, O almighty God, that we who have celebrated the paschal solemnity, may by Thy bounty show forth its effects in our life and conduct. Through Christ our Lord. Amen.

Second Sunday after Easter

The Mass

Since the joyful return of the alleluia in the Mass of Holy Saturday, we have been celebrating the Easter season (*tempus paschale*). It is a period in which the Church rejoices in the resurrection and ascension of Christ, and in the perfect redemption consummated by the descent of the Holy Ghost. In this holy season we consider ourselves as having risen with Christ. We are redeemed, freed from all sin and from all earthly servitude. "Therefore, if you be risen with Christ, seek the things that are above, where Christ is sitting at the right hand of God. Mind the things that are above, not the things that are upon the earth" (Col 3:1 f.).

Formerly it was the custom of the Christians of Rome to assemble in the church of St. Peter on the second Sunday after Easter. This is the Sunday of the Good Shepherd, who, after His Resurrection and before His Ascension into heaven, appointed Peter to be the visible shepherd of His sheep and His lambs. In spirit we gather today in St. Peter's, safe under the protection of the Good Shepherd. In the Introit we sing His praise with grateful hearts, remembering all that He has done for us by His death, His Resurrection, and by sharing His divine life with us through holy baptism. "The earth is full of the mercy of the Lord.... Rejoice in the Lord, O ye just" (Introit).

The Prince of the Apostles, in whose church we assemble today, tells us what Christ did for us: "Dearly beloved: Christ suffered for us, leaving you an example that you should follow in His steps.... [He] bore our sins in His body upon the tree; that we, being dead to sins, should live to justice" (Epistle). To this prevailing thought of the Christian at Easter time, St. Peter joins the concept of Christ as the Good Shepherd, "by whose stripes you were healed. For you were as sheep going astray; but you are now converted to the shepherd and bishop of your souls" (Epistle).

Christ introduces Himself in the Gospel as the Good Shepherd. "I am the Good Shepherd. The good shepherd giveth his life for his sheep.... I am the Good Shepherd, and I know Mine, and Mine know Me.... I lay down My life for My sheep" (Gospel). We acknowledge gratefully Christ's description of Himself, as we recall what we have experienced during Holy Week. We acknowledge this blessed announcement of Christ with a firm *Credo:* "I believe." He is indeed the true shepherd, the Savior of our souls. In the Offertory we cry out to Him, "O God, my God, to Thee do I watch at break of day," that I may be united to Thee; "and in Thy name I will lift up my hands." Thus in spirit we make our offering, and bring our gifts, and subject our will to Christ, the Good Shepherd, so that we may follow in His footsteps to the altar of sacrifice.

In the Consecration the Good Shepherd will be personally present on our altar with His self-sacrificing love. There He will renew in a mystical manner the offering of His life for His sheep, and will confer on them the benefits and the fruit of His death. "I lay down My life for My sheep." Here in the Mass these words are realized. "I know Mine, and Mine know Me." It is a recognition full of efficacious and life-giving grace. Through the instrumentality of this most sacred offering, all mercy, all grace, and all supernatural life come to us.

"And Mine know Me." In the Mass we renounce all false gods and all perversity, and join ourselves to Christ in a most intimate union, that we may become part of His sacrifice and thus become one with Him in spirit and in intention. Having been united with Him, we live His life and follow the path on which He has gone before us. Thus we shall be led to green pastures in the sacrificial banquet of Holy Communion. He is the Good Shepherd who nourishes us with His glorified substance and makes Himself entirely ours. "I am the Good Shepherd, and I know My sheep, and Mine know Me" (Communion). Could He unite Himself to us in a more intimate and loving way than He has done?

Meditation

Easter, the day of the Lord's victory over sin and hell, the day of our resurrection to a new life (through baptism and penance), today receives a new meaning. The risen Lord is the Good Shepherd who lays down His life for His sheep. With her heart filled with gratitude, the Church recognizes Jesus as the Good Shepherd. "The earth is full of the mercy of the Lord, alleluia; by the word of the Lord [I baptize thee; I absolve thee from thy sins; this is My body, and this is My blood] were the heavens [the redeemed] made, alleluia, alleluia. Rejoice in the Lord, O ye just [the redeemed, the Church]" (Introit).

Jesus is the Good Shepherd. "The good shepherd giveth his life for his sheep. But the hireling and he that is not the shepherd, whose own the sheep are not, seeth the wolf coming and leaveth the sheep and flieth; and the wolf catcheth and scattereth the sheep; and the hireling flieth because he is a hireling and he hath no care for the sheep. I am the Good Shepherd; and I know Mine, and Mine know Me, as the Father knoweth Me and I know the Father; and I lay down My life for My sheep" (Gospel).

The mark by which the good shepherd is to be recognized is his selfless zeal for the welfare of the flock that has been entrusted to him. His zeal makes him willing to sacrifice his life for his flock. It is otherwise with the hireling, who works for a fee, for he is a hireling whose own the sheep are not. When he sees the enemy, the wolf, coming, he does not place himself on guard. He will not risk his own life; he assures first his own safety, for he lacks a personal interest in the flock. There is still another mark by which the true shepherd may be recognized. He knows personally each of the sheep committed to his care. For him the individual sheep is not just one among many, as would be the case with the hireling. There exists between the individual soul and Jesus a union so personal and so intimate and trusting, that the union of the Father and Son in the Blessed Trinity is mirrored in it. The mutual understanding and love of the Father and Son are reflected also by this relationship between the Good Shepherd and His flock. Blessed are we, the baptized, the children of the Church, who have been entrusted to Jesus, the Good Shepherd. He lays down His life for His sheep. He guides each one of them, cares for them, and loves them with an intimate love, as though each sheep were His only care. What unquestioning faith and confidence we should have in the Good Shepherd!

"The Good Shepherd giveth His life for His sheep." As a matter of fact He is so concerned for our salvation that He descended from heaven, subjected Himself to suffering, and became obedient unto death for our sake. How zealously He has sought us out! He comes daily in the Mass in search of us; seeking us out, He enters our hearts each day in Holy Communion. He lives and prays for us unceasingly in the solitude of the tabernacle. He inspires us and enlightens us without ceasing, and is continually knocking at the door of our hearts with His grace. He consoles us, reproaches us, delights us, admonishes us, allows us to fall, and then raises us up; He protects us from ourselves and from our own evil inclinations, desires, and passions. "I am the Good Shepherd; and I know Mine." This assurance sustains us; for He is the Good Shepherd of my soul, and I am His chief concern. He knows me, all that is in me, both the good and the evil. His eyes follow me wherever I wander. When my way is through briars or painful thorns, He helps me; when I am in need, when I am troubled or in darkness, He comes to me. His heart beats for me, and He is always near me, even when I am obliged to go forth into a hostile world, and when I cry out in vain for love and sympathy.

"I am the Good Shepherd." He has risen; He, the Good Shepherd who seeks me so lovingly, lives. The man who possesses this living faith can never be poor, or homeless, or alone. There can never again be for him a sterile period, either in his heart or in his work. Let us live with the liturgy in the spirit of faith.

"I know Mine, and Mine know Me." Where? In the offering of true love. Only the spirit of sacrificial love can build a bridge between the Shepherd and His sheep. Only when love has been purified of all selfishness, can a true interior and vital union, based on perfect mutual understanding, be realized between the Shepherd and His sheep. No one can remain faithful unless he bears the imprint of the Lord's wounds in his heart. That is the mystery of the true shepherd, Jesus Christ.

Prayer

O God, who by the humility of Thy Son hast raised up a fallen world, grant to Thy faithful people abiding joy; that those whom Thou hast delivered from the perils of eternal death, Thou mayest cause to enjoy eternal happiness. Through the same Christ our Lord. Amen.

Monday

"You were as sheep going astray. But you are now converted to the Shepherd and Bishop of your souls" (Epistle). What a wonderful Easter message!

"But you are now converted to the Shepherd and Bishop of your souls." Through baptism you have found your way back to the Shepherd in the Church. You were without guidance, without suitable pasture, and destined for perdition. At Easter, through the holy sacraments of baptism and penance, you were restored to the Good Shepherd. He directs and guides you with divine wisdom and love; He leads you without error; He directs you with ineffable goodness and strength. How fortunate you are in having found your way back at Easter to the Good Shepherd of your soul! You are fortunate to be placed under His direction and guidance, for those who follow His direction and guidance cannot go astray or be lost.

He and He alone is able, by His divine power, to defend us against the enemy, however powerful that enemy may be. Neither hell, nor the world, nor the flesh can have any part in us as long as we are under His protection. Any other guide is uncertain and treacherous, and any measures we may take to protect ourselves against such false leadership will lead us to perdition. Only when we subject ourselves to Christ can we proceed with perfect certitude and assurance. How deceived we are when we depend on any other guide, on our own judgment or our own personal desires, submitting to the rule of our passions! Rather, we must give ourselves to Jesus with complete confidence and with an unshakable trust in Him to whom we have been restored.

Jesus has already trod the path over which He leads His sheep. The Epistle points out the way for us. "Dearly beloved: Christ suffered for us, leaving you an example that you should follow in His steps. Who did no sin, neither was guile found in His mouth. Who, when He was reviled, did not revile; when He suffered, He threatened not [to avenge Himself], but delivered Himself to him that judged Him unjustly; who His own self bore our sins in His body upon the tree, that we, being dead to sins, should live to justice; by whose stripes you were healed" (Epistle). The path is the way of self-sacrificing love, the way of suffering, the way of perfect submission to the will of the Father in heaven. By this path Jesus reached the glory of His Resurrection and His exaltation in heaven. This is the way of salvation; there is no other way.

In the Gospel today Christ assures us that "Mine know Me." They know Him not only in prayer, in the celebration of the liturgy, in spiritual meditation, or in the momentary consolations and sensible graces they receive; they know Him also in practical life, with all its hardships and its many trials and tribulations. They follow in the footsteps of the cross-laden Savior; they follow the Lord who was unjustly condemned and humiliated; they follow Him "who, when He was reviled, did not revile, when He suffered, He threatened not, but delivered Himself to him that judged Him unjustly" (Epistle). These are the true sheep of the divine Shepherd.

"But you are now converted to the Shepherd and Bishop of your souls." Christ desires to be our shepherd. If we take our Christianity seriously, we shall place ourselves under His direction. All human prudence is treacherous, all human plans fail, and all true progress in the spiritual life is impossible unless we are united to Christ. He guides us by means of His word and His commandments, which are given to us in the holy Gospels. He guides us by the example He gave us during His earthly life, and which He continues to give unceasingly in the secrecy of the tabernacle and in the Holy Sacrifice of the Mass. He guides us by means of the Church, by means of her doctrines and her teaching office, by means of her laws and her commandments, and finally, by means of her priesthood. He guides us who are striving for Christian perfection through the spiritual directors which He provides for us. The more perfectly we submit ourselves to these directors and the more confidently we follow their direction, the more certainly we shall experience that He is "the Good Shepherd." "He that heareth you, heareth Me; and he that despiseth you, despiseth Me" (Lk 10:16).

Why are we so reluctant to believe that our way, and the way of the Church, is the way of renunciation, the way of the cross, the way of humiliation, the way of nothingness in the eyes of the world? It is because we have not yet understood that our portion is to "follow His steps" and to drink of His chalice (cf. Mt 20:22).

"I am the Good Shepherd." If our faith in Christ as the Good Shepherd, as our leader and protector, were only a living faith, we should live in the consciousness that He is guiding us and protecting us, that He is solicitous for our well-being every instant of our lives. If we could so live, how much more peaceful our lives would be, how free from solicitude! How confidently, how safely, we should pursue our way! How happy we should be knowing that the wisdom, love, and power of the Good Shepherd guides us to the goal of eternal life! Even in the darkest hours we should feel confident. But we are too concerned with ourselves, with our works, and with our miseries. Therefore we become pessimistic and dispirited. O Lord, increase our faith in Thee, our Good Shepherd.

Prayer

O God, who by the humility of Thy Son hast raised up a fallen world, grant to Thy faithful people abiding joy; that those whom Thou hast delivered from the perils of eternal death, Thou mayest cause to enjoy eternal happiness. Through the same Christ our Lord. Amen.

Tuesday

"I am the Good Shepherd, alleluia" (Communion). With these words of the Lord the liturgy distributes Holy Communion to the faithful on the second Sunday after Easter: "I am the Good Shepherd, alleluia; and I know My sheep, and Mine know Me, alleluia."

He knows and loves us, and we know and love Him in the mystery of the Holy Eucharist and in the Sacrifice of the Mass.

The Holy Sacrifice of the Mass. God could not have conferred on us a more marvelous gift than the Sacrifice of the Mass. In this sacrifice He gives us His very self, a priceless treasure, more desirable than all the riches of the world. By this sacrifice we can bring joy to an eternal and holy God; by it we are enabled to render God a perfect recompense for all that He has done for us. If we had not this Holy Sacrifice, how could we ever worthily thank and honor God for the forgiveness of our sins? Without it, how would we be able to obtain from Him the graces, the strength, and the light that we need? How could we ever reach our goal of eternal life?

To give us the Holy Eucharist, the Holy Sacrifice of the Mass, the Son of God must first descend from heaven and assume our human nature. After thirty years spent in secluded preparation, He goes forth to seek us, to search out His wandering sheep, that He may rescue and redeem them. He accomplishes this redemption through fasting, prayer, sacrifice, and through hardships of all kinds, and finally through the sacrifice of His own body and blood. All this He does that He may leave us the Holy Eucharist. "Having loved His own who were in the world, He loved them unto the end" (Jn 13:1) through the institution of the Holy Eucharist. "This is My body.... This is My blood.... This do in commemoration of Me." The Holy Sacrifice of the Mass embraces the entire life of Christ: His suffering, His subjection to His Father, His love for us, His merits, and His prayers. All this is brought down upon the altar in the Holy Sacrifice and becomes entirely ours. We in turn offer it up to the heavenly Father as a sacrifice of praise, thanksgiving, petition, and satisfaction.

"I am the Good Shepherd.... I lay down My life for My sheep." In the Holy Sacrifice of the Mass I offer Myself up for them with the same love, with the same intense longing for their redemption, with which I offered Myself up on the cross. "I am the Good Shepherd."

The sacrificial banquet of Holy Communion. "Alleluia, alleluia. The disciples recognized the Lord Jesus in the breaking of bread." In this Alleluia verse the liturgy has in mind the two disciples who met our Lord on the way to Emmaus. While walking from Jerusalem to Emmaus on Easter night, they are discussing the events of the last few days, and Jesus overtakes them on the way. He joins them, but they do not recognize Him. They do not know Him even when He explains the Scriptures to them. Only when they are seated at table and He takes bread in His hands, blesses it, breaks it, and gives it to them to eat, do they recognize Him. We are these disciples. We, too, recognize Him in the breaking of bread, in the reception of Holy Communion. Thus, by becoming the food of our souls, He shows His great love for us. He could not exercise His mission on earth as the pastor of our souls in a manner more perfect.

"I know My sheep, and Mine known Me" (Communion). They know their Shepherd in the grace received in Holy Communion. Each day they receive the Holy Sacrament, and each day they do so with a purer and more fervent heart. Through the reception of Holy Communion they daily kindle in their hearts the fire of love for Christ. He becomes all things to them. They recognize Him and love Him in His person, in His sacraments, in His doctrines, in His commandments, and in His members. They recognize Him and love Him in days of prosperity as well as in days of adversity, trial, and suffering.

"I know My sheep." Yes, Lord, you know all things. You know me, not with a knowledge that is cold and impersonal, but with a love that is full of compassion and understanding. You love me with a heart that is loving, self-sacrificing, and filled with unspeakable condescension and goodness. You know me in the Blessed Eucharist.

"And Mine know Me." O Lord, that I might truly know You, the Good Shepherd, in the Holy Sacrifice of the Mass, in Holy Communion, in Thy tabernacle! If I could only know You perfectly! If I could only bring myself to recognize You in Your pastoral mission and in the trials that each day brings! If only I could conceive You as the one great reality and allow myself to be completely governed by that knowledge! "And Mine know Me," and love Me, hearken to Me, look to Me for guidance, depend on Me, believe in Me, and offer themselves up for Me.

"O God, my God, to Thee do I watch at break of day; and in Thy name I will lift up my hands, alleluia" (Offertory). I fly to You and look up to You at the break of day, bringing You the offering of my prayers, my adoration, my works, and my sufferings. To Thee, the Good Shepherd, I subject all the powers and movements of my soul.

Prayer

The Lord ruleth me, and I shall want nothing. He hath set me in a place of pasture. He hath brought me up on the water of refreshment. He hath converted my soul. He hath led me on the paths of justice for His own name's sake. For though I should walk in the midst of the shadow of death, I will fear no evils, for Thou art with me. Thy rod and Thy staff, they have comforted me, Thou hast prepared a table before me against them that afflict me. Thou hast anointed my head with oil, and my chalice which inebriateth me, how goodly is it! And Thy mercy will follow me all the days of my life. And that I may dwell in the house of the Lord unto length of days. (Psalm 22.)

Wednesday
Solemnity of St. Joseph, Patron of the Universal Church

In March we celebrated a feast in memory of St. Joseph's sanctity and holiness. Today he is presented to us as the patron and protector of the Church. On this day we should thank this mighty protector and renew our faith in him. This day should bring us renewed confidence in the efficacy of his help and protection. It should spur us on to seek his help in the many dangers that threaten us. "Go to Joseph."

St. Joseph was the head of the Holy Family and its protector. From all eternity he was selected to be the guardian of God's most precious possessions on earth, Jesus and Mary. God entrusted to him His rarest treasure, and Joseph discharged his duties with perfect fidelity. With serene unselfishness he accepted the responsibility for Mary and concealed from the prying eyes of the world the mystery of her miraculous conception of the Son of God. As the legitimate spouse of Mary, he accompanied her to Bethlehem, and there joined her in adoring the divine child. Jesus, the son of his legitimate spouse, is also his child and his responsibility. Joseph was faced with an unfathomable mystery, but he accepted it on faith. Like the child's mother, Mary, he lived now only to serve Him, to act as His protector, provider, and father. God gave him all the rights and duties of a father with regard to Jesus. Faithful to his duty, and true to his responsibility, Joseph withdrew into Egypt for the safety of Mary and the child. During those bitter years of exile, he provided for the needs of his little family. Eventually he returned to Galilee, and there in the seclusion of Nazareth he continued his role as provider, guide, and protector of Jesus and Mary.

Joseph is also the protector and patron of Holy Mother the Church. In 1870, when the Church was in great peril, Pius IX selected St. Joseph as the patron of the universal Church; the Holy Family of Nazareth has become the family of God, the Church Universal.

The duties which Joseph once performed for Jesus and Mary he now performs for Holy Mother the Church and all her children. He performs these functions for us with the same love, the same fidelity, the same strength which he once displayed with respect to Jesus and Mary. The liturgy of the day presents him in this way. We gratefully accept his protection as we recite the words of the Introit: "The Lord is our helper and protector; in Him our heart shall rejoice, and in His holy name we have trusted, alleluia, alleluia." Then we make this request: "Give ear, O Thou that rulest Israel [Holy Mother the Church], Thou that leadest Joseph like a sheep." St. Joseph in turn assures us: "In whatever tribulation they shall cry to me, I will hear them, and be their protector always" (Alleluia verse). Then in the name of Holy Mother the Church we beg of St. Joseph: "Do thou, O Joseph, make us lead an innocent life; may it ever be shielded by thy patronage" (Alleluia verse).

The Church has great confidence in the protection of St. Joseph. "If armies in camp should stand together against me, my heart shall not fear. If a battle should rise up against me, in this will I be confident. I praise thee forever, for thou art a mighty protector" (Responsory at Matins). Holy Mother the Church places these words in the mouth of St. Joseph: "The Lord has made me to be as the father of a king, and the ruler over all His possessions. He has exalted me that He might save many peoples. Come unto me, and I will give you all the riches of Egypt, that you may eat of the fat of the land" (*ibid.*). "The people cried out to the king seeking nourishment, to whom he responded: Go to Joseph." We, too, have been directed to seek the help of St. Joseph. We cry out to him. "Our salvation is in thy hand. Only glance at us, and we will gladly serve the king" (Responsory at Matins). Thus we understand the admonition of the Church, "Go to Joseph."

We know that St. Joseph will care for us with the same solicitude and love with which he cared for Jesus and Mary. That is the ground for our implicit faith in him. He assures us: "In whatever tribulation they shall cry to me, I will hear them, and be their protector always." St. Joseph hears in our prayers the voice of the Savior who prays in us. Can he refuse to give ear to us? Can he leave our petition unanswered? He cannot if we have the confidence which the liturgy has in his burning zeal. It would have us honor him and fly to his patronage in all matters of our external life and in our exertions to acquire virtue and sanctity.

PRAYER

O God, who in Thy ineffable providence hast willed to select the blessed Joseph as the spouse of Thy holy mother, we beseech Thee that we who honor him as our protector on earth, may deserve to have him for our intercessor in heaven. Who livest and reignest for all eternity. Amen.

Thursday
St. Joseph

The Church devotes the entire octave of this feast to the honor of St. Joseph, the patron of the universal Church and the protector of the Holy Family. She stands in awe at the abundance of grace which God has showered upon this great saint.

The Epistle describes the plentiful graces which God bestowed on the Joseph of the Old Testament. We stand in spirit at the deathbed of the venerable patriarch Jacob, whose twelve stalwart sons are gathered around him. With prophetical insight Jacob looks into the future and sees the destiny of his sons and their progeny. He passes on to them their inheritance — that is, the blessing of the God of Abraham. Joseph he blesses with the words recorded in the Epistle of today's Mass: "Joseph is a growing son, a growing son [Joseph means growing] and comely to behold. The daughters [his progeny] run to and fro upon the wall. But they that held darts [Joseph's brethren, evil men] provoked him and quarreled with him and envied him. His bow rested upon the strong [Joseph triumphs and overcomes them], and the bands of his arms and his hands were loosed by the hands of the mighty one of Jacob [by the marvelous intervention of God]. Thence he came forth [from prison and from slavery] a pastor, the stone of Israel. The God of thy father shall be thy helper, and the Almighty shall bless thee with the blessings of heaven above, with the blessings of the deep that lieth beneath, with blessings of the breasts and of the womb. The blessings of thy father are strengthened with the blessings of his fathers [Abraham and Isaac] until the desire of the everlasting hills shall come [Christ the Savior]. May they be upon the head of Joseph, upon the crown of the Nazarite among his brethren." This is an apt description of the abundance of grace bestowed on the Joseph of the New Testament.

"The blessings of thy father are strengthened with the blessings of his fathers until the desire of the everlasting hills shall come." The events foreseen by Jacob on his deathbed were fulfilled in a marvelous way in St. Joseph. The blessing with which God enriched Joseph came in the form of the Messias, the Son of God in human form. Jesus is the fullness of divine blessings, the source of all salvation, of all riches, of all that is of lasting value in heaven and on earth. He is a blessing of God that surpasses immeasurably all the blessings that were given by God to the patriarchs and saints of the Old Testament. This is the blessing which is received by Joseph, "the chosen one among his brethren," a blessing which surpasses that of all men. He was selected in preference to all other men to be the spouse of Mary, the mother of Jesus. Since he is her legitimate spouse, Jesus, her son, the Son of God, and even Mary herself belong to him as their father and their protector. The holy liturgy stands in awe at the singular graces with which God has enriched St. Joseph. With the single exception of Mary herself, his graces exceed those of all other men. The Church considers herself fortunate to be placed, like Jesus and Mary, under the protection of this blessed man. In his hands God has placed the power necessary for victory over Herod and over all the enemies of the Holy Family and of the Church. This is the belief of the Church, and we confidently acquiesce in this belief.

In the mind of the liturgy, St. Joseph was, of all men, endowed with the greatest measure of grace, with the single exception of Mary. He is a fountain of grace, to whom we are directed to apply. During the great famine in Egypt, the people cried out to the king (Pharao) for bread. He replied: "Go to Joseph." God gives us a similar command, "Go to Joseph." Through his mediation we shall obtain the graces necessary for salvation and protection against our internal and external enemies, and against the persecutors and oppressors of Holy Mother the Church. Thus God honors him upon whom He has bestowed the prerogatives of a father.

Since he is the foster father of Jesus, St. Joseph possesses a singular power and authority over his son even now in heaven. After Mary, his power of intercession is greater than that of any other saint. Do we not all too often forget his power of intercession? Would it not be well for us to acquire that faith and confidence in St. Joseph which the liturgy teaches us and to go to him as it recommends? "Our salvation is in thy hands. Only glance at us, and we will gladly serve the king" (Responsory at Matins). "Praise the Lord, O Jerusalem," the Church, the Christian soul; for He has appointed St. Joseph to be thy protector. "He hath strengthened the bolts of thy gates; He hath blessed thy children within thee" through the intercession of St. Joseph (Offertory).

Prayer

If armies in camp should stand together against me, my heart shall not fear. If a battle should rise up against me, in this will I be confident. I shall praise Thee forever, for Thou art a mighty protector. (Responsory at Matins.)

Friday
St. Joseph

The Gospel of the Mass concludes the account of the baptism of Jesus in the Jordan with the words: "And Jesus Himself was beginning about the age of thirty years, being (as it was supposed) the son of Joseph."

Jesus was thought to be the son of Joseph. Joseph was in a real sense the father of Jesus, and it was just and proper that he should be called the father of Jesus. It is true that Jesus was conceived by the power of the Holy Ghost, and Jesus had no real human father by natural generation. Nevertheless, Joseph is the father of Jesus. On earth he takes the place of the heavenly Father, by whom Christ was generated from all eternity. Joseph's foremost claim to be the father of Jesus rests on the fact that he is "the husband of Mary, of whom was born Jesus, who is called Christ" (Mt 1:16). By virtue of his marriage to Mary, the child which Mary conceived by the Holy Ghost and brought forth in a stable, belongs also to Joseph, her legitimate spouse. Because He is Mary's son, Jesus is also the son of Joseph and subject to his paternal care and authority. Joseph knew that as the father of Jesus he was charged with the responsibility of providing for Him. For this reason he shares the anxiety of Mary when Jesus remains behind them in the temple, and he accompanies her back to the city to search for Him. "Son, why hast Thou done so to us? Behold, Thy father and I have sought Thee sorrowing.... And He went down with them and came to Nazareth, and was subject to them" (Lk 2:48, 51).

"And [He] was subject to them." Jesus, the Son of God, subjects Himself to St. Joseph as a child and a son. The Son of the omnipotent God obeys, as His legitimate father on earth, St. Joseph, who is a mere creature. The liturgy of the day places great emphasis on this truth. St. Joseph exercises paternal authority over the Son of God. Even in heaven Jesus shows great deference to the wishes and petitions of St. Joseph, for these are also the commands of His father; "and [He] was subject to them." Jesus does not ignore or refuse the requests of St. Joseph. How fortunate the Church is to have this powerful saint as her patron, her mediator, and her protector! How fortunate the soul who adopts him for the same purpose! "Go to Joseph."

Jesus has been entrusted to St. Joseph. God engendered in the soul of St. Joseph a true paternal love and devotion, that he might take a real fatherly interest in Jesus and live but to serve Him. Joseph is true to that love. He exercises this paternal solicitude, not only for the person of Jesus, but also for the Church which He instituted, and for all its members. The Church is nothing else but the visible form of Christ on earth, the body of Christ with all His members. For this reason the heart of St. Joseph burns with love for the Church just as it did for Jesus. Joseph is also the true father, the mighty protector and patron of the Church. "Go to Joseph."

Today we offer up the Holy Sacrifice to the eternal Father for having given us St. Joseph as the protector and intercessor of the Church. We place the merits and the prayers on the paten at Mass and lift them up to God saying: "Accept, O holy Father, almighty and everlasting God, this spotless host which I offer to Thee." Relying on the patronage of St. Joseph, we pray in the Secreta for grace to "make our hearts despise all earthly things, and love Thee, the true God, with perfect charity." On the feast of St. Joseph we petition that we too may be Josephs, "growing sons," increasing in our love for God.

The Church has great faith and trust in St. Joseph because Jesus has given him the heart of a father. From the day of Christ's birth we find St. Joseph tireless and consistently true in his paternal love. God seems to have wished to put this fatherly love to a test, for Joseph is obliged to exchange his home in Nazareth for the stable in Bethlehem, to forsake his fatherland for the exile in Egypt, and to sacrifice the security of his life as a tradesman for the uncertain life of a wanderer. But Joseph never falters. He is always prompt in the observance of God's will. We can place ourselves in his care with full confidence.

Prayer

O God, who in Thy ineffable providence hast willed to select the blessed Joseph as the spouse of Thy holy mother, we beseech Thee that we who honor him as our protector on earth, may deserve to have him for our intercessor in heaven. Who livest and reignest for all eternity. Amen.

Saturday
St. Joseph

In one of the lessons used at Matins during the octave of St. Joseph, our Holy Mother the Church makes use of one of the sermons of St. Bernardino of Siena. We follow the thought of this great client of St. Joseph.

Joseph and Mary. By divine inspiration Joseph and Mary entered into a true and legitimate marital union. This union binds them together in heart and soul so intimately that they are perfectly one in spirit. How could the Holy Ghost bind St. Joseph so intimately to Mary in spirit, if he were not like to her also in virtue? For this reason it was necessary that St. Joseph, too, possess virginal purity, be firmly grounded in humility, be inflamed with the love of God, and be a man of perfect modesty. Mary knew that St. Joseph had been selected by the Holy Ghost to be her husband and the faithful protector of her virginity. She knew that God had selected him to share her love and solicitude for the divine child. Could she fail, then, to entertain for St. Joseph the most pure and devoted love?

Joseph and Jesus. Joseph possessed a tender love for Christ. When he bore the divine child in his arms and spoke to Him, must Christ not have made the most precious revelations to him and filled his heart with unspeakable joy, as He did in later years? And to all this was added the happiness of seeing and gazing upon Jesus. What a joy it must have been for St. Joseph to hear the sweet name of "father" from the lips of Jesus! What exertions he must have undergone during the flight to Egypt, on the return journey to Nazareth, during the pilgrimages up to the temple in Jerusalem, in his arduous toil in his shop in Nazareth in order to provide for Jesus! All this he did out of love for Him whom Mary, the bride of the Holy Ghost, had given him for a child. Mary herself refers to this singular love of St. Joseph for the child when they found Him teaching in the temple: "Son, why hast Thou done so to us? Behold, Thy father and I have sought Thee sorrowing" (Lk 2:48).

To Joseph, who is closer to Jesus and Mary than any of the other saints in heaven, we have been entrusted. He fulfills the same duties for Holy Mother the Church and for all of us that he fulfilled for Jesus and Mary. He performs his duties with the same devotion and love with which he served Jesus and Mary. "Praise the Lord, O Jerusalem [the Church], because He hath strengthened the bolts of thy gates" through the intercession of St. Joseph (Offertory).

For the liturgy, Holy Communion is the guarantee that we shall obtain the protection of St. Joseph. "But Jacob begot Joseph, the husband of Mary, of whom was born Jesus, who is called Christ, alleluia" (Communion). In Holy Communion, He who was the most precious possession of Joseph and Mary becomes ours also. By Holy Communion we are daily incorporated in a more intimate union with Christ, who is our head. St. Joseph, seeing that we who are entrusted to him form with Jesus one Christ, will perform for us the same functions which he performed for Jesus. Must he not shower the same love and solicitude upon the Church and upon us who are members of that Church? Such an interpretation the liturgy gives to our reception of Holy Communion. By the daily reception of Holy Communion we are bound more closely to the Church, and thus acquire a new and better claim to the protection and intercession of the mighty St. Joseph.

Today we must renew our faith and confidence in St. Joseph and in the love he bears for Christ and for us who are His members. We should endeavor to receive Holy Communion worthily every day, and thus become more closely united to the Church, so as to share in the protection of St. Joseph.

Prayer

O God, who in Thy ineffable providence hast willed to select the blessed Joseph as the spouse of Thy holy mother, we beseech Thee that we who honor him as our protector on earth, may deserve to have him for our intercessor in heaven. Who livest and reignest for all eternity. Amen.

Third Sunday after Easter

The Mass

The resurrection leads to the glorification of Christ and to His ascension. In His ascension the words of the Apostle are verified: "He humbled Himself, becoming obedient unto death, even to the death of the cross. For which cause God also hath exalted Him, and hath given Him a name which is above all names. That in the name of Jesus every knee should bow, of those that are in heaven, on earth, and under the earth. And that every tongue should confess that the Lord Jesus Christ is in the glory of God the Father" (Phil 2:8–11). Likewise that mysterious pronouncement made by Christ after the Last Supper finds its fulfillment in the Ascension: "If I go not, the Paraclete will not come to you; but if I go, I will send Him to you" (Jn 16:7). Christ is eager to assure us of His abiding presence among us. He sends us the Spirit, the Holy Ghost, through whom He can be near to us to lead us and guide us. "It is the Spirit that quickeneth" (Jn 6:64). After the departure of Christ, the apostles and all those who have died and risen with Him in baptism, receive from the Holy Spirit the strength and courage to bear witness to Christ. Filled with this power and light of the Holy Spirit, they are able to overcome the world. They find it possible to endure persecution and suffering without faltering, and to live in the world and yet to be not of the world. This is the fruit of Easter. The spirit of Easter is the spirit of resurrection by means of baptism. It gives us unconquerable faith in the new powers that are given to us. It makes us conscious of the fact that we are stronger than Satan and sin, stronger than the world, the flesh, and even our own fallen nature. This spirit binds us to Him who, as the victorious conqueror, sits at the right hand of the Father and operates in all those whom He has called to His kingdom. He frees us from all attachment to the world, and directs our thoughts and our desires to where Christ sits at the right hand of His Father and where He has prepared a place for us in the house of His Father.

This Easter spirit fills our hearts, and guides and enlightens us in darkness and the necessities of our earthly life, thus preparing us for the baptism of the Spirit on the feast of Pentecost. The Mass for this Sunday must be interpreted in the light of this principle.

In the Mass of this Sunday the risen Christ announces for the first time His approaching departure. He is to ascend to His Father, but He must leave us behind in the world with all its dangers. However, the Easter spirit and the Easter light will guide us safely through the dangers and trials of our earthly life. Filled with this Easter spirit, we rejoice at the thought of the departure of Christ, and in spite of the certainty of our separation from Him, we break forth in a joyous Easter song, the Alleluia. "Shout with joy to God all the earth, alleluia; sing ye a psalm to His name, alleluia" (Introit). Ah, would that we were filled and vivified by this Easter spirit! For that grace we pray in the Kyrie and in the Collect: "O God,... grant to all those who profess to be Christians the grace to reject those things which are contrary to that name, and to follow such things as are agreeable to it." That is the spirit of Easter, the spirit of baptism, whose marvelous power the Epistle explains. Have we really acquired this spirit? Has Easter really created this spirit and this attitude in our souls? If it has, then the Alleluia verse can be applied to us: "The Lord hath sent redemption to His people." Then we shall have no fear of that which must be true of every Christian: "It behooved Christ to suffer... and so to enter into His glory" (Alleluia).

Now Christ speaks in the Gospel: "A little while, and now you shall not see Me; and again a little while, and you shall see Me.... And you shall be made sorrowful, but your sorrow shall be turned into joy." By means of the Easter spirit we are consoled in the suffering which results from our being thus left behind. Having the Easter spirit, we know that there will be an eventual victory and an eternal resurrection. Through darkness into light! Thus we courageously sing our Credo and our joyful Offertory song: "Praise the Lord, O my soul." Eventually we shall see Him face to face, and we shall possess Him for all eternity.

But even now we behold Him daily for a moment, living among us in a mystical manner. Not the senses of man, but only the eyes of faith behold the risen Christ living in our midst at the Consecration. Christ keeps a joyful reunion with us. He gives Himself to us as our offering; He lives and prays with us; He offers Himself to the Father for us and with us, and we offer with Him and through Him. He unites us in His unending sacrificial life, lifts us up in His pure hands, satiates us at Holy Communion with His risen life, and draws our hearts with Him into heaven. "A little while, and you shall not see Me, alleluia; and again a little while, and you shall see Me" (Communion). Indeed this is a blessed reunion which we experience in every Mass. And when the Holy Sacrifice is finished we speak our *Deo gratias* with hearts filled with gratitude. We have seen the Lord, alleluia.

Meditation

The liturgy already directs our attention to the ascension of the Lord. Still we are not sad at this departure of the Master. We have never felt that the earth was our true home, for our true home is in heaven. "A little while," and we, too, shall follow Him and there we shall be with Him always.

"A little while, and now you shall not see Me" (Gospel). We are to remain on earth for only a short time as pilgrims and strangers. Woe to us, if the earth becomes our home! The more complete our resurrection with Christ, the more we shall find that all our desires are on "the things that are above, where Christ is sitting at the right hand of God" (Col 3:1); they are fixed on that which is eternal, on our heavenly home. The life which we received from Christ through baptism, penance, and the reception of Holy Communion, requires that we reject firmly but gladly all the pleasures, joys, and riches of the world. It requires of us a life of mortification and renunciation, a continual battle against flesh and blood, against the movements and desires of our fallen nature. It requires that we be continually crucified with Christ by sharing His poverty, His humiliations, and His sufferings. The man who is truly risen with Christ will no longer be understood by the world. His manner of acting, his deeds, his speech, will be misunderstood. Yes, even God Himself has prepared for him humiliations, misunderstandings, sufferings, dryness, bitterness, and sickness. Those who live with Christ find this world an unfriendly place; whereas those who never pray, who pay no heed to God or the Church, often acquire much of this world's goods. Such men laugh and enjoy life. But the Lord reassures us, "a little while."

"And again a little while, and you shall see me." Easter and our resurrection with Christ are merely the introduction to our eventual ascension with Him. After our resurrection with Christ we shall return to Him in heaven, and there we shall see Him and share His life and His inheritance. "Your sorrow shall be turned into joy.... You now indeed have sorrow; but I will see you again, and your heart shall rejoice, and your joy no man shall take from you." Only a little while longer and death will come to call us to our home, where there will be no tears and no want. There we shall enjoy happiness, perfect happiness in the possession of God the Father, God the Son, and God the Holy Ghost. This happiness will be eternal, enjoyed without the fear that anyone can ever take it from us.

"It behooved Christ to suffer ... and so to enter into His glory, alleluia" (Alleluia verse). Suffering is past; it has been exchanged for the joy of heaven, alleluia. "You now indeed have sorrow; but I will see you again, and your heart shall rejoice." The law that Christ fulfilled must be fulfilled also by all those who are incorporated in Him. Christ is the key that makes it possible to understand our life. "For unto you it is given for Christ, not only to believe in Him, but also to suffer for Him" (Phil 1:29). He whom God desires to free from this miserable world with its dangers and its deceits, and to lead to the possession of eternal goods, must be prepared for privations, misfortunes, and suffering during the "little while" of his life on earth. "But your sorrow shall be turned into joy."

The life of the Christian here on earth is really a life of sorrow, a life of suffering and hardship, a life of renunciation of his own wishes and desires, a life of crucifixion with Christ. Woe be to us if we have no sorrows. How can our sorrow be changed into joy if we have no sorrow? Eternal joy is the daughter of the sorrow which is our portion here on earth. "A little while, ... and your sorrow shall be turned into joy."

We approach now to celebrate the Holy Sacrifice of the Mass. There we renew our resolve to embrace Christian sorrow. There we stir up our desires for sacrifice, for renunciation, for suffering, and for being crucified together with Christ, our victim on the altar. Holy Communion disposes us and gives us the strength to embrace Christian sorrow. The Eucharist is the guarantee of our reunion with Christ. "I will see you again, and your heart shall rejoice, and your joy no man shall take from you."

Prayer

O God, who dost show to them that are in error the light of Thy truth, that they may return to the way of righteousness: grant to all those who profess to be Christians the grace to reject those things which are contrary to that name, and to follow such things as are agreeable to it. Through Christ our Lord. Amen.

Monday

"Yet a little while," for you are only pilgrims and strangers on earth. The liturgy wishes to center our attention and our efforts on what is right and enduring, and on those things in which we can find true peace. That alone has permanent value.

"Yet a little while" (Gospel). Everything that exists on earth is temporal and passing. Our goods, our pleasures and our joys, our health, beauty, strength, youth, wealth, honors, friendships, even our suffering and misfortune, are of short duration and soon pass away. Man's life on earth is like a gust of wind, and his "days [are] measurable" (Ps 38:6). "All flesh is grass, and all the glory thereof as the flower of the field. The grass is withered, and the flower is fallen because the spirit of the Lord hath blown upon it" (Is 40:6 f.). Every creature on earth bears this stamp on its forehead, "yet a little while." Why do we cling to the things of this earth? Why do we rely on them so persistently? What peace can we find in them? We are pilgrims on the earth for "a little while." He who can grasp this truth understands life. He who heeds this warning of our Lord, need fear no evil, for he can weather every storm. He is a pilgrim and a stranger, and is left undisturbed by the uneasy ebb and flow of life. We are "deceivers, and yet true; as unknown, and yet known; as dying, and behold we live; as chastised and not killed; as sorrowful, yet always rejoicing; as needy, yet enriching many; as having nothing and possessing all things" (2 Cor 6:8–10).

Only one thing is permanent, our faith and our hope. "I will see you again, and your heart shall rejoice, and your joy no man shall take from you" (Gospel). The true Christian, the Christian who has risen with Christ, lives by faith and in the hope of those things that are to come. "I believe in life everlasting."

"But our conversation is in heaven; from whence also we look for the Savior, our Lord Jesus Christ. Who will reform the body of our lowness, made like to the body of His glory, according to the operation whereby also He is able to subdue all things unto Himself" (Phil 3:20 f.). Our Lord is already preparing Himself for His ascension into heaven. "Let not your heart be troubled. You believe in God, believe also in Me. In My Father's house there are many mansions. If not, I would have told you; because I go to prepare a place for you. And if I shall go and prepare a place for you, I will come again and will take you to Myself, that where I am you also may be. And whither I go you know, and the way you know.... I am the way, the truth, and the life" (Jn 14:1 ff.). "Heaven and earth shall pass, but My words shall not pass" (Mt 24:35). "The word of our Lord endureth forever" (Is 40:8).

Our souls must meditate on our heavenly home that they may become strong. Only when buoyed up by such thoughts will they maintain the proper attitude and become strong enough to overcome the world, to despise worldly things, and remain true to their ideals. By virtue of this strength, Christians live for the future. They long for martyrdom, and with St. Paul they desire "to be dissolved and to be with Christ" (Phil 1:23). They rejoice at the privilege of being allowed to suffer for their faith. "If you be reproached for the name of Christ, you shall be blessed; for that which is of the honor, glory, and power of God, and that which is of His Spirit, resteth upon you" (1 Pt 4:14).

"But the things that were gain to me, the same I have counted loss for Christ. Furthermore, I count all things to be but loss for the excellent knowledge of Jesus Christ my Lord; for whom I have suffered the loss of all things and count them but as dung that I may gain Christ.... That I may know Him and the power of His resurrection and the fellowship of His sufferings, being made conformable to His death. If by any means I may attain to the resurrection which is from the dead.... Forgetting the things that are behind and stretching forth myself to those things that are before, I press towards the mark to the prize of the supernal vocation of God in Christ Jesus" (Phil 3:7 ff.).

"Be ye followers of me, brethren, and observe them who walk so as you have our model. For many walk, of whom I have told you often (and now tell you weeping) that they are enemies of the cross of Christ. Whose end is destruction; whose God is their belly; and whose glory is in their shame; who mind earthly things. But our conversation is in heaven" (Phil 3:17–20). Even St. Paul had to complain of this worldly attitude. What would he say of our disposition? Let us not be counted among those "whose glory is their shame."

Prayer

Grant, O Lord, by these mysteries, that we may learn to subdue our worldly desires and love the things of heaven. Through Christ our Lord. Amen. (Secreta.)

Tuesday

"Alleluia. The Lord hath sent redemption to His people, alleluia." The Mass of the third Sunday after Easter is built on this theme; it is permeated by the spirit of gladness. "Shout with joy to God, all the earth, alleluia. Sing ye a psalm to His name, alleluia" (Introit). Easter, the Resurrection of the Lord, is our awakening to a new life of grace. It brings us the promise that we shall one day awaken to a life of glory. "How terrible are Thy works, O Lord!" (Introit.) "Praise the Lord, O my soul. In my life I will praise the Lord" (Offertory).

"The Lord hath sent redemption to His people." This deliverance is first of all from the tyranny of the flesh. "Dearly beloved, I beseech you, as strangers and pilgrims, to refrain yourselves from carnal desires, which war against the soul" (Epistle). "Therefore, brethren, we are debtors, not to the flesh to live according to the flesh, for if you live according to the flesh, you shall die; but if by the spirit you mortify the deeds of the flesh, you shall live.... The wisdom of the flesh is an enemy to God, for it is not subject to the law of God; neither can it be. And they who are in the flesh cannot please God" (Rom 8:12 f., 7 f.). Through the holy sacraments of baptism, penance, and the Eucharist, the Lord has made it possible for us to "refrain from carnal desires." Mary and Joseph are shining examples of unsullied purity and perfect chastity and virginity; they were perfectly detached from all inordinate worldly desires. They overcame the unruly tendencies toward pride, impatience, anger, envy, self-love, and self-seeking. Their lives were pure and devoted to the love of God and of Christ. Their one concern in life was to do the will of God and what was pleasing to Him. They were victorious over the desires and the movements of the flesh. They were truly redeemed.

"The Lord hath sent redemption to His people." God has given us also the power to overcome our lower sensual nature, our passions and our evil inclinations. We are redeemed. Though by ourselves we are weak and helpless, we are yet able to overcome our evil inclinations and to conquer in the struggle for purity and holiness. "I can do all things in Him who strengtheneth me" (Phil 4:13). Ah, had we but the deep living faith so evident in the liturgy of today's Mass! "The Lord hath sent redemption to His people, alleluia."

"Have your conversation good among the gentiles." That is the admonition given by St. Peter in the Epistle. In truth, "you are the light of the world" (Mt 5:14). "For you were heretofore darkness, but now light in the Lord. Walk, then, as children of the light" (Eph 5:8). "So let your light shine before men that they may see your good works and glorify your Father, who is in heaven" (Mt 5:16); that is, may they learn to know God and Christ and be led to them. A holy mission indeed! "For so is the will of God, that by doing well you may put to silence the ignorance of foolish men." The Epistle further commands us explicitly to obey our legitimate rulers: "Be ye subject, therefore, to every human creature for God's sake." Christian freedom does not release us from the authority of the state or the Church, or from the obligations of our state of life. Furthermore, this Epistle admonishes us to honor everyone and to practice fraternal charity: "Honor all men; love the brotherhood; fear God; honor the king." Finally we are commanded to be subject to authority, whether that authority treat us justly or unjustly: "Servants, be subject to your masters with all fear, not only to the good and gentle but also to the forward. For this is thankworthy." How diligently Joseph and Mary followed such a life of perfect submission! They feared God, prayed, rendered perfect obedience externally and internally to legitimate authority, were humbly subject to all men, often under the most trying circumstances. Such a life of submission is the fruit of Easter, the fruit of baptism, of the Eucharist, and of the grace we received through our resurrection with Christ. Why should not this life be possible to me? "The Lord hath sent redemption to His people."

"The Lord hath sent redemption to His people." Therefore "shout with joy to God, all the earth, alleluia; sing ye a psalm to His name, alleluia, alleluia" (Introit).

Though man is weak and helpless, the Christian can become mighty. He has only to learn the secret of his strength and his greatness, which lies in the light, the grace, the power, the new life, which results from his incorporation in the risen Christ. We know that we have been redeemed, that we are living branches united to the vine and growing by virtue of this union with Christ in His Church. I am not an isolated branch, torn from the vine and choked to death by enveloping thorns; I am a living branch of a great, living organism which shoots its roots deep into the earth, and whose limbs reach upward until they touch the very throne of God. I am a member of that great community which comprises all the strong, pure, noble souls in whom Christ lives, and who share His strength, His spirit, and His life. Indeed, "The Lord hath sent redemption to His people."

How I should rejoice, thank God, and trust in Him! How I should pray and strive to conquer the tyranny of carnal lusts by becoming strong, holy, and perfect before God and men!

Prayer

O God, who dost show to them that are in error the light of Thy truth, that they may return to the way of righteousness: grant to all those who profess to be Christians the grace to reject those things which are contrary to that name, and to follow such things as are agreeable to it. Through Christ our Lord. Amen.

Wednesday
Octave of the Solemnity of St. Joseph

Today we celebrate the octave of the Solemnity of St. Joseph. The lessons at Matins, taken from the Book of Genesis, tell the story of the Old Testament. Let us consider for a moment this story.

The first type. Joseph is sold by his brethren to the Ismaelites and is carried by them into Egypt. There he becomes the slave of Putiphar, an official of the king of Egypt. "And the Lord was with him, and he was a prosperous man in all things; and he dwelt in his master's house, who knew very well that the Lord was with him and made all that he did to prosper in his hand. And Joseph found favor in the sight of his master and ministered to him; and being set over all by him, he governed the house committed to him and all things that were delivered to him. And the Lord blessed the house of the Egyptian for Joseph's sake, and multiplied all his substance, both at home and in the fields" (Gn 39:2–5). Here we have a type of the Joseph of the New Testament, chosen by God as the protector of the Holy Family at Nazareth, of the holy family of God, the Church, and of every Christian family. For St. Joseph's sake the blessing and the protection of God rests on the Church and on the Christian family. With confidence we should appeal to St. Joseph in all our needs and place our trust in him.

The second type. The king of Egypt had a dream that caused him great uneasiness. Seven kine, very fat and beautiful, came up out of the river Nile. Then seven other kine, very lean and ill-favored, also came up and they devoured the seven fat kine. And the king sent for his interpreters, but they could not declare the meaning of the dream. Then by chance Pharao heard of Joseph in prison, and ordered him to be brought. Joseph explained the dream, and then Pharao said to him: "Seeing that God hath shown thee all that thou hast said, can I find one wiser and one like unto thee? Thou shalt be over my house, and at the commandment of thy mouth all the people shall obey.... Behold, I have appointed thee over the whole land of Egypt" (Gn 41:39–41). Then Pharao placed his signet ring on Joseph's finger and a golden chain about his neck. A herald went before him and declared him to be over the whole land of Egypt. Joseph was charged with the responsibility of seeing that provision was made for the seven lean years. Joseph discharged this duty well. He arranged matters so that during the seven years of want which followed the seven years of plenty, there was no shortage of bread. "And the famine prevailed in the whole world, but there was bread in all the land of Egypt" (Gn 41:54). Where St. Joseph rules, where he has been made the protector of the Church and the family, there is never any spiritual famine. In the realm of St. Joseph there is never a lack of bread, even when all other lands are laid waste by famine. How many thousands have experienced that Joseph never refuses their request for spiritual aid! With Holy Mother the Church we should go to Joseph to "buy food."

We recognize in St. Joseph the fulfillment of the words of today's Mass: "Alleluia, alleluia. In whatever tribulation they shall cry to me, I will hear them and be their protector always." We shall take St. Joseph at his word. We believe in him, trust in him, and seek him out in all our needs.

"And the famine prevailed in the whole world, but there was bread in all the land of Egypt." There is no want wherever St. Joseph rules. Yet how much hunger there is today in the hearts of men, even in those who come from Christian families, and even in the souls of those consecrated to God! The Church directs us to apply to St. Joseph. "As Thou dost make us rejoice in the protection of blessed Joseph, so by his merits and prayers make us partakers of everlasting glory" (Postcommunion). In the Mass he obtains for us the grace to "make our hearts despise all earthly things, and love Thee, the one true God, with perfect charity" (Secreta).

Prayer

It is truly meet and just, right and profitable for us at all times and in all places to give thanks to Thee, O holy Lord, the Father Almighty, everlasting God. And with due praises magnify Thee, bless, and proclaim Thee on the feast of blessed Joseph, who, as a just man, was given by Thee as the spouse of the virgin Mother of God, and, as a faithful and prudent servant, was set over Thy family, that with fatherly care he might guard Thy only-begotten Son, who was conceived by the Holy Ghost, Jesus Christ, our Lord. (Preface of St. Joseph.)

Thursday

"Alleluia. It behooved Christ to suffer... and so to enter into His glory" (Alleluia verse). "Christ, rising again from the dead, dieth now no more; death shall no more have dominion over Him" (Rom 6:9). Thus the glorified Christ stands before us and prays for us to His Father. "Father, I will that where I am, they also whom Thou hast given Me may be with Me [as My brethren, as members of My body], that they may see My glory which Thou hast given Me" (Jn 17:24).

The glory of the risen Christ. Christ gave us a glimpse of His glory through the three apostles whom He took with Him to Mount Tabor, where "He was transfigured before them. And His face did shine as the sun, and His garments became white as snow" (Mt 17:2). Now, after the resurrection, the splendor of the victor becomes visible on Tabor. The soul of Jesus, from the plenitude of the light of divine life with which it is flooded, sheds its heavenly beauty and strength upon His body also. Even though He was wounded, scourged, spat upon, and mocked, even though He suffered the pains and tortures of His passion, and was put to death and robbed of all beauty, yet He now shines with the brilliancy of the sun (gift of clarity). He can no longer suffer pain or death (gift of impassibility). He has shed all the defects of mortal human nature. The fulfillment of every wish and command follows the act of the will with the speed of light, penetrating all things like thought, like a spirit; He is like a spirit, yet possesses a true body (gift of agility). For the risen Christ, walls, towers, and locks are no longer an obstacle. On Easter morning the glorified body of Jesus rises from the grave and penetrates the door of the room where the disciples were gathered with the ease with which light penetrates glass. Such was the glory of the risen Christ. "Shout with joy to God all the earth, alleluia; sing ye a psalm to His name, alleluia" (Introit).

The glory of those who rise with Christ. "When Christ shall appear [on the last day], who is your life, then you also shall appear with Him in glory" (Col 3:4). Christ is risen, and we, too, shall one day rise from the dead. We are bound to Him by a most intimate union, for we have already risen with Him. The beginning of our resurrection is to be found in our baptism, by which we receive sanctifying grace, and in Holy Communion, by which we receive actual grace. This is the source of our eventual resurrection. "Who will reform the body of our lowness, made like to the body of His glory, according to the operation whereby also He is able to subdue all things unto Himself" (Phil 3:21). "Then shall the just shine as the sun" (Mt 13:43).

All the noble and holy saints who have ever lived on earth will rise and live again, and they will be honored and acclaimed in heaven for all eternity. For them there will be no more wailing, no more sorrow, no more pain. "Behold, I make all things new" (Apoc 21:5; 2 Cor 5:17). This miserable body which we now have will share in eternal life, in the glory and the immortality of the resurrection. "It is sown in corruption; it shall rise in incorruption. It is sown in dishonor; it shall rise in glory. It is sown in weakness; it shall rise in power. It is sown a natural body; it shall rise a spiritual body.... And when this mortal hath put on immortality, then shall come to pass the saying that is written: Death is swallowed up in victory. O death, where is thy victory? O death, where is thy sting?" (1 Cor 15:42–44, 54 f.)

"A little while" (Gospel). If Christ is risen, then we, too, shall rise. After our residence on earth for a little while, the life "in My Father's house" awaits us (Jn 14:2). That life will not be an empty existence, a dull, shadowy life such as the pagans considered the afterlife; it will be a life full of activity, a full, eternal life spent in company with the blessed and with God, who is the fountainhead of all life and happiness. After this "little while" we shall experience complete satisfaction, we shall have every desire fulfilled, and be perfect in God. "Father, I will that where I am, they also whom Thou hast given Me may be with Me" (Jn 17:24). A future of perfect bliss lies infallibly ahead of me. What, then, are the momentary trials and difficulties I suffer now? Two things are absolutely certain: that life on earth is brief and transient; and that after a little while there will be an eternal life of glory (cf. Rom 8:18). Indeed, they are inseparably connected. By means of this short life I earn my eternal glory. "These that are clothed in white robes, who are they? And whence came they?" John is asked in the Apocalypse. When he is unable to answer, he is told: "These are they who are come out of great tribulation and have washed their robes and have made them white in the blood of the lamb" (7:13 f.). "Out of great tribulation." That is the surest pledge and the best guarantee of a happy eternity.

Should not our hearts be filled with joy and blessed hope? We are one with the risen Christ. This union is the source of all our good fortune. If we truly believed and had full confidence, we would exclaim, "I look for the resurrection of the dead and the life of the world to come." The Christian may expect such a resurrection. "A little while … and I will see you again, and your heart shall rejoice."

Prayer

O God, who hast willed that Thy Son be crucified that we might be freed from the power of the devil, grant unto Thy servants that they may obtain the grace of the resurrection. Through the same Jesus Christ our Lord. Amen.

Friday

"A little while, and you shall not see Me; and again a little while, and you shall see Me, because I go to the Father" (Gospel). The risen Christ must present Himself to the Father. He belongs, not in this world, but in the realm of heaven. Therefore He must "go to the Father."

The risen Christ, our head, stands before us. "I go to the Father." In Christ there is an inner sanctuary, a holy of holies, which none can approach except the Father. In the inmost depths of His soul He is free from all that is merely human, from all earthly things, and is consecrated exclusively to the Father. "I am not alone, because the Father is with Me" (Jn 16:32). The life of Christ is one of complete preoccupation with the Father. He is one in heart with the Father; completely at rest with Him. In all things the eyes of Christ see the Father. His most urgent desire is to serve the Father, to live for Him, and to offer Himself up to the Father. With perfect devotion and love, with childlike trust and confidence, He abandons Himself to the will of the Father. In the Garden of Olives, He prays, "Not as I will, but as Thou wilt" (Mt 26:39). "I go to the Father," and will be united to Him in an inseparable union of life and love. For this reason His soul is so full of confidence, so detached, courageous, calm, mild, and steadfast. "I go to the Father."

We, the baptized, are the members of the risen Christ. "Therefore, if you be risen with Christ, seek the things that are above, where Christ is sitting at the right hand of God" (Col 3:1). "Lift up your hearts." We answer, "We have lifted them up to the Lord." Christ has taken up His abode in the inmost sanctuary of our soul, together with the Father and the Holy Spirit.

This, then, is our world, our entire inheritance, our sole good. There, in our soul, He listens to our petitions and speaks to our hearts. In that sanctuary I can approach Him and speak to Him.

"I will go and see this great sight" (Ex 3:3). This sanctuary is a holy place. Like Moses, we must first put off our shoes before approaching; that is, we must put aside all the inordinate desires of our hearts. We must leave all things behind, and seek nothing from this world; we must be truly spiritual, truly detached from all things of this world, no matter how much they may attract us. We must "salute no man by the way" (Lk 10:4), and be dependent on no creature. We must not be slaves either of our work or of our prayer. We must not be disturbed by what our neighbor does, nor become dejected when we are deserted by others or when others ridicule us. Humiliations and sickness must not dismay us. Even our own will we must renounce. Our petty thoughts and desires, our pride, and all self-love, self-conceit, and self-satisfaction must be suppressed. "I go to the Father," casting aside all things and leaving behind me all that is not of God, even if this renunciation cause me pain, and even if I feel myself most strongly attracted by the world. Our thoughts, our feelings, our desires, our ambitions, must all be centered on the Lord. We must let "the dead bury their dead" (Mt 8:22), and pursue our course courageously in the land of the living. We should not allow ourselves to become attached to anything, or to become dependent on anything. We must see through unworldly eyes, rise above all the vanities of the world, and free ourselves from that restless activity which is the driving force in the lives of worldly men. "I go to the Father." This is the mystery of our resurrection with Christ.

"I go to the Father" when I offer the Mass. There upon the golden paten I place all that this day may bring of labor, or suffering, or hardship, and offer it all to the Father. This is the precious offering of love. "Not as I will, but as Thou wilt" (Mt 26:39). "Thy will be done." Thus again at the beginning of the day we separate ourselves from the old man, the man of selfishness, the man who is attached to the fleeting things of this world. In this spirit of sacrifice we free our souls from every inordinate appetite and inclination, and beg the Lord that we may belong entirely to Him.

"I go to the Father" under all circumstances, and not merely in times of trial and difficulty. I go to Him even with the mistakes I have made. These mistakes should not make us uneasy, sad, depressed, or angry with ourselves. We should rather hasten to our Father and humble ourselves before Him, recognizing and acknowledging our own weakness and unworthiness. Then we should ask for forgiveness and for the strength to be more faithful and more circumspect in the future.

"I go to the Father" with a steadfast petition that He may liberate me completely from myself, and grant me to be truly poor in spirit, that He may grant me a deep and all-embracing faith, that He may grant me an ardent love for Christ, that He may grant me perfect conformity of my will to the eternal, divine will. This is the life that is proper to one who is risen with Christ. Such a Christian may look forward to a blessed ascension.

Prayer

O God, grant to Thy people to love that which Thou commandest and to desire that which Thou dost promise; so that amid the changing things of this world, our hearts may be set where true joys are to be found. Through Christ our Lord. Amen. (Collect for the Fourth Sunday after Easter.)

Saturday

"You shall lament and weep, ... but your sorrow shall be turned into joy" (Gospel). That is the lot of all those on earth who belong to Christ and to the Church. "You shall lament and weep" on earth; that is, the Christian must expect suffering, for "it behooved Christ to suffer ... and so to enter into His glory" (Alleluia verse). But what, after all, are the sufferings of this life compared to the glory to come?

This is the portion of the members of Christ: "For whom He foreknew, He also predestinated to be made conformable to the image of His Son" (Rom 8:29). Here on earth man can have no true good, no real good fortune, no authentic virtue or holiness, apart from a living union with Christ. "I am the vine, you the branches; he that abideth in Me and I in him, the same beareth much fruit; for without Me you can do nothing" (Jn 15:5). The lot of Jesus on earth was one of poverty, lowliness, deprivation, misunderstanding, calumny, persecution, the cross, and death. Can the lot of the disciple of Christ be otherwise? If we consider our lives in the light of faith, must not such suffering of our present life make us like Christ, and must we then not look upon them as our highest and most precious possession? Would the Son of God, eternal Wisdom Himself, have chosen and sought out such suffering had it not been the highest good? Consider how ardently the saints have longed for suffering. They have even gone in search of it. "Suffering, not death." We, too, should look upon our lives in the same light.

"And if sons [of God], heirs also; heirs indeed of God and joint heirs with Christ; yet so, if we suffer with Him, that we may be also glorified with Him" (Rom 8:17). Let us suffer that we may be glorified with Him. The two are inseparably connected. "For that which is at present momentary and light of our tribulation, worketh for us above measure, exceedingly an eternal weight of glory" (2 Cor 4:17). "Your sorrow shall be turned into joy" (Jn 16:20). Yes, it must ever be so. There is surely no more certain sign of predestination than our similarity to Christ, our crucified head. In this belief the liturgy celebrates during the Easter cycle the feasts of certain martyrs, who are the true disciples of the King of martyrs, Christ. By His own suffering and death Christ exalted the crown of martyrdom, and in the same way He sanctified all suffering. Through their suffering and death for Christ, the holy martyrs merited eternal life and made their eternal salvation certain. Fortunate indeed, then, are they who suffer. Suffering corrects all spiritual blindness and makes us see the specious goods of this life in their true light. It cleanses the heart from all that is inordinate and worldly, from the love of gold, honor, and human praise, and from all self-love. Yet we all fear suffering and strive to avoid it. When a small suffering overtakes us, we cry out and complain. A harsh word, a small slight, a disappointment in something we sought, and we become dissatisfied, angry, and unhappy. Yet we know it is a disgrace to be a Christian if we are unwilling to be crucified with Christ.

In the naves of our Churches the cross hangs from an arch of triumph. Here the Christian comes to pray and seek consolation and strength. But what does he pray for? Very often that he and his dear ones may be relieved of their crosses. Is this the lesson taught by Him who gazes down from the cross on him who prays? We have not yet learned the true meaning of the cross. We see only the cross and not the resurrection that follows; we see only the sorrow, the poverty, the persecution, but not the glory given as a reward. "Blessed are the poor.... Blessed are they that mourn.... Blessed are they that suffer persecution" (Mt 5:3 ff.). How we lack the true spirit of Christ! How poorly we understand!

When we participate in the Mass, we see Christ in His suffering and death. We believe with firm faith that by His suffering and death He redeemed the world, opened heaven for us, and earned for us the grace of eternal life. But once we have returned to our homes it seems that we forget all that we saw and believed during the Mass. We do not yet properly understand the mystery of the crucifixion and the resurrection. "O foolish and slow of heart, to believe in all things which the prophets have spoken. Ought not Christ to have suffered these things and so to enter into His glory?" (Lk 24:25 f.) "I am the way, the truth, and the life" (Jn 14:6). Lord, increase our faith.

Prayer

O God, who bringest blessings out of all things for those who love Thee, grant us to be disposed to love Thee with a love that is unfailing so that no temptation may destroy the longing that Thou hast awakened in our hearts. Through Christ our Lord. Amen.

Fourth Sunday after Easter

The Mass

The unfolding of the Easter mysteries presses forward with steady stride. Now already we catch a glimpse of the coming of the Holy Spirit, who will bring the Easter season to a close with an all-pervading baptism of the spirit. "It is expedient to you that I go; for if I go not, the Paraclete will not come to you" (Gospel). He will come and complete the victory of Christ in the world, in the Church, and in the souls of men. He will convince the world of sin, of righteousness, and of judgment; He will make known all truth to the Church and to the faithful.

The Introit strikes a joyful Easter note: "Sing ye to the Lord a new canticle, alleluia; for the Lord hath done wonderful things, alleluia. He hath revealed [by His Resurrection] His justice in the sight of the Gentiles." He has revealed His justice by making complete satisfaction for us to the Father, and by having given new life through the sacrament of baptism. We are now justified, justified even in the holy eyes of God. We are now pure and clothed in the garment of justifying and sanctifying grace. We shine in the brilliancy of our divine adoption and in our supernatural holiness. This is the fruit of the Easter mysteries. Full of gratitude for all that Christ has done for us by His death and resurrection, we break forth in a joyous *Gloria in excelsis Deo*. After this joyous thanksgiving follows the petition: "Grant to Thy people to love that which Thou commandest and to desire that which Thou dost promise; so that amid the changing things of this world, our hearts may be set where true joys are to be found" (Collect). Thus we pray united in spirit, each praying for the other in the spirit of true Christian brotherhood. This true Easter spirit for which we pray, is the "best gift," the perfect gift that comes to us from above. It is the result of the divine love and grace we share through our baptism. "Wherefore, casting away all uncleanness and abundance of naughtiness, with meekness receive the ingrafted word, which is able to save your souls" (Epistle).

With grateful hearts we recognize what God has done for us by the mysteries of Easter and baptism; and therefore, after the Epistle we sing, "Alleluia, the right hand of the Lord hath wrought strength, [by awakening us from the death of sin], the right hand of the Lord hath exalted me [by baptism and sanctifying grace], alleluia. Christ [and in Christ, the Church and all the baptized] rising again from the dead, dieth now no more. Death shall no more have dominion over Him, alleluia." Christ, and with Him the Church, lives as an eternal witness that the world sins terribly by its unbelief, that He is sinless and holy, for otherwise He could not go to the Father; He testifies that Satan, and with him all his followers, are already judged (Gospel). We, the members of the Church, place ourselves at the side of Christ and joyfully sing the Credo.

Just as Christ presented Himself to His disciples on Easter evening, so, too, He comes among us at the Consecration of the Mass. He abides with us. The offering which the Church, guided and enlightened by the Comforter, offers continually to God, is a positive witness that Christ lives, and that the world is convinced of sin if it refuses to believe in Him. It bears witness to the fact that Christ is pure and holy and that He has overcome the prince of this world in Himself and in His spiritual children.

This testimony of the Holy Ghost becomes more vital when we are united with Christ in His sacrifice, in His life, and in His death. The Holy Ghost enables the Church, her priests, and her faithful to unite themselves to Christ in His sacrifice so that their wills and their lives are changed like the bread on the altar. Their manner of life and action is thus vivified by the life and action of Christ. Thus the world can see and know through their actions that Christ lives in them. Christ is a reality, and not a mere phantasy. He is pure and holy. He is stronger than death and sin and Satan. He overcomes evil in all those who become a sacrifice with Him, and who take on His spirit and life through the reception of Holy Communion. Thus they are transformed so that their lives become a witness of Christ and of His holiness and His victory. Thus at the Consecration is fulfilled what we heard in the earlier part of the Mass: Christ lives, and the Holy Ghost will bear witness to Him and glorify Him (Gospel). And the Holy Ghost will do the same for us who take part in this Holy Sacrifice. In the celebration of the Mass, He brings about a marvelous transformation. He brings Christ down upon our altars and makes His presence in the hearts of men a reality. He renews Christ, His real presence, His life, and His victory.

Meditation

The glorification of Christ was not completed by His resurrection from the dead. He goes to the Father also as man, that He may take possession of His throne and, as the glorified Savior, share with God dominion over the world. "Sing ye to the Lord a new canticle" (Introit). He withdraws His visible presence from His disciples and from His Church that He may send them the Holy Spirit in His place. But by means of the Holy Spirit, He will always remain with them invisibly and spiritually. "If I go not, the Paraclete will not come to you; but if I go, I will send Him to you" (Gospel).

"I go to Him that sent Me" (Gospel). Jesus withdraws His visible presence from His disciples and from His Church. They must free themselves from their attachment to His human form; they must give up the comfort and the solace of having Him physically near them and associating with Him. They, too, must become spiritualized. Then only can He send them His Holy Spirit and make them bearers of the Spirit. They must acquire the strength of the Spirit if they are to become the rulers of the world and comfort mankind in all its trials and difficulties. "I go to Him that sent Me." This is a call to become more spiritual, to become detached from all that is worldly.

In our piety we all too often act in a manner that is not spiritual, even with our Lord. We long for His sensible presence, for sensible devotion. We wish to have Him speak to us audibly and give us real visions or some tangible manifestation of His love; we long for sensible graces and consolations of many sorts. This is an unsound sort of spirituality, based on sensible devotion. But Christ tells us, "It is expedient to you that I go." We must become more spiritual: that is the lesson taught by the liturgy during the time before Pentecost. We are taught that we must lift up our hearts to the glorified, heavenly Christ, and free ourselves from all that is perceptible to the senses, and live for the life above. We must seek a spirituality based on the spirit of faith and on a determined effort to overcome all our selfish desires and tendencies. Our spirituality must be based on a love that attends to God alone and occupies itself entirely with what comes from Him and leads to Him. "It is expedient to you that I go; for if I go not, the Paraclete will not come to you."

"I will send Him to you." Jesus leaves us; but since He is no longer bodily present, He sends us His Holy Spirit. He merited for us this greatest of all God's gifts, the Holy Spirit, through His sufferings and death. Now He ascends into heaven that He may send Him to us as our comforter to take His place. But the Holy Spirit has not come to protect us from all suffering and adversity, from temptation and difficulties. He comes rather to fill us with the strength to live and work for Jesus under all circumstances; that is, to work in the spirit of truth and humility. He comes to help us live in voluntary poverty, humility, and suffering. In a word, the Holy Spirit comes to help us conform our lives perfectly to the life of Christ. The Holy Ghost induces us to live in Jesus and for Jesus. He makes us witnesses (martyrs), and in this spirit we gladly embrace ridicule, injustice, suffering, the loss of our possessions, and even the loss of our life. How much we stand in need of such a helper and comforter! How fervently we should pray during this week that God may send this blessed comforter to us and to His Church!

With the newly baptized we perceive the sensible presence of the Lord in the great festivities and symbols of Easter day. Now the liturgy seeks to lead us from the joy of Easter back to the struggle and the sufferings of the world. She seeks to anchor our hearts in heaven, to elevate them above attachment to the world and the love of mere temporal things. She seeks to lift our hearts to heaven, "where true joys are to be found" (Collect). For us who are Christians, a higher world, a world of eternity, is the one reality. To help us reach that world, the glorified Lord sends us the Holy Ghost. We long for His coming and cry without ceasing: *Veni, Sancte Spiritus:* "Come, Holy Ghost, and fill the hearts of Thy faithful."

The most effective means of acquiring true Christian spirituality is through participation in the Mass. We must renounce our personal, human, egotistical spirit, and rid ourselves of all that is worldly and transient. For this reason we receive the Holy Eucharist, which is the spiritualized and glorified flesh and blood of the Lord, who pours forth the wealth and the riches of the Holy Ghost upon us.

Prayer

O God, who makest the minds of Thy faithful to be of one will, grant to Thy people to love that which Thou commandest and to desire that which Thou dost promise; so that amid the changing things of this world, our hearts may be set where true joys are to be found. Through Christ our Lord. Amen.

Monday

In the Epistle, St. James, the first bishop of Jerusalem, speaks to us. He addresses himself first to the Jewish Christians, then to all the rest of us.

"Let no man, when he is tempted, say that he is tempted by God. For God is not a tempter of evils, and He tempteth no man. But every man is tempted by his own concupiscence, being drawn away and allured" (Jas 1:13 f.). Only that which is good can come from God. Whatever God can give and does give is always a perfect gift. Thus, "of His own will He hath begotten us [the baptized] by the word of truth, that we might be some beginning of His creatures" (Epistle). This is the good gift, the perfect gift, which God gives us: the gift of rebirth by water and the Holy Spirit. We are first and above all the predestined, the consecrated children of God. Today we thank God for this perfect gift of His love and mercy. In humility we ask why God gives this perfect gift to us in preference to millions of others who were more deserving of it than we were. Why does He not tire of continually giving this precious gift to me, who am so unworthy? He renews this gift continually in the sacraments of penance and the Eucharist, and in many other channels of grace. It is His love that prompts Him to do this.

"Let every man be swift to hear, but slow to speak, and slow to anger. For the anger of man worketh not the justice of God. Wherefore, casting away all uncleanness and abundance of naughtiness, with meekness receive the ingrafted word, which is able to save your souls" (Epistle). "Be slow to speak and slow to anger"; be not easily aroused and easily vexed; become not easily embittered or irritated. What is pleasing to God cannot be produced in anger. This good gift of God produces in each soul a love of silence and seclusion, so that the soul rests in God. It produces in the soul a meekness and a supernatural calm and peace which is far removed from all animosity and evil. It excludes and overcomes all impatience and irritation. This meekness springs from the fire of love, from self-conquest, from the peace that envelops the soul that is possessed and enlightened by Christ.

In such a soul the sensitiveness of the easily irritated, impatient man, with his degraded and unspiritual inclinations, is replaced by Christian meekness, which gives strength and mastery over one's evil tendencies, and victory over self-love and that sensitiveness so characteristic of the worldly man. Such heroic meekness is born of God; but anger, impatience, and sensitiveness are not born of God, nor of grace, nor are they the fruit of regeneration. Anger is a weakness which attempts to hide behind violent words or deeds, which are unworthy of one who is reborn through Christ. "Blessed are the meek" (Mt 5:4).

With the liturgy of the fourth Sunday after Easter we recognize the "perfect gift," which comes down to us from the Father of light, to be the Holy Ghost, whose coming we await. Through His Word, God has made us His children. Through His Word, that is, through Christ, He gives us the Holy Ghost. On our part we must prepare our souls for His coming through prayer, through the practice of silence, and through an ardent longing for Him.

When we bring our gifts to the altar at the Offertory of the Mass, we repeat with grateful hearts the words of the Offertory prayer: "Shout with joy to God all the earth, sing ye a psalm to His name; come and hear, and I will tell you, all ye that fear God, what great things the Lord hath done for my soul, alleluia." Among the great things the Lord hath done for my soul is the regeneration of that soul. Then, too, He has bestowed on me the sonship of God, making me share the spirit of Christ; He has given me membership in His Church, and has sent to me the Holy Ghost.

Prayer

O God, who makest the minds of Thy faithful to be of one will, grant to Thy people to love that which Thou commandest and to desire that which Thou dost promise; so that amid the changing things of this world, our hearts may be set where true joys are to be found. Through Christ our Lord. Amen.

Tuesday

"And when He is come, He will convince the world of sin, . . . because they believed not in Me" (Gospel). Unbelief was the great sin of the Jews. In spite of the prophecies of the Old Testament which Christ manifestly fulfilled, in spite of His evident miracles, in spite of His resurrection on Easter morning, of which they themselves were the reluctant witnesses, the Jews refused to believe. Therefore, after our Lord's Ascension into heaven, it was part of the mission of the Holy Ghost to convince the world that the Jews erred in not accepting Christ. This was their great sin: the sin of unbelief.

The Holy Ghost worked through the apostles. On Pentecost He descended upon the apostles and called them to act as witnesses of Christ's Resurrection. Emboldened by the power of the Holy Ghost, Peter faces the multitude of people in Jerusalem and declares: "This Jesus hath God raised again, whereof all we are witnesses" (Acts 2:32). The Holy Ghost brings about a complete transformation in the apostles. They had been timid, but now they are filled with indomitable courage and holy daring. They had been slow of understanding, but now they are filled with divine wisdom and speak a language which they had not learned. They had deserted their Lord and Master during His passion, and Peter had even denied Him; but now they are the intrepid teachers of His doctrine and the heralds of His resurrection. But the Holy Ghost assists them in other ways, too; for He gives them the power to work miracles, the reality of which no one can deny, and the significance of which no one can misconstrue. Thus the Holy Ghost convinces the world that the failure to accept the Christ whom the apostles preach is a terrible sin. We stand amazed at these works of the Holy Ghost in the apostles, and rejoice for Christ, whom the apostles bear witness to by the power of the Holy Spirit. "This is the stone which was rejected by you the builders, which is become the head of the corner. Neither is there salvation in any other. For there is no other name under heaven given to men whereby we must be saved" (Acts 4:11 f.).

The Holy Ghost operates in the Church of Christ. He gives her holiness and the gift of miracles. A Church which produces saints bears the stamp of God's approval. The Holy Ghost has placed this unmistakable seal on the Church of Christ, for He produces in the Church the heroism of perfect love for God and man. "By this shall all men know that you are My disciples, if you have love one for another" (Jn 13:35).

The doctrine of the Church is holy; her moral practices are holy; her sacraments are holy; her prayer and her liturgy are holy. The life of her children is saintly, and she has produced millions of saints for heaven. Many of her children on earth have reached a high degree of sanctity, and all of this holiness is due to the operation of the Holy Ghost. Every man must acknowledge this Church as the true Church, as the Church established by Christ and sanctified by the Holy Ghost.

The second stamp of approval which the Holy Ghost places on the Church is the gift of miracles. Christ Himself refers to this gift of miracles and offered His miracles as a proof of His divine mission. They are a means by which men can recognize the true Church and distinguish it from others. "But they, going forth, preached everywhere, the Lord working withal and confirming the word with signs that followed" (Mk 16:20).

The Acts of the Apostles and the history of the Church are little more than the fulfillment of this prophecy of Christ: "Behold, I am with you all days" (Mt 28:20). The Church is the visible, ever-present, and easily understood proof of the testimony of the Holy Ghost to the world, that failure to believe in Christ is a sin. "And when He is come, He will convince the world of sin [the great sin of unbelief],... because they believed not in Me." We recognize and thank God with joy for the work of the Holy Ghost in the apostles and in the Church. We acknowledge with unshakable faith that our Lord is "Christ the Son of the living God,... the way, the truth, and the life" (Jn 11:27; 14:6). "I do believe, Lord; help my unbelief" (Mk 9:23).

"He that believeth and is baptized shall be saved; but he that believeth not, shall be condemned" (Mk 16:16). There are so many men in our times who, like the Jews of old, refuse to believe in Jesus. They can hardly ignore the work of the Holy Ghost; in fact they can almost feel it with their hands. The holiness of the Church, her marvelous unity of doctrine, the miracles which even today are worked by the saints in the Church, all speak eloquently of the fruitful and living presence of the Holy Ghost in the Church. It is a sin and terrible oversight not to believe in Christ. We pity the poor, blinded people who have been cheated of their faith. We pray and intercede for them that they may come to understand that they sin if they fail to come to Jesus and to see that He is the only source of salvation.

The Church lives in each one of us. I, too, must bear personally the stamp of the Holy Ghost in my thinking, in my speech, in my actions. I, too, must be a living and effective witness for Christ. Everyone must see in me what miracles of grace and holiness the Christian faith can produce in men; and through my life others must be forced to acknowledge that Jesus is the truth. This model life should be the result of my participation in Mass, the fruit of my Holy Communions, the result of my prayers and meditations.

Prayer

Send forth from heaven, O Lord, Thy assistance to Thy people, that they may seek Thee with all their hearts, and may thus merit to obtain what they worthily seek. Through Christ our Lord. Amen.

Wednesday

"And when He [the Holy Ghost] is come, He will convince the world... of justice, because I go to the Father" (Gospel). This is the second part of the mission of the Holy Ghost to the world.

Men of the world judged Christ as an unholy and unjust man, and crucified Him on the cross between two thieves. They cast Him aside and placed Him on a plane with a criminal, Barabbas; indeed, they preferred Barabbas to Him, as though Christ were the greater evildoer. They brand Him even today, no less than they did during His lifetime, as a liar and a tremendous impostor. They reject and condemn His doctrine even as they rejected and condemned His person. He still commands us to serve and love God, and our neighbor as ourself; the world preaches self-love and practices it even to the exclusion of God, and it ridicules all those who seek to serve God. Christ preaches submission to the will of God; the world urges independence and self-sufficiency apart from God. Jesus preaches humility; but the world teaches man to assert himself and recognize no power but his own will and no law but the fulfillment of his own desires. Jesus preaches poverty of spirit, meekness, and separation from all that is worldly and passing, and He demands the rejection of all the vanities and idle things of the world; He has pronounced those "blessed" who are pure of heart, who suffer hunger and want for the sake of justice, and who suffer persecution for His name. The world ridicules such principles and such ideals, and sets up her maxims in opposition to the doctrines of Christ; she takes the same attitude toward those things established by Christ: His Church, His priesthood, His moral code, the liturgical worship and the authority of His Church. What is the long line of heresies and schisms but a denial of the Church of Christ? Are they not degenerate deceivers who seek not the will of Christ and the things of God, but are accompanied by a mad thirst for power and honor, and an uncontrollable greed?

"He will convince the world ... of justice, because I go to the Father." How could Christ go to the Father and be accepted into the presence of God if He were the wicked, unjust, and sinful man the Pharisees of ancient times and the modern world would make Him out to be? "I go to the Father"; but when the Holy Ghost, the Paraclete, is come, He will testify that Christ, who was crucified by men, cast off by the world, and branded as a deceiver, is actually with the Father. Christ has been received by the Father, elevated and crowned with glory; God has placed His seal of approval on Christ's holiness, on His justice, on His teaching, and on His life. Christ is acknowledged by God as His Son, as the way, the truth, and the life.

God will also fulfill the promises made by Christ. "Every one therefore that shall confess Me before men, I will also confess him before My Father who is in heaven" (Mt 10:32). On divine authority rests the prophecy: "Heaven and earth shall pass, but My words shall not pass" (Mt 24:35). Divinely approved, too, is Christ's teaching of voluntary poverty, humility, and self-denial, Christ's love for God and for souls, and finally, His complete self-effacement on the cross. It follows, then, that God must approve the Church which Christ founded, that He must endorse the dogmas it teaches and the moral standards it maintains; He must approve of its spirit, the saints it produces, and the interior and exterior life that it leads.

"He will convince the world ... of justice." This justice is embodied in Christ, who "alone art holy." "Sing a new canticle to the Lord, alleluia, for the Lord hath done wonderful things, alleluia. He hath revealed [by sending the Holy Ghost] His justice in the sight of the Gentiles, alleluia, alleluia" (Introit).

The justice which the Holy Ghost brings is not the justice of the world. Christ has been acknowledged by God to be the only truly just one. In Christ alone can true virtue and true holiness be found; that is, true holiness is found only in Christ and in those who live in union with Him, who live and grow by virtue of that union. True Christian virtue is found only in the Church which is filled with the Spirit of Christ.

Now we understand the liturgy when it sings the Communion chant: "When the Paraclete, the Spirit of truth is come, He shall convince the world of sin, and of justice, and of judgment, alleluia, alleluia." With each worthy reception of Holy Communion, Christ implants His spirit deeper in our souls. We leave the Communion table and return to our work, to our family, to our customary occupations, convinced of the heinousness of sin, and we hate it and condemn it. We are "convinced of justice," and we reason and conduct ourselves according to its dictates. We live according to the spirit which Christ has given us.

Prayer

May the Holy Ghost penetrate our hearts, O Lord, and cleanse them. May He penetrate them to their depths with His dew and make them fruitful. Through Christ our Lord. Amen.

Thursday

"When He [the Holy Ghost] is come, He will convince the world of sin, and of justice, and of judgment, because the prince of this world is already judged" (Gospel). The third part of the Holy Ghost's mission is to convince the world that the prince of this world, Satan, and with him his domain, the entire world, has been judged. The world is unjust; in Christ alone is there justice and truth.

Jesus has passed sentence on the prince of this world. This first sentence was given by Christ on the cross. "Now is the judgment of the world; now shall the prince of this world be cast out. And I, if I be lifted up from the earth, will draw all things to Myself" (Jn 12:31 f.). Christ allowed Himself to be unjustly sentenced and put to death by the world. Thus, fixed to the cross, He is a living judgment written in the blood which poured forth from His wounds. The blood of this innocent victim stands as a contradiction to the judgment which Satan, the prince of this world, and his servants, Pilate and the Jews, passed upon the innocent, unspotted Son of God.

Christ has passed judgment on the prince of this world a second time by His Resurrection from the dead, through which He has proved the falsity of the charges made against Him by the Jews. He was accused of being a blasphemer, of working His miracles and wonders with the help and by the power of the devil. These infernal lies are now unmasked. God Himself has proved through the Resurrection that Christ was the Son of God. "That in the name of Jesus every knee should bow, . . . and that every tongue should confess that the Lord Jesus Christ is in the glory of God the Father" (Phil 2:10 f.). Thus sentence has been passed on Satan and upon the whole world. The judgment of the world concerning Christ, the gospel, the Church, the Christian faith, Christian morals, the meaning of life, the value of material things, is thus proved to be false. "Now is the judgment of the world; now shall the prince of this world be cast out" (Jn 12:31), that is, through the resurrection of Christ. Satan is dethroned. Justice is on the side of the Lord. The world is filled with lies, treachery, and falsehood. Grant me the light, O Lord, to recognize the world for what it is and to avoid it and all its abominations.

The Holy Ghost, too, passes judgment on the prince of this world. After Christ ascended to His Father, the Holy Ghost came to confirm the judgment passed by Christ on the world, and to maintain that judgment through the many centuries of the Church's history. The world mistakenly thought that with His burial, Christ's doctrines and teachings had been buried with Him. But the Holy Ghost came to supply for the crucified Christ. The gospel of Christ spread with incredible speed through the cities and towns of the empire, and captured the hearts and minds of the people. Although the Jews rejected the gospel, it was accepted by the Gentiles, who believed and were admitted to baptism. They rallied to the standard of Christ and made their abjuration of Satan. They renounced Satan and the world with all its vanities, its specious maxims, its deceptive power. The Holy Ghost is to construct a new world founded on Christ. All who believe are to live in the greatest harmony. Men no longer consider their possessions their own; all is held in common. No longer are there any needy ones among them; all dwell together in peace. "And all they that believed were together, and had all things common. Their possessions and goods they sold, and divided them to all, according as every one had need" (Acts 2:44 f.).

The disciples of Christ were not troubled by covetousness, envy, and discord; harmony, charity, joy, and devotion to God reigns in their midst. They were not proud or egotistical, but they submitted in all humility to the guidance of the apostles and of the Church. "The prince of this world is already judged." He has been judged and sentenced. Judgment had been passed upon his maxims, his spirit, his way of life, not only in the ancient Church, but in the Church of all times. This judgment has been accepted by millions of faithful Christians in the East and in the West, in the past and in the present. Moreover, the Church of Christ is never without its saints. Thus again the Holy Ghost passes judgment on the prince of this world. "For all that is in the world, is the concupiscence of the flesh, and the concupiscence of the eyes, and the pride of life, which is not of the Father, but is of the world. And the world passeth away, and the concupiscence thereof" (1 Jn 2:16 f.). Satan has been judged, sentenced, and condemned; he has been proved a liar. We, too, pass this same judgment on Satan and the world, for we will have no part in them.

"The prince of this world is already judged." This is the song of the Church and of the Christian soul at Easter time. Satan has been overpowered and dethroned. But nevertheless the Lord has given him an hour of grace for our own good. He still wanders about in the world, using the hours given him by God with the greatest zeal, to deceive and mislead the world. He propagates his lies, which the world mistakes for pronouncements of truth. The hearts of many men, which should be raised to heaven, Satan manages to turn again to the earth. Many Christians, having been deceived by him, turn to material and transitory things.

"The prince of this world is already judged." He is judged, not only by the risen Christ Himself, but also by His members who are risen with Him. The condemnation of the prince of this world must be verified in us also, just as it is in Christ. We must condemn him with our thoughts, our words, and our speech. Each of our actions must pass judgment on Satan. We pass judgment on him through our faith in Christ, the crucified and risen Lord, and through the love which we manifest for Him "who loved me and delivered Himself for me" (Gal 2:20). We condemn him by our confidence in Christ, by our faithfulness to the vows we made at the time of our baptism, by the nobility of our ideals, by our opposition to evil, its influence, and its illusions.

"The prince of this world is already judged." The fruitfulness of the work of the Holy Ghost in the Church, in the baptized, is also evidence of the judgment passed on Satan and the world.

The Holy Ghost continually justifies, confirms, and glorifies Jesus in His members. He offers proof that Christ is the Son of God, that His words are true, that His virtue was genuine. His promises are not false but true. Through the power of Holy Communion, He will be glorified in me. He will form me and reshape me into a spiritual man, so that in my daily life I, too, may stand as a judgment against the world and Satan (Communion).

Prayer

O Lord, who by the sacred communion of this sacrifice hast made us partakers of the one supreme divine nature, grant, we beseech Thee, that as we know Thy truth, so we may follow it by a worthy life. Through Christ our Lord. Amen. (Secreta.)

Friday

"O God, grant to Thy people to love that which Thou commandest" (Collect). It is the command of the Church that we love God and His holy will. In this manner the Church wishes the baptized to rise to a new life with Christ. This grace we implore for one another.

"The fear of the Lord is the beginning of wisdom" (Ps 110:10). The fear of God forms the very foundation of the spiritual life. As long as we have to struggle with sin, the fear of the justice of God occupies the most important place in our spiritual life. The just punishments of God visited on sinners, the anger of God, the everlasting pain of hell, are ever before our eyes. We must never forget our moral weakness, the attraction of sinful actions, the ever-present possibility that we may fall. Nor can we forget that we are too little concerned about the graces of God, that we often act from purely natural motives rather than from supernatural ones. We know from experience that we are careless, easily provoked, impatient, and unpleasant toward our fellow men. We know that we are self-centered and have many faults. All these things should inspire us with a continual and secret fear of God. The fear of God should accompany us throughout our lives, influence all our thoughts and acts, and take a firm hold on us. "Blessed is the man that feareth the Lord" (Ps 111:1). "Fear God and depart from evil.... The fear of the Lord hateth evil" (Prv 3:7; 8:13). "The fear of the Lord is the beginning of wisdom."

"Thou shalt love the Lord, Thy God" (Mt 22:37). The fear of the Lord is necessary, but the proper basis and the chief motivating force of Christianity is love. Love alone is worthy of God, who is entitled to our love because of His infinite perfection and goodness. He deserves our love because of His many benefactions and the wealth He will bestow on us in eternal life. "Thou shalt love the Lord, Thy God," is the first and the greatest commandment. God demands all our love, and He alone deserves it. Love for God shapes our heart, disentangles it from the world, and turns it to God. Love alone can make our hearts big enough and strong enough to endure sacrifice in the service of God. Fear can cause us to avoid evil, but it cannot elevate us to the performance of good. Love effects both at one and the same time. It draws us away from what is evil, or from what is only apparently evil, and inspires us to do good. It draws us from what is merely good to that which is better, and, in spite of all difficulties and hardships, from that which is better to that which is perfect. Fear causes us to think too much of ourselves; it cannot inspire us with generosity. It keeps us within the commandments, it keeps us faithful to our duty, and then feels that it has done enough. Charity is quite different, for it always gives beyond the measure of duty. It looks on all that it has done as nothing. Charity alone can understand the full significance of that saying of the Word, "So you also, when you shall have done all these things that are commanded you, say: We are unprofitable servants; we have done that which we ought to do" (Lk 17:10).

When the Holy Ghost has endowed a soul with charity, He enlarges the heart also, so that it has room for a larger understanding of those things which are permitted. He implants in the soul the gift of piety, that is, the desire and the longing to please God and to fulfill His will. "My meat is to do the will of Him that sent Me" (Jn 4:34). Such a soul makes no distinction between the bond and the free, between what is merely permitted and what is perfect. Whenever an opportunity occurs for nourishing the flame of charity, that opportunity will be embraced by such a soul with a burning zeal. It no longer asks what its obligation is. It has discovered the secret; it does all that it can; then it is certain that it has fulfilled its obligation. It loves both the commandments of God and the will of God. Such a soul is free even though it is bound by the commandments. It does not live under restraint, it does not sigh under its burden as does a slave, it never tries to release itself even when it might do so. He who possesses charity says with the Psalmist: "O Lord my portion, I have said, I would keep Thy law" (Ps 118:57). Such a soul knows itself to be a child of God, and therefore it tries to do much more than is required by the commandments, and thus gives pleasure to its Father.

The liturgy implores God for the virtue of charity for all the faithful. Charity is the greatest of the Christian virtues. It fulfills perfectly the commandments of God. "For this is the charity of God, that we keep His commandments" (1 Jn 5:3). But charity keeps the commandments, not because of a fear of punishment, nor because of compulsion, as a slave keeps them, nor because of a desire for merit; but rather to please Him to whom the Christian subjects himself freely and joyfully at the time of his baptism.

Charity and the works of charity go hand in hand. Only those are perfect works which are done out of love. Charity is the soul and the root of all virtue. Works, such as the fulfillment of the law, are the food, the nourishment, the essential condition for the existence of charity. He who would fulfill the commandments perfectly must do so out of love. He who would acquire the virtue of charity must perform works of charity. He who would reach perfection must endeavor with all his strength to exercise himself incessantly in works of charity.

Prayer

O God, who makest the minds of Thy faithful to be of one will, grant to Thy people to love that which Thou commandest and to desire that which Thou dost promise; so that amid the changing things of this world, our hearts may be set where true joys are to be found. Through Christ our Lord. Amen.

Saturday

"Grant to Thy people to love that which Thou commandest and to desire that which Thou dost promise; so that amid the changing things of this world, our hearts may be set where true joys are to be found" (Collect). We should long to ascend to heaven and should be absorbed by the desire for eternity.

As our high priest our Savior recited this prayer: "Father, I will that where I am, they also whom Thou hast given Me may be with Me. That they may see My glory which Thou hast given Me, because Thou hast loved Me before the creation of the world" (Jn 17:24). The Father promised that we shall be taken to that place where Jesus is in the glory of the Father. Through our baptism we have become the children of God, "and if sons, heirs also, heirs indeed of God and joint heirs with Christ" (Rom 8:17). The Lord has prepared a place for us in heaven, that "our fellowship may be with the Father and with His Son Jesus Christ" (1 Jn 1:3); that is, we are to possess and enjoy the life and the fruits of the three divine persons, to see God, to repose eternally in the presence of God, to love Him. The joy of God will then be our joy; the life of God will be our life. We shall share a perfect life, in which all our powers will find their most perfect exercise and complete fulfillment. If we could only perceive what things God has prepared for us, what great efforts we would exert to obtain this one thing necessary! Father, grant us to desire with all the powers of our soul the things which Thou hast promised us. Let us forget all worldly things, all that is temporal and passing, and exert ourselves to obtain those things that await us.

"Grant that our hearts may be set where true joys are to be found" (Collect). The baptized soul must linger here on earth, but he allows transitory things to pass by as if they were no concern of his. He possesses them and he makes use of them as if he possessed them not and used them not. All his powers and thoughts and endeavors are concentrated on eternity, on the world above the stars. He lives entirely for the things that are to come when this world has passed away. His mind is occupied with the consideration of future joys, and of the perfect and glorious happiness of eternity. He is assured of possessing it because he possesses the Holy Ghost, and because he has become the son of God through his baptism. It is guaranteed to him by the resurrection and ascension of the Lord, who is the head of the body into which he has been incorporated. "But God (who is rich in mercy), for His exceeding charity wherewith He loved us, even when we were dead in sins, hath quickened us together in Christ (by whose grace you are saved) and hath raised us up together and hath made us sit together in the heavenly places, through Christ Jesus. That He might show in the ages to come the abundant riches of His grace in His bounty towards us in Christ Jesus" (Eph 2:4–7).

What value can the things of this world have for him who is firmly rooted in a world that is above all transitory, temporal things? He can afford to wait, for the world can never give him peace or enjoyment. He exerts his energies and directs his impulses to rise to higher things, to obtain the one thing necessary, to obtain those things which have a lasting value. Earthly possessions, difficulties and hardships, pain and disappointments, cannot deter him. His treasure is buried in the field of heaven; he has discovered one precious pearl, and he sacrifices all else to purchase this field, this pearl, this blessed eternity. The thought of eternity gives him the strength to sacrifice and struggle, to pardon injuries, and to suffer in patience. He acquires a zeal for the salvation of immortal souls. He learns to sacrifice himself in works of charity, to acquire for his brothers and sisters in Christ the riches of eternal life. The thought of eternity gives him a driving force that is stronger than the memory of earthly joys, more insistent than the cravings of nature, more persistent than self, more enduring than death. "Grant to Thy people ... to desire that which Thou dost promise."

"Blessed are the poor in spirit.... Blessed are the meek.... Blessed are they that hunger and thirst after justice.... Blessed are the merciful.... Blessed are the clean of heart" (Mt 5:3 ff.). These are the true Christians, heroic souls who are firmly fixed on heaven.

The worldly man delights in "the concupiscence of the flesh, and the concupiscence of the eyes, and the pride of life" (1 Jn 2:16). Unfortunately so many Christians are completely occupied with the things of this world. Easter should find them new men, risen from the dead, with their hearts firmly set on heaven, men of heroism. And yet they will still be lost in the abyss of the old man, spiritual weaklings, worldly men. Thus with the liturgy we pray for them from the depths of our souls, that "our hearts may be set where true joys are to be found."

Before we approach the sacred moment of consecration at Mass, the priest admonishes us, *Sursum corda:* "Lift up your hearts." And we answer, *Habemus ad Dominum*. Have we indeed lifted up our heart to the Lord? Or have we lifted it up only to earthly affairs, good health, or worthless trifles? Let us consider all things in the light of eternity and ask ourselves under all circumstances: "Of what value is this for eternal life?"

Prayer

O God, who makest the minds of Thy faithful to be of one will, grant to Thy people to love that which Thou commandest and to desire that which Thou dost promise; so that amid the changing things of this world, our hearts may be set where true joys are to be found. Through Christ our Lord. Amen.

Fifth Sunday after Easter

The Mass

In a few days the paschal season, taken in the narrowest sense of the word, will come to a close with the feast of the Ascension. What wonder, then, that the liturgy for Easter and for the Ascension are combined in the Mass for this Sunday.

The Introit of the Mass rings with the joy of Easter. It is as though our gratitude for our resurrection with Christ through baptism would well up again to the very heavens in all its splendor and power. "The Lord hath delivered His people [through baptism], alleluia." And as we pour forth our thanks for having risen with Christ in baptism, we pray also that the graces of Easter may remain with us when the season itself has passed. This petition we make as we recite fervently the Kyrie. The Collect for the day expresses this sentiment even more clearly and forcefully. "O God, from whom all good things proceed, grant to Thy suppliants that by Thy inspiration we may think what is right and with Thy guidance carry out the same" (Collect). Lent and Easter have given the faithful a vivid realization of their duties, but this knowledge must be carried out in their lives. "Dearly beloved, be ye doers of the word and not hearers only, deceiving your own selves" (Epistle). Thus the apostle James admonishes us in his earnest and matchless way. That is the obligation laid on us by our baptism, by our celebration of Easter. We must live according to our belief. "Religion pure and undefiled before God and the Father is this: to visit the fatherless and widows in their tribulation, and to keep one's self unspotted from this world"

(Epistle). We must practice charity and break away completely from the world. The task which Easter places upon us is not an easy one.

Our obligation to renounce the world is emphasized by the Gospel: "I go to the Father." We, too, must go to the Father; we must withdraw from the handicaps and the restrictions imposed on us by Original Sin. That is the real significance of Easter and of the baptism which we have received. He who now is about to go to the Father, goes not for His own benefit alone, nor to reap all the profit for Himself. There He is to act as our intermediary, and by praying in His name we may expect to find salvation. Through Christ, our intermediary, our prayers and desires also ascend to the Father.

When we sing the Credo, we ask resolutely and confidently for the grace to act always in the spirit of Easter. We express our faith in the Credo, and our consciousness of victory in the Offertory: "O bless the Lord our God, ye Gentiles, and make the voice of His praise to be heard; who hath set my soul to live, and hath not suffered my feet to be moved."

"I came forth from the Father and am come into the world. Again I leave the world and go to the Father." What is here said in the Gospel becomes a reality in the Mass. During the Consecration of the Mass He descends into the world as God, mystically and sacramentally. We greet Him joyfully by singing, "Holy, holy, holy. Blessed is He that cometh in the name of the Lord." Now we take the place of the disciples in the Gospel, and receive with joy the comforting message of the Lord: "If you ask the Father anything in My name, He will give it you. Hitherto you have not asked anything in My name." Hitherto, that is, before you received baptism, before it became possible for you to pray with Him and through Him in the Mass, you had not asked anything in His name. But now the prayer of the sacrificing Christian becomes one with the prayer of Christ in the Sacrifice of the Mass; it becomes substantially united to that of Christ. Just as the bread is changed by the prayer of Christ, so our prayer is changed into Christ's prayer and carried by His pure hands to the throne of the Father. For this reason the Father, in the Holy Sacrifice of the Mass, pours forth the love which He bears for Christ upon us also who sacrifice with Him. The Father carries out the promise made by Christ: "The Father Himself loveth you, because you have loved Me" (Gospel). Therefore after the Consecration we can say with childlike confidence: "Our Father, who art in heaven." Thus we can lay aside and forget all that is earthly and unimportant, and arise with Christ to a new life; and when He offers Himself, we, too, can daily "go to the Father."

Through Christ and in Christ we become children of the Father and of His love. "The Father Himself loves you" and gives proof of this love, not only in the Holy Sacrifice of the Mass, but also in Holy Communion. "Sing ye to the Lord, alleluia." Holy Communion is God's answer to the prayer we offer in union with Christ, His Son. It is His reply to our resolve: "I will go to the Father." "The Father Himself loveth you because you have loved Me and have believed that I came out from God" (Gospel).

Meditation

"Declare it with the voice of joy and let it be heard, alleluia; declare it even to the ends of the earth: The Lord hath delivered His people, alleluia" (Introit). From the Christian point of view the most important of all truths is the fact that men have been redeemed and that they are the children of God. Now heaven has been opened again to us, and so, too, the heart of the Father. "Amen, amen, I say to you, if you ask the Father anything in My name, He will give it you" (Gospel).

"Hitherto you have not asked anything in My name." It is true that the apostles had asked the Lord: "Lord, teach us to pray" (Lk 11:1), and He had taught them how to say the Our Father. And indeed, they had asked Him for an increase of faith. But as yet they had not prayed to the Father in the name of Jesus, basing their request on the fact of His death or on the merits of the blood that He had shed. This was not possible for them, since it was necessary that the Lord first pour forth His blood and sacrifice His life on the cross. It was necessary that He first, as the high priest of the New Covenant "having obtained eternal redemption" by His own blood, enter once into the holy of holies (Heb 9:12). The Lord begins to exercise His office as our intermediary at the time of His ascension. Thus previous to that time the apostles could not ask in His name.

But there was still another reason why they could not pray in His name. Previous to His passion and death Christ had not revealed to them entirely the nature of His mission. They had always had visions of a temporal kingdom and throne of glory. That He was to die on the cross they could not comprehend. How could they pray in His name as long as they believed Him to be something other than what He actually was? They came to the correct concept of Him and His mission only after His death and resurrection and ascension, only after the descent of the Holy Ghost at Pentecost. Only then did they begin to understand that no one can pray in the name of Jesus unless he bases his prayers on Christ's merits, on His suffering and death, and offers his prayers to the Father through the merits of the blood of Christ. Only he can come to the Father who is one in spirit with the crucified Christ. Only he can expect to be heard who, like the Lord, is willing to be obedient even to death, and who can say with Jesus, "My meat is to do the will of Him that sent Me" (Jn 4:34). Only when we have acquired the spirit of Christ, His point of view, conformity to the will of God, can we actually pray in the name of Jesus. Then our prayers will be united to His prayers and incorporated in them, to be acknowledged by Him as His own and offered by Him to His Father. Such prayers will certainly be answered.

"Ask and you shall receive, that your joy may be full" (Gospel). Our Savior has given the solemn promise, in His own name and in the name of His Father, that "whatsoever you shall ask the Father in My name, that will I do" (Jn 14:13). In prayer we have an unfailing means for obtaining light, power, and grace from God. "For every one that asketh, receiveth; and he that seeketh, findeth; and to him that knocketh, it shall be opened" (Lk 11:10). He who fails to ask, will not receive; he who asks little, shall receive but little; while he who asks much, will receive much. This divine rule in the order of grace is borne out by experience and by the history of the Church. It is the law that "to the humble [God] giveth grace" (1 Pt 5:5); and "He hath filled the hungry with good things; and the rich He hath sent empty away" (Lk 1:53). In prayer we abandon ourselves and go to the Father. Why? We become conscious of our own nothingness and misery; in all humility we acknowledge our nothingness and our insufficiency; we humbly confess that we are unable to help ourselves, that we cannot live by ourselves, and that of ourselves we can accomplish nothing. For this reason we lift our hearts to God, for "every best gift and every perfect gift is from above, coming down from the Father of lights" (Jas 1:17). Thus we throw open the doors of our being to the infinity of God, that His light and power may stream in.

Prayer is the respiration of the soul; the soul exhales its own nothingness and inhales God. Prayer is the abandonment of self and a dedication to God. If we would preserve and nourish the life of God which we received in baptism, then we must breathe forth ourselves into God and inhale the light and the power of God. This we do in prayer. There is no grace without prayer. Only he who casts himself down in humility, only he who can abandon himself and his own nothingness, only he who absorbs God — only he can be helped. Only those who ask shall receive.

"If you ask the Father anything in My name, He will give it you" (Gospel). We ask the Father in the name of Jesus principally when we celebrate the Holy Sacrifice of the Mass in the proper spirit. This we do by taking into our hands His sacred body and His precious blood, the price of our salvation, and offering them up to the Father. "We Thy servants [the priest], and also Thy holy people,... offer up to Thy most excellent majesty, from among Thy gifts and presents, a pure victim, a holy victim, a spotless victim, the holy bread of life everlasting and the chalice of eternal salvation" (Canon). Here His sufferings, His blood, and His death speak for us. Here He acts as our advocate and makes our needs the object of His priestly prayer, a prayer which is all-powerful with God. He is our intercessor and intermediary. Now His promise is fulfilled: "Ask and you shall receive, that your joy may be full." Then the Lord who was sacrificed for us comes into our hearts at Holy Communion. Our hearts now become His dwelling place, where He lives and prays. He elevates our prayers with His own and makes them a part of His adoration, His thanksgiving, His praise. The small grain of incense which is our prayer He puts into the thurible of His praying heart. Thus it becomes a part of His own perfect prayer and rises up to the Father like the smoke of incense. "Through Him and with Him and in Him" the Father receives from us also "all honor and glory."

"Alleluia, I came forth from the Father and am come into the world; again I leave the world and I go to the Father, alleluia" (Alleluia verse). He is our advocate with the Father, He has opened heaven to us again and made our approach to the Father possible. Now since we are children of the Father, we are free to speak and say, "Our Father." Christ, who is our elder brother, prays with us and in us. We pray with Him and in Him and in His name, basing our claims on His merits. Thus our prayer becomes all-powerful, but only under one condition: "If any man think himself to be religious, not bridling his tongue but deceiving his own heart, this man's religion is vain. Religion clean and undefiled before God and the Father is this: To visit the fatherless and widows in their tribulation, and to keep one's self unspotted from this world" (Epistle).

Prayer

O God, from whom all good things proceed, grant to Thy suppliants that by Thy inspiration we may think what is right and with Thy guidance carry out the same. Through Christ our Lord. Amen.

Monday, Rogation Day

Today we observe the first of the three rogation days which immediately precede the feast of the Ascension. In the mind of the liturgy our petitions are to accompany the Lord when He ascends into heaven. Christ in His Ascension is our emissary, our messenger, our advocate. With this thought in mind the Church holds her rogation processions. "Arise, O Lord, help us and redeem us for Thy name's sake" (Processional antiphon). "Lord have mercy on us. Christ have mercy on us." May all the saints pray for us that we may obtain forgiveness and protection from our enemies and from the enemies of the Church; that there may be concord and harmony among all peoples; that there may be but one fold and one shepherd; that all men may be saved. The Church places these petitions on the paten, in the hands of the Lord, who is about to offer Himself up to the Father with her and for her.

"For where there are two or three gathered together in My name, there am I in the midst of them" (Mt 18:20). The prayer of the Christian is necessarily a catholic (universal) prayer, made with and for the rest of the community. He who has once learned to pray in the spirit of Christ, knows that his prayer belongs to the whole Church. He knows that nothing is so foreign to the spirit of Christ and to a child of God as a narrow isolationism. "Woe to him that is alone" (Eccles 4:10). The Christian knows that when he prays he is supported and abetted by his brethren. If he loves God with all his heart, he means not with his own heart alone, but with those of all his brethren. He feels that Jesus, Mary, the saints in heaven, and all earnest Christians on earth have but one heart, the heart of Jesus. By virtue of the power of the Holy Ghost, they have but one soul. When he prays, he knows that all the blessed in heaven and the baptized on earth pray with him, joining in one "Our Father," in one "Glory be to the Father, and to the Son, and to the Holy Ghost"; all join in the same "Hail Mary." When he prays, he has a deep consciousness of these others praying with him, and he joins his prayers to those of the whole community, even when he prays alone, knowing that no one by himself dares to approach the Father. One can approach God only in company with the other children of God, united to them, as it were, with one heart and one soul. All must approach the Father together and present themselves as one; otherwise the Father is not pleased with them.

He who prays alone is narrow, egotistical, and isolated. Separated from the community, he cannot ask "our Father" to "give us this day our daily bread, and forgive us our trespasses." He has failed to understand that this promise has been made only to the community of men, praying with one another and for one another. "Where there are two or three gathered together in My name, there am I in the midst of them," supporting their petition, supplementing it, and presenting it to the Father.

"No man cometh to the Father but by Me" (Jn 14:6). Only in communion with Him and through Him can we gain admission to God with our prayers. He leads us, since we are joined to Him, into the sacred presence of God. Through Him we have become the children of God and may now gain admission to the Father. Through Him and in Him we live, we feel, we work as children of God and fulfill the duties which are ours by reason of our being members of the family of God. We perceive also our obligation of approaching God as children when we pray.

In truth we can be said to be really praying only when we do so with Christ and through Christ. He must be in our midst. Wherever two or three are assembled in His name, there He is to be found among them if they are of one soul and one mind, united by mutual love. They are one in the measure in which they are one in their prayer, in heart, and in spirit. He stands in the midst of those who pray as their leader and guide. Now the Father hears the voice of His Son mingled with the prayers of the community. For this reason our prayers are answered. Through this union of prayer we establish contact with Christ and with His prayers. He assimilates and unites the entire Church with Himself. God does not look with pleasure nor bestow His grace on those separated from the community, but only on the Church and on those in communion with the Church. The individual can hope to receive from Him only in the measure in which he unites himself to the community and to the Church. The more intimately we associate ourselves with the community, with the Church, with our parish, with our family, with the various religious families, the more pleased God will be with us, and the more fruitful becomes our prayer. "For where there are two or three gathered together in My name, there am I in the midst of them" (Mt 18:20).

But what if we should be living at odds with our brethren? What if we are given to hatred and are guilty of a lack of charity both in word and in action? Can our prayer then be truly a prayer of the community, made in the name of Christ? It could hardly be so.

During the rogation processions the Church prays the Litany of the Saints. The Church militant unites with the Church triumphant, with Mary, the Queen of all saints, with the holy angels, with the apostles and martyrs, with the confessors and virgins. This union provides a vast multitude of holy souls praying as one. Joining her prayer to those of the saints, the Church cries out to the Lord, "be merciful," "deliver us from all evil," "we beseech Thee, hear us." Then she adds many prayers addressed to the Father. All these she offers to God through her intermediary, Jesus Christ. "For where there are two or three gathered together in My name, there am I in the midst of them." How fruitful these rogation processions must be, for the Church is sure to be heard! "He heard my voice from His holy temple, alleluia" (Introit).

Prayer

Grant, we beseech Thee, O almighty God, that we who in our affliction confide in Thy mercy, may be ever defended by Thy protection against all adversity. Through Christ our Lord. Amen.

Tuesday, Rogation Day

"Ask, and it shall be given you; seek, and you shall find; knock, and it shall be opened to you" (Gospel). This solemn promise was made by the Lord to those who pray. Confiding in this promise, we join in the rogation procession and the Mass.

"The continual prayer of a just man availeth much. Elias was a man passible like unto us; and with prayer he prayed that it might not rain upon the earth, and it rained not for three years and six months. And he prayed again, and the heaven gave rain, and the earth brought forth her fruit" (Epistle). Thus we see how efficacious and how fruitful were the prayers of the just man Elias. And the Lord has also promised us in the Gospel: "Ask, and it shall be given you." How great, then, must be the intercessory power of the Church! How great must be the power of that prayer if all members of the Church and the saints in heaven lift their hands to the Father in supplication! The Church prays incessantly through her priests, through her religious, through the saints, through Mary, the most powerful of all intercessors, and through her Head, who is Christ Jesus. Christ is with the Father; He is also in our tabernacles, "always living to make intercession for us" (Heb 7:25). We join our prayers to those of the Church, and we have the assurance: "Ask, and it shall be given you." We place our trust in the intercessory power of the Church, of which we are living members. We also place great confidence in the power of our prayer, because of the fact that we are supported and abetted by the prayers of many holy and

God-fearing brothers and sisters in Christ. What a precious possession such prayers are! How we should prize and treasure them!

"Ask, and it shall be given you." What the Church wants today, above all else, is souls devoted to prayer. All of us in some way share a responsibility for our fellow Christians. God wishes the salvation of all men. But if this goal is to be realized, men must themselves desire salvation and work to obtain it. Moreover, men must will the salvation of their fellow men and work to accomplish it. Every man is master of his own destiny. But even so, each one of us is in some measure the master of the destiny of others. We all contribute to the good fortune (or ill fortune), the salvation and eternal destiny, of our fellow men. Because we are all branches of the same living vine, Christ, our lives are intertwined. Necessarily, therefore, we can and do promote or hamper the progress of other branches of the vine. There is no such thing as a neutral position.

To a certain extent even the eternal salvation of our fellow men lies in our hands. This responsibility we discharge by means of our example and our prayers. By means of our prayers we prevent the just wrath of God from being visited upon His people. The sins of men in our day call out to heaven for vengeance. How frightful are the sins of unbelief! How horribly men revile God; how rashly they deny Him; how foolishly they blaspheme against Him and His Church! The world is drenched in sins of hatred — hatred between nations, hatred between social classes, hatred between individuals. For that reason we are admonished in today's Epistle: "Dearly beloved,... pray one for another that you may be saved.... If any of you err from the truth and one convert him, he must know that he who causeth a sinner to be converted from the error of his way, shall save his soul from death, and shall cover a multitude of sins."

To save souls through the power of prayer is the great occupation of the Church during the rogation days and at other times also. She prays that souls may be saved, and that is the purpose of our prayer also. We pray with the tenacity of the beggar mentioned in today's Gospel: "Yet if he shall continue knocking, I say to you, although he will not rise and give him because he is his friend; yet because of his importunity he will rise and give him as many as he needeth." We must pray much, pray diligently, and pray without ceasing. "Ask, and it shall be given you."

We place too little trust in the promise that has been made to us and too little dependence on the value and the power of prayer. That is why our prayers lack confidence and zeal. And yet, precisely to those who possess zeal and confidence the promise has been made: "All things whatsoever you ask when ye pray, believe that you shall receive" (Mk 11:24), and "If thou canst believe, all things are possible to him that believeth" (Mk 9:22). Moreover, the closer our union with the Church, the more effective our prayers will be. This union with the Church will manifest itself in the firmness of our faith, in our obedience to her commands, in our devotion to her service, in our participation in her prayer, in our sharing of her sacrifice. Under these circumstances our prayers will have the quality that every effective prayer must have: they will be devout, zealous, unceasing, childlike, and persevering. Therefore pray with the Church.

"Ask, and it shall be given you." Today the liturgy associates this admonition with our reception of Holy Communion, for at that time we are most intimately bound to Christ the vine, to the other members of the community, and to the Church herself. At this most holy moment Christ, who has sacrificed Himself for us, prays with us and for us, together with the whole Church, to which He is intimately united; and we pray with Him and through Him. Then we shall receive, we shall find, it will be opened to us.

PRAYER

Kindly grant our prayers, we beseech Thee, O Lord, that while we receive Thy gifts in tribulation, we may increase in love for Thee through our consolation. Through Christ our Lord. Amen. (Postcommunion.)

Wednesday
Vigil of the Ascension

Today we live with our Lord and Savior. The thought that concerns Him most today is the realization: "I come to Thee," to the Father. The Son knocks at the door of the Father and begs admission for Himself and for His disciples.

"Father, the hour is come; glorify Thy Son, that Thy Son may glorify Thee.... I have glorified Thee on earth: I have finished the work which Thou gavest Me to do; and now glorify Thou Me, O Father, with Thyself, with the glory which I had before the world was" (Gospel). Christ asks His Father to let His human nature share in that glory which He possessed as the Son of God from all eternity. How completely He has humbled Himself! Although He was God, at the moment of His Incarnation He took on our lowly human nature and "emptied Himself, taking the form of a servant.... He humbled Himself, becoming obedient unto death, even to the death of the cross" (Phil 2:7 f.). By a life of poverty, humility, and suffering, and by complete subjection to the will of the Father, He has fulfilled the task which was given to Him. Now He returns to the Father, and we share His feelings and His joy. We join in His prayer to the Father: "Father,... glorify Thy Son" as He has glorified Thee. Give also to His humanity the glory that is justly His. Exalt Him above the world and above the highest heavens. Take Him to Thyself and set His throne at the right hand of Thy majesty. Let the scepter of His power extend to the ends of the earth. Let Him rule in the human nature He has assumed as King and Master, and let every knee bow to Him, "of those that are in heaven, on earth, and under the earth" (Phil 2:10). Let His name and His gospel be made known to all mankind. Let all men be incorporated in Him, that they may feel the power of His salvation and may be saved through Him. Prepare for Him a spouse pure and spotless, a holy and blessed Church. Make that Church holy, universal, mighty, and invincible. Give Him power over souls, over hearts, over peoples, and over all ages. Let all offer sacrifice to Him, and may He extend His sway over all men. May He save all men and give them life, that they may possess it in its fullness.

"I have manifested Thy name to the men whom Thou hast given Me out of the world. Thine they were, and to Me Thou gavest them, and they have kept Thy word. Now they have known that all things which Thou hast given Me are from Thee; because the words which Thou gavest Me, I have given to them; and they have received them, and they have known in very deed that I came out from Thee, and they have believed that Thou didst send Me. I pray for them; I pray not for the world, but for them whom Thou hast given Me; because they are Thine and all My things are Thine, and Thine are Mine" (Gospel). We belong to Him as the members of the body belong to the head. He cannot go to His Father without us. He desires that we, His brothers, share in His eternal inheritance. "I pray for them ... whom Thou hast given Me." He prays for us because we have been united to Him through our baptism, through our daily Holy Communion. How shall we measure this ineffable love of the Savior? How intense is His desire that the gates of heaven be opened to all men, and that in the mansion of His heavenly Father a place be prepared for us! O Lord I believe in You, and I trust and confide entirely in You.

"Declare it with the voice of joy and let it be heard, alleluia; declare it even to the ends of the earth: The Lord hath delivered His people, alleluia, alleluia" (Introit). We have been delivered. He will take us with Him to His Father. "Shout with joy to God, all the earth, sing ye a psalm to His name; give glory to His praise. Glory be to the Father and to the Son and to the Holy Ghost" (Introit). The Lord has delivered His people. He goes now to prepare a place for them in heaven, and very soon we shall join Him there. "It is truly meet and just, right and profitable to salvation, to extol Thee indeed at all times, O Lord, but especially with the highest praise to magnify Thee at this time, when Christ our Pasch was sacrificed. For He is the true lamb who hath taken away the sins of the world. Who by dying hath overcome our death, and by rising again hath restored our life" (Preface for Easter). We have been delivered.

"Sing ye to the Lord, alleluia; sing unto the Lord and bless His name; show forth His salvation from day to day, alleluia, alleluia" (Communion). Praise Him from day to day for the work of salvation which He has accomplished for us, and which He will one day bestow on us at our entrance into heaven.

Prayer

O God, from whom all good things proceed, grant to Thy suppliants that by Thy inspiration we may think what is right and with Thy guidance carry out the same. Through Christ our Lord. Amen.

Feast of the Ascension

On this day Christ's triumph is complete. The victory which He gained by His resurrection from the dead is today made perfect. The Lord, together with the human nature He assumed, has ascended to the Father. He now shares in the dominion of heaven and earth; He now rules all hearts and all souls.

Forty days have elapsed since Easter. During this period it was the intention of divine providence that our faith in the resurrection of Christ should be confirmed and strengthened. The disciples had been bewildered by the fact that their Master had died on the cross. He had breathed forth His spirit, and His body had been buried. All this had weakened their faith and aroused doubts in the minds of the dejected disciples. During the forty days that followed, the apostles and disciples acquired such a firm and steadfast faith that they were not saddened by our Lord's Ascension, but were rather filled with joy.

And indeed the Ascension was a cause for joy. Human nature had been exalted above the highest heavens and placed above the angels and archangels. It had been allowed to approach the very throne of God. The apostles knew now that they would be allowed to share in the glory of Him whose nature they shared.

Since the Ascension of Christ is our exaltation, and whither the glory of the head has gone first, there the hope of the body is also called, let us rejoice with gladness and delight in giving thanks. For today not only have we been confirmed as the possessors of paradise, but in Christ we have even penetrated the heights of heaven, having gained far more through the ineffable grace of Christ than we had lost through the malice of the devil. For those whom the virulent enemy cast down from the happiness of their first state, these the Son of God has placed as one body with Himself at the right hand of the Father, who lives and reigns in the unity of the Holy Ghost for all eternity. Amen.[17]

Christ, our head, "hath raised us up together, and hath made us sit together in the heavenly places" (Eph 2:6). We are "heirs indeed of God and joint heirs with Christ" (Rom 8:17), called to share the inheritance of Christ. "Now you are the body of Christ, and members of member" (1 Cor 12:27), "For no man ever hated his own flesh; but nourisheth and cherisheth it, as also Christ doth the Church" (Eph 5:29). Now the members and the body share in that which belongs to the head. Thus we possess even today the riches and glory and exaltation of the Ascension in Christ our head.

Christ's victory and triumph is not His personal victory and triumph, but belongs to the whole Christ, to the entire Church. When He died on the cross He embodied the whole of mankind, and the whole of mankind shared in His death. As the second Adam, He includes the whole of mankind also in His resurrection and ascension. He won the victory and has triumphed, not only for Himself, but for us also, for the whole Church. Our head has been taken up into heaven, where He reserves a place also for us. That place already belongs to us and is secured for us by Christ. That does not mean that God will one day take us to Himself in heaven, but rather that God has already brought us to heaven in Christ.

"And if I shall go and prepare a place for you, I will come again and will take you to Myself, that where I am you also may be. And whither I go you know, and the way you know" (Jn 14:3 f.).

How could we do anything else but rejoice, at least to the extent of our belief? Our joy as Christians on this occasion will be in direct proportion to our faith.

What must we do that we may be certain to share in the Ascension later on? We need do only one thing, remain united to Christ. How can we remain united to Him? By becoming members of His body, His Church, and by living in harmony with its teachings.

Prayer

Grant, we beseech Thee, O almighty God, that we who believe Thy only-begotten Son, our Redeemer, has this day ascended into heaven, may ourselves also dwell in spirit on heavenly things. Through Christ our Lord. Amen.

Feast of the Ascension (2)

Today we ascend the Mount of Olives (the stational church of St. Peter) with Peter and the other apostles to witness Christ's Ascension. "And it came to pass, whilst He blessed them, He departed from them and was carried up into heaven. And they adoring went

[17] St. Leo the Great; lesson at Matins.

back into Jerusalem with great joy. And they were always in the temple praising and blessing God" (Lk 24:51–53).

Today we rejoice with Christ, who, after His many trials and hardships on earth, can now take His repose. Today He "sitteth on the right hand of the majesty on high" (Heb 1:3) and takes possession of the glory, dignity, and power that belong to Him properly as the man Christ Jesus, the Son of God and the "Lord of glory" (1 Cor 2:8). Today the man Jesus takes possession of His royal power and assumes jurisdiction over all the goods and riches of God; today He begins to exercise His supreme authority over all creatures, both living and dead. Today He is crowned King of kings. Today He receives authority to judge the living and the dead. Today He is made a "quickening spirit" (1 Cor 15:45). Henceforth Jesus does not belong to one nation, as He did heretofore. He now belongs to all nations and to the Church in all her parts and members. He embraces all men, filling them with His life and His spirit. Today He transfers the capital of His world-wide empire, the Church, from earth to heaven; He begins to give His "gifts to men" (Eph 4:8). Do we not have good reason for rejoicing with Him today? Should we not congratulate Him on His Ascension? Should we not submit to Him and choose Him for our King again? Should we not place all our trust and hope and love in Him?

We rejoice also in our own good fortune. Christ is sitting at the right hand of the Father, but He has not deserted us; He thinks of us with love. He has gone, but He has gone "into heaven itself, that He may appear now in the presence of God for us" (Heb 9:24); He lives there always "to make intercession for us" (Heb 7:25). He knows our nothingness, and He is solicitous for us. He does not allow us to wander from His eyes even for a moment. He makes our business His business, our needs His needs, and He is our surety before the Father. "But if any man sin, we have an advocate with the Father, Jesus Christ, the just" (1 Jn 2:1). He is our high priest, sacrificing Himself always for us. He offers His body, the blood which He poured out on the cross, His most Sacred Heart, His adoration and veneration of the Father. He offers His love in the Holy Sacrifice of the Mass, substituting for us and supplying for what is lacking in our service. He is our head, and He draws His members after Himself by the power of His example, by His inspirations, by His exhortations to good, by His grace, and by His surpassing goodness. All this He does, that where the head is, the members may also be. He goes "to prepare a place" for us (Jn 14:3). The place He prepares for us is with the Father in His eternal home in heaven. He sends us the Holy Ghost, the Consoler, from on high, that He may fill us with grace, strengthen us, sanctify us, and prepare us for our return to the Father. Do we not, then, have good reason for rejoicing today?

Now we approach the altar for the celebration of Mass. While we are thus assembled the risen Christ appears in our midst. We are like the apostles gathered around Peter. The Lord comes to strengthen our faith. He says to us, as He said to them, "Go ye into the whole world and preach the gospel to every creature" (Gospel). He gives us strength to resist all that might endanger our salvation, and He draws us after Him into heaven. "Sing ye to the Lord, who mounteth above the heaven of heavens to the east, alleluia" (Communion).

By means of Holy Communion, Christ the head unites all the members of His mystical body to Himself and draws them after Him. The reception of Holy Communion is our assurance and, as it were, the first stage of our eventual resurrection, ascension, and glorification. Alleluia.

Prayer

Grant, we beseech Thee, O almighty God, that we who believe Thy only-begotten Son, our Redeemer, has this day ascended into heaven, may ourselves also dwell in spirit on heavenly things. Through Christ our Lord. Amen.

Friday after the Ascension

"The Lord is in Sinai, in the holy place" (Alleluia verse). "Let us praise the King of kings" (Antiphon at Lauds). The feast of the Ascension is a day of triumph for Christ. He is the Lord.

Christ is the Lord, the *Kyrios* (Phil 2:11). He has accomplished man's deliverance from sin, and has taken His seat "on the right hand of the Majesty on high, being made so much better than the angels, as He hath inherited a more excellent name than they. For to which of the angels hath He [God] said at any time: Thou art My Son, today have I begotten Thee.... Sit on My right hand until I make Thy enemies Thy footstool?" (Heb 1:3–5, 13.) It was not to the angels that He subjected the world of the future (the Church of the New Testament), but to Christ, His Son. "What is man that Thou art mindful of Him? Or the son of man that Thou visitest him?... Thou hast crowned Him with glory and honor [through His Ascension].... Thou hast subjected all things under His feet" (Ps 8:5 ff.; Heb 2:6 ff.). If it is said, "Thou hast subjected all things under His feet," then there is nothing that is not subject to Him (Heb 2:8). He Himself has assured us: "All power is given to Me in heaven and in earth" (Mt 28:18). When we sing the gloria we joyfully acknowledge His dominion: "Thou who sittest at the right hand of the Father, have mercy on us. For Thou alone art holy; Thou alone art the Lord; Thou alone, O Jesus Christ, art most high, together with the Holy Ghost, in the glory of God the Father." We firmly believe that Christ, God Incarnate, is the Lord. We thank God that He has thus exalted our Lord and that He has subjected all things to His dominion. We, too, will be subject to Him, to His will, to His commandments, to His Church and its ministers.

The reign of Christ gives Him the right to rule over all that has been made subject to Him, in heaven and on earth, in time and eternity. Men and angels and all created things, both now and throughout all eternity, must obey the will of the Father and of His risen Son, our Savior, and honor Them. "Thou alone art the Lord." Christ is the Lord, not only of the Sabbath, but of all days; not only of a part of the day, but of the whole day; not only of one locality, but of the whole world. All our internal and external acts, all of our actions and deeds, must be performed to serve Him and promote His honor; they must preach Christ and be subject to His will and pleasure. Our most personal desires, our most secret ambitions, our very essence and being belong to Him. "Thou alone art the Lord." He is the absolute Master of all things. His is a supremacy to which all else is subdued. God has made us completely and entirely dependent on Christ in all our desires and actions. This dependence embraces not only individuals, but the whole community; it includes all nations and all races. Today heaven and earth and hell must all confess, now and forever, that Christ is the Lord (cf. Phil 2:10 ff.). We willingly accept this domination of Christ over us, over all mankind, over all creation. We pray that all may be subject to Him and confess Him as their Master. "Thy kingdom come."

"He that shall humble himself shall be exalted" (Mt 23:12). He "emptied Himself, taking the form of a servant, being made in the likeness of men, and in habit found as a man. He humbled Himself, becoming obedient unto death, even to the death of the cross. For which cause God also hath exalted Him and hath given Him a name which is above all names. That in the name of Jesus, every knee should bow, of those that are in heaven, on earth, and under the earth" (Phil 2:7 ff.). We may often feel that Satan is still the true lord of the world. Often we are faced with the baffling riddle of sin, and are overawed by the overwhelming power of Satan, by the infidelity, evil, and sin we see about us. Yet our faith in the power and dominion of Christ over sin remains firm, even though it is not apparent. We place our trust entirely in His strong arm, in His wise providence, in His love which moves Him to work for the salvation of all men. We cannot comprehend the secrets of His wisdom any more than we can understand the love, power, and wisdom of God. "Blessed are they that have not seen and have believed" (Jn 20:29).

Prayer

Grant, we beseech Thee, O almighty God, that we who believe Thy only-begotten Son, our Redeemer, has this day ascended into heaven, may ourselves also dwell in spirit on heavenly things. Through Christ our Lord. Amen.

Saturday after the Ascension

"After He had spoken to them, He was taken up into the heavens, and sitteth on the right hand of God" (Gospel). The period of Christ's visible residence on earth has been completed. Nevertheless He remains among us through His word: "Behold, I am with you all days, even to the consummation of the world" (Mt 28:20).

"And they, adoring, went back into Jerusalem with great joy. And they were always in the temple praising and blessing God" (Lk 24:52 f.). Although the Savior had departed, the disciples were not saddened, but were rather filled with joy. One of the greatest and most inspiring joys of the Church is the knowledge that now, even though the Master has withdrawn His visible presence, she is united to Him by a more intimate union. She is now joined to Him in the unity of the mystical body as the members are joined to the head. From this moment on, she realizes that the words of the Master apply to her: "I am the vine, you the branches" (Jn 15:5). Now He lives in us and among us. We in turn live by Him as His members, as the branches live by the vine. During the time of His visible presence on earth, Christ completed the work of redemption. But He still continues with this work and perfects it in each one of us, although He Himself is sitting at the right hand of His Father in heaven.

By Christ's death on the cross we were enabled to become members of His body; but we have been incorporated, not in the physical body which He possessed on earth, but in the glorified mystical body which became a reality with His ascension. He found it necessary to withdraw from us in order to get closer to us, in order to live in us, to be one with us, to share with us the fruit of His life on earth and of His death on the cross. Of what advantage for us would the death of Christ be, or His teachings, or the example He gave us, or the exertions He underwent for us, had He not risen and ascended into heaven? Of what profit would all these things be to us, if He had not been exalted, if He had not ascended on high that we might share

His glorified life with Him? He is the head of the mystical body, and we are the members. Why, then, should we be grieved by His departure? "It is expedient to you that I go" (Jn 16:7). "And He hath subjected all things under His feet, and hath made Him head over all the Church, which is His body, and the fullness of Him who is filled all in all" (Eph 1:22 f.). His body possesses the fullness of all gifts and graces, which He acquired at the time of His Ascension. "He that descended is the same also that ascended above all the heavens, that He might fill all things" (Eph 4:10). Thus Christ's ascension is not a day of sadness for us, but rather a day of joy. So, like the infant Church, which was a witness of the Ascension, we return from the memory of the Ascension "with great joy,... praising and blessing God" (Lk 24:52 f.).

"Behold, I am with you all days." He looks after us and cares for us, and even returns to us in the Holy Sacrifice of the Mass. Had He not been glorified, had He not ascended into heaven, had He not been given a place at the right hand of the Father, we should now have no Sacrifice of the Mass, no Holy Communion, no sacrament of baptism, no sacrament of penance, no priesthood, and no Church. But now that He sits at the right hand of the Father, He finds a way to be present among us in body and soul, to return to us as God and man, to truly give Himself to us under the appearance of bread and wine, to be at once the priest and the victim of our sacrifice. The whole community gathered about the altar is united with Him and offers itself also in the sacrifice, thus becoming with Him a holocaust to the Father. Love, devotion, and the spirit of sacrifice stream from that altar and envelop the sacrificing, praying community. Here at the altar men gain the courage and the strength to suffer their daily cares and difficulties. Here, through the reception of Holy Communion, during those moments of silent adoration at the steps of the altar, they gain the courage and the strength to endure the burdens of their state of life and the hardships imposed on them by the obligations of family life and fraternal charity. Here they feel the enlivening, consoling presence of the glorified Lord. "Behold, I am with you all days."

"Sing ye to the Lord who mounteth above the heaven of heavens to the east, alleluia." Thus the Church today bursts forth in joy at the time of Holy Communion. He who ascended in glory and sat at the right hand of the Father, now descends again to earth and comes to us in Holy Communion, and nourishes us with His glorified flesh and blood. In this manner He plants in us the seed of the resurrection of the body, and prepares us for the resurrection which we confidently expect.

Christ the risen Lord reposes now with His human nature in the bosom of the Father. And in a sense we also repose there with Him, for, "ascending on high, He hath led captivity captive" (Alleluia verse). Thus He freed us from the captivity of sin and the devil.

Where the head is, there the members must also be. And although our Head is in heaven, He is simultaneously on earth at all times. He lives, prays, works and suffers in the baptized, in us who are His members. "And I live, now not I; but Christ liveth in me" (Gal 2:20). He lives among us in the Blessed Sacrament, loving us, coming close to us, nourishing our souls with His life. "Come to me all you that labor and are burdened, and I will refresh you" (Mt 11:28).

Prayer

Grant, we beseech Thee, O almighty God, that we who believe Thy only-begotten Son, our Redeemer, has this day ascended into heaven, may ourselves also dwell in spirit on heavenly things. Through Christ our Lord. Amen.

Sunday within the Octave

The Mass

Christ ascended into heaven to enter into His glory. The Church which He left behind on earth gazes fondly after Him and longs to see again and be united with the one to whom her heart and her love belong. Without Him she is desolate and lonely, for she still lingers here on earth.

This mood causes her to cry out to her absent bridegroom in the Introit of today's Mass: "I have sought Thy face, Thy face, O Lord, I will seek; turn not away Thy face from me, alleluia, alleluia. The Lord is my light and my salvation; whom shall I fear?" (Introit.) It is we, the Church, who prays thus. Each of us says, "I have sought Thy face." Our incessant search for the absent Lord is expressed eloquently in the repeated Kyrie; the same idea is expressed in the Collect. Our life should be the expression of our devotedness to God, and of our longing for purity of heart and for freedom from all that may displease Him. "Thy face, O Lord, I will seek" in earnest prayer, in patient and merciful love, in selfless devotion to others, in loyalty to the Church, in zeal for souls, and in the quest for the grace of God (Epistle). "As long as you did it to one of these My least brethren, you did it to Me" (Mt 25:40). Thus the longing of the Church and of Christians for heaven will draw down the grace of God and of Christ upon the world. When a soul is fired by such a noble aim, it will not seek the face of Christ in vain. "I will not leave you orphans; I will come to you" (Jn 14:18) in the person of the Paraclete, the Holy Ghost, "whom I will send you from the Father" (Gospel). We receive this promise gratefully and profess our belief in Him in the Credo.

In the Offertory we are reminded of the triumphal entry of Christ into His sanctuary in heaven. This triumphal entry symbolizes the approach of the eternal high priest to the heavenly altar, upon which Christ offers Himself for our eternal union with the Father (Offertory). Together with our gifts of bread and wine we also offer to God ourselves: our wills, our inclinations, all our faculties, and all our actions. We make an all-embracing holocaust of ourselves, we make our action a living *sursum corda,* imitating the ascension of Christ.

The moment of consecration approaches. What Christ has promised now becomes a reality: "I will come to you." What a blessed coming! "I have sought Thy face." Now He descends among us, enters into a most real and intimate union with us, a union of prayer and spirit, a sacrifice offered to God. Here in the Holy Sacrifice of the Mass He unites us to Himself in His sacrificial mission. Just as He, through the almighty power of His word, changes the substance of the bread into that of His body, so, too, if we allow Him to make of us a holocaust, He will penetrate our inmost depths with His life and His spirit. Thus through an intelligent and active participation in the Holy Sacrifice of the Mass, our lives become ever a more certain expression of the spirit of Christ in us. If we participate in the Holy Sacrifice in spirit and truth, if daily we die and rise with Christ, we shall become living and invincible witnesses of Christ, a personified testimony of Him (Gospel). That is the prime fruit of the sacrifice of the altar.

The daily devout celebration of the Holy Sacrifice of the Mass emphasizes ever more and more, not only the opposition between the Christian and the "old man" within him, but also between the Christian and the world about him, between the Christian and the enemies of the cross. "They will put you out of the synagogues; yea, the hour cometh that whosoever killeth you will think that he doth a service to God" (Gospel). But the devout participation in the Mass makes the Christian not only a heroic witness to Christ, but also a victorious hero with Christ. "I will come to you" in Holy Communion.

"I pray, not that Thou shouldst take them out of the world" with its illusions, its deceptions, its mockery, and its persecutions, "but that Thou shouldst keep them from evil" (Jn 17:15). This is the noble fruit of sacrifice and of the Holy Sacrifice of the Mass. We are given the grace to persevere, to conquer the world and sin and hell.

Prayer

Almighty and eternal God, grant that our will may be ever devoted to Thee, and that we may serve Thy majesty with a sincere heart. Through Christ our Lord. Amen.

Meditation

The Lord has ascended into heaven. The Church gazes fondly upward and promises, "Thy face, O Lord, I will seek" (Introit).[18] But the Church does not forget the commission given her by the Lord: "You shall give testimony [to Me]" (Gospel). The Church bears testimony to Christ by the fact that she loves Him and suffers for Him.

The Church loves. Her very being and existence consists in her accomplishment of this task of fraternal charity assigned to her by God. Because the Church is the kingdom of God on earth, it is an organism of fraternal love. "This is My commandment, that you love one another as I have loved you" (Jn 15:12). "By this shall all men know that you are My disciples, if you have love one for another" (Jn 13:35). By this same characteristic it will be clear to all men that she is the Church of Christ. "Dearly beloved, be prudent and watch in prayers. But before all things have a constant mutual charity among yourselves; for charity covereth a multitude of sins. Using hospitality one towards another without murmuring; as every man hath received grace, ministering the same one to another, as good stewards of the manifold grace of God. If any man speak, let him speak the words of God. If any minister, let him do it as of the power which God administereth; that in all things God may be honored, through Jesus Christ our Lord" (Epistle). What more noble vocation could one have than that of giving testimony to Christ? We fulfill this vocation to the degree that we practice charity in our thoughts, in our words, and in our works.

The Church suffers. "And you shall give testimony, because you are with Me from the beginning. These things have I spoken to you that you may not be scandalized. They will put you out of the synagogues; yea, the hour cometh that whosoever killeth you will think that he doth a service to God. And these things will they do to you because they have not known the Father nor Me. But these things I have told you, that when the hour shall come you may remember that I told you of them" (Gospel). The Church indeed suffers. She shares the lot of her bridegroom. "If they have persecuted Me, they will also persecute you" (Jn 15:20).

St. Peter was crucified; St. Paul was beheaded. Uncounted thousands, champions of Christian faith and virtue, have given their lives in testimony of Christ. Bishops, priests, deacons,

[18] Formerly the Mass today was celebrated in the church of St. Mary of the Martyrs in Rome, which was once the Roman Pantheon. Here the veil of Veronica, which bears the image of our Lord's face and is now preserved in St. Peter's, was once kept.

laymen, young men and old men and virgins, young boys like St. Pancratius, and young girls like St. Agnes have sacrificed all to be witnesses to Christ. The Church suffered ten severe persecutions during the first three centuries. In the centuries which followed, great heresies arose, and these caused new sufferings for the Church. New enemies arose, new martyrs were born. The kings and the mighty ones of earth demand that the Church abandon her position on the sanctity of marriage and allow the passions of a fallen human nature to control our actions. But the Church continues to give testimony to Christ and His law even though whole nations abandon her. Modern ideologies and modern theories are born and demand a hearing. They ask that the Church accommodate her dogmas and her teachings to the spirit of the times. But the Church will not compromise; she clings to Christ. She is denounced, and her name is dragged down into the mire; but she suffers patiently, giving testimony to Christ and the immutability of His laws. O holy Church, thou hast been faithful to the commission given thee by thy departing bridegroom: "You shall give testimony [of Me]." Thou surely art the true Church of Christ. I cling to thee, and by my loyalty to you I also give testimony to Christ. This I shall do, even at the cost of worldly honors and esteem, even at the cost of my life.

"But before all things have a constant mutual charity among yourselves." By our charity all men may know whether the spirit of Christ has been fruitful in us or not. For this reason the liturgy never tires of reminding us of the necessity of charity. "This is My commandment, that you love one another as I have loved you" (Jn 15:12).

"The hour cometh that whosoever killeth you will think that he doth a service to God" (Gospel). We do not anticipate any other treatment, and we would not have it otherwise. "And these things I have told you, that when the hour shall come, you may remember that I told you" (Gospel). Yet often we refuse to understand that this hour must come. We are ready to accept anything but suffering. How little of Christ's life and spirit must be in us!

PRAYER

Almighty and eternal God, grant that our will may be ever devoted to Thee, and that we may serve Thy majesty with a sincere heart. Through Christ our Lord. Amen.

Monday within the Octave

In the Holy Sacrifice of the Mass we take part in a worldwide procession which follows Christ's Ascension into heaven. "God is ascended with jubilee, and the Lord with the sound of a trumpet, alleluia" (Offertory). He enters heaven to sit at the right hand of His Father. His function as high priest, which began with His assumption of human nature, is to continue and to be fruitful for all eternity. "The Lord said to my Lord: Sit thou at My right hand.... Thou art a priest forever according to the order of Melchisedech" (Ps 109:4).

Christ's heavenly priesthood is not a mere repetition or summation of His sacrifice on the cross. It is the perpetuation of that sacrifice, continued out of His zeal for the honor of the Father and for the salvation of souls. It is the eternal, efficient, representation of the sacrifice of the cross. As long as there remain souls on earth that are in need of salvation and to whom the salutary merits of Christ's work must be applied, He continues to exercise His priesthood on their behalf.

This He does in a twofold way: first of all, through His continuous sacrificial prayer. He is like another Moses praying with outstretched arms while His people fight against their adversaries. If Moses lowered his hands, Amalec overcame; and when he lifted them up, Israel overcame (Ex 17:11). Likewise Christ is "always living to make intercession for us" (Heb 7:25). "Christ Jesus that died; yea, that is risen also again, who is at the right hand of God, who also maketh intercession for us" (Rom 8:34).

He also exercises His priesthood through His sacrificial life in the Eucharist on our altars. There the divine high priest offers Himself through the hands of His ordained minister. In the midst of His people He offers His body and His blood, His life with its inexhaustible merits, His acts, His adoration, His praise, His obedience, and His love. "This holy and unspotted victim" He places in the hands of His Church at the offertory, that all those who are in heaven and on earth may have an offering to make to the Father which is entirely worthy of Him. "This is My body.... This is My blood"—the fruit of the Lord's Ascension into heaven.

"Thou art a priest forever according to the order of Melchisedech" (Ps 109:4). Not after the manner of the bloody sacrifices of the Old Testament is He a priest, but after the manner of the unbloody sacrifice of the New, after the manner of the mystical priest-king, Melchisedech, who offered bread and wine. Christ, the divine high priest, by means of His omnipotence transforms the bread and wine into His sacred body and His most precious blood. The Eucharistic sacrifice celebrated by the divine high priest becomes the foundation on which His kingdom is established and extended here on earth. This is the source of the efficacy of the life-giving waters of baptism and of the graces furnished by the other sacraments. It is the eternally pulsating heart which circulates the streams of life and light and love throughout the members of the mystical body. By means of this offering the high priest makes the most complete satisfaction for sin, the most adequate return for benefits received from God, the most effective intercession for further needs, the worthiest adoration for all creatures. Through this Holy Sacrifice the priestly spirit of Christ is stirred up in all His members. By means of the Mass, Christ lives in His Church, in His members on earth, being persecuted in them, doing penance in them, accomplishing good through them, and adoring His father by means of them. By means of this offering He unites those whom He has redeemed more closely to Himself, incorporates them in His own sacred offering, and offers them to the Father, a "holy and unspotted victim."

"The Lord will send forth the scepter of Thy power out of Sion. Rule Thou in the midst of Thy enemies. With Thee is the principality in the day of strength, in the brightness of the saints.... Thou art a priest forever" (Ps 109:2 ff.). Through the power of Your holy priesthood You rule over the powers of darkness and of evil. Rule the hearts of men, make them Your own. Make them to be with You at the Holy Sacrifice of the Mass a pure, holy, and unspotted victim to be offered to the Father. Fill them with the power and the spirit of Your own sacred priesthood.

Our high priest possesses an eternal priesthood because He Himself is eternal. For this reason He is able to redeem perfectly all those who come to God through Him, for He makes continual intercession for them. "For it was fitting that we should have such a high priest, holy, innocent, undefiled, separated from sinners, and made higher than the heavens" (Heb 7:26). How fortunate we are to have such a divine high priest! We will "go in to the altar of God" and pray "through Christ our Lord." We shall celebrate the Sacrifice of the Mass with Him, and allow ourselves to become part of His offering. He is able to redeem us completely and to sanctify us through His prayer and sacrifice.

An eternal high priest! The sacrificial intention of Christ is eternal. Eternal, too, is that divine compassion which sympathizes with the poor, fallen nature of man with its infirmities, for He is like unto us in all things except sin (Heb 4:15). Through His eternal saving Christ continues to live His temporal life forever. His self-denial, His tears, His sufferings, His labors, His humility, are continued in this way; for He is the sacrificial lamb, the victim offered by the high priest. Rich indeed are those who live on earth according to the spirit and poverty of Christ.

"For we have not a high priest who cannot have compassion on our infirmities; but one tempted in all things like as we are, without sin. Let us go therefore with confidence to the throne of grace; that we may obtain mercy, and find grace in seasonable aid" (Heb 4:15 f.).

Prayer

O Lord, having been filled with Thy holy gifts (the Holy Eucharist), we beseech Thee to grant that we may always persevere in giving thanks to Thee. Through Christ our Lord. Amen. (Postcommunion, Sunday after the Ascension.)

Tuesday within the Octave

"Father, the hour is come, glorify thy Son.... As thou hast given Him power over all flesh" (Jn 17:1 f.). The Father heard this prayer of His Son and glorified Him through His Ascension into heaven. "Sit Thou at My right hand" (Ps 109:1). Now He shares in the dominion and the glory of the Father. To Him "all power is given ... in heaven and in earth" (Mt 28:18). He has been given the power to rule and to judge.

The power to rule. Behind the gentle sweetness of the gospel there stands also the royal power of the lawgiver. Christ does not preach merely to edify; He states the law. He supports His laws with sanctions of eternal happiness or eternal damnation. "Go ye into the whole world and preach the gospel to every creature. He that believeth and is baptized shall be saved, but he that believeth not shall be condemned" (Gospel). Under the law of Christ there is no distinction of persons, no privileged persons, no one against whom discrimination is made, but only the just and the unjust. No one has power over the law of Christ, not even the Church, and everyone must accept it with respect and humility. No earthly lawgiver, no parliament, no king, no minister, no science, can dispense from the law of Christ nor ignore it with impunity. He has made His law known through the gospel and through His Church so that no one can excuse himself on the plea of ignorance; and this applies especially to those who belong to the Church. "All power is given to Me in heaven and in earth." This power extends to me also, to my body and my soul, to my very life. I gladly acknowledge His power over me, His law, His command.

The power to judge. "This Jesus, who is taken up from you into heaven, shall so come as you have seen Him going into heaven" (Epistle). He shall come again as the judge at the end of time. That will be the crowning act of the glorified Christ. The glory of that day is before His eyes as He stands before the high council at Jerusalem. "Nevertheless I say to you, hereafter you shall see the Son of Man sitting on the right hand of the power of God, and coming in the clouds of heaven" (Mt 26:64). "For neither doth the Father judge any man, but hath given all judgment to the Son" (Jn 5:22). To Him He has given the power to inflict punishment on the whole race, on individual peoples and states, on individual persons, on false science, on passing whims and notions, as the history of mankind testifies. He "hath given all judgment to the Son, that all men may honor the Son as they honor the Father" (Jn 5:22 f.). Every soul must appear before Him as its judge as soon as it has left the body. It must give an account to Him; it must answer to Him who knows its most secret thoughts, its hidden motives, its every action, both good and bad. An account must be given to Him whose sentence is eternal. Later all must appear again before the Judge of the world. Then He will separate them as the shepherd separates the sheep from the goats. To the former He will say, "Come, ye blessed of My Father"; and to the latter, "Depart from Me, ye cursed, into everlasting fire.... And these shall go into everlasting punishment, but the just into life everlasting" (Mt 25:34 ff.).

Jesus, who was condemned by the council of the Jews to be crucified, is the Judge of the world. Before Him must bow all who "are in heaven, on earth, and under the earth" (Phil 2:10). Even those who now deny Him or reject Him will have to confess and acknowledge Him. Christ will eventually triumph and put all His enemies to silence. How we shall rejoice that we have lived for Him! How happy we shall be when He says to us, "Well done, good and faithful servant. Because thou has been faithful over a few things, I will place thee over many things; enter thou into the joy of thy Lord" (Mt 25:23)! How glad we shall be that while on earth we lived according to the teaching and example of Christ, that we have loved poverty and humility, that we have clung to the cross and despised the world! How great will be our joy when we shall hear the sentence of the judge: "Come, ye blessed of My Father, possess you the kingdom prepared for you from the foundation of the world" (Mt 25:34)!

Jesus, our Savior and Redeemer, has been enthroned at the right hand of the Father as Master and Judge. He cannot and will not be our Redeemer if we fail to accept His laws and to subject ourselves to them. The more perfectly we conform to His law, the more certain we become that He is truly our Redeemer.

Today we pay Him homage on His high throne in heaven. We honor Him by our faith in Him. Even though we may not understand all that He has revealed, we nevertheless submit to the spirit and the letter of everything that He has said. We pay Him homage by the submission of our will when we fulfill His commandments faithfully. "This is My commandment, that you love one another as I have loved you" (Jn 15:12). "You have heard that it hath been said: Thou shalt love thy neighbor and hate thy enemy. But I say to you: Love your enemies; do good to them that hate you" (Mt 5:43 f.). We pay homage to the glorified Redeemer by our love. He wants our hearts and our love. He will not accept the cold, enforced service of the servant or the slave, but insists on the service of a voluntary and holy love. To fear the command of Christ is good, but to love it is much better. We honor Him by our life. Whatever befalls us each day in our work, whatever problems confront us, whatever obligations are imposed on us, we should accept them as the will of the Lord. Our motto should ever be: "Thy will be done."

Prayer

Almighty and eternal God, grant that our will may be ever devoted to Thee, and that we may serve Thy majesty with a sincere heart. Through Christ our Lord. Amen. (Collect, Sunday after the Ascension.)

Wednesday within the Octave

The Lord has ascended into heaven. The apostles return from Mount Olivet into the city of Jerusalem. In the upper room, the room of the Last Supper, we find "all these were persevering with one mind in prayer with the women and Mary, the mother of Jesus" (Acts 1:14). Thus the Lord "commanded them that they should not depart from Jerusalem, but should wait for the promise of the Father" (Acts 1:4). During these days the Church also, with Mary and the apostles and the holy women, awaits the promise of the Father, the coming of the Holy Ghost.

But an unholy spirit of the world lives and works in us, in spite of the religious exercises which we undertake, in spite of the prayers we say, and in spite of our confessions and our daily Holy Communion. A more dangerous enemy than the world, the flesh, or the devil is the so-called human spirit, our own spirit. This spirit is the enemy of all those who try seriously to practice piety or make progress in the spiritual life. It is full of treason and treachery and falsehood. It is unstable, curious, restless, and destroys all repose and tranquility. Sometimes our spirit appears to be completely subdued and subjected to God, but it is merely masquerading under the guise of righteousness and a pretended zeal, and is really directed by a satanic spirit. Pretending to promote the honor of God and to strive after perfection, it is really just hiding its own selfishness and narrowness. It inspires us to act out of purely human and natural motives, to act apart from the movements of grace and independently of the will and intentions of God. It cries out for peace, that is, for ease and untrammeled freedom, and unceasingly strives for bodily comfort. It seeks itself even in religious matters, although often under the pretense of searching for perfection. When it strives against evil, or when it serves God or attempts to save souls, it is really only seeking itself. This natural, human spirit still lives and works all too powerfully in us. Even after the coming of the Holy Spirit we may with good reason cry out, "Come, Holy Spirit." "Create a clean heart in me, O God, and renew a right spirit within my bowels" (Ps 50:12).

The Holy Spirit is the spirit of true life. He gives light and faith; He inspires noble ambitions and undying hope. The fire of the Holy Spirit warms the soul and creates enthusiasm. It consumes all that is ignoble and evil, and suppresses the spirit of selfishness and worldliness. It directs all our actions to God and passes a condemnatory sentence on everything in us that is common or ordinary. It sharpens our ability to detect evil in ourselves, and removes all drowsiness from our members and from our soul. It gives us freedom of spirit that detaches us from all that is transitory, and binds our hearts firmly to God. It helps us to face life with a holy indifference and a noble simplicity, and gives us a freedom that is satisfied with the bare necessities of life. It uses the goods of the earth and of the world, even the advantages of culture, only to bring the life of the soul to maturity. We stand very much in need of such a spirit. During these days, in company with Mary and the apostles, we beg that we may receive this spirit. *Veni, Sancte Spiritus:* "Come, Holy Spirit; fill the hearts of Thy faithful and inspire them with the fire of Thy divine love."

"Come, Holy Ghost." He will come to us in the measure in which we desire Him and long for Him. Our desire and our longing for Him will increase as we become conscious of the degree to which we are slaves to the spirit of worldliness. How little true spiritual freedom we possess! How small our degree of living faith! How purely natural our manner of thinking, of judging, of deciding our problems. How little insight we possess in spiritual matters! How can we be lifted up to the level of spiritual men? Certainly not by our own effort and desire. Only the grace of God and the power of the Holy Ghost can do this. "Open thy mouth wide and I will fill it" (Ps 80:11). The more we desire and ask for, the more we shall receive. "For every one that asketh, receiveth" (Mt 7:8). He that does not ask will not receive. "He hath filled the hungry with good things; and the rich He hath sent empty away" (Lk 1:53).

"And I send the promise of My Father upon you; but stay you in the city till you be endued with power from on high" (Lk 24:49). That is the command of the Father for these days which precede Pentecost. We continue in prayer with Mary and the apostles. Even while we are occupied with the duties of our state of life and the care of our families, we can keep our hearts fixed on God and free to commune with God in prayer. We wish to be prepared when the Holy Spirit descends from heaven at Pentecost and seeks admission to our souls. God grant that He may not pass us by.

Prayer

O God, our refuge and our strength, who art the Author of all true piety, give ear to the pious prayers of Thy Church, and grant that we may in truth receive what we so earnestly seek. Through Christ our Lord. Amen.

Octave of the Ascension

"Grant, we beseech Thee, O almighty God, that we who believe Thy only-begotten Son, our Redeemer, has this day ascended into heaven, may ourselves also dwell in spirit on heavenly things" (Collect). In this prayer which the Church offers to God she seeks to make our life harmonize with our faith.

Sursum corda. We must lift up our hearts to dwell in heaven in spirit. We are to live with the glorified Christ, who is our head, our exemplar, the way and the truth. All our hopes and expectations should be placed in Him. We must concentrate only on what is yet to come, on what is eternal. *Sursum corda.* The incidents of our lives, the misfortunes we suffer, the men with whom we associate, the works we perform, the duties we must fulfill, the sufferings we must undergo, should all be considered in the light of eternity and through the eyes of God and our glorified Redeemer. To dwell in heaven means to accept all our misfortunes and difficulties after the example of Him who was unjustly condemned to death, who was executed in the most shameful manner, and whom the Father exalted above the highest heavens. It means not to wish to be acclaimed and honored by men, but to submit our deeds and omissions to Him who sees all our actions from heaven, and provides that nothing we do with the proper intention is ever lost or without its proper reward.

He who dwells in heaven in spirit considers all his actions in the light of his eternal destiny. He is not, however, shiftless or disinterested. On the contrary, he takes a more intense interest and uses greater insight than others. He lives in the peace of God and does not pass from one excitement to another. He lives on a higher plane of life and works quietly and in peace with his eyes fixed on heaven. He takes misfortunes as coming from the hand of God, and follows faithfully in the footsteps of Him whom he knows to be now in heaven sitting at the right hand of the Father. "In your patience you shall possess your souls" (Lk 21:19). Such a man uses the temporal things for his eternal salvation. This is the true wisdom which confounds all worldliness, lifts us up from the mire, rescues us from the narrowness and selfishness of our fallen nature with all its vanity and confusion.

Christ took immense pains to save us. He descended from heaven into the womb of the Virgin, from the womb of the Virgin to the crib, from the crib to the cross, from the cross to the grave; from the grave He returned to heaven. The incarnate Son of God underwent all of these things for us that we might follow Him. We beg Him from the depths of our hearts, "Draw us after Thee." We must follow in His footsteps. We must follow Him with our hearts to where He has ascended in the body.

Let us fly from earthly desires; let nothing here below now please us who have a Father in heaven. And certainly we must consider well the fact that He who was so mild on His ascent, on His return will be so terrible; and whatever He has commanded us with meekness, He will require of us with severity. Let no one, then, disregard the allotted time for his repentance; let no one neglect the care of himself while he is able, because our Redeemer will then be all the more strict in judgment in proportion as He has shown greater patience before judgment.[19]

"Father I will that where I am, they also whom Thou has given Me may be with Me" (Jn 17:24). Bossuet's reflections on this passage are well worth quoting:

Thou hast sent Me that they may be perfectly one. Therefore, Father, since you have given them to Me, not only as fellow soldiers, not only as brothers, but also as My members, I will that they be perfectly one as members of My body. Just as you have given Me perfect mastery over Myself, so, too, make Me master of My members. Therefore, Father, I will that where I am they also may be. If I am in glory, they should be also. They should be there in perfect unity with Me.

"That they may see My glory which Thou hast given Me" (Jn 17:24). In their own bodies they should witness this glory. They should see its magnitude and know its source. I have received it from Thee. Thou hast loved Me before the world was made and hast given Me such great glory that I can share it with others. "For them do I sanctify Myself" (Jn 17:19). They had become the victims of Your anger. I substituted Myself for them; since I sanctify Myself and offer Myself to Thee with complete devotion, and consecrate Myself to Thee, they also should be holy and devoted to Thee. "For them do I sanctify Myself." This I did principally on the cross, but continue now daily in the Holy Sacrifice of the Mass. I continue to do this that they may be consecrated and offered to the Father, and while still on earth may live a heavenly life completely devoted to God.

Prayer

Grant, we beseech Thee, O almighty God, that we who believe Thy only-begotten Son, our Redeemer, has this day ascended into heaven, may ourselves also dwell in spirit on heavenly things. Through Christ our Lord. Amen.

Friday after the Octave of the Ascension

"Almighty and eternal God, grant that our will may be ever devoted to Thee, and that we may serve Thy majesty with a sincere heart." (Collect). We pray for a submissive will and for purity of heart for all those who are devoutly preparing for Pentecost.

[19] St. Gregory, lesson at Matins.

A submissive will. For the reception of grace and the efficacious application of it, we can best dispose ourselves by imitating Mary. We should pronounce a perfect fiat to all that grace asks of us. We must maintain such an attitude even if it implies our crucifixion or seems to threaten our destruction. This disposition of soul excludes all egotism and all attachment to our own earthly desires. If the Holy Spirit is to fructify us and renew us as He did the apostles, we must prepare the ground of our soul to the best of our ability for His coming. We make such a preparation by forsaking our own desires and ridding ourselves of everything that is not in accord with God's will and honor. Then our souls will be truly free. Then we shall respond to every impulse and inspiration of the Holy Spirit with a fervent, "Thy will be done." God works best, if one may use the expression, on the ground of nothingness. He created all things out of nothing. As long as we have not completely effaced ourselves to prepare for the reception of His grace, as long as we are not entirely submissive to His will and design and completely dependent on His grace, as long as we depend on ourselves and seek to carry out our own desires, we hinder His work in us; for we lack the submissiveness of will necessary for the free operation of His grace.

Purity of heart. Purity of heart is opposed to sin, to faults, and to imperfections. We know that before the Holy Ghost will enter the heart of man, it must at least be free from sin and from willful imperfections and faults, or it must at least have the sincere desire to achieve such purity of heart. But there is also a purity of heart with regard to the reception of the grace which God gives us. This purity of heart makes us purer, more enlightened, and more humble in proportion to the degree by which we are enriched and elevated by grace. The greater the graces God gives, the more purity of the affections required of the soul. The soul should possess something of that purity of heart which Mary possessed when she was congratulated by Elizabeth and raised her eyes to Him from whom she had received so much grace: "My soul doth magnify the Lord ... He hath regarded the humility of His handmaid.... He that is mighty hath done great things to me" (Lk 1:46 ff.). Mary is elevated too far above the motive of selfish love to become proud over the distinction that has been given to her. She rejoices only in what God has wrought in her; she sees only Him and not herself. She possessed perfect purity of soul and was ready for the reception of grace. But how different it is with us! How great is our secret pride! What idle self-complacency we indulge in when God gives us grace! How often we take a foolish pride in the graces we receive, and think ourselves something great because of them. The honor and the good pleasure of God is seldom our primary motive in our quest of holiness. Our thoughts and actions and designs are often primarily concerned with ourselves. Our selfish pride instills a subtle poison into all our actions and infects even our love of God, so that what we should do purely for the love of God, we do for ourselves. We have, then, good grounds for asking God: "Grant that our will may be ever devoted to Thee, and that we may serve Thy majesty with a sincere heart" (Collect).

Pentecost will be fruitful in graces. But a perfectly pure and unselfish heart is required to profit by them. Not without reason Mary met with the apostles in the upper room. She is the exemplar of all those to whom God gives great graces; we must imitate her example. She teaches us that we should not long for special favors; that we should not believe that we have been given any special graces because of our own worthiness and excellence; that we should not ascribe to our own deserts any of the graces which we receive; that in matters of the spirit we should be humble; that we should never undertake works of piety or self-abnegation in order to obtain sensible consolations. All such things are based on self-love and only hinder the work of God. Such motives turn the gifts of heaven into a deadly poison.

To approach God we must efface ourselves and understand our own nothingness. "He that humbleth himself shall be exalted" (Lk 14:11).

Prayer

Almighty and eternal God, grant that our will may be ever devoted to Thee, and that we may serve Thy majesty with a sincere heart. Through Christ our Lord. Amen.

Pentecost

"But I tell you the truth; it is expedient to you that I go; for if I go not, the Paraclete will not come to you; but if I go, I will send Him to you" (Jn 16:7). When Christ ascended into heaven, He went to His Father. Today He fulfills His promise of sending to His apostles and to His Church the Paraclete, the Holy Ghost. This coming is further proof that He has been glorified and that He sits at the right hand of the Father.

At Christmas, God became incarnate; He came to share with us His participation in the divine life and in the grace of God. Easter is the feast of the resurrection of the soul from sin and of the incorporation of man in the mystical body of the glorified Christ through the sacraments of baptism and the Eucharist. Pentecost is the feast of the visible mission of the Holy Ghost to the apostles, to the Church, to each Christian family, and to each individual soul. By virtue of His death on the cross, the Lord has merited the grace of the sending of the Holy Ghost. Now that He is in heaven He prays for and effects the coming of the Holy Ghost, that we may grow in grace and holiness, that we may be strong and firm in faith, that we may reach perfection and share in the inheritance of Christ our head.

The Holy Ghost seals and perfects the unity of the Father and the Son in the godhead. For this reason He also effects the living union between Christ and us, between the head and the members. The life and the work of Christ the head and the Holy Ghost the Sanctifier are not to be separated from one another in us. Thus in the mind of St. Paul, "to live in Christ" means the same thing as "to live in the Spirit." "In this we know that we abide in Him, and He in us; because He hath given us of His Spirit" (1 Jn 4:13). We have been elevated to the divine life by Christ; but the Holy Ghost also took part in this operation. Where the Holy Ghost is not operating, there can be no body of Christ. "The faithful become members of the body of Christ when they attain life through the Spirit of Christ," the Holy Ghost (St. Augustine). The divine life is always given through Christ, the incarnate God. When we allow Him to do so, He always sends us the Holy Ghost, the Spirit of love. This Spirit always binds us again firmly to the Father, so that we long and strive with all our strength to be true children of the Father and to attain to perfect love. Therefore the life of Christ which was implanted in our souls by baptism (Easter) cannot be made perfect without the coming of the Holy Ghost (Pentecost).

Pentecost is the complement and the completion of Easter. Easter gives us the beginning of supernatural life and incorporation in Christ. But this new life must unfold; it must be strengthened and enkindled into a burning fire which can resist all things; it must be imbued with a love which is stronger than death, so that we are prepared to suffer all things for Christ, even the sacrifice of our life. This strengthening of our spirit is brought about by our baptism with the Holy Ghost at Pentecost. The spirit of Pentecost is the spirit that makes the confessors and martyrs. It gives light, power, and unconquerable strength. This effect is visible in the apostles, who "went from the presence of the council, rejoicing that they were accounted worthy to suffer reproach for the name of Jesus" (Acts 5:41).

Pentecost is the birthday of the Church and of Christianity, the beginning of the New Dispensation. Man, having been touched by the Spirit, no longer lives according to the flesh, according to the principles and ideals of fallen human nature; he lives in the Spirit. He is filled with the light of truth and is guided by the Spirit of truth Himself, the Holy Ghost. The new generation of men now sees all things in their proper place in the plan of divine providence and in their relationship to eternity. In the spirit of truth and love the new generation is called to act for good and upright motives, to do only what is pleasing to the Father. It is a generation of spiritual men. Since they "live in the spirit," they must also "walk in the spirit" (Gal 5:25). They belong to Christ, and with Him they crucify their flesh, together with its passions and lusts. They are not envious of one another, but practice mildness, patience, and charity (Gal 5:26 f.). "The fruit of the spirit is charity, joy, peace, patience, benignity, goodness, longanimity, mildness, faith, modesty, continency, chastity" (Gal 5:22 f.).

In the baptism of the Spirit, which the Church receives at Pentecost, she is washed clean in the blood of Christ; she arises with Him; she is imbued with the fullness of new life. Today she stands with the divine dowry which Christ earned for her and gave to her. She is bright with the glow of eternal youth and fertility as she stands at the side of her heavenly bridegroom. Now she has been prepared for that arduous life for which she is destined upon earth. She has been prepared to share the life of her bridegroom and to remain faithful to Him in spite of all that may befall her; she is prepared to represent Him under all circumstances, and joyfully to bring forth new generations of children. The Holy Ghost, the Spirit of love and truth, dwells within her and operates in her. He is the soul of the body of the Church. He guides her and leads her to her eternal nuptials with her divine spouse, Jesus Christ. That is the meaning of the mission of the Holy Ghost and of the feast of Pentecost.

The feast of Pentecost is a day of thanksgiving for the foundation of the Church, in which is contained all the treasures of supernatural riches, and through which all grace and redemption is given to men. Pentecost is a day of thanksgiving for the coming of the Holy Ghost and for the establishment of the sacrament of confirmation. It is a day on which we place a joyful and grateful trust in the operation of the Holy Ghost within us, and thank Him for His inspiration and guidance. On this day we again place ourselves in the hands of the Holy Ghost with complete confidence. He should be the soul of our soul; He should reign in us, amid the ruins of our own fallen nature. Pentecost is a day of petition, a day on which we should implore the Holy Ghost for a full measure of His graces and gifts. With the Church we pray:

Come, Thou Holy Spirit, come,
And from Thy celestial home
Send Thy light and brilliancy.

Come, Thou father of the poor,
Come, Thou source of gifts secure,
Come, our heart's true radiancy.

Thou, of all consolers best,
Thou, the soul's most welcome guest,
Sweet refreshment constantly.

In our labor, rest most sweet,
Grateful coolness in the heat,
Solace in adversity.

O Thou light most pure and blest,
Shine within the inmost breast
Of Thy faithful company.

Lacking Thy divinity
Nothing good in man can be,
Nothing but iniquity.

What is sordid, make Thou pure,
What is wounded, do Thou cure,
Slake now our aridity.

What is rigid, gently bend;
What is frigid, warmly tend;
Strengthen what goes erringly.

Fill Thy faithful who confide
In Thy power to guard and guide,
With Thy sevenfold mystery.

Give them virtue's sure reward,
Give them Thy salvation, Lord,
Give eternal felicity. Amen.

Vigil of Pentecost

In ancient Rome those who for some reason or other had not been able to receive baptism at Easter, received the sacrament on the vigil of Pentecost, which is similar to the vigil of Easter. It expresses the idea of our baptism by the Holy Ghost.

The Epistle relates that St. Paul came to Ephesus and found there certain disciples who had already been baptized, and he inquired whether they had received the Holy Ghost after their baptism. They, however, said that they had not so much as heard of the Holy Ghost. Paul concluded from this reply that they had not received the baptism of Jesus, otherwise they would have received the Holy Ghost. As a matter of fact, they had received the baptism of John; that is, the baptism which John had given at the Jordan, and not the sacrament of baptism established by Christ. Then "they were baptized in the name of the Lord Jesus. And when Paul had imposed his hands on them, the Holy Ghost came upon them, and they spoke with tongues and prophesied."

Besides giving Himself, the Holy Ghost gave them various gifts and charismata, thus making His presence known by sensible signs. In recalling this event, the liturgy has us in mind. We have received both the baptism of Christ and the sacrament of confirmation. We are bearers of the Spirit, filled with the Holy Ghost.

The Introit applies to us: "When I shall be sanctified in you, I will gather you together out of all the countries [into the fold of the Church], and I will pour upon you clean water [baptism] and you shall be cleansed from all your filthiness." There can be no doubt that we have received the Holy Ghost. The Holy Ghost, together with the Father and the Son in the inseparable unity of the divinity, has come to us to abide in us. He is most intimately bound to our souls in a living union. "The Spirit of truth, whom the world cannot receive because it seeth Him not nor knoweth Him, shall abide with you and shall be in you" (Gospel). He lives and works in us who have been incorporated in the body of Christ.

"He that loveth Me shall be loved of My Father; and I will love him and will manifest Myself to him" (Gospel). With what a love He has loved us! He has loved us with that same love which binds the Father and the Son and the Holy Ghost together in the Blessed Trinity. We Christians can boast that the love with which the Father and the Son love us, and with which we love them, is God. "God is charity" (1 Jn 4:8). It is the Holy Ghost, the Love of God, who binds the Father and the Son together and completes their love. It is the same Holy Ghost who binds us to Christ, as head and members, so that as one we love, work, pray, suffer, and adore the Father. Through His miraculous entry into our souls and His marvelous union with them, He effects our union with Christ and binds us to the fountainhead of all grace. We are incorporated in Christ through the Holy Ghost, who lives in us. And the Holy Ghost, the Love of God, dwells in us because we are incorporated in Christ.

O marvelous unity! O union of love! As surely as we are incorporated in Christ through baptism and are organically bound to Him and become one with Him, just as truly the Holy Ghost, the essence of divine love, dwells in us. What an elevation of our human nature, since the Holy Ghost, so to speak, becomes incarnate in us! What love on the part of God, that the Father and the Son and the Holy Ghost should bind us to themselves in such unending blessedness! The same Holy Ghost, the expression of the love of the Father and the Son, binds us to the Son and, through the Son, to the Father.

How unfortunate that we should always merely skim the surface of our souls! Into the inner sanctuary where You reside, O Holy Ghost, we seldom penetrate. O God, at Pentecost give us a view of those unfathomable depths in which You dwell. From this day on let our gaze be fixed on Thee. Draw us away from the turmoil and distractions of our daily life into the depths of our soul where the Holy Ghost lives and works, that we may listen to His inspirations and live by His spirit.

We dissipate our energies by distractions and allow ourselves to become slaves to our duties and obligations. We allow ourselves no moments of silence and meditation in which we might be led to the Holy Ghost, who lives in us. We forget His presence entirely. He lingers in the dark recesses of our soul and waits in vain for a glance or a word from us.

Let us withdraw more into our own hearts, into their very depths. Let us listen to His inspirations and obey them promptly. Let us hearken to the voice that speaks within us and stirs us to action. Let us be more conscious of the sublime presence of God within us.

Prayer

O almighty God, grant, we beseech Thee, that we who keep the festival of the coming of the Holy Ghost may ever burn with the desire of heavenly things, and ever thirst after the waters of life eternal. Through Christ our Lord. Amen.

Pentecost Sunday

The Mass

The brilliant sun of Easter, our Lord Jesus Christ, rose to the highest heavens at the time of His Ascension. Just as at Pentecost the natural sun has normally reached the highest point of its orbit and begins to pour forth the full force of its rays upon the earth so that the earth may bring forth its fruits, in like manner Christ sends forth His rays from the heavenly heights upon His people and warms them with the glow and the fire of the Holy Ghost. Just fifty days after Easter, on that day when the Jews celebrated the feast of their deliverance from Egypt and the reception of the law on Mount Sinai, the Church is perfected through the power and the strength of the Holy Ghost.

The infant Church was gathered together in the supper room at Jerusalem; today the supper room is the great basilica of St. Peter, which now encloses men of all languages and of all races. At the third hour the Holy Ghost descended upon the apostles in the form of tongues of fire, thus completing the first step in their sanctification, thus bringing them to spiritual maturity. The Holy Ghost excludes no one. Men of all nations and of all peoples unite to confess: "The Spirit of the Lord hath filled the whole world, alleluia; and that which containeth all things hath knowledge of the voice, alleluia" (Introit). He lives in the hearts of those who will receive Him. He is the source and the bond of unity, of mutual understanding and reciprocal love. Sin and its author, the evil spirit, breed disharmony and strife and contention. Therefore we pray in the Introit, "Let God arise and let His enemies be scattered." This plea for action on the part of God is continued in the Kyrie and in the Collect of the Mass. The Epistle gives us the historical account of the events that occurred on Pentecost. But the work begun on Pentecost is not yet complete and must be renewed and repeated in us. Therefore we kneel after the Epistle and sing: "Come, Holy Ghost, fill the hearts of Thy faithful, and enkindle in them the fire of Thy love" (Alleluia verse). Then we rise to our feet and sing:

Come, Thou Holy Spirit, come,
And from Thy celestial home
Send Thy light and brilliancy.

Come, Thou father of the poor,
Come, Thou source of gifts secure,
Come, our heart's true radiancy.

The Holy Ghost comes to us to dwell in our hearts with the Father and the Son, truly and personally. He is our teacher; He brings peace.

At the Offertory we sing Psalm 67, which sings of the victory of Christ and His Church. We join in this victorious procession, decked out in the royal livery of Christ (through baptism and confirmation). Having conquered evil within ourselves and in our surroundings, we proceed like glorious victors to the "temple which is in Jerusalem," that is, to the altar. We pray that God may confirm and perfect in us what we received at Easter through baptism, and that it may be renewed and strengthened by the Holy Ghost (Secreta). In the Holy Sacrifice of the Mass the wonderful things related in the Epistle are re-enacted in us. As we offer our sacrifice, we turn from self-love and offer our own souls to God. Thus we make room for the entry of the Holy Ghost. We receive Holy Communion and thus receive a new and more perfect incorporation in Christ. We will become more perfectly united to the body of Christ than ever before if we live by the Spirit of Christ, the Holy Ghost. This thought is presented to us in the Communion chant, for if we devoutly receive Holy Communion, we shall be "filled with the Holy Ghost."

Meditation

Seven times seven days, a complete jubilee octave, have passed since Easter. Now the Holy Ghost, the Third Person of the Blessed Trinity, the eternal expression of the mutual love of the Father and the Son, comes to us. He comes with the sound of a mighty wind, appearing to the apostles in the form of tongues of fire which rest upon each of them. Made bold by this baptism of fire, they go forth into the world and proclaim by word and deed, even by the sacrificing of their lives, that Christ the crucified One is truly risen.

The first Pentecost. The historical event of Pentecost is related in the Epistle. The apostles and Mary, the Mother of Jesus, are gathered together in one place. About the third hour (about nine o'clock) they hear a mighty rush of wind as if a storm were approaching. Then tongues of fire appear above the heads of each of them. They are all filled with the Holy Ghost and begin to speak in various tongues, according as the Holy Ghost inspired them. Outside the house a great crowd of people has gathered, who cannot imagine what has happened. Then they hear the disciples and the apostles speaking in various languages, and each one, in the language in which he was born, hears of the wonderful things which God has done. A new Pentecost! In ancient times God confirmed His covenant with Israel to the accompaniment of thunder and lightning. But the law He gave was the law of fear, the law of severity, the law of servitude. This is a new Pentecost, a Pentecost that fills the hearts of men with love, freedom, and holy joy. The Holy Ghost appears with a mighty wind, penetrating and filling the hearts of the disciples. They are freed from their former timidity and hesitancy. The Holy Ghost enlightens men, guides their thoughts, provides for their needs, controls their desires, inspires their affections, adjusts their motives, and elevates them to the kingdom of the spirit. He teaches them a new manner of life. He gives them courage, strength of character, stability, inexhaustible patience, a readiness for sacrifice, a will to suffer for the sake of Christ. They are indeed a new creation.

Our Pentecost. In the mind of the liturgy, Pentecost is not merely the commemoration of a past event; the wonders related in the Epistle are repeated today in us. We also gather in one place during the celebration of the Holy Sacrifice of the Mass and unite in prayer, awaiting the coming of the Holy Ghost. For this reason we pray at the end of the Epistle: "Come, Holy Ghost, fill the hearts of Thy faithful, and kindle in them the fire of Thy love." When the glorified Savior appears in our midst at the Consecration of the Mass, He will bring the Holy Ghost with Him.

In our reception of Holy Communion the events of Pentecost will take visible form. The Holy Ghost comes to each of us and fills us with His fire and His power. He does not come to us in the form of fiery tongues, but in the form of a fragile host which is the glorified body of Christ and contains also the Spirit of Christ, the Holy Ghost. When we receive Holy Communion, we receive again the baptism of the Spirit. Having been filled with the Holy Ghost, having become bearers of the Spirit and apostles of the Lord, we announce the marvelous works of the Lord. During the distribution of Holy Communion the Church sings: "Suddenly there came a sound from heaven as of a mighty wind coming, ... and they were all filled with the Holy Ghost, speaking the wonderful works of God, alleluia, alleluia." Pentecost has been repeated in the present.

"If any one love Me, he will keep My word, and My Father will love him, and We will come to him and will make Our abode with him" (Gospel). Thus our Lord describes the love of the Father, and of the Son, and of the Holy Ghost, the love which binds us all together. God is never very far from us; He is actually within us. This is the joyful message of Pentecost: God is within us! The Father loves us, not only for today or for tomorrow, but for all eternity. God is within us and we are filled with light and warmth. We must let His rays shine into our hearts; we must let Him come and make His abode within us. We are filled with His power and fire, which will consume all evil and all sin within us. This fire is our holy zeal to serve God and our Savior.

Pentecost is the seal and the perfection of the mystery of Easter. If Easter is baptism, Pentecost is confirmation. Easter gives us a new birth; Pentecost brings us to maturity. At Pentecost we reach our full stature, we are brought to man's estate, to perfection by the power of the Holy Ghost. The baptism of the Spirit prepares us for heroic deeds, sanctifies our thoughts, purifies our motives. It makes us perfect Christians.

Prayer

O God, who hast this day taught the hearts of the faithful by the light of the Holy Ghost; grant that by the same Spirit we may always be truly wise and ever rejoice in His holy consolation. Through Christ our Lord. Amen.

Monday

Today the Church addresses herself to the newly baptized and the newly confirmed, and also to the rest of us who renew the grace of our baptism and confirmation. She calls us together at the church of St. Peter in Chains.

St. Peter once had a vision in which he saw a great linen sheet, as it were, being let down from heaven, which contained all kinds of beasts of the earth and birds of the sky. A voice from heaven addressed him saying: "Arise, Peter: kill and eat. But Peter said: Far be it from me, for I never did eat any thing that is common and unclean" (Acts 10:13 f.). But while he was thinking of these things, legates came from a Roman officer, Cornelius, begging him to come to Cornelius, who was a pagan. Now Peter understood the meaning of the vision, for God showed him that no man may be called common or unclean. Even the pagan has value in the eyes of God. Cornelius informed Peter that he had been bidden in a vision to summon the apostle. Then Peter preached the crucifixion and the resurrection of Christ.

And while Peter was yet speaking, the Holy Ghost came down upon all those who listened to him, upon Cornelius and the heathens who were with him (Acts 10:44 f.). The Jewish Christians who accompanied Peter were astonished that the Holy Ghost had been given also to the Gentiles, and Peter ordered that the heathens be baptized (Epistle). The Holy Ghost will be given also to the Gentiles who come to the Church. The Spirit of God makes no distinction between Hebrew and Gentile, nor between nation and nation. "God so loved the world as to give His only-begotten Son, that whosoever believeth in Him may not perish, but may have life everlasting" (Gospel). We are invited today by the liturgy to thank God that we have been called to Christ, to the Church, to baptism and confirmation.

"God so loved the world as to give His only-begotten Son, that whosoever believeth in Him may not perish, but may have life everlasting. For God sent not His Son into the world to judge the world, but that the world may be saved by Him. He that believeth in Him is not judged; but he that doth not believe is already judged, because he believeth not in the name of the only-begotten Son of God" (Gospel). Baptism gives us the gift of faith. We are saved by faith, for "whosoever believeth in Him may not perish, but may have life everlasting," In so far as it depends on Him, the divine physician comes to heal the sick. But those who will not follow His instructions take their lives in their own hands. Those who will not allow Him to save them are responsible for their own damnation. "He that believeth in Him is not judged; but he that doth not believe is already judged, because he believeth not in the name of the only-begotten Son of God."

"He is already judged." The judgment hath not yet appeared, but the judgment has already been made. For the Lord knew who were His; He knew who would persevere unto a crown and who would continue unto the flame. He knew the wheat on His threshing floor, and He knew the chaff. He knew the grain and He knew the cockle. "He that doth not believe is already judged." Why judged? "Because he believeth not in the name of the only-begotten Son of God."[20]

"Without faith it is impossible to please God" (Heb 11:6).

"He fed them with the fat of wheat, alleluia; and filled them with honey out of the rock, alleluia, alleluia" (Introit). This is the thanksgiving song of the baptized, and it is also our hymn of thanksgiving. We have been fed with the wheat of the Eucharist and filled with the honey from the rock of Christ. His flesh and His blood, His love, are all ours as the result of our baptism. "Rejoice to God our helper; sing aloud to the God of Jacob, alleluia" (Introit). The Lord hath done great things for us; now we must make some return to Him.

In Holy Communion, God gives us the Holy Ghost and an increase of sanctifying grace. "The Holy Ghost will teach you," the Communion prayer tells us. The more devout our reception of Holy Communion, the more the Holy Ghost will increase our faith and strengthen it and make it live. "But he that doth truth, cometh to the light" (Gospel); that is, he will acquire an active and vigorous faith. The more truly Christian we make our lives, the deeper and more pure and more active will be our faith.

Today we gratefully recall our baptism and confirmation. "The Lord thundered from heaven, and the Most High gave His voice [at the descent of the Holy Ghost], and the fountains of waters appeared, alleluia" (Offertory).

[20] St. Augustine; lesson at Matins.

We thank God for the precious gift of faith. It is our most valuable and treasured possession. "And this is the judgment: Because the light is come into the world, and men loved darkness rather than the light" (Gospel). This is the great sin, the sin of unbelief. "For every one that doth evil hateth the light."

PRAYER

O God, who didst send the Holy Ghost to Thy apostles, listen favorably to the prayers of Thy people, that Thou mayest bestow peace upon those to whom Thou hast given faith. Through Christ our Lord. Amen.

Tuesday

The glory of the Church was perfected by the descent of the Holy Ghost. In the sacrament of baptism her children received the "fullness of life." Therefore the Church calls out to the baptized and the confirmed: "Receive the joy of your glory, alleluia; giving thanks to God, alleluia, who hath called you to a heavenly kingdom, alleluia, alleluia" (Introit). She also warns us with maternal solicitude not to squander the riches we have received in baptism and confirmation. "Attend, O My people, to My law; incline your ears to the words of My mouth" (Introit).

"I am come that they may have life, and may have it more abundantly" (Gospel). When the apostles received word that Samaria had accepted the Gospel, they made haste to confer the Holy Ghost upon those who had been baptized. Peter and John were sent into Samaria and both apostles prayed over the baptized. "Then they laid their hands upon them, and they received the Holy Ghost" (Epistle). In the normal course of events, the sacrament of baptism is completed by the sacrament of confirmation. The new life given by the sacrament of rebirth must be strengthened, confirmed, and completed by the sacrament of the Spirit, the sacrament of confirmation. That life must develop into a vigorous maturity, untroubled by the violent turbulence of human passion, and characterized by the quiet, harmonious, overwhelming power of the divine Spirit.

The soul which is to be called and prepared by the sacrament of confirmation for deeds of Christian heroism, rises by a gradual and steady growth to the heights of Christian perfection. It acquires perfect detachment from the world, a pure and holy love of God, of Christ, and of its neighbor. It is prepared to practice heroic virtue, humility, patience, sacrifice, and daily suffering. Baptism alone restores supernatural life to the soul, and is sufficient for salvation. Through baptism the soul is reborn; but it is the will of God that this life be brought to perfection through the sacrament of confirmation. The Lord desires heroic and perfect Christians. It is His will to give us not merely life and a precarious escape from sin and eternal death, but also the fullness of life, as He says, "I am come that they may have life and may have it more abundantly." This fullness of life is attained through the descent of the Holy Ghost. Therefore the apostles were so zealous in seeing that the faithful received the Holy Ghost through the reception of confirmation: the sacrament of growth and strength, the sacrament of religious and moral maturity, the sacrament which completes baptism and brings the soul to Christian perfection.

Jesus is the shepherd of those who have been baptized and confirmed. "To him the porter openeth, and the sheep hear his voice, and he calleth his own sheep by name and leadeth them out. And when he hath led out his own sheep he goeth before them; and the sheep follow him because they know his voice" (Gospel). Christ is likewise the gate for all His sheep, the only gate by which the sheep can enter into the fold to spend the night in the enclosure. Anyone who would seek to lead and pasture the sheep of Christ without His authorization "is a thief and a robber," who leads the sheep to destruction. He who comes to the sheep through Christ and with the proper authorization will be saved. He will find the best pasture for the sheep, since he acts in the name of Christ and by His authority. Only in Christ and through His properly authorized minister may we find life and find it more abundantly. Such life can be had only from him to whom Christ said, "All power is given to Me in heaven and in earth. Going, therefore, teach ye all nations; baptizing them in the name of the Father and of the Son and of the Holy Ghost. Teaching them to observe all things whatsoever I have commanded you" (Mt 28:18–20). Such life can be had only from Christ living in His Church, in His apostles, in His bishops, and in His priests. "Amen, I say to you, whatsoever you shall bind upon earth shall be bound also in heaven; and whatsoever you shall loose upon earth shall be loosed also in heaven" (Mt 18:18).

The life given by baptism must grow; it is strengthened and brought to perfection by the reception of confirmation. By means of this life we are incorporated in Christ and in the living organism of the Church. Nowhere else and in no other way can we find life, experience growth, or achieve perfection. Everywhere else we find only empty pretense, evil, and death. How fortunate we are to be members of the true Church of Christ, and to be under the protection of the shepherds appointed by Christ! How thankful we should be! But we should also pray and offer the Holy Sacrifice for all who remain outside the fold of the Church, and we should act as apostles to all who are in the hands of those who have not entered the sheepfold through the right gate. Our own spiritual riches obliges us to practice charity toward those who are spiritually destitute.

"The Lord opened the doors of heaven and rained down manna upon them to eat; He gave them the bread of heaven; man ate the bread of angels, alleluia" (Offertory). Baptism, confirmation, and the Eucharist provide us with the abundance of life.

"The Spirit who proceedeth from the Father, alleluia; He shall glorify Me, alleluia, alleluia" (Communion). At the time of Holy Communion Jesus pours forth the Holy Ghost into our hearts. He is the Spirit of life, of love, of strength, of sanctity. He forms us very much in the same manner as He did the apostles at Pentecost. Our life, guided and formed by the action of the Holy Ghost, becomes holy and virtuous, and thus we glorify the glorified Christ who sent the Holy Ghost to us. By the devout reception of Holy Communion, "the Holy Ghost renews our souls" (Postcommunion). How careful, then, we should be to receive Communion as worthily as possible.

Prayer

Grant we beseech Thee, O Lord, that the power of the Holy Ghost may abide in us; may it mercifully cleanse our hearts and defend us from all danger. Through Christ our Lord. Amen.

Ember Wednesday

Gathered at the feet of Mary (the stational church for the day is that of St. Mary Major), we contemplate the fruitfulness of the Holy Ghost in the Church of Christ. "O God, when Thou didst go forth in the sight of Thy people, making a passage for them,... the earth was moved, and the heavens dropped [manna], alleluia. Let God arise, and let His enemies be scattered; and let them that hate Him flee from before His face" (Introit). This Introit gives us a picture of the power and the efficacy of the operations of the Holy Ghost among the Israelites of the Old Testament as they wandered through the desert to the Promised Land.

The visible works of the Holy Ghost in the Church. On the feast of Pentecost the prophecy made by the prophet Joel was fulfilled: "And it shall come to pass after this that I will pour out My Spirit upon all flesh; and your sons and your daughters shall prophesy; your old men shall dream dreams, and your young men shall see visions.... And I will show wonders in heaven; and in earth, blood, and fire, and vapor of smoke. The sun shall be turned into darkness, and the moon into blood before the great and dreadful day of the Lord doth come. And it shall come to pass that every one that shall call upon the name of the Lord shall be saved" (Jl 2:28 ff.).

At Pentecost God poured forth His Spirit upon the Church, and He continues to send forth the Spirit at all times and in all ages, as has been visibly manifested by the miracles which have been worked in the Church from the beginning even until now. This visible manifestation of the power of the Holy Ghost is described in the Epistle. "And by the hands of the apostles were many signs and wonders wrought among the people. And they were all with one accord in Solomon's porch. But of the rest no man durst join himself unto them; but the people magnified them. And the multitude of men and women who believed in the Lord was more increased; insomuch that they brought forth the sick into the streets and laid them on beds and couches, that when Peter came, his shadow at the least might overshadow any of them, and they might be delivered from their infirmities. And there came also together to Jerusalem a multitude out of the neighboring cities bringing sick persons and such as were troubled with unclean spirits, who were all healed" (Acts 5:12–16).

The Church has never lacked miracles. They are a continual witness of the presence and of the fruitfulness of the Holy Ghost in the Church. There is much human weakness in the Church, many faults and many scandals; but in spite of this human element with its imperfections and sins, we find everywhere the effects of the work of the Holy Ghost. We can place our full trust and confidence in the Church in which the Holy Ghost lives and works, in spite of all the faults and the mistakes of its human members.

The invisible work of the Holy Ghost in the Church has been described by the Lord: "No man can come to Me except the Father, who hath sent Me, draw him" (Jn 6:44). The essential element in the work of the Church is the grace of the Holy Ghost. It is the Holy Ghost who unites the Father and the Son; He also joins us to the Son and, through the Son, to the Father. Everything depends on His operation in us. The more fully we allow ourselves to be drawn and guided by the Holy Ghost, the closer we shall come to Jesus and His mysteries and His graces. The Holy Ghost must draw us to every good thought and word and deed. Every act of faith, of hope, and of love for God requires the inspiration and the help of the Holy Ghost. If our virtues and our deeds are to be truly perfect and worthy of God, they need the special and continual touch of the Holy Ghost. Even though we are endowed with all the supernatural virtues, we still remain mere apprentices in the spiritual life. We know what we must do; and yet lack the virtue and the faculty to perform these things with ease. The Holy Ghost must guide us. He must seize our intellect and our wills and guide us in prayer, in work, in the decisions we have to make, and in the difficulties we encounter every day. He must share with us His manner of seeing, of loving, of thinking, and of working.

Our works and our conduct will be perfect only when the Holy Ghost has taken complete possession of us. Therefore, in addition to the supernatural virtues of faith, hope, charity, justice, fortitude, temperance and wisdom, He gives us also His seven gifts. Thus He equips the tiny boat of our soul with sails upon which He Himself, the Spirit of God, blows. Our progress across the sea of life is then no longer slow and painful. We are propelled and guided by the Spirit. If the Spirit of God breathes upon the sails of our boat, then our journey will be a happy one. Then through the work and the help of the Holy Ghost, who lives in our soul, we shall come to the Father. But woe to us if we prefer to work alone, if we withdraw from the help and guidance of the Holy Ghost, and place our trust in our own efforts and abilities. We shall then certainly fall behind and be lost.

We pay too little heed to the approach and the knocking of the Holy Ghost. We do not live in the spirit, and therefore the Holy Ghost cannot operate perfectly within us. If we only had eyes to see!

If the Holy Ghost is to work successfully in us, He must find in us a great purity of heart, a simplicity and humility of soul, an active love of recollection and prayer, and finally, a burning love of God and of one's neighbor. But actually He finds us careless about venial sin, about certain infidelities and imperfections. We neglect inward and outward mortification, and refuse to be completely detached from our worldly works and actions. Our heads are filled with curiosity and are occupied with other people. We are too solicitous about our honor, our temporal progress, our relatives, our health, our spiritual progress, our former life. We are not yet completely detached from ourselves. How, then, can the Holy Ghost work unhampered in our soul and draw us to the Father? "Come, Holy Ghost, fill the hearts of Thy faithful, and kindle in them the fire of Thy love."

Prayer

Grant, we beseech Thee, almighty and merciful God, that the Holy Ghost may come to us and make us the temple of His glory. Through Christ our Lord. Amen.

Thursday

Philip the Deacon (Epistle) and the apostles (Gospel) wrought great signs and wonders by the power of the Holy Ghost, whom they had received. We also have received the Holy Ghost, and we still receive Him daily. We must therefore be spiritual men, men who work, not in their own way, but in the spirit of Christ and the Holy Ghost.

The spirit of independence, the human spirit, judges all things and thinks in a purely natural and earthly way. It considers those blessed who possess and enjoy great riches. It calls those great who possess worldly wisdom and enjoy the respect and esteem of their fellow men, who occupy positions of rank, and who wield great power and influence. It seeks always its own interests; it knows well the art of making profit at all times and under all circumstances; it is a master at carrying out its own designs and serving its own interests. It usurps a large part of the life even of pious and spiritual persons. Under the pretense of serving God, it is continually seeking itself and its own natural desires, its own comfort, its own honor. In all matters of the spirit it follows the prudence of the flesh and preaches moderation and mediocrity. It is one of the chief causes of negligence, and is a fruitful source of quarrels, disputes, coolness towards others, envy, and of an unwarranted solicitude for its own good reputation. It destroys tranquility, peace of soul. It gives men an exaggerated sense of their own importance. With good reason the masters of the spiritual life have called it "the greatest evil" on earth. What a host of men there are who are ruled by this tyrannical spirit of independence!

The Holy Ghost is the Spirit of Christ, and He has communicated Himself to the soul of man with all His gifts and graces. "The spirit of the Lord is upon Me. Wherefore He hath anointed Me to preach the gospel to the poor; He hath sent Me to heal the contrite of heart" (Lk 4:18). By the "spirit of Christ" we understand especially the principle that moved and motivated His will and His judgment. All of His actions were controlled by His burning desire to accept the will of His Father and perform it at all times. He was driven by the urge to overcome all things and accomplish all that was necessary for fulfilling the will of the Father and for redeeming mankind. In Christ the head and in us the members, the "spirit of Christ" is the spirit of love for the Father, the spirit of humility, of obedience, of recollection, of prayer, of suffering, and of sacrifice. This spirit causes the Christian to live and act according to the eight beatitudes, to rejoice in God, to desire to be as nothing in the eyes of the world, to be spurned and rejected by the world. This spirit inspires us to desire a life of renunciation and detachment, and complete union with God. It makes us seek only God's will and honor. This is the Spirit "whom the world cannot receive because it seeth Him not nor knoweth Him" (Jn 14:17).

"The Spirit of the Lord hath filled the whole world, alleluia" (Introit). This is the joyful message of Pentecost. Let us cast off, then, the spirit of independence, the spirit of the world, with its purely natural inclinations. The Holy Ghost, the Spirit of Christ, will take possession of us, guide us, inspire us, and direct us. He will give us the treasures of His light. He will give our wills a Christian nobility, an unconquerable strength, and the stability which we will need in order to live a life of virtue. He will overcome the resistance of our self-will, and subdue our rebellious nature. He will make us the willing instruments of the will of God and the salvation of souls. How foolish of us to refuse to lay aside the treacherous spirit of worldliness! "Come, Holy Ghost, fill the hearts of Thy faithful."

"And they were all filled with the Holy Ghost," with the Spirit of Christ (Acts 2:4). This was true of the apostles; it is likewise true of the priest at his ordination; it is true of all of us at our confirmation. The spirit of Christ must live in us. We Christians, especially the priests and religious, must conform ourselves to the great concepts of Christ as laid down in the gospel.

We must form our lives according to His principles and motives, and make them evident in our own personality. If only we were filled with faith in the abiding presence of the Holy Ghost, and with trust in His assistance! If we but had a clear vision of the efficacious life of the

Holy Ghost within our souls, we would be zealous in the service of the Church and energetic in subjecting our own spirit and in seeking to lead a holy life.

Prayer

May the outpouring of the Holy Ghost cleanse our hearts, O Lord, and may they be made fruitful by the intimate sprinkling of His dew. Through Christ our Lord. Amen.

Ember Friday

In the church of the Twelve Apostles, the church of the penitents, the Mass for Ember Friday is celebrated. It is a day of penance and a day on which to give thanks for the remission of sins.

"Thy sins are forgiven thee" (Gospel). Today we celebrate the Mass in the church in which on Holy Thursday the penitents were reconciled with the Church after having been absolved from their sins. During Easter time we have received rich and powerful graces. Have we fully cooperated with them? Must we not still reproach ourselves for our many sins, our infidelities, negligences, faults, and imperfections? Today we attend the Holy Sacrifice to express our contrition, to make amends, and to do penance. We are like the paralytic mentioned in the Gospel, who was totally paralyzed. His friends tried to bring him in on a stretcher and lay him at the feet of Jesus. But "when they could not find by what way they might bring him in because of the multitude, they went up upon the roof and let him down through the tiles with his bed into the midst before Jesus. Whose faith when He saw, He said: Man, thy sins are forgiven thee.... Arise, take up thy bed and go into thy house" (Gospel).

"O children of Sion, rejoice and be joyful in the Lord your God; because He hath given you a teacher of justice and He will make the early and the latter rain to come down to you as in the beginning. And the floors shall be filled with wheat, and the presses shall overflow with wine and oil. And you shall eat in plenty and shall be filled; and you shall praise the name of the Lord your God, who hath done wonders with you. And My people shall not be confounded forever. And you shall know that I am in the midst of Israel" (Epistle). This prophecy of Joel has been fulfilled in us. All our sins have been destroyed by the sacrificial death of Christ; we have been redeemed. We are children of God, loved by God with a divine love. Therefore, "let my mouth be filled with Thy praise, alleluia; that I may sing alleluia, alleluia" (Introit). This day is marked by great rejoicing, for the Holy Ghost has indeed been given to us. He is the teacher of justice. "He will teach you all things and bring all things to your mind, whatsoever I shall have said to you" (Jn 14:26). He lives in our soul and leads us to an upright, God-fearing life. He is given to us as the love which joins the Father to the Son, the Son to the Father, and us to both of Them; He elevates us so that we can have a certain participation in the life of the Holy Trinity. He is the fructifying rain which brings forth in us a multitude of spiritual and supernatural goods. Have we not good reason for rejoicing? Today we have seen wonderful things. "Praise the Lord, O my soul; in my life I will praise the Lord; I will sing to my God as long as I shall be, alleluia" (Offertory).

"Alleluia, alleluia. O how good and sweet is Thy Spirit, O Lord, within us, alleluia. Come, Holy Ghost, fill the hearts of Thy faithful, and kindle in them the fire of Thy love."

What is sordid, make Thou pure;
What is wounded, do Thou cure;
Slake now our aridity.
What is rigid, gently bend;
What is frigid, warmly tend;
Strengthen what goes erringly.

Fill Thy faithful who confide
In Thy power to guard and guide,
With Thy sevenfold mystery.

By a devout participation in the Holy Sacrifice, we receive, as the fruit of our work, the forgiveness of our sins and the remission of the temporal punishment due to sin. As an assurance of the forgiveness of our sins and of the graces and the help we are to receive, the Lord personally enters into our souls. "I will not leave you orphans; I will come to you again, alleluia; and your heart shall rejoice, alleluia."

"And your heart shall rejoice." This is the characteristic mark of the Christian; he is ever joyful and thankful to God, who has done such great things for him. Ah, if we could only be fully aware of the great truth: we are saved. God has taken away our sins. He loves us, and as a guarantee of His love and forgiveness, He pours forth His Spirit into our soul. "Praise the Lord, O my soul; in my life I will praise the Lord; I will sing to my God as long as I shall be, alleluia." From paralytics we have been made new men through the operation of the Holy Ghost in our soul.

Prayer

O merciful God, suffer not Thy Church, gathered together in the Holy Ghost, to be troubled by any assault of her enemies. Through Christ our Lord. Amen.

Ember Saturday

Today we assemble in the church of St. Peter. Just as the Christians of an earlier age offered tithes of their crops in thanksgiving to God for a bountiful harvest, so we, too, during the final days of the Easter cycle offer our thanks to God for the rich harvest of spiritual fruits we have received. For the liturgy this is a day of great festivity (Second lesson), a holy day, a day for fervent spiritual thanksgiving.

In retrospect. "Brethren, being justified by faith, let us have peace with God, through our Lord Jesus Christ, by whom also we have access through faith into this grace wherein we stand, and glory in the hope of the glory of the sons of God" (Epistle). We have been saved, we have been reconciled to God. We have been saved, not through any works which we have performed, not through our own natural powers and efforts, but through the grace of God which He has given us in baptism. We have been reconciled to God through faith in Jesus Christ, who was crucified, who rose from the dead, and who redeemed us with His most precious blood. We are saved; we have been justified. The first result of our justification is the fact that we are now at peace with God. We can now approach God with ease and confidence, because we know that He loves us and that nothing can separate us from Him.

We have been reconciled to Him through our Lord Jesus Christ, the Second Person of the Blessed Trinity. Heretofore we were the children of wrath; but now we are His friends, members of His family, members of the elect.

The second fruit of our justification is the fact that through the death and resurrection of Christ we have received and now live a life of grace. By virtue of the grace we have received, we share the life of God, a life of unspeakable blessedness and riches. The "eye hath not seen, nor ear heard, neither hath it entered into the heart of man what things God hath prepared for them that love Him" (1 Cor 2:9). We are made "partakers of the divine nature" (2 Pt 1:4). By reason of the grace we possess, we have an assurance and guarantee of the glory which we anticipate even now as children of God. "Dearly beloved, we are now the sons of God; and it has not yet appeared what we shall be. We know that when He shall appear, we shall be like to Him, because we shall see Him as He is" (1 Jn 3:2). We shall see Him, no longer as in a mirror, but face to face; we shall rest lovingly in His heart; we shall share His habitation and His blessedness for all eternity. That is our hope, the hope in which we glory.

The prospect of the future. "And not only so, but we glory also in tribulations, knowing that tribulation worketh patience, and patience trial, and trial hope; and hope confoundeth not" (Epistle). Such hope is possessed by the Christian who has lived through Easter and Pentecost in the spirit of the Church. He rejoices even in the trials and tribulations of life. He knows that tribulation gives him an opportunity to practice patience. By suffering patiently he will gain strength; his virtue will be tried and proved, and he will acquire a firm hope, which will not deceive. This hope is the third fruit of the justification which Christ won for us through His suffering and resurrection. With it we find joy in the tribulations and afflictions of life, for we know that they effect our eternal reward. The unbeliever, the pagan, is a pessimist. He flies from tribulations and curses them. We, however, rejoice if we are allowed to suffer. We do not look on affliction as an evil, but rather as the path to eternal glory. For us suffering carries in its bosom eternal salvation.

Certainty. "Hope confoundeth not; because the charity of God is poured forth in our hearts by the Holy Ghost, who is given to us" (Epistle). We are certain of the life that awaits us. This confidence rests on our awareness that God loves us. This is the sweetest mystery of Christianity: God loves us with a divine love. The Father loves the Son and the Son loves the Father through the Holy Ghost. This Holy Ghost is the love through which and in which God loves Himself. Nor does He reserve this love entirely for Himself. He pours it into our hearts also like a healing, nourishing, strengthening oil. In the Holy Ghost we love God in the way that is most pleasing to Him and most fitting for us who are the children of God; that is, we love Him with the love of the Holy Ghost, whom we possess and through whom we return the kiss of paternal love. Could our hope betray us, since God sees the image of the Holy Ghost in us, and therefore loves Himself in us? Must not the promise of Christ be fulfilled in us, "As the Father hath loved Me, I also have loved you" (Jn 15:9)? Joyfully aware of God's love, the liturgy sings: "Hope confoundeth not; because the charity of God is poured forth in our hearts by the Holy Ghost, who is given to us" (Epistle).

These are the priceless gifts of the Easter season which closes today: We are saved, we are justified, we have been reconciled with God, and are at peace. We possess sanctifying grace and share

God's life with Him. We rejoice in tribulations because they unite us to our crucified and risen Savior, and give us the hope of attaining to the glory of the children of God in heaven. And in addition to all this, we possess within our souls the Holy Ghost, the infallible guarantee of the things we hope for. Why should we not rejoice? Should we not have great confidence? Are we not immensely rich in God and in the Church?

The Easter cycle ends with the Mass today. With grateful hearts we recall all the gifts and benefits which the risen Lord has given us through His Church during the past eight weeks. "The charity of God is poured forth in our hearts, alleluia; by His Spirit dwelling within us, alleluia, alleluia. Bless the Lord, O my soul; and let all that is within me bless His holy name" (Introit).

Prayer

May the Holy Ghost enkindle in us, O Lord, that same fire which our Lord Jesus Christ sent down upon earth and willed should fiercely burn in our hearts. Who livest and reignest with Thee in the unity of the same Holy Ghost, world without end. Amen.

PART THREE

The Time After Pentecost

Introduction

With the celebration of the feast of Pentecost, the mystery of the actual redemption of mankind comes to an end. Through Christ we have received a new life, and the Holy Spirit has been infused into our hearts in order that the life which we received at our resurrection at Easter may be protected, developed, and brought to perfection. During the Sundays after Pentecost this work of the Holy Spirit is accomplished. During this time we have the obligation of cooperating with the Holy Spirit so that He may operate in us and heal us. We must fully cooperate with Him and allow ourselves to be guided by Him so that we may be brought to spiritual maturity. The chief means placed at our disposal for this work is the devout celebration of Mass and the fruitful reception of Holy Communion.

Unlike the Sundays of Advent, the Sundays after Epiphany, and the Sundays of Lent, which stand in close relationship to Easter, these Sundays after Pentecost are not closely bound together by a close relationship. Each of these Sundays is, in a sense, a little Easter all by itself. The central point of each of these Sundays is the celebration of the Eucharist. Throughout the week we are occupied with our daily tasks and the obligations of our vocation in life. Thus we are necessarily brought into contact with the world and its spirit, and can scarcely escape being somewhat infected by that spirit. But on Sunday we withdraw from the world for the celebration of the Holy Eucharist. We seek to stir up within our souls the graces and the blessings we received at Easter, and through our baptism and our confirmation, by means of the reception of the Eucharist. We wish to arise again in Christ and with Christ, and become more intimately and more perfectly united to Him. We renew our renunciation of sin and of the spirit of the world and our fallen nature. Through the devout celebration of the Mass we obtain renewed strength, a new joy, and an increased courage for the struggle to live in Christ and through Christ during the weeks that lie ahead of us.

These twenty-four Sundays fit perfectly in that great procession of events which leads from Christ's Resurrection at Easter to His coming at the Last Judgment. Easter brought us the grace of redemption and initiated us into the mystery of life in Christ and our incorporation in Him and in His Church. The Lord has withdrawn from us and has ascended into heaven in order to prepare a dwelling place for us there. "And if I shall go and prepare a place for you, I will come again and will take you to Myself; that where I am, you also may be" (Jn 14:3). We have been left behind in the world; but we are prepared through the reception of the Holy Spirit at Pentecost, and called to fulfill our mission in the world as men of the Spirit, depending on the strength of the Holy Ghost, the Spirit of Christ, and the gospel. We recall the promise that was made to us by Christ: "I will come again and will take you to Myself." Our hearts are filled with longing for this return of the Lord, and we stand with our lamps in readiness. Soon the day will come when we shall be told, "Behold the bridegroom cometh, go ye forth to meet Him" (Mt 25:6). He shall come to take us to Himself, that we may all be where He is. Thus the time after Pentecost is for the Church the period of the growth and completion of the kingdom of God on earth, and thus is appropriately affixed to the feast of Pentecost, the day on which the Church was founded.

Three thoughts dominate the Masses said during the period after Pentecost: the remembrance of Easter, the expectation of the return of Christ, and the battles and the sufferings that are to be expected in the present life. We call to mind the feast of Easter and our resurrection from the grave of sin; we look forward with longing to our final redemption and to our eventual resurrection to the eternal life which has been promised to us. The perfect redemption which we await will be accomplished in the "day of Christ," the day on which He will return with power and majesty to judge both the living and the dead. We plunge into the battle between the spirit and the flesh, between the new man and the old man, between the kingdom of God and the kingdom of sin. The strength required for this battle will be furnished by the Eucharist. "I live, and you shall live" (Jn 14:19).

Trinity Sunday

The Mass

The first Sunday after Pentecost is dominated by the feast of the Holy Trinity. Ever since the beginning of the ecclesiastical year, the liturgy has kept us conscious of the great mystery of our redemption, the mystery of God's love and mercy. Today the Church turns gratefully to contemplate the great mystery on which our redemption depends. The source and the final end of all the graces she has received, of all the mysteries she has celebrated during the past year, is the mystery of the Holy Trinity.

Today the Church lifts her heart, overflowing with love, in a grateful *Gloria Patri, et Filio, et Spiritui Sancto.* Thus she sings in memory of the mystery and the blessings of Christmas, Easter, and Pentecost; and in the Introit of the Mass these words bear aloft to the very throne of the Holy Trinity her joy and her gratitude: "Blessed be the Holy Trinity and undivided unity; we will give glory to Him because He hath shown His mercy to us." Today the Kyrie may be understood to mean: "Graciously accept our thanks, O Father, Son, and Holy Ghost." Our gratitude is further expressed in the Gloria and in the Epistle, especially by the significant words with which the Epistle ends: "For of Him and by Him and in Him are all things; to Him be glory forever." The same sentiment is repeated in the Gradual and in the Alleluia verse. The mystery of the Holy Trinity is the subject of the Gospel also. That mystery we shall never fully understand, — one God in three persons — yet we believe it firmly and express that belief in the Credo: "I believe."

At the Offertory we sing: "Blessed be God the Father and the only-begotten Son of God, and also the Holy Spirit; because He hath shown His mercy to us." The Holy Trinity is revealed to us in a tangible manner in the Holy Sacrifice of the Mass, through which the work of our redemption is repeated and grace is imparted to us. God manifests His grace to us by placing Christ in our hands as our offering, so that together with Christ we become a gift pleasing to the Divinity. With Christ and in Christ we are able to approach the very throne of the Holy Trinity. There, since we are the brothers of Christ, we may address the Father as His children: "Our Father,... hallowed be Thy name.... Give us this day our daily bread, and forgive us our trespasses,... [and] deliver us from evil." But the remission of our sins is not enough. In the offering of Holy Communion the Father gives us as our daily bread the most Holy Eucharist, the most tangible expression and the surest guarantee of His love and His mercy. For this reason we sing the beautiful Communion hymn: "We bless the God of heaven, and before all living we will praise Him; because He hath shown His mercy to us." Then we pray that "the reception of this sacrament and the confession of the holy and eternal Trinity... may profit us to the salvation of body and soul" (Postcommunion). Today our *Deo Gratias* has a special significance, for "He hath shown His mercy to us" in the Holy Sacrifice. "Glory be to the Father, and to the Son, and to the Holy Ghost."

Meditation

Today's feast is celebrated in honor of the Father and the Son and the Holy Ghost, the Triune God, in thanksgiving for His eternal mercy, because of which He has created us, redeemed us, and sanctified us.

"O the depth of the riches of the wisdom and of the knowledge of God" (Epistle). With St. Paul and with Holy Mother the Church we stand in awe at the depth of the divine mercy, of the divine wisdom, and of the divine knowledge. We are amazed at the great wisdom and love of God as manifested in His selection of men, particularly in His selection of the Gentiles in preference to the chosen people of Israel, as the recipients of His grace and redemption. The heathens were the first to wander away from God, and God selected the Israelites as His chosen people. But Israel in turn rejected Christ and salvation, and because of the infidelity and the unbelief of the Jews, the gospel was given to the Gentiles. "For God hath concluded all in unbelief (both Jews and heathens) that He may have mercy on all" (Rom 11:32). At the end of time both the Jews and the heathens will belong to Christ. "O the depth of the riches of the wisdom and of the knowledge of God. How incomprehensible are His judgments, and how unsearchable His ways! For who hath known the mind of the Lord? Or who hath been His counsellor? Or who hath first given to Him, and recompense shall be made him? For of Him and by Him and in Him are all things; to Him be glory forever" (Epistle). "Blessed be the Holy Trinity and undivided unity; we will give glory to Him because He hath shown His mercy to us" (Introit).

This is the God to whom we are consecrated. He has in His infinite mercy made us sharers of His divine life. We have been baptized "in the name of the Father and of the Son and of the Holy Ghost" (Gospel), and we share in the inexhaustible riches of the life of the Holy Trinity; we have even been made "partakers of the divine nature" (2 Pt 1:4). Therefore by virtue of our baptism we belong, not to ourselves, not to created things, not to men, not to the world nor to Satan, but to God. At the time of our baptism we renounced all these things, and since then we believe in the Father, and in the Son, and in the Holy Ghost. We have been consecrated to Them, and we belong entirely to Them. Anything less than God is unworthy of us, and God alone can satisfy us, not only during our earthly sojourn, but also in heaven, where we shall one day share the inexhaustible riches of the holy and blissful life of the Father and the Son and the Holy Ghost. This life comes to us entirely through the mercy of God. "Blessed be the Holy Trinity and undivided unity; we will give glory to Him because He hath shown His mercy to us" (Introit).

This is a day for giving thanks to the Father and the Son and the Holy Ghost. During the course of the Church year we have been made aware of the innumerable blessings of love and mercy conferred by God on us, on the Church, and on all mankind. "For God so loved the world as to give His only-begotten Son; that whosoever believeth in Him may not perish, but may have life everlasting" (Jn 3:16).

This is a day for renewing our consecration to God. We should renounce the world with our whole heart, and break away effectually from all that can be displeasing to Him. As on the day of our baptism, we should repeat, "I believe in the Father, and in the Son, and in the Holy Ghost." This belief implies more than the admission that the Father and the Son and the Holy Ghost exist and constitute one God in three Persons. It implies that I live for the Father and the Son and the Holy Ghost, by whom I have been sanctified, and to whom I have been consecrated by my baptism. This consecration we renew again today, and we should ratify it daily and make it more effective through the devout participation in the Mass. When we say the preliminary prayers at the foot of the altar, we rid ourselves of all attachment to the world, reject all infidelity, and renounce all that is alien to our state as creatures consecrated to God. At the Offertory we lay our hearts at the side of the bread and wine that we may make a new consecration and dedication of ourselves to the Father and to the Son and to the Holy Ghost. During the Consecration of the Mass, the sacrificial fire of our Lord and Savior will descend from heaven upon our offering, enkindling it with the fire of His love, and He will bear it up to heaven. We, too, are consecrated and offered up to the Father. We live, now no longer for ourselves, but for God alone.

This dedication of ourselves to God is strengthened and sealed by the Lord at the time of Holy Communion. This earthly consecration extends through Holy Communion to the eternal *communio* in heaven, where we shall enjoy the companionship of God the Father, and of God the Son, and of God the Holy Ghost. Then we shall see Him just as He is, face to face. For all eternity we shall share His life, His glory, His divine knowledge, and the mansions of His eternal love. This glorious reward the Son of God earned for us while on earth, by His life, His suffering, and His death. "We bless the God of heaven, and before all living we will praise him; because He hath shown His mercy to us" (Communion).

Prayer

Almighty and everlasting God, who hast given Thy servants, in their confession of the true faith, to bear witness to the glory of the eternal Trinity, and to adore the unity in the might of its majesty: we beseech Thee that by our steadfastness in that same faith we may be ever defended from all adversity. Through Christ our Lord. Amen.

Monday

The spirit of Pentecost, the spirit of Christ, is a spirit of love for God and for one's neighbor. The new life which has been given us through the redemption is protected by this spirit of charity. Therefore we are admonished in the Mass for the first Sunday after Pentecost to love one another.

"God is charity." "He that loveth not, knoweth not God, for God is charity. By this hath the charity of God appeared towards us, because God hath sent His only-begotten Son into the world that we may live by Him. In this is charity; not as though we had loved God, but because He hath first loved us and sent His Son to be propitiation for our sins.... And we have known and have believed the charity which God hath to us. God is charity; and he that abideth in charity abideth in God and God in him. In this is the charity of God perfected with us, that we may have confidence in the day of judgment; because as He is, we also are in this world" (1 Jn

4:8 ff.; Epistle). God is love. Our possession of this love makes us resemble God. If we possess something in common with the Judge already in this world, we need not fear that on the Day of Judgment, the day of our death, we shall be sentenced and cast off by Him. Charity gives us this assurance: "Fear is not in charity; but perfect charity casteth out fear, because fear hath pain. And he that feareth is not perfected in charity" (Epistle).

"If God hath so loved us; we also ought to love one another. No man hath seen God at any time. If we love one another, God abideth in us, and His charity is perfected in us.... If any man say: I love God; and hateth his brother, he is a liar. For he that loveth not his brother whom he seeth, how can he love God, whom he seeth not? And this commandment we have from God, that he who loveth God love also his brother" (Epistle). "He that saith he is in the light, and hateth his brother, is in darkness, even until now. He that loveth his brother abideth in the light.... But he that hateth his brother is in darkness [in sin] and walketh in darkness, and knoweth not whither he goeth; because the darkness hath blinded his eyes" (1 Jn 2:9 f.).

At the head of the Epistles for the many Sundays which follow Pentecost, the liturgy places that one which promulgates the great commandment of the love of God and of one's neighbor. Christian perfection consists essentially in the perfect love of God and of one's fellow men. The final end and aim of all the commandments is charity. Without this love for God and for one's neighbor, none of the commandments and none of the duties of a Christian life can be perfectly fulfilled. Charity is the root, the life, and the soul of all the virtues. It is the essence of virtue, for if it is lacking, there is no true virtue; whereas if there is charity, no virtue is wanting. Charity is infused in our hearts through the Holy Ghost, who has been given to us. Not every man can give great alms to the poor or practice heroic mortification, but everyone is able to practice charity.

The Mass for the first Sunday after Pentecost emphasizes the duty of fraternal charity. This great commandment is emphasized especially in the Epistle, to which we reply: "I said, O Lord, be Thou merciful to me; heal my soul, for I have sinned against Thee" (Gradual). Christianity breathes the spirit of love for God and for one's neighbor. It is in this duty of practicing fraternal charity that we fail most often, in spite of all our piety.

"Hearken to the voice of my prayer, O my King and my God: for to Thee will I pray, O Lord" (Offertory), now in the Offertory of this Mass, while celebrating this Holy Sacrifice with Thee. This prayer asks for forgiveness and pardon for our many offenses against charity, and implores strength to develop a perfect love. "Charity is patient, is kind; charity envieth not, dealeth not perversely; is not puffed up; is not ambitious, seeketh not her own, is not provoked to anger, thinketh no evil" (1 Cor 13:4 f.). How far removed we are from such dispositions! Our self-love and our pride make this perfect charity difficult to attain. With strength obtained through the reception of Communion we trust that we shall fulfill our duties of fraternal charity more perfectly than has been our wont. The liturgy has great confidence in the power of the Eucharist to produce this effect in us, for we receive the Spirit of the Lord when we partake of His flesh and blood. In a sense, the reception of Holy Communion is a renewal of Pentecost, for through its use we become spiritual men, having a great capacity for the love of God and our fellow man. For this reason we rejoice with the words of the Communion prayer: "I will speak of all Thy marvelous works; I will be glad and rejoice in Thee. I will sing unto Thy name,

O Thou Most High." We shall praise God by our inward struggles and by our active life. But in all things, charity.

Prayer

O God, the strength of those that hope in Thee, favorably hear our supplications; and since without Thee mortal infirmity can do nothing, grant the help of Thy grace that, in fulfilling Thy commandments, we may please Thee both in will and in action. Through Christ our Lord. Amen.

Tuesday

Christmas, Easter, Pentecost, all are eloquent expressions of the mystery of God's mercy to men. "By this hath the charity of God appeared towards us, because God hath sent His only-begotten Son into the world that we may live by Him" (Epistle). "I will sing unto the Lord, who giveth me good things" (Introit). I will sing to the Lord, not only with words, not only in my heart, but also by the works which I perform. I will show mercy to those who are my brothers in Christ, and do good unto them.

"Be you merciful, as your Father also is merciful. Judge not, and you shall not be judged. Condemn not, and you shall not be condemned. Forgive, and you shall be forgiven" (Gospel). What is the work of the Incarnation of the Son of God but a magnificent expression of the merciful love of God? "For God so loved the world as to give His only-begotten Son" (Jn 3:16). And since the Father has willed the Incarnation of the Son in order that He might offer Himself up for us and destroy our guilt, what is the motive of the Father but merciful love, which does not spare even His Son in order that the servant may be rescued? Oh, the mercy of the love of God! How often we have broken faith with God since our baptism! How often we have grieved Him, spurned Him, and left Him in our pursuit of sin! On hundreds of occasions He has had reason to let us fall and to cast us off forever. Yet He has always had mercy on us and has forgiven us again and again. "Not by the works of justice which we have done, but according to His mercy He saved us" (Ti 3:5). "As I live, saith the Lord God, I desire not the death of the wicked, but that the wicked turn from his way and live" (Ez 33:11). "Can a woman forget her infant, so as not to have pity on the son of her womb? And if she should forget, yet will not I forget thee" (Is 49:15). "Be you merciful, as your heavenly Father also is merciful." We must be merciful to all men, and particularly to all those who have injured us. "Father, forgive them for they know not what they do" (Lk 23:34). We must be merciful to sinners. We must hate sin, yet love the sinner. We must be merciful toward the poor and the needy, and this mercy must exist not only in our hearts but also in our actions. "Blessed are the merciful, for they shall obtain mercy" (Mt 5:7).

"Give, and it shall be given unto you; good measure, and pressed down, and shaken together, and running over, shall they give into your bosom. For with the same measure that you mete withal, it shall be measured to you again" (Gospel). These words were spoken by our Lord Himself and are both a command and a promise. This is a promise that is fulfilled thousands of times in life, and a commandment only too often completely ignored. It is a cardinal point in the divine economy that "with the same measure that you mete withal, it shall be measured to you again." "He that hath the substance of this world and shall see his brother in need and shall shut up his bowels from him, how doth the charity of God abide in him?" (1 Jn 3:17.) "And whosoever shall give to drink to one of these little ones a cup of cold water only in the name of a disciple, amen I say to you, he shall not lose his reward" (Mt 10:42).

"When we pray," says St. Augustine in explaining this Gospel, "we are all God's beggars. We stand before the door of the great Father ... desiring to receive something; and that something is God Himself. What does the beggar ask of you? Bread. And what do you ask of God but Christ, who says: 'I am the living bread which came down from heaven'?" When we approach the Father and ask Him for something, we may be sure that "with the same measure that you mete withal, it shall be measured to you again." "Give, and it shall be given to you." Give generously, and you will receive in abundance; give sparingly, and your return will be small. Have we considered earnestly this law of giving and receiving?

"Seekest thou mercy from God? Then be thou merciful.... Seekest thou something from God? Then give, and it shall be given to you" (St. Augustine). Give and forgive, that is the spirit of Christ and the spirit of Christianity.

Prayer

O God, the strength of those that hope in Thee, favorably hear our supplications; and since without Thee mortal infirmity can do nothing, grant the help of Thy grace that, in fulfilling Thy commandments, we may please Thee both in will and in action. Through Christ our Lord. Amen.

Wednesday

"I pray ... for them also who through their word [the preaching of the apostles] shall believe in Me. That they all may be one as Thou, Father, in Me and I in Thee; that they also may be one in Us" (Jn 17:20 f.). The Holy Trinity, the trinity in unity and the unity in trinity, is the model and the source of our unity in love.

The Holy Trinity is a type of the union of love which exists in the Christian family. The life of the three persons of the Blessed Trinity is a life of most intimate unity. Apart from the distinction of persons, they are one in nature, in knowledge, in understanding, and in love. For them there can be no isolation, no consideration of self apart from the other persons, no life for themselves apart. In the bosom of the Holy Trinity there is only the closest community of interest in one another, for one another, and to one another. "As Thou, Father, in Me and I in Thee." The Christian family, the religious community, the Christian community, should all pattern their life of unity after this example of multiplicity in unity and unity in multiplicity. This unity of His members is the cherished wish of the Savior, expressed in His priestly prayer the night before He died: "That they may be one." In what manner are they to be one? "As Thou, Father, in Me and I in Thee." What a sublime and divine model! "I in them, and Thou in Me." And to what purpose? "That they may be made perfect in one." The main purpose, however, of this Christian unity is that "the world may know that Thou hast sent Me and hast loved them, as Thou hast also loved Me" (Jn 17:23). In life we honor and acknowledge the divine Trinity principally by living in perfect unity and harmony with one another. In the same manner we bear witness to Christ, living the life of Christ. In this way we show ourselves to be the true children of the Father and win His love for us. But unfortunately, when it comes to being "one in heart and soul," we often fail miserably.

The strength necessary for establishing this Christian unity comes to us from the Holy Trinity. Our poor, fallen human nature does not easily accommodate itself to such unity. It is hindered by envy, ambition, and selfishness; it is hampered by individual habits and customs; it is fettered by our unchecked love of the trivial pleasures of the world. Moreover, true Christian unity is made difficult by the diversity of temperaments and the persistence of self-will. All these human weaknesses make an almost irresistible obstacle to that wish of our Lord, "that they may be one." A true unity, stripped of all hypocrisy and superficiality, can be achieved only by grace. Grace is given to us precisely for the purpose of helping us to overcome all narrowness and selfishness inherent in our fallen nature, that we may find it possible to live with one another and for one another.

"And the glory which Thou hast given Me, I have given to them; that they may be one as We also are one" (Jn 17:22). The glory which is given to us is the glory of divine sonship, the result of sanctifying grace. Why is this life of God, this life of the Blessed Trinity, given to us? In order that we may be one as the Father and the Son and the Holy Ghost are one. Sanctifying grace is the result of our participation in the life of the Blessed Trinity. Such a participation must result in the unity of heart and spirit. When sanctifying grace resides in the soul, all narrowness of spirit and all isolation must be destroyed. We share in the glory of God, in the sonship of God, to the degree that we separate ourselves from the world and acquire the generosity necessary for sacrificing our own interests and our own wishes for those of our neighbor.

"That they may be one." We all form one body with Christ. "Wherefore receive one another, as Christ also hath received you, unto the honor of God" (Rom 15:7). "And if one member suffer anything, all the members suffer with it; or if one member glory, all the members rejoice with it" (1 Cor 12:26). But are we truly conscious that we form one body? Who of us can say that he is ill when his neighbor is ill? Who of us is vexed when his neighbor is distressed? Who of us has suffered because others have suffered misfortune? All about us there are so many in spiritual, moral, and physical need, and yet we seem to be scarcely aware of it. Our consciousness of our unity is so meager! Should we not feel our brother's need? Should we not assist him in carrying his burdens? To do so would indeed be in the true spirit of Christianity.

"Be ye merciful, as your Father also is merciful" (Gospel). The Lord has commanded us not to judge, nor to condemn, nor to pass sentence on anyone. But how do we obey this command? We cannot overlook the splinter in our brother's eye; yet we are incapable of seeing the beam in our own eye (Gospel). Are we, then, really merciful? As long as we act in such a manner, can we reasonably expect to receive mercy ourselves on the day of judgment? Are we unaware that we may expect the grace of God and share in the divine sonship only in the measure in which the zeal of charity burns in our soul?

"O Lord, be Thou merciful to me; heal my soul, for I have sinned against Thee" (Gradual). The liturgy directs our attention to the Eucharist and to our incorporation in Christ. From these sources the spirit of Christ, the spirit of charity, must find its way into our souls. "I will speak of all Thy marvelous works; I will be glad and rejoice in Thee; I will sing unto Thy name, O Thou Most High" (Communion).

Prayer

Pour forth the spirit of Thy love into our hearts, O Lord, that all they whom Thou hast nourished with this heavenly bread may, through Thy paternal goodness, be of one heart and mind. Through Christ our Lord. Amen.

Thursday
Feast of Corpus Christi

The feast of Corpus Christi was established as a day of thanksgiving for the institution of the Holy Eucharist as a sacrifice and a sacrament. "He fed them [the faithful] with the fat of wheat, and filled them with honey out of the rock [Christ], alleluia, alleluia, alleluia" (Introit). Christ in His humanity and in His divinity, in body and soul, has become both our high priest and our sacrifice, our food and our friend, and resides in our tabernacles.

The promise of the Holy Eucharist (Gospel). The multitude which followed Christ into the desert and lingered with Him on the shore of the Sea of Galilee, was fed with a miraculous bread. During the following night Christ astonished His disciples by walking on the water, showing them that He was the master of nature and the elements. The following day the people flocked to Him again, for they hoped that He would again provide them with food. Christ spoke to them in the synagogue at Capharnaum. "My flesh is meat indeed, and My blood is drink indeed. He that eateth My flesh and drinketh My blood, abideth in Me and I in him. As the living Father hath sent Me, and I live by the Father; so he that eateth Me, the same also shall live by Me. This is the bread that came down from heaven. Not as your fathers did eat manna and are dead. He that eateth this bread, shall live forever" (Jn 6:56–59). Many of the Jews complained, "This saying is hard, and who can hear it?" and at once they left Him. We, however, accept this teaching of Christ, as did St. Peter: "Lord, ... Thou hast the words of eternal life" (Jn 6:69). We believe, for we know that Thou art God.

The institution of the Holy Eucharist. "Brethren, I have received of the Lord that which also I delivered to you, that the Lord Jesus, the same night in which He was betrayed, took bread, and giving thanks, broke, and said: Take ye and eat, this is My body which shall be delivered for you; this do for the commemoration of Me. In like manner also the chalice, after He had supped, saying: This chalice is the new testament in My blood; this do ye, as often as you shall drink, for the commemoration of Me. For as often as you shall eat this bread and drink this chalice, you shall show the death of the Lord until He come. Therefore whosoever shall eat this bread or drink of the chalice unworthily, shall be guilty of the body and the blood of the Lord. But let a man prove himself, and so let him eat of that bread, and drink of the chalice. For he that eateth and drinketh unworthily, eateth and drinketh judgment to himself, not discerning the body of the Lord" (Epistle).

The Lord promised the Eucharist and gave it to us. That which we preserve in our tabernacles, that which we worship and adore on our altars, is not mere bread and wine, but the real flesh and blood of the Lord. He is present there entire and undivided, with the fullness of His divinity and of His humanity. He is there "full of grace and truth.... And of His fullness we all have received" (Jn 1:14, 16). Christ lives and remains with us in the Blessed Sacrament. He is there, not merely symbolically, but actually and in person. In the Eucharist there really resides He who was born of Mary, who was crucified and died for us, who arose from the dead and was glorified.

"I believe ... in Jesus Christ, His only Son, our Lord," who is actually present here in the Blessed Sacrament. He was "born of the Father before all ages; God of God, light of light, true God of true God; begotten, not made; consubstantial with the Father; by whom all things were made. Who for us men and for our salvation, came down from heaven; and was incarnate by the Holy Ghost of the Virgin Mary; and was made man. He was crucified also for us, suffered under Pontius Pilate, and was buried. And the third day He rose again according to the Scriptures; and ascended into heaven. He sitteth at the right hand of the Father; and He shall come again with glory to judge the living and the dead; and His kingdom shall have no end" (Credo).

Our God dwells among us. He has appeared among us and revealed Himself to us, not merely in word or in the spirit or by virtue of the grace He imparts; but He has appeared in visible form for men who depend so utterly on their senses. In Paradise God appeared to our first parents in visible form, and again He made His presence known to Moses by means of the burning bush. When the chosen people were being led through the wilderness, He made His presence known in a visible manner by means of the cloud which appeared over the Ark of the Covenant by day, and the pillar of fire which appeared by night. Then, finally, He appeared in new visible form, God and man in one person, as the Son of God, born of the Virgin Mary. "And we saw His glory, the glory as it were of the only-begotten of the Father, full of grace and truth" (Jn 1:14). "The Word was made flesh and dwelt among us," not only for the few short years of His earthly life, but forever in the most Blessed Sacrament, the miracle of His love. "Behold, I am with you all days, even to the consummation of the world" (Mt 28:20). We believe in this work of the infinite mercy of God. We are grateful, and we rejoice in the possession of the Blessed Eucharist.

Today we renew our faith in the presence of Christ in the tabernacle. We renew also our trust in Him, our love for Him, and our consecration to His service. "How lovely are Thy tabernacles, O Lord of Hosts. My soul longeth and fainteth for the courts of the Lord" (Ps 83:2 f.).

Prayer

O God, who in this wonderful sacrament has left us a memorial of Thy passion, grant us, we beseech Thee, so to reverence the sacred mysteries of Thy body and blood that we may ever perceive within us the fruit of Thy redemption. Who livest and reignest world without end. Amen.

Friday after Corpus Christi

"O God, who in this wonderful sacrament has left us a memorial of Thy passion!" (Collect.) The Holy Sacrifice of the Mass and the Blessed Sacrament are the memorial of the passion of Christ.

The Holy Eucharist recalls the suffering and death of Christ. "This is My body, which is given for you.... This is ... My blood, which shall be shed for you" (Lk 22:19 f.). The Holy Eucharist is the fruit of the suffering and death of Christ. It embraces the bloody sacrifice on the cross and all the actions and all the suffering that went to make up His passion. The Eucharist commemorates the suffering in the Garden of Olives, the scourging, the crowning with thorns, the unjust condemnation, and the bitter journey to Golgotha. It includes especially the salutary offering with which our Lord and Savior consummated His sacrifice on the cross. It embraces His perfect obedience to the Father, His thirst for humiliations, His acceptance of suffering and death, His love for the Father and for sinners, whom He seeks to redeem and reconcile with the Father. All these were the price at which the Eucharist was bought, the price He paid in order to remain near us in the Eucharist and to offer on the altar the Holy Sacrifice to the Triune God. With the eyes of faith we should see all these sufferings of Christ in the Eucharist.

The Holy Eucharist commemorates the suffering and death of Christ. In the Holy Sacrifice of the Mass, the death of Christ on the cross is commemorated and renewed through the separation of the bread and wine, the visible species under which He offers Himself up to the Father. After His resurrection Christ could no longer suffer or die. As the risen and glorified Christ on the altar, He is entirely incapable of suffering or of death. But through the celebration of the Mass, He renews before our eyes in an unbloody manner His death on the cross. He appears personally among us, the same divine being who offered Himself up for us on the cross. He appears with the sacrificial intention and with the same inward disposition which made His offering on the cross a perfect sacrifice, and which makes perfect also the sacrifice which He now makes upon the altar. Just as He expressed His complete submission to the Father through His death, that is, through the separation of His body and blood on the cross; so now He renews daily that perfect disposition of soul in a visible manner through the Holy Sacrifice of the Mass. Just as His blood was separated from His body on the cross, so now the visible elements of His sacrifice, the bread and wine, are separately consecrated upon the altar. Thus the celebration of the Holy Sacrifice of the Mass becomes a visible representation and a commemoration of the suffering and death of Christ. We should recall daily through this Holy Sacrifice the precious price which Christ has paid for our salvation. We should recall how complete was His dedication to the work of our redemption, how unceasingly He thought of our salvation. "The Son of God . . . loved me and delivered Himself for me" (Gal 2:20).

The Eucharist is not a mere empty symbol that simply reminds us of the suffering of the Lord. It is a symbol which embraces the entire reality of the passion: Christ, His true body and blood, His soul, His sacrificial purpose, His internal and constant will to sacrifice. It is both a representation and a type given to us that, by considering it in remembrance of the suffering and death of our Lord, we also may learn to become a daily and perfect sacrifice to the Father. Daily we should unite ourselves to Christ our head, and offer ourselves up in union with the sacrificial action of Christ.

The celebration of the Holy Sacrifice of the Mass with Christ is the center of all true Christian piety. This sacrifice points to the bloody sacrifice of Christ on the cross. The devout participation in the Holy Sacrifice of the Mass necessarily produces in us a deeper understanding of the sacrificial life of Christ and makes us conscious of our Christian duty of participating in that sacrificial life. Here in the Sacrifice of the Mass we shall learn that sacrifice is the root of all that is great, the heart of all that is noble, and the crown of all that is worth while in the life of a Christian. Here we obtain the knowledge, the courage, and the strength to make a complete offering of ourselves to God. Unless we gain from our celebration of Mass the strength, courage, and spirit of sacrifice necessary to make our lives a joyful and uninterrupted holocaust for the love of God, we have not yet learned to celebrate Mass fruitfully.

For Christ the Eucharist is a sacrament which offers Him an opportunity for perfect self-immolation and self-sacrifice. Can it be anything less for us? Should not the Eucharistic Lord be the very soul of my existence also? Should not I become unreservedly His, filled with His spirit of sacrifice, an integral part of His offering to the Father? An Eucharistic soul is of necessity a soul consumed with the desire of sacrificing itself for the love of God and of Christ.

PRAYER

O God, who in this wonderful sacrament has left us a memorial of Thy passion, grant us, we beseech Thee, so to reverence the sacred mysteries of Thy body and blood that we may ever perceive within us the fruit of Thy redemption. Who livest and reignest world without end. Amen.

Saturday after Corpus Christi

"The priests of the Lord offer incense and loaves to God, and therefore they shall be holy to their God and shall not defile His name, alleluia" (Offertory). The Holy Eucharist is the sacrifice of the New Testament, the Holy Sacrifice of the Church.

The essence of Christianity and all Christian piety lies in the fulfillment of the prayer, "Hallowed be Thy name." The first duty of the Christian is to sanctify the name of God, to worship Him, to acknowledge His dominion, and serve Him perfectly, as is His due. But who is capable of honoring Him and serving Him in a manner that is truly worthy of Him? There is only one who is capable of this: the Son of God made man, Jesus Christ, our Lord. He is one in essence with the Father. He is at the same time one of us. Since He is both God and man, He can offer to the Father an adoration and homage which is of infinite value and worthy of Him. This same homage, the divinity of Christ, we can and must pay to the Father. Christ's divinity is the reflection of the glory of the Father; it is an eternal and perfect hymn of praise to the Father; it is the means by which God has honored Himself from all eternity. Only through Christ and in Christ can we sanctify the name of God and pay Him an homage that is truly worthy of Him. The very essence of our religion, then, consists in our offering of Christ to the Blessed Trinity. To this offering we must add the offering of ourselves, with every fiber of our being. The essence of our piety consists in our offering of Christ to the Father, and with Him our very being, in order that we may be able to "offer up spiritual sacrifices, acceptable to God by Jesus Christ" (1 Pt 2:5).

In the Holy Sacrifice of the Mass we offer up Christ. What we do by our own strength alone, is valueless in the sight of God, and can never rise above the level of our own insignificance. And yet we have the duty of offering to God an eternal homage. In view of our nothingness, how can we offer such a homage? "Through Him [Christ], and with Him, and in Him is to Thee, God the Father Almighty, in the unity of the Holy Ghost, all honor and glory." Through the Holy Sacrifice of the Mass it becomes possible for us to offer Christ to His Father—the acme of the eternal and perfect worship of the divinity. God gave us His Son through the mystery of the Incarnation, not that we should retain Him for ourselves, but that we should give Him back to the Father in the Holy Sacrifice of the Mass as an expression of our filial love. In the Mass we offer Christ as our gift to the Father. His heart, His body, His soul, His most precious blood,

His infinite merits, His adoration and veneration of the Father, His love, His obedience, His humility, we lay at the feet of the Father as part of our gift. With outstretched hands we offer up to the Father everything Christ has that is pleasing to the Father to supply for all those things in which we ourselves are lacking, so that we may praise and thank God for His favors in a manner that is worthy of Him. This offering is the most noble action of a Christian.

By virtue of our baptism are we able to offer the Holy Sacrifice of the Mass. Only we the baptized have the precious privilege of making this unique offering to God our own personal gift. "Receive, O holy Father, almighty and eternal God, this spotless host.... Through Him, and with Him, and in Him, is to Thee, God the Father Almighty, in the unity of the Holy Ghost, all honor and glory."

Our blessed Lord and Savior came down upon earth, and comes again daily in the Holy Sacrifice, not primarily that He might give Himself to us, but rather that we might be able to give Him to His Father. He who confines his attention to the host, who prays only to the Lord without at the same time considering the fact that Christ is offering Himself to the Father, fails to understand the precious gift which Christ has left behind in the Holy Eucharist.

The sum and substance of all Christian piety is contained in the devout celebration of the Holy Sacrifice of the Mass. Through our baptism we become capable of taking an active part in the celebration of the Holy Sacrifice, which is our first and most solemn duty, the most important and most meritorious act of our lives. In assisting at Mass we exercise that participation in the priesthood which is conferred upon us through our baptism. Therefore the participation in Mass is the most precious and the most significant function of our spiritual life.

Prayer

Graciously receive, O Lord, this offering which we Thy servants and Thy entire family make unto Thee. Grant peace in our day, and deliver us from eternal damnation, and count us in the number of Thy elect. Through Christ our Lord. Amen.

Second Sunday after Pentecost

The Mass

The parable of the "great supper" furnishes the theme for the liturgy of this week. We are accustomed to associate the parable of the "great supper" with the feast of Corpus Christi as though it referred specifically to that feast, since it happens that this Sunday falls within the octave of Corpus Christi. As a matter of fact, however, this Gospel was read on the second Sunday after Pentecost hundreds of years before the feast of Corpus Christi was established. In the mind of the liturgy the "great supper" refers not merely to the banquet of the Eucharist, but to all those good things to which God in His love invites us, such as His Incarnation, our baptism, our redemption, the Eucharist, grace, and eternal beatitude.

With hearts filled with gratitude, we are reminded in the Introit of the fact that at Easter time we were given an invitation to the banquet of supernatural life and eternal beatitude. "The Lord became my protector, and He brought me forth into a large place; He saved me because He was well pleased with me.... The Lord is my firmament, and my refuge, and my deliverer" (Introit). With joy and gratitude we now approach the marvelous banquet that is now being prepared for us in the Holy Eucharist. In this sacrifice and in Holy Communion Christ becomes our firmament, our refuge, and our deliverer. To Him we cry, "O Christ have mercy on us." "Grant, O Lord, that we may have a perpetual fear and love of Thy holy name" (Collect); then we can participate most fruitfully in the supernatural banquet of salvation, the Holy Eucharist.

The Epistle summons the faithful to Christian unity, and to a close union with the Church. Together they form one body, one organism vivified and enlivened by one soul and bound together by one love. The community of the Church is the banquet hall in which the banquet is to be prepared. In her is contained the fullness of grace and salvation. "We know that we have passed from death to life, because we love the brethren. He that loveth not abideth in death" (Epistle). We pray that God may deliver us from everything which might prevent our participating in the heavenly banquet, and that we may not suffer the misfortune of those unhappy guests mentioned in the Gospel. Many guests are invited to the banquet; but many of those first invited decline the invitation because of their attachment to worldly things. For this reason the poor, the sick, the beggars, the despised, and the downtrodden also receive the invitation; and they accept it. In place of those who were first invited (the Jews), these others (the Gentiles) are accepted. The great ones of the earth, the complacent ones, lose their place to the poor and the outcast. "Blessed are the poor in spirit; ... blessed are they that mourn; ... blessed are they that hunger and thirst after justice" (Mt 5:3 ff.). Blessed indeed are those who hunger and thirst after the supernatural goods of the heavenly banquet.

The Offertory prayer expresses our intense desire to participate in the heavenly banquet. In the Holy Sacrifice of the Mass we can take part in that feast to which we were invited at the time of our baptism. Woe be to us if, because of our worldliness or sensuality, we fail to respond to this invitation. "None of these men that were invited shall taste of my supper" (Gospel). Let us place ourselves among the poor, the feeble, the sick, the despised, and the needy of the Gospel. For these, because of their membership in the Church, are called to the banquet of salvation.

In the Holy Sacrifice of the Mass we renounce the concupiscence of the eyes, the concupiscence of the flesh, and the pride of life, just as we once did in our baptism. We offer ourselves up with Christ and receive His grace and His redemption as our share of His banquet. With hearts filled with gratitude we sing the beautiful Communion hymn: "I will sing to the Lord, who giveth me good things; and I will sing to the name of the Lord the Most High." He has given to me His flesh and His blood as a guarantee of my eventual participation in the great banquet of eternal life.

Meditation

We approach the Holy Sacrifice today with great joy and gratitude. We recall the great graces given us on the feasts of Christmas, Easter, and Pentecost; and joyfully cry out in the Introit: "The Lord became my protector, and He brought me forth into a large place; He saved me because He was well pleased with me." I have been redeemed because God loved me. "The Lord [in the Holy Eucharist] is my firmament, and my refuge, and my deliverer" (Introit).

"A certain man made a great supper and invited many. And he sent his servant at the hour of supper to say to them that were invited, that they should come, for now all things are ready" (Gospel). Those who had been invited, however, made excuses to their host. One had bought a farm, and another a yoke of oxen, and a third had just taken a wife; and therefore they could not come. "Then the master of the house, being angry, said to his servant: Go out quickly into the streets and lanes of the city, and bring in hither the poor, and the feeble, and the blind, and the lame.... Go out into the highways and hedges, and compel them to come in, that my house may be filled. But I say unto you, that none of these men that were invited shall taste of my supper" (Gospel).

The banquet is prepared today and every day for us in the Holy Eucharist. The rich, that is, those who have no interest except in worldly, material things, persist in declining this invitation to the Eucharistic banquet. They have no taste for such food. The poor, however, those who are free of earthly encumbrances, the sick, the weak, and those who have little of this world's goods, all are satisfied at the Eucharistic table. We rejoice that we are among those who have been invited to the Eucharistic banquet. We lift ourselves above earthly goods and desires and long for the eternal goods supplied by the Eucharist. "He hath filled the hungry with good things; and the rich he hath sent empty away" (Lk 1:53). In our hunger for the Holy Eucharist and in our longing for Holy Communion we shall want nothing. A great blessing is our realization that we are the poor, the weak, the blind, and the lame, and that we stand so much in need of the strength and help of the Holy Eucharist.

The special fruit of a devout participation in the Eucharistic banquet is the spirit, the will, and the strength necessary to love as God wishes us to love (Epistle). "Dearly beloved, wonder not if the world hate you. We know that we have passed from death to life because we love the brethren. He that loveth not, abideth in death. Whosoever hateth his brother is a murderer; and you know that no murderer hath eternal life abiding in himself. In this we have known the charity of God, because He hath laid down His life for us; and we ought to lay down our lives for the brethren. He that hath the substance of this world, and shall see his brother in need, and shall shut up his bowels from him, how doth the charity of God abide in him? My little children, let us not love in word nor in tongue, but in deed and in truth" (Epistle). "By their fruits you shall know them" (Mt 7:16). By the fruits of fraternal charity, by our willingness to sacrifice ourselves for the good of the brethren, in great things and in small, others will be able to judge us, and we shall be able to judge ourselves. By this means we shall be able to determine how fruitful our reception of Holy Communion has been. Nothing in the life of a Christian is more difficult than the consistent practice of fraternal charity. The more closely we are associated with others in life, the more heavily the burdens of others weigh upon us (Gal 6:2), and the greater is the strain placed upon our love. But from the reception of Holy Communion we shall obtain the strength to practice fraternal charity, to master ourselves, and to suppress our personal desires and ambitions. There we shall find the strength to forgive others, to understand their difficulties, and to treat them with charity and deference under all circumstances. By the strength gained from Holy Communion we shall be able to avoid all bitterness and uncharitableness. By this means we shall be able to maintain peace of soul in spite of all internal and external disturbances, and become "one bread, one body, all that partake of one bread" (1 Cor 10:17).

"I will love Thee, O Lord my strength. The Lord is my firmament, my refuge, and my deliverer" (Introit). Such must be our reply to God's love in the Holy Eucharist. "In this we have known the charity of God, because He hath laid down His life for us" (Epistle). He laid down His life for us once in a bloody manner on the cross, and He continues to do so daily in an unbloody manner in the Eucharist. Should we also not love Him from the depths of our hearts? "I will sing to the Lord, who giveth me good things; and I will sing to the name of the Lord the Most High" (Communion), who remains here below with us in the Holy Eucharist, and who gives Himself to us as our food.

There are many who remain cold and unresponsive to His love. They have been invited to the delightful banquet of the Eucharist, but they excuse themselves on the pretext that they have more important things to attend to. How mistaken is their estimate of the value of the Eucharist! They lack a vital and living faith.

But there are many who present themselves for the banquet which the Lord has prepared for them, but who approach in a manner that is mechanical and casual. They approach without the ardor which would make their Communions fruitful; they lack that living faith, that deep veneration, and that ardent longing to be united with the Lord in a most intimate union and to be filled with His life.

Prayer

Grant, O Lord, that we may have a perpetual fear and love of Thy holy name, for Thou never ceasest to direct and govern by Thy grace those whom Thou instructest in the steadfastness of Thy love. Through Christ our Lord. Amen.

Monday after Corpus Christi

"This is My body which shall be delivered for you.... This chalice is the new testament in My blood" (Epistle). With these words our Lord established the Holy Sacrifice of the Mass. The blood "which shall be shed for many unto remission of sins" (Mt 26:28) is, in the words of Holy Scripture, a sacrificial offering, a true and efficacious sacrifice. The celebration of Mass is the offering which Christ makes of Himself to the Father.

The victim which is offered to God in the Holy Sacrifice is Christ our Lord. Just as He once offered Himself to the Father on the cross in a bloody manner and with unspeakable pain and suffering, so now He offers Himself to the Father in an unbloody manner in the Holy Sacrifice of the Mass, as the glorified and impassible Lord now triumphant over all suffering. This second offering truly contains Christ Himself with all His inexhaustible capacity for offering homage and praise to God. This sacrifice is infinite in its power to obtain grace from God, pardon for sins, and forgiveness for offenses. Christ offers to His Father His sacred body, His most precious blood, the life which He lived while upon earth, the merits He obtained, the virtues He practiced, His sufferings and His death. He includes in His sacrifice every action that He performed from the moment of His entrance into this world, together with the prayers He said and the sufferings He endured. He offers a "pure victim, a spotless victim," which the Father has found most pleasing. Ever since the time of Cain and Abel, men have built altars and sacrificed their victims upon them, for they knew they were guilty of sin and separated from God. They desired to return to God and to obtain His grace and forgiveness, for which purpose they offered the blood of countless animals, and even the blood of fellow men. But with these offerings God could not be satisfied, though they were well meant. "Sacrifice and oblation Thou wouldst not.... Then said I: Behold I come to do Thy will, O God" (Heb 10:5, 9). On the cross the only-begotten of the Father offered Himself with love and perfect obedience, and now He continues that same offering on our altars in an unbloody manner. In the Holy Sacrifice of the Mass the prediction of the Prophet is fulfilled in Him: "And I will not receive a gift of your hand," that is, from the hand of the priests of the Old Testament. "For from the rising of the sun even to the going down, My name is great among the Gentiles, and in every place there is sacrifice, and there is offered to My name a clean oblation" (Mal 1:10 f.). This clean oblation is the sacrifice of the Church, the sacrifice of the New Testament, the Holy Sacrifice of the Mass.

The priest who offers the Holy Sacrifice of the Mass "is one and the same as He who offered the sacrifice on the cross" (Council of Trent). From the beginning of time priests have stood at the altar of God to offer sacrifice, but the words of the Prophet are applicable to all of them: "I have no pleasure in you, saith the Lord of hosts; and I will not receive a gift of your hand" (Mal 1:10). The hands and hearts of human priests are stained with sin. Because He had compassion on our unworthiness and our impotence, the Son of God became one of us. He became man, and as the God-man He acts as our high priest from the first moment of His entrance into the world. "Behold I come." It is He who with divine and unstained hands offers Himself to the Father in the Holy Sacrifice of the Mass, through the instrumentality of the human priest, who acts as His minister. The real priest who offers the sacrifice, however, is Christ Himself. For this reason the Holy Sacrifice of the Mass is always a pure and holy sacrifice, pleasing at all times to the Father, ever efficacious and meritorious.

With the eyes of faith we acknowledge Christ to be really and personally present under the appearance of bread and wine. We acknowledge Him to be present here, in body and soul, with His life and His suffering, in this sacrifice which He again offers to the Father. The same love for the Father and for us which He proved so conclusively through His death on the cross is present in this sacrifice also. Since Christ is the real priest who makes the offering, the sacrifice must always be worthy of the three divine persons, the Father, the Son, and the Holy Ghost, and it must always render to them a perfect act of praise and honor. Since the offering is made by Christ Himself, it must always ascend to heaven and plead for us in words which the Father cannot refuse. Through this sacrifice full and perfect satisfaction is also made to God for the countless sins and offenses of men which cry to heaven for vengeance. The altar is the sanctuary of the Church and of mankind, the spring of living waters. All that is sublime and noble, all that is elevated and divine, flows from the altar to the souls of men.

In the Holy Sacrifice of the Mass, Jesus is both the victim and the high priest. St. Gertrude relates that in one of her visions she saw Christ acting as the real priest and offerer. He stood upon His throne in heaven and with His own hands offered His most holy heart to His Father, thus acting both as priest and as victim. "At the very moment when God the Son was offering His divine heart to the Father, the bell of the tower rang, announcing the moment of the consecration."

Jesus is our high priest in the Holy Sacrifice of the Mass. He offers Himself with the same love, with the same subjection to His Father, with the same desire of honoring the Father and of satisfying for our sins, that He manifested when He offered Himself on the cross. He can say now, as truly as He did on the cross, "I thirst." He is still consumed with the same desire to love, honor, and thank the Father in a manner worthy of the Father. At the same time His heart is absorbed in us, so that in our stead He may praise, honor, and love the Father, and perform for us all those things of which we ourselves are incapable.

The wealth of the Christian consists in this, that we possess "a great high priest,... Jesus the Son of God;... holy, innocent, undefiled, separated from sinners, and made higher than the heavens" (Heb 4:14; 7:26). We have at the same time an eternally worthy victim, the most holy heart of the Savior.

Prayer

Protect us, O Lord, that we who avail ourselves of Thy holy mysteries in the Holy Sacrifice of the Mass, may dedicate ourselves to heavenly things and serve Thee with body and soul. Through Christ our Lord. Amen.

Tuesday after Corpus Christi

"This is My body which shall be delivered for you.... This chalice is the new testament in My blood" (Epistle). Holy Mother the Church is the sole custodian of the Eucharistic sacrifice, which is the center and the consummation of Christian worship and Christian piety.

The Mass is the sacrifice of the Church. Day after day the Church approaches the altar through thousands of her ordained priests. "Receive, O holy Father, almighty and eternal God, this spotless host which I [the priest], Thy unworthy servant, and all Thy faithful [those assembled here and the whole Church] offer to Thee." The Church holds in her virgin hands the pure, holy, and spotless victim, "the holy bread of eternal life, the chalice of eternal salvation," the body and blood of the Lord, together with His merits, His satisfactions, and His prayers. "Through Him, and with Him, and in Him," the Church offers unceasingly to the Father, the Son, and the Holy Ghost, a worthy adoration, homage, thanksgiving, love, and satisfaction for sin. With the Church each one of us also may offer up his sacrifice in every Mass that is celebrated throughout the world. We take part in every Mass that is said, and thus our offering to the Father never ceases.

The Sacrifice of the Mass is offered by the whole Church, and not merely by the priest who is actually celebrating the Mass, or by those who are actually physically present. "We offer to Thee, O Lord, the chalice of salvation." "Receive, O holy Father, almighty and eternal God, this spotless host which ... all Thy faithful offer to Thee." What a wonderful grace it is that, by virtue of our membership in the Church, we may make to God, both day and night, an unceasing offering of adoration, thanksgiving, satisfaction, and petition! What a consolation it is to know that each time this offering is made not only by the whole Church, but also for the whole Church. The chalice is offered that it may "rise up in the sight of Thy divine majesty as a sweet savor for our own salvation and for that of the whole world." Daily the Church, through the hands of her priests, raises to heaven the sacred bread and the chalice of blood to implore God for grace, pardon, light, protection, and assistance for us and for all men. Even though all others have forgotten us, the Church continues to pray for us and to offer sacrifice for us.

The Holy Sacrifice of the Mass is also our offering. At baptism the indelible character of the sacrament was imprinted on our soul, which confers on us all the rights and privileges of membership in the Church. By virtue of this character we have the right to approach the altar and exercise our so-called priesthood of the laity. The right to sacrifice is ours. We have the privilege of offering to the Father in heaven the body and blood of Christ. We are no longer confined to the offering of the blood of animals or the common bread of sacrifice, as were the men of the Old Testament. We are like Mary, who appears in the temple with Jesus in her arms. We have an adequate means of supplying for all of our own deficiencies through the offering of the heart of our Savior together with all His sufferings, His death, His merits, and His virtues. All these belong to us. In the Holy Sacrifice of the Mass, His heart, His life, His merits, His virtues, belong entirely to us. He supplies for us in the Mass; He prays, loves, offers thanksgiving and satisfaction in our stead. We act through Him, with Him, in Him, with His love and with His zeal for accomplishing the will of the Father. We pray to the Father through the heart of Jesus, we love the Father with the love of Christ, we address Him in the prayers of Christ, which must always be heard. We offer to the Father the blood of Christ in satisfaction for our sins. This is the most excellent kind of piety, the most efficacious kind of prayer and work. We act through Him, with Him, and in Him when we participate in the Holy Sacrifice of the Mass. Our offering is made in union with Christ, our high priest, and in union with His mystical body, the Church.

We, Thy people sanctified through holy baptism, offer to Thy divine Majesty a pure, holy, and spotless victim, the body and blood of Thy beloved Son. Since we hold in our hands the heart and the blood of Jesus, and offer them up to the Father, He will surely hear us and grant our prayers. Inspired by this confidence, and depending not upon our own merits but upon the sacrifice of Christ, we pray with the priest after the Consecration for our beloved dead, for ourselves, and for all our brethren. Joining with the priest we recite that most precious of all prayers, the Our Father. We say it "through Him, and with Him, and in Him." He prays it again through us, and with us, and in us. He is the head, and we are the members; but we form one body, one Christ.

It is our privilege to offer Christ to His Father as our own gift. What a royal priesthood is given us through our baptism, in that we are made living members of the Lord our head! In offering the Savior to His Father we include ourselves also. The head cannot be offered without the body and its members. If we were to exclude ourselves from this offering, we should maim the body of Christ, for we are a part of Jesus Christ. In the bread and wine of the Offertory at Mass we include ourselves. We desire to become victims of the holy will of God, like an animal that is sacrificed to the Lord. We wish to die, to die to ourselves, to our passions, to sin, and to all that may in any way be displeasing to God. We wish to be consumed by the fire of divine love. We wish to make of our lives a complete holocaust to the Divinity, a sacrifice of thanksgiving, of adoration, of satisfaction, and of petition. In this manner when we offer Christ, we offer ourselves also.

"Be mindful, O Lord, of Thy servants and handmaids and of all here present, whose faith and devotion are known to Thee...." According to the measure of our faith and our spirit of sacrifice, we reap the fruits of our offering.

Prayer

We beseech Thee, O Lord, sanctify these our gifts of bread and wine, and through them cause us also to become eternal and worthy victims to Thee. Through Christ our Lord. Amen.

Wednesday after Corpus Christi

"Do this in commemoration of Me." At the Last Supper, Christ offered Himself to the Father under the appearance of bread and wine. To the apostles He gave the command: "Do this in commemoration of Me"; that is, He commanded them to do precisely as He had done. By this command He appointed and ordained them to the priesthood, conferring on them the power to offer the Eucharistic sacrifice. This they were to do, not for themselves alone, but with us and for us in the name of the whole Christian community. We, too, are to offer and participate in this sacrifice. For that purpose we were baptized. Participation in the Eucharistic sacrifice is the most fundamental act of Christian life and Christian piety. "Do this in commemoration of Me," is a command given us by the Lord which applies to all Christians, although not in the same measure and in the same sense.

"Glory to God in the highest" (Lk 2:14). Nothing in this world is more important than the glorification of God. This was the primary purpose of the creation of the world, the redemption of man, the Incarnation of the Son of God, and our eventual glorification in heaven. But who can glorify God in a manner worthy of Him, and in the measure that is His due? No one but the incarnate Son of God, Jesus Christ. Although He was the Son of God, He humbled Himself and became obedient unto death. Since His human nature is united to the divinity in the unity of one person, Christ can offer homage to God that is authentically human. How can other men fulfill the commandment laid upon them to glorify God? How can they ever hope to glorify Him in a becoming manner? They can so glorify Him by offering to the Father, His only-begotten Son, Jesus Christ, together with His flesh and blood, His heart, His merits, His adoration of the Father, His subjection to the will of the Father, His love of the Father. We can glorify God by offering Him ourselves in union with Christ, our head, with complete subjection to Him and with unselfish dedication to Him. Our glorification of the Father is essentially a priestly act, an uninterrupted will to offer, a continuous act of sacrifice. The sacrifice that is offered is not merely that of Christ Himself, but is the offering of the whole Christ, the head and the members. In baptism the "holy priesthood" was conferred upon us that we might offer "spiritual sacrifices, acceptable to God by Jesus Christ" (1 Pt 2:5). We become a living *Gloria Patri* sung to the honor of God, a living hymn of praise that is worthy of the Father. To make that possible the Son of God became man, making us part of Himself. He gave Himself to us that we might give Him back to His Father with a childlike love as our gift to God, thus supplying for our own nothingness, our abject poverty, our complete unworthiness. He made it possible for us to hallow eternally the name of God.

"Do this in commemoration of Me." We fulfill our priestly function of honoring the name of God most perfectly when we offer the Holy Sacrifice of the Mass. There, through the consecration performed by the priest, Christ becomes the victim of our sacrifice. He is given to us that we may consecrate Him to the Father. "Through Him, and with Him, and in Him, is to Thee, God the Father Almighty, in the unity of the Holy Ghost, all honor and glory, for ever and ever." "Do this." We do the very same thing that Jesus did. We take Him in our hands as He took bread and wine, and offer Him to the Father, His flesh and blood, His life, His sufferings, His death, all that He did, all that He is. We offer to the Father this victim of inexhaustible worth, a victim which renders to God infinite praise and honor. We assist at the celebration of Mass, not primarily to venerate the Lord who has appeared on our altar or to be enriched and enlivened by Him, but first of all that we may offer Him to His Father. Similarly, He comes down upon our altar, not primarily that He Himself may be glorified or that He may be of assistance to us, but principally to glorify the majesty of God. If we were to confine our participation in the Mass to the adoration of Christ or to the quest of some grace for ourselves, we should demonstrate clearly that we misunderstand the purpose of Christ's coming, the true meaning of the Eucharist, and we should not be fulfilling that command of the Lord, "Do this in commemoration of Me." In the Holy Sacrifice of the Mass the Father and the Blessed Trinity are the principal objects of our worship. Christ is the intermediary, and He desires that we offer Him to His Father.

Many Christians believe they have discharged their obligations at Mass when they say their prayers, either orally or mentally, when they express their love for Christ, when they prepare themselves properly for the reception of Holy Communion. But that is not sufficient. That which is most essential in the eyes of Christ and in the mind of God appears to us to be so unimportant that we often forget it or neglect it altogether. On the other hand, that which is in no way essential, we make the most important. How, then, can we manage to approach the celebration of Mass with the proper spirit and with the joy that should characterize our participation?

We are burdened with the realization that we are incapable of offering to God the homage that is His due, and we bewail our impotence. We strive for a greater love for God, and make great efforts to overcome our deficiency. We may be willing even to sacrifice everything for this purpose. And yet, all our efforts would amount to practically nothing. We live in a fool's paradise if we hope to be able to honor God properly with anything that is entirely our own, with anything that we can accomplish by our own effort. If we are so disposed, we can make very little progress; and if we do manage to make some progress, it is without joy. But once we understand what has been given to us in the person of Christ, what an infinite power for good was placed at our disposal when Christ commanded us, "Do this in commemoration of Me"; then we will be able to participate in the celebration of the Holy Sacrifice of the Mass worthily and with the proper spirit.

Prayer

O Lord, may the sacrifice which we offer to Thy name purify us and confirm us more each day in a truly heavenly life. Through Christ our Lord. Amen.

Thursday
Octave of Corpus Christi

"He that eateth My flesh and drinketh My blood, abideth in Me, and I in him" (Gospel). The Holy Eucharist is the sacrament of union.

"He abideth in Me, and I in him." Through the reception of the Holy Eucharist, a living and fruitful union of Christ with the soul is accomplished. "When melted wax is poured into melted wax, both portions become perfectly intermingled. When we partake of the body and blood of Christ, something very similar occurs. Christ becomes part of us, and we become part of Him" (St. Cyril of Jerusalem). "The fellowship of the body and blood of Christ, of Holy Communion, aims at nothing else but that we be transformed into that of which we partake, and that we bear the spirit and the flesh of Him in whom we have died, with whom we have been buried, and with whom we have risen" (St. Leo the Great). By partaking of this food we become incorporated in Christ, and for this reason it is necessary that we be taken up to where Christ is, there to be associated with Him in a community of life inexpressibly rich in its spirit and possessions, since He is the Son of God. He will be in us, and we in Him.

Now we are the object of the eternal and supernatural love of the Father, which makes us, more than ever before, children of God, which sweeps us up to the bosom of the Blessed Trinity. Now we are enveloped by the fullness of the godhead, by the life of God, and at the same time made partakers of the glory which the Son has received from the Father. Now the words of Christ are fulfilled, "And the glory which Thou hast given Me, I have given to them" (Jn 17:22). Now we become one in body and blood with Him. Now we become "Christophers," bearers of Christ, since we have partaken of His flesh and blood, and thus become partakers of the divine nature and possessors of the divine life. (St. Cyril of Jerusalem.) This participation in the life of God accomplishes at the same time our perfect possession of the Holy Ghost, who dwells in a special way in the body of Christ, of which we have partaken. He diffuses Himself in the richest measure in those who are united to Christ as one body. Since we have been bound to our Lord so as to form one body, we shall be filled with His Spirit and with His divine life. We shall become one in spirit with Him just as truly and as intimately as we have become one in body with Him in the Holy Eucharist.

"As ... I live by the Father, so he that eateth Me, the same also shall live by Me" (Gospel). This life in Christ is the marvelous result of the Eucharistic union. It does not consist principally in the fact that we fashion and shape our will after that of the Lord who operates in us; neither does it consist in the fact that Christ's spirit guides and controls ours. The unity of spirit which results from the reception of Holy Communion is based on the fact that our spirit is permeated with the Spirit that lives in Christ. God in His innermost essence places Himself in our soul and fills us with His divine life. He grasps the soul like an enveloping flame to penetrate it with His light and His warmth, and to clothe it in His own glory. Now that we have become one in spirit with God through the Holy Eucharist, the Son of God lives His divine life within us. "And I live, now not I; but Christ liveth in me" (Gal 2:20). "And all My things are Thine, and Thine are Mine" (Jn 17:10). His love is our love, His thoughts are our thoughts; His will and our will are one; His love, His thoughts, His desires, and ours are like particles of incense which melt and intermingle and send a single column of incense up to heaven. The Lord destroys in our souls our purely human way of thinking, seeing, and acting, and plants in us His way of thinking, seeing, and acting. He tears us away from our selfish blindness and elevates us to an understanding of His spirit, of His poverty, of His love of the Father, of His humility, of His obedience, and of His love of the cross. We begin to forsake our selfish, personal wishes, plans, ambitions, and desires, and by means of His spirit begin to live after His manner of life. "He that eateth Me, the same also shall live by Me."

"If thou didst know the gift of God" (Jn 4:10). How inestimably precious is the wealth of the soul that has received Holy Communion! But such a soul must indeed be pure if it presumes to receive this sacrament. "But let a man prove himself; and so let him eat of that bread and drink of that chalice. For he that eateth and drinketh unworthily, eateth and drinketh judgment to himself, not discerning the body of the Lord" (Epistle).

The oftener we receive Holy Communion, the more we must die to the natural man, the more we must be possessed by the spirit and the sentiments of Christ. The oftener we receive, the more we must love, treasure, and seek what He loves, treasures, and seeks. Christ loves poverty, prayer, insignificance in the eyes of the world, humility, simplicity, the cross, and sacrifice. If we do not gradually come to love the things that He loved on earth and live as He lived while on earth, must we not admit that our Holy Communions are not producing in us the fruit that they should? Wherein lies the fault?

"He that seeth Me, seeth the Father" (Jn 14:9). Christ is so intimately united with the Father that he who sees the one sees the other. Since we receive Holy Communion so frequently, must not, then, everyone who sees and hears us, see and hear Christ also? Must they not recognize Christ in our manner of thinking, speaking, and acting? Must they not through these our words and actions recognize Christ who lives, prays, works, and suffers in us?

Prayer

O God, who in this wonderful sacrament has left us a memorial of Thy passion, grant us, we beseech Thee, so to reverence the sacred mysteries of Thy body and blood that we may ever perceive within us the fruit of Thy redemption. Who livest and reignest world without end. Amen.

Friday
Feast of the Sacred Heart of Jesus

The liturgy associates the feast of the Sacred Heart of Jesus with the feast of Corpus Christi as a sort of continuation of the latter. The object of our worship on this feast is the physical heart of the God-man together with the humanity and the divinity of Christ — the heart of Jesus as a living member of this living organism. We adore the physical heart of Jesus as a symbol and expression of Christ's love for men, particularly in the redemption on the cross, and as an expression of the mystery of the Holy Eucharist. By the heart of Jesus we mean, in the last analysis, the divine person of Jesus, which reveals His divine and human love for us by the symbol of His Sacred Heart. The mysteries of the Incarnation, of the redemption, of the coming of the Holy Ghost, of the final resurrection, and of our participation in the life of God, depend ultimately on the mystery of the Savior's love for us. All these mysteries are embodied in the heart of Jesus, and we wish to honor and appreciate them more fully on the feast of the Sacred Heart.

The concept which the liturgy presents of the Sacred Heart of Jesus is outlined for us in the Introit, in the Gospel, and in the Preface of the Mass. "The thoughts of His heart are to all generations; to deliver their souls from death and feed them in famine" (Introit). "Come to Me all you that labor and are burdened, and I will refresh you" (Alleluia). The Gospel leads us to the cross of Christ: "But after they [the soldiers] were come to Jesus, when they saw that He was already dead, they did not break His legs, but one of the soldiers with a spear opened His side, and immediately there came out blood and water" (Gospel). The mystery which is contained in this opening of Christ's side is explained to us in the Preface. His side was pierced, "that from His opened heart, as from a sanctuary of divine bounty, might be poured out upon us streams of mercy and grace; and that in His heart always burning with love for us, the devout may find a haven of rest and the penitent a refuge of salvation" (Preface). The opening in the side of Jesus was prefigured by the door of Noe's ark, through which all were obliged to pass who were to be rescued from the destruction of the Deluge (Hymn at Lauds). The wound in the side of Jesus is the door of salvation.

Our obligations toward the Sacred Heart of Jesus are explained in the Collect of the Mass. We are obliged to render to the Sacred Heart a becoming homage (our adoration, praise, and thanksgiving) and at the same time make a worthy reparation for our sins. These thoughts are presented for our consideration on this feast. We acknowledge and honor in the Sacred Heart of Jesus the summation of Christ's divine and human inner life, with all His virtues, affections, and emotions, all His ambitions and desires. We venerate and honor especially the unspeakable love of Jesus for us, which He has revealed by His death on the cross and by His establishment of the Holy Eucharist. We have countless other reasons for thanking Him, worshiping Him, and adoring Him. We likewise wish to acknowledge the ingratitude we have shown Him, the many repeated infidelities with which we have responded to His love and His countless graces. We wish to make recompense for our neglect of His love and the graces which He earned for us on the cross and which He has manifested in the Eucharist. We wish to compensate for our coldness and lack of interest in Him. What a multitude of offenses we have each day to regret, to repent of, and to satisfy for!

"My heart hath expected reproach and misery; and I looked for one that would grieve together with me, but there was none; and for one that would comfort me, and I found none" (Offertory). Not so with me; for in me He will find one that will grieve with Him. In me He will find one to console Him, as did the angel who came to Him in the Garden. Jesus can be consoled by expiation, by satisfaction, by love.

Behold the heart that has loved men so much, the heart that has loved men in the Incarnation, in the crib, and on the cross. Who can comprehend the love of the heart of Jesus, especially when we consider who we are and who He is? Truly we have no claim upon Him and His love except that which He in His infinite mercy has given to us. Who could be more unworthy of His love than we have been? And yet He has loved us with an abundance of love. How can we ever forget this thought or take an interest in anything other than the eternal love of God for us, who have been so undeserving of that love? Should we not, like an earthly lover, forget even food and drink and sleep so that every hour of the day and night we may devote our attention to Jesus as the object of our love? Graces have been heaped upon us in such abundance that we can scarcely bear them or enumerate them; Christ's mercy appears anew each day. And still more, He will grant me the reward that eye hath not seen, nor ear heard, nor the heart of man hath conceived. Yet we remain cold and unmoved, having many interests in life that seem far more important than Christ Himself. Sacred Heart of Jesus, how Thou hast loved us! Teach us to love Thee more and more.

PRAYER

O God, who in the heart of Thy Son, wounded by our transgressions, dost mercifully vouchsafe to bestow upon us the infinite wealth of Thy love; grant, we beseech Thee, that revering it with meet devotion, we may make a worthy reparation for our sins. Through the same Christ our Lord. Amen.

Saturday after the Feast of the Sacred Heart

To St. Paul was given the privilege of revealing to the Gentiles the "unsearchable riches of Christ," that is, the wealth of grace and salvation which are given to us through Christ. He falls on his knees and begs God that we may comprehend the "breadth, and length, and height, and depth" of God's mercy in calling us to the faith, and Christ's love, "which surpasseth all knowledge" (Epistle).

Oh, "the breadth, and length, and height, and depth" of God's mercy for us! That mercy is expressed in the mystery of the Incarnation: "And the Word was made flesh and dwelt among us" (Jn 1:14). Christ further expresses His mercy for men in the mystery of His life of voluntary poverty, in His humility, His subjection to the Father, and His willingness to do whatever the Father desires of Him. "The breadth, and length, and height, and depth" of the mercy of God are expressed with infinite forcefulness by His suffering in the Garden, at the pillar, and on the way to Calvary, and especially by His crucifixion and death on the cross. All these sufferings He endured for our sake, to render satisfaction to God in our stead. He has withheld nothing. There is not a single act of His will that is not directed toward our redemption; there was not a single member of His adorable body that did not suffer for us. There was no suffering, no humiliation, no injustice that He did not endure for us. He shed every drop of His precious blood for us. Who can fathom the breadth, and length, and height, and depth of the mercy of the Sacred Heart of Jesus? Who can measure it as it is revealed in our vocation to grace and salvation and to membership in the Church? Or who can measure it as expressed in our call to receive the sacrament of baptism, or in our participation in the Holy Sacrifice of the Mass and Holy Communion? What divine mercy is expressed in our incorporation in the mystical body of Christ, since we thereby become branches of Christ, the vine, now through grace, but eventually through the possession of the glory of heaven! Other men He has passed by. Why has He selected me in preference to others? Certainly not because I was more worthy. Only because of pure mercy and compassion has He chosen me. Oh, the depth and the height of divine mercy!

"The charity of Christ which surpasseth all knowledge." Why does Christ lavish His mercy upon us? What is the source from which this infinite mercy springs? His love. Love is His very essence. Love is the secret of His being. He loves us with a love that no words can express and no created intellect can comprehend. Love makes as one the lovers. For them they are no longer two persons, but a perfect unity of the two in one. "And all My things are Thine, and Thine are Mine" (Jn 17:10). Christ has removed the barrier that separates us from Him, for by baptism He has called us to a living union with Himself, who is our head. By virtue of this mystical union, Christ's merits, satisfactions, and prayers become ours. And everything that was ours becomes His. When we suffer, He suffers in us and with us. When we humble ourselves, He offers satisfaction through us to the Father. If we emulate the spirit of Christ and practice the poverty of Christ, He uses this power to pay homage to His Father. "All My things are Thine, and Thine are Mine." Christ was not satisfied with having once paid the price of our redemption; He is not satisfied with being merely our exemplar and teacher. Love unites. He draws us to Himself and unites us to Himself in a mysterious but efficacious participation in His life and merits. He could not have done more. He could not have given us His love more completely or more perfectly. And all this love, "which surpasseth all knowledge," He has revealed to us in the symbol of His Sacred Heart.

What is meant by the veneration of the Sacred Heart? It means a living faith in the mercy and love of Jesus; it means a consciousness and understanding of the mystery of Christ's love for us. It means especially a devout and grateful regard for that living union between Christ and the soul, between the head and the members. It implies an abiding joy in the realization that we are united to Him, that we have been elevated by Him to share His life and His riches.

"That being rooted and founded in charity, you may be able to comprehend with all the saints what is the breadth, and length, and height, and depth; to know also the charity of Christ which surpasseth all understanding, that you may be filled unto all the fullness of God" (Epistle). We should dwell on the infinity of Christ's mercy and love. We must place Him before all else. We must be conscious of our mystical union with Him. Then, indeed, we shall be filled with the fullness of God.

Prayer

O almighty and eternal God, look down upon the heart of Thy beloved Son, and upon the praise and satisfaction which it renders to Thee in the name of sinners and such as seek Thy mercy, and do Thou graciously grant pardon in the name of Thy divine Son, Jesus Christ, who liveth and reigneth with Thee in the unity of the Holy Ghost, world without end. Amen.

Third Sunday after Pentecost

The Mass

The memory of Easter dominates the texts and prayers of the Mass for this Sunday. First of all we are reminded of Christ the Redeemer, the restorer of life. "What man is there of you that hath a hundred sheep, and if he shall lose one of them, doth he not leave the ninety-nine in the desert and go after that which was lost, until he find it; and when he hath found it, lay it upon his shoulders rejoicing?" (Gospel.) Did we not also experience this attention of the Good Shepherd at Easter? Our first rescue by the Good Shepherd, at our baptism, has not yet been completed. We are still exposed to danger; we may still wander away from His vigilant care, become lost in the wilderness and the thicket of sin. We still must struggle against the powers of evil working within us and the temptations which assail us from without.

Because of these many dangers, like the straying sheep of the Gospel, we turn sorrowfully to the Good Shepherd at the beginning of the Mass today. "Look Thou upon me, O Lord, and have mercy on me; for I am alone and poor. See my abjection and my labor; and forgive me all my sins, O my God. To Thee, O Lord, have I lifted up my soul" (Introit). The Kyrie and the Gloria have the same theme: "Thou who takest away the sins of the world, have mercy upon us. Thou who takest away the sins of the world, receive our prayer. Thou who sittest at the right hand of the Father, have mercy upon us." In the Collect we pray: "Multiply Thy mercies upon us, that having Thee for our ruler and Thee for our guide, we may so make use of temporal goods that we lose not those which are everlasting." We are lambs which have become entangled in the thorns of temporal goods. It is the duty of the Christian to turn away from temporal things and turn toward the eternal, to look to the provident hand of God for guidance. "Cast all your care upon Him, for He hath care of you" (Epistle).

"But the God of all grace who hath called us in baptism unto His eternal glory, ... after you have suffered a little, will Himself perfect you, and confirm you, and establish you" (Epistle). The things of this world serve to prepare us for the life hereafter. They all have a value for eternity. Is not God the highest good of man? He is the Good Shepherd, who takes special care of those sheep who have gone astray and are lost. In the liturgy today we are the lost sheep whom He takes upon His shoulders and carries back to the fold of the Church. There, in the gathering of the faithful, He calls together His friends, the baptized, and invites them to rejoice with Him in the Eucharistic banquet. "Or what woman having ten groats, if she lose one groat, doth not light a candle, and sweep the house, and seek diligently until she find it?" (Gospel.) This woman is also a symbol of the Church, who carries a light in her hand (Christ) and goes about in the world seeking those souls which are entangled in worldliness and sin. How she rejoices at the sight of a sinner doing penance, leaving his former evil ways and turning wholeheartedly to Christ!

At the Offertory those things which we heard in the Epistle and Gospel become realities. We are the sheep, lost in worldliness, trivialities, temporal things, and sin. We are indeed lost groats. In the Holy Sacrifice of the Mass we disengage ourselves from our ill-advised absorption in temporal things and sin. We resign ourselves and allow ourselves to be found and taken up by Christ, who by His suffering and death has come forth in search of us. We repent of our waywardness and infidelity, which have caused us to seek worldly things instead of following Christ. In the spirit of sacrifice we surrender to Christ and become sacrificial victims with Him, seeking thus to be freed from our perverted love of the things of this world. We long to be changed from enemies of God to His friends, and to serve Him faithfully, and to belong to Him entirely. When we return to Him in the Holy Sacrifice, He prepares for us, the sheep who were lost, the joyful banquet of the Holy Eucharist.

Meditation

At Easter we were reborn. Pentecost brought us the Holy Ghost, and with Him the maturity, courage, and strength of manhood. Now we are faced with the difficulties of life, with its temptations, and trials, and needs. On our way through the difficulties of life we come to the Lord and pray: "Look Thou upon me, O Lord, and have mercy upon me" (Introit). "Multiply Thy mercies upon us, that having Thee for our ruler and Thee for our guide, we may so make use of temporal goods that we lose not those which are everlasting" (Collect).

"Cast all your care upon Him, for He hath care of you" (Epistle). We are in danger because of temporal wealth and worldly affairs. Once we made this renunciation: I renounce the world and its vanities. But what is our attitude now? Even more than we ourselves suspect or admit, we busy ourselves in the search for worldly possessions and become absorbed in temporal things. We are given so much to these things and we are so concerned with worldly affairs and worldly possessions and cares, that we are in danger of forgetting the one thing most necessary, our eternal salvation. Many men are so absorbed with their daily tasks, with duties of their state of life, and with the care of their family, that they give little heed to their spiritual progress and to the condition of their soul. Even the graces which God gives them through the sermons they hear and the instructions they receive, or through the inner inspirations which He gives them, produce very little effect. In their case the seed cast down by the sower falls among thorns. They hear the word of God, but "the care of this world and the deceitfulness of riches choketh up the word, and he becometh fruitless" (Mt 13:22). "Cast all your care upon Him, for He hath care of you." How utterly lacking we are in confidence! How little trust we place in Him with regard to our spiritual and corporal needs, or to our family and those dear to us! We want to make all the necessary provisions ourselves; so great is our trust in our own abilities.

"For He hath care of you." This is the picture of the Sacred Heart of Jesus which the liturgy presents to us. "What man is there of you that hath a hundred sheep, and if he shall lose one of them, doth he not leave the ninety-nine in the desert and go after that which was lost until he find it; and when he hath found it, lay it upon his shoulders rejoicing, and coming home call together his friends and neighbors, saying to them: Rejoice with me because I have found my sheep that was lost?" Then the liturgy gives us a second image of the Lord's tender solicitude: "Or what woman having ten groats, if she lose one groat, doth not light a candle, and sweep the house, and seek diligently until she find it; and when she hath found it, call together her friends and neighbors, saying: Rejoice with me because I have found the groat which I had lost?" These parables present a telling picture of the loving solicitude which the Lord shows for our salvation. How completely we can depend on His love and His constancy! "Let them trust in Thee who know Thy name, O Lord; for Thou hast not forsaken them that seek Thee" (Offertory).

"Cast all your care upon Him." Does this mean that we are to have no solicitude whatever for our own welfare? No, indeed! There is a necessary solicitude which we must have. The Lord Himself teaches us that we are to pray and work for our daily bread. He desires that to the five talents we have been given, we add another five. He reproaches the slothful servant for not having placed the money entrusted to him where it might draw interest (Mt 25:27). We must exercise a certain amount of solicitude for the necessities of life and make efforts to procure them. But there is also an unjustified and perverted solicitude. Many people exercise such an intense solicitude and expend so much energy in providing for their temporal needs that they live and think as though there were no such thing as divine providence. Such unwonted solicitude is condemned both by our Lord and by the liturgy, which tells us to "cast your care upon Him." Put aside all anxious and unwonted solicitude. Trust in the Lord and His love, "for He hath care of you."

"Cast all your care upon Him." We have only one obligation about which we must be solicitous, and that is to do at this moment what God at this moment wants us to do. All other cares we may cast upon the Lord, trusting with a blind faith, leaving all else in His hands.

"Cast all your care upon Him." The care of that which is temporal and of that which is eternal, the care of our past and of our future, we place with supreme confidence in His hands. "He hath care of you."

Prayer

O God, the protector of all who hope in Thee, without whom nothing is strong, nothing is holy; multiply Thy mercies upon us, that having Thee for our ruler and Thee for our guide, we may so make use of temporal goods that we lose not those which are everlasting. Through Christ our Lord. Amen.

Monday

"At that time, the publicans and sinners drew near unto Jesus, to hear him; and the Pharisees and scribes murmured, saying: This man receiveth sinners and eateth with them" (Gospel).

Jesus receiveth sinners. The Son of God "for us men and for our salvation came down from heaven." This truth we acknowledge in the Credo of the Mass. Many men are of the opinion that the Son of God came down from heaven principally in order that He might redeem mankind from sin. If Adam had not sinned, the Son of God would never have appeared on earth; in that event there would never have been a Christ, a Christmas, an Easter, a tabernacle, or the Mass. But "the Son of Man is come to seek and to save that which was lost" (Lk 19:10). He came for the benefit of those who needed a physician (Lk 5:31). In His loving mercy He receives the publicans and the penitent Magdalen. Even for the adulterous woman whom the Pharisees cast at His feet, He had words of mercy. How graphically He described His love of sinners in the parable of the Good Shepherd and the prodigal son! What a holocaust He made of Himself for sinners through His suffering and death! We should not wonder, then, that He received sinners. He had been risen from the dead only a short while when He gave us on that first Easter evening the sacrament of penance. Christ hates sin with a divine hatred, but He loves the sinner and desires to save him. How often we also have experienced the fact that He receives sinners! He has shown us this mercy in the sacrament of baptism, in the sacrament of penance, and in the multitude of inspirations and graces He has given us. What would have become of us had He not been disposed to receive sinners with such a divine and infinite love? What would have happened to us if He had abandoned us? Indeed, we have so much for which to be thankful.

"Gather from this fact that true justice has compassion, but false justice has scorn. Although even the just are rightly aroused against the sinner, it is one thing when done as a mark of pride and another when done out of zeal for discipline.... They inflict punishment, but in the spirit of love. Although outwardly they treat them severely, yet inwardly they preserve sweetness through charity. They prefer to themselves those whom they must correct, and hold them whom they judge to be better than themselves.... On the contrary, they who are accustomed to pride themselves on their false justice, despise everyone else, having no compassion on the weak. The more they believe themselves to be just, the greater sinners they become. The Pharisees who reproached the Lord because He received sinners, were of this number" (St. Gregory; lessons at Matins).

"Let them trust in Thee who know Thy name, O Lord, for Thou hast not forsaken them that seek Thee; sing ye to the Lord, who dwelleth in Sion [the tabernacle]; for He hath not forgotten the cry of the poor" (Offertory).

He "receiveth sinners and eateth with them." Now, at the Sacrifice of the Mass, He offers Himself to the Father in order that we may receive the remission of our sins and obtain the grace to overcome temptations. In Holy Communion He prepares a banquet for us, for His love for sinners is inexhaustible.

"So I say to you, there shall be joy before the angels of God upon one sinner doing penance" (Gospel). Let us examine ourselves earnestly to see whether or not we possess that Pharisaical spirit, which believes that it needs no penance, which passes judgment on others, which criticizes with a bitter zeal the faults of others, and looks down with disdain on "sinners." Piety can so easily become pride or self-complacency and can lead us to disparage others. It sometimes believes that it has no need of penance, and thus departs from the true way of self-abnegation and mortification.

Prayer

O God, the protector of all who hope in Thee, without whom nothing is strong, nothing is holy; multiply Thy mercies upon us, that having Thee for our ruler and Thee for our guide, we may so make use of temporal goods that we lose not those which are everlasting. Through Christ our Lord. Amen.

Tuesday

"O holy banquet in which Christ is received!" At the moment of Holy Communion we receive the incarnate Son of God with all that He has and all that He is. "In all things you are made rich in Him" (1 Cor 1:5).

We possess Christ in His human nature. Holy Communion diffuses in our soul the blessed and heavenly life of His most sacred humanity. We receive His divine and human heart and glorified soul. Once Blessed Angela of Foligno saw in a vision the splendor of the glorified humanity of Christ. There remained with her throughout her lifetime, as a result of this experience, a sublime light, an unspeakable delight, and a boundless joy more beatific than all the other delights which can please the heart of man. This sacred humanity of Jesus, this most precious body, this heart, which contains an abundance of grace, wisdom, and love, we actually receive at Holy Communion. This beautiful, holy soul bathed in a dazzling light, this source of all peace and joy, this foretaste of sanctity and of the paradise of God, we receive at the Eucharistic banquet.

We possess Christ in His divinity. "Having loved His own who were in the world, He loved them unto the end" (Jn 13:1); that is, He loved them until He had exhausted all the possibilities of love. Jesus comes to us in Holy Communion as God, as the Son of the eternal Father, that we might share and live with Him that divine life. "He that eateth Me, the same also shall live by Me" (Jn 6:58). We will live with Christ the life which He possesses from His Father. From all eternity the Father gives life to the Son, entire, undiminished, in such perfection and with such an outpouring of love that the Father and Son are one God with the same life and the same fullness of love, joy, peace, and blessedness. This same life which overflows from the Father to the Son, and which is communicated by the Son to His assumed humanity, permeates our souls also when we receive Holy Communion. We shall never be able to appreciate fully what Christ has given to us in the Holy Eucharist.

Where the Father and the Son are, there also is the Holy Ghost. When we receive Holy Communion, our soul is placed in an unspeakably wonderful state. The Father, the Son, and the Holy Ghost live their mysterious life in us in blessed silence, just as They do in heaven. At that moment we ourselves become the heaven of God. In our soul the Father declares, "Thou art My Son, this day have I begotten Thee" (Ps 2:7). In His Word the Father expresses in our soul the fullness of His essence. Through His Word, through His Son, He produces in our soul the image of His perfection and His essence. "God of God, light of light, true God of true God, begotten not made" (Credo). He showers upon the Son divine and blessed love. The Son responds to the Father with a similar eternal love. The Holy Ghost is the expression of this mutual divine love, which binds the Father to the Son. All this takes place within our soul. We are united to this life of the three divine persons in Holy Communion, so that we share their life through sanctifying grace, supernatural virtues, and particularly through the possession of the theological virtues of faith, hope, and charity. As yet we possess this life only imperfectly and in the obscurity of faith; one day we shall possess it perfectly, in the immediate vision of God the Father, God the Son, and God the Holy Ghost. "O holy banquet in which Christ is received!"

How unworthy we are of the grace of Holy Communion! It should give us an ever fuller participation in the life of God. "He that eateth My flesh and drinketh My blood, abideth in Me, and I in Him" (Jn 6:57). No closer union between Christ and us exists or is conceivable. His body is joined to our body, His soul to our soul, His operations to our operations, and this union is achieved in a supernatural manner that our sanctification and perfection in Him may be assured. In this union our complete self, with all that we are, excepting our sins and our evil inclinations, is drawn into the life of Jesus. This is a union which in the intention of the Lord is never to be broken, and should endure for eternity.

Why is this union often less perfect than Jesus would have it be? The fault lies in us. We do not treasure the privilege of Holy Communion highly enough. We fail most often in making an adequate preparation for it. This preparation should consist primarily in our remaining united with Christ from the time of one Holy Communion to the next. It should consist in our permitting ourselves to be guided and directed by Him and by His spirit from day to day. It implies that we avoid every thought, word, and action which He could not accept and acknowledge as His own. But how often we fail to be sufficiently vigilant! How often we fail to carry out His wishes and desires! We seem to be always following our own will, fulfilling our own desires, and satisfying our self-love.

Prayer

Grant, we beseech Thee, O Lord, that we may be satiated through the eternal enjoyment of Thy divinity, for which the reception of Thy precious body and blood in this world prepares us. Who livest and reignest for all eternity. Amen.

Wednesday

We are now within the octave of the feast of the Sacred Heart of Jesus. With the holy liturgy we pray: "Grant, we beseech Thee, that revering with meet devotion [the infinite wealth of Thy love], we may make a worthy reparation for our sins" (Collect). We have a twofold duty to the Sacred Heart of Jesus: the duty of loving surrender and the duty of atonement.

The duty of love. Love requires a return of love. To the love of Christ, which we venerate under the symbol of His Sacred Heart, we reply with a loving self-surrender, which implies an ardent longing that He be known, loved, and honored; it implies deep grief at the sight of sin and a joyful delight in the promotion of His interests and in the triumph of His love, His Church, and His grace. This love constrains us to come to Him with full confidence, to pour forth our hearts before Him, to bewail our coldness, our faults, and our imperfections, to present to Him in a childlike spirit our toils, our troubles, and our trials, and to commit all things into His hands. It goes even one step further and makes us living images of Jesus, both inwardly and outwardly. Such a love drives us to embrace a life of penance and self-denial. We reduce our needs and conquer our senses. We limit ourselves even in permissible delights. We detach ourselves inwardly and even outwardly, as far as our calling allows, from worldly things. We conform our will in perfect harmony to His good pleasure. We live, now no longer by our own spirit, but by a conscious dependence on His spirit and under the influence of His grace. Happy is the soul that is so deeply wounded by the love of Christ that it loses all taste for anything that is not Christ or does not lead to Christ. Happy is the soul which is so penetrated by His love that it rules all its affections, words, and works, so that the soul no longer knows or seeks anything except Him. Blessed is the soul that is so absorbed in Him that it renounces all other love and thinks of Him alone and is completely possessed by Him. "And I live, now not I; but Christ liveth in me" (Gal 2:20).

The duty of atonement for our own sins and for those of others. He who lives by the spirit of Christ naturally feels the injuries which are done to Christ. The same love which makes the interests of Christ our interests, causes us to be sad when we see Christ persecuted and despised. We take all His injuries as our own, and they cause us pain because of our great love for Him. The more we see Him despised and treated with coldness and indifference, the more we are constrained to express our own love for Him. In like manner we strive to exert special care to prevent faults and unfaithfulness in ourselves and to avoid anything that could give Him pain. Therefore we undertake fresh penances and renunciations in order to give Him an authentic proof of our love. In the same measure we adore Him, worship Him, praise Him in His glory, and beg of Him mercy and grace. We strive to perform our works more perfectly, to accept with perfect resignation from His hand all the trials and temptations that come to us in life. All these things we do out of love for Christ, who has loved us with an eternal love.

"Poor Jesus," St. Alphonsus Liguori would say, "Poor Jesus! Who is concerned about you or your interests?" How He longs to be loved by us! We contemplate the crucifix, and yet we remain unmoved. We read the cruel story of His suffering and death, and yet we remain cold and indifferent. We kneel to pray, but we can scarcely hold out for fifteen minutes. We see others falling into sin, and yet we are not disturbed at knowing that Jesus is being injured, so long as our own soul is not placed in danger. Strange signs of love indeed! Jesus seems to occupy a very unimportant corner of our heart.

Even on the feast of the Sacred Heart we go our own way and seek our own will. All our energies are bent on satisfying our own desires, on making all things easy and pleasant for ourselves. We are ever in search of physical satisfaction and comfort, and we want our spiritual life to consist in a rich measure of interior consolations. We praise the Sacred Heart of Jesus with our lips, but in reality seek ourselves in all things. Where is our love? Where is our spirit of atonement?

Prayer

O God, who in the heart of Thy Son, wounded by our transgressions, dost mercifully vouchsafe to bestow upon us the infinite wealth of Thy love; grant, we beseech Thee, that revering it with meet devotion, we may make a worthy reparation for our sins. Through the same Christ our Lord. Amen.

Thursday

This week the Church prays that God may ever pour forth upon us a greater measure of His mercy, so that under His guidance and direction we may make use of temporal things in such a way as not to lose those which are eternal. Temporal things are given to us that we may serve the eternal God.

Temporal things are given for our use. We are obliged to "pass through" such things and yet remain detached from them. This obligation extends to all things that are not God: to all created things, animate and inanimate, physical and spiritual, the things of nature and those above nature, whatever the day may bring. All these things are given to us for our use. But we are to use them only as means and instruments in the work of God, that we may serve Him and accomplish our own salvation. With good reason God attached much pleasure and satisfaction to man's use of creatures, but He did not mean that man should seek his final end in them. These pleasures were to serve as a fine oil does for the machine: they were to be a benefit which man was to accept gratefully from the hand of God, and thus out of gratitude serve God more faithfully, devotedly, and joyfully.

Holy Mother the Church knows how prone we men are to make use of created things, not merely as a means to an end, but as an end in themselves; she knows how apt we are to rest in them, to seek our joy in them, and even to make them our God. She knows how many men say secretly to themselves: Man must indeed fear God, respect Him, and adore Him at a respectful distance. But actually they seek their enjoyment in created things such as a comfortable life, sports, travel, great works of art, beauty, health, honor, renown, good fortune, and prosperity. For these things they live, and in them they find their happiness. With great sadness Holy Mother the Church, during these weeks that follow Pentecost, thinks of these her children who are so poorly enlightened by the spirit of the Holy Ghost. She prays God most earnestly that He may have mercy on these wayward children, that He may show them even greater mercy than hitherto, and pour forth the Holy Spirit upon them, so that they may learn to make use of created things as a means of serving Him, and that they may pass through them in such a manner that their hearts, their desires, their longings, and their love may not remain attached to them. We, too, share this sadness of Holy Mother the Church and join her in beseeching God from the depths of our hearts that He may give us all the grace so to make use of all these created things that we may eventually attain the eternal God.

God alone is to be our final end: God the Father, the unfathomable source of divinity; God the Son, the eternal, resplendent Word; God the Holy Ghost, the eternal and blessed expression of the mutual love of the Father and the Son; the blessed humanity of Jesus; the Sacred Heart of Jesus. In God we will find our joy and our rest. The mighty and holy God entered our souls at the hour of our baptism, and He lives there within us in order that we may enjoy Him, possess Him, and share His divine life with Him. He gives Himself to us as a loving Father, with whom we may speak with the greatest confidence and trust. He gives Himself to us that we may live with the living God in our souls and find our joy and our habitation in Him rather than in anything else that is not God. Happy are we, the sons of the Church, who know Christ, who possess Him as our offering in the Holy Sacrifice of the Mass, as the food of our souls in Holy Communion, as our friend and companion in the tabernacle, as the life-giving vine, to which we are engrafted as branches through the mystery of the communion of saints. He has given Himself to us for our enjoyment, that we might find happiness and rest in Him. As we pass through life, in everything we meet on the way, in everything the day may bring, welcome or unwelcome, we see Him, His continual presence, His holy will, His wisdom, His goodness, His love, and His providence. In all our labors, trials, sufferings, and temptations, we see God before us and the working of His love in us. Thus we rest in God's good pleasure, in His wisdom, His goodness, and His eternal love for us. Therefore we are not disturbed by the injustice and injuries done to us by other men. Neither are we too concerned about our health, our existence, or our earthly goods; for we have found peace in God. But this is only a small beginning and a foretaste of the blessed peace that we shall enjoy when we attain the final and complete possession of God.

"The time is short. It remaineth that they also who have wives be as if they had none; and they that weep as though they wept not; and they that rejoice as if they rejoiced not; and they that buy as though they possessed not; and they that use this world as if they used it not; for the fashion of this world passeth away" (1 Cor 7:29, 31).

We are to pass by all created things. They have been given to us only as instruments and means for attaining God. We are to use them only for the purpose for which they were given; we may use them only so long and to the extent that they are useful to us in the service of God. In a holy freedom of the spirit and the heart, we must lift ourselves above created things and never allow ourselves to become the slaves to them. We are to possess God alone, Christ Jesus alone, and therefore we must seek only those things that are dear to Him and lead to Him.

Prayer

O God, the protector of all who hope in Thee, without whom nothing is strong, nothing is holy; multiply Thy mercies upon us, that having Thee for our ruler and Thee for our guide, we may so make use of temporal goods that we lose not those which are everlasting. Through Christ our Lord. Amen.

Friday
Octave of the Feast of the Sacred Heart

"To me, the least of all the saints, is given this grace, to preach among the Gentiles the unsearchable riches of Christ" (Epistle). With these words the Apostle addresses us. These unsearchable riches of Christ the liturgy finds buried in the Sacred Heart of Jesus, which contains all the treasures of wisdom and knowledge, and in which dwells the fullness of divinity. In the Sacred Heart of Jesus, God bestows upon us, through His infinite mercy, the inexhaustible treasures of His love (Collect).

The unsearchable riches of Christ are hidden in His Sacred Heart, which is the symbol and summation of His inexhaustible sanctity and loving mercy. It contains the inexhaustible fullness of His life: His thoughts, His intentions, His desires, His feelings. It contains the entire prayer life of Jesus, and His holy, divinely perfect, and unbroken adoration of the Divinity; it contains His praise, His thanksgiving, His subjection to the Father in heaven and in our tabernacles on earth. It contains the inexhaustible plenitude of His graces, virtues, and holiness. There, too, is concentrated the perfection of His life of obedience, His voluntary emptying of Himself, His sublime humility, His love of poverty and of suffering. In this heart He lives His life of love for the Father and for us sinners; here the fire of His zeal for our eternal salvation burns most brightly. The Sacred Heart contains all the merits which Christ earned from the moment of His first entrance into the world to His last breath of life on the cross. In the Sacred Heart is concentrated all the wealth of atonement and satisfaction which the Son offered to the eternal Father during His life on earth. The Sacred Heart wields irresistible power over Satan and the elements, and over the spirits and hearts of men; He Himself has declared: "All power is given to Me in heaven and in earth" (Mt 28:18). In Christ, in His Sacred Heart, "we have redemption through His blood, the remission of sins, according to the riches of His grace" (Eph 1:7). All these riches belong to us. The Sacred Heart of Jesus belongs to us, for God has given it to us, as we are assured in the Collect of the feast: "O God, who in the heart of Thy son, dost mercifully vouchsafe to bestow upon us the infinite wealth of Thy love." With the Sacred Heart of Jesus the wealth of His prayers, His merits, and His satisfactions also belongs to us.

It is our privilege to take in our hands this Sacred Heart and offer it to the Father in the Holy Sacrifice of the Mass. Thus we can adore the Holy Trinity in a worthy manner and make a worthy offering of praise; thus we can offer a perfect act of thanksgiving and make full reparation and atonement for our sins. We can make these offerings of praise, thanksgiving, and reparation even apart from the Holy Sacrifice of the Mass, for there is not a single moment of our lives in which we cannot make use of the Sacred Heart of Jesus and offer it up to the Father. Every moment of the day and night Jesus loves us, prays for us, thanks the Father for us, and offers up satisfaction for us. Thus we can always pray in union with the prayers of the Sacred Heart of Jesus and unite our prayers to His. So, too, when we have been guilty of faults, we can offer up to the Father the merits of Jesus in satisfaction for our sins. Whenever we stand in need of grace, we can offer to the Father the Sacred Heart of Jesus with its power of intercession. If we should have to undergo some suffering, we can unite it to the suffering of Jesus, who at that very moment is offering up His sufferings and death to the Father on some altar somewhere in the world. Through Christ we can work, pray, and suffer; through Him we can love God with the love of the Sacred Heart. The Sacred Heart belongs entirely to us. Through the Sacred Heart we can pray for those who do not worship Him themselves. Through the Sacred Heart of Jesus we can love the Father in the name of those who do not love Him, but rather hate Him and revile Him. Through the Sacred Heart of Jesus we can offer satisfaction for the sinners of the whole world. How rich and powerful we have become through our possession of the Sacred

Heart of Jesus! "O God, who in the heart of Thy Son dost mercifully vouchsafe to bestow on us the infinite wealth of Thy love."

We who by nature are so poor, may become rich at the moment we cease to depend on ourselves and attach ourselves completely to Jesus and make use of His Sacred Heart. "I no longer pray for anything, nor even offer anything. I simply unite myself to the Savior and say: 'O God, I offer Thee, in thanksgiving for all the benefits Thou has bestowed upon me, Thy beloved Son as my gift, as my adoration, instead of all my own works. I offer Him to Thee in place of all my love and everything else I have. Take Him, heavenly Father, in place of all the things Thou couldst have from me. For I have nothing that would be worthy of Thee, but Him whom out of such great love for me Thou has given me'" (St. Margaret Mary Alacoque).

"If any man thirst, let him come to Me and drink" (Jn 7:37). Do we not thirst to love God and honor Him as He deserves to be loved and honored and adored? If we exerted ourselves to the utmost, by ourselves we could not worthily love and honor Him. Therefore we must entirely forget our own inefficacious efforts and offer Jesus to the Father, together with His heart, His love, and His adoration; we can make this offering every moment of the day through the Holy Sacrifice of the Mass. That is the best method of honoring the Sacred Heart of Jesus.

Prayer

Teach us, O Lord, who have tasted the sweetness of Thy most dear heart, to despise what is temporal and to love what is eternal. Thou who livest and reignest for all eternity. Amen.

Saturday

At Pentecost we receive the Holy Ghost. Through the reception of the Holy Ghost we become mature Christians fortified for Christian life, for struggle and suffering. In order to fortify us and strengthen us for suffering, the Epistle today admonishes us: "Be ye humbled under the mighty hand of God, that He may exalt you in the time of visitation.... But the God of all grace, who hath called us unto the eternal glory in Christ Jesus, after you have suffered a little, will Himself perfect you, and confirm you, and establish you" (Epistle). The way of all perfection is this: "Be ye humbled under the mighty hand of God," for "God resisteth the proud, but to the humble He giveth grace" (1 Pt 5:5).

"God resisteth the proud." He is proud who lives by his own spirit and who will not subject his own will to the commands, ordinances, and plans of God, and who sets up his own plans and his own will against the will of God. He is proud who wishes to be his own master, and who wishes to be in no way responsible to God. Pride is the source of all sin and the root of all evil in men. Pride is at the bottom of man's every departure from God, and it is the most formidable obstacle in his return to God. It is the real cause that prevents man from being united to God and from subjecting himself to God. And pride thrives, not only in the world, but in the hearts of the baptized, and even in the hearts of many good Christians. Pride is the cockle in the wheat. Like all weeds, pride needs no cultivation. Every gust of wind spreads its seeds abroad, and the better the ground, the deeper the roots sink into it. It may be torn up a thousand times, but it will always spring to life again if the slightest root is left behind. This fact is especially true for those who wish to live an intensive religious life. The more they live the life of the spirit, the more they are tempted to imagine that because of their spirituality they are superior to others. They take pleasure in their severe asceticism, and they are flattered if they are looked upon with a reverential fear by others. They are tempted to look down upon "the others" and consider them inferior to themselves. They are always ready with a false zeal to criticize others, to correct them, to condemn them, and to speak uncharitably of them. They are often impatient with the leisurely way in which God works. They linger with great pleasure on the good they have accomplished, which all too often they exaggerate. Such a pride is an obstacle to grace and to union with God. Does Christ the true vine then really live in us? Should we wonder that we do not make greater progress in holiness? "God resisteth the proud."

"But to the humble He giveth grace." This is the law of the dominion of grace: "He that shall humble himself shall be exalted" (Mt 23:12). According to all the rules of justice, this autocratic resistance to God, this pride, this source of all evil in man, can be subdued only through subjection to God through humility. "Suffer the little children to come unto Me, ... for of such is the kingdom of heaven" (Mk 10:14). The spirit of Christ is a spirit of humility. "Learn of Me, because I am meek and humble of heart" (Mt 11:29). We are to learn from Christ, not to work wonders, not to be glorious in the eyes of the world, not to accomplish great deeds, but to be meek and humble of heart. Humility is the essence of all that Christ taught by word and example. Humility is the summation of His whole life, the virtue most characteristic of Christ. It is the foundation of the spiritual structure, the base upon which all other virtues must rest. Humility is the root and the beginning of all good, the door to the kingdom of heaven. Our progress in union with God and in union with Christ depends in large measure on our progress in humility. The higher the structure of our holiness rises, the deeper must be the foundation of humility on which it rests. Without humility there can be no life of faith, no truth and sincerity, no nobility of soul, no spirit of sacrifice, no self-sacrificing love. If we are truly humble, we give little thought to ourselves. The opinion of men, one's own honor, one's own advantage, one's own satisfaction, one's own wishes and desires, are spurned by the man who is truly humble. He is concerned only with God's will and God's honor. Whatever is not in some way concerned with God leaves him cold. What comes from God and leads to God interests him, elevates him, inspires him, even though in itself it has no particular attraction. There is no greater courage than in humility. Threats, mockery, slander, do not disturb the humble man. All flattery is lost on him. And when for the sake of God or His work he must sacrifice all things, he does so gladly. Humility seeks God and His will alone. It shrinks from no task, or sacrifice, or suffering. The humble man knows that he will find the source of all strength in being humble, in completely subjecting himself to God and His will, in observing minutely the regulations of the Church or of the religious community, in fulfilling the duties of his state in life. He takes to heart that saying of the Apostle: "I can do all things in Him who strengtheneth me" (Phil 4:13).

"Be you humbled under the mighty hand of God that He may exalt you in the time of visitation." This is the most earnest admonition of the liturgy during the fourth week after Pentecost. The Holy Ghost, the Spirit of Christ, will establish His rule in us and extend it. But He can do so only if our souls are humble, submissive, and conformed to His will. In the measure in which we know and acknowledge our nothingness and unworthiness, and come to Him in humility and confidence, in the same measure will He exalt us "in the time of visitation"; that is, in the time of prayer, at Mass, and at Holy Communion. To live for Christ is to love humility, to be despised by the world, to be subject to the will of the Father, to love the cross, suffering, reverses, and difficulties of all sorts. We are but branches of Christ, who is the vine. We must live just as Christ lives. Our life cannot be other than a life of humility and of joyful dependence on God and His will and His providence. "He that shall humble himself shall be exalted" (Mt 23:12).

Prayer

O God, the protector of all who hope in Thee, without whom nothing is strong, nothing is holy; multiply Thy mercies upon us, that having Thee for our ruler and Thee for our guide, we may so make use of temporal goods that we lose not those which are everlasting. Through Christ our Lord. Amen.

Fourth Sunday after Pentecost

The Mass

The thought of Easter appears clearly in the Mass of this Sunday. Around us is the mighty ocean with its storms and its dangers; around us are enemies, sickness, and death. Therefore we fly to Christ. "The Lord is my light and my salvation. Whom shall I fear?" (Introit.) We cling to the Lord. He holds the scepter of the world in His hand. He will bring it about that "the course of this world may be so peaceably ordered" that we may serve God "in quiet devotion" (Collect). It is true that suffering and want must come; but for those who have given themselves to Christ, these sufferings are not to be compared to the glory that will be revealed in us (Epistle). As all creation longs for deliverance from the slavery and the corruption of sin, so, too, we await the moment when our adoption as the sons of God will be accomplished with all its glory. We await our entry into the bliss of eternity, the resurrection of our flesh to life everlasting. This longing, however, can be satisfied only by our Lord Himself. We must cling to Him.

During this week the Church sometimes celebrates the feast of SS. Peter and Paul. Therefore we find our Lord today in the boat of Peter (Gospel). We press close to Him to hear His word, which He speaks to the world from the bark of Peter, the Church. We are those fish who were enclosed in Peter's net in the early morning (in baptism), and there, having been enclosed in the net of the Church, we found salvation. We were rescued by the bark of Peter. Let us remain true to the salvation which we obtained in baptism and in the Church. It is for this grace that we pray in the Offertory.

As we approach to make our offering, we place ourselves at the side of Christ, as we did on the day of our baptism. Today in the Holy Sacrifice of the Mass, which we celebrate with Him, we enter into the closest union with Him and become one victim with Him. We have chosen the way of Christ, the way of the cross, the way of renunciation of sin and of the world with all its attractions and temptations. We know that the suffering entailed by the renunciation of sin, the flesh, and the world, are not to be compared with the glory of the children of God, to which we have been called. On the paten at Mass we must lay our rebellious nature and our rebellious wills, which shrink from suffering and renunciation. Here we renew the previous renunciation we made at the time of our baptism (Secreta).

Through our participation in the suffering and death of Christ, which is made possible to us through our offering of the Holy Sacrifice of the Mass, we also enter into the glory of the new life of which the Epistle speaks, the life of the children of God. Participation in the Holy Sacrifice of the Mass signifies our sharing not only in the suffering and death of Christ, but also in His resurrection. Offering ourselves with Christ, we, like the substance of the bread and wine, will undergo a change in spirit and life. That supernatural life which was planted in our souls in baptism will be deepened and inspired. The Spirit of the Son of God descends into our soul and accomplishes with irresistible power the final glorification and redemption of body and soul.

This sanctification, however, Christ accomplishes only in the bark of Peter, that is, in His holy Church, in which through Peter and his successors He appears and teaches. He accomplishes it in all those who, like the fishes of today's Gospel, are caught in the net of Peter which was cast out at the command of the Lord. Only where Christ is, is there light, salvation, and redemption; that is, in the bark of Peter, the Church. In her custody is placed the sacrifice from which all redemption and grace flow. Blessed be the day that brought us to Christ in baptism and made us members of His Church. "The Lord is my firmament, and my refuge, and my deliverer" (Communion).

Meditation

Today we see two small boats moored at the bank of the Lake of Genesareth. The fishermen have left them and are washing their nets. Christ enters one of these boats, the one belonging to Peter. Peter stands by Him in the boat and pushes it off a short distance from the shore. Jesus begins to instruct the people, and after He has finished speaking to them, He works the miracle of the draught of fishes. Peter and his companions obey the command of Christ and catch such a multitude of fish that their nets threaten to break. Then Christ appoints Peter to be a fisher of men. "Fear not, from henceforth thou shalt catch men."

"And when they had done this, they enclosed a very great multitude of fishes; and their net broke" (Gospel). What an unexpected catch! For the liturgy this draught of fish is a symbol and figure: the fish which Peter caught at the command of the Lord are the souls of the faithful. "We fishes have been born [by baptism] in the water" (Tertullian). Through Peter, and through the Church founded upon him, we have been drawn by baptism out of the sea of sin and perdition, and we have found Christ and salvation. Christ's command to Peter still applies: "Let down your nets." It is carried out in the preaching of the word of God, in the celebration of Mass, and in the administration of the holy sacraments. Peter and His Church and her priests may often complain, "Master, we have labored all the night and have taken nothing." But the Lord insists on His command, "Let down your nets"; and Peter and His Church and her priests, who experience so many reversals and misfortunes, take up the work anew, — "at Thy word" — in blind faith, in humble obedience to His word, even though human prudence can see no chance of success. Peter, the Church, and her priests exert themselves to the utmost, but the results accomplished depend not on their efforts, but solely and entirely on His grace. "But at Thy word I will let down the net." It often appears as though the Lord wished to do all the work by Himself and put His Church and His priests to shame. He humbles them that He may later exalt them. When the day of eternity dawns, they will see the "very great multitude of fishes" they have taken, and will be amazed at the power of the Lord, which has made their humble efforts so fruitful and successful.

"The multitude pressed upon Jesus to hear the word of God" (Gospel). And Jesus entered into a boat that was Peter's and taught them from the boat. We are the people of the Gospel who press upon Jesus to hear the word of God, and He speaks to us from the bark of Peter. If we would have the word of God preached to us with fidelity and fruitfulness, then we must come to the bark of Peter, the Catholic Church. She is infallible, "the pillar and ground of the truth" (1 Tm 3:15). The Holy Ghost resides in the Church, and He has been given to her in order that He may teach her "all truth" (Jn 16:13). Behind Peter and his successors and assistants there stands the imposing figure of the Lord Himself. We cannot be misled by the Church, by the popes, bishops, and priests, for the Lord Himself is with them. He speaks through them to us: "He that heareth you, heareth Me" (Lk 10:16).

We may with confidence entrust ourselves to the net which Peter and his helpers cast out to take us. In this net we shall be brought to the Lord, and we shall find "the way, the truth, and the life" (Jn 14:6). There, too, we shall find a life of grace and the right to eternal life in heaven. With Peter and the Church we may rejoice while we sing, "The Lord is my light and my salvation; whom shall I fear? The Lord is the protector of my life; of whom shall I be afraid? My enemies that trouble me have themselves been weakened and have fallen" (Introit). In the Church, the net of Peter, we find the holy mysteries, the sacraments of baptism and the Eucharist, by means of which we shall be cleansed from our sins (Postcommunion), and shall receive an increase of grace and the possession of divine life. In the Church "the Lord is my firmament, and my refuge, and my deliverer; my God is my helper" (Communion).

Today we should thank God, who, through Peter and His Church and His priesthood, has rescued mankind from the perdition into which it had fallen through Adam's sin. We should thank Peter and the Church and the priesthood that they have so faithfully complied with the commission given to them by Christ to "catch men."

On this day we should commit ourselves in loving confidence to Peter and the Church over which he has been placed. Through Peter we obtain the truth, the forgiveness of our sins, grace, and salvation. "Thou art Peter and upon this rock I will build My Church" (Mt 16:18). "He that heareth you, heareth Me; and he that despiseth you, despiseth Me" (Lk 10:16). "I believe in the one, holy, catholic, and apostolic Church."

Prayer

Grant, we beseech Thee, O Lord, that the course of this world may be so peaceably ordered by Thee that Thy Church may joyfully serve Thee in quiet devotion. Through Christ our Lord. Amen.

Monday

At one time the fourth Sunday after Pentecost was called the Sunday before the feast of SS. Peter and Paul. It is somewhat like a feast in preparation for that of the apostles. The Gospel relates the story of the miraculous draught of fishes, the appointment of the apostles to be fishers of men, and the heroic action of Peter, James, and John: "And having brought their ships to land, leaving all things they followed Him" (Gospel).

We wait "for the adoption of the sons of God, the redemption of our body" (Epistle). What is a Christian? He is a man who waits for the glory to come, that shall be revealed to us. We have good reason to count on this revelation of glory: "For the expectation of the creature waiteth for the revelation of the sons of God. For the creature was made subject to vanity, not willingly, but by reason of him that made it subject in hope; because the creature also itself shall be delivered from the servitude of corruption into the liberty of the glory of the children of God. For we know that every creature groaneth and travaileth in pain, even till now; and not only it, but ourselves also, who have the first fruits of the Spirit, even we ourselves groan within ourselves, waiting for the adoption of the sons of God, the redemption of our body" (Epistle). This redemption of the body we expect in the resurrection from the dead, in the assumption of our bodies into heaven, and in the eternal possession and enjoyment of God.

The important part of our vocation as Christians lies in the other world. We are confident we shall attain the happiness of heaven, and today we celebrate a feast in our anticipation of attaining it. In the hope of that eternal Easter lies the fountainhead of our happiness, our continual joy, our Christian optimism. Our good fortune arises from the fact that the Son of God became man for our sake. God loves the man Christ as His Son. We have been incorporated in Him, we are one with Him, the Son of God, and with Him we become sons of God. For this reason the Father extends also to us the love which He lavishes on His Son. The love with which He loves us is the same love which He has for His Son, and it gives our hope its certainty and its blessedness. The Father does not separate us from His Son. Where the Son is, there we shall be also, since with Him and in Him we, too, are sons of God. Just as the day of glory and of eternal life is certain for the Son, so too will the day of glory for our bodies and souls be certain. We await, then, what is to come; that is, the unspeakable glory that is to be revealed to us, the sons of God. We lift up our hearts and minds and "reckon that the sufferings of this time are not worthy to be compared with the glory to come, that shall be revealed in us," when, after this life, we attain our eternal reward (Epistle). In this hope we pass by earthly pleasures and joys, and press forward toward those that are eternal, the true and perfect happiness. Our destiny is to see God, to possess Him, and to enjoy Him.

"In Christ Jesus our Lord." On Christ is the certainty and the beatitude of our hope founded; it has its source in Him. The more closely we are bound to Him in a living union of faith, trust, and love, and the more intimately we unite ourselves to His spirit and life, the more certain we are of the revelation of the glory of the Son of God in us. But Christ is to be found only in the bark of Peter, in the Church that is founded on Peter, to whom Christ said, "Launch out into the deep and let down your nets for a draught.... Fear not, from henceforth thou shalt catch men" (Gospel). The vocation of Peter and of his successors and their representatives is to catch men by the order of Christ and with the power of Christ. They are to catch men so that they may be led to Christ and thus share in the adoption of the sonship of God. "And if sons, heirs also; heirs indeed of God and joint heirs with Christ" (Rom 8:17). We acknowledge the authority of St. Peter and his successors in the Catholic Church and its holy priesthood. We see in Peter and in his successors and helpers, not the "sinful man" mentioned in the Gospel nor the merely natural men who "have labored all the night and have taken nothing," but the representatives of the Lord, who commissioned them to go forth into the whole world and fish for men. The Church has the right to rule men for Christ and for eternal life. We likewise have the duty to allow ourselves to be caught by Peter in the net of the Catholic Church. "All power is given to me in heaven and in earth; going, therefore, teach ye all nations, baptizing them in the name of the Father, and of the Son, and of the Holy Ghost" (Mt 28:18 f.). "He that heareth you, heareth Me; and he that despiseth you, despiseth Me; and he that despiseth Me, despiseth Him that sent Me" (Lk 10:16). The road to Christ and eternal life is directly through Peter and the Church.

"Thine they were, and to Me Thou gavest them" (Jn 17:6). But we were given to Christ, not merely as companions of His struggles and sufferings, but as very members of His body. "Father, I will that where I am, they also whom Thou hast given Me may be with Me; that they may see My glory which Thou hast given Me" (Jn 17:24). We shall see and in our own body experience and enjoy His glory with Him. We await with great longing this revelation of the glory of our sonship in God, which will be made to us in Christ and in His Church. There we shall learn "what the hope is of the glory of His inheritance in the saints" (Eph 1:18).

Prayer

Grant, we beseech Thee, O Lord, that the course of this world may be so peaceably ordered by Thee that Thy Church may joyfully serve Thee in quiet devotion. Through Christ our Lord. Amen.

Tuesday

Pentecost has made us strong in the Christian life. "Launch out into the deep and let down your nets" (Gospel). We have taken up our work each day and have exerted ourselves. But what have we accomplished? Why have we not made some progress? What good results have we to show for our labor? Sins, mistakes, errors, and imperfections. In Peter we recognize ourselves; we come to our Lord and we say, "Master, we have labored all the night and have taken nothing" (Gospel).

"Master, we have labored all the night and have taken nothing." Why is it that we have made so little progress in spite of all the graces we have received, in spite of all our efforts, our abnegations, prayers, meditations, examinations of conscience, confessions, and Communions? What is wanting to us? We have been working "in the night"; we have been working without that clear and brilliant light of a living spirit of faith, and have done all our reasoning, willing, and acting without that necessary light. We have been living mechanically, in a routine manner, and without a definite supernatural point of view. We have been performing our work with predominantly natural motives: for self-love, pride, self-seeking, vanity. Like Peter, we labor during the night and without the help of Jesus. That which guides us in our actions and intentions is not the spirit of Jesus, His example, His love, and His operation in us and through us. We work, pray, and suffer without a clear consciousness of our organic union with Him who is the vine. What wonder, then, if we experience little growth and increase! "Abide in Me and I in you. As the branch cannot bear fruit of itself unless it abide in the vine, so neither can you unless you abide in Me.... Without Me you can do nothing" (Jn 15:4 f.). We work, just as Peter did, chiefly on our own initiative and according to our own judgment and will; we decide for ourselves what we are to do and how it is to be done. For this reason our labor is unfruitful. Only if the Lord gives the word, directing us where, when, and how we are to cast out our nets, and only if we can say with St. Peter, "At Thy word I will let down the net," only then will our efforts bear fruit. We are wanting in the spirit of faith and in a living consciousness of our union with Christ and the necessity of making our will and our intentions depend entirely on those of Christ. Therefore we must make the sorry confession: "Master, we have labored all the night and have taken nothing."

"But at Thy word I will let down the net." Shall we be discouraged when we reflect on our own weakness and ineffectiveness? We find the answer in the prayers of today's Mass: "The Lord is my light and my salvation; whom shall I fear? The Lord is the protector of my life; of whom shall I be afraid?" (Introit.) Christ is with us. In the Holy Sacrifice of the Mass He comes to us to strengthen us in our weakness, to aid us in our helplessness, and to give efficacy to our petitions and our prayers. Having become our offering, He presents Himself to the Father and begs for light and strength for us, that we may again pursue with steadfastness the way of Christian perfection and salvation; He draws near to us in Holy Communion. By this means He incorporates us in His own life. We know ourselves to be filled with Christ, to be made one with Him, and with Him, the true vine, to be elevated to the world of divine grace. We are the few drops of water that are added to the wine in the chalice, the chalice of salvation. Why, then, should we fear? Every day He comes to us with renewed love, offering Himself anew for us, giving us new graces in Mass and in Holy Communion. Every moment of the day we can in spirit return to Him in His blessed tabernacle and warm ourselves in the sun of the Holy Eucharist. Let us no longer consider our own powerlessness, but rather His continual presence, His life and power operating in us. "I am the vine and you the branches; he that abideth in Me and I in him, the same beareth much fruit" (Jn 15:5). He lives in us, He fights and conquers in us. "I can do all things in Him who strengtheneth me" (Phil 4:13). "The Lord is my firmament, and my refuge, and my deliverer; my God is my helper" (Communion).

"At Thy word I will let down the net." Whenever we seek to act by ourselves and depend on ourselves, we invite and deserve failure. We thus cut ourselves off from the living vine, from Him without whom we can do nothing. Therein lies the mystery of all failure and all defeat. He who depends on himself is bound to fail. For this reason there is only one path for us to follow. We must depend on Christ and on His grace; since we are branches, we must depend on the strength imparted to the branches by the vine. "He that abideth in Me and I in him, the same beareth much fruit; for without Me you can do nothing" (Jn 15:5).

In the Gospel we see how Peter's failure was followed by success. He understood why he failed; he had sought success relying on his own efforts. But then he acknowledges his error and expresses his confidence in the Lord: "At Thy word I will let down the net." As a result he experiences a striking success. "They enclosed a very great multitude of fishes."

Prayer

We beseech Thee, O Lord, that we may be reconciled to Thee; inform our wills so that they may be submissive to Thee. Through Christ our Lord. Amen.

Wednesday

"Master, we have labored all the night and have taken nothing." The work has been long and tiring. But it was nocturnal work, work without Jesus, done without the command of the Lord and not dependent on His will and intentions. How could it have been successful?

"We have labored all the night and have taken nothing." These words sound as if they had been spoken by ourselves. Work is the battle cry of the age. Day and night men are consumed by the frantic press of business. Work is also the watchword of those who try to live a life of piety. We make martyrs of ourselves and groan under burdens which we are not able to carry (Mt 23:4). We begin a thousand good works and scarcely bring one to completion. We assume numerous spiritual exercises and regulations, yet we do not approach true holiness. We make trial of every new fashion in the spiritual life, and yet we are not satisfied. We set out in search of new methods, new meditations, and new saints; we keep accounts and make frequent inventories, and we know that all is not well.

Work is also the battle cry of all those who work for the salvation of souls, who live a life of charity and Catholic action. They work feverishly in their offices and pound furiously on their typewriters. They found new organizations and start new projects; new members are sought and new guilds started. Innumerable books are written, and countless periodicals are prepared and distributed. Conventions meet on every hand. All has been splendidly organized, and yet, where are the fruits of all these industrious works of piety? What have we to show for all our charitable undertakings? What harvest have we reaped from our apostolate? What results have we obtained from all our social and religious activity? Must we not often approach the Master and confess with Peter, "Master, we have labored all the night and have taken nothing?

"But at Thy word." At the command of Jesus, Peter again cast forth his net. He acted at the express command of the Master, conformed entirely to His will. His second attempt is crowned with astonishing success. Only work that is blessed by the Lord Himself will be successful. "Seek ye first the kingdom of God, … and all these things shall be added unto you" (Lk 12:31). A multitude of external works and projects and an ever increasing activity are no guarantee of success. Not the number of our pious undertakings makes us holy, but the power springing from our interior life, from our attempts at union with Christ, from our search for true holiness, gives us the guarantee of success. The breath of life must go forth from our interior life into our external works, just as the sap must flow from the heart of the tree into the branches and the blossoms. The source of this interior life is, first of all, the interior virtues, such as a vivifying faith, humble subjection to the will of God, the spirit of self-denial, the spirit of prayer, the love of God and of Christ. Our efforts must first of all be centered on strengthening this inner life. We must cooperate with the Holy Spirit, who dwells within us, with God, who lives and works in us; we must listen to His voice speaking to us and guiding us.

Only when inordinate passion has been subjected within us, when the spirit of God and of Christ has conquered in us, when our actions proceed from a spirit of self-detachment, then shall we be able to work with a selfless love, with a pure intention, and for the sake of God alone. Only then will our work be blessed and be fruitful. Only such an interior life can make us generous in adversity, patient in suffering, magnanimous and persistent; only such an interior life gives us the strength to conquer self, to be faithful to our obligations, to perform our duties perfectly both interiorly and exteriorly, and to subject ourselves entirely to the will of God.

This life gives us the ability to bear our trials and adversities with calmness and resignation for the love of God, and to make use of them for our own improvement. This cultivation of the interior life is our best guarantee that God's blessing will rest upon our work, and that our efforts will bear fruit.

"The Lord is my light and my salvation; whom shall I fear? The Lord is the protector of my life; of whom shall I be afraid? My enemies that trouble me have themselves been weakened and have fallen" (Introit). Thus speaks the man who lives a true interior life. He sees God in everything that happens to him. By his intentions he directs all his actions to God; he never relies on himself, but depends entirely and completely on God, trusting in His merciful protection.

"Enlighten my eyes that I may never sleep in death" (Offertory). Give us a wholesome understanding of the true interior life, which sees God in everything, which directs all its actions to God and for the love of God. This prayer we place on the paten at the Mass today: "Draw our rebellious wills unto Thee" (Secreta), that in all our actions and works we may live for Thee; that we may seek Thee and Thy holy will and Thy glorification.

The Lord wishes to continue His life in us — the vine living in its branches. He comes to us in Holy Communion in order to fill us yet more with His life and His spirit. He desires to make our souls His mansion. In His earthly mission He performs a threefold task: He lives His life of seclusion in the tabernacle, He lives in the prayers and virtues of His saints, He lives a life of continuous suffering in the souls of men. To cultivate this interior life is our primary task, for the fruitfulness of our activity depends on it. A worthy reception of Holy Communion spurs us on to a higher interior life.

Prayer

Grant, we beseech Thee, O Lord, that the course of this world may be so peaceably ordered by Thee that Thy Church may joyfully serve Thee in quiet devotion. Through Christ our Lord. Amen.

Thursday

"And going up into one of the ships that was Simon's, He desired him to draw back a little from the land; and sitting He taught the multitudes out of the ship" (Gospel).

Jesus teaches the multitudes, who are always attracted to Him. Do they not have scribes and Pharisees to teach them? Yes, indeed; but Christ teaches in a manner quite different from that of the scribes and Pharisees. "He was teaching them as one having power," and all "were in admiration at His doctrine" (Mt 7:28 f.). He accommodates Himself to the simple by the use of parables. The kingdom of heaven He likens to a sower who went out to sow his seed, and as he sowed, some fell by the wayside and was devoured by the birds of the air; some fell upon a rock and could not grow; some fell among thorns and was choked; some fell upon good ground and brought forth fruit a hundredfold (Mt, chap. 13). Christ spoke of merciful love: "You have heard that it was said to them of old: Thou shalt not kill. And whosoever shall kill, shall be in danger of the judgment. But I say unto you, that whosoever is angry with his brother shall be in danger of the judgment" (Mt 5:21 f.). "And you have heard that it was said to them of old: Thou shalt not commit adultery. But I say to you, that whosoever shall look on a woman to lust after her hath already committed adultery with her in his heart" (Mt 5:27 f.). He tells us how we can gain the kingdom of heaven and what is the true meaning of life. The world cannot supply the real answer to the purpose of life. It cannot be the enjoyment of earthly possessions or worldly goods, which can be taken away from us against our will by force or fraud. The true purpose of human life is to be found only in the striving for spiritual perfection and the proper direction of human acts in their relationship to God. The true task of man in this world is to struggle for justice, mercy, and purity in the midst of a world which is swayed by injustice, selfishness, impurity, and neglect of God. "Lay not up to yourselves treasures on earth.... Lay up to yourselves treasures in heaven" (Mt 6:19 f.). "Enter ye at the narrow gate; for wide is the gate and broad is the way that leadeth to destruction, and many there are who go in thereat. How narrow is the gate and straight is the way that leadeth to life; and few there are that find it" (Mt 7:13). These are the principles and the lessons which Christ taught the multitudes who followed Him. These are the words of eternal life.

Jesus teaches us also, coming as He does daily in the Sacrifice of the Mass. He ever abides in His Church. "Behold, I am with you all days, even to the consummation of the world" (Mt 28:20). He, the Lord and Master, is the power that supports St. Peter and the priests and doctors of the Church. The pope, the bishops, and the priests are the instruments which Christ uses to instruct us; He, the Lord, the divine truth that never fails, teaches, commands, and works through them. The priests and the various officials of the Church work in the name and at the command of the Lord, for they derive all their power and authority from Him. There is but one properly constituted authority in the Church, and that is the authority founded on St. Peter. Christ has said, "He that heareth you, heareth Me; and he that despiseth you, despiseth Me" (Lk 10:16). The Catholic priest preaching the word of God speaks not as a mere man, not as the mere human creature we see standing before us, but as the representative of Christ. It is not Peter, nor Gregory, nor Pius who speaks from the bark of Peter, but Christ the Lord. The Church is guided in her teaching by Christ Himself, and she can endure no compromise with the spirit of the world. "Jesus Christ, yesterday, and today, and the same forever" (Heb 13:8). This thought gives us confidence and consolation. We are listening to the word and the preaching of Christ. It is really He who teaches us through His priests and bishops.

"He that heareth you, heareth Me." Why is it that since the days of the apostles the world has persecuted the priesthood of the Church? Because it hates Christ, whom it sees in the priesthood. It is always He whom they seek to persecute when they molest the priest. In union with St. Peter the priesthood answers in the name of Christ: "We ought to obey God rather than men. The God of our fathers hath raised up Jesus, whom you put to death, hanging Him upon a tree. Him hath God exalted with His right hand, to be prince and Savior, to give repentance to Israel and remission of sin. And we are witnesses of these things and the Holy Ghost, whom God hath given to all that obey Him" (Acts 5:29 ff.).

We must be prepared to support Christ in the person of His priests. We are not to be misled by human frailties, nor scandalized by any moral shortcomings we may find in the person of individual priests. We know that these deficiencies do not touch the Lord, who is the real Master and who works through His priests. "All things therefore whatsoever they shall say to you, observe and do; but according to their works do ye not" (Mt 23:3).

Even a man like St. Peter could make mistakes, but in spite of this fact Christ founded His Church on him. By his fall Peter was drawn closer to the Lord. "Simon, son of John, lovest thou Me?... Lord, Thou knowest all things; Thou knowest that I love Thee" (Jn 21:17).

Prayer

Almighty and eternal God, whose Spirit sanctifieth and penetrateth the entire body of Thy Church, answer our prayer for all ranks of Thy priesthood, that with the assistance of Thy grace they may all serve Thee faithfully. Through Christ our Lord. Amen.

Friday

In the mystery of Pentecost we received the baptism of the Spirit in order that we might preserve the life of grace, which we received at our baptism and which we are to bring to maturity in our daily lives. The Masses for the Sundays following Pentecost offer us a powerful means for accomplishing this perfection of grace in us, for they admonish us to desire the coming of the Lord. On the day when the Lord comes, He will renew within us the brightness of grace and remind us that we are the sons of God.

The Epistle for the fourth Sunday after Pentecost reminds us of the beauty of Christian virtue and of a life of self-sacrifice and suffering. To live the Christian life means to expect the coming of the Lord.

"We ourselves groan within ourselves, waiting for the adoption of the sons of God" (Epistle). "For we are saved by hope" (Rom 8:24). Our hope is well founded. The fact that we are the sons of God is our pledge of the glory that is to come. There are four witnesses who pledge that our hopes will be fulfilled: First, there is the visible creation, which, though it is subject to many infirmities because of our sins, bears testimony to the hope that some day it will be delivered from corruption and will share in the glory of the sons of God; but now it "groaneth and travaileth in pain," expecting to bring forth a new creation, a new heaven and a new earth.

The second witness is the Holy Spirit, who has been poured forth into our hearts, who "helpeth our infirmity... [and] asketh for us with unspeakable groanings" (Rom 8:26), putting the necessary prayers on our lips. Being within us, He bears witness to the glory that will be revealed in us. It is by sanctifying grace, by the grace received in the sacraments, by the illuminations and inspirations which He gives us daily, that He operates within our souls and we possess the "first fruits of the spirit" (Rom 8:23).

The third witness is the Father, He who in unmistakable terms has promised us the glorification that awaits us. "To them that love God all things work together unto good.... For whom He foreknew, He also predestined to be made conformable to the image of His Son.... And whom He predestined, them He also called. And whom He called, them He also justified. And whom He justified, them He also glorified" (Rom 8:28 ff.).

The fourth witness is Christ Jesus, who died, "yea, that is risen also again; who is at the right hand of God, who also maketh intercession for us" (Rom 8:34). Since Christ's love for us places our hope on such a firm foundation, it is only we who can fail. Nothing "shall be able to separate us from the love of God, which is in Christ Jesus our Lord" (Rom 8:39). The Father himself loves us, since we are branches of the vine, who is Christ Jesus. As the children of God we are entitled to share in His eternal glory, for since we are children, we are heirs, heirs of God and coheirs of Christ. The glory to come has not been made manifest to us, but we have the infallible hope of being made the children of God. We therefore await with fervent longing the day when the Lord will come, who will vest us, even according to our flesh, with the garments of His eternal glory. We are to be elevated above all things temporal and above the things of this world. We were made for eternity, for the life of eternal glory.

But "we suffer with Him that we may be also glorified with Him" (Rom 8:17). Here we see a picture of the Church on earth. "If they have persecuted Me, they will also persecute you" (Jn 15:20). Jesus continues His life in us. His life on earth was one of suffering, of humiliation, and of misrepresentation. Men did not cease to persecute and calumniate Him until they had crucified Him. He died and was buried, and on the third day He arose from the dead vested in the garments of His glory. That life He continues to live in His Church and in us who are the members of His mystical body. The more we become one with Him, the more we must share His suffering. "We suffer with Him that we may be also glorified with Him." Let us bear our cross cheerfully and in the spirit of fortitude, expecting the glory that will be revealed in us and being grateful that we have been allowed to walk the way of the cross with Christ. The crosses which we must carry are those of poverty, self-denial, humiliation, and rejection by the world. But Christ will return to fill us with His glory, and the promise of His coming will enlighten us and support us.

Let us accept the invitation of the Lord to "launch out into the deep," to go forth into the storms, and struggles, and trials of life. But we are not alone. "The Lord is my light and my salvation; whom, shall I fear?" (Introit.) We are convinced that "neither death, nor life, nor angels, nor principalities, nor powers, nor things present, nor things to come … shall be able to separate us from the love of God" (Rom 8:38 f.). His love for us is unfailing. He is with us, keeping His hand on the helm of our fragile bark. Therefore we can set sail with full confidence.

"We groan within ourselves, waiting for the adoption of the sons of God, the redemption of our body." Such is the attitude of the liturgy during the season after Pentecost. During this season the Church awaits the coming of her bridegroom and the time of her heavenly nuptials. Accepting the invitation of the Church, we raise our eyes above all that is temporal and fix them on the Lord, longing for His coming and for the brightness of His glorified body. "I expect the resurrection of the dead, and the life of the world to come" (Credo).

The daily descent of our Lord in the Sacrifice of the Mass gives us a pledge of His second coming and of the manifestation of the glory that shall be revealed to us as the children of God. He comes in the fullness of His majesty, hidden as yet to our mortal eyes. During Holy Communion He impresses His glorified nature ever more deeply upon our souls, and we wait patiently and with holy longing for the day of the eternal communion, when we shall participate in the revelation of His glory. "The Lord is my firmament, and my refuge, and my deliverer; my God is my helper" (Communion).

Prayer

We beseech Thee, O Lord, deign to accept our sacrifices so that having been reconciled to Thee, all our desires may by Thy mercy be conformed to Thy will. Through Christ our Lord. Amen.

Saturday

This week is a preparation for the feast of SS. Peter and Paul. As we follow them through their arduous apostolic careers, and when we see them suffering their cruel martyrdom at Rome, we become aware that their life of suffering for Christ was the source of their eternal glory. "The sufferings of this time are not worthy to be compared with the glory to come, that shall be revealed in us" (Epistle).

The liturgy for the fourth Sunday after Pentecost tells us that the Church is hard pressed, for she herself speaks of being troubled by her enemies (Introit). The spirit of the world is restless and uneasy, and it resists the work of the Church. Although the Church labors ceaselessly, casting out her nets for the souls of men through the hands of her priests, missionaries, lay apostles, and manifold institutions, she yet appears to encounter failure after failure. She seeks to capture the souls of men that she may sanctify them and save them; but humanly speaking, she, like Peter, appears to have failed in her fishing. "We have labored all night and have taken nothing." Among her own children there are many scandals, many apostates, much unfaithfulness, many traitors, many faithless ones, many sinners. These are some of the sufferings of the Church, the "sufferings of this time." How manifold are the sufferings of her children! How great are the trials that beset the Christian from the cradle to the grave! Sometimes those who are least deserving of pain suffer the most. The nearer they approach God, the more thoroughly they are purified by the fire of suffering. The more earnestly they strive to serve God, the more they are misunderstood, despised, repudiated, and persecuted by the world. Sometimes they receive like treatment even from their friends. "Because ... I have chosen you out of the world, therefore the world hateth you" (Jn 15:19). Even those who are nearest to us and whom we justly hold in high esteem, desert us. Even those in whom we trusted consider themselves justified in deserting and rejecting us. These sufferings are certainly the deepest and most bitter.

Sometimes God Himself seems to have taken the side of our enemies. He often allows those who strive most honestly to serve Him to succumb to human frailty, commit foolish mistakes, contract imperfections, and compromise themselves in the eyes of others, so that their few remaining friends begin to waver. Within their souls they experience that fearful condition which makes them think that evil has reentered their souls and brought ten other devils with it, and all good seems to have fled. Their power of resistance seems to have vanished; their imagination is plagued with vile pictures; their understanding of God and things spiritual is weakened; their will is indolent; their mind is dull; and their heart is devoid of devotion. To all this there is often added the feeling of having been forsaken by God. Such sufferings cannot be understood by anyone who has not experienced them; but we should not be surprised if they should come to us, for by our baptism we have committed ourselves to suffer and die with Christ that we might also rise with Him.

Compared to the glory we are to experience in the next world, the sufferings of this world are insignificant. Let us consider the life of St. Peter. During his earthly pilgrimage there was little in his life that was pleasing or beautiful. After the hard years of his life as a poor fisherman, he enjoys for a short time his close association with Christ. Those were his best years. His life as a missionary in Jerusalem, Antioch, and Rome was difficult, filled with bitter disappointments, beset by humiliation and persecution. Under the Emperor Nero his career is culminated by the crucifixion which Christ had foretold to him. "When thou wast younger, thou didst gird thyself and didst walk where thou wouldst. But when thou shalt be old, thou shalt stretch forth thy hands, and another shall gird thee and lead thee whither thou wouldst not" (Jn 21:18). But today he triumphs in the glory of eternal life, and the time of suffering is past. What he once considered a loss, has become his most precious gain. Through his crosses and sufferings he has merited a crown of everlasting glory. Therefore he stands before us and encourages us: "The sufferings of this time are not worthy to be compared with the glory to come." In the same spirit the Church believes and hopes, and in the same spirit we, too, must believe and hope.

In Holy Communion our Lord seeks to draw us to Himself. He asks us at the time of Holy Communion, as He did at the time of our baptism: "Can you drink the chalice that I shall drink?" (Mt 20:22.) Relying on His power, we desire to drink it. "The sufferings of this time are not worthy to be compared with the glory to come."

Having been crucified with Christ in baptism, we offer ourselves daily, while assisting at Mass, as living sacrifices together with our Lord. His power is communicated to us daily in Holy Communion and in the many actual graces which we receive. Opportunities for taking up the cross and following Him are never wanting. As yet perhaps we have not learned how to embrace cheerfully the sufferings of Christ, how to share the chalice of the Lord, how to love the cross as Christ loved it. And yet, with every cross comes grace and strength. The interior life, the life of the religious community, thrives on the cross. The cross is our salvation.

PRAYER

Grant, we beseech Thee, O Lord, that the course of this world may be so peaceably ordered by Thee that Thy Church may joyfully serve Thee in quiet devotion. Through Christ our Lord. Amen.

Fifth Sunday after Pentecost

THE MASS

The Spirit of Christ, which was poured out on the Church at Pentecost, is the Spirit of love, and it urges us to practice charity. This spirit of God and of Christ will attain a dominant position in the Church and in every member of the Church to the extent in which it is cultivated. This seed was planted in the soul at baptism and should grow to maturity. Today's liturgy seeks to instill into our hearts the spirit of love for God and for our fellow men. Charity opens the path to heavenly treasures that surpass our fondest desires. It frees the soul from the bonds of the world and even from itself. It gives wings to the soul, that it may soar above this present world and attain that goal for which it was reborn through baptism.

Imbued with this spirit, we enter the holy dwelling of the Lord, singing the Introit and lifting up our eyes to almighty God, who is our light and our salvation. We lift up our hands and pray: "Pour forth Thy love into our hearts" (Collect). We seek a love like that pictured for us in the

Epistle of the Mass, a love for God that is inseparably connected with love for our neighbor. "Dearly beloved, be ye all of one mind, having compassion one of another, being lovers of the brotherhood, merciful, modest, humble; not rendering evil for evil, nor railing for railing, but contrariwise, blessing" (Epistle). Since we need a powerful means of grace for putting this heroic love into practice, we pray in the Gradual: "Behold, O God our protector, … give ear to the prayers of Thy servants." The Alleluia verse assures us that our prayers for the spirit of charity will be answered: "In Thy strength, O Lord, the king [the baptized] shall joy; and in Thy salvation he shall rejoice exceedingly." The Gospel also announces a message of Christian charity, and is addressed especially to those who participate in today's celebration of the Sacrifice of the Mass: "If, therefore, thou offer thy gift at the altar, and there thou remember that thy brother hath anything against thee, leave there thy offering before the altar, and go first to be reconciled with thy brother; and then coming thou shalt offer thy gift." This impressive lesson we learn in the Mass shows us the great value the Church places on the spirit of charity.

Enlightened by the instruction we have received, we prepare for the Holy Sacrifice, imploring our Lord to give us the strength to follow the principles He has given us. With the visible elements of the sacrifice, the bread and wine, we lay on the altar our wills, that they may be formed in true Christian charity. There before our eyes the new Calvary becomes really and truly present, where Christ sacrifices once again the last drop of His precious blood. We hear Him utter His astounding confession of love: "Father, forgive them, for they know not what they do" (Lk 23:34). In the Consecration of the Mass the message of the Gospel and the Epistle are realized, for here is a love that renders good for evil, blessing for railing, making no reply to the most cruel persecutors except one of mercy and forgiveness. Taking this magnificent sacrifice of love into our hands, we offer it up to the heavenly Father in thanksgiving for all the graces we have received since our baptism. We offer it in expiation for our many offenses against charity, imploring our Lord that through this Holy Sacrifice our hearts may be united to His. We ask that we may share in His spirit and in the love of His heart. Like Christ, we forgive all those who have offended us, and during this sacrifice we pray with the Redeemer and in His spirit: "Father, forgive them, for they know not what they do."

Since our prayers, our sacrifices, our merits and graces belong to every other member of the mystical body, being contained, as it were, in the heart of Christ, we pray: "Our Father, … give us this day our daily bread, and forgive us our trespasses as we forgive those who trespass against us; … deliver us from evil." We reach the climax of Christian charity when we receive Holy Communion, for there we find one food, one spirit, one thought, one goal. "For we, being many, are one bread, one body, all that partake of one bread" (1 Cor 10:17). Here Christ is "our peace" (Eph 2:14), permeating us with His spirit, the spirit of love. Here at His holy table, "in the house of the Lord" (Communion), Christian charity is taught and implanted in the hearts of Christians. Here we learn to love, and our love is renewed and strengthened for the search for supernatural love. It is our duty to put into practice in our daily lives what we have received through the Holy Sacrifice.

Meditation

Today we commemorate the Sunday after the feast of SS. Peter and Paul. In times past this feast of Peter and Paul was one of the greatest feasts of the year, and in Rome all the bishops of the so-called Roman Patriarchate gathered with many pilgrims to celebrate this feast with the pope and to hold the yearly Roman council. It was a feast of harmonious love of the family of God, united with their father at the tomb of the Prince of the Apostles.

"Be ye all of one mind." With these words the Prince of the Apostles preaches the gospel of love to the congregation gathered around his tomb. "Be ye all of one mind, having compassion one of another, being lovers of the brotherhood, merciful, modest, and humble; not rendering evil for evil, nor railing for railing, but contrariwise, blessing; for unto this are you called, that you may inherit a blessing" (Epistle). This ardent wish of the Apostle is also the wish of our Holy Mother the Church; but it is more than that, it is the longing desire of the Savior Himself. It is He who prays to the Father during the Last Supper: "That they all may be one, as Thou, Father, in Me, and I in Thee; that they also may be one in Us; that the world may believe that Thou hast sent Me" (Jn 17:21). Christ wishes us to be one in faith, one in charity, one in prayer, one heart and soul, especially when partaking of the Holy Sacrifice of the Mass. We do not pray as isolated individuals, each for himself. We do not say, "O God, hear *me*"; but, "*Our* Father"; "Give *us* this day *our* daily bread"; "Let *us* pray"; "Pour forth Thy love into *our* hearts." It is clear that our prayer must be a prayer with the community, for the interests of the community, and according to their intentions and desires, their needs and wants. We must pray with the Church and her liturgy. We follow St. Peter's admonition most perfectly when, uniting ourselves with the liturgy, we subordinate our "I" to "we."

In order to be one in prayer, it is necessary, of course, that in our daily life we are one in heart and soul, "having compassion one of another, being lovers of the brotherhood, merciful, modest, humble." Such a life will be impossible without abundant grace and a spirit of charity that suppresses self and is willing to suffer everything for Christ's sake, speaking no guile, forgiving injuries, blessing all men. We shall live as we pray, and we shall pray as we live.

"Sanctify the Lord Christ in your hearts" (Epistle). When we recall the time of Nero in Rome, we see how this cruel tyrant, thirsting for the blood of the Christians, accuses them of having set fire to the city of Rome. He calls them enemies and haters of humanity, of culture, and of the state; he has them murdered in a most cruel way, and amuses himself with the sight of their agonies. But St. Peter consoles his congregation of Christians: "Who is he that can hurt you if you be zealous of good? But if also you suffer anything for justice's sake, blessed are ye. And be not afraid of their fear, and be not troubled; but sanctify the Lord Christ in your hearts" (Epistle). Look upon Christ and believe in Him. Him they accused of the worst crimes, but He held His peace and submitted humbly and patiently to the unjust condemnation to death. He did not threaten nor curse His enemies, but, asking grace and forgiveness from His Father, He prayed: "Father, forgive them, for they know not what they do" (Lk 23:34). "Sanctify the Lord Christ in your hearts"; believe in Him, follow Him, and persecution will be unable to harm you. In eternity you will be glorified with Him, as you have suffered injustice with Him. There always will be those who calumniate and persecute Christ in His Church and her members. If only we persevere in doing good, if only we are just and holy, preserving a good conscience, believing in Christ, adhering to His teachings, and following His example, that is sufficient. "The Lord is my light and my salvation; whom shall I fear?" (Introit.)

"Be ye all of one mind." "If, therefore, thou offer thy gift at the altar, and there thou remember that thy brother hath anything against thee, leave there thy offering before the altar, and go first to be reconciled to thy brother; and then coming thou shalt offer thy gift" (Gospel). How can we participate in the sacrifice of Him who offers Himself out of love for us and our brethren, while we foster anger, aversion, grudges, and uncharity in our heart? How can we, sacrificing with Him, become a holy sacrifice to the Father, while envy and jealousy, hatred and disdain contaminate our souls?

The liturgy of the Mass strongly emphasizes the fact that we can offer the Eucharistic sacrifice and share its graces and blessings only in so far as we, having renounced our own self, are devoted to each other in sincere charity. "Be ye all of one mind, having compassion one of another, being lovers of the brotherhood, merciful, modest, humble; not rendering evil for evil, … but contrariwise, blessing." Such is the spiritual disposition necessary for a fruitful celebration of the Holy Sacrifice. We therefore pray in the Agnus Dei: "Grant us peace" and a mutual harmony, that we, being one heart and one soul, may be free from any shadow of deliberate aversion, hatred, and discord. Only then are we allowed to accept the fruit of the Holy Sacrifice, Holy Communion.

Prayer

O God, who hast prepared invisible goods for those who love Thee, pour forth Thy love into our hearts, that loving Thee in all things and above all things, we may be worthy to receive Thy promises, which exceed all our desires. Through Christ our Lord. Amen.

Monday

The spirit of man separates and isolates; it is a spirit of selfishness and pride. The spirit of God, however, unites hearts in an understanding love and sincere benevolence. No sooner had the Holy Ghost come down upon the apostles and the young Church in Jerusalem on the day of Pentecost, than "the multitude of believers had but one heart and one soul; neither did any one say that aught of the things which he possessed was his own; but all things were common unto them" (Acts 4:32). "They were persevering in the doctrine of the apostles, and in the communication of the breaking of the bread, and in prayers; … praising God, and having favor with all the people" (Acts 2:42, 47). When the Spirit of God guides the hearts of men, He unites them in a holy and selfless love. His Church, therefore, receiving her life from the Spirit of Christ, must necessarily be "a covenant of love" (St. Ignatius of Antioch) and harmony, a community of love.

The model of the community of love is the triune God. "That they all may be one, as Thou, Father, in Me, and I in Thee; that they also may be one in Us" (Jn 17:21), the Father, Son, and Holy Ghost, who are a trinity of persons in a perfect unity of essence and being, of will, love, action, power, wisdom, beatitude, and glory. Likewise we also, the children of His Church, are to be one as the Father and the Son are one. "And the glory which Thou hast given Me, I have given to them; that they may be one, as We also are one" (Jn 17:22). The glory of this sonship of God has been imparted to us by Christ in the grace of our being children of God; that is, in sanctifying grace. By sanctifying grace we possess the life of the Blessed Trinity, illuminating us and working within us. Thus we also, though being many, become "one body in Christ" (Rom 12:5), one sublime community like that of the three divine Persons in God. Sanctifying grace, the sonship of God, therefore, establishes the community-forming spirit by uniting hearts and souls and by always and everywhere renouncing isolation, all self-centeredness, and the inclination to praise and sacrifice to God alone. Since it is the aim of grace that we be one as the Father, the Son, and the Holy Ghost are one, our attainment of the community spirit will be a sign of the efficaciousness of grace in us, indicating how far the Holy Ghost, the Spirit of Christ, is working within us. Practically it will be recognized by our impulse and efforts to become united with the thoughts, feelings, and efforts of the whole Church, the diocese, the parish, the family, or the religious community. The more that grace (divine life) becomes efficacious within us, the more shall we, united with Christ in the community of His Church, be able to live the life of the Father, the Son, and the Holy Ghost.

The way to community love is of a threefold nature. First it is the way of a hard, continuous, and consistent asceticism. Sunday's Epistle instructs us: "Be ye all of one mind, having compassion one of another, being lovers of the brotherhood, merciful, modest, humble; not rendering evil for evil, ... but contrariwise, blessing." The second way is set forth in the Collect: we must pray for the spirit of community love. Although our fallen nature is given to pride, selfishness, and self-sufficiency, it is, like grace itself, God's gift. The Christian community spirit is born of God in the depths of the unity of the three divine persons. The Church, therefore, has us pray: "Pour forth Thy love into our hearts, that loving Thee in all things and above all things, we may be worthy to receive Thy promises." Genuine love towards God and Christ necessarily calls for love towards our neighbor and towards the community. The third way to community love is in the Eucharistic sacrifice and Holy Communion. When we, celebrating Christ's sacrifice, become united with Him in Holy Communion, we must necessarily grow into the community of the Church. For the Holy Sacrifice is the sacrifice of the whole Church, of the community of the body of Christ and all His members. The meal of sacrifice is a real communion, a union of all in the living and life-giving bread that they eat. The more sincerely and the more perfectly we offer ourselves as victims during the Sacrifice of the Mass, the purer will be our sacrifice and the sacrifice of the Church, and the more intimate will be our union in Christ, the vine, in the community of the Church.

"Be ye all of one mind." That is the great objective of Holy Mother the Church during the weeks after Pentecost. How wonderfully fruitful was the descent of the Holy Ghost on that first Christian community! "The multitude of believers had but one heart and one soul" (Acts 4:32). How fruitful should the yearly celebration of Pentecost be in our days too, in the Church, in religious societies, and in Christian homes. But to say that the baptized of our day have "but one heart and one soul" has little meaning. Even those who should be devoted to piety, who multiply their prayers and devotions, and celebrate daily the Holy Sacrifice and partake of the holy meal, too frequently have little of that spirit. "The fruit of the Spirit is charity, joy, peace, patience, benignity, goodness, longanimity, mildness, faith, modesty, continency, chastity" (Gal 5:22 f.). Do I possess these fruits of Pentecost?

We pray that this spirit may be born in all of us. "Hear, O Lord, my voice with which I have cried to Thee; be Thou my helper, forsake me not, nor do Thou despise me, O God my Savior" (Introit). "Behold, O God our protector, and look on Thy servants" (Gradual). Destroy in all of us the great enemy of the interior unity of the members of Thy body: pride and self-love. Give us a new spirit, the spirit of selflessness and humility, that we may devote ourselves to Thee in the community of Thy body, the Church.

Prayer

O God, who hast prepared invisible goods for those who love Thee, pour forth Thy love into our hearts, that loving Thee in all things and above all things, we may be worthy to receive Thy promises, which exceed all our desires. Through Christ our Lord. Amen.

Tuesday

While in spirit we bring our gift to the altar during the Sacrifice of the Mass, the Church places these words on our lips: "I set God always in my sight; for He is at my right hand that I be not moved" (Offertory).

"I set God always in my sight." Such is the attitude of our Holy Mother the Church as she recalls all the sorrows and miseries she has experienced on her hard pilgrimage through the centuries. Always hard pressed, she is often misunderstood, hated, betrayed, forsaken, and denied even by her own children. Though she suffers terribly, she keeps her peace without being troubled. She sees the Lord in all her sufferings, and she finds Him in all her defeats, losses, and failures, as well as in her victories. He gave her the understanding that He works in and through all happenings, that all things are in His hand, that to Him is given "all power ... in heaven and in earth" (Mt 28:18), that He guides everything, governing and directing everything for the good and advantage of His Church. She trusts His wisdom and power, His love for her and for every human soul. He gave His life for His Church and for souls, He prayed, worked, and toiled during thirty-three years for His Church. And, as if this were not enough, He daily offers on innumerable altars during the Holy Sacrifice of the Mass, His body, His blood, and His heart to His Father for the salvation of the world. Praying, imploring, expiating in the tabernacle without end, He lifts up His immaculate hands to heaven. "I set God always in my sight" in the mysteries of His Incarnation, His passion and death, His life with the Father, since He is "always living to make intercession for us" (Heb 7:25). He lives among us in the mystery of the Eucharistic sacrifice and by means of His continual presence in the tabernacle. He works within the souls of men through His priesthood, through the ceaseless prayer of the Church, through the sacraments, and by interior illuminations.

"He is at my right hand that I be not moved" (Offertory). Rejoicing with these words, the Church is well aware of the fact that Christ Jesus our Lord is living and working within her, permeating His mystical body with His life. She is confident, for "the gates of hell shall not prevail against" her (Mt 16:18); "Behold, I am with you all days, even to the consummation of the world (Mt 28:20). "I will bless the Lord, who hath given me understanding" (Offertory), the faithful understanding of the mystery of her being filled and united with Christ. This understanding gives her that calm and victorious confidence in the ceaseless battles she has to fight. "He is at my right hand that I be not moved"; thus also rejoices the soul that is united with the Church. "I am the vine; you the branches" (Jn 15:5). For us He is not only the truth we must accept, not only the way, the model, and example after whom we must model our lives; He is, first of all, our life. We are to be coheirs of the life of Jesus. We are His members, His branches; He is our head; He is the vine. He feeds and nourishes us with His power that we may conquer evil and be virtuous. He lives within us that He may guide our thinking, guard, strengthen, and guide our will; that He may pray, fight, work, and suffer within us and through us, His members. "And I live, now not I; but Christ liveth in me" (Gal 2:20). "I will bless the Lord, who hath given me understanding, . . . for He is at my right hand that I be not moved" (Offertory).

"I set God always in my sight," not only as a model and example, as the teacher of truth, as all-knowing, before whose judgment seat I shall some day have to give an account of my stewardship, but also as the Lord who loves, protects, and guides me, who works, fights, and conquers within me by the power of His almighty hand. Why do I fear the difficulties of my daily life? Why do I get discouraged when I consider my own weaknesses, the power of temptation, my passions, and my bad habits? If only we would lift our eyes more to the Lord and trust His power to work within us, our lives would be happier, more joyful, more free, and more fruitful.

"I set God always in my sight" that I may serve Him, devoting myself to Him without hesitation, and trying to discover His will, that I may fulfill it.

"I set God always in my sight" that I may go to Him with everything I have to face during the day, thanking Him, confessing my helplessness before Him, and asking for His power and assistance. Every problem of my soul should find its solution in a look upon Him, in a short prayer to Him, in an act of thanksgiving, or love, or confidence, or repentance, or intercession. "He is at my right hand that I be not moved."

Prayer

O God, who hast prepared invisible goods for those who love Thee, pour forth Thy love into our hearts, that loving Thee in all things and above all things, we may be worthy to receive Thy promises, which exceed all our desires. Through Christ our Lord. Amen.

Wednesday

With the Church we pray to God that He may pour forth His love into our hearts, so that we may love Him in all things and above all things. The Spirit of Pentecost, which we have received, is a spirit of love. But in order to love God in all things, we must, first of all, see Him in all things.

We should see God in all things. Being engaged in many works and duties, we have to deal with many different kinds of people; some of these are kind to us, some are indifferent, and some are even hostile toward us. We are subjected to various sufferings, weaknesses, inconveniences, ailments, trials, and temptations. Wherever we are, we encounter puzzling problems and disasters that spell tragedy in our own life or in that of others. We enjoy health, nature, culture, the gifts of the spirit, of the heart, of the body, and prosperity and grace; we mourn the loss of those who are dear to us and of things that we treasure. We torture ourselves with the fear of evils that may befall us, of inconveniences that may come upon us, of insults that may be inflicted upon us, of work that may be too hard for us. We are anxious about our well-being, our health, the development of our business, our relationship with other people, our reputation, and our standing with those in high positions. We wish to enjoy the pleasures of life, those that are noble and those that are less so, devoting much of our time and energy to them. But we do not see the most important element, both in men and occurrences; we do not see God who operates in all things. We overlook God's plan, His all-wise, all-loving, and all-powerful providence; we fail to perceive His nearness, His hand working in all things. That we see God in all things is the first and most important step to an interior life. Our very purpose on earth is to know God, to see Him in everything, in all happenings and experiences, be they small or great. We should see the hand of God in all our trials, whether they come directly from God or by means of men. Nothing can happen to us without God's permission. If we wish to reach God, we must learn to see Him working in every creature. We must see in Him a Father who loves us, and then the way to the love of God will be open to us.

We should love God in all things. If we live only according to the suggestions of our fallen nature, then we love only ourselves in things about us. If we seek only our own pleasures, our own honor, our own interests and enjoyments, we make ourselves the center of life and accommodate ourselves to things and men that we may get the most with the least effort. That spirit is our own depravity and egotism expressing itself, that spirit is the result of a deeply ingrained pride. The grace of the Holy Spirit will destroy this depravity in us and teach us to pursue a higher aim, the love of almighty God. To love God in everything is to accept everything that life may have in store for us as coming from the holy, all-wise, benevolent hand of God. It is to submit our will to the dispensations of divine providence with humility and a loving devotion, and to surrender unconditionally to the will and commands of God, as expressed in the sufferings, losses, inconveniences, and disturbances which befall us. Thus we acquire an honest desire never to follow our own will, our own whims, our own wishes, but to accept and do whatever pleases God and whatever corresponds to His holy will. We must embrace our sufferings and difficulties, first of all, because such an acceptance of suffering is pleasing to Him. We accept them because they come from His hand, knowing that the Lord gives and the Lord takes away. When we attain this spirit, we can truly say that we love God in all things, that we embrace His will in all things, that we will only what He wills. In this manner we shall truly live for the honor and glory of God.

The feast of Pentecost teaches us that we must see and love God in all things. God wishes to lift us above all that is purely human, above all human desires and ambitions, and to establish us in the realm of the spirit. When once the soul has been stripped of its blindness and egotism, it is impervious to restlessness, worry and excitement. It is then no longer conscious of anything but the love, honor, and interests of God. It finds peace and rest and protection in God, and prays: "Come, Holy Ghost, fill the hearts of Thy faithful. Teach us to see and love God in all things."

Let us, therefore, try to see and love God in all things and to surrender to His will in all things. Only in this way can we be freed from our inordinate attachment to men, from undue attention to our work, from an unseemly devotion to the things of this world. Only in this way can we achieve freedom of soul and shake off our dependence on the joys and pleasures of this life. Only in this way can we acquire a holy indifference to the sufferings, difficulties, and trials of this life. We must seek to acquire fortitude for the sufferings, sacrifices, and difficulties that may befall us. We must achieve complete domination over all our natural inclinations, over our impatience, our sensuality, our pride, our ambition, and our lack of charity. We should walk continually in the presence of God, speaking to Him from a heart that is free, calm, and united to Him. "Come Holy Ghost, fill the hearts of Thy faithful."

Prayer

O God, who hast prepared invisible goods for those who love Thee, pour forth Thy love into our hearts, that loving Thee in all things and above all things, we may be worthy to receive Thy promises, which exceed all our desires. Through Christ our Lord. Amen.

Thursday

The Collect expresses the great desire of the Church: "Pour forth Thy love into our hearts" that we may love Thee "in all things and above all things." The Spirit of Christ living and working within our souls urges us to this love. So we, too, making the intention of the community our own personal intention, beseech God that He may give us the grace to truly love Him above all things.

May we love Thee "in all things and above all things." We aspire to love. It is our only sentiment worthy of God, who made it the great commandment. It is the only sentiment that can truly change our heart by directing it towards God and disengaging it from creatures, by enlarging and strengthening it to do and suffer everything for God. When we truly love God, we are determined to sacrifice and lose everything rather than offend or displease Him; we desire nothing more than what He wills and as He wills it. Placing our one happiness above all earthly values, pleasures, and riches, we are willing to leave father and mother, to renounce earthly love, to postpone everything agreeable life might offer us, in order to live for Him, to promote His honor, to please Him. We say with the Apostle: "The things that were gain to me, the same I have counted loss for Christ. Furthermore I count all things to be but loss for the excellent knowledge of Jesus Christ my Lord,... and count them but as dung, that I may gain Christ" (Phil 3:7 f.). We understand what Christ meant when He said: "He that loveth father or mother more than Me, is not worthy of Me; and he that loveth son or daughter more than Me, is not worthy of Me" (Mt 10:37). God must be preferred in all things and above all things. His holy will must be sought always. God and His holy will should be our only thought, our only desire, the world around which everything centers. If we place Him and His will and honor above everything else, we forget ourselves, embracing pain as well as joy, poverty as well as abundance, sickness as well as health.

Love is above any other motive. The natural man acts from purely natural motives: a noble man from noble motives, an egoistic and wicked one from egoistic, perverted, and sinful motives. But even the Christian, trying to achieve the perfection of a Christian life, finds within himself a frightening tendency to place the consideration of his ego before all his motives. Even he is always tempted to think first of his own advantage, his own satisfaction instead of God, His will, and His honor; the habit of thinking of himself first and of seeking himself first is so deep-rooted even in the good and spiritual minded, that he is hardly aware how much he is moved by reasons other than the love of God. To love God above all things does not mean we must exclude other noble motives. It means only that other motives, however noble and good, must be subordinated to the motive of the love of God. The first and decisive motive governing all other motives in the true Christian is the love of God. The true Christian accepts whatever befalls him because such a happening is ordained by God and is permitted by Him. But we all have the bad habit of seeking ourselves first. We must oppose to this bad habit, not merely an occasional act or intention, but a good habit of seeking God first. In all things we should look to Christ and to God first, accepting all sacrifices and trials as coming from His hand.

"Pour forth Thy love into our hearts." Love makes us forgetful of ourselves and ready to sacrifice everything rather than displease God in the smallest matter. Love values the happiness of pleasing Him above every other good, and renders us more jealous of our friendship with Him than of that with anyone else in this world. Such a love considers His slightest wish as a command. Such a love disregards mere human considerations, despises the threats or enticements of those who would turn it away from the will of God, which it wishes to see accomplished in all things.

Who can lead us to the possession of such a love? Holy Mother the Church teaches us that we must pray and sacrifice with her in order to obtain it. Let us place this petition on the paten which our Lord holds in His hands as He offers Himself with us and for us today. His prayer will make our petition efficacious with the Father, for during Holy Communion the ardor of His divine love for the Father will be ours also.

The more intensely and the more purely we love, the more we sanctify Christ in our hearts and lives, showing forth His nature and His spirit.

Prayer

O God, who hast prepared invisible goods for those who love Thee, pour forth Thy love into our hearts, that loving Thee in all things and above all things, we may be worthy to receive Thy promises, which exceed all our desires. Through Christ our Lord. Amen.

Friday

"If therefore thou offer thy gift at the altar, and there thou remember that thy brother hath anything against thee, leave there thy offering before the altar, and go first to be reconciled to thy brother; and then coming thou shalt offer thy gift" (Gospel).

"Blessed are the peacemakers" (Mt 5:9). Our Lord and Savior knows no "eye for an eye, and a tooth for a tooth." Rather He came into this world as the Prince of Peace. "On earth peace to men of good will" (Lk 2:14), sang the angels on the holy night of His birth. "Peace be to you" (Jn 20:21), He greets His apostles. When leaving this world He leaves His peace with us. He commands His apostles to bring peace into the houses they enter (Mt 10:12). Their feet should be "shod with the preparation of the gospel of peace" (Eph 6:15). "The peace of God, which surpasseth all understanding" (Phil 4:7), is the end of their apostolic work. Christ Himself is the living peace. His soul knows no storms, but only the strong and deep peace of being safe in God. Even when His enemies speak evil against Him, even when they annoy Him and offend Him, even when they scourge Him, and crown Him with thorns, and crucify Him, He is neither excited nor disturbed. His life always is a life of peace. In His presence turbulent minds grow calm, and even those possessed by evil spirits become peaceful. The rage of the furious sea subsides in His presence, tears are dried, and even God's just anger with the wickedness of humanity is disarmed. His peace-loving soul and His message of peace are the weapons wherewith He conquers His enemies and protects His followers. How much injustice they inflicted on Him! With how much evil they pursued Him! What good reason

He had to be angry, to demand justice, to ask the Father to send Him legions of angels that they might destroy His enemies! But instead He covers all the iniquity and blindness of men with His mantle of love, impressing the sign of peace on them: "Father, forgive them, for they know not what they do" (Lk 23:34). Indeed, "Blessed are the peacemakers."

"If thou offer thy gift at the altar." We daily offer our gift of bread and wine at the altar, and with bread and wine we offer ourselves and our will to live entirely for God. We are most sincere in our self-immolation. We expect, therefore, His countenance to shine graciously upon us, as it once shone upon Abel's sacrifice. "For God loveth a cheerful giver" (2 Cor 9:7). But there is another dark shadow on our soul; perhaps we are troubled by some tension, some ill-feeling, some discord with our brother, perhaps on account of a mere trifle. The guilt is, to some degree at least, on our side. Neither will speak the first word of peace. The world is big enough that we can avoid each other and find our way to God without our brother. One enmity or friendship more or less can hardly matter. Thus we come to the altar asking God's blessing; but there awaits us an unexpected reception: "Leave there thy offering before the altar, and go first to be reconciled to thy brother."

"Blessed are the peace-makers." They alone will reap the full blessing of the Holy Sacrifice. No one can celebrate the Sacrifice of the Mass and gain its blessing for his own self alone without his brother. The Mass is, by its very essence, the sacrifice of the entire body of Christ united in holy love, a sacrifice of the community. Together we pray; together we sacrifice; together the priest and the entire congregation offer to God this divine gift. We offer this sacrifice for all here present, for the entire Catholic Church in the whole world. How could we possibly offer this sacrifice worthily if we, through our own guilt, are the cause of discord with only one member of this community. If, during the day, we want to offer our efforts, work, and sufferings to God, but live, through our own guilt, in disharmony with a brother in Christ, we shall hear again: "Leave there thy offering. I am not inclined to accept it." And coming to the tabernacle, offering Him our heart, we shall hear again: "Leave there thy offering. It cannot please Me. Go first to be reconciled to thy brother. Make peace." The altar is a place of peace. He who lives in discord is not allowed to approach it.

How few there are who take the Lord's warning seriously! "If thou offer thy gift at the altar, and there thou remember that thy brother hath anything against thee, leave there thy offering before the altar, and go first to be reconciled to thy brother." There is too much excitement, nervousness, tension, and discord among those who sacrifice even daily, too much of the "eye for an eye, tooth for a tooth" attitude of the Old Testament. Is it not time for us to take our Lord's warning seriously? Is He not bound to tell us, when we come to the Holy Sacrifice: Either have peace with thy brother, or keep thy offering? It is love toward our neighbor that counts.

"Except your justice abound more than that of the scribes and Pharisees, you shall not enter into the kingdom of heaven" (Gospel). Wherein is our justice and piety tested? It is tested in our will to love our brother and work with him. Love opens the door to the altar, to the common sacrifice of Christ and His Church, to the reception of Holy Communion.

Prayer

We beseech Thee, O Lord, to look down upon our prayers and graciously accept these gifts of Thy servants and handmaids, that what each has offered to the honor of Thy name may profit all unto salvation. Through Christ our Lord. Amen.

Saturday

Today's liturgy combines the love of God and of our neighbor. The prayers of the Church earnestly ask for a love of God by which we can love Him above all things and in all things. The Epistle and Gospel urge us to love our neighbor, for the love of God and of our neighbor cannot be separated.

"If any man say: I love God, and hateth his brother; he is a liar. For he that loveth not his brother, whom he seeth, how can he love God, whom he seeth not?" (1 Jn 4:20.) Why must this be so? Because the love of God and of neighbor are one and the same love. We love our brother for the sake of God, that is, with the same love with which we love God and Christ. Taking more than a merely human viewpoint, we look at man with the eyes of God and see in him a child of God, in whom the Father is well pleased. We see in him the soul redeemed by the blood of the Savior, the soul for which the Son of God became man and was lifted up on the cross, the soul for which He instituted the Church and the sacraments. Seeing in our fellow man a member of the body of Christ, we know that whatever we do to the member we do to the head, which is Christ the Lord. "Amen I say to you, as long as you did it to one of these My least brethren, you did it to Me." And likewise: "Amen I say to you, as long as you did it not to one of these least, neither did you do it to Me" (Mt 25:40, 45). This is the chief characteristic of Christian charity: it is inseparably united with our love for God and Christ. Reminding us of this unity, the Mass for the fifth Sunday after Pentecost tells us that we can love God and the Savior only in so far as we love our brother. For he who does not love his brother, cannot love God.

"This is My commandment, that you love one another as I have loved you" (Jn 15:12). How faithfully and devotedly Jesus has loved us! So we, too, must love our brother and our sister, both as regards their temporal welfare and as regards the care of their soul and their eternal salvation. Who will fulfill this commandment of the Lord? Since self-love is evidently the greatest foe of charity, only he can fulfill this command who has conquered self-love, which makes us so self-centered that it causes us to look upon our neighbor as a stranger for whom we need have no concern. It stirs within us the spirit of egoism, jealousy, pride, envy, and hatred, rendering impossible any perfect love towards our fellow man. It leads us to commit a thousand offenses against charity, for it makes us insensible, cold, ill-disposed, unjust, partial, bitter. If we, therefore, wish to fulfill the commandment of Christian charity, we must die to the love of self; this we will do only in so far as we are filled with love for God and Christ. The love of God and the love of self are like the two arms of a scale; the one can go up only if the other goes down. The love of self disappears in the same degree as the love for God fills our soul. For this reason the love of our neighbor can be practiced only if we have true love for God. The more perfectly we possess this love of God, the more perfectly we will also practice the love of our neighbor; these two belong so inseparably together that the love of our neighbor will be possible only if we have the love of God within us.

"Pour forth Thy love into our hearts" that we may love Thee "in all things and above all things" (Collect). If the love of God is within us, we will also love our neighbor. Then we will be "all of one mind, having compassion one of another, being lovers of the brotherhood, merciful, modest, humble; not rendering evil for evil, nor railing for railing, but contrariwise blessing" each other, "for unto this [we] are called, that [we] may inherit a blessing." Then we shall also "refrain [our] tongue from evil, and [our] lips that they speak no guile" (Epistle).

"Except your justice abound more than that of the scribes and Pharisees, you shall not enter into the kingdom of heaven" (Gospel). What is it that makes Christian justice and perfection tower so far above the so-called justice of the scribes and Pharisees? Is it not that we take the proper attitude toward charity? "You have heard that it was said to them of old: Thou shalt not kill. And whosoever shall kill, shall be in danger of the judgment. But I say to you, that whosoever is angry with his brother, shall be in danger of the judgment.... And whosoever shall say: Thou fool, shall be in danger of hell fire" (Gospel). "A new commandment I give unto you: That you love one another, as I have loved you, that you also love one another" (Jn 13:34).

The measure of our love for God and our Savior, of our entire interior life, and of our piety, is determined by the degree of our charity towards our fellow man. "We know that we have passed from death to life, because we love the brethren. He that loveth not, abideth in death" (1 Jn 3:14).

Prayer

O God, who hast prepared invisible goods for those who love Thee, pour forth Thy love into our hearts, that loving Thee in all things and above all things, we may be worthy to receive Thy promises, which exceed all our desires. Through Christ our Lord. Amen.

Sixth Sunday after Pentecost

The Mass

On this Sunday the Easter motif resounds through the texts and songs of the Mass. The graces given to us through baptism and the Holy Eucharist at Easter and planted in our hearts as living seeds, are to grow and ripen under the breath of the Spirit of Pentecost.

Filled with gratitude as we enter the house of God, we look back at all the aids to salvation we received on Easter. Through holy baptism we became "His people," "His anointed," and He became our "strength," "the protector of [our] salvation" (Introit). How could we ever preserve the wonderful gift of supernatural life without His aid? To our gratitude for the past days of grace we add our prayers for the future: "Save, O Lord, Thy people, and bless Thy inheritance, and rule them forever" (Introit). Here we ask that the supernatural goods of Easter may be preserved and increased. We fortify this prayer with our *Kyrie eleison* and *Gloria in excelsis:* "Thou who takest away the sins of the world, receive our prayer." "Implant in our hearts the love of Thy name, increase in us true religion" (Collect).

The first and most fundamental of the supernatural gifts is the grace of baptism, by which we are made Christians. "All we who are baptized in Christ Jesus are baptized in His death; for we are buried together with Him by baptism unto death" (Epistle). We are buried, but only in order to rise with Him to a truly supernatural and divine life that is not of this world. That is the meaning of baptism and the essence of our Christian life. "If we be dead with Christ, we believe that we shall live also together with Christ" (Epistle). When the natural man within us has been changed and we become other Christs, the supernatural food given us by Christ bears fruit a hundredfold. Baptism is the door that leads to the Holy Eucharist. Christ still has "compassion on the multitude," on those liable to succumb in the desert of their earthly pilgrimage. When Christ, moved by loving compassion, deals out the bread of life to His people, we gratefully answer the message of the Gospel announcing the Eucharist with our Credo, and implore Him again: "Perfect Thou my goings in Thy paths, … show forth Thy wonderful mercies" (Offertory), as Thou didst show forth Thy mercies toward the hungry people in the Gospel.

Repeating the miracle of His mercy and love for us during the Sacrifice of the Mass, Christ revives the wonderful scene we witnessed in the Epistle and Gospel. We are again mysteriously "buried together with Him … unto death" in the renewal of the sacrifice of the cross on our altar. There "our old man is crucified with Him, that the body of sin may be destroyed, and that we may serve sin no longer" (Epistle). For we are baptized and came to celebrate Mass that we, being sacrificed with our crucified Lord, might be one with Him in death and resurrection. "If we have been planted together in the likeness of His death, we shall also be in the likeness of His resurrection" (Epistle). Being sacrificed with Christ, we have, as it were, stepped out of the realm of earthly things, escaped the allurements and pleasures of the world, and established ourselves in the kingdom of God, thinking His thoughts, seeking His interests, searching for His goodness and beatitude. Here we wish to live through Christ, with Him, and in Him, rendering in eternity all honor to God, who alone is worthy of all praise.

We must now live for God alone, obeying His holy commandments, seeking His holy will, and performing the duties He assigns to us in everyday life. We are like the people of the Gospel, retiring with Him from the world to go into the desert, where He plans to enrich us with a wonderful food, the sacrificial meal of Holy Communion. Through the power of this food we are enabled to keep aloof from the world in the desert where we have been led by baptism and where we are to be "alive to God, in Christ Jesus our Lord" (Epistle). Verily, "the Lord is the strength of His people, and the protector of the salvation of His anointed" (Introit).

Meditation

We have been baptized (Epistle), and we are partakers of the Holy Eucharist (Gospel). Both baptism and the Holy Eucharist, having been planted as seeds in our souls, are to grow and ripen into a Christian life under the warmth of the Spirit of Pentecost.

"All we who are baptized in Christ Jesus are baptized in His death. For we are buried together with Him by baptism unto death.… Knowing this, that our old man is crucified with Him, that the body of sin may be destroyed, and that we may serve sin no longer.… Now if we be dead with Christ, we believe that we shall live also together with Christ, knowing that Christ, rising again from the dead, dieth now no more.… For in that He died to sin, He died once; but in that He liveth, He liveth unto God" (Epistle). St. Paul gives us a description of the Christian as God and His Church want him to be, a man dead to sin. Sin is no longer to have dominion over him. Because he died to sin with Christ, he now lives with Christ, having become a living branch of the vine which is Christ. He lives as another Christ, devoted to God and loved by Him. If we could only realize the importance of baptism as the Christians of the first centuries did; if we would live, as they did, only for the things given us in baptism, we also would die to sin, living Christ's life and experiencing the sublime dignity and riches of the Christian way of life.

"A great multitude" followed our Lord into the solitude of the desert that they might hear His word. They have now been with Him three days and have nothing to eat. Therefore, calling His disciples together, He tells them; "I have compassion on the multitude.... If I shall send them away fasting to their home, they will faint in the way." Seeing no solution to this problem, the disciples ask Him: "From whence can anyone fill them here with bread in the wilderness?" They have only seven loaves of bread left. Taking the loaves and giving thanks, He broke the bread and gave it to His disciples to set before the people. "And they did eat, and were filled" (Gospel). The liturgy sees in us the multitude that followed Christ into the desert. In baptism we have avowed: "I renounce Satan and all his works. I believe in God the Father. I believe in Jesus Christ, His Son, our Lord. I believe in the Holy Ghost, the Holy Catholic Church, the communion of saints, the resurrection of the body, and life everlasting." Having made up our mind to live for God and for Christ, we have followed Him. "In the desert," removed from the world and from its principles and all it stands for, we listen to Christ, partaking of His spirit, of His love of poverty, of His humility, of His crosses and sufferings. Lest we faint on the rough road through the desert, each morning He offers us the Holy Eucharist through the hand of His disciples, the priests. By the strength of this food we live the new life into which we have been baptized. Having died to sin, we live together with God in Christ Jesus, sharing His life as branches on the vine.

"So do you also reckon yourselves to be dead indeed to sin, but alive to God; in Christ Jesus our Lord" (Epistle). Having become members of Christ, we relive Christ's death and resurrection during our earthly pilgrimage. "Christ is our way; let us observe Him. He suffered to enter into His glory. He embraced being despised in order to be exalted. He died, but rose again" (St. Augustine).

"He was delivered up for our sins, and rose again for our justification" (Rom 4:25). We also repeat in our lives the mysteries of Christ, which unite us with Him in His life and death. "Buried with Him in baptism, in whom also you are risen again by the faith of the operation of God, who hath raised Him up from the dead. And you, when you were dead in your sins and the uncircumcision of your flesh, He hath quickened together with Him, forgiving you all offenses" (Col 2:12 f.).

All our greatness, all our supernatural dignity, derives from baptism, which enriched us with divine life by uniting us with Christ. Whatever excellence natural human life may appear to have, it is really night, death, and vanity compared with that life we received in baptism. Only through the grace of baptism does our life receive its dignity and value for eternity. On the day of our baptism we were born for life eternal. Through sanctifying grace, which we received at baptism, we carry within ourselves the pledge of the glorious life to come. It is our foremost duty to be ever thankful for God's mercy and grace.

Prayer

O God of power, from whom are all good things, implant in our hearts the love of Thy name, increase in us true religion, nourish us with all goodness, and by Thy mercy keep us in the same. Through Christ our Lord. Amen.

Monday

"The Lord is the strength of His people, and the protector of the salvation of His anointed" (Introit). We are His people in the community of the Church; we are His "anointed" (Christians), having been anointed with holy chrism in baptism: "I anoint thee with the oil of salvation in Christ Jesus our Lord, that thou mayest have life everlasting." The Sunday Gospel explains how He is "the strength of His people and the protector of the salvation of His anointed."

"There was a great multitude with Jesus" in the desert, and they had nothing to eat. They followed Him, eager to listen to His words and happy to be in His presence. We are that multitude. We were united with Jesus in baptism, when, with joyful devotion, we confessed: "I believe in Jesus Christ, and in the communion of saints." Today we also acknowledge Him, His gospel, His principles, and His example; we try to keep faithfully what we promised in baptism. Daily we renounce again, even more perfectly than we did yesterday, Satan, sin, self-love, and the vanities and pleasure of life. The world has many followers, even among the baptized, who do not keep the promises they made to Christ, refusing, more or less, to follow Him, because to follow Him is too hard for them, too uncomfortable, too much out of date, and offers too few advantages. Let us follow our Lord all the more faithfully into the desert, on the rough roads of voluntary renunciation and poverty, rejoicing in hard work, sufferings of all kind, and humiliations and offenses inflicted by our fellow men. To be with Him and to have Him is all that matters. "Seek ye therefore first the kingdom of God and His justice" (Mt 6:33). As members of Christ we know that we are united with Him in the most intimate communion of life. His salvation and His grace have been poured forth into our souls in abundance. "He that followeth Me, walketh not in darkness" (Jn 8:12). We have been delivered "from the power of darkness, and translated into the kingdom of the Son of His love" (Col 1:13). Thus we become "fellow citizens of the saints," of the strong and the pure of heart, "domestics of God" (Eph 2:19), in order to become hereafter "joint heirs with Christ," the Son of God (Rom 8:17). We follow Him, knowing no one else to whom we may give our hearts, our mind, our strength, and our life.

"I have compassion on the multitude." The multitude had already been with the Lord three days and had nothing to eat. His compassionate and merciful heart urges Him to provide for them, that they may go home contented. We are this multitude. Following the Lord on the hard and rough road of this life, we must face a long journey which leads us through desert trails, over hot sand and under burning sun, with hardly a single oasis to offer us shade and refreshing water. How are we to reach our home with the heavenly Father? Are we not sure to faint in the way? But "the Lord is the strength of His people, and the protector of the salvation of His anointed." Being miraculously nourished by the bread of the Holy Eucharist, we shall attain our goal, fortified by this food. We daily witness on our altars the miracle of the consecration of bread into His holy body and of wine into His holy blood. Commanding His disciples, the priests of the Church, to administer this bread to the baptized, He works the miracle of His omnipotence daily at the Consecration during the Mass. Through the miracle of love and self-sacrifice for us in Holy Communion, He is indeed "the strength of His people, and the protector of the salvation of His anointed." Blessed are they that follow the Lord into the desert; He takes care of them through the manna of the Holy Eucharist.

During the Sacrifice of the Mass we offer the few loaves of bread which the Gospel speaks of, and He works in them a marvelous miracle. He changes the few pieces of bread, the hosts, into His own body, feeding therewith the souls of those who hunger after Him and His life.

He asks so little of us: a small renunciation, the abandonment of some reading we like or some curious look or question; or He may wish us to overcome some inordinate affection or to control our impatience. For some small sacrifice made out of love for Him, He will work in our souls the wonder of interior enlightenment, of deliverance from some evil, of an increase of grace.

"Alleluia, alleluia. In Thee, O Lord, have I hoped, let me never be confounded; deliver me in Thy justice, and release me; bow down Thy ear to me, make haste to deliver me. Alleluia." We must have confidence, for the Lord has "compassion on the multitude." "Save, O Lord, Thy people, and bless Thy inheritance, and rule them forever" (Introit).

Prayer

O Lord, who hath nourished us with Thy gifts in Holy Communion, grant, we beseech Thee, that they may be efficacious in our souls, purifying and protecting us with the help of Thy grace. Amen.

Tuesday

We are emphatically reminded today of the meaning of our Christian faith. Our "old man," ruined by Adam's fall and born in sin, has been buried with Christ in baptism. He lies in the tomb as one dead. The new man, coming forth from the waters of baptism, an image of our Lord rising out of the sepulcher, carries within himself the life of grace and the sonship of God. The baptism which we once received means death and life.

"We are buried together with Him by baptism unto death" (Epistle). God originally intended that we should enter this life as sons of God and partakers of the divine life, possessing sanctifying grace, the virtues, and the gifts of the Holy Spirit. Thwarting this plan of God, Adam through his sin lost for himself and all mankind, whose head and representative he was, the grace and right to the heritage awaiting us in heaven. But God had mercy on us. He sent His Son that He, as the new head of humanity, might atone for man's offense against God. The entire earthly life of the Savior until the consummation of His sacrifice on the cross, bears the character of death and sacrifice. Since He was the lamb that takes upon Himself the sins of the world, God placed the whole burden of man's sins upon Him. From the first moment of His earthly existence He consents to whatever the Father has prepared for Him. Thus His life becomes a continual sacrifice. His humiliation in Bethlehem, the flight from the persecution of Herod, the hatred of His enemies during His public life, His passion and death on the cross, prove Him to be the lamb of sacrifice that is carried to be a victim (Jer 11:19), the worm that is trod upon, according to the words of the Psalmist (Ps 21:7).

"We are buried together with Him by baptism unto death." By our baptism we have been united with His life of continuous sacrifice, suffering, and renunciation. We always bear "about in our body the mortification of Jesus" (2 Cor 4:10). Being crucified with Him, we drink the chalice of suffering with Him. What has been written of Him has to be said of us too: "Ought not Christ to have suffered these things and so to enter into His glory?" (Lk 24:26.) "We are buried together with Him by baptism unto death." Having been immersed in His death, we became partakers of His sacrifice and death.

"As Christ is risen from the dead by the glory of the Father, so we also may walk in newness of life" (Epistle). Through His resurrection our Lord began a new life. Having only one guiding principle, "I do always the things that please Him" (Jn 8:29), Christ lived during His mortal life only for the Father. But whereas His passion and death were necessary, since during His earthly life the sins of humanity lay upon Him, after His resurrection He can neither die nor suffer any longer. Humanity's indebtedness to God has been discharged and atoned for. Now He has the fullness of life, stability, and security. "Death shall no more have dominion over Him.... In that He liveth, He liveth unto God" (Epistle). In His risen body everything combines to show forth the fullness of life. This glorious life has the fullness of liberty and spirituality, of impassibility and incorruptibility; it is occupied by incessant thanksgiving and praise of the Father, and will be crowned after forty days by His Ascension into heaven, where Christ shall sit at the right hand of the Father. "So we also may walk in newness of life." For just as Christ, rising from the dead, left in the sepulcher the linen cloth, the symbol of His ability to suffer and die, and proceeded from death to a new life; so, too, our souls, having been purified by the waters of baptism, were freed from sin and embellished with the life of grace and the splendor of divine life. We walk "in newness of life," in the power and glory of the life of grace. Having been planted like a mustard seed in our souls, grace must grow and must be kept alive in the fight against evil concupiscence within us and in the world around us, gaining strength by our striving daily more effectively after all virtue and sanctity.

Death and life! The more complete our death, the fuller our life will be. No man can serve two masters, God and mammon. Neither can any one serve God and sin, the new man and the old man within himself. Christianity demands character, steadfastness of principles, clear thinking, and manliness.

Celebrating the Holy Sacrifice with our Lord, we die unto ourselves, sacrificing ourselves with the bread to obtain the newness of life. By this union in sacrifice with our self-sacrificing Lord, we re-enact daily within ourselves the mystery of death and life. Thus we have died to sin and live for God in Christ Jesus, in the power of the Holy Sacrifice and of Holy Communion.

Thus we struggle day after day to die completely to ourselves in order to gain a perfect life. This life will be ours for all eternity when the Lord will address us: "Well done, good and faithful servant;... enter thou into the joy of thy Lord" (Mt 25:21).

Prayer

O God of power, from whom are all good things, implant in our hearts the love of Thy name, increase in us true religion, nourish us with all goodness, and by Thy mercy keep us in the same. Through Christ our Lord. Amen.

Wednesday

The divine life, which we first received through baptism, has been implanted in us as a seed. We must develop it by continuously cooperating with the grace of the Holy Spirit.

The death of sin was effected in baptism. But the law of salvation demands that the life of grace be incessantly fostered, renewed, and confirmed. Through Adam's sin we lost all supernatural goods with one stroke. Though God returns to us through the sacrament of baptism the divine gift of His grace and sonship, we do not receive it with the perfection and strength that was given to Adam. Despite the fact that Original Sin and all personal sins are forgiven by baptism, and that sanctifying grace is again poured into our soul, evil concupiscence remains within us, and as the source of sin it threatens to destroy the divine life within us. By impairing the judgment, it makes us amenable to the allurements of this world and of the flesh, and places us in continual danger of being unfaithful to God and our baptism. Even after baptism evil concupiscence remains in our hearts that we may always remember our fallen state and learn to understand what bottomless depths of moral corruption and depravity there are within us. This understanding should help us to recognize our helplessness and sinfulness so that we may cling to God and seek His grace. It should aid us, furthermore, in our continual struggle against sin, passion, and the allurements of the world, so that we may, of our own accord, determine to adhere to God and a virtuous life.

Though we are really dead to sin, our dying to ourselves must continue because of the concupiscence we carry within us, which captivates us as "the law of sin that is in my members" (Rom 7:23). We must maintain a persevering and unyielding resistance to Satan and a continual renunciation of the insinuations of the devil and the allurements of the flesh and the world.

"Be renewed in the spirit of your mind; and put on the new man, who according to God is created in justice and holiness of truth" (Eph 4:23 f.). Grace, the source of our supernatural life, urges us to become men of action. The kingdom of God is within us. Being but a germ, however, like the mustard seed of the Gospel, it must grow into a great tree. "He that is just, let him be justified still" (Apoc 22:11). No one in this world is so perfect that he cannot attain greater perfection. We have an obligation to strive for perfection. There is no fixed measure of virtue or faith or love for God and men, to which more cannot still be added. If we stop striving after perfection in grace and virtue, we cease to be perfect; that is, we no longer are what we ought to be according to the commandment of God. For this is our perfection on earth, that we make the life of grace and virtue within us grow each day. Such growth requires continual progress. Once we lag behind or start losing ground, it is our duty to take up our struggle with renewed zeal. To stand still is impossible for us, for nothing created remains unchanged. Either it grows or it languishes; we either go ahead, or we fall back. We must either penetrate deeper into God and Christ, or God and Christ will withdraw. With good reason, then, many saints bound themselves by vow to progress unceasingly in grace and virtue. Knowing the weakness of human nature, its cowardice and inconstancy, they were aware how easily they might start to waste time and grace, and fall far short of their fixed goal. "Be renewed in the spirit of your mind, and put on the new man, who according to God is created in justice and holiness of truth" (Eph 4:23 f.). By baptism we become members of the body of Christ, called upon to live His life so that we are gradually "transformed into the same image" (2 Cor 3:18). To reflect the fullness of Christ's grace and virtue is our foremost obligation.

Death and life renew themselves again and again in our life since the hour of our baptism. We must put life to death for life's sake. "He must increase, but I must decrease" (Jn 3:30). "As many of you as have been baptized in Christ, have put on Christ" (Gal 3:27), not like a garment, exteriorly, but interiorly. "I am the vine, you the branches" (Jn 15:5). Within His Church He will continue to live in each Christian by transmitting to them His spirit, His purity, His devotion to the Father, His life of humility and prayer.

If we would conform ourselves to God's plan, we must die to sin once and for all. Since, unfortunately, we can through our own fault relapse into the death of sin, a strict asceticism is necessary. The purpose of such an asceticism is to foster the growth of the seed planted in our soul in baptism. Christian life is merely the continuation of that life implanted in us at our baptism. We must continue to die to sin and live to Christ. The liturgy especially helps us attain this end. Associating us daily, during the Sacrifice of the Mass, with the life and death of Christ, the liturgy urges us to "be renewed in the spirit."

In heaven we shall be perfectly free from sin, from death and sorrow, and we shall see the full growth of the seed of grace planted in our hearts at baptism.

Prayer

Perfect Thou my goings in Thy paths, that my footsteps be not moved. Incline Thy ear, and hear my words; show forth Thy wonderful mercies, Thou who savest them that trust in Thee, O Lord. (Offertory.)

Thursday

"We are baptized in Christ Jesus" (Epistle). We are, to use the vigorous language of the Apostle, immersed in the person of Christ our Lord, and are thus intimately associated with the life of Christ. We have been lifted up to become partakers of the life of Christ and His mystical body. This inscrutable mystery initiates us into the Christian life.

Baptism is the one supremely important event in the life of the individual Christian and compares in importance with the Incarnation of the Son of God with regard to humanity as a whole. This work of God, applied to us in baptism, laid the foundation stone of "God's building" within us (1 Cor 3:9). Whatever we achieve in our struggle toward perfection, is very slight compared to this work of God. The task, however, proposed to us by God's salvific will, is of an immense importance. Baptism places the Christian under the strictest obligation of striving after Christian perfection. It binds us personally to strive for salvation, and leaves us no alternative. Baptism, correctly understood and fully appreciated, offers us a motive for striving after perfection which surpasses all others in power or value. It forms the starting point for our Christian struggle and Christian life, points out the direction, and governs and directs our entire Christian life. "So do you also reckon yourselves to be dead indeed to sin, but alive to God, in Christ Jesus our Lord" (Epistle).

Baptism gives birth to Christ in our hearts. Although it is a transitory act, it establishes an enduring spiritual relationship between us and Christ in His mystical body, His holy Church. The grace of baptism is the greatest of all graces, and it urges us to cultivate the union with Christ which was established at baptism. We must exert ourselves daily to perfect our union with Him, gratefully and joyfully acknowledging His divine guidance. How is this to be done? We must die to sin and live to God in Christ Jesus. Most of us do strive for perfection, but we do not fully realize the divine change God worked within us at baptism. We have too little appreciation of the fact that baptism is the beginning and the foundation of all our endeavors to achieve salvation, and that these endeavors are nothing but the organic growth of the supernatural seed planted within us in that holy sacrament. Our endeavors would be much more joyful and energetic if we were more mindful of the change God wrought within us at baptism. Our struggle would be much more consistent if we realized vividly how immensely important is this first of the sacraments and how insignificant in comparison are our own efforts toward perfection. If we were mindful of these facts, how much more courageously we would work, and how much more persevering and energetic would be our spiritual endeavors! The Church, therefore, places the thought of baptism in the center of her liturgy; thus, for example, baptism is mentioned in the Masses during Lent, on Holy Saturday, and in the Masses of the Sundays after Easter and Pentecost. Every Sunday at the Asperges the Church reminds us of the great sacrament which we have received as the principal means of our salvation.

In our struggle for perfection we are to obey God's commands and imitate His example, especially in the so-called evangelical counsels, which the Lord has taught us by His word and example. "If thou wilt be perfect, go sell what thou hast, and give to the poor, and thou shalt have treasure in heaven; and come follow Me" (Mt 19:21). But even if we follow perfectly the evangelical counsels, it is possible to overlook the fundamental idea that through baptism we are incorporated in Christ and receive a share in His life and power. Concentrating on our obligations and duties, we are apt to overlook the power and fullness of life that sustains us, which was given us in baptism. We are often too occupied with ourselves, with our insufficiency and sinfulness, and too little concerned about the power working within us, the vine whose little branches we are and by whom we are sustained, fed, and formed.

"So do you also reckon yourselves to be dead indeed to sin, but alive to God, in Christ Jesus our Lord," being incorporated in Christ, the head, whose spirit and power replenishes you and lives in you.

Prayer

O God of power, from whom are all good things, implant in our hearts the love of Thy name, increase in us true religion, nourish us with all goodness, and by Thy mercy keep us in the same. Through Christ our Lord. Amen.

Friday

The Lord leads His friends into the desert, far from the conveniences, allurements, and pleasures of the world. "All we who are baptized in Christ Jesus are baptized in His death" (Epistle). The life of a baptized Christian is, in its truest essence, a continual process of dying. He will reproduce and perfect the life of Christ within himself only in so far as he takes up his cross, denies himself through unceasing mortification, and gains dominion over himself. Today's liturgy reminds us again of this basic truth.

"We ... are baptized in His death." To be united with Christ in baptism means to die in Christ, to be crucified and buried with Christ. Dying to Christ means imitating His life of poverty and accepting His crosses and mortifications. If we want to live the new life in Him and with Him and His Church, we must die daily, hourly. God, the one true God, must be always before the eyes of the baptized, as the only goal of his striving and longing. After the Son of God became man by embracing human nature, His human will had to be in perfect conformity with His divine will. Such a perfect harmony of His wills could be achieved only through a continuous and unreserved devotion of His human will and desires to the will of the Father, which He accomplished through continual mortification and His voluntary acceptance of a bitter and ignominious death on the cross. Through His acts of mortification and self-denial, through His death on the cross, He perfected the union of the human nature with the divine nature.

The way of Christ, the head, must also be the way of His members, the baptized. Having been united with Him in baptism, grafted onto Him, as it were, we must perfect this fundamental union through moral actions. The way leading to this union requires that we overcome our ego, mortify and deny ourselves after the example of Christ, our head, so that we become one with the life and death of Christ. "If thou wilt be perfect, go sell what thou hast, and give to the poor, and thou shalt Have treasure in heaven; and come follow Me" (Mt 19:21). "Every one of you that doth not renounce all that he possesseth cannot be My disciple" (Lk 14:33). Mortification and self-denial are the fundamental principles in our life with Christ. Without them no truly Christian life is possible. "We ... are baptized in His death."

"We are debtors, not to the flesh to live according to the flesh. For if you live according to the flesh, you shall die; but if by the Spirit you mortify the deeds of the flesh, you shall live" (Rom 8:12 f.). To be united with Christ means, fundamentally, to fight against the concupiscence of the lower man. We are assured that our body, by our baptism, is the temple of the Holy Ghost (1 Cor 6:19), that through the life of God within us, through sanctifying grace, it is sanctified by our union with Christ, that it is called, to be "made like to the body of His glory" (Phil 3:21). Concupiscence, however, is still alive within it, and sin desires to reign in the mortal body (Rom 6:12). Because we live in the flesh, concupiscence seeks to "work in our members, to bring forth fruit unto death" (Rom 7:5): "Another law [works] in my members, fighting against the law of my mind" (Rom 7:23). It urges us to follow the flesh: "fornication, uncleanliness, immodesty, luxury" (Gal 5:19). The life in Christ, therefore, which has been established in us through baptism, demands necessarily that concupiscence be mortified. "They that are Christ's have crucified their flesh with the vices and concupiscences" (Gal 5:24). No weed dies of itself, least of all the weeds of the soul. Neither does virtue and the perfect life of Christ within us grow by itself. We must work continuously, pulling out the weeds, digging the ground of our soul with a sharp spade. This necessitates the mortification of the lusts of the flesh and a tempering of the demands of our senses, our mind, our inclinations, and our passions. It requires a continual battle against the defects of our nature and character. "If any man will come after Me, let him deny himself" (Mt 16:24). That is the fundamental law of living with Christ.

"All we who are baptized in Christ Jesus are baptized in His death." It is an unalterable law of Christian life that there is no salvation except in carrying the cross of Christ and in following the Crucified. We Christians today can be justly reproached for being too calmly optimistic and for looking too much to our own comfort. Men reproach us for living a Christian life which has become entirely too worldly. Christ gives His choicest graces to those who follow Him into the desert, who walk the way of Christian self-denial.

Would that we might understand the language of the liturgy, which teaches us that mortification and self-denial are the way of Christ, and that they must also be the way of the members of Christ.

Prayer

O God of power, from whom are all good things, implant in our hearts the love of Thy name, increase in us true religion, nourish us with all goodness, and by Thy mercy keep us in the same. Through Christ our Lord. Amen.

Saturday

"We ... are baptized in His death" (Epistle). By means of voluntary and joyful participation in our Lord's passion and cross, Christian self-denial attains to its highest perfection.

"If any man will come after Me, let him deny himself and take up his cross and follow Me" (Mt 16:24). The Son of God came to us on this earth to share His life with us. He became man and toiled incessantly to care for souls. He was insulted and opposed by men until at last they condemned Him to death and crucified Him. His life was a life of suffering; He Himself so willed it. Voluntarily, with complete subjection to the will of the Father, He drank the chalice the Father had commanded Him to drink for our salvation. He spent His life in suffering, sorrow, and self-denial in order to reconcile us with His Father, to open heaven for us, and to save us from eternal damnation. A "man of sorrows" (Is 53:3) from the manger to the cross, He embraced the cross, poverty, and mortification. When He was led out to be scourged, He offered no resistance. He suffered in silence, perfectly resigned to the will of the Father, even when He was scoffed at in a most rude and humiliating way and mockingly crowned with thorns. Silent and resigned to the will of the Father, He took up His cross and carried it up to the heights of Calvary, where He suffered unutterable agony. After three hours, during which He shed the last drop of His precious blood, He consummated His life of sacrifice. The life of the Son of God was a life of suffering leading to the cross.

"We ... are baptized in His death." Many Christians like to meditate on our Lord's passion, whether by means of a meditation book, the Stations of the Cross, or by frequent glances at a crucifix. Our being Christians, however, our being "baptized in His death," requires more than the mere meditation on His passion. It calls for a real union of suffering with Christ, an efficacious union which we must experience in actual life. To this union of suffering we have been baptized, and by this union we are called to possess and enjoy with Christ His transfiguration. In order to become coheirs of His glory, however, we must follow in the way He walked and win glory as He won His: we must share His suffering. In being "nailed [with Christ] to the cross" (Gal 2:19), and in being "planted together in the likeness of His death" (Rom 6:5), we have the only assurance of attaining this glory. "We ... are baptized in His death"; and "we who live are always delivered unto death for Jesus' sake; that the life also of Jesus may be made manifest in our mortal flesh" (2 Cor 4:11). Our suffering is a suffering with Christ. We long to be found in Him in "the fellowship of His sufferings, being made conformable to His death" (Phil 3:10).

With St. Paul we do not want "to know anything, . . . but Jesus Christ, and Him crucified" (1 Cor 2:2). Our life of renunciation, mortification, and suffering is a vital and joyful life with Christ, a partaking of His death in order that we may live with Him. We love His cross and poverty, the mortifications and trials He sends us. Imparting to us His own strength in suffering, He leads us, by means of our union with Him in His passion, upward to Himself, to the heights of His victory, to His resurrection and glory.

Whomsoever God wills to raise up to sanctity, He first nails to the cross. For this reason those who have been entirely crucified with Christ, are also those to whom God gives the greatest graces. As sufferings were for Christ the head, so they are for us His members, the gate through which we must enter into the bliss of His transfiguration. From Christ's point of view, the lack of suffering is a great evil. If we are immersed in Christ's death and suffer with Christian endurance, we are pleasing to Him. If we suffer patiently when we are sick and abandoned by others, when we are unable to devote ourselves to spiritual exercises as we wish, we please Him more than we would by great works. The highest of all human achievements is to know how to suffer with Christ. "We . . . are baptized in His death."

The liturgy introduces us daily into the school of the cross during the Sacrifice of the Mass. Here we enter more and more deeply into union with Christ's sacrifice and passion in order that in Holy Communion we may be united with Him in a new and more perfect union of life.

Prayer

Perfect Thou my goings in Thy paths, that my footsteps be not moved. Incline Thy ear, and hear my words; show forth Thy wonderful mercies, Thou who savest them that trust in Thee, O Lord. (Offertory.)

Seventh Sunday after Pentecost

The Mass

How to increase and perfect the supernatural life we received in baptism (Easter) through the descent of the Holy Ghost (Pentecost) is the theme of today's Mass. Today, as we enter the house of God to attend Mass, the liturgy directs our gaze to the risen Christ reigning with heavenly majesty and glory as God and King: "The Lord is most high, He is terrible; He is a great King over all the earth." He has extended His dominion over me, too, and over anything that belongs to me, since in baptism He wrested me from the power of sin and hell. Gratefully and with the voice of joy I acknowledge His benign providence and His dominion over me.

By baptism we are called to a great work: "As you have yielded your members to serve uncleanness and iniquity unto iniquity, so now yield your members to serve justice unto sanctification" (Epistle). Great is the fruitfulness arising from a life which is in accordance with the grace of baptism: "Sanctification and . . . life eternal. For the wages of sin is death. But the grace of God is life everlasting; in Christ Jesus our Lord" (Epistle). Thus St. Paul portrays the unbaptized and the baptized, the unredeemed and the one redeemed through grace, the slave of sin and the servant of justice. With open eyes the liturgy realizes that even among the baptized, even among those who are called to the Holy Sacrifice, there are "false prophets," Christians in name only, who wear the garments and have the appearance of the sheep belonging to the flock of Christ, but who are inwardly ravening wolves. "By their fruits you shall know them" (Gospel). The decisive factor is not that they have been washed in the waters of baptism, or that they have been anointed with holy oil, or that they have promised to renounce Satan and his works; decisive will be the works that bear witness to the interior character of the whole man. Neither are words, nor religious exercises, nor the mere attendance at church services, nor membership in Christian organizations decisive. "Not every one that saith to Me: Lord, Lord, shall enter into the kingdom of heaven; but he that doeth the will of My Father who is in heaven, he shall enter into the kingdom of heaven" (Gospel). The kingdom of Christ in our souls cannot be built up by pious words only; but convictions and works are more important.

"As in holocausts of rams and bullocks, and as in thousands of fat lambs, so let our sacrifice be made in Thy sight this day" (Offertory). May it be a sacrifice which implies real hardship for those who sacrifice; but we have only one real gift of sacrifice, one infinitely more valuable than the most expensive holocaust of the Old Covenant. This gift is Christ. If we truly wish to share in the sacrifice offered at Mass, it is not enough that we utter a few formulas, repeating, "Lord, Lord." Sacrificing means offering one's self, one's will, one's inclinations to the "will of [the] Father who is in heaven." It means forsaking everything that is not compatible with God's holy will, such as sin, proximate occasions of sin, evil inclinations, evil intentions, improper words, sinful relations, and bad company of any kind. Sacrificing means becoming one with Christ in one's thinking and judging, striving and willing, talking and acting; it means entering into Christ's spirit, making good the promises of our baptism. It means living for God and His holy commandments in our occupations and in our everyday life, yielding the good fruits of a good tree.

While assisting at Mass today, we avow this sentiment and this will. Placing not merely empty words and meaningless formulas on the paten, we sacrifice ourselves, our wills, our hearts, and determine to seek in all things only what God wills just as He wills it. We must be determined not to permit our "members to serve uncleanness and iniquity unto iniquity," but "to serve justice unto sanctification." Then God, bowing down His ear from heaven, stretches out His fatherly hand in order to make us partakers of His salvation, to which He has called us in baptism, and the pledge of which He gives us in Holy Communion.

Meditation

The liturgy of this Sunday draws a sharp contrast between the old man and the new. The old man is the man without God, without Christ, man on a purely natural level; the new man is the one born of God in baptism, filled with the Holy Ghost in confirmation, hastening toward the goal of eternal life — a new, spiritual man enlivened by God and Christ.

The old man. "You have yielded your members to serve uncleanness and iniquity unto iniquity" (Epistle), following the concupiscence of the flesh, which is inclined towards evil. Feeling unfettered and free, you neglected the commandments of God and the natural law, which He has written into every man's heart. "When you were the servants of sin, you were free from justice" (Epistle). With somber colors the Apostle paints the picture of unredeemed man. "When they knew God, they have not glorified Him as God; ... but became vain in their thoughts, and their foolish heart was darkened.... And as they liked not to have God in their knowledge, God delivered them up to a reprobate sense, to do those things which are not convenient; being filled with all iniquity, malice, fornication, avarice, wickedness, full of envy, murder, contention, deceit, malignity; whisperers, detractors, hateful to God, contumelious, proud, haughty, inventors of evil things, disobedient to parents, foolish, dissolute, without affection, without fidelity, without mercy" (Rom 1:21, 28- 31). What St. Paul saw and experienced, modern man has confirmed, whose first principle is: Away with God and with belief in Him, in Christ, in things supernatural, in the life beyond. There is only one god: man himself, humanity. Man is his own law-giver, his own law, his own judge. It would be immoral for man to fulfill a law not made by himself, even if it were the revealed will of God. Away, therefore, with the doctrine of Original Sin, of a hereditary corruption. Human nature, as it is, is good, is beautiful, is pure, is holy. What need man do besides follow his nature and live his life fully by surrendering to his instincts and desires? Why should we need a Redeemer, a God become man, a Church, divine help and grace? Such is the spirit of modern man, autonomous and liberated from God. He is a god and a law to himself. We need not be surprised when we hear of injustice, untruthfulness, egoism, corruption, and boundless moral misery on every hand in the world today. "As they liked not to have God in their knowledge, God delivered them up to a reprobate sense." Thus they are slaves of sin and unbelief, of the denial and hatred of God, making gods of themselves. "The end of them is death."

The new man. "Now yield your members to serve justice unto justification.... But now being made free from sin and become servants to God, you have your fruit unto sanctification, and the end life everlasting" (Epistle). In virtue of our baptism and of our having become united with Christ, who is the vine, we have become the "good tree," living branches of Christ. "Every good tree bringeth forth good fruit," not merely useless leaves (Gospel). Our Lord demands fruit. "Not every one that saith to Me: Lord, Lord, shall enter into the kingdom of heaven; but he that doeth the will of My Father who is in heaven, he shall enter into the kingdom of heaven" (Gospel). This is the new man, the Christian man. But this new man must die to concupiscence, to the allurements and desires of the flesh, to inordinate devotion to earthly goods and pleasures, and to the desire for worldly honors. Instead of these things, the new man must be a good tree that brings forth good fruit, living for God in all things. He must first of all seek God and His will alone.

The liturgy today wishes us to examine ourselves seriously. "By their fruits you shall know them" — the old man and the new man. "Now the works of the flesh [the old man] are manifest, which are fornication, uncleanness, immodesty, luxury, idolatry, witchcrafts, enmities, contentions, emulations, wraths, quarrels, dissensions, sects, envies, murders, drunkenness, revellings, and such like.... They who do such things shall not obtain the kingdom of God. But the fruit of the Spirit [the new man] is charity, joy, peace, patience, benignity, goodness, longanimity, mildness, faith, modesty, continency, chastity. Against such there is no law" (Gal 5:19–23).

"As you have yielded your members to serve uncleanness and iniquity unto iniquity, so now yield your members to serve justice unto justification." In baptism we yielded ourselves, soul and body, to serve justice and the will of God. This devotion of ours to God and His holy will we deepen and renew every day in the Sacrifice of the Mass. We put whatever we may have or be on the paten, that nothing may belong to us any longer, neither worldly goods nor our own will, but everything may be entirely at the disposal of God. In Holy Communion we deepen our union with Christ and become ever more perfectly filled with His holy spirit in order that, yielding our "members to serve justice unto sanctification," we may be able to say with Him: "My meat is to do the will of Him that sent Me" (Jn 4:34).

Prayer

O God, whose providence in the ordering of all things never fails, we humbly beseech Thee to put away from us all harmful things and to give us those things which are profitable for us. Through Christ our Lord. Amen.

Monday

Through baptism we become branches of Christ, who is the fruitful vine. "Every branch in Me that beareth not fruit, He will take away; and every one that beareth fruit, He will purge it that it may bring forth more fruit" (Jn 15:2). We have been called to bring forth good fruit. "Every good tree bringeth forth good fruit.... By their fruits you shall know them" (Gospel).

"Not every one that saith to Me: Lord, Lord, shall enter into the kingdom of heaven" (Gospel). We pray, perhaps we pray much; but too often we do not pray in the right manner. We are much like those who say, "Lord, Lord," following our own ideas and indulging in our own fancies. How many there are who pray for hours and meditate daily, who regularly examine their conscience and perform all kinds of exercises of piety, but who, nevertheless, harbor ill feeling against those around them, who are peevish, reckless, and egoistic! They pray, but in their everyday life they become indignant at trifling offenses. They are without self-control, they make hasty, uncharitable judgments in thought and word. Is such conduct the fruit of Christian prayer? Their kind of prayer is not true prayer and can hardly be agreeable to almighty God. It is a prayer which is not even pleasing to men, for it can even become repulsive and cause men to treat true piety with contempt. No blessing rests on one who thus cries, "Lord, Lord"; but only a curse. They shall not enter into the kingdom of a fully Christian life. "Every tree that bringeth not forth good fruit shall be cut down and shall be cast into the fire."

"He that doeth the will of My Father who is in heaven, he shall enter into the kingdom of heaven" (Gospel). "Every good tree bringeth forth good fruit." God expects of us, not merely words, no empty "Lord, Lord," but real fruit, since we have been united with Christ. The fruit, however, is to do the will of the Father. Our everyday life proves whether or not our prayers are genuine. If our prayers do not detach us from ourselves, if they do not make us more ready to make sacrifices, more faithful to God, they are not genuine. If they do not make us day by day more vigilant in our fight against our perverted affections, more patient and tolerant of our neighbor's faults and weaknesses, if they do not render us more courageous in self-denial and more faithful to duty, they are not genuine. If our meditations and prayers do not make us daily more perfect, urging us to acquiesce more readily in God's visitations, in suffering, sickness, inconveniences, temptations, and spiritual trials, then they are not genuine. Genuine prayers urge us, unfailingly and with an inner necessity, to accept God's will in everything, no matter how much our human nature may have to suffer. We pray only as well as we love. Loving God, however, means accepting and doing His will. "He that doeth the will of My Father who is in heaven, he shall enter into the kingdom of heaven."

True piety does not exhaust itself in the performance of exercises of piety and does not consist in our praying often and willingly; piety is an attitude of our will embracing and determining our entire life. It means striving to accept whatever the day may have in store for us as His will and as sent to us by His providence and love; it means seeing God in all things and looking up to Him, suffering all things for His pleasure and honor. Breaking away from everything by which we might offend God or incur His displeasure, true piety anxiously avoids voluntary faults and imperfections. It is as solicitous for the love of our fellow man and for the fulfillment of one's duty as it is for prayer. "Not every one that saith to Me: Lord, Lord, shall enter into the kingdom of heaven; but he that doeth the will of My Father who is in heaven." We are truly pious, devoted to interior life, perfect, only in so far as we endeavor to do the will of the Father who is in heaven.

"As you have yielded your members to serve uncleanness and iniquity unto iniquity, so now yield your members to serve justice unto sanctification.... You have your fruit unto sanctification, and the end life everlasting" (Epistle). This is our fruit: to become holy by fulfilling the will of the Father who is in heaven, "and the end life everlasting." "Every good tree bringeth forth good fruit."

Prayer

O God, whose providence in the ordering of all things never fails, we humbly beseech Thee to put away from us all harmful things and to give us those things which are profitable for us. Through Christ our Lord. Amen.

Tuesday

Easter presented us with a new life. The Spirit of Pentecost brings it to full maturity, as summer makes the growing crops ripen with its light and warmth. Today's liturgy reminds us of a husbandman who inspects his crops during the summertime to see whether they are growing and ripening. He is looking forward to the fruit. "By their fruits you shall know them" (Gospel), those who are truly Christians, truly pious and devoted to God. To have been baptized is not enough; neither is it sufficient to belong to a religious society or to wear the robe of a religious. God wants fruit. "Every tree that bringeth not forth good fruit shall be cut down and shall be cast into the fire" (Gospel). The liturgy takes seriously the growing and ripening of the divine life.

"The evil tree bringeth forth evil fruit." The evil tree brings forth fruit too, but it is evil fruit that cannot be used and is cast away. They are the evil trees who live according to their instincts and passions and do the works of fallen nature, who live apart from the life of God, rejecting baptism and sanctifying grace. However hard we may work and toil under such conditions, even though we astonish the world with our deeds, we produce nothing but empty fruits, wild fruits that have no value for eternal life, to which we are called. We are evil trees when, having been united with God through baptism, we become unfaithful to our baptismal vows, separating ourselves from Him and His life through mortal sins. The very nature of baptism and our faith make us still a part of Christ; but we are as branches on Christ that have withered away, barren of good fruits and bearing only evil fruits of sinful thoughts, desires, and works. We are evil trees when, though united with God and Christ through sanctifying grace, we do not take seriously the cultivation of the divine life within us. We do not commit any grave sins, perhaps, but we are not greatly interested in our growth in the interior life. We want to live comfortably without effort, without being bothered by any fixed order of life. Being lukewarm, we prefer to confine our religion to absolute necessities. "I would thou wert cold or hot. But because thou art lukewarm, and neither cold nor hot, I will begin to vomit thee out of my mouth" (Apoc 3:15 f.). We are evil trees as long as we do not honestly take pains to grow interiorly in virtue and perfection. We are a tree that produces leaves and blossoms, but does not bring forth any real fruit. Our search for perfection, our Christian life, is motivated by our longing for honor and esteem, by our desire for success, by our pride, which makes us want to be better than others. We bring forth fruits, but the fruits are evil.

"A good tree cannot bring forth evil fruit." The Church is a good tree. She is the tree "which is planted near the running waters, which shall bring forth its fruit in due season. And his leaf shall not fall off" (Ps 1:3). The roots of this sublime tree lie in Christ. Out of Him and the infinite wealth of His life, the Church in her sacraments continually draws fresh life, new strength and fruitfulness. The Church throughout all ages has added new branches to her tree, bearing pure and holy souls, and presenting them to her heavenly bridegroom. We also can be good trees in the garden of the Church. Ezechiel saw us when he beheld the fountain going forth from the temple, becoming a life-giving river along whose banks trees were planted, all richly laden with fruits. The temple from which the fountain sprang is Christ the Lord. "And of His fullness we all have received" (Jn 1:16). We have grown together with Him, being His living branches. "I am the vine; you the branches" (Jn 15:5). The river is the grace going forth from Christ, the Redeemer, being poured out over us by means of the Church and the sacraments. We are the trees, bringing forth fruit in due time: the fruit of good works. Though the storms of temptations, trials, and suffering may sweep over us, they are unable to lessen our vitality and fruitfulness as long as our strength is rooted in Christ. We must draw our strength and fruitfulness from Him, the holy fountain, the fullness of all that is holy, noble, pure, and strong.

"A good tree cannot bring forth evil fruit." It is supremely important that we maintain a vital union with Christ the vine and grow daily by becoming more intimately united with Him. We must renounce with joy and determination everything that might be an obstacle to our becoming another Christ. "Know, O Christian, thy dignity" (St. Leo the Great). Be a good tree that brings forth only good fruit.

Having been planted in the garden of the Church as good trees, we have at our disposal everything necessary for growth and fruitfulness. We must bring forth good fruit, fruit of a sincere repentance and conversion, fruit of charity towards our neighbor. If anyone believes that he loves God, but does not love his neighbor, he deceives himself; he is a tree that brings forth no fruit. There can be no good tree which does not help others and does not practice charity; a good tree shares its fruit with the poor and suffering, and is ready at all times to give even of the little it may call its own.

"Every tree that bringeth not forth good fruit shall be cut down and shall be cast into the fire." Having been baptized, we belong to the Church and we must yield fruit. God does not want empty trees; He wants fruitful trees.

Prayer

May Thy healing work in our souls mercifully free us from our perverse inclinations, O Lord, and lead us ever to do that which is right in Thy sight. Through Christ our Lord. Amen.

Wednesday

The Church admonishes us: "Come, children, hearken to me; I will teach you the fear of the Lord. Come ye to Him and be enlightened; and your faces shall not be confounded" (Gradual). These words are, as it were, the answer of our Holy Mother the Church to the words of the Epistle: "Being made free from sin and become servants to God, you have your fruit unto sanctification, and the end life everlasting."

Having "become servants to God," and therefore His entire and exclusive property, our whole being, thinking, willing, and doing can belong only to Him. In baptism we have declared: "I believe in God"; I believe that I am God's, with all that I am and possess. We are servants of God. Therefore only one thing matters: the will of our heavenly Father. Our life is Christian only in so far as it has been made to serve God's will. We must therefore renounce our own will and the desires of our heart, and overcome our inordinate passions and our self-love. We must do solely whatever God desires, accept what He sends, suffer what He permits, and submit to His commands. Neither may we refuse to accept the humiliations He sends us or the troubles, inconveniences, disappointments, and sufferings we encounter. "Not as I will, but as Thou wilt" (Mt 26:39). As the drop of water which the priest pours into the chalice at the Offertory becomes one with the wine, so the will of the Christian likewise must become one with the will of God in all things and under all conditions. "Unless the grain of wheat falling into the ground die, itself remaineth alone. But if it die, it bringeth forth much fruit" (Jn 12:24 f.). Unless our entire seeking and striving has become one with the divine will, it cannot bring forth much fruit. Easter and Pentecost seek to lift us up to these heights. "Come, children, hearken to me; I will teach you the fear of the Lord. Come ye to Him and be enlightened; and your faces shall not be confounded" (Gradual). We are taught how to strive after a life of unspeakable happiness and holy peace in union with God.

"God hath sent the Spirit of His Son into your hearts, crying: Abba, Father. Therefore now he is not a servant, but a son" (Gal 4:6 f.). So we are sons of God, not servants or slaves. A slave serves out of fear of being punished. He obeys his master, but not out of love; he obeys because he is forced to do so, but reluctantly and without interest for his master's cause. The son, however, serves the father because he loves him, because it pleases him to make his father happy. He is sincerely interested in everything that might be his father's business, knowing only one fear: that he may fail to do everything to his father's satisfaction. We serve God as His children out of love for Him, not because we fear the terrible threat of eternal punishment. Fear is wholesome and necessary in order to keep alive within us the spirit of penance and mortification. Fear is necessary since we too often are exposed to dangerous occasions and temptations; but holy love must be the predominant motive in all our actions. Our Lord and Father deserves to be obeyed out of nobler and more sublime motives than fear. We have been baptized in the love of God; and we are commanded to "love the Lord Thy God" (Mt 22:37). Fear restrains us from doing evil; but love prompts us to do only what is pleasing to the Father, what may best serve

His interests and honor. It is never satisfied with the thought of having done enough; it urges us to render an even greater service of love and greater sacrifices.

God, on His part, answers with even greater proofs of His love. He draws the soul towards Himself; the fear which until now plagued the soul, hindering its loving conversation with God, gives way to an unspeakably blissful intimacy with Him and an unshakable confidence in His love. Even the fear of not loving Him enough, of not pleasing Him, is no longer a torturing fear; but it incites the soul to watch more carefully, to fight more courageously, and to break with everything that is not of God. If it fears that it has offended the Father, it hurries to Him full of humility, repentance, and confidence, knowing that He will not refuse the kiss of peace. The longing to give Him everything continues to live in the soul. "Perfect charity casteth out fear" (1 Jn 4:18). We have been baptized in this love.

How well the Father has arranged everything for us! Whereas once we yielded our members "to serve uncleanness and iniquity unto iniquity" (Epistle), God through His love and mercy has delivered us from sin. From "servants of sin" we have "become servants to God," having received the vocation and the power "to yield [our] members to serve justice unto sanctification." The fruit of our transformation: "life everlasting." Are we not to be thankful from the depths of our heart? Let us thank Him with words, with the offering of our sacrifice, which is Christ our Lord; but above all, let us thank Him with our life.

"Clap your hands, all ye nations; shout unto God with the voice of joy" (Introit). These words are an invitation to us, the baptized, the children of God, to give thanks at all times and in all places, but especially during the Holy Sacrifice of the Mass. "As in holocausts of rams and bullocks, and as in thousands of fat lambs; so let our sacrifice be made in Thy sight this day, that it may please Thee" (Offertory): a sacrifice of thanksgiving through Christ our Lord.

Prayer

May Thy healing work in our souls mercifully free us from our perverse inclinations, O Lord, and lead us ever to do that which is right in Thy sight. Through Christ our Lord. Amen.

Thursday

"Now being made free from sin and become servants to God, you have your fruit unto sanctification, and the end life everlasting" (Epistle). With these brief words the Apostle represents our entire life. From sin we turn to a life in union with God, to a life of sanctity. This is the law of our life: to do the will of God in all things, to fulfill His commandments as faithful servants. We must therefore learn to see His holy will in all things.

We must learn to see God's will in anything that may happen to us during our life: in difficulties, sufferings, and humiliations, in whatever may occur, be it agreeable or painful; for His providence manifests itself in all things. A deep and living faith is needed for this view of life, an eye that is not deceived by the mere outward appearance of things. A Christian should observe life with an eye that searches into the deeper reasons for everything, finding in all things the hand of God and His infinitely wise and loving providence guiding and providing for all creatures. He sees with the eye of faith; his judgment is not formed by merely natural considerations and principles. Neither does he seek first his own advantage or his own will before the will of God. The care for his own welfare comes second. The preservation of his health, the fulfillment of his desires, the longing to be delivered from disagreeable situations and persons, from difficulties and pains, from trials, temptations, and suffering, are always made dependent on the will of God. Such a man sees God's will first in all things. Blessed is the soul for whom everything else recedes into nothingness before the splendor and beauty of the divine will.

Not only must we see God's will in all things, we must love and fulfill it. We shall undoubtedly find that the will of God hedging our life about like a law and regulating it in all its details is uncomfortable and repellent to our nature and its desires and appetites. It is a yoke that often appears hard and oppressing; it will crush him who embraces it reluctantly or unwillingly. But whoever embraces it wholeheartedly, it will lift up to the pure and holy love of God. He who lives according to Christ's spirit loves the law and yoke of God's will. He loves his work, his duties, the commands of his parents, and the orders of his superiors; he loves the commandments of God and the Church, the rules and discipline of the order to which he belongs. He loves the will of God, which he seeks and sees in all things, even when his nature recoils from the difficulties, renunciations, humiliations, and trials of life. For this reason he grows strong in fulfilling his duties with devotion and a noble constancy; he regards nothing so insignificant that it may be neglected. To him all his efforts become a blessed and gratifying cooperation with the will of God, a sharing of His life. He accepts God's will in all his undertakings. Everything, even the seemingly least important of his duties, becomes holy and awe-inspiring. The true Christian is no longer guided by merely human conceptions and motives: his life is imbued with a pure and strong love of the things that please God. He no longer asks: How far am I bound to go? How far am I free to do what I like? How far can I go without committing a serious sin? He simply loves with a love that recognizes no such distinctions and questions. His love is the measure of his fulfillment of the divine will. He obeys cheerfully and unreservedly. Such a man is indeed a good tree that brings forth good fruit.

We are here on earth to know God, to see Him in all things, to love and serve Him, and thereby to merit eternal life. God comes first; His glory is to be preferred to our well-being and our happiness.

"Come, children, hearken to me; I will teach you the fear of the Lord" (Gradual). "As you have yielded your members to serve uncleanness and iniquity unto iniquity, so now yield your members to serve justice unto sanctification"; that is, the fulfillment of the will of God. "He that doeth the will of My Father who is in heaven, he shall enter into the kingdom of heaven."

In fulfilling his duties, the good Christian does not devote a meticulous attention to the outward appearance of things. He does not stand behind a veil, as it were, to look for God from afar off. Knowing that God is very near, he discovers Him in his work and in the fulfillment of his duties. Being fully aware of God's omnipresence, he realizes that where God's will is, there also is His grace and His aid. Knowing that he serves God when fulfilling his duties, he tries to fulfill them wholeheartedly in order to find his Maker and become united with Him. Thus he finds God and His kingdom in all things.

Prayer

O God, whose providence in the ordering of all things never fails, we humbly beseech Thee to put away from us all harmful things and to give us those things which are profitable for us. Through Christ our Lord. Amen.

Friday

"Clap your hands, all ye nations; shout unto God with the voice of joy. For the Lord is most high, He is terrible; He is a great King over all the earth" (Introit). Now being made free from sin, we have become "servants to God" (Epistle), ready to accept and do His will. To do whatever God wills, and to do it lovingly, is the perfect road leading to sanctity and life eternal. "Being made free from sin and become servants to God, you have your fruit unto sanctification, and the end life everlasting" (Epistle).

God guides us in two ways. He either takes our hand and bids us follow Him, or He carries us in His arms as a mother carries her child. In the first instance He manifests His will in the commands, duties, and demands of nature and social life (the revealed will of God). While fulfilling His will, we cling to His hand by following His intentions, commandments, and desires, thus "taking our little steps" (St. Francis de Sales). The second, a more passive way of fulfilling God's will, is "the will of God's good pleasure." This loving, powerful, and gentle operation of God within us accompanies us wherever we are, under all conditions and circumstances. God is always at work purifying and sanctifying our soul, and filling it with His life. "Are not five sparrows sold for two farthings, and not one of them is forgotten before God?... Fear not, therefore; you are of more value than many sparrows.... A hair of your head shall not perish" (Lk 12:6 f.; 21:18). Thus God takes care of us. Everything, whether small or great must serve His purpose. He guides, rules, and directs all things in such a way that they become a help to each and every one of us, leading us on towards Him and His grace. "We know that to them that love God, all things work together unto good" (Rom 8:28). With His infinite wisdom and love, God works within us for our salvation, making use of the best possible means at the most opportune time and in the most perfect manner. His loving providence guiding and directing our ways of life is certain "to put away from us all harmful things and to give us those things which are profitable for us" (Collect). Such is our faith and our hope.

"Commit thy way to the Lord and trust in Him, and He will do it" (Ps 36:5). We trust in God's plans concerning us; we have confidence "that to them that love God, all things work together unto good." We believe that all His plans for us have a divinely good intention, that His love always and in all things rules His plans, and that His hand guides even when it strikes. Behind the suffering, injustice, and bitterness about us, we do not merely see men and human intentions; looking deeper we see God and His work. We believe. We submit to His holy will and the cross He imposes on us, to whatever He permits, mysterious and dark though it may sometimes appear. Submitting faithfully to all plans, trials, and afflictions, we are fully prepared to let Him do with us whatever He pleases. "Commit thy way to the Lord," let Him freely enter and work in your soul. Learn to take life in full harmony with God's providence. Give up your own anxiety and solicitude. "Trust in Him, and He will do it." Once we have given ourselves unreservedly to God's will and have become entirely His servants, our fruit will be life everlasting.

"He that humbleth himself, shall be exalted" (Lk 18:14). "Suffer the little children and forbid them not to come to Me; for the kingdom of heaven is for such" (Mt 19:14). "Amen, I say to you, unless you be converted and become as little children, you shall not enter into the kingdom of heaven" (Mt 18:3).

"He that doeth the will of My Father who is in heaven, he shall enter into the kingdom of heaven." This is our way: the fulfilling of God's will. By fulfilling the duties God imposes on us, we have active piety; by submitting to everything His providence may send us, we have passive piety.

God leads, we follow. His will and operation come first; our will and work come next. God gives, we accept. When He enters our interior life, we unite ourselves with Him and become active. The more perfectly we become united with His will, abandoning ourselves to His good pleasure, the more fruitful becomes our life. Once we are dead to our own thinking and willing, God's will and operations within us can be efficacious and life-giving.

Prayer

May Thy healing work in our souls mercifully free us from our perverse inclinations, O Lord, and lead us ever to do that which is right in Thy sight. Through Christ our Lord. Amen.

Saturday

"He that doeth the will of My Father who is in heaven, he shall enter into the kingdom of heaven" (Gospel). This declaration is an unequivocal, infallible promise, since it comes from infallible truth itself. By fulfilling the will of God we shall find a sure and straight road leading to heaven.

"The kingdom of heaven" is to be found wherever God is, wherever He is adored, recognized, praised, and glorified. It is in us in so far as we are united to the Church in faith, hope, and charity, and we separate ourselves from earthly and created things. We find the kingdom of God wherever His infinitely holy, wise, and just will is recognized and obeyed. Beginning on earth in His Church and in the souls of Christians, it will be eternal in the glory of the Father, the Son, and the Holy Ghost. There it will be the kingdom of the clear and the unveiled recognition of God, of a never-ending bliss in His presence, the realm where God is enjoyed, and where eternal homage of praise and thanksgiving is paid unto Him. There will resound a jubilant "Glory be to the Father, and to the Son, and to the Holy Ghost."

We enter into the kingdom of heaven when we recognize God by acknowledging His nearness, His operation within us, His providence, His will in all things in our daily lives. Whenever we renew our devotion to Him and His holy will, lovingly embracing this will and sincerely trying to fulfill it, we enter a new and more perfect mansion of this kingdom. Christ told us, "In My Father's house there are many mansions" (Jn 14:2). At last, despising this earthly life, we shall enter the one which will be our abode forever. Then the kingdom of God will be within us, ravishing our souls with the unspeakable bliss and joys of God's glory. "Eye hath not seen, nor ear heard, neither hath it entered into the heart of man, what things God hath prepared for them that love Him" (1 Cor 2:9).

The road leading to the kingdom of God is the will of God. There is only this one road. The prayers and graces offered to us by God, the inspirations, encouragements, and various opportunities that present themselves in daily life, are but means towards the end. They effectually serve us only after we are moving on the sure way to God. They can be correctly used only by him who "doeth the will of My Father who is in heaven." This is the correct and sure way; it is the only way which we are bound to search out and follow. In order to find God's will and to follow it, we must know it. It reveals itself to us in our reason and in the dictates of common sense. Revelation speaks of it in the Ten Commandments, and it is further made known to us in the commandments of the Church: in the commandments of fasting and abstinence, the obligation of attending Mass on Sundays, of receiving the sacraments of penance and the Holy Eucharist at least once a year. It is made known to us in the regulations of Canon Law and the rules and constitutions of religious communities. We fulfill the will of God in the duties of our profession, whatever it may be. We find it in our vocation as a father, a mother, an official, an employer or employee, as a working man or a maid servant. God's will has been revealed to each one of us; it is the road that leads to heaven. All that matters is our will to seek it and follow it. "He that doeth the will of My Father who is in heaven, he shall enter into the kingdom of heaven."

In baptism the Lord has lifted us up to His level in order that He may continually live His life within us. "I am the vine, you the branches" (Jn 15:5). His life was one of continuous and unswerving devotion to the will of the Father. "Not as I will, but as Thou wilt" (Mt 26:39). "My meat is to do the will of Him that sent Me" (Jn 4:34). We also live our lives in harmony with His if we unite our desires, plans, and intentions with whatever the Father wills.

"Come ye to Him" by uniting your wills with His will. "Come ye to Him and be enlightened; and your faces shall not be confounded" (Gradual). The complete subjection of our will to His good pleasure must be the fruit of our attendance at Mass and of our reception of Holy Communion. In Holy Communion, He daily kindles anew within us the holy fire of His spirit and of His loving devotion to the Father. Through us, His members, "the world may know that I love the Father" (Jn 14:31). We should so live that the world may see in us Christ's love for the Father.

Prayer

O God, whose providence in the ordering of all things never fails, we humbly beseech Thee to put away from us all harmful things and to give us those things which are profitable for us. Through Christ our Lord. Amen.

Eighth Sunday after Pentecost

The Mass

The call to Christianity in baptism has placed tremendous responsibilities on man, obliging him to discharge duties that go with him through his entire life, daily and hourly. God has given us the lifetime duty to develop within ourselves the divine life we received from Christ at baptism. Whence is man to draw the strength and courage to preserve this supernatural life of the children of God and to overcome the obstacles and resist the hostility of the powers of this world? How can he preserve the goods of supernatural life and increase them? He surely stands in need of continual inspiration, help, and understanding. The liturgy will provide these, especially through our assistance at Mass.

The Introit of today's Mass recalls the hour of our baptism, the mystery of Easter: "We have received Thy mercy, O God.... Thy right hand is full of justice. Great is the Lord and exceedingly to be praised, in the city of God, in His holy mountain"; that is, in the Church, through which the holy fountains of sacramental graces reach us and open to us the waters of salvation. Our gratitude and jubilation find their expression in our prayer to God to preserve within us the graces of baptism and to enable us to live according to His will.

In striking phrases the Epistle explains what baptism demands of a Christian: "Brethren, we are debtors, not to the flesh to live according to the flesh"; but we are called, as children of God and coheirs of Christ, "to mortify the deeds of the flesh" and to be "led by the Spirit of God," to live according to the dictates of our supernatural life. A fierce battle is required of us if our spirit is to conquer the flesh by making it subject to the divine powers within us. Today's Gradual, however, tells us that we are not left alone in this battle of the spirit against the flesh: "In Thee, O God, have I hoped; O Lord, let me never be confounded." How much effort is expended by men who think only of this world to take care of worldly interests and to attain to a material goal! The unjust steward exemplifies man's concern for worldly prosperity; for though he is unjust, a man who lives according to the flesh and the wisdom of the flesh, though in his ways and means he is a man full of zeal and earthly wisdom, he provides a model for Christians, the children of light: a model of zeal and prudent energy in the pursuit of their higher, supernatural goals. But unfortunately wisdom and experience teach us that "the children of this world are wiser in their generation than the children of light" (Gospel).

Instructed anew in our duties as Christians, we are ready for the Holy Sacrifice. Uniting ourselves with Christ, offering with Him one sacrifice, we fulfill what the Epistle asks of us. Sacrificing ourselves, as we once did when we received baptism, we refuse "to live according to the flesh." Instead we are determined to live according to the spirit and to build anew on the foundation laid in baptism. Thus we again commit ourselves to the duties and obligations placed on us in baptism. We likewise renew our faith in our adoption as the children of God and our unshakable trust in our eternal heritage in heaven. In the sacrificial meal the glorified Son of God imparts His life to our souls, assuring us that together with Him, the first-born, we are children of the Father, called to a blessed heritage in heaven, of which an unfailing pledge has been given to us in Holy Communion. "Taste and see that the Lord is sweet; blessed is the man that hopeth in Him" (Communion).

Meditation

The eighth Sunday after Pentecost is a day of grateful jubilation for the graces of Easter and Pentecost. "We have received Thy mercy, O God, in the midst of Thy temple [through the reception of baptism]. According to Thy name, O God, so also is Thy praise unto the ends of the earth; Thy right hand is full of justice" (Introit). Easter and Pentecost have greatly enriched us; God is our Father, Christ is our brother, and the Holy Ghost dwells within us. We are children of God and therefore heirs of God and coheirs with Christ. Can anything be wanting? In order to make us realize fully our greatness in Christ, this Sunday's liturgy puts before our eyes two types of men, the man of the flesh and the man of the spirit, the child of this world and the child of God, the man living in communion with Christ and the one separated from Him.

The man of the flesh is worldly; his outlook is very worldly. All that matters to him are temporal things. The Gospel portrays him under the figure of the unjust steward. What counts first with him are the means by which he can get ahead in the affairs of this world; whether he uses the right means, those that comply with the demands of justice, matters little to him. He belongs to the children of this world who have little interest in a life to come and who are not greatly concerned about the commandments of God or a life modeled on Christ's life and the principles of the gospel. "If any man love the world, the charity of the Father is not in him. For all that is in the world is the concupiscence of the flesh and the concupiscence of the eyes and the pride of life, which is not of the Father but is of the world. And the world passeth away and the concupiscence thereof; but he that doeth the will of God abideth forever" (1 Jn 2:15–17).

"They that are according to the flesh, mind the things that are of the flesh.... The wisdom of the flesh is death,... because the wisdom of the flesh is an enemy to God; for it is not subject to the law of God.... And they who are in the flesh, cannot please God" (Rom 8:5 ff.). For this reason "we are debtors, not to the flesh to live according to the flesh; for if you live according to the flesh, you shall die" (Rom 8:12 f.; Epistle). In baptism and through the mission of the Holy Ghost, God's grace saved us from the slavery of the concupiscence of the flesh and made us men according to the spirit, who mind the things that are of the spirit. "We have received Thy mercy, O God, in the midst of Thy temple," the Church.

In the man who lives according to the spirit, who lives in Christ and does not live according to the flesh, the justification of the law is fulfilled. For the law of the spirit is life, and we have been freed from the law of sin and death in Christ Jesus. If we live according to the spirit and not according to the flesh, we mortify the deeds of the flesh by the spirit. The Spirit of God that filled and guided Christ, lives in every one baptized in His name. It is God Himself and His Spirit, the living flame of God, the eternal love being poured out from the Father to the Son, from the Son to the Father. This Spirit causes us to glow with His divine life, and burning with the fire of love for God, we come to the Father with childlike confidence. The Spirit of Christ causes us to see life with the eyes of God and according to the values He places on things, making us love and rejoice in whatever He desires. It urges us to renounce our attachment to earthly goods and interests, and to regard as nothing the things of the world and whatever honors or pleasures they may have to offer.

Blessed are the poor in spirit, those who renounce the things of this world. Blessed are the meek, those who patiently submit themselves to all the hard and disagreeable things of life for Christ's sake. Blessed are they that mourn, that willingly renounce the pleasures and vanities of this life. Blessed are the clean of heart. Blessed are they that suffer persecution for justice's sake, that are reviled and slandered by evil men. We should be these blessed ones of whom Christ spoke, since we have been made free in baptism and have received the Holy Ghost in the sacrament of confirmation. We must be men of the spirit.

"We have received Thy mercy, O God, in the midst of Thy temple"; that is, through the sacrament of baptism. We thank the Lord for what He has done for us.

The life of the spirit is great and exalted. Poor in its outward appearance, it is inwardly rich in blessing; for even though it is unpretentious and hidden, it nevertheless exceeds all things which are not of God. It makes us grow in the life of God and brings God Himself into our hearts. Its fruits are a holy freedom, peace and security in God. Who could be happier, freer, stronger, and more at peace with himself and his fellow men than the man who is governed by the Spirit? He lives God's life.

Prayer

Grant to us, O Lord, we beseech Thee, the spirit to think and do always such things as are right; that we who cannot exist without Thee, may be able to live according to Thy will. Through Christ our Lord. Amen.

Monday

"We are debtors, not to the flesh, to live according to the flesh" (Epistle). In baptism and confirmation we have received the Spirit that dwells within us, the Spirit of Christ, the Holy Spirit. He renews within us that mind and direction of will which makes us look up to God and His goodness. It is especially He who united us in baptism with the living Christ, so that our communion with Christ is determined according to our possession of the Holy Spirit. If anyone does not possess the Spirit of Christ, he cannot belong to Him.

"You have received the spirit of adoption of sons" (Epistle). The very moment we received baptism, sanctifying grace entered into our soul, which meant that the Holy Ghost took up His abode there. He produced within us the life of grace just as He produced the miracle of the Incarnation by descending upon the Virgin of Nazareth. Christ must again be born within us. "How shall this be done?... The Holy Ghost shall come upon thee, and the power of the Most High shall overshadow thee" (Lk 1:34 f.) at the hour of grace, the moment of our baptism. From now on He dwells in our souls, drawing them into the stream of love that goes forth from the Father to the Son and from the Son to the Father. The Holy Ghost directs that stream of love, which is Himself, to us mortal beings. "The charity of God is poured forth in our hearts by the Holy Ghost, who is given to us" (Rom 5:5). By virtue of that love given to us, we become members of Christ and are incorporated in Him, who is the head, that we may live a new life in Christ. We become children of the Father and go to the Father through Christ. The Spirit given to us transforms us, drawing us into the love with which Christ, the Son of God, loves the Father and makes us partakers of the life of the Father. We also can say: "I love the Father" (Jn 14:31), for the Spirit living within us is the Spirit of love, Christ's love for the Father. Henceforth the law of our life is the same law which guides the life of Christ: "I love the Father."

"The children of this world are wiser in their generation than the children of light" (Gospel). They live a life on a natural plane, thinking in a human and worldly way. They regard as happy those who have the money to buy the pleasures and honors of life, who are respected by their fellow men and have influential positions in society. Guided by such a worldly attitude of mind, they strive to obtain wealth, prosperity, and honor, and live only according to the dictates of their temporal interests. They are symbolized by the unjust steward of the Gospel. But those who have received the spirit of sonship, the baptized and the confirmed, are determined and guided in their actions and thoughts by the Spirit of God. In the power of the Holy Ghost dwelling and working within them, they mortify the deeds of the flesh, avoid sin, and shun this worldly spirit and its works. The spirit of sonship is the spirit of love, a childlike love of the Father. Wherever this love has taken possession of the soul, it subdues natural and earthly thoughts, considerations, and motives. Such a soul is filled with the light of God; it reckons the value of things according to the principle of faith and according to the teaching and the example of Christ. Those who placed their confidence in the flesh, in their education and knowledge, their character, their faculties, and their efficiency, are trained by the Spirit so that they can say with St. Paul: "The things that were gain to me, the same I have counted loss for Christ. Furthermore I count all things to be but loss for the excellent knowledge of Jesus Christ my Lord; for whom I have suffered the loss of all things, and count them but as dung, that I may gain Christ and may be found in Him" (Phil 3:7–9).

"If you live according to the flesh, you shall die; but if by the Spirit you mortify the deeds of the flesh, you shall live" (Epistle). Through the Holy Spirit we shall gain life everlasting. The Lord pours Him forth into our souls if only we do not bar His entrance by mortal sins. This Spirit of love urges us to go to the Father, in order that in Christ we may live and serve the Father and His interests with childlike, joyful, and trusting devotion.

The Holy Ghost crowns and seals the eternal communion existing between Father and Son. In a similar manner He is the guiding principle and the cause of Christ's intimate union with His members. Thus head and members live in intimate union in the power of the Holy Spirit. We have, therefore, every reason to rejoice in the Holy Spirit, who has been given to us. With gratitude to Him we should open our souls and do everything in our power to make it possible for Him to work in us.

Prayer

Grant to us, O Lord, we beseech Thee, the spirit to think and do always such things as are right; that we who cannot exist without Thee, may be able to live according to Thy will. Through Christ our Lord. Amen.

Tuesday

"We are debtors, not to the flesh to live according to the flesh; for if you live according to the flesh, you shall die; but if by the Spirit you mortify the deeds of the flesh, you shall live" (Epistle). The Spirit creates life and liberty; His law is "the perfect law of liberty" (Jas 1:25).

"When I have a will to do good, evil is present with me.... I see another law in my members, fighting against the law of my mind, and captivating me in the law of sin, that is in my members" (Rom 7:21 ff.). There is much within us that is sordid, corrupt, and sensual, which wages war against our soul; but beneath these evil inclinations the soul struggles and strives for light. The soul wants to lift herself up spiritually. If she does not succeed in rising upwards with a pure, noble, and holy mind, the features of the bestial and carnal man will become visible in her. She is forced either to abandon herself to brutish instincts and become a slave of the flesh, or to wage the fight against them unceasingly. If she neglects this fight, she must needs become a traitor to herself, misunderstanding her very nature. She must fight, or abandon all hope of being a child of God, destined some day to participate in the nobility, liberty, and happiness of the sons of God. "Whosoever are led by the Spirit of God, they are the sons of God" (Epistle). Only by fighting against the law of sin, against the concupiscence of the flesh, the concupiscence of the eyes, and the pride of life, can the child of God be born within us. "If you live according to the flesh, you shall die," being slaves to the law of sin. "Unhappy man that I am, who shall deliver me from the body of this death?" (Rom 7:24.) The law of God and His Holy Spirit make it clear to us that the only way to achieve true spirituality is by a continual struggle, by an earnest asceticism and self-denial. The Holy Ghost, whom we received in confirmation as the Spirit of fortitude, will lead us to victory over the law of the flesh and to the perfect sonship of God.

"If by the Spirit you mortify the deeds of the flesh, you shall live." The law of the Holy Spirit is the law of liberty. Like the rays of the sun it illuminates and warms and nourishes life. It is the part of a flower to be beautiful. It is the duty of man to live according to the norms given to him by his Creator, and to cherish and increase the nobility planted in him by God. This law of the Spirit frees him from faults and sins. It makes his soul clear-sighted, helping him to see the divine will in all things and to direct himself towards all that is noble and divine. Wresting him from the fetters of selfishness and passion, it leads him to the liberty of the children of God.

"If by the Spirit you mortify the deeds of the flesh, you shall live." The law of the Spirit is the law of liberty, "the royal law" (Jas 2:8), which, lifting us beyond the limits of our fallen nature, fills us with the consciousness of superiority and victory, with a truly royal mind. It frees us from the bonds of natural indolence and sloth in doing good, from our natural dislike of things religious, and from our aversion to spirituality. Now we love the law of the Spirit, fulfilling it not as slaves, but freely, out of the love for God which has been poured forth into our hearts by the Holy Spirit. We realize that life comes to us through the law of the Spirit. Meeting the deepest demands of our nature, which yearns for God, for truth and goodness, it frees us and lifts us up, filling us with divine life and power. With the law of the Spirit we receive the life and liberty of the sonship of God. "We have received Thy mercy, O God, in the midst of Thy temple; according to Thy name, O God, so also is Thy praise unto the ends of the earth; Thy right hand is full of justice" (Introit).

"The fruit of the Spirit is charity, joy, peace, patience, benignity, goodness, longanimity, mildness, faith, modesty, continency, chastity.... They that are Christ's have crucified their flesh, with the vices and concupiscences. If we live in the Spirit, let us also walk in the Spirit" (Gal 5:22–25).

"Come, Holy Ghost, and fill the hearts of Thy faithful."

Prayer

Grant to us, O Lord, we beseech Thee, the spirit to think and do always such things as are right; that we who cannot exist without Thee, may be able to live according to Thy will. Through Christ our Lord. Amen.

Wednesday

"You have received the spirit of adoption of sons, whereby we cry: Abba, Father" (Epistle). The Holy Spirit is with us at the beginning of our life in Christ and effects our union with Christ, our head. Thus He makes us the children of God in union with Christ. He regulates our communion with Christ, with the Church, and with other members of the Church.

The Spirit of our union with the Son. We are united with Christ, the Son of God, in so far as we have "the communication of the Holy Ghost" (2 Cor 13:13). For St. Paul "living in Christ" means the same as "living in the Spirit." For him baptism is baptism in Christ and in the Holy Spirit. This is the fundamental law of Christian life: "If any man have not the Spirit of Christ, he is none of His" (Rom 8:9). The Spirit of Christ is the Holy Ghost, who draws us into such an intimate communication with the Son that St. Paul can say: "Know you not that your bodies are the members of Christ?" and he adds: "Know you not that your members are the temple of the Holy Ghost, who is in you?" (1 Cor 6:15, 19.) "He who is joined to the Lord, is one spirit" (1 Cor 6:17). It follows that we cannot be in Christ without being simultaneously in union with the Holy Spirit. We can be united with Christ, the only-begotten Son of God, and children of the Father only so far as we are filled with the Holy Spirit and live in Him. "In this we know that we abide in Him, and He in us: because He hath given us of His Spirit" (1 Jn 4:13). For "the incarnate Son of God has not received the Holy Spirit for Himself, the only-begotten Son of God, but for us" (St. Cyril of Alexandria). "The faithful become Christ's mystical body in so far only as they are determined to live by the Spirit of Christ. Only the body of Christ lives by the Spirit of Christ" (St. Augustine). Therefore we begin to possess and live Christ's life the very moment when we possess the Holy Spirit and live by Him. We are growing in Christ, living His life, in the same degree as we become spiritual. The liturgy of the Sundays after Pentecost wishes to bring home to us that we are to become more spiritual, more enlightened by the Spirit of God, filled with Him and guided by Him.

The Spirit of our union with the body of Christ. "Now there are diversities of graces, but the same Spirit; and there are diversities of ministries ... [and] operations, but the same God, who worketh all in all.... To one indeed, by the Spirit, is given the word of wisdom; and to another, the word of knowledge,... to another, faith in the same Spirit.... But all these things one and the same Spirit worketh, dividing to every one according as He will" (1 Cor 12:4 ff.). As the vitality of the various members and organs in a natural organism can work fruitfully only if these various organs cooperate in the unity of the organism, so likewise in the organism of the body of Christ, the Church, the variety of the members, offices, and graces has to be coordinated in the unity of the organism, the entire body. The Holy Ghost accomplishes this unity by directing the different operations and members towards the growth and perfection of the body of Christ. We belong to Christ not as individuals or single members, but only as members of the community, of the entire body. We are of necessity connected with the other members and related to them; for the member does not live its own separate existence, but only in connection with the life of the organism. So we, too, living not for ourselves, but for the organism, have to be united not only with the living head, but also with each single member in the communion of the Holy Spirit, who is the principle of unity in the variety of the different members, operations, and offices of the Church.

The Church is a community wrought by the Holy Ghost and living in Him. She is "one body and one spirit" (Eph 4:4) in communion with the Holy Spirit, who links the individual member with Christ and, through Christ, with the Father. She is one in spirit and also one in body. The more we consider ourselves members of the organism and responsible for the welfare of the mystical body, the more charity grows within us. We attain a greater love for souls, for the poor, for those who have gone astray, for all our brethren who have been seduced or have fallen away. The Spirit of love will make us live and understand what St. Paul puts so emphatically before our eyes as the gift to be preferred before all other gifts: "If I speak with the tongues of men, and of angels, and have not charity, I am become as sounding brass or a tinkling cymbal. And if I should have prophecy and should know all mysteries and all knowledge, and if I should have all faith, so that I could remove mountains, and have not charity, I am nothing.... And now there remain faith, hope, and charity, these three; but the greatest of these is charity" (1 Cor 13:1 f., 13).

"We have received Thy mercy, O God, in the midst of Thy temple" (Introit). We have received through God's mercy union with the Son of God and with the body of Christ, gifts of infinite value. We gratefully proclaim: "Let us give thanks to the Lord our God." The celebration of today's Mass is to be a *Eucharistia*, a sacrifice of thanksgiving, offered in the name of all those who live in union with the Son of God and His mystical body. It must be a sacrifice of petition for all who belong to this body in order that all of us may recognize the grace given to us in baptism (Easter) and confirmation (Pentecost), and that we may live as Christians, as bearers of the Spirit of Christ. We certainly are no longer debtors to the flesh. Having received the Holy Spirit we are of one spirit with our Lord Jesus Christ. We live by the Spirit of God and the Spirit of Christ. Our Lord gives us His special graces when, in Holy Communion, He pours out upon us His Holy Spirit. "Taste and see that the Lord is sweet; blessed is the man that hopeth in Him" (Communion).

Prayer

May this heavenly mystery, O Lord, heal us both in soul and body; and may we ever feel within us the power of the sacraments we celebrate. Through Christ our Lord. Amen.

Thursday

"You have not received the spirit of bondage again in fear, but ... the spirit of adoption of sons, whereby we cry: Abba, Father" (Epistle). "Behold what manner of charity the Father hath bestowed upon us, that we should be called and should be the sons of God" (1 Jn 3:1).

God comes to us in the person of a child. He does not come to us as an angel, nor as Lord and Judge, not even as a loving Father; but He prefers the humble simplicity and helplessness of a child. He brings nothing with him, neither nobility of birth nor the splendor of His majesty, nothing but His life; He chooses the helplessness and sweetness of a child, though He could have come in the splendor of a king. He is well aware of the fact that there is no greater moral power among men than the weakness of a child. It conquers the most hardened heart and has power over every good spirit. God, of course, could force men to do His will; He could tread upon them, but He wants to win their hearts to Himself, and therefore He comes as a child, not as an omnipotent God; His helplessness bespeaks His desire for us. The divine child wants us to forget our timidity and fear, and desires that we come to Him with a childlike simplicity. "We have received Thy mercy, O God, in the midst of Thy temple" (Introit).

"Suffer the little children and forbid them not to come to Me" (Mt 19:14). As God became the Son of Man, so men become the sons of God. "You have received the spirit of adoption of sons." In becoming children before God, we find the road that leads to Him and to the possession of Christ's life and heritage. All true Christianity consists in our being called and being the sons of God (1 Jn 3:1). A child knows instinctively that it will be well taken care of by its father and mother. Having experienced no worries, no grief, and no fear of life, a child sees only sunny skies and is full of hope and expectation of wonderful things to come. A child is satisfied with what it sees and can lay its hands on; it has a faith that explains and brightens everything. It has a heaven and a father and a mother; it wants to believe and to pray, to reach beyond itself to God the Father and to Mary, its mother. A child has faults and weaknesses too, but these, too, do not cause it great worry. If the father punishes his child, it will be love only that wields the rod, for he means only well with his child.

"You have received the spirit of adoption of sons." We are aware of our being children of God. We therefore stand at the mysterious gates of life without fear and without undue solicitude. Knowing that we are being taken care of by His love and providence, we leave our ways and our destiny entirely to the direction of this loving Father. We are resigned to His dispensations, for we know that they are the work of a loving, well-meaning Father; He does not permit anything to befall us without having first measured it so that we may be able to bear it. We are satisfied to be guided along the road He has destined for us, throwing ourselves into the arms of God, like a child whose only desire is to be carried by its mother that it may rest at her bosom and be caressed by her. Every desire of the Father, every sign coming from Him, is holy, is a command to us. Whatever we do, we do to show our love for the Father and our desire to please Him. We have our faults and behave badly sometimes, but realizing what we have done, we regret having offended Him. We ask His pardon, and He in His mercy gives us new graces and new proofs of His love.

"You have received the spirit of adoption of sons." There is much piety which does not recognize God with a childlike disposition, which knows only the service of fear, of servitude, of oppressing and paralyzing anxiety. Who can serve God out of feelings of love if he does not know Him to be lovable? For this reason even many Christians are cold and tepid toward God, because they see in Him nothing but the fearful Lord, the Lawgiver and Judge. From this attitude spring many feelings that are foreign to the usual disposition of children; they are the source of all listlessness in religious life. The lack of childlike confidence and simplicity is the reason for so many temptations against faith and the many anxieties that impede a tender devotion toward God and the spirit of joyful sacrifice.

God wishes us to be as children before Him. He has implanted the gift of piety in our souls in baptism in order that we may offer Him a childlike disposition of mind. If we are truly children, we simply believe what He commands, submitting ourselves to His holy will and commandments. Then we are guided by His divine leadership in all things with that spirit of faith which lifts us beyond the merely human point of view in our thinking and judging. Forgetting ourselves, we rest on the heart of the Father, without worry or unrest, guided by a spirit of love and confidence. Renouncing our own will, we let Him, the Father, work within us whatever He wills. Placing no obstacles in His way, we become His children, dying to ourselves in order to be free for His spirit, His will, His working within us. "Out of the mouths of infants and of sucklings Thou hast perfected praise" (Ps 8:3).

PRAYER

Grant to us, O Lord, we beseech Thee, the spirit to think and do always such things as are right; that we who cannot exist without Thee, may be able to live according to Thy will. Through Christ our Lord. Amen.

Friday

"You have received the spirit of adoption of sons" (Epistle). We therefore are no mere strangers and guests who pass by, but members of the family of God, of that house whose foundation has been laid by Christ. These inexhaustible riches of supernatural sonship have been bestowed upon us through baptism and confirmation. Unfortunately we think too little of them.

Our being children of God is the root and foundation of all virtues and of all sanctity. The gifts of nature are many and differ in each person. Grace builds upon nature, ennobling our natural faculties, talents, and abilities. Grace, therefore, differs in each soul. "To every one of us is given grace, according to the measure of the giving of Christ" (Eph 4:7). In Christ's flock every sheep has its own name. The Lord knows each one and calls His own sheep by name. Each soul receives proper graces, and each has to comply, in its own way, with the graces and intentions of God.

The more the soul gives itself up to the tender working of the Holy Ghost in a way appropriate to its individual nature, the more it will be transformed into Christ, the Son of God, and become like Him. If it has heeded the call of the Holy Spirit by making good use of the graces bestowed upon it, it has attained sanctity. The first link in the chain of graces and gifts which God gives us, however, is that merciful regard for us by which He predestined us from all eternity to become His children. This predestination is the dawn of all the mercies God wills and intends to bestow on us. The grace of supernatural sonship with which God enriched us, the foundation of which the Son of God laid through His Incarnation and which He bestowed upon each one of us at the moment of our baptism, is the basis for all God's communications with the soul and for all the subsequent illuminations and inspirations of grace. Without this grace even a wealth of natural gifts, the most splendid accomplishments, and admirable spiritual greatness is worthless for eternal life. The one grace of being a child of God is worth more than the whole universe (St. Thomas); it is our boast and our pride. By making us His children, God has made us participants in His own divine nature. Being born of God, we possess His nature in so far as the divine nature can be imparted to a created being. Transcending our own nature, we share God's life, His knowledge and truth, His love, His perfections, His bliss, His beatitude, and His glory; now, indeed, only as in a mirror, but someday in the perfection of the beatific vision.

To be the children of God means to be His friends. Friendship calls for intimacy, the communion of hearts. The friend reproduces, as it were, his own person in his friend. Wishing his friend the same good he desires for himself, the friend does everything possible for him. He wants to see him and exchanges ideas with him, and he talks with him about matters of common interest. Friends understand each other, sharing joys and sorrows; they grow into one, as it were, and are animated by one soul. We are the children of God, not merely friends. The grace of sonship renders us so beautiful, pure, and great in God's eyes that He finds Himself reproduced in us; therefore He loves us with that unspeakable love with which He loves Himself. In order to assure us of the sincerity and earnestness of His love for us, God became like us by the Incarnation of His Son. As He condescended to become like us in His Incarnation and His life on earth, sharing all the pains, troubles, and sufferings that fall to the lot of men, so He invites us to share the bliss and happiness of the friendship of God.

Friendship is one of the deepest needs of a human heart. It will not rest until it has found another heart to share its joys and suffering. It can rest only when it finds understanding interest and loving sympathy. "Blessed is he that findeth a true friend" (Ecclus 25:12). Human hearts, however, are too narrow, too finite. Even if two kindred souls meet, they cannot satisfy each other's needs completely in all the storms of life. The heart of God alone can satisfy all human needs. By reason of the grace of sonship, God's heart is so intimately united to our hearts that it permeates them, joining them so that virtually only one soul lives in them, one spirit, the Holy Ghost. This heart contains the fullness of all that is noble, beautiful, pure, strong, and amiable: it is a heart full of love, faithfulness, and unselfishness. As far as God is concerned, a disappointment or a breach of friendship is impossible; His friendship is enduring. He is the only friend who is always near us, who dwells continually in our soul with a divine concern and a divine fidelity and devotion. He knows every thought, every desire, every beat of our heart, and understands all our impulses so that we need not look for the correct words or the right expressions to state our needs. Here we have a friend who understands all our needs, our troubles, and difficulties even better than we do ourselves. This friend has no faults, He makes no mistakes; He is perfection itself. He desires nothing for Himself, but everything for us. He wants only to give Himself to us in an ever more perfect way, that He may make us happy with His love: "Taste and see that the Lord is sweet; blessed is the man that hopeth in Him" (Communion).

"You have received the spirit of adoption of sons." By this spirit we are the children and friends of God. "We have received Thy mercy, O God, in the midst of Thy temple; according to Thy name, O God, so also is Thy praise unto the ends of the earth; Thy right hand is full of justice. Great is the Lord and exceedingly to be praised, in the city of God, in His holy mountain" (Introit).

Being children of God and friends of God obliges us to become like Christ, to live for Him and the Father, to do great things for Him, and to suffer for Him. To be friends of God means to be of one mind, of one will, of one spirit with Him, aloof from everything that is sinful or not in accord with His will.

Prayer

May this heavenly mystery, O Lord, heal us both in soul and body; and may we ever feel within us the power of the sacraments we celebrate. Through Christ our Lord. Amen.

Saturday

"You have received the spirit of adoption of sons, whereby we cry: Abba, Father" (Epistle). The spirit of the sonship of God opens to us the sanctuary of true prayer, be it vocal prayer or silent prayer.

"We know not what we should pray for as we ought" (Rom 8:26). The most important element in prayer is the method of contacting God. Prayer is the source of the divine life that is to fill the soul and lead us toward sanctity. Our contact with God, however, is neither the fruit of our own efforts nor the searching of our intellect nor a mere natural exertion of our will and faculties. "I give you to understand that no man, speaking by the Spirit of God, saith Anathema to Jesus. And no man can say the Lord Jesus, but by the Holy Ghost" (1 Cor 12:3). Only the believing and loving soul will be able to enter into fruitful communion with God. Faith and charity are meaningless unless they live and work under the guidance of the Holy Ghost. Only in the spirit of the Holy Ghost can the soul go to the Father and talk with Him with a feeling of intimacy and with the liberty of a child of God. "We know not what we should pray for as we ought" (Rom 8:26). Prayer is a work of the supernatural man who in Christ has been lifted up by the Holy Ghost and has become united with Christ, the Son of God.

"The Spirit Himself asketh for us with unspeakable groanings. And He that searcheth the hearts knoweth what the Spirit desireth; because He asketh for the saints according to God" (Rom 8:26 f.). "You have received the spirit of adoption of sons, whereby we cry: Abba, Father." We pray as children of the Father. So our prayer is the expression of our innermost feelings, desires, strivings, yearnings, and we express ourselves in the spirit of sonship given to us. It is the Holy Spirit dwelling within us, who prays for us. He inspires our prayers, awakening in us faith, hope, and charity, and the affections of reverence, gratitude, and devotion. With sanctifying grace He infused into our soul His seven gifts, and whenever He urges us to pray and intends to lead us to the Father, He strikes the strings of this living harp. He employs those faculties of our soul which render us children before God. He touches the string of holy fear, that we may approach the Father reverently. He awakens the grace of piety, that our reverence may be that of the liberty and intimacy of a child. By means of the gift of knowledge He makes us see and appraise natural truths and experiences in the light of God. By the gift of understanding He reveals to us in our prayers the deep truths of our holy faith, of the gospel, of the life of God. Through the gift of wisdom He imparts to us an interior urge to taste of God and His mysteries; it is He who makes us experience the bliss and solace of knowing God. Thus the Holy Spirit produces within us the feelings and sentiments of a child wherewith we may go to the Father in our prayers. He asks us to adore the Father with childlike feelings, to thank and praise Him, to offer Him our heart and soul, our mind and body, and to beseech Him that He may hear our prayers and listen to our needs.

"The Spirit Himself asketh for us.... And He that searcheth the hearts knoweth what the Spirit desireth." Being pleased with these prayers made in the spirit of sonship, the Father benevolently accepts the thanksgiving, adoration, devotion, and petitions of His child. It is for this reason that our prayers, if they are offered in the spirit of sonship, are so valuable and fruitful, and that the soul praying in this spirit will be able to draw many great graces from this conversation with the Father.

No one is guided more accurately by the Spirit of God in his prayers than he who prays with the Church. Guided by the Holy Ghost, the Church is the great *ecclesia orans,* the praying Church. When we follow the leadership of the Church, there is less danger that we shall pray according to our own intentions, which are often purely mundane and merely the expression of our own spirit and mind. The more we are guided in our prayers by the Church, by her prayers and religious ceremonies, by her needs and sentiments, the more we are guided by the

Spirit of God and the more perfect is our prayer. The Spirit of God directs us to community prayer; He urges us to pray: "Our Father . . . Give us this day our daily bread, and forgive us our trespasses . . . Deliver us from evil." The Spirit of God urges us to pray in the plural form. The more perfectly we practice this kind of prayer, the more our devotion will assume the spirit of sonship, the spirit of the Holy Ghost.

Prayer

Grant us, O Lord, we beseech Thee, the spirit to think and do always such things as are right; that we who cannot exist without Thee, may be able to live according to Thy will. Through Christ our Lord. Amen.

Ninth Sunday after Pentecost

The Mass

The liturgy of this Sunday presents to us a very impressive procession: that of the children of Israel wandering through the desert. The great and inspiring experience of the departure from Egypt and the passing through the Red Sea belong to the past. Now the chosen people have settled down to the monotony and hardship of everyday life in the desert, and this dull life weighs so heavily on their hearts that their boredom is evident even in their faces. The pilgrims in the desert yearn for the pleasures of Egypt; many of them dance around a golden calf and engage in disgraceful idolatry; others commit adultery, while some even grumble against God and Moses. On account of this infidelity there fell in one day twenty-three thousand who committed fornication; others perished, bitten by serpents; those who murmured were destroyed by the destroyer (Epistle). The liturgy also presents another scene. From the height of Mt. Olivet, Christ looks down upon the city of Jerusalem. Seeing the proud and beautiful city with its majestic temple, He wept over it saying: "If thou also hadst known, and that in this day, the things that are to thy peace" (Gospel).

"Now all these things happened to them in figure, and they are written for our correction. . . . Wherefore he that thinketh himself to stand, let him take heed lest he fall" (Epistle). The things that happened to Israel in the desert and to Jerusalem might be repeated even in us who are baptized in Jesus Christ. It is not enough for us to have left, by baptism in Jesus Christ, the Egypt of a world fallen away from God and to have passed through the Red Sea (to have escaped the powers of Satan and hell); it is just as important for us to live according to the obligations of baptism and the principles of our faith by submitting ourselves to the long and arduous wandering through the desert of this life. It is just as important that we cease to yearn for the pleasures of Egypt (the world), that we give up the worship of false gods, avoid fornication, and refrain from murmuring against the Lord.

Was not Israel chosen before all other nations? Did it not have the promises of God, the patriarchs, divine revelation, the worship of the true God, and the sacrifices? Jerusalem possessed a splendid temple, newly erected by Herod. There the holy fire burned unceasingly on the altar, and God Himself dwelt in the holy of holies in the temple. For this reason Jerusalem believed that it could stand — and yet it fell. Did not the people themselves have God as their leader in the desert in the pillar of fire; did they not have the ark of the covenant, sacrifices, and a divinely appointed leader, Moses? Yet despite all this, the people fell in the wilderness. Can we expect, therefore, that baptism and our membership in the Church of Christ, our Christian name, will protect us from mishaps and eternal perdition? "He that thinketh himself to stand, let him take heed lest he fall."

With this thought in mind we proceed gravely today to the celebration of Mass. What was planted in our souls in baptism and confirmation must be preserved, tested, and employed in severe struggles. On entering the house of God we realize our weakness and the necessity of fighting; but looking up to the majestic picture of our Lord greeting us, His children, we say: "Behold, God is my helper, and the Lord is the protector of my soul; turn back the evils upon my enemies, and cut them off in Thy truth, O Lord my protector" (Introit). We pray that He may help us against those enemies who, according to the Epistle, felled the people of Israel—worldliness, idolatry, fornication, and murmuring. Putting this request into the Kyrie, the Gradual, and the Offertory, we are aware that we ourselves are the wanderers in the desert mentioned in the Epistle.

We humbly profess that the Savior has often good reason to weep over our faithlessness, too, telling us: "If thou also hadst known, and that in this day, the things that are to thy peace." We believe in His merciful love for our souls, professing, therefore, in the Credo that "for us men and for our salvation He came down from heaven, . . . was crucified also for us, . . . and was buried." At the Consecration He comes to us and on the altar renews His death on the cross. We now lay our hearts on the paten, renouncing all perverted desires, all idolatry, all fornication, and all murmuring. Thus we sincerely turn to our Lord, confessing: "The justices of the Lord are right, rejoicing hearts, and His judgments sweeter than honey and the honeycomb; for Thy servant keepeth them" (Offertory).

Meditation

An exalted dignity has come to us in baptism and confirmation. The liturgy of the week after Easter and after Pentecost never tires of reminding us of the riches of our state. Today it incites us to be faithful to the baptismal graces and our Christian name. "He that thinketh himself to stand, let him take heed lest he fall" (Epistle). We are free to misuse graces and become faithless to our call and election; but the result of such action will be eternal death.

"He that thinketh himself to stand, let him take heed lest he fall." The Epistle and the gospel direct our view to the chosen people made rich in graces by the Lord. By the power of His word the Lord brought to an end their slavery in Egypt and protected them with special providence, helping them with many miracles. He led the people through the Red Sea. He made His covenant with them at Mount Sinai, revealing His will in the Ten Commandments; He protected them from the parching heat of the sun in the desert by the pillar of a cloud, and guided them at night by means of a pillar of fire. He provided them with an abundant supply of water coming forth from the rock, and fed them daily with manna. When at last they reached the Jordan, they witnessed new miracles; without being hampered by the waters of the river they crossed the bed of the Jordan. Praying and praising God, they marched around the walls of Jericho and conquered the city; they saw how the power of God delivered their enemies, the Canaanites, into their victorious hands. Thereafter they took possession of the Promised Land. Theirs was the ark of the covenant, the law, the priesthood of the true God; later on, instead of the simple tent for the ark, they had the wonderful temple in Jerusalem, where God showed His mercy and protection again and again. Becoming more and more aware of their being the chosen people, they became proud and self-reliant, thinking themselves saved because they were the children of Abraham (Mt 3:9; Jer 7:4). They became so confirmed in their self-sufficiency that the representatives and the leaders of the people, the priests and scribes, refused to acknowledge the Messias promised by their prophets.

The chosen people did not comply with their divine election. "Let us not covet evil things, as they also coveted. Neither become ye idolaters, as some of them; as it is written: The people sat down to eat and drink, and rose up to play. Neither let us commit fornication, as some of them committed fornication, and there fell in one day three and twenty thousand. Neither let us tempt Christ, as some of them tempted, and perished by the serpents. Neither do you murmur, as some of them murmured, and were destroyed by the destroyer. Now all these things happened to them in figure, and they are written for our correction.... Wherefore he that thinketh himself to stand, let him take heed lest he fall" (Epistle). Israel fell; God rejected the Jewish people.

Yet how eagerly the Lord sought them! How deep was His affection for Jerusalem! He wept over the city, saying: "If thou also hadst known, and that in this day, the things that are to thy peace; but now they are hidden from thy eyes. For the days shall come upon thee, and thy enemies shall cast a trench about thee, and compass thee round, and straighten thee on every side; and beat thee flat to the ground, and thy children who are in thee; and they shall not leave in thee a stone upon a stone, because thou hast not known the time of thy visitation" (Gospel). Forty years later this prophecy was fulfilled literally; Jerusalem, preferred and elected by God, fell because it had not known the time of its visitation and had misused God's graces. Its destruction is a warning for us Christians. It is not enough to belong to the chosen people, to be a Christian; what matters is the fact that we must accept the graces offered us in baptism and confirmation, in Mass and Holy Communion, and that we be faithful members of the Church, denying ourselves ever more that the kingdom of God may be perfected within us.

"All these things happened to them in figure, and they are written for our correction, upon whom the ends of the world are come. Wherefore he that thinketh himself to stand, let him take heed lest he fall," lest he meet the fate of Jerusalem, which did not make use of the graces given to it. "Thou hast not known the time of thy visitation."

The baptized must be tempted, too, that their fidelity to God and Christ be tested and strengthened. Temptations threaten us from within and from without: from concupiscence, love of the world, and our self-love, which cause us to follow our own desires and oppose the working of grace and the Holy Ghost.

Prayer

Let Thy merciful ears, O Lord, be open to the prayers of Thy suppliant people; and that Thou mayest grant them their petitions, make them ask such things as shall please Thee. Through Christ our Lord. Amen.

Monday

The theme of today's Mass is emphasized particularly through the Introit, the Collect, the Offertory, and the Communion. We hear loud supplications for help, together with a prayer of gratitude for the help we received. "Save me, O God, by Thy name, and deliver me in Thy strength" (Introit). "Deliver me from my enemies, O my God; and defend me from them that rise up against me" (Gradual). We also hear: "Behold, God is my helper, and the Lord is the protector of my soul; turn back the evils upon my enemies, and cut them off in Thy truth, O Lord my protector" (Introit). These are the characteristics of the prayer of the Church. The people of Israel, once chosen by God but later rejected by Him, make themselves the implacable opponents and enemies of Christ and His Church. The never-ending fight of darkness against light, of the Synagogue against the Church, of the realm of Antichrist against Christianity, is typified by the fight of Saul against David (Psalm 53: Introit and Gradual).

"Save me, O God, by Thy name." David flees before Saul into a hiding place in the desert of Ziph, southeast of Hebron. The people of that district betray the hiding place of the refugee to King Saul and offer to lead Saul with his army to the place. David has no refuge but his God. With his growing need his belief in the power and love of God also grows, and so does his confidence in God's nearness and willingness to help. "Save me, O God, by Thy name, and deliver me in Thy strength." His confidence is the better founded since his persecutors do not care about God and His commandments, about truth and justice. They do not heed God's judgments and do not attempt to refrain from injustice. And behold! God is there and helps. "Behold, God is my helper, and the Lord is the protector of my soul."

When Saul and his men had surrounded David so that an escape was impossible, Saul was informed that the Philistines had invaded his country. The disaster Saul wished to inflict on David now fell back on himself. Saul had to return without delay in order to save his people and his crown. "Behold, God is my helper, and the Lord is the protector of my soul; turn back the evils upon my enemies, and cut them off in Thy truth."

The fight between Saul and David symbolizes the fight between the Synagogue and the Church. Christ will always be persecuted in His Church and in His members. But "God is faithful, who will not suffer you to be tempted above that which you are able; but will make also with temptation issue, that you may be able to bear it" (Epistle). "God is my helper," the Church proclaims triumphantly. For two thousand years her own experience has taught her this truth. "God is my helper," we, the children of the Church, also sing with joy. We cannot be spared a continual struggle, but God is faithful; He is our helper. We also have frequently experienced His help.

"Turn back the evils upon our enemies, and cut them off in Thy truth, O Lord my protector." The Synagogue has been the natural enemy of Christ and His Church from the time of the first Pentecost until this day. It wanted to destroy the young Church; money was not wanting, neither was influence with Caesar in Rome. The Synagogue inspired the terrible persecutions of the Christians under Nero and Domitian; it has been allied with all the powers of Antichrist to this day. The Church has only God and the weapon of prayer, but she will conquer. A striking pledge of her victory over Antichrist and those powers that seek to dig her grave is the punishment of the city of Jerusalem threatened in today's Gospel: "The days shall come upon thee, and thy enemies shall cast a trench about thee; ... [they] shall beat thee flat to the ground, and thy children who are in thee; and they shall not leave in thee a stone upon a stone." The destruction of Jerusalem in the year 70 A.D. is the sure sign, manifest to all, of the protection the Lord affords His Church and, through the Church, all her children. All of us have cause to rejoice: "Behold, God is my helper; . . . turn back the evils upon my enemies, and cut them off, . . . O Lord my protector." He has shown His loving protection again and again in the history of the Church and her children.

"The justices of the Lord are right, rejoicing hearts, and His judgments sweeter than honey and the honeycomb; for Thy servant keepeth them" (Offertory). In the Sacrifice of the Mass we unite ourselves with the Lord and live for Him and His will, desiring nothing for ourselves but everything for Him, His honor, and His holy will.

"He that eateth My flesh and drinketh My blood, abideth in Me, and I in him, saith the Lord" (Communion). The Holy Eucharist unites us to the Church and to the Lord; therefore He is my helper. Although He makes us and His Church participants of His trials, sufferings, and persecutions, although we drink "His chalice," nevertheless in the Holy Eucharist He imparts to us His Spirit and the powerful means for conquering all our adversaries. "Behold, God is my helper." He is faithful. He will not suffer His Church and us to be tempted above that which we are able to bear; "but will make also with temptation issue, that [we] may be able to bear it" (Epistle).

Strengthened by this belief and assured of our final victory, we exclaim, "Behold, God is my helper and . . . the protector of my soul." I stand by Him and His holy Church with her sacrifice and her sacraments. He turns the evil upon my enemies and cuts them off in His truth. We can sing with joy: "O Lord our Lord, how admirable is Thy name in the whole earth. For Thy magnificence is elevated above the heavens" (Gradual).

Prayer

Let Thy merciful ears, O Lord, be open to the prayers of Thy suppliant people; and that Thou mayest grant them their petitions, make them ask such things as shall please Thee. Through Christ our Lord. Amen.

Tuesday

"The people sat down to eat and drink, and rose up to play" (Epistle). It is hard to understand how the chosen people could act in this manner after all the great miracles God had wrought in their behalf, after they had been saved and guided by Him, fed on heavenly manna, and unceasingly blessed with graces. Now forgetting all these graces and the land promised them, the people sit down to eat and drink and to enjoy the pleasures of life. "All these things . . . are written for our correction" (Epistle).

"Jerusalem, Jerusalem, thou that killest the prophets and stonest them that are sent unto thee, how often would I have gathered together thy children, as the hen doth gather her chickens under her wings, and thou wouldest not?" (Mt 23:37.) How many benefits God heaped upon His chosen people! How often He sent His prophets to instruct and to warn them, to lead them back to the right path, and to dissuade them from their idolatry! Jerusalem's reply to all these graces was to stone and kill the prophets, those messengers of God. "I will sing to my beloved the canticle of my cousin concerning his vineyard. My beloved had a vineyard on a hill in a fruitful place. And he fenced it in, and picked the stones out of it, and planted it with the choicest vines, and built a tower in the midst thereof, and set up a winepress therein; and he looked that it should bring forth grapes, and it brought forth wild grapes.... What is there that I ought to do more to my vineyard, that I have not done to it?" (Is 5:1 ff.) This parable of the vineyard is a picture of the graces which God showers upon us, especially helping grace.

Despite the splendor of sanctifying grace, it is, nevertheless, but the supernatural foundation of the soul's vitality. In whatever degree supernatural faculties and powers have been planted in our soul together with sanctifying grace, in order to become efficacious they need to be awakened by additional supernatural influences and helps. Although we have received the seven gifts of the Holy Ghost together with sanctifying grace, these gifts are but the sails by means of which the little ship of our soul hastens toward the shores of heaven. Since these sails have to be swelled and moved by the powerful breath of the Holy Ghost, we need helping graces. Despite the fact that the branch is not without life, it must be continually fed by the vine if it is not to lose its life. Now, we are branches on Christ, the vine. From Christ life and power flow unceasingly into the members of His mystical body, just as the life-giving sap flows from a vine into its branches. This is the power which precedes all good works of the members, which accompanies and follows them, bestowing that supernatural value without which they are neither acceptable nor meritorious before God. (Cf. Council of Trent, Session VI, chap. 16.) But the Lord, wishing to provide for their salvation and their interior growth and sanctification, has connected some helping grace with whatever may happen to them in life. This help may take the form of an illumination, a warning, a suggestion, or an inspiration to make an act of love, thanksgiving, or contrition. Every moment the Lord waits at the door of our heart with some helping grace, eager to knock and enter. It is a consoling thought that we live in an atmosphere of grace and are surrounded by graces everywhere and at all times.

"Jerusalem, Jerusalem, thou that killest the prophets, and stonest them that are sent unto thee, how often would I have gathered together thy children,... and thou wouldest not?" (Mt 23:37.) The destruction of Jerusalem is a warning example of misused graces. "If thou also hadst known ... the things that are to thy peace" (Gospel). What is to our peace is a firm acceptance of the graces of the Lord, of the understanding He imparts to us, of the interior inspirations with which He urges us to act. "But now [the things that are to thy peace] are hidden from thy eyes." We misunderstand and neglect God's graces and inspirations and follow our own will, opposing God's gifts and invitations with indifference or even an obstinate and defiant "no." Now God's help, protection, and blessings will be taken away. Now the enemy, Satan, self-love, and concupiscence, will have an easy victory. "[They] shall cast a trench about thee, and compass thee round, and straiten thee on every side,... because thou hast not known the time of thy visitation" (Gospel).

"All these things happened to them in figure, and they are written for our correction" (Epistle). The liturgy of this Sunday entreats and warns us: "He that thinketh himself to stand, let him take heed lest he fall" (Epistle).

To make light of grace and to underestimate its importance is our grievous sin. "How often would I ..., and thou wouldest not" (Mt 23:37). We need helping grace every moment, no matter what we do, whether we pray or sacrifice and suffer in the discharge our duties. Is it not almost a habit with us to meet the suggestions of grace with reluctance or refusal? Do we not often answer: It is not my duty to do this or that; I need not renounce this pleasure, for I am not commanded to do so; I am not bound to undergo this kind of mortification? Grace is calling and drawing us; but we despise it. "If thou also hadst known . . . the things that are to thy peace."

"What doth it profit a man if he gain the whole world and suffer the loss of his own soul?" (Mt 16:26.) With every misused grace man's soul suffers some damage. "If thou also hadst known" what treasures can be stored up with the help of grace, how each grace is followed by another one, how each grace of which we make a good use makes us grow in sanctifying grace, in divine life, making us richer in graces during life and richer in merits for all eternity.

Prayer

Let Thy merciful ears, O Lord, be open to the prayers of Thy suppliant people; and that Thou mayest grant them their petitions, make them ask such things as shall please Thee. Through Christ our Lord. Amen.

Wednesday

"The people sat down to eat and drink, and rose up to play" (Epistle). Such frivolity could happen even at Mount Sinai shortly after God had appeared in His majesty in thunder and lightning. The Israelites had soon forgotten the miracles God had wrought for them: the passing of the Red Sea, His presence in the pillar of a cloud and in the pillar of fire, and the miraculous manna which God gave them daily. The people at the foot of the mountain eat and drink and dance, paying homage to a golden calf, the idol of the Egyptians. "All these things . . . are written for our correction, upon whom the ends of the world are come" (Epistle).

"If thou didst know the gift of God" (Jn 4:10), the value of sanctifying grace! Sanctifying grace lifts us beyond the merely natural man and his way of perceiving, and makes us participants in the life of the triune God. Being closely connected with God and immersed in the light and fire of the divinity, the soul takes on the splendor, ardor, and spirituality of God, receiving a beauty, nobility, and life resembling divine beauty and life. Thus the soul assumes a form of existence corresponding to the purity and spirituality of the divine nature, to which is attached as a reward the virtues of faith, hope, and charity. By the virtue of faith we see God, the world and its events, and the actions of men with the eyes of God: we see correctly. Hope lifts us above all created things: we repose in the lap of God, our loving Father, and aided by His power we endeavor to strive for the highest good, which no created power can attain by itself. Love alone can reach God: we love God because He is God, after the manner in which He loves us and the eternal Son loves Him. By the virtue of holy love we become immersed in God as if we were one nature with Him. Can there be any possession in this world equal to sanctifying grace and the divine virtues immediately flowing from it?

"If thou also hadst known . . . the things that are to thy peace; but now they are hidden from thy eyes" (Gospel). These words are also addressed to us. The greatest evil we can suffer is that of underestimating grace and supernatural values. "The people sat down to eat and drink, and rose up to play." We place a higher value on worldly accomplishments than we do on grace.

Sometimes even without noticing how frivolously we act, we prefer earthly pleasures and goods, perhaps even forbidden and sinful things, to the gifts of grace, and we thus reject this precious gift of God. Failing to understand the importance of judging in the light of faith, we think and judge according to merely natural human principles, and thus adjust our standards to those of the world. We likewise underestimate grace when we act out of merely natural human motives, when we fulfill our duties and take up our crosses without the support of faith and the ideals of grace. We make light of prayer, which alone can assure us of the graces necessary for our eternal salvation, and as a result our hearts, like trees, wither away for want of nourishment, even though outwardly our work flourishes. Above all, we neglect to sanctify our thoughts, our words, and our works by supernatural intentions, thus failing to make them meritorious for ourselves, for the Church, and for our fellow men. "If thou also hadst known ... the things that are to thy peace; but now they are hidden from thy eyes." Because we underestimate the necessity of grace and things supernatural, — the sacraments, the Church, her doctrines, and her precepts — we remain sterile and make no headway toward our heavenly destiny. Thus we oppose the interests of God, of His Church, of the souls of others, and of our own soul as well. We have good reason to fear that the Lord will weep over us, too, when we disregard His grace and love, preferring instead the vanities of this world.

Let us beseech the Lord to deliver us from the misfortune of underestimating the value of grace and the sonship of God. "Deliver me from my enemies, O my God; and defend me from them that rise up against me" (Alleluia). These enemies are our worldliness and our lack of faith. Praying thus, we implore the Lord for all our brethren in Christ.

"My house is the house of prayer, but you have made it a den of thieves" (Gospel). We are this house and temple of God as long as we are in possession of the sonship of God. By virtue of this intimate relationship to God, the Father, the Son, and the Holy Ghost dwell within us, rendering our soul a house of prayer. We, on our part, glorify the divine guest dwelling in our soul by our service of charity, homage, and devotion. "But you have made it a den of thieves." This sad state of affairs has occurred to us if we prefer worldly things to the grace of being a child of God and of living for the Father. Then we profane and desecrate this sanctuary by worldly, vain, and sinful thoughts and desires, by bad conduct towards the God living within us, by our many infidelities, and by our disobedience towards His holy will. "He that thinketh himself to stand, let him take heed lest he fall" (Epistle).

Prayer

Let Thy merciful ears, O Lord, be open to the prayers of Thy suppliant people; and that Thou mayest grant them their petitions, make them ask such things as shall please Thee. Through Christ our Lord. Amen.

Thursday

As Jesus rides solemnly into Jerusalem, the multitude cries: "Hosanna to the son of David: Blessed is He that cometh in the name of the Lord" (Mt 21:9). Jesus, however, weeps over the city. He loves Jerusalem, and because He loves it He is deeply grieved that it has not known the time of its visitation.

"The days shall come upon thee, and thy enemies shall cast a trench about thee, and compass thee round, and straiten thee on every side; and beat thee flat to the ground, and thy children who are in thee; and they shall not leave in thee a stone upon a stone, because thou hast not known the time of thy visitation" (Gospel). Did Jerusalem have no opportunity to recognize the time of its visitation? When the three Magi came from the East to seek the newborn king of the Jews, were not the priests and scribes able to direct them to Bethlehem? When a deputation of the priests in Jerusalem came to John the Baptist at the Jordan asking him who he was and why he baptized, did not John answer in unmistakable terms: "I am the voice of one crying in the wilderness, make straight the way of the Lord, as said the prophet Isaias.... I baptize with water; but there hath stood one in the midst of you, whom you know not. The same is He that shall come after me:... the latchet of whose shoe I am not worthy to loose" (Jn 1:23 ff.)? Did not the Lord during the time of His public life work enough miracles before the eyes of all the people of Galilee and Jerusalem, deeds that testified to His divinity? Only a few days had passed since He raised Lazarus to life, and now a few days later He enters the gates of Jerusalem.

It is Jerusalem's own fault that it did not know the time of its visitation. It had expected a national and political Messias who would fulfill its earthly dreams; it did not know the time of its merciful visitation and did not acknowledge the real Messias sent by God. Now Jerusalem has incurred just punishment. In a few days the veil of the temple will be rent; God's covenant with His people will be torn asunder. Pentecost will be the birthday of a new chosen people, of the New Covenant, of the Church of Christ; salvation will be taken from the chosen people and given to the Gentiles. Scarcely one generation will pass before the Romans will come and cast a trench about Jerusalem, will conquer and utterly destroy it. Truly they will not leave a stone upon a stone, because Jerusalem has not known the time of its visitation. "All these things ... are written for our correction" (Epistle). The visitation of the Lord, which we did not recognize through our own fault, and the grace which we refused and misused, cry out for vengeance, for punishment and expiation. Yet the Lord loves us still; He wishes to save us. But if we will not receive Him, He makes use of the rod of correction in order to make us understand that we must walk in His ways.

"Thou hast rejected the word of the Lord, and the Lord hath rejected thee" (1 Kgs 15:26). King Saul heard the word of God, yet he despised it and acted against God's command. He therefore is rejected by God, and the crown of kingship is bestowed on another man. Whenever we resist grace or abuse it, we are in danger of losing our eternal salvation. One grace is always linked to another one, to a whole series of graces. If we make good use of one grace, it is followed by another, greater one; this grace, in its turn, is followed by a series of new and more perfect graces. If we make light of one grace and lose it, we lose with this one grace a whole series of graces connected with it. It is possible that our salvation may depend upon this present grace. At all times and in all places this law holds good as a punishment for one misused grace: God deprives us of new graces. When the Holy Ghost knocks at the door of our soul and we refuse Him entrance, He will depart. When He speaks within us and we do not listen to His word, He will be silent. When He makes His light rise upon us and we close our eyes, He will withdraw.

"Neither let us tempt Christ, as some of them tempted and perished" (Epistle). The Israelites knew God's command, yet they ignored Him in order to find out, as it were, whether His commands were seriously meant. "Neither let us tempt Christ." Let us not despise His grace, His call, His inspirations, His will, presuming, perhaps, that the Lord will not insist on His word and inspirations.

Let us resolve now to be faithful to His grace and to manifest our esteem for it. "The justices of the Lord are right, rejoicing hearts, and His judgments sweeter than honey and the honeycomb; for Thy servant keepeth them" (Offertory). This promise of fidelity to the Lord and His grace we place on the paten during Mass.

"He that eateth My flesh and drinketh My blood, abideth in Me, and I in him" (Communion). The fruit of the Mass and Holy Communion is the union of our souls and hearts with Christ the Lord. We are of one heart and one soul with Him, one love and one will. When He gives Himself to us, He permeates us with His light, that we may know the time of His visitation. He gives us strength that we may lovingly comply with the inspirations of His grace. "Behold God is my helper, and the Lord is the protector of my soul" (Introit).

Prayer

Let Thy merciful ears, O Lord, be open to the prayers of Thy suppliant people; and that Thou mayest grant them their petitions, make them ask such things as shall please Thee. Through Christ our Lord. Amen.

Friday

"When Jesus drew near to Jerusalem, seeing the city, He wept over it." He loves the city of His people. "If thou also hadst known, and that in this day, the things that are to thy peace.... And entering into the temple, He began to cast out them that sold therein.... And He was teaching daily in the temple" (Gospel). Here we witness merciful love and love punishing and judging. The liturgy wants to impress deeply upon our minds that the Lord will come to judge the living and the dead. The love with which He wants to save and redeem us, "the living," is a love of justice.

Jesus loves Jerusalem. He rides solemnly into the city, and many of its inhabitants cordially welcome Him today. He is well aware, however, that today's "hosanna" will be followed within a few days by the cry, "Crucify Him." He knows that the Jews are going to condemn Him to death during these days, and that even before a week has passed He will hang on the Cross on the heights of Calvary, rejected and murdered by the people He has loved so much. He weeps, not only over the things that are to happen to Him in Jerusalem, but also over the poor city, which is destined to be destroyed. Less than forty years hence it will be in ruins. It has made itself unworthy; it is no longer the Holy City with its magnificent temple, the house of God. Even now it is planning the murder of the Lord. "How often would I have gathered together thy children,... and thou wouldest not" (Mt 23:37). Jesus shed tears because Jerusalem has rejected and refused the grace of God; it will therefore be rejected by God. It has let itself be deceived by its hope and desire of obtaining earthly splendor and glory.

Jesus judges. "Entering into the temple, He began to cast out them that sold therein, and them that bought, saying to them: It is written, My house is the house of prayer, but you have made it a den of thieves" (Gospel). Christ loves, and because He loves, He judges, for genuine love is a judging love. When the sun appears, it drives away all obscurity and darkness, and all things can be recognized in their real contours. So it is with love. Wherever it appears, egoism in all its forms and camouflages is clearly recognized. Where divine love appears, it delves down into the most hidden impulses and thoughts of men, condemning all that is obscure, dark, unrefined, and impure in man's heart. If the presence of a very noble and truly affectionate man makes us aware of our own egoism and want of charity, how much more must that be the case when Christ appears with His divine love? Is not each word He speaks to us a judgment, a judgment delving into our most secret impulses and thoughts? Then the soul cannot help judging itself from His point of view. The more lovingly the Lord approaches a soul, the more thoroughly He makes His light permeate it in order to purify that soul from everything that is unholy and may impair its peace and salvation. His love condemns everything that is unjust, egoistic, and opposed to God. Permeating the soul, this love makes it recognize clearly all the powers of destruction working within it, and reject everything that is unholy and displeasing to God.

God's love cannot be separated from His justice; for only one who loves judges us truly and works sincerely and efficaciously for our salvation. If our salvation is to be established, judgment must be passed on all that is impure, unholy, and unjust. This rule obtains for matters of great importance as well as for those of lesser concern. We must die in order to grow, for it is only through death that we can reach life. Whenever the Lord visits His judgment upon us, in the catastrophes of world events, in the various tests and trials He sends us, in difficulties and temptations, in illness and sufferings, He wants to heal and save us by His judgment. "If thou also hadst known."

Love without judgment is love without truth; it cannot redeem us. Only that love which brings us self-knowledge, humiliation, contrition, and repentance, can deliver us from the fetters of our impurity and corruption, our pride and egoism, and can lift us out of the darkness to the light.

The Lord is the judge of the living and the dead. He judges us because He loves us. He condemns everything within us that displeases Him. The more He loves us, the more unsparingly He judges us.

Prayer

Let Thy merciful ears, O Lord, be open to the prayers of Thy suppliant people; and that Thou mayest grant them their petitions, make them ask such things as shall please Thee. Through Christ our Lord. Amen.

Saturday

"At that time, when Jesus drew near to Jerusalem, seeing the city, He wept over it.... And entering into the temple, He began to cast out them that sold therein, and them that bought, saying to them: It is written, My house is the house of prayer, but you have made it a den of thieves. And He was teaching daily in the temple" (Gospel). This Gospel gives us a picture of Christ working within the soul. He loves the soul, but His love is a severe, jealous love. If He is to enter into the sanctuary of the soul, everything else must leave.

"I am the Lord thy God, mighty, jealous" (Ex 20:5). "The Lord, His name is Jealous; He is a jealous God" (Ex 34:14). He loved His people with divine love, and He did everything to assure them of His love. With the power of His miracles He delivered the people out of Egypt, led them into the Promised Land, and revealed Himself in various ways. Time and again He chastised the people in order to bring them back to the right path. But the majority of the poor people of Israel did not understand the chastisement, the jealous love of their God. Forgetting Him, they turned their thoughts to vanities, to the idols of the heathens, and to worldly goods and interests. They came to the temple year after year to offer sacrifices, but they honored God with their lips only; their hearts were far from Him (Mt 15:8). "If thou also hadst known . . . the things that are to thy peace." The jealous love of God becomes, after so many fruitless efforts, the love of justice and punishment, leaving no stone upon a stone in Jerusalem. God's love does not spare His people. He permits the enemy to cast a trench about Jerusalem and surround it. Thus His avenging love takes up the scourge, purging away everything that does not belong in the sanctuary, and then He Himself takes possession of the temple.

"I am jealous of you with the jealousy of God" (2 Cor 11:2). Just as the Lord was jealous of Jerusalem, as He demonstrated in today's Gospel, so He is also jealous of the soul which He has lovingly drawn to Himself and made the object of His love. He is jealous of us and desires that our heart and mind pay homage to Him. He wants our entire being. He wants our thoughts, our judgments, and wills, that these faculties of our soul may be lifted above flesh and blood, beyond the merely natural way of thinking and judging; He desires us to think the thoughts of God and Christ, and to see all things in the light of eternity. He desires that we value whatever He values, love what He loves, renounce and despise what He renounces and despises. He desires the homage of our hearts; He wishes to become the center of our plans, desires, and inclinations, of whatever we do or omit. He wants us to look at Him first of all, and at Him alone, rendering love and homage to Him at all times. Thus He jealously asks us to die to our own desires and wishes, knowing only His good pleasure and looking for nothing in heaven or on earth but God and His holy will. He wishes to be "the God of [our] heart, and the God that is [our] portion forever" (Ps 72:26). His jealousy knows no bounds. Only after we have given Him all that He asks, the sum of our own desires and wishes, will He be satisfied. He knows no rest until we are entirely His.

Since we ourselves, however, are unwilling to sacrifice our self-love, He undertakes to destroy it. Showing no mercy or consideration, He breaks all the ties that link our hearts and our spirits to anything that is not Himself. He sends us interior trials, spiritual dryness, humiliating experiences, temptations of a kind we may never have known before; there will be exterior trials, sickness, suffering, humiliations, and calumny. Sometimes He does not even spare us that bitterest of all spiritual trials, the feeling of being left in darkness, of being abandoned and repudiated by God. By these means God works with His jealous love within our souls. Thus the soul becomes purified and freed from all the fetters of egoism. Now it is ready to accept whatever God may send, sorrow as well as joy, poverty no less than abundance, death as well as life. The soul knows only Him, who now enters into the sanctuary of its innermost being. "He was teaching daily in the temple." The soul is His property, His abode. Now when He talks to it, it listens like Mary did at the feet of the Master. It experiences the inexpressible sweetness of the jealous love of the Lord: "I am jealous of you with the jealousy of God."

"Behold God is my helper, and the Lord is the protector of my soul." He loves me with a jealous love. "If thou also hadst known, and that in this day," in these times when love is tried, when Christ, seeking entrance, leaves no stone upon a stone, but calls upon suffering, hardships, sickness, and both interior and exterior trials to perfect the work within the soul. They, on their part, purge it of its stains and make it a fit sanctuary for the Lord. This is the way of jealous love.

In the Mass today we gladly place our entire being on the altar, into His hands. He must be Lord in the temple of our soul. Our heart and spirit must pay homage to Him. We must give everything to Him.

Prayer

Let Thy merciful ears, O Lord, be open to the prayers of Thy suppliant people; and that Thou mayest grant them their petitions, make them ask such things as shall please Thee. Through Christ our Lord. Amen.

Tenth Sunday after Pentecost

The Mass

Two facts determine the growth of the kingdom of God within us: the grace of God, and the attitude the soul takes toward the working of that grace. "There are diversities of graces, but the same Spirit; and there are diversities of ministries, but the same Lord; and there are diversities of operations, but the same God, who worketh all in all.... To one indeed, by the Spirit, is given the word of wisdom; and to another the word of knowledge ...; to another the grace of healing in one Spirit.... But all these things one and the same Spirit worketh, dividing to every one according as He will" (Epistle). To this all-powerful working of grace entirely independent of man corresponds, on the part of man, a humble recognition of his utter helplessness. "No man can say: The Lord Jesus, but by the Holy Ghost" (Epistle). Today's liturgy teaches us that wherever man's weakness and inability to fulfill by himself the demands of the supernatural life are acknowledged, there alone is possible the development of the life of grace in man.

Therefore acknowledging the insufficiency of our own human and natural faculties, we go today to the celebration of Mass. The Pharisee stands before us. With proud composure he prays: "O God, I give Thee thanks that I am not as the rest of men." He ponders his worth, well aware of his apparent superiority over other men. His proud prayer, however, becomes his undoing: "I say to you, this man [the publican] went down to his house justified rather than the other [the Pharisee]; because every one that exalteth himself shall be humbled, and he that humbleth himself shall be exalted" (Gospel). We share the humble and repentant sentiments of the publican, hardly daring to lift up our eyes towards heaven. Our prayer is a sincere *mea culpa*, a loud, "O God, be merciful to me a sinner." Acknowledging our unworthiness and weakness, we confidently go to our Lord, beseeching Him: "O God, who dost manifest Thy almighty power chiefly in showing mercy and pity; increase Thy mercy towards us" (Collect). We know that all the work of salvation depends primarily on His mercy.

During Mass today we ourselves are the humble and repentant publican. During the Holy Sacrifice we are to learn that we, too, shall be exalted and find pardon and grace whenever we present ourselves in humility and repentance before God. Acknowledging our own insufficiency, during Mass we cling to a superior power: "To Thee, O Lord, have I lifted up my soul; in Thee, O my God, I put my trust" (Offertory). Convinced of the inefficaciousness of our own prayers and sacrifices, we confidently depend on our communion with Christ and our intimate union with His prayers and sacrifice, which are of infinite value. During Mass we are exalted because He becomes our sacrifice and, being the mediator between the Father and humanity, takes up our cause before God. Thus, "through Him, with Him, and in Him," we are enabled to honor the Father worthily in the Holy Sacrifice, to adore, love, and thank Him, to expiate for our sins, and to beseech Him in our prayers in a worthy manner that makes them acceptable to Him. The reception of Holy Communion enhances our exaltation, when the living, glorified, and exalted Christ Himself becomes our food, pouring into our souls the fullness of His divine life. "He that humbleth himself shall be exalted" (Gospel).

Meditation

Christ the Lord, the Judge, stands before our eyes in today's liturgy. "Let my judgment come forth from Thy countenance; let Thy eyes behold the things that are equitable" (Gradual). Christ judges self-righteousness, as represented by the Pharisee, and the humble and repentant acknowledgment of guilt, as represented by the publican. "O God, be merciful to me, a sinner" (Gospel). He decides in favor of the humble and repentant acknowledgment of guilt against the conceited self-righteousness of the proud Pharisee.

"Two men went up into the temple to pray; the one a Pharisee, and the other a publican. The Pharisee, standing, prayed thus with himself: O God, I give Thee thanks that I am not as the rest of men, extortioners, unjust, adulterers; as also is this publican. I fast twice in the week; I give tithes of all that I possess. And the publican, standing afar off, would not so much as lift up his eyes towards heaven, but struck his breast saying: O God, be merciful to me, a sinner" (Gospel). Here we have two persons, two representatives of religion and piety, men from different worlds, appearing in judgment before the face of God. Christ the Judge passes the judgment: "I say to you, this man [the publican] went down to his house justified rather than the other." And He the Judge gives reasons for His judgment: "Every one that exalteth himself shall be humbled, and he that humbleth himself shall be exalted" (Gospel). The sinner finds pardon with God as long as he confesses himself to be a sinner and unworthy of God's graces, and as long as he implores forgiveness from the Lord and strength for leading a good life. But woe to the proud self-righteousness that needs no penance, no conversion. Woe to the kind of piety that thinks well of itself, of its good works, its mortifications, and its virtues, while it despises others as extortioners, unjust, and adulterers. The prayers of such men cannot be pleasing to God, neither can their works. "God resisteth the proud, but to the humble He giveth grace" (1 Pt 5:5).

"To Thee, O Lord, have I lifted up my soul; in Thee, O my God, I put my trust" (Offertory). Behold the Church humbly beseeching her divine Master. The Pharisee in today's Gospel is to the liturgy the representative of the Jews, whereas the publican represents the Gentiles, the Church. Again we are confronted with that astonishing fact from the history of salvation: the chosen people are rejected, and the Gentiles are mercifully received into the Church. "O God, Thou dost manifest Thy almighty power chiefly in showing mercy and pity" (Collect). The Church, called out of the midst of the Gentiles, knows that she was a sinner, entirely unworthy of being called to God's mercies. She went up into the temple, seeking God; like the publican of the Gospel, she stood off at a distance hardly daring to lift up her eyes towards heaven. She could but pray: "O God, be merciful to me, a sinner." There was nothing she could offer, no works of which she could boast in the sight of God; she could bring only her misery and unworthiness and the confession of her sinfulness. God accepted this confession with mercy and love. He sent His only-begotten Son to lift her out of the misery and filth of sin, to purify her in His blood, and to make her His virginal bride and queen. "This man went down to his house justified rather than the other."

Israel, once the chosen people, by boasting of its loyalty and fidelity to the law, causes its own rejection: "Every one that exalteth himself shall be humbled, and he that humbleth himself shall be exalted." But the Church knows herself to be the recipient of God's mercy; whatever she calls her own in the way of graces, virtues, and blessings, she knows is only the product of God's purest mercy and undeserved love. "O God, Thou dost manifest Thy almighty power chiefly in showing mercy and pity" (Collect). Day after day she is the repentant publican who makes his pilgrimage to the temple. She is well aware of the fact that her children are bound by the fetters of sin and concupiscence, unworthy of grace and pardon. Day after day, however, she recalls the power of God's mercy and, together with her children, prays for all: "O God, be merciful to me, a sinner."

With the Church we approach the Holy Sacrifice with the sentiments of the humble and repentant publican. Bowing down at the Confiteor we confess: *mea culpa, mea culpa, mea maxima culpa.* At the Kyrie we ask pardon and mercy for our many sins and infidelities. At the Offertory we bring our gifts to the altar: a repentant heart, which places its confidence in God's mercy alone, and not in its own faculties of intellect or will: "To Thee, O Lord, have I lifted up my soul: in Thee, O my God, I put my trust." For "I can do all things in Him who strengtheneth me" (Phil 4:13). "Receive, O holy Father, almighty and eternal God, this spotless host which I, Thy unworthy servant, offer unto Thee, my living and true God, for my own countless sins, offenses, and negligences, and for all here present."

With the Church we come to adore and to sacrifice, and, together with the sacrifice of Christ, to be received by God. Christ the Lord celebrated His sacrifice on Golgotha in the spirit of humility. In like manner we will be able to partake of it only in so far as we enter into the spirit of Christ's humility. The more we enter into that spirit during Mass, professing ourselves worthy of death and willing to die with Jesus, the better we shall be able to celebrate a resurrection with Him at Communion, when we shall be exalted and glorified by His life within us. "He that humbleth himself shall be exalted."

Prayer

O God, who dost manifest Thy almighty power chiefly in showing mercy and pity; increase Thy mercy towards us, that we, seeking the way of Thy promises, may be made partakers of Thy heavenly treasures. Through Christ our Lord. Amen.

Monday

The Pharisee and the publican represent pride and humility. In a more general way we can identify the Pharisee with the proud, self-assured agnostic who sees no need for God, a Redeemer, a Church, or prayer. Similarly the Church is the publican who humbly and fervently beseeches God to grant her light and grace for doing good, who does not trust in herself, but expects everything from Him and His mercy. She, the Church, "went down to [her] house justified rather than the other," the unbeliever, the proud; "because every one that exalteth himself shall be humbled, and he that humbleth himself shall be exalted" (Gospel).

"Every one that exalteth himself shall be humbled." The proud man trusts in his ability to do everything by his own strength. He needs neither God nor man; he is self-sufficient. But what is the consequence of such a point of view? He is bound daily to experience how little man is able to do by himself, how many mistakes he makes, how often he is a failure. Because he suffers grievous disappointments daily, he becomes peevish and impatient. Seeking only his own honor, his plans and changing interests center around his own advantage; following the ideas of the moment, he is continually kept in a state of excitement, tension, and unrest. Pride is always narrow-minded and centers entirely around its own petty interests. Being its own reward, it shall be humbled. For the proud man not only is rejected by God, he is despised by his fellow men as well, even when they flatter and serve him; besides, he becomes his own burden and punishment. There is no blessing on the proud. "God resisteth the proud" (1 Pt 5:5). Thus pride leads to interior unrest and remorse; it weakens a man's strength because he will not rely on God's power. The proud man relies entirely on his own talents, knowledge, prowess, and efforts, which are but a "broken staff of a reed, ... upon which if a man lean, it will go into his hand and pierce it" (Is 36:6). Pride is weakness. "The foolish things of the world hath God chosen, that He may confound the wise; and the weak things of the world hath God chosen, that He may confound the strong" (1 Cor 1:27).

"He that humbleth himself shall be exalted." In humility there is strength. It is always and everywhere accompanied by generosity. Humility is the ornament of all the other virtues; it is never satisfied with the outward appearance of things, with things done by halves; neither does it long for the satisfaction of trivial and passing success. Never tired of doing good, it is most happy when it brings a sacrifice; it is resourceful in giving proofs of its charity. The humble man does not think of himself. He does not care much about the opinions of the world and of men, about his own honor and advantages, about the satisfaction of his own desires. He is concerned only about God's holy will and His glory; he counts nothing important except God, and heeds only what comes from God and leads to Him. A humble man is unselfish, and therefore without envy and jealousy. His concern is "that by all means ... Christ be preached" (Phil 1:18). The misdeeds of his fellow men do not discourage him; on the contrary, they are an incitement for him to be all the more faithful by serving the community and his neighbor. A humble man is also courageous. Threats, mockery, and calumny do not disturb him; flatteries cannot seduce him. He is ready to do whatever God's will demands of him. When difficult and humiliating tasks are entrusted to him, he fears neither the efforts nor the sacrifices involved; he knows he can do all things in Him who is his strength. The less a humble man trusts in himself, the more unshakable is his confidence that God's power will render all things possible. How often it happens that great men, working unceasingly, leave hardly a trace of their efforts to posterity, while others, whose talents and endeavors appear almost negligible, are blessed with tremendous success in their undertakings! Such is the mystery of humility, of distrust of self, of trust in God and His grace. God imparts His grace to the humble. "He that humbleth himself shall be exalted."

In humility we must look for the secret of strength; herein lies the strength and invincibility of the Church. Living by the Spirit of the Lord and in the spirit of humility and submission to God, she expects everything from God. "To Thee, O Lord, have I lifted up my soul; in Thee, O my God, I put my trust; . . . for none of them that wait on Thee shall be confounded" (Offertory). Oppressed on all sides, persecuted and calumniated, she is confident of victory. She knows only one source of power: prayer and humble submission to God, "who worketh all in all" (Epistle). She is the praying Church, relying on God's mercy, grace, and aid: "When I cried to the Lord, He heard my voice" (Introit). The prayers of the humble overpower God; He cannot leave them unheard.

The secret of our strength lies in the spirit of humility; for God gives His grace to the humble. The more humble we are, the more room is there for God to work in our soul. Whatever is good and great in a man's soul can grow and thrive only under the cloak of humility.

The cause of our weakness, our faults, and relapses is our self-reliance, which causes us to forget that God worketh "both to will and to accomplish, according to His good will" (Phil 2:13). "He that humbleth himself shall be exalted."

Prayer

O God, who dost manifest Thy almighty power chiefly in showing mercy and pity; increase Thy mercy towards us, that we, seeking the way of Thy promises, may be made partakers of Thy heavenly treasures. Through Christ our Lord. Amen.

Tuesday

"Every one that exalteth himself shall be humbled, and he that humbleth himself shall be exalted" (Gospel). Let us return again to the picture of the Pharisee and the publican. The one exemplifies self-love, boasting of its own excellence and ignoring God and His grace; the other exemplifies the love for God which makes man forget himself because of God and causes him to put his whole trust in God's mercy and grace. It is the picture of pride and humility in another form. Pride is the spirit of this world; humility, the spirit of Christ and His Church.

Pride is the spirit of this world, the pagan spirit. Whoever follows his own spirit and will, is a proud man. A man in his pride turns away from God, refusing to place the talents, faculties, and powers of his body and soul at the disposal of God. He wants to be his own master; not even God may claim any right over him. Pride, the refusal to submit to God, is the beginning of every sin; pride is the beginning and the root of all evil. It is the leaven which infects the good in man and, as it grows, corrupts the whole. It is the greatest obstacle to union with God; it encourages the passions and human concupiscence. These are the characteristics of worldliness: neglect of God, self-love, and pride. The world has no need for God, no need for a Redeemer, a Church, prayer, or the sacraments. It considers itself able to remain pure, patient, and charitable by its own strength. This spirit of the world, of pride and self-glorification, often enters even the hearts of Christians.

Despite the fact that they solemnly renounced the world when they received the Holy Ghost, they long for praise and favors from men in high positions, and they like to be honored by the world. We, too, are often servile in our attitude towards the powerful ones of this world; we fail utterly to understand the need for Christian humility; we are entirely lacking in the spirit of Christ and His Church. No wonder, then, that Christian life suffers so greatly, that we deny our Christian ideals and principles so easily, that we sacrifice our convictions for philosophical novelties.

Humility is the spirit of Christ. "Learn of Me," He tells us, "because I am meek and humble of heart" (Mt 11:29). We need not work miracles or create new worlds; we need not raise the dead to life. But one thing is necessary: to be humble of heart. Pride is such a devastating poison that it can be counteracted only by a very strong antidote. The remedy our Lord offers is the most powerful that could ever be: the deepest humiliation of the Son of God. Entering into this world, Christ chose submission, poverty, humiliation, and finally the most disgraceful death on the cross. We see Him rejected by men, condemned to die as a criminal on the cross. Such is the humility of Jesus. Humility is the beginning and end of all He does for our salvation, the very essence of what He has taught us in word and deed.

Humility is the most characteristic virtue of Jesus. Therefore humility is also the first virtue of Christ's mystical body, the Church, and of every true Christian who is a member of this body. It is the only foundation on which virtues can safely be built; it is the root and the beginning of salvation and all good. The growth of virtue and grace depends on the progress of humility. The entire structure of the life of grace rests on the two fundamental pillars of the power of Christ's cross and the working of the Holy Ghost; but only he whose spiritual life is founded in humility will be able to carry the burden of Christ's cross and live a Christian life. The Holy Ghost, on the other hand, will never dwell in a soul that is not humble. This humility is the foundation upon which the Christian supernatural life must rest. A humble submission to God's will and the acknowledgment of our nothingness before Him remove the obstacles which a heart corrupted by pride puts in the way of faith, hope, and charity. "Learn of Me, because I am meek and humble of heart."

We are branches of Christ, the vine. With St. Paul we say: "I can do all things in Him who strengtheneth me" (Phil 4:13). Of ourselves we are nothing, but we are strong in Him.

Whatever supernatural good we possess comes to us from without, from Christ, who is the vine, the head. "Of His fullness we all have received, and grace for grace" (Jn 1:16). Whatever we are and whatever we have, we are and have only because we are branches of Christ, the vine, members of His mystical body. To Him, therefore, we owe all honor and glory. As far as we are concerned, we can please ourselves only in our infirmities. "Gladly, therefore, will I glory in my infirmities, that the power of Christ may dwell in me. For which cause I please myself in my infirmities, in reproaches, in necessities, in persecutions, in distresses, for Christ. For when I am weak, then I am powerful" (2 Cor 12:9 f.).

Prayer

O God, who resisteth the proud and granteth Thy grace to the humble of heart, grant, we beseech Thee, the virtue of true humility, the model of which Thy only-begotten Son hath deigned to be before our eyes. Never permit us to invite Thy anger through our pride, but may we receive the mercy of Thy grace through obedience. Through Christ our Lord. Amen.

Wednesday

"God worketh all in all" (Epistle). God's grace is the foundation of Christian humility. "By the grace of God, I am what I am; and His grace in me hath not been void, but I have labored more abundantly than all they; yet not I, but the grace of God with me" (1 Cor 15:10). What is the Apostle by himself? He calls himself "one born out of due time," unworthy of the vocation of an apostle of Christ. "For I am the least of the apostles, who am not worthy to be called an apostle, because I persecuted the Church of God" (1 Cor 15:9). God gives His grace to the humble of heart: to the publican, who repentantly strikes his breast, to those men who, like St. Paul, think little of themselves. God works great wonders in a humble heart.

It is "God who worketh in you, both to will and to accomplish, according to His good will" (Phil 2:13). For sin we are sufficient in ourselves, for our whole nature was inclined to evil once it had been weakened through Original Sin. Our reason lacks clear vision in many important questions if light from above is not given to it through the channels of grace. Our will is paralyzed, weakened, and inclined to evil. The passions pervert the spirit, dragging it all too often down to their own level; concupiscence has an uncanny power over the imagination, the thoughts, the instincts, and the inclinations of man. So man is self-sufficient for sinning, but not for avoiding and conquering sin. He is equally unable to perform works of supernatural value, works that please God. We are not "sufficient to think any thing of ourselves as of ourselves; but our sufficiency is from God" (2 Cor 3:5). We are unable to work anything at all supernaturally good, for it is "God who worketh all in all." If He does not awaken and stir our will, we never shall be able to perform even the slightest good work. His spirit must move and direct our will; the first impulse, the very beginning of every good work and action, is not from ourselves, but is the result of God's grace and mercy towards us. The right will must be given to us by God. "What hast thou that thou hast not received? And if thou hast received, why dost thou glory as if thou hadst not received it?" (1 Cor 4:7.) It is God who worketh all in all; we are entirely impotent and helpless by ourselves.

It is "God who worketh all in all." He works at the beginning, during the performance, and at the completion of the work. Every act of ours receives its existence, measure, direction, and duration from God. Where He is not present, there are no good works. Our actions are determined by God in two ways: God ordains them and inspires us to perform them; God's action gives our actions duration and value. Our activity can neither precede God's activity nor continue without it, being in every respect dependent upon Him. If we perform good works, God has given us not only the will to do this particular good work, but also the power to accomplish it. This grace has in no way been merited by us. How, therefore, can we ever boast of the good we have done? Can we justly ascribe it to our own powers? How can we extol our own work as if we had done anything good by our own power? "God worketh all in all." "No flesh should glory in His sight" (1 Cor 1:29). If the Lord must give us the will as well as the power to do good, if "it is not of him that willeth, nor of him that runneth, but of God that showeth mercy" (Rom 9:16), how can we in any way rely on our own will and strength? With the Apostle we must confess humbly and gratefully: "By the grace of God, I am what I am" (1 Cor 15:10).

"Unless the Lord build the house, they labor in vain that build it. Unless the Lord keep the city, he watcheth in vain that keepeth it. It is vain for you to rise before light" (Ps 126:1 f.). It is God's work that matters. If He is not the co-worker, the work of man is in vain; without God it is without blessing and fruit. "It is vain for you to rise before light," preferring to act and work first before He starts with His work. Actions that are the work of man's spirit and powers and are not moved by God's grace, actions that are not dependent on His will and work, will be without fruit.

"He that humbleth himself shall be exalted." This is the secret of true piety. If we humbly submit ourselves to God's will, we have started on the right path. "Rise ye after you have sitten" (Ps 126:2). First of all we must sit, rest, accept wholeheartedly God's working within our souls; then we must rise and work with the power of God's help. With His help we are confident that we can accomplish all things. "To Thee, O Lord, have I lifted up my soul; in Thee, O my God, I put my trust" (Offertory).

PRAYER

O God, who dost manifest Thy almighty power chiefly in showing mercy and pity; increase Thy mercy towards us, that we, seeking the way of Thy promises, may be made partakers of Thy heavenly treasures. Through Christ our Lord. Amen.

Thursday

The Gospel shows us two men praying in the temple. One of them begins thus: "O God, I give Thee thanks that I am not as the rest of men.... I fast twice in the week; I give tithes of all that I possess." The other stands afar off, and "would not so much as lift up his eyes towards heaven." He strikes his breast, saying: "O God, be merciful to me, a sinner." The one boastfully asserts that there is nothing he must pray for. Sufficient in himself, he remains within himself, expecting to receive everything from himself and believing himself able to fulfill all his needs by himself. The other man prays, going outside of himself; he opens his heart that God may give him something, thus lifting himself beyond his self to God.

"To Thee, O Lord, have I lifted up my soul; in Thee, O my God, I put my trust" (Offertory). When we pray we go outside of ourselves, lifting our heart towards God. But who can lift us towards Him, unless He does so Himself? Of our own power we are unable to escape from ourselves. As long as we rely on ourselves, like the Pharisee in the temple, we are unable to transcend our own being; we remain within ourselves, excluding the influence of God's grace. With such pride we cannot truly pray: "To Thee, O Lord, have I lifted up my soul." Pride does not pray; only humility prays, because it does not feel sufficient in itself. Abandoning itself, humility professes its dependence on God. Thus it can truly say: "To Thee, O Lord, have I lifted up my soul." He who speaks in such a way receives nothing from himself; but he receives everything from God. All that he has received he returns to God without retaining anything for himself or ascribing anything to his own powers. Having nothing of himself, keeping nothing for himself, he admits that he has received everything he possesses from God and for God. He can truly say: "To Thee, O Lord, have I lifted up my soul." This is a genuine prayer to God and denotes a true union with Him. It requires the giving up of one's self in order to adhere to God, in order to will and love only what God wills and what is pleasing to Him. Such an attitude of, mind is founded on humility.

"In Thee, O my God, I put my trust; let me not be ashamed" (Offertory); that is, I shall be heard. "When I cried to the Lord, He heard my voice, from them that draw near to me"

(Introit). Genuine and humble prayer is always accepted by God. "He that humbleth himself shall be exalted" (Gospel). Such is a fundamental law of the spiritual life. The word of the Baptist will always be true: "He must increase, but I must decrease" (Jn 3:30). In the measure we go outside of ourselves in prayer, God enters into our souls, filling us with His gifts and graces. The more we renounce ourselves in prayer, the more we grow in love for God. The more we decrease, the more He increases within us until that day when, humility and self-renunciation having become perfect, everything we are is from God and for God. Genuine prayer enlarges our hearts, enabling us to receive all the gifts of God, even God Himself. When He is within us, He will be also for us; and "if God be for us, who is against us?" (Rom 8:31.) "When I cried to the Lord, He heard my voice, from them that draw near to me; and He humbled them, who is before all ages, and remains forever" (Introit).

The publican prayed and went down to his house justified. Such is the power of genuine, humble prayer. We experience this power of prayer all the more intimately when we unite our prayers with those of the praying Church. Through liturgical prayers we increase our power, we renounce our individuality and enter into communion with the praying Church. "To Thee, O Lord, have I lifted up my soul" in union with the praying Church. Then it can be truly said of us: "This man went down to his house justified."

We shall pray well and fruitfully to the extent to which we humbly forget ourselves and renounce our own will and desires. Sometimes we feel unhappy if we do not obtain what we desire and pray for. It is our pride and self-will that is wounded. Our prayer, however, will be all the better and more efficacious the more humbly we acknowledge our failures and our weakness and let the Lord direct our ways as He pleases. Only of the man who sincerely prays with humility did the Lord say: "This man went down to his house justified."

PRAYER

O God, who dost manifest Thy almighty power chiefly in showing mercy and pity; increase Thy mercy towards us, that we, seeking the way of Thy promises, may be made partakers of Thy heavenly treasures. Through Christ our Lord. Amen.

Friday

"To Thee, O Lord, have I lifted up my soul; in Thee, O my God, I put my trust; let me not be ashamed" (Offertory). "When I cried to the Lord, He heard my voice" (Introit). The Church believes that God graciously hears her prayers. Knowing the power and the value of prayer, she prays full of confidence in the Lord; she prays through Him in a humble way.

The Church prays full of confidence in the Lord. Having paid for our guilt through His life and death, our Lord has rendered the most perfect satisfaction to the Father, thus meriting all the graces necessary for our salvation. In heaven and in the tabernacle He unceasingly implores the Father for us. The Church knows that she is too weak of herself, for many of her children are still subject to sin and unable to do good works without the help of God. For this reason she feels all the more obliged to call upon the satisfaction, merits, and prayers of the Lord. "I can do all things in Him who strengtheneth me" (Phil 4:13). Daily and without interruption she offers the Father during Mass the blood, merits, and satisfaction the Lord has made for us during His earthly life. These merits and satisfactions are of infinite value, and by this sacrifice the Church renders infinite homage, praise, and glory to almighty God. By virtue of the Mass she offers to divine justice the most complete satisfaction and expiation for our sins and the punishment due to them. By the Mass the Church gains abundant actual graces which illuminate the sinner and induce him to make acts of penance and contrition, thus leading him back to the friendship of God in the sacrament of penance. In the Mass she also gains the graces that incite and strengthen the just man to do good works, to make sacrifices, and to lift up his soul to perfect love for God and his neighbor. Offering Himself as a gift of sacrifice for His Church in the Mass, the Lord is the high priest and mediator before the Father, pleading the cause of His beloved bride, the Church. Can it be possible that the Father will deny anything to the Son, in whom He is well pleased? Will He disregard the prayers which His Son submits to Him in the name of His Church and for the Church? Assuredly God will not disregard the prayers of His Son. With confidence the Church prays in union with Christ: "In Thee, O my God, I put my trust; let me not be ashamed."

The Church prays through Christ, the Lord. She concludes all her prayers with the words, "through Christ our Lord." Since He is the mediator ordained by God to mediate between Himself and us, the Church, full of confidence, puts her prayers and intentions, her thanksgivings and praises in the hands of this mediator. He accepts them, uniting them with the adoration, thanksgiving, and praises of His own Heart, making them His own in such a way that He offers them to His Father as if they really were His own. Small wonder, then, that the Church rejoices: "When I cried to the Lord, He heard my voice" (Introit). For this reason she never wearies of praying and fears nothing, though she is surrounded by her enemies on all sides and is ever oppressed and persecuted. "To Thee, O Lord, have I lifted up my soul; in Thee, O my God, I put my trust; let me not be ashamed." Now we understand why the Church repeatedly sings songs of triumph and victory: she is sure that her prayers will be heard through Christ, the mediator who makes them part of His all-powerful prayers.

We pray with the Church. By virtue of our communion with the Church we also pray relying on Christ, the mediator, who ascended into heaven as our precursor and sits at the right hand of the Father "that He may appear now in the presence of God for us" (Heb 9:24). Having become one with Him, we also may go to the Father and say: "I am Thy first-begotten one." We are allowed to speak to the Father in the name of His Son, asking of Him with fullest confidence for whatever we may stand in need of.

We possess sanctifying grace, the grace of the sonship of God, by virtue of which the features of Christ, the Son of God, have been imprinted upon our soul. When, therefore, the Father sees us clothed with the robe of sanctifying grace, in the likeness of His Son, He cannot refuse us what we ask of Him; for in asking of Him we rely not on ourselves but on Him in whom the Father is well pleased.

Prayer

O God, who dost manifest Thy almighty power chiefly in showing mercy and pity; increase Thy mercy towards us, that we, seeking the way of Thy promises, may be made partakers of Thy heavenly treasures. Through Christ our Lord. Amen.

Saturday

"When I cried to the Lord, He heard my voice" (Introit). The Church is always going up to the temple to pray. Her basic attitude is one of homage towards God, of littleness before Him, of adoration and humility.

The Church pays homage to God. The first duty the Church of Christ performs is the adoration of God and humble submission to Him. In all humility she bows down to submit herself to God. Every page of the Holy Scriptures, both the Old and the New Testament, is holy to her; she believes in every word of the Gospels. Believing requires humility. In her priests and religious she stands in the sanctuary day and night paying homage to God. "It is truly meet and just, right and availing unto salvation, that we should at all times and in all places give thanks unto Thee, O Lord" (Preface). Unceasingly the Church chants the psalms in honor of her Lord and God, continuing her avowal in the Gloria: "We adore Thee, we glorify Thee, we give thanks to Thee for Thy great glory." Out of her mouth goes forth an unending "Glory be to the Father, and to the Son, and to the Holy Ghost." Daily and hourly she celebrates the Sacrifice of the Mass, offering to God in her gift of sacrifice an infinitely valuable adoration and homage. "Through Him, and with Him, and in Him, be unto Thee, O God the Father Almighty, in the unity of the Holy Ghost, all honor and glory."

The Church receives every gift from God. What could she do by herself, without God, without Christ? What can the body achieve without the head, which enlivens and directs all the other members? What is the branch without the vine? The Church knows that "no man can say: The Lord Jesus, but by the Holy Ghost" (Epistle). She knows the many gifts and graces which are operative in her children. "To one indeed, by the Spirit, is given the word of wisdom; and to another, the word of knowledge; . . . to another, the grace of healing; . . . to another, the working of miracles; to another, prophecy; to another, the discerning of spirits" (Epistle). "It is God who worketh in you, both to will and to accomplish" (Phil 2:13). The Church knows that she has nothing of herself, but has received from God the fullness of all good things. "Of His fullness we all have received, and grace for grace" (Jn 1:16). Therefore she expects and requests everything from the Lord. "When I cried to the Lord, He heard my voice" (Introit).

The Church returns all things to God. She does not retain for herself what she has received through her prayers to Him. His gifts and graces she returns as homage, adoration, praise, and thanksgiving, especially during the Sacrifice of the Mass. "A hymn becometh Thee in Sion; and a vow shall be paid to Thee in Jerusalem" (Gradual). Whatever the Church has received in gifts and graces, she turns to good use with her members, — into works of charity, of zeal for souls, of love towards God and men — rendering it fruitful for God and His interests, for His glory and the salvation of souls. She is like another virgin of Nazareth who, after her blessed conception of the Son of God, retained nothing for herself, but returned everything she had received to Him from whom she received it, as we learn from her admirable Magnificat and the words of devoted love to Elizabeth and John.

We unite our prayers with those of the Church. The more we abandon our own way of praying by humbly submitting them to the prayers of the Church, the more our prayers will be assured of being heard.

Nothing for oneself, but everything for God: that is the language of humility. He who prays in the right spirit asks nothing for his own sake, but acknowledges that whatever he has, he has received it from God and for God, for Christ and His Church. Genuine prayer urges the soul to work for God, for Christ, and for souls. It necessarily unites our soul with God and Christ, with the Church, and with our fellow men.

He who prays in the right spirit neither ignores God's gifts nor denies any of the rights of his fellow men. Well aware of the fact that he did not receive these gifts and graces to be used for his own ends, he tries to make good use of them for God and His glory.

Prayer

O God, who dost manifest Thy almighty power chiefly in showing mercy and pity; increase Thy mercy towards us, that we, seeking the way of Thy promises, may be made partakers of Thy heavenly treasures. Through Christ our Lord. Amen.

Eleventh Sunday after Pentecost

The Mass

The liturgy of the Mass for the eleventh Sunday after Pentecost is entirely dominated by the thought of Easter and by the remembrance of that unforgettable event of Easter night, the reception of baptism. By today's Mass the grace and the obligations of baptism are renewed.

The sixty-seventh psalm gives us a splendid picture of Easter by showing us the children of Israel on their march to the Promised Land. Having left the captivity and slavery of Egypt, they march, full of joy, through the Red Sea, where their enemies perish. At Sinai they receive the Ten Commandments; they are fed by the manna, and at last come into possession of the land of Canaan. Jahve goes with His people from Sinai to the heights of Mt. Moria, where, in the temple of Jerusalem, He has chosen the dwelling place where He would draw to Himself those that were of a just mind and would offer their prayers and sacrifices to Him. They would be united in one faith and one cult. From here power and grace was to go out to His people.

What the Introit thus reproduces before our eyes has been repeated in baptism. On Easter we were brought out of Egypt, that life of separation from God. We then marched through the waters of the Red Sea (baptism); we received Christ's new law, and, having been nourished with the manna of Holy Communion, we were introduced into the new Jerusalem. Here, in the Church, symbolized by the house of God, God has His holy dwelling place; here we can seek and find Him in His holy Church, in the community of His mystical body. Full of gratitude for the inexpressible grace of baptism and membership in the Church we rejoice: "God [is] in His holy place" (Introit). Here in the church, on the altar of the Catholic house of prayer, He is enthroned in the midst of His people, the baptized, who, being of one faith and one mind and animated by the same desire of sacrifice, gather around Him during the Sacrifice of the Mass. Here in the Eucharistic sacrifice lies a source of strength and blessing for all those who have devoted themselves to Christ in baptism.

"Brethren: I make known unto you the gospel which I preached to you, which also you have received and wherein you stand, by which also you are saved, if you hold fast after what manner I have preached unto you" (Epistle). The things that came to pass centuries ago become a reality again during the celebration of the Mass, though in a mystical way: Christ again dies and rises again. With Him we died in baptism to rise again to a new life. In celebrating Mass we not only renew Christ's death and Resurrection, we also renew our own death and resurrection, which began with our baptism. Today we are the deaf and dumb man of the Gospel who is healed by the touch of Christ's hand; a similar healing we experienced at our baptism. In the Offertory we gratefully confess: "I will extol Thee, O Lord, for Thou hast upheld me and hast not made my enemies to rejoice over me." Devoting our entire being to Him, during the Holy Sacrifice we renew our baptism by renouncing during the coming week everything that is not pleasing to Christ. We again consecrate everything to Him without reserve, devoting to Him our time and our bodily and spiritual strength, our thoughts, desires, and wishes. Belonging thus to Him, we live His life in accordance with the admonition of the Communion: "Honor the Lord with thy substance,... and thy barns shall be filled with abundance."

Meditation

"He that humbleth himself shall be exalted" (Gospel of the tenth Sunday). During the past week the Church made it clear that we, her children, are by ourselves like the publican who struck his breast and said, "O God, be merciful to me a sinner." Today the Church knows herself to be exalted by the grace of God; therefore she is full of power and life. Because she trusted in God, she can now pray: "I have been helped; and my flesh hath flourished again" (Gradual); "Thou hast upheld me and hast not made my enemies to rejoice over me" (Offertory). The joy of Easter permeates today's liturgy. The holy joy of jubilation and of resurrection must fill our souls, too.

"Unto Thee will I cry, O Lord" (Gradual). "At that time, Jesus going out of the coasts of Tyre, came by Sidon to the Sea of Galilee.... And they bring to Him one deaf and dumb, and they besought Him that He would lay His hand upon him. And taking him from the multitude apart, He put His fingers into his ears, and spitting, He touched his tongue; and looking up to heaven, He groaned and said to him: *Ephpheta,* which is, Be thou opened; and immediately his ears were opened, and the string of his tongue was loosed, and he spoke right" (Gospel). In this picture the Church recognizes herself and us, her children, as the deaf and dumb man. What did any of us amount to before the Savior came down to us and filled us with His light and life in baptism? All of us were deaf and dumb to things divine, unable to speak a single word that could be pleasing to God, unable to call Him our Father. Such was our condition and our sad plight after Original Sin. We would still be in this desperate state if God had not saved us, if He had not, with divine mercy, accepted us as His children.

"I will extol Thee, O Lord, for Thou hast upheld me" (Offertory). In baptism we, the deaf and dumb ones, were brought to the Lord. Holy Mother the Church prayed for us to the Lord that He might lay His hand upon us. He appeared visibly in the person of His priest, who put his fingers into our ears and touched them with spittle, saying: "*Ephpheta,* which is, Be thou opened." And immediately our ears were opened to hear the voice of God, and the strings of our tongues were loosed; deaf and dumb before, we began now to understand and to speak right.

"Dost thou renounce Satan?" we were asked; and we replied: "I do renounce him." Then we were anointed with holy oil and were asked: "Dost thou believe in God, the Father Almighty, Creator of heaven and earth? Dost thou believe in Jesus Christ, His only Son our Lord?... Dost thou believe in the Holy Ghost, the holy Catholic Church, the communion of saints, the remission of sins, the resurrection of the body, and life everlasting?" We who had been deaf and dumb before, now understood and spoke right: "I believe." Again we were asked: "Wilt thou be baptized?" and we answered: "I will." We then were immersed in death with Christ. By dying with Him we were able to receive life with Him, the life of the risen Christ, who lives within us as the head lives with the members. "My flesh hath flourished." It has been reanimated by the power and life of the risen Christ. So together with the risen Lord, who lives within us, we rejoice: "I will extol Thee, O Lord, for Thou hast upheld me and hast not made my enemies to rejoice over me; O Lord, I have cried to Thee, and Thou hast healed me" (Offertory). "God [is] in His holy place; God who maketh men of one mind to dwell in a house; He shall give power and strength to His people" (Introit). He truly has given us life.

"I delivered unto you first of all, which I also received, how that Christ died for our sins according to the Scriptures; and that He was buried, and that He rose again the third day" (Epistle). The death and resurrection of Christ are the source of life for us who are the members of His mystical body. Christ lives, and with Him we also live, in so far as we die with Him. This is the meaning of Mass and Holy Communion: if we die with Him in spirit, He will instill His immortal life into us, now in Holy Communion and later in the eternal bliss of the life to come. "He shall give power and strength to His people" (Introit).

"By the grace of God I am what I am; and His grace in me hath not been void" (Epistle). This grateful confession of the Church is our confession also; for of ourselves we are deaf and dumb, but through grace Christ lives in us. "The mercies of the Lord I will sing forever" (Ps 88:2).

Prayer

O almighty and eternal God, who in the abundance of Thy loving kindness art wont to give beyond the deserts and desires of those who humbly pray; pour down upon us Thy mercy, forgiving us those things of which our conscience is afraid, and granting us those blessings which we dare not presume to ask. Through Christ our Lord. Amen.

Monday

"He hath done all things well; He hath made both the deaf to hear and the dumb to speak" (Gospel). Thus rejoicing, the Church never wearies of gratefully recognizing what the Lord did for her and her children in the sacrament of baptism. If we do not belong to Him, we are deaf and dumb; if we do belong to Him, however, our ears are opened and we speak right. "I will extol Thee, O Lord, for Thou hast upheld me" (Offertory).

"He hath made the deaf to hear." Before we had been received into Christ's life, we had an ear only for the voice of our fallen nature, of our self-love, and of the world. Searching for the things that please the natural man, our thoughts and feelings were according to those of men of the world; we knew only the natural struggle for existence. We were deaf to God, for our ears were not attuned to the things that are God's. When He restored the power of hearing to us who were deaf, we became Christians and listened attentively for the voice from above, for the whisperings of God dwelling within us, and for the inspirations of the Holy Spirit. From then on we understood the language of God. We came to look at life from the viewpoint of God and the gospel; we suddenly realized that the wisdom of this world and its judgment and principles are foolishness, and that the ideals that the world despises and condemns are true wisdom in the sight of God. "The wisdom of the flesh is an enemy to God" (Rom 8:7). "The Lord chose not them [men of renown], neither did they find the way of knowledge.... And because they had not wisdom, they perished through their folly" (Bar 3:27 f.). He gave us the spirit of wisdom and understanding of the things that are God's. We therefore count earthly things for nothing; we bear with patience the vicissitudes and sufferings of life. Our foremost desire is to be united with God, who dwells, loves, and works within us, to listen to His inspirations and suggestions, and to draw ever nearer to our heavenly goal. "Rejoice to God our helper; sing aloud to the God of Jacob" (Gradual).

"He hath made ... the dumb to speak." While we were yet separated from Christ and His life, the Lord loosed our tongue in the sacrament of baptism and united us to Himself. From now on we are allowed to approach the Father as children. "You have received the spirit of adoption of sons, whereby we cry: Abba, Father" (Rom 8:15). In baptism the word of the prophet has been fulfilled in us: "I will pour out upon the house of David and upon the inhabitants of Jerusalem the spirit of grace and of prayers" (Zac 12:10). United with Christ, we may speak to the Father with confidence, but even more: as the deaf and dumb man in the Gospel "spoke right," we likewise have been granted the grace of speaking to the Father in a manner that is pleasing to Him. Since the Lord has united us with Himself, He makes our prayers a part of His intercessions with the Father; thus we pray and speak to the Father in Christ, with Christ, and through Christ. It is not our voice, however, which the Father hears; it is rather the voice of Him in whom He is well pleased. We pray in the name of Jesus (Jn 14:13); that is, in closest unity with Him and through Him. When we pray and speak to the Father, the word of the Lord is fulfilled: "If you abide in Me, and My words abide in you, you shall ask whatever you will, and it shall be done unto you" (Jn 15:7). We have no reason to fear that our praying and speaking will not please the Father, for we pray in Jesus Christ. The power of our prayer is the result of our baptism, of our union with Christ. "He hath made ... the dumb to speak."

"I will extol Thee, O Lord, for Thou hast upheld me and hast not made my enemies to rejoice over me" (Offertory). The sacrifice of today's Mass must be a sacrifice of thanksgiving to Him who has cured us in baptism and has poured out His gifts to us in abundance. "Let us give thanks to the Lord our God."

"God in His holy place; God who maketh men of one mind to dwell in a house; He shall give power and strength to His people" (Introit). These words taken from the sixty-seventh psalm are a hymn of triumph, the triumph of the Church. God's place is heaven, whither He will lead us, His people, with wonderful power and strength. Though the road will pass through the desert of this earthly life, and enemies will oppress us from all sides, He will be our protection. The Lord bestows unity, perfection, and strength on His Church. Through baptism we have become members of God's people. In the Mass let us again profess our fidelity to Him. In communion with Him we shall find the right way to heaven under His loving protection and guidance.

PRAYER

O almighty and eternal God, who in the abundance of Thy loving kindness art wont to give beyond the deserts and desires of those who humbly pray; pour down upon us Thy mercy, forgiving us those things of which our conscience is afraid, and granting us those blessings which we dare not presume to ask. Through Christ our Lord. Amen.

Tuesday

"God in His holy place; God who maketh men of one mind to dwell in a house" (Introit). The Lord guides those who are of one mind towards their eternal destiny in His Father's house. You are "one body and one spirit; as you are called in one hope of your calling. One Lord, one faith, one baptism" (Eph 4:4 f.); the unity of God's Church is founded on the unity of the faith (Epistle).

"I make known unto you the gospel which I preached to you" (Epistle). The Apostle wishes to assure the Corinthians: You have accepted the gospel; you stand by it staunchly; you want to keep it, thus saving your souls; but if it does not lead you to eternal happiness, you have accepted it in vain. "I delivered unto you first of all, which I also received, how that Christ died for our sins according to the Scriptures, and that He was buried, and that He rose again the third day" (Epistle). The whole structure of our faith depends on the fact of Christ's resurrection. What leads us to heaven and matters most of all is our faith. We must have blind faith in the gospel as preached by the apostles and announced to us by the Church. There is but "one faith." In this matter the Church admits no different opinion. What God has revealed to us and what Christ the Lord in His gospel or through His apostles and His Church has required us to believe, we must accept with unquestioning faith. Reason must give its assent to supernatural truth. As children of the Church we give our assent, even in the twentieth century, to the immutable teachings of God, of Christ, and of His Church. We accept the sacraments, Holy Scripture, belief in eternal life and the resurrection, just as did the early Christians of Jerusalem and Rome, of Corinth and Ephesus, of Philippi and Thessalonike. There is no difference between our faith today and the faith of antiquity, when persecution made so many glorious martyrs. It is the same faith whether it is preached to the people of Europe, America, Africa, or Australia; there is but one creed in all the languages of the world, one *Gloria Patri et Filio et Spiritui Sancto,* which the Church confesses with all her children everywhere. To those who are of one mind the Lord gives a dwelling in His holy place in heaven. In this one faith of the Church, if we accept it, we shall gain life eternal, providing that we live up to it after the manner preached to us by Christ and His apostles. The one faith of the Church is, therefore, the only way to our Father's house.

"You stand ... in the gospel which I preached to you" (Epistle). In today's Epistle the Church expresses her concern that we stand in the faith which we once accepted and to which we swore fidelity at our baptism. In the ages of faith Catholics felt as safe in their faith as a child walking at the side of its mother. To them God's existence admitted no doubt; He was near at hand like an earthly father. Christ with His saints was near at hand like a friend and brother; the Church had a place in their everyday life, and they loved her like a mother. The will of God was the law written in their hearts, and consequently the dawn of eternity beckoned to them like the warm sun on a serene spring day. The supernatural world was almost as familiar to them as this world.

Today, however, the whole world fights against our faith. Sometimes Christ is dismissed as a myth; sometimes God is looked upon as a fiction of human whims and desires. In some places the Church is considered a natural development growing out of the combination of Greek culture, Roman imperialism, oriental mysticism, and medieval piety; in other places divine providence is confused with chance and fate. A "new faith" is promulgated, calling into doubt the immortality of the soul and many other doctrines fundamental to Christianity. This "new faith" has so dominated modern thinking and modern education that he who accepts the creed of the apostles and the Church is opposed by the world. Our Catholic faith demands of us character, sacrifice, and heroism. If we seek the approval of the multitude, if we wish to be considered liberal, educated, and modern, we must renounce our faith, for it is out of fashion. Whoever wishes to keep his faith in our day must be a hero ready to withstand the secularism and atheism which pervades the modern world. The Christian of our time has become a martyr; he is a victim of prejudice, persecution, and contempt. Not without reason the Apostle admonishes us in the Epistle to stand in "the gospel which I preached to you."

"I make known unto you the gospel which I preached to you, … and wherein you stand" (Epistle). These words implore us to stand firm in our faith and to live according to it. For "what shall it profit, my brethren, if man say he hath faith, but hath not works? Shall faith be able to save him?" (Jas 2:14.) "Every one therefore that shall confess Me before men, I will also confess him before My Father who is in heaven. But he that shall deny Me before men, I will also deny him before My Father who is in heaven" (Mt 10:32 f.).

We are men of one mind and of one faith in our devotion to the Church. It is her office to teach us the faith. The more faithfully we stand by her, the deeper and more fruitful our faith will become. Though the Church conveys the faith to us in various ways, she does so especially by means of the liturgy. Let us pray with her, thus making use of the surest means of preserving our faith.

Prayer

We beseech Thee, O Lord, that we may feel supported in soul and body, that being saved in both, we may glory in the fullness of the heavenly remedy. Through Christ our Lord. Amen.

Wednesday

"And taking him from the multitude apart, He put His fingers into his ears … and said to him: *Ephpheta*, which is, Be thou opened. And immediately his ears were opened" (Gospel). The Church recalls gratefully that moment when the Lord, approaching her children, endowed them, as it were, with a new and spiritual ear, that they may perform acts of supernatural faith. Without this mysterious *Ephpheta* we never would be able to truly say, "I believe"; nor could we ever reach Christ, our salvation.

"I make known unto you the gospel which I preached to you, … by which also you are saved, if you hold fast after what manner I preached unto you" (Epistle). With these words of the Apostle the Church today addresses us, her children. The faith which she preaches to us is the starting point: "the substance of things to be hoped for, the evidence of things that appear not.... Without faith it is impossible to please God" (Heb 11:1, 6) and to come to the sonship of God and to be partakers of the divine life (Council of Trent, Sess. VI, chap. 8). Faith unites us with Christ, making us partakers of the life of the body of which Christ is the head. Through acts of faith we move towards Christ, the head, mysteriously joined to Him in such a way that we, being members of His body, are enabled to partake of the life of the head. Through faith and baptism together we become members of Christ.[21] If the body of Christ, the Church, is to be continually formed anew through the acquisition of new members for the mystical body of Christ, faith together with the sacrament of baptism is essentially necessary. For Christ dwells in our hearts by faith (Eph 3:17). Only by faith in the revealed word of God, as proposed to us by the Church of Christ, do we have life in Christ. Only by faith and the gospel which the Church received from Christ and His apostles, and which she preaches without error, can we be saved. The Lord planted this faith in our souls that by believing we may be joined to Christ and His salvation. "And taking him from the multitude apart, He put His fingers into his ears and said to him: *Ephpheta,* which is, Be thou opened."

"Hold fast after what manner I preached unto you" (Epistle). The Apostle means to tell us that the only thing that matters is that both in spirit and in practical life we hold fast to our faith after the manner he and the Church continually preach it to us. Our spiritual point of view has to become ever more like that of the mystical body, the Church. We must accept her faith and her moral doctrines, and join her in prayer and sacrifice, realizing that we are one with Christ, the head, united with Him in a true communion of being, sustained by His strength, and permeated by His life. From this consciousness our faith gains strength and vitality. The greater and more lively is our faith, the more intimately we become united with Christ and His Church. The more this faith is the guiding principle of our thoughts and struggles, the more deeply we grow into Christ, the head, and the more profoundly the life of the body flows down into us, the members. It is, therefore, our most urgent duty to "hold fast [to the gospel] after what manner I [the Church] preached unto you."

"God in His holy place; God who maketh men of one mind to dwell in a house; He shall give power and strength to His people" (Introit). "He hath done all things well; He hath made both the deaf to hear, and the dumb to speak" (Gospel). With such sentiments of gratitude we address God today. We thank Him sincerely for the grace of baptism and the gift of faith. Today we must gratefully acknowledge and confirm our faith, which the Lord freely gave to us, together with the other members of His Church.

When we for the first time came in contact with our Holy Mother the Church, she asked us: "What dost thou ask of the Church of God?" We answered: "Faith." "What doth faith bring thee?" the Church asked again. We replied: "Life everlasting." "If then thou desirest to enter into

[21] The operation of grace differs in the case of a child and in that of an adult who is being baptized. The child becomes united with Christ through the sacrament of baptism, and as it grows older the child perfects this union through acts of faith. When an adult is baptized, the act of faith constitutes the beginning of the union with Christ. In this case it is perfected through the sacrament of baptism.

life, keep the commandments. Thou shalt love the Lord thy God with thy whole heart, and with thy whole soul, and with thy whole mind; and thy neighbor as thyself."

Prayer

I will extol Thee, O Lord, for Thou hast upheld me and hast not made my enemies to rejoice over me. O Lord, my God, I have cried to Thee, and Thou hast healed me. Thou hast brought forth, O Lord, my soul from hell; Thou hast saved me from them that go down into the pit. Sing to the Lord, O ye His saints; and give praise to the memory of His holiness. (Ps 29:2 ff.)

Thursday

"I delivered unto you first of all, which I also received, how that Christ died for our sins according to the Scriptures, and that He was buried, and that He rose again the third day according to the Scriptures; and that He was seen by Cephas, and after that by the eleven.... And last of all He was seen also by me" (Epistle). This apostolic sermon is simple, strong, and clear. The central theme is the fact that Jesus, the Son of Man, is the Son of God, and that He was sent into this world for our redemption and sanctification, as a victim for our sins.

"He that believeth in the Son, hath life everlasting; but he that believeth not the Son, shall not see life; but the wrath of God abideth on him" (Jn 3:36). In this life already God's wrath abides on him who does not believe in Jesus, His Son. Belief in His Son is considered a matter of highest concern in the eyes of God. "For God so loved the world as to give His only-begotten Son, that whosoever believeth in Him may not perish, but may have life everlasting." And as an explanation the Evangelist adds: "For God sent not His Son into the world to judge the world, but that the world may be saved by Him. He that believeth in Him is not judged. But he that doth not believe, is already judged: because he believeth not in the name of the only-begotten Son of God" (Jn 3:17 ff.). In vain will he try to save his soul if he does not believe in Jesus, the Son of God.

One truth is clear: the first condition for sharing in the divine life and for being saved is the belief in the Son of God, "who for us men and for our salvation came down from heaven," who died for us and rose again. Three times the Father announced to mankind that Jesus is His Son in whom He is well pleased (Mt 3:17; 17:5; Jn 12:28). The Father gives this testimony of His Son before men that they may believe in Jesus. To verify this testimony, the Father gave Christ power over the elements, over sickness and death, and raised Him from the dead on the third day. Everyone who sees the Son and believes in Him has life everlasting (Jn 6:40). All revealed truth is contained in the testimony of the Father: "This is My beloved Son." Our whole faith, likewise, consists in our acceptance of this testimony of the Father. If we believe in Jesus, the Son of God, who became man for us, we believe implicitly in the entire revelation of the Old and New Testaments, in all the teachings of the apostles and the Church. Our faith is simply the development of the Father's testimony: "This is My beloved Son." Our supernatural life is based on our vivid realization of Christ's divinity.

"If we receive the testimony of men, the testimony of God is greater. For this is the testimony of God, which is greater, because He hath testified of His Son. He that believeth in the Son of God, hath the testimony of God in himself. He that believeth not the Son, maketh Him a liar; because He believeth not in the testimony which God hath testified of His Son. And this is the testimony that God hath given to us, eternal life. And this life is in His Son. He that hath the Son, hath life" (1 Jn 5:9–12). The life of the Father is this, that in one eternal act He begets His Son, giving Him the fullness of His perfections. By this act the Father expresses Himself, His essence and being, in this one eternal Word. Every testimony which the Father manifests to the world when pronouncing, "This is My beloved Son," is but the audible reproduction of this interior life of the Deity: "Thou art My Son, this day have I begotten Thee" (Ps 2:7). "He that believeth in the Son of God, hath the testimony of God in himself." Whenever we accept the testimony of the Father, believing and confessing that the babe in the manger, the youth in the carpenter shop at Nazareth, the man of sorrows who was condemned to death, scourged, crowned with thorns, and crucified, is the Son of God, then we proclaim with the Father the divinity of His Son. Whenever we bend our knees before the Holy Eucharist and believe that the Son of God is present on the altar with body and soul, with divinity and humanity, then we act like the Father's true children, proclaiming the divinity of His Son. If we consecrate all our love to Jesus, placing all our strength and service at His disposal, then our life is a reproduction of the life of the Father, and we are united with that life, possessing and sharing it. "He that believeth in the Son of God, hath the testimony of God in himself." With this testimony he also has the life of God in himself.

The Church firmly believes in the testimony of the Father. Her entire life and being is a realization of her creed: "I believe in Jesus Christ, the only-begotten Son of God, who was conceived by the Holy Ghost, born of the Virgin Mary, suffered under Pontius Pilate, was crucified, died, and was buried.... He rose again from the dead." She steadfastly testifies to the divinity of Christ. We must remain faithful to her testimony and her faith in Jesus, the Son of God, who became man for our salvation.

To be a Christian means to believe in Jesus and in all that He taught and did for our salvation. The more courageously we confess our adherence to the teaching of Jesus, to His example, and to His Church, the more the kingdom of God and His life will take root in our souls. The profound persuasion that Jesus is God and that He became man for our salvation is the foundation and essence of our entire spiritual life. It makes us bow down our head in reverent adoration and devotion to Him and His holy will.

Prayer

O almighty and eternal God, who in the abundance of Thy loving kindness art wont to give beyond the deserts and desires of those who humbly pray; pour down upon us Thy mercy, forgiving us those things of which our conscience is afraid, and granting us those blessings which we dare not presume to ask. Through Christ our Lord. Amen.

Friday

The liturgy of the eleventh Sunday after Pentecost connects the healing of the deaf and dumb man with the conversion of St. Paul. "And last of all He was seen also by me, as one born out of due time. For I am the least of the apostles, who am not worthy to be called an apostle, because I persecuted the Church of God; but by the grace of God I am what I am; and His grace in me hath not been void" (Epistle). Encountering Christ while hurrying to Damascus to destroy the Church of Christ, Saul received through the mercy and power of the Lord the new interior ear; he understood Jesus. From then on "he spoke right"; he preached Jesus crucified, "unto the Jews indeed a stumbling block, and unto the Gentiles foolishness; but unto them that are called, both Jews and Greeks, Christ the power of God and the wisdom of God" (1 Cor 1:23 f.).

"By the grace of God I am what I am" (Epistle). Paul is truly a miracle of the grace of God. Who thought less of becoming a Christian than Saul on his way to Damascus? Who was, humanly speaking, less prepared for the reception of such a grace than this persecutor of the Christians? His heart was burning with hatred for the Galilean. And yet, just at that moment when Saul least expects it, the mercy of the Lord descends upon him. Touched by grace, he fell on the ground, and from that moment on he was deaf and dumb to his former thoughts and ideas, to his entire former way of living. Having broken with his past entirely, after three days of peace and recollection Saul becomes Paul. He is baptized in Damascus, and his soul having been opened to the light and the truth of Christ, he eagerly listens to the inspirations of grace. Then the Lord looses his tongue, and he preaches Christ crucified and the mercy of God towards him: "By the grace of God I am what I am." Now he delivers himself up entirely to the working of grace within his soul, and grace instructs him. He labors more abundantly than all the other apostles and disciples. "His grace in me hath not been void."

We are astonished at this miracle of grace, this miracle of the power of the Lord, who makes the deaf hear and the dumb speak. Together with St. Paul, the apostle of grace, we confess: "In God hath my heart confided, and I have been helped; and my flesh hath flourished again; and with my will I will give praise to Him" (Gradual). The Lord gives His graces in abundance. "God,... Thou art wont to give beyond the deserts and desires of those who humbly pray" (Collect). Saul did not pray to the Lord; and yet the Lord gave him an abundance of His powerful love and grace.

"His grace in me hath not been void; but I have labored more abundantly than all they; yet not I, but the grace of God with me" (1 Cor 15:10). No sooner has he been baptized than he goes to the synagogues of Damascus, preaching Christ, whom shortly before he had persecuted. He is not afraid to confess Christ, even when facing those who knew that he had come to Damascus for the express purpose of seizing Christians so that he might bring them bound to Jerusalem. Paul did not stop to consider what they might think of him. Grace works in him, urging him to make good use of all his powers to preach Christ. It urges him to undertake three laborious missionary voyages to Greece and Asia Minor, to suffer hunger and thirst, cold and nakedness, scourging and imprisonment for the sake of Christ. Thrice he suffered shipwreck, being a night and a day in the depth of the sea, in danger lest he perish in the waters. Persecution followed him everywhere, from the Jews and the Gentiles, in the cities and in the sea (2 Cor 11:23 ff.). But God's grace urges him to take loving care of the churches and communities which he founded. He instructs, exhorts, and consoles them in his epistles; he is jealous of them "with the jealousy of God, for I have espoused you to one husband that he may present you as a chaste virgin to Christ" (2 Cor 11:2). "Who is weak, and I am not weak? Who is scandalized, and I am not on fire?" (2 Cor 11:29.) Paul indeed has labored more for the Lord than all the others. "Yet," he corrects himself, "not I, but the grace of God with me." Depending entirely on God's grace which works all things, Paul considers himself only an instrument. "God in His holy place; ... He shall give power and strength to His people" (Introit). He is "wont to give beyond the deserts and desires of those who humbly pray." It is God "who worketh in you both to will and to accomplish, according to His good will" (Phil 2:13). Paul is what he is by the grace of God, who determined his future work on the road to Damascus without his prayers and merits; Paul merely cooperated with God's grace. Thus Paul has become a shining example of what God is willing and able to do with a man who gives himself up entirely into His hands.

In Saul and in Paul we recognize ourselves. By ourselves we are but another Saul; but God's mercy is able to make of us another Paul. "My flesh hath flourished" when touched by the almighty hand of the Lord, who makes the deaf hear and the dumb speak. "I will extol Thee, O Lord, for Thou hast upheld me" (Offertory). If only we also could say with St. Paul: "His grace in me hath not been void."

Prayer

O almighty and eternal God, who in the abundance of Thy loving kindness art wont to give beyond the deserts and desires of those who humbly pray; pour down upon us Thy mercy, forgiving us those things of which our conscience is afraid, and granting us those blessings which we dare not presume to ask. Through Christ our Lord. Amen.

Saturday

"I make known unto you the gospel which I preached to you: ... how that Christ died for our sins, ... and that He rose again the third day" (Epistle). The Church never tires of announcing in all the rites of her liturgy this message of life for all those who die with Christ in baptism and in the celebration of Mass.

"My flesh hath flourished again; and with my will I will give praise to Him" (Gradual). This victorious Easter chant, filled with feelings of gratitude, should be sung by Christians every Sunday. Every Sunday, through the liturgy of the Mass, we should become more vividly aware of the fact that we possess life, because, having died with Christ, we arose with Him to a new life. The celebration of Mass is for us a renewal and continuation of our baptism, when we were "buried together with Him ... into death" (Rom 6:4). The Apostle instructs us that through baptism we were buried with Him that we might arise to a new life with Him. Our old man was also crucified that the body of sin might be destroyed and serve sin no longer. We believe that we, the members of Christ's mystical body, the branches of the vine, share the life of the risen Christ because we also died with Him.

"My flesh hath flourished again." It has been deeply humiliated under the curse and servitude of sin and the concupiscence of the flesh; but now in baptism it has become, through the power of the Lord, a vessel of divine life. Being a branch of Christ, the true Christian, fortified by the power of the risen Christ, is able to resist the assaults of the tempter and the allurements of the flesh and the world. Lifting up his mind and heart to God, he tries continually to fill his soul with divine life, thus becoming ever more perfectly the spiritual, risen man, who out of the fullness of his union with God and Christ is enabled to diffuse light and strength over others also. "My flesh hath flourished again," for it possesses the life of divine sonship, of Christian virtue and union with God. "With my will I will give praise to Him" (Gradual). "In His holy place, ... He shall give power and strength to His people," who live in the union of love within the Church (Introit).

"In the abundance of Thy loving kindness [Thou] art wont to give beyond the deserts and desires of those who humbly pray" (Collect). The Jews bring a deaf and dumb man to the Lord, asking that He impose His hands upon him. The Lord does more than they dare ask of Him. He puts His fingers into the poor man's ears, and spitting, He touches his tongue, saying, "*Ephpheta,* which is, Be thou opened" (Gospel). In this act He shows the superabundance of His love. Soon after we were born, devoted hearts and hands brought us to the Lord, imploring Him to deliver us from the power of sin. He received us, washing us in the laver of regeneration that our soul might be free from sin. But that was not enough for His love. He filled us with His life, the immortal life of the risen one, planting in our soul, and even in our weak flesh, the seed of the resurrection to come and preparing us for the blessed transfiguration of our eternal happiness with God. "My flesh hath flourished again." "I shall not die, but live" (Ps 117:17). "Eye hath not seen, nor ear heard, neither hath it entered into the heart of man, what things God hath prepared for them that love Him" (1 Cor 2:9). Already here on earth He gives a foretaste of this happiness to them that love Him, and the fulfillment of it in the land of promise. "O God, ... in the abundance of Thy loving kindness [Thou] art wont to give beyond the deserts and desires of those who humbly pray."

The resurrection of our Lord is the central truth of our Christian faith. It is the source of the supernatural life of the baptized, an inexhaustible fountain of grace. "I make known unto you the gospel which I preached to you: ... that Christ died for our sins, ... and that He rose again the third day" (Epistle).

The Church announces this message to us when she celebrates the Eucharistic sacrifice, which is the representation of the death and resurrection of the Lord. If we share His death, we shall also be partakers of His life. The Mass is the fountain from which we can draw that strength which He has promised. Here we shall be healed and "feel supported in soul and body" (Postcommunion).

When celebrating the Mass we honor the Lord with our gifts "and with the first of all [our] fruits" (Communion): we offer to Him all we have, placing it all as a gift of sacrifice on the altar. Thus sacrificing all we have without reserve, we die a sacred death indeed. But our "barns shall be filled with abundance and [our] presses shall run over with wine" (Communion); for Christ lives in us, and we also shall live because we have died with Him in the spirit of sacrifice, renunciation, and love.

Prayer

O almighty and eternal God, who in the abundance of Thy loving kindness art wont to give beyond the deserts and desires of those who humbly pray; pour down upon us Thy mercy, forgiving us those things of which our conscience is afraid, and granting us those blessings which we dare not presume to ask. Through Christ our Lord. Amen.

Twelfth Sunday after Pentecost

The Mass

"Blessed are the eyes that see the things which you see. For I say to you, that many prophets and kings have desired to see the things that you see, and have not seen them; and to hear the things that you hear, and have not heard them" (Gospel). We Christians who have come today to celebrate the Holy Sacrifice of the Mass are the people of the New Covenant to whom are addressed the words: "Blessed are the eyes that see the things which you see." The people of the Old Covenant, those living before the time of Christ, are the "many prophets and kings." In this manner the liturgy of the twelfth Sunday after Pentecost recalls again the splendor of the Easter mystery, revealing to us our happy lot in belonging to Christ and His kingdom through the sacrament of baptism. It reminds us also of the duties which we assumed through the reception of this sacrament.

During the holy night of Easter we found the way to Christ again in the sacrament of rebirth, and we received the first beginnings of our new life through our union with Christ. This life is a seed which must grow and mature slowly, but which is threatened by dangers and is hemmed in by difficulties which retard its development and endanger its very existence. Realizing these conditions, we ask for help from above in the Introit of today's Mass: "Incline unto my aid, O God; O Lord, make haste to help me. Let my enemies be confounded and ashamed, who seek my soul." In the Kyrie and the Collect we continue our entreaties: "Grant, we beseech Thee, that we may run without hindrance toward the attainment of Thy promises."

Baptism has enriched us immeasurably in the union of life with Christ. The Old Testament was a "ministration of death," since it could make clear to us only the nature of death (sin) and could pass judgment by punishing sin and sinners; it was, however, unable by itself to restore the Spirit, the supernatural life of grace. How different is the New Covenant, the Covenant of the life-giving Spirit, the giver of graces! How different the new state of interior justification of the soul before God! We have become members of this Covenant, and for this privilege "I will bless the Lord at all times" (Gradual). By means of this union life is given again to man, wounded and tortured unto death by sin. Like the priest in today's Gospel, the Old Testament passes by the wounded man. But Christ, the New Covenant, pours oil and wine into the wounds (baptism and the Eucharist), brings the half-dead man to an inn, the inn of the Church, and takes care of him so that he may regain full strength and a robust life.

The parable of the good Samaritan is fulfilled in us, the children of the Church. We ourselves are the wanderer who fell among robbers and upon whom Christ looked down full of compassion, taking him into His Church in the sacrament of baptism. In view of this wonderful condescension on the part of the Savior we say: "I believe in one holy Catholic Church; I believe in one baptism." During the Sacrifice of the Mass, Christ, the good Samaritan, appears personally in our midst to continue His presence with us and to perfect His work of healing and restoration. A second Moses, He implores God on our behalf, offering with His prayers His own flesh and blood, His heart, Himself wholly to the Father as a gift of sacrifice. We are allowed to take Him into our hands as our own gift of sacrifice, offering Him up to God through the hands of the priest as a victim for our sins. "Blessed are the eyes that see the things which you see" and the hands that offer what you offer. How much more acceptable is the sacrifice and prayer of Christ than that of Moses, the mediator of the Old Covenant! How much more acceptable is our sacrifice, the sacrifice of the baptized, than the sacrifices of men of ancient times who did not possess Christ! "Blessed are the eyes that see the things which you see."

"The earth shall be filled with the fruit of Thy works" (Communion). In Holy Communion Christ truly is the good Samaritan who comes to us with a most perfect devotion, full of love, carrying wine and oil in His hands, "that wine may cheer the heart of man, and that he may make the face cheerful with oil, and that bread may strengthen man's heart" (Communion). In Holy Communion He instills new life into our soul: life of His life, spirit of His Spirit, love of His love. Let us try to be "good Samaritans," too, mindful of the fact that, when we come down from the Holy Sacrifice and Holy Communion to discharge our duties in everyday life, we also must fulfill Christ's words: "Go and do thou in like manner" (Gospel).

Meditation

God wishes to fill our souls with a consciousness of the glory and magnificence of all those graces that have fallen to our lot through Christ, the good Samaritan, in His holy Church. "Blessed are the eyes that see the things which you see" (Gospel).

"I say to you, that many prophets and kings have desired to see the things that you see, and have not seen them; and to hear the things that you hear, and have not heard them" (Gospel). They had circumcision, the law of Moses, the temple, the daily sacrifices in Jerusalem, the psalms, the holy books; they were God's chosen people enjoying God's special protection. And yet they desired to see and hear what we, the baptized, the children of the Church of the New Covenant, see and hear: Jesus Christ. They were not granted this privilege, however, for the Old Covenant with its law, its rites, and its ceremonies was unable to redeem humanity.

"A certain man went down from Jerusalem to Jericho and fell among robbers, who also stripped him, and having wounded him, went away, leaving him half dead. And it chanced that a certain priest went down the same way, and seeing him, passed by. In like manner also a Levite, when he was near the place and saw him, passed by" (Gospel). This picture of poor, unredeemed humanity, robbed by the devil and beaten half to death, is also a picture of the Old Testament, which, with its priests and Levites, was unable to save fallen humanity. It contained laws, prescribed prayers and sacrifices, and the observance of "days, and months, and times, and years" (Gal 4:10); it imposed many washings and penances. At its disposal were but "weak and needy elements" (Gal 4:9) unable to give true supernatural life. It was a "ministration of death" without means of communicating the life of grace.

"Blessed are the eyes that see the things which you see." Blessed are we who are members of the New Covenant, the union of grace. The priests and the Levites of the Old Covenant pass by the man who fell among robbers; they are unable to help him. "But a certain Samaritan, being on his journey, came near him, and seeing him, was moved with compassion, and going up to him, bound up his wounds, pouring in oil and wine; and setting him upon his own beast, brought him to an inn, and took care of him" (Gospel). The good Samaritan is none other than Christ the Lord. A good Samaritan, the Son of God, came down from the eternal abode of heaven to take care of poor, lost humanity. Full of compassion, He bows down daily to our misery to heal our wounds and renew life within us by means of the sacraments. He pours oil (baptism) and wine (Holy Eucharist) into our wounds and delivers us up to our Holy Mother the Church, commanding her to take care of us until He returns. It is He whom the prophets and kings of the Old Testament desired. Now He appears and founds the covenant of glory. The service of this covenant is a service that leads to justification. There is no salvation except in Christ and His Church.

It is granted to us "to hear" and "to see" the good Samaritan, who is Christ the Savior. He deigns to come down to us in the holy sacraments of baptism and penance, and particularly in the sacrament of the Holy Eucharist. He is joined to all of us as closely as the vine is to its branches, as the head is to the members, filling us with His life. "Blessed are the eyes that see the things which you see": Christ, with whom we are united in baptism and the Holy Eucharist. "I will bless the Lord at all times; His praise shall ever be in my mouth. In the Lord shall my soul be praised" (Gradual).

"Blessed are the eyes that see the things which you see." The center of all life is Christ, the healing and life-giving Samaritan. We see Him in His successors: the pope, the bishops, and the priests. "He that heareth you, heareth Me; and he that despiseth you, despiseth Me; and he that despiseth Me, despiseth Him that sent Me" (Lk 10:16). The Catholic priest through his ordination has become for us another Christ.

He "hath made us fit ministers of the New Testament.... Now if the ministration of death ... was glorious, so that the children of Israel could not steadfastly behold the face of Moses, for the glory of his countenance,... how shall not the ministration of the spirit [the priesthood of the New Covenant] be rather in glory?" (Epistle.) It is not so much the priest who speaks the words, "This is My body," over the bread as it is Christ Himself. The priest is but His instrument. We should see in the priest not so much the human person; we should rather see Christ in him, whose instrument he is. In the priest we should see, respect, hear, and love Christ the Lord, the eternal high priest.

Prayer

Almighty and merciful God, of whose gift it cometh that Thy faithful people do unto Thee true and laudable service; grant, we beseech Thee, that we may run without hindrance toward the attainment of Thy promises. Through Christ our Lord. Amen.

Monday

On this day we should cry: "Incline unto my aid, O God; O Lord, make haste to help me" (Introit). This is the cry of the man who fell among robbers. On the other hand, this is also a day of sincere thankfulness: "I will bless the Lord at all times; His praise shall ever be in my mouth" (Gradual). This hymn of praise is an expression of gratitude to the good Samaritan (Christ), who restored life to the man who had fallen among robbers.

"A certain man went down from Jerusalem to Jericho and fell among robbers, who also stripped him, and having wounded him, went away, leaving him half dead" (Gospel). The man who went down from Jerusalem to Jericho is Adam, the father and head of humanity.

He leaves Jerusalem, the state of the grace, the gifts he had possessed in Paradise, the child-like and intimate companionship with God, and goes down to Jericho, the state of fallen nature. The robbers are the devils who seduce him to sin, depriving him of sanctifying grace, the sonship of God, and the other graces of life in Paradise. Human nature, which heretofore enjoyed peace and order, becomes unsettled and restless. "When I have a will to do good, evil is present with me. For I am delighted with the law of God, according to the inward man. But I see another law in my members, fighting against the law of my mind, and captivating me in the law of sin, that is in my members" (Rom 7:21 ff.). In Adam we recognize the whole of humanity: in Adam all of us went down from Jerusalem to Jericho and fell among robbers. How many of us went down from the Jerusalem of childhood with its innocence to the Jericho of manhood and fell among robbers? How many, however, found our way back to the holy city of Jerusalem, to the state of sanctifying grace, in the sacrament of penance during a mission or retreat? But then we left it again for the sake of worldly and material interests. Those of us who went down from Jerusalem to Jericho and fell among robbers, thus losing their innocence, their interior happiness, even their God or their faith, are a matter of gravest concern to the Church. With motherly love she has compassion on all these unfortunate ones, and in their name she beseeches the Lord: "Incline unto my aid, O God; O Lord, make haste to help me. Let my enemies be confounded and ashamed, who seek my soul" (Introit). Entering into the spirit of the liturgy, we also share her concern and, feeling the need of our brethren, we implore the Lord from the bottom of our hearts: "Lord, have mercy. Christ, have mercy. Lord, have mercy."

"And it chanced that a certain priest went down the same way, and seeing him, passed by. In like manner also a Levite" (Gospel). The priest and the Levite represent the Old Testament. Unable to save suffering humanity, it passed by. "But a certain Samaritan, being on his journey, came near him, and seeing him, was moved with compassion, and going up to him, bound up his wounds, pouring in oil and wine; and setting him upon his own beast, brought him to an inn." The Samaritan is Christ the Lord. The beast of burden is His holy humanity, which the Son of God embraced for our salvation. He laid the wounded man upon His beast of burden by carrying our sins in His body in order to atone for them on the cross. The oil and wine He poured into the wounds are the holy sacraments of the New Covenant. The inn is the Church. Before ascending into heaven, this Samaritan gives His Church two pence, His doctrine and His sacraments, commanding her to take care of the sick man. "Blessed are the eyes that see the things which you see"; that is, God's mercy in the Incarnation of the eternal Word, in the redemption on the cross, in the foundation of the Church, and in the institution of the hierarchy and the sacraments of the Church. God answered the cries of humanity fallen among robbers: "Incline unto my aid, O God; O Lord, make haste to help me. Let my enemies be confounded and ashamed, who seek my soul. Let them be turned backward and blush for shame, who desire evils to me" (Introit).

"Incline unto my aid, O God; O Lord, make haste to help me." We pray with the Church that He may help us now when He comes down upon the altar in the Holy Sacrifice. We desire Him to come down to us and not to pass us by. "Show us, O Lord, Thy mercy, and grant us Thy salvation" (prayers at the foot of the altar), now, during this hour of sacrifice. Be our good Samaritan, and "let them be turned backward and blush for shame, who desire evils to me."

The kingdom of God, as willed and instituted in this world by Christ, is a kingdom of charity, and comes to us by means of a fraternal and merciful love. It carries oil and wine in its hands. "By this shall all men know that you are my disciples, if you have love one for another" (Jn 13:35). The Church is charity. She is the enduring and visible presence of the good Samaritan, who works, heals, and saves through her. She is also the expression of God's love for immortal souls, a love that leads each man and entire nations to God. For this reason the Lord gave her the two pence, His doctrine and the sacraments, and implanted in her heart the spirit of the good Samaritan. The more she is misunderstood, and the more her mercy, her charity, and her work are misinterpreted, the more we must endeavor to understand her and to follow her.

Prayer

Almighty and merciful God, of whose gift it cometh that Thy faithful people do unto Thee true and laudable service; grant, we beseech Thee, that we may run without hindrance toward the attainment of Thy promises. Through Christ our Lord. Amen.

Tuesday

Christ, the Son of God, is the good Samaritan who came down upon this earth and poured oil and wine into the wounds of humanity. The holy liturgy expresses this thought by the words which accompany the reception of Holy Communion: "The earth shall be filled with the fruit of Thy works, O Lord, that Thou mayest bring bread out of the earth, and that wine may cheer the heart of man; that he may make the face cheerful with oil, and that bread may strengthen man's heart" (Communion).

"The earth shall be filled with the fruit of Thy works." It is now harvest time. In the name of humanity the Church offers her thanks to heaven in this Sunday's Communion prayer. God's hands have given a blessed harvest: bread and wine and oil are the gifts of His wisdom, power, and mercy. "All expect of Thee that Thou give them food in season. What Thou givest to them they shall gather up; when Thou openest Thy hand, they shall all be filled with good" (Ps 103:27 f.). Year after year the Lord commands nature, and it brings forth the food needed by the innumerable creatures on earth. We hardly stop to consider what a miraculous work it is to sustain humanity by means of the few seeds which are sowed in the ground year after year. It is the miraculous work of the wisdom, power, and love of God. The good Samaritan bows down each year, each day, and each hour, to our weakness and temporal needs, lovingly granting us the daily bread that sustains our lives. "The earth shall be filled with the fruit of Thy works." How much we have to be thankful for!

"That Thou mayest bring bread out of the earth, and that wine may cheer the heart of man." The earth and its fruit are symbols for the liturgy. The earth which brings forth the bread and wine represents the human nature of Jesus Christ, the Son of God. This exalted human nature, most intimately united with the person of the divine Word, is the fruitful soil that brings forth the Eucharistic gifts of bread and wine. The merits of His death on the cross ripened the precious, abundant grain and the grapes, out of which the new generation of the baptized is to gain supernatural food for the soul. "I am the bread of life. Your fathers did eat manna in the desert, and are dead.... I am the living bread which came down from heaven. If any man eat of this bread, he shall live forever; and the bread that I will give, is My flesh, for the life of the world.... He that eateth My flesh and drinketh My blood, hath everlasting life" (Jn 6:48 ff.). Bread and wine are the gifts of the good Samaritan. They heal, they produce strength and life, a life of harmony between spirit and nature, a life of sanctity and justice pleasing to God. In virtue of the Holy Eucharist we are anointed with holy oil; that is, with the Spirit of the Lord, the Holy Ghost. He is light and life, knowledge and charity, faith and strength; He is "the oil of gladness" (Ps 44:8) that protects us from death, that heals the wounds of our life and pours over us the fullness of sanctity. "That Thou mayest bring bread out of the earth, and that wine [the wine of the Holy Eucharist] may cheer the heart of man." All these gifts come to us from the boundless love of the good Samaritan.

"The earth shall be filled with the fruit of Thy works, O Lord, that Thou mayest bring bread out of the earth, and that wine may cheer the heart of man; that he may make the face cheerful with oil, and that bread may strengthen man's heart" (Communion). Gratitude for a blessed temporal harvest immediately leads the liturgy to think of the supernatural blessings which have come to us as members of Christ in the bread and wine of the Holy Eucharist. The liturgy has in mind both the temporal and the supernatural blessings. It does not, however, view the temporal blessings as something distinct from the spiritual ones, since its faith is so deep that the temporal and natural gifts become immediately and of themselves a type and symbol of spiritual and supernatural gifts.

"That bread may strengthen man's heart." We think at once of the bread of the Holy Eucharist, the bread of life come down from heaven, which heals our weakness and our infirmities, and renews the forces worn out by the struggle of life. Fortifying us against the power of concupiscence and of our passions, it stimulates the soul to take up again the road of virtue and perfection with renewed and unconquerable courage and zeal. "As the living Father hath sent Me, and I live by the Father; so he that eateth Me, the same also shall live by Me" (Jn 6:58). Christ's power works within all of us. "I can do all things in Him who strengtheneth me" (Phil 4:13).

We do not pray in vain: "Incline unto my aid, O God; O Lord, make haste to help me. Let my enemies be confounded and ashamed, who seek my soul" (Introit). "If God be for us, who is against us? He that spared not even His own Son, but delivered Him up for us all, how hath He not also, with Him, given us all things?" (Rom 8:31 f.) Since we possess Christ, who has more reason to be confident than we?

Prayer

Almighty and merciful God, of whose gift it cometh that Thy faithful people do unto Thee true and laudable service; grant, we beseech Thee, that we may run without hindrance toward the attainment of Thy promises. Through Christ our Lord. Amen.

Wednesday

When thinking of the New Covenant, the liturgy of this week is full of jubilation. It is the covenant of the Spirit, the covenant whose service leads to justification. Blessed are they that belong to this covenant.

"Therefore receiving an immovable kingdom, we have grace; whereby let us serve, pleasing God, with fear and reverence" (Heb 12:28). This immovable kingdom has been given to us in the New Covenant, into which, without effort or merit, we have been received in baptism. It embraces the fullness of the spiritual, supernatural world created by God in Jesus Christ. "We saw His glory, the glory as it were of the only-begotten of the Father, full of grace and truth" (Jn 1:14). This covenant is our participation in Christ's redemption: the debt which we had to pay to divine justice has been rescinded; adequate atonement has been made for our sins. Sin has been conquered, the power of hell has been broken, death has met its conqueror, and heaven has been opened. "God, who is rich in mercy, for His exceeding charity wherewith He loved us, even when we were dead in sins, hath quickened us together in Christ... and hath raised us up together and hath made us sit together in the heavenly places, through Christ Jesus.... For by grace you are saved through faith, and that not of yourselves, for it is the gift of God" (Eph 2:4 ff.). All these glories are part of the New Covenant, into which we have been received. This covenant also embraces the riches and treasures of the Church: the divine truth entrusted to the Church, the sacraments, the fullness of grace, the virtues, prayers, and merits of the Church on earth and in heaven. "We have received an immovable kingdom," full of riches and supernatural glory. We Christians have been placed in a kingdom, a spiritual order, the possession of which can make us rich and happy beyond our fondest hopes.

"We all beholding the glory of the Lord with open face, are transformed into the same image from glory to glory, as by the Spirit of the Lord" (2 Cor 3:18). In place of the earthly Moses with his veiled face (Epistle) we Christians are allowed to look upon the Lord Himself, whose face is unveiled and shining in glory. This face takes hold of us in the very depths of our being and forms us into its own image. Christ's image is being formed in us as His glory is reflected in ours. Continual meditation on the person and work of Christ, and our unceasing efforts to imitate Him, realizing what He has done and is still doing for us, change us completely into other Christs. We feel urged to continually thank and praise Him who did everything for us even before we knew Him, when we were still children of God's wrath, and who made us heirs of God without any personal merits of our own. Thus despite all the troubles and sufferings of this earthly life, we must endeavor never to lose sight of the unmerited glories of the New Covenant. Once it has become our first and sincere endeavor to meditate on the interior perfections of the Lord and on His work and His Church, to believe and trust in them, and to praise them, we will have a true understanding of the essentials of a Christian life. Here we have the roots and the fertile soil of genuine fruitfulness in the Christian life, which result from our meditation on Christ. Our fruitfulness cannot be anything but the superabundance of the perfections and glories of the New Covenant, into which we have been received. It must consist in the reflection of the glory of the Lord within our soul, the consideration of which changes us ever more perfectly into His image "by the Spirit of the Lord."

"Blessed are the eyes that see the things which you see" (Gospel). We are the privileged ones who see all these things "with open face" through the revelation and the graces of the New Testament. Unfortunately we exert ourselves too little to become aware of the glory of Christ, of His person, of His work, and of His Church. We are not grateful enough for the exalted kingdom (the New Covenant) into which we have been received. Trusting too little in the interior fullness and power of this covenant and the glory it contains, we lose much of this power and the courage and confidence which once made St. Paul say: "Who shall accuse against the elect of God? God that justifieth. Who is he that shall condemn? Christ Jesus that died yea that is risen also again, who is at the right hand of God, who also maketh intercession for us" (Rom 8:33 f.). If only we, too, could speak with St. Paul the language of a courageous and confident Christianity, how blessed we would be.

Prayer

Almighty and merciful God, of whose gift it cometh that Thy faithful people do unto Thee true and laudable service; grant, we beseech Thee, that we may run without hindrance toward the attainment of Thy promises. Through Christ our Lord. Amen.

Thursday

The liturgy of the Mass for the twelfth Sunday after Pentecost presents to us Moses, the mediator of the Old Covenant, interceding before God's majesty and imploring His mercy for a faithless and sinful people. "And the Lord was appeased from doing the evil which He had spoken of doing against His people" (Offertory).

"If the ministration of condemnation be glory, much more the ministration of justice aboundeth in glory" (Epistle). Moses, the mediator of the Old Covenant, remained on Mount Sinai, conversing intimately with God. Since he remained so long on the mountain, the people waiting at the foot of the mountain thought they had been deceived. The people took the golden earrings from their ears and brought them to Aaron. "And when he had received them, he fashioned them by founder's work, and made of them a molten calf. And they said: These are thy gods, O Israel, that have brought thee out of the land of Egypt" (Ex 32:4). They then sacrificed to the false god, and "sat down to eat and drink, and rose up to play. And the Lord spoke to Moses, saying: Go, get thee down, thy people ... have made to themselves a molten calf, and have adored it, and sacrific[ed] victims to it.... See that this people is stiff-necked. Let Me alone that My wrath may be kindled against them, and that I may destroy them.... But Moses besought the Lord his God, saying: Why, O Lord, is Thy indignation enkindled against Thy people, whom Thou hast brought out of the land of Egypt? ... Let not the Egyptians say, I beseech Thee: He craftily brought them out that He might kill them in the mountains and destroy them from the earth. Let Thy anger cease.... Remember Abraham, Isaac, and Israel, Thy servants, to whom Thou sworest by Thy own Self, saying: I will multiply your seed as the stars of heaven.... And the Lord was appeased from doing the evil which he had spoken against His people" (Ex 32:6 ff.). The glory of the service which Moses, the mediator of the Old Covenant, rendered was that he, by his intercession before God and by his prayers, saved his people from the wrath of God and the terrible punishment they had merited because of their apostasy. Even the ministration of the Old Covenant, "the ministration of death," was able to achieve so much.

"If the ministration of condemnation be glory, much more the ministration of justice aboundeth in glory": this ministration of the Holy Sacrifice which we possess in the New Covenant and which we daily celebrate. Here it is no longer Moses, but rather Christ, the high priest, the Son of God, who intercedes for His people, the faithful, before His Father. Offering an infinitely more valuable gift of sacrifice, His own blood, His passion and death, He implores the Father to grant His people grace and forgiveness, thus appeasing God's anger which we, the baptized, have so often deserved. How often do we not commit daily infidelities against the commandments of God in spite of the powerful and abundant graces given to us! How often do we not deserve God's punishment! Woe unto us if the Lord, our Moses, raises not His hands daily to the Father, if He does not pray for us and offers not His gift of sacrifice. He does so during the Holy Sacrifice of the Mass, offering up His life as He did once on the cross. Looking down upon us with compassion, He implores the Father: "Father, forgive them, for they know not what they do" (Lk 23:34). The Father cannot resist the prayers and sacrifices of His Son. By the Sacrifice of the Mass He allows Himself to be appeased from doing the evil which He had threatened against His people. This "ministration of justice" leads to justification, salvation, and eternal happiness; it is a ministration more wonderful and efficacious than the ministration of the Old Covenant, in the same degree as the life, passion, and death of the Lord are exalted above the prayers of Moses, a mere man. We are indeed blessed in the ministration of the New Covenant, in the Holy Sacrifice of the Mass, in our high priest, Jesus Christ. "Blessed are the eyes that see the things which you see. For I say to you, that many prophets and kings have desired to see the things that you see, and have not seen them" (Gospel).

This "ministration of the Spirit" that leads to justification the Lord has entrusted to the priesthood of His Church. The priest is "taken from among men, is ordained for men in the things that appertain to God, that he may offer up gifts and sacrifices for sins" (Heb 5:1), thus obtaining for us justification before God and the remission of sins. He is endowed with the same mission and power that the Lord gave His apostles when He said: "As the Father hath sent me, I also send you.... Receive ye the Holy Ghost. Whose sins you shall forgive, they are forgiven them; and whose sins you shall retain, they are retained" (Jn 20:21 ff.). To His apostles and their successors and assistants, the bishops and priests, He gives also the power of changing bread and wine into His body and blood. This "ministration of the Spirit," of the New Covenant, leads to justification. "Blessed are the eyes that see the things which you see."

"But [Jesus], for that He continueth forever, hath an everlasting priesthood, whereby He is able also to save forever them that come to God by Him; always living to make intercession for us" (Heb 7:24 f.). Our high priest not only performed the ministration of the Spirit once while dying on the cross, but He continually renews it during the Sacrifice of the Mass and by His continuous prayers in heaven. "Blessed are the eyes that see the things which you see."

Prayer

May we be quickened, O Lord, by participation in this holy mystery, and may it grant us both the expiation of our sins and the strengthening of our souls. Through Christ our Lord. Amen.

Friday

"Master, what must I do to possess eternal life?" asked the lawyer in the Gospel. Jesus answered with a counter-question: "What is written in the law? How readest thou?" And the lawyer replied: "Thou shalt love the Lord thy God with thy whole heart, and with thy whole soul, and with all thy strength, and with all thy mind; and thy neighbor as thyself." Jesus said to him: "Thou hast answered rightly; this do, and thou shalt live." But the lawyer wished to justify himself, and therefore he asked: "Who is my neighbor?" Jesus then related the parable of the good Samaritan and at the end asked the lawyer: "Which of these three, in thy opinion, was neighbor to him that fell among robbers?" He said: "He that showed mercy to him." Jesus said to him: "Go and do thou in like manner." This, then, is the commandment of the Lord: Go and be also a good Samaritan.

"The earth shall be filled with the fruit of Thy works, O Lord" (Communion). The bread and wine of the Holy Eucharist give the Church the power and the obligation to be a good Samaritan to suffering humanity. Man is not called to merely an earthly goal, to attain which he must fulfill his duties on earth and make use of his natural powers and talents; but beyond that he is destined for a heavenly goal, for which he must develop his supernatural powers and faculties in order to share in the divine life. He is to be permeated with divine and sanctifying powers of life, that he may be lifted up into the fullness of life in God. This elevation of man to share the divine life, however, cannot be the work of man himself. It is the work of God, of His free and merciful love and grace.

When God created man in Paradise, He made him a partaker of this divine life through grace. Both grace and nature had been bestowed on Adam for all of us. But Adam sinned and, as the head and representative of the entire human race, lost for all mankind the life of grace. Thus humanity is the man who fell among robbers. Who will save him and restore to him the life of the sonship of God? It can be restored to him only by God Himself through Christ and His Church. To the latter God has entrusted the wine of the Holy Eucharist and the oil of the graces of salvation. With all the power of her divine Master she ministers to humanity. She feels obliged to render her service to those who fall among robbers, for she performs the service of the good Samaritan when she fulfills the command of her Master: "Going therefore, teach ye all nations; baptizing them in the name of the Father, and of the Son, and of the Holy Ghost; teaching them to observe all things whatsoever I have commanded you" (Mt 28:19 f.). With unmoved courage and heroic perseverance, the Church for two thousand years has fulfilled her commission, strengthened by the power which the good Samaritan provided for her when He gave her the two pence: the power of teaching and the sacraments, especially the Holy Eucharist.

Our Lord commanded His Church to "take care of him," but first of all, of the salvation of his soul. He wants her to practice the works of mercy, particularly the spiritual works of mercy. Therefore the Church prays for the living and the dead, and prays especially for those who are dead in sin, that they may rise again to the life of grace. To show sinners the right way and to instruct the ignorant were always important duties of the Church. She never wearies of caring for sinners and the ignorant through instruction and admonition, but especially through the administration of the sacrament of penance. In this sacrament of mercy the Church, full of understanding, mercy, and love, bows down to the man fallen among robbers. Into his wounds she pours the oil of grace and forgiveness through the power of God. New life and new joy will return to the soul which before was full of fear and despair. When a new will and a new strength for doing good, a powerful longing for God, and a healing peace come back into such a man's soul, it can be truly asserted that no power on earth is able to console, heal, and show mercy as does the Church in the sacrament of penance. "Which of these three, in thy opinion, was neighbor to him that fell among robbers?" The Levite, the priest of the Old Testament, or the Church of the New Testament with her sacrament of penance? She has the ministration that leads to justification, life, and union with God; no one but she possesses it. "Blessed are the eyes that see the things which you see" (Gospel): the Church, the mystical body of Christ, full of the powers of salvation, giving life to those who come to her dead in sin.

The program leading to justification has been given to the Church. "Whose sins you shall forgive, they are forgiven them; and whose sins you shall retain, they are retained" (Jn 20:23). The Church has the power of the heavenly Judge: to forgive and to retain sins. In this judgment we are at the same time the prosecutor and the witness. Its effectiveness depends on the sincerity of our self-accusation and on our firm purpose to amend our ways of life. Only if our disposition is right can the Church make good use of her vocation of being the good Samaritan.

"Many prophets and kings have desired to see the things that you see, and have not seen them; and to hear the things that you hear, and have not heard them" (Gospel). We see, we hear, we possess the things of which Christ spoke; yet we neither think of them nor are we as thankful for them as we should be.

PRAYER

Almighty and eternal God, of whose gift it cometh that Thy faithful people do unto Thee true and laudable service; grant, we beseech Thee, that we may run without hindrance toward the attainment of Thy promises. Through Christ our Lord. Amen.

Saturday

"Go and do thou in like manner" (Gospel). Let us also imitate the conduct of the good Samaritan. Such charity is the service of the New Covenant, of the baptized, who in such abundant measure experience the mercy of the good Samaritan, the Son of God become man. The sacraments of baptism, the Holy Eucharist, and penance oblige us to "go and do thou in like manner."

"Which of these three, in thy opinion, was neighbor to him that fell among robbers?" Jesus asks the lawyer in the Gospel. True Christian charity is merciful with a mercy that springs from a living compassion for the need of our fellow men; it is the desire to help him as far as possible. "Go and do thou in like manner." We have become members of Christ in baptism; with each Mass and Holy Communion we perfect our union with Christ, the head. Understanding more deeply His spirit and His power of love, we also feel urged, by virtue of this union with Christ, to practice mercy and charity. "Be ye therefore merciful, as your Father also is merciful" (Lk 6:36). "Blessed are the merciful; for they shall obtain mercy" (Mt 5:7). The spirit of Christ, if it truly lives within us, forbids us to pass by another's need coldly and without compassion. We cannot act like the Levite and the priest of the Gospel, who saw their fellow man's need, but passed by. Woe be to us if we act in such a manner; we would be sorely wanting in the spirit of Christ. "If any man have not the Spirit of Christ, he is none of His" (Rom 8:9). "Amen, I say to you, as long as you did it to one of these My least brethren, you did it to Me" (Mt 25:40).

"Go and do thou in like manner." The Lord demands both the spirit and the works of charity. These are the corporal works of mercy: to feed the hungry, to give drink to the thirsty, to cover the naked, to shelter the homeless, to visit the imprisoned, to care for the sick, to bury the dead. And these are the spiritual works of mercy: to guide sinners, to instruct the ignorant, to counsel the doubting, to comfort the sorrowing, to suffer injustice patiently, to forgive those who have injured us, to pray for the living and the dead. According to the above works we shall be judged at the hour of our death and on the last day. These works of mercy, which we performed with the desire to help our fellow men for Christ's sake, to aid the members of Christ's mystical body, and to render to them in the spirit of Christ the service of the good Samaritan, shall determine our place in heaven or hell. "Come, ye blessed of my Father, possess you the kingdom prepared for you from the foundation of the world. For I was hungry, and you gave Me to eat; I was thirsty, and you gave Me to drink; I was a stranger, and you took Me in; naked, and you covered Me; sick, and you visited Me; I was in prison, and you came to Me.... Then He shall say to them also that shall be on His left hand: Depart from Me, you cursed, into everlasting fire which was prepared for the devil and his angels. For I was hungry, and you gave Me not to eat; I was thirsty, and you gave Me not to drink; I was a stranger, and you took Me not in; naked, and you covered Me not; sick and in prison, and you did not visit Me" (Mt 25:34 ff.). The works of mercy open heaven; the lack of mercy leads to eternal hell.

"Moses prayed in the sight of the Lord his God, and said: Why, O Lord, is Thy indignation enkindled against Thy people? Let the anger of Thy mind cease.... And the Lord was appeased from doing the evil which He had spoken of doing against His people" (Offertory). Such is the power of God's mercy. Did not Moses have reason enough for being angry with his people dancing around a golden calf at the foot of the mountain? But he has compassion on the infatuated, misled people, and his prayer, born out of this compassion, is answered by God. Thus can God's anger be allayed. "Blessed are the merciful; for they shall obtain mercy" for themselves and for others (Mt 5:7).

So we also, who are going to offer the Holy Sacrifice, are full of mercy and compassion concerning the temporal and spiritual needs of our brethren. With a heart full of compassion we lift up our offering to heaven: "Why, O Lord, is Thy indignation enkindled against Thy people? Let the anger of Thy mind cease.... And the Lord was appeased from doing the evil which He had spoken of doing against His people."

In Holy Communion we are filled with the Spirit of Christ. He is the Spirit of compassion who, viewing our misery, says with the words of the Gospel: "I have compassion on the multitude" (Mk 8:2). "Put ye on, therefore, as the elect of God, holy, and beloved, the bowels of mercy, benignity, humility, modesty, patience" (Col 3:12).

Prayer

Almighty and merciful God, of whose gift it cometh that Thy faithful people do unto Thee true and laudable service; grant, we beseech Thee, that we may run without hindrance toward the attainment of Thy promises. Through Christ our Lord. Amen.

Thirteenth Sunday after Pentecost

The Mass

Today the liturgy again compares the Old Covenant with the New; in the former we see life without Christ; in the latter, life in Him and with Him. In the Old Testament the law of sin and death prevails; in the New Testament the word of life holds sway. This comparison admonishes us to acknowledge our privilege of having been united with Christ in baptism and of having become one with Him, the living vine. "To Abraham were the promises made and to his seed," St. Paul tells us in the Epistle. This blessed seed and bringer of salvation, however, is not Moses (the Old Covenant); for the Mosaic law neither redeems from sin nor does it restore life. The promises of life are fulfilled by Christ alone and are given only "to them that believe" (Epistle). Redemption from sin is given to us in Christ alone and through faith in Him. We therefore have to go to Him, devoting ourselves entirely to faith in Christ and thanking Him with our whole heart for having been called to Him in baptism and the Holy Eucharist.

We are Christians, the Lord's covenant (Introit). He has freed us from the leprosy of Original Sin and planted in our souls the seeds of supernatural life and eternal salvation. Being without gratitude for the grace of healing (Gospel), however, we gave way to the man of sin and the passions within us, thus becoming faithless to our holy covenant with Christ through our faults. During today's Mass, therefore, we realize our weakness and sinfulness and with remorse for our unfaithfulness we implore the Lord in the Introit: "Have regard, O Lord, to Thy covenant, and forsake not to the end the souls of Thy poor; arise, O Lord, and judge Thy cause, and forget not the voices of them that seek Thee." "Lord, have mercy on us; Christ, have mercy on us; Lord, have mercy on us." "Grant unto us an increase of faith, hope, and charity; and that we may obtain what Thou dost promise, make us love that which Thou dost command" (Collect). These promises will be given to us by our faith in Jesus Christ (Epistle). "Have regard, O Lord, to Thy covenant.... Thou hast been our refuge from generation to generation" (Gradual). For two thousand years He has ever renewed His Church interiorly and exteriorly; He has fortified her anew; He has guided and protected her, sanctified and saved her.

What the Gospel relates becomes true in us at the time when we received baptism; during the celebration of Mass it becomes again a blessed reality and a Real Presence. Now, at this hour, the Savior is again going "into a certain town," into His Church, into our house of worship. We are lepers covered with the leprosy of sin and are going to meet Him. "Jesus, Master," we cry out, "have mercy on us" (Gospel). He sees us and refers us to the priest, who is the mediator between the altar (Christ) and the sacrificing community. Through the hands of the priest Christ offers Himself up, pouring His graces, redemption, and life from the heights of the altar down into the hearts of the sacrificing community. We participate in these graces to the same degree that we become one sacrifice with the Savior, who offers Himself up to the Father by renewing His death on the cross. How few there are, however, out of the community who return after their baptism, rendering their service of gratitude in the Mass by renewing the graces and the true spirit of baptism, by renouncing sin, Satan, and the world! How few there are who thus show true gratitude for the grace of baptism! "Were not ten made clean?

And where are the nine?" (Gospel.) This reproachful question is addressed to us ungrateful Christians who follow worldly pleasures. Blessed are they who know how to be grateful and appreciate the privilege of being Christians. "Thou hast given us, O Lord, bread from heaven" (Communion). How grateful we should be for our baptism and for being privileged to participate in the Sacrifice of the Mass!

Meditation

The liturgy of this Sunday again calls to our attention the relationship between the Old Covenant and the New. It presents the old problem of whether Christ and His Church alone shall be the foundation of our eternal salvation, or whether besides Him and His Church, the law of Moses, the Old Testament, shall be necessary and binding. The answer of the liturgy is unmistakable and clear: Christ and Christ alone is the source of our salvation. "Neither is there salvation in any other. For there is no other name under heaven given to men whereby we must be saved" (Acts 4:12).

"To Abraham were the promises made, and to his seed" (Epistle). "Go forth out of thy country and from thy kindred and out of thy father's house, and come into the land which I shall show thee. And I will make of thee a great nation, and I will bless thee.... In thee shall all the kindred of the earth be blessed" (Gn 12:1 ff.). Abraham had to wait many years before a son was born to him, Isaac, the son of promise. Now he is commanded by God to sacrifice this son of promise, his only child, by his own hand. Yet Abraham obeys. When he lifts the sword to sacrifice his son, the Lord orders him to cease, and instead of Isaac he sacrifices a ram provided by God. Now the Lord repeats His promises to Abraham: "Because thou hast done this thing and hast not spared thy only-begotten son for My sake, I will bless thee.... And in thy seed shall all the nations of the earth be blessed, because thou hast obeyed My voice" (Gn 22:16 ff.). God does not say, as St. Paul stresses in today's Epistle, "To his seeds, as of many; but as of one, and to thy seed, which is Christ," in whom alone all the nations of the earth shall be blessed and shall have salvation from the Lord: "That the blessing of Abraham might come on the Gentiles through Christ Jesus; that we may receive the promise of the spirit by faith" (Gal 3:14). "He that believeth and is baptized shall be saved; but he that believeth not, shall be condemned" (Mk 16:16).

"At that time, as Jesus was going to Jerusalem,... as He entered into a certain town, there met Him ten lepers," who cried to Him for help and healing. He commanded them: "Go, show yourselves to the priests" (Gospel). They obey, and while they go they are made clean. The law of Moses, the Old Covenant with its priesthood and sacrifices, is unable to heal those poor people from their leprosy. Through Christ alone can a sinful world receive salvation; for in Him alone all the nations of the earth are blessed. Only one of the ten lepers who were cured returned to the Lord. Praising God with a loud voice, he ascribes his healing to God, to Jesus, acknowledging thereby that Jesus is the Savior and that salvation cannot be found in men's own works or in the fulfillment of the law of the Old Testament. Forsaking the Old Testament, he becomes a child of the Church, having been called from among the pagans and sinners "by the faith of Jesus Christ" (Epistle). The Church believes and teaches that there is no salvation but in Christ alone. "There is no other name under heaven given to men whereby we must be saved" (Acts 4:12).

Without interruption she sings the praises of the Lord, rendering to Him her gratitude for the Eucharist, the Holy Sacrament of His love.

We must understand what today's Mass wishes to convey to us. We believe in Christ and we wish to stand by Him, for in Christ, and in Christ alone, can we be saved. Faith in Christ alone makes us partakers of the fruit of redemption and assures us of eternal life. It must be a faith, however, "that worketh by charity" (Gal 5:6). "Without faith it is impossible to please God" (Heb 11:6). But it still remains ever true that the greatest virtue is charity. "If I should have all faith so that I could remove mountains, and have not charity, I am nothing" (1 Cor 13:2).

In the ten lepers of the Gospel, we recognize ourselves. In baptism the Lord, out of pure mercy and without any merit of ours, cleansed us from the leprosy of our sins; and time and again He has repeated our cleansing through His priests in the second baptism, the sacrament of penance. "Go, show yourselves to the priests."

Today we come to the Holy Sacrifice in order to thank God worthily for the infinite love which He has shown us through so many graces. He never ceases to shower us with His graces, even when we do not think of them or even when we have made ourselves unworthy of new graces because of our pride and self-esteem.

We thank the heavenly Father for all His love and graces especially by offering to Him in the Mass the flesh and blood of our Savior. "Through Him, and with Him, and in Him, be unto Thee, O God, the Father Almighty, in the unity of the Holy Ghost, all honor and glory, world without end."

We thank the Lord for the grace of baptism, for the sacrament of penance, and for the Holy Eucharist with our prayers, but especially with our lives: with the resolution to be faithful to the graces and promises of baptism. We promise to be faithful in fulfilling our duties of praying and working, by sincerely endeavoring to keep ourselves undefiled by sin and free from voluntary faults and imperfections, trying to spend our lives in pure love for Him.

Prayer

Almighty and everlasting God, grant unto us an increase of faith, hope, and charity; and that we may obtain what Thou dost promise, make us love that which Thou dost command. Through Christ our Lord. Amen.

Monday

The Church, in grave distress, cries to heaven: "Have regard, O Lord, to Thy covenant" (Introit). It is a cry appealing God to be faithful to His covenant, for the Lord Himself made this covenant with His chosen people, the Church, wherein He bound Himself to take care of them. The cause of the Church is God's own cause. "Have regard, O Lord, to Thy covenant, and forsake not to the end the souls of Thy poor" (Introit).

"This is the blood of the covenant which the Lord hath made with you concerning all these words" (Ex 24:8). From the beginning God made a covenant with humanity. When Adam had sinned, He supported fallen humanity with His infinite compassion and promised the

Redeemer. "I will put enmities between thee and the woman, and thy seed and her seed; she shall crush thy head, and thou shalt lie in wait for her heel" (Gn 3:15). God made this covenant with humanity that the serpent, sin, might be vanquished and that fallen humanity might be redeemed and saved. When men's sins became unbearable, the Lord sent the Deluge. After the flood, however, He renewed His covenant with Noe, the second father of the human race, and later with Abraham, the father of the Israelites. He again made a covenant with the chosen people, whom He had brought out of Egypt, when on Mount Sinai, amidst thunder and lightning, He solemnly proclaimed the law of the covenant. Moses wrote down the law and erected an altar. The people sacrificed to the Lord and promised to observe the law and the Ten Commandments given to them by God. Moses then took some of the sacrificial blood and sprinkled it on the people, saying: "This is the blood of the covenant which the Lord hath made with you concerning all these words."

"This is My blood of the New Testament" (Mt 26:28). God makes a perfect covenant with humanity in Christ Jesus our Lord. It is an immutable covenant, full of grace and glory. "Sacrifice and oblation thou wouldst not.... Holocausts for sin did not please Thee.... Then said I: Behold, I come to do Thy will, O God" (Heb 10:5 ff.). Here we have the covenant of the Father with His only-begotten Son, who became man for our redemption. The Son enters this world and takes upon Himself in His Incarnation our human nature in order to fulfill the great work He has chosen to undertake. He has come to fulfill the Father's will in the poverty of the stable of Bethlehem, through a life of prayer and work at Nazareth, through the pains and privations of His public life, and in the sufferings and humiliations of the Passion. "I came down from heaven, not to do My own will, but the will of Him that sent Me" (Jn 6:38). "This is My blood of the New Testament." The New Covenant has been made and sealed with His blood. The anger of the Father has been appeased, the power of sin and hell has been broken, and heaven has been reopened. We are children of God again, His "holy and beloved" (Col 3:12). "The charity of God is poured forth in our hearts by the Holy Ghost, who is given to us" (Rom 5:5). Ours are the sacraments with their graces; ours is the Church with her inexhaustible riches of truth, life, and power. All these gifts have been founded on the covenant which God made with us in Christ and through Him, without any work or merit of ours. God showed this mercy to us even before we had been called into existence.

To us, as to the Israelites of old, God addresses His promise: "I will take you to Myself for My people, I will be your God" (Ex 6:7). "Happy is that people whose God is the Lord" (Ps 143:15). We are the people of the New Covenant, the covenant of grace and redemption that has been assured us through a holy legacy. We are happy and grateful to be the people of the New Covenant.

"To Abraham were the promises made and to his seed," which is Christ, the head of the Church. Through the Church we also receive these promises. In the New Covenant, sealed by the blood of Christ, the fullness of truth and grace is deposited. Since we have become members of the New Covenant in baptism, all the riches of redemption are ours. It is therefore our first duty to become ever more closely united with Christ and His Church. He is the fullness of grace, the ocean of divine life; He is the source of all true holiness and strength.

The blood of the New Covenant, mysteriously flowing on our altars during the celebration of the Mass, is placed in our hands as a gift of sacrifice that we may offer it to God in atonement for our sins and as a pledge of future grace and help for ourselves, for our brethren in Christ, and for the whole world. "Have regard, O Lord, to Thy covenant, and forsake not to the end the souls of Thy poor; arise, O Lord, and judge Thy cause, and forget not the voices of them that seek Thee" (Introit). As a consequence of God's covenant with us, we are His people; His cause is our cause. When we receive Holy Communion, the blood of the covenant is poured into our souls, and the Lord confirms anew this holy covenant. In Holy Communion we also confirm and renew our devotion to God. "Thou art my God; my times are in Thy hands" (Offertory). I want to be yours for time and eternity.

PRAYER

Almighty and everlasting God, grant unto us an increase of faith, hope, and charity; and that we may obtain what Thou dost promise, make us love that which Thou dost command. Through Christ our Lord. Amen.

Tuesday

"To Abraham were the promises made, and to his seed. [God] saith not: And to his seeds, as of many; but as of one, and to thy seed, which is Christ" (Epistle), that is, the whole Christ, the mystical body, the Church and all her members. Now, if the Old Covenant was founded on promises which no Israelite could doubt would be fulfilled, even if his reason and experience in life might demur, how much more may we expect of the New Covenant that has been made in Christ. Of Christ the Apostle testifies: "All the promises of God are in Him; ... therefore also by Him" (2 Cor 1:20). This is to the Apostle the message of salvation: "That the Gentiles should be fellow heirs, and of the same body, and copartners of His promise in Christ Jesus" (Eph 3:6). We are "the children of promise" (Gal 4:28).

"All the promises of God are in Him." Whatever blessings, graces, and heavenly rewards God promised the fathers of the Old Testament, were also promised to us in Christ. In Christ, and in Him alone, salvation and all the means of salvation have been given to humanity and to each man. This is God's plan of salvation: "By this hath the charity of God appeared towards us, because God hath sent His only-begotten Son into the world, that we may live by Him" (1 Jn 4:9). God gave "His only-begotten Son" (Jn 3:16) that He may become our brother and we may become His coheirs, possessing with Him His grace and glory, and "that He might shew in the ages to come the abundant riches of His grace, in His bounty towards us in Christ Jesus" (Eph 2:7). God gives us all things in His Son, Christ Jesus; through Him alone does God communicate with us and we with Him. "No man cometh to the Father but by Me" (Jn 14:6). Christ is the way, the only way, that leads to the Father. Without Him we can do nothing. The branch cannot bring forth fruit or even have life at all if it does not remain connected with the vine. "If any one abide not in Me, he shall be cast forth as a branch, and shall wither, and they shall gather him up and cast him into the fire, and he burneth" (Jn 15:6): Nobody can lay any other foundation than the one that has been laid in Christ Jesus. We must keep building on this foundation. "Now if any man build upon this foundation, gold, silver, precious stones, wood, hay, stubble, every man's work shall be manifest" (1 Cor 3:12 f.).

God gives the fullness of His life to the humanity of Christ, thereby making the Incarnation of His Son the fountain of grace in His Church and her members "according to the measure of the giving of Christ" (Eph 4:7). Either we are holy in Christ or we are not holy at all. We have been chosen "not according to our own works, but according to His own purpose and grace, which was given us in Christ Jesus before the times of the world" (2 Tm 1:9). Christ is the center, the fountain, the fulfillment of all the promises. In Him is salvation and every means of salvation; in Him is all grace, redemption, and faith.

Christ on His part also gave us wonderful promises, which are to be fulfilled in the time to come. To His Church He makes the promise that the gates of hell shall never prevail against her. He promises her that He will be with her all days, even to the consummation of the world (Mt 28:20). To us He makes the promise that some day He will return with much power and majesty. "The hour cometh wherein all that are in the graves shall hear the voice of the Son of God. And they that have done good things, shall come forth unto the resurrection of life; but they that have done evil, unto the resurrection of judgment" (Jn 5:28 f.). He makes us some other promises, too, which are of a more general nature and are directed to each of us individually as an aid for our personal Christian life and endeavors. "He that abideth in Me, and I in him, the same beareth much fruit" (Jn 15:5). "He that loveth Me, shall be loved of My Father; and I will love him, and will manifest Myself to him" (Jn 14:21). "Blessed are the poor in spirit, for theirs is the kingdom of heaven. Blessed are the meek, for they shall possess the land. Blessed are they that mourn, for they shall be comforted. Blessed are they that hunger and thirst after justice, for they shall have their fill. Blessed are the merciful, for they shall obtain mercy. Blessed are the clean of heart, for they shall see God. Blessed are the peacemakers, for they shall be called the children of God. Blessed are they that suffer persecution for justice's sake, for theirs is the kingdom of heaven. Blessed are ye when they shall revile you, and persecute you, and speak all that is evil against you, untruly for my sake" (Mt 5:3 ff.).

Christ also gives promises meant for those who leave everything out of love for Him. "Amen, I say to you . . . every one that hath left house, or brethren, or sisters, or father, or mother, or wife, or children, or lands for My name's sake, shall receive an hundredfold, and shall possess life everlasting" (Mt 19:28 f.). These are no empty words; they are unfailing, divinely sure promises, which we are not allowed to minimize or belittle in any way. Christ is infinite truth; we therefore must believe and joyfully accept these promises.

The promises given to the fathers have been fulfilled in Christ and in Him alone. In Him alone we have grace and through Him alone can we expect the heavenly heritage. With the words of the Apostle we stand with Christ: "I know whom I have believed, and I am certain that He is able to keep that which I have committed unto Him, against that day" (2 Tm 1:12).

The promises made by Christ are so exalted and all-embracing that nothing on earth can be compared with them.

PRAYER

Almighty and everlasting God, grant unto us an increase of faith, hope, and charity; and that we may obtain what Thou dost promise, make us love that which Thou dost command. Through Christ our Lord. Amen.

Wednesday

Christ had cleansed ten lepers; only one, however, returned to Him to thank Him for having been healed (Gospel). This one who returned is a type of the Church, which, having been cleansed in the blood of the Lord and the waters of baptism, returns to the Lord to thank Him. "Let us give thanks to the Lord our God."

"It is truly meet and just, right and availing unto salvation, that we should at all times and in all places give thanks unto Thee, O holy Lord, Father Almighty and everlasting God, through Christ our Lord" (Preface of the Mass). The praise of God is the first object of the prayers of the Church; she adores, praises, and thanks Him. Every morning at sunrise she remembers that blessed moment when her children were born to light through the reception of the sacrament of baptism, when they rose out of the darkness of sin to a new life. In gratitude for these graces the Church sends her praises heavenward, especially in the Canticle of Lauds and the Benedictus, thanking the heavenly Father for having wrought in her children the miracle of spiritual resurrection from death to life. When the sun has risen, the priests of the Church go to the altar to celebrate the Holy Sacrifice of the Mass, which is a sacrifice of thanksgiving for the benefits of creation and of God's providence in governing the world, and for the grace of the Incarnation, the redemption, and the descent of the Holy Ghost. It is the sacrifice of thanksgiving for the grace of divine sonship, for God's dwelling within our souls, for our union with Christ, the head, and for membership in His mystical body. The Church feels urged to give thanks to God for having preserved and governed her throughout the centuries, for having multiplied her children throughout the earth, and for having unceasingly poured forth His assisting grace upon her children, illuminating and admonishing them, stimulating and aiding them with His divine wisdom.

At the beginning of dusk, at Vespers, the Church gratefully looks back at the past, recalling all the graces she and her children have received, especially the greatest of all, the approach of God Himself to His children in Holy Communion. She jubilantly expresses her gratitude through the Magnificat of Mary, the Virgin Mother of God: "My soul doth magnify the Lord. And my spirit hath rejoiced in God, my Savior. Because He that is mighty hath done great things to me; and holy is His name. And His mercy is from generation unto generation, to them that fear Him" (Lk 1:46 ff.). At Compline she expresses her gratitude in the words of the aged Simeon: "Now Thou dost dismiss Thy servant, O Lord, according to Thy word in peace; because my eyes have seen Thy salvation" (Lk 2:29 f.).

The Church is aware that her debt of gratitude to God is so great that she never will be able to pay it by herself. Even if all the choirs of the angels and the blessed concurred, they would not be able to make a worthy return of gratitude for all the graces and gifts which God has bestowed upon the children of His Church. She therefore thanks Him "through Christ our Lord." Making the cause of the Church His own, Christ, the mediator between God and men, unites the thanksgiving of His spouse and all her children with the infinitely meritorious acts of thanksgiving which unceasingly arise from His most Sacred Heart to the Father. He permeates the thanksgivings given to God by the Church with the fragrance and power of His human-divine thanksgiving. Through Him the Church is enabled to give to God thanks that are worthy of His love and graces. In return God gives to the Church and her children new graces and blessings.

The spirit of the Church is a spirit of gratitude. The more we unite ourselves in prayer with the liturgy of the Church, the more we become like the good leper who returned to Christ and gave glory to God.

"Were not ten made clean? And where are the nine?" (Gospel.) With deep sorrow the liturgy recognizes in these nine that were cleansed but did not return to the Lord, a great number of her children who have been cleansed in baptism and have experienced the love of the Lord in their first Holy Communion, but who have forgotten His love, the gift which, without any merits of theirs, they received from the Lord's boundless charity, and do not return to praise God and thank Him. If we listen to the Gospel, we witness a sad scene: Ten lepers have been cleansed, but only one of them returns to the Lord to give thanks for having been healed, and this one is a Samaritan, a foreigner who does not even belong to the Lord's chosen people. The children of predilection have been showered with graces and benefits by God and have been cared for day after day by the Lord's providence; and yet they are ungrateful. They pay no attention to the privilege of having been chosen. They live under one roof with the Lord; the tabernacle is near at hand; they have the Sacrifice of the Mass, the blessings of the sacraments, and many other graces. And yet they do not appreciate these blessings and do not make any use of the graces offered; they are ungrateful. "Where are the nine?" Only one out of ten gives thanks to the Lord. Do I belong to the ungrateful nine?

Prayer

Almighty and everlasting God, grant unto us an increase of faith, hope, and charity; and that we may obtain what Thou dost promise, make us love that which Thou dost command. Through Christ our Lord. Amen.

Thursday

The liturgy of the Church works for Christ with zeal and consistency. It proves that He is the Lord; it urges the faithful to remember that Christ must be the center of their life and that the good they find within themselves they must ascribe to Him and the work of His grace. "Of His fullness we all have received" (Jn 1:16).

"Man is justified ... by the faith of Jesus Christ" (Gal 2:16). We are not justified by the observance of the law of Moses nor by our own poor human struggles and endeavors. "For all have sinned and do need the glory of God. Being justified freely by His grace through the redemption that is in Jesus Christ, whom God hath proposed to be a propitiation, through faith in His blood, to the showing of His justice.... Where is then the boasting? It is excluded. By what law? Of works? No, but by the law of faith. For we account a man to be justified by faith, without the works of the law" (Rom 3:23 ff.). "You are all the children of God by faith in Christ Jesus. For as many of you as have been baptized in Christ, have put on Christ. There is neither Jew nor Greek; there is neither bond nor free; there is neither male nor female. For you all are one in Christ Jesus. And if you be Christ's, then you are the seed of Abraham, heirs according to the promise" (Gal 3:26 ff.). Here we have the essence of God's plan of redemption: We receive the graces He intends to give us, the sonship of God, by faith in Jesus Christ. "You are all the children of God by faith in Christ Jesus" (Gal 3:26). And St. John assures us that it is by faith that we receive the incarnate Word of God

(Jn 1:12). By faith we become one with Christ; by faith we devote ourselves to Him, and He leads us to the Father, making us with Him possessors of divine life. The more perfect, solid, and deep our faith in Jesus, the Son of God, the more we shall be entitled to be sons of God and to be participants in the divine life. The Council of Trent justly says: "Without faith it is impossible to please God and to attain to the fellowship of His Son" (Sess. VI, chap. 8). We have this faith through the teaching mission of the Church.

"Arise, go thy way; for thy faith hath made thee whole" (Gospel). The Samaritan who was cleansed by Jesus of his leprosy and came back to Jesus, "fell on his face before His feet, giving thanks." But the Lord says to him: "Arise, go thy way; for thy faith hath made thee whole." The Lord repeatedly asks us to think of Jesus, the Son of God. "According to your faith be it done unto you," He tells the two blind men who wanted to be healed by Him. "And their eyes were opened" (Mt 9:29 f.). "Fear not; believe only," He says to the ruler of the synagogue, whose daughter had already died. "Believe only, and she shall be safe" (Lk 8:50). Faith is the first condition He asks for; it is the indispensable presupposition of His miracles. To faith, on the other hand, He cannot deny anything; because of her faith he forgives the sinful woman her sins (Lk 7:50); for the same reason He opens to the good thief the gates of eternal life: "Amen I say to thee, this day thou shalt be with Me in paradise" (Lk 23:43).

The faith God demands is faith in His Son, Jesus, who became man for our redemption. We must have faith in the testimony that came down from heaven and was heard three times above Jesus: "This is My beloved Son, in whom I am well pleased; hear ye Him" (Mt 3:17; 17:5; Jn 12:28). "The Father Himself who hath sent Me, hath given testimony of Me" (Jn 5:37). "Every one who seeth the Son and believeth in Him, may have life everlasting" (Jn 6:40). "God so loved the world as to give His only-begotten Son; that whosoever believeth in Him, may not perish, but may have life everlasting.... He that believeth in Him is not judged. But he that does not believe, is already judged; because he believeth not in the name of the only-begotten Son of God" (Jn 3:16, 18). Faith in Jesus Christ, the Son of God, is the first condition for eternal life. Faith in His divinity embraces all other revealed truths. The Samaritan, the representative of the Church of the Gentiles, believes and hears the words: "Arise, go thy way; for thy faith hath made thee whole."

The Church believes in Jesus, the Son of God. During the course of the centuries many heretics denied the divinity of Christ; the Church, however, stands steadfastly by her faith in Christ, the Son of God. We join the Church in her faith. "Every one who seeth the Son and believeth in Him, may have life everlasting" (Jn 6:40).

"This is my beloved Son." This testimony of the Father contains all revealed truths; the acceptance of this truth embraces our entire faith. When professing our faith in Jesus, the Son of God, we also believe in all the revelation of the Old Testament, which is fulfilled in Christ. This faith contains also our belief in the revelations of the New Testament, in the doctrines of the apostles and the Church, for the teaching of the apostles and the Church is nothing but the exposition of the revelation announced by Christ.

The firm conviction that Christ is the Son of God is essential for supernatural life and holiness. On this foundation our Holy Mother the Church builds her doctrine. To her, therefore, "is given the promise" because she believes.

Prayer

Almighty and everlasting God, grant unto us an increase of faith, hope, and charity; and that we may obtain what Thou dost promise, make us love that which Thou dost command. Through Christ our Lord. Amen.

Friday

"We account a man to be justified by faith, without the works of the law" (Rom 3:28). The only way of justification is through faith in Jesus Christ, the Son of God. "He that believeth and is baptized, shall be saved; but he that believeth not, shall be condemned" (Mk 16:16).

"Go, show yourselves to the priests" (Gospel). The Mosaic law ordained that whoever was healed of leprosy must show himself to the priest. The priest, by virtue of his authority, confirmed the fact that the afflicted person had been cured of the dreaded disease. The lepers in the Gospel, therefore, betake themselves to a nearby town in search of a priest in order to have their cure verified. Nine of the ten show themselves to the priest, thus fulfilling the commands of the Mosaic law. Believing that they owe their healing to the works of this law, they do not even think of returning to the Lord to thank Him. Here we have proof of the tragic delusion and blindness of the people of Israel, who believed that the works, sacrifices, washings, and prayers commanded by the law of Moses "could give life" (Epistle). It is a delusion to believe that the life of grace and true salvation can come from anyone or anything but faith in Christ Jesus. We meet the same blindness and delusion in those who rely on merely native talents and natural strength and efforts, believing that they need no supernatural help through faith in Jesus Christ, the Son of God. "If there had been a law given which could give life, verily justice should have been by the law. But the Scripture hath concluded all under sin, that the promise by the faith of Jesus Christ might be given to them that believe" (Epistle). "He that believeth not, shall be condemned." There is no salvation but in Jesus Christ. "For there is no other name under heaven given to man whereby we must be saved" (Acts 4:12).

"One of them, when he saw that he was made clean, went back with a loud voice glorifying God; and he fell on his face before His feet, giving thanks" (Gospel). He does not go to the priests, for he understands that he does not owe his healing to the works of the law or his own endeavors. He believes in Jesus, who commands him: "Arise, go thy way, for thy faith hath made thee whole." Having become aware of the fact that he has been cleansed, he went back "with a loud voice glorifying God; and ... giving thanks." To the liturgy this man is the type of those who believe and to whom has been given "the promise by the faith of Jesus Christ" (Epistle). To them the Lord gives the promise: "Thy faith hath made thee whole." To them, however, that rely on the works of the law, on merely human efforts, expecting salvation from natural powers, the fearful word is said: "He that believeth not the Son, shall not see life; but the wrath of God abideth on him" (Jn 3:36).

What the Gospel relates about the ten lepers is to the liturgy a categorical: "without faith it is impossible to please God" (Heb 11:6). "He that believeth in the Son, hath life everlasting; but he that believeth not the Son, shall not see life; but the wrath of God abideth on him" (Jn 3:36).

In baptism the faith has been planted in our soul. We daily strengthen it by praying and by making acts of faith. The deeper this faith in Jesus becomes, the safer and more solid and fruitful will be our spiritual life. Our spiritual life and sanctity derive their strength and growth from the living faith in the Son of God given to us by the Father. Whether Jesus shows Himself to us as a helpless child in the manger, as a working man in His father's shop, or as a teacher continually exposed to the contradiction of His enemies, He is always Christ, God and man. Whether we see Him in disgrace and humiliation in His passion and death on the cross, whether we believe in Him, hidden and forgotten in the tabernacle, He remains always the same, the Son of the eternal Father, equal in substance with the Father, equal in majesty, power, and wisdom. If we have this vivid faith in Him, it must of necessity constrain us to make acts of adoration and urge us to devote ourselves to the will of Him who, though human, nevertheless remains forever God, the Son of the eternal Father.

True faith in Jesus, the Son of God, will necessarily be perfected in love, urging us to take upon ourselves the sacrifices Jesus asks of us, to remain unshaken in times of temptation, and to be strong in all the trials and sufferings of life. "In Thee, O Lord, have I hoped; I said, Thou art my God; my times are in Thy hands" (Offertory).

Prayer

Almighty and everlasting God, grant unto us an increase of faith, hope, and charity; and that we may obtain what Thou dost promise, make us love that which Thou dost command. Through Christ our Lord. Amen.

Saturday

It is now harvest time; God has blessed the farmer's work. The seeds planted in the soil in spring have sprung up; they grew slowly at first, but then after some months they became a waving field of grain. At the sight of these growing and ripening fields the liturgy reminds us of the necessity of our interior growth in faith, hope, and charity: "Grant unto us an increase of faith, hope, and charity" (Collect).

"Grant unto us an increase of faith, hope, and charity." The nine men of the Gospel who have been healed of leprosy accept the cure the Lord has given them; but they are absorbed by the thought of their cure; of being able to return to their families and to work again. They are a picture of the many Christians who accept our Lord's gifts and benefits: life, health, and the powers of body and soul; yet do not regard the giver of these gifts. Eternal and supernatural things are of no interest to them. They dedicate their life only to worldly and natural interests, concentrating their efforts on one goal alone: how they may progress in their worldly undertakings. Often this attitude is true not only in individuals, but even in whole communities. To this one-sided natural point of view, the Church opposes the striving after spiritual and supernatural values, "the increase of faith, hope, and charity." She wishes us to strive first after supernatural life, the life of grace. "Seek ye first the kingdom of God and His justice, and all these things shall be added unto you" (Lk 12:31). "What shall it profit a man if he gain the whole world and suffer the loss of his soul?" (Mk 8:36.) What matters first of all is God and a life for God, built on the virtues of faith, hope, and charity; we must seek first the supernatural life of the soul, a life of union with

God; and then only may we seek temporal things. The Church sees with sorrow how many of her children become worldly and strive after natural and temporal things alone, thus neglecting the life of grace and the works of faith. She prays for all these that the Lord may grant them "an increase of faith, hope, and charity." Let us unite our prayers also with those of the Church.

"Make us love that which Thou dost command" (Collect). "Man must fear obedience more than disobedience," was a favorite saying of St. Francis de Sales. If we love that which God commands, we shall be safe against faithlessness and transgressions of His commands. The commands of God are often unwelcome and unpleasant. But happy are we if we do what God commands us to do. "My yoke is sweet and My burden light" (Mt 11:30). If we submit ourselves to the will of God because we feel forced to do so, the burden will crush us; but if we embrace His commands with a ready and joyful heart, they will support us. It is important that we make a distinction between what is hard and severe and what is sweet and light. Commands and duties are hard; sweet, however, is the holy will of God, for love makes sweet and light all things which God wants us to do.

Love also urges us to do cheerfully the things God asks of us; it causes us to embrace our cross with a generous and persevering will, to fulfill our duties conscientiously even in minor details. This faithfulness sees behind even trifling matters the infinitely wise and holy will of God and the opportunity of drawing closer to God by the proper use of little things. Let us look at the saints in this regard. How joyful, light, and cheerful were their souls! We may justly assert that they were as free as they were obedient and faithful. Devoting themselves to God and to Him alone, they were not bound by any creature. They knew neither the severity of the Pharisees nor the scrupulous narrow-mindedness of the scribe; but, being free, they are exact in all things. We observe in them a conscientiousness in the smallest detail; yet they never lose their adaptability to their surroundings. The wisdom of many of their actions, inspired by the love of God, helps them to overcome many difficulties which seem an insurmountable obstacle to us. The saints understand that it is our duty, not only to act in accordance with the will of God, but also to act from motives inspired by love for God. Thus they find the right way of combining broad-mindedness with exactitude, ease with fidelity. The liturgy wishes us to have this spiritual attitude. The Church prays God that we may "love that which Thou dost command."

"Grant unto us an increase of faith, hope, and charity," of wisdom, understanding, and an appreciation of grace and things supernatural. This is the great need of our times: an understanding of supernatural values. These should govern our thinking, our speech, our acts, our families, and our nations. The science of our age must also come to acknowledge the supernatural sphere. But we often prefer earthly and temporal things, even sinful things, to those supernatural; we act out of merely natural motives in accordance with the supposed wisdom of our own spirit. We especially underestimate the power of prayer, which is the fountain from which all graces come to us. We neglect to spiritualize our thoughts, words, and actions; we do not properly esteem or make use of the Church and her sacraments. "Grant unto us an increase of faith, hope, and charity."

Prayer

Almighty and everlasting God, grant unto us an increase of faith, hope, and charity; and that we may obtain what Thou dost promise, make us love that which Thou dost command. Through Christ our Lord. Amen.

Fourteenth Sunday after Pentecost

The Mass

"No man can serve two masters" (Gospel). This is an impressive admonition to the baptized to renounce all half-heartedness and the thought that, after all, it may be possible to serve two masters, rather than to serve God exclusively. When we received baptism, we declared ourselves for Christ; it is our duty to renew frequently the solemn declaration we then made, thus sealing our baptismal vow with our lives. Two powers oppose each other: the spirit and the flesh (Epistle), God and mammon (Gospel). Nobody can be loyal to both these masters.

Renouncing indecision and half-heartedness, in today's Mass we must stand with God and Christ. "How lovely are Thy tabernacles, O Lord of hosts! My soul longeth and fainteth for the courts of the Lord." Here in the Catholic house of worship, the baptized find their home; here they implore the Lord: "Behold, O God, our protector, and look on the face of Thy Christ; for better is one day in Thy courts above thousands" (Introit). Today we again draw a line of separation between ourselves and the world and make up our minds to follow Christ and to seek the kingdom of God and the Spirit. "Behold, O God,... and look on the face of Thy Christ." Give us grace to separate ourselves from the world and mammon.

The Epistle gives us a vivid description of the realm of the flesh. It is "fornication, uncleanness, immodesty, luxury, idolatry, witchcrafts, enmities, contentions, emulations, wraths, quarrels, dissensions, sects, envies, murders, drunkenness, revellings, and such like.... They who do such things shall not obtain the kingdom of God," for they are contradicting their baptismal vow. Granting that they may to some extent be Christians, they nevertheless try to serve two masters; but "no man can serve two masters."

The Epistle also describes the kingdom of the spirit. It is the kingdom of "charity, joy, peace, patience, benignity, goodness, longanimity, mildness, faith, modesty, continency, chastity.... They that are Christ's have crucified their flesh with the vices and concupiscences." A true Christian can serve only one cause, that of Christ and the kingdom of God; with all his strength he tries to avoid the dangers threatening from the realm of the evil one. For this reason he is not solicitous for the goods of this world and bodily necessities; but he seeks the kingdom of God first, trying to live in justice before God, full of confidence that all other things shall be added unto him. Good Christians live for their God and His service. They also strive, it is true, after cultural values; but they do not lose themselves entirely in these things, nor are they separated from God while trying to earn a livelihood for themselves and their families. They realize that there are higher goods and values than these. "O taste and see that the Lord is sweet" (Offertory).

The liturgy reminds us that during the celebration of the Mass, God looks favorably on the face of His Christ; that is, His community. During the Consecration He comes down into our midst, sacrificing Himself for our salvation. "O taste and see that the Lord is sweet." "It is good to trust in the Lord rather than to trust in princes" (Gradual). The Lord understands our needs, even our temporal cares and solicitude, and during the Holy Sacrifice He gathers them into His most Sacred Heart, making them His own and the object of His prayers before His Father in heaven. "Therefore I say to you, be not solicitous for your life, what you shall eat, nor for your body, what you shall put on.... Your Father knoweth that you have need of all these things. Seek ye therefore first the kingdom of God" (Gospel). Having received in Holy Communion the fullness of the Spirit and of the life of God, we can also be sure that "all these things shall be added unto [us]."

Meditation

"Be not solicitous for your life, what you shall eat, nor for your body, what you shall put on.... Your Father knoweth that you have need of all these things" (Gospel). Divine providence feeds the birds of the skies and clothes the lilies of the field. Do we not have even more reason for believing that it will feed and clothe man, the child of God?

"Thy providence, O Father, governeth [the universe]" (Ws 14:3). Absolutely nothing that happens either in the universe or in the life of men is not directly willed by God or at least permitted by Him. Whatever is sinful God cannot, of course, will or approve; He can only permit it to occur; but He wills, orders, and governs all other things. His providence works with a divine, all-embracing wisdom, with a boundless power, with a goodness and love that is always intent on doing the best for each individual as well as for mankind and His creation in general. "Are not five sparrows sold for two farthings, and not one of them is forgotten before God?... You are of more value than many sparrows" (Lk 12:6 f.). The way God takes care of us is comparable to the way a hen takes care of her young ones, or a tireless mother looks after her child. "You shall be carried at the breasts, and upon the knees they shall caress you. As one whom the mother caresseth, so will I comfort you" (Is 66:12 f.). "Can a woman forget her infant, so as not to have pity on the son of her womb? And if she should forget, yet will not I forget thee" (Is 49:15).

Besides the general providence of God, there is a particular providence, too, which extends to all those who sincerely seek God, who love Him and live for Him, who truly are His children. The Father in heaven guards them with an attentive and watchful eye, proving Himself particularly good and benevolent towards them. He works continually within them, being especially intent on sanctifying their souls day and night. Whatever happens to them in this world, must serve for their good. God, in His wisdom, power, and goodness, has ordered and joined everything in such a way that it leads to their greater sanctification. He makes no exception in this regard, but seeks to lead those whom He loves to continuous interior growth and to perfect union with Him, their true goal and happiness. How astonished and full of gratitude and admiration we shall some day be, when we finally come to understand in the light of eternity how divinely wise, powerful, and good has been God's work within our souls here on earth, how He ordered and governed our lives for our own best interest. "Thy providence, O Father, governeth [the universe]."

"O ye of little faith!" (Gospel.) In the past we have experienced many evident proofs of God's loving care, both for our spiritual life and our material well-being. If we examine our lives even superficially, we shall realize how much mercy He has shown us, how He has protected us from many dangers of body and soul, and how He was our strength in countless temptations. If we have eyes to see, we ought to be aware of how much patience He has had with us, how many enlightenments and inspirations for doing good He planted in our souls, how many wonderful gifts of spirit, of heart, and of body He has bestowed upon us. But how often we rejected His guidance! Yet He took our hand and did not refuse His love and grace, even after we had stubbornly broken away from Him. Do we not have reason enough to put all our confidence in Him? Yet it is precisely this confidence that is particularly wanting in us; we have too little confidence.

We deserve the reproach of the Lord, "O ye of little faith!" When will we understand and follow the Lord's word, "Be not solicitous therefore, saying, what shall we eat, or what shall we drink, or wherewith shall we be clothed, for after all these things do the heathen seek" (Gospel)? Where is our Christian faith? When will we finally accept His advice, "Seek ye therefore first the kingdom of God and His justice; and all these things shall be added unto you"? If only we would obey God and in all things accept His will, He would take care of the rest.

"The angel of the Lord shall encamp round about them that fear Him, and shall deliver them. O taste and see that the Lord is sweet" (Offertory).

The fundamental principle of Christian piety is a joyful confidence in God, which should also be the foundation of our Christian faith. We need it especially when our vocation entails disappointments and failures, when exterior sufferings threaten to deprive us of our former confidence, when interior sufferings, temptations, difficulties, faults, and sins are about to lead us astray and discourage us. "Behold the birds of the air; for they neither sow nor do they reap, nor gather into barns, and your heavenly Father feedeth them. Are you not of much more value than they?" (Gospel.) The birds are only His creatures. We are His children, and He is our Father. Are we not of much more value than they?

PRAYER

Keep, we beseech Thee, O Lord, Thy Church with perpetual mercy; and because the frailty of man without Thee cannot but fall, keep us ever by Thy help from all things hurtful, and lead us to all things profitable to our salvation. Through Christ our Lord. Amen.

Monday

This week the liturgy expresses the faith of the Church in divine providence as the power which governs the lives of the faithful. We are weak human beings and we lack the strength to keep away from the things that are injurious; we are incapable of doing the things that are for our spiritual good. But the infinitely wise and powerful providence of God watches over our frailty and weakness, ruling and governing all our affairs. Protecting us from what might be injurious, leading us to the things that are useful and wholesome, this providence watches over the Church and her children.

God's providence protects us from things that are injurious to us, for He knows the frailty of man. We do not know what lies ahead of us; we do not know what the next hour may bring. We deliberate, we decide on this step or that, not knowing whether it will be for the good of our soul or not. Dangers threaten us from within and without. Within us there is our weakness, which consists in a lack of wisdom or even in blindness; we are always in danger of being deceived by men, by the world, by our own passions, by self-love, by the fear of men, and by the spirit of the world, which always wants us to follow our baser instincts. We are threatened from without by the devil, by our associations with men, by our worries over the necessities of daily life; there are a thousand occasions of sin and of infidelities of all kinds; we must reckon with countless dissipations and allurements placed before us by the world and our own concupiscence. Wherever we are, there lurk the things that are injurious to us, threatening to divert our soul from God, the only true goal. How shall we protect ourselves from the things that are injurious to us? Our own insight and watchfulness and efforts fail us almost entirely. Woe unto us unless someone else intervenes, unless someone full of compassion on our blindness and frailty grasps our hands and keeps us away from the things that could lead to our perdition. The providence of God does intervene to keep us from things hurtful. We do not fully realize how much we owe to the protection of our heavenly Father.

God's providence leads us to the things that are wholesome. God never ceases to work within our soul for our salvation; with untiring care He tries to lead us to the things that are conducive to salvation. What is the Incarnation of the Son of God, His death on the cross, His Ascension into heaven, His sitting at the right hand of the Father, His never-ceasing compassion on us, asking mercy for us, but the uninterrupted work of God within our soul? What else could He have intended when He instituted the sacraments of baptism and confirmation, the Sacrifice of the Mass, the sacraments of penance and the Holy Eucharist, but to lead us to things that are wholesome for us? He commands us to discharge the duties of our vocation; He orders us to fulfill our obligations of prayer, the special commands and regulations He gave us, our vows. And what can all that mean to us if it is not intended for our purification and sanctification? What does He wish to achieve by the daily trials and difficulties, the sufferings, temptations, and humiliations in our interior and exterior life? What can be His intention when He sends us sicknesses and illnesses, and when He suffers us to fall into sin? The only possible explanation is that He desires to lead us to the things that are conducive to our salvation. We ourselves do not know what will be conducive to our salvation; nor do we know how to make good use of the right means. We are never sure that we are tending in the right direction at a given moment. Only God, the Father in heaven, by His infinite wisdom and love is able to lead us unerringly to our heavenly goal. "Commit thy way to the Lord and trust in Him, and He will do it" (Ps 36:5). This is our faith, our grateful confidence: God's providence leads us to those things that are conducive to our salvation.

How wonderful is God's providence despite the fact that we cannot understand His ways! "Are not two sparrows sold for a farthing? And not one of them shall fall on the ground without your Father. But the very hairs of your head are all numbered. Fear not, therefore; better are you than many sparrows" (Mt 10:29 ff.). What can we fear? When the Lord takes care of us, when He leads us to the things that might be conducive to our salvation, we can have no reason whatsoever to be afraid. The only fear we ought to have is that our weak will may rely upon itself and lead us to pride, false confidence, and our own perdition. Let us, therefore, abandon ourselves, our soul, and our salvation into the hands of the Father in heaven, that He and His will may rule our destiny.

God's ways generally are entirely different from the ways of men, which are based on human plans that often depart from the plans of God's providence. Yet His providence alone can protect us from the things that are injurious to us and lead us to those that serve our salvation. The Apostle admonishes us to "walk in the spirit" of an unshaken faith in God's divine providence. "It is good to confide in the Lord rather than to have confidence in man. It is good to trust in the Lord rather than to trust in princes" (Gradual). We might add that it is good to trust in the Lord rather than in our own human knowledge and faculties and our puny efforts.

Prayer

Keep, we beseech Thee, O Lord, Thy Church with perpetual mercy; and because the frailty of man without Thee cannot but fall, keep us ever by Thy help from all things hurtful, and lead us to all things profitable to our salvation. Through Christ our Lord. Amen.

Tuesday

"Behold the birds of the air; for they neither sow nor do they reap, nor gather into barns, and your heavenly Father feedeth them" (Gospel). Our Lord says very emphatically that God is our "heavenly Father." We ought not be solicitous about what we shall eat or drink or wherewith we shall be clothed, "for your heavenly Father knoweth that you have need of all these things" (Gospel). God is our Father; it is important for our life and way of thinking that we always and everywhere look upon God as our Father. Otherwise the fountains of our piety are bound to dry up.

God is our Creator and therefore our Lord. We belong to Him with all we have. Our life is entirely in His hands, entirely given over to His providence. As our Creator, He is the God of terrible majesty and power, of infinite omniscience and sanctity, before whom we are as dust, mere nothingness. Since He is our Lord, it is our duty to serve Him; since He is our Lord, He is also our Judge, who knows all our thoughts, words, and works. The terrifying exactness of His knowledge and judgment makes us tremble; the splendor of His infinite holiness dazzles us. If we look at God from one of these points of view, we shall always remain cringing and terrified. Under such conditions we cannot serve Him out of love; we remain cold and dry in our attitude towards Him, being able, at best, to utter some frightened words of recognition. Then we become lax in our religious duties and despondent if temptations against our faith arise within our soul or if we are tortured by uneasiness and scruples which undermine our devotion without leaving any place for a joyful imitation of our Lord. It is unfortunately true that we Christians too often look upon God only as our Creator and Judge, thus placing between ourselves and God a wall which hinders us from coming to Him with the feelings of a child, full of filial love and confidence. Here we meet with one of the main hindrances to an interior life in union with God.

God is our Father. Day after day the believing Christian experiences the fact that God is his Father and acts like a father towards him. God sent His only-begotten Son into the world that "we might receive the adoption of sons. And because you are sons, God hath sent the Spirit of His Son into your hearts;... therefore now he is not a servant, but a son" (Gal 4:5–7). God is our Father; whatever tender and loving meaning the word "father" connotes, it is contained with infinite fullness in the word "heavenly Father." Our becoming aware of the fact that He is our Father lifts up our soul and consoles and strengthens it. Faith in God the Father does away with the feelings of loneliness and abandonment. It casts in a new light the chastisements and visitations which the Lord sends us. This faith strengthens and encourages us during hours of temptation, gives us light and security in darkness, and makes us confide blindly in God despite the problems we have to face. Out of this faith in God the Father there arise filial feelings, and with these feelings peace of mind enters the soul, even if a man cannot entirely forget his previous sins and wasted life. With unshaken confidence we commend our eternity into His hands.

Even indifferent actions become an occasion for gaining that sweet interior liberty which protects us from worry and anxiety. With such filial feelings towards God we more easily acquire forgetfulness of self, love of prayer, calmness in difficult situations, serenity in trials, and resignation in afflictions; and the sacraments operate more fruitfully than they did before. Our life is changed entirely, for now we have found in God a Father. Being aware of His fatherly solicitude, we see Him near us with His love, His help, and His grace. The various affairs of life take on a different aspect; they lose their restless and depressing character, and we no longer find them distressing and torturing. They seem to have become peaceful, sweet; they bring us joy and happiness, because we have found in them our Father.

There is something tragic in the fact that we are always inclined to see God under some aspect other than that of a Father. It is unfortunate for us that we fail to look upon Him as a Father, for He loves us, pardons us, and is near us in all our temptations. He wishes us well in all conditions of life. If we but realized His goodness, we could not doubt that He hears our prayers, that He blesses all those who are dear to us and those for whom we pray. He always remains the Father who bears our neglect and coldness with infinite patience.

Our Father in heaven knows everything that happens to us. How much consolation and peace this faith brings! Whatever happens to us, be it through misfortune or the folly of men, or even through malice, cannot disturb our peace as long as we look upon God as our Father. He wills that we carry the crosses that come to us, because He is the Father who loves us. We should find supreme happiness in fulfilling His will.

If we remember in all the events of life that God is our Father and is ever near with His guidance and love, we will always be full of joy. Our religion is a religion of love and joy, and one of the characteristic traits of a Christian is a love for God the Father. May we always look upon Him as our loving Father.

Prayer

Keep, we beseech Thee, O Lord, Thy Church with perpetual mercy; and because the frailty of man without Thee cannot but fall, keep us ever by Thy help from all things hurtful, and lead us to all things profitable to our salvation. Through Christ our Lord. Amen.

Wednesday

Formerly the fourteenth Sunday after Pentecost was called the Sunday of divine providence. The spirit of this Sunday announces the glad tidings of the loving providence of God, which cares for the birds and clothes the lilies of the field, and which, even more important, watches over His children, those redeemed by Christ, with loving care. "O taste and see that the Lord is sweet" (Offertory).

"How lovely are Thy tabernacles, O Lord of hosts! My soul longeth and fainteth for the courts of the Lord" (Introit). This prayer of the Church indicates that we long to be with God and Christ. Our striving aims at being one with Christ, the head, sharing His life with Him. Christ the holy and sinless One, imparts to us His spirit, His purity, His domination over the lower instincts and inclinations of our fallen nature. Walking "in the spirit," we have a foretaste of the bliss of heaven already here on earth, a foretaste of the life which awaits those who truly belong to Christ. We "taste and see that the Lord is sweet"; we seek "first the kingdom of God," that life which is in Christ. "How lovely are Thy tabernacles, O Lord of hosts!" How delightful and satisfying is this life in Christ! "He that abideth in Me, and I in him, the same beareth much fruit; for without Me you can do nothing. If any one abide not in Me, he shall be cast forth as a branch, and shall wither" (Jn 15:5 ff.). Therefore "my soul longeth and fainteth for the courts of the Lord," for union with Christ; "for better is one day in Thy courts above thousands" (Introit).

"Walk in the spirit." The Epistle knows the way both of the flesh and of the spirit. Because life means a long struggle, the Holy Spirit has been given to us on Pentecost, on the day of our confirmation, in order that He may help us in the fight against the flesh with its concupiscences. He gives us strength to enable us to crucify the flesh, thus to harvest the fruits of the Spirit, which are "charity, joy, peace, patience, benignity, goodness, longanimity, mildness, faith, modesty, continency, chastity" (Epistle). It is impossible to serve two masters; we will serve either the flesh or the spirit. At the hour of our baptism we determined to walk in the spirit; for us there is, therefore, only a life for God, in Christ and His Spirit. Though we must live in the world, take care of our family and community, work for our daily bread, we must always "walk in the spirit."

"Seek ye first the kingdom of God and His justice; and all these things shall be added unto you.... Your Father knoweth that you have need of all these things" (Gospel). We must seek first the things that belong to the kingdom of God; but "the kingdom of God is within you" (Lk 17:21). This kingdom consists in a living union with God dwelling and working within our souls and in a filial and intimate conversation with the Father, who is so near to us. "Your Father knoweth that you have need of all these things." If we have no reason to worry about material things, our only duty should be to look after the things of our spiritual life. Material things, however, "shall be added unto you," as the fruitfulness and blessings of the interior life. Everything depends on God's blessing. "Unless the Lord build the house, they labor in vain that build it" (Ps 126:1).

"Be not solicitous therefore, saying, what shall we eat, or what shall we drink, or wherewith shall we be clothed, for after all these things do the heathens seek" (Gospel). To be solicitous about life is a pagan attitude. A Christian has faith. The chief difference between a Christian and a non-Christian is that the Christian has faith in the loving providence of God the Father. To be a Christian means to have a blind confidence in God by despising the world and material goods, and by trusting instead in that seemingly uncertain, yet divinely safe providence of the Father. "Blessed are they that have not seen, and have believed" (Jn 20:29).

"Seek ye first the kingdom of God and His justice; and all these things shall be added unto you." It is our blessed duty to seek this kingdom of God by blindly committing our life to His providence, by trusting that He will arrange all things for our good. When we have reached the point where God and His will alone determine our actions, where our will and desires have become one with His, we will have reached a state which is happier and more satisfying than any other happiness in this world. This state of resignation we can reach only by faith and confidence, by childlike devotion and love.

Our Holy Mother the Church is our model, for she walks in this spirit despite the fact that she is oppressed on all sides. Without solicitude she seeks first the kingdom of God. Day after day, year after year, she celebrates the liturgy calmly and joyfully. She daily administers Holy

Communion to us that we may be able to thrust ourselves blindly into the arms of our Father, seeking the kingdom of God without solicitude. "Come, let us praise the Lord," the Church sings every day at Matins.

Prayer

Keep, we beseech Thee, O Lord, Thy Church with perpetual mercy; and because the frailty of man without Thee cannot but fall, keep us ever by Thy help from all things hurtful, and lead us to all things profitable to our salvation. Through Christ our Lord. Amen.

Thursday

"If we live in the Spirit, let us also walk in the Spirit" (Gal 5:25). Through the Holy Ghost and His operation within us we received the life of the children of God; let us therefore "walk in the Spirit," whom we have received in baptism and confirmation.

"If we live in the Spirit." At the moment of our baptism the Father and the Son infused the Holy Spirit into our souls. He is the great gift of God to us, the gift of our espousal to the Son of God, a gift that enriches our soul, making it beautiful and lovable in the sight of God. When the Holy Ghost descends into our unworthy soul, He enriches it with divine beauty, decorating it with His gifts, and making it resplendent with delightful purity in the eyes of God. It is He who now lives and works within our soul: He, the Paraclete, the Consoler, the love of God, who proceeds from the Father and the Son as the substantial expression of that perfect love that unites Father and Son; and we also are drawn into this mystical life of love within the deity. As the consequence of our being partakers of this mystical life, we are permeated by the divine life and are bearers of the fire of divine love. Thus fortified we go to the Father with warm and childlike affection, yearning with unspeakable longing to meet our heavenly bridegroom.

The Holy Ghost urges us to think, talk, act, and suffer in a way that is pleasing to God. He prepares our body and soul for the blessed embrace of Jesus which we experience in Holy Communion; He engenders the life of sanctifying grace within our soul, thereby laying the foundation for our eventual perfection and eternal happiness in heaven. While enriching us with the precious gift of sanctifying grace, He also pours into our soul supernatural powers and gifts, the virtues of faith, hope, charity, justice, prudence, fortitude, temperance. Together with these virtues He enriches us with His special gifts; the fear of the Lord, piety, wisdom, fortitude, counsel, knowledge, and understanding. The entire natural life within us is the result of His work. He also guides and forms our interior and religious life.

"Let us also walk in the Spirit." We walk in the Spirit as long as we live in the state of sanctifying grace. If we commit a mortal sin, the Holy Ghost is forced to leave us; for then we render our soul unfit as a further dwelling place for Him. In addition to driving Him out of our soul, we deprive ourselves of the source and principle of our interior life as well as the life of grace itself. We walk in the Spirit, on the other hand, if we follow faithfully and humbly the illuminations and inspirations and admonitions of the Holy Spirit living and working within us. It is absolutely necessary that we generously deny ourselves, renouncing our human way of thinking and judging, that we continuously and willingly listen to the inspirations of the Holy Ghost working within our soul, and especially that we try to preserve a great purity of heart;

"for wisdom will not enter into a malicious soul, nor dwell in a body subject to sins" (Ws 1:4). We must endeavor without ceasing to reach that height of purity of heart that excludes any voluntary venial sin, even an imperfection that has been recognized as such. It is also necessary to live a life of recollection, silencing unnecessary thoughts and cares, and to subject our will in all things and under all circumstances to the holy will of God, being resigned to anything that may happen to us as being willed or permitted by God's providence.

There are three obstacles to our walking in the Spirit: the human spirit of man, the spirit of the world, and the evil spirit. Man's own spirit induces him to act out of purely natural motives without dependence on the operation of the Holy Spirit and His grace within us. The spirit of the world is the spirit of the concupiscence of the eyes; it is the atmosphere surrounding us everywhere and influencing our actions. Then there is the evil spirit, the devil, trying to seduce and ruin us with his temptations.

The power of the Holy Ghost gives us the strength to resist our own human spirit, the spirit of the world, and the devil. These spirits have been destined by divine providence to molest us, but only in order that we may be all the more willing to unite ourselves with the true Spirit, the Holy Ghost, working within our souls.

Unfortunately, we pay too little attention to the presence of the Holy Ghost within our soul, and we do not live in a close enough union with Him. We are not grateful enough towards Him who deigns to dwell within our soul, making our body His temple and unerringly guiding our soul if only we are willing to be led by Him.

Prayer

Keep, we beseech Thee, O Lord, Thy Church with perpetual mercy; and because the frailty of man without Thee cannot but fall, keep us ever by Thy help from all things hurtful, and lead us to all things profitable to our salvation. Through Christ our Lord. Amen.

Friday

We live in Christ since we have been united with Him in baptism; living in Christ has almost the same meaning to St. Paul as walking "in the Spirit." "In this we know that we abide in Him," says St. John, "and He in us; because He hath given us of His Spirit" (1 Jn 4:13). "We are Christ's body if we live of the Spirit of Christ; only the body of Christ lives of His Spirit" (St. Augustine). After we have received the Holy Spirit, the Spirit of Christ, we must "walk in the Spirit" (Epistle).

"The flesh lusteth against the spirit,... so that you do not the things that you would.... [But] they that are Christ's have crucified their flesh with the vices and concupiscences" (Epistle). They are no longer guided by the desires of their corrupt nature; they are new men, risen with Christ. Therefore they live the life of Christ and do not work "the works of the flesh, which are fornication, uncleanness, immodesty, luxury, idolatry, witchcrafts, enmities, contentions, emulations, wraths, quarrels, dissensions, envies, sects, murders, drunkenness, and revellings, and such like.... They who do such things shall not obtain the kingdom of God" (Epistle). The way of a Christian is of necessity the way of Christ; with Him we must fight and carry our cross. In order to help us and to live within us, He has become one with us. He came to destroy

Adam's sin and to lead the world back to God through His self-denial and death on the cross. Christ made us members of His mystical body that we might continue His self-denial and death by denying ourselves. As members of the body whose head is Christ, we become ever more closely united with Him by sharing His life and sufferings. We therefore are not allowed to do the things that we would like to do (Epistle), to which our fallen nature, concupiscence, passions, and self-love entice us. Because of the dangers arising from the flesh we must crucify the flesh with its vices and concupiscences; only then can the Spirit perfect His work within us.

We must "walk in the Spirit" of the new and supernatural life given to us in union with Christ. The Spirit lifts us above the powers of darkness and our own passions, above the desires of worldly-minded man; He never grows weary of destroying the works of the flesh within us by making the thoughts, inclinations, and intentions of our heart submissive to the working of His grace. He has been promised and sent to us by Christ to remain with us forever. By His very nature He is intent on God and His will, and urges us to be good children of the Father in heaven by trying to please Him through our actions and sacrifices, thus proving our reverence, gratefulness, and love towards Him. The Spirit urges us to strive after virtue and to devote ourselves to prayer and holy recollection; He teaches us to love Christ, poverty, obedience, self-denial, and chastity. He awakens within us the desire to become holy and zealous for the interests of God and for the salvation of souls; He therefore imparts to us love of the cross, courage to be faithful in little things, strength to live a heroic life. The fruits of His works are wonderful: "Charity, joy, peace, patience, benignity, goodness, longanimity, mildness, faith, modesty, continency, chastity" (Epistle). By these fruits we shall recognize whether or not we walk in the Spirit.

"Walk in the spirit, and you shall not fulfill the lusts of the flesh" (Epistle). It is most important for us that we walk in the spirit, being guided by the Spirit of Christ. As far as our works have been done in the Spirit of Christ, they are good, holy, and pleasing to God; without this Spirit they are worthless in the sight of God.

"As the living Father hath sent Me, and I live by the Father, so he that eateth Me, the same also shall live by Me" (Jn 6:58). This exalted promise is the great means that enables us, through the Holy Eucharist, to walk in the Spirit. "He that eateth My flesh and drinketh My blood, abideth in Me and I in him" (Jn 6:57). The oftener and more worthily we receive Holy Communion, the more intimately we become united with the Spirit. Our walking "in the Spirit" must be the fruit of our assistance at Mass and of our reception of Holy Communion.

Prayer

Keep, we beseech Thee, O Lord, Thy Church with perpetual mercy; and because the frailty of man without Thee cannot but fall, keep us ever by Thy help from all things hurtful, and lead us to all things profitable to our salvation. Through Christ our Lord. Amen.

Saturday

"No man can serve two masters.... You cannot serve God and mammon" (Gospel). There is no alternative: we live either for God or for mammon. A divided allegiance is impossible, for we would be divided against ourselves. "Be not solicitous therefore, saying, what shall we eat, or what shall we drink, or wherewith shall we be clothed, for after all these things do the heathens seek.... Seek ye therefore first the kingdom of God and His justice; and all these things shall be added unto you" (Gospel).

"Seek ye therefore first the kingdom of God." A Christian's first duty is to live for God and to obey His will and commandments, that he may try to please Him before all things. God made us for Himself; He is the source of our being and the only true goal of our life. "Thou hast created us for Thyself, O Lord, and our hearts are restless until they rest in Thee" (St. Augustine). In order that we may live for God again, He sent His only-begotten Son into this world; for when through sin we had turned to the world and worldly interests, our life and our best efforts were without any real meaning; they were without God. God then sent His Son that He might lead us back to God, that we might find Him again and as His children live entirely for the Father. In order that we may serve God more perfectly, He unceasingly pours into our souls power and light; He desires to free us from attachments to the world and to the vanities of life, which are our main obstacles to fulfilling the will of the Father in heaven. Day after day He invites us to the Holy Sacrifice and gives Himself to us as the food for our souls in Holy Communion, that we may leave all things and live for the Father. He thus permeates our spirit more and more with His spirit and thoughts, making us strong to renounce faithfully and perseveringly all that is not God's, and to live for Him alone. To live for God must be our only care; for here not merely our honor and our temporal welfare are at stake, but our fate for all eternity. To live for God, therefore, must be our one concern, compared with which all other matters and interests are of secondary importance. We cannot postpone this matter a single day, not even a single hour; for it is a matter most pressing. The entire life of man is to live for God. Whatever does not serve this goal is vanity and death, and whatever within our soul may be opposed to God and His will, is an evil, an aversion from the right purpose, the destruction of life. "Seek ye therefore first the kingdom of God." There is no other alternative.

"All these things shall be added unto you." "Be not solicitous therefore, saying, what shall we eat, or what shall we drink, or wherewith shall we be clothed." We have only this one care: to live for God. If we live for God, we do whatever God asks of us and suffer whatever He wishes us to suffer; and we fulfill His will as He desires us to, motivated particularly by the thought that it is He who wills it. God wills that we do our part by fulfilling His will, and He will take care of the rest; all other things "shall be added unto [us]." "Behold the birds of the air; for they neither sow nor do they reap, nor gather into barns, and your heavenly Father feedeth them." They do what God expects them to do by virtue of the instincts given to them; God takes care of what may be wanting. "Consider the lilies of the field, how they grow; they labor not, neither do they spin; but ... not even Solomon in all his glory was arrayed as one of these" (Gospel). God determined for them the laws of growth, and they develop according to these laws, thus producing their fruits. God provides the conditions necessary for their growth. "Are you not of much more value than they?" If we have lived to the best of our ability for God and His holy will, we have done our part; God the Father will take care of what may be wanting in our life. "For your Father knoweth that you have need of all these things. Seek ye therefore first the kingdom of God and His justice [His desires and commands], and all these things shall be added unto you."

"Be not solicitous" does not mean that we ought not to be careful and conscientious in fulfilling the duties of our vocation or our state of life; but we should not pursue them in such a manner that we lose ourselves in the troubles and works imposed on us, neglecting thereby our first duty, to seek God and His justice; that is, to fulfill first of all God's holy will.

"After all these things do the heathens seek." We Christians have a different attitude towards the things of this world than have non-Christians. They are dominated by solicitude for the things of this world. The thought of food and clothing, of health and position in business, of success and honor, is the most important factor in their lives. The Christian, however, has a different outlook on life. He also must care for all these things, but not in a "solicitous" way, becoming engrossed in their pursuit. He rather has an unshaken and childlike confidence in God that determines and guides his life and gives it a supernatural meaning. "Your Father knoweth that you have need of all these things." He will give them to us, since He gives even the animals in the field, the birds of the air, the grass and the lilies in the field, whatever they need for their existence. "It is good to confide in the Lord rather than to have confidence in man" (Gradual).

Prayer

Keep, we beseech Thee, O Lord, Thy Church with perpetual mercy; and because the frailty of man without Thee cannot but fall, keep us ever by Thy help from all things hurtful, and lead us to all things profitable to our salvation. Through Christ our Lord. Amen.

Fifteenth Sunday after Pentecost

The Mass

"I am come that they may have life and may have it more abundantly" (Jn 10:10). Christ gives life, both to the soul and to the body. Once He has raised the soul from the death of sin through baptism, He imparts to us a more vigorous and fruitful life through His grace, especially through the Holy Sacrifice of the Mass. He lays the foundation for our bodily resurrection through the Holy Sacrifice and through Holy Communion, which are the fruits of our baptism.

The principal thought of today's Mass is contained in the Gospel. Jesus arrives at the city of Naim as a young man is being carried to his grave. The mother of this young man, a widow of Naim, follows the procession, weeping. Many Christians are like this young man, for they have lost through their lapses into sin the gift of life which they received in baptism. The mother, who represents the Church, stands sorrowing at the side of the lifeless body. In the Introit of the Mass she prays for her unfortunate children: "Bow down Thy ear, O Lord, to me and hear me: Save Thy servant, O my God, that trusteth in Thee; have mercy on me, O Lord, for I have cried to Thee all the day. Give joy to the soul of Thy servant." Give joy and consolation to Thy Church, O Lord, as you once gave consolation to the sorrowing mother mentioned in today's Gospel. Lord have mercy on us. "Cleanse and defend Thy Church, we beseech Thee, O Lord, because it cannot continue in safety without Thee" (Collect).

The demands made upon the members of the Church are eloquently explained by St. Paul in the Epistle. The Gradual and the Alleluia verse speak of the wealth of the baptized, who are privileged to participate in the Holy Sacrifice: "It is good to give praise to the Lord, and to sing to Thy name, O Most High.... For the Lord is a great God and a great King over all the earth, alleluia." He is the master of life and death. All things are subject to His will, and nothing can resist His power. The Gospel bears witness to this truth.

When Jesus was passing by the city of Naim, He was accompanied by His disciples and a great multitude of the Jews. As He approached the gate of the city, He met the funeral cortege of a young man, the only son of a widow, who was being carried to the burial place. "And when the Lord saw her, He had compassion on her and said to her: Weep not" (Gospel). As He approached the bier, He commanded the bearers to halt. Then He spoke to the young man, saying: "Young man, I say to thee, arise." The young man sat up on his bier and Jesus delivered him to his mother.

Jesus gives life, and He alone can give it. We, too, were once children of death because of Original Sin; but Jesus met us on the way. Our mother, the Church, was mourning over us. Christ was touched with pity and approached us through His representatives, His priests, and by their hands the life-giving waters of baptism were poured upon us. In this way we received spiritual life and were united to our mother, the Church. With gratitude in our hearts we today recall the occasion of our baptism. "With expectation I have waited for the Lord, and He had regard to me; and He heard my prayer, and He put a new canticle into my mouth, a song to our God" (Offertory). Christ will come again to our grave and will say to us, "I say to thee, arise." The gates of the grave will be flung open, and we shall arise from the dead. With joy the glorified soul will embrace its body, revivify it with its blessed life, usher it into the realm of the living, and unite it to the happy and glorified Church in heaven. "With expectation I have waited for the Lord.... He put a new canticle into my mouth." He who gives life to the dead enters into our midst today in the Holy Sacrifice of the Mass, as the all-merciful and all-powerful God. Death still holds sway over many members of the Church, who are ruled by sin, passion, worldliness, and indifference to God, and who have forgotten the day of their baptism. But even for these the Church prays, weeping; and our Lord touches them by His grace and says to them: "Young man, I say to thee, arise."

Christ has given Himself as a sacrifice for the dead. He prays to the Father for mercy and pardon. With unspeakable groanings He prays for grace and power that life may be restored to these who are spiritually dead. "I have come that they may have life and have it more abundantly." For this purpose, too, Christ offers Himself up in the Holy Sacrifice of the Mass and in Holy Communion. "The bread that I will give is My flesh for the life of the world" (Communion prayer).

Meditation

The liturgy of this Sunday is dominated by the picture of the raising to life of the young man of Naim. We ourselves have been called to life through our baptism. Having restored us to life, Christ gives us back to our sorrowing mother, the Church. The thought of Easter also enters prominently into the liturgy of the day. Today we are to be grateful for the grace of baptism and the sacrament of penance.

"Young man, I say to thee, arise" (Gospel). For the liturgy, this young man who was dead represents those spiritually dead: the heathen, the apostate, the renegade, the enemy of God, the Christian who has fallen into sin, the unfaithful one who has forsaken his vocation. At the foot of the bier stands the sorrowing mother, weeping and praying. She is the Church lifting her hands to the Lord and imploring grace and mercy for her many children who are spiritually dead. "Have mercy on me, O Lord, for I have cried to Thee all the day" (Introit). *Kyrie eleison, Christe eleison, Kyrie eleison!* What would become of these children who are spiritually dead, did not our Holy Mother the Church remain at their side praying unceasingly for them? Our Lord sees this sorrowing mother, and has compassion on her, and says to her, "Weep not." And as He approaches the bier, those who carry it stand still, and He says: "Young man, I say to thee, arise." And he that is dead sits up and speaks, and is delivered to his mother. She has regained life for her dead child through her sorrow and through her prayer.

This restoration to life is repeated today and every day in the Holy Sacrifice of the Mass. There are many Christians who are spiritually dead. They appear to be alive, but they are actually spiritually dead and laid out on their biers. Only our Holy Mother the Church is aware of their miserable condition. During the Holy Sacrifice she cries out to Him who alone can restore them to life. She asks for mercy and for the grace of God, that the sinner may recognize his error, that he may break the bonds of sin, and that he may turn finally to do good. Our Holy Mother the Church believes that her tears and her prayers, supported by the Holy Sacrifice of the Mass, are effective, for at that time Christ does come to restore life and strength to those dead in sin. We are members of this praying and sacrificing Church. Our prayers and sacrifices are effective in so far as we are united to the Church. "Have mercy on me, O Lord, for I have cried to Thee all the day." Our cries to the Lord will be heard if we in our charity remember to pray for the dead and offer the Holy Sacrifice for them.

"Young man, I say to thee, arise." We have already arisen, for we possess the life of grace. As living creatures of God, we celebrate the Holy Sacrifice. But with most of us the Lord has still to make the life that is in us fruitful. We can still arise to a more active and fruitful life. There is still within us much that hinders and checks the growth of Christ's life in us. We still long for empty honors, envy one another, and deceive ourselves by imagining ourselves to be greater than we really are. We see the faults of our neighbor, but neglect to instruct them in the spirit of charity. We refuse to share the burdens of our neighbor, and thus fail to fulfill the law of Christ. We allow ourselves to be flattered by others and misled by them, instead of following our own conscience and the will of God. We refuse to live by the spirit, and we forget that he who sows in the flesh, "of the flesh also shall reap corruption, but he that soweth in the spirit, of the spirit shall reap life everlasting" (Epistle). Woe unto us if our Holy Mother the Church did not lift up her hands in prayer for us, beseeching the Lord to restore the dead to life! She prays for us in the Divine Office, through the prayers of her holy priests and religious; she prays for us in the Holy Sacrifice of the Mass. There the Lord says to us, "Young man, I say to thee, arise." Christ in the company of His Church stands before the throne of the Father, offering sacrifice and working in us through the power of grace, that we may this day apply ourselves to the things of God in the spirit of charity, devotion, and sacrifice. At Holy Communion He communicates to us His own divine life.

"It is good to give praise to the Lord, and to sing to Thy name, O Most High. To show forth Thy mercy [Thy grace] in the morning, and Thy truth in the night. Alleluia, alleluia. For the Lord is a great God and a great King over all the earth, alleluia" (Gradual). The Lord is more powerful than death or sin. He has called us from death through baptism, and has recalled us often through the sacrament of penance.

"He had regard to me" (Offertory), who am so unworthy, so tepid. He hath had regard for me in the Holy Sacrifice and in the prayers of the Church. "He put a new canticle into my mouth," for He has so often refreshed me through Holy Communion and the sacrament of penance. Woe to me if He had not looked upon me with mercy.

"The bread that I will give is My flesh for the life of the world" (Communion). He touches me and nourishes me with His flesh and His blood. He fills me with zeal for the glory of His Father and for the salvation of souls. When He is near, all spiritual weakness and depression vanish. With Him we live the life of the blessed. "I can do all things in Him who strengtheneth me" (Phil 4:13).

Prayer

Let Thy continual pity cleanse and defend Thy Church, we beseech Thee, O Lord; and because it cannot continue in safety without Thee, govern it evermore by Thy help. Through Christ our Lord. Amen.

Monday

As Jesus is approaching the little village of Naim, He meets, as it were by chance, a funeral procession transporting the body of a young man. Seeing the sorrow of the afflicted mother, who is a widow, He approaches and restores the young man to life.

The story is related very briefly in the Gospel. "At that time, Jesus went into a city called Naim; and there were with Him His disciples and a great multitude. And when He came nigh to the city, behold a dead man was carried out, the only son of his mother, and she was a widow. And a great multitude of the city was with her. Whom when the Lord had seen, being moved with mercy toward her, He said to her: Weep not. And He came near and touched the bier, and they that carried it stood still. And He said: Young man, I say to thee, arise. And he that was dead sat up and began to speak. And He delivered him to his mother" (Gospel). The Lord sees the mother's tears, and these touch His heart. He cannot refuse to help when He sees her sorrow. But first He speaks a word of consolation: "Weep not." And then He proceeds to act: "Young man, I say to thee, arise." Then He delivers to the mother the son who has been restored to life. Thus Christ shows that He is the Lord of mercy. He is charity, He has compassion; He speaks a word and performs a deed. When charity requires it, He will work wonders; He will even recall the dead to life. The mother had not expected this miracle; the Lord does infinitely more than man dares to hope for. We, on the other hand, are mean and selfish in contrast to the plenitude of His goodness and love.

This incident has a deep meaning in the eyes of the liturgy. We, too, were once spiritually dead because of our sins, but our mother, the Church, wept and prayed for us. Every day she prayed to the Lord in the Masses said by the multitude of her priests, in which she remembers all her children. "Be mindful, O Lord, of Thy servants … and of all here present, whose faith and devotion are known to Thee, for whom we offer … this sacrifice of praise.… We beseech Thee, O Lord, graciously to receive this oblation. Dispose our days in Thy peace and command that we be delivered from eternal damnation and numbered among the flock of Thine elect" (Canon of the Mass). Now He comes. With divine power He changes the bread into His flesh and the wine into His blood, and offers them to the eternal Father in order that we and all who desire it may obtain the gift of life, and that this life may increase and grow. If our mother were to fail us, if she stood not at the side of her dead children, praying and offering up sacrifice for them, there would be no resurrection to life for these miserable ones. But this merciful service is rendered to us by Holy Mother the Church. Many of her children reject her, cast her aside, deceive her, and hate her; but she will not be prevented from standing at the bier of her dead children. She will go forth to meet the Lord, and He will approach the bier full of compassion. He will touch it and awaken the dead one to life. This work is accomplished by the Church as often as she offers the Holy Sacrifice and as often as she takes the book of the Divine Office into her hands and prays in the name of sinners and unbelievers, who will not pray for themselves. If only she stands at our bier and prays over us, we are safe. The prayer of the Church restores us to life and saves mankind from destruction.

"I desire therefore, first of all, that supplications, prayers, intercessions, and thanksgivings be made for all men, for kings and for all that are in high station, that we may lead a quiet and peaceable life in all piety and chastity. For this is good and acceptable in the sight of God our Savior, who will have all men to be saved and to come to the knowledge of the truth" (1 Tm 2:1–4).

We follow the widow of Naim. "A great multitude of the city were with her." We are members of that throng. We share the sadness and tears of this good mother during the celebration of the Holy Sacrifice, during the recitation of the Divine Office, and during our private devotions. The privilege of praying is given to us, not merely that we should pray for ourselves, but rather that we may promote the welfare of the Church and the spiritual good of others.

We unite ourselves with this mother and join our prayers to hers. The more intimate our union with her in prayer and sacrifice, the more perfectly our duty of promoting the welfare of others will be performed, and the more perfectly we will carry out our obligation of awakening life in others and of increasing their spiritual growth.

Prayer

Let Thy continual pity cleanse and defend Thy Church, we beseech Thee, O Lord; and because it cannot continue in safety without Thee, govern it evermore by Thy help. Through Christ our Lord. Amen.

Tuesday

"And when He came nigh to the city, behold a dead man was carried out, the only son of his mother, and she was a widow. And a great multitude of the city was with her" (Gospel). For the liturgy, the widow of Naim is a type of the Church at prayer. The same is true of the multitude of people who accompanied the widow and mourned and prayed with her. They are a type of the multitude of parents, priests, and teachers who mourn for and pray for their errant children, for those who are spiritually dead, for those who are in error, for those who are wicked, and for those who are dead. The Lord meets them also in the way and consoles them: "Weep not." He meets them during the Holy Sacrifice of the Mass, and this meeting is made possible through the sacrificing priest.

"Be mindful O Lord of Thy servants . . . and of all here present, whose faith and devotion are known to Thee" (Memento of the Living). This moment is filled with mystery. In this memento the priest includes all those whom he wishes to be included in the fruits of the Mass and in the merits of the sacrifice of the cross, which is the sun from which all light and life proceeds. If the sun is to work its beneficent influence upon men, its warmth and light must be brought to them through some medium. If the sun is to fill a room with its light, the rays of the sun must in some way be directed into the room. Similarly, if the sacrifice of Christ on the cross is to become our sacrifice, it must in some direct way be applied to us. Only then can we participate in the reconciliation effected by Christ between His heavenly Father and us. Such a participation is made possible through the Holy Sacrifice of the Mass; only in this way can we really share in the adoration, prayers, and thanksgiving offered by Christ the eternal high priest. However, it is necessary that the Holy Sacrifice of the Mass itself become in some sense our sacrifice. It does so since the sacrificing priest offers the Mass for us. Christ could have enabled each person to offer this sacrifice, but He did not do so. He has given the power of offering it solely to His priests. The priest is charged with the duty of offering this sacrifice, of allowing it to produce its fruits, and, through his free choice, of applying it as he sees fit. This privilege gives the priesthood its immense importance and dignity. If he is "mindful" of me, if in his intention the Mass is to be applied to me, then that sacrifice becomes my sacrifice; then it is I whom Christ meets during the Holy Sacrifice of the Mass. Of great importance, then, is the moment when the priest prays: "Be mindful, O Lord, of Thy servants . . . and of all here present." At this moment we meet the Lord as did the widow at the gates of Naim.

"For whom we offer, or who offer up to Thee, this sacrifice of praise for themselves and all those dear to them, for the redemption of their souls, the hope of their safety and salvation; who now pay their vows to Thee, the eternal living and true God" (Memento of the Living). After the priest, through his application of his intention in the Mass, has thus identified us and our intentions with Christ, who is offering Himself in the Holy Sacrifice, we can indeed offer up this Mass as our own, for ourselves and for those dear to us, and for all those for whose salvation and sanctity we are solicitous: "For the redemption of their souls, the hope of their safety and salvation." In offering up the Lord as the victim of our sacrifice, we exercise a unique power over the heart of God; for we offer to Him His own beloved Son through the miracle of transubstantiation. We offer to God the heart of Jesus with its inexhaustible fountain of love. He bears in that heart our sacrifice and our prayers for all those who are dear to us, and offers them to the Father.

Through the power of this Holy Sacrifice we shall receive help and consolation. The prayers that we lay upon the paten for the salvation and sanctification of our beloved ones will be answered. In a mysterious manner the dew of grace will refresh the soul for whom we are solicitous. The hour will come when the Lord will approach the bier of our dead and recall them to the life of grace. "I say to thee, arise." How rich we are in the possession of the Holy Sacrifice of the Mass!

In order that we may be effectively united to the sacrifice of Christ, it is required on our part that we have faith and the spirit of self-sacrifice. "Be mindful, O Lord, . . . of all here present, whose faith and devotion are known to Thee." We approach with the desire of taking part in the offering of the priest, of arousing in our souls the sacrificial spirit of Christ's heart, of offering to God works of charity and acts of devotion, adoration, praise, and thanksgiving. The priest can unite us to his sacrifice by means of his memento only in so far as we possess a living faith and a spirit of self-sacrifice, for "faith . . . worketh by charity" (Gal 5:6).

What a precious possession, then, is the memento of the priest made for our intention. We can assure ourselves of this blessing by a devout and fruitful participation in the Mass; for during the Mass the priest makes a memento for "all here present," and thus makes it possible for them to offer the Mass with him and to share in its fruits.

Prayer

Let Thy continual pity cleanse and defend Thy Church, we beseech Thee, O Lord; and because it cannot continue in safety without Thee, govern it evermore by Thy help. Through Christ our Lord. Amen.

Wednesday

Once again the baptized are admonished to "walk in the spirit." "Brethren, if we live in the spirit, let us also walk in the spirit" (Epistle). The feast of Pentecost has brought us the Holy Spirit with His gifts and His graces. It becomes us, therefore, to walk in the spirit and to sow in the spirit.

"For he that soweth in his flesh, of the flesh also shall reap corruption" (Epistle). The flesh and its concupiscences are indeed fertile soil. He who sows in this ground will reap an abundant harvest of corruption. Who are they who sow in the flesh? The Apostle explains clearly in the Epistle: He who seeks worldly honors; he who through his vanity and ambition provokes quarrels with his neighbors; he who is envious of others and covetous of their property; he who imagines himself to be something, whereas he is not; he who compares himself with others, and passes an invidious judgment on their thoughts, words, and actions rather than leave all such judgments to God; he who has no sympathy and understanding for the frailty, misery, and weaknesses of his fellow men; he who refuses to carry the burdens of others; he who fails to pray for his brother and admonish him; he who fails to perform corporal and spiritual works of mercy. Such a man is worldly, acts from purely natural motives, and is absorbed in himself, untouched by the supernatural power of the Holy Spirit.

"But he that soweth in the spirit, of the spirit shall reap life everlasting" (Epistle). The field of the spirit is also a fertile field. Happy indeed are they who sow in this field. He sows in this field who does not seek honors, who does not yield to envy and jealousy, who admonishes his erring brother in the spirit of meekness and charity and guides him back to God; such a man is humble and knows his own frailty, and he examines his own life in the light of God's will and the dictates of his own conscience. They sow in the spirit who "bear one another's burdens" and practice charity toward their neighbor in word and deed, who do good while there is yet time, realizing that they are bound to the body of Christ and united with all His members through the sacrament of baptism. Such as these "shall reap life everlasting."

"For he that soweth in his flesh, of the flesh also shall reap corruption." All those works which are performed from purely natural and worldly motives are sown in the flesh. The same is true of all works that are not performed for the love of Christ. They may be good works in themselves, but they are without value for eternity; their end is corruption.

"But he that soweth in the spirit, of the spirit shall reap life everlasting." That is, he shall reap a reward that is of eternal value: the reward of the spirit, the reward of faith, the reward of grace, the reward promised by Christ. And every action performed in this spirit, no matter how insignificant it is in itself, is meritorious for eternity. How foolish of us not to exercise more zeal to sow in the spirit!

Jesus approaches the city of Naim. There He finds a dead man accompanied by his weeping mother. So, too, when He comes to a Christian family or to a parish, He finds some who are dead. They are sowing in the flesh and they will reap corruption of the flesh. But their distracted mother, the Church, stands weeping over them; she carries the burdens of her children who are spiritually dead. She has compassion on them and ceases not to pray for them, to offer sacrifice for them, and to make satisfaction for them. We must unite ourselves to this mother who prays: "Bow down Thy ear, O Lord, to me and hear me; save Thy servant, O my God, that trusteth in Thee,... for I have cried to Thee all the day" (Introit).

The more we sow in the spirit with our Holy Mother the Church, the more certain we can be of helping those who sow in the flesh. Through our prayers united with hers, we may obtain for them the grace to sow in the spirit so that they may reap life eternal.

Prayer

Let Thy continual pity cleanse and defend Thy Church, we beseech Thee, O Lord; and because it cannot continue in safety without Thee, govern it evermore by Thy help. Through Christ our Lord. Amen.

Thursday

"Brethren if we live in the spirit, let us also walk in the spirit.... Bear ye one another's burdens, and so you shall fulfill the law of Christ" (Epistle). To walk in the spirit, therefore, means to bear one another's burdens. Christ bore the burden of our sins, and we must likewise bear the burdens of others.

"Bear ye one another's burdens." Our Lord gives us an example in the Sunday Gospel. The only son of a widow of the city of Naim is being carried out to his burial. Many of the people of the city accompany her and share her sorrow, thus sharing her burden. Our Lord meets the procession as it leaves the city. As it approaches Him near the gates of the city, He has compassion on the mother. He wishes to share her burden and in charity lighten her grief. "Weep not," He tells her. The widow feels that the Lord understands her grief and that He wishes to take part in her suffering. He approaches the bier and touches it, and they that carry it stand still. Then the Lord addresses the young man, "Young man, I say to thee, arise"; and the young man sits up. Then Jesus delivers him to his mother. Thus the Lord bore his neighbor's burden, shared her misery and pain, and left an example for us.

"Bear ye one another's burdens." Everyone has a burden to bear during his life on earth; one in this manner, another in that. Each one of us receives his cross from the Lord; everyone has his difficulties and his trials. For one it may be poverty, sickness, or misfortune; for another it may be professional or business reverses, the loss of property, family troubles, or the death of a dear one. In these circumstances Christian charity must rule. Christian charity cannot ignore the sufferings of others, or treat them with levity or indifference. Christian charity looks upon the misfortunes of others as its own. It suffers with those who suffer; it seeks to offer consolation and counsel. It seeks to lighten the weight of the cross on the shoulders of its neighbor who is bowed down with his burden of sorrow. A sorrow shared is a sorrow halved. What a splendid spectacle it would be if in our parishes, dioceses, and families, we who call ourselves Christians could really rise to such a heroic level of charity. Such charity requires a deep sympathy with the sufferings of others, an understanding heart, and a spirit of self-sacrifice. Moreover, it requires a faith that can see Christ in each of its neighbors, in the poor, the afflicted, the sorrowing, the sick, and the unfortunate. It requires that they keep ever in mind the words of the Lord, "As long as you did it to one of these My least brethren, you did it to Me" (Mt 25:40).

Christ Himself comes down upon the earth each day in order that He may share our needs, our sufferings, our burdens, and our crosses. "Come to Me all ye that labor and are burdened, and I will refresh you" (Mt 11:28). He comes to us daily in the Holy Sacrifice as our high priest in order that He may assume our burdens, present them to the Father, and obtain from the Father strength for us to bear our burdens faithfully and fruitfully, and thus win for ourselves the rewards of eternal life. He comes to us in Holy Communion in order to arouse in us His own sacrificial spirit and sacrificial power. Strengthened by His spirit, we are capable of bearing our daily burdens and crosses, and of drinking the chalice which He drank (Mt 20:22). He enlightens us from the cross, from the altar, and from the tabernacle. We must enter daily more deeply into the mystery of His sufferings and learn the secret of suffering with Him, "yet so, if we suffer with Him, that we may be also glorified with Him" (Rom 8:17). This is the law of Christ: "Where I am, there also shall My minister be. If any man minister to Me, him will My Father honor" (Jn 12:26). Thus the Lord shares our burdens.

We believe in the mystery of the indwelling of God in our souls. The Holy Trinity dwells with us and shares its divine life with us. The Holy Trinity operates in our souls that we may progress in this union, and helps us bear our miseries, our burdens, our trials, and our never-ending difficulties. But with each cross that is laid upon our shoulders, we receive added light and strength to bear our crosses patiently. God Himself bears our burdens. If it were not so, how could we bear the cross and sustain the difficulties and the trials of Christian life, the perfect life? Since God so faithfully helps us bear our burdens, we should also bear one another's burdens.

"Bear ye one another's burdens"; thus you will fulfill the law of Christ. "If you keep My commandments, you shall abide in My love; as I also have kept My Father's commandments and do abide in His love" (Jn 15:10). And yet, where Christian charity is concerned, we fail most frequently, even when our closest neighbors and friends should be the object of our charity. We have no care whatever for the needs of strangers, no compassion on those who are poor and hungry. As long as we suffer no want ourselves, we are content. We have hardly a word of sympathy for those who are in need or in difficulties; we certainly have no time to assist them. Are we, then, really "walking in the spirit"? Where is that faith that should cause us to see Christ bearing His cross in each of our afflicted neighbors? "He that hath the substance of this world, and shall see his brother in need, and shall shut up his bowels from him, how doth the charity of God abide in him?" (1 Jn 3:17.)

Prayer

Let Thy continual pity cleanse and defend Thy Church, we beseech Thee, O Lord; and because it cannot continue in safety without Thee, govern it evermore by Thy help. Through Christ our Lord. Amen.

Friday

"Brethren, if we live in the spirit, let us also walk in the spirit.... Bear ye one another's burdens" (Epistle). When the Apostle was admonishing the Galatians to bear one another's burdens, he had in mind particularly the burden of faults and sins, which they so easily noticed in their neighbors. He has in mind, first of all, those who are being tempted to prove unfaithful to their God, to their faith, and to their Church. He has in mind, too, those who have already given way to temptation. Even the latter he would urge, "Bear ye one another's burdens" lest they continue to fail. If they have already fallen, they may still be helped to rise, "and so you shall fulfill the law of Christ" (Epistle).

Throughout the year at the hour of Sext, except during Advent, Lent, and Eastertide, the liturgy admonishes us: "Bear ye one another's burdens, and so you shall fulfill the law of Christ." It was at the sixth hour, the hour of Sext, that Christ ascended His cross on Good Friday, where He bore all of our burdens and sins, "blotting out the handwriting of the decree that was against us, which was contrary to us. And He hath taken the same out of the way, fastening it to the cross" (Col 2:14). He has taken upon Himself the sins and the burdens of the whole world, and has done penance in our stead and redeemed us from sin. Thus the liturgy continually represents Him to us, urging us: "Bear ye one another's burdens" after the example of your crucified Savior, "who for us men and for our salvation came down from heaven" (Credo) to do penance for us. He came to offer to God an infinite satisfaction which we could not offer for ourselves; He is our representative, "the Lamb of God... who taketh away the sin of the world" (Jn 1:29). He takes upon Himself our sins just as if they were His own. How heavily our sins press upon Him! If you would know how bitter was that burden, contemplate the scene at the Mount of Olives, at the pillar of the scourging, on the cruel journey to Calvary, and during the final bitter hours on the cross. He has truly borne the burden of our sins.

"Go, and do thou in like manner" (Lk 10:37). What is our attitude toward our brother in Christ, whom we find in danger of falling into sin? We well know his weakness in this crisis or that temptation. We see that he is threatened by a grave danger, but do we help him? We live with others and know their weakness, their unfaithfulness and their faults, but we are impatient with them because of their faults; we despise them and their conduct. We presume to judge them with a lack of fraternal charity, and we go out of our way to make our displeasure with them evident. Is this the way to "bear one another's burdens"? Should we not concern ourselves more with the spiritual needs of our fellow men? Should we not rather have compassion on them, and seek to lead them in the right way, and strive to win them for God? Yet how seldom we offer them a word of encouragement in the spirit of meekness and charity! Why should I care for him? we ask ourselves; he is old enough to take care of himself. But we should have more concern for his condition.

"Bear ye one another's burdens." A great misfortune has overtaken our neighbor, for he has become the victim of passion, the dupe of his own imprudence and unchecked evil tendencies. And what do we do about it? How do families react to the fall of one of its members, even a religious family? Very often the poor sinner is greeted only with words of condemnation and contempt. He is often shunned as being unclean, unworthy to sit at table with his brethren or to associate with them. He is stoned on every hand, and men see only his sins and his weaknesses. Is that what the Apostle meant when he admonished us: "Bear ye one another's burdens"? Certainly not! Precisely at such times, when our brother has met with calamity, he stands in need of help, "so that on the contrary, you should rather forgive him and comfort him lest perhaps such a one be swallowed up with overmuch sorrow. Wherefore I beseech you, that you would confirm your charity towards him" (2 Cor 2:7 f.). Especially at such times we should show our interest in his welfare and devise ways and means of approaching him in the matter, of assisting him and helping him. "Bear ye one another's burdens." We must pray for our brother; we must know how to share his trials with him; we must do penance with him and for him, just as Christ did penance for us and sacrificed Himself for us. That is true Christian charity.

"So you shall fulfill the law of Christ." Hate sin but love the sinner. We are to hate all sin and wrongdoing, yet love the sinner with a merciful and benevolent charity. But do we act thus? We distinguish between the sin and the sinner, but we are so severe with the sin that we despise the sinner also. Instead of bearing patiently the sins and faults of others, we use them as an occasion for despising our brother and for exalting ourselves.

Let us consider seriously the example left us by our Lord. How did He bear our burdens? He poured out His blood on the cross that He might obtain pardon for all our sins and infidelities. He offers His body and blood to the Father each day for us in the Holy Sacrifice. With what patience, meekness, and longsuffering He endures sinners! He prays for them in His tabernacle without ceasing. In spite of our continued neglect of Him, He continues to give Himself to us with perfect charity in Holy Communion.

Prayer

Let Thy continual pity cleanse and defend Thy Church, we beseech Thee, O Lord; and because it cannot continue in safety without Thee, govern it evermore by Thy help. Through Christ our Lord. Amen.

Saturday

The Church cries out from the depths of her misery, and we cry out with her: "Bow down Thy ear, O Lord, to me and hear me; save Thy servant, O my God, that trusteth in Thee; have mercy on me, O Lord, for I have cried to Thee all the day. Give joy to the soul of Thy servant" (Introit). "Let Thy continual pity cleanse and defend Thy Church, ... and because it cannot continue in safety without Thee, govern it evermore by Thy help" (Collect).

"Let Thy continual pity cleanse and defend Thy Church." "Christ also loved the Church, and delivered Himself up for it that He might sanctify it, cleansing it by the laver of water in the word of life. That He might present it to Himself a glorious Church, not having spot or wrinkle or any such thing; but that it should be holy and without blemish" (Eph 5:25–27). The children of that Church are to live and walk by the power of the Holy Spirit, who descended upon the Church at Pentecost. They are to be men of the spirit, men not desirous of vainglory, men who do not provoke each other to envy. They are to be men of the spirit; men conscious of their own weakness and instability, who are to teach the sinner the practice of meekness. They are to bear one another's burdens and to be tireless in the pursuit of good (Epistle). The Church is the spotless bride of Christ. Since she herself is without blemish, she longs to see this same quality in all her children. She suffers from the consciousness that many of her children, perhaps the greater part of them in this world, are not what they ought to be. She knows their weakness, their sinfulness, their lack of true spirituality. She knows how she is dishonored and disgraced by their conduct. She cries out to the Lord from the depths of her misery with the voice of the widow of Naim, "Have mercy on me, O Lord, for I have cried out to Thee all the day." "Let Thy continual pity cleanse and defend Thy Church."

"Let Thy continual pity cleanse and defend Thy Church." "I will put enmities between thee and the woman, and thy seed and her seed; she shall crush thy head, and thou shalt lie in wait for her heel" (Gn 3:15). Christ and His Church stand on one side and the devil and his adherents on the other. The enmity between these two factions has endured through the ages; they are engaged in a battle unto death. This battle has continued from the beginning of the history of the Church. Powerful enemies against the Church have arisen among the Jews, among the heathens, among the heretics. The Christian doctrine of the Trinity has been denied; the divinity of Christ and the unity of His person have been attacked; Original Sin has been denied, and the doctrine of grace and salvation has been rejected. In later times the Eucharist was abandoned and the efficacy of the sacraments and the value of the Mass were impugned. The temporal power of the world was used to attack the Church in an attempt to destroy her. For three centuries the Roman emperors used every means at hand to persecute bishops and laity, torturing them with unspeakable cruelty. When Rome failed, the nations of the North and the South, the powers of the East and the West sought to destroy the Church. As the centuries passed, the persecutions continued; she was betrayed and maligned, violated and tortured. But "the gates of hell shall not prevail against it" (Mt 16:18).

The mercy of God protects and defends the Church; His grace guides her. Without God's help she could not resist and overcome the continual persecutions and attacks of the evil one and his supporters. The fact that she has been able to resist all attacks from without and from within, and that she has survived all dangers and persecutions, is due primarily to the enduring mercy of God. The Church herself acknowledges her indebtedness to the goodness of God. "It is good to give praise to the Lord; and to sing to Thy name, O Most High. To show forth Thy mercy in the morning and Thy truth in the night" (Gradual).

The Church suffers from the sins and the faults committed by her members. Still she always remains the holy Church of Christ. We also suffer from such sins and with the Church we reject them as evil. But we love the Church. We can prove our devotion to our Holy Mother the Church by walking in the spirit, and by eradicating all sinful thoughts, deeds, and desires from our own lives, and by striving for true holiness. Thus we must work for the cleansing and sanctification of the Church.

Today we pray that God may cleanse and sanctify His Church. We pray that all the members of the Church will make use of the means placed at their disposal for this purpose. These means are principally the celebration of Mass, the sacrament of penance, and the practice of prayer. This prayer we lay on the paten today:

Prayer

Let Thy continual pity cleanse and defend Thy Church, we beseech Thee, O Lord; and because it cannot continue in safety without Thee, govern it evermore by Thy help. Through Christ our Lord. Amen.

Sixteenth Sunday after Pentecost

The Mass

Today the joyful theme of Easter recedes into the background. The fall season has come. The days are shorter, the nights longer; the darkness is increasing in nature as well as in the soul of the praying Church. By mere chance the Epistles for this Sunday and the following Sundays present those letters which St. Paul wrote during his captivity in Rome. Also today for the first time in the Gradual the Lord appears as the one who will come in glory at the end of time, a thought which is characteristic of the following Sundays after Pentecost.

On the day of our rebirth a wonderful seed was sown in our soul. In the warmth of the Church year it should grow and mature; it should ripen into a rich, full life of grace for the soul and for the Church militant. "Be strengthened by His [Christ's] Spirit with might into the inward man, that Christ may dwell by faith in your hearts; that being rooted and founded in charity, . . . you may be filled unto all the fullness of God" (Epistle). But the seed has not grown in many who received the grace of rebirth and in whom the precious roots of a supernatural life were planted. Where a fruitful return was expected, there is the prospect of failure. Such a fear burdens the soul of the Church today, and therefore she cries out in the Introit: "Have mercy on me, O Lord, for I have cried to Thee all the day. . . . Bow down Thy ear to me, O Lord, and hear me; for I am needy and poor." The same fear impels her to cry out to heaven in the Kyrie and again in the Collect: "Let Thy grace . . . ever go before us and follow us." Then only can it awaken the supernatural seed of life and make it develop into a crop rich "in good works." God "is able to do all things more abundantly than we desire or understand" (Epistle). He can send new life and make us grow to spiritual maturity so that when Christ returns we shall be worthy to accompany Him to the realm of His glory. "Alleluia. Sing ye to the Lord a new canticle because the Lord hath done wonderful things. Alleluia."

On a certain Sabbath, Jesus was invited to dine at the home of a respectable Pharisee. A man afflicted with dropsy approached Him, and the Lord touched him, cured him, and sent him away. Thus the liturgy would have us understand that today during the Mass the same Lord comes to us to cure us. It sees us in the person of the sick man. In humility we acknowledge and confess our sickness and unworthiness. "Look down, O Lord, to help me; let them be confounded and ashamed that seek after my soul to take it away; look down, O Lord, to help me" (Offertory).

In the Holy Sacrifice Christ shares His life with us; He approaches the Father and intercedes and prays for us. In Holy Communion He becomes the food of our souls. There we shall obtain the strength to live a Christian life as described in the Epistle. The soul now prays with firm resolution and hope. "O Lord, I will be mindful of Thy justice alone"; that is, I will think only of Thy justice as I walk before Thee. "O Lord, Thou hast taught me from my youth"; Thou hast strengthened me through this Eucharistic food, and Thou hast guided me since my early youth. "And unto old age and gray hairs, O God, forsake me not" (Communion).

Meditation

"The Gentiles shall fear Thy name, O Lord, and all the kings of the earth Thy glory. For the Lord hath built up Sion and He shall be seen in His majesty" (Gradual). The liturgy now turns its gaze away from the turmoil of this transitory world to the return of the Lord on the day when He will come again "with great power and majesty" (Lk 21:27). At the resurrection of the dead, Sion (the Church) will arise to the new and perfect life of the blessed in heaven.

"Have mercy on me, O Lord, for I have cried to Thee all the day; for Thou, O Lord, art sweet and mild and plenteous in mercy to all that call upon Thee. Bow down Thy ear to me, O Lord, and hear me; for I am needy and poor" (Introit). The fall has come and the Lord comes, too, to gather His crops. During the course of the ecclesiastical year He has "done wonderful things" for His Church (Alleluia verse) at Christmas, Easter, and Pentecost. Day by day He gave it new instructions and new graces; continually He worked in it that it might be fortified in the faith through His spirit, that it might grow in charity and be filled with the plenitude of divine life. What fruit it should have produced! But from so many of her children the Church does not receive the rich harvest she expected. Her pains have been wasted on so many of her children, even in the case of those who are especially consecrated to God. They have not grown spiritually strong and robust; they have no sense of the infinite riches of the knowledge of Christ and of life in Christ. They have no appreciation of the infinite riches of God which could be theirs. The Church views with deep sorrow the many who produced practically no fruit.

"He that humbleth himself shall be exalted" (Gospel). The humble shall be filled with "all the fullness of God" (Epistle). If our growth in grace has not flourished, it is because we laid no foundation in humility. This fact the liturgy wishes to teach us through today's Gospel. Jesus is invited to the house of a respectable Pharisee, where He meets a man who is suffering from dropsy. Jesus touches him and heals him, and then turns to the Pharisees who are at table with Him. He has noticed how "they chose the first seats at the table." "When thou art invited to a wedding, sit not down in the first place, lest perhaps one more honorable than thou be invited by him.... Sit down in the lowest place, that when he who inviteth thee cometh, he may say to thee: Friend, go up higher. Then shalt thou have glory before them that sit at table with thee." This was the sin of the Pharisees: they wished to be honored and highly esteemed. This is also our sickness, our dropsy: we are proud, we esteem ourselves better than others. As long as we maintain this attitude, the life of faith and charity cannot strike deep roots in our soul, the Lord cannot impart His life to us in its fullness. We are filled only with ourselves, "For God resisteth the proud" (1 Pt 5:5). "Every one that exalteth himself shall be humbled, and he that humbleth himself shall be exalted" (Gospel).

True progress and growth in the life of grace depends on humility and on our willingness to be among the least. Only the humble can understand "the breadth and length and height and depth" of the mystery of our life in Christ. Only the humble comprehend "the charity of Christ, which surpasseth all knowledge." Only the humble have room to be filled with "all the fullness of God" and with the divine life of grace. Only the power of Christ "is able to do all things more abundantly than we desire or understand," and Christ thus acts only in the humble. Only the humble know their own unworthiness and helplessness, and come to the Lord's supper, the Holy Eucharist, in this spirit, where Christ touches these who are sick and heals them.

Who will heal us of our pride, which is symbolized by the man with dropsy as well as by the Pharisees of the Gospel? The Lord and His grace will heal us at the table of the Holy Eucharist, at Holy Communion. Although we have done great damage to ourselves through our pride, all is not lost. It is not too late yet, if only we come to the Lord. He touches us in Holy Communion with His pure flesh and blood. He inflames our infirm soul with His clean, healthy soul, our heart with His heart, our charity with His charity; He joins our endeavors to His holy endeavors and offers them to God. We are healed and become new men through the power of the Holy Eucharist. We trust in Him, and we are nourished by our daily reception of the holy Sacrament.

Humility is the only remedy for our infirmity of soul and the only avenue to grace. Christ Himself gives us an example of humility in the daily celebration of the Mass. The Lord becomes present to us each day under the appearance of bread and wine, just as two thousand years ago He became man, humbling Himself that He might become our priest, our sacrifice, and our food. He takes the lowest place in this banquet, as once in the same spirit He took the last place by suffering and dying for us. We also must learn to take the last place, to be humble, to die with the Lord, by the complete submission of our will to the will and designs of the Father.

"Have mercy on me, O Lord, for I have cried to Thee all the day" (Introit). Give me the light and the grace to walk the way of Christian humility, unhampered by pride and self-will.

Prayer

Let Thy grace, we beseech Thee, O Lord, ever go before us and follow us, and may it make us to be continually zealous in doing good works. Through Christ our Lord. Amen.

Monday

Today the Church prays for the spiritual stability of her children. The sky is darkened. Persecutions from without and conflicts, crises, difficulties from within, press upon the Church. The Apostle is imprisoned in Rome. The Christians of Ephesus, he fears, may have fallen into error concerning the doctrine that he taught them; persecution and his imprisonment may scandalize them and cause them to abandon Christ. The Apostle in his chains can only pray for them that they find grace to remain faithful despite persecutions and his apparent failure.

"Brethren, I pray you not to faint at my tribulations for you" (Epistle). The Apostle has just reminded his converts at Ephesus that we have access to the Father in the faith of Christ, the mediator. We are His children, He is our Father. Therefore the Apostle prays that we become not fainthearted at the tribulations which he and the Church must suffer for us, the baptized. These sufferings, this abuse, these persecutions of the Church, of religion, of the clergy, give us no cause for faintheartedness, as if the Church had erred in her doctrines, her commandments, or her sacraments. On the contrary these sufferings and persecutions of the Church "are your glory"; they are like the wounds of the crucified Lord; they are the wounds of the visible Church on earth. They are an unmistakable proof that this is the Church of Christ and possesses the spirit of Christ; for like its founder, it is despised and persecuted, scourged and fettered. "If the world hate you, know ye that it hath hated Me before you. If you had been of the world, the world would love its own; but because you are not of the world, but I have chosen you out of the world, therefore the world hateth you.... If they have persecuted Me, they will also persecute you" (Jn 15:18 ff.). The sufferings of the Church make us strong in faith and establish our unity with the Church and with Christ, our head. They give us the assurance that we possess Christ in His Church, and with Him redemption and life.

"My tribulations for you ... are your glory" (Epistle). The Apostle suffers his tribulations for the Ephesians; the Church suffers her persecutions for us. She consoles us: "I pray you not to faint at my tribulations for you." The Church is filled with the spirit of Christ, "who loved me and delivered Himself for me" (Gal 2:20). He who will save souls with Christ must necessarily go with Him the way of the cross, the way of suffering and humility. The Church does so; she is happy to go with the Lord and "to suffer for us." She tells us that God loves us so much that He not only has given His only-begotten Son for us, but He also wills that the apostles, the saints, the whole Church, should suffer for each one of us and so be united with Christ our Savior. The days of the persecution of the Church of Christ are days of grace and blessing for us. They incite us to do penance and show us that the prayers of the Church are not enough to conciliate God; she must suffer, she must be persecuted "for us" that we may find pardon and grace through the tribulations which she suffers for us, "which are your glory." She thus proves how she cares for us, how seriously she takes upon herself the task to save us for eternal life. She continually drinks the chalice of the Lord with us, full of motherly solicitude for our welfare.

"Have mercy on me, O Lord, for I have cried to Thee all the day" (Introit). Thus the Church prays for mercy for us sinners, apostates, and ungrateful Christians. She cries all the day: in the continual prayer offered up by her priests and religious, in her sufferings, in her continual tribulations and persecutions. She cries to Him in the Holy Sacrifice which she celebrates, when she joins the crucified Lord and through His sacrifice is enabled to suffer with Him and to obtain pardon and grace for us. "I [the church] pray you not to faint at my tribulations for you." She knows why she is blasphemed and persecuted and suffers tribulations. "If any one preach to you a gospel besides that which you have received, let him be anathema. For do I now persuade men or God? Or do I seek to please men? If I yet pleased men, I should not be the servant of Christ" (Gal 1:9 f.). The more she is persecuted and suffers tribulations, the more we are persuaded that she does not serve the world, that she therefore suffers contumely because she is faithful to Christ.

Prayer

Let Thy grace, we beseech Thee, O Lord, ever go before us and follow us, and may it make us to be continually zealous in doing good works. Through Christ our Lord. Amen.

Tuesday

The Apostle bows his knee to the Father and prays for five graces for his beloved Ephesians. The first grace, that they may "be strengthened by His Spirit with might unto the inward man." The second, "that Christ may dwell by faith in [their] hearts." The third, that they may be "rooted and founded in charity." The fourth, that they may comprehend the "charity of Christ, which surpasseth all knowledge." The fifth, that they "may be filled unto all the fullness of God" (Epistle).

"To be strengthened by His Spirit with might unto the inward man," is the first petition of the Apostle; and in a certain sense it is the foundation of all that follows. The Christian life necessarily is a life of spirituality; it is nothing else but the living of the life of the only-begotten Son of God, who causes us to think His thoughts, to take His principles as maxims of our lives, to carry out His intentions. He would have us love what He has loved: poverty, humility, submission to God's will, sufferings, and the cross. The spiritual life lifts us above the thoughts and ambitions of the man of sin; it frees us from egoism and uncontrolled passions and habits, and elevates us to the realm of faith, where we have confidence in God and love God and our fellow creatures. The spiritual man has his senses, his imagination, and his passions under control so that they never drag his will down to their level. He is always turned inward upon himself, where God the Holy Ghost lives and works in the depths of his soul. He knows no curiosity, no haste, no excitement, no dejection, no distractions. He does not interfere with the affairs of others, he flees criticism of others, and abstains from judging others. He knows no fear of men and shows deference only to the will of God. In all things he makes himself dependent on God and the operation of grace. He does his duty as demanded and never refuses to submit to the will and demands of God; he accepts his trials and tribulations as coming from divine providence, and greets them with a resigned and confident fiat: As Thou wilt. That we lead such a life, that we "be strengthened ... with might unto the inward man," is the prayer of the Apostle and the wish of the Church.

"By His Spirit." An interior life cannot be attained through any purely natural power, nor by any natural effort, nor by any advance in training or culture. We may use our natural talents and natural virtues, we may exercise our intellect and will, our mind and character, and bring them to a natural perfection; but these natural powers alone will not make us real Christians. True Christian spiritual life means an intensive life of grace. However, such a life implies a new order of being which far excels that of nature and can come into existence only by the power of the Holy Ghost. It is He who gives birth to the interior life, who preserves and unfolds it and carries it up to the heights of union with God. It is He who penetrates our soul always more with His beauty, with His purity, and with the fire of charity, just as the rays of the sun shine on the dewdrop and pierce it, causing it to reflect the beauty of the sun. The more we yield to the operation of the Holy Ghost, the more powerful will our interior life become.

A more intense interior life in all Christians is the need of the hour. This need becomes more urgent as we march towards the time of the harvest, the end of life. As we go forward with the sacred liturgy, we more clearly perceive this need, for the time when the glorified Lord will return to judge the living and the dead, is swiftly approaching. He comes to us personally at the hour of our death, at the time of the particular judgment. How we shall regret that we did not work diligently to intensify our interior life when we yet had the time!

Our growth in the interior life is to be achieved without slighting or neglecting the duties and obligations of our state in life. In the first place we must cultivate a life of prayer and meditation, of abstinence and self-denial, of purity of the heart and the awareness of the presence of God. If we achieve such an interior life, all the external duties to which we are obliged will reflect the spirit of our interior life and will be enlivened and made fruitful by it.

Prayer

Let Thy grace, we beseech Thee, O Lord, ever go before us and follow us, and may it make us to be continually zealous in doing good works. Through Christ our Lord. Amen.

Wednesday

"The Father of our Lord Jesus Christ [grant you] ... that Christ may dwell by faith in your hearts" (Epistle) is the second prayer addressed by the Apostle to God. The Church joins in this prayer of the Apostle for us.

"Christ may dwell in your hearts," not as He is in the tabernacle, not as He becomes ours in Holy Communion, but "by faith." The Apostle means that Christ should be in our hearts as the Lord explained in the parable of the vine and the branches: Christ must live in us as the vine lives and works in its branches, as it causes them to grow and flourish and bear fruit. So He, the glorified Lord, lives in us, the baptized; and we become the living branches united to Him, possessing and bearing His spirit. "And I live, now not I, but Christ liveth in me" (Gal 2:20). If we pray to the Father, then Christ prays in us. If we practice poverty as the Lord taught us to, He lives His life of poverty in us and sanctifies our poverty. If we deny ourselves in this or that, then His spirit of self-denial supports us and gives full value before God to our sacrifice. If we become apostles for the salvation of souls, then our zeal is the expression of the zeal of the Lord, who lives in us and works through us for the salvation of others. If we suffer, then He suffers mystically in us, His members. He bears part of the pains because He lives in us, the vine in the branches. "I live, now not I, but Christ liveth in me." In me Christ prays, works, suffers, and loves. These words, "Christ may dwell in your hearts," give our life a new meaning and value, one immensely sublime and surpassing all that is human. Of ourselves we are nothing, full of human weaknesses, capable only of failures; therefore we trust in the Lord, in His prayers, in His charity, in which all the treasures of wisdom and knowledge are contained and in which the Father is well pleased. How fitting, then, is the Apostle's prayer "that Christ may dwell ... in your hearts."

"By faith." Without faith all mere human knowledge, all human effort, all natural endeavor, is useless. That Christ may dwell in our hearts is possible only through faith. When we confessed our faith in Christ at our baptism, the Lord began to dwell in our hearts. The more we live by faith in Christ through the exercise of charity, the more the life of Jesus becomes our life. "I live, now not I, but Christ liveth in me." The more we see Him living in us by faith, and the more attentively we listen to Him and allow Him to work in us, the more we lose ourselves. Then we no longer lean on the feeble, bending reed of self, but on the Strong One, the Holy One, who lives in us and prays, loves, and glorifies the Father in us. The more intensely we live this life of faith, the more vividly we realize our own misery and nothingness. But as we look and see Him living in us, we can use His love of the Father, His virtues, His merits, His sufferings and death, His blood, and His heart as our own. We offer Him as our sacrifice to the Father. We can offer His pure and loving heart to the Father in reparation for our deficiency in charity and purity. All we need is a living faith; in such a faith we are immensely rich. God grant "that Christ may dwell by faith in [our] hearts," that we may see Him in ourselves through faith and know our inestimable riches.

Why do we so often turn to the creatures which are about us? Must we not fear that every moment we are separated from Christ we are in danger of being lost, since He is not living and working in us? A single look upon Him heals our weakness, banishes the darkness, drives away sadness, and fills the soul with unspeakable joy. Are we depressed because of our sinfulness, are we afraid of the difficulties which accumulate before us? Then let us look upon Jesus, who lives and works in us, and we shall find peace. Should we lose heart or give up the struggle because of our instability and weakness? We should remember that "I can do all things in Him who strengtheneth me" (Phil 4:13).

"The Lord is nigh. Be nothing solicitous, but in everything, by prayer and supplication with thanksgiving, let your petitions be made known to God. And the peace of God which surpasseth all understanding, keep your hearts and minds in Christ Jesus" (Phil 4:5–7).

Prayer

Let Thy grace, we beseech Thee, O Lord, ever go before us and follow us, and may it make us to be continually zealous in doing good works. Through Christ our Lord. Amen.

Thursday

"The Father of our Lord Jesus Christ [grant that you be] ... rooted and founded in charity" (Epistle). In the last analysis everything depends on charity. "And now there remain faith, hope, and charity, these three; but the greatest of these is charity" (1 Cor 13:13).

"Love therefore is the fulfilling of the law" (Rom 13:10). "Thou shalt love the Lord thy God with thy whole heart, and with thy whole soul, and with thy whole mind, and with thy whole strength. This is the first commandment" (Mk 12:30). "If I speak with the tongues of men and of angels, and have not charity, I am become as sounding brass or a tinkling cymbal. And if I should have prophecy and should know all mysteries and all knowledge, and if I should have all faith so that I could remove mountains, and have not charity, I am nothing. And if I should distribute all my goods to feed the poor, and if I should deliver my body to be burned, and have not charity, it profiteth me nothing" (1 Cor 13:1–3). "God is charity; and he that abideth in charity, abideth in God, and God in him" (1 Jn 4:16). "Now the end of the commandment is charity, from a pure heart and a good conscience and an unfeigned faith" (1 Tm 1:5). All good deeds are deeds of charity. It is the root, the life, the soul, the sum of all virtues, the first and last of the virtues; it is perfection itself. Where love fails, all fails; where love is, there is everything. It fulfills the commandments and the will of God, not out of fear, not out of force, not for the sake of reward, but to please Him to whom it is devoted. It gives the least of our actions an immense value in the sight of God, which by far surpasses their natural value. And such works profit not only us, but the whole Church, and are of greater value than any other works, no matter how great they may appear to men. "Now there remain faith, hope, and charity, these three; but the greatest of these is charity" (1 Cor 13:13). "Follow after charity" (1 Cor 14:1).

"You may be able to comprehend ... the breadth and length and height and depth" of the mystery of Christ's humility and self-denial, as well as the mystery of His Incarnation and His sufferings and death. God's love explains the mystery of our vocation and that of the heathens, our membership in His Church, and our possession of the divine life. Charity explains the mystery of our incorporation in Christ, who is the head, "who loved me and delivered Himself for me" (Gal 2:20). Who can comprehend the height and depth, the breadth and length of the charity of God? "For God so loved the world as to give His only-begotten Son, that whosoever believeth in Him, may not perish but may have life everlasting" (Jn 3:16). Charity gives a clarified vision. He who lacks charity does not walk in the full light.

"To know also the charity of Christ, which surpasseth all knowledge" (Epistle). Human reason, human speculation, and human knowledge cannot comprehend the love of Christ's heart, but only charity, or rather the knowledge that is born of charity, can do so. With such a knowledge the little child knows its mother. It is not a knowledge of the intellect, for the child has it before he comes to the use of reason. It is not knowledge obtained through faith or through the word or authority of others. It is knowledge of another kind: the knowledge of love. The child loves and knows himself to be loved. Instinctively it returns love for love. If it is taken away from its mother, it cries and it is not to be satisfied till it reposes again on its mother's breast. The mother is everything to it, the whole world. Such also is the knowledge of the loving soul of God's chosen ones. Such a soul may be unlearned, unable to say or to think great things about Him; but who will say this soul does not know God? He knows himself to be loved by God; he knows Him to be always near embracing his soul with the arms of His love. The soul feels instinctively that God is solicitous about it. God leads, protects, and supports; the soul finds in Him its whole pleasure, its all; it longs for God and sacrifices all for Him. God reveals Himself to such a loving soul and lets it see and taste how sweet and good He is. Such is the knowledge which the Apostle and the liturgy ask for us.

"Follow after charity" (1 Cor 14:1). Are we firmly rooted and grounded in charity? We can easily test our degree of charity. The love of God expresses itself in our charity toward our fellow men. "Charity is patient, is kind; charity envieth not, dealeth not perversely, is not puffed up, is not ambitious, seeketh not her own, is not provoked to anger, thinketh no evil; rejoiceth not in iniquity, but rejoiceth with the truth; beareth all things, ... endureth all things" (1 Cor 13:4–7). "He that hath My commandments and keepeth them, he it is that loveth Me. And he that loveth Me shall be loved of My Father; and I will love him and will manifest Myself to him.... If any one love Me, he will keep My word, and My Father will love him, and We will come to him and will make Our abode with him" (Jn 14:21, 23).

Prayer

Let Thy grace, we beseech Thee, O Lord, ever go before us and follow us, and may it make us to be continually zealous in doing good works. Through Christ our Lord. Amen.

Friday

May He grant you "to be strengthened by His Spirit with might unto the inward man." For this grace the Apostle first prays in this Sunday's Epistle. "That Christ may dwell in your hearts," is the second grace. "That being rooted and founded in charity, you may be able to comprehend . . . what is the breadth and length and height and depth" of the grace of your vocation is the third grace; and "to know also the charity of Christ" is the fourth grace. These four graces have but one purpose: "That you may be filled unto all the fullness of God" (Epistle).

"If any one love Me, . . . My Father will love him, and We will come to him and will make Our abode with him" (Jn 14:23). The fullness of the Godhead — of the Father, Son, and Holy Ghost — becomes ours through the power of baptism and our incorporation in Christ. "For in Him [Christ] dwelleth all the fullness of the Godhead corporeally. And you are filled in Him" (Col 2:9 f.). "The charity of God is poured forth in our hearts" (Rom 5:5). God descends to us, who are but dust, and abides in our soul. He Himself is in us, He speaks to us, He watches our steps, He inspires us, He admonishes and guides us with infinite benevolence, with divine wisdom and deep love, with a clear vision and with a strong arm, which nothing can resist. We may speak to Him any time, come to Him as His beloved children, seek His help, reveal the inmost feelings of our hearts. We can express our gratitude, our affections, our love, our contrition, our needs. We need not await the dawn of eternity to possess God; we bear Him within us. And with Him we have a foretaste of the perfect blessedness which awaits us in eternity. Tribulations and miseries are easily borne when we are conscious of the nearness and love of God, our devoted Father. His nearness makes us joyful and happy and immensely rich. We must be more keenly aware of the presence of God living in us.

"Filled unto all the fullness of God." From this original fountain of divine life, from which we receive all things, we receive a new source of life, the fountain of grace. It operates like an overflow of God's infinite love for us. It gives us the unspeakable fullness of God; it elevates our human nature to a state which far surpasses all our natural powers and abilities; it lifts our will, heart, and mind into the world of God, and plants a new love in us, the love of the child for its father, the childlike confidence which makes us cry out, "Abba, Father." We glow with the light of purity and the holiness of God, and penetrated with this divine life, we are endowed with the divine virtues of faith, hope, and charity. The so-called moral virtues, which are conferred upon us with sanctifying grace, serve these three theological virtues. We receive also the virtues of prudence, justice, fortitude, and temperance. All are a participation in the divine life which we possess through the power of sanctifying grace and by virtue of the indwelling of the Father, Son, and Holy Ghost. In these virtues God gives us the rudders with which we must steer the small ship of our soul to the shores of eternity through the stormy sea of time. The journey is fatiguing, the way is far, our own strength is not enough. Therefore to develop and protect these virtues He gives us the sails of the seven gifts — wisdom, knowledge, understanding, counsel, piety, fortitude, strength, and fear of the Lord — which the Holy Ghost, who lives in us, swells and drives as a powerful blowing wind. The same Spirit of God who hovered above the human nature of Christ and filled it, steadily moves above our soul, enlivens it with His power, enlightens it through His divine light, and urges it to perfect, heroic charity.

Besides being "filled unto all the fullness of God," we are given endless graces of counsel, graces which clarify the intellect and incite and strengthen the will. We also receive the grace of the special guidance and providence of God, which saves us from the insidious plots of the devil and from sin, and gives us courage and power to continue in the performance of good deeds. It helps us to perform acts pleasing to God and to bring forth more abundantly the fruits of the Holy Ghost: charity, joy, peace, patience, benignity, goodness, longanimity, mildness, faith, modesty, continency, chastity (Gal 5:22 ff.). Thus filled with God, we ever grow in grace and in the participation of divine life. The more we grow in grace, the more fruitful become our prayers, our works, our acts of self-denial, our sufferings, and our sacrifices made for our brethren in Christ. Truly, "in all things you are made rich in Him" (1 Cor 1:5).

"Sing, ye, to the Lord a new canticle, because the Lord hath done wonderful things" (Alleluia verse). The liturgical year will soon end. With deep seriousness the liturgy calls upon us to grow and to be ripe for the harvest, to attain to the fullness of God. We are likened to the servants of a man who is about to go on a journey. He calls his servants and delivers his goods to them. He gives five talents to one of them, two talents to another, and one talent to a third. After a long time the master will return. The one who got five talents must gain five more; the one with two must have two more; otherwise they will be judged. "Wicked and slothful servant.... For to every one that hath, shall be given, but from him that hath not, that also which he seemeth to have shall be taken away. And the unprofitable servant cast ye out into the exterior darkness" (Mt 25:26 ff.).

Prayer

Let Thy grace, we beseech Thee, O Lord, ever go before us and follow us, and may it make us to be continually zealous in doing good works. Through Christ our Lord. Amen.

Saturday

The Church reminds us of the coming of the Lord at the Last Judgment. Then He will take her home. But the Church is grieved at the thought of the many souls who must be left behind in spite of all the graces they received and in spite of her prayers, pains, sacrifices; for they will not be ripe for harvest. For these she implores: "Have mercy on me, O Lord" (Introit); "Look down, O Lord, to help me" (Offertory); "Let Thy grace ... ever go before us and follow us, and may it make us to be continually zealous in doing good works" (Collect).

"Have mercy on me, O Lord, for I have cried to Thee all the day" (Introit). "With fear and trembling work out your salvation. For it is God who worketh in you, both to will and to accomplish, according to His good will" (Phil 2:12 f.). If He left us to ourselves, we should be borne down continually by the heavy weight of our fallen nature into the depth of evil, and to estrangement from God. "So then it is not of him that willeth nor of him that runneth, but of God that showeth mercy" (Rom 9:16). We are branches of Christ, the vine. "He that abideth in Me and I in him, the same beareth much fruit; for without Me you can do nothing.... As the branch cannot bear fruit of itself, unless it abide in the vine, so neither can you unless you abide in Me.... If any one abide not in Me, he shall be cast forth as a branch and shall wither" (Jn 15:4 ff.). If we the branches would bear the fruit of eternal salvation, we must remain in living contact with the vine. Only thus can we absorb His living sap and life. The living sap is grace, without which we cannot do anything which has value for eternity. "No man can come to Me except the Father... draw him" (Jn 6:44) through grace. Without the help of grace there can be no perfect contrition, no pardon for sins, no improvement of life, no good thoughts pleasing to God; no works, prayers, or sufferings that can have any value. All depend on the help of grace and the mercy of God; for man of himself can do nothing. Even the greatest talents and the most perfect knowledge have no value in themselves for eternal salvation. God gives His grace out of pure mercy and charity; we can never have a just claim to it because of our merits or efforts. How insignificant indeed is man!

"Let Thy grace, we beseech Thee, O Lord, ever go before us and follow us" (Collect). His grace comes first, not our will. Our will is, in a sense, sleeping and dead. It must be awakened by His helping grace, which moves our will that it may turn to God. If God's grace is not first given, then our will cannot move. If the will is awakened and aroused, it moves freely but under the inspiration of grace. Even when the work has been begun, the will still needs the help of grace. Grace accompanies our work and permeates it, making it supernatural and meritorious; that is, worthy of eternal reward. Thus the grace works in a twofold way: it precedes our will and helps us to determine the act; when we have begun to act, it follows our will and our act, continually supporting us so that we will and act, pray, and suffer in a way that is conducive to our salvation. God works in us the will and work; we are incapable of either by ourselves. "Unless the Lord build the house, they labor in vain that build it" (Ps 126:1). By ourselves alone we are incapable of good and have only the ability to commit sin. From God alone we have the power to think, to will, to do good.

How insignificant and ineffectual are man's efforts! After God has given us the fullness of supernatural riches, He must still give us aid every moment; otherwise we cannot accomplish anything with all these riches; we can only lose them.

We are children of God, branches of Christ the vine, through sanctifying grace. But Christ, says the Council of Trent, pours this power into the just, as the head into the members and the vine into the branches; this power continually precedes their good works, accompanies them, and follows them, and gives them a value without which they cannot be pleasing to God and without which they are not meritorious (Sess. VI, chap. 16). Helping grace comes more readily to us who possess the divine life through sanctifying grace. It is given to us as a staff in our hands; it will not be taken away unless we throw it away ourselves. It surrounds us continually as the light of the sun surrounds our eyes and does not vanish unless the eye is closed. Grace continually knocks at our heart to entice us to do good; it speaks to us to teach us; it admonishes us to what is good and keeps us out of sin; it strengthens us in danger, and supports us if we have sanctifying grace. "Now all good things came to me together with her, and innumerable riches through her hands" (Ws 7:11). How poor, how unfortunate we are if we lose sanctifying grace!

How many graces the Lord has given us, at the hour of baptism, during childhood, in the years of our youth, during our manhood! How many each day, each hour! How holy we would now be if we had only valued these graces and used them!

Prayer

Let Thy grace, we beseech Thee, O Lord, ever go before us and follow us, and may it make us to be continually zealous in doing good works. Through Christ our Lord. Amen.

Seventeenth Sunday after Pentecost

The Mass

The ecclesiastical year is drawing to an end. Now the Church looks for its perfection in eternity, for its home, its last end, and its rest. She knows that there Christ the Lord reigns in glory. The Church left behind on earth makes a long and weary journey to Him.

In former times the bishop with his clergy proceeded from the sacristy to the altar through the aisles of the church in solemn procession; the chanters also walked in this procession. Above the altar the picture of the glorified Christ shone in splendid mosaics in the apse. While the procession proceeded to the altar, the chanters began the Introit, their pilgrimage-song. Hearts and eyes are directed to Christ, who looks down from the height of the apse. "Thou art just, O Lord, and Thy judgment is right; deal with Thy servant according to Thy mercy. Blessed are the undefiled in the way, who walk in the law of the Lord" (Introit). Blessed are we who dare approach the Lord on this day at the Holy Sacrifice of the Mass. But the celebration of the Holy Sacrifice of the Mass requires that we be "undefiled," that we walk "in the law of the Lord"; that we abstain from "the defilements of the devil and with pure hearts follow Thee, the only God" (Collect). Our life must be worthy of the Mass; it must be a preparation for the celebration of the Holy Sacrifice. What is especially demanded of us, says the Epistle, is a charity which forgets itself and wishes to work for the community, in the union of the spirit, in thought and deed: "One body and one spirit.... One Lord, one faith, one baptism, one God and Father of all."

We must become one with the community, avoiding all disputes and quarrels, one in heart and soul walking with the Lord. If we have become one in charity, then the praise of the beatitude given in the Gradual refers to us: "Blessed is the nation whose God is the Lord [Christ], the people whom He hath chosen for His inheritance." This precious inheritance, already ours on this earth, is perfected in eternity, where the Lord Christ is enthroned in His glory, which He will communicate to His elect. How the soul and the Church long for the day which will give her that glory: the day of the resurrection of Christ! "Alleluia. O Lord, hear my prayer and let my cry come to Thee. Alleluia." This is the cry of the ancient Church: Maran-atha. Come, O Lord, to the Last Judgment, to fetch us to the kingdom of glory! He comes in the Gospel as the teacher of the great commandment of charity. He comes as the risen Lord, of whom David sang: "The Lord said to my Lord: Sit Thou at My right hand" (Ps 109:1).

We go to the glorified Lord at the sacrifice and implore Him: "Show Thy face upon Thy sanctuary" (Offertory), upon the sacrificing community, which puts upon the altar its gifts of bread and wine, its prayers and works, its power, its time, its willingness to renounce sin, the flesh, and the world, and to live during the coming week with Christ, and to be to Him a pleasing sacrifice. Christ becomes our sacrifice. In Him and with Him we are sacrificed, that is, consecrated to God. Thus we fulfill the commandment of the Gospel: "Thou shalt love the Lord thy God with thy whole heart"; we love Him through Christ, with Christ, and in Christ, and give Him "all honor and glory." Taken up in the sacrifice of Christ, we recite our *Pater noster* with a heart enkindled with charity. Soon Christ will come to us in Holy Communion. He becomes the life-giving food of our soul, sets up the throne of His glory in it, commands His enemies to flee, and infuses some of the fullness of His life and power into our souls.

Meditation

"What think you of Christ; whose Son is He?" Jesus asked the Pharisees. They answered Him, "David's." But He replied, "How, then, doth David, in spirit, call Him Lord, saying: The Lord said to my Lord: Sit on My right hand until I make thy enemies thy footstool? If David, then, call Him Lord, how is He his son?" The Pharisees were silenced. We confess Him to be the Lord who sits at the right hand of the Father in majesty and glory, the King who will return at the end time to judge the living and the dead.

The Lord said, "Sit on My right hand." Thus Christ today appears to the Church and its liturgy. He is the Lord, the supreme ruler of the world. He has accomplished the redemption of men on earth; now He has been made King of them all. Such was the will of the Father. "Ask of Me and I will give Thee the Gentiles for Thy inheritance and the utmost parts of the earth for Thy possession" (Ps 2:8). "Sit Thou at My right hand until I make Thy enemies Thy footstool" (Ps 109:1). The man Christ has received the fullness of power from the Father. He will conquer His enemies. The day will come when there will be no enemy; Christ will be the victor. "That in the name of Jesus every knee should bow, of those that are in heaven, on earth, and under the earth" (Phil 2:10). The Church, surrounded by enemies and persecuted on all sides, faithfully looks upon Him for protection. She knows that He will defeat her enemies; He will pass a just judgment upon all the evils which have accumulated in the history of mankind. He will take up the Church and all of us who are members of the Church in glory on His return. "Thou art just, O Lord, and Thy judgment is right" (Introit). Justice will be established and evil destroyed. In this judgment all untruth will be defeated and falsehood revealed. Peoples and states will be cleansed of evil, and the innocence, virtue, justice, and holiness of the Church will be established. The Church awaits this day on which the Lord will come again with great glory and power. He is the Lord. All knees shall bow before Him. All will have to acknowledge His word and His judgment.

Christ shows His power and glory by filling His faithful with His spirit and uniting them "in the bond of peace" (Epistle). He gives us the royal commandment to love God and our fellow man. He fills all His faithful with His spirit. He cleanses them of whatever may separate them from Him, such as their egoism, their pride, their self-love. They become one with Him, inflamed by one spirit, established in one faith and in the one baptism, inspired by one hope. All are children of the one Father, "who is above all, and through all, and in us all" (Epistle). Our unity is proof of His supremacy. The more united we are in heart, in soul, and in spirit, the more surely we give testimony for Him. "Thou alone art holy. Thou alone art the Lord. Thou alone, O Jesus Christ, art the Most High, with the Holy Ghost, in the glory of the Father" (Gloria). Therefore the Epistle exhorts us to "walk worthy of the vocation in which you are called. With all humility and mildness, with patience, supporting one another in charity, careful to keep the unity of the Spirit in the bond of peace." This is the greatest commandment: "Thou shalt love the Lord thy God with thy whole heart... [and] thy neighbor as thyself" (Gospel). Having such a love we become one people in "the unity of the Spirit," in the unity of Christ's love.

"Blessed is the nation whose God is the Lord, the people whom He hath chosen for His inheritance" (Gradual). Christ is our Lord. He has chosen us as His own. He, who was the Son of God, had no need of us; yet He descended from heaven out of pure mercy, and because of our misery He came in search of us, His lost sheep. He wants us for His own. That He might possess us and make us happy, He accepted the cross and bought us with His own blood. At baptism He made us children of God and received us into His Church. Gratefully we exclaim: "Blessed is the nation whose God is the Lord."

"I am the Lord thy God.... Thou shalt not have strange gods before Me" (Ex 20:2 f.). He alone is God. We must do all for Him and according to His holy will. We can have no desire or ambition that is opposed to His will. "Vow ye, and pray to the Lord your God, all you that round about Him bring presents: to Him that is terrible, even to Him who taketh away the spirit of princes" (Communion). He is my Lord, He alone. We must walk worthy of our vocation as Christians, in charity and in love of our fellow man. Charity is humble, mild, and patient; it tolerates the mistakes of others. It preserves unity of the spirit through peace, benevolence, concord, and holy love. Do we walk thus?

Prayer

Grant Thy people, we beseech Thee, O Lord, to shun the defilements of the devil and with pure hearts to follow Thee, the only God. Through Christ our Lord. Amen.

Monday

"Blessed is the nation whose God is the Lord" (Gradual). Christ, enthroned at the right hand of the Father and living in His Church, protects, supports, and guides her with His powerful hand. What have we to fear?

"Sit on My right hand" (Gospel). The glorified Lord now participates in the glory of the Father, even according to His human nature, thus sharing with His human and divine nature the majesty and power of the triune God. "All power is given to Me in heaven and in earth" (Mt 28:18). He has become "obedient unto death, even to the death of the cross, for which cause God also hath exalted Him and hath given Him a name which is above all names" (Phil 2:8 f.). He is "the Lord." But the Church announces throughout all countries and all ages that He has suffered and died, that He rose from the dead, ascended into heaven, and is now enthroned at the right hand of the Father. In union with the Church we believe in Him and pay homage to Him. We rejoice that the Father has made Him Master and King of the world, of the angels, and of men, Master also of the powers that are under the earth — the devils and the damned. He governs all things; He rules the course of history; He guides the nations and the Church. He permits the evil, injustice, and catastrophes which visit mankind and single nations, families, and individuals, because He has the power to guide everything for the best. We believe in Him and trust His rule of the world, of spirits, and of souls. "Thou alone art the Lord" (Gloria).

"Daniel prayed to God" (Offertory). The liturgy recognizes the Lord in the praying Daniel. The Lord is in His Church, although He sits at the right hand of the Father. He is the same praying high priest who places Himself at the disposal of the praying and sacrificing community. He prays together with the faithful to the Father: "Hear, O Lord, the prayers of Thy servant; show Thy face upon Thy sanctuary, and look down favorably upon this people, upon whom Thy name is invoked, O God" (Offertory). The Lord is united with His people, with His Church, with each one of us, praying, sacrificing, leading us all to the Father, that through the power of the Holy Sacrifice we may receive the forgiveness of our sins, and that the holy and triune God may be merciful to us and pour out the fullness of light and grace into our hearts. It is His great and unspeakable love towards us that does not forget us when He has entered into His glory. He has promised: "I am with you all days, even to the consummation of the world" (Mt 28:20). This promise He keeps and fulfills. Invisibly He comes into our midst in the Holy Sacrifice, giving Himself as the food of our souls: He, the Lord, to whom all power is given in heaven and on earth. To such an extent the almighty God humbles Himself—whose power nothing can resist, who is stronger than flesh and passion and the old man within us, stronger than the world and Satan with his pomps—that He dwells in the tabernacle to be near us at all times with the power of His prayers and the wisdom of His Spirit whenever we need help against the enemies of our salvation. "Blessed is the nation whose God is the Lord, the people whom He hath chosen for His inheritance. By the word of the Lord the heavens were established; and all the power of them by the Spirit of His mouth" (Gradual). Should we not in all things depend on Him who is near us with the fullness of His might and His love?

We approach "the day of the Lord" when He shall return for judgment. "Thou art just, O Lord, and Thy judgment is right" (Introit). "If Thou, O Lord, wilt mark iniquities, Lord, who shall stand it" (Ps 129:3). You come down to us in the Sacrifice of the Mass and in Holy Communion with innumerable graces and proofs of charity to bring us Your salvation: a continually repeated granting of grace and mercy. "Deal with Thy servant according to Thy mercy" (Introit). "Lord have mercy on us, Christ have mercy on us, Lord have mercy on us." "O Lord, hear my prayer, and let my cry come to Thee" (Alleluia verse). "Hear my prayer" for the grace to love Thee, the Lord, with my whole heart, with my whole soul, with my whole mind, and my neighbor as myself (Gospel). Grant, O Lord, that we all may walk worthy of our vocation, in the unity of the Spirit, in humility, patience, and charity (Epistle). "All power is given to Me in heaven and in earth" (Mt 28:18), even over our hearts. Penetrate them with Thy Spirit, Thy purity, and Thy power, that they may overcome all things opposed to Thy working within us.

Prayer

Grant Thy people, we beseech Thee, O Lord, to shun the defilements of the devil and with pure minds to follow Thee, the only God. Through Christ our Lord. Amen.

Tuesday

Viewing the day of the Lord, the Last Judgment, the Church prays for the grace that we may withstand the temptations of the devil and may follow God alone with pure hearts.

"Your adversary, the devil, as a roaring lion, goeth about seeking whom he may devour" (1 Pt 5:8). "Our wrestling is not against flesh and blood; but against principalities and powers, against the rulers of the world of this darkness, against the spirits of wickedness in the high places" (Eph 6:12). The devil "was a murderer from the beginning, and he stood not in the truth;... for he is a liar and the father thereof" (Jn 8:44). However, his power over sinful mankind has been broken by Christ. "For this purpose the Son of God appeared, that He might destroy the works of the devil" (1 Jn 3:8). But with God's permission and subject to His power and will, the devil is still allowed to show us his power in different ways. He does so specially by means of temptations, troubling us with many evil desires. By stirring up our imagination he awakens in us wrong, sinful thoughts. By working on our lower nature he tries to seduce us to sin; he influences our exterior senses by inducing us to see, hear, feel, and experience sinful things. He also tries to harm us by inflicting misfortunes on us through the power granted him by God. To what extent the devil is able to exert his troubling and disturbing influence in this respect, the Church teaches us in her exorcisms and blessings and by her use of holy water.

Sometimes it happens that the devil is given the power to take possession of the bodies of men and to use them as if he himself were the soul of such bodies, or to interfere with a man's actions. We know of cases in the lives of saints when the devil persecuted and tortured them, trying to wean them from their faithfulness to God and Christ. Thus we are all exposed to the influence of the devil and are always in danger of being deceived by the father of lies and of being dragged into sin. How many have been deceived and misled, thus walking on the road that leads to eternal damnation! Not without reason the Church prays to God for us that He may give us the grace to withstand the temptations of the devil. She does not expect us to escape all temptations, but she prays that we may not be deceived by him and become unfaithful to God.

The only way that we can follow God is through holy love. "Thou shalt love the Lord thy God with thy whole heart, and with thy whole soul, and with thy whole mind. This is the greatest and the first commandment" (Gospel). This commandment contains all other commandments; it is the great duty that includes all other duties. Love is the highest expression of man's efforts. Whenever I love, I devote my whole being and all my faculties to the service and interests of him whom I love. We are obliged to love. "Thou shalt love the Lord, thy God." Nothing else matters; all other things are to be loved only in Him and for His sake. "Thou shalt love the Lord thy God with thy whole heart." A weakhearted charity does not satisfy the Lord; we have to love Him with our whole heart and with every part of our being, with our intellect and will, with our heart and all our affections and passions, with all the strength even of our bodies. We have to love God at every moment. He asks for a pure intention, an intention without any selfish consideration of our own profit, honor, or satisfaction. All things that life gives us we are obliged to use for God's interests and honor. That means we have to love God in all things for His sake; we have to seek Him and do everything for His honor. That is real piety, for it means seeking God alone with a pure intention. That we may obtain this grace, the Church this week asks for us the grace to follow God with pure hearts (Collect). It is our duty to seek God with a pure intention and with pure love.

Two masters are contending for us for time and eternity: Christ and Antichrist (the devil). With our free will we have to decide which one we will serve. On one side stands the Lord, who shall return some day for judgment; on the other side the devil tries to win us over to him. We must renounce the devil, as we did on the day of our baptism; we must cling to the Lord.

The more we seek God and live in accordance with His commandment of love, the safer we are against the temptations and persecutions of the devil. It is not necessary that we see the devil in everything and fear him; we should rather see the Lord in everything and love Him. When we seek only the love of God, we have the power to overcome Satan and his pomps. Therefore we should strive, first of all, to "follow after charity" (1 Cor 14:1). "Thou shalt love the Lord thy God." We secure the love of God through the Holy Eucharist, which is the sacrament of love, the fire which the Lord brought down from heaven to this earth (Lk 12:49), and with which He wishes to inflame our hearts that we learn to love the Father with the love of Jesus. The liturgy therefore leads us every morning to the Holy Eucharist, the source of divine love.

"Thou shalt love the Lord thy God with thy whole heart, and with thy whole soul, and with thy whole mind.... Thou shalt love thy neighbor as thyself. On these two commandments dependeth the whole law and the prophets" (Gospel). Do I love the Lord? Do I love Him in all things with an undivided love? Do I love all other things in Him and for His sake? Love is the measure of our sanctity.

Prayer

Grant Thy people, we beseech Thee, O Lord, to shun the defilements of the devil and with pure hearts to follow Thee, the only God. Through Christ our Lord. Amen.

Ember Wednesday in September

In southern countries the Ember days of autumn are days of thanksgiving for the completed harvest of fruits and grapes. The liturgy connects them with the solemn commemoration of the New Year's celebration of the Old Testament and the great Day of Atonement. These Ember days, therefore, have become days of thanksgiving and of atonement.

A day of atonement. The Gospel tells us of a father whose son was possessed by the devil. The father brings the poor boy to Jesus that He may cast out the evil spirit; Jesus complies with this request. "And when He was come into the house, His disciples secretly asked Him: why could not we cast him out? And He said to them: This kind can go out by nothing but by prayer and fasting." The liturgy presents here a picture of our soul. Although through Original Sin our soul had fallen into the power of the devil, we were rescued through the reception of baptism. Nevertheless the devil has not been left without any power over us; for in us lives the evil spirit of pride, lust, egoism, and worldliness. We ourselves have too often been ruled by evil spirits in our solicitude for our daily needs, in our seeking for earthly and temporal things. This day is a day of recollection, when these spirits must be banished again. We therefore go to the Eucharistic Lord, who can and will banish them, provided we pray and fast. "This kind can go out by nothing but by prayer and fasting." The Lord's words are an earnest admonition that this day is a day of atonement and of fasting, a day of contrition and repentance for the evil we have done, for the many acts of faithlessness and negligence.

A day of rejoicing in the Lord. The second lesson relates how Esdras read the law of Moses from morning until midday before the men and women and all those that could understand; and all the people listened attentively. Then Esdras spoke to the people: "This is a holy day to the Lord our God; do not mourn nor weep,... for the joy of the Lord is our strength." In the liturgy we ourselves are the people that attentively listen to the words of the law. This day is a day of holy reading, a day to be occupied with God, with the Gospel and its doctrines, with the joy of the Lord, when we meditate on His love shown to us in His incarnation, in the redemption on the cross, in the Eucharist, and in the innumerable graces given to us. We rejoice in the Lord and in His loving providence and guidance, recalling the grace of our having become children of God, of the indwelling of God in our souls, of having been destined to become heirs of heaven.

A day of thanksgiving for blessings of the spiritual and supernatural harvest which God has given us. An impressive picture of these blessings is given us by the prophet Amos in the first lesson: "Behold, the days come when the ploughman shall overtake the reaper, and the treader of grapes him that soweth seed, and the mountains shall drop sweetness and every hill shall be filled." Looking back over the past months since Pentecost, we think of the rich temporal blessings which God has given us; but even more precious are the spiritual blessings which we have received. We have been blessed in the daily fulfillment of our holy calling, either in the world or in the religious life: in our daily prayers and meditations, in the daily Mass and Communion, in the many inspirations of grace. We have received many graces through exterior and interior tribulations, through our purification and redemption from the spirit of the world and from pride and egoism.

Ember Wednesday is a day of recollection. We follow the intentions of the Church by abstaining from bodily food and also by abstaining from sin (second Collect). Strengthened anew, we leave the Ember days as the young man of the Gospel, fortified through the power of the Eucharistic Lord.

"I will meditate on Thy commandments, which I have loved exceedingly; and lift up my hands to Thy commandments, which I have loved" (Offertory). I am resigned to Thy holy will in all things. When we receive Holy Communion, the Church prays: "Eat fat meats and drink sweet wine, and send portions to them that have not prepared for themselves." The fruit of Holy Communion is that charity which spends itself by helping others and giving to others. "Be not sad, for the joy of the Lord is our strength" (Communion). "Blessed is the nation whose God is the Lord, the people whom the Lord hath chosen for His inheritance" (Gradual).

Prayer

O Lord, may the remedies of Thy mercy uphold our weakness, we beseech Thee; and in pity renew our strength, which by its nature is ever failing. Through Christ our Lord. Amen.

Thursday

A doctor of the law approached our Lord to tempt Him, asking: "Master, which is the great commandment of the law?" Jesus answered Him: "Thou shalt love the Lord thy God with thy whole heart, and with thy whole soul, and with thy whole mind. This is the greatest and the first commandment. And the second is like to this: Thou shalt love thy neighbor as thyself" (Gospel).

"Thou shalt love the Lord thy God." Not all love of God is perfect. Sometimes we love God because we have received some good from Him or hope to receive some good from Him. We love Him that we may escape eternal damnation and may be eternally happy with Him. Such love is imperfect because we love God first of all for our own sake and for the sake of our eternal salvation. Such love is naturally good and supernaturally effective, but it is not perfect love. Perfect love seeks God for His own sake without thinking of self. Through perfect love the soul is so attached to God that he who is joined to the Lord, is one spirit with Him (1 Cor 6:17). With perfect love God and the soul are so united that they become as it were one.

God penetrates the soul with the fullness of His light and His goodness. He gives Himself to the soul so completely that He communicates His life to it so that it shares His knowledge, His will, and His love, which become the object of the soul's blessedness. He belongs to the soul completely and it dwells in Him and loses itself in Him; it loves the beloved more than itself. It is elevated above its own nature and is so closely united to the beloved that it shares the nature of the beloved and receives a new life. "He who is joined to the Lord is one spirit" (1 Cor 6:17). This love is the essence of Christian perfection, the highest reach to which a soul can attain, the perfect fulfillment of all the commandments, the end and object of all our striving. This fact is true because through such a love we achieve perfect union with God and complete victory over sin, particularly over our besetting sin of self-love. Moreover, through such a love we conquer our inordinate desires and our attachment to all that is worldly and transitory. If we give God our love, then we have given Him all. If we give ourselves entirely up to Him, then He gives Himself entirely to us in the fullness of His love in time and eternity.

"With thy whole heart, and with thy whole soul, and with thy whole mind." God wills to have our whole love, otherwise He is not satisfied. He is jealous of the devotion of our spirit. "I am the Lord thy God, mighty, jealous" (Ex 20:5). We must subject our spirit to Him in humility, seeing as He sees, judging as He judges; we must subject our intellect to faith and accept all that the day may bring, as the dispensation of a kindly providence. God is jealous of the love of our heart, for He must be the center of all our wishes and movements; He wishes us to love Him above all else, and to subordinate the love we have for other creatures to our love for Him. God is jealous of our powers and our works. He desires that we put them at His service at all times, that we use them for fulfilling His holy will, and that we avoid all willful infidelity. God is jealous of our intentions and motives, and desires that we make Him the center of all our actions. We must never allow self to be our chief motive, but always God and God alone. God is jealous of our thoughts and desires, and in so far as it is humanly possible in our daily life, we must direct them all to Him, that even while we work they may center upon Him and give Him assurance of our love. He wishes to have our whole and undivided love.

"Thou art just, O Lord," when Thou dost demand of us all our love; all the rest that we can give to Thee is so little. "Vow ye, and pray to the Lord your God, all you that round about Him bring presents" (Communion). But all our vows and presents have value only in the degree in which they express our love.

"Thou shalt love the Lord thy God." Do we love Him with a perfect love that really seeks Him for His own sake? Does our love abhor every willful venial sin, every willful infidelity, every slight omission? Does our love seek for nothing but that which will give joy to God? Does it seek His holy will and good pleasure in all things? Is it prepared to accept all that He sends simply because He sends it? Does our love produce works and actions that express our devotion to God? Does our love also manifest charity towards our friends and enemies? "Follow after charity" (1 Cor 14:1).

Prayer

O God, Thou dost make all things a blessing for those who love Thee. Grant that our hearts may be bound to Thee by an immovable love, that no temptation may harm the life that Thou hast awakened in us. Through Christ our Lord. Amen.

Ember Friday in September

At the church of the Twelve Apostles we were absolved of our sins on Holy Thursday and received again into the community of the Church and reconciled with God. Today we assemble again at this stational church to do penance for the sins and infidelities of the last three months and to obtain pardon. We come with Magdalen, the sinner and penitent, to hear from Christ Himself the words: "Thy faith hath made thee safe; go in peace" (Gospel). "Let the heart of them rejoice that seek the Lord; seek ye the Lord and be strengthened" (Introit).

"Return, O Israel, to the Lord thy God; for thou hast fallen down by thy iniquity. Take with you words and return to the Lord and say to Him: Take away all iniquity and receive the good, and we will render the calves of our lips.... Neither will we say anymore: The works of our hands are our gods" (Epistle). Thus we are called to do penance with a contrite and humble heart and to confess to the Lord. Magdalen is an example for us. She comes to the Lord and throws herself at His feet. She washes His feet with tears, kisses them, and anoints them with the ointment she has brought with her. She comes with a heart full of shame, full of contrition, full of courage, in self-accusation and humility. She is determined to amend her life. The Lord responds to this contrition and love which He Himself through His mercy planted in the heart of the sinful woman. "Many sins are forgiven her, because she hath loved much; but to whom less is forgiven, he loveth less. And He said to her: Thy sins are forgiven thee" (Gospel). We, too, are sinners. We, too, are penitent. We come to Him in the Holy Sacrifice, when He appears in our midst. We confess to Him that we have sinned and have offended God. We accuse ourselves in the presence of His representative. We hear the consoling words: "I absolve thee of thy sins. Go in peace." We obtain pardon in proportion to our contrition and love. "To whom less is forgiven, he loveth less." But on the other hand, less is forgiven to Him who loves less.

"I will heal their breaches, I will love them freely; for My wrath is turned away from them. I will be as the dew; Israel shall spring as the lily, and his root shall shoot forth as that of Libanus. His branches shall spread, and his glory shall be as the olive tree, and his smell as that of Libanus.... They shall live upon wheat [the Eucharist], and they shall blossom as a vine" (Epistle). With great tenderness and charity the Lord accepts the contrite, penitent soul, as is clear from His reception of the sinner Magdalen. Simon the Pharisee is a witness against the sinner who entered and threw herself at the feet of Jesus. He says to himself, "This man, if He were a prophet, would know surely who and what manner of woman this is that toucheth Him, that she is a sinner" (Gospel). But the Lord has come in search of sinners that He may save them. He has no word of blame for Magdalen. He does not wait until He is begged before she is allowed to appear before Him. He draws her with the power of His love and grace, and He forgives her entire debt. She renounces the false gods she has served till now, and follows the Lord. She is the first of the holy women to see the risen Savior. She receives special graces and becomes a great saint, whom we may all admire and imitate.

The self-righteous Pharisee who has invited the Lord for dinner and the sinful, penitent, contrite Magdalen present a striking contrast. The Pharisee is a type of the Jewish people, while Magdalen represents those converted from the Gentiles. In the mind of the liturgy, we are the contrite Magdalen, for the first step to grace and holiness is penitence.

We give expression to our repentance when we fast on Ember days. We sanctify our fast through the celebration of the Eucharistic sacrifice. At this sacrifice we unite our fasting and penance to the suffering and death of the Lord, and we beseech God that He may be pleased with the sacrifice of our fast and make us worthy of His grace, which we expect from the Mass. This grace will lead us to the promises of eternal life (Secreta).

A special fruit of repentance is the reception of the Holy Eucharist. "Remove from me reproach and contempt" (Communion). How else may I hope to participate worthily in the holy Sacrament of Thy body and blood? At Holy Communion we receive the power to seek "out Thy commandments, O Lord, for Thy testimonies are my meditation" (Communion). The final fruits of penitence are "blessings yet more excellent" (Postcommunion); that is, our union with the Lord in heaven, where He will take us up to share His joy, His light, His glorified life, forever.

Today we willingly undertake to do penance and propose for ourselves a life of self-denial so that we may participate in the fruits of penitence. With Magdalen we forsake a life of sin for one of friendship with the Lord; as friends we are changed into saints and become heirs of the joy of the Lord.

Prayer

Grant, O almighty God, we beseech Thee, that by our devout keeping of the holy observances year by year, we may in body and in soul give pleasure to Thee. Through Christ our Lord. Amen.

Ember Saturday in September

At Matins today the liturgy connects the celebration of the Feast of Atonement (first lesson) with that of the Feast of Tabernacles (second lesson). The Feast of Atonement, celebrated by the Israelites for seven days, was a feast of thanksgiving for the guidance which God had given His people during the forty years of wandering in the desert. Thus our Ember days are marked as days of penance and thanksgiving.

Christ is the "high priest of the good things to come" (Epistle). The Feast of Atonement in the Old Testament was only a type and a symbol. The high priest entered the holy of holies to sprinkle the blood of the slaughtered animals on the Ark of the Covenant. But this ceremony could not obtain forgiveness of sins. It is different with Christ, our high priest. Through His death on the cross He has won for us an eternal inheritance, and at His Ascension He goes into the heavenly holy of holies, not with the blood of animals, but with His own precious blood which He shed for us and by which He cleansed us of our sins and reconciled us with God (Epistle). Although the Feast of Atonement in the Old Testament is only a figure, a feeble symbol of what is given to us in the New Testament, the admonition given to the people of Israel applies to us as well. "The tenth day of this month shall be the day of atonement. It shall be most solemn.... You shall afflict your souls,... because it is a day of propitiation, that the Lord your God may be merciful unto you. Every soul that is not afflicted on this day, shall perish from among His people" (first lesson). How much more important to us are the Ember days, days of penance, on which we pray, afflict ourselves, fast, and abstain in order to obtain pardon! "Forgive us our sins, O Lord.... Help us, O God our Savior, and for the glory of Thy name, O Lord, deliver us" (first Gradual).

"A certain man had a fig tree planted in his vineyard, and he came seeking fruit on it, and found none; and he said to the dresser of the vineyard: . . . Cut it down, therefore; why cumbereth it the ground? But he answering, said to him: Lord, let it alone this year also, until I dig about it and dung it; and if happily it bear fruit. . . . And He was teaching in their synagogue on the Sabbath; and behold there was a woman who had a spirit of infirmity eighteen years, and she was bowed together, neither could she look upwards at all. Whom when Jesus saw, He called her unto Him and said to her: Woman, thou art delivered from thy infirmity. And He laid His hands upon her, and immediately she was made straight and glorified God" (Gospel). This is a day of atonement, a day of forgiveness, a day of grace, a day of help from the Lord, who comes to us in the Mass. We are the unfruitful fig tree, the bowed woman who could not look upwards.

We are approaching the end of the ecclesiastical year. Already the Lord is preparing for His return at the moment of our death and again at the end of the world. Still we have not borne the fruit which the Lord expects of us. The soil is not at fault, for we are planted in the vineyard of the Lord, His holy Church. Light and air — counsel, admonitions, graces — are not wanting. Because the conditions are so favorable the Lord returns so often, for He hopes to find fruit sometime. But we have not made a good use of grace, and thus we have remained an unfruitful fig tree. We are like the bowed woman of the Gospel, totally absorbed in perishable and transitory things, unable to stand erect and lift our thoughts to God. In spite of our baptism, in spite of our vocation, in spite of the fact that we are heirs of God, in spite of our prayers, our readings, our meditations, in spite of our religious enclosure, we remain unfruitful. "Therefore if you be risen with Christ [through baptism], seek the things that are above, where Christ is, sitting at the right hand of God. Mind the things that are above, not the things that are upon the earth" (Col 3:1 f.). Indeed we are the bowed woman. What remains for us but to do penance and return to Jesus?

This day is a day of grace. Christ comes into our midst at Mass. He pities us and He begs the Lord of the vineyard, the Father: "Let it alone this year also, until I dig about it and dung it; and if happily it bear fruit." With this prayer He goes to the Father at the Holy Sacrifice. But even this is not enough. With pity He calls the sick woman (us) to Him. "Woman, thou art delivered from thy infirmity." In the sacrament of penance and in the Eucharist He lays His hands upon us and lifts us up. He gives us His Spirit; we become strong enough to lay aside all worldliness, to break our chains and live for God. We thank Him for this grace which He has given us and we glorify God.

"In the seventh month shall you celebrate this feast, as I made the children of Israel to dwell in tabernacles when I brought them out of the land of Egypt. I am the Lord your God" (Communion). In the mind of the liturgy the celebration of this day is the preparation for the glory of the life to come. God has destined us for the repose of eternal life through the power of the Holy Eucharist. There we shall glorify God and celebrate the feast of gratitude eternally.

"These, then, are the things which you shall do: Speak ye the truth every one to his neighbor, . . . and let none of you imagine evil in your hearts against his friend. Only love ye truth and peace" (fourth lesson).

Prayer

Almighty and everlasting God, who by means of wholesome abstinence dost heal us in soul and in body; we humbly beseech Thy majesty that appeased by the fervent devotion of those who fast, Thou wouldst grant us help now and in the time to come. Through Christ our Lord. Amen.

Eighteenth Sunday after Pentecost

The Mass

Ideas that the last two Sundays merely suggested are now brought out in bold relief. After the Ember days of autumn, the end of the Church year approaches. The approaching end of the year is apparent even in nature, for fall is here and life is dying. Christ prepares to return on the last day, and the liturgy longs for redemption, for the return of the spouse who at last will lead her home to the peace of heaven.

The eighteenth Sunday after Pentecost has quite a different character from those that precede. It must be studied in the light of the celebration of the preceding Ember Saturday and the associated ordination of priests. In ancient Rome the Christian community marched to St. Peter's late in the evening of that Saturday for the night service, during which the pope performed the ordination rite. Early in the morning the newly ordained priests were taken to the various churches of the city to celebrate their first Masses. Thus the eighteenth Sunday was originally without its proper liturgy. The present Mass for this day bears the character of a Mass of ordination, however thoroughly it may be preoccupied with thoughts of Christ's return.

At the Introit we direct our eyes to the newly ordained priests entering the church. They rejoice at their first sacrifice: "I rejoiced at the things that were said to me: We shall go into the house of the Lord." We pray for grace and for the blessing of God on the newly ordained priests. "Give peace, O Lord, to them that patiently wait for Thee [the newly ordained priests] that Thy prophets [the priests] may be found faithful" (Introit). At the same time we think of the house of eternal glory: "Give peace [final salvation, eternal blessing], O Lord, to them that patiently wait for Thee.... I rejoiced at the things that were said to me: We shall go into the house of the Lord," into heaven. This Introit is a wonderful pilgrim song placed in the mouth of Christians going to heaven. We sing the Kyrie for the new priests and for ourselves, pilgrims on the way to heaven. In the Collect we pray: "Let the operation of Thy mercy direct our hearts," for our salvation depends primarily on the mercy of God.

In the Epistle we look back gratefully to what we have received during the ecclesiastical year. "I give thanks to my God always for you, for the grace of God that is given you in Jesus Christ, that in all things you are made rich in Him,... so that nothing is wanting to you in any grace." Then we are instructed to look forward, "waiting for the manifestation of our Lord Jesus Christ, who also will confirm you unto the end without crime, in the day of the coming of our Lord Jesus Christ." This "manifestation of our Lord Jesus Christ" is made daily at the Mass, again at the hour of our death, and finally on Judgment Day. The words of the Gradual apply to this threefold manifestation of the Lord. "I rejoiced at the things that were said to me: We shall go into the house of the Lord." In the Alleluia we greet the Lord in His glory as He will appear at that day of His last manifestation. Now at Mass He manifests Himself to us as He did to the man sick of palsy, as the gentle physician of soul and body. He tells us: "Be of good heart, son, thy sins are forgiven thee.... Arise, take up thy bed" (Gospel).

We ourselves, who celebrate the sacrifice today, are the sick man of the Gospel. At the Sacrifice of the Mass we are brought to Christ through the priest. He sends us His salvation and His grace, an anticipation of the perfect salvation of the world to come. Through the celebration of the Mass we are healed and receive the power to arise and go into the house of the Lord, into heaven. Thankfully we answer the Gospel with our Credo: I believe in eternal life.

At the Offertory Moses appears at the altar offering upon it holocausts and victims — a figure of Christ, who now celebrates His sacrifice at the altar for the remission of all sins. Now we make our offering. We unite ourselves with the sacrificing Christ on our altar, and thus we crucify the old man of sin; during the sacrifice we die to sin and to the world and all its vanities. The more closely we unite ourselves to the sacrifice of Christ, the more perfectly He shares His grace with us and the more fully He makes "us partakers of the one supreme Godhead" (Secreta). Thus we the more surely "come into His courts" (Communion) in the kingdom of His glory. "I rejoiced at the things that were said to me: We shall go into the house of the Lord."

Meditation

"Give peace, O Lord" (Introit). Give us that perfect redemption which the Savior has merited for us, and the eternal blessing which is promised in the Old Testament, in the Gospels, and in the writings of the apostles. "I rejoiced at the things that were said to me: We shall go into the house of the Lord" (Introit), into our eternal home. We, the baptized, await eternal life.

"I give thanks to my God always for you, for the grace of God that is given you in Christ Jesus" (Epistle). This Sunday we look with grateful hearts at our life and at the ecclesiastical year, which is now drawing to its close. We remember the many great graces which the Lord has given us during our life and during the many weeks which have passed since the beginning of the Church year. We confess "that in all things you are made rich in Him," Jesus Christ (Epistle). Although we are poor and sinful, He has generously given us blessings and graces. What would we be without Him, without our union with Him as the head of the Church? Through Him we share in the divine intellect and life, being heirs of God, and receive an unbroken series of graces from the Father, Son, and Holy Ghost. "Nothing is wanting to you in any grace" (Epistle). Should we not therefore rejoice? We are "waiting for the manifestation of our Lord, Jesus Christ" (Epistle), for His return personally to us at the hour of our death, and to the whole of mankind on the last day. The Christian awaits His return in eager expectation of what is to come. He sees beyond the present day and beyond the fleeting events of tomorrow, and looks to eternity, "waiting for the manifestation of our Lord," just as the virgins in our Lord's parable await the bridegroom (Mt 25:1 ff.). Meanwhile "in all things you are made rich in Him, . . . who also will confirm you unto the end without crime, in the day of the coming of our Lord Jesus Christ" (Epistle). Thus the Church will be without crime when the Lord comes, entirely spotless for her spouse, clothed in the beauty of the graces and virtues of her spouse. Thus she desires and expects us to be when the Lord appears, now in the Sacrifice of the Mass and later on at the hour of our death and on the last day. The Lord strengthens us that we may endure until the end, clean, without sin, adorned with graces, in the garment of the bridegroom. We possess all grace and continual help from the Lord. Have we not cause enough to give thanks?

The beginning and source of all our hopes of salvation lies in the baptism which we have received. It is the greatest event in our life. The Gospel account of the man sick with the palsy reminds us of our baptism. When Jesus had come to Capharnaum, "they brought Him one sick of the palsy." Jesus performs a twofold favor for him. First He forgives him his sins: "Thy sins are forgiven thee." Then He heals him of his palsy: "Arise, take up thy bed and go into thy house." And the sick man got up and went home. A similar cure was wrought in us. The Lord has healed us from the sickness of Original Sin through baptism. Through the sacrament of penance and the Holy Eucharist, He removes our personal sins and detaches us from the world, freeing us from the flesh and from evil and indifference. To heal us more perfectly and to free us from innate weakness, the Lord comes to us in the Mass and in Holy Communion. He will free us from the consequences of sin when we are eventually raised from the dead. Then He will command us: "Go into thy house," our heavenly home, where we shall rejoice with Him for all eternity.

The liturgy rejoices: "I rejoiced at the things that were said to me: We shall go into the house of the Lord." At baptism, in the sacrament of penance, and especially in the celebration of Mass and the reception of Holy Communion we are healed of our sicknesses and the seed of the eternal resurrection is planted in our body. This is our hope; this is what the revelation of the Lord Jesus will bring: final salvation, eternal life for soul and body. "He arose and went into his house"; that is the resurrection of the body and life everlasting in the home of the Father. "I rejoiced at the things that were said to me: We shall go into the house of the Lord," into heaven.

This is a day of thanksgiving, a day on which we seek heaven. We go into the house of the Lord. "Bring up sacrifices," the Communion admonishes us. Celebrate the Holy Sacrifice; "come into His courts." He Himself comes into His house, the Christian house of worship. "Adore ye the Lord in His holy court," which He has built upon our altars. However, the material house of God is only a symbol and an antechamber. Through the power of the Holy Sacrifice and Holy Communion the way is opened for us into the house of heaven. "I rejoiced at the things that were said to me: We shall go [through the power of the Holy Sacrifice and Holy Communion] into the house of the Lord."

Although by ourselves we are poor and helpless, although, like the man of the Gospel, we are sick with the palsy, we have become rich through Christ by being united to Him through baptism. "Nothing is wanting to you in any grace" for reaching your goal, your eternal home. "Take up thy bed and go into thy house."

Prayer

Let the operation of Thy mercy, we beseech Thee, O Lord, direct our hearts; for without Thee we cannot please Thee. Through Christ our Lord. Amen.

Monday

Returning from His mission, the Lord has just reached the city of Capharnaum in Galilee. He is teaching in the house of Simon Peter, and He is surrounded by a dense crowd. The house is crowded even to the door. "They brought Him one sick of the palsy." Four men carry him, but they cannot bring him into the house because of the dense crowd. Their confidence in the power and goodness of the Lord and their love for the sick man is so great that they lower him through an opening in the roof (Mk 2:4). Jesus, seeing their faith, says to the man sick of the palsy, "Son, thy sins are forgiven thee." He also heals him of the bodily sickness and commands him, "Arise, take up thy bed and go into thy house" (Gospel).

"Be of good heart, son, thy sins are forgiven thee." Gratefully we recall the moment when we also were brought to the Savior at the time of our baptism. We were carried into the house of Peter, the Church. Our faithful parents sought to provide for the welfare of our soul. When we received baptism, the Lord said to us: "Son, thy sins are forgiven thee. Arise and go into thy house," to thy eternal home; thou art a child of God, an heir of God and coheir with Christ. With gratitude we recall that hour of grace, when, after we had lost the grace of baptism, we returned to the Lord, to the house of Peter, the Church. We had sinned and lost the divine life which was given to us at baptism. We were as one sick of the palsy. We came to the Lord in the person of His priest, and Jesus saw our faith, our contrition, our confidence, our desire to regain divine life. "Be of good heart, son, thy sins are forgiven thee. Arise and go into thy house." The door of our eternal home is open again.

We are as one sick of the palsy. Who can give us new and vigorous life again? Only Jesus the Lord, and only in the house of Simon Peter, the Church. The sacraments of baptism and penance belong to the Church. In His Church He gives peace and forgiveness, reconciliation with God, and grace to those who follow Him, who believe in Him, who believe and glorify God, "who had given such power to men," the power to forgive sins on earth (Gospel). He grants forgiveness and grace to those who believe that He has given this power to His apostles and their successors, the bishops and priests. "All power is given to Me in heaven and in earth. Going, therefore, teach ye all nations, baptizing them" (Mt 28:18 f.). "Whose sins you shall forgive, they are forgiven them" (Jn 20:23). "Son, thy sins are forgiven thee. Arise, take up thy bed and go into thy house." Eternal life awaits you. "And he arose and went into his house" (Gospel). The way of Christian life is to arise from the palsy of sin and proceed to our heavenly home. At baptism we promised to renounce Satan, sin, and the world. We renounce them again in the sacrament of penance. We must arise, free ourselves from lust and passion, and break the bonds of evil habits; we must lift ourselves up from the mire of self-love and of sloth as we vowed to do at our baptism.

"I believe in God, the Father Almighty, . . . and in Jesus Christ, His only Son. . . . I believe in the Holy Ghost, the holy Catholic Church." I subject myself to God, to His commandments, to His Church. I wish to be filled and guided by the Spirit of God, the Holy Ghost. I live for God, I go to God.

What we have already vowed at our baptism we confirm every time we receive the sacrament of penance. We confirm all this especially when we offer the Holy Sacrifice of the Mass. We arise, cast aside everything that is displeasing to God, and offer ourselves, together with our sacrificing Lord, in perfect dedication to God.

We give thanks; we rejoice, for we have been assured that we shall go into the house of the Lord, our eternal home. Here, in the house of the Lord made of stones, we await the blessed arrival of the Lord in the celebration of the Eucharistic Sacrifice and in the reception of Holy Communion; for then "Thou dost make us partakers of the one supreme Godhead" (Secreta). Here He forgives us our sins and our faults, and He fills us with His own Spirit and life. Through the power of the food which He offers us we shall be able to make our way to our eternal home.

The sick man begs the Lord for bodily health; but first the Lord heals his soul. The bodily disease is only of secondary importance; it is less harmful to him than the disease of the soul.

First provision must be made for the soul and its eternal life. "For what doth it profit a man if he gain the whole world and suffer the loss of his own soul" (Mt 16:26).

Prayer

Let the operation of Thy mercy, we beseech Thee, O Lord, direct our hearts; for without Thee we cannot please Thee. Through Christ our Lord. Amen.

Tuesday

"Behold the bridegroom cometh, go ye forth to meet him" (Mt 25:6). As if the Church heard this call today, she is solicitous that her children be ready and prepared: rich in grace, in virtue, in the knowledge of the Christian life, and in good works. She wants to obtain the grace to be steadfast and faithful to the end; she wishes us to be perfect and without blemish at the arrival of our Lord Jesus Christ, at the hour of our death and at the Last Judgment.

The Apostle sees the young community of Corinth producing abundant fruit. He gives thanks for the grace which his new converts in Christ Jesus have received. "In all things you are made rich in Him, in all utterance and in all knowledge," in the praiseworthy achievement of Christian doctrine and in the deeper comprehension of it. "As the testimony of Christ was confirmed in you": the testimony which the Apostle has given for Christ in Corinth, his sermons and his efforts, have struck deep roots and promise a good crop. "So that nothing is wanting to you in any grace": the grace of Christ has been fruitful in the Church of Corinth and in each one of us. What else is wanting? Only the manifestation of the glory of the Lord, His second coming, which the Church of Corinth awaits; and God will "confirm you unto the end without crime in the day of the coming of our Lord Jesus Christ" (Epistle). The young Christian community at Corinth is ripe for the arrival of the Lord, rich in grace, in knowledge, in virtue, and in good works. The liturgy holds up this community as an example. It desires that we be "without crime in the day of the coming of our Lord Jesus Christ." It urges us to compare the grace and virtues of the young Christian community of Corinth with our Christian communities and families today and with our own personal lives.

"In all utterance and in all knowledge." The Apostle does not fail to point out how he has reaped such rich fruit from his Corinthians. He had preached a year and half at Corinth, but they are rich "in all things." They possess the whole apostolic doctrine; the doctrines and maxims of the gospel are their laws and principles. They adhere to the doctrine of Christ; they look upon the example of Christ; they walk in the light of Christ. Therefore they are rich in fruit, not merely external fruit, but also "in all knowledge." They imbibed all the Christian truth; they take the pains and the time to comprehend spiritually all that they have heard, and they are so convinced of what they believe that they carry it out practically in their lives. They live an interior life in the spirit of faith. Thus they gain a new and truly Christian outlook on life and turn away from the heathen and worldly point of view. They live as they swore to do at baptism: "I renounce the devil and all his works and pomps." A splendid example for our Christians of the twentieth century!

"Nothing is wanting to you in any grace" (Epistle). Must not we also bear rich fruit? "I... have appointed you that you should go and should bring forth fruit; and your fruit should remain" for eternal life (Jn 15:16). The day of the return of the Lord is near; He warns us earnestly: "Give an account of thy stewardship" (Lk 16:2). Now is the time of grace. At the Mass the Lord anticipates His eventual return. He comes to us now as the Savior: "Be of good heart, son, thy sins are forgiven thee" (Gospel).

At Holy Communion the Lord perfects His redemptive work in us. We come to Him with the faith and confidence of the man sick with the palsy. He touches us with His life-giving flesh and blood. "Arise" to a new and better life, "and go into thy house" (Gospel). Our place is in heaven above. The Lord returns daily at Communion to prepare us for His final coming at our death and on the last day.

Prayer

Let the operation of Thy mercy, we beseech Thee, O Lord, direct our hearts; for without Thee we cannot please Thee. Through Christ our Lord. Amen.

Wednesday

The Apostle admits with great satisfaction: "Nothing is wanting to you in any grace" (Epistle). There are extraordinary spiritual gifts, the so-called charisms, which were found in abundance in the young community of Corinth (1 Cor 12). There are also certain ordinary gifts of God which are necessary and useful for all of us, the so-called spiritual gifts and spiritual consolations, which are given to us as precious helps on the way to our eternal home. "You are made rich in Him" (Epistle).

"Nothing is wanting to you in any grace." There is no lack of anything in God. He gives the necessary help and grace to each of us according to his needs. He gives us, moreover, many consolations and favors of sensible devotion as an incentive and support to our efforts. These are all graces of God, signs of His love for us, by which we receive a deeper knowledge of Him and of Christ. They give us the strength to overcome the devil and all worldliness. They lighten the hardships of our profession and the bitterness of our difficulties. They enliven our charity, strengthen us in temptation, give us confidence in God, increase our faith, and make us a consolation to our brethren. Should we not give thanks for these graces also?

The fruits of the spiritual gifts are great and useful. They calm our distracted and worldly thoughts and reveal a wealth and plentitude of divine gifts which we had not heretofore conceived. Acts of virtue are no longer painful and difficult, but come spontaneously and easily. Conquering our temptations, external and internal, no longer presents any great difficulty. On the contrary we overcome them with an ease and assurance unknown before. The conflict between the flesh and the spirit suddenly subsides. We feel the results: The spirit again regains the mastery over the rebellious movements of fallen nature. "In all things you are made rich."

With grateful hearts we confess, "In all things you are made rich." Nothing is wanting to us. The Lord has left nothing undone. He sowed His seed with generous hands. If the seed has fallen upon good ground, it should yield fruit a hundredfold (Lk 8:8).

"The Gentiles shall fear Thy name, O Lord" (Alleluia verse). We, the Gentiles, "are made rich … in all things." The Lord has given us the riches of His graces through His divine mercy.

"Nothing is wanting to you in any grace" (Epistle). So with confidence we await the return of the Lord. He "will confirm you unto the end" (Epistle). He will crown His graces and consolations with the grace of final perseverance. We shall lose what we have, but we expect with confidence that He "will confirm [us] unto the end." We are joyfully confident that "we shall go into the house of the Lord" (Introit). Heaven is open to us.

"Give peace, O Lord, to them that patiently wait for Thee" (Introit), to us who are waiting for Thy return now in the celebration of the Mass and at Holy Communion, and likewise at the hour of our death. "I rejoiced at the things that were said to me: We shall go into the house of the Lord" (Introit).

Prayer

Let the operation of Thy mercy, we beseech Thee, O Lord, direct our hearts; for without Thee we cannot please Thee. Through Christ our Lord. Amen.

Thursday

"Nothing is wanting to you in any grace, waiting for the manifestation of our Lord Jesus Christ. Who also will confirm you unto the end without crime, in the day of the coming of our Lord Jesus Christ" (Epistle). The grace of God is given to us in Christ. God will also complete what He has commenced in us; He will give us the greatest of all graces, the grace of perseverance until the end, the grace to enter eternal life through a happy death. "I rejoiced at the things that were said to me: We shall go into the house of the Lord" (Introit).

He "will confirm you unto the end" (Epistle). We have received rich graces from God. The ecclesiastical year that is slowly drawing to an end has been a year of blessing to us. May we expect further graces from God in spite of our abuse, neglect, and misuse of many graces? May we count on perseverance unto the end? Must not the word of the Apostle fill us with fear: "He that thinketh himself to stand, let him take heed lest he fall" (1 Cor 10:12)? And again, "I will have mercy on whom I will have mercy, and I will show mercy to whom I will show mercy. So then it is not of him that willeth nor of him that runneth, but of God that showeth mercy" (Rom 9:15 f.). It would be futile to try to learn whether or not we should persevere without crime unto the end. We need not worry about the future; let us provide for the present. We cannot merit the grace of final perseverance, although we may with good reason expect that God in His mercy will give us the grace of counsel, which will lead us safely through the temptations of life. The more faithfully we cooperate with grace, the more assurance we have that God will give us more effectual graces and helps. Do we, then, doubt His providence? Did not the Son of God die for each one of us? Would not He be willing to relive His difficult life on earth and suffer His passion once more for us only to save us? "He that spared not even His own Son, but delivered Him up for us all, how hath He not also, with Him, given us all things?" (Rom 8:32.) We may well believe: "He will confirm you unto the end." "For I know whom I have believed" (2 Tm 1:12). "Who will have all men to be saved" (1 Tm 2:4).

"But he that shall persevere unto the end, he shall be saved" (Mt 10:22). Perseverance to the end is an unmeritable grace of God. However, we can and we must work for this most precious of all God's graces. The first means for obtaining the grace of final perseverance is continual prayer for this favor. We pray for it in the Our Father: "Deliver us from evil," from an unhappy death. It is as if we prayed, "Give us the grace to continue in grace unto the end." The second means is the faithful performance of our religious duties, especially the devout assistance at Mass. A life of prayer makes our days rich and full; it gives us strength and light, and keeps us well disposed; therefore it is of the essence of perseverance. If we perform our religious duties irregularly and unfaithfully, then our spiritual stability and perseverance are in grave danger. Another means for obtaining the grace of perseverance is the practice of zeal and earnestness in overcoming sin, even the slightest sin and infidelity. To secure perseverance we have to avoid the occasions of sin and keep a close watch over our thoughts and senses. A fourth means for obtaining perseverance is the regular and devout use of the sacraments of penance and Holy Communion. Our interior development, our progress in virtue, our eternal salvation, and our perseverance to the end is conditioned to a great extent by our use of the sacraments, which are a source of grace.

"Nothing is wanting to you in any grace.... [Christ] will confirm you unto the end." "For I desire not the death of him that dieth, saith the Lord God, return ye and live" (Ez 18:32). We believe in His mercy and in His charity. "And Jesus, seeing their faith, said to the man sick of the palsy: Be of good heart, son, thy sins are forgiven thee" (Gospel). Will He act differently with us if we believe in Him, trust Him, and perform our duties faithfully?

"Give peace, O Lord, to them that patiently wait for Thee" (Introit). Give them the grace of a happy death, the grace of perseverance. We cannot merit it even though we are most faithful. We can obtain it only from Thy mercy. We "wait for Thee" and Thy grace.

The blessed arrival of the Lord at Mass and Holy Communion is the sign of His merciful return at the hour of our death. This is His promise: He "will confirm you unto the end" (Epistle). "Bring up sacrifices and come into His courts" (Communion) at the celebration of the Mass, and come into the dwellings of heaven. "I rejoiced at the things that were said to me: We shall go into the house of the Lord."

Prayer

Let the operation of Thy mercy, we beseech Thee, O Lord, direct our hearts; for without Thee we cannot please Thee. Through Christ our Lord. Amen.

Friday

"Waiting for the manifestation of our Lord Jesus Christ" (Epistle). Earnestly we pray: "Give peace, O Lord, to them that wait for Thee" (Introit); give them the peace of eternal life in God. "I rejoiced at the things that were said to me: We shall go into the house of the Lord," our heavenly home (Introit).

"For the fashion of this world passeth away" (1 Cor 7:31). "Behold, Thou hast made my days measurable and my substance is as nothing before Thee. And indeed all things are vanity, every man living. Surely man passeth as an image; yea and he is disquieted in vain. He storeth up and he knoweth not for whom he shall gather these things" (Ps 38:6 ff.). Everything that surrounds us and pleases and delights us is like a shadow that passes or a wisp of smoke that disappears.

Even the longest life passes quickly and, when gone, is like a dream in the night. All that is dear to us — our family, our home, pleasure, knowledge, talent — all is transitory: our work, our profession, our business, the body which we pampered, even our sufferings, our pains, and our miseries all pass and leave us with empty hands. "All flesh is grass and all the glory thereof as the flower of the field. The grass is withered and the flower is fallen because the spirit of the Lord hath blown upon it. Indeed the people is grass. The grass is withered" (Is 40:6 ff.). Every day before our very eyes we see that all that surrounds us becomes dust; death changes all, death disrupts all and tramples all underfoot. All that surrounds us vanishes and perishes. We ourselves shall vanish like smoke. "For we have not here a lasting city, but we seek one that is to come" (Heb 13:14). "Remember man, that thou are dust, and to dust thou shalt return."

"Waiting for the manifestation of our Lord Jesus Christ." We Christians labor for that which is eternal. We know that "whosoever will save his life, shall lose it; and whosoever shall lose his life for My sake and the gospel, shall save it. For what shall it profit a man if he gain the whole world and suffer the loss of his soul? Or what shall a man give in exchange for his soul?" (Mk 8:35 ff.) We know that "every one that hath left house, or brethren, or sisters, or father, or mother, or wife, or children, or lands for My name's sake, shall receive a hundredfold, and shall possess life everlasting" (Mt 19:29). We know the reply of the Lord to the rich young man: "If thou wilt be perfect, go sell what thou hast and give to the poor, and thou shalt have treasure in heaven" (Mt 19:21). "Lay not up to yourselves treasures on earth, where the rust and the moth consume and where thieves break through and steal" (Mt 6:19). "The time is short; it remaineth that they also who have wives be as if they had none; and they that weep, as though they wept not; and they that rejoice, as if they rejoiced not; and they that buy, as though they possessed not; and they that use this world, as if they used it not. For the fashion of this world passeth away" (1 Cor 7:29 ff.). We are risen with Christ through baptism. Therefore we "seek the things that are above, where Christ is sitting at the right hand of God; mind the things that are above, not the things that are upon the earth" (Col 3:1 f.). In this way we await the manifestation of the Lord.

When we recall the imminent return of the Lord at our death, we understand the beatitudes of Christ's sermon upon the mount. "Blessed are the poor in spirit.... Blessed are the meek.... Blessed are they that mourn.... Blessed are they that hunger and thirst after justice.... Blessed are the clean of heart, for they shall see God" (Mt 5:3 ff.). Their thoughts dwell on eternal life, which they look forward to. That is Christian wisdom. They are "waiting for the manifestation of our Lord Jesus Christ." We Christians do not fear the day of our Lord's coming; rather we rejoice and long for it. Men who have clung to the nothingness of this world fear the loss of that nothingness; there remains for them only a great, eternal emptiness. But we, since we are Christians, have long since learned to value only what is divine and eternal. We have endeavored to make the seed of eternal life spring to life in a handful of loam taken from the earth. When the Lord returns and calls us, our work will bear fruit. Should we therefore not rejoice? "I rejoiced at the things that were said to me: We shall go into the house of the Lord." We may die, but we shall go home to heaven.

"Bring up sacrifices and come into His courts" (Communion). The Christian finds the way to his eternal home in the celebration of the Mass. From the Sacrifice we receive the necessary grace by which we shall merit eternal life.

PRAYER

Let the operation of Thy mercy, we beseech Thee, O Lord, direct our hearts; for without Thee we cannot please Thee. Through Christ our Lord. Amen.

Saturday

We are "waiting for the manifestation of our Lord Jesus Christ" (Epistle). "In the day of the coming of our Lord Jesus Christ" we should be "without crime," without faults (Epistle). We must be healed of all our infirmities, as was the man sick of the palsy, who was healed by the Lord in soul and body (Gospel).

We must be "without crime" in regard to our soul when the Lord comes to us at the hour of our death. For this end "in all things [we] are made rich in Him" when we receive baptism, when we partake of the Holy Sacrifice, when we receive the graces of the sacraments of confirmation and of penance, when we receive the gifts that the Lord incessantly showers on our soul. He "also will confirm you unto the end, without crime, in the day of the coming of our Lord Jesus Christ." "Behold I stand at the gate and knock. If any man shall hear My voice and open to Me the door, I will come in to him, and will sup with him, and he with Me" (Apoc 3:20). As long as we are here on earth, He overwhelms all uncleanness and imperfection in us when He enters our soul. If we open to Him, He enters with all the riches of His graces, and gives them to us. He establishes His kingdom in us and helps us live His clean and holy life. In holy unity He sups with us and we sup with Him one and the same food, the food of God Himself, the divine life which we possess with Him. This life will become strong in us and rule us. It does not tolerate sin, false principles, conscious imperfections, or disorderly inclinations. If there be anything of selfishness or willfulness of thought or deed, the Lord destroys it through the painful but necessary tribulations which He sends us. Thus we will be "without crime in the day of the coming of our Lord," thanks to the powerful efficacy of His grace. We must not let Him knock in vain; we must let Him enter and do with us as He likes; we must let Him work His will in us. "Whosoever abideth in Him, sinneth not" (1 Jn 3:6).

We must be "without crime" in regard to the body. "In the day of the coming of our Lord Jesus Christ," at His return in power and glory, He will repeat in our body the wonder He worked on the man sick of the palsy. "Arise ... and go into thy house." This is not only a cure, but an awakening to life. "It is sown in corruption, it shall rise in incorruption. It is sown in dishonor, it shall rise in glory. It is sown in weakness, it shall rise in power. It is sown a natural body, it shall rise a spiritual body.... Therefore as we have borne the image of the earthly, let us bear also the image of the heavenly.... For this corruptible must put on incorruption; and this mortal must put on immortality" (1 Cor 15:42 ff.). The Lord "will reform the body of our lowness, made like to the body of His glory" (Phil 3:21). "When Christ shall appear [on the last day], who is your life, then you also shall appear with Him in glory" (Col 3:4). "I believe in the resurrection of the body and life everlasting."

"Nothing is wanting to you in any grace, waiting for the manifestation of our Lord Jesus Christ" (Epistle). "Give peace, O Lord, to them that patiently wait for Thee"; give also grace, holiness of soul, and the blessed resurrection of the body. "Hear the prayers of Thy servant and of Thy people Israel," the holy Church (Introit).

We give thanks to the Lord for holiness of soul as well as for the resurrection of the body; we give thanks to the Lord who today appears at the celebration of the Eucharistic Sacrifice. He cleanses us of our sins and fills us with His life. Here He sows the seed of a blessed resurrection in our body. "He that eateth My flesh and drinketh My blood, hath everlasting life; and I will raise him up in the last day.... He that eateth My flesh and drinketh My blood, abideth in Me and I in him" (Jn 6:55, 57).

Prayer

Let the operation of Thy mercy, we beseech Thee, O Lord, direct our hearts; for without Thee we cannot please Thee. Through Christ our Lord. Amen.

Nineteenth Sunday after Pentecost

The Mass

"Give peace, O Lord, to them that patiently wait for Thee," we prayed last Sunday (Introit). Today we receive the answer of the Lord: "I am the salvation of the people" (Introit). Then before our eyes the gates of heaven are opened, and we see the immense throngs which move forward in an unbroken procession toward heaven. To all these who are called He will bring salvation.

The hall of the marriage feast is open, the banquet is ready. For us this means the sacrifice which is prepared at this hour at the celebration of the Mass. The banquet hall is the Christian Church. At Mass the Lord (Christ) enters the hall and goes about to welcome His guests, to espouse their souls as His bride in an intimate union of prayer and sacrifice. But in order to take part in the banquet it is not enough that one merely enter the hall, that one is baptized; it is essential that one possess also the wedding garment, "the new man who according to God is created in justice and holiness of truth" (Epistle) — freedom from sin and a disposition to obey the commandments of God (Communion). This parable issues a serious warning to all of us who wish to offer the Mass with the priest.

But the banquet of the Mass is not the final meal; it is the introduction to the banquet of eternal communion; that is, of our eternal union with God. We have received the grace of baptism; we are called to His banquet and are granted admission to the hall of the Church. Through our participation in the Eucharistic banquet we prepare the way for the true, heavenly banquet. But there is a condition: "Attend, O My people, to My law, incline your ears to the words of My mouth" (Introit). At Holy Communion we must be able to say: "Thou hast commanded Thy commandments to be kept most diligently. Oh that my ways may be directed to keep Thy justifications."

It must be our serious endeavor to be "prepared in soul and body ... [to] perform the works that are Thine" (Collect). Therefore the Epistle admonishes us: "Be ye renewed in the spirit of your mind and put on the new man, who according to God is created in justice and holiness of truth. Wherefore, putting away lying, speak ye the truth every man with his neighbor, for we are members one of another.... Let not the sun go down upon your anger." Such is the wedding garment, the new man. He who does not wear this garment, cannot take part in the banquet of heaven. He may have found a place on earth in the hall of the Church, but when the King comes (for judgment at the last day) He will ask: "Friend, how camest thou in hither, not having on a wedding garment?" And then He will command His waiters: "Bind his hands and feet, and cast him into the exterior darkness" (Gospel). The return of Christ at the end of the world will bring the separation of the cockle and the wheat.

"I am the salvation of the people," the salvation of all those who perform their duties faithfully, as they promised to do at their baptism, and who daily "put on the new man." While celebrating Mass they bury the old man, the man of sin, the man of passion, the man of evil habits; and they devote themselves to Christ, to God, to God's will and commandments. They live according to the will of God and for His honor. Thus they daily put on the new man through celebration of the Mass. They enrich their wedding garment always more and more, and they make themselves ready to partake of the Holy Sacrifice. Here the words of the Offertory are fulfilled, "Thou wilt quicken me, O Lord;... and Thy right hand shall save me."

Meditation

The liturgy today leads us into the brilliantly lit and festively decorated banquet hall, which is thronged with guests dressed in resplendent wedding garments, awaiting eagerly the arrival of the King. The hall is the Church; we, the baptized, are the guests. The wedding garment is the garment of sanctifying grace. We are all waiting for the arrival of the Lord, the King.

"Be ye renewed in the spirit of your mind and put on the new man, who according to God is created in justice and holiness of truth" (Epistle). The nearer the day of the return of the Lord approaches, the more insistent become the admonitions of the Church: "You know not the day nor the hour" (Mt 25:13). "As in the days of Noe, so shall also the coming of the Son of Man be. For as in the days before the flood they were eating and drinking, marrying and giving in marriage, even till that day in which Noe entered into the ark, and they knew not till the flood came and took them all away; so also shall the coming of the Son of Man be.... Watch ye, therefore, because ye know not what hour your Lord will come" (Mt 24:37 ff.). The Church wishes that we be ready when the Lord comes at the hour of our death. We shall be ready if we wear the wedding garment of sanctifying grace. We shall be ready if we renew our inner disposition, if at each Mass, at each Holy Communion, at each sincere prayer, at each stimulation of grace, we put on the new man in our thoughts, our judgment, our will, and our actions.

In the Christian life there is only one direction, forward and upward. If we fail to progress, if we cease to exert ourselves every day and every moment, we shall lose ground, we shall revert to the old man, to separation from God. We shall be ready to meet the King if we strive incessantly and do not weaken. That is what the Epistle means when it admonishes: "Be ye renewed." The Church fears that we might become weak, that we might neglect grace and thus lose our wedding garment of sanctifying grace. She fears that, like the foolish virgins, we may go to meet the Lord without the necessary oil in our lamps. She fears lest, when the bridegroom comes, we shall not be ready and we shall be excluded. "I know you not."

"The kingdom of heaven is likened to a king who made a marriage for his son.... And the marriage was filled with guests. And the king went in to see the guests, and He saw there a man who had not on a wedding garment, and he saith to him: Friend, how camest thou in hither, not having on a wedding garment? But he was silent" (Gospel). It is not sufficient that we have come to the banquet hall of the Church; a wedding garment is also required. It is not enough that we have received baptism and have accepted the Christian faith; we must live according to the gospel; we must live a life of justice and holiness; we must possess sanctifying grace and Christian virtues. "Wherefore, putting away lying, speak ye the truth every man with his neighbor, for we are members one of another. Be angry and sin not. Let not the sun go down upon your anger. Give not place to the devil. He that stole, let him now steal no more, but rather let him labor, working with his hands the thing which is good, that he may have something to give to him that suffereth need. Let no evil speech proceed from your mouth, but that which is good, to the edification of faith, that it may administer grace to the hearers.... Let all bitterness, and anger, and indignation, and clamor, and blasphemy be put away from you, with all malice. And be ye kind one to another, merciful, forgiving one another, even as God hath forgiven you in Christ.... But fornication and all uncleanness or covetousness, let it not so much as be named among you, as becometh saints" (Eph 4:25–29, 31; 5:3).

The wedding banquet to which we are invited is Holy Communion. But the Apostle gives us a grave warning: "Therefore whosoever shall eat this bread or drink the chalice of the Lord unworthily, shall be guilty of the body and of the blood of the Lord. But let a man prove himself, and so let him eat of that bread and drink of the chalice. For he that eateth and drinketh unworthily, eateth and drinketh judgment to himself, not discerning the body of the Lord" (1 Cor 11:27–29).

The wedding to which we are invited is the blessed possession of God. "That My joy may be in you and your joy may be filled" (Jn 15:11). We will be granted admission to the eternal banquet only if we are clothed in the wedding garment of sanctifying grace and have overcome every fault of our former lives, having done full penance for our sins, either in this life or in purgatory. With the liturgy during these weeks we long for the wedding banquet of eternal life. We put on the new man; we strive for perfect charity in all our acts.

Prayer

Almighty and merciful God, in Thy loving kindness shield us from all adversity, that being prepared in soul and body, we may with free minds perform the works that are Thine. Through Christ our Lord. Amen.

Monday

The Church now looks forward to the end of time. In those days "shall many be scandalized and shall betray one another and shall hate one another. And many false prophets shall rise and shall seduce many. And because iniquity hath abounded, the charity of many shall grow cold" (Mt 24:10–12). The Church will be ridiculed, derided, and persecuted. She will await in her white garments the coming of the Lord. She looks up to Him, and He reassures her: "I am the salvation of the people, saith the Lord; in whatever tribulation they shall cry to Me, I shall hear them; and I will be their Lord forever" (Introit).

"I am the salvation of the people." We hear a great deal today about "self-redemption" and about the exploration of our inner self, that from such an experience we may expect all the redemption and rebirth that is necessary. Many persons therefore seek to construct their spiritual life on a purely natural basis and hope by this means to triumph over their lower nature. This reliance on self can lead only to their destruction, for the will unconsciously but most certainly becomes the prey of self-deception. Such self-reliant persons fail to perceive the weaknesses of human nature. They cannot understand how even our highest aspirations are vitiated by so much vanity, selfishness, covetousness, and greed for power. They do not realize how much hypocrisy, harshness, and violence is contained even in our desire for righteousness; how much sensuality there is even in our spirituality. How erroneous it is to suppose that we can depend on our own spiritual strength and ability, or that we can form ourselves into perfect men by our own powers, and triumph over the weaknesses and disabilities of our fallen nature! With good reason, then, the liturgy beseeches God today that we may be protected from adversities from within and from without. It prays that by means of His all-powerful grace He may protect us from all that could injure us in body or soul, and that we may devote ourselves to whatever is according to His will (Collect). It is not our own spirituality, nor our own nature, nor our own will, nor our own ideals, nor our own plans and provisions, nor flesh and blood that can save us and redeem us; but only the grace of God, which reaches us through Christ our head. "I am the salvation of the people; ... in whatever tribulation they shall cry to Me, I shall hear them."

"Come to Me all you that labor and are burdened, and I will refresh you" (Mt 11:28). He will give us light, understanding, fortitude, joy, peace, strength, inner freedom, purity, and victory over all that springs from the world below and that could overcome our souls. Christ, whose human nature is filled with the purity and the holiness of the divinity, possesses the fullness of life, of holiness, of strength, of purity and immortality. He possesses these things not only in Himself and for Himself, but for us also. He is for us a model of holiness. By taking Christ as our model we come to know the "new man" which we must become and the ideal toward which we must strive — the new man free of sin, "who according to God is created in justice and holiness of truth" (Epistle). He is, moreover, our salvation through His teaching and commandments. "Attend, O My people, to My law; incline your ears to the words of My mouth" (Introit). He is our salvation also through the operation of His grace in us. He, the vine, lives His life in us the branches. His life enlivens our spirit, our will, our very being. He makes us strong, pure, and holy. He is the strength of the wine and the nourishment of the bread that sustains us. By our use of the Eucharist, His divine life is renewed, increased, and strengthened in us, and we tend toward the fullness of all sanctity. The Holy Eucharist is the guarantee of our eventual resurrection in the body and that salvation which is made certain through the merits of our divine Savior. To whom shall we go that we may have the fullness of life and the fulfillment of all desires? "Come to Me all you that labor and are burdened."

As long as we hold fast to Christ, our salvation is assured. Separation from Christ means the loss of our salvation. If we refuse to accept His doctrine, if we refuse to obey His commands, if we refuse to follow His counsels, if we fail to cooperate with the operation of His grace in us, we shall not be saved. Only when we give ourselves to Him completely will He work in us the fullness of His salvation, the fullness of His grace and blessing. Christ desires our entire being.

"I am the salvation of the people." We place our complete trust in the salvific will of the Savior for all sinners, for He will give us salvation. In this we place our confidence in spite of our many infidelities, in spite of our half-heartedness, in spite of our frequent misuse and neglect of grace. Great as is our sinfulness and our need, greater still is His mercy, His love, and His will to save. For this reason we approach the Holy Sacrifice with great courage and confidence. "If I shall walk in the midst of tribulation, Thou wilt quicken me, O Lord; and Thou wilt stretch forth Thy hand against the wrath of my enemies; and Thy right hand shall save me" (Offertory).

Prayer

May the healing power of Thy grace, O Lord, mercifully rid of us all perverseness of heart and make us ever cleave to Thy commandments. Through Christ our Lord. Amen.

Tuesday

"The kingdom of heaven is likened to a king who made a marriage for his son" (Gospel). He has invited many guests and called them to his banquet, but they do not come. He calls them a second time, and still they do not appear. They even kill some of the servants whom the king has sent to them. Then the king sends his servants into the streets to invite whomsoever they find. "The marriage indeed is ready, but they that were invited were not worthy."

"Come ye to the marriage." The king calls the nobles, the great, the officials of the city; but they do not accept the invitation. One goes to his farm, another to his merchandise. Now the poor and lowly are invited. They are allowed to enter the banquet hall and sit at the royal table. This is a figure of our call to the faith. Those first invited are the people of Israel, to whom God sent the patriarchs and the prophets and finally His own Son. But Israel will have nothing to do with the Messias sent by God; nor will it enter the kingdom of grace founded by the Messias. Because Israel will not enter the banquet hall, the Church founded by Christ, God now invites the poor who have wandered in the darkness of heathendom, and the Gentiles who erred without the light of revelation, to partake of His banquet: "Come ye to the marriage," to the good things of Christ and the Church: grace, the sacraments, the Holy Eucharist. "For many are called, but few are chosen." We are called and admitted to the wedding feast in the kingdom of God, the Church.

Baptism has been for us the entrance into the Church, but the Church also invites us to the wedding feast of eternal life in heaven. "For many are called, but few are chosen." Not all who are admitted to membership in the Church are certain of being admitted to the eternal wedding feast. God has called us to the Church without any merit of ours, but He does not bless us without our cooperation and effort. The warning that "many are called, but few are chosen" is explained by the Epistle: "Be ye renewed in the spirit of your mind and put on the new man." We are called to eternal life; there is no lack of good will on the part of God, and the assistance of His grace is assured us. But it is our task to cooperate with grace and to put on the new man through a firm faith in the light and inspiration of grace. We must fulfill the commandments of God and of Christ under the leadership and guidance of the Church. If we fail to do our part by neglecting or abusing the grace of God, we belong to the number of those who are called but are not chosen. We are like the foolish virgins who were indeed chosen by the bridegroom, but who had no oil in their lamps and were not ready when the gates of the banquet hall were opened. The doors are closed, and they who were called but were not prepared, are excluded. "I know you not" (Mt 25:12).

"For many are called, but few are chosen." Israel was called, but by its own fault it missed that call. "For if God hath not spared the natural branches, fear lest perhaps He also spare not thee" (Rom 11:21) if you make yourself unworthy of election.

"Our fathers were all under the cloud and all passed through the sea. And all in Moses were baptized in the cloud and in the sea; and did all eat the same spiritual food [the manna]. And all drank the same spiritual drink [the water which Moses struck from the rock by the command of God],... but with most of them God was not well pleased; for they were overthrown in the desert. Now these things were done in a figure of us, that we should not covet evil things, as they also coveted. Neither become ye idolators as some of them.... Neither let us commit fornication as some of them committed fornication.... Neither do you murmur as some of them murmured and were destroyed by the destroyer. Now all these things happened to them in figure; and they were written for our correction.... Wherefore he that thinketh himself to stand, let him take heed lest he fall" (1 Cor 10:1–12).

Prayer

Almighty and merciful God, in Thy loving kindness shield us from all adversity, that being prepared in soul and body, we may with free minds perform the works that are Thine. Through Christ our Lord. Amen.

Wednesday

The king makes a marriage feast for his son and calls the guests, but those whom he invited do not come. They despise the wedding dinner that the king has prepared for them and turn to other occupations. One goes to his farm, another to his business; and thus they are excluded from the wedding dinner of the king.

"All things are ready; come ye to the marriage" (Gospel). The King is God the Father. He makes a marriage feast for His only-begotten Son, whom He has sent into the world that He, too, may become a man. The Son of God assumes our human nature in the womb of the Virgin, and draws our human nature into an intimate union with His divine person. Through the human nature which He assumed at His Incarnation, we also, in a certain sense, share the nature of Christ. Through His union with the human nature which He received from Mary, He wedded Himself to the whole of mankind and to each one of us. Thus we are espoused to the Son of God. He has espoused us with an infinite love, and He will pour out the riches of His Godhead upon us and upon all mankind.

"Come ye to the marriage." The primary purpose of man's life on earth is to seek Christ and to become daily more intimately united to Him through faith and love. The King "sent His servants," the teachers, the priests, the Church, outward tribulations and inward lights and graces, "to call them that were invited to the marriage, and they would not come." He called again. "But they neglected, and went their ways, one to his farm, and another to his merchandise" (Gospel). Poor wayward humanity of antiquity! Poor wayward men of today! They go their own way, disregarding the invitation of the King. The besetting sin of our day is indifference. Men speak, write, and rule without Christ, without God. The world is emancipated from its God; it is godless. Men have lost their supernatural center and have turned to what is not God. Indeed, many even actively preach and promote hatred of God and Christ. What a privilege, if we understand the intentions of God, is this invitation to the marriage feast! What a grace to be allowed to enter into so intimate a union with Christ, the spouse of the soul!

"Come ye to the marriage." The wedding feast of the King is presented to us Catholics at the time of Holy Communion. Holy Communion is essentially a wedding feast. Its object is to establish a unity of love between ourselves and Christ and the other members of His Church. Its end is our living, fruitful growth in Christ, the vine. At Holy Communion the Lord is the sole spouse of our soul, yielding Himself up with the most complete and intimate surrender to us, embracing our soul and penetrating our very essence. This wedding feast rejoices, consoles, and strengthens us every morning anew and inflames us with fervent mutual love: love for love, heart for heart, sacrifice for sacrifice. We know that today is our wedding day, and tomorrow is our wedding day. But not all understand this word, but only they to whom it is given (Mt 19:11). Many Catholics, unfortunately despise this wedding feast "and [go] their ways, one to his farm, and another to his merchandise." They do not understand that Communion is a wedding banquet of the King; they have other interests. We on our part must, therefore, welcome the invitation of Jesus the more eagerly.

The incarnation of the Son of God and Holy Communion were both prepared for us by the King who makes a wedding feast for His Son. We are the ones invited to the marriage. We accept the invitation every day with still deeper faith, with greater appreciation and deeper humility, with more fervent love. Let it never be said of us: "They neglected, and went their ways." Daily we must work for the renewal of our spirit and mind that we may put on the new man, that we may appear, at the wedding banquet in the "wedding garment" of grace, virtue, love, and holiness.

PRAYER

Almighty and merciful God, in Thy loving kindness shield us from all adversity, that being prepared in soul and body, we may with free minds perform the works that are Thine. Through Christ our Lord. Amen.

Thursday

"The kingdom of heaven is likened to a king who made a marriage for his son" (Gospel). The King, God the Father, sends His Son into the world that He may become our spouse. The union is fulfilled most perfectly in a union of love effected through Holy Communion, when we are bodily united with Him and He with us.

"He that eateth My flesh and drinketh My blood, abideth in Me and I in him" (Jn 6:57). The primary object of this union with the flesh and blood of Christ is the union of spirit and heart. From the mouth to the heart! Such a sublime union should result in an intimate union of body and spirit in a union of love. The Lord, therefore, nourishes us with the bread of the Eucharist that He may lower Himself to our level and fill us with His spirit. In this way our spirit should be strengthened, filled with the fullness of God. But all growth in grace and virtue, all union of man with Christ, is conditioned by the increase and growth of charity. It is charity that changes us into Christ; it is the fire that purges all worldliness from our soul. Holy Communion aims at the increase, purification, and perfection of charity, which is the most beautiful and most precious gift of Holy Communion. Under the warm rays of the sun the hard green berries become soft and sweet; in like manner the Sun of the Eucharist brings about a tremendous change of the inner man in us, because of Christ's limitless love poured forth upon us. The thoughts, acts, sentiments, and endeavors of the natural man give way to those of Jesus. His truth becomes the light of our spirit; His love becomes the life-stream of our heart. We go out of ourselves, forsake ourselves, and enter into Him, united to Him as to a spouse.

At the moment of Holy Communion we become Christ-bearers, absorbing His flesh and His blood in our veins; and thus we partake of the divine nature (St. Cyril of Jerusalem). This partaking of the divine nature is true not only as long as the Eucharistic gifts are present in us, but even when they are gone He remains in us as God, knowing all about us, watching over us, giving us His love and grace. His love, the love of His divine-human heart, remains with us. The union of His heart with our heart is the real purpose of Holy Communion. If the hearts of earthly lovers remain united even when they are physically separated, if they are always near each other, thinking of each other and longing for each other in love, then it must be clear that the loving heart of Jesus must continue to love us even when we are physically separated. It is His desire to espouse our soul according to His human nature also. "With desire I have desired to eat this pasch with you" (Lk 22:15). "Having loved His own who were in the world, He loved them unto the end" (Jn 13:1). The Eucharist unites us with Christ in a durable bond of unity, a community of interests, a mutual possession, which will be knitted firmly by the power of love. How fortunate we should consider ourselves to be thus so closely united to our God!

"He that eateth My flesh and drinketh My blood, abideth in Me and I in him" in a holy espousal. Love draws the beloved to itself and changes him into itself. What is more natural than that as often we receive Holy Communion worthily, we are renewed in our thinking and become new men who are created after God and Christ in true justice and holiness. "Thou hast commanded Thy commandments to be kept most diligently. Oh that my ways may be directed to keep Thy justifications" (Communion). The espoused soul knows only what will please the Lord. It has become one spirit with Him, one in desire and endeavor. That is the fruit of Holy Communion.

Prayer

Almighty and merciful God, in Thy loving kindness shield us from all adversity, that being prepared in soul and body, we may with free minds perform the works that are Thine. Through Christ our Lord. Amen.

Friday

"Put on the new man.... Wherefore, putting away lying, speak ye the truth.... Be angry and sin not. Let not the sun go down on your anger. Give not place to the devil" (Epistle).

"Be angry and sin not." There lies in man both a justified and an unjustified anger: anger against himself, against men, against conditions in which he lives. Anger has its origin in one's consciousness of having been injured. As far as it is directed against other persons, the anger is founded on the idea that others underestimate our worth or fail to show us the respect we feel is due to us. Anger results from the desire to revenge some real or supposed injury that has been inflicted on us. Anger easily combines with hate, at least when the desire for revenge appears reasonable and justified. In this case we do not desire that he who has done us harm be punished out of charity, or out of justice, or solicitude for his soul, but rather out of the evil desire to be avenged on the person who has harmed us. Anger often prompts us to act unjustly and to punish one who has not merited punishment, or to punish far above the proper measure someone who merited it. Anger and the desire of revenge and punishment are sins against meekness and mercy. They destroy the mutual peace of men and give rise to many sins against charity by causing unrest and rash judgments in words and works. With good reason the Epistle admonishes us: "Be angry and sin not." Be not aroused to anger; cling not to anger; do not show your anger outwardly, but restrain and control your irritation. Never make a decision in anger; for at such a time reason is impaired and we cannot judge correctly. But, above all, when your anger is aroused, turn your eyes to God and seek to do His will. Seek God's will in all the disagreeable things and all the bitter things that disturb you, for they come from the hand of God. If we consciously turn to God when disagreeable occasions threaten us, we shall easily overcome our anger.

"Blessed are the meek" (Mt 5:4) does not mean that Christian meekness consists in our having deep distrust of ourself; nor does it mean that we should never assert ourselves, nor that we should allow others to treat us as they will. That is not the meekness of Christ; that is spinelessness. Indeed such a negative attitude that shows indifference even against evil has nothing to do with true Christian meekness. Christ's meekness springs from strength, not from weakness. It is born of an ardent love for God and neighbor, and is an index of self-control. It flourishes in the silence of the soul possessed and blessed by God, in which the egoism of the spiteful and impatient man and the low instincts of fallen nature are replaced by a higher life. It is a new reaction to adversity. Christian meekness requires humanity, tenderness, sympathy, and love for our neighbor. But it follows an unmerciful logic in the use of all these emotions and cleans them of all self-love, pride, meanness, and servility. Christian meekness is the product of a thoughtful, conscious, vital heroism carried to its logical end. It seeks perfection and the divine union. Therefore it alone can use the strong, sublime virtue of meekness and tenderness as the law of its own perfection. Only Christian meekness can uncover the weakness which lies behind every outburst of anger and behind every ill-advised and spiteful word or deed. True Christian meekness is to be found only in the regenerated man who is created after the image of God in true justice and holiness.

"Be angry and sin not." Jesus Himself became angry at the sight of the buyers and sellers in the temple. "And when He had made, as it were, a scourge of little cords, He drove them all out of the temple, the sheep also and the oxen; and the money of the changers He poured out, and the tables He overthrew. And to them that sold doves He said: Take these things hence and make not the house of My Father a house of traffic" (Jn 2:15 ff.). He is not indifferent to the desecration of the temple. He cannot be. He opposes the evil with His very soul. Should not we also be angry at times and oppose evil with all our strength and with our whole soul? Yes, indeed! But we must not resort to force; we must not shed blood to avenge blood; we must not seek bitter revenge.

"Be angry and sin not." "Be not overcome by evil, but overcome evil by good" (Rom 12:21). True Christianity gains all its strength from within. It begins with a thorough self-reformation, with the establishment of the new man, and only then turns to the reform of others. Because we are not so regenerated, our anger is unholy and unfruitful.

When we have put on the new man, who is meek in the spirit of Christ, we become spiritually strong. Then we turn to the reform of others with firmness, yet without bitterness. Then only may we safely apply the outward means of correction to others without sacrificing principles, and yet with discretion. "Blessed are the meek, for they shall possess the land."

Prayer

Almighty and merciful God, in Thy loving kindness shield us from all adversity, that being prepared in soul and body, we may with free minds perform the works that are Thine. Through Christ our Lord. Amen.

Saturday

The Judge shall come. Therefore, "Be ye renewed in the spirit of your mind, and put on the new man, who according to God is created in justice and holiness of truth. Wherefore, putting away lying, speak ye the truth every man with his neighbor; for we are members one of another" (Epistle). We are, as it were, clothed by nature in a lie, by reason of Original Sin — a lie which like a garment covers us and makes us appear otherwise than we are. The new man, the one baptized, puts away this deceptive garment and speaks the truth.

"Putting away lying." "The mouth that belieth killeth the soul" (Ws 1:11). "Lie not one to another" (Col 3:9). "Keep thy tongue from evil, and thy lips from speaking guile" (Ps 33:14). Such is the unchangeable law of God. And yet there is in the world, even among Christians, so much untruth, dishonesty, deception, and deceit. Dishonesty is the essence of the world's maxims and of worldly actions. The so-called polish of the world is at best little else than an attempt to cover the inward man with a pleasing veneer, an attempt to veil the sense of words so as to make the right seem wrong and the wrong seem right. The spirit of the world is the prudence of the flesh. Its maxim is: Do what you like, but do not get caught in your wrongdoing. Keep up appearances, protect your honor. Faults you may commit, but do not admit them. You may sin and dishonor God and your conscience, but you should never through an honest confession seek to restore the honor of God and of your own self-respect.

The world thinks a man stupid and silly who would suppose that his outward actions should be a mirror of his heart. To the world such an attitude is only a new proof that Christianity is naive and outmoded, unfit to compete with the culture of our modern world. There is much conscious deception of one's neighbor, parents, and superiors in the pursuit to achieve personal ambitions and aims. Such is the world; and even we have gone so far that we cannot bear the truth. If someone tries to point out a cheap deception, to tell us the truth in a kind way, we condemn him for a lack of culture and delicacy. We who daily perform our devotions, partake in the Mass, and receive Holy Communion, have wandered far from the spirit of Christ. "Be ye renewed in the spirit of your mind, and put on the new man."

"Speak ye the truth every man with his neighbor." How simple and natural Christ was in His words and His conduct! Every child understood Him. The saints of the Church have imitated the example of Christ. They are characterized by a spirit of truth, righteousness, and simplicity. Righteousness and honesty of the heart are the root of all virtue in them, a criterion of perfection. A man may work miracles, he may be venerated as a saint; but if only once he is caught in an untruth or in an act of deceit, he is condemned by every serious man. "For the Holy Spirit ... will flee from the deceitful" (Ws 1:5). "His will is in them that walk sincerely" (Prv 11:20). Our God is a God of truth. "Heaven and earth shall pass away, but My words shall not pass away" (Lk 21:33). Truth demands that our words be in conformity with our thoughts, that we speak exactly as we think, that we conform our actions to our mind. Our conduct must be the expression of our inner thoughts. "Speak ye the truth,... for we are members one of another." The Christian community needs to respect the truth. What would result if we questioned every word of our neighbor, our brother in Christ? How could any community so exist? Misunderstandings would arise, confidence would be destroyed; anger, unjust prejudice, hate, and enmity will rule when we can no longer depend on the word of others. How essential to love and mutual understanding is truthfulness!

God gives us the key of truth: "My eyes are ever towards the Lord" (Ps 24:15). As long as we adopt the attitude of the world, as long as we make use of deception, ignoring our conscience and neglecting our duties, as long as we still have in mind any object other than the will of God, we shall never walk the way of Christian truth. But the Epistle today exhorts us: "Put ye on the new man."

"Thou hast commanded Thy commandments to be kept most diligently. Oh, that my ways may be directed to keep Thy justifications!" (Communion.) All our thoughts must be directed to the observing of God's commandments. Uprightness and truth may at times be inconvenient, but if we look to God and observe His commandments, we will rise above all difficulties.

PRAYER

Almighty and merciful God, in Thy loving kindness shield us from all adversity, that being prepared in soul and body, we may with free minds perform the works that are Thine. Through Christ our Lord. Amen.

Twentieth Sunday after Pentecost

THE MASS

"Upon the rivers of Babylon there we sat and wept, when we remembered thee, O Sion." These words of the Offertory express the theme of today's Mass. The Church feels that she is exiled, far from home, far from her Lord. She is oppressed, despised, persecuted, in her head and in her members. The life of exile is hard and bitter. Therefore at the end of the ecclesiastical year she longs for the peace of her heavenly home. Continually she directs her gaze to the Lord to see whether He will not soon come to take possession of His kingdom.

We, too, live in exile. With hearts full of contrition and humility we confess with the three children in the furnace of Babylon: "All that Thou hast done to us, O Lord, Thou hast done in true judgment, because we have sinned against Thee; ... but give glory to Thy name and deal with us according to the multitude of Thy mercy" (Introit). With great devotion we cry in the Kyrie for mercy, forgiveness, and peace. We have determined to respond to the admonition of the Epistle and to remain without sin throughout our life. We do not cling to the world and its goods, but "the eyes of all hope in Thee, O Lord" (Gradual). Our whole desire is centered on heaven, our true home. All our thoughts belong to the Lord. "Thou openest Thy hand and fillest every living creature with Thy blessing" (Gradual). He shows mercy to the distracted father and answers his prayers with the consoling assurance: "Go thy way, thy son liveth" (Gospel). He also grants mercy at the request of the Church, who implores Him: Come down and heal my erring sons. But He has not yet come. The hour of His arrival has not yet dawned; but He guarantees it: "Thy son liveth." The Church believes and continues her journey towards the great day of salvation. With joy she sings her Credo. She is not deceived.

"There we sat and wept" (Offertory). We are the sick son of the ruler in the Gospel story; but we hope in the Lord: "Thou givest them meat in due season. Thou openest Thy hand and fillest every living creature with Thy blessing" (Gradual). We are determined to be "undefiled in the way" (Introit), to realize in our life the admonition of the Epistle. We renounce sin and malice and our inordinate desires during the Sacrifice of the Mass; we resolve to mortify our will, our desires, our unruly passions, and bad habits. We renounce the world and all that is transitory, our ambitions and desires, in the hope of a blessed eternity. "My heart is ready" (Alleluia). Soon He will come at the Consecration and bring life and salvation; the Consecration is the fulfillment of the promise of the Gradual: "The eyes of all hope in Thee, O Lord, and Thou givest them meat in due season."

Now during the Mass He will permit us to join Him in His sacrifice in the measure in which we have renounced sin, the world, and ourselves. He puts Himself at our disposal as our sacrifice. He gives us His heart, His adoration, His virtues, His merits and graces, that we may come to the Father in Him and with Him. He gives us Himself, His rich, glorified life in Holy Communion. "The eyes of all hope in Thee." Thus our misery is consoled by hope and confidence. Through this participation in the divine life, we are given strength to bear our life in exile till the Lord appears again at His second coming to summon each of us and the entire community to the heavenly home. Then He will open His hand and fill us who have hoped in Him with the blessing of everlasting life. "Be mindful of Thy word [Thy promises] to Thy servant, O Lord, in which Thou hast given me hope; this has comforted me in my humiliation" (Communion).

Meditation

The Church year is drawing to a close. The end of this year recalls to the Church the end of the world and of the long period of waiting that intervenes before the coming of the Savior. "Thy kingdom come," the kingdom of blessed salvation and our rescue from exile.

"We have sinned against Thee, and we have not obeyed Thy commandments" (Introit). Thus prayed Azarius, one of the three children in the furnace, as "they walked in the midst of the flame praising God and blessing the Lord" (Dn 3:24). The Church is in the furnace of persecution and suffering. She praises the Lord: "All that Thou hast done to us, O Lord, Thou hast done in true judgment, because we have sinned against Thee" (Introit). Daily the Church begs God for mercy in the Kyrie at Mass and at Lauds: "Have mercy on me, O God" (Ps 50:3). Today, because the ecclesiastical year is drawing to an end, this cry has a special significance. We look back upon the graces of the current year that is now near its end. We recall all that God has done and has wanted to do to us, the children of the Church, the brethren in Christ. Daily He came into our midst to sacrifice Himself for us and to supply us with the graces and fruits of the sacrifice of the cross. He invited us to become a sacrifice with Him, to be crucified with Him, to die with Him. Daily in His sacrifice He gives us forgiveness for our sins and fills us with His risen, immortal life. We, however, have neglected His help and have failed to establish ourselves firmly in this life; we have not allowed it to produce its full effect on us. We have sinned and have deserved punishment.

"But give glory to Thy name and deal with us according to the multitude of Thy mercy" (Introit). The evil that we as members of the Church have wrought will be turned against the Lord by His enemies. A Church, they will say, which harbors sinners and uses them as its servants, a Church which cannot change them, is not the Church of Christ; it has failed in its task; it should give way to a new and more effective religion. "Give glory to Thy name." For Thy sake forgive us our trespasses and deal with us according to Thy mercy. Withhold Thy judgment, for the evil slander us: "Who is your God?" they say. Defend Thy Church, show Thy power so that the enemies of the Church may see and believe in Thee. "Give glory to Thy name."

The Church cries for a sign from the Lord. She does not ask for signs and wonders, but for a spiritual change in the souls of her children: "That they may be cleansed from all offenses and serve Thee with a quiet mind" (Collect); that they may see and do the will of God; that they may be "filled with the Holy Spirit, . . . being subject one to another in the fear of Christ" (Epistle).

"Give glory to Thy name." Holy Mother the Church sees with sorrow that many of her children, born to her by baptism, are sick unto death. She hastens to the Lord as did the ruler in the Gospel and begs Him "to come down and heal his son for he [is] at the point of death." This is the agonized cry of the Church for the hour of the Lord's return in glory. "Come down." Heal my child. Bring salvation. But His time is not yet come. He imposes upon His spouse new trials of faith. He comes silently, invisibly, mysteriously in the host. During Mass He sacrifices Himself and places at the disposal of the faithful the fruits of His sacrifice on the cross. At Holy Communion He gives Himself as the spiritual nourishment of the soul and assures the Church, "Thy son liveth" (Gospel). The Church "believeth the word which Jesus said" to her and goes her way, believing in Him and His healing power. She presses on towards the day of His return and her eternal salvation.

The Church is aware of the sins and faults of her ministers and members. She confesses and deplores them; but she does not stop at sin and the sinner. She acknowledges the faults before the Lord and confesses them to the Lord, thereby singing a hymn to His glory, justice, holiness, and mercy. Through her faith in His mercy and love she expects the remission of all faults and the grace necessary for the reformation of the sinner. "Go thy way, thy son liveth." The Church consoles and encourages her children to make new, more energetic, and more faithful efforts. She points out to them the power of the Holy Sacrifice and of Holy Communion for such effort.

"The eyes of all hope in Thee, O Lord; and Thou givest them meat in due season. Thou openest Thy hand and fillest every living creature with Thy blessing" (Gradual). The Lord filled with His blessings the ailing son of the royal officer. So, too, at the celebration of the Mass, He bestows His blessings on the ailing children of the Church. So, too, will He bless His Church at His return, when He will come to summon her to the eternal nuptials of heaven.

Prayer

Graciously grant to Thy faithful, we beseech Thee, O Lord, forgiveness and peace, that they may be cleansed from all offenses and serve Thee with a quiet mind. Through Christ our Lord. Amen.

Monday

The son of a ruler at Capharnaum has become desperately sick. The father, hearing that Jesus is passing from Judea into Galilee, travels two days to beseech Him to come down at once to Capharnaum and heal his son. "Lord, come down before my son die." The Lord fulfills the desire of the ruler, but not in the manner he had expected. He does not go to Capharnaum Himself, but heals the sick boy from a distance. He tells the ruler: "Go thy way, thy son liveth." The ruler believes; when he reaches his home, he finds that his son has recovered. The fever had left him at the moment when Jesus said to him, "Thy son liveth" (Gospel).

"Unless you see signs and wonders, you believe not" (Gospel). The father of the dying boy has heard of Jesus and believes that He has the power to save his son from death, otherwise he would not have traveled so far to meet the Lord. But his was not the kind of faith Jesus required. The ruler thinks the Lord must visit his house at Capharnaum to effect the cure. He believes the power of the Lord to be local and to depend on His personal presence. He expects Him to lay His hands upon His son and to make him well by a miracle visible to all. For this reason the Lord admonished him saying, "Unless you see signs and wonders, you believe not." The officer is so absorbed by his desire to save his child that he takes no further notice of the admonition. With the urgency of a man in desperate straits, he repeats his prayer, "Come down before my son die." Jesus does not go to Capharnaum, for it is more important to inspire in this man faith of a higher kind. He heals the sick boy from afar without laying His hands upon him, without a sign or motion. The officer allows himself to be led to the heights of perfect faith by the Lord. "Go thy way, thy son liveth." He believes the words Jesus has spoken to him. "Blessed are they that have not seen and have believed" (Jn 20:29). Thus the Lord teaches His people to have faith in His love, in His divine providence, in His almighty, hidden power. His ways are not our ways.

"Lord, come down before my son die." In the anxious officer with his weak and imperfect faith, the liturgy sees us Christians of today. We know by experience how many of our brethren in Christ live entirely for this world and what it has to offer, losing themselves more and more in things that are transitory. The Christian faith suffers much from these unfaithful brethren. The maxims of the world are continually gaining ground. This worldly attitude, with all its false ideals and goods, and its denial of Christ and His Church, is growing by leaps and bounds. We know the dangers to which our own souls and those of our beloved ones are exposed. We fear for their salvation. With the officer of the Gospel we approach the Lord and say, "Lord, come down before my son die." Intervene as You have often done in the history of Israel and of the Church. Come down for judgment with a strong arm, with burning anger, with a judgment terrible on evil. Work some wonder that they may believe again and return to You, and thus save their souls. Thus secretly we look for some sign or wonder of the Lord. But He warned us: "Unless you see signs and wonders, you believe not"; therefore He does not fulfill our wish. He rather leads us on to the heights of faith. "Behold, I am with you all days, even to the consummation of the world" (Mt 28:20). He wishes us to trust in His love, His wisdom, His will, and His power, and to believe firmly in His power to save souls and to conquer evil. "But have confidence, I have overcome the world" (Jn 16:33). What the Lord wants of us is faith; as yet He does not come for judgment. Daily He gives us new grounds for faith, and thus He strengthens our faith and increases it. We believe, just as did the officer of the Gospel, and proceed on our way to our eternal home with a strong, blind faith. There we shall learn that "thy son liveth."

We are continually looking for a sign from the Lord. We seek proofs of His reality, of His Godhead and incarnation, of His divine providence, of His mysterious and effective operation in our hearts, of His power to bend our stubborn wills with His gentle inspirations. Faith in His promises is not sufficient for us. We listen avidly to prophecies and to fortune tellers, and believe implicitly the senseless talk about strange things which are to befall us personally and the world in general. We well deserve that reproach of the Lord, "Unless you see signs and wonders, you believe not."

"The days are evil" (Epistle), and for this reason we should all the more trust the providence and power of Christ's love. We must not fear. The more that cares oppress us and dangers threaten us, the closer should we draw to the Lord, praying, repenting of our sins, confiding in His kind love. "The eyes of all hope in Thee, O Lord; and Thou givest them meat in due season. Thou openest Thy hand and fillest every living creature with Thy blessing" (Gradual). Thus we believe and trust. If we trust in the word of the Lord, we will not be deceived as the officer of the Gospel was not deceived.

Prayer

Graciously grant to Thy faithful, we beseech Thee, O Lord, forgiveness and peace, that they may be cleansed from all offenses and serve Thee with a quiet mind. Through Christ our Lord. Amen.

Tuesday

"Brethren: See how you walk circumspectly, not as unwise, but as wise" (Epistle). This timely admonition to live for the one thing necessary, the salvation of our souls, becomes the more urgent as we recall with the liturgy the approach of the Lord at the time of our death.

"Not as unwise." The first step in the Christian way of life is to free ourselves from the folly of sin and from all evil; that is, to purify our soul. He who wishes to climb a ladder, must start with the lowest rung. Our first task as Christians is to fight against our faults and to root out our own vices. To accomplish this end we must work diligently. Although the beginnings may be difficult, the task later becomes easier, since grace operates ever more readily in our soul once a beginning has been made. "See how you walk circumspectly, not as unwise," not as those who think that they can make progress without purifying the heart, without a struggle against their evil inclinations and prevailing faults, against temptation and the power of the passions. All virtue must be built on the foundation of self-denial and the mortification of the outward and inward senses, of our inclination to pride and uncharitableness. Virtue must be based on an earnest spirit of self-denial, either through a willing acceptance of those sufferings and trials sent to us by God, or through voluntary imposition of mortifications upon ourselves. We must overcome our purely natural manner of thinking and reasoning about events and people, about trials and difficulties. We must daily seek a greater detachment from our own will and from the power of self-love, which poisons and destroys the value of all our work and effort.

"But as wise." The Apostle could have boasted of many advantages: his ancestry, his talents, his learning, his zeal for the law. "But the things that were gain to me, the same I have counted loss for Christ. Furthermore, I count all things to be but loss for the excellent knowledge of Jesus Christ, my Lord; for whom I have suffered the loss of all things and count them but as dung, that I may gain Christ and may be found in Him, not having my justice, which is of the law, but that which is of the faith of Christ Jesus, which is of God, justice in faith; that I may know Him and the power of His Resurrection and the fellowship of His sufferings, being made conformable to His death, if by any means I may attain to the resurrection which is from the dead. Not as though I had already attained, or were already perfect; but I follow after, if I may by any means apprehend, wherein I am also apprehended by Christ Jesus. Brethren, I do not count myself to have apprehended, but one thing I do; forgetting the things that are behind and stretching forth myself to those that are before, I press towards the mark, to the prize of the supernal vocation of God in Christ Jesus" (Phil 3:7–14). What excellent advice! With every step we draw nearer to the final coming of Christ, to our death and judgment.

"As in the days of Noe, so shall also the coming of the Son of Man be. For as in the days before the flood, they were eating and drinking, marrying and giving in marriage, even till that day in which Noe entered into the ark; and they knew not till the flood came and took them all away; so also shall the coming of the Son of Man be. Then two shall be in the field; one shall be taken and one shall be left. Two women shall be grinding at the mill; one shall be taken and one shall be left. Watch ye, therefore, because you know not what hour your Lord will come. But know this ye, that if the goodman of the house knew at what hour the thief would come, he would certainly watch and would not suffer his house to be broken open. Wherefore be you also ready, because at what hour you know not the Son of Man will come" (Mt 24:37–44).

"Then shall the kingdom of heaven be like to ten virgins who, taking their lamps, went out to meet the bridegroom and the bride. And five of them were foolish, and five wise. But the five foolish, having taken their lamps, did not take oil with them. . . . And the bridegroom tarrying, they all slumbered and slept. And at midnight there was a cry made: Behold the bridegroom cometh, go ye forth to meet him. Then all those virgins arose and trimmed their lamps. And the foolish said to the wise: Give us of your oil, for our lamps are gone out. The wise answered, saying: Lest perhaps there be not enough for us and for you, go ye rather to them that sell, and buy for yourselves. Now whilst they went to buy, the bridegroom came; and they that were ready went in with him to the marriage, and the door was shut. But at last came also the other virgins, saying: Lord, Lord, open to us. But he answering, said: Amen I say to you, I know you not. Watch ye therefore, because you know not the day nor the hour" (Mt 25:1 ff.).

"Walk ye circumspectly, not as unwise, but as wise, redeeming the time, because the days are evil. Wherefore, become not unwise, but understanding what is the will of God." The Epistle here has in mind an effective and practical understanding of the will of God, by virtue of which we make use of every moment to carry out what God expects of us, and especially to bear the burdens he sends us. That is true Christian wisdom.

Prayer

Graciously grant to Thy faithful, we beseech thee, O Lord, forgiveness and peace, that they may be cleansed from all offenses and serve Thee with a quiet mind. Through Christ our Lord. Amen.

Wednesday

The Epistle admonishes us to be "redeeming the time, because the days are evil." The end is drawing near. We may look upon our lifetime as a market from which we are to buy and carry away all that we can for God and for our soul. We can easily misuse the time that is allotted to us, or use it to the detriment of our own soul. "Wherefore, become not unwise."

"Redeeming the time." The years are hastening by. Before we realize it our allotted time will be exhausted and we shall stand at the brink of the grave. Every day and every moment of the day is given to us to be used for God, and thus to prepare for ourselves a happy eternity. Of all the time that is given to us, we can be certain of only the present brief moment. And before we have time to reflect on it, that moment is also gone. The past is gone forever and will never return. The future does not yet belong to us, and perhaps it never will. And so we possess only the present brief moment, and even this will be gone in an instant. Our whole eternity depends on whether or not we make use of the present moment. We can lose it or let it pass by unused. We may even make use of it for sin. But we can also make use of it to obtain precious graces. Death or life, happiness or unhappiness, heaven or hell, depend on the use we make of the present moment. Should we, then, not make use of every moment of the life that is given us, which may end at any moment, for the purpose of gaining heaven? Can we afford to let a single minute pass by unused? Do we dare give a single minute to living for this world or for sin? Should we not rather strive zealously to gain all that can be gained for God and for our soul?

"For whether we live, we live unto the Lord; or whether we die, we die unto the Lord" (Rom 14:8). We are Christians dedicated to God by virtue of our baptismal vows and perhaps by religious profession. Our whole being, our bodies and souls, our gifts and talents, our health and strength, belong to Him. Our time also belongs to Him. It is not we who have the right to determine and decide how the days, hours, and minutes given to us are to be used, but He to whom we are dedicated. He should determine the use of our free time and every moment of our life. Only one thing is left to us to do: to seek to know at every moment of the day what God desires of us, so that we may speak a ready fiat to all that He commands or desires. Since He is the complete master of every moment of our life, it should be a matter of complete indifference to us whether He assigns us to this task or to that. We should be prepared at every moment to undertake and perform whatever He wills and desires. God does not allow us a single moment for idleness. He determines all things, controls, rules, and ordains all our actions. If He assigns us no outward work to do, then He occupies us inwardly. At every moment He draws us to Himself to love Him, to thank Him, to praise Him, and to subject ourselves completely to His holy will. Every moment of the day should be an expression of the child's love for its Father in an unbroken elevation of the soul which loves Him and delivers itself confidently into the hands of its Father. At every moment we should contemplate God and His holy will and His grace. At every moment we can gather rich and grace-laden sheaves for the barns of eternity.

We can be certain of only the present moment, and we must make the best use of it. During that one moment we must do well what God desires of us. But instead we are so fond of living for the future; we make plans and are unnecessarily anxious about the things that are to occur tomorrow. Or we are preoccupied with the past, with unnecessary and injurious recollections, doubts, and scruples, and allow the present moment of grace to pass unused.

All too often we postpone to a later time what we ought to do at the present moment to fulfill the will of God. Eventually these deferred duties catch up with us and we find them an intolerable burden. Thus we can no longer perform such duties as we should. We hurry through them with an unbecoming haste merely to get them finished, not because we see in them the will of God. And all this time we should be performing every duty as it comes, with ease and confidence, with our eyes always fixed on God. Only one who is deeply grounded in the faith and who is absorbed in God can make the proper use of his time.

Since we waste so much of the time that is given to us, our faith urges us to recall our Lord's return for the judgment, and in the words of the Epistle it reminds us of the day of our death: "Redeeming the time." We have much to atone for.

What shall I, frail man, be pleading,
Who for me be interceding,
When the just are mercy needing?

Guilty, now I pour my moaning,
All my shame with anguish owning;
Spare, O God, Thy suppliant groaning.[22]

PRAYER

Graciously grant to Thy faithful, we beseech Thee, O Lord forgiveness and peace, that they may be cleansed from all offenses and serve Thee with a quiet mind. Through Christ our Lord. Amen.

Thursday

"Brethren: See how you walk circumspectly, not as unwise, but as wise, redeeming the time, because the days are evil" (Epistle). The times indeed are evil, filled with temptations, allurements,

[22] Sequence of the Requiem Mass, trans. from *The Saint Andrew Daily Missal.*

and dangers for our unstable supernatural aspirations and efforts. The chief danger and difficulty lies in our natural inclination toward spiritual sloth, which hinders us in our attempts to make use of our time for God and for the cultivation of a deep spirituality. The three chief forms of spiritual sloth are distraction, melancholy or depression of spirit, and occupation with unnecessary things.

Distraction is a state in which we are occupied with things which should not occupy us at the time. It is a "sin without a body." Distractions work in silence and call no attention to themselves. In fact, one of the most dangerous aspects of distractions is the fact that we scarcely notice that we are distracted. They are like a cancerous growth on our spiritual life, which gives birth to many unwholesome conditions, such as dissatisfaction with ourselves, a critical attitude toward others, a restless desire to justify ourselves, and an unhealthy tendency to criticize others. It destroys our recollection in prayer, makes us listless after our Holy Communion, causes us to fulfill our duties without zeal, and fills us with an overpowering distaste for mortification. This condition causes us to postpone till later deeds which we should do this very day and this very moment. We fall into a state of unrest and spiritual sloth, and we no longer see God in our duties, but only an intolerable burden. Distraction prevents us from beginning a work which we have long been about to commence. Distraction causes us to overburden ourselves with too many oral prayers and too many outward practices of piety.

Spiritual melancholy. No other condition in the spiritual life can lead to so many grievous sins as melancholy. It is opposed to humility, since it makes us quarrelsome and contentious rather than patient. It is in no sense contrition, but rather a secret anger with ourselves; it is not a true sorrow because we have offended God. It is, in the last analysis, a species of self-love. We become melancholy because we are too slothful to be faithful to our duties and to act properly. We have lost the courage necessary to break with our faults and imperfections. We inwardly turn to creatures and seek consolation from them. We want to be noticed and recognized, and we think that others ought to know how we feel and how we travail and suffer. Such spiritual melancholy gives the devil power over our soul. It weakens and impedes the effectiveness of the sacraments. It makes sweet things bitter, and causes the salutary instruments of the spiritual life to act like poison. We lose our courage for struggle and renunciation. We can no longer find God, and this very difficulty plunges us into a deeper melancholy. How effectively all this checks us in our attempts to make good use of the graces that God gives us! The chief source of such deep melancholy is the tendency to be less concerned with God and His honor and will than with our own will and what is pleasing to us. This tendency is true even in practices of piety; even many religious set as the goal of their spiritual effort, not God's honor, but rather their own spiritual progress. They are more concerned about themselves than they are about God's glory.

Preoccupation with unnecessary things. There perhaps never was a time when men were so prone to become absorbed in unnecessary things as now. They are tempted on all sides to waste their precious time in an inordinate and excessive preoccupation with lectures, newspapers, radio programs, movies, sports, celebrations, and new sensations. Not only worldly people give themselves to this intemperate concern with the things of this world, which prevents them from attending to the one thing necessary; but even we who are consecrated and dedicated to the service of God, have become absorbed in these unnecessary things, and thus impair our spirit of prayer and recollection, and prevent ourselves from giving ourselves entirely to God. How many unnecessary distractions we allow ourselves! How many unnecessary and even sinful thoughts and plans we harbor! How much time we devote to secular reading! Truly the liturgy has good reason to urge us to be "redeeming the time, for the days are evil."

An unusual degree of holiness and mortification is not required for our making the best use of every moment that is given to us. One of the greatest advantages of the religious life is this, that it protects and guards us against spiritual sloth. But even in the religious state, as well as in the world, one must have an appreciation of the value of every moment, an intense life of faith, a burning love for Christ, a generous detachment from the world, and a love for mortification.

Prayer

Graciously grant to Thy faithful we beseech Thee, O Lord, forgiveness and peace, that they may be cleansed from all offenses and serve Thee with a quiet mind. Through Christ our Lord. Amen.

Friday

"Redeeming the time, because the days are evil.... Wherefore, become not unwise, but understanding what is the will of God" (Epistle). The wisdom of the Christian life consists in understanding what is the will of God. God and His holy will must be respected under all circumstances. We shall redeem the time in the measure in which we are accustomed to regard all things in the light of God's holy will and good pleasure, and to suffer and accept all things in conformity with His will.

"Understanding what is the will of God." The Lord had but one concern: to do the will of His Father in all things. At all times He saw and understood the will of the Father with perfect clarity and certainty. When He came into this world as the incarnate Son of God, He had from the very beginning the clear vision of God. "For I do always the things that please Him" (Jn 8:29). "My meat is to do the will of Him that sent Me" (Jn 4:34). He knows only the will of the Father. His life is completely absorbed in God.

We share the life of Christ, for we are incorporated in Him. For us, too, everything must depend on the will of the Father. Our progress and our perfection depends on our "conforming ourselves with our whole heart to the will of God, never seeking anything for ourselves, either great or small, either for time or for eternity" (*Imitation of Christ,* III, chap. 25). Perfection consists in love; and love consists in our conforming ourselves to the will of God. "Thy will be done." We can fulfill the will of God, however, only in so far as we know and recognize it. We shall have made the first step in the Christian life and in the life of perfection when we begin to see the provident hand of God in all the situations and happenings of our life. We should not allow ourselves to become absorbed by these events and happenings, but we should look beyond them to the ultimate reality, almighty God Himself, "who worketh all in all" (1 Cor 12:6).

We can know and recognize the will of God by certain signs by which He makes known to us what He wills and desires. These signs are, first of all, the express word of God, as made known to us in the revelations of the Old and the New Testament, which tell us what God commands and forbids, what He advises and expects of us beyond His express commandments. Another sign of the will of God is manifested in His providence and His creation. Every creature proclaims the power and wisdom and love of God, and urges us to show the greatest respect for Him and to love and serve Him. God's providence is made manifest in everything that happens, from the greatest to the least. Every event of our lives, no matter how insignificant it may seem to us, is directed by the wisdom of God and ordained for our best interests. Our spiritual duties, nature, the social obligations arising from our membership in society, the duties of our state of life, are but so many manifestations of the will of God in our regard.

A third indication of the will of God may be found in the inspirations which He gives to us, which are not as easily recognized as the openly manifested will of God. If we achieve and maintain a close union with God, these inspirations will become increasingly clear and certain. A fourth sign of the will of God will be found in the enlightenment of our understanding. It is the will of God that we turn to Him in the spirit of faith and allow our intellect to be enlightened by His divine intellect. In many circumstances this is the only source from which we may seek enlightenment. As we grow in grace and increase in charity, our intellect becomes so enlightened by the Holy Spirit that we come to know instinctively what is the will of God. This is the gift of counsel.

"Understanding what is the will of God." There can be no more blessed knowledge than knowing what is the will of God. In the light of such knowledge we say: It is His will; He has ordained it so; He has allowed this to come to pass. Thus all our duties become light and sweet. Whatever befalls us we offer to Him as a prayer, saying: I accept this out of love for thee; or in the words of the Introit: "Blessed are the undefiled in the way, who walk in the law of the Lord."

"Understanding what is the will of God," we confess: "All that Thou hast done to us, O Lord, Thou hast done in true judgment; because we have sinned against Thee, and we have not obeyed Thy commandments" (Introit). In all the sufferings that God imposes on us we must recognize the hand of the just, merciful, and loving Father. We should humble ourselves beneath the hand of God, and with unshakable confidence in His justice and mercy cry out, "Give glory to Thy name, and deal with us according to the multitude of Thy mercy." Thus we should consider and accept the sufferings of this life in the spirit of our Holy Mother the Church.

Prayer

Graciously grant to Thy faithful, we beseech Thee, O Lord, forgiveness and peace, that they may be cleansed from all offenses and serve Thee with a quiet mind. Through Christ our Lord. Amen.

Saturday

The liturgy is concerned today with the approaching end of all things, and particularly with the proximity of our own death. Holy Mother the Church is filled with sorrow to see so many of her baptized children living worldly lives, totally absorbed by worldly cares and interests, and devoting themselves so completely to temporal goods and pursuits. They are totally lacking in "understanding what is the will of God; and be not drunk with wine, wherein is luxury; but be ye filled with the Holy Spirit" (Epistle).

"Be ye filled with the Holy Spirit," as Mary was and as the apostles were after the descent of the Holy Ghost. Be filled with the Holy Spirit, who inspired awe and reverence in all who saw them who had been transformed by His coming. Instinctively men recognized that some divine power was operating in them. The very purpose of our receiving baptism and confirmation is to be filled with this same Holy Spirit. Before our baptism the priest breathed upon us and said: "Depart, thou unclean spirit, and give place to the Holy Ghost, the Paraclete." Then the priest traced the sign of the cross on our forehead. After putting blessed salt on our tongue, he prayed: "I command thee, thou impure spirit, in the name of the Father, and of the Son, and of the Holy Ghost, to depart from this servant of God. May He who walked upon the waters and extended His right hand to the sinking Peter, command thee to go forth, thou accursed and damned spirit." The Holy Spirit entered our soul at the moment of our baptism and filled it with His light and sanctity.

When we were led to the sacrament of confirmation, the bishop received us with the words: "May the Holy Spirit descend upon thee, and may the power of the Most High defend thee from sin. Amen." What was accomplished in the apostles at Pentecost, was repeated again in us at confirmation. We received the Holy Ghost as a protection in our fight with the devil, as a means of coming to the full knowledge of Christ and His doctrine, as a means of developing and perfecting ourselves in Christian virtue and holiness. The bishop extended his hand over us and called down upon us the Spirit of truth and understanding, the Spirit of wisdom and strength, the Spirit of knowledge and piety, and the Spirit of the fear of the Lord, which is the foundation of all true spiritual life. Then the bishop anointed us with chrism and prayed: "Establish and confirm what Thou hast wrought in Thy holy temple." We have become temples of the Holy Ghost; we should daily increase in perfection.

"Be ye filled with the Holy Spirit." The evil spirit no longer has any claim over us. The spirit of worldliness and our purely natural outlook on life must also be put aside. We may no longer act from purely natural motives and for purely selfish ends, or for the satisfaction of our purely natural feelings, ambitions, and desires. Our guiding principle must now be the Holy Spirit, who dwells within us and rules us. Our purely natural way of thinking and living must now be replaced by a deeper and more vital faith. Our hope now rests on a joyful and unshakable trust in the love of God our Savior, and on our childlike trust in the powerful and all-embracing providence of our heavenly Father. Our will becomes so absorbed by the divine will that the latter becomes the mainspring of all our thoughts, desires, and actions. Filled with the Holy Spirit, we live continually in the fear of the Lord. We fear sin and flee from it and from the slightest negligence and unfaithfulness; we know that we belong entirely to God and that we must save and sanctify our soul at any cost. Filled with the Holy Spirit, we live in the love of Christ. We maintain a tender and vital communion with God, our Father and friend. We live always in His presence and devote ourselves completely to His praise in thanksgiving and complete surrender. We forget ourselves entirely and devote ourselves with burning zeal to Him and His interests. We believe that our highest good and our most precious possession is to be pleasing to Him and to live according to His will and good pleasure. We cling to Christ with a tender and childlike love, considering His incarnation and the mysteries of His life on earth. We are devoted to Holy Mother the Church and all that the Holy Spirit works through her in her sacraments, her life, and her prayer.

Filled with the Holy Spirit, we are contented. In spite of external and internal sufferings and trials, a deep and unshakable peace and sense of security resides in our hearts. Even temptation does not confuse or dishearten us. In our contacts with the world about us we preserve our peace of soul, even when others intrude on our rights. Filled with the Holy Spirit, we lift ourselves above the purely natural manner of thinking and acting. Instinctively and without great difficulty we free ourselves from our indolence and uncertainty, and tend naturally (we ourselves hardly know how) to seek what is right. We feel ourselves strengthened to avoid all mediocrity and routine, and are enabled to perform acts that are heroic. A more than human principle is at work in us, and this is the Holy Spirit. Filled with the Holy Spirit, we sing and rejoice in our hearts to the Lord (Epistle). We are united with the universal praying Church in thanksgiving, adoration, love, and praise, and in the Sacrifice of the Mass.

"Be ye filled with the Holy Spirit," is the wish of the liturgy and the fruit of the feast of Pentecost during the weeks that follow. In order that we may be filled with the Holy Spirit, we must separate ourselves from all sin and infidelity. We must be careful to cooperate with grace, and must strive to avoid all routine and negligence; we must seek to avoid all self-seeking, all worldly desires and ambitions. We must seek to crush our hidden pride and our misguided self-confidence, avoiding all concessions to the senses and to the flesh.

Prayer

Graciously grant to Thy faithful, we beseech Thee, O Lord, forgiveness and peace, that they may be cleansed from all offenses and serve Thee with a quiet mind. Through Christ our Lord. Amen.

Twenty-First Sunday after Pentecost

The Mass

The year of grace is rapidly drawing to a close. The Church lives in fear lest the enemy, by redoubling his efforts, destroy for the faithful the fruit of the fleeting year. For this reason she admonishes her children to renew their struggle and to be steadfast in goodness and truth, resisting Satan and his cohorts. The Christian is by nature a soldier. The life of the Christian is a warfare in defense of the ideals of Christ the King, our Lord and God. In Holy Scripture this Christian warfare is prefigured in Esther, who, strengthened by fasting and prayer, presents herself before the king and overcomes the cruel and cunning Aman, the enemy of her people. Job, too, prefigures this same ideal through his faith and patience in his persecutions and his struggle against Satan. The example of Job and Esther, and the thought of the approaching judgment all spur us on to a valiant struggle against evil.

Esther, that is, the Church and the Christian soul, is hated, persecuted, and oppressed by Aman, who is the figure of Satan and all his helpers. She seeks an escape in prayer. "All things are in Thy will, O Lord; and there is none that can resist Thy will" (Introit). Rise up then in Thy power, O Lord, and "watch over Thy household" (Collect). The enemies that rise up against the Church and the Christian soul are not only those of flesh and blood (human weakness), but the struggle is "against the principalities and powers, against the rulers of the world of this darkness, against the spirits of wickedness in the high places" (Epistle). For this struggle God provides us with strong armor: "your loins girt about with truth, and having on the breastplate of justice, and your feet shod with the preparation of the gospel of peace; in all things taking the shield of faith, wherewith you may be able to extinguish all the fiery darts of the most wicked one. And take unto you the helmet of salvation and the sword of the spirit, which is the word of God" (Epistle).

The Gradual resumes the theme of the Introit. By gazing on the majesty of God, who existed "before the mountains were made, or the earth and the world was formed," the Christian soul acquires strength and stability. What is man in comparison to such a God? Only a miserable sinner. Yet God willingly forgives us our sins if we ask Him; but we must also freely forgive others (Gospel). Then we may hope for strength and help from God in overcoming the enemy of our salvation, as Job, an upright and God-fearing man, victoriously and persistently waged his fight against Satan with heroic patience. Satan tried by all manner of oppression and misfortune to make him curse God; but Job was stronger than Satan. He put on the armor of God and remained true and faithful to Him (Offertory).

With a firm faith in God, the Ruler of all creation, and strengthened by fasting and prayer, Esther, the bride and queen, the Church, makes her entrance into the presence of the King. We accompany her. With her we offer our gifts to the King. The gifts that we offer are the body and blood of Christ, "the bread of life and the chalice of eternal salvation"; and to this, our principal gift, we add ourselves, that we may love God and serve Him and belong to Him entirely. With Job, who is also a type of the suffering and humiliated Christ, we are prepared to submit completely to the will of God and to suffer whatever difficulties or crosses He may send to us. For the armor and the protection we need in this struggle with the powers of evil, we go to the Holy Sacrifice of the Mass. We receive the breastplate of justice and holiness, the shield of faith, the helmet of invincible conviction that we shall conquer and be saved. At Holy Communion we receive salvation in Christ. Christ, who was not found wanting in trials and tribulations, lives in His Church and in us. He, like another Job, conquers and overcomes all His enemies through His patient subjection to the will of God. He conquers the evil spirits, the princes of this world, and the enemies of the Church through us, who are His members. Through the reception of Communion and our union with Christ, we obtain repose of soul and eternal salvation. Christ has solemnly promised: "He that eateth Me, the same also shall live by Me" (Jn 6:58). This is the "food of immortality" (Postcommunion). At Mass we shall gain the strength necessary to forgive and pardon those who have offended us, that we ourselves may await the Day of Judgment with faith and confidence in the mercy of God.

Meditation

The Church is the new Israel, which, departing from the land of Egypt (this present world) is being led into the promised land of eternity (Alleluia verse). Between the time of our departure from Egypt (our baptism) and the time of our entrance into the promised land (the hour of our death) we are beset on all sides by the enemies of our salvation. But we shall be victorious. We have in our hands the weapons which give us the assurance of victory.

The hostile powers which oppose us, the people of God, are presented to us today in the liturgy in the person of the enemies of Job and Esther. Job lived a simple and upright life in the fear of God. Therefore, "Satan besought that he might tempt [him]; and power was given him from the Lord over his possessions and his flesh" (Offertory). Esther was informed of Aman's cruel plan to kill the Israelites in the Persian empire all in one day. She prayed to the Lord, and He delivered them (Introit). With the liturgy we see ourselves and Holy Mother the Church surrounded and oppressed on all sides, for we are like Job and the Israelites for whom Aman had planned a terrible destruction. Persecution is the portion of all those who adhere to God. Because they walk upright in the way of God, Satan seeks permission to tempt them. The Lord has given Satan a certain amount of power over them. A people which is not tempted is not the people of God. A Church which does not suffer continual persecution and oppression is not the Church of Christ. The watchword of that Church is "fight," for "our wrestling is not against flesh and blood, but against principalities and powers, against the rulers of the world of this darkness, against the spirit of wickedness in the high places" (Epistle). God gives the wicked spirits power over the Church and over Christians, that, being tempted, they may prove their strength and valor under temptation. Satan, however, cannot go further than God permits. Christ is Lord even over Satan and hell.

We shall conquer all our enemies and we need have no fear, for the Lord "hast been our refuge from generation to generation" (Gradual). Through His holy Church we have received the armor of God at our baptism. With this armor we can resist and "stand in all things perfect. Stand, therefore, having your loins girt about with truth, and having on the breastplate of justice, and your feet shod with the preparation of the gospel of peace; in all things taking the shield of faith, wherewith you may be able to extinguish all the fiery darts of the most wicked one. And take unto you the helmet of salvation and the sword of the Spirit, which is the word of God" (Epistle). Other weapons placed in our hands are those of abstinence and prayer. Esther made use of fasting and prayer (Introit). When Job was tempted by the devil, he gave himself to prayer. St. Paul at the end of his Epistle to the Ephesians adds the admonition: "By all prayer and supplication, praying at all times in the spirit; and in the same, watching with all instance and supplication for all the saints" (Eph 6:18). In the Gospel our attention is called to another useful weapon, the practice of mercy and charity toward our neighbor. "Forgive us our trespasses as we forgive those who trespass against us." This weapon of fraternal charity and mercy gives us certain power even over God, for if we are merciful, God will be merciful also to us; for to the extent that we show mercy to others, we shall ourselves receive mercy. "Forgive and you shall be forgiven" (Lk 6:37). But on the other hand, "so also shall My Father do to you, if you forgive not every one his brother in your hearts" (Gospel).

Today's Gospel is filled with consolation. God does indeed give Satan and evil men a certain power over the Church and her virtuous children. The evil they inflict on the Church is taken into account in the plans of God's providence. Godless men and their leader, Satan, are made to serve the ends of almighty God. We are at all times under the powerful protection of God, even though it may appear that we have been delivered into the hands of our enemies.

"Israel went out of Egypt, the house of Jacob from a barbarous people" (Alleluia). We, too, have departed from a barbarous people having idols and false gods. Just as we once did at the time of our baptism, so now in the celebration of the Mass we renounce all that is not godly and persevere in walking in the ways of God. With holy Job, at the Offertory we abandon ourselves into the hands of God, even though He may deliver us into the hands of our enemies, send us tribulations, deprive us of our possessions, and inflict bodily sufferings upon us. His will be done. We are a complete holocaust in the hands of God and we wish to remain so. The more completely we abandon ourselves into His hands, the more certain we can be that He will take us to Himself and save us (Communion).

Prayer

Watch over Thy household, we beseech Thee, O Lord, with continual mercy, that through Thy protection it may be freed from all adversities and be devoted to good works. Through Christ our Lord. Amen.

Monday

Today the Church presents to us the figure of Job, a just man who has been delivered over to the power of Satan, surrounded by unfaithful friends, afflicted with a dread disease, deprived of his possessions, and ridiculed by his friends and neighbors. Armed with faith and confidence in God, and inspired by holy patience, he lifts up his eyes to God and remains steadfast in all his trials and afflictions. Job is a type of the innocent Savior: suffering, yet victorious in all His afflictions. He is a type of the persecuted but victorious Church. Although with the permission of God she and her children are subjected to trials and persecutions, they are still victorious.

Our fight "is not against flesh and blood," against the men of this world, "but against principalities and powers, against the rulers of the world of this darkness," that is, against evil men and malicious spirits. It is the will of God that the Church fight continually. We who are members of the militant Church are soldiers committed to battle. "The kingdom of heaven suffereth violence, and the violent bear it away" (Mt 11:12). Our enemies and the enemies of the Church are not the men about us, but the evil and malicious spirits who by far surpass men in their intelligence and power. "My name is legion, for we are many" (Mk 5:9). These spirits are utterly malicious, deceitful, and unfaithful. Their objective is the destruction and eternal damnation of the precious souls that Christ has purchased by His blood. These spirits are the complete masters of "the world of this darkness" and the leaders of the infidels, the evil and godless men of this world, who make war on Christ. They accomplish their work through men like Nero and Domitian and Arius; they work through all those who mock, malign, and oppress Christ and His Church. As long as the Church remains on earth, it will be a fighting Church, a Church militant. Through the Church, Christ fights against the Antichrist. We are the soldiers of the Church militant, and St. Peter admonishes us: "Be sober and watch, because your adversary, the devil, as a roaring lion goeth about seeking whom he may devour" (1 Pt 5:8). The Church reminds us of this danger every evening at Compline and urges us: "Whom resist ye, strong in faith" (1 Pt 5:9). We are to resist the devil with the faith of Esther, the faith of the Church. "All things are in Thy will, O Lord, and there is none that can resist Thy will; for Thou hast made all things, heaven, and earth, and all things that are under the cope of heaven; Thou art Lord of all" (Introit). The Lord is more powerful than Satan and all the powers of darkness. "Lord, Thou hast been our refuge" (Gradual).

"Whom resist ye, strong in faith" (1 Pt 5:9), that is, in the armor of God: "Having your loins girt about with truth, and having on the breastplate of justice, and your feet shod with the preparation of the gospel of peace; in all things taking the shield of faith,... the helmet of salvation and the sword of the Spirit, which is the word of God" (Epistle). The Apostle is solicitous lest the soldiers of Christ neglect any of the weapons which the Lord has provided for them. The whole armor of the Christian soldier consists of six pieces: a girdle, a breastplate, sandals, a shield, a helmet, and a sword. The girdle of truth is the virtue of faith and our oath of allegiance given to the Lord at the time of our baptism. The "breastplate of justice" is our dedication to a good and virtuous life. The sandals with which the feet of the Christian soldier must be shod are our promptness in living at all times in the spirit and doctrine of Christ, our imitation of the example of the Lord, our application of His teachings to our own life, and the example of a virtuous Christian life that we give to the world. On our left arm we carry the "shield of faith": our firm confidence in His abiding presence, in His power, His grace, His operation within our souls. On our heads we wear the "helmet of salvation," that is, our hope and trust in the eternal salvation which awaits us. With the right hand we wield the "sword of the Spirit, which is the word of God." Imitating Christ's example in the desert, we are to reply to all the suggestions of Satan: "Begone, Satan! For it is written: The Lord thy God shalt thou adore, and Him only shalt thou serve" (Mt 4:10).

The life of the Church and of her children is a continual struggle to establish the ideals of Christ in the world. Christ relives His earthly life in us and conquers in us. He fights and conquers in us all days, "even to the consummation of the world" (Mt 28:20); for He is the risen Lord, the King of the world, who lives in His members. In order that He might live in us and conquer through us, He united us to Himself as His members through baptism. He gives us Himself as the food for our souls, and from this food we gain power and strength. With His power and strength we fight and conquer; on Him we depend for all things. "All things are in Thy will, O Lord; and there is none that can resist Thy will; for Thou hast made all things" (Introit). "Lord, Thou hast been our refuge from generation to generation. Before the mountains were made, or the earth and world was formed,... Thou art God" (Gradual). Thou fightest within Thy Church and conquerest within Thy members.

We are to put on the armor of God and maintain a firm confidence in Christ, who lives within us. We must be faithful to the oath of allegiance we took at baptism, keeping alive the spirit of faith, our zeal for the gospel, and our spirit of penance and abstinence.

Prayer

Watch over Thy household, we beseech Thee, O Lord, with continual mercy, that through Thy protection it may be freed from all adversities and be devoted to good works. Through Christ our Lord. Amen.

Tuesday

"The kingdom of heaven is likened to a king who would take an account of his servants" (Gospel). We are waiting for the Lord to appear for the so-called particular judgment, which follows immediately after death. This judgment will decide our lot in eternity; that is, whether we shall spend our eternity in heaven or in hell. "It is appointed unto men once to die, and after this the judgment" (Heb 9:27).

The particular judgment. The Mass for the Dead gives us a startling picture of the judgment of the world. The day of the coming of the Lord, the day of death, the day of our particular judgment, is a day of reckoning, a day on which we shall have to render an account of the sins and faults of our past life. It is a day of reckoning on which we shall have to give an account of all our talents and graces, of our health, our bodies, and our faculties, of our thoughts, words, and deeds, and of every moment of time.

Lo! the book exactly worded
Wherein all hath been recorded;
Thence shall judgment be awarded.

When the Judge His seat attaineth,
And each hidden deed arraigneth,
Nothing unavenged remaineth.[23]

"Give an account of thy stewardship" (Lk 16:2), give an account of thy whole life. At the moment of our death the good and the evil which we have done, the things that we have neglected or done imperfectly, will stand out before our soul as clearly as the light of the sun. Then the Judge will pass an eternal sentence, saying either, "Come, ye blessed of My Father," or "Depart from Me, you cursed, into everlasting fire" (Mt 25:34, 41). What will be the sentence that will be passed on me? It will be the sentence which I have prepared for myself by my actions while living in this world. How terrible and how important is that moment of death! But every moment of my life is just as important. Each one may be my last, the moment of my judgment.

Our Holy Mother the Church presents her children to the Judge. She identifies herself with her anxious child and implores the Lord on its behalf:

Think, good Jesus, my salvation
Caused Thy wondrous incarnation.
Leave me not in reprobation.

Faint and weary Thou hast sought me,
On the cross of suffering bought me.
Shall such grace be vainly brought me?

Thou the sinful woman savedst;
Thou the dying thief forgavest;
And to me a hope vouchsafest.[24]

[23] Ibid.
[24] Ibid.

In the Offertory of the Mass for the Dead, the Church entreats the Lord: "O Lord Jesus Christ, King of Glory, deliver the souls of all the faithful departed from the pains of hell and from the deep pit; deliver them from the lion's mouth, that hell may not swallow them up.... We offer Thee sacrifices and prayers of praise, O Lord; do Thou accept them for those souls for whom we this day make commemoration; cause them, O Lord, to pass from death to life." This prayer expresses the anxiety of a mother for her children. When all others have deserted the imperiled soul, Holy Mother the Church remains faithfully at its side, praying and offering sacrifice for it. Her prayers ascend to the very throne of God, and there she influences God to be merciful in His judgment.

While we remain in this life we may earn for ourselves a merciful judgment. In the celebration of the Mass we possess the means of making satisfaction to God for our sins and negligences. But we must offer this sacrifice to God with sincerity, zeal, and a spirit of contrition. We must perform works of penance for our own sins, and forgive readily the offenses committed against us. We must perform works of Christian charity, for much will depend on the charity and mercy we have shown to our offending neighbor (Mt 25:31–46). Through the reception of Holy Communion the soul finds strength and protection from the dangers arising from evil spirits and from the flesh and the world. Holy Communion is an "antidote which saves us from mortal sin" (Council of Trent). It augments the grace in our soul, strengthens our virtues, and inflames charity and the love of one's neighbor. It heals the soul of its weaknesses and gives it spiritual joy, strength, zeal, and enthusiasm. Through Holy Communion we are intimately united to our Blessed Lord. He has conquered sin, death, and Satan. He will "execute judgment on them that persecute me" and will conquer them (Communion). He lives, fights, and conquers in us. Through the power of Holy Communion we shall experience a merciful judgment and receive the reward of eternal life (Jn 6:57).

Prayer

Watch over Thy household, we beseech Thee, O Lord, with continual mercy, that through Thy protection, it may be freed from all adversities and be devoted to good works. Through Christ our Lord. Amen.

Wednesday

"And as he had not wherewith to pay it, his lord commanded that he should be sold, and his wife and children, and all that he had, and payment to be made. But that servant, falling down, besought him, saying: Have patience with me, and I will pay thee all. And the lord of that servant, being moved with pity, let him go and forgave him the debt" (Gospel).

"And forgave him the debt." How marvelous is God's mercy! The miserable servant realizes that his lord is angry and now he hears him give the order to the officers of justice, that he and all his family be sold into slavery. He throws himself at the feet of the master and begs for mercy and promises to pay the entire debt. Was not that master fully aware that his servant would never be able to pay the whole debt of ten thousand talents? Then what did the servant mean by saying that he would pay the debt in full? Undoubtedly the master was moved by his servant's plea for mercy and considered only the willingness of the servant to pay a debt that was entirely beyond his power to satisfy. He forgave him the debt "because thou besoughtest me." Such is God's way. When the erring sinner humbles himself and acknowledges his sin, repents of it and resolves to do better, God forgives his sin, no matter how great it may be. How powerful is the prayer of sorrow and repentance when it seeks mercy and forgiveness! "But thou hast mercy upon all, because thou canst do all things and overlookest the sins of men for the sake of repentance" (Ws 11:24). "As I live, saith the Lord God, I desire not the death of the wicked, but that the wicked turn from his way and live" (Ez 33:11). "The Lord dealeth patiently for your sake, not willing that any should perish, but that all should return to penance" (2 Pt 3:9).

"Shouldst not thou then have had compassion also on thy fellow servant, even as I had compassion on thee?" (Gospel.) Our God is a merciful God, but He is also just. The master had forgiven the wicked servant his entire debt. "But when that servant was gone out, he found one of his fellow servants that owed him a hundred pence; and laying hold of him he throttled him, saying: Pay what thou owest. And his fellow servant, falling down, besought him, saying: Have patience with me, and I will pay thee all. And he would not; but went and cast him into prison till he paid the debt" (Gospel). The master heard of this harsh act and summoned the unmerciful servant before him, and said: "Thou wicked servant, I forgave thee all the debt, because thou besoughtest me; shouldst not thou then have had compassion also on thy fellow servant even as I had compassion on thee?" When God is merciful to us, He expects that we extend mercy and forgiveness to those who injure us or cause us sorrow or pain. "But I say to you: Love your enemies; do good to them that hate you; and pray for them that persecute and calumniate you, that you may be the children of your Father who is in heaven, who maketh His sun to rise upon the good and the bad, and raineth upon the just and the unjust" (Mt 5:44 f.). "And when you shall stand to pray, forgive if you have aught against any man, that your Father also, who is in heaven, may forgive you your sins" (Mk 11:25). It is only just, then, that we who have so often experienced the mercy of God should extend a like mercy to those who offend us. But how sadly we fail in thus being the children of our heavenly Father! How often we utter our own sentence of condemnation when we fail to forgive others!

This, then, is a preliminary condition for those who wish to obtain mercy and dispose themselves for forgiveness: they must be prepared to show a merciful and forgiving love for their brother. "For if you will forgive men their offenses, your heavenly Father will forgive you also your offenses" (Mt 6:14). "If therefore thou offer thy gift at the altar, and there thou remember that thy brother hath anything against thee, leave there thy offering before the altar and go first to be reconciled to thy brother; and then coming thou shalt offer thy gift" (Mt 5:23 f.). The Kiss of Peace immediately before the Communion of the Mass is our pledge that we forgive our brethren from the bottom of our heart and cast all bitterness and resentment aside: "May the peace of the Lord be with you." Only when we have signified our union with our brethren do we dare approach to receive the sacrament of the Holy Eucharist, "the sacrament of brotherly love, the symbol of unity and the bond of charity" (St. Augustine).

"[He] forgave him the debt." How abundant is God's mercy in the sacrament of penance! We repent of our sins, we confess them humbly to the representative of God in the confessional, we beg for forgiveness, and we are prepared to perform the penance that is assigned to us. And then God forgives us our entire debt and the punishment which we have so keenly deserved. He restores us to the state of grace and receives us again among His beloved children.

Prayer

Watch over Thy household, we beseech thee, O Lord, with continual mercy, that through Thy protection it may be freed from all adversities and be devoted to good works. Through Christ our Lord. Amen.

Thursday

The liturgy last Sunday directed our attention to the last days. We now await the return of the Lord, the day of judgment, and our final sentence. "The kingdom of heaven is likened to a king who would take an account of his servants" (Gospel). The king is both merciful and just. To the servant who asks to be forgiven his debts, he grants mercy. But the servant who is unmerciful toward his fellow servant, he delivers to the torturers "until he paid all the debt."

The Lord is merciful. The indebtedness of His servant is immense, and He has the right to demand full payment. But He shows mercy to him and cancels the whole debt: "I forgave thee all the debt because thou besoughtest me" (Gospel). When God forgives, He forgives completely. When He finds a sinner penitent, contrite, and disposed to amend his life, He forgives the whole debt. If the sinner is capable of an act of perfect contrition, a perfect act of love, it is apparent that he is prepared to do whatever God requires, and God forgives his entire debt, his sins and the temporal punishment due to them. God is a merciful God. With justice He could leave us in our sins. But He bears patiently with us until the very hour of our death, continually inviting us to repentance and amendment. Because of His mercy He gives us time to confess our sins, to repent, and to amend our lives. If we comply, He forgives us our debts and adds His grace. With this grace He gives us His abiding presence and the right to eternal happiness. "God (who is rich in mercy) for His exceeding charity wherewith He loved us, even when we were dead in sins, hath quickened us together in Christ (by whose grace you are saved), and hath raised us up together and hath made us sit together in the heavenly places, through Christ Jesus. That He might show in the ages to come the abundant riches of His grace in His bounty towards us in Christ Jesus" (Eph 2:4–7).

The Lord is just. The servant whose immense debt had been entirely forgiven goes out and meets a fellow servant. The amount this servant owes him is trifling in comparison with that which he owed his master. His fellow servant falls on his knees and beseeches him, "Have patience with me, and I will pay thee all." But the wicked servant will show no mercy to his fellow servant. Cruelly and without hesitation he has him cast into prison until he pays the entire debt. Now the master hears of this wicked act and is grieved, so that he delivers the wicked servant to the torturers "until he paid all the debt."

God is thorough in His administration of justice as well as in His mercy. We, too, must make complete satisfaction for the temporal punishment due to sin, either in this world or in purgatory. "Thou shalt not go out from thence [from the pains of purgatory] till thou repay the last farthing" (Mt 5:26). And should a soul have the misfortune to appear before God in the state of mortal sin, God is still thorough in His justice and condemns that soul to hell for all eternity. Such a sinner will never be able to pay all his debt. He must remain eternally separated from

God; for his debt will never be satisfied. He has been condemned for all eternity and thrown into the pit, "where their worm dieth not, and the fire is not extinguished" (Mk 9:43). "It is a fearful thing to fall into the hands of the living God" (Heb 10:31). The condemned sinner is no longer a child of God and no longer receives grace; he has lost his right to eternal life, and he is cast into exterior darkness, where there is "weeping and gnashing of teeth" (Mt 22:13). The poor wretch cannot lift a hand to ward off his fate; he cannot make the slightest movement to escape hell. Repentance and sorrow and even prayer are now in vain. It is too late. Hell is eternal.

God is just. "It is a fearful thing to fall into the hands of the living God." For this reason we pray daily and hourly in preparation for the coming judgment. We strive to keep our hearts and our minds free from every stain of sin. We pass judgment on ourselves each day by an earnest examination of our past life, our thoughts, our desires, our deeds, and we stand in fear of the just anger of God. We have a salutary fear of hell. Hell is only for those who spurn God, who are unfaithful to God, who are lacking in virtue. We strive to do penance, for God is merciful and we trust in that mercy. Although we are weak, inclined to evil, full of faults and frailties, we do not lose courage, for we have been humbled by our sins and we are sorry for them. We approach the sacrament of penance asking for grace and forgiveness in the firm hope that we shall receive a merciful judgment. We shall find mercy in proportion to the mercy we have shown to others. "Be ye therefore merciful as your heavenly Father also is merciful" (Lk 6:36). "Blessed are the merciful, for they shall obtain mercy" (Mt 5:7).

God is both just and merciful. In the celebration of the Mass we make complete satisfaction to the justice of God through the blood of Christ Jesus. In Holy Communion He gives us Jesus, the incarnate mercy of God.

Prayer

Watch over Thy household, we beseech Thee, O Lord, with continual mercy, that through Thy protection it may be freed from all adversities and be devoted to good works. Through Christ our Lord. Amen.

Friday

"The kingdom of heaven is likened to a king who would take an account of his servants. And when he had begun to take the account, one was brought to him that owed him ten thousand talents" (Gospel). We ourselves are this debtor.

"One was brought to him that owed him ten thousand talents." The poor man was unable to repay such a great debt. In this servant we see ourselves. We owe the Lord a debt that we can never pay. We are indebted to Him for our creation, for God preferred us to so many others whom He might have created but did not. We are indebted to Him for the grace of preservation on the earth; He could allow us to sink back into nothingness if He willed. We are indebted to Him for our body and our soul, for our powers and abilities, our health, our life, and for whatever good we possess. We are indebted to Him for the gift of His divine Son, for the grace of salvation, for our dignity as children of God, for the grace of sharing in the life of God already here on earth and eventually in eternity, and for the glorification of our bodies and souls. To

Him we owe the grace of union with Christ the vine, the grace of membership in the Church, the gift of faith. We are indebted to Him for the Church, the sacraments, the Mass and Holy Communion. Through God's generosity we participate in the good works of the other members of the Church, in the intercession of the blessed in heaven, in the meritorious works of the Blessed Mother. We are indebted to Him for the innumerable graces which we receive daily, which help us to resist sin and the temptations of the devil. We owe to Him the countless inspirations and enlightenments which cause us to perform acts of virtue. We are His debtors for any progress we have made in grace and virtue. If we are priests or religious, we are indebted to Him above all for the precious grace of our vocation, which has preserved us from so many dangers and temptations and which has permitted us to spend so much time in prayer and in union with God. Our debt to God our Savior is indeed great. Ten thousand talents hardly describes the amount of our indebtedness to God.

"Have patience with me, and I will pay thee all" (Gospel). Is it possible that we can repay God in full for all His graces? Yes, indeed, we shall make full payment through the Holy Sacrifice of the Mass. The Mass is essentially a "eucharist," a sacrifice of thanksgiving, a payment for a debt of gratitude. In that sacrifice we take the "spotless host," Christ, the lamb of the sacrifice, in our hands and offer Him up to His Father. Since our own prayers of thanksgiving are so feeble, we take this host, this body of Jesus, this blood of the Redeemer, and offer it to heaven, an infinite prayer of thanksgiving. "Vouchsafe to look upon them with a gracious and tranquil countenance and to accept them [our gifts] even as thou wert pleased to accept the offerings of Thy just servant Abel." "Through Him, and with Him, and in Him is to Thee, God the Father Almighty, in the unity of the Holy Ghost, all honor and glory" (Canon of the Mass). The Mass is a perfect sacrifice of thanksgiving. As often as the Church offers this Sacrifice, all her children offer it with her in payment for their debt of gratitude, which we hope to satisfy "through Christ our Lord." "Have patience with me, and I will pay thee all."

"Have patience with me, and I will pay Thee all," is the petition of the Church through her liturgy. She will make this payment through the Holy Eucharist, the sacrifice of thanksgiving. "Let us give thanks to the Lord our God" (let us celebrate the Eucharist), says Holy Mother the Church; and we answer, "It is meet and just." The Church, through the mouth of her priest, confirms our assertion, "It is truly meet and just, right and profitable for us at all times and in all places to give thanks to Thee, O holy Lord, the Father Almighty and everlasting God, through Christ our Lord." In these words of the Preface the prayer of praise and thanksgiving of the oldest Christian liturgy is preserved and in it is expressed the spirit of the sacrificing Church in its earliest form. By participating in the Mass we acquire the spirit of the Church and apply that spirit to our daily lives. Our life should not be a life devoted primarily to seeking things from God, but rather to offering Him acts of thanksgiving, adoration, and praise. Our life should be one continual hymn of praise. "We praise Thee; we bless Thee; we adore Thee; we glorify Thee. We give Thee thanks for Thy great glory, O Lord God, heavenly King, God the Father Almighty. O Lord Jesus Christ, the only begotten Son.... For Thou alone art holy, Thou alone art the Lord, Thou alone, O Jesus Christ, art most high, together with the Holy Ghost, in the glory of God the Father" (Gloria).

"Prayers are few enough, but prayers of thanksgiving are still more rare" (W. Faber). Daily men send thousands of Our Fathers and Hail Marys up to heaven, but they are directed chiefly to obtain favors or to escape difficulties. If these petitioners receive their requests, do they offer up prayers of thanksgiving? "Were not ten made clean? And where are the nine? There is no one found to return and give glory to God but this stranger" (Lk 17:17 f.). This complaint of the Lord could very well be applied to us Christians also. We are so sparing in our thanks because our love is so meager. Gratitude is so much a work of love that we shall spend our whole eternity giving thanks to God as we gaze upon Him and love Him eternally. Here on earth our Holy Mother the Church renders thanks to God in the Holy Sacrifice of the Mass. We should join her in this spirit.

Prayer

Watch over Thy household, we beseech Thee, O Lord, with continual mercy, that through Thy protection it may be freed from all adversities and be devoted to good works. Through Christ our Lord. Amen.

Saturday

"The kingdom of heaven is likened to a king who would take an account of his servants. And when he had begun to take the account, one was brought to him that owed him ten thousand talents" (Gospel). The liturgy has us in mind when it speaks of the debtor who owed ten thousand talents.

"One was brought to him that owed him ten thousand talents," that is, an immense sum of money. Such an immense debt we owe to God because of our sins; for even one mortal sin far surpasses such a debt to God. A single mortal sin is such a heinous offense against God that man could never make satisfaction for it. Even the severest and most excruciating penance could not satisfy for such a sin. The gravity of an offense is always measured by the dignity of the one offended. Sin is an offense of infinite gravity because the infinite God is the one who is offended. How can man, who is finite, make amends for an offense against the infinite majesty of God? It is absolutely impossible for a sinner himself to make reparation for the injury he has done through his sin. Not even the merits and satisfactions of all the men who have ever lived could make amends for one single sin. We who are sinners are, then, debtors who owe to God a debt of ten thousand talents. We have contracted an immense debt with God through Original Sin and through our personal sins, through our violations of the laws of God and the Church in thought, word, and deed.

"Have patience with me, and I will pay thee all" (Gospel). We can pay our debt to God, however, by making use of the merits and satisfactions of Christ our Savior. He who is both God and man is alone capable of paying our debt to God. This debt He has paid through His suffering and death. Through baptism He has united us with His sufferings and death so that they become ours, "just as if we ourselves had suffered and died" (St. Thomas Aquinas). Daily during the Holy Sacrifice of the Mass we can offer the sufferings and death of Christ for our sins. We can offer His merits, His satisfactions, His precious blood to the Father as full payment for the debt that we owe. The Mass is a propitiatory sacrifice. "Receive, O holy Father, almighty and eternal God, this spotless host, which I thine unworthy servant offer unto Thee, my living and true God, for my countless sins, offenses, and negligences" (prayer at the Offertory). "Graciously receive, O Lord, the sacrifices with which Thou hast willed that Thou shouldst be appeased and our salvation by Thy powerful mercy be restored" (Secreta). "Lord, Thou has been our refuge from generation to generation" (Gradual). The Lord, in His bloody death on the cross and in the unbloody sacrifice on the altar, is our refuge. Through the celebration of the Mass, God is reconciled and grace and forgiveness are given even for the greatest crime (Council of Trent, Sess. XXII, chap. 2). We can, then, with full confidence cry out, "Have patience with me, and I will pay thee all." I will give the full satisfaction for my sins through the Holy Sacrifice of the Mass.

"Have patience with me, and I will pay thee all," through the merits of Jesus Christ, which are offered to Thee in the Holy Sacrifice of the Mass. However, the merits of Christ can supply for our defects only to the extent that we unite ourselves with His intentions, and only if we are resolved to amend our lives and to do penance for our sins. By His death on the cross the Lord has made satisfaction for our sins; but this fact does not free us from the obligation of doing penance ourselves. At the Holy Sacrifice we can claim the merits of Christ as our own only if we ourselves practice penance and offer good works to God. If we do this we can be assured that the Father will forgive us our sins.

But that we be forgiven, a second condition is laid down. "Forgive us our trespasses as we forgive those who trespass against us." If we are unwilling to forgive our fellow servants, the Lord will say to us when we are called upon to give an account: "Thou wicked servant, I forgave thee all the debt, because thou besoughtest me. Shouldst not thou then have had compassion also on thy fellow servant, even as I had compassion on thee? And his lord, being angry, delivered him to the torturers, until he paid all the debt. So shall My heavenly Father do to you if you forgive not every one his brother from your hearts" (Gospel). We may obtain forgiveness for our sins through the Holy Sacrifice of the Mass only if we are prepared to forgive "every one his brother from [his] heart."

We are approaching the day of judgment, the day on which we will be called on to give an account. The nearer the day of our death approaches, the more urgent is our need for penance and repentance. "Forgive and you shall be forgiven" (Lk 6:37).

Prayer

Graciously receive, O Lord, the sacrifices with which Thou hast willed that Thou shouldst be appeased and our salvation by Thy powerful mercy be restored. Through Christ our Lord. Amen.

Twenty-Second Sunday after Pentecost

The Mass

A deep seriousness characterizes the liturgy for this week. Christ is about to return to us at the Consecration of the Mass, and we are reminded of His return for the Last Judgment. We are conscious that a life filled with many faults and sins lies behind us. Our faults press heavily upon us. Fully aware of the misery of our condition, we cry out to the Lord whose return we expect, "If Thou, O Lord, wilt mark iniquities, Lord, who shall stand it?" (Introit.) We repeat this sentiment in the Kyrie and in the Collect and Secreta.

The theme of this Sunday is given in the Epistle: "We are confident in the Lord Jesus, that He who hath begun a good work in you, will perfect it unto the day of Christ Jesus." The good work of our Christian life began at the time of our baptism. The seed that was planted in our soul then is the source of our supernatural life and must be brought to maturity and perfection. When this end is accomplished, we shall be prepared for the "day of Christ Jesus," that is, for the day of His return, for the day of our particular judgment, and for the general judgment. It is the prayer of the Church and of the Apostle that "you may be sincere and without offense unto the day of Christ, filled with the fruit of justice through Jesus Christ" (Epistle).

The best preparation for the return of Christ is the practice of fraternal charity and a life dedicated to the service of the community and our fellow men. Charity "is the bond of perfection" (Col 3:14), "the fulfilling of the law" (Rom 13:10), the mark of the true Christian, and a guarantee of mercy for its possessor when Christ returns. St. Paul today exhorts his hearers: "That your charity may more and more abound." "Where there are two or three gathered together in My name, there am I in the midst of them" (Mt 18:20). The Christian community gathered together to offer the Holy Sacrifice is united by a spirit of true Christian charity. Such a community is one in heart and soul, and it sings the song of brotherhood in the bonds of love: "Behold how good and how pleasant it is for brethren to dwell together in unity" (Gradual). The spirit of love for our brethren is the best preparation for a fruitful celebration of the Holy Sacrifice. We readily and willingly obey the command of Christ, "Render therefore to Caesar the things that are Caesar's, and to God the things that are God's" (Gospel).

"Render ... to God the things that are God's." We carry out this duty at the celebration of Mass. At the Consecration, Christ, the Son of God, appears in our midst. He places Himself at our disposal as a pure offering to be made to His heavenly Father. In offering Him we "render ... to God the things that are God's," for we offer to Him His own Son; we offer God to God, we offer the Son to the Father with all His merits and riches. "Through Him, and with Him, and in Him is to Thee, O God, ... all honor and glory."

To this unspotted offering we join ourselves, our bodies, our souls, our hearts, our wills, our prayers, our works, our virtues, our miseries, our sacrifices, our difficulties, and those of the whole Church. "Behold how good and how pleasant it is for brethren to dwell together in unity." God showers His blessings upon such a community. This blessing is given to us particularly at the time of Holy Communion. We have not asked in vain: "If Thou, O Lord, wilt mark iniquities, Lord, who shall stand it? For with Thee is merciful forgiveness" (Introit). "I have cried, for Thou hast heard me" (Communion). My resolution is made. I will offer to the one God a loving sacrifice with the community, with the whole Church. "Render therefore to Caesar the things that are Caesar's, and to God the things that are God's."

Meditation

Two thoughts are expressed by the Church today with regard to the certain and imminent return of the Lord: we must attain perfection before the "day of Christ" (Epistle), and we, the members of the Church, still are far from perfect.

The liturgy expects that we will have reached perfection by the time the Lord returns. On the day of our death the work which God began in us at the time of our baptism should be complete. With tender love God implanted "the good work" of Christian life in us. He provided all the graces and powers which we needed to reach perfection. Daily and each hour of the day He gave us inspirations and new graces, that our "charity may more and more abound in knowledge and understanding; that [we] may approve the better things; that [we] may be sincere and without offense unto the day of Christ, filled with the fruit of justice [of a holy and perfect life], through Jesus Christ," who has merited for us, through His sufferings and death, the grace and the strength to lead a holy life (Epistle). We are bound to strive after perfection, and we must reach it individually and as a community. In the liturgy Holy Mother the Church expects us to attain this goal. "Brethren, we are confident... that He who hath begun a good work in you, will perfect it unto the day of Christ Jesus," that is, unto the day of our death and judgment (Epistle).

In reality, however, we have not attained the perfection expected of us. The Church looks with anxiety on the multitude of her children whom she has borne to her spouse through the sacrament of baptism. How great was her joy on Laetare Sunday, on Easter night, and during Easter week, as she led the newly baptized in their white garments to the altar! How fervently she prayed for them that these, her "newborn children," might walk in the way which they had begun at the time of their baptism! How earnestly she prayed that they might preserve their baptismal garment without stain, that they might never make themselves unworthy of it! Today she looks back over the course of the year. How often her hopes and expectations were disappointed! There has been so much unfaithfulness, so many and such grievous sins in these her children. She is inspired to cry out with the Psalmist: "If Thou, O Lord, wilt mark iniquities, Lord, who shall stand it?" (Introit.) The heart of the Church is moved to shame and humble contrition. As she prepares to appear before her spouse today at Mass, like Esther she trembles with the consciousness of her unworthiness as she approaches her King. "Remember me, O Lord, Thou who rulest above all power, and give a well-ordered speech in my mouth, that my words may be pleasing in the sight of the prince" (Offertory). "Grant, O merciful God, that this saving oblation may unceasingly cleanse us of our faults and defend us from all adversities" (Secreta). "I have cried to Thee, for Thou, O God, hast heard me. O incline Thy ear unto me and hear my words" pleading for grace and forgiveness. Today we unite ourselves to the Church and make her sentiments our own.

The liturgy expects of us perfection and spiritual maturity. Supported and assisted by the grace of God, we must attain perfection; for Christ Himself desires it. Our task is to grow continually in faith, in our dependence on His divine providence, in the love of God, in charity. It is God who carries the principal burden of bringing us to perfection. He leads us to perfection by sending us trials, tribulations, humiliations, and opportunities to practice fraternal charity. He perfects us by making us endure spiritual dryness, temptations, and troubles of soul; He sends us daily crosses and allows us to fall into faults, that we may be humbled. Sometimes He sends us sickness, failure, and misfortunes. We approach perfection when we allow Him to do with us as He wills, when we submit willingly to everything that He sends, when we commit ourselves into His hands without reservation and without fear. When we reach such a point we shall be "sincere and without offense unto the day of Christ, filled with the fruit of justice" (Epistle). But how far we still are from such a high degree of perfection!

"Filled with the fruit of justice through Jesus Christ" (Epistle). That is the perfection which the Church expects of us by the time Christ returns. She expects us to make use of the talents and graces that have been given to us. We become perfect through the operation of Christ, who is the head working in His members. We shall be perfect to the extent that we grow in Christ, and to the extent that we can truthfully say, "I live, now not I, but Christ liveth in me" (Gal 2:20). Christ is the head working in His members, the vine working in His branches. The best means of growing in Christ will be found in the devout use of the Holy Eucharist.

"Behold how good and how pleasant it is for brethren to dwell together in unity" (Gradual). We know ourselves to be members of Christ, members of the Church, members of the communion of saints. The more devoutly we pray, work, and sacrifice with the other members of the community, the more rapidly and the more surely we shall reach perfection, and the more spotless we shall be on "the day of Christ." Union with Christ is the only means of attaining perfection and eternal salvation, for we are not sufficient by ourselves.

Prayer

O God, our refuge and strength, the very Author of godliness, hear the devout prayers of Thy Church and grant that what we confidently ask we may efficaciously obtain. Through Christ our Lord. Amen.

Monday

"That you may be sincere and without offense unto the day of Christ" (Epistle). This is the intention and the favor for which the Church prays in the canonical hours of the Divine Office and in every Mass throughout the year, but especially now that the coming of the day of Christ is recalled to us by the end of the Church year. Now the Church, the Esther of the New Covenant, cries out to the Lord: "Give a well-ordered speech in my mouth, that my words may be pleasing in the sight of the prince" (Offertory).

"Give a well-ordered speech in my mouth." The Church prays that Christ, the Word of God, may espouse her to Himself again and become entirely hers. She prays that in the Holy Sacrifice He may offer Himself to the Father as her offering, and enter into His presence as her intercessor, laying her prayers and her petitions before the Father. She prays that by means of the reception of Holy Communion, Christ may unite Himself to her and all her members, that they may all be purified and sanctified. It is the prayer of the Church that in the Mass the Word of God may speak, through the offering of His blood, in the name of all His sinful brethren and ask: "If Thou, O Lord, wilt mark iniquities, Lord, who shall stand it? For with Thee is merciful forgiveness, O God of Israel. Out of the depths I have cried to Thee, O Lord; Lord, hear my voice" (Introit). "I have cried, for Thou, O God, hast heard me; O incline Thy ear unto me, and hear my words" (Communion). It is the fact that she prays with a "well-ordered speech" that gives the Church confidence that her prayer will be answered favorably. When she prays, it is Christ, the Son, "in whom the Father is well pleased," who prays in her. She prays through Christ, who can always say, "I give Thee thanks that Thou hast heard Me" (Jn 11:41). Can God refuse to hear the prayer of Him who intercedes for us and offers Himself up for us with such unutterable love? When we pray and make our offering with the Church, "a well-ordered speech" is placed in our mouth also, for we offer to the Father the soul, the body, and the blood of His Son. What we offer to the Father is the praise, the thanksgiving, and the satisfaction made by the Son. "You are made rich in Him, ... who also will confirm you unto the end without crime, in the days of the coming of our Lord Jesus Christ" (1 Cor 1:5, 8).

"Behold how good and how pleasant it is for brethren to dwell together in unity. It is like the precious ointment on the head, that ran down upon the beard, the beard of Aaron" (Gradual). In the Mass, Christ, the well-ordered Word, is present in the midst of His brethren, praying and offering sacrifice with them. The head and the members form one Christ. It is only when we are united by a vital union with the Church, who prays, suffers, and offers sacrifice with her head, that we shall grow in knowledge and understanding. Only through such a union will we achieve the power to choose what is right and remain clean and unspotted until the day of Christ, filled with the fruits of justice. But to do this we must avoid spiritual isolation; we must unite ourselves to the mystical body, to the Christian community as a whole, through which Christ now operates. The grace of Christ comes to us as individuals through the Church, which is the whole body of the faithful united in Him. "We must be engrafted in Christ in order to share His life" (St. Augustine). "Behold how good and how pleasant it is for brethren to dwell together in unity"; that is, to pray together and to praise and thank the Lord in union with Christ, the "firstborn amongst many brethren" (Rom 8:29). We are many, yet we have but one heart and one soul. What a grace to have been made members of the mystical body! How blessed we shall be if we live in perfect harmony with the Church! If we live thus, grace will flow down upon us like oil from the head who is Christ; His life, the life of the vine, shall flow in us, the branches.

"Give a well-ordered speech in my mouth." Blessed art thou, O holy mother Church, the Esther of the new covenant. The Lord has placed a well-ordered speech in thy mouth. Christ the Lord lives and prays in you. He cries out to His Father and prays for you. When you pray, it is He who prays in you. How powerful, how moving, how effective is your exhortation, "Let us pray," and the offering you make "through Christ our Lord"! You offer to God that which is God's, the sacrifice which alone is perfect, the Holy Sacrifice of the Mass.

"Give a well-ordered speech in my mouth." We pray with a well-ordered speech when we make use of the liturgical prayer of the Church, than which there can be no more effective or fitting prayer. Through the mouth of the Church the incarnate Son of God continually sounds forth the praise of His heavenly Father. In the prayer of the Church we give to God what is God's.

"Give a well-ordered speech in my mouth." God places such a speech in our mouth through Holy Communion. The eternal Word becomes our food in the Eucharist. Through us He prays to the Father. He prays to the Father in our stead and for our needs. How fortunate we are! What prayer could be more precious and more effective? "Behold how good and how pleasant it is for brethren to dwell together in unity." The most perfect union is effected by Christ in Holy Communion.

Prayer

O God, our refuge and strength, the very Author of godliness, hear the devout prayers of Thy Church and grant that what we confidently ask we may efficaciously obtain. Through Christ our Lord. Amen.

Tuesday

On a certain occasion the Jews approached Christ and proposed a question, asking Him to judge and give them guidance. Is it lawful for a Hebrew to pay tribute to the pagan emperor in Rome? Had not the Roman emperor destroyed their national independence? Is he not of the uncircumcised and an unbeliever? How, then, can a Jew pay tribute to him?

This question of paying tribute to Caesar raised two problems — the problem of the tribute itself and the problem of the political subjection of the Jews. The Jews were violently opposed to the rule of the Romans. For almost a hundred years they had borne the hard yoke imposed on them by the Romans. Moreover, this question involved a touchy political issue with which the Pharisees were particularly concerned. Jesus had won the hearts of the common people of the nation, and the Pharisees, who had come to look upon themselves as the leaders of the nation, saw their influence waning. Fearing that He would expose them before the people, they asked themselves how they might get rid of Him. With this in view they held counsel to determine how they might trap Him in His speech, and they hit upon this ingenious plan. They will confront Him with a religious question that is closely bound up with a political issue. "Is it lawful to pay tribute to Caesar?" If He says yes, He will offend the Jews; if He says no, He will be considered a revolutionary and will become involved with the Roman authorities. Behold how the plots, rivalries, and intrigues of men operate. See how men love money, play politics, and ruthlessly plot the ruin of their adversaries. This is true not only of the Pharisees of old, nor only of pagans and infidels, but at times even of Christians who take part in such plots and intrigues. Among men there is no end of scheming, plotting, and intrigue.

"Is it lawful to pay tribute to Caesar?" Christ's answer presents not the human but the divine point of view. Christ understands the duplicity of His questioners and will not allow Himself to become involved in their intrigue. With divine majesty and sovereign foresight He evades their cleverly laid plot. "Show Me the coin of the tribute.... Whose image and inscription is this?" When they tell Him that both belong to Caesar, He draws the fine distinction: "Render therefore to Caesar the things that are Caesar's, and to God the things that are God's" (Gospel). He commands them to deal justly in all things both with the emperor and with God, with the state and with the Church, in matters of politics and religion. Christ is far above the intrigues of men. His interest is in God and His law, the law of justice and charity. How easily and simply the problems and difficulties of men might be solved if there were no passion, no prejudice, no selfishness! If men would only look to God and His commandments, to His laws and designs, the world would be a better place to live in.

The liturgy explains what the Gospel announces, that the day of Christ is near at hand. She sees in the Lord divine knowledge and divine wisdom which can distinguish in the problems presented to Him. He is the divine Judge before whose wisdom all must be amazed. In the story of the Gospel we recognize a figure of the Last Judgment, which Christ will hold at His coming.

"Render ... to God the things that are God's," especially now during the Holy Sacrifice of the Mass. At the Offertory we render "to God the things that are God's" and lay upon the paten our very selves, with all that we are and all that we possess: our time, our talents, our will, our heart, our freedom, our health, our works, our miseries, and all our needs. "Receive, O holy Father, this spotless host." Through this mysterious union with Him in the Sacrifice of the Mass and in Communion we return to the tasks of the day and give "to Caesar the things that are Caesar's, and to God the things that are God's."

"Render therefore to Caesar the things that are Caesar's, and to God the things that are God's." In the first place we owe to God the service of piety, a life lived for God. "Godliness is profitable to all things, having promise of the life that now is and of that which is to come" (1 Tm 4:8). The life of God makes us strong and versatile in solving the problems of the community and of the state. It makes us stronger, more self-sacrificing, more patient, more generous, more conscious of our duty, and more trustworthy in its execution. It teaches us to do all things with calmness and self-assurance. It gives us strength for the tasks that lie before us, courage for self-denial and sacrifice, energy for a fruitful life. If man does not give to God the things that are God's, if he works without God, without religion, without Christ, the word of the Scriptures will be fulfilled in him: "Cursed is the earth in thy work" (Gn 3:17). How can he give to Caesar, to society, those things that are Caesar's? Christ demands absolute justice in our thoughts, our speech, our actions; He expects us to act properly toward our friends and our enemies, toward individuals and society.

Prayer

O God, our refuge and strength, the very Author of godliness, hear the devout prayers of Thy Church and grant that what we confidently ask we may efficaciously obtain. Through Christ our Lord. Amen.

Wednesday

With renewed earnestness the liturgy reminds us of the approaching "day of Christ" (Epistle). During the present week it is absorbed by the thought of the return of the Lord. It wishes us to perform all our actions on earth keeping in mind the thought of death, eternity, and the life that is to come. "In all thy works remember thy last end, and thou shalt never sin" (Ecclus 7:40).

The day of judgment is approaching. "If Thou, O Lord, wilt mark iniquities, O Lord, who shall stand?" (Introit.) If Thou didst not pour out Thy mercy upon us during our earthly life; if Thou should not defer judgment upon our sins until the last day, who, O Lord, would escape Thy anger? If we were to be judged only by the world with its loose morals and flexible moral standards, if judgment were left to our enemies and those who slander us, if we were to be judged only by our superiors or our confessors, who are usually indulgent and lenient, if we were to be judged only by men, then we might say with St. Paul: "But to me it is a very small thing to be judged by you or by man's day; but neither do I judge my own self.... He that judgeth me is the Lord,... who both will bring to light the hidden things of darkness and will make manifest the counsels of the hearts" (1 Cor 4:3 ff.). "For we shall all stand before the judgment seat of Christ" (Rom 14:10), both in the particular judgment and at the Last Judgment. "And in the end of a man is the disclosing of his works" (Ecclus 11:29). "For nothing is covered that shall not be revealed, nor hid that shall not be known" (Mt 10:26). "For we must all be manifested before the judgment seat of Christ, that every one may receive the proper things of the body, according as he hath done, whether it be good or evil" (2 Cor 5:10). This much is certain: "He that judgeth me is the Lord," the all-wise, all-holy, and the most just God. We must all make answer to Him who "searcheth the reins and the hearts" (Apoc 2:23). "Lord, Thou has proved me and known me; Thou hast known my sitting down and my rising up. Thou hast understood my thoughts afar off" (Ps 138:1–3). The liturgy reminds us that if we keep the thought of the coming judgment in mind, we shall perform our duties more correctly, form a much more correct appraisal of our trials, sufferings, joys, and successes in life.

He who redeemed us on the cross because of His love for us, is also to be our Judge. He has done all that He could do to draw us to His love and to induce us to model our lives after His own holy life. During our life on earth He keeps Himself concealed from us and maintains a continual silence whether men serve Him faithfully or sin against Him. But He cannot and will not remain forever silent. At the moment when our life is at an end, when the union between body and soul is broken, He will assert His complete dominion over the soul. He will appear then as the Lord and Master. Fortunate will we be if we can appear before Him clean and unspotted and say to Him: "Show us Thy face, and we shall be saved" (Ps 79:4). Woe, then, to all those who have forgotten Him; His appearance will strike terror into their hearts. Woe to those who have transgressed His commandments, to those who have rejected His truth and His grace, who have been unfaithful to His Church, and who have slandered and maligned it. Woe to those who have lived after the fashion of this world. They will tremble with fear when He takes into His royal hand the scepter and passes judgment upon them.

Those things in which we have failed, whatever we have omitted or done out of self-will, whatever we have done out of pride or self-interest, will have to be submitted to the scrutiny of the judge. In so far as we have allowed our heart to become attached to creatures, we shall be obliged to acknowledge the emptiness and vanity of all creatures. In those things in which our hearts have wandered away from God, they must now return to Him. If our heart has found its rest in a life that knew no prayer or self-denial, it will now awaken to a sense of confusion and abandonment. If in our present life there is much injustice, if virtue is not rewarded but is rather penalized while vice triumphs, in that day the right order will be restored. The Lord will set everything in its proper place.

The Lord will come also as the rewarder. Then the just will receive the reward of their faith and of their patience, and they shall look upon the gentle face of Christ. Then those who have followed Him and have daily borne His cross, those who have fought for Him, suffered and mortified themselves for Him, will enter into peace. Woe to those who have resisted God and His holy will, and who die in that state. God will have no choice but to punish them. All those who have resisted God will be banished from His presence (Ps 9:4).

"Be sincere and without offense unto the day of Christ" (Epistle). The Lord Himself has pointed out the way that we are to follow: "Judge not and you shall not be judged" (Lk 6:37). And the Apostle exhorts us: "But if we would judge ourselves, we should not be judged" (1 Cor 11:31). We should pass judgment on ourselves in our examination of conscience, in our daily meditation, and in the confessional. Woe to us for our unrepented sins, for our failures in fraternal charity, for the false judgments we have made, for our sinful speech, for our dishonest dealing, for our neglect of meditation and self-examination. "If we would judge ourselves, we should not be judged."

PRAYER

O God, our refuge and strength, the very Author of godliness, hear the devout prayers of Thy Church and grant that what we confidently ask we may efficaciously obtain. Through Christ our Lord. Amen.

Thursday

"And this I pray, that your charity may more and more abound in knowledge and in all understanding; that you may approve the better things; that you may be sincere and without offense unto the day of Christ" (Epistle). The "day of Christ," the day of our death and of the Last Judgment, is near at hand. Not a minute should be lost. It is imperative that we grow in the love of Christ Jesus.

God desires from us perfect love. "He, answering, said: Thou shalt love the Lord thy God with thy whole heart, and with thy whole soul, and with all thy strength, and with all thy mind; and thy neighbor as thyself" (Lk 10:27). God has commanded us to love Him. Indeed, the commandment to love God is the first and most important of all the commandments. This commandment knows no limits. Love is an insatiable good; it has no measure, it never rests satisfied. Man, of course, can never love God as He deserves to be loved, he will never be able to fulfill perfectly the command to love. He must always strive to increase in love, to "love with [his] whole soul, and with all [his] strength." That love must steadily increase until our death. We are making a pilgrimage to heaven, a pilgrimage that involves a continual wandering. As long as we have not reached our goal in eternity, continual progress in virtue is a sacred duty. Woe to us should we ever reach the point where we say I shall love God just so much and no more! With such an attitude we could not fulfill the first and greatest of commandments; and if we neglect this first of the commandments, how shall we fulfill the others? That is why the liturgy is so insistent on our continual growth in charity.

Perfect charity requires the complete conquest of all self-seeking, the destruction of indolence and envy, of all impatience and false judgment. It requires the complete abandonment of all purely natural ways of thinking and acting. It permits no routine or worldly manner of acting. It demands the conquest of pride and of all inordinate desires; it requires the sacrifice of all that is opposed to a godly spirit, or that hinders our progress in the spiritual life and in the perfect love of God. However, perfect love involves not merely the mortification of our senses and of our spirit; it requires also the powerful operation of God in our soul by means of spiritual dryness, temptation, suffering, and humiliation. Once God begins to operate in a soul, that soul undertakes all its works and actions for God. It then attributes nothing to itself, but everything to God. In all things it looks to Him, to His continual presence, and to His love. "But he who is joined to the Lord is one spirit" (1 Cor 6:17). Such a soul knows only love, and its works are the works of a pure and perfect love. The Lord brings it about that such a perfect soul knows everything that it should know, thinks as it should think, forgets what it should forget, loves what it should love, and loves nothing outside of God or apart from God. O precious life of love! One act of perfect love is of greater value in the eyes of God and of greater benefit to the Church than all the imperfect works of the entire world. "And this I pray, that your charity may more and more abound" (Epistle).

"That your charity may more and more abound." It is for the accomplishment of this end that the liturgy has been instituted. Our growth in charity is the very purpose of the Mass and of Holy Communion, which nourishes the inner life of man. By this means the measure of our charity is increased, the powers of the soul are invigorated through the infusion of sanctifying grace and the infused virtues, and man is thus given the strength to strive for a holier and more perfect life.

Our growth in the love of God gives unerring direction to our practice of fraternal charity, unites us more closely to the mystical body, and disposes us to live for one another and at peace with one another. For this reason the Epistle and the Gradual of the Mass remind us, "Behold how good and how pleasant it is for brethren to dwell together in unity." A truly supernatural love of our neighbor is not only most intimately connected with the love of God, but may be even more properly said to be identical with the love of God. Growth in the love of God means a growth in fraternal charity, a closer union with the body of the Church, and a participation in the sufferings, prayers, and sacrifices of our brethren. Such is the mind of the Church. May we so live "that your charity may more and more abound." This must be accomplished primarily by Christ. He alone can extinguish in us what is harmful to the spirit of fraternal charity. Only He is strong enough to stifle in us the spirit of self-love. "Unless the Lord build the house, they labor in vain that build it" (Ps 126:1).

In all His operations within our soul the Lord has but one object, and that is to destroy self-love in us that He may make room for the love of God. He can and He will accomplish this in us. It is for this purpose that the Church prays that we may grow in charity. We may place our trust in the prayer of the Church, for Christ prays through her.

Prayer

O God, our refuge and strength, the very Author of godliness, hear the devout prayers of Thy Church and grant that what we confidently ask we may efficaciously obtain. Through Christ our Lord. Amen.

Friday

The Church prays that we may abound in charity. This "first and greatest commandment" which the Lord gave us is continually before her eyes. "Thou shalt love the Lord thy God with thy whole heart, and with thy whole soul, and thy whole mind.... Thou shalt love thy neighbor as thyself" (Mt 22:37, 39). Love is the essence of perfection and the highest reach of Christian virtue. Whether we are "upright and unspotted in the day of Christ" will depend on the measure of our love. Love decides our destiny.

"He that abideth in charity, abideth in God and God in him" (1 Jn 4:16). Love rises above the awareness of "me and you"; the language of love says, "And all my things are thine, and thine are mine" (Jn 17:10). Love gives everything. It is the supreme expression, the summation of all that one can do for another. Through love we are united and identify ourselves with the one we love. Because we love God, we adore Him, we glorify Him, and we honor Him as best we can. "For he that loveth his neighbor hath fulfilled the law" (Rom 13:8). "Charity... is the bond of perfection" (Col 3:14). All commandments are based on the precept of charity. There is, after all, only one commandment, since all commandments have only one objective, which is charity. As the many twigs and branches of a tree are offshoots of the same root, so the various acts of virtue grow out of the one root, charity. The commandments of the Lord are many, and yet they are one. They are many in a multiplicity of works, but they are one in their source, which is charity (St. Gregory the Great). Charity is the motive force behind all the commandments, and it is charity and charity alone which unites us with God and makes us like unto Him. It makes us objects of divine love and children of God, and draws God Himself to us. God the Father, God the Son, and God the Holy Ghost dwell in us and share with us their divine and blessed life. "He that abideth in charity, abideth in God and God in him."

There are certain marks of growth in charity. The more we love, the more conscious we become of our own imperfection, of our own sinfulness, of our own impurity, of our own perversity. We become acutely aware of our lack of progress because of our attachment to worthless things that prevent us from giving ourselves up completely to the love of God and of our Savior. How selfish we are, how reluctant to give up all for God, to submit to Him entirely and completely! When we realize this we are not hindered and checked, but we are humbled and inspired to strive for a more perfect love of God. This is the feeling that urged the saints to long for humiliations and suffering. Previously the consciousness of sin was a torture to them and the source of their zeal; now their inability to love Him sufficiently, to consume themselves by sacrifices for Him, is an incomparably greater torture. They wish to give God a superabundant love because of their vivid consciousness of the feebleness of all that they do. This is a sign that they are growing in charity. The more we grow in charity, the more dissatisfied we are with our present state. Such a dissatisfaction does not prostrate us, or discourage us, or make us despondent; it urges us rather to greater and better things. It awakens in us a need for greater perfection, a need to be more pure and holy. It makes us grateful to God and gives us an unshakable confidence in His help and grace; at the same time we acquire a deep remorse for not having responded to the graces already offered. The more we grow in charity, the more insatiable becomes our desire to make use of all that life brings for the greater honor and glory of God. The greater our love for God, the closer we draw to Him, the more we desire to suffer for Him, the more we desire to bear all things for Him out of pure and perfect love.

"Behold how good and how pleasant it is for brethren to dwell together in unity" (Gradual). By these words the sacred liturgy directs us to unite ourselves to the Church and to Christ our head. By this union with the body of Christ and with our brethren our love will grow more and more till it reaches perfection. Only by such a union does the Lord, the "first-born among many brethren," unite Himself to us. He makes us His members and makes it possible for us to join our prayers, works, sufferings, which are in themselves worthless, to His prayers, works, and sufferings. Now our prayers and works become a vital part of His, which are of infinite value. Our works and sufferings are transformed by His spirit, His love, His purity, and His perfection, and thus acquire a value in the sight of God which by themselves they would lack. Thus we grow rapidly in grace, virtue, and love. This power of growth is acquired by virtue of our baptism and our union with Christ our head. "Behold how good and how pleasant it is for brethren to dwell together in unity." What would we be without this union with Christ our head and with His Church? Let us give thanks to the Lord our God.

Prayer

O God, our refuge and strength, the very Author of godliness, hear the devout prayers of Thy Church and grant that what we confidently ask we may efficaciously obtain. Through Christ our Lord. Amen.

Saturday

The Church prays that "your charity may more and more abound in knowledge and in all understanding, that you may approve the better things, that you may be sincere and without offense unto the day of Christ" (Epistle).

"That your charity may more and more abound in knowledge." The more intense our love of God, the deeper will be our understanding of divine things. To abound in charity means to acquire a deeper and more perfect knowledge of God, of His salvation, of His holiness, and of His redemption. Charity unites the soul to God. The charitable soul reposes in the heart of Jesus as the child reposes on the breast of its mother. It finds its only joy in God. The more it desires God, the more closely God draws it to Himself and manifests Himself to it so that it can see and taste how sweet He is. It has a profound knowledge of God and of His mysteries, a knowledge which God Himself provides personally and directly. He reveals Himself to such a soul in a mystical way and manifests His lovableness through the instrumentality of men. He dwells in the loving soul to be its sole love and consolation. It may approach Him, touch Him, speak to Him with confidence, and turn to Him as a flower turns to the sun to receive the full benefit of the light. This light given by God develops our understanding of God and of His essence. In this sense Holy Mother the Church prays that our charity may abound more and more in knowledge and understanding, "that you may approve the better things."

Knowledge born of charity makes us understand that we still are not what we ought to be. It gives us a desire for what lies before us and sets before us the ideal of perfect union with God; it makes us wish to submit perfectly to His holy will and good pleasure. The soul thirsts to share His perfect life and to become enraptured by His inexhaustible holiness. Knowledge born of charity urges us to a greater purity and holiness in thought, word, and deed. Steeped in the glow of this divine purity and holiness, the loving soul is stripped of all uncleanness, of all imperfection, of all selfishness. It becomes pure in its intentions, in its motives, in its works, in its deeds. Finally, knowledge born of charity fills our hands with the fruit of good works, for charity and good works are so dependent on one another that the one cannot exist without the other. Charity in the soul is the root of all good works. On the other hand, charity decreases and disappears if it is not nourished by good works, just as a fire languishes unless fuel is supplied. Good works are the fuel for charity. If charity abides in our souls, we are "filled with the fruit of justice" (Epistle), we are clean and "without offense unto the day of Christ," prepared for the hour of death and judgment.

The liturgy is concerned with our growth in charity, which is the foundation and source of all other virtues; indeed, it includes all the other virtues. Where charity is lacking, all else fails. Where charity exists, there also are the other virtues. Where charity exists, man gives to God the things that are God's and to Caesar the things that are Caesar's.

Charity gives without reservation. It will suffer hardships and reverses. Charity renounces the world, its goods, its honors, its pleasures. It crucifies the flesh, sacrifices its time, its powers, its health, and even its life for the sake of God. It places the love of God above all things, even above its own well being and its own satisfaction. Charity is strong; it despises the world with its trials and dangers, the devil with his plots and his temptations. Charity subjects the passions and breaks evil habits. It is strong in the hour of trial and causes us to suffer crosses and sufferings, injustices and humiliations, trials and temptations with equanimity. Charity is unselfish. It loves God not for the sake of His gifts but for Himself alone. It directs all its energies to God and knows no desire but God's good pleasure.

The love of God is closely bound up with the love of neighbor. How can one love God without loving his neighbor, since God's love embraces all men? How can one love God and not love those for whom He suffered and died, for whom He established His Church and its sacraments, and in whom the Blessed Trinity lives and works? The test of true charity is our love for our neighbor. "Behold how good and how pleasant it is for brethren to dwell together in unity" (Gradual).

"Give a well-ordered speech in my mouth"; give me Christ in the Holy Eucharist. This is the way to perfection in love. At the Holy Sacrifice the Lord, the Word of God, places His gifts in our hands. His heart, His prayers, His limitless charity, His praise, devotion, and thanksgiving belong to us. "Through Him, and with Him, and in Him is to Thee, O God," a meet and perfect praise, even from us poor sinners. We love God with the loving heart of Jesus Himself. At Holy Communion the sacrificial victim, glowing with love for the Father, plants in our hearts the fire of love which consumes His heart. God puts the "well-ordered speech" into our mouth. Must not our charity grow strong and be perfected? If only we possessed the spirit of the sacred liturgy, with how much courage and confidence we should be inspired! "I can do all things in Him who strengtheneth me" (Phil 4:13). Do we not depend too much on ourselves, and too little on Him who works in us? "And I live, now not I, but Christ liveth in me" (Gal 2:20).

Prayer

O God, our refuge and strength, the very Author of godliness, hear the devout prayers of Thy Church and grant that what we confidently ask we may efficaciously obtain. Through Christ our Lord. Amen.

Twenty-Third Sunday after Pentecost

The Mass

The theme of the Mass for this Sunday is given in the Gospel. A certain ruler, Jairus by name, approaches the Lord and reports, "My daughter is even now dead, but come lay Thy hand upon her, and she shall live." In the liturgy this dead child is a symbol of dying Judaism, which rejected Jesus Christ and His Church. Jesus accompanies the ruler to restore his child to life. But just as He is about to leave, a woman full of faith steps forward and touches the hem of His garment. "If I shall touch only His garment, I shall be healed" (Gospel). This heathen woman who was troubled with an issue of blood is a type of paganism seeking Christ. Christ cured her even before He entered the house of Jairus. The pagans became the first to reap the benefits of salvation; only when the pagans have all entered the Church, will Israel as a people accept the faith. When Israel has come into the Church, the final coming of Christ will not be far distant.

Today the Church rejoices in the fact that Christ has called His once chosen people to salvation and restores it to life as He did the daughter of Jairus. She trusts in the promise of God, "I think thoughts of peace and not of affliction.... I will bring back your captivity" (Introit); that is, I will bring you back to share in the graces and blessings of Christ's redemption. "Lord, Thou hast blessed Thy land; Thou hast turned away the captivity of Jacob" (Introit). The Jews will share the sonship of God with the pagans and will partake of the inheritance of the children of God. In that day there will be but one flock and one shepherd, one kingdom, one Church, one eternal communion of saints, united in one head, Christ. Such is Christ's victory, the victory of grace. Thus the Church feels, hopes, and prays. The Church desires the salvation of all men, whether Jew or Gentile. We share in this desire of the Church and pray to God for that end in the Kyrie during Mass.

Like the daughter of Jairus and the woman troubled with the issue of blood, we await the touch of Christ. When He will return, when we shall arise again in the flesh, "He will reform the body of our lowness" (Epistle) even more effectively than He did for this woman and for the daughter of Jairus. With the liturgy today we are absorbed in the thought of Christ's return, which will be such a joyful day for the Church. In that day she will be gathered together in all her members; all of her children and all those masses of mankind who have died in the state of sanctifying grace will be lifted up "out of the depths" of earthly misery to the heights of the heavenly happiness, where they will behold God face to face and enjoy eternal rest and blessedness. What Christ did for the dead girl and the ailing woman, He does today and every day to men without number, when He brings them back from their exile to the house of their heavenly Father. Therefore we sing in the Gradual: "In God shall we glory all the day." O blessed return of Christ at the end of time, at the end of our earthly pilgrimage! It will be the day of our salvation. "I think thoughts of peace."

Today Christ enlightens us in the Holy Sacrifice of the Mass. Today, in company with the ruler of the synagogue and the sick woman, we approach Christ at the Offertory of the Mass. What can we offer Him? Like Jairus and the ailing woman, we have nothing but our sickness, our misery, and our death. We have all been wounded by Original Sin and by personal sins; we are all sick, weak, and dying. "Out of the depths [of our sins] I have cried to Thee" (Alleluia verse).

In the Holy Sacrifice of the Mass we find Christ. At the Consecration He comes to meet us and is touched by our misery and distress. Not only does He listen to our troubles, but He makes them His own and unites Himself to us most intimately in His most pure sacrifice. Offering Himself to His Father, He offers also our distress, our prayers, and our desires, supporting them by His love, His merits, His purity, and His holiness. With us He prays, "Give us this day our daily bread and forgive us our trespasses.... Lead us not into temptation; but deliver us from evil." At the time of Holy Communion He comes directly to us. This is He who cured the woman of the Gospel and who took the sick daughter of Jairus by the hand and restored her to life. When He touches us, too, we shall observe that power goes out of Him and heals us. "I think thoughts of peace and not of affliction." "Amen I say to you, whatsoever you ask when you pray, believe that you shall receive, and it shall be done to you" (Communion). Those who meet Christ at Mass and in Holy Communion will make the same experience as Jairus, the ruler of the synagogue, and the sick woman of the Gospel, whose prayers were answered.

Meditation

"The Lord saith, I think thoughts of peace and not of affliction. You shall call upon Me, and I will hear you; and I will bring back your captivity from all places" (Introit). The coming of Christ at the time of our death and at the end of time means more than judgment; it means especially the end of our captivity, merciful redemption, and the entrance of the soul into its eternal and heavenly home. The liturgy directs our gaze to heaven and the blessed life of eternity, a life that has already begun through our reception of sanctifying grace and through our incorporation in Christ.

"From whence also we look for the Savior, our Lord Jesus Christ, who will reform the body of our lowness, made like to the body of His glory, according to the operation whereby also He is able to subdue all things unto Himself" (Epistle). Still we cry out to God "out of the depths" of our misery in this earthly life. We must still struggle and fight, be subject to temptation and the occasion of sin at every step. We must still live a life of lowliness and need, the life which Christ once led on earth and which He still lives here in His members. Just as Christ our head was not glorified until He had first suffered and died on the cross, so, too, we who are His members will not see the day of glorification until we have fought the fight of our early life to the end.

Life on earth is a struggle. Only when the last member of the mystical body has fought and suffered like Christ its head, will perfect redemption be accomplished according to the example of our Lord. During these last days of the ecclesiastical year, the liturgy awaits and longs for the day of salvation, the day of our resurrection from the dead, the day which will introduce the Church to the eternal happiness of heaven. During these last weeks of the Church year we also lift our thoughts to the true life for which we were redeemed, for which we received baptism, and for which we received so many powerful graces. "We look for the Savior, our Lord Jesus Christ, who will reform the body of our lowness, made like to the body of His glory."

"Our conversation is in heaven" (Epistle). Let us not be numbered among those "of whom I have told you often (and now tell you weeping) that they are enemies of the cross of Christ; . . . whose God is their belly, and whose glory is in their shame; who mind earthly things" (Epistle). At the end of the Church year we should feel that we are on the threshold of our heavenly home. We are indeed still in this world, but actually we have no concern with this world, at least with its manner of living and thinking. We must live in the spirit of the Apostle: "This therefore I say, brethren: The time is short, it remaineth that they also who have wives be as if they had none. And they that weep, as though they wept not; and they that rejoice, as if they rejoiced not; and they that buy, as though they possessed not; and they that use this world, as if they used it not. For the fashion of this world passeth away" (1 Cor 7:29–31). If we take seriously our Christianity, our membership in the Church and the mystical body, our liturgical life, we do not really live for time or for this world, but rather for heaven and for eternity. Our thoughts and our desires and ambitions soar far above all earthly and temporal concerns. We are motivated by our expectation of the resurrection from the dead and by our hope for eternal life. That is what we are working for.

We work, not so much in dread of the coming judgment, as with a consciousness of our unity with our Redeemer, who will one day clothe our miserable bodies in the garments of His glory. Of what value are money, riches, earthly pleasures and joys, honor and distinction, in comparison to those things that await us in eternity? Of what importance are the sufferings, sacrifices, humiliations, and trials of this present life when we remember the things that are promised us in heaven? "For I reckon that the sufferings of this time are not worthy to be compared with the glory to come that shall be revealed in us" (Rom 8:18). "Eye hath not seen, nor ear heard, neither hath it entered into the heart of man, what things God hath prepared for them that love Him" (1 Cor 2:9).

There are two types of Christians: those who "are enemies of the cross of Christ; ... whose God is their belly, who mind earthly things," and those whose "conversation is in heaven" with the glorified Redeemer. These latter await His coming with desire. "For to me to live is Christ, and to die is gain.... Having a desire to be dissolved and to be with Christ" (Phil 1:21, 23).

"From whence also we look for the Savior, our Lord Jesus Christ." This thought applies not only to the end of time, which is perhaps in the far distant future, but to this very day, particularly in the Holy Sacrifice of the Mass. Christ comes in the Holy Sacrifice of the Mass and in Holy Communion with the same power and strength that He demonstrated in today's Gospel in curing the woman with the issue of blood and in raising to life the daughter of Jairus.

The Mass is a prelude to our glorification in heaven. The eventual resurrection and glorification which we await as members of His mystical body, will be the more surely ours, the more firmly and the more deeply we become incorporated in Him through Holy Communion. "He that eateth My flesh and drinketh My blood hath everlasting life, and I will raise him up in the last day.... He that eateth this bread shall live forever" (Jn 6:55, 59).

Prayer

Remit, we beseech Thee, O Lord, the sins of Thy people, that by Thy kindness we may be delivered from the trammels of our sins, in which through our frailty we have become entangled. Through Christ our Lord. Amen.

Monday

Holy Mother the Church is mindful of all her children and loves them all. It is her desire that all of them attain eternal life, and in this desire she includes even the people of Israel, once God's chosen people. In the last days they are to return to the Lord, for He is a God of mercy and peace.

"At that time, as Jesus was speaking to the multitudes, behold a certain ruler came up and adored Him, saying: Lord, my daughter is even now dead; but come lay Thy hand upon her, and she shall live. And Jesus, rising up, followed him with His disciples. And behold a woman, who was troubled with an issue of blood twelve years, came behind Him and touched the hem of His garment. For she said within herself: If I shall touch only His garment, I shall be healed.... And the woman was made whole from that hour. And when Jesus was come into the house of the ruler and saw the minstrels and the multitude making a tumult, He said: Give place; for the girl is not dead, but sleepeth. And they laughed Him to scorn. And when the multitude was put forth, He went in and took her by the hand. And the maid arose" (Gospel). How kind and merciful the Lord is! How effective was the prayer of Jairus and the woman afflicted with the issue of blood! Jesus is the Lord of life and death.

For the liturgy the dead girl is a symbol of the people of Israel, dead to the graces of salvation since they rejected the Lord (Mt 27:20–25). The Lord, however, "thinks thoughts of peace" (Introit), thoughts of mercy and salvation. When appealed to, He rises and goes to restore an unhappy people again to the life of grace. While He is on His way to restore life to the dead girl, an ailing woman intervenes. In the mind of the liturgy the woman with the issue of blood represents the pagans who come to Christ. The Lord pauses to cure the ailing woman before He enters the house of Jairus to restore life to his daughter. The liturgy implies that the pagans will receive salvation through Christ first, and then only will the people of Israel submit to Him. "For I would not have you ignorant, brethren, of this mystery,... that blindness in part has happened in Israel, until the fullness of the Gentiles should come in" (Rom 11:25). But God "will have all men to be saved and to come to the knowledge of the truth" (1 Tm 2:4). Men are guilty of innumerable sins and defects; but at the end of time there will be peace. The Lord will forgive the sins of His children, and they shall return to the house of their Father. "You shall call upon me and I will hear you; and I will bring back your captivity from all places" (Introit). How good and how merciful is our God!

"I think thoughts of peace," thoughts of mercy, reconciliation, and salvation, although the people have been unfaithful and have crucified and rejected their high priest, Jesus Christ. These words apply to us the baptized, who are represented in the Gospel by the woman who was troubled with the issue of blood. How many and what rich graces have been given to us during the year of grace which is now drawing to an end! Our conscience urges us to repentance for our lack of cooperation with these graces. How negligent we have been in the use of the rich graces that have been given to us! Has God not had ample reason for rejecting us, as He once rejected His chosen people? But He has not done so, and He gives us the assurance: "I think thoughts of peace and not of affliction" (Introit). In spite of the vast number of sins, negligences, and faults of the past year, we still hear His message of peace. The Lord will forgive us all our sins if we but call upon Him.

"You shall call upon Me, and I will hear you; and I will bring back your captivity from all places." Our plea is for mercy and for forgiveness. With penitent and contrite hearts we cry out: "Out of the depths I have cried to Thee, O Lord; Lord, hear my prayer; out of the depths I have cried out to Thee" (Offertory). Without contrition and penance on our part, the Lord cannot grant us the forgiveness we seek.

"If I shall touch only His garment, I shall be healed." We touch the hem of His garment as often as we contritely confess our sins to His representative, the priest. We touch Him, His very flesh and blood, when we receive Holy Communion. How fortunate we are in being members of the Church of the New Testament! We are healed of our infirmities and receive the gift of eternal life.

On this day we pray with Holy Mother the Church: "Remit, we beseech Thee, O Lord, the sins of Thy people, that by Thy kindness we may be delivered from the trammels of our sins, in which through our frailty we have become entangled. Through Christ our Lord." At the moment of Holy Communion the Lord unites us to Himself. He prays in us and in His holy Church, to whom He gives the assurance: "Amen I say to you, whatsoever you ask when you pray, believe that you shall receive, and it shall be done to you" (Communion). The Church believes this promise of the Lord, who assures her, "Be of good heart, daughter, thy faith hath made thee whole" (Gospel).

PRAYER

Remit, we beseech Thee, O Lord, the sins of Thy people, that by Thy kindness we may be delivered from the trammels of our sins, in which through our frailty we have become entangled. Through Christ our Lord. Amen.

Tuesday

"Our conversation is in heaven, from whence also we look for the Savior, our Lord Jesus Christ" (Epistle). Holy Mother the Church awaits lovingly the return of the Lord, her bridegroom. Ever since that eventful day when He ascended into heaven, she has kept her vigil, expecting Him presently to reappear to summon her to her eternal nuptials. She prays in the Credo of the Mass: "I confess one baptism for the remission of sins. And I expect the resurrection of the dead."

"Then shall the kingdom of heaven be like to ten virgins, who, taking their lamps, went out to meet the bridegroom and the bride" (Mt 25:1). The Lord gave us many beautiful descriptions of the Church while He was still upon earth, but none surpasses in beauty and charm the one in which He describes the kingdom of God in the parable of the ten virgins who go forth to meet the bridegroom. One thought possesses their souls, and all their attention is directed to one end: not to miss the coming of the bridegroom. How eagerly they look forward to his coming! They are swept away with the desire to greet the bridegroom and to enter with him into the bridal feast. Yes, indeed, that is a true picture of the Church, which is the bride of Christ. She awaits with eager longing the coming of the Lord. What has the world to offer her? Her attention is fixed on her eternal goal. "Our conversation is in heaven, from whence also we look for the Savior, our Lord Jesus Christ."

The Church is filled with desire and longing for the coming of this Savior. Her children greet one another with the salutation, Maran-atha — "May the Lord come" (1 Cor 16:22); and she often sighs, "Amen, come Lord Jesus" (Apoc 22:20). With eager desire she prays: "Lord, remember to deliver Thy Church from all evil and to perfect it in Thy love, and from the four winds gather it together, the sanctified one, into Thy kingdom, which Thou hast prepared for it. For Thine is the power and the glory forever. Let grace come, and let this world pass away."[25] Even the terrible disasters of the last days will only serve to increase the longing of the Church.

"And I expect the resurrection of the dead." The Church awaits the resurrection of the dead with absolute confidence and without dread. This she does with good reason, for Christ her head has already risen to eternal life, thus giving His mystical body unshakable confidence in its own resurrection. If we remain living members of the mystical body, our resurrection is likewise assured. Indeed, the fulfillment of this desire has already begun, for even here on earth we share already in the divine life, which will be unfolded in its perfection in heaven. Likewise

[25] *Didache*, chap. 10.

our resurrection and our glorification in heaven have already begun in the person of Christ our head. "In God shall we glory all the day long; and in Thy name we will give praise forever" (Gradual). We trust in God's assurance: "I think thoughts of peace and not of affliction.... I will bring back your captivity from all places" (Introit).

"Our conversation is in heaven." A future of happiness and blessing awaits us. Of what importance, then, are the trials of this present life? What wonder, then, that in those ages of the Church when men lived in continual expectation of the coming of Christ, a generation of martyrs arose, which with true heroism despised the goods and honors of this world and trampled them under foot, and gave their life and their blood in order to gain Christ and eternal life! What wonder that such an age could produce a generation of virgins, strong, mortified, and pure, such as Cecilia, Agnes, and Agatha! They understood well what it meant to go forth to meet Christ. Do we understand as well?

"And if I shall go and prepare a place for you, I will come again, and will take you to Myself; that where I am, you also may be.... These things I have spoken to you that My joy may be in you, and your joy may be filled" (Jn 14:3; 15:11). We who are incorporated in Christ will experience the fulfillment of these promises in the time that is to come.

The day of Christ's coming, the day of our death, may be sooner than we expect. Are we prepared for it? Are we prepared to meet the bridegroom with burning lamps? Or have our lamps gone out for want of oil? We must always be prepared for the coming of the bridegroom, for we "know not the day nor the hour" when He will come to call us to the bridal feast of heaven.

Prayer

Remit, we beseech Thee, O Lord, the sins of Thy people, that by Thy kindness we may be delivered from the trammels of our sins, in which through our frailty we have become entangled. Through Christ our Lord. Amen.

Wednesday

The liturgy takes great pains during the last weeks of the Church year to keep alive in the hearts of all Christians the thought of the day when the bridegroom will return, and it inspires them with great hope in that day. It strengthens men in the hope that He "also will confirm you unto the end without crime, in the day of the coming of our Lord Jesus Christ";[26] it would have us always prepared, that we "may be sincere and without offense unto the day of Christ."[27] We are invited to celebrate the joyful feast of All Saints for eight days, and we are also allowed to share that ardent longing for heaven which possesses the souls of those in purgatory. The Church then prays for us that "we may be delivered from the trammels of our sins" (Collect) and not be "overcome by human dangers" (Postcommunion). She admonishes us always to stand fast in the Lord" (Epistle). She knows well how easy it is to desert Christ and to fix our attention on the things of this world.

[26] Epistle for the Eighteenth Sunday after Pentecost.

[27] Epistle for the Twenty-Second Sunday after Pentecost.

"Stand fast in the Lord." We are incorporated in Christ through baptism. From that moment on Christ relives His life in us. His thoughts and desires are not centered on earthly things, on lust and uncleanness, on honors, pleasures, and luxurious living. All that is sinful or displeasing to His father is entirely foreign to Him; Christ has the will of His Father always before His eyes. Christ lives in us here on earth the life that we shall live in eternity, a life of continual union with God. Thus His conversation is in heaven. This "conversation" consists in the contemplation of the Father, a continual devotion to what the Father loves and to the unbroken adoration and praise of the Father. It is in effect an eternal "I go to the Father" (Jn 14:28).

Christ has joined us to Himself through baptism in order that He may be able to live His life again in us, and live it to the end. By means of Holy Communion, He daily deepens this union in order that we may be filled with His spirit and His strength, that we who are the members of the mystical body may share more perfectly in the life of the head. The more perfectly we become united to Him, the more perfectly is our conversation in heaven. Thus we also become more perfectly detached from worldly goods through a joyful self-abnegation and a renunciation of inordinate occupations, possessions, desires, honors, and worldly esteem. In Christ the things of this world lose their value for us. We become like the Apostle who, once he had caught a glimpse of the glory of heaven (2 Cor 12:1 ff.), considered as dung all that he had heretofore valued and trusted in. He is now "in Christ"; he is possessed by Christ, and he forgets all that lies behind him, all that is earthly. He longs only for the things that await him, and attends only to the mission to which God has called him through Christ Jesus (Phil 3:5 ff.). Today the liturgy directs our attention to him: "Brethren, be followers of me" (Epistle).

"Many walk that are enemies of the cross of Christ" (Epistle). They have renounced Satan and his works, and have received the impression of the sign of the cross on their breasts and foreheads to show that they belong to Christ crucified. Through their baptism they were engrafted as branches on the vine which is Christ, in order that they might live by Him. "The flesh that is reborn through baptism is the flesh of the Crucified" (St. Leo the Great). "With Christ I am nailed to the cross" (Gal 2:19). "But God forbid that I should glory save in the cross of our Lord Jesus Christ; by whom the world is crucified to me, and I to the world" (Gal 6:14). But today some Christians walk as "enemies of the cross of Christ," for they "mind earthly things" (Epistle). The Apostle wept bitterly over these wayward Christians, and today the Church does the same. "Out of the depths I have cried to Thee, O Lord; Lord hear my prayer" (Offertory). But she also prays for them: "Remit, we beseech Thee, O Lord, the sins of Thy people, that by Thy kindness we may be delivered from the trammels of our sins" (Collect), from the trammels of earthly goods and possessions.

In the person of the ruler of the synagogue the Church approaches the Lord, "My daughter is even now dead; but come, lay Thy hand upon her, and she shall live" (Gospel). And He assures her: "I think thoughts of peace and not of affliction" (Introit). "Amen I say to you, whatsoever you ask when you pray, believe that you shall receive, and it shall be done to you" (Communion).

"Stand fast in the Lord." We must stand fast in the Lord through our continual consciousness of our living union with Him who is our head. We have been elevated above all that is merely natural or temporal, for "our conversation is in heaven" (Epistle).

After having received so many graces, should we not be entirely possessed by Christ? Should we not by this time consider all that is precious in the eyes of worldly men but as dung? Are we to be numbered among those who walk as "enemies of the cross of Christ; ... who mind earthly things? But our conversation is in heaven."

Prayer

We beseech Thee, almighty God, that Thou wilt not permit to be overcome by human dangers those whom Thou grantest to rejoice in the participation in the divine mysteries. Through Christ our Lord. Amen. (Postcommunion.)

Thursday

This joyful message the Church brings us today: "I will bring back your captivity from all places" (Introit). The Lord has ascended into heaven to prepare a place for us. "If I shall go and prepare a place for you, I will come again and will take you to Myself, that where I am, you also may be" (Jn 14:3).

"He shall come again," the Church assures us in the Credo. The Lord Himself has to return. "And then shall appear the sign of the Son of Man in heaven.... All tribes ... shall see the Son of Man coming in the clouds of heaven with much power and majesty. And He shall send His angels with a trumpet and a great voice; and they shall gather together His elect from the four winds, from the farthest parts of the heavens to the utmost bounds of them" (Mt 24:30 ff.). "But when these things begin to come to pass, look up and lift up your heads, because your redemption is at hand" (Lk 21:28). He will come to judge the wicked and "to be glorified in His saints [the baptized] and to be made wonderful in all them who have believed" (2 Thes 1:10). "All that are in the graves shall hear the voice of the Son of God. And they that have done good things, shall come forth unto the resurrection of life; but they that have done evil, unto the resurrection of judgment" (Jn 5:28 f.). "And as in Adam all die, so also in Christ all shall be made alive. But every one in his own order: the first fruits, Christ; then they that are of Christ, who have believed in His coming. Afterwards the end, when He shall have delivered up the kingdom to God and the Father, when He shall have brought to nought all principality and power and virtue. For He must reign until He hath put all His enemies under His feet. And the enemy, death, shall be destroyed last" (1 Cor 15:22–26). Once He has subjected all things to Himself, He will take us by the hand and lead us to the Father, saying, "Come, ye blessed of My Father, possess you the kingdom prepared for you from the foundation of the world" (Mt 25:34). Then the promise will be fulfilled, "I shall come again and will take you to Myself." We trust in this promise of the Lord, and in His will and His ability to fulfill it. "Lift up your heads, because your redemption is at hand."

"That where I am, you also may be" (Jn 14:3). "Father, I will that where I am, they also whom Thou hast given Me may be with Me" (Jn 17:24), not only as My brethren, but as members of My mystical body. Therefore if I am in glory, they also shall be there with Me as My members. "That they may see My glory, which Thou hast given Me" (Jn 17:24). Yes, they shall receive this glory themselves; for I "will reform the body,... made like to the body of [My] glory" (Epistle). Father, "I in them, and Thou in Me" (Jn 17:23). Therefore the love which Thou hast for Me must be given to them also. And the joy and glory and blessing which Thou hast given Me, must be given to them also, that My joy may be made perfect in them.

Who indeed can comprehend "what things God hath prepared for them that love Him" (1 Cor 2:9)? All these things have been prepared for us, who are the members of Christ, who are members of His spouse, the Church.

O marvelous mystery of our union with Christ through baptism and the Holy Eucharist! O marvelous mystery of the communion of saints! "I will that where I am, they also whom Thou hast given Me may be with Me" (Jn 17:24). I am the head, you are the members. "I am the vine, you the branches. He that abideth in Me, and I in him, the same beareth much fruit; for without Me you can do nothing. If any one abide not in Me, he shall be cast forth as a branch and shall wither, and they shall gather him up and cast him into the fire, and he burneth" (Jn 15:5 f.).

"Thou hast delivered us, O Lord, from them that afflict us; and hast put them to shame that hate us. In God shall we glory all the day; and in Thy name we will give praise forever" (Gradual).

PRAYER

Remit, we beseech Thee, O Lord, the sins of Thy people, that by Thy kindness we may be delivered from the trammels of our sins, in which through our frailty we have become entangled. Through Christ our Lord. Amen.

Friday

"I will bring back your captivity from all places" (Introit). The time of our exile is drawing to a close. Our home in heaven awaits us. We are "fellow citizens with the saints, and the domestics of God" (Eph 2:19). We are "heirs indeed of God, and joint heirs with Christ" (Rom 8:17).

"He will dwell with them and they shall be His people; and God Himself with them shall be their God. And God shall wipe away all tears from their eyes; and death shall be no more; nor mourning, nor crying, nor sorrow shall be any more; for the former things are passed away" (Apoc 21:3 f.). The time of our imprisonment, the time of our exile, is at an end. We are home at last. The time of tribulation and trouble, of labor and suffering, is past. The days of our exile are over, and the way of the cross, which we had to walk in this world, has been completed. We have entered "into the joy of the Lord" (Mt 25:21), into the land of light and plenty, into the land of perfect happiness and bliss. We are allowed to join our voices with the redeemed and with the seraphim and sing "Holy! Holy! Holy!" Our soul sinks in the unfathomable depths of light and glory. We have regained the inheritance which we lost, the inheritance which Christ reclaimed for us through His sufferings and death. We have obtained that which "eye hath not seen, nor ear heard, neither hath it entered into the heart of man what things God hath prepared for them that love Him" (1 Cor 2:9).

"Fellow citizens with the saints, and the domestics of God" (Eph 2:19), we are home at last with God. God Himself is our heaven and our inheritance. "We shall live in Him and at the same time we shall be the dwellings of God" (St. Augustine). "We shall see Him as He is," "face to face" (1 Jn 3:2; 1 Cor 13:12). We shall see God and all things in

Him. We shall love Him, cling to Him, and receive all the blessings of His love. We shall possess God and be overwhelmed through the joy of that love. O life of inexpressible joy! We shall behold the beauty of God unveiled. We shall contemplate the infinite truth with perfect clarity. We shall possess all good things without measure and without any fear of ever losing them or ever becoming satiated with them. And this happiness we experience in one eternal, unbroken act. Yes, we shall be at home with God, enjoying the eternal and blessed possession of the divinity. And God will be within us, enlightening us by direct intuition. We shall all be as tiny suns, reflecting the glorious light of the mighty Sun that has risen upon us. We shall be at home, at rest, in the heart of our Father. We shall be at home, enjoying the most delightful and the most intimate union with the bridegroom of our souls. We shall be in possession of His glory, His blessing, His riches. "They shall be inebriated with the plenty of Thy house, and Thou shalt make them drink of the torrent of Thy pleasure" (Ps 35:9). We shall be at home with all the blessed of heaven, in company with our brothers and sisters in Christ, in company with all that are pure, strong, and noble. There will be no envy and no selfishness amongst us; we shall know only an all-embracing and universal charity. We shall be united one with the other, possessing but one heart and one soul in the love of God and of Christ. We shall be at home and shall have all that we desire: all truth, all knowledge, all virtue, all holiness, all honor, and the love of God and of the angels and the saints. We shall possess the love of God, of Mary, of all who are good and noble. O blessed home!

"Let us always embrace that vision with perfect faith. Let us strive for it with all our hearts and achieve it by the continual practice of charity. Whether we achieve it or not depends entirely on us. Heaven suffers violence. Heaven can be purchased by no price less than yourself, O man. The measure of its value is the value of your very being. Give yourself completely, and you will possess it" (St. Bede).

"For I reckon that the sufferings of this time are not worthy to be compared with the glory to come" (Rom 8:18). "Blessed are the poor in spirit.... Blessed are the meek.... Blessed are they that mourn.... Blessed are they that hunger and thirst after justice.... Blessed are they that suffer persecution for justice's sake.... Blessed are ye when they shall revile you and persecute you, and speak all that is evil against you, untruly, for my sake. Be glad and rejoice, for your reward is very great in heaven" (Mt 5:3–12).

God has promised us, "I will bring back your captivity." We have been united to Christ and the Church through baptism. How precious, then, should the Church and sacraments of baptism and the Eucharist be to us! "He that eateth Me, the same also shall live by Me" (Jn 6:58). How wretchedly poor are those who do not possess Christ, the Church, and the sacraments! How wretched are those who, though baptized, do not live as members of the Church! These are those who "walk as enemies of the cross of Christ,... whose God is their belly;... who mind earthly things" (Epistle).

Prayer

We beseech Thee, almighty God, that Thou wilt not permit to be overcome by human dangers those whom Thou grantest to rejoice in the participation in the divine mysteries. Through Christ our Lord. Amen. (Postcommunion.)

Saturday

"I expect the resurrection of the dead" (Credo). But before heaven is opened to us and before we can be with Christ, we must conquer death with Him. "It is appointed unto men once to die" (Heb 9:27).

"Dust thou art and into dust thou shalt return" (Gn 3:19). "Wherefore as by one man sin entered into this world, and by sin death, and so death passed upon all men in whom all have sinned" (Rom 5:12). Death is the punishment for Original Sin, which all men contract through Adam. It is a severe punishment, a punishment which no man can escape, but which the natural man would avoid if he could. Death means the loss of all that man possessed on earth, the loss of all that he treasured and prized. It means the separation from the friends he loved, the occupations he enjoyed, the works in which he gloried, and the habits and tastes which he acquired. But death also means an end of all temptations and occasions of sin, the ceasing of the danger of losing God and His grace; it means also the end of the time for merit, for after death we cannot add one iota to our reward in eternity. With death our status is fixed for all eternity, for after that there will be no change. Whatever has not been finished then, will never be finished. Death decides all issues permanently. Opportunities neglected while on earth will never come again.

"For to me to live is Christ; and to die is gain" (Phil 1:21). For us who have been incorporated in Christ, death has lost its terror. For us death is a gain, a release. It opens to us the door that leads to our Father and our heavenly home. Death will mark our last opportunity for consecrating ourselves to God by a perfect act of love. We accept death willingly, as a means of uniting ourselves to God, as a necessary condition imposed on us by God for that union. We could never give to God more than we can give in that moment; that is, ourselves and all that we have.

"All we who are baptized in Christ Jesus, are baptized in His death" (Rom 6:3). In our death Christ continues His death and His sacrifice on the cross until the end of time. When Christ offered Himself on the cross, He also offered us who are members of His mystical body. Through our death we complete and "fill up those things that are wanting of the sufferings of Christ, in [our] flesh, for His body which is the Church" (Col 1:24). Our death is a death in Christ, a death with Christ, a consummation of that sacrifice to which we were dedicated by our baptism. Sacrificed with Christ, drinking the chalice of His suffering, we, too, become a sacrifice acceptable to the Father, effective for the salvation of our own souls and for those of our brethren, for the salvation of the whole Church and for the whole of mankind.

The Christian is Christ living, Christ suffering, Christ dying. He is the vine, we are the branches; but we are one "mystic being" (St. Thomas). When we are dying, we are like Him, the victim and the priest who is offering the sacrifice. We are the sacrifice because we have been subjected to suffering and death by God; we are the offering priests because we accept willingly and with complete resignation the death He has imposed upon us. Thus we offer our last sacrifice to God.

"May I enjoy the wild beasts that are prepared for me; and I pray that they may be found eager to rush upon me, which also I will entice to devour me speedily, and not deal with me as with some, whom out of fear they have not touched. But if they be unwilling to assail me, I will compel them to do so.... Now I begin to be a disciple. And let no one, of things visible or invisible, envy me that I should attain to Jesus Christ. Let fire and the cross; let the crowds of wild beasts; let tearings, breakings, and dislocations of bones; let cutting off of members; let shatterings of the whole body; and let all the dreadful torments of the devil come upon me. Only let me attain to Jesus Christ."[28] Such is the spirit in which St. Ignatius of Antioch went to meet his death. Ignatius was a Christian of heroic stature.

St. Charles Borromeo was obliged to pass daily in his palace a picture which represented death holding a sickle. But the saint had a golden key substituted for the sickle. Such is the Christian attitude toward death: it is a key and not an instrument of destruction.

"I think thoughts of peace and not of affliction.... I will bring back your captivity" (Introit). Death marks our release from this life of temptation and sorrow and the beginning of our glorified life. The liturgy looks upon the day of death as our birthday, our *dies natalis,* the day on which the Christian is born into eternal life.

Prayer

Remit, we beseech Thee, O Lord, the sins of Thy people, that by Thy kindness we may be delivered from the trammels of our sins, in which through our frailty we have become entangled. Through Christ our Lord. Amen.

Twenty-Fourth and Last Sunday after Pentecost

The Mass

We have arrived at the last Sunday after Pentecost, the end of the ecclesiastical year. "The day of Christ" is about to dawn. At the moment when the night seems darkest, at the moment when the spirits of evil seem to have reached the height of their power, at the moment when evil men seem to have wandered away from God as far as possible, the Son of Man will appear suddenly in the clouds. Every knee shall bend and acknowledge that He is the Lord, that it is He who has overcome the powers of evil, and that He comes now to call His faithful ones to their kingdom. For this reason the liturgy looks upon the day of the coming of Christ as a day of joy, a day to be longed for, a day of victory for Christ, a day which will see the triumph of the Church and her entry into the rest and peace of her eternal home with God.

Today we bear witness to the arrival of Christ and His eventual victory, to the day when Christ will bring his Church, composed of all nations and tribes, to the peace and joy of heaven. At the thought of all this our hearts rejoice and are glad. We catch a glimpse of our Redeemer, clothed in the power and majesty of His glorified body, coming down to us from the heavens. "I think thoughts of peace," He tells us, "and not of affliction.... I will bring back your captivity" (Introit). We press forward eagerly to meet Him and sigh for the revelation of the glory of the children of God. We cry out *Kyrie eleison:* "Lord have mercy." Then we find ourselves sitting at the feet of the Apostle who, though bound in chains at Rome, does not cease to pray for us that we may be worthy of God, may please Him in all things, and bring forth fruits worthy of Him, thanking Him that he "hath made us worthy to be partakers of the lot of the saints in light" (Epistle). These are the precious fruits of the blessed year of grace which we are just now bringing to a close. He "hath delivered us from the power of darkness and hath translated us into the kingdom

[28] St. Ignatius, *Epistle to the Romans*, chap. 5; trans. from *The Ante-Nicene Fathers*, I, 75 f.

of the Son of His love" (Epistle). We cry out with joy: "Thou hast delivered us, O Lord, from them that afflict us.... In Thy name we will give praise forever" (Gradual). Then the marvelous scene of the return of Christ is spread out before our eyes. When His time has come, the Son of Man will return with great power and glory. "He shall send His angels; and they shall gather together His elect from the four winds, from the farthest parts of the heavens to the utmost bounds of them" (Gospel). We receive this joyful message with a devout Credo: "I believe.... I expect the resurrection of the dead and the life of the world to come."

Now we come to the Offertory, and our sentiments are expressed in the Secreta: "Be propitious, O Lord, to our supplications, and accepting the offerings and prayers of Thy people, turn all our hearts unto Thee, that being delivered from earthly desires, we may pass on to heavenly desires." Together with our offerings of bread and wine, we lay our hearts upon the paten. When we make this offering we detach our hearts from all "earthly desires," from all evil inclinations, from all inordinate attachment to earthly goods, be they money, possessions, honors, position, or health. The bread, which was confected from many grains of wheat, and the wine, which is mixed with a few drops of water, are symbols of our union with Christ and the Church to form one unified and perfect sacrifice to the Father. We have been "delivered from earthly desires" and "pass on to heavenly desires" through the offering of this Holy Sacrifice. We wish to conform to the will of God in thought and in inclination, in wish and desire, in will and work, and to be "filled with the knowledge of the will of God in all wisdom and spiritual understanding; that [we] may walk worthy of God, in all things pleasing, being fruitful in every good work, and increasing in the knowledge of God, strengthened with all might according to the power of His glory" (Epistle). The Lord comes to us at the time of the consecration in power and glory, to fill us with His spirit and life, and to offer us as a "pure, holy, and unspotted victim" to the Father. In this sacrifice we become one bread, one body, one kingdom of Christ, offered to the Father. In this kingdom we shall be united in thought and desire to form one kingdom of grace and love.

Meditation

"They shall see the Son of Man coming in the clouds of heaven with much power and majesty" on the day when Christ returns to judge the world (Gospel). It is the day of the general judgment.

"He shall come to judge the living and the dead" (Apostles' Creed). The Lord still lives. He is not only the Redeemer of men; He is also the end of all creation. Once He appeared in the world in poverty and lowliness; but He will come again with power and majesty. "The moon shall not give her light and the stars shall fall from heaven, and the powers of heaven shall be moved; and then shall appear the sign of the Son of Man in heaven [the cross], and then shall all the tribes of the earth mourn; and they shall see the Son of Man coming in the clouds of heaven with much power and majesty" (Gospel). It is the day of Christ's triumph, and He will be glorified before all men. First He will recall the dead to life by the power of His word, and they shall rise from their graves to appear before His judgment seat. They will not appear as individuals, for their fate has been settled at the time of the particular judgment and will not be changed; they will appear rather as part of the whole human race; they will be grouped according to their ideologies, politics, errors, according to their culture and age. They will be obliged to reveal their true character, whether they are good grain or useless chaff. They will have to confess whether they have been for God or against Him, whether they have loved Christ or hated Him, whether they have served the Church or worked against her. It will then be clear whether as fathers, mothers, superiors, state officials, scientists, writers, priests, shepherds of souls, laymen, or hermits, they have been a good or bad influence on others; whether they have advanced the kingdom of God, or whether they have hindered it.

All men will be subject to the judgment of Christ, whom the world today despises and ignores. All will have to bend their knees before Him and submit to His decisions. "Thou alone art holy. Thou alone art the Lord. Thou alone are most high, O Jesus Christ, together with the Holy Ghost, in the glory of God the Father" (Gloria). On the day of Christ's triumph the world will fully acknowledge Him. How the Church longs for that day! On that day Christ and His Church, and all who have been faithful to Him, will receive full justice. "Maran-atha," Come, O Lord.

In the midst of the confusion of the elements, in the midst of a terrifying darkness, a light will appear suddenly in the sky, "the sign of the Son of Man," a cross formed of brilliant rays, the despised and hated cross of Christ. All men will be forced to behold it and to acknowledge that from it alone comes salvation. This fiery cross will announce the return of the Lord. Just as He ascended into the heavens with His glorified body, so will He come again in the clouds of heaven "in the glory of His Father" (Mt 16:27), surrounded by His angels. All will behold and will acknowledge the glory that He won for them through His blessed death. They will have to acknowledge what Christ accomplished for their bodies and souls through His incarnation, His cross and resurrection, His ascension, through the descent of the Holy Ghost, through His Church and her dogmas and her sacraments. They will acknowledge and confess that if any have been lost, it is not the fault of God. And those who have won salvation will admit and confess that they must thank God and His grace, and that "it is God who worketh in you, both to will and to accomplish" (Phil 2:13). "Not that we are sufficient to think any thing of ourselves, as of ourselves; but our sufficiency is from God" (2 Cor 3:5).

The second coming of Christ on the Day of Judgment will set the seal of God's final approval on Christ's first coming in the stable at Bethlehem, on the truth of His incarnation, on the truth of His doctrine and the holiness of His life, on the truth taught by His Church and the authenticity of her mission, her authority, her pronouncements, her doctrines, and the validity of her sacraments. Happy shall we be if while on earth we have acknowledged the Lord, if we have believed and obeyed Him and His Church.

The Lord comes to us in a mystical manner during the Holy Sacrifice of the Mass, with power and majesty, although for the present this glory is hidden from our eyes. He gathers His elect about Him and fills them with His spirit. He associates them with Himself in offering to the Father a sacrifice which alone is "pure, holy, and unspotted." During Holy Communion they will be translated "into the kingdom of the son of His love" (Epistle). They will be united to Him most intimately. This coming is but a prelude to His final coming; it is a coming in grace and a pledge of His coming on the Day of Judgment. Full of faith and confidence we go forth to meet Him when He comes to us in the Holy Sacrifice of the Mass. From the celebration of this sacrifice we acquire the strength to "walk worthy of God, in all things pleasing, being fruitful in every good work, strengthened with all might" (Epistle). We trust that at His return we may be worthy to hear the words, "Come ye blessed of My Father" (Mt 25:34).

Prayer

Arouse, we beseech Thee, O Lord, the wills of Thy faithful, that by more earnestly seeking the fruit of the divine work, they may receive more abundantly the gifts of Thy loving kindness. Through Christ our Lord. Amen.

Monday

"Heaven and earth shall pass away" (Gospel). "This therefore I say, brethren, the time is short,... for the fashion of this world passeth away" (1 Cor 7:29, 31). How rapidly the days slipped by during the past Church year. They will never come again. The graces and the opportunities they offered me are gone forever.

"The time is short. It remaineth that they also who have wives be as though they had none; and they that weep, as though they wept not; and they that rejoice, as if they rejoiced not; and they that buy, as though they possessed not; and they that use this world, as if they used it not; for the fashion of this world passeth away" (1 Cor 7:29–31). The trials and the troubles of this world are hardly worth the worry they cause. All that we experience in this world, all that surrounds us, is subject to corruption and decay. In conflict of soul the Psalmist prays: "And what is the number of my days.... Behold, Thou hast made my days measurable, and my substance is as nothing before Thee. And indeed all things are vanity, every man living. Surely man passeth as an image; yea, and he is disquieted in vain. He storeth up, and he knoweth not for whom he shall gather these things" (Ps 38:5–7).

"The fashion of this world passeth away." There is far less in this world than we suppose. We gain nothing by spending so much of our time in the occupations and interest of this world. "Therefore, if you be risen with Christ [in baptism], seek the things that are above, where Christ is sitting at the right hand of God; mind the things that are above, not the things that are upon the earth. For you are dead, and your life is hid with Christ in God" (Col 3:1–3). Therefore "it remaineth that they also who have wives be as if they had none;... and they that use this world, as if they used it not; for the fashion of this world passeth away" (1 Cor 7:29, 31). Thus the Christian believes and thinks.

Be "solicitous for the things that belong to the Lord" (1 Cor 7:32). Observe that the Church has but one thought, the will of the Lord. She is possessed by one great passion, and this rules her heart: "The things that pertain to God." For that reason her life is so genuine, so upright, so unified, so peaceful, so recollected. What else has been the concern of the Church during the past year but the things of God? Holy Mother the Church has withdrawn us daily from the streets of the world into the holy of holies that we might learn to be solicitous for the things of God. How diligently she has taught us through her instructions, through the Gospels, through her liturgical song! How often she has admonished us to withdraw farther and farther from the world and to be united to Christ! How diligent she has been in making sacrifices for us! How instant in prayer! She can indeed say with truth, "We cease not to pray for you and to beg that you may be filled with the knowledge of the will of God, in all wisdom and spiritual understanding; that you may walk worthy of God in all things pleasing, being fruitful in every good work, and increasing in the knowledge of God; strengthened with all might,... giving thanks to God the Father, who hath made us worthy to be partakers of the lot of the saints in light" (Epistle).

How much power and grace the Church has given us during the past year through her sacrifice and her sacraments! She has done so much for us that we might die to the things of this world and begin to live for the things that pertain to God.

"Turn all our hearts unto Thee, that being delivered from earthly desires, we may pass on to heavenly desires" (Secreta). The Lord must accomplish this transformation. "For it is God who worketh in you, both to will and to accomplish, according to His good will" (Phil 2:13). However, we and the Church may pray for the grace to be delivered from earthly desires. "Out of the depths I have cried to Thee, O Lord; Lord, hear my prayer" (Offertory). In the Holy Sacrifice of the Mass, Christ prays with His Church and in us and with us; and when we are united to Him in Holy Communion, He gives us the assurance, "Amen, I say to you, whatsoever you ask when you pray, believe that you shall receive, and it shall be done to you" (Communion).

"The fashion of this world passeth away. Unless a man be disengaged from all creatures, he cannot freely attend to divine things. Therefore there are so few people of interior life, because so few know how to free themselves completely from the passing and created things of this world. For this a great grace is required, which lifts the soul above created things, above itself. Unless a man be elevated in spirit, and freed from attachment to all creatures, and wholly united to God, whatever he knows and whatever he possesses is of little value.... Whatever is not God, is nothing and must be looked upon as nothing" (*Imitation of Christ*, III, chap. 31).

Prayer

Arouse, we beseech Thee, O Lord, the wills of Thy faithful, that by more earnestly seeking the fruit of the divine work, they may receive more abundantly the gifts of Thy loving kindness. Through Christ our Lord. Amen.

Tuesday

"You shall call upon Me, and I will hear you; and I will bring back your captivity from all places" (Introit). Our Lord and Savior is one day to return in power and glory. "For the hour cometh wherein all that are in the graves shall hear the voice of the Son of God. And they that have done good things shall come forth unto the resurrection of life; but they that have done evil, unto the resurrection of judgment" (Jn 5:28 f.). The evil shall rise to be judged and confined to the eternal misery of hell. "The heavens shall pass away with great violence,... and the earth and the works which are in it shall be burnt up" (2 Pt 3:10). The Day of Judgment will make manifest the power of the Crucified.

The power of Christ will be manifested in the resurrection of the dead. The prophet Ezechiel saw in a vision a field filled with the bones of the dead. But the Spirit of the Lord passed over this field, and a voice said: "I will lay sinews upon you and will cause flesh to grow over you, and will cover you with skin; and I will give you spirit, and you shall live and you shall know that I am the Lord.... Behold, I will open your graves and will bring you out of your sepulchers, O My people;... and you shall live" (Ez 37:6 ff.). What the prophet saw in a vision will come to pass at the Last Judgment. Christ the Lord will open the graves of the dead and lead them forth that they may live again. Then they will all acknowledge that He is the Lord, "for He must reign until He hath put all His enemies under His feet. And the enemy death shall be destroyed last" (1 Cor 15:25 f.). When He calls, everyone without exception will rise from his grave; no one will be able to resist His powerful word. All must obey Him and resume the body which they laid aside at death. The power of the word of Christ will unite again the elements that had returned to dust, that had decayed and had been scattered to the four winds. The power of death will finally be conquered by the power of Christ, which on this day will be made manifest to all the world. How the Church rejoices in this victory of Christ! It will indeed be the "day of Christ."

The power of Christ will also be manifested in the destruction of the world. "Heaven and earth will pass away, but My words shall not pass away" (Gospel). "But the heavens and earth which are now,... [are] reserved unto fire against the Day of Judgment.... But we look for new heavens and a new earth according to His promises, in which justice dwelleth" (2 Pt 3:7, 13). The resurrection of a single soul is the guarantee of the redemption of the universe. "For the expectation of the creature waiteth for the revelation of the sons of God.... Because the creature also itself shall be delivered from the servitude of corruption, into the liberty of the glory of the children of God" (Rom 8:19, 21). What God intended for humanity and for the whole of creation, but which is now obscured by the mire of sin and death and which sighs under the curse of vanity, will in that day be restored to its pristine beauty and harmony; and the excellence and the beauty of God's plan will be revealed.

"I saw a new heaven and a new earth.... And I, John, saw the holy city, the new Jerusalem, coming down out of heaven from God, prepared as a bride adorned for her husband" (Apoc 21:1 f.). The new Jerusalem, heaven, will descend to the earth from above. This new Jerusalem will appear as a bride adorned and going to meet her spouse. Heaven will then no longer be the secret dwelling place of God, but the revelation of God to man. The heavens above and the earth below, appearances and reality, will be one. What is earthly will become heavenly, and what is of the body will be but a mirror for the spirit. Creation will be perfected in God; it will know no decline, no change, no distress. Nothing will be altered; but creation will take on the beauty of God Himself and enjoy an eternal spring. It will be always young and always new. Healed will be the conflict between the flesh and the spirit which sin caused in man and in all creation, and harmony and order will be re-established, not only in individual men, but in all creation, "that God may be all in all" (1 Cor 15:28). Salvation and final redemption will be granted to the body and the soul of man, to heaven and earth, and to all that exists, through the incarnate Son of God. "Thy kingdom come."

"The day of Christ" will be a day of victory, the day of triumph for Christ's truth, humility, and love. Glory to Thee, O Christ, the Victor, the King in whom all things live.

"The day of Christ" will be a day of triumph for the Church, for her beliefs, for her sacraments, for her sufferings borne for Christ, for her prayer, for her work for souls. The Church will conquer and live triumphant, and we shall triumph with her.

"The day of Christ" will be a day of victory for the Holy Eucharist, which has nourished the germ of life in us. "He that eateth My flesh and drinketh My blood, hath everlasting life. And I will raise him up in the last day" (Jn 6:55). "The day of Christ" will be a day of triumph for our faith in the Eucharist and our devotion to It.

"The day of Christ" will be a day of triumph for the first-born from the dead, and for us, whom He has recalled to life, giving us a proof of His justice and mercy, of His power and holiness.

Prayer

Arouse, we beseech Thee, O Lord, the wills of Thy faithful, that by more earnestly seeking the fruit of the divine work, they may receive more abundantly the gifts of Thy loving kindness. Through Christ our Lord. Amen.

Wednesday

Christ is coming to judge the heavens and the earth; "For we must all be manifested before the judgment seat of Christ, that every one may receive the proper things of the body according as he hath done, whether it be good or evil" (2 Cor 5:10). The liturgy beseeches almighty God to give us the grace to "walk worthy of God, in all things pleasing" (Epistle). If we have done so, we can go to meet our judge without fear.

"Walk worthy of God, in all things pleasing." The Epistle instructs us how we may thus walk: "Be filled with the knowledge of the will of God, in all wisdom and spiritual understanding." It is the will of Holy Mother the Church that we be filled with a spiritual and supernatural wisdom and foresight. She wishes us to understand what she intends for us and does for us. She would have us grow in our understanding of the mysteries of the incarnation, the redemption, the operation of grace in our souls, our incorporation in Christ, and our participation in divine life, grace, and eternal life. According to the mind of the liturgy, the Christian should live in a world of the spirit, so "that the God of our Lord Jesus Christ, the Father of glory, may give unto you the Spirit of wisdom and of revelation in the knowledge of Him" (Eph 1:17). Through this wisdom and understanding we have "knowledge of the will of God"; that is, knowledge of the benevolent providence of God, which determined from all eternity to send His divine Son, that He might through His suffering and death reconcile us to the Father and adopt us as the very sons of God. Inspired by such a knowledge, we "walk worthy of God, in all things pleasing." A profound knowledge of what God is, and what He did for us, and what He will yet do for us in eternity, cannot but influence our lives. It will make us "fruitful in every good work,... strengthened with all might according to the power of His glory, in all patience and long suffering with joy" (Epistle). We should first know God, what He is, and what He means to us, and then only should we look upon ourselves. Only then shall we acquire a joyful consciousness of our participation in the life of God.

"Giving thanks to God the Father, who hath made us worthy to be partakers of the lot of the saints in light; who hath delivered us from the power of darkness, and hath translated us into the kingdom of the Son of His love, in whom we have redemption through His blood, the remission of sins" (Epistle). We have received three great graces from God. Though born into the world as children of anger and destruction, we become partakers of the lot of the saints in light, since we share the light of faith here on earth and are one day to share in the light of glory and blessedness in heaven. Although we were born into the world as the slaves of Satan, God has freed us from the domination of the powers of darkness and has made us members of the kingdom of His beloved Son and of His Church. As members of the Church, we become members of the body of Christ, branches of the living vine, living by the Spirit of Christ, filled with Christ, and destined one day to share His inheritance in heaven. Finally, Christ has redeemed us through His suffering and death, and has obtained for us the remission of sins. We should give "thanks to God the Father" by our continual consciousness of the graces He has poured forth upon us in Christ Jesus. Our lives should be an unbroken "Thanks be to God," an uninterrupted eucharist, a continual act of gratitude to God the Father.

The object of the liturgy during the past year has been to give us a better understanding of the benefits God has bestowed on us in the incarnation of His only-begotten Son and in His life and teaching, in His suffering and death, in His resurrection, ascension, and glorification; she has striven to teach us the meaning of our incorporation in Christ and to induce us to live the life of the sons of God. She has sought to make us understand the importance of the Eucharist, which is offered by the priest each day and given to us as our spiritual nourishment. She would have us understand that Christ still operates in us and will continue to do so until we are finally prepared to share with Him His eternal glory and blessedness. We should continually meditate on these truths.

"Brethren, we cease not to pray... that you may be filled with the knowledge of the will of God in all wisdom" (Epistle). Once we are able to live in the knowledge of what God is and what He has done for us, and we are absorbed by this thought in spite of all the bitter trials that come to us, in spite of all misfortunes, difficulties, failures, and setbacks, then we are truly perfect Christians. Such a knowledge of God is not easily acquired. To keep one's gaze fixed on God and Christ throughout the day is not an easy task. The world about us tends to distract our attention from the part that Christ and God play in our redemption and sanctification. Our own efforts to work out our salvation tend to take the place of primary importance. In a world in which evil is so predominant, the grace and work of Christ and God appear remote and unreal. We are occupied too much with ourselves and too little with God, our Savior; we therefore are no longer able to view life in its proper perspective. Thus, too, we lose that spirit of Christian joy and confidence which characterized the life of St. Paul. "For I am sure that neither death nor life,... nor things present nor things to come, nor might... nor any other creature shall be able to separate us from the love of God which is in Christ Jesus" (Rom 8:38). God should occupy the first place in our lives.

Prayer

Arouse, we beseech Thee, O Lord, the wills of Thy faithful, that by more earnestly seeking the fruit of the divine work, they may receive more abundantly the gifts of Thy loving kindness. Through Christ our Lord. Amen.

Thursday

"Then shall appear the sign of the Son of Man in heaven.... They shall see the Son of Man coming in the clouds of heaven with much power and majesty" (Gospel). When evil has reached its climax, the Lord will appear, "and then that wicked one shall be revealed, whom the Lord Jesus shall kill with the spirit of His mouth, and shall destroy with the brightness of His coming" (2

Thes 2:8). The good shall be separated from the wicked as "the shepherd separateth the sheep from the goats" (Mt 25:32). Then the number of the elect shall be filled. This day of the harvest, the Last Judgment, is at hand.

"Suffer both to grow until the harvest" (Mt 13:30). The growth of the wheat and the cockle side by side is a type of good and evil, of the children of light and the children of darkness, of the kingdom of Satan and the kingdom of Christ. These two kingdoms, each commanded by its king, will oppose each other until the end of time. In the one kingdom the law of the flesh rules supreme, and in the other the law of the spirit. In the one, men devote themselves to the search for fortune and transitory pleasure; in the other they live for the hope of a blessed eternity. In the kingdom of Satan men place a high value on the things of this earth; in the kingdom of Christ only that which is supernatural is important. Although these two kingdoms exist side by side here on earth, they are separated in their ideals and objectives by an immense chasm. The same sun rises upon the members of these two kingdoms, and they breathe the same air; their fields are made fruitful by the same rains, but the two kingdoms are as far apart as day and night. The cockle and the wheat grow side by side, and as they reach maturity the difference between them becomes more acute. Evil is gathering its forces for one last effort, for the decisive battle. But when Christ will appear for judgment, those who were opposed spiritually will also be separated physically: "Depart from Me, you cursed, into everlasting fire" (Mt 25:41). But to His own He will say: "Come, ye blessed of My Father" (Mt 25:34). Christ has known His own from the beginning, and He has remained with them in the world, there redeeming and blessing them. He has permitted the evil ones to continue also, either that He might convert them from their evil, or that they may be the cause of the increase of virtue in the good. "Suffer both to grow until the harvest."

"In the time of the harvest I will say to the reapers: Gather up first the cockle and bind it into bundles to burn; but the wheat gather ye into my barn" (Mt 13:30). The Day of Judgment is the day of the return of the Lord, the day of reckoning, the day when a clear and decisive distinction will be made between the good and the evil, between the kingdom of Christ and the kingdom of Satan. The Last Judgment will conclude the work of divine providence, which has watched over the course of the world for thousands of years. The Last Judgment will perfect the work of divine providence and will confirm and make final all the judgments of God from the beginning. Then the history of the world and all the events that have occurred since the beginning of time will be laid before us like an open book. This is the day on which the justice of God's decisions will be confirmed, and they who accuse Him of having been harsh, will be confounded (Mt 25:24). On that day the wisdom of God will triumph, for all men will see how mildly, wisely, and justly God has governed the world. All will then see that God has treated every one according to his just due. "Thou hast delivered us, O Lord, from them that afflict us, and hast put them to shame that hate us" (Gradual).

At the Last Judgment we shall see the triumph of the charity of God, who has always lent a willing ear to the petitions of men, who has entertained only thoughts of peace and good will, and who has turned away from thoughts of bitterness and affliction. (Introit). It will be apparent that God has left nothing undone to save those who have gone astray. The Day of Judgment will be a day of triumph for the power of God, who bends even the powers of evil to His own purpose and allows it to exist, although He despises it, that He may show His mercy to sinners and lead the virtuous to greater virtue through the molestations of evil men. On the Day of Judgment all will be forced to confess: "Thou art just, O Lord, and Thy judgment is right" (Ps 118:137); "All the ways of the Lord are mercy and truth" (Ps 24:10). The Day of Judgment will see the separation of all that is unclean, false, and unjust from all that is good, true, clean, and sublime. In that day truth will triumph over falsehood, justice over injustice, faith over unbelief, adherence to Christ over apostasy. The cockle shall be gathered into bundles to be burned, and the wheat into the barns of the Lord.

Christus vincit; Christus regnat; Christus imperat. "Christ conquers; Christ reigns; Christ commands." In this belief we await His coming. "Thy kingdom come." Because of our faith in His return in power and glory, we accept willingly the difficulties we meet in the world, many of which are hard for us to understand. Our faith is tested without ceasing; but we shall not go astray. We know that the day of the harvest is to come, the day when darkness will be separated from the light. "Walk then as children of the light" (Eph 5:8) with Christ and His Church.

Prayer

Be propitious, O Lord, to our supplications and ... turn all our hearts unto Thee, that being delivered from earthly desires, we may pass on to heavenly desires. Through Christ our Lord. Amen. (Secreta.)

Friday

During the final week of the ecclesiastical year the language of the liturgy becomes very earnest and impressive. The Last Judgment with all its terrors is approaching. It is foreshadowed by the destruction of the city of Jerusalem seventy years after Christ's death. Do penance; "walk worthy of God, in all things pleasing; ... strengthened with all might according to the power of His glory" (Epistle).

Christ once passed judgment on the city of Jerusalem: "If thou also hadst known, and that in this thy day, the things that are to thy peace; but now they are hidden from thy eyes. For the days shall come upon thee; and thy enemies shall cast a trench about thee, and compass thee round, and straiten thee on every side, and beat thee flat to the ground, and thy children who are in thee; and they shall not leave in thee a stone upon a stone" (Lk 19:42–44). "When therefore you shall see the abomination of desolation, which was spoken of by Daniel the prophet standing in the holy place; ... then they that are in Judea, let them flee to the mountains; and he that is on the house top, let him not come down to take anything out of his house," but make his flight at once. "For there shall be then great tribulation, such as hath not been from the beginning of the world until now, neither shall be; and unless those days had been shortened, no flesh should be saved" (Gospel). Such is the sentence Christ passed on Jerusalem. The armies of Titus surrounded the city, and those who tried to flee the doomed city, perished with fearful pain and anguish on crosses. Within the city, mothers driven mad by hunger slaughtered their own children. The terrible siege continued for two years, until finally the Romans broke into the city, slaughtered the people, destroyed the temple, and leveled the city. This judgment of God should be a warning to us.

Christ also predicted that God would pass judgment on the world. "The sun shall be darkened, and the moon shall not give her light, and the stars shall fall from heaven, and the powers of heaven shall be moved" (Gospel). Both heaven and earth were created by the word of God, who commanded the dry land to appear and the waters to be gathered together in one place. The same God commanded the waters to flood the earth at the Deluge. On the last day the same almighty God will command His creation to be destroyed because of man's sin. "The sun shall be darkened, and the moon shall not give her light, and the stars shall fall from heaven." God made all creation for man's use; but man, corrupted by sin, injustice, and covetousness, has used the things of this world for his own pleasure and not for the purpose intended by God. Man has deserted his God and has attached himself to creatures, making them his God and his last end. Instead of being a means toward reaching God, they have become a hindrance that prevents man from reaching his last end. Nature, which was created by God and which is decked out in such wondrous beauty each year, becomes for man an occasion of sin that leads him into a final apostasy. For this reason nature, too, must be purged by fire from all perversion and uncleanness to satisfy justice and holiness. "Heaven and earth shall pass away" because of the sins of men.

"Then shall all of the earth mourn" (Gospel). The day of Christ's return will be a day of reckoning, a "dread day," a day on which all creation will be purged with fire. That will be a day of fear, of great misery, of terrible bitterness.

> Death and nature will be quaking,
> When creation is awaking,
> To its Judge an answer making.
> —*Dies irae*

The liturgy directs our attention to the Last Judgment and admonishes us in all things to remember the day of reckoning that is to come. "In all things consider the end; how you shall stand before the strict Judge from whom nothing is hidden.... He who learned to be a fool in this world and to be scorned for the sake of Christ, will then appear to have been most wise. Then the mortified body will rejoice far more than if it had been pampered with every pleasure.... Then shall simple obedience be more exalted than all worldly cleverness. Then a good and clear conscience will bring more joy than the philosophy of the learned. Then contempt for riches will have more value than all the treasures of this earth. Then you will find more consolation in having prayed devoutly than in having fared daintily; you will be happy that you preferred silence to prolonged gossip.... Strict penance will be more pleasing than all earthly delights. All, therefore, is vanity, except to love God and to serve Him only" (*Imitation of Christ*, I, chap. 24).

Prayer

Out of the depths I have cried to Thee, O Lord; Lord hear my voice. Let Thy ears be attentive to the voice of my supplication. If Thou, O Lord, wilt mark iniquities, Lord, who shall stand it? For with Thee there is merciful forgiveness, and by reason of Thy law, I have waited for Thee, O Lord. My soul has relied on His word, my soul hath hoped in the Lord. From the morning watch even until night, let Israel hope in the Lord. Because with the Lord there is mercy; and with Him plentiful redemption. And He shall redeem Israel from all his iniquities. (Ps 129.)

Saturday

"When the Son of Man shall come in His majesty, and all the angels with Him, then shall He sit upon the seat of His majesty. And all nations shall be gathered together before Him, and He shall separate them one from another as the shepherd separateth the sheep from the goats. And He shall set the sheep on His right hand, but the goats on His left" (Mt 25:31–33).

"Then shall the King say to them that shall be on His right hand: Come ye blessed of My Father, possess you the kingdom prepared for you from the foundation of the world. For I was hungry, and you gave Me to eat; I was thirsty, and you gave Me to drink; I was a stranger, and you took Me in; naked, and you covered Me; sick, and you visited Me; I was in prison, and you came to Me. Then the just shall answer Him: Lord, when did we see Thee hungry and feed Thee; thirsty, and gave Thee drink? And when did we see Thee a stranger and took Thee in? or naked, and covered Thee? Or when did we see Thee sick or in prison, and came to Thee? And the King answering shall say to them: Amen I say to you, as long as you did it to one of these My least brethren, you did it to Me.

"Then He shall say to them also that shall be on His left hand: Depart from Me, you cursed into everlasting fire, which was prepared for the devil and his angels. For I was hungry, and you gave Me not to eat; I was thirsty, and you gave Me not to drink. I was a stranger, and you took Me not in; naked, and you covered Me not; sick and in prison, and you did not visit Me. Then they also shall answer Him, saying: Lord, when did we see Thee hungry, or thirsty, or a stranger, or naked, or sick, or in prison, and did not minister to Thee? Then He shall answer them, saying: Amen I say to you, as long as you did it not to one of these least, neither did you do it to Me. And these shall go into everlasting punishment; but the just, into life everlasting" (Mt 25:34–46).

"And these shall go into everlasting punishment; but the just, into life everlasting." This separation will be for all eternity. After the Last Judgment there will be only heaven and hell, and these will last for eternity. God will be blessed for eternity by the just in heaven and cursed for eternity by the wicked in hell. The godless man will be cast, body and soul, into everlasting fire (Mt 10:28).

The poor Lazarus, who once sat at the door of the rich man, covered with sores and plagued by hunger, was carried by the angels to the bosom of Abraham. But the rich man, "who was clothed in purple and fine linen, and feasted sumptuously every day," died and "was buried in hell." Seeing Lazarus afar off, he cried out: "Father Abraham, have mercy on me and send Lazarus that he may dip the tip of his finger in water to cool my tongue; for I am tormented in this flame. And Abraham said to him: Son, remember thou didst receive good things in thy lifetime, and likewise Lazarus evil things, but now he is comforted and thou art tormented" (Lk 16:19 ff.).

On the last day God will separate the good and the bad for all eternity. On the one side will be the sheep and on the other the goats. On one side the redeemed and on the other the damned. What saved the one and condemned the other? It was the practice or lack of charity toward one's neighbor; that is, the love of one's neighbor in whom one saw Christ. "As long as you did it to one of these My least brethren, you did it to Me." The love of neighbor is an expression of our love for Christ. We love Christ to the extent that we love our neighbor, in whom we see Christ. We oppose Christ if we oppose our neighbor. If we show coldness, injustice, harshness, or a lack of charity toward our neighbor, we show it to Christ. It is our charity that will decide our fate.

"Heaven and earth shall pass away, but My words shall not pass away" (Gospel). Whatsoever you have done to one of My brethren, or have neglected to do with regard to them, you have done it to Me.

Prayer

Be propitious, O Lord, to our supplications, and … turn all our hearts unto Thee, that being delivered from earthly desires, we may pass on to heavenly desires. Through Christ our Lord. Amen. (Secreta.)

Special Feasts

June 29, SS. Peter and Paul

The feast of SS. Peter and Paul is important for the Church. "On this day Simon Peter ascended the gibbet of the cross, alleluia. Today the bearer of the keys to the kingdom joyfully went to Christ. Today the apostle Paul, the light of the world, bent his head and received the crown of martyrdom for the name of Christ, alleluia" (Magnificat antiphon).

"Thou art Peter, and upon this rock I will build My Church" (Gospel). With these words the Lord rewards the confession which Simon Peter made in the name of the other apostles: "Thou art Christ, the Son of the living God." Christ had asked His disciples: "Whom do men say that the Son of Man is?" And His disciples replied, "Some, John the Baptist, and other some, Elias, and others, Jeremias, or one of the prophets" (Gospel). There are still many false opinions about Christ; but only one true answer has ever been given to the question, "Who is Christ?" That was the answer of Simon Peter: "Thou art Christ, the Son of the living God." With this answer of Peter and the apostles we also agree. With them we acknowledge Christ's divinity. For two thousand years the Church has repeated this answer in spite of the ridicule of pseudo-scientists: "Thou art Christ, the Son of the living God."

"Thou art Peter, and upon this rock I will build My Church." Peter and the Church are inseparable. Peter is the foundation upon which the Church is built: Peter, the man of faith, the man who left all things to follow Christ (Mt 19:27). The Church is founded on Peter, who sacrificed his life for his faith under the emperor Nero, and who shared the crucifixion of the Lord. To Peter the Lord said: "I will give to thee the keys of the kingdom of heaven; and whatsoever thou shalt bind upon earth, it shall be bound also in heaven; and whatsoever thou shalt loose on earth, it shall be loosed also in heaven" (Gospel). To him, the Prince of the Apostles, is given the greatest power on earth. The Church of Christ can be only where Peter is, either in person or in his successors. Although the powers of hell are to attack Peter and the Church, the "gates of hell shall not prevail against it" (Gospel), for it is built on Peter, the rock. We are one with Peter; we are established on this rock, and we have no cause for fear. We are grateful that we have been established on so firm a foundation. We have only to remain united with Peter and the Church founded on him, and we shall draw ever closer to Christ.

"And the gates of hell shall not prevail against it." "In those days [in the year 42 or 43] Herod the king stretched forth his hand to afflict some of the Church; and he killed James, the brother of John, with the sword. And seeing that it pleased the Jews, he proceeded to take up Peter also" (Epistle). Thus the Church of Christ falls for the first time into the hands of her enemies. But "the gates of hell shall not prevail against it." "Peter, therefore, was kept in prison; but prayer was made without ceasing by the Church unto God for him. And when Herod would have brought him forth, the same night Peter was sleeping between two soldiers, bound with two chains.... And behold, an angel of the Lord stood by him ... [and] raised him up, saying: Arise quickly. And the chains fell off from his hands." Peter put on his sandals, cast his garment about him, and followed the angel. "Passing through the first and second ward, they came to an iron gate that leadeth to the city, which of itself opened to them; and going out they passed on through one street; and immediately the angel departed from him. And Peter, coming to himself, said:

Now I know that in very deed the Lord hath sent His angel and hath delivered me out of the hand of Herod, and from the expectation of the people of the Jews" (Epistle).

In Peter the Church sees herself today. Just as God freed Peter from his enemies, so, too, He has often delivered her in time of trial. She sees Peter's delivery repeated in her own history. She has been persecuted by men, taken prisoner, oppressed, and persecuted; and yet she has been wonderfully saved by the angel of the Lord. Thankfully the Church rejoices in the Introit: "Now I know in very deed that the Lord hath sent His angel, and hath delivered me out of the hand of Herod." This Introit refers not to Peter alone, but to the whole Church.

This incident is repeated likewise in the life of every Christian who is faithful to Christ and to the Church and her teachings. "The gates of hell shall not prevail against it." We are founded on Peter and, through Peter, on Christ the Lord. We shall overcome all evil if we cling obediently and faithfully to Peter: to the Church and her sacraments, her moral doctrines, and her priesthood.

"Whom do men say that the Son of Man is?" Whatever men may say today concerning Christ, we stand with Peter and confess, "Thou art Christ, the Son of the living God." "Thou alone art holy, Thou alone art the Lord, Thou alone art most high, O Jesus Christ, together with the Holy Ghost in the glory of God the Father" (Gloria).

Our power and safety lies in our union with Peter, with the Church, with Rome, with our bishops and priests. When we celebrate the Holy Eucharist, we enter into the deepest and most intimate union with Christ and His Church. Thus united with Peter, we ourselves become a rock, and on this rock the Lord will build His Church and the kingdom of His glory and grace.

Prayer

O God, who hast consecrated this day to the martyrdom of Thy apostles Peter and Paul, grant that Thy Church may in all things follow their teaching, from whom it first received the faith. Through Christ our Lord. Amen.

July 1, The Most Precious Blood of Our Lord

The month of July is dedicated to the Most Precious Blood, just as the month of June is dedicated to the Sacred Heart of Jesus. The entire wealth and value of redemption is contained in the precious blood of Christ. Therefore the feast of the Most Precious Blood is one on which we should express our gratitude for the redemption we have received through Jesus Christ.

"Thou hast redeemed us, O Lord, in Thy blood, out of every tribe and tongue, and people and nation, and hast made us to our God a kingdom" (Introit). We have been redeemed. The liturgy already counts us among the blessed in heaven. With the Church triumphant we cast ourselves down on our faces before the Lamb; "and they sang a new canticle, saying: O Lord,... Thou wast slain, and hast redeemed us to God in Thy blood, out of every tribe and tongue,... and hast made us to our God a kingdom and priests" (Apoc 5:9 f.). "The mercies of the Lord I will sing forever; I will show forth Thy truth with my mouth to generation and generation" (Introit). What our Lord did was something quite different from that done by the high priest of the Old Testament. Once a year the high priest entered into the temple where the Ark of the Covenant was kept, "not without blood, which he offereth for his own and the people's ignorance" (Heb 9:7). But "Christ being come, a high priest of the good things to come,... by His own blood entered once into the Holies, having obtained eternal redemption" (Epistle). The redemption of Christ lasts for eternity. It was a redemption quite different from that of the Old Testament. It shall "cleanse our conscience from dead works," that we "may receive the promise of eternal inheritance" (Epistle). "Being now justified by His blood, shall we be saved from wrath through Him" (Rom 5:9). We are redeemed through the blood of Christ and through the merits of His death. "The mercies of the Lord I will sing forever."

"At that time Jesus, when He had taken the vinegar, said: It is consummated. And bowing His head, He gave up the ghost.... The soldiers, therefore, came; and ... one of the soldiers with a spear opened His side, and immediately there came out blood and water" (Gospel). Christ was only eight days old when He shed His blood for us at His circumcision. He shed blood a second time on the Mount of Olives, when He saw the terrible sufferings that awaited Him. He shed blood a third time during the scourging at the pillar, and again when He was cruelly crowned with thorns by the soldiers. His blood flowed again when His garments were torn from Him on Calvary, thus reopening the wounds of the scourging. He shed His blood for us again when His hands were pierced with the cruel nails. He hung on the cross shrouded in the garment of His own blood. But even after He had bowed His head and given up the ghost a few drops of blood still remained in His body. He would shed this for us, too, that He might give His blood to the very last drop. "Having loved His own who were in the world, He loved them unto the end" (Jn 13:1). Christ wished to give men this final proof of His love. In the Credo of the Mass we confess our faith in His saving death: "I believe ... in one Lord Jesus Christ, the only-begotten Son of God; ... who for us men and for our salvation came down from heaven.... He was crucified also for us, suffered under Pontius Pilate and was buried." "Thou hast redeemed us, O Lord, in Thy blood, and hast made us to our God a kingdom."

"This is He that came by water and blood, Jesus Christ; not by water only, but by water and blood. There are three who give testimony in heaven: the Father, the Word, and the Holy Ghost; and these three are one. And there are three that give testimony on earth: the spirit, the water, and the blood; and these three are one" (Gradual). We have three witnesses that Jesus is the promised Savior, the Son of God. The witness of the water, that is, the voice of the Father, who acknowledged Him as His Son at the baptism in the Jordan; the witness of the blood, that is, the blood of the Son which was shed on Calvary; the witness of the Spirit, that is, the testimony of the Holy Ghost, who acknowledged Christ to be the Son of God through His descent upon the faithful on Pentecost. We believe in Him who has redeemed us in His blood.

The precious blood of Jesus is placed in our hands as our offering at the Holy Sacrifice of the Mass. "The chalice of benediction which we bless, is it not the communion of the blood of Christ?" (Offertory.) That which we offer after the Consecration and which we consume in Holy Communion, is no longer mere wine, but the most precious blood of Christ; it is the price of our atonement and the surest guarantee of our salvation when the Lord shall return (Communion).

We have been redeemed. Heaven is again open to us through the precious blood of Christ. "Let us draw near with a true heart in the fullness of faith, having our hearts sprinkled from an evil conscience. . . . Let us hold fast the confession of our hope" (Heb 10:22 f.), that we may receive the promise of the inheritance in the kingdom of God.

Prayer

O almighty and everlasting God, who didst appoint Thy only-begotten Son to be the Redeemer of the world, and hast willed to be appeased by His blood; grant unto us, we beseech Thee, so to venerate with solemn worship the price of our salvation, and by its power be so defended against the evils of this life, that we may enjoy its everlasting fruit in heaven. Through Christ our Lord. Amen.

July 2, The Visitation of the Blessed Virgin Mary

The feast of the birth of St. John, the octave of which is celebrated on July 1, is immediately followed by that of the Visitation of the Blessed Virgin. In confirmation of the assertion that "no word is impossible with God," the angel assures the Virgin at Nazareth: "Behold thy cousin Elizabeth, she also hath conceived a son in her old age, and this is the sixth month with her" (Lk 1:36). Mary understands. Although she has just conceived the Son of God, although her soul is sunk in contemplation of the mystery of the Son whom she is to bear, she hurries across the mountains to her cousin Elizabeth to offer her services for the last three months of her confinement. Her first act after having conceived the Son of God is to go forth into the world on a mission of mercy, to be of service to Elizabeth and John, to place herself at the service of man.

The Gospel relates the event as follows: "At that time Mary, rising up, went into the hill country with haste to a city of Juda. And she entered into the house of Zachary and saluted Elizabeth. And it came to pass that when Elizabeth heard the salutation of Mary, the infant leaped in her womb [John the Baptist]. And Elizabeth was filled with the Holy Ghost; and she cried with a loud voice and said: Blessed art thou among women and blessed is the fruit of thy womb. And whence is this to me, that the mother of my Lord should come to me? For behold, as soon as the voice of thy salutation sounded in my ears, the infant in my womb leaped for joy. And blessed art thou that hast believed, because those things shall be accomplished that were spoken to thee by the Lord." And Mary said, "My soul doth magnify the Lord, and my spirit has rejoiced in God my Savior" (Gospel). Mary is the mother of Christ, the vessel that produced the Savior. She brings the Lord and, with Him, salvation to the house of Zachary. Elizabeth is filled with the Holy Spirit at her approach. John is cleansed from Original Sin in his mother's womb; Christ brings salvation to all men through the instrumentality of His mother. Mary on her part, blessed as she is by the Lord and elect above all men, places herself at the disposal of the Lord who works through her. Were it left to her she would doubtless have preferred to remain in her house at Nazareth, in silence and isolation, absorbed in the contemplation of the Son whom she bore. But the news of her cousin's condition hardly reaches her before she arises and, forgetting herself, hastens to the call of grace. In imitation of her example we should never neglect the needs of our neighbor, but should hasten to perform whatever charity, justice, or politeness demands.

The Epistle gives us the meaning of this event related in the Gospel. John the Baptist is a type of mankind and of the Church. Christ is the bridegroom of our soul, who comes to us through His holy mother. Mary is the intermediary who brings the bridegroom to us, and the sponsor of the compact between Him and our soul. The events related in the Gospel today are repeated continually in the lives of all of us. The Church beholds Mary, the mother of Christ, hastening into the hill country to bring salvation to the Precursor (to us), and she cries out in joy: "Arise, make haste, my love, my dove, my beautiful one, and come. For winter is now past; … the flowers have appeared in our land; … the fig tree hath put forth her green figs, the vines in flower yield their sweet smell. Arise, my love, my beautiful one, and come. … Show me thy face, let thy voice sound in my ear" (Epistle). The Lord can hardly wait until He has reached John and us to sanctify us. He is eager to cleanse us from our sins and to sanctify us with His grace, to elevate us to the level of His divine life. He is eager to be the bridegroom of our soul, and to share His gifts and His grace with us, and to make us the children of God and heirs of His eternal inheritance. But He will do this only through Mary, only through her who brought Him into this world, only through her who is a figure of His Church, only through Mary.

Happy are we who hear His voice in the teachings and doctrines of the Church, and blessed are we if we follow them. "Blessed art thou, that thou hast believed." We are blessed through Christ, through the Church. We, too, may well lift our voices each day and exclaim: *"Magnificat*—My soul doth magnify the Lord; and my spirit hath rejoiced in God, my Savior," who wishes to espouse us in love. He will be espoused to us through baptism and Holy Communion. Through these we shall be united with Him who is our head, and later we shall ascend with Him into heaven to share His glory and power. "My soul doth magnify the Lord."

All this we have received through Mary, the mediatrix of all grace. How precious she should be in our sight, this most gracious virgin who bore a Savior for us. All these blessings we receive through our membership in the Church, through our faith in Christ, through the liturgy of the Church, through the sacraments and the Holy Sacrifice.

Prayer

Impart to Thy servants, we beseech Thee, O Lord, the gift of Thy heavenly grace, so that we for whom the childbearing of the Blessed Virgin was the beginning of salvation, may receive an increase of peace on this joyful festival of her Visitation. Through Christ our Lord. Amen.

August 6, The Transfiguration of Our Lord Jesus Christ

"The exalted King of Glory, come let us adore Him." With these words the Invitatory of the Divine Office introduces today's feast. The Transfiguration of Christ is a feast which celebrates the exaltation of Christ the Lord. The patriarchs and prophets of the Old Testament, represented by Moses and Elias, give testimony on Tabor and confess Him to be the Messias predicted in the Old Testament. The voice of the Father is heard from heaven saying, "This is My beloved Son; … hear ye Him" (Gospel). Christ's transfiguration on Mount Tabor assures us of His divinity and confirms us in our faith and our hope.

We believe firmly in Jesus, the King of Glory, who will come again with power and glory to judge the living and the dead. "We have not followed cunningly devised fables when we made known to you the power and presence of our Lord Jesus Christ [His second coming with great power]; but having been made eyewitnesses of His majesty [transfiguration].

For He received from God the Father honor and glory; this voice coming down to Him from the excellent glory: This is My beloved Son, in whom I am well pleased, hear ye Him. And this voice we heard brought from heaven when we were with Him in the holy mount" (Epistle). The glory in which Peter saw the transfigured Lord on the mountain, gives Peter and all of us the certainty that the Lord will later reappear in His glory, and that even as man He is the King of Glory. "Glory and wealth are in His house, and His justice remaineth forever and ever" (Offertory).

Although He was the Son of God, "He humbled Himself, becoming obedient unto death, even to the death of the cross. For which cause God also hath exalted Him and hath given Him a name which is above all names. That in the name of Jesus every knee should bow,... in heaven, on earth, and under the earth. And that every tongue should confess that the Lord Jesus Christ is in the glory of God the Father" (Phil 2:8–11). The prophets of the Old Testament also give testimony of Him (Acts 10:43). We who see Him in His glory on Tabor through Peter "have the more firm prophetical word, where-unto you do well to attend, as to a light that shineth in a dark place, until the day dawn, and the day star arise in your hearts" (Epistle). We believe; we adore the King of Glory. "I speak my words to the King" (Gradual). My thoughts, my wishes, my time, my strength, my love, my sacrifices, all center on Him.

Christ's divinity is the source of our hope. "We look for the Savior, our Lord Jesus Christ, who will reform the body of our lowness, made like to the body of His glory" (Phil 3:20–21). We have confidence that our body will be made like the body of the Lord, which was transfigured on Tabor. The liturgy reminds us, "Behold what manner of charity the Father hath bestowed upon us, that we should be called and should be the sons of God.... We know that when He shall appear, we shall be like to Him" (1 Jn 3:1 f.). In the transfiguration of the Lord on Tabor we possess a visible image as well as a guarantee of our eventual transfiguration in body and soul. Through the transfiguration on Tabor, O Father, "Thou didst wonderfully foreshow the perfect adoption of sons by a voice coming down in a shining cloud" (Collect). These words of the Father, "This is My beloved Son, in whom I am well pleased" (Gospel), are spoken also to us who are joined to Christ through baptism. Because we are children, we are heirs, heirs of God and co-heirs of Christ, "the King of Glory, and sharers in that same glory" (Collect).

"Thou art beautiful above the sons of men; grace is poured abroad in Thy lips. My heart hath uttered a good word. I speak my works to the King. Alleluia, alleluia. He is the brightness of eternal light, the unspotted mirror, and the image of His goodness" (Gradual).

"In this transfiguration it was indeed intended principally to take away from the hearts of the disciples the scandal of the cross, lest the degradation of His voluntary passion should shake the faith of those men to whom had been revealed the excellence of His hidden majesty" (St. Leo). In times when the kingdom of Satan displays its power and the kingdom of Christ is most hard pressed, the Church lifts up her eyes to Tabor to see the splendor of the hidden glory of God. "Thou alone art the Lord. Thou alone art most high," the King of Glory.

Prayer

O God, who in the glorious transfiguration of Thy only-begotten Son didst confirm the mysteries of faith by the testimony of the Fathers, and who didst wonderfully foreshow the perfect adoption of sons by a voice coming down in a shining cloud, mercifully grant that we be made coheirs of the King of Glory Himself and sharers in that same glory. Through Christ our Lord. Amen.

August 15, The Assumption of the Blessed Virgin Mary

"Sing ye to the Lord a new canticle, because He hath done wonderful things" (Introit). The feast of the Assumption is a great feast of Mary. In the assumption of Mary the Church sees her own future assumption into heaven, and her heart is filled with joy at the thought.

Although she was conceived without sin and was therefore exempt from punishment and the consequences of Original Sin, Mary accepted death in imitation of her divine Son. "Amazed at this wonderful mystery, they could only think that He who had been pleased to take flesh from the Virgin Mary, to be made man, and to be born, though He was God the Word, and Lord of glory, who had preserved her virginity without stain after childbirth, should also have been pleased to honor her pure body after her death, keeping it incorrupt and translating it to heaven before the general resurrection" (St. John Damascene). A few days after her death the Lord took up her body and united it to the soul in the glory of heaven. The humble virgin who asked only to be "the handmaid of the Lord" (Lk 1:38) ascends the glorious throne which her Son has prepared for her. She is crowned Queen of heaven and earth. Now she is "established in Sion"; "my power was in Jerusalem, and I took root in an honorable people [the saints and blessed of heaven] and in the portion of my God,... and my abode is in the full assembly of saints" (Ecclus 24:15 f.).[29]

"Mary hath chosen the best part" (Lk 10:42). When Jesus arrived at Bethany, "a certain woman named Martha received Him into her house; and she had a sister called Mary, who, sitting also at the Lord's feet, heard His word" (Lk 10:38 f.). Martha, who was busy serving her guest, became impatient with Mary, who sat idle at the feet of the Lord. She even displayed her anger by complaining to the Lord that Mary should help her with the serving. But Jesus took the part of Mary: "Mary hath chosen the best part." In Mary of Bethany the liturgy sees the virgin Mother of God. Her life centers about Christ. She sees Him, hears Him, and is wholly filled with Him. She lives in His mysteries; she shared in His first public miracle at Cana (Jn 2:1 ff.), and she carefully observes each of His words and works. In spirit and often in body she accompanies Him during the time of His public life, listening to His doctrine and witnessing His miracles. When all the others leave Him, she remains with Him in her love. After His Ascension her thoughts follow Him, and she is consumed by a loving desire to be with Him. She has indeed "chosen the best part," a life absorbed in Jesus. She is conscious of Him alone, and all her interest is centered on Him. Now Mary dwells with Him in heaven. What she had begun on earth, has now been perfected. She is with Jesus; she shares His glory and power. "Mary hath chosen the best part, which shall not be taken away from her."

"Mary hath chosen the best part," the part of the handmaid, the way of humility, of interior life, of devotion to God, of subjection to the will of God. "Hearken, O daughter, and see and incline

[29] Epistle from the Common of the Blessed Virgin, formerly read on the feast of the Assumption. The Gospel for this feast formerly was from Luke 10:38–42. –Fr. Malone

thy ear; for the King hath greatly desired thy beauty" (Gradual). "He that humbleth himself, shall be exalted" (Lk 18:14).

"Mary hath chosen the best part." Mary is the community of the faithful; she chooses the best part in Holy Communion, for she chooses Christ and in Him the life of grace. Holy Communion is a guarantee and foretaste of the eternal blessing which Mary today enjoys.

Prayer

Almighty and everlasting God, who hast taken up the immaculate Virgin Mary, the mother of Thy Son, with body and soul into heavenly glory: grant, we beseech Thee, that intent on higher things we may always deserve to be partakers of her glory. Through the same Christ our Lord. Amen.

September 8, The Nativity of the Blessed Virgin Mary

Today we celebrate the birth of the Virgin Mary, the Mother of God. "Out of Thee hath risen He who sitteth on the throne, alleluia" (Benedictus antiphon). This is a day of joy and happiness. The morning star appears in the person of Mary and announces the approach of Christ the Savior. "Out of thee the Sun of Justice hath risen, Christ our God, who taking away the curse, hath bestowed blessing, and confounding death, hath given us eternal life" (Magnificat antiphon). We possess Him through Mary.

"Hail, holy mother, giving birth to thy child thou didst bring forth the King who ruleth heaven and earth forever and ever" (Introit). The Church on earth, together with the Church in heaven and the choirs of angels and saints, greets her. They see in her not a helpless, feeble child reposing in the arms of St. Anne, but the woman selected by God to bring the Savior into the world. "Happy art thou, O holy Virgin Mary, and most worthy of praise, for out of thee the Sun of Justice hath risen, Christ our God" (Alleluia). She was born of a human father and mother, like every other human being. She is of the house of David, a house once highly honored, but later humbled, bereft of power, forgotten and despised. A member of this house of David is elected by God to "bear the Creator of all things; Him who made thee, thou didst bring forth" (Offertory). "He whom the whole world cannot contain, enclosed Himself in thy womb" (Gradual). "But the foolish things of the world hath God chosen, that He may confound the wise; and the weak things of the world hath God chosen, that He may confound the strong" (1 Cor 1:27). With wonder the Church contemplates the mystery of the birth of the Mother of God. "Hail, holy mother, giving birth to thy child thou didst bring forth the King who ruleth heaven and earth." "Blessed is the womb of the Virgin Mary, which bore the Son of the eternal Father" (Communion).

"The Lord possessed me in the beginning of His ways, before He made anything from the beginning. I was set up from eternity and of old, before the earth was made. The depths were not as yet, and I was already conceived.... When He prepared the heavens, I was there; when with a certain law and compass He enclosed the depths,... I was with Him, forming all things, and was delighted every day, playing before Him at all times, playing in the world; and my delight is to be with the children of men" (Epistle). This passage describes the birth of Mary as she was conceived in the mind of God even before the creation of the world. Mary is pictured as the seat and bearer of the eternal Wisdom of God. Wisdom is born of God, a child of God, a most perfect copy of God, His companion and helper in the work of creation. Mary is most intimately associated with this divine Wisdom. She is like a cloud that conceals and contains the sun, the hidden Wisdom of God: "A woman clothed with the sun" (Apoc 12:1). She is the Seat of Wisdom, the Vessel of Honor, the House of God, the spouse and helpmate of divine Wisdom in the person of Christ. She is to share in renewing all things in Christ, in freeing the world from sin, and in filling it with the grace, light, and life of God. Today she is born to us, the daughter of God, the Seat of Wisdom, the earthly reflection of the Wisdom of God, the queen of the universe, an instrument of our salvation. Reverently we approach this child who is destined to bear Him "whom the whole world cannot contain," "the Sun of Justice, Christ our God." We believe; we give thanks to God for having given us Mary and, through Mary, Christ our King.

"Now, therefore, ye children, hear me: Blessed are they that keep my ways. Hear instruction and be wise, and refuse it not. Blessed is the man that heareth me and that watcheth daily at my gates and waiteth at the posts of my doors. He that shall find me shall find life, and shall have salvation from the Lord" (Epistle). Mary is herself wholly absorbed in the wisdom of God. Her thoughts, her judgments, her will, her actions, her whole life are permeated by that wisdom. "Hear me," she exhorts us, follow my example of charity, poverty, humility, obedience, devotion to God, love of neighbor, prayer, and holy solitude. Thus should the wisdom of God govern the man who "shall have salvation from the Lord."

"Happy art thou, O holy Virgin Mary, and most worthy of praise, for out of thee the Sun of Justice hath risen, Christ, our God" (Alleluia). You gave Him to us that holy night at Bethlehem. You give Him again to us today at the Consecration and in Holy Communion.

"Blessed is the womb of the Virgin Mary, which bore the Son of the eternal Father" (Communion). Blessed are all they who at Holy Communion, like Mary, receive Him "whom the world cannot contain." "Hear instruction and be wise, and refuse it not."

Prayer

Impart to Thy servants, we beseech Thee, O Lord, the gift of Thy heavenly grace, so that we for whom the childbearing of the Blessed Virgin was the beginning of salvation, may receive an increase of peace on this joyful festival of her nativity. Through Christ our Lord. Amen.

September 14, The Exaltation of the Holy Cross

The season of autumn has arrived; the days are growing shorter, and the light of evening fails rapidly. Holy Mother the Church lifts up the sign of victory, the sign of the cross, as a barrier against the powers of darkness. The sign of the cross will be "the sign of the Son of Man" (Mt 24:30) when He comes to pass judgment on the living and the dead. The thought of the coming judgment has occurred frequently during the time after Pentecost. The world celebrates the advance of culture and science, the triumphs of technology, and its military victories; but Holy Mother the Church exalts the sign of her victory, the holy cross, the sign of salvation.

Christ "humbled Himself, becoming obedient unto death; even the death of the cross" (Epistle). The Son of God became man that He might humble Himself. He laid aside the glory of the Godhead and took on the form of man that He might be like unto us in all things except sin.

His whole life was one conscious and voluntary progress toward death on the cross. "For which cause God also hath exalted Him and hath given Him a name which is above all names; that in the name of Jesus every knee should bow, of those that are in heaven, on earth, and under the earth; and that every tongue should confess that the Lord Jesus Christ is in the glory of God the Father" (Epistle). Even according to His sacred humanity He now shares with the Father the ruling of the world. "Thou alone art the Lord. Thou alone art most high, O Jesus Christ, together with the Holy Ghost in the glory of God the Father" (Gloria).

Jesus Christ our Savior was humbled on the cross, but He was also exalted through the cross. "It behooves us to glory in the cross of our Lord Jesus Christ, in whom is our salvation, life, and resurrection; by whom we are saved and delivered" (Introit). Through the Cross we obtain the forgiveness of our sins, the fullness of God's grace, union with Christ, and the fullness of the Holy Ghost, who is poured out in our hearts. Through the Cross our acts become fruitful, our prayers and sacrifices become meritorious, our hope and faith in the eternal promises become firm. The Cross should be more dear to us than anything on this earth, and we should cling to it faithfully.

"And I, if I be lifted up from the earth, will draw all things to Myself. Now this He said," adds St. John, "signifying what death He should die" (Gospel). "Now shall the prince of this world be cast out" (Gospel). Through Christ's death on the cross the power of Satan was broken. Everyone who belongs to the kingdom of Christ, to the Church, possesses the power to escape from the power of Satan and sin. Grace flows to him steadily from Christ on the cross.

"And I, if I be lifted up from the earth, will draw all things to Myself." Through His death on the cross, Christ has become the King and center of all hearts. The force of His love as exhibited on the cross conquers the hearts of men. The grace which He merited through His death is so powerful that it can sway and control the strongest will. Through the sermon which He preached from the cross, Christ conquered the world. To those who are not Christ's, the cross is foolishness; but to the elect it is a sign of power. "For the word of the cross to them indeed that perish is foolishness; but to them that are saved, . . . it is the power of God. For it is written: I will destroy the wisdom of the wise, and the prudence of the prudent I will reject. Where is the wise? Where is the scribe? . . . Hath not God made foolish the wisdom of this world? For seeing that in the wisdom of God the world by wisdom knew not God, it pleased God by the foolishness of our preaching [of the cross] to save them that believe. For both the Jews require signs, and the Greeks seek after wisdom. But we preach Christ crucified, unto the Jews indeed a stumbling block and unto the Gentiles foolishness; but unto them that are called, both Jews and Greeks, Christ, the power of God and the wisdom of God" (1 Cor 1:18–24). Therefore the Apostle, the Church, and the true servant of the Lord know nothing "but Jesus Christ and Him crucified. . . . That your faith might not stand on the wisdom of men, but on the power of God" (1 Cor 2:2, 5).

In the Cross is our salvation; in the Cross is life; in the Cross is our protection against the enemy; in the Cross is the strength of the spirit and the progress of holiness. There is no other way to life, no other way to the heights of perfection, except the Cross. "If I be lifted up from the earth [I] will draw all things to Myself." Woe to those who seek another Christ, a Christ who was not crucified. "But God forbid that I should glory save in the cross of our Lord Jesus Christ; by whom the world is crucified to me and I to the world" (Gal 6:14).

The cross is the sign of our salvation. It was traced on our forehead and on our breast at the time of our baptism. By this sign we are recognized as the disciples of the Crucified. "But it behooves us to glory in the cross of our Lord, Jesus Christ, ... by whom we are saved and delivered" (Introit).

The priest blesses us with the sign of the cross, and at this sign the devils are seized with terror. By making use of the sign of the cross we receive grace, power, light, and strength. Our forefathers in the faith would not begin a single task without first making the sign of the cross, so deep was their faith in the power of this sign. Do we hold the sign of the cross in such high esteem? Do we exalt the cross in our daily life? "In this sign you shall conquer." There is no other way to holiness, resurrection, and eternal life except the way of the cross.

Prayer

O God, who dost gladden us this day by the annual solemnity of the Exaltation of the Holy Cross, grant, we beseech Thee, that as we have known its mystery on earth, we may deserve in heaven the reward which it has purchased. Through Christ our Lord. Amen.

September 15, The Seven Sorrows of the Blessed Virgin Mary

Forty days after Christ's birth, Mary carried Him to the temple of Jerusalem to present Him to God. The aged Simeon blessed her and repeated the words of the prophet, "Behold this child is set for the fall and for the resurrection of many in Israel, and for a sign which shall be contradicted. And thy own soul a sword shall pierce" (Lk 2:34 f.). This prophecy is fulfilled in Mary as she stands beneath the cross on Golgotha in an intimate union of suffering and pain with her Son, who sacrificed Himself on the cross for sinners. For many centuries the liturgy has honored Mary as Queen of Martyrs.

"At that time, there stood by the cross of Jesus, His mother, and His mother's sister, Mary of Cleophas, and Mary Magdalen. When Jesus therefore had seen His mother and the disciple standing whom He loved [John], ... He saith to the disciple: Behold thy mother. And from that hour the disciple took her to his own" (Gospel). Mary had waited a long time for the fulfillment of Simeon's prophecy. She was well acquainted with the words of the Psalmist. She knew that her Son was the Son of God, who had become man that He might sacrifice His life voluntarily for the salvation of men. Now that dread moment had come. Mary, who was so intimately united to the Lord, was to take part in this work of salvation and share all His sufferings with Him. Such was her vocation as His mother. God showed her no mercy, as He had shown none to His Son. She could not depart from Calvary, but felt that she must share His anguish and pain. His dishonor and sufferings were hers too, and she stood beneath the cross to unite her own sacrifice with the sacrifice of Christ. She offered up to the Father that which was most dear to her, her divine Son. She suffered unspeakably. In a sense her desolation was complete when she heard her Son give her away to be the mother of another: "Woman, behold thy son."

From now on another man would call her mother, John, the son of Zebedee. Are the bonds which bound her to the fruit of her womb to be torn asunder? Is it not enough that she has shared the tortures and humiliation of her Son? No, she must also share His final desolation, His abandonment by the Father: "My God, My God, why hast Thou forsaken Me?" (Mt 27:46.)

"Sorrowful and tearful art thou, O Virgin Mary, standing by the cross of the Lord Jesus, thy Son and Redeemer" (Gradual). The Church shares the desolation of the sorrowful mother.

"The Lord hath blessed thee by His power, who by thee hath brought our enemies to nought. Blessed art thou, O daughter, by the Lord the most high God, above all women upon the earth.... For that thou hast not spared thy life by reason of the distress and tribulation of thy people, but hast prevented our ruin in the presence of our God" (Epistle). Mary is another Judith in the mind of the liturgy. In spite of great danger to her own life, Judith went forth boldly to cut off the head of Holofernes, the leader of the enemy, in order to save her people from destruction. Mary, the mother of sorrow, sacrifices her own Son on Golgotha, thus crushing the head of the serpent. She shared in the work of our redemption through her sufferings. Thankfully we greet her with the Church: "Blessed art thou, O daughter, by the Lord the most high God, above all women." On Golgotha she also earned the palm of martyrdom (Communion). On Golgotha she participated in our redemption and merited for us a life of grace and eternal glory with her Son. On Golgotha she accepted us all as her children in the person of John. "Woman, behold thy son"; love him as you loved Me. We are grateful for this adoption, and we trust in her motherhood and maternal love. With John we take her as our own and thus comply with the command of Jesus, "Behold thy mother."

Like our Lord Himself, Mary was obliged to walk the way of the cross. She followed Him till the end, and stood beneath the cross to suffer with Him, to share His sorrow and dishonor. She does not excuse herself or seek to escape. She desires to share His disgrace, His humiliation, His rejection by His own people. We, too, should imitate her example. Although she is the mother of the disfigured and crucified Savior, she stands bravely beneath His cross. Her eyes are fixed on Him. She forgets herself completely. Because she lives entirely in Him, she finds the strength to remain till the last and to sacrifice all.

We acknowledge Mary as the one to whom, after Christ, we owe our salvation. At the celebration of the Mass we, the sacrificing community, the family, the parish, the Church, are like Mary beneath the cross, sacrificing the Lord for the glory of God and the salvation of souls. At Holy Communion we receive the strength to share the sufferings and humiliations of Jesus with a steadfast and loyal heart.

Prayer

O God at whose passion a sword of sorrow pierced the most sweet soul of the glorious virgin and mother, Mary, mercifully grant that we who reverently commemorate her sorrows, may obtain the happy effect of Thy passion. Who livest and reignest forever. Amen.

October 11, The Maternity of the Blessed Virgin Mary

Many centuries have passed since Nestorius, a Patriarch of Constantinople, launched the heresy which taught that the person of Christ was different from the person of the Son of God. Nestorius asserted that Mary did not conceive nor bring forth the Second Person of the Blessed Trinity, but only the man Christ. According to his teaching she was not the Mother of God, not a God-bearer, but only the mother of a mere man, in whom God dwelt only as in a temple. A few years after the beginning of the Nestorian heresy, a council was assembled at Ephesus (431

A.D.), which proclaimed that Mary had given birth to Jesus, who was, at one and the same time, God and man, having two natures but one person. God does not live in Him merely as in a temple, but the man Jesus is at the same time God. Mary is mother, not only of the humanity of Christ, but of the Son of God also. She is the Mother of God. The people of Ephesus awaited the decision of the council with breathless expectation. When the doors of the council hall were opened and the decision was made known, the people greeted the Fathers with great rejoicing and accompanied them to their dwellings with flaming torches, crying out: "Mary is the bearer of God; Mary is the Mother of God." Today, more than fifteen hundred years later, we make the same joyful confession.

Mary is the mother of Jesus, the Son of God. The Gospel recounts an incident of His childhood during which He first refers to His divine origin. When Jesus was twelve years old, Joseph and Mary went to Jerusalem to offer sacrifice. "When they returned, the child Jesus remained in Jerusalem, and His parents knew it not." They believed Him to be in the company of relatives. But they were mistaken. After a long and anxious search they found Him in the temple, sitting among the doctors of the law. "And His mother said to Him: Son, why hast Thou done so to us? Behold Thy father and I have sought Thee sorrowing." This rebuke shows the concern of a mother who has borne suffering with love. But Jesus meekly answers: "Did you not know that I must be about My Father's business?" He refers to His heavenly Father, for He is Son of God. He was conceived, not by the power of man, but by the power of God (Offertory). When the angel had first brought the message to Mary, she had answered, "Behold the handmaid of the Lord; be it done to me according to thy word" (Lk 1:38). And at her word, the only-begotten Son of God was made flesh in the womb of the Virgin Mother. We pay tribute to this mystery at the Communion, when we confess, "Blessed is the womb of the Virgin Mary, which bore the Son of the eternal Father." Blessed art thou, O holy Mother of God, who wert united to the Son of God in a most intimate union when thou didst bear Him in thy womb.

Mary provided the body for the Son of God, and in return Christ filled the soul of Mary with the fullness of His spirit. Mary became wholly absorbed in Him and became like Him. She became united to Him in a most intimate union. "Alleluia, alleluia. Virgin Mother of God, He whom the whole world cannot contain, enclosed Himself in thy womb, being made man, Alleluia." "Hail Mary, full of grace, the Lord is with thee; blessed art thou among women, and blessed is the fruit of thy womb, Jesus."

"As the vine, I have brought forth a pleasant odor, and my flowers are the fruit of honor and riches" (Epistle). The blossoms on this vine are the precious virtues of faith and humility which the Virgin exhibited when she received the message of the angel. She was resolute in her attachment to her virginity: "I know not man" (Lk 1:34). Yet she is obedient to the will of God and speaks her fiat: "Behold the handmaid of the Lord; be it done to me according to thy word" (Lk 1:38). "My flowers are the fruit of honor and riches," Christ the Lord. "There shall come forth a rod out of the root of Jesse," Mary, who is sprung from the house of David; "and a flower shall rise up out of his root," Christ, the Son of Mary (Gradual). Humanity and divinity are united in this one person. "Come over to me, all ye that desire me, and be filled with my fruits" (Epistle). Mary does not keep her child for herself; she bequeathes Him to us when He is born at Bethlehem, when He is offered in the temple, and when He offers Himself up on the cross. She gives Him to us again daily in Holy Communion. Mary has borne Christ for us.

Together with her divine Son, she has given us salvation and an abundance of grace. She stands even today at the throne of God as our advocate and our all-powerful intercessor, armed with irresistible intercessory power, the mother of all those who are in the state of sanctifying grace.

We renew our faith in the mystery of Mary's divine motherhood. "Hail, Mary, full of grace, the Lord is with thee." God is thy child, having taken His humanity from thy flesh.

"Come over to me ... and be filled with my fruits," for it is Christ Jesus whom I give you. He was first given to us when we were reborn through baptism; He is given to us today at Mass and Holy Communion: "Hath He not also with Him given us all things?" (Rom 8:32.) Since Mary has given us all things through Christ, we today express our gratitude to her.

Prayer

O God, who didst will that at the message of the angel Thy Word should take flesh in the womb of the Blessed Virgin Mary, grant to Thy suppliants that we who believe her to be truly the Mother of God, may be aided by her intercession with Thee. Through Christ our Lord. Amen.

Feast of Christ the King

Today is a day of thanksgiving to the Father for having made His Son the King and Lord of all things. It is a day of homage to the God-man, Jesus Christ, to whom is given all power in heaven and on earth. "He shall rule from sea to sea, and from the river [Euphrates] to the ends of the earth. And all kings of the earth shall adore Him; all nations shall serve Him" (Gradual). We, too, adore and serve Him today and forever.

"I am a King." One of the great events in the history of mankind was the appearance of Jesus before the representative of the pagan Roman empire. "Art Thou the King of the Jews?" Pilate asked Him; and later, "Art Thou a King then?" Jesus answered him, "Thou sayest that I am a King. For this was I born, and for this came I into the world, that I should give testimony to the truth." But He also assured Pilate "My kingdom is not of this world" (Gospel). His is the kingdom of God, in which the sick are healed, the blind receive their sight, and the oppressed are freed. His is the kingdom of God which destroys the power of Satan and sin, which gives us divine life, divine freedom, and divine gifts. His is "a kingdom of truth and life, a kingdom of holiness and grace, a kingdom of justice, love, and peace" (Preface): the joyful kingdom of God in our soul. Christ's divine kingdom consists of the personal presence of God within us, governing our thoughts, our intellect, our will, our whole spiritual life, through our union with Christ our head. The kingdom of God has been brought by Jesus upon this earth. He established it through His doctrines, His example, and especially through His death on the cross. He is the Ruler of this kingdom; He makes its laws and commandments. God "hath given all judgment to the Son" (Jn 5:22), "that in the name of Jesus every knee should bow, of those that are in heaven, on earth, and under the earth; and that every tongue should confess that the Lord Jesus Christ is in the glory of God the Father" (Phil 2:10 f.). Joyfully we adore Him; for "the Lamb that was slain [on the cross] is worthy to receive power, and divinity, and wisdom, and strength, and honor. To Him be glory and empire forever and ever" (Introit). "The Lord shall sit a King forever. The Lord will bless His people with peace" (Communion).

God "hath translated us into the kingdom of the Son of His love, in whom we have received redemption through His blood, the remission of sins" (Epistle). Through Christ we receive the life of grace and become children of God; we acquire power over the world, the flesh, and our evil passions; we achieve victory over Satan and the eternal death of hell; we receive freedom of the spirit and heart through the possession of the divine life and sanctifying grace. Thus, too, we acquire a right to share in the kingdom of eternal glory. We give "thanks to God the Father, who hath made us worthy to be partakers of the lot of the saints in light; who hath delivered us from the power of darkness, and hath translated us into the kingdom of the Son of His love,... who is the image of the invisible God, the first-born of every creature. For in Him were all things created in heaven and on earth;... all things were created by Him and in Him" (Epistle). All that the universe contains of wonder and beauty is His, and was created by Him and in Him. He is the true Master of the will and minds of men, of their bodies and souls, their thoughts, inclinations, and desires. Heaven and earth, spirit and body, belong to Him. He has the power and the right to use all earthly things in the service of His spiritual kingdom. "He may hold the primacy; because in Him it hath well pleased the Father that all fullness should dwell" (Epistle). The man Jesus Christ is the King. May He rule over me also, over my thoughts, my will, and my whole being. I adore Him, I serve Him, and seek only that which He wishes and desires.

We rejoice with the Church that the Father has made Him the King and Lord of all things. "Ask of Me," the Father says to Christ, "and I will give Thee the Gentiles for Thy inheritance, the utmost parts of the earth for Thy possession" (Offertory).

The Lord is King. He rules and guides His kingdom, the Church, and supports our souls with a strong arm. The hostile powers will fight in vain against His kingdom. "Fear not, little flock, for it hath pleased your Father to give you a kingdom" (Lk 12:32). We consecrate ourselves and all we possess to Christ the King.

Christus vincit; Christus regnat; Christus imperat.
Christ conquers; Christ reigns; Christ commands.

Prayer

Almighty and eternal God, who hast willed to restore all things through Thy beloved Son, the King of the universe, graciously grant that all the families of the Gentiles separated by the wound of sin may be subjected to His most loving dominion. Who with Thee liveth and reigneth forever and ever. Amen.

November 1, Feast of All Saints

Gaudeamus! "Let us all rejoice in the Lord, celebrating a feast in honor of all the saints, at whose solemnity the angels rejoice and join in praising the Son of God" (Introit). Today we rejoice with the angels and saints in praising Christ, the "King of all the saints." We rejoice in the knowledge that we belong to the communion of saints through our membership in the body of Christ.

"I saw a great multitude which no man could number, of all nations, and tribes, and peoples, and tongues, standing before the throne and in sight of the Lamb, clothed with white robes, and palms in their hands; and they cried with a loud voice, saying: Salvation to our God, who sitteth upon the throne, and to the Lamb. And all the angels stood round about the throne, ... and they fell down before the throne upon their faces, and adored God saying: Amen. Benediction, and glory, and wisdom, and thanksgiving, honor, and power, and strength to our God forever and ever. Amen" (Epistle). O blessed creatures! They have all been saved and now praise God. Indeed, "there is no want to them that fear Him. They that seek the Lord shall not be deprived of any good" (Gradual). They now possess God and, in God, the plenitude of all good things. In God they are eternally blessed. "Come to Me, all you that labor and are burdened, and I will refresh you" (Alleluia verse). We rejoice with our brethren who have been saved, and congratulate them on having achieved the end of their existence.

We, too, are destined for heaven. The way that led them to salvation and to blessedness is the way explained in the Sermon on the Mount and in today's Gospel, which relates the eight beatitudes. "The kingdom of heaven suffereth violence, and the violent bear it away" (Mt 11:12). "If any man will come after Me, let him deny himself, and take up his cross, and follow Me" (Mt 16:24). Anyone who thinks he can reach heaven without exerting himself, without daily mortification, without subduing his will, is deceiving himself. Heaven is made up of those who are "poor in spirit," that is, those who have detached themselves from all that is not God. It is the meek, and those who suffer injury and injustice without resentment, and those who return love for hatred and repay evil with good, who attain to the kingdom of heaven. Heaven is for those who resist the allurements of pleasure and of the world, and who find their joy in God. Heaven is for those who thirst after justice and who strive to be holy. It is the merciful, and those who show compassion for the corporal and spiritual misery of their fellow men for the love of Christ, who will be blessed in the world to come. The joys of the blessed are promised to those who are pure of heart and who fly from the least imperfection and fault. Heaven is the reward of the peacemakers, who strive always to please God, and who preserve equanimity of spirit in spite of provocation and the promptings of their own passions. Blessed, too, are those who suffer persecution for the sake of Christ, and who are reviled and despised because of Him. The promises of the Sermon on the Mount are guaranteed to all of these, and to them it is said: "Be glad and rejoice, for your reward is very great in heaven" (Gospel).

"These are they who are come out of great tribulation and have washed their robes and have made them white in the blood of the Lamb. Therefore they are before the throne of God.... They shall no more hunger nor thirst.... For the Lamb ... shall rule them and shall lead them to the fountains of the waters of life; and God shall wipe away all tears from their eyes" (Apoc 7:14–17). "And they shall see His face, and His name shall be on their foreheads.... The Lord God shall enlighten them, and they shall reign forever and ever" (Apoc 22:4 f.). Truly, "The souls of the just are in the hand of God, and the torment of malice shall not touch them; in the sight of the unwise they seemed to die [here on earth], but they are in peace [in heaven]. Alleluia" (Offertory). How wonderful is the Christian life!

The feast of All Saints is a feast which celebrates the triumph of grace over nature. It is an apology for the effectiveness of the Church and her work; it is the triumph of her doctrine, her teachings, her sacraments, her priesthood, and particularly her Holy Sacrifice. Through the power of the Eucharistic sacrifice and Holy Communion, the Church has turned sinners into saints. Through the Holy Eucharist our brethren in Christ, although weak and sinful by nature, have walked the way of the eight beatitudes, and have thus sanctified themselves. We, too, must cling to the Church, to her doctrine, and to her sacraments. These means provide the one safe way to heaven. At the Offertory of the Mass, the liturgy sees the souls of the just as they lay themselves on the paten to be offered as a sacrifice to God. "In the sight of the unwise they seemed to die, but they are in peace." They understood the necessity of uniting themselves to the offering of Christ, and now they possess the precious fruit of that union: peace and the eternal communion of the blessed in heaven.

Prayer

O almighty and eternal God, who hast granted us to venerate the merits of all Thy saints in one solemnity, vouchsafe to us, we beseech Thee, through the multitude of our intercessors, that abundance of Thy mercy which we have desired. Through Christ our Lord. Amen.

November 2, All Souls' Day

"On this day the commemoration of all the faithful departed [is celebrated], on which our Holy Mother the Church . . . strives to give help to all those who are still suffering in purgatory, through powerful prayers to her Lord and spouse, that they may soon be joined to the community of the heavenly blessed" (Roman Martyrology), On this day the Church exercises her charity in thought and in deed for her departed dead.

Charity in thought. Holy Mother the Church knows the suffering of her children in the flames of purgatory and sympathizes with them. Their chief suffering is their exclusion from the presence of God. These souls repose "in Christ" and are intimately united with Him; they are in the state of grace and realize that eventually they will attain the sight of God. But still they are detained; they do not enjoy "eternal rest." "The perpetual light" does not yet shine upon them. They are still in the "bonds of sin," suffering temporal punishment due to their sins. They have "still the spots of their daily sins," although they long for God and for a "place of refreshment, light, and peace" (Memento of the Dead). They still suffer the pain of separation from God. They love God, and they love Him alone; but they cannot possess Him, see Him, or repose in Him. They are not as yet worthy of associating with Him. Their sins, their unfaithfulness, their want of contrition and penance, have caused this temporary separation from God. How fervently they repent of their sins and negligences now! But their contrition, their tears, their prayers, cannot help them. The time for such repentance ended with death. "The night cometh, when no man can work" (Jn 9:4). They can expiate their sins only through suffering, and they will be detained until God's justice is satisfied. The Church knows the misery and helplessness of the souls in purgatory. Today she takes pity on them and wishes that we also be touched by this pity.

Charity in deed. The Church knows that she can bring help to the souls in purgatory through her prayers and especially through the Sacrifice of the Mass. Today she prays for the poor souls and permits each priest to celebrate the Holy Sacrifice three times, that grace may flow from the altar and be poured forth in abundance on the souls in purgatory, thus enabling many of them to enter into heaven today. Today the Church makes it possible for the faithful to gain plenary indulgences for the deceased in purgatory as often as they wish. We are conscious of our unity in the Church, and we should joyfully join her in this work of mercy. We dedicate this day and this whole month to the poor souls. We pray for them, offer up to God the sacrifice of the Mass for them, and endeavor to gain plenary indulgences for them.

At the Holy Sacrifice of the Mass we take the Sacred Heart of Jesus and the precious blood of the Savior into our hands and offer them to the Father as a means of satisfaction for the debt that the souls in purgatory may still owe to divine justice. We pay the debt of our brethren in purgatory with the blood of Jesus. Taking the precious blood of Jesus in our hands we pray: "Be mindful also, O Lord, of Thy servants who have gone before us with the sign of faith and who sleep the sleep of peace. To these, O Lord, and to all who rest in Christ, grant, we beseech Thee, a place of refreshment, light, and peace."

"We offer Thee, O Lord, sacrifices and prayers of praise; do Thou accept them for those souls whom this day we commemorate. Grant them, O Lord, to pass from death [their separation from God in purgatory] to life, which Thou didst promise to Abraham and to his seed" (Offertory).

Prayer

Mercifully look down, we beseech Thee, O Lord, upon the sacrifices which we offer Thee for the souls of Thy servants and handmaids, that to those on whom Thou didst confer the merit of Christian faith, Thou mayest also grant its reward. Through Christ our Lord. Amen. (Secreta.)

All Souls' Day (2)

Every day we pray with the holy liturgy that God may be indulgent to our sins and to the souls in purgatory. We pray that they may be cleansed from all sin through the power of the Holy Sacrifice, and that they may be released from "every bond of sin." We pray that they may be "purged by this sacrifice and obtain both forgiveness and everlasting rest" (Postcommunion of the second Mass). We pray that whatever blemishes the soul may have contracted from its contact with the world may be washed away by the mercy of God's pardon.

"Grant to the souls of Thy servants and handmaids the remission of all their sins" (Collect of the first Mass). The souls in purgatory may still have to satisfy for venial sins. It is true that a Christian at the approach of death may make an act of perfect love for God and by this act be forgiven all his sins, but if a Christian should die suddenly and without the opportunity of making such an act of love, he would enter purgatory with venial sins yet unforgiven. In purgatory he will be freed from these venial sins; thus the Church prays: "Grant to the souls of Thy servants and handmaids the remission of all their sins." In the liturgy of the Mass for the Dead, the Church has in mind the moment of death. She asks God for the "remission of all sins," that the soul may have the grace to make an act of perfect love before death or at the moment of death, and so be freed from every stain of sin. The prayer of the Church for the moment of death is accepted by God, and even the prayers she offers for the departed weeks and years after their death have been considered in the plan of salvation for those souls. The prayers which Holy Mother Church offers for the faithful departed today, benefit even those who have died many years ago. Should we not join Holy Mother the Church, then, in her prayers and implore fervently, "Grant to the souls of Thy servants and handmaids the remission of all their sins"?

"Absolve, O Lord, the souls of all the faithful departed from every bond of sin." The souls in purgatory are perfectly conformed to the will of God. They love only Him; they love Him with their whole heart and soul. Their will coincides with His will, and they desire nothing but what He desires. They subject themselves voluntarily to the sufferings of purgatory, and they do so out of love, for they now wish to please God. They will suffer what He imposes upon them just as long as it is His will that they should do so, for they know that God is holy and just. Every sin, even the smallest conscious imperfection, demands satisfaction. If these faults have not been satisfied for on earth, they must be expiated in purgatory. In purgatory the poor souls suffer a twofold punishment. There is first of all the punishment caused by their separation from God, which is the principal punishment of purgatory. It is also the most severe suffering of purgatory, so severe that it surpasses human understanding. But there are other punishments. God's justice demands that they suffer by other means also, such as external fire. Souls have separated themselves from God in the search for external things, and it is the will of God that they should suffer by means of created objects also. This, too, is a terrible punishment. The soul which is separated from its body becomes doubly sensitive, and these external tortures are truly excruciating. But we who still live in this world can relieve them of these burdens and free them from the temporal punishments due to sin by our prayers.

"Grant to the souls of Thy servants and handmaids the remission of all their sins." Absolve them "from every bond of sin," from all punishment. "Eternal rest grant unto them, O Lord."

God is holy; nothing unclean can exist in His presence. God is just; no one will ever escape from His prison "till thou repay the last farthing" (Mt 5:26). God is merciful; He desires that we pay the debts of the poor souls in purgatory, which they cannot pay themselves. He loves these souls. He will shorten the days of their detention if we who are united to them by the communion of saints offer our suffrages for them. Should we not do all that we can for the poor souls in purgatory? Should we not make a specific memento for our departed brethren, and through the Holy Sacrifice of the Mass offer for them the satisfactions of the Savior? Let us pray for them more diligently and undertake works of penance for them.

Prayer

O God, the Creator and Redeemer of all the faithful, grant to the souls of Thy servants and handmaids the remission of all their sins, that by devout prayers they may obtain the forgiveness which they have always desired. Through Christ our Lord. Amen.

All Souls' Day (3)

In the Mass for the Dead the Church pictures herself as standing at the bedside of him for whom she is celebrating the Holy Sacrifice. She is consoled by the thought that the soul of the departed child is to receive the desired redemption and glorification in heaven through this Sacrifice of the Mass. For the Church the Mass is a sacrifice of adoration, thanksgiving, satisfaction, and petition. In this sacrifice the Lord offers to the Father His own propitiatory works, together with those of His Church and its members, for the living and the dead. "Eternal rest grant unto them, O Lord, and let the perpetual light shine upon them" (Introit, Gradual, Communion) through the power of this Holy Sacrifice which we offer for them.

"A hymn, O God, becometh Thee in Sion; and a vow shall be paid to Thee in Jerusalem" (Introit). The psalm was a hymn of thanksgiving sung at the time of harvest in the Old Testament. The Church sees in the death of one of her children an occasion for thanksgiving. She is harvesting the fruits of the grace and the mercy of God, the fruits of her own labors and prayers. This soul is the fruit of her teaching and her sacraments, and now she offers it to almighty God at this Mass. Now with joy and gratitude in her heart she carries the fruit of her labor like a golden sheaf of wheat to the altar, and places it upon the paten to be offered to God. At the Consecration this offering will be joined to the sacrifice of the Lord and will be lifted up as an eternal hymn of praise to God for His mercy, and as a hymn of thanksgiving for the many graces received. Such is the attitude taken by the Church on the occasion of the death of one of her children. Her Mass for the Dead does not breathe the spirit of mourning for the departed, but rather one of praise and joy and thanksgiving to God, who has "perfected" one of her children and has taken him up to his glory. For this reason the ancient liturgy of the dead added this psalm to the Introit: "Blessed is he whom Thou hast chosen and taken to Thee; he shall dwell in Thy courts. We shall be filled with the good things of Thy house" (Ps 64:5). These blessings are the result of the power of the Holy Sacrifice which this departed one celebrated so often during his life and with which he is now being offered to God. Such is the mind of the sacred liturgy at the hour of death. By the power of the Holy Sacrifice the departed come "unto the resurrection of life" and eternal glory (Gospel).

"All that the Father giveth to Me shall come to Me; and him that cometh to Me I will not cast out" (Jn 6:37; Gospel of the second Mass). At the Offertory the Church offers to Christ, the King of Glory, the gifts of bread and wine together with the prayers of the faithful and the soul of the departed one (Offertory). The decisive moment for this soul is the moment of death, when it must appear before the Lord and King, who will decide whether or not it should be admitted to heaven. Holy Mother the Church piously implores: "O Lord, Jesus Christ, King of Glory, deliver the souls of all the faithful departed from the pains of hell and from the deep pit. Deliver them from the lion's mouth.... Grant them, O Lord, to pass from death to life, which Thou didst promise to Abraham and to his seed" (Offertory). The Church, praying and sacrificing, now awaits the coming of the Lord at the Consecration. What a blessed coming this is! He comes to receive the soul recommended to Him by the Church. He places in its hands the price of its redemption, His precious blood, that it may make complete its satisfaction for the temporal punishment due to its sins. The Church offers to the Father the prayers and satisfactions, the sufferings and death of the Lord as a perfect propitiatory sacrifice for all that this soul may yet owe by way of satisfaction. "Mercifully look down ... upon the sacrifice which we offer Thee for the souls of Thy servants" (Secreta of the first Mass). At Communion the Church prays: "May the perpetual light shine upon them, O Lord, with thy saints forever."

Holy Mother the Church esteems the Sacrifice of the Mass so highly because she is persuaded of its value for the salvation of the living and for the relief of the souls in purgatory. She depends on the merits of Christ and His saints, which are offered to God in this Holy Sacrifice. How sadly lacking we are in this spirit of the Church! We tend to place the emphasis on our own works of satisfaction rather than on those of Christ and the saints. For this reason we lack faith in the power of the Holy Sacrifice which the Church possesses.

Happy the man who is a member of the communion of saints and who lives according to the spirit of the Church! If we live in the spirit of the Church, we shall bear much fruit during our life. The fruit of the good works we have performed during our life will be offered up to God at the hour of our death as an offering of thanksgiving. Blessed are we, then, if we devote ourselves wholly to this life of the Church. She is our best friend during life and our most faithful companion in the hour of death.

Prayer

Absolve, O Lord, the souls of all the faithful departed from every bond of sin, that in the glory of the resurrection they may rise to a new and better life with Thy saints and Thy elect. Through Christ our Lord. Amen.

All Souls' Day (4)

Two thoughts are emphasized in the liturgy of the Mass for the Dead: the utter helplessness of the poor souls in purgatory, and the assurance of their eventual salvation, the resurrection of their bodies to life eternal.

"Eternal rest grant unto them, O Lord" (Introit). Although the faithful departed are in the state of grace, they suffer because they are separated from God. They love Him; they cling to Him with their whole soul; they have lost interest in all that is not God; they know how empty and vain life is without God. They see now how foolishly they acted while on earth by being so careless about sin, about their imperfections, their infidelities, their disobedience, and their inordinate attachment to men and the things of this world. They know now the folly of their indifference toward their duties, the danger of temporizing with their evil desires and thoughts, the penalty of neglect, the loss suffered through carelessness in their duties and through their reluctance to bring sacrifices. All their so-called petty offenses become heavy chains which now bind them for a time in the confines of purgatory and separate them from God. The greatest sorrow of the poor souls is that they are separated from God by their own fault. They have no other desire but to be with God, who is their joy, their love, their life, and their last end. Their hunger for Him grows and consumes them ever more as they are cleansed in the flames of purgatory. Just as a stone falling from on high gains acceleration the nearer it comes to earth, so the desire and longing of the souls in purgatory increases every moment and is accentuated in proportion to their nearness to God. This painful, tormenting, consuming hunger of the poor souls is in the mind of the sacred liturgy when it prays: "Eternal rest grant unto them, O Lord, and let the perpetual light shine upon them"; that is, fulfill their desire to be united to Thee; grant that they may see Thee face to face.

"I came down from heaven, not to do My own will, but the will of Him who sent Me. Now this is the will of the Father, who sent Me, that of all that He has given Me, I should lose nothing, but should raise it up again in the last day; and this is the will of my Father that sent Me, that every one who seeth the Son and believeth in Him, may have life everlasting, and I will raise him up in the last day" (Gospel of the second Mass). In the heart of the Church there lives a hope of the speedy entrance of the poor souls into eternal life, for she has the assurance of the blessed resurrection of her children who depart from this life. The severity of the sufferings of the poor souls is alleviated and made bearable by this hope. In view of this fact even the Mass for the Dead becomes a "eucharist," a prayer of thanksgiving to God. "It is truly meet and just, right and profitable, that we should at all times and in all places give thanks to Thee, O holy Lord, Father Almighty, everlasting God, through Christ our Lord. In whom the hope of a blessed resurrection has shone upon us.... For unto Thy faithful, O Lord, life is changed, not taken away [by death]; and the abode of this earthly sojourn being destroyed, an eternal dwelling is prepared in heaven. And therefore ... with all the heavenly hosts we sing a hymn to Thy glory, saying without ceasing: Holy, Holy, Holy" (Preface).

The Church remembers her children as long as they remain in purgatory; she knows that they have been saved and redeemed. Eternal life is assured them, and there is no possibility of their being lost, since they can no longer sin. They love God above all things with a perfectly pure love, and they are loved by God. He has already prepared a place for them in heaven. Yet a little while and they will repose in the heart of God eternally.

"Eternal rest grant unto them, O Lord, and let the perpetual light shine upon them." "Absolve, O Lord, the souls of all the faithful departed from every bond of sin. And by the help of Thy grace may they be worthy to escape the sentence of vengeance and enjoy the beatitude of eternal light" (Tract).

Through the sacred liturgy we may share the burden of the poor souls in purgatory. We firmly believe that all who died in Christ are saved in Christ, "in whom the hope of a happy resurrection has shone on us.... For unto Thy faithful, O Lord, life is changed, not taken away." Our salvation depends on our incorporation in Christ, on our being filled by His life and His Spirit through our common faith, our common sacrifice, and the other sacraments of the Church.

Prayer

O God, the Creator and Redeemer of all the faithful, grant to the souls of Thy servants and handmaids the remission of all their sins, that by devout prayers they may obtain the forgiveness which they have always desired. Through Christ our Lord. Amen.

All Souls' Day (5)

"Eternal rest grant unto them, O Lord, and let the perpetual light shine upon them.... Absolve, O Lord, the souls of all the faithful departed from every bond of sin. And by the help of Thy grace may they be worthy to escape the sentence of vengeance and enjoy the beatitude of eternal light" (Gradual and Tract). Thus we beseech the Lord on behalf of the poor souls. We know that we can still be of assistance to our beloved departed even beyond the grave. The holy bonds which have bound us together during our life are not destroyed by death. There is between us a spiritual, supernatural intercourse in the community of the saints.

"Now you are the body of Christ, and members of member" (1 Cor 12:27). God "hath subjected all things under His [Christ's] feet and hath made Him head over all the Church, which is His body" (Eph 1:22 f.). Whoever is united to this body of Christ belongs to the community of saints, to that supernatural, living community which unites all the redeemed in Christ and with Christ. All are united one with another: the saints of heaven, the suffering souls in purgatory, and the members of the militant Church on earth. We all form the one body of Christ, and are called to support each other that we may all attain eternal life. We all enjoy a living relationship as members of one body. "And if one member suffer anything, all the members suffer with it; for if one member glory, all the members rejoice with it" (1 Cor 12:26). Through this vital connection as members of the one body, we are in a position to help the souls in purgatory reach perfection in Christ and attain the happiness of eternal life. "God hath tempered the body . . . that there might be no schism in the body; but the members might be mutually careful one for another" (1 Cor 12:24 f.). We must be solicitous for our brothers and sisters in purgatory. It is the will of God that we help and assist them.

"Bear ye one another's burdens" (Gal 6:2). The souls of our brethren in purgatory bear the "burden" of the temporary punishment which is due to sins, faults, and infidelities committed during their life, and for which they have not yet made full satisfaction. In this communion of saints we are given the power to carry part of their burden. Because of our membership in the communion of saints we can apply our good works to the poor souls and do for them what they cannot do for themselves. We can offer to God satisfaction for the temporal punishment due to sin which God may still demand of them. We lighten the burden of the poor souls as often as we offer the Holy Sacrifice of the Mass for them. In the Mass we possess the most profitable and most effective means of helping our departed brethren (Council of Trent, Sess. XXV). We bear their burden whenever we gain indulgences and apply them to their souls. All the prayers, sacrifices, good works, mortifications, and sufferings which we undertake for God's sake, have a propitiatory value. With all these works we can lessen the burden of the poor souls and ameliorate their sufferings. The more intimately we associate ourselves with the communion of saints, the more efficient our efforts become. Is it not a sublime task to bear the burden of the poor souls and thus console them in their suffering? How thankful they will be to us!

Our ability to help the poor souls does not arise from our physical relationship with them, or from our connections and circumstances, but rather from our union with Christ and His Church. Our union in Christ, our head, is the basis of this power. It is charity that binds us to the community of brothers and sisters in Christ. In the measure we possess this charity we shall also be able to help our departed brethren.

"If I should have all faith so that I could remove mountains, and have not charity, I am nothing. And if I should distribute all my goods to feed the poor, and if I should deliver my body to be burned, and have not charity, it profiteth me nothing" (1 Cor 13:2 f.). We must practice charity in the communion of saints, in the Church, in the parish, in the religious community, and in the family.

Prayer

Absolve, O Lord, the souls of all the faithful departed from every bond of sin. And by the help of Thy grace may they be worthy to escape the sentence of vengeance and enjoy the beatitude of eternal light. Amen. (Tract.)

The Dedication of a Church

The feast of the Dedication of a Church commemorates the day when a bishop consecrated to the service of God a building of stone, which thus became the dwelling place of Christ and the property of God. Having recited the Seven Penitential Psalms, the bishop blessed the water and sprinkled the exterior walls of the building. Then he entered the Church to take possession of it in the name of Christ. The bishop then went about the interior of the Church three times, sprinkling the altars and the walls. He called down from heaven upon this temple the grace that sanctifies, and bore the relics of the saints in solemn procession to the altar, where they were entombed. The church now became a place of sacrifice, the dwelling of God with man, a house of prayer, a place of blessing.

"How lovely are Thy tabernacles, O Lord of hosts!" (Introit.) God is omnipresent. He dwells in the room in which we live, and in every stone and blade of grass on which we tread. He personally lives in our soul, drawing it to Himself with love. He fills it with light and power; He speaks to it, admonishes it, enlightens it; He inspires it to do good and to avoid evil. But in our church God dwells in a particular and singular manner. Here alone the incarnate Son of God dwells in the tabernacle with His divinity and His humanity, His body and soul. Here upon this altar He offers His sacrifice of adoration, praise, thanksgiving, and petition. Here in this tabernacle He lives and prays continually on our behalf. Here we may approach Him, exchange confidences with Him, open our hearts to Him, express our love for Him, and explain our trials and difficulties. Here we may seek help for the needs and cares of those dear to us, help for those who are ill or in danger, help for those who are on the point of losing their faith or their virtue. Here He continues His work of sanctifying us through the sacraments of baptism, confirmation, penance, holy orders, and matrimony. Here each day He provides sweet nourishment for our souls in Holy Communion. God the Father and God the Holy Ghost dwell here with Him in a mysterious and intimate union. "Terrible is this place; it is the house of God and the gate of heaven" (Introit). "Behold the tabernacle of God with men, and He will dwell with them. And they shall be His people, and God Himself with them shall be their God" (Epistle).

"Illuminate this temple by the virtue of Thy indwelling, and grant that all who assemble here to pray, from whatsoever tribulation they shall call upon Thee, may obtain the blessings of Thy consolation." This prayer the bishop says as he dedicates the church, begging God to hear the prayers which we shall offer up in this holy temple. God does not let such prayers go unanswered. Such is the firm belief of the Church, and for this reason she reminds us on the anniversary of the dedication of a church: "My house shall be called the house of prayer, saith the Lord: in it every one that asketh receiveth, and he that seeketh findeth" (Communion). "My eyes also shall be open and My ears attentive to the prayer of him that shall pray in this place. For I have chosen and have sanctified this place that My name may be there forever, and My eyes and My heart may remain there perpetually" (2 Par 7:15 f.). In this place God is especially attentive to the prayers of men; here "every one that asketh receiveth." A consecrated church is a sacramental, a holy place dedicated to God, in which we may expect especially to be heard because of the prayer which was said over it on the day of its dedication. "This day is salvation come to this house" (Gospel), since Christ Himself has entered it personally to dispense to His members the fullness of His grace.

"Grant that all who assemble here to pray, . . . may obtain the blessings of Thy consolation." When we come to the church to pray, we do not pray alone. This church, through its dedication to God, connects us with the prayers of the Church and the Christian community. Prayers offered in this consecrated church of stone are supported by the Church and will be heard.

"This day salvation is come to this house" (Gospel). Salvation was brought to the house of God on the day of its dedication, when the Lord first celebrated His sacrifice in it. But every day the Lord reappears upon the altar at the Consecration of the Mass. The church then becomes like the house of Zachaeus, who "received Him with joy" (Gospel). What is said of the church is said of us also: We receive Him with joy at the Consecration of the Mass and in Holy Communion.

PRAYER

O God, who year by year dost renew the day of the consecration of this Thy holy temple, and dost ever bring us again in safety to the holy mysteries, hear the prayers of Thy people and grant that whosoever entereth this temple to seek blessings may rejoice to obtain all that he seeketh. Through Christ our Lord. Amen.

The Dedication of a Church (2)

In the language of the liturgy, the word church means more than the sacred edifice. It means the living Church on earth as well as the Church in heaven. The word church means the house of God made of stone, it is true; but it also means that living organism which is the body of Christ with all its perfection and all its faults. The word church implies the faults and miseries of men as well as their virtues and perfections; it connotes the misery and poverty of men as well as the inexhaustible riches of God. It suggests the place where it is the pleasure of God to dwell: the altar and the tabernacle. All these thoughts are suggested to the mind of the Christian on the feast of the Dedication of a Church, which is really a feast of the communion of all the saints.

"Behold the tabernacle of God with men" (Epistle), in the house of stone, in the Church, in the community of saints, in our own soul. "For you are the temple of the living God" (2 Cor 6:16). "The temple of God is holy, which you are" (1 Cor 3:17). The consecration of the temple of our soul took place at the moment of our baptism. There we received sanctifying grace and became children of God. "The charity of God is poured forth in our hearts, by the Holy Ghost, who is given to us" (Rom 5:5). "If any one love Me, he will keep My word, and My Father will love him, and We will come to him and will make Our abode with him" (Jn 14:23).

"This day is salvation come to this house, because he also is a son of Abraham" (Gospel). We ourselves are like Zachaeus, who in the eyes of the Jews was a great sinner. "He was gone to be a guest with a man that was a sinner" (Gospel). Christ became our guest at the hour of our baptism. The unwelcome tenant of our soul, Satan, was cast out. Our sins were forgiven, grace entered our soul, and with grace, God Himself, the Father, the Son, and the Holy Ghost. We became "sons of Abraham," children of election, who before were children of wrath. "For the Son of Man is come to seek and to save that which was lost" (Gospel).

"You are the temple of the living God," a most holy tabernacle. God has come into our soul to make us rich and happy, to take possession of us as He takes possession of the temple built of stone. If we are the dwelling place, the temple of God, then we are God's property. "He will dwell in them; and they shall be His people" (Epistle). We are a holy place where God Himself dwells and works. We are the temple of the Holy Ghost, who loves good and hates evil; we are the children of almighty God, who protects us, takes us by the hand, and leads us safely through the perilous way of life. God lives in us through His inexhaustible love. He forgives us; He gives us power to do good; He makes our sacrifices sweet and the burden of life easy. What have we to fear? Why should we be anxious if we believe that God dwells in our heart? "This day is salvation come to this house."

Let us be most grateful. "The half of my goods I give to the poor; and if I have defrauded any man of anything, I restore him fourfold" (Gospel). The presence of the Lord in his house makes Zachaeus so happy that he loses his taste for earthly goods and treasures. He accepts joyfully the favor Christ shows him. As we become aware of the indwelling of God, we withdraw ourselves from worldly pursuits ever more and more. We become men of the spirit, communing with God in intimate prayer and listening intently to His voice. We receive His inspirations and admonitions with joy. We live in the light which God gives us, and we see in all that the day brings the hand of His providence, shaping all things to our best interest. He speaks to us, consoles us, and gives us light and grace. He takes us under His special care that we may escape the dangers which menace us. He gives us delight in His mysteries and "the peace of God, which surpasseth all understanding" (Phil 4:7). Truly has "salvation come to this house." God Himself has made His abode in us. How empty and vain are all other goods in comparison to the possession of God!

"This day is salvation come to this house," the temple of my soul. "This day," in the celebration of the Holy Eucharist and in Holy Communion, He enters our house and we are renewed. In gratitude for such a favor we should be able to say with Zachaeus: "The half of my goods I give to the poor." Filled with the Spirit of Christ, we should be generous and charitable to the poor, to our brethren in Christ. That must be the fruit of Holy Communion.

"You are a temple of the living God." We are not sufficiently conscious of our dignity as baptized Christians, as tabernacles of the most holy Trinity, as thrones of the Godhead. How pure and how well ordered must be the tabernacle of the Most Holy! "Holiness becometh Thy house, O Lord" (Ps 92:5). Holy must be our thoughts, our passions, our wishes, our words, our works, our motions, our whole conduct. "For the temple of God is holy, which you are" (1 Cor 3:17).

"You are the temple of the living God." Our fellow men are also temples of God, and we must see God in all men: in our fellow workers, in children, in the poor, in the wretched and despised. And we must also treat them with respect and reverence, "For the temple of God is holy, which you are."

Prayer

O God, who from living and chosen stones dost prepare an eternal dwelling place for Thy majesty, assist Thy suppliant people, that Thy Church, while benefiting by material enlargement, may also expand by spiritual increase. Through Christ our Lord. Amen. (Postcommunion.)

Index

Our mission is to publish authentically Catholic books that are traditional, accessible, and beautiful.

Benedictus Books takes its name from the opening Latin phrase of the Canticle of Zechariah, prayed daily in the Catholic Church since the earliest centuries. Our logo evokes the antiquity of Gregorian chant and the illuminated manuscript tradition, emphasizing continuity with the faith and worship of the past and the continuing relevance of our sacred patrimony today.

Benedictus Books was established in 2021 with the launch of our acclaimed periodical *Benedictus*, the "Traditional Catholic Companion" — a daily devotional drawing on the theological riches and customs of the ancient Roman Rite, and allowing for a deeper experience of the traditional Latin Mass, liturgical calendar, and writings of countless saints and theologians. This periodical reflects the three core values of Benedictus Books:

Traditional. We are committed to preserving and handing on the Faith of our forefathers without diminution or change, publishing works that are both inspired by and conformable to traditional Catholic doctrine, liturgy, and spirituality. Our primary focus is on republishing reliably orthodox works that help to promote the interior life and sanctification of the domestic church through classical forms of prayer and worship.

Accessible. Recognizing that many aspects of Catholic doctrine, liturgy, and custom have become obscured in recent decades, we place an emphasis on texts that explain and assist readers in mining the vast theological wealth that is contained and expressed in the traditional Roman Rite, as well as those writings of saints and scholars that have been profoundly shaped by the same.

Beautiful. Rooted in the perennial tradition of Western sacred art, we believe that texts treating such exalted subjects deserve a truly beautiful and durable presentation. We invest extensive time and meticulous care to create inspiring new typesettings with rich ornament and illustration, crisp typography, clean layouts, and classic bindings to make every book as pleasing to hold and look at as it is to read.

In order to be worthy of the noble content they contain, all of our books are crafted to the most exacting standards, allowing these priceless treasures from our Catholic tradition to be cherished for years to come.